The Official

SCRABBLE®

Crossword Game

Players

DICTIONARY

SIXTH EDITION

The Official

SCRABBLE® BRAND

Crossword Game

Players

SIXTH EDITION

Merriam-Webster, Incorporated

Springfield, Massachusetts

Library of Congress Cataloging-in-Publication Data

Names: Merriam-Webster, Inc.
Title: The official Scrabble players dictionary.
Description: Sixth Edition. I Springfield, Massachusetts : Merriam-Webster,
    Incorporated, [2018]
Identifiers: LCCN 2018024087 I ISBN 9780877794226 hardcover
Subjects: LCSH: Scrabble (Game)—Glossaries, vocabularies, etc.
Classification: LCC GV1507.S3 O36 2018 I DDC 793.734—dc23
LC record available at https://lccn.loc.gov/2018024087

Made in the United States of America

1st Printing   Quad Graphics, Versailles, KY   August 2018

P₃ REFACE • This is the sixth edition of the enormously popular *The Official SCRABBLE Players Dictionary*, and it includes the new qualified entries found in *Merriam-Webster's Online Dictionary* not previously entered in *The Official SCRABBLE Players Dictionary*. This dictionary has been prepared especially for lovers of SCRABBLE crossword games and is endorsed by the North American SCRABBLE Players Association (NASPA) for recreational and school use.

It is important to remember that *The Official SCRABBLE Players Dictionary* was edited solely with this limited purpose in mind. It is not intended to serve as a general dictionary of English; thus, such important features of general dictionaries as definitions of multiple senses, pronunciation respellings, etymologies, and usage labels are omitted. It is also important to remember that this specialized dictionary contains words of up to eight letters and their inflections.

It is the intention of the makers of SCRABBLE crossword games that they be enjoyed by children and adults alike. With this consideration in mind, words likely to offend players of the game have been omitted from this edition. The words omitted are those that would qualify for a warning usage note on the basis of standards applied in Merriam-Webster™ dictionaries.

The detailed organization and special features of the dictionary are explained in the Introduction which follows. It should be read with care by all who use the dictionary. Now that this new updated work is available, we are confident that it will afford satisfaction and enjoyment to SCRABBLE crossword game players everywhere.

We gratefully acknowledge the contributions of the members of the North American SCRABBLE Players Association, who, with Jim Pate as cochairman, culled and compiled all the SCRABBLE-qualified words from the latest standard dictionaries. Their painstaking efforts have been invaluable to the preparation of this edition. Their names are as follows: Timothy Bottorff, Ross Brown, James Cherry, John Chew, Chris Cree, Kurt Davies, Robert Gillis, Adam Henderson, Peter R. Huszagh, Dallas Johnson, Chris Lipe, Bob Lipton, George MacAulay, Anna Miransky, Paul Mulik, and Matthew Tunnicliffe. In addition, special thanks go to Merriam-Webster Production Editor Emily Vezina and Merriam-Webster Editorial Database Specialist Anne McDonald for their assistance in the production of this edition.

Benjamin Korzec
General Editor

Every letter counts in SCRABBLE, the classic word game with the iconic game board.

And every word that counts is right here in *The Official SCRABBLE Players Dictionary* by Merriam-Webster. The SCRABBLE game has always been a case of "your word against mine," and when you go for a challenge, you want to be sure you're not going to be the player to lose their turn! The game of SCRABBLE might be seen by some as just a little friendly competition, but to win, you've got to choose your words and your spaces very carefully to get those high scores. Look for hooks, shuffle the tiles on your rack and use your letters well. May the best words win!

For more information on all things SCRABBLE, go to https://scrabble.hasbro.com.

The Official SCRABBLE Players Dictionary has been endorsed by the North American SCRABBLE Players Association (NASPA).

NASPA is a community of tournament, club, and avid home players of the SCRABBLE Brand Crossword Game. We foster an atmosphere for people of all skill levels to play their favorite game, improve their abilities, and above all, meet people who share a similar love of the game. For more information about our clubs, tournaments, and other activities, please find us on Facebook or Twitter (@NASPA), or contact us at:

info@scrabbleplayers.org
www.scrabbleplayers.org

NTRODUCTION ● **MAIN ENTRIES** ● Main entries are listed in boldface type and are set flush with the left-hand margin of each column. Except for an occasional cross-reference (such as **UNDERLAIN** past participle of underlie), main entries contain from two to eight letters, since words within this range are considered to be most useful to SCRABBLE crossword game players. Words that are not permissible in SCRABBLE crossword games have not been included in this dictionary. Thus, proper names, words requiring hyphens or apostrophes, words considered foreign, and abbreviations have been omitted. Because dictionaries have different criteria for selecting entries, several American and Canadian standard dictionaries were consulted in preparing the list of main entries for this book. Obsolete, archaic, slang, and nonstandard words are included because they are permitted by the rules of the game. All variant forms of a main entry are shown at their own alphabetical places and defined in terms of the principal form. **Words that exceed eight letters in length and are not inflected forms of main entries in this dictionary should be looked up in a standard dictionary.** *Merriam-Webster's Collegiate® Dictionary, Eleventh Edition,* is recommended as a reference for longer words.

PARTS OF SPEECH ● An italic label indicating a part of speech follows each main entry except cross-references, for which the label is given at the root word. The eight traditional parts of speech are indicated as follows:

n	noun
v	verb
adj	adjective
adv	adverb
pron	pronoun
prep	preposition
conj	conjunction
interj	interjection

When a word can be used as more than one part of speech, each part of speech is entered separately if the inflected forms are not spelled alike. For example, both the adjective *humble* and the verb *humble* are entered because the inflected forms vary.

HUMBLE *adj* **-BLER, -BLEST** modest
HUMBLE *v* **-BLED, -BLING, -BLES** to reduce the pride of

On the other hand, the verb *rage* is entered while the noun *rage* is not because the inflected form *rages* at the verb is spelled the same as the plural form of the noun. In a dictionary for SCRABBLE crossword game players, entry of the noun is therefore redundant. Homographs (words spelled alike) which may be used as the same part of speech are treated in the same way. For example, *lie* is entered as a verb twice because the inflected forms are spelled differently.

LIE	*v* **LAY, LAIN, LYING, LIES** to be in or get into a horizontal position
LIE	*v* **LIED, LYING, LIES** to speak falsely

If both sets of inflected forms were spelled alike, only one *lie* would be entered in this dictionary. In this way the dictionary includes as many different spellings as possible yet avoids wasting space with repeated entry of words spelled in the same way. The SCRABBLE crossword game player, after all, needs only one entry to justify a play.

INFLECTED FORMS ● Inflected forms include the past tense, past participle, present participle, and present tense third person singular of verbs, the plural of nouns, and the comparative and superlative of adjectives and adverbs. They are shown in boldface capital letters immediately following the part-of-speech label. Irregular inflected forms are listed as main entries when they fall four or more alphabetical places away from the root word (see **Cross-References** below). All inflected forms are allowable for play in SCRABBLE crossword games.

The principal parts of the majority of verbs are shown as **-ED, -ING, -S** (or **-ES** when applicable). This indicates that the past tense and past participle are formed simply by adding *-ed* to the entry word, that the present participle is formed simply by adding *-ing* to the entry word, and that the present third person singular is formed simply by adding *-s* (or *-es*) to the entry word.

SWARM	*v* **-ED, -ING, -S** to move in a large group

When inflection of an entry word involves any spelling change in addition to the suffixal ending (such as the dropping of a final *-e*, the doubling of a final consonant, or the changing of a final *-y* to *-i-*) or when the inflection is irregular, the inflected forms given indicate such changes.

MOVE	*v* **MOVED, MOVING, MOVES** to change from one position to another
DOT	*v* **DOTTED, DOTTING, DOTS** to cover with dots (tiny round marks)
CRY	*v* **CRIED, CRYING, CRIES** to weep
BREAK	*v* **BROKE, BROKEN, BREAKING, BREAKS** to reduce to fragments

For verbs of more than one syllable, either the last syllable or the last two syllables are shown to indicate spelling changes.

CANCEL	*v* **-CELED, -CELING, -CELS** or **-CELLED, -CELLING, -CELS** to annul
INDICATE	*v* **-CATED, -CATING, -CATES** to point out

The plurals of nouns are preceded by the abbreviation "pl." Most plurals are shown as **-S** (or **-ES** when applicable) to indicate that the plural is formed simply by adding the given suffix to the entry word.

PIZZA	*n* pl. **-S** an Italian open pie

When pluralizing a noun involves any spelling change in addition to the suffixal ending (such as the changing of a final -y to -i- or a final -f to -v-) or when the plural is irregular, the plural form shown indicates such change.

LEFTY	*n* pl. **LEFTIES** a left-handed person
CALF	*n* pl. **CALVES** or **CALFS** a young cow or bull
INDEX	*n* pl. **INDEXES** or **INDICES** a type of reference guide at the end of a book

In such cases involving polysyllabic nouns at least the last syllable is shown.

AVIARY	*n* pl. **-ARIES** a large enclosure for live birds

For the sake of clarity, two groups of nouns that are confusing to many, those ending in -o and those ending in -y, are always indicated in this dictionary by showing at least the last syllable, even though no spelling change is involved.

POLO	*n* pl. **-LOS** a game played on horseback
TURKEY	*n* pl. **-KEYS** a large American bird

Variant plurals are shown wherever they add another word permissible in SCRABBLE crossword games.

DODO	*n* pl. **-DOS** or **-DOES** an extinct flightless bird

Plurals which have the same form as the singular are shown only when they are the only plural for that entry. This is done to show that for the entry in question it is not permissible to add **-S** (or **-ES**) to the singular to create a plural.

SHEEP	*n* pl. **SHEEP** a ruminant mammal
MOOSE	*n* pl. **MOOSE** a ruminant mammal

Otherwise, they are omitted and only the plural with the inflection is shown.

HADDOCK	*n* pl. **-S** a food fish

The italic label *n/pl* is given to two kinds of nouns. One is the plural noun that has no singular form.

MORES	*n/pl* the customs of a particular group

The other is the plural noun of which the singular form contains more than eight letters and is not entered in this dictionary.

> **SENSORIA** *n/pl* the parts of the brain concerned with the reception and interpretation of sensory stimuli

Sensorium, the singular form, has nine letters and therefore is not entered.

The comparative and superlative forms of adjectives and adverbs are shown, when applicable, immediately following the part-of-speech label. Any spelling changes are indicated in the forms shown.

> **NEAR**   *adj* **NEARER, NEAREST** situated within a short distance
>
> **FAR**   *adv* **FARTHER, FARTHEST** or **FURTHER, FURTHEST** at or to a great distance
>
> **GLUEY**   *adj* **GLUIER, GLUIEST** resembling glue

Not all adjectives or adverbs can be inflected, and only those inflected forms shown are acceptable. None of the adjectives and adverbs listed as run-on entries in this dictionary have inflected forms.

RUN-ON ENTRIES   ●   A main entry may be followed by one or more derivatives in boldface type with a different part-of-speech label. These are run-on entries. Run-on entries are not defined since their meanings are readily derivable from the meaning of the root word.

> **PLAY**   *v* **-ED, -ING, -S** to engage in amusement or sport **PLAYABLE** *adj*
>
> **HAMULUS**   *n* pl. **-LI** a small hook **HAMULAR, HAMULATE, HAMULOSE, HAMULOUS** *adj*

No entry has been run on at another if it would fall alphabetically four or more places from the entry. **When you do not find a word at its own place, it is always wise to check several entries above and below to see if it is run on.**

CROSS-REFERENCES   ●   A cross-reference is a main entry that is an inflected form of another word (such as the plural form of a noun, the past tense form of a verb, or the comparative form of an adjective). An inflected form is entered as a main entry if it undergoes a spelling change in addition to or instead of suffixation *and* if it falls alphabetically four or more places away from the root word.

For example, in the entries reproduced below, **SCARING** is a main entry because it involves a spelling change (the final *-e* of *scare* is dropped) besides the addition of the **-ING** ending and because it falls four or more places from the entry **SCARE**. On the other hand, *scares* is not a main entry because it involves no spelling change beyond the addition of the ending **-S**. **SCARIER** and **SCARIEST** are main entries because they involve a spelling change (the *-e-* is dropped and the final *-y* is changed to *-i-*) besides the addition of the **-ER**, **-EST** endings and they fall more four or more places from the entry **SCARY**.

SCARE   *v* **SCARED, SCARING, SCARES** to
              frighten

. . .

SCARIER   comparative of scarey and scary
SCARIEST   superlative of scarey and scary
SCARING   present participle of scare

. . .

SCARY   *adj* **SCARIER, SCARIEST** frightening

This policy is intended to make the word desired as easy to find as possible without wasting space. Nevertheless, many inflected forms will appear only at the main entry. **You should always look at several entries above and below the expected place if you do not find the desired word as a main entry.**

Cross-reference entries for present tense third person singular forms of verbs use the abbreviation "sing."

DEFINITIONS ●

In most cases, only one very brief definition is given for each main entry since definitions do not play a significant role in the SCRABBLE crossword game. This definition serves only to orient the player in a general way to a single meaning of the word. It is not intended to have all the precision and detail of a definition in a good general dictionary.

When a word consisting of eight or fewer letters appears in a definition but is not an entry in this dictionary, it is glossed in parentheses. For example, at the entry for the verb *plank*, the noun "planks" is used in the definition and is glossed because the noun *plank* is not a separate entry.

PLANK   *v* **-ED, -ING, -S** to cover with planks (long,
              flat pieces of lumber)

A main entry that is a variant form of another entry is defined in terms of the most common form, which is entered and defined at its own alphabetical place.

PEROGI   *n* pl. **-ES** or **-S** pierogi
PEROGIE   *n* pl. **-S** pierogi
PEROGY   *n* pl. **-GIES** pierogi

. . .

PIEROGI   *n* pl. **-ES** a small dumpling with a filling

SCRABBLE crossword game players in Canada will be pleased to learn that variant forms such as *honour*, *centre*, and *cheque*, which are often omitted from general dictionaries, have also been included in this book.

LISTS OF UNDEFINED WORDS ● Two separate lists of
undefined words appear below the entries that begin with RE- and with
UN-. These words are not defined because they are self-explanatory:
their meanings are simply the sum of a meaning of the prefix *re-* or *un-*
and a meaning of the root word. All of their inflected forms are given,
however.

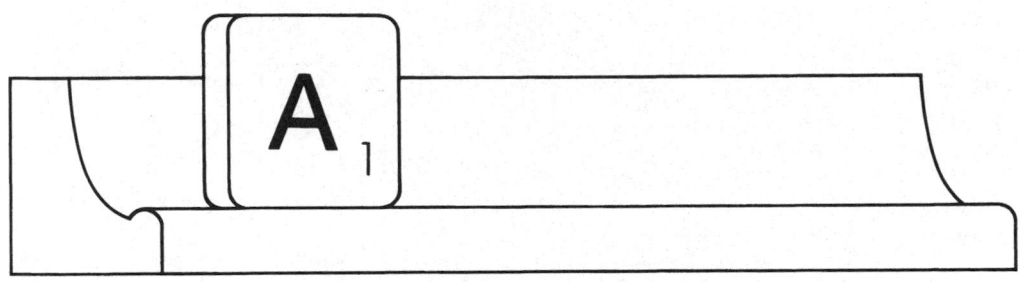

AA *n* pl. **-S** rough, cindery lava

AAH *v* **-ED, -ING, -S** to exclaim in amazement, joy, or surprise

AAL *n* pl. **-S** an East Indian shrub

AALII *n* pl. **-S** a tropical tree

AARDVARK *n* pl. **-S** an African mammal

AARDWOLF *n* pl. **-WOLVES** an African mammal

AARGH *interj* — used to express disgust

AARRGH *interj* aargh

AARRGHH *interj* aargh

AASVOGEL *n* pl. **-S** a vulture

AB *n* pl. **-S** an abdominal muscle

ABA *n* pl. **-S** a sleeveless garment worn by Arabs

ABACA *n* pl. **-S** a Philippine plant

ABACK *adv* toward the back

ABACUS *n* pl. **-CUSES** or **-CI** a calculating device

ABAFT *adv* toward the stern

ABAKA *n* pl. **-S** abaca

ABALONE *n* pl. **-S** an edible shellfish

ABAMP *n* pl. **-S** abampere

ABAMPERE *n* pl. **-S** a unit of electric current

ABANDON *v* **-ED, -ING, -S** to leave or give up completely

ABAPICAL *adj* directed away from the apex

ABASE *v* **ABASED, ABASING, ABASES** to lower in rank, prestige, or esteem **ABASEDLY** *adv*

ABASER *n* pl. **-S** one that abases

ABASH *v* **-ED, -ING, -ES** to make ashamed or embarrassed

ABASIA *n* pl. **-S** a defect in muscular coordination in walking

ABASING present participle of abase

ABATE *v* **ABATED, ABATING, ABATES** to reduce in degree or intensity **ABATABLE** *adj*

ABATER *n* pl. **-S** one that abates

ABATIS *n* pl. **-TISES** a barrier made of felled trees

ABATOR *n* pl. **-S** one that unlawfully seizes an inheritance

ABATTIS *n* pl. **-TISES** abatis

ABATTOIR *n* pl. **-S** a slaughterhouse

ABAXIAL *adj* situated away from the axis

ABAXILE *adj* abaxial

ABAYA *n* pl. **-S** a long loose robe worn by Arab women

ABBA *n* pl. **-S** father — used as a title of honor

ABBACY *n* pl. **-CIES** the office of an abbot

ABBATIAL *adj* pertaining to an abbot

ABBE *n* pl. **-S** an abbot

ABBESS *n* pl. **-ES** the female superior of a convent of nuns

ABBEY *n* pl. **-BEYS** a monastery or convent

ABBOT *n* pl. **-S** the superior of a monastery

ABBOTCY *n* pl. **-CIES** abbacy

ABDICATE *v* **-CATED, -CATING, -CATES** to give up formally

ABDOMEN *n* pl. **-MENS** or **-MINA** the body cavity containing the viscera

ABDUCE *v* **-DUCED, -DUCING, -DUCES** to abduct

ABDUCENS *n* pl. **-CENTES** a cranial nerve

ABDUCENT *adj* serving to abduct

ABDUCING present participle of abduce

ABDUCT *v* **-ED, -ING, -S** to draw away from the original position

ABDUCTEE *n* pl. **-S** one that has been abducted

ABDUCTOR *n* pl. **-S** or **-ES** an abducent muscle

ABEAM *adv* at right angles to the keel of a ship

ABED *adv* in bed

ABEGGING *adj* begging

ABELE *n* pl. **-S** a Eurasian tree

ABELIA *n* pl. **-S** an Asian or Mexican shrub

ABELIAN *adj* being a commutative group in mathematics

ABELMOSK *n* pl. **-S** a tropical herb

ABERRANT *n* pl. **-S** a deviant

ABET *v* **ABETTED, ABETTING, ABETS** to encourage and support

ABETMENT *n* pl. **-S** the act of abetting

ABETTAL *n* pl. **-S** abetment

ABETTED past tense of abet

ABETTER *n* pl. **-S** abettor

ABETTING present participle of abet

ABETTOR *n* pl. **-S** one that abets

ABEYANCE *n* pl. **-S** temporary inactivity

ABEYANCY *n* pl. **-CIES** abeyance

ABEYANT *adj* marked by abeyance

ABFARAD *n* pl. **-S** a unit of capacitance

ABHENRY *n* pl. **-RYS** or **-RIES** a unit of inductance

ABHOR *v* **-HORRED, -HORRING, -HORS** to loathe

ABHORRER *n* pl. **-S** one that abhors

ABIDANCE *n* pl. **-S** the act of abiding

ABIDE *v* **ABIDED** or **ABODE, ABIDING, ABIDES** to accept without objection

ABIDER *n* pl. **-S** one that abides

ABIGAIL *n* pl. **-S** a lady's maid

ABILITY *n* pl. **-TIES** the quality of being able to do something

ABIOSIS *n* pl. **-OSES** absence of life **ABIOTIC** *adj*

ABJECT *adj* sunk to a low condition **ABJECTLY** *adv*

ABJURE *v* **-JURED, -JURING, -JURES** to renounce under oath

ABJURER *n* pl. **-S** one that abjures

ABLATE *v* **-LATED, -LATING, -LATES** to remove by cutting

ABLATION *n* pl. **-S** surgical removal of a bodily part

ABLATIVE *n* pl. **-S** a grammatical case

ABLATOR *n* pl. **-S** one that ablates

ABLAUT *n* pl. **-S** a patterned change in root vowels of verb forms

ABLAZE *adj* being on fire

ABLE *adj* **ABLER, ABLEST** having sufficient power, skill, or resources

ABLE *n* pl. **-S** a communications code word for the letter A

ABLED *adj* capable of unimpaired function

ABLEGATE *n* pl. **-S** a papal envoy

ABLEISM *n* pl. **-S** prejudice or discrimination against disabled people

ABLEIST *n* pl. **-S** one that practices ableism

ABLER comparative of able

ABLEST superlative of able

ABLINGS *adv* ablins

ABLINS *adv* perhaps

ABLOOM *adj* blooming

ABLUENT *n* pl. **-S** a cleansing agent

ABLUSH *adj* blushing

ABLUTED *adj* washed clean

ABLUTION *n* pl. **-S** a washing

ABLY *adv* in an able manner

ABMHO *n* pl. **-MHOS** a unit of electrical conductance

ABNEGATE *v* **-GATED, -GATING, -GATES** to deny to oneself

ABNORMAL *n* pl. **-S** a mentally deficient person

ABOARD *adv* into, in, or on a ship, train, or airplane

ABODE *v* **ABODED, ABODING, ABODES** to forebode

ABOHM *n* pl. **-S** a unit of electrical resistance

ABOIDEAU *n* pl. **-DEAUS** or **-DEAUX** a type of dike

ABOIL *adj* boiling

ABOITEAU *n* pl. **-TEAUS** or **-TEAUX** aboideau

ABOLISH *v* **-ED, -ING, -ES** to do away with

ABOLLA *n* pl. **-LAE** a cloak worn in ancient Rome

ABOMA *n* pl. **-S** a South American snake

ABOMASAL *adj* pertaining to the abomasum

ABOMASUM *n* pl. **-SA** the fourth stomach of a ruminant

ABOMASUS *n* pl. **-MASI** abomasum

ABOON *adv* above

ABORAL *adj* situated away from the mouth **ABORALLY** *adv*

ABORNING *adv* while being born

ABORT *v* **-ED, -ING, -S** to bring forth a fetus prematurely

ABORTER *n* pl. **-S** one that aborts

ABORTION *n* pl. **-S** induced expulsion of a nonviable fetus

ABORTIVE *adj* failing to succeed

ABORTUS *n* pl. **-ES** an aborted fetus

ABOUGHT past tense of aby and abye

ABOULIA *n* pl. **-S** abulia **ABOULIC** *adj*

ABOUND *v* **-ED, -ING, -S** to have a large number or amount

ABOUT *adv* approximately

ABOVE *n* pl. **-S** something that is above (in a higher place)

ABRACHIA *n* pl. **-S** a lack of arms

ABRADANT *n* pl. **-S** an abrasive

ABRADE *v* **ABRADED, ABRADING, ABRADES** to wear away by friction

ABRADER *n* pl. **-S** a tool for abrading

ABRASION *n* pl. **-S** the act of abrading

ABRASIVE *n* pl. **-S** an abrading substance

ABREACT *v* **-ED, -ING, -S** to release repressed emotions by reliving the original traumatic experience

ABREAST *adv* side by side

ABRI *n* pl. **-S** a bomb shelter

ABRIDGE *v* **ABRIDGED, ABRIDGING, ABRIDGES** to reduce the length of

ABRIDGER *n* pl. **-S** one that abridges

ABROACH *adj* astir

ABROAD *adv* out of one's own country

ABROGATE *v* **-GATED, -GATING, -GATES** to abolish by authoritative action

ABROSIA *n* pl. **-S** a fasting from food

ABRUPT *adj* **ABRUPTER, ABRUPTEST** rudely brief **ABRUPTLY** *adv*

ABSCESS *v* **-ED, -ING, -ES** to form an abscess (a localized collection of pus surrounded by inflamed tissue)

ABSCISE *v* **-SCISED, -SCISING, -SCISES** to cut off

ABSCISIN *n* pl. **-S** a regulatory substance found in plants

ABSCISSA *n* pl. **-SAS** or **-SAE** a particular geometric coordinate

ABSCOND *v* **-ED, -ING, -S** to depart suddenly and secretly

ABSEIL *v* **-ED, -ING, -S** to rappel

ABSEILER *n* **-S** one that abseils

ABSENCE *n* pl. **-S** the state of being away

ABSENT *v* **-ED, -ING, -S** to take or keep away

ABSENTEE *n* pl. **-S** one that is not present

ABSENTER *n* pl. **-S** an absentee

ABSENTLY *adv* in an inattentive manner

ABSINTH *n* pl. **-S** absinthe

ABSINTHE *n* pl. **-S** a bitter liqueur

ABSOLUTE *adj* **-LUTER, -LUTEST** free from restriction

ABSOLUTE *n* pl. **-S** something that is absolute

ABSOLVE *v* **-SOLVED, -SOLVING, -SOLVES** to free from the consequences of an action

ABSOLVER *n* pl. **-S** one that absolves

ABSONANT *adj* unreasonable

ABSORB *v* **-ED, -ING, -S** to take up or in

ABSORBER *n* pl. **-S** one that absorbs

ABSTAIN *v* **-ED, -ING, -S** to refrain voluntarily

ABSTERGE *v* **-STERGED, -STERGING, -STERGES** to cleanse by wiping

ABSTRACT *adj* **-STRACTER, -STRACTEST** difficult to understand

ABSTRACT *v* **-ED, -ING, -S** to take away

ABSTRICT *v* **-ED, -ING, -S** to form by cutting off

ABSTRUSE *adj* **-STRUSER, -STRUSEST** difficult to understand

ABSURD *adj* **-SURDER, -SURDEST** ridiculously incongruous or unreasonable **ABSURDLY** *adv*

ABSURD *n* pl. **-S** the condition in which man exists in an irrational and meaningless universe

ABUBBLE *adj* bubbling

ABULIA *n* pl. **-S** loss of willpower **ABULIC** *adj*

ABUNDANT *adj* present in great quantity

ABUSE *v* **ABUSED, ABUSING, ABUSES** to use wrongly or improperly **ABUSABLE** *adj*

ABUSER *n* pl. **-S** one that abuses

ABUSIVE *adj* characterized by wrong or improper use

ABUT *v* **ABUTTED, ABUTTING, ABUTS** to touch along a border

ABUTILON *n* pl. **-S** a flowering plant

ABUTMENT *n* pl. **-S** something that abuts

ABUTTAL *n* pl. **-S** an abutment

ABUTTED past tense of abut

ABUTTER *n* pl. **-S** one that abuts

ABUTTING present participle of abut

ABUZZ *adj* buzzing

ABVOLT *n* pl. **-S** a unit of electromotive force

ABWATT *n* pl. **-S** a unit of power

ABY *v* **ABOUGHT, ABYING, ABYS** to pay the penalty for

ABYE *v* **ABOUGHT, ABYING, ABYES** to aby

ABYSM *n* pl. **-S** an abyss

ABYSMAL *adj* immeasurably deep

ABYSS *n* pl. **-ES** a bottomless chasm **ABYSSAL** *adj*

ACACIA *n* pl. **-S** a flowering tree or shrub

ACADEME *n* pl. **-S** a place of instruction

ACADEMIA *n* pl. **-S** scholastic life or environment

ACADEMIC *n* pl. **-S** a college student or teacher

ACADEMY *n* pl. **-MIES** a secondary school

ACAI *n* pl. **-S** a purple berrylike fruit of a tropical palm

ACAJOU *n* pl. **-S** a tropical tree

ACALEPH *n* pl. **-LEPHS** or **-LEPHAE** a jellyfish

ACALEPHE *n* pl. **-S** acaleph

ACANTHA *n* pl. **-THAE** a sharp spiny part

ACANTHUS *n* pl. **-THUSES** or **-THI** a prickly herb

ACAPNIA *n* pl. **-S** a lack of carbon dioxide in blood and tissues

ACARBOSE *n* pl. **-S** a drug for treating diabetes

ACARI pl. of acarus

ACARID *n* pl. **-S** a type of arachnid

ACARIDAN *n* pl. **-S** acarid

ACARINE *n* pl. **-S** acarid

ACAROID *adj* resembling an acarid

ACARPOUS *adj* not producing fruit

ACARUS *n* pl. **-RI** a mite

ACAUDAL *adj* having no tail

ACAUDATE *adj* acaudal

ACAULINE *adj* having no stem

ACAULOSE *adj* acauline

ACAULOUS *adj* acauline

ACCEDE *v* **-CEDED, -CEDING, -CEDES** to consent

ACCEDER *n* pl. **-S** one that accedes

ACCENT *v* **-ED, -ING, -S** to pronounce with prominence

ACCENTOR *n* pl. **-S** a songbird

ACCEPT *v* **-ED, -ING, -S** to receive willingly

ACCEPTEE *n* pl. **-S** one that is accepted

ACCEPTER *n* pl. **-S** one that accepts

ACCEPTOR *n* pl. **-S** accepter

ACCESS *v* **-ED, -ING, -ES** to get at

ACCIDENT *n* pl. **-S** an unexpected or unintentional occurrence

ACCIDIA *n* pl. **-S** acedia

ACCIDIE *n* pl. **-S** acedia

ACCLAIM *v* **-ED, -ING, -S** to shout approval of

ACCOLADE *v* **-LADED, -LADING, -LADES** to praise

ACCORD *v* **-ED, -ING, -S** to bring into agreement

ACCORDER *n* pl. **-S** one that accords

ACCOST *v* **-ED, -ING, -S** to approach and speak to first

ACCOUNT *v* **-ED, -ING, -S** to give an explanation

ACCOUTER *v* **-ED, -ING, -S** to equip

ACCOUTRE *v* **-TRED, -TRING, -TRES** to accouter

ACCREDIT *v* **-ED, -ING, -S** to give official authorization to

ACCRETE *v* **-CRETED, -CRETING, -CRETES** to grow together

ACCRUAL *n* pl. **-S** the act of accruing

ACCRUE *v* **-CRUED, -CRUING, -CRUES** to come as an increase or addition

ACCURACY *n* pl. **-CIES** the quality of being accurate

ACCURATE *adj* free from error

ACCURSED *adj* damnable

ACCURST *adj* accursed

ACCUSAL *n* pl. **-S** the act of accusing

ACCUSANT *n* pl. **-S** an accuser

ACCUSE *v* **-CUSED, -CUSING, -CUSES** to make an assertion against

ACCUSER *n* pl. **-S** one that accuses

ACCUSTOM *v* **-ED, -ING, -S** to make familiar

ACE *v* **ACED, ACING, ACES** to score a point against in a single stroke

ACEDIA *n* pl. **-S** apathy

ACELDAMA *n* pl. **-S** a place of bloodshed

ACENTRIC *adj* having no center

ACEQUIA	*n* pl. **-S** an irrigation ditch or canal
ACERATE	*adj* acerose
ACERATED	*adj* acerose
ACERB	*adj* **ACERBER, ACERBEST** sour
ACERBATE	*v* **-BATED, -BATING, -BATES** to make sour
ACERBIC	*adj* acerb
ACERBITY	*n* pl. **-TIES** sourness
ACEROLA	*n* pl. **-S** a West Indian shrub
ACEROSE	*adj* needle-shaped
ACEROUS	*adj* acerose
ACERVATE	*adj* growing in compact clusters
ACERVULI	*n/pl* spore-producing organs of certain fungi
ACESCENT	*n* pl. **-S** something that is slightly sour
ACETA	pl. of acetum
ACETAL	*n* pl. **-S** a flammable liquid
ACETAMID	*n* pl. **-S** an amide of acetic acid
ACETATE	*n* pl. **-S** a salt of acetic acid **ACETATED** *adj*
ACETIC	*adj* pertaining to vinegar
ACETIFY	*v* **-FIED, -FYING, -FIES** to convert into vinegar
ACETIN	*n* pl. **-S** a chemical compound
ACETONE	*n* pl. **-S** a flammable liquid **ACETONIC** *adj*
ACETOSE	*adj* acetous
ACETOUS	*adj* tasting like vinegar
ACETOXYL	*n* pl. **-S** a univalent radical
ACETUM	*n* pl. **-TA** vinegar
ACETYL	*n* pl. **-S** a univalent radical **ACETYLIC** *adj*
ACHE	*v* **ACHED, ACHING, ACHES** to suffer a dull, continuous pain
ACHENE	*n* pl. **-S** a type of fruit **ACHENIAL** *adj*
ACHIER	comparative of achy
ACHIEST	superlative of achy
ACHIEVE	*v* **ACHIEVED, ACHIEVING, ACHIEVES** to carry out successfully
ACHIEVER	*n* pl. **-S** one that achieves
ACHILLEA	*n* pl. **-S** yarrow
ACHINESS	*n* pl. **-ES** the state of being achy
ACHING	present participle of ache
ACHINGLY	*adv* in an aching manner
ACHIOTE	*n* pl. **-S** a yellowish red dye
ACHIRAL	*adj* pertaining to a symmetrical molecule
ACHOLIA	*n* pl. **-S** a lack of bile
ACHOO	*interj* ahchoo
ACHROMAT	*n* pl. **-S** a type of lens
ACHROMIC	*adj* having no color
ACHY	*adj* **ACHIER, ACHIEST** aching
ACICULA	*n* pl. **-LAS** or **-LAE** a needlelike part or process **ACICULAR** *adj*
ACICULUM	*n* pl. **-LUMS** or **-LA** a bristlelike part
ACID	*n* pl. **-S** a type of chemical compound
ACIDEMIA	*n* pl. **-S** a condition of increased acidity of the blood
ACIDHEAD	*n* pl. **-S** one who uses LSD
ACIDIC	*adj* sour
ACIDIFY	*v* **-FIED, -FYING, -FIES** to convert into an acid
ACIDITY	*n* pl. **-TIES** sourness
ACIDLY	*adv* sourly
ACIDNESS	*n* pl. **-ES** acidity
ACIDOSIS	*n* pl. **-DOSES** an abnormal condition of the blood **ACIDOTIC** *adj*
ACIDURIA	*n* pl. **-S** a condition of having excessive amounts of acid in the urine
ACIDY	*adj* sour
ACIERATE	*v* **-ATED, -ATING, -ATES** to turn into steel
ACIFORM	*adj* needle-shaped
ACING	present participle of ace
ACINUS	*n* pl. **-NI** a small, saclike division of a gland **ACINAR, ACINIC, ACINOSE, ACINOUS** *adj*
ACKEE	*n* pl. **-S** akee
ACLINIC	*adj* having no inclination
ACME	*n* pl. **-S** the highest point **ACMATIC, ACMIC** *adj*
ACNE	*n* pl. **-S** a skin disease **ACNED** *adj*
ACNODE	*n* pl. **-S** an element of a mathematical set that is isolated from the other elements
ACOCK	*adj* cocked
ACOELOUS	*adj* lacking a true body cavity
ACOLD	*adj* cold
ACOLYTE	*n* pl. **-S** an assistant
ACONITE	*n* pl. **-S** a poisonous herb **ACONITIC** *adj*

ACONITUM *n* pl. **-S** aconite

ACORN *n* pl. **-S** the fruit of the oak tree **ACORNED** *adj*

ACOUSTIC *n* pl. **-S** a hearing aid

ACQUAINT *v* **-ED, -ING, -S** to cause to know

ACQUEST *n* pl. **-S** something acquired

ACQUIRE *v* **-QUIRED, -QUIRING, -QUIRES** to come into possession of

ACQUIREE *n* pl. **-S** one that is acquired

ACQUIRER *n* pl. **-S** one that acquires

ACQUIT *v* **-QUITTED, -QUITTING, -QUITS** to free or clear from a charge of fault or crime

ACRASIA *n* pl. **-S** a lack of self-control **ACRATIC** *adj*

ACRASIN *n* pl. **-S** a substance secreted by the cells of a slime mold

ACRE *n* pl. **-S** a unit of area

ACREAGE *n* pl. **-S** area in acres

ACRED *adj* owning many acres

ACRID *adj* **-RIDER, -RIDEST** sharp and harsh to the taste or smell

ACRIDINE *n* pl. **-S** a chemical compound

ACRIDITY *n* pl. **-TIES** the state of being acrid

ACRIDLY *adv* in an acrid manner

ACRIMONY *n* pl. **-NIES** sharpness or bitterness of speech or temper

ACRO *n* pl. **ACROS** a skiing event in which a skier performs acrobatic moves to music

ACROBAT *n* pl. **-S** one skilled in feats of agility and balance

ACRODONT *n* pl. **-S** an animal having rootless teeth

ACROGEN *n* pl. **-S** a plant growing at the apex only

ACROLECT *n* pl. **-S** a high form of a language

ACROLEIN *n* pl. **-S** a flammable liquid

ACROLITH *n* pl. **-S** a type of statue

ACROMION *n* pl. **-MIA** the outward end of the shoulder blade **ACROMIAL** *adj*

ACRONIC *adj* occurring at sunset

ACRONYM *n* pl. **-S** a word formed from the initials of a compound term or series of words

ACROSOME *n* pl. **-S** a thin sac at the head of a sperm

ACROSS *prep* from one side of to the other

ACROSTIC *n* pl. **-S** a poem in which certain letters taken in order form a word or phrase

ACROTISM *n* pl. **-S** weakness of the pulse **ACROTIC** *adj*

ACRYLATE *n* pl. **-S** an acrylic

ACRYLIC *n* pl. **-S** a type of resin

ACT *v* **-ED, -ING, -S** to do something

ACTA *n/pl* recorded proceedings

ACTABLE *adj* suitable for performance on the stage

ACTIN *n* pl. **-S** a protein in muscle tissue

ACTINAL *adj* having tentacles

ACTING *n* pl. **-S** the occupation of an actor

ACTINIA *n* pl. **-IAS** or **-IAE** a marine animal

ACTINIAN *n* pl. **-S** actinia

ACTINIC *adj* pertaining to actinism

ACTINIDE *n* pl. **-S** any of a series of radioactive elements

ACTINISM *n* pl. **-S** the property of radiant energy that effects chemical changes

ACTINIUM *n* pl. **-S** a radioactive element

ACTINOID *n* pl. **-S** an actinide

ACTINON *n* pl. **-S** an isotope of radon

ACTION *v* **-ED, -ING, -S** to bring a lawsuit against

ACTIONER *n* pl. **-S** a film with exciting action

ACTIVATE *v* **-VATED, -VATING, -VATES** to set in motion

ACTIVE *n* pl. **-S** a participating member of an organization

ACTIVELY *adv* with activity

ACTIVISM *n* pl. **-S** a doctrine that emphasizes direct and decisive action

ACTIVIST *n* pl. **-S** an advocate of activism

ACTIVITY *n* pl. **-TIES** brisk action or movement

ACTIVIZE *v* **-IZED, -IZING, -IZES** to activate

ACTOR *n* pl. **-S** a theatrical performer **ACTORISH, ACTORLY** *adj*

ACTRESS *n* pl. **-ES** a female actor **ACTRESSY** *adj*

ACTUAL *adj* existing in fact **ACTUALLY** *adv*

ACTUARY *n* pl. **-ARIES** a statistician who computes insurance risks and premiums

ACTUATE *v* **-ATED, -ATING, -ATES** to set into action or motion

ACTUATOR *n* pl. **-S** one that actuates

ACUATE — *adj* sharp

ACUITY — *n* pl. **-ITIES** sharpness

ACULEATE — *n* pl. **-S** a stinging insect

ACULEUS — *n* pl. **-LEI** a sharp-pointed part

ACUMEN — *n* pl. **-S** mental keenness

ACUTANCE — *n* pl. **-S** a measure of photographic clarity

ACUTE — *adj* **ACUTER, ACUTEST** marked by sharpness or severity **ACUTELY** *adv*

ACUTE — *n* pl. **-S** a type of accent mark

ACYCLIC — *adj* not cyclic

ACYL — *n* pl. **-S** a univalent radical

ACYLATE — *v* **-ATED, -ATING, -ATES** to introduce acyl into

ACYLOIN — *n* pl. **-S** a type of chemical compound

AD — *n* pl. **-S** an advertisement

ADAGE — *n* pl. **-S** a traditional saying expressing a common observation **ADAGIAL** *adj*

ADAGIO — *n* pl. **-GIOS** a musical composition or movement played in a slow tempo

ADAMANCE — *n* pl. **-S** adamancy

ADAMANCY — *n* pl. **-CIES** unyielding hardness

ADAMANT — *n* pl. **-S** an extremely hard substance

ADAMSITE — *n* pl. **-S** a lung-irritating gas

ADAPT — *v* **-ED, -ING, -S** to make suitable

ADAPTER — *n* pl. **-S** one that adapts

ADAPTION — *n* pl. **-S** the act of adapting **ADAPTIVE** *adj*

ADAPTOR — *n* pl. **-S** adapter

ADAXIAL — *adj* situated on the same side as

ADBOT — *n* pl. **-S** a specialized computer program

ADD — *v* **-ED, -ING, -S** to combine or join so as to bring about an increase **ADDABLE** *adj*

ADDAX — *n* pl. **-ES** a large antelope

ADDEDLY — *adv* additionally

ADDEND — *n* pl. **-S** a number to be added to another

ADDENDUM — *n* pl. **-DUMS** or **-DA** something added or to be added

ADDER — *n* pl. **-S** a venomous snake

ADDIBLE — *adj* capable of being added

ADDICT — *v* **-ED, -ING, -S** to devote or surrender to something habitually or compulsively

ADDITION — *n* pl. **-S** something added

ADDITIVE — *n* pl. **-S** a substance added to another to impart desirable qualities

ADDITORY — *adj* making an addition

ADDLE — *v* **-DLED, -DLING, -DLES** to confuse

ADDRESS — *v* **-DRESSED** or **-DREST, -DRESSING, -DRESSES** to speak to

ADDUCE — *v* **-DUCED, -DUCING, -DUCES** to bring forward as evidence

ADDUCENT — *adj* serving to adduct

ADDUCER — *n* pl. **-S** one that adduces

ADDUCING — present participle of adduce

ADDUCT — *v* **-ED, -ING, -S** to draw toward the main axis

ADDUCTOR — *n* pl. **-S** an adducent muscle

ADEEM — *v* **-ED, -ING, -S** to take away

ADELGID — *n* pl. **-S** a small insect

ADENINE — *n* pl. **-S** an alkaloid

ADENITIS — *n* pl. **-TISES** inflammation of a lymph node

ADENOID — *n* pl. **-S** an enlarged lymphoid growth behind the pharynx

ADENOMA — *n* pl. **-MAS** or **-MATA** a tumor of glandular origin

ADENOSIS — *n* pl. **-NOSES** abnormal growth of glandular tissue

ADENYL — *n* pl. **-S** a univalent radical

ADEPT — *adj* **ADEPTER, ADEPTEST** highly skilled **ADEPTLY** *adv*

ADEPT — *n* pl. **-S** an adept person

ADEQUACY — *n* pl. **-CIES** the state of being adequate

ADEQUATE — *adj* sufficient for a specific requirement

ADHERE — *v* **-HERED, -HERING, -HERES** to become or remain attached or close to something

ADHEREND — *n* pl. **-S** the surface to which an adhesive adheres

ADHERENT — *n* pl. **-S** a supporter

ADHERER — *n* pl. **-S** one that adheres

ADHERING — present participle of adhere

ADHESION — *n* pl. **-S** the act of adhering

ADHESIVE — *n* pl. **-S** a substance that causes adhesion

ADHIBIT *v* **-ED, -ING, -S** to take or let in

ADIEU *n* pl. **ADIEUS** or **ADIEUX** a farewell

ADIOS *n* pl. **-OSES** goodbye

ADIPOSE *n* pl. **-S** animal fat **ADIPIC** *adj*

ADIPOSIS *n* pl. **-POSES** obesity

ADIPOUS *adj* pertaining to adipose

ADIT *n* pl. **-S** an entrance

ADJACENT *adj* next to

ADJOIN *v* **-ED, -ING, -S** to lie next to

ADJOINT *n* pl. **-S** a type of mathematical matrix

ADJOURN *v* **-ED, -ING, -S** to suspend until a later time

ADJUDGE *v* **-JUDGED, -JUDGING, -JUDGES** to determine judicially

ADJUNCT *n* pl. **-S** something attached in a subordinate position

ADJURE *v* **-JURED, -JURING, -JURES** to command solemnly

ADJURER *n* pl. **-S** one that adjures

ADJUROR *n* pl. **-S** adjurer

ADJUST *v* **-ED, -ING, -S** to bring to a more satisfactory state

ADJUSTER *n* pl. **-S** one that adjusts

ADJUSTOR *n* pl. **-S** adjuster

ADJUTANT *n* pl. **-S** an assistant

ADJUVANT *n* pl. **-S** an assistant

ADLAND *n* pl. **-S** the world of advertising

ADMAN *n* pl. **-MEN** a man employed in the advertising business

ADMASS *n* pl. **-ES** mass-media advertising

ADMIN *n* pl. **-S** an administration

ADMIRAL *n* pl. **-S** a high-ranking naval officer

ADMIRE *v* **-MIRED, -MIRING, -MIRES** to regard with wonder, pleasure, and approval

ADMIRER *n* pl. **-S** one that admires

ADMIT *v* **-MITTED, -MITTING, -MITS** to allow to enter

ADMITTEE *n* pl. **-S** one that is admitted

ADMITTER *n* pl. **-S** one that admits

ADMIX *v* **-MIXED** or **-MIXT, -MIXING, -MIXES** to mix

ADMONISH *v* **-ED, -ING, -ES** to reprove mildly or kindly

ADNATE *adj* joined to another part or organ

ADNATION *n* pl. **-S** the state of being adnate

ADNEXA *n/pl* conjoined anatomical parts **ADNEXAL** *adj*

ADNOUN *n* pl. **-S** an adjective when used as a noun

ADO *n* pl. **ADOS** bustling excitement

ADOBE *n* pl. **-S** an unburnt, sun-dried brick

ADOBO *n* pl. **-BOS** a Philippine dish of fish or meat

ADONIS *n* pl. **-ISES** a handsome young man

ADOPT *v* **-ED, -ING, -S** to take into one's family by legal means

ADOPTEE *n* pl. **-S** one that is adopted

ADOPTER *n* pl. **-S** one that adopts

ADOPTION *n* pl. **-S** the act of adopting **ADOPTIVE** *adj*

ADORABLE *adj* worthy of being adored **ADORABLY** *adv*

ADORE *v* **ADORED, ADORING, ADORES** to love deeply

ADORER *n* pl. **-S** one that adores

ADORN *v* **-ED, -ING, -S** to add something to for the purpose of making more attractive

ADORNER *n* pl. **-S** one that adorns

ADOWN *adv* downward

ADOZE *adj* dozing

ADRENAL *n* pl. **-S** an endocrine gland

ADRIFT *adj* drifting

ADROIT *adj* **ADROITER, ADROITEST** skillful **ADROITLY** *adv*

ADSCRIPT *n* pl. **-S** a distinguishing symbol written after another character

ADSORB *v* **-ED, -ING, -S** to gather on a surface in a condensed layer

ADSORBER *n* pl. **-S** one that adsorbs

ADSUKI *n* pl. **-S** adzuki

ADULARIA *n* pl. **-S** a mineral

ADULATE *v* **-LATED, -LATING, -LATES** to praise excessively

ADULATOR *n* pl. **-S** one that adulates

ADULT *n* pl. **-S** a fully developed individual

ADULTERY *n* pl. **-TERIES** voluntary sexual intercourse between a married person and someone other than his or her spouse

ADULTLY *adv* in a manner typical of an adult

ADUMBRAL *adj* shadowy

ADUNC *adj* bent inward

ADUNCATE *adj* adunc

ADUNCOUS   *adj* adunc

ADUST   *adj* scorched

ADVANCE   *v* **-VANCED, -VANCING, -VANCES** to move or cause to move ahead

ADVANCER   *n* pl. **-S** one that advances

ADVECT   *v* **-ED, -ING, -S** to convey or transport by the flow of a fluid

ADVENT   *n* pl. **-S** arrival

ADVERB   *n* pl. **-S** a word used to modify a verb, adjective, or other adverb

ADVERSE   *adj* acting in opposition

ADVERT   *v* **-ED, -ING, -S** to call attention

ADVICE   *n* pl. **-S** recommendation regarding a decision or action

ADVISE   *v* **-VISED, -VISING, -VISES** to give advice to

ADVISEE   *n* pl. **-S** one that is advised

ADVISER   *n* pl. **-S** one that advises

ADVISING   present participle of advise

ADVISOR   *n* pl. **-S** adviser

ADVISORY   *n* pl. **-RIES** a report giving information

ADVOCAAT   *n* pl. **-S** a liqueur consisting of brandy, sugar, and eggs

ADVOCACY   *n* pl. **-CIES** the act of advocating

ADVOCATE   *v* **-CATED, -CATING, -CATES** to speak in favor of

ADVOWSON   *n* pl. **-S** the right of presenting a nominee to a vacant church office

ADWARE   *n* pl. **-S** computer software that is provided free but has advertisements

ADWOMAN   *n* pl. **-MEN** a woman employed in the advertising business

ADYNAMIA   *n* pl. **-S** lack of physical strength **ADYNAMIC** *adj*

ADYTUM   *n* pl. **-TA** an inner sanctuary in an ancient temple

ADZ   *v* **-ED, -ING, -ES** to shape (wood) with an adz (a cutting tool)

ADZE   *v* **ADZED, ADZING, ADZES** to adz

ADZUKI   *n* pl. **-S** the edible seed of an Asian plant

AE   *adj* one

AECIA   pl. of aecium

AECIAL   *adj* pertaining to an aecium

AECIDIAL   *adj* pertaining to an aecium

AECIDIUM   *n* pl. **-IA** an aecium

AECIUM   *n* pl. **-IA** a spore-producing organ of certain fungi

AEDES   *n* pl. **AEDES** any of a genus of mosquitoes

AEDILE   *n* pl. **-S** a magistrate of ancient Rome

AEDINE   *adj* pertaining to an aedes

AEGIS   *n* pl. **-GISES** protection

AEGROTAT   *n* pl. **-S** a certificate excusing an ill student from an examination

AENEOUS   *adj* having a greenish gold color

AENEUS   *adj* aeneous

AEOLIAN   *adj* eolian

AEON   *n* pl. **-S** eon

AEONIAN   *adj* eonian

AEONIC   *adj* eonian

AEQUORIN   *n* pl. **-S** a protein secreted by jellyfish

AERADIO   *n* pl. **-DIOS** a Canadian radio service for pilots

AERATE   *v* **-ATED, -ATING, -ATES** to supply with air

AERATION   *n* pl. **-S** the act of aerating

AERATOR   *n* pl. **-S** one that aerates

AERIAL   *n* pl. **-S** an antenna

AERIALLY   *adv* in a manner pertaining to the air

AERIE   *n* pl. **-S** a bird's nest built high on a mountain or cliff **AERIED** *adj*

AERIER   comparative of aery

AERIES   pl. of aery

AERIEST   superlative of aery

AERIFORM   *adj* having the form of air

AERIFY   *v* **-FIED, -FYING, -FIES** to aerate

AERILY   *adv* in an aery manner

AERO   *adj* pertaining to aircraft

AEROBAT   *n* pl. **-S** one that performs feats in an aircraft

AEROBE   *n* pl. **-S** an organism that requires oxygen to live **AEROBIC** *adj*

AEROBICS   *n/pl* exercises for conditioning the heart and lungs by increasing oxygen consumption

AEROBIUM   *n* pl. **-BIA** aerobe

AERODUCT   *n* pl. **-S** a type of jet engine

AERODYNE   *n* pl. **-S** an aircraft that is heavier than air

AEROFOIL   *n* pl. **-S** airfoil

AEROGEL   *n* pl. **-S** a highly porous solid

AEROGRAM	*n* pl. **-S** an airmail letter
AEROLITE	*n* pl. **-S** a meteorite containing more stone than iron
AEROLITH	*n* pl. **-S** aerolite
AEROLOGY	*n* pl. **-GIES** the study of the atmosphere
AERONAUT	*n* pl. **-S** one who operates an airship
AERONOMY	*n* pl. **-MIES** the study of the upper atmosphere
AEROSAT	*n* pl. **-S** a satellite for use in air traffic control
AEROSOL	*n* pl. **-S** a gaseous suspension of fine solid or liquid particles
AEROSTAT	*n* pl. **-S** an aircraft that is lighter than air
AERUGO	*n* pl. **-GOS** a green film that forms on copper
AERY	*adj* **AERIER, AERIEST** airy
AERY	*n* pl. **AERIES** aerie
AESTHETE	*n* pl. **-S** esthete
AESTIVAL	*adj* estival
AETATIS	*adj* of the age of
AETHER	*n* pl. **-S** the upper region of the atmosphere **AETHERIC** *adj*
AFAR	*n* pl. **-S** a great distance
AFEARD	*adj* afraid
AFEARED	*adj* afeard
AFEBRILE	*adj* having no fever
AFF	*adv* off
AFFABLE	*adj* easy to talk to **AFFABLY** *adv*
AFFAIR	*n* pl. **-S** anything done or to be done
AFFAIRE	*n* pl. **-S** a brief amorous relationship
AFFECT	*v* **-ED, -ING, -S** to give a false appearance of
AFFECTER	*n* pl. **-S** one that affects
AFFERENT	*n* pl. **-S** a nerve that conveys impulses toward a nerve center
AFFIANCE	*v* **-ANCED, -ANCING, -ANCES** to betroth
AFFIANT	*n* pl. **-S** one who makes a written declaration under oath
AFFICHE	*n* pl. **-S** a poster
AFFINAL	*adj* related by marriage
AFFINE	*n* pl. **-S** a relative by marriage
AFFINED	*adj* closely related
AFFINELY	*adv* in the manner of a type of mathematical mapping
AFFINITY	*n* pl. **-TIES** a natural attraction or inclination
AFFIRM	*v* **-ED, -ING, -S** to state positively
AFFIRMER	*n* pl. **-S** one that affirms
AFFIX	*v* **-ED, -ING, -ES** to attach
AFFIXAL	*adj* pertaining to a prefix or suffix
AFFIXER	*n* pl. **-S** one that affixes
AFFIXIAL	*adj* affixal
AFFLATUS	*n* pl. **-ES** a creative inspiration
AFFLICT	*v* **-ED, -ING, -S** to distress with mental or physical pain
AFFLUENT	*n* pl. **-S** a stream that flows into another
AFFLUX	*n* pl. **-ES** a flowing toward a point
AFFORD	*v* **-ED, -ING, -S** to have sufficient means for
AFFOREST	*v* **-ED, -ING, -S** to convert into forest
AFFRAY	*v* **-ED, -ING, -S** to frighten
AFFRAYER	*n* pl. **-S** one that affrays
AFFRIGHT	*v* **-ED, -ING, -S** to frighten
AFFRONT	*v* **-ED, -ING, -S** to insult openly
AFFUSION	*n* pl. **-S** an act of pouring a liquid on
AFGHAN	*n* pl. **-S** a woolen blanket or shawl
AFGHANI	*n* pl. **-S** a monetary unit of Afghanistan
AFIELD	*adv* in the field
AFIRE	*adj* being on fire
AFLAME	*adj* flaming
AFLOAT	*adj* floating
AFLUTTER	*adj* nervously excited
AFOOT	*adv* on foot
AFORE	*adv* before
AFOUL	*adj* entangled
AFRAID	*adj* filled with apprehension
AFREET	*n* pl. **-S** an evil spirit in Arabic mythology
AFRESH	*adv* anew
AFRIT	*n* pl. **-S** afreet
AFRO	*n* pl. **AFROS** a curly or frizzy hairstyle
AFT	*adv* toward the stern
AFTER	*prep* behind in place or order
AFTERS	*n/pl* dessert

AFTERTAX *adj* remaining after payment of taxes

AFTMOST *adj* nearest the stern

AFTOSA *n* pl. **-S** a disease of hoofed mammals

AG *n* pl. **-S** agriculture

AGA *n* pl. **-S** a high-ranking Turkish military officer

AGAIN *adv* once more

AGAINST *prep* in opposition to

AGALLOCH *n* pl. **-S** the fragrant wood of a tropical tree

AGALWOOD *n* pl. **-S** agalloch

AGAMA *n* pl. **-S** a tropical lizard

AGAMETE *n* pl. **-S** an asexual reproductive cell

AGAMIC *adj* asexual

AGAMID *n* pl. **-S** an Old World lizard

AGAMOUS *adj* agamic

AGAPE *n* pl. **-PES** or **-PAE** or **-PAI** a communal meal of fellowship **AGAPEIC** *adj*

AGAR *n* pl. **-S** a viscous substance obtained from certain seaweeds

AGARIC *n* pl. **-S** any of a family of fungi

AGAROSE *n* pl. **-S** a sugar obtained from agar

AGATE *n* pl. **-S** a variety of quartz **AGATOID** *adj*

AGATIZE *v* **-IZED, -IZING, -IZES** to cause to resemble agate

AGAVE *n* pl. **-S** a tropical plant

AGAZE *adj* gazing

AGE *v* **AGED, AGING** or **AGEING, AGES** to grow old

AGEDLY *adv* in the manner of an old person

AGEDNESS *n* pl. **-ES** oldness

AGEE *adv* to one side

AGEING *n* pl. **-S** aging

AGEISM *n* pl. **-S** discrimination based on age

AGEIST *n* pl. **-S** an advocate of ageism

AGELESS *adj* never growing old

AGELONG *adj* lasting for a long time

AGEMATE *n* pl. **-S** a person of the same age as another

AGENCY *n* pl. **-CIES** an organization that does business for others

AGENDA *n* pl. **-S** a list of things to be done

AGENDUM *n* pl. **-S** an item on an agenda

AGENE *n* pl. **-S** a chemical compound used in bleaching flour

AGENESIA *n* pl. **-S** agenesis

AGENESIS *n* pl. **AGENESES** absence or imperfect development of a bodily part **AGENETIC** *adj*

AGENIZE *v* **-NIZED, -NIZING, -NIZES** to treat with agene

AGENT *v* **-ED, -ING, -S** to act as a representative for **AGENTIAL** *adj*

AGENTING *n* pl. **-S** the business or activities of an agent

AGENTIVE *n* pl. **-S** a word part that denotes the doer of an action

AGENTRY *n* pl. **-RIES** the office or duties of an agent

AGER *n* pl. **-S** one that ages

AGERATUM *n* pl. **-S** a flowering plant

AGGADA *n* pl. **-DAS** or **-DOT** or **-DOTH** haggadah

AGGADAH *n* pl. **-DAHS** or **-DOT** or **-DOTH** haggadah

AGGADIC *adj* haggadic

AGGER *n* pl. **-S** a mound of earth used as a fortification

AGGIE *n* pl. **-S** a type of playing marble

AGGRADE *v* **-GRADED, -GRADING, -GRADES** to fill with detrital material

AGGRESS *v* **-ED, -ING, -ES** to commit the first act of hostility

AGGRIEVE *v* **-GRIEVED, -GRIEVING, -GRIEVES** to distress

AGGRO *n* pl. **-GROS** a rivalry or grievance

AGHA *n* pl. **-S** aga

AGHAST *adj* shocked by something horrible

AGILE *adj* able to move quickly and easily **AGILELY** *adv*

AGILITY *n* pl. **-TIES** the quality of being agile

AGIN *prep* against

AGING *n* pl. **-S** the process of growing old

AGINNER *n* pl. **-S** one that is against change

AGIO *n* pl. **AGIOS** a premium paid for the exchange of one currency for another

AGIOTAGE *n* pl. **-S** the business of a broker

AGISM *n* pl. **-S** ageism

AGIST *v* **-ED, -ING, -S** to feed and take care of for a fee, as livestock

AGITA *n* pl. **-S** a feeling of agitation

AGITATE *v* **-TATED, -TATING, -TATES** to move with a violent, irregular action **AGITABLE** *adj*

AGITATO *adj* fast and stirring — used as a musical direction

AGITATOR *n* pl. **-S** one that agitates

AGITPROP *n* pl. **-S** pro-Communist propaganda

AGLARE *adj* glaring

AGLEAM *adj* gleaming

AGLEE *adv* agley

AGLET *n* pl. **-S** a metal sheath at the end of a lace

AGLEY *adv* awry

AGLIMMER *adj* glimmering

AGLITTER *adj* glittering

AGLOO *n* pl. **AGLOOS** an air hole through the ice made by a seal

AGLOW *adj* glowing

AGLU *n* pl. **-S** agloo

AGLY *adv* agley

AGLYCON *n* pl. **-S** a type of chemical compound

AGLYCONE *n* pl. **-S** aglycon

AGMA *n* pl. **-S** eng

AGMINATE *adj* clustered together

AGNAIL *n* pl. **-S** a piece of loose skin at the base of a fingernail

AGNATE *n* pl. **-S** a relative on the father's side **AGNATIC** *adj*

AGNATHAN *n* pl. **-S** one of a group of jawless vertebrates

AGNATION *n* pl. **-S** the relationship of agnates

AGNIZE *v* **-NIZED, -NIZING, -NIZES** to acknowledge

AGNOMEN *n* pl. **-MENS** or **-MINA** an additional name given to an ancient Roman

AGNOSIA *n* pl. **-S** loss of ability to recognize familiar objects

AGNOSTIC *n* pl. **-S** one who disclaims any knowledge of God

AGO *adv* in the past

AGOG *adv* in a state of eager curiosity

AGON *n* pl. **-S** or **-ES** the dramatic conflict between the main characters in a Greek play

AGONAL *adj* pertaining to agony

AGONE *adv* ago

AGONIC *adj* not forming an angle

AGONIES pl. of agony

AGONISE *v* **-NISED, -NISING, -NISES** to agonize

AGONISM *n* pl. **-S** a contest or struggle

AGONIST *n* pl. **-S** one that is engaged in a struggle

AGONIZE *v* **-NIZED, -NIZING, -NIZES** to suffer extreme pain

AGONY *n* pl. **-NIES** extreme pain

AGORA *n* pl. **-RAS** or **-RAE** a marketplace in ancient Greece

AGORA *n* pl. **AGOROT** or **AGOROTH** a monetary unit of Israel

AGOUTI *n* pl. **-S** or **-ES** a burrowing rodent

AGOUTY *n* pl. **-TIES** agouti

AGRAFE *n* pl. **-S** agraffe

AGRAFFE *n* pl. **-S** an ornamental clasp

AGRAPHA *n/pl* the sayings of Jesus not found in the Bible

AGRAPHIA *n* pl. **-S** a mental disorder marked by inability to write **AGRAPHIC** *adj*

AGRARIAN *n* pl. **-S** one who favors equal distribution of land

AGRAVIC *adj* pertaining to a condition of no gravitation

AGREE *v* **AGREED, AGREEING, AGREES** to have the same opinion

AGRESTAL *adj* growing wild

AGRESTIC *adj* rural

AGRIA *n* pl. **-S** severe pustular eruption

AGRIMONY *n* pl. **-NIES** a perennial herb

AGRO *n* pl. **AGROS** a student of agricultural science

AGROLOGY *n* pl. **-GIES** the science of soils in relation to crops

AGRONOMY *n* pl. **-MIES** the application of scientific principles to the cultivation of land

AGROUND *adv* on the ground

AGRYPNIA *n* pl. **-S** insomnia

AGUACATE *n* pl. **-S** an avocado

AGUE *n* pl. **-S** a malarial fever **AGUED** *adj* **AGUELIKE, AGUISH** *adj* **AGUISHLY** *adv*

AGUEWEED *n* pl. **-S** a flowering plant

AGYRIA *n* pl. **-S** a disease of the brain

AH *v* **-ED, -ING, -S** aah

AHA *interj* — used to express surprise, triumph, or derision

AHCHOO *interj* — used to represent the sound of a sneeze

AHEAD *adv* at or to the front

AHEM *interj* — used to attract attention

AHI *n* pl. **-S** a marine food fish

AHIMSA *n* pl. **-S** the Hindu principle of nonviolence

AHOLD *n* pl. **-S** a hold or grasp of something

AHORSE *adv* on a horse

AHOY *interj* — used in hailing a ship or person

AHULL *adj* abandoned and flooded, as a ship

AI *n* pl. **-S** a three-toed sloth

AIBLINS *adv* ablins

AID *v* **-ED, -ING, -S** to help

AIDE *n* pl. **-S** an assistant

AIDER *n* pl. **-S** one that aids

AIDFUL *adj* helpful

AIDLESS *adj* helpless

AIDMAN *n* pl. **-MEN** a corpsman

AIGLET *n* pl. **-S** aglet

AIGRET *n* pl. **-S** aigrette

AIGRETTE *n* pl. **-S** a tuft of feathers worn as a head ornament

AIGUILLE *n* pl. **-S** a sharp, pointed mountain peak

AIKIDO *n* pl. **-DOS** a Japanese art of self-defense

AIL *v* **-ED, -ING, -S** to cause pain or discomfort to

AILERON *n* pl. **-S** a movable control surface on an airplane wing

AILMENT *n* pl. **-S** a physical or mental disorder

AIM *v* **-ED, -ING, -S** to direct toward a specified object or goal

AIMER *n* pl. **-S** one that aims

AIMFUL *adj* full of purpose **AIMFULLY** *adv*

AIMLESS *adj* lacking direction or purpose

AIN *n* pl. **-S** ayin

AINSELL *n* pl. **-S** own self

AIOLI *n* pl. **-S** garlic mayonnaise

AIR *adv* **AIRER, AIREST** early

AIR *v* **-ED, -ING, -S** to expose to the air (the mixture of gases that surrounds the earth)

AIRBAG *n* pl. **-S** an inflatable safety device in an automobile

AIRBALL *v* **-ED, -ING, -S** to miss the goal in basketball

AIRBASE *n* pl. **-S** a military base for aircraft

AIRBOAT *n* pl. **-S** a boat used in swampy areas

AIRBORNE *adj* flying

AIRBOUND *adj* stopped up by air

AIRBRUSH *v* **-ED, -ING, -ES** to apply in a fine spray by compressed air, as paint

AIRBURST *n* pl. **-S** an explosion in the air

AIRBUS *n* pl. **-BUSES** or **-BUSSES** a passenger airplane

AIRCHECK *n* pl. **-S** a recording made from a radio broadcast

AIRCOACH *n* pl. **-ES** the cheaper class of accommodations in commercial aircraft

AIRCRAFT *n* pl. **AIRCRAFT** any machine or device capable of flying

AIRCREW *n* pl. **-S** the crew of an aircraft

AIRDATE *n* pl. **-S** the scheduled date of a broadcast

AIRDROME *n* pl. **-S** an airport

AIRDROP *v* **-DROPPED, -DROPPING, -DROPS** to drop from an aircraft

AIRER *n* pl. **-S** a frame on which to dry clothes

AIRFARE *n* pl. **-S** payment for travel by airplane

AIRFIELD *n* pl. **-S** an airport

AIRFLOW *n* pl. **-S** a flow of air

AIRFOIL *n* pl. **-S** a part of an aircraft designed to provide lift or control

AIRFRAME *n* pl. **-S** the framework and external covering of an airplane

AIRGLOW *n* pl. **-S** a glow in the upper atmosphere

AIRHEAD *n* pl. **-S** a stupid person

AIRHOLE *n* pl. **-S** a hole to let air in or out

AIRIER comparative of airy

AIRIEST superlative of airy

AIRILY *adv* in an airy manner

AIRINESS *n* pl. **-ES** the state of being airy

AIRING *n* pl. **-S** an exposure to the air

AIRLESS *adj* having no air

AIRLIFT *v* **-ED, -ING, -S** to transport by airplane

AIRLIKE *adj* resembling air

AIRLINE *n* pl. **-S** an air transportation system

AIRLINER *n* pl. **-S** a large passenger aircraft

AIRLOCK *n* pl. **-S** a blockage in a pipe caused by an air bubble

AIRMAIL *v* **-ED, -ING, -S** to send mail by airplane

AIRMAN *n* pl. **-MEN** an aviator

AIRN *n* pl. **-S** iron (a mineral element)

AIRPARK *n* pl. **-S** a small airport

AIRPLANE *n* pl. **-S** a winged aircraft propelled by jet engines or propellers

AIRPLAY *n* pl. **-PLAYS** the playing of a record on a radio program

AIRPORT *n* pl. **-S** a tract of land maintained for the landing and takeoff of aircraft

AIRPOST *n* pl. **-S** a system of conveying mail by airplane

AIRPOWER *n* pl. **-S** the military strength of a nation's air force

AIRPROOF *v* **-ED, -ING, -S** to make impermeable to air

AIRSCAPE *n* pl. **-S** a view of the earth from an aircraft or a high position

AIRSCREW *n* pl. **-S** an airplane propeller

AIRSHED *n* pl. **-S** the air supply of a given region

AIRSHIP *n* pl. **-S** a lighter-than-air aircraft having propulsion and steering systems

AIRSHOT *n* pl. **-S** an aircheck

AIRSHOW *n* pl. **-S** an exhibition of aircraft stunts

AIRSICK *adj* nauseated from flying in an airplane

AIRSIDE *n* pl. **-S** the side of an airport terminal facing the aircraft

AIRSOME *adj* cold

AIRSPACE *n* pl. **-S** the portion of the atmosphere above a particular land area

AIRSPEED *n* pl. **-S** the speed of an aircraft with relation to the air

AIRSTRIP *n* pl. **-S** a runway

AIRT *v* **-ED, -ING, -S** to guide

AIRTH *v* **-ED, -ING, -S** to airt

AIRTIGHT *adj* not allowing air to escape or enter

AIRTIME *n* pl. **-S** the time when a broadcast begins

AIRTRAM *n* pl. **-S** an aerial cable car

AIRVAC *n* pl. **-S** evacuation by air ambulance

AIRWARD *adv* toward the sky

AIRWAVE *n* pl. **-S** the medium of radio and television transmission

AIRWAY *n* pl. **-WAYS** a passageway in which air circulates

AIRWISE *adj* skillful in aviation

AIRWOMAN *n* pl. **-WOMEN** a female aviator

AIRY *adj* **AIRIER, AIRIEST** having the nature of air

AISLE *n* pl. **-S** a passageway between sections of seats **AISLED** *adj*

AISLEWAY *n* pl. **-WAYS** an aisle

AIT *n* pl. **-S** a small island

AITCH *n* pl. **-ES** the letter H

AIVER *n* pl. **-S** a draft horse

AIYEE *interj* — used to express great alarm

AJAR *adj* partly open

AJEE *adv* agee

AJI *n* pl. **-ES** or **-S** a type of chili pepper

AJIVA *n* pl. **-S** inanimate matter

AJOWAN *n* pl. **-S** the fruit of an Egyptian plant

AJUGA *n* pl. **-S** a flowering plant

AKEBIA *n* pl. **-S** a climbing shrub

AKEE *n* pl. **-S** a tropical tree

AKELA *n* pl. **-S** a leader of a cub scout pack

AKENE *n* pl. **-S** achene

AKIMBO *adj* having hands on hips and elbows bent outward

AKIN *adj* related by blood

AKINESIA *n* pl. **-S** loss of muscle function **AKINETIC** *adj*

AKRASIA *n* pl. **-S** acrasia **AKRATIC** *adj*

AKVAVIT *n* pl. **-S** aquavit

AL *n* pl. **-S** an East Indian tree

ALA *n* pl. **ALAE** a wing or winglike part

ALACHLOR *n* pl. **-S** an herbicide

ALACK *interj* — used to express sorrow or regret

ALACRITY *n* pl. **-TIES** cheerful promptness

ALAE pl. of ala

ALAMEDA *n* pl. **-S** a shaded walkway

ALAMO	*n* pl. **-MOS** a softwood tree	**ALBUM**	*n* pl. **-S** a book for preserving photographs or stamps
ALAMODE	*n* pl. **-S** a silk fabric	**ALBUMEN**	*n* pl. **-S** the white of an egg
ALAN	*n* pl. **-S** a large hunting dog	**ALBUMIN**	*n* pl. **-S** a simple protein
ALAND	*n* pl. **-S** alan	**ALBUMOSE**	*n* pl. **-S** a proteose
ALANE	*adj* alone	**ALBURNUM**	*n* pl. **-S** sapwood
ALANG	*adv* along	**ALCADE**	*n* pl. **-S** alcalde
ALANIN	*n* pl. **-S** alanine	**ALCAHEST**	*n* pl. **-S** alkahest
ALANINE	*n* pl. **-S** an amino acid	**ALCAIC**	*n* pl. **-S** a type of verse form
ALANT	*n* pl. **-S** alan	**ALCAIDE**	*n* pl. **-S** the commander of a Spanish fortress
ALANYL	*n* pl. **-S** a univalent radical	**ALCALDE**	*n* pl. **-S** the mayor of a Spanish town
ALAR	*adj* pertaining to wings		
ALARM	*v* **-ED, -ING, -S** to frighten by a sudden revelation of possible injury	**ALCAYDE**	*n* pl. **-S** alcaide
		ALCAZAR	*n* pl. **-S** a Spanish fortress or palace
ALARMISM	*n* pl. **-S** the practice of alarming others needlessly	**ALCHEMY**	*n* pl. **-MIES** a medieval form of chemistry **ALCHEMIC** *adj*
ALARMIST	*n* pl. **-S** one who alarms others needlessly	**ALCHYMY**	*n* pl. **-MIES** alchemy
ALARUM	*v* **-ED, -ING, -S** to alarm	**ALCID**	*n* pl. **-S** a diving seabird
ALARY	*adj* alar	**ALCIDINE**	*adj* pertaining to a family of seabirds
ALAS	*interj* — used to express sorrow or regret	**ALCOHOL**	*n* pl. **-S** a flammable liquid
ALASKA	*n* pl. **-S** a heavy fabric	**ALCOOL**	*n* pl. **-S** an alcoholic liquor
ALASTOR	*n* pl. **-S** an avenging deity in Greek tragedy	**ALCOPOP**	*n* pl. **-S** a flavored beverage containing 4-6 percent alcohol
ALATE	*n* pl. **-S** a winged insect	**ALCOVE**	*n* pl. **-S** a recessed section of a room **ALCOVED** *adj*
ALATED	*adj* having wings		
ALATION	*n* pl. **-S** the state of having wings	**ALDEHYDE**	*n* pl. **-S** a type of chemical compound
ALB	*n* pl. **-S** a long-sleeved vestment	**ALDER**	*n* pl. **-S** a shrub or small tree
ALBA	*n* pl. **-S** the white substance of the brain	**ALDERFLY**	*n* pl. **-FLIES** a winged insect
ALBACORE	*n* pl. **-S** a marine food fish	**ALDERMAN**	*n* pl. **-MEN** a member of a municipal legislative body
ALBATA	*n* pl. **-S** an alloy of copper, nickel, and zinc	**ALDICARB**	*n* pl. **-S** a pesticide
ALBEDO	*n* pl. **-DOS** or **-DOES** the ratio of the light reflected by a planet to that received by it	**ALDOL**	*n* pl. **-S** a chemical compound
		ALDOLASE	*n* pl. **-S** an enzyme
ALBEIT	*conj* although	**ALDOSE**	*n* pl. **-S** a type of sugar
ALBICORE	*n* pl. **-S** albacore	**ALDRIN**	*n* pl. **-S** an insecticide
ALBINAL	*adj* albinic	**ALE**	*n* pl. **-S** an alcoholic beverage
ALBINIC	*adj* pertaining to albinism	**ALEATORY**	*adj* pertaining to luck
ALBINISM	*n* pl. **-S** the condition of being an albino	**ALEC**	*n* pl. **-S** a herring
ALBINO	*n* pl. **-NOS** an organism lacking normal pigmentation	**ALEE**	*adv* toward the side of a vessel sheltered from the wind
ALBITE	*n* pl. **-S** a mineral **ALBITIC** *adj*	**ALEF**	*n* pl. **-S** aleph
ALBIZIA	*n* pl. **-S** a tropical tree	**ALEGAR**	*n* pl. **-S** sour ale
ALBIZZIA	*n* pl. **-S** albizia	**ALEHOUSE**	*n* pl. **-S** a tavern where ale is sold

ALEMBIC   *n* pl. **-S** an apparatus formerly used in distilling

ALENCON   *n* pl. **-S** a needlepoint lace

ALEPH   *n* pl. **-S** a Hebrew letter

ALERT   *adj* **ALERTER, ALERTEST** ready for sudden action **ALERTLY** *adv*

ALERT   *v* **-ED, -ING, -S** to warn

ALEURON   *n* pl. **-S** aleurone

ALEURONE   *n* pl. **-S** protein matter found in the seeds of certain plants

ALEVIN   *n* pl. **-S** a young fish

ALEWIFE   *n* pl. **-WIVES** a marine fish

ALEXIA   *n* pl. **-S** a cerebral disorder marked by the loss of the ability to read **ALEXIC** *adj*

ALEXIN   *n* pl. **-S** a substance in the blood that aids in the destruction of bacteria

ALEXINE   *n* pl. **-S** alexin

ALFA   *n* pl. **-S** a communications code word for the letter A

ALFAKI   *n* pl. **-S** alfaqui

ALFALFA   *n* pl. **-S** a plant cultivated for use as hay and forage

ALFAQUI   *n* pl. **-S** a teacher of Muslim law

ALFAQUIN   *n* pl. **-S** alfaqui

ALFORJA   *n* pl. **-S** a leather bag

ALFREDO   *adj* served with a white cheese sauce

ALFRESCO   *adv* outdoors

ALGA   *n* pl. **-GAS** or **-GAE** any of a group of primitive aquatic plants **ALGAL** *adj*

ALGAROBA   *n* pl. **-S** the mesquite

ALGEBRA   *n* pl. **-S** a branch of mathematics

ALGERINE   *n* pl. **-S** a woolen fabric

ALGICIDE   *n* pl. **-S** a substance used to kill algae

ALGID   *adj* cold

ALGIDITY   *n* pl. **-TIES** coldness

ALGIN   *n* pl. **-S** a viscous substance obtained from certain algae

ALGINATE   *n* pl. **-S** a chemical salt

ALGOID   *adj* resembling algae

ALGOLOGY   *n* pl. **-GIES** the study of algae

ALGOR   *n* pl. **-S** coldness

ALGORISM   *n* pl. **-S** the Arabic system of arithmetic notation

ALGUACIL   *n* pl. **-S** a constable in a Spanish-speaking country

ALGUAZIL   *n* pl. **-S** alguacil

ALGUM   *n* pl. **-S** almug

ALIAS   *v* **-ED, -ING, -ES** to assign an assumed name to

ALIASING   *n* pl. **-S** the appearance of distortions in computer graphics

ALIBI   *v* **-BIED, -BIING, -BIS** or **-BIES** to make excuses for oneself

ALIBLE   *adj* nourishing

ALIDAD   *n* pl. **-S** alidade

ALIDADE   *n* pl. **-S** a device used in angular measurement

ALIEN   *v* **-ED, -ING, -S** to transfer to another, as property

ALIENAGE   *n* pl. **-S** the state of being foreign

ALIENATE   *v* **-ATED, -ATING, -ATES** to make indifferent or unfriendly

ALIENEE   *n* pl. **-S** one to whom property is transferred

ALIENER   *n* pl. **-S** alienor

ALIENISM   *n* pl. **-S** alienage

ALIENIST   *n* pl. **-S** a physician who treats mental disorders

ALIENLY   *adv* in a foreign manner

ALIENOR   *n* pl. **-S** one that transfers property

ALIF   *n* pl. **-S** an Arabic letter

ALIFORM   *adj* shaped like a wing

ALIGHT   *v* **ALIGHTED** or **ALIT, ALIGHTING, ALIGHTS** to come down from something

ALIGN   *v* **-ED, -ING, -S** to arrange in a straight line

ALIGNER   *n* pl. **-S** one that aligns

ALIKE   *adj* having close resemblance

ALIMENT   *v* **-ED, -ING, -S** to nourish

ALIMONY   *n* pl. **-NIES** an allowance paid to one spouse by the other after divorce

ALINE   *v* **ALINED, ALINING, ALINES** to align

ALINER   *n* pl. **-S** aligner

ALIPED   *n* pl. **-S** an animal having a membrane connecting the toes

ALIQUANT   *adj* not dividing evenly into another number

ALIQUOT   *n* pl. **-S** a number that divides evenly into another

ALIST   *adj* leaning to one side

ALIT   a past tense of alight

ALIUNDE	*adv* from a source extrinsic to the matter at hand
ALIVE	*adj* having life
ALIYA	*n* pl. **-S** aliyah
ALIYAH	*n* pl. **-YAHS** or **-YOS** or **-YOT** or **-YOTH** the immigration of Jews to Israel
ALIZARIN	*n* pl. **-S** a red dye
ALKAHEST	*n* pl. **-S** the hypothetical universal solvent sought by alchemists
ALKALI	*n* pl. **-LIS** or **-LIES** a type of chemical compound **ALKALIC** *adj*
ALKALIFY	*v* **-FIED, -FYING, -FIES** to alkalize
ALKALIN	*adj* alkaline
ALKALINE	*adj* containing an alkali
ALKALISE	*v* **-LISED, -LISING, -LISES** to alkalize
ALKALIZE	*v* **-LIZED, -LIZING, -LIZES** to convert into an alkali
ALKALOID	*n* pl. **-S** a type of chemical compound
ALKANE	*n* pl. **-S** a type of chemical compound
ALKANET	*n* pl. **-S** a European plant
ALKENE	*n* pl. **-S** a type of chemical compound
ALKIE	*n* pl. **-S** alky
ALKIES	pl. of alky
ALKINE	*n* pl. **-S** alkyne
ALKOXIDE	*n* pl. **-S** a type of chemical salt
ALKOXY	*adj* containing a univalent radical composed of alkyl united with oxygen
ALKY	*n* pl. **-KIES** one who is habitually drunk
ALKYD	*n* pl. **-S** a synthetic resin
ALKYL	*n* pl. **-S** a univalent radical **ALKYLIC** *adj*
ALKYLATE	*v* **-ATED, -ATING, -ATES** to combine with alkyl
ALKYNE	*n* pl. **-S** a type of chemical compound
ALL	*n* pl. **-S** everything that one has
ALLANITE	*n* pl. **-S** a mineral
ALLAY	*v* **-ED, -ING, -S** to reduce in intensity or severity
ALLAYER	*n* pl. **-S** one that allays
ALLEE	*n* pl. **-S** a tree-lined walkway
ALLEGE	*v* **-LEGED, -LEGING, -LEGES** to assert without proof or before proving
ALLEGER	*n* pl. **-S** one that alleges
ALLEGORY	*n* pl. **-RIES** a story presenting a moral principle
ALLEGRO	*n* pl. **-GROS** a musical passage played in rapid tempo
ALLELE	*n* pl. **-S** any of several forms of a gene **ALLELIC** *adj*
ALLELISM	*n* pl. **-S** the state of possessing alleles
ALLELUIA	*n* pl. **-S** a song of praise to God
ALLERGEN	*n* pl. **-S** a substance capable of inducing an allergy
ALLERGIC	*adj* pertaining to allergy
ALLERGIN	*n* pl. **-S** allergen
ALLERGY	*n* pl. **-GIES** a state of hypersensitive reaction to certain things
ALLEY	*n* pl. **-LEYS** a narrow passageway
ALLEYWAY	*n* pl. **-WAYS** an alley
ALLHEAL	*n* pl. **-S** a medicinal herb
ALLIABLE	*adj* capable of being allied
ALLIAK	*n* pl. **-S** an Inuit sledge
ALLIANCE	*n* pl. **-S** an association formed to further the common interests of its members
ALLICIN	*n* pl. **-S** a liquid compound
ALLIED	past tense of ally
ALLIES	present 3d person sing. of ally
ALLIUM	*n* pl. **-S** a bulbous herb
ALLOBAR	*n* pl. **-S** a change in barometric pressure
ALLOCATE	*v* **-CATED, -CATING, -CATES** to set apart for a particular purpose
ALLOD	*n* pl. **-S** allodium
ALLODIUM	*n* pl. **-DIA** land held in absolute ownership **ALLODIAL** *adj*
ALLOGAMY	*n* pl. **-MIES** fertilization of a flower by pollen from another
ALLONGE	*n* pl. **-S** an addition to a document
ALLONYM	*n* pl. **-S** the name of one person assumed by another
ALLOPATH	*n* pl. **-S** one who treats diseases by producing effects incompatible with those of the disease
ALLOSAUR	*n* pl. **-S** a large dinosaur
ALLOT	*v* **-LOTTED, -LOTTING, -LOTS** to give as a share or portion

ALLOTTEE _n_ pl. **-S** one to whom something is allotted

ALLOTTER _n_ pl. **-S** one that allots

ALLOTYPE _n_ pl. **-S** a type of antibody

ALLOTYPY _n_ pl. **-TYPIES** the condition of being an allotype

ALLOVER _n_ pl. **-S** a fabric having a pattern extending over the entire surface

ALLOW _v_ **-ED, -ING, -S** to put no obstacle in the way of

ALLOXAN _n_ pl. **-S** a chemical compound

ALLOY _v_ **-ED, -ING, -S** to combine to form an alloy (a homogenous mixture of metals)

ALLSEED _n_ pl. **-S** a plant having many seeds

ALLSORTS _n/pl_ assorted small candies

ALLSPICE _n_ pl. **-S** a tropical tree

ALLUDE _v_ **-LUDED, -LUDING, -LUDES** to make an indirect reference

ALLURE _v_ **-LURED, -LURING, -LURES** to attract with something desirable

ALLURER _n_ pl. **-S** one that allures

ALLUSION _n_ pl. **-S** the act of alluding **ALLUSIVE** _adj_

ALLUVIA _a_ pl. of alluvium

ALLUVIAL _n_ pl. **-S** soil composed of alluvium

ALLUVION _n_ pl. **-S** alluvium

ALLUVIUM _n_ pl. **-VIUMS** or **-VIA** detrital material deposited by running water

ALLY _v_ **-LIED, -LYING, -LIES** to unite in a formal relationship

ALLYL _n_ pl. **-S** a univalent radical **ALLYLIC** _adj_

ALMA _n_ pl. **-S** almah

ALMAGEST _n_ pl. **-S** a medieval treatise on astrology or alchemy

ALMAH _n_ pl. **-S** an Egyptian girl who sings and dances professionally

ALMANAC _n_ pl. **-S** an annual publication containing general information

ALMANACK _n_ pl. **-S** almanac

ALME _n_ pl. **-S** almah

ALMEH _n_ pl. **-S** almah

ALMEMAR _n_ pl. **-S** a bema

ALMIGHTY _adj_ having absolute power over all

ALMNER _n_ pl. **-S** almoner

ALMOND _n_ pl. **-S** the edible nut of a small tree **ALMONDY** _adj_

ALMONER _n_ pl. **-S** one that distributes alms

ALMONRY _n_ pl. **-RIES** a place where alms are distributed

ALMOST _adv_ very nearly

ALMS _n_ pl. **ALMS** money or goods given to the poor

ALMSMAN _n_ pl. **-MEN** one who receives alms

ALMUCE _n_ pl. **-S** a hooded cape

ALMUD _n_ pl. **-S** a Spanish unit of capacity

ALMUDE _n_ pl. **-S** almud

ALMUG _n_ pl. **-S** a precious wood mentioned in the Bible

ALNICO _n_ pl. **-COS** an alloy containing aluminum, nickel, and cobalt

ALODIUM _n_ pl. **-DIA** allodium **ALODIAL** _adj_

ALOE _n_ pl. **-S** an African plant **ALOETIC** _adj_

ALOFT _adv_ in or into the air

ALOGICAL _adj_ being outside the bounds of that to which logic can apply

ALOHA _n_ pl. **-S** love — used as a greeting or farewell

ALOIN _n_ pl. **-S** a laxative

ALONE _adj_ apart from others

ALONG _adv_ onward

ALOOF _adj_ distant in interest or feeling **ALOOFLY** _adv_

ALOPECIA _n_ pl. **-S** baldness **ALOPECIC** _adj_

ALOUD _adv_ audibly

ALOW _adv_ in or to a lower position

ALP _n_ pl. **-S** a high mountain

ALPACA _n_ pl. **-S** a ruminant mammal

ALPHA _n_ pl. **-S** a Greek letter

ALPHABET _v_ **-ED, -ING, -S** to arrange in the customary order of the letters of a language

ALPHORN _n_ pl. **-S** a wooden horn used by Swiss herdsmen

ALPHOSIS _n_ pl. **-SISES** lack of skin pigmentation

ALPHYL _n_ pl. **-S** a univalent radical

ALPINE _n_ pl. **-S** a plant native to high mountain regions

ALPINELY _adv_ in a lofty manner

ALPINISM _n_ pl. **-S** mountain climbing

ALPINIST _n_ pl. **-S** a mountain climber

ALREADY _adv_ by this time

ALRIGHT _adj_ satisfactory

ALSIKE _n_ pl. **-S** a European clover

ALSO	*adv* in addition	**AM**	present 1st person sing. of be
ALT	*n* pl. **-S** a high-pitched musical note	**AMA**	*n* pl. **-S** amah
		AMADAVAT	*n* pl. **-S** an Asian songbird
ALTAR	*n* pl. **-S** a raised structure used in worship	**AMADOU**	*n* pl. **-S** a substance prepared from fungi for use as tinder
ALTER	*v* **-ED, -ING, -S** to make different	**AMAH**	*n* pl. **-S** a Chinese nurse
ALTERANT	*n* pl. **-S** something that alters	**AMAIN**	*adv* with full strength
ALTERER	*n* pl. **-S** one that alters	**AMALGAM**	*n* pl. **-S** an alloy of mercury with another metal
ALTERITY	*n* pl. **-TIES** the state of being other or different	**AMANDINE**	*adj* prepared with almonds
ALTHAEA	*n* pl. **-S** althea	**AMANITA**	*n* pl. **-S** any of a genus of poisonous fungi
ALTHEA	*n* pl. **-S** a flowering plant		
ALTHO	*conj* although	**AMANITIN**	*n* pl. **-S** a chemical compound
ALTHORN	*n* pl. **-S** a brass wind instrument	**AMARANTH**	*n* pl. **-S** a flowering plant
ALTHOUGH	*conj* despite the fact that	**AMARELLE**	*n* pl. **-S** a variety of sour cherry
ALTITUDE	*n* pl. **-S** the vertical elevation of an object above a given level	**AMARETTI**	*n/pl* macaroons made with bitter almonds
ALTO	*n* pl. **-TOS** a low female singing voice	**AMARETTO**	*n* pl. **-TOS** a kind of liqueur
ALTOIST	*n* pl. **-S** one who plays the alto saxophone	**AMARNA**	*adj* pertaining to a certain historical period of ancient Egypt
ALTRUISM	*n* pl. **-S** selfless devotion to the welfare of others	**AMARONE**	*n* pl. **-S** a dry red wine
		AMASS	*v* **-ED, -ING, -ES** to gather
ALTRUIST	*n* pl. **-S** one that practices altruism	**AMASSER**	*n* pl. **-S** one that amasses
ALUDEL	*n* pl. **-S** a pear-shaped vessel	**AMATEUR**	*n* pl. **-S** one that engages in an activity for pleasure
ALULA	*n* pl. **-LAE** a tuft of feathers on the first digit of a bird's wing **ALULAR** *adj*		
		AMATIVE	*adj* amorous
ALUM	*n* pl. **-S** a chemical compound	**AMATOL**	*n* pl. **-S** a powerful explosive
ALUMIN	*n* pl. **-S** alumina	**AMATORY**	*adj* pertaining to sexual love
ALUMINA	*n* pl. **-S** an oxide of aluminum	**AMAUTI**	*n* pl. **-S** amautik
ALUMINE	*n* pl. **-S** alumina	**AMAUTIK**	*n* pl. **-S** an Inuit woman's parka
ALUMINUM	*n* pl. **-S** a metallic element **ALUMINIC** *adj*	**AMAZE**	*v* **AMAZED, AMAZING, AMAZES** to overwhelm with surprise or wonder **AMAZEDLY** *adv*
ALUMNA	*n* pl. **-NAE** a female graduate		
ALUMNUS	*n* pl. **-NI** a male graduate	**AMAZON**	*n* pl. **-S** a tall, powerful woman
ALUMROOT	*n* pl. **-S** a flowering plant	**AMBAGE**	*n* pl. **-S** a winding path
ALUNITE	*n* pl. **-S** a mineral	**AMBARI**	*n* pl. **-S** ambary
ALVAR	*n* pl. **-S** an area of exposed limestone	**AMBARY**	*n* pl. **-RIES** an East Indian plant
		AMBEER	*n* pl. **-S** tobacco juice
ALVEOLAR	*n* pl. **-S** a sound produced with the tongue touching a place just behind the front teeth	**AMBER**	*n* pl. **-S** a fossil resin
		AMBERINA	*n* pl. **-S** a type of glassware
ALVEOLUS	*n* pl. **-LI** a small anatomical cavity	**AMBEROID**	*n* pl. **-S** ambroid
ALVINE	*adj* pertaining to the abdomen and lower intestines	**AMBERY**	*n* pl. **-BERIES** ambry
		AMBIANCE	*n* pl. **-S** ambience
ALWAY	*adv* always	**AMBIENCE**	*n* pl. **-S** the character, mood, or atmosphere of a place or situation
ALWAYS	*adv* at all times		
ALYSSUM	*n* pl. **-S** a flowering plant	**AMBIENT**	*n* pl. **-S** ambience

AMBIT   *n* pl. **-S** the external boundary of something

AMBITION   *v* **-ED, -ING, -S** to seek with eagerness

AMBIVERT   *n* pl. **-S** a person whose personality type is intermediate between introvert and extravert

AMBLE   *v* **-BLED, -BLING, -BLES** to saunter

AMBLER   *n* pl. **-S** one that ambles

AMBO   *n* pl. **AMBOS** or **AMBONES** a pulpit in an early Christian church

AMBOINA   *n* pl. **-S** amboyna

AMBOYNA   *n* pl. **-S** the mottled wood of an Indonesian tree

AMBRIES   pl. of ambry

AMBROID   *n* pl. **-S** a synthetic amber

AMBROSIA   *n* pl. **-S** the food of the Greek and Roman gods

AMBRY   *n* pl. **-BRIES** a recess in a church wall for sacred vessels

AMBSACE   *n* pl. **-S** bad luck

AMBULANT   *adj* ambulating

AMBULATE   *v* **-LATED, -LATING, -LATES** to move or walk about

AMBUSH   *v* **-ED, -ING, -ES** to attack from a concealed place

AMBUSHER   *n* pl. **-S** one that ambushes

AMEBA   *n* pl. **-BAS** or **-BAE** amoeba **AMEBAN, AMEBIC, AMEBOID** *adj*

AMEBEAN   *adj* alternately responding

AMEER   *n* pl. **-S** amir

AMEERATE   *n* pl. **-S** amirate

AMELCORN   *n* pl. **-S** a variety of wheat

AMEN   *n* pl. **-S** a word used at the end of a prayer to express agreement

AMENABLE   *adj* capable of being persuaded **AMENABLY** *adv*

AMEND   *v* **-ED, -ING, -S** to improve

AMENDER   *n* pl. **-S** one that amends

AMENITY   *n* pl. **-TIES** the quality of being pleasant or agreeable

AMENT   *n* pl. **-S** a mentally deficient person

AMENTIA   *n* pl. **-S** mental deficiency

AMENTUM   *n* pl. **-TA** ament

AMERCE   *v* **AMERCED, AMERCING, AMERCES** to punish by imposing an arbitrary fine

AMERCER   *n* pl. **-S** one that amerces

AMESACE   *n* pl. **-S** ambsace

AMETHYST   *n* pl. **-S** a variety of quartz

AMI   *n* pl. **-S** a friend

AMIA   *n* pl. **-S** a freshwater fish

AMIABLE   *adj* having a pleasant disposition **AMIABLY** *adv*

AMIANTUS   *n* pl. **-ES** a variety of asbestos

AMICABLE   *adj* friendly **AMICABLY** *adv*

AMICE   *n* pl. **-S** a vestment worn about the neck and shoulders

AMICUS   *n* pl. **AMICI** one not party to a lawsuit but permitted by the court to advise it

AMID   *n* pl. **-S** amide

AMIDASE   *n* pl. **-S** an enzyme

AMIDE   *n* pl. **-S** a type of chemical compound **AMIDIC** *adj*

AMIDIN   *n* pl. **-S** the soluble matter of starch

AMIDINE   *n* pl. **-S** a type of chemical compound

AMIDO   *adj* containing an amide united with an acid radical

AMIDOGEN   *n* pl. **-S** a univalent chemical radical

AMIDOL   *n* pl. **-S** a chemical compound

AMIDONE   *n* pl. **-S** a chemical compound

AMIDSHIP   *adv* toward the middle of a ship

AMIDST   *prep* in the midst of

AMIE   *n* pl. **-S** a female friend

AMIGA   *n* pl. **-S** a female friend

AMIGO   *n* pl. **-GOS** a friend

AMIN   *n* pl. **-S** amine

AMINE   *n* pl. **-S** a type of chemical compound **AMINIC** *adj*

AMINITY   *n* pl. **-TIES** the state of being an amine

AMINO   *n* pl. **-NOS** a chemical group present in amines

AMIR   *n* pl. **-S** a Muslim prince or governor

AMIRATE   *n* pl. **-S** the rank of an amir

AMISS   *adj* being out of proper order

AMITIES   pl. of amity

AMITOSIS   *n* pl. **-TOSES** a type of cell division **AMITOTIC** *adj*

AMITROLE   *n* pl. **-S** an herbicide

AMITY   *n* pl. **-TIES** friendship

AMMETER   *n* pl. **-S** an instrument for measuring amperage

AMMINE *n* pl. **-S** a type of chemical compound

AMMINO *adj* pertaining to an ammine

AMMO *n* pl. **-MOS** ammunition

AMMOCETE *n* pl. **-S** the larva of a lamprey

AMMOLITE *n* pl. **-S** the fossilized shell of an ammonite

AMMONAL *n* pl. **-S** a powerful explosive

AMMONIA *n* pl. **-S** a pungent gas

AMMONIAC *n* pl. **-S** a gum resin

AMMONIC *adj* pertaining to ammonia

AMMONIFY *v* **-FIED, -FYING, -FIES** to treat with ammonia

AMMONITE *n* pl. **-S** the coiled shell of an extinct mollusk

AMMONIUM *n* pl. **-S** a univalent chemical radical

AMMONO *adj* containing ammonia

AMMONOID *n* pl. **-S** ammonite

AMNESIA *n* pl. **-S** loss of memory

AMNESIAC *n* pl. **-S** one suffering from amnesia

AMNESIC *n* pl. **-S** amnesiac

AMNESTIC *adj* pertaining to amnesia

AMNESTY *v* **-TIED, -TYING, -TIES** to pardon

AMNIO *n* pl. **-NIOS** a surgical insertion of a needle into the uterus

AMNION *n* pl. **-NIONS** or **-NIA** a membranous sac enclosing an embryo **AMNIC, AMNIONIC, AMNIOTIC** *adj*

AMNIOTE *n* pl. **-S** a vertebrate that develops an amnion during the embryonic stage

AMOEBA *n* pl. **-BAS** or **-BAE** a unicellular microscopic organism **AMOEBAN, AMOEBIC, AMOEBOID** *adj*

AMOEBEAN *adj* amebean

AMOK *n* pl. **-S** a murderous frenzy

AMOLE *n* pl. **-S** a plant root used as a substitute for soap

AMONG *prep* in the midst of

AMONGST *prep* among

AMORAL *adj* lacking a sense of right and wrong **AMORALLY** *adv*

AMORETTO *n* pl. **-TOS** or **-TI** a cupid

AMORINO *n* pl. **-NI** an amoretto

AMORIST *n* pl. **-S** a lover

AMOROSO *n* pl. **-SOS** a type of wine

AMOROUS *adj* pertaining to love

AMORT *adj* being without life

AMORTISE *v* **-TISED, -TISING, -TISES** to amortize

AMORTIZE *v* **-TIZED, -TIZING, -TIZES** to liquidate gradually, as a debt

AMOSITE *n* pl. **-S** a type of asbestos

AMOTION *n* pl. **-S** the removal of a corporate officer from his or her office

AMOUNT *v* **-ED, -ING, -S** to combine to yield a sum

AMOUR *n* pl. **-S** a love affair

AMP *v* **-ED, -ING, -S** to amplify

AMPACITY *n* pl. **-TIES** the largest amount of current that a wire can carry

AMPERAGE *n* pl. **-S** the strength of an electric current expressed in amperes

AMPERE *n* pl. **-S** a unit of electric current strength

AMPHIBIA *n/pl* organisms adapted for life both on land and in water

AMPHIOXI *n/pl* lancelets

AMPHIPOD *n* pl. **-S** a small crustacean

AMPHORA *n* pl. **-RAS** or **-RAE** a narrow-necked jar used in ancient Greece **AMPHORAL** *adj*

AMPLE *adj* **-PLER, -PLEST** abundant **AMPLY** *adv*

AMPLEXUS *n* pl. **-ES** the mating embrace of frogs

AMPLIFY *v* **-FIED, -FYING, -FIES** to make larger or more powerful

AMPOULE *n* pl. **-S** ampule

AMPUL *n* pl. **-S** ampule

AMPULE *n* pl. **-S** a small glass vial

AMPULLA *n* pl. **-LAE** a globular bottle used in ancient Rome **AMPULLAR** *adj*

AMPUTATE *v* **-TATED, -TATING, -TATES** to cut off by surgical means

AMPUTEE *n* pl. **-S** one that has had a limb amputated

AMREETA *n* pl. **-S** amrita

AMRIT *n* pl. **-S** amrita

AMRITA *n* pl. **-S** a beverage that bestows immortality in Hindu mythology

AMTRAC *n* pl. **-S** a military vehicle equipped to move on land and water

AMTRACK *n* pl. **-S** amtrac

AMTRAK *n* pl. **-S** amtrac

AMU *n* pl. **-S** a unit of mass

AMUCK *n* pl. **-S** amok

AMULET   *n* pl. **-S** an object worn to protect against evil or injury

AMUSE   *v* **AMUSED, AMUSING, AMUSES** to occupy pleasingly **AMUSABLE** *adj* **AMUSEDLY** *adv*

AMUSER   *n* pl. **-S** one that amuses

AMUSIA   *n* pl. **-S** the inability to recognize musical sounds

AMUSIVE   *adj* amusing

AMYGDALA   *n* pl. **-LAE** an almond-shaped anatomical part

AMYGDALE   *n* pl. **-S** amygdule

AMYGDULE   *n* pl. **-S** a small gas bubble in lava

AMYL   *n* pl. **-S** a univalent radical

AMYLASE   *n* pl. **-S** an enzyme

AMYLENE   *n* pl. **-S** a flammable liquid

AMYLIC   *adj* pertaining to amyl

AMYLOGEN   *n* pl. **-S** amylose

AMYLOID   *n* pl. **-S** a hard protein deposit resulting from degeneration of tissue

AMYLOSE   *n* pl. **-S** the relatively soluble component of starch

AMYLUM   *n* pl. **-S** starch (a solid carbohydrate)

AN   *indefinite article* — used before words beginning with a vowel sound

ANA   *n* pl. **-S** a collection of miscellaneous information about a particular subject

ANABAENA   *n* pl. **-S** a freshwater alga

ANABAS   *n* pl. **-ES** a freshwater fish

ANABASIS   *n* pl. **-ASES** a military advance

ANABATIC   *adj* pertaining to rising wind currents

ANABLEPS   *n* pl. **-ES** a freshwater fish

ANABOLIC   *adj* pertaining to a process by which food is built up into protoplasm

ANACONDA   *n* pl. **-S** a large snake

ANADEM   *n* pl. **-S** a wreath for the head

ANAEMIA   *n* pl. **-S** anemia **ANAEMIC** *adj*

ANAEROBE   *n* pl. **-S** an organism that does not require oxygen to live

ANAGEN   *n* pl. **-S** a period of hair growth

ANAGLYPH   *n* pl. **-S** a type of carved ornament

ANAGOGE   *n* pl. **-S** a spiritual interpretation of words **ANAGOGIC** *adj*

ANAGOGY   *n* pl. **-GIES** anagoge

ANAGRAM   *v* **-GRAMMED, -GRAMMING, -GRAMS** to transpose the letters of a word or phrase to form a new one

ANAL   *adj* pertaining to the anus

ANALCIME   *n* pl. **-S** analcite

ANALCITE   *n* pl. **-S** a mineral

ANALECTA   *n/pl* analects

ANALECTS   *n/pl* selections from a literary work or group of works

ANALEMMA   *n* pl. **-MAS** or **-MATA** a type of graduated scale

ANALGIA   *n* pl. **-S** inability to feel pain

ANALITY   *n* pl. **-TIES** a type of psychological state

ANALLY   *adv* at or through the anus

ANALOG   *n* pl. **-S** analogue

ANALOGIC   *adj* pertaining to an analogy

ANALOGUE   *n* pl. **-S** something that bears an analogy to something else

ANALOGY   *n* pl. **-GIES** resemblance in some respects between things otherwise unlike

ANALYSE   *v* **-LYSED, -LYSING, -LYSES** to analyze

ANALYSER   *n* pl. **-S** analyzer

ANALYSIS   *n* pl. **-YSES** the separation of a whole into its parts

ANALYST   *n* pl. **-S** one that analyzes

ANALYTE   *n* pl. **-S** a substance being analyzed

ANALYTIC   *adj* pertaining to analysis

ANALYZE   *v* **-LYZED, -LYZING, -LYZES** to subject to analysis

ANALYZER   *n* pl. **-S** one that analyzes

ANANDA   *n* pl. **-S** extreme happiness

ANANKE   *n* pl. **-S** a compelling necessity in ancient Greek religion

ANAPAEST   *n* pl. **-S** anapest

ANAPEST   *n* pl. **-S** a type of metrical foot

ANAPHASE   *n* pl. **-S** a stage of mitosis

ANAPHOR   *n* pl. **-S** a word or phrase that takes reference from a preceding word or phrase

ANAPHORA   *n* pl. **-S** the repetition of a word or phrase at the beginning of several successive verses or sentences

ANARCH   *n* pl. **-S** an advocate of anarchy

ANARCHY   *n* pl. **-CHIES** absence of government **ANARCHIC** *adj*

ANASARCA *n* pl. **-S** a form of dropsy

ANATASE *n* pl. **-S** a mineral

ANATHEMA *n* pl. **-MAS** or **-MATA** a formal ecclesiastical ban or curse

ANATOMY *n* pl. **-MIES** the structure of an organism **ANATOMIC** *adj*

ANATOXIN *n* pl. **-S** a toxoid

ANATTO *n* pl. **-TOS** annatto

ANCESTOR *v* **-ED, -ING, -S** to be an ancestor (a person from whom one is descended) of

ANCESTRY *n* pl. **-TRIES** a line or body of ancestors

ANCHO *n* pl. **-CHOS** a chili pepper

ANCHOR *v* **-ED, -ING, -S** to secure by means of an anchor (a device for holding a floating vessel in place)

ANCHORET *n* pl. **-S** a recluse

ANCHOVY *n* pl. **-VIES** a small food fish

ANCHUSA *n* pl. **-S** a hairy-stemmed plant

ANCHUSIN *n* pl. **-S** a red dye

ANCIENT *adj* **-CIENTER, -CIENTEST** of or pertaining to time long past

ANCIENT *n* pl. **-S** one who lived in ancient times

ANCILLA *n* pl. **-LAS** or **-LAE** a helper

ANCON *n* pl. **-ES** the elbow **ANCONAL, ANCONEAL, ANCONOID** *adj*

ANCONE *n* pl. **-S** ancon

ANCRESS *n* pl. **-ES** a female recluse

AND *n* pl. **-S** an added condition or stipulation

ANDANTE *n* pl. **-S** a moderately slow musical passage

ANDESITE *n* pl. **-S** a volcanic rock

ANDESYTE *n* pl. **-S** andesite

ANDIRON *n* pl. **-S** a metal support for holding wood in a fireplace

ANDRO *n* pl. **-DROS** a steroid sex hormone

ANDROGEN *n* pl. **-S** a male sex hormone

ANDROID *n* pl. **-S** a synthetic man

ANE *n* pl. **-S** one

ANEAR *v* **-ED, -ING, -S** to approach

ANECDOTE *n* pl. **-DOTES** or **-DOTA** a brief story

ANECHOIC *adj* neither having nor producing echoes

ANELE *v* **ANELED, ANELING, ANELES** to anoint

ANEMIA *n* pl. **-S** a disorder of the blood **ANEMIC** *adj*

ANEMONE *n* pl. **-S** a flowering plant

ANEMOSIS *n* pl. **-MOSES** separation of rings of growth in timber due to wind

ANENST *prep* anent

ANENT *prep* in regard to

ANERGIA *n* pl. **-S** anergy

ANERGY *n* pl. **-GIES** lack of energy **ANERGIC** *adj*

ANEROID *n* pl. **-S** a type of barometer

ANESTRUS *n* pl. **-TRI** a period of sexual dormancy

ANETHOL *n* pl. **-S** anethole

ANETHOLE *n* pl. **-S** a chemical compound

ANEURIN *n* pl. **-S** thiamine

ANEURISM *n* pl. **-S** aneurysm

ANEURYSM *n* pl. **-S** an abnormal blood-filled dilation of a blood vessel

ANEW *adv* once more

ANGA *n* pl. **-S** any of the eight practices of yoga

ANGAKOK *n* pl. **-S** an Inuit medicine man

ANGARIA *n* pl. **-S** angary

ANGARY *n* pl. **-RIES** the right of a warring state to seize neutral property

ANGEL *v* **-ED, -ING, -S** to support financially

ANGELIC *adj* pertaining to an angel (a winged celestial being)

ANGELICA *n* pl. **-S** an aromatic herb

ANGELUS *n* pl. **-ES** a Roman Catholic prayer

ANGER *v* **-ED, -ING, -S** to make angry

ANGERLY *adv* in an angry manner

ANGINA *n* pl. **-S** a disease marked by spasmodic attacks of intense pain **ANGINAL, ANGINOSE, ANGINOUS** *adj*

ANGIOMA *n* pl. **-MAS** or **-MATA** a tumor composed of blood or lymph vessels

ANGLE *v* **-GLED, -GLING, -GLES** to fish with a hook and line

ANGLEPOD *n* pl. **-S** a flowering plant

ANGLER *n* pl. **-S** one that angles

ANGLICE *adv* in readily understood English

ANGLING *n* pl. **-S** the sport of fishing

ANGLO *n* pl. **-GLOS** a white North American of non-Hispanic or non-French descent

ANGORA *n* pl. **-S** the long, silky hair of a domestic goat

ANGRY *adj* **-GRIER, -GRIEST** feeling strong displeasure or hostility **ANGRILY** *adv*

ANGST *n* pl. **-S** a feeling of anxiety or dread

ANGSTROM *n* pl. **-S** a unit of length

ANGSTY *adj* **ANGSTIER, ANGSTIEST** feeling anxiety or dread

ANGUINE *adj* resembling a snake

ANGUISH *v* **-ED, -ING, -ES** to suffer extreme pain

ANGULAR *adj* having sharp corners

ANGULATE *v* **-LATED, -LATING, -LATES** to make angular

ANGULOSE *adj* angular

ANGULOUS *adj* angular

ANHEDRAL *n* pl. **-S** the downward inclination of an aircraft's wing

ANHINGA *n* pl. **-S** an aquatic bird

ANI *n* pl. **-S** a tropical American bird

ANIL *n* pl. **-S** a West Indian shrub

ANILE *adj* resembling an old woman

ANILIN *n* pl. **-S** aniline

ANILINE *n* pl. **-S** a chemical compound

ANILITY *n* pl. **-TIES** the state of being anile

ANIMA *n* pl. **-S** the soul

ANIMACY *n* pl. **-CIES** the state of being alive

ANIMAL *n* pl. **-S** a living organism typically capable of voluntary motion and sensation **ANIMALIC** *adj*

ANIMALLY *adv* physically

ANIMATE *v* **-MATED, -MATING, -MATES** to give life to

ANIMATER *n* pl. **-S** animator

ANIMATO *n* pl. **-TOS** or **-TI** a musical passage played in a lively manner

ANIMATOR *n* pl. **-S** one that animates

ANIME *n* pl. **-S** a resin obtained from a tropical tree

ANIMI *n* pl. **-S** anime

ANIMISM *n* pl. **-S** the belief that souls may exist apart from bodies

ANIMIST *n* pl. **-S** an adherent of animism

ANIMUS *n* pl. **-ES** a feeling of hostility

ANION *n* pl. **-S** a negatively charged ion **ANIONIC** *adj*

ANISE *n* pl. **-S** a North African plant

ANISEED *n* pl. **-S** the seed of the anise used as a flavoring

ANISETTE *n* pl. **-S** a liqueur flavored with aniseed

ANISIC *adj* pertaining to an anise

ANISOLE *n* pl. **-S** a chemical compound

ANKERITE *n* pl. **-S** a mineral

ANKH *n* pl. **-S** an Egyptian symbol of enduring life

ANKLE *v* **-KLED, -KLING, -KLES** to walk

ANKLET *n* pl. **-S** an ornament for the ankle

ANKUS *n* pl. **-ES** an elephant goad

ANKUSH *n* pl. **-ES** ankus

ANKYLOSE *v* **-LOSED, -LOSING, -LOSES** to unite or grow together, as the bones of a joint

ANLACE *n* pl. **-S** a medieval dagger

ANLAGE *n* pl. **-GES** or **-GEN** the initial cell structure from which an embryonic organ develops

ANLAS *n* pl. **-ES** anlace

ANNA *n* pl. **-S** a former coin of India and Pakistan

ANNAL *n* pl. **-S** a record of a single year

ANNALIST *n* pl. **-S** a historian

ANNATES *n/pl* the first year's revenue of a bishop paid to the pope

ANNATTO *n* pl. **-TOS** a yellowish-red dye

ANNEAL *v* **-ED, -ING, -S** to toughen

ANNEALER *n* pl. **-S** one that anneals

ANNELID *n* pl. **-S** any of a phylum of segmented worms

ANNEX *v* **-ED, -ING, -ES** to add or attach

ANNEXE *n* pl. **-S** something added or attached

ANNONA *n* pl. **-S** a tropical tree

ANNOTATE *v* **-TATED, -TATING, -TATES** to furnish with critical or explanatory notes

ANNOUNCE *v* **-NOUNCED, -NOUNCING, -NOUNCES** to make known publicly

ANNOY *v* **-ED, -ING, -S** to be troublesome to

ANNOYER *n* pl. **-S** one that annoys

ANNUAL *n* pl. **-S** a publication issued once a year

ANNUALLY *adv* once a year

ANNUITY *n* pl. **-TIES** an allowance or income paid at regular intervals

ANNUL	*v* **-NULLED, -NULLING, -NULS** to make or declare void or invalid
ANNULAR	*adj* shaped like a ring
ANNULATE	*adj* composed of or furnished with rings
ANNULET	*n* pl. **-S** a small ring
ANNULI	a pl. of annulus
ANNULLED	past tense of annul
ANNULLING	present participle of annul
ANNULUS	*n* pl. **-LUSES** or **-LI** a ring or ringlike part **ANNULOSE** *adj*
ANOA	*n* pl. **-S** a wild ox
ANODE	*n* pl. **-S** a positively charged electrode **ANODAL, ANODIC** *adj* **ANODALLY** *adv*
ANODISE	*v* **-ISED, -ISING, -ISES** to anodize
ANODISER	*n* pl. **-S** anodizer
ANODIZE	*v* **-IZED, -IZING, -IZES** to coat with a protective film by chemical means
ANODIZER	*n* pl. **-S** one that anodizes
ANODYNE	*n* pl. **-S** a medicine that relieves pain **ANODYNIC** *adj*
ANOINT	*v* **-ED, -ING, -S** to apply oil to as a sacred rite
ANOINTER	*n* pl. **-S** one that anoints
ANOLE	*n* pl. **-S** a tropical lizard
ANOLYTE	*n* pl. **-S** the part of an electricity-conducting solution nearest the anode
ANOMALY	*n* pl. **-LIES** a deviation from the common rule, type, or form
ANOMIE	*n* pl. **-S** a collapse of the social structures governing a given society **ANOMIC** *adj*
ANOMY	*n* pl. **-MIES** anomie
ANON	*adv* at another time
ANONYM	*n* pl. **-S** a false or assumed name
ANOOPSIA	*n* pl. **-S** a visual defect
ANOPIA	*n* pl. **-S** anoopsia
ANOPSIA	*n* pl. **-S** anoopsia
ANORAK	*n* pl. **-S** a parka
ANORETIC	*n* pl. **-S** anorexic
ANOREXIA	*n* pl. **-S** loss of appetite
ANOREXIC	*n* pl. **-S** one affected with anorexia
ANOREXY	*n* pl. **-OREXIES** anorexia
ANORTHIC	*adj* denoting a certain type of crystal system
ANOSMIA	*n* pl. **-S** loss of the sense of smell **ANOSMIC** *adj*
ANOTHER	*adj* one more
ANOVULAR	*adj* not involving ovulation
ANOXEMIA	*n* pl. **-S** a disorder of the blood **ANOXEMIC** *adj*
ANOXIA	*n* pl. **-S** absence of oxygen **ANOXIC** *adj*
ANSA	*n* pl. **-SAE** the projecting part of Saturn's rings
ANSATE	*adj* having a handle
ANSATED	*adj* ansate
ANSATZ	*n* pl. **-ES** a possible solution to a problem
ANSERINE	*n* pl. **-S** a chemical compound
ANSEROUS	*adj* silly
ANSWER	*v* **-ED, -ING, -S** to say, write, or act in return
ANSWERER	*n* pl. **-S** one that answers
ANT	*n* pl. **-S** a small insect
ANTA	*n* pl. **-TAS** or **-TAE** a pilaster formed at the termination of a wall
ANTACID	*n* pl. **-S** a substance that neutralizes acid
ANTALGIC	*n* pl. **-S** an anodyne
ANTBEAR	*n* pl. **-S** an aardvark
ANTE	*v* **ANTED** or **ANTEED, ANTEING, ANTES** to put a fixed stake into the pot before the cards are dealt in poker
ANTEATER	*n* pl. **-S** any of several mammals that feed on ants
ANTECEDE	*v* **-CEDED, -CEDING, -CEDES** to precede
ANTEDATE	*v* **-DATED, -DATING, -DATES** to be of an earlier date than
ANTEFIX	*n* pl. **-FIXES** or **-FIXAE** or **-FIXA** an upright ornament at the eaves of a tiled roof
ANTELOPE	*n* pl. **-S** a ruminant mammal
ANTENNA	*n* pl. **-NAS** or **-NAE** a metallic device for sending or receiving radio waves **ANTENNAL** *adj*
ANTEPAST	*n* pl. **-S** an appetizer
ANTERIOR	*adj* situated in or toward the front
ANTEROOM	*n* pl. **-S** a waiting room
ANTES	present 3d person sing. of ante
ANTETYPE	*n* pl. **-S** an earlier form
ANTEVERT	*v* **-ED, -ING, -S** to displace by tipping forward

ANTHELIA	*n/pl* halolike areas seen in the sky opposite the sun
ANTHELIX	*n* pl. **-LIXES** or **-LICES** the inner curved ridge on the cartilage of the external ear
ANTHEM	*v* **-ED, -ING, -S** to praise in a song
ANTHEMIA	*n/pl* decorative floral patterns used in Greek art
ANTHEMIC	*adj* pertaining to an anthem (a song of praise)
ANTHER	*n* pl. **-S** the pollen-bearing part of a stamen **ANTHERAL** *adj*
ANTHERID	*n* pl. **-S** a male reproductive organ of certain plants
ANTHESIS	*n* pl. **-THESES** the full bloom of a flower
ANTHILL	*n* pl. **-S** a mound formed by ants in building their nest
ANTHODIA	*n/pl* flower heads of certain plants
ANTHOID	*adj* resembling a flower
ANTHRAX	*n* pl. **-THRAXES** or **-THRACES** an infectious disease
ANTHRO	*n* pl. **-THROS** anthropology
ANTI	*n* pl. **-S** one that is opposed
ANTIACNE	*adj* effective against acne
ANTIAIR	*adj* directed against attacking aircraft
ANTIAR	*n* pl. **-S** an arrow poison
ANTIARIN	*n* pl. **-S** antiar
ANTIATOM	*n* pl. **-S** an atom comprised of antiparticles
ANTIBIAS	*adj* opposed to bias
ANTIBODY	*n* pl. **-BODIES** a body protein that produces immunity against certain microorganisms or toxins
ANTIBOSS	*adj* opposed to bosses
ANTIBUG	*adj* effective against bugs
ANTIC	*v* **-TICKED, -TICKING, -TICS** to act in a clownish manner
ANTICAR	*adj* opposed to cars
ANTICITY	*adj* opposed to cities
ANTICK	*v* **-ED, -ING, -S** to antic
ANTICLY	*adv* in a clownish manner
ANTICOLD	*adj* effective against the common cold
ANTICULT	*n* pl. **-S** a group opposed to a cult
ANTIDORA	*n/pl* holy breads
ANTIDOTE	*v* **-DOTED, -DOTING, -DOTES** to counteract the effects of a poison with a remedy
ANTIDRUG	*adj* opposed to illicit drugs
ANTIFA	*n* pl. **-S** a person or group opposing fascism
ANTIFAT	*adj* preventing the formation of fat
ANTIFLU	*adj* combating the flu
ANTIFOAM	*adj* reducing or preventing foam
ANTIFOG	*adj* preventing the buildup of moisture on a surface
ANTIFUR	*adj* opposed to the wearing of animal furs
ANTIGANG	*adj* opposed to gangs
ANTIGAY	*adj* opposed to homosexuals
ANTIGEN	*n* pl. **-S** a substance that stimulates the production of antibodies
ANTIGENE	*n* pl. **-S** antigen
ANTIGUN	*adj* opposed to guns
ANTIHERO	*n* pl. **-ROES** a protagonist who is notably lacking in heroic qualities
ANTIJAM	*adj* blocking interfering signals
ANTIKING	*n* pl. **-S** a usurping king
ANTILEAK	*adj* preventing leaks
ANTILEFT	*adj* opposed to leftism
ANTILIFE	*adj* opposed to life
ANTILOCK	*adj* designed to prevent the wheels of a vehicle from locking
ANTILOG	*n* pl. **-S** the number corresponding to a given logarithm
ANTILOGY	*n* pl. **-GIES** a contradiction in terms or ideas
ANTIMALE	*adj* opposed to men
ANTIMAN	*adj* antimale
ANTIMASK	*n* pl. **-S** a comic performance between the acts of a masque
ANTIMERE	*n* pl. **-S** a part of an organism symmetrical with a part on the opposite side of the main axis
ANTIMINE	*adj* effective against mines
ANTIMONY	*n* pl. **-NIES** a metallic element
ANTING	*n* pl. **-S** the deliberate placing, by certain birds, of living ants among the feathers
ANTINODE	*n* pl. **-S** a region between adjacent nodes
ANTINOME	*n* pl. **-S** one that is opposite to another
ANTINOMY	*n* pl. **-MIES** a contradiction between two seemingly valid principles

ANTINUKE *n* pl. **-S** a person who opposes the use of nuclear power plants or nuclear weapons

ANTIPHON *n* pl. **-S** a psalm or hymn sung responsively

ANTIPILL *adj* opposing the use of contraceptive pills

ANTIPODE *n* pl. **-S** an exact opposite

ANTIPOLE *n* pl. **-S** the opposite pole

ANTIPOPE *n* pl. **-S** one claiming to be pope in opposition to the one chosen by church law

ANTIPORN *adj* opposed to pornography

ANTIPOT *adj* opposing the use of pot (marijuana)

ANTIPYIC *n* pl. **-S** a medicine that prevents the formation of pus

ANTIQUE *v* **-TIQUED, -TIQUING, -TIQUES** to give an appearance of age to

ANTIQUER *n* pl. **-S** one that antiques

ANTIRAPE *adj* concerned with preventing rape

ANTIRED *adj* opposed to communism

ANTIRIOT *adj* designed to prevent or end riots

ANTIROCK *adj* opposed to rock music

ANTIROLL *adj* designed to reduce roll

ANTIRUST *n* pl. **-S** something that prevents rust

ANTISAG *adj* designed to prevent sagging

ANTISERA *n/pl* serums that contain antibodies

ANTISEX *adj* opposed to sexual activity

ANTISHIP *adj* designed for use against ships

ANTISKID *adj* designed to prevent skidding

ANTISLIP *adj* designed to prevent slipping

ANTISMOG *adj* designed to reduce pollutants that cause smog

ANTISMUT *adj* opposed to pornography

ANTISNOB *n* pl. **-S** one that is opposed to snobbery

ANTISPAM *adj* designed to block spam (unsolicited email)

ANTISTAT *n* pl. **-S** an agent for preventing the buildup of static electricity

ANTITANK *adj* designed to combat tanks

ANTITAX *adj* opposing taxes

ANTITYPE *n* pl. **-S** an opposite type

ANTIWAR *adj* opposing war

ANTIWEAR *adj* designed to reduce the effects of long or hard use

ANTIWEED *adj* concerned with the destruction of weeds

ANTLER *n* pl. **-S** the horn of an animal of the deer family **ANTLERED** *adj*

ANTLIKE *adj* resembling an ant

ANTLION *n* pl. **-S** a predatory insect

ANTONYM *n* pl. **-S** a word opposite in meaning to another

ANTONYMY *n* pl. **-MIES** the state of being an antonym

ANTRA *a* pl. of antrum

ANTRAL *adj* pertaining to an antrum

ANTRE *n* pl. **-S** a cave (a hollow place in the earth)

ANTRORSE *adj* directed forward or upward

ANTRUM *n* pl. **-TRUMS** or **-TRA** a cavity in a bone

ANTSY *adj* **-SIER, -SIEST** fidgety

ANURA *n/pl* frogs and toads

ANURAL *adj* anurous

ANURAN *n* pl. **-S** a frog or toad

ANURESIS *n* pl. **-RESES** inability to urinate **ANURETIC** *adj*

ANURIA *n* pl. **-S** absence of urine **ANURIC** *adj*

ANUROUS *adj* having no tail

ANUS *n* pl. **-ES** the excretory opening at the end of the alimentary canal

ANVIL *v* **-VILED, -VILING, -VILS** or **-VILLED, -VILLING, -VILS** to shape on an anvil (a heavy iron block)

ANVILTOP *n* pl. **-S** an anvil-shaped cloud mass

ANXIETY *n* pl. **-ETIES** painful or apprehensive uneasiness of mind

ANXIOUS *adj* full of anxiety

ANY *adj* one, no matter which

ANYBODY *n* pl. **-BODIES** a person of some importance

ANYHOW *adv* in any way

ANYMORE *adv* at the present time

ANYON *n* pl. **-S** a subatomic particle

ANYONE *pron* any person

ANYPLACE *adv* in any place

ANYTHING *n* pl. **-S** a thing of any kind

ANYTIME *adv* at any time

ANYWAY *adv* in any way

ANYWAYS *adv* anyway

ANYWHERE *n* pl. **-S** any place

ANYWISE *adv* in any way

AORIST *n* pl. **-S** a verb tense **AORISTIC** *adj*

AORTA *n* pl. **-TAS** or **-TAE** a main artery **AORTAL, AORTIC** *adj*

AOUDAD *n* pl. **-S** a wild sheep

APACE *adv* swiftly

APACHE *n* pl. **-S** a Parisian gangster

APAGOGE *n* pl. **-S** establishment of a thesis by showing its contrary to be absurd **APAGOGIC** *adj*

APANAGE *n* pl. **-S** appanage

APAREJO *n* pl. **-JOS** a type of saddle

APART *adv* not together

APATETIC *adj* having coloration serving as natural camouflage

APATHY *n* pl. **-THIES** lack of emotion

APATITE *n* pl. **-S** a mineral

APE *v* **APED, APING, APES** to mimic

APEAK *adv* in a vertical position

APEEK *adv* apeak

APELIKE *adj* resembling an ape (a large, tailless primate)

APEMAN *n* pl. **-MEN** an extinct apelike primate

APER *n* pl. **-S** one that apes

APERCU *n* pl. **-S** a brief summary

APERIENT *n* pl. **-S** a mild laxative

APERITIF *n* pl. **-S** an alcoholic drink taken before a meal

APERTURE *n* pl. **-S** an opening

APERY *n* pl. **-ERIES** the act of aping

APETALY *n* pl. **-ALIES** the state of having no petals

APEX *n* pl. **APEXES** or **APICES** the highest point

APHAGIA *n* pl. **-S** inability to swallow

APHANITE *n* pl. **-S** an igneous rock

APHASIA *n* pl. **-S** loss of the ability to use words

APHASIAC *n* pl. **-S** one suffering from aphasia

APHASIC *n* pl. **-S** aphasiac

APHELION *n* pl. **-ELIONS** or **-ELIA** the point in a planetary orbit farthest from the sun **APHELIAN** *adj*

APHESIS *n* pl. **-ESES** the loss of an unstressed vowel from the beginning of a word **APHETIC** *adj*

APHID *n* pl. **-S** any of a family of small, soft-bodied insects

APHIDIAN *n* pl. **-S** an aphid

APHIS *n* pl. **APHIDES** an aphid

APHOLATE *n* pl. **-S** a chemical used to control houseflies

APHONIA *n* pl. **-S** loss of voice

APHONIC *n* pl. **-S** one affected with aphonia

APHONY *n* pl. **-NIES** aphonia

APHORISE *v* **-RISED, -RISING, -RISES** to aphorize

APHORISM *n* pl. **-S** a brief statement of a truth or principle

APHORIST *n* pl. **-S** one that aphorizes

APHORIZE *v* **-RIZED, -RIZING, -RIZES** to write or speak in aphorisms

APHOTIC *adj* lacking light

APHTHA *n* pl. **-THAE** a small blister in the mouth or stomach **APHTHOUS** *adj*

APHYLLY *n* pl. **-LIES** the state of being leafless

APIAN *adj* pertaining to bees

APIARIAN *n* pl. **-S** an apiarist

APIARIST *n* pl. **-S** a person who raises bees

APIARY *n* pl. **-ARIES** a place where bees are kept

APICAL *n* pl. **-S** a sound articulated with the apex (tip) of the tongue

APICALLY *adv* at or toward the apex

APICES *a* pl. of apex

APICULUS *n* pl. **-LI** a sharp point at the end of a leaf

APIECE *adv* for each one

APIMANIA *n* pl. **-S** an excessive interest in bees

APING present participle of ape

APIOLOGY *n* pl. **-GIES** the study of bees

APISH *adj* slavishly or foolishly imitative **APISHLY** *adv*

APLANAT *n* pl. **-S** a type of reflecting or refracting surface

APLASIA *n* pl. **-S** defective development of an organ or part

APLASTIC *adj* not plastic

APLENTY *adj* being in sufficient quantity

APLITE *n* pl. **-S** a fine-grained rock **APLITIC** *adj*

APLOMB *n* pl. **-S** self-confidence

APNEA *n* pl. **-S** temporary cessation of respiration **APNEAL, APNEIC** *adj*

APNOEA *n* pl. **-S** apnea **APNOEAL, APNOEIC** *adj*

APO *n* pl. **APOS** a type of protein

APOAPSIS *n* pl. **-APSIDES** or **-APSES** the high point in an orbit

APOCARP *n* pl. **-S** a fruit having separated carpels

APOCARPY *n* pl. **-PIES** the state of being an apocarp

APOCOPE *n* pl. **-S** an omission of the last sound of a word **APOCOPIC** *adj*

APOCRINE *adj* pertaining to a type of gland

APOD *n* pl. **-S** an apodal animal

APODAL *adj* having no feet or footlike appendages

APODOSIS *n* pl. **-OSES** the main clause of a conditional sentence

APODOUS *adj* apodal

APOGAMY *n* pl. **-MIES** a form of plant reproduction **APOGAMIC** *adj*

APOGEE *n* pl. **-S** the point in the orbit of a body which is farthest from the earth **APOGEAL, APOGEAN, APOGEIC** *adj*

APOLLO *n* pl. **-LOS** a handsome young man

APOLOG *n* pl. **-S** apologue

APOLOGAL *adj* pertaining to an apologue

APOLOGIA *n* pl. **-GIAS** or **-GIAE** a formal justification or defense

APOLOGUE *n* pl. **-S** an allegory

APOLOGY *n* pl. **-GIES** an expression of regret for some error or offense

APOLUNE *n* pl. **-S** the point in the orbit of a body which is farthest from the moon

APOMICT *n* pl. **-S** an organism produced by apomixis

APOMIXIS *n* pl. **-MIXES** a type of reproductive process

APOPHONY *n* pl. **-NIES** ablaut

APOPHYGE *n* pl. **-S** a concave curve in a column

APOPLEXY *n* pl. **-PLEXIES** a sudden loss of sensation and muscular control

APORIA *n* pl. **-S** an expression of doubt for rhetorical effect

APORT *adv* on or toward the left side of a ship

APOSPORY *n* pl. **-RIES** a type of reproduction without spore formation

APOSTACY *n* pl. **-CIES** apostasy

APOSTASY *n* pl. **-SIES** an abandonment of one's faith or principles

APOSTATE *n* pl. **-S** one who commits apostasy

APOSTIL *n* pl. **-S** a marginal note

APOSTLE *n* pl. **-S** a disciple sent forth by Christ to preach the gospel

APOTHECE *n* pl. **-S** a spore-producing organ of certain fungi

APOTHEGM *n* pl. **-S** a maxim

APOTHEM *n* pl. **-S** the perpendicular from the center to any side of a regular polygon

APP *n* pl. **-S** a computer program for a major task

APPAL *v* **-PALLED, -PALLING, -PALS** to appall

APPALL *v* **-ED, -ING, -S** to fill with horror or dismay

APPANAGE *n* pl. **-S** land or revenue granted to a member of a royal family

APPARAT *n* pl. **-S** a political organization

APPAREL *v* **-ELED, -ELING, -ELS** or **-ELLED, -ELLING, -ELS** to provide with outer garments

APPARENT *adj* easily seen

APPEAL *v* **-ED, -ING, -S** to make an earnest request

APPEALER *n* pl. **-S** one that appeals

APPEAR *v* **-ED, -ING, -S** to come into view

APPEASE *v* **-PEASED, -PEASING, -PEASES** to bring to a state of peace or contentment

APPEASER *n* pl. **-S** one that appeases

APPEL *n* pl. **-S** a feint in fencing

APPELLEE *n* pl. **-S** the defendant in a type of judicial proceeding

APPELLOR *n* pl. **-S** a confessed criminal who accuses an accomplice

APPEND *v* **-ED, -ING, -S** to add as a supplement

APPENDIX *n* pl. **-DIXES** or **-DICES** a collection of supplementary material at the end of a book

APPESTAT *n* pl. **-S** the mechanism in the central nervous system that regulates appetite

APPETENT *adj* marked by strong desire

APPETITE *n* pl. **-S** a desire for food or drink

APPLAUD *v* **-ED, -ING, -S** to express approval by clapping the hands

APPLAUSE   *n* pl. **-S** the sound made by persons applauding

APPLE   *n* pl. **-S** an edible fruit

APPLET   *n* pl. **-S** a computer program for a simple task

APPLEY   *adj* **APPLIER, APPLIEST** resembling or suggestive of an apple

APPLIED   past tense of apply

APPLIER   *n* pl. **-S** one that applies

APPLIQUE   *v* **-QUED, -QUEING, -QUES** to apply as a decoration to a larger surface

APPLY   *v* **-PLIED, -PLYING, -PLIES** to bring into contact with something

APPOINT   *v* **-ED, -ING, -S** to name or assign to a position or office

APPOSE   *v* **-POSED, -POSING, -POSES** to place side by side

APPOSER   *n* pl. **-S** one that apposes

APPOSITE   *adj* relevant

APPRAISE   *v* **-PRAISED, -PRAISING, -PRAISES** to set a value on

APPRESS   *v* **-ED, -ING, -ES** to press close to something else

APPRISE   *v* **-PRISED, -PRISING, -PRISES** to notify

APPRISER   *n* pl. **-S** one that apprises

APPRIZE   *v* **-PRIZED, -PRIZING, -PRIZES** to appraise

APPRIZER   *n* pl. **-S** one that apprizes

APPROACH   *v* **-ED, -ING, -ES** to come near or nearer to

APPROVAL   *n* pl. **-S** the act of approving

APPROVE   *v* **-PROVED, -PROVING, -PROVES** to regard favorably

APPROVER   *n* pl. **-S** one that approves

APPULSE   *n* pl. **-S** the approach of one moving body toward another

APRAXIA   *n* pl. **-S** loss of the ability to perform coordinated movements **APRACTIC, APRAXIC** *adj*

APRES   *prep* after

APRICOT   *n* pl. **-S** an edible fruit

APRON   *v* **-ED, -ING, -S** to provide with an apron (a garment worn to protect one's clothing)

APROPOS   *adj* relevant

APROTIC   *adj* being a type of solvent

APSE   *n* pl. **-S** a domed, semicircular projection of a building **APSIDAL** *adj*

APSIS   *n* pl. **-SIDES** an apse

APT   *adj* **APTER, APTEST** suitable

APTERAL   *adj* apterous

APTERIUM   *n* pl. **-RIA** a bare area of skin between feathers

APTEROUS   *adj* having no wings

APTERYX   *n* pl. **-ES** the kiwi

APTITUDE   *n* pl. **-S** an ability

APTLY   *adv* in an apt manner

APTNESS   *n* pl. **-ES** the quality of being apt

APYRASE   *n* pl. **-S** an enzyme

APYRETIC   *adj* having no fever

AQUA   *n* pl. **AQUAS** or **AQUAE** water (a transparent, tasteless, odorless liquid)

AQUACADE   *n* pl. **-S** a swimming and diving exhibition

AQUAFABA   *n* the liquid that results when beans are cooked in water

AQUAFARM   *v* **-ED, -ING, -S** to cultivate food fish

AQUAFIT   *n* pl. **-S** an exercise class in water

AQUANAUT   *n* pl. **-S** a scuba diver trained to live in underwater installations

AQUARIA   a pl. of aquarium

AQUARIAL   *adj* pertaining to an aquarium

AQUARIAN   *n* pl. **-S** a member of the old sects that used water rather than wine in religious ceremonies

AQUARIST   *n* pl. **-S** one who keeps an aquarium

AQUARIUM   *n* pl. **-IUMS** or **-IA** a water-filled enclosure in which aquatic animals are kept

AQUATIC   *n* pl. **-S** an organism living or growing in or near water

AQUATINT   *v* **-ED, -ING, -S** to etch, using a certain process

AQUATONE   *n* pl. **-S** a type of printing process

AQUAVIT   *n* pl. **-S** a Scandinavian liquor

AQUEDUCT   *n* pl. **-S** a water conduit

AQUEOUS   *adj* pertaining to water

AQUIFER   *n* pl. **-S** a water-bearing rock formation

AQUILINE   *adj* curving like an eagle's beak

AQUIVER   *adj* quivering

AR   *n* pl. **-S** the letter R

ARABESK	*n* pl. **-S** a design of intertwined floral figures	**ARC**	*v* **ARCED, ARCING, ARCS** or **ARCKED, ARCKING, ARCS** to move in a curved course
ARABIC	*adj* derived from gum arabic	**ARCADE**	*v* **-CADED, -CADING, -CADES** to provide with an arcade (a series of arches)
ARABICA	*n* pl. **-S** an evergreen shrub that produces coffee beans		
ARABIS	*n* pl. **-ES** a mat-forming plant	**ARCADIA**	*n* pl. **-S** a region of simple pleasure and quiet
ARABIZE	*v* **-IZED, -IZING, -IZES** to cause to acquire Arabic customs	**ARCADIAN**	*n* pl. **-S** one who lives in an arcadia
ARABLE	*n* pl. **-S** land suitable for cultivation	**ARCADING**	*n* pl. **-S** an arcade
ARACEOUS	*adj* belonging to the arum family of plants	**ARCANE**	*adj* mysterious **ARCANELY** *adv*
		ARCANUM	*n* pl. **-NUMS** or **-NA** a mystery
ARACHNID	*n* pl. **-S** any of a class of segmented invertebrate animals	**ARCATURE**	*n* pl. **-S** a small arcade
ARAHUANA	*n* pl. **-S** arowana	**ARCH**	*v* **-ED, -ING, -ES** to bend like an arch (a curved structure spanning an opening)
ARAK	*n* pl. **-S** arrack		
ARAME	*n* pl. **-S** an edible seaweed	**ARCHAEA**	*n/pl* a large group of microorganisms **ARCHAEAL** *adj*
ARAMID	*n* pl. **-S** a type of chemical compound		
		ARCHAEAN	*n* pl. **-S** a microorganism of the archaea
ARANCINI	*n/pl* balls of cooked rice		
ARANEID	*n* pl. **-S** a spider	**ARCHAEON**	*n* pl. **-CHAEA** archaean
ARAPAIMA	*n* pl. **-S** a large food fish	**ARCHAIC**	*adj* pertaining to an earlier time
ARAROBA	*n* pl. **-S** a Brazilian tree	**ARCHAISE**	*v* **-ISED, -ISING, -ISES** to archaize
ARAWANA	*n* pl. **-S** arowana	**ARCHAISM**	*n* pl. **-S** an archaic word, idiom, or expression
ARB	*n* pl. **-S** a type of stock trader		
ARBALEST	*n* pl. **-S** a type of crossbow	**ARCHAIST**	*n* pl. **-S** one that archaizes
ARBALIST	*n* pl. **-S** arbalest	**ARCHAIZE**	*v* **-IZED, -IZING, -IZES** to use archaisms
ARBELEST	*n* pl. **-S** arbalest		
ARBITER	*n* pl. **-S** one chosen or appointed to judge a disputed issue **ARBITRAL** *adj*	**ARCHDUKE**	*n* pl. **-S** an Austrian prince
		ARCHER	*n* pl. **-S** one that shoots with a bow and arrow
ARBOR	*n* pl. **-ES** a tree when contrasted with a shrub	**ARCHERY**	*n* pl. **-CHERIES** the sport of shooting with a bow and arrow
ARBOR	*n* pl. **-S** a shady garden shelter	**ARCHFOE**	*n* pl. **-S** a principal foe
ARBOREAL	*adj* living in trees	**ARCHI**	pl. of arco
ARBORED	*adj* having trees	**ARCHIL**	*n* pl. **-S** orchil
ARBORETA	*n/pl* places for the study and exhibition of trees	**ARCHINE**	*n* pl. **-S** a Russian unit of linear measure
ARBORIST	*n* pl. **-S** a tree specialist	**ARCHING**	*n* pl. **-S** a series of arches
ARBORIZE	*v* **-IZED, -IZING, -IZES** to form many branches	**ARCHIVE**	*v* **-CHIVED, -CHIVING, -CHIVES** to file in an archive (a place where records are kept) **ARCHIVAL** *adj*
ARBOROUS	*adj* pertaining to trees	**ARCHLY**	*adv* slyly
ARBOUR	*n* pl. **-S** a shady garden shelter **ARBOURED** *adj*	**ARCHNESS**	*n* pl. **-ES** slyness
		ARCHON	*n* pl. **-S** a magistrate of ancient Athens
ARBUSCLE	*n* pl. **-S** a dwarf tree		
ARBUTE	*n* pl. **-S** an evergreen tree **ARBUTEAN** *adj*	**ARCHWAY**	*n* pl. **-WAYS** a passageway under an arch
		ARCIFORM	*adj* having the form of an arch
ARBUTUS	*n* pl. **-ES** an evergreen tree	**ARCING**	*n* pl. **-S** the curved form of an arc

ARCKED a past tense of arc

ARCKING a present participle of arc

ARCO *n* pl. **ARCHI** a note or passage played with the bow of a stringed instrument

ARCSINE *n* pl. **-S** the inverse function to the sine

ARCTIC *n* pl. **-S** a warm, waterproof overshoe

ARCUATE *adj* curved like a bow

ARCUATED *adj* arcuate

ARCUS *n* pl. **-ES** an arch-shaped cloud

ARDEB *n* pl. **-S** an Egyptian unit of capacity

ARDENCY *n* pl. **-CIES** ardor

ARDENT *adj* characterized by intense emotion **ARDENTLY** *adv*

ARDOR *n* pl. **-S** intensity of emotion

ARDOUR *n* pl. **-S** ardor

ARDUOUS *adj* involving great labor or hardship

ARE *n* pl. **-S** a unit of surface measure

AREA *n* pl. **-S** a particular extent of space or surface **AREAL** *adj* **AREALLY** *adv*

AREA *n* pl. **AREAE** a section of the cerebral cortex having a specific function

AREAWAY *n* pl. **-WAYS** a sunken area leading to a basement entrance

ARECA *n* pl. **-S** a tropical tree

AREG *n/pl* areas of shifting desert sand dunes

AREIC *adj* pertaining to a region of the earth contributing little surface drainage

ARENA *n* pl. **-S** an enclosed area for contests

ARENE *n* pl. **-S** an aromatic compound

ARENITE *n* pl. **-S** rock made up chiefly of sand grains

ARENOSE *adj* sandy

ARENOUS *adj* arenose

AREOLA *n* pl. **-LAS** or **-LAE** a small space in a network of leaf veins **AREOLAR, AREOLATE** *adj*

AREOLE *n* pl. **-S** areola

AREOLOGY *n* pl. **-GIES** the study of the planet Mars

AREPA *n* pl. **-S** a cornmeal cake

ARETE *n* pl. **-S** a sharp mountain ridge

ARETHUSA *n* pl. **-S** a flowering plant

ARF *n* pl. **-S** a barking sound

ARGAL *n* pl. **-S** argol

ARGALA *n* pl. **-S** a type of stork

ARGALI *n* pl. **-S** a wild sheep

ARGENT *n* pl. **-S** silver **ARGENTAL, ARGENTIC** *adj*

ARGENTUM *n* pl. **-S** silver

ARGH *interj* aargh

ARGIL *n* pl. **-S** a white clay

ARGINASE *n* pl. **-S** an enzyme

ARGININE *n* pl. **-S** an amino acid

ARGLE *v* **-GLED, -GLING, -GLES** to argue

ARGOL *n* pl. **-S** a crust deposited in wine casks during aging

ARGON *n* pl. **-S** a gaseous element

ARGONAUT *n* pl. **-S** a marine mollusk

ARGOSY *n* pl. **-SIES** a large merchant ship

ARGOT *n* pl. **-S** a specialized vocabulary **ARGOTIC** *adj*

ARGUABLE *adj* capable of being argued about **ARGUABLY** *adv*

ARGUE *v* **-GUED, -GUING, -GUES** to present reasons for or against

ARGUER *n* pl. **-S** one that argues

ARGUFIER *n* pl. **-S** one that argufies

ARGUFY *v* **-FIED, -FYING, -FIES** to argue stubbornly

ARGUING present participle of argue

ARGUMENT *n* pl. **-S** a discussion involving differing points of view

ARGUS *n* pl. **-ES** an East Indian pheasant

ARGYLE *n* pl. **-S** a knitting pattern

ARGYLL *n* pl. **-S** argyle

ARHAT *n* pl. **-S** a Buddhist who has attained nirvana

ARIA *n* pl. **-S** an elaborate melody for a single voice

ARIARY *n* pl. **ARIARY** a monetary unit of Madagascar

ARID *adj* **-IDER, -IDEST** extremely dry **ARIDLY** *adv*

ARIDITY *n* pl. **-TIES** the state of being arid

ARIDNESS *n* pl. **-ES** aridity

ARIEL *n* pl. **-S** an African gazelle

ARIETTA *n* pl. **-S** a short aria

ARIETTE *n* pl. **-S** arietta

ARIGHT *adv* rightly; correctly

ARIL   *n* pl. **-S** an outer covering of certain seeds **ARILED, ARILLATE, ARILLOID** *adj*

ARILLODE   *n* pl. **-S** a type of aril

ARIOSE   *adj* characterized by melody

ARIOSO   *n* pl. **-SOS** or **-SI** a musical passage resembling an aria

ARISE   *v* **AROSE, ARISEN, ARISING, ARISES** to get up

ARISTA   *n* pl. **-TAS** or **-TAE** a bristlelike structure or appendage **ARISTATE** *adj*

ARISTO   *n* pl. **-TOS** an aristocrat

ARK   *n* pl. **-S** a large boat

ARKOSE   *n* pl. **-S** a type of sandstone **ARKOSIC** *adj*

ARLES   *n/pl* money paid to bind a bargain

ARM   *v* **-ED, -ING, -S** to supply with weapons

ARMADA   *n* pl. **-S** a fleet of warships

ARMAGNAC   *n* pl. **-S** a French brandy

ARMAMENT   *n* pl. **-S** a military force equipped for war

ARMATURE   *v* **-TURED, -TURING, -TURES** to furnish with armor

ARMBAND   *n* pl. **-S** a band worn around an arm (an upper appendage of the human body)

ARMCHAIR   *n* pl. **-S** a chair with armrests

ARMER   *n* pl. **-S** one that arms

ARMET   *n* pl. **-S** a medieval helmet

ARMFUL   *n* pl. **ARMFULS** or **ARMSFUL** as much as the arm can hold

ARMGUARD   *n* pl. **-S** a covering to protect the arm

ARMHOLE   *n* pl. **-S** an opening for the arm in a garment

ARMIES   pl. of army

ARMIGER   *n* pl. **-S** one who carries the armor of a knight

ARMIGERO   *n* pl. **-GEROS** armiger

ARMILLA   *n* pl. **-LAS** or **-LAE** a thin membrane around the stem of certain fungi

ARMING   *n* pl. **-S** the act of one that arms

ARMLESS   *adj* having no arms

ARMLET   *n* pl. **-S** an armband

ARMLIKE   *adj* resembling an arm

ARMLOAD   *n* pl. **-S** an armful

ARMLOCK   *n* pl. **-S** a hold in wrestling

ARMOIRE   *n* pl. **-S** a large, ornate cabinet

ARMONICA   *n* pl. **-S** a type of musical instrument

ARMOR   *v* **-ED, -ING, -S** to furnish with armor (a defensive covering)

ARMORER   *n* pl. **-S** one that makes or repairs armor

ARMORIAL   *n* pl. **-S** a treatise on heraldry

ARMORY   *n* pl. **-MORIES** a place where weapons are stored

ARMOUR   *v* **-ED, -ING, -S** to armor

ARMOURER   *n* pl. **-S** armorer

ARMOURY   *n* pl. **-MOURIES** armory

ARMPIT   *n* pl. **-S** the hollow under the arm at the shoulder

ARMREST   *n* pl. **-S** a support for the arm

ARMSFUL   a pl. of armful

ARMURE   *n* pl. **-S** a woven fabric

ARMY   *n* pl. **-MIES** a large body of men trained and armed for war

ARMYWORM   *n* pl. **-S** a destructive moth larva

ARNATTO   *n* pl. **-TOS** annatto

ARNICA   *n* pl. **-S** a perennial herb

ARNOTTO   *n* pl. **-TOS** a tropical tree

AROID   *n* pl. **-S** a flowering plant

AROINT   *v* **-ED, -ING, -S** to drive away

AROMA   *n* pl. **-S** a pleasant odor

AROMATIC   *n* pl. **-S** a fragrant plant or substance

AROSE   past tense of arise

AROUND   *prep* on all sides of

AROUSAL   *n* pl. **-S** the act of arousing

AROUSE   *v* **AROUSED, AROUSING, AROUSES** to stimulate

AROUSER   *n* pl. **-S** one that arouses

AROWANA   *n* pl. **-S** a large, tropical fish

AROYNT   *v* **-ED, -ING, -S** to aroint

ARPEGGIO   *n* pl. **-GIOS** a technique of playing a musical chord

ARPEN   *n* pl. **-S** arpent

ARPENT   *n* pl. **-S** an old French unit of area

ARQUEBUS   *n* pl. **-ES** an early portable firearm

ARRACK   *n* pl. **-S** an Oriental liquor

ARRAIGN   *v* **-ED, -ING, -S** to call before a court of law to answer an indictment

ARRANGE   *v* **-RANGED, -RANGING, -RANGES** to put in definite or proper order

ARRANGER   *n* pl. **-S** one that arranges

ARRANT   *adj* outright **ARRANTLY** *adv*

ARRAS   *n* pl. **-ES** a tapestry **ARRASED** *adj*

ARRAY   *v* **-ED, -ING, -S** to place in proper or desired order

ARRAYAL   *n* pl. **-S** the act of arraying

ARRAYER   *n* pl. **-S** one that arrays

ARREAR   *n* pl. **-S** an unpaid and overdue debt

ARREST   *v* **-ED, -ING, -S** to seize and hold by legal authority

ARRESTEE   *n* pl. **-S** one that is arrested

ARRESTER   *n* pl. **-S** one that arrests

ARRESTOR   *n* pl. **-S** arrester

ARRHIZAL   *adj* rootless

ARRIBA   *interj* — used to express pleasure

ARRIS   *n* pl. **-RISES** a ridge formed by the meeting of two surfaces

ARRIVAL   *n* pl. **-S** the act of arriving

ARRIVE   *v* **-RIVED, -RIVING, -RIVES** to reach a destination

ARRIVER   *n* pl. **-S** one that arrives

ARROBA   *n* pl. **-S** a Spanish unit of weight

ARROGANT   *adj* overly convinced of one's own worth or importance

ARROGATE   *v* **-GATED, -GATING, -GATES** to claim or take without right

ARROW   *v* **-ED, -ING, -S** to indicate the proper position of with an arrow (a linear figure with a wedge-shaped end)

ARROWY   *adj* moving swiftly

ARROYO   *n* pl. **-ROYOS** a brook or creek

ARROZ   *n* pl. **ARROCES** or **ARROZES** rice

ARSENAL   *n* pl. **-S** a collection or supply of weapons

ARSENATE   *n* pl. **-S** a chemical salt

ARSENIC   *n* pl. **-S** a metallic element

ARSENIDE   *n* pl. **-S** an arsenic compound

ARSENITE   *n* pl. **-S** a chemical salt

ARSENO   *adj* containing a certain bivalent chemical radical

ARSENOUS   *adj* pertaining to arsenic

ARSES   pl. of arsis

ARSHIN   *n* pl. **-S** archine

ARSINE   *n* pl. **-S** a poisonous gas

ARSINO   *adj* containing a certain univalent chemical radical

ARSIS   *n* pl. **ARSES** the unaccented part of a musical measure

ARSON   *n* pl. **-S** the malicious or fraudulent burning of property **ARSONOUS** *adj*

ARSONIST   *n* pl. **-S** one that commits arson

ART   *n* pl. **-S** an esthetically pleasing and meaningful arrangement of elements

ARTAL   a pl. of rotl

ARTEFACT   *n* pl. **-S** artifact

ARTEL   *n* pl. **-S** a collective farm in Russia

ARTERIAL   *n* pl. **-S** a type of highway

ARTERY   *n* pl. **-TERIES** a vessel that carries blood away from the heart

ARTESIAN   *adj* pertaining to a type of well

ARTFUL   *adj* crafty **ARTFULLY** *adv*

ARTICLE   *v* **-CLED, -CLING, -CLES** to charge with specific offenses

ARTIER   comparative of arty

ARTIEST   superlative of arty

ARTIFACT   *n* pl. **-S** an object made by man

ARTIFICE   *n* pl. **-S** a clever stratagem

ARTIGI   *n* pl. **-S** atigi

ARTILY   *adv* in an arty manner

ARTINESS   *n* pl. **-ES** the quality of being arty

ARTISAN   *n* pl. **-S** a trained or skilled workman

ARTIST   *n* pl. **-S** one who practices one of the fine arts

ARTISTE   *n* pl. **-S** a skilled public performer

ARTISTIC   *adj* characteristic of art

ARTISTRY   *n* pl. **-RIES** artistic quality or workmanship

ARTLESS   *adj* lacking cunning or guile

ARTMAKER   *n* pl. **-S** one that produces art

ARTSIE   *n* pl. **-S** a student in an arts program

ARTSY   *adj* **-SIER, -SIEST** arty

ARTWORK   *n* pl. **-S** illustrative or decorative work in printed matter

ARTY   *adj* **ARTIER, ARTIEST** showily or pretentiously artistic

ARUANA   *n* pl. **-S** arowana

ARUGOLA   *n* pl. **-S** arugula

ARUGULA   *n* pl. **-S** a European annual herb

ARUM   *n* pl. **-S** a flowering plant

ARUSPEX *n* pl. **-PICES** haruspex

ARVAL *adj* pertaining to plowed land

ARVO *n* pl. **-VOS** afternoon

ARYL *n* pl. **-S** a univalent radical

ARYTHMIA *n* pl. **-S** an irregularity in the rhythm of the heartbeat **ARYTHMIC** *adj*

AS *adv* to the same degree

ASANA *n* pl. **-S** a posture in yoga

ASARUM *n* pl. **-S** a perennial herb

ASBESTOS *n* pl. **-ES** a mineral **ASBESTIC** *adj*

ASBESTUS *n* pl. **-ES** asbestos

ASCARED *adj* afraid

ASCARID *n* pl. **-S** a parasitic worm

ASCARIS *n* pl. **-RISES** or **-RIDES** ascarid

ASCEND *v* **-ED, -ING, -S** to go or move upward

ASCENDER *n* pl. **-S** one that ascends

ASCENT *n* pl. **-S** the act of ascending

ASCESIS *n* pl. **-CESES** the conduct of an ascetic

ASCETIC *n* pl. **-S** one who practices extreme self-denial for religious reasons

ASCI pl. of ascus

ASCIDIAN *n* pl. **-S** a small marine animal

ASCIDIUM *n* pl. **-DIA** a flask-shaped plant appendage

ASCITES *n* pl. **ASCITES** accumulation of serous fluid in the abdomen **ASCITIC** *adj*

ASCOCARP *n* pl. **-S** a spore-producing organ of certain fungi

ASCON *n* pl. **-S** a type of sponge **ASCONOID** *adj*

ASCORBIC *adj* relieving scurvy

ASCOT *n* pl. **-S** a broad neck scarf

ASCRIBE *v* **-CRIBED, -CRIBING, -CRIBES** to attribute to a specified cause, source, or origin

ASCUS *n* pl. **ASCI** a spore sac in certain fungi

ASDIC *n* pl. **-S** sonar

ASEA *adv* at sea

ASEISMIC *adj* not subject to earthquakes

ASEPSIS *n* pl. **-SEPSES** the condition of being aseptic

ASEPTIC *adj* free from germs

ASEXUAL *adj* occurring or performed without sexual action

ASH *v* **-ED, -ING, -ES** to convert into ash (the residue of a substance that has been burned)

ASHAMED *adj* feeling shame, guilt, or disgrace

ASHCAKE *n* pl. **-S** a cornmeal cake

ASHCAN *n* pl. **-S** a metal receptacle for garbage

ASHEN *adj* consisting of ashes

ASHFALL *n* pl. **-S** a deposit of volcanic ash

ASHIER comparative of ashy

ASHIEST superlative of ashy

ASHINE *adj* shining

ASHINESS *n* pl. **-ES** the condition of being ashy

ASHLAR *v* **-ED, -ING, -S** to build with squared stones

ASHLER *v* **-ED, -ING, -S** to ashlar

ASHLESS *adj* having no ashes

ASHMAN *n* pl. **-MEN** one who collects and removes ashes

ASHORE *adv* toward or on the shore

ASHPAN *n* pl. **-S** a tray under a grate to catch the ashes

ASHPLANT *n* pl. **-S** a walking stick

ASHRAM *n* pl. **-S** a secluded dwelling of a Hindu sage

ASHRAMA *n* pl. **-S** a stage of life in Hinduism

ASHTANGA *n* pl. **-S** a type of yoga

ASHTRAY *n* pl. **-TRAYS** a receptacle for tobacco ashes

ASHY *adj* **ASHIER, ASHIEST** covered with ashes

ASIAGO *n* pl. **-GOS** a type of cheese

ASIDE *n* pl. **-S** a comment by an actor intended to be heard by the audience but not the other actors

ASININE *adj* obstinately stupid or silly

ASK *v* **-ED, -ING, -S** to put a question to

ASKANCE *adv* with a side glance

ASKANT *adv* askance

ASKARI *n* pl. **-S** a soldier or police officer of eastern Africa

ASKER *n* pl. **-S** one that asks

ASKESIS *n* pl. **ASKESES** ascesis

ASKEW *adv* to one side

ASKING *n* pl. **-S** the act of one who asks

ASKOS *n* pl. **ASKOI** an oil jar used in ancient Greece

ASLANT	*adj* slanting
ASLEEP	*adj* sleeping
ASLOPE	*adj* sloping
ASLOSH	*adj* covered with water
ASOCIAL	*n* pl. **-S** one that avoids the company of others
ASP	*n* pl. **-S** a venomous snake
ASPARKLE	*adj* sparkling
ASPECT	*n* pl. **-S** appearance of something to the eye or mind
ASPEN	*n* pl. **-S** any of several poplars
ASPER	*n* pl. **-S** a Turkish money of account
ASPERATE	*v* **-ATED, -ATING, -ATES** to make uneven
ASPERGES	*n* pl. **ASPERGES** a Roman Catholic rite
ASPERITY	*n* pl. **-TIES** acrimony
ASPERSE	*v* **-PERSED, -PERSING, -PERSES** to spread false charges against
ASPERSER	*n* pl. **-S** one that asperses
ASPERSOR	*n* pl. **-S** asperser
ASPHALT	*v* **-ED, -ING, -S** to coat with asphalt (a substance used for paving and roofing)
ASPHERIC	*adj* varying slightly from an exactly spherical shape
ASPHODEL	*n* pl. **-S** a flowering plant
ASPHYXIA	*n* pl. **-S** unconsciousness caused by lack of oxygen
ASPHYXY	*n* pl. **-PHYXIES** asphyxia
ASPIC	*n* pl. **-S** the asp
ASPIRANT	*n* pl. **-S** one that aspires
ASPIRATA	*n* pl. **-TAE** a type of plosive
ASPIRATE	*v* **-RATED, -RATING, -RATES** to pronounce with an initial release of breath
ASPIRE	*v* **-PIRED, -PIRING, -PIRES** to have an earnest desire or ambition
ASPIRER	*n* pl. **-S** an aspirant
ASPIRIN	*n* pl. **-S** a pain reliever
ASPIRING	present participle of aspire
ASPIS	*n* pl. **-PISES** aspic
ASPISH	*adj* resembling an asp
ASPRAWL	*adj* sprawling
ASQUINT	*adv* with a sidelong glance
ASRAMA	*n* pl. **-S** ashram
ASS	*n* pl. **-ES** a hoofed mammal
ASSAGAI	*v* **-GAIED, -GAIING, -GAIS** to pierce with a light spear
ASSAI	*n* pl. **-S** a tropical tree
ASSAIL	*v* **-ED, -ING, -S** to attack
ASSAILER	*n* pl. **-S** one that assails
ASSASSIN	*n* pl. **-S** a murderer
ASSAULT	*v* **-ED, -ING, -S** to attack
ASSAY	*v* **-ED, -ING, -S** to attempt
ASSAYER	*n* pl. **-S** one that assays
ASSEGAI	*v* **-GAIED, -GAIING, -GAIS** to assagai
ASSEMBLE	*v* **-BLED, -BLING, -BLES** to come or bring together
ASSEMBLY	*n* pl. **-BLIES** the act of assembling
ASSENT	*v* **-ED, -ING, -S** to express agreement
ASSENTER	*n* pl. **-S** one that assents
ASSENTOR	*n* pl. **-S** assenter
ASSERT	*v* **-ED, -ING, -S** to state positively
ASSERTER	*n* pl. **-S** one that asserts
ASSERTOR	*n* pl. **-S** asserter
ASSESS	*v* **-ED, -ING, -ES** to estimate the value of for taxation
ASSESSOR	*n* pl. **-S** one that assesses
ASSET	*n* pl. **-S** a useful quality or thing
ASSIGN	*v* **-ED, -ING, -S** to set apart for a particular purpose
ASSIGNAT	*n* pl. **-S** one of the notes issued as currency by the French revolutionary government
ASSIGNEE	*n* pl. **-S** one to whom property or right is legally transferred
ASSIGNER	*n* pl. **-S** one that assigns
ASSIGNOR	*n* pl. **-S** one who legally transfers property or right
ASSIST	*v* **-ED, -ING, -S** to give aid or support to
ASSISTER	*n* pl. **-S** one that assists
ASSISTOR	*n* pl. **-S** assister
ASSIZE	*n* pl. **-S** a session of a legislative or judicial body
ASSLIKE	*adj* resembling an ass
ASSOIL	*v* **-ED, -ING, -S** to pardon
ASSONANT	*n* pl. **-S** a word or syllable that resembles another in sound
ASSONATE	*v* **-NATED, -NATING, -NATES** to use a word or syllable that resembles another in sound

ASSORT	v **-ED, -ING, -S** to distribute into groups according to kind or class
ASSORTER	n pl. **-S** one that assorts
ASSUAGE	v **-SUAGED, -SUAGING, -SUAGES** to make less severe
ASSUAGER	n pl. **-S** one that assuages
ASSUME	v **-SUMED, -SUMING, -SUMES** to take on
ASSUMER	n pl. **-S** one that assumes
ASSURE	v **-SURED, -SURING, -SURES** to insure
ASSURED	n pl. **-S** an insured person
ASSURER	n pl. **-S** one that assures
ASSURING	present participle of assure
ASSUROR	n pl. **-S** assurer
ASSWAGE	v **-SWAGED, -SWAGING, -SWAGES** to assuage
ASTANGA	n pl. **-S** ashtanga
ASTASIA	n pl. **-S** inability to stand resulting from muscular incoordination
ASTATIC	adj unstable
ASTATINE	n pl. **-S** a radioactive element
ASTER	n pl. **-S** a flowering plant
ASTERIA	n pl. **-S** a gemstone cut to exhibit asterism
ASTERISK	v **-ED, -ING, -S** to mark with an asterisk (a star-shaped printing mark)
ASTERISM	n pl. **-S** a property of certain minerals of showing a starlike luminous figure
ASTERN	adv at or toward the rear of a ship
ASTERNAL	adj not connected to the sternum
ASTEROID	n pl. **-S** a type of celestial body
ASTHANGA	n pl. **-S** ashtanga
ASTHENIA	n pl. **-S** lack of strength
ASTHENIC	n pl. **-S** a slender, lightly muscled person
ASTHENY	n pl. **-NIES** asthenia
ASTHMA	n pl. **-S** a respiratory disease
ASTIGMIA	n pl. **-S** a visual defect
ASTILBE	n pl. **-S** an Asian perennial
ASTIR	adj moving about
ASTOMOUS	adj having no stomata
ASTONISH	v **-ED, -ING, -ES** to fill with sudden wonder or surprise
ASTONY	v **-TONIED, -TONYING, -TONIES** to astonish
ASTOUND	v **-ED, -ING, -S** to amaze

ASTRAGAL	n pl. **-S** a convex molding
ASTRAL	n pl. **-S** a type of oil lamp
ASTRALLY	adv in a stellar manner
ASTRAY	adv off the right course
ASTRICT	v **-ED, -ING, -S** to restrict
ASTRIDE	adv with one leg on each side
ASTRINGE	v **-TRINGED, -TRINGING, -TRINGES** to bind or draw together
ASTUTE	adj shrewd **ASTUTELY** adv
ASTYLAR	adj having no columns
ASUNDER	adv into pieces
ASURA	n pl. **-S** a Hindu demon
ASWARM	adj swarming
ASWIM	adj swimming
ASWIRL	adj swirling
ASWOON	adj swooning
ASYLUM	n pl. **-LUMS** or **-LA** an institution for the care of the mentally ill
ASYNDETA	n/pl omissions of certain conjunctions
AT	prep in the position of
ATABAL	n pl. **-S** a type of drum
ATABRINE	n pl. **-S** a drug to treat malaria
ATACTIC	adj showing no regularity of structure
ATAGHAN	n pl. **-S** yataghan
ATALAYA	n pl. **-S** a watchtower
ATAMAN	n pl. **-S** a hetman
ATAMASCO	n pl. **-COS** a flowering plant
ATAP	n pl. **-S** the nipa palm tree
ATARAXIA	n pl. **-S** peace of mind
ATARAXIC	n pl. **-S** a tranquilizing drug
ATARAXY	n pl. **-RAXIES** ataraxia
ATAVIC	adj pertaining to a remote ancestor
ATAVISM	n pl. **-S** the reappearance of a genetic characteristic after several generations of absence
ATAVIST	n pl. **-S** an individual displaying atavism
ATAXIA	n pl. **-S** loss of muscular coordination
ATAXIC	n pl. **-S** one suffering from ataxia
ATAXY	n pl. **ATAXIES** ataxia
ATE	n pl. **-S** blind impulse or reckless ambition that drives one to ruin
ATECHNIC	adj lacking technical knowledge

ATELIC   *adj* pertaining to a type of verb form

ATELIER   *n* pl. **-S** a workshop or studio

ATEMOYA   *n* pl. **-S** a fruit of a hybrid tropical tree

ATENOLOL   *n* pl. **-S** a drug to treat hypertension

ATHANASY   *n* pl. **-SIES** immortality

ATHEISM   *n* pl. **-S** the belief that there is no God

ATHEIST   *n* pl. **-S** a believer in atheism

ATHELING   *n* pl. **-S** an Anglo-Saxon prince or nobleman

ATHENEUM   *n* pl. **-S** a literary institution

ATHEROMA   *n* pl. **-MAS** or **-MATA** a disease of the arteries

ATHETOID   *adj* affected with a type of nervous disorder

ATHIRST   *adj* having a strong desire

ATHLETE   *n* pl. **-S** one skilled in feats of physical strength and agility **ATHLETIC** *adj*

ATHODYD   *n* pl. **-S** a type of jet engine

ATHWART   *adv* from side to side

ATIGI   *n* pl. **-S** a type of Inuit parka

ATILT   *adj* being in a tilted position

ATINGLE   *adj* tingling

ATISHOO   *interj* ahchoo

ATLAS   *n* pl. **ATLASES** or **ATLANTES** a male figure used as a supporting column

ATLATL   *n* pl. **-S** a device for throwing a spear or dart

ATMA   *n* pl. **-S** atman

ATMAN   *n* pl. **-S** the individual soul in Hinduism

ATOLL   *n* pl. **-S** a coral island

ATOM   *n* pl. **-S** the smallest unit of an element **ATOMIC, ATOMICAL** *adj*

ATOMICS   *n/pl* the science dealing with atoms

ATOMIES   pl. of atomy

ATOMISE   *v* **-ISED, -ISING, -ISES** to atomize

ATOMISER   *n* pl. **-S** atomizer

ATOMISM   *n* pl. **-S** the theory that the universe is composed of simple, indivisible, minute particles

ATOMIST   *n* pl. **-S** an adherent of atomism

ATOMIZE   *v* **-IZED, -IZING, -IZES** to reduce to a fine spray

ATOMIZER   *n* pl. **-S** a device for atomizing liquids

ATOMY   *n* pl. **-MIES** a tiny particle

ATONAL   *adj* lacking tonality **ATONALLY** *adv*

ATONE   *v* **ATONED, ATONING, ATONES** to make amends or reparation **ATONABLE** *adj*

ATONER   *n* pl. **-S** one that atones

ATONIA   *n* pl. **-S** atony

ATONIC   *n* pl. **-S** an unaccented syllable or word

ATONING   present participle of atone

ATONY   *n* pl. **-NIES** muscular weakness

ATOP   *adj* being on or at the top

ATOPY   *n* pl. **-PIES** a type of allergy **ATOPIC** *adj*

ATRAZINE   *n* pl. **-S** an herbicide

ATREMBLE   *adj* trembling

ATRESIA   *n* pl. **-S** absence or closure of a natural bodily passage **ATRESIC, ATRETIC** *adj*

ATRIA   a pl. of atrium

ATRIAL   *adj* pertaining to an atrium

ATRIP   *adj* aweigh

ATRIUM   *n* pl. **ATRIUMS** or **ATRIA** the main room of an ancient Roman house

ATROCITY   *n* pl. **-TIES** a heinous act

ATROPHIA   *n* pl. **-S** a wasting away of the body or any of its parts **ATROPHIC** *adj*

ATROPHY   *v* **-PHIED, -PHYING, -PHIES** to waste away

ATROPIN   *n* pl. **-S** atropine

ATROPINE   *n* pl. **-S** a poisonous alkaloid

ATROPISM   *n* pl. **-S** atropine poisoning

ATT   *n* pl. **ATT** a monetary unit of Laos

ATTABOY   *n* pl. **-BOYS** an expression of encouragement or approval to a man or boy

ATTACH   *v* **-ED, -ING, -ES** to connect as an associated part

ATTACHE   *n* pl. **-S** a diplomatic official

ATTACHER   *n* pl. **-S** one that attaches

ATTACK   *v* **-ED, -ING, -S** to set upon violently

ATTACKER   *n* pl. **-S** one that attacks

ATTAGIRL   *interj* — used to express encouragement or approval to a woman or girl

ATTAIN   *v* **-ED, -ING, -S** to gain or achieve by mental or physical effort

ATTAINER   *n* pl. **-S** one that attains

ATTAINT   *v* **-ED, -ING, -S** to disgrace

ATTAR   *n* pl. **-S** a fragrant oil

ATTEMPER   *v* **-ED, -ING, -S** to modify the temperature of

ATTEMPT   *v* **-ED, -ING, -S** to make an effort to do or accomplish

ATTEND   *v* **-ED, -ING, -S** to be present at

ATTENDEE   *n* pl. **-S** an attender

ATTENDER   *n* pl. **-S** one that attends

ATTENT   *adj* heedful

ATTEST   *v* **-ED, -ING, -S** to affirm to be true or genuine

ATTESTER   *n* pl. **-S** one that attests

ATTESTOR   *n* pl. **-S** attester

ATTIC   *n* pl. **-S** a story or room directly below the roof of a house

ATTICISM   *n* pl. **-S** a concise and elegant expression

ATTICIST   *n* pl. **-S** one who uses atticisms

ATTICIZE   *v* **-CIZED, -CIZING, -CIZES** to use atticisms

ATTIRE   *v* **-TIRED, -TIRING, -TIRES** to clothe

ATTITUDE   *n* pl. **-S** a state of mind with regard to some matter

ATTORN   *v* **-ED, -ING, -S** to acknowledge a new owner as one's landlord

ATTORNEY   *n* pl. **-NEYS** a lawyer (a member of the legal profession)

ATTRACT   *v* **-ED, -ING, -S** to cause to approach or adhere

ATTRIT   *v* **-TRITTED, -TRITTING, -TRITS** to lose by attrition

ATTRITE   *v* **-TRITED, -TRITING, -TRITES** to attrit

ATTUNE   *v* **-TUNED, -TUNING, -TUNES** to bring into harmony

ATWAIN   *adv* in two

ATWEEN   *prep* between

ATWITTER   *adj* twittering

ATYPIC   *adj* atypical

ATYPICAL   *adj* not typical

AUBADE   *n* pl. **-S** a morning song

AUBERGE   *n* pl. **-S** an inn

AUBRETIA   *n* pl. **-S** aubrieta

AUBRIETA   *n* pl. **-S** a flowering plant

AUBURN   *n* pl. **-S** a reddish brown color

AUCTION   *v* **-ED, -ING, -S** to sell publicly to the highest bidder

AUCUBA   *n* pl. **-S** a shrub of the dogwood family

AUDACITY   *n* pl. **-TIES** boldness

AUDAD   *n* pl. **-S** aoudad

AUDIAL   *adj* aural

AUDIBLE   *v* **-BLED, -BLING, -BLES** to call a substitute play in football

AUDIBLY   *adv* in a way so as to be heard

AUDIENCE   *n* pl. **-S** a group of listeners or spectators

AUDIENT   *n* pl. **-S** one that hears

AUDILE   *n* pl. **-S** one whose mental imagery is chiefly auditory

AUDING   *n* pl. **-S** the process of hearing, recognizing, and interpreting a spoken language

AUDIO   *n* pl. **-DIOS** sound reception or transmission

AUDISM   *n* pl. **-S** discrimination or prejudice against deaf people

AUDIST   *n* pl. **-S** one that practices audism

AUDIT   *v* **-ED, -ING, -S** to examine with intent to verify

AUDITEE   *n* pl. **-S** one that is audited

AUDITION   *v* **-ED, -ING, -S** to give a trial performance

AUDITIVE   *n* pl. **-S** an auditory

AUDITOR   *n* pl. **-S** one that audits

AUDITORY   *n* pl. **-RIES** a group of listeners

AUGEND   *n* pl. **-S** a number to which another is to be added

AUGER   *n* pl. **-S** a tool for boring

AUGH   *interj* — used to express despair or frustration

AUGHT   *n* pl. **-S** a zero

AUGITE   *n* pl. **-S** a mineral **AUGITIC** *adj*

AUGMENT   *v* **-ED, -ING, -S** to increase

AUGUR   *v* **-ED, -ING, -S** to foretell from omens

AUGURAL   *adj* pertaining to augury

AUGURER   *n* pl. **-S** one that augurs

AUGURY   *n* pl. **-RIES** the practice of auguring

AUGUST   *adj* **-GUSTER, -GUSTEST** inspiring reverence or admiration **AUGUSTLY** *adv*

AUK   *n* pl. **-S** a diving seabird

AUKLET   *n* pl. **-S** a small auk

AULD   *adj* **AULDER, AULDEST** old

AULIC   *adj* pertaining to a royal court

AUMBRY   *n* pl. **-BRIES** ambry

AUNT   *n* pl. **-S** the sister of one's father or mother

AUNTHOOD   *n* pl. **-S** the state of being an aunt

AUNTIE   *n* pl. **-S** aunt

AUNTIES   pl. of aunty

AUNTLIKE   *adj* resembling an aunt

AUNTLY   *adj* **-LIER, -LIEST** of or suggesting an aunt

AUNTY   *n* pl. **AUNTIES** aunt

AURA   *n* pl. **-RAS** or **-RAE** an invisible emanation

AURAL   *adj* pertaining to the sense of hearing **AURALLY** *adv*

AURALITY   *n* pl. **-TIES** the quality of being aural

AURAR   pl. of eyrir

AURATE   *adj* having ears

AURATED   *adj* aurate

AUREATE   *adj* golden

AUREI   pl. of aureus

AUREOLA   *n* pl. **-LAS** or **-LAE** a halo

AUREOLE   *v* **-OLED, -OLING, -OLES** to surround with a halo

AURES   pl. of auris

AUREUS   *n* pl. **-REI** a gold coin of ancient Rome

AURIC   *adj* pertaining to gold

AURICLE   *n* pl. **-S** an ear or ear-shaped part **AURICLED** *adj*

AURICULA   *n* pl. **-LAS** or **-LAE** an auricle

AURIFORM   *adj* ear-shaped

AURIS   *n* pl. **AURES** the ear

AURIST   *n* pl. **-S** a specialist in diseases of the ear

AUROCHS   *n* pl. **-ES** an extinct European ox

AURORA   *n* pl. **-RAS** or **-RAE** the rising light of the morning **AURORAL, AUROREAN** *adj*

AUROUS   *adj* pertaining to gold

AURUM   *n* pl. **-S** gold

AUSFORM   *v* **-ED, -ING, -S** to subject steel to a strengthening process

AUSPEX   *n* pl. **-PICES** a soothsayer of ancient Rome

AUSPICE   *n* pl. **-S** a favorable omen

AUSTERE   *adj* **-TERER, -TEREST** grave in disposition or appearance

AUSTRAL   *n* pl. **-ES** or **-S** a former monetary unit of Argentina

AUSUBO   *n* pl. **-BOS** a tropical tree

AUTACOID   *n* pl. **-S** a hormone

AUTARCH   *n* pl. **-S** an absolute ruler

AUTARCHY   *n* pl. **-CHIES** absolute rule

AUTARKY   *n* pl. **-KIES** national economic self-sufficiency **AUTARKIC** *adj*

AUTECISM   *n* pl. **-S** the development of the entire life cycle of a parasitic fungus on a single host

AUTEUR   *n* pl. **-S** the creator of a film

AUTHOR   *v* **-ED, -ING, -S** to write

AUTISM   *n* pl. **-S** extreme withdrawal into fantasy

AUTIST   *n* pl. **-S** an autistic

AUTISTIC   *n* pl. **-S** one who is affected with autism

AUTO   *v* **-ED, -ING, -S** to ride in an automobile

AUTOBAHN   *n* pl. **-BAHNS** or **-BAHNEN** a German superhighway

AUTOBODY   *n* pl. **-BODIES** the shell of a motor vehicle

AUTOBUS   *n* pl. **-BUSES** or **-BUSSES** a bus

AUTOCADE   *n* pl. **-S** a parade of automobiles

AUTOCOID   *n* pl. **-S** autacoid

AUTOCRAT   *n* pl. **-S** an absolute ruler

AUTODIAL   *v* **-DIALED, -DIALING, -DIALS** or **-DIALLED, -DIALLING, -DIALS** to dial a telephone number automatically

AUTODYNE   *n* pl. **-S** a type of electrical circuit

AUTOGAMY   *n* pl. **-MIES** fertilization of a flower by its own pollen

AUTOGENY   *n* pl. **-NIES** the production of living organisms from inanimate matter

AUTOGIRO   *n* pl. **-ROS** a type of airplane

AUTOGYRO   *n* pl. **-ROS** autogiro

AUTOHARP   *n* pl. **-S** a type of zither

AUTOLOAD   *adj* self-loading

AUTOLYSE   *v* **-LYSED, -LYSING, -LYSES** to autolyze

AUTOLYZE   *v* **-LYZED, -LYZING, -LYZES** to break down tissue by the action of self-contained enzymes

AUTOMAN   *n* pl. **-MEN** an automobile maker

AUTOMAT   *n* pl. **-S** a type of cafeteria

AUTOMATA   *n/pl* robots

AUTOMATE   *v* **-MATED, -MATING, -MATES** to convert to a system of automatic control

AUTOMEN   *n* pl. of automan

AUTONOMY   *n* pl. **-MIES** the state of being self-governing

AUTONYM   *n* pl. **-S** a name by which a people refers to itself

AUTOPEN   *n* pl. **-S** a device for imitating signatures

AUTOPSIC   *adj* pertaining to an autopsy

AUTOPSY   *v* **-SIED, -SYING, -SIES** to examine a dead body to determine the cause of death

AUTOSAVE   *v* **-SAVED, -SAVING, -SAVES** to save on a computer at regular intervals

AUTOSOME   *n* pl. **-S** a type of chromosome

AUTOTOMY   *n* pl. **-MIES** the shedding of a damaged body part

AUTOTYPE   *n* pl. **-S** a type of photographic process

AUTOTYPY   *n* pl. **-TYPIES** autotype

AUTUMN   *n* pl. **-S** a season of the year **AUTUMNAL** *adj*

AUTUNITE   *n* pl. **-S** a mineral

AUXESIS   *n* pl. **AUXESES** an increase in cell size without cell division

AUXETIC   *n* pl. **-S** a substance that promotes auxesis

AUXIN   *n* pl. **-S** a substance used to regulate plant growth **AUXINIC** *adj*

AVA   *adv* at all

AVADAVAT   *n* pl. **-S** a small songbird

AVAIL   *v* **-ED, -ING, -S** to be of use or advantage to

AVANT   *adj* culturally or stylistically new

AVARICE   *n* pl. **-S** greed

AVAST   *interj* — used as a command to stop

AVATAR   *n* pl. **-S** the incarnation of a Hindu deity

AVAUNT   *interj* — used as an order of dismissal

AVE   *n* pl. **-S** an expression of greeting or farewell

AVELLAN   *adj* having the four arms shaped like filberts — used of a heraldic cross

AVELLANE   *adj* avellan

AVENGE   *v* **AVENGED, AVENGING, AVENGES** to exact retribution for

AVENGER   *n* pl. **-S** one that avenges

AVENS   *n* pl. **-ES** a perennial herb

AVENTAIL   *n* pl. **-S** ventail

AVENUE   *n* pl. **-S** a wide street

AVER   *v* **AVERRED, AVERRING, AVERS** to declare positively

AVERAGE   *v* **-AGED, -AGING, -AGES** to calculate the arithmetic mean of

AVERMENT   *n* pl. **-S** the act of averring

AVERRED   past tense of aver

AVERRING   present participle of aver

AVERSE   *adj* opposed; reluctant **AVERSELY** *adv*

AVERSION   *n* pl. **-S** a feeling of repugnance

AVERSIVE   *n* pl. **-S** a punishment

AVERT   *v* **-ED, -ING, -S** to turn away

AVERTER   *n* pl. **-S** one that averts

AVGAS   *n* pl. **-GASES** or **-GASSES** gasoline for airplanes

AVIAN   *n* pl. **-S** a bird

AVIANIZE   *v* **-IZED, -IZING, -IZES** to make less severe by repeated culture in a chick embryo, as a virus

AVIARIST   *n* pl. **-S** the keeper of an aviary

AVIARY   *n* pl. **-ARIES** a large enclosure for live birds

AVIATE   *v* **-ATED, -ATING, -ATES** to fly an aircraft

AVIATION   *n* pl. **-S** the act of aviating **AVIATIC** *adj*

AVIATOR   *n* pl. **-S** one that aviates

AVIATRIX   *n* pl. **-TRICES** or **-TRIXES** a female aviator

AVICULAR   *adj* pertaining to birds

AVID   *adj* eager

AVIDIN   *n* pl. **-S** a protein found in egg white

AVIDITY   *n* pl. **-TIES** the state of being avid

AVIDLY   *adv* in an avid manner

AVIDNESS   *n* pl. **-ES** avidity

AVIFAUNA   *n* pl. **-NAS** or **-NAE** the bird life of a particular region

AVIGATOR   *n* pl. **-S** one that navigates aircraft

AVION   *n* pl. **-S** an airplane

AVIONICS   *n/pl* the science of electronics applied to aviation **AVIONIC** *adj*

AVISO   *n* pl. **-SOS** advice

AVO   *n* pl. **AVOS** a monetary unit of Macao

AVOCADO   *n* pl. **-DOS** or **-DOES** the edible fruit of a tropical tree

AVOCET   *n* pl. **-S** a shore bird

AVODIRE   *n* pl. **-S** an African tree

AVOID   *v* **-ED, -ING, -S** to keep away from

AVOIDER   *n* pl. **-S** one that avoids

AVOSET   *n* pl. **-S** avocet

AVOUCH   *v* **-ED, -ING, -ES** to affirm

AVOUCHER   *n* pl. **-S** one that avouches

AVOW   *v* **-ED, -ING, -S** to declare openly **AVOWABLE** *adj* **AVOWABLY, AVOWEDLY** *adv*

AVOWAL   *n* pl. **-S** an open declaration

AVOWER   *n* pl. **-S** one that avows

AVULSE   *v* **AVULSED, AVULSING, AVULSES** to tear off forcibly

AVULSION   *n* pl. **-S** the act of avulsing

AW   *interj* — used to express protest, disgust, or disbelief

AWA   *adv* away

AWAIT   *v* **-ED, -ING, -S** to wait for

AWAITER   *n* pl. **-S** one that awaits

AWAKE   *v* **AWAKED** or **AWOKE, AWOKEN, AWAKING, AWAKES** to wake up

AWAKEN   *v* **-ED, -ING, -S** to awake

AWAKENER   *n* pl. **-S** one that awakens

AWAKING   present participle of awake

AWARD   *v* **-ED, -ING, -S** to grant as due or merited

AWARDEE   *n* pl. **-S** one that is awarded something

AWARDER   *n* pl. **-S** one that awards

AWARE   *adj* having perception or knowledge

AWASH   *adj* covered with water

AWAY   *adv* from a certain place

AWAYNESS   *n* pl. **-ES** the state of being distant

AWE   *v* **AWED, AWING** or **AWEING, AWES** to inspire with awe (reverential fear)

AWEARY   *adj* weary

AWEATHER   *adv* toward the windward side of a vessel

AWED   past tense of awe

AWEE   *adv* awhile

AWEIGH   *adj* hanging just clear of the bottom — used of an anchor

AWELESS   *adj* lacking awe

AWESOME   *adj* inspiring awe

AWFUL   *adj* **-FULLER, -FULLEST** extremely bad or unpleasant **AWFULLY** *adv*

AWHILE   *adv* for a short time

AWHIRL   *adj* whirling

AWING   a present participle of awe

AWKWARD   *adj* **-WARDER, -WARDEST** lacking skill, dexterity, or grace

AWL   *n* pl. **-S** a pointed tool for making small holes

AWLESS   *adj* aweless

AWLWORT   *n* pl. **-S** an aquatic plant

AWMOUS   *n* pl. **AWMOUS** alms

AWN   *n* pl. **-S** a bristlelike appendage of certain grasses **AWNED, AWNLESS, AWNY** *adj*

AWNING   *n* pl. **-S** a rooflike canvas cover **AWNINGED** *adj*

AWOKE   a past tense of awake

AWOKEN   a past participle of awake

AWOL   *n* pl. **-S** one who is absent without leave

AWRY   *adv* with a turn or twist to one side

AX   *v* **-ED, -ING, -ES** to work on with an ax (a type of cutting tool)

AXAL   *adj* axial

AXE   *v* **AXED, AXING, AXES** to ax

AXEL   *n* pl. **-S** a jump in figure skating

AXEMAN   *n* pl. **-MEN** axman

AXENIC   *adj* free from germs

AXES   pl. of axis

AXIAL   *adj* pertaining to or forming an axis **AXIALLY** *adv*

AXIALITY   *n* pl. **-TIES** the state of being axial

AXIL   *n* pl. **-S** the angle between the upper side of a leaf and its supporting stem

AXILE   *adj* axial

AXILLA   *n* pl. **-LAE** or **-LAS** the armpit

AXILLAR   *n* pl. **-S** a feather on the undersurface of a bird's wing

AXILLARY   *n* pl. **-LARIES** an axillar

AXING   present participle of axe

AXIOLOGY   *n* pl. **-GIES** the study of values and value judgments

AXIOM	*n* pl. **-S** a self-evident truth
AXION	*n* pl. **-S** a hypothetical subatomic particle
AXIS	*n* pl. **AXES** a straight line about which a body rotates **AXISED** *adj*
AXIS	*n* pl. **AXISES** an Asian deer
AXITE	*n* pl. **-S** a fiber of an axon
AXLE	*n* pl. **-S** a shaft upon which a wheel revolves **AXLED** *adj*
AXLETREE	*n* pl. **-S** a type of axle
AXLIKE	*adj* resembling an ax
AXMAN	*n* pl. **-MEN** one who wields an ax
AXOLOTL	*n* pl. **-S** a salamander of Mexico and western United States
AXON	*n* pl. **-S** the central process of a neuron **AXONAL** *adj*
AXONE	*n* pl. **-S** axon
AXONEMAL	*adj* pertaining to an axoneme
AXONEME	*n* pl. **-S** a part of a cilium
AXONIC	*adj* pertaining to an axon
AXOPLASM	*n* pl. **-S** the protoplasm of an axon
AXSEED	*n* pl. **-S** a European herb
AY	*n* pl. **AYS** aye
AYAH	*n* pl. **-S** a native maid or nurse in India
AYAYA	*n* pl. **-S** a type of singing among the Inuit
AYE	*n* pl. **-S** an affirmative vote
AYIN	*n* pl. **-S** a Hebrew letter
AYURVEDA	*n* pl. **-S** a Hindu system of medicine
AZALEA	*n* pl. **-S** a flowering shrub
AZAN	*n* pl. **-S** a Muslim call to prayer
AZIDE	*n* pl. **-S** a type of chemical compound **AZIDO** *adj*
AZIMUTH	*n* pl. **-S** an angle of horizontal deviation
AZINE	*n* pl. **-S** a type of chemical compound
AZLON	*n* pl. **-S** a textile fiber
AZO	*adj* containing nitrogen
AZOIC	*adj* pertaining to geologic time before the appearance of life
AZOLE	*n* pl. **-S** a type of chemical compound
AZON	*n* pl. **-S** a radio-controlled aerial bomb
AZONAL	*adj* pertaining to a type of a soil group
AZONIC	*adj* not restricted to any particular zone
AZOTE	*n* pl. **-S** nitrogen **AZOTED** *adj*
AZOTEMIA	*n* pl. **-S** an excess of nitrogenous substances in the blood **AZOTEMIC** *adj*
AZOTH	*n* pl. **-S** mercury
AZOTIC	*adj* pertaining to azote
AZOTISE	*v* **-TISED, -TISING, -TISES** to azotize
AZOTIZE	*v* **-TIZED, -TIZING, -TIZES** to treat with nitrogen
AZOTURIA	*n* pl. **-S** an excess of nitrogenous substances in the urine
AZUKI	*n* pl. **-S** adzuki
AZULEJO	*n* pl. **-JOS** a type of ceramic tile
AZURE	*n* pl. **-S** a blue color
AZURITE	*n* pl. **-S** a mineral
AZYGOS	*n* pl. **-ES** an azygous anatomical part
AZYGOUS	*adj* not being one of a pair

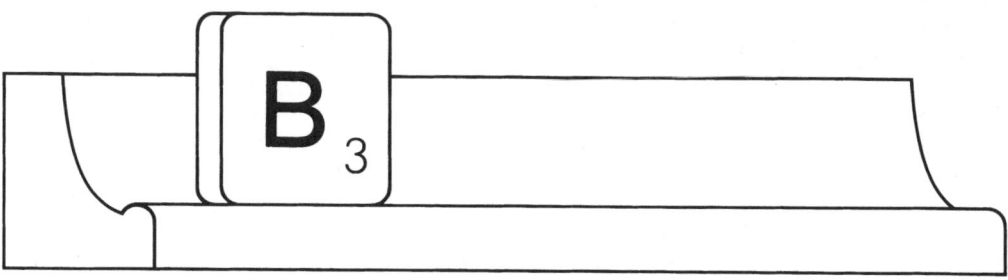

BA   *n* pl. **-S** the eternal soul, in Egyptian mythology

BAA   *v* **-ED, -ING, -S** to bleat

BAAL   *n* pl. **BAALS** or **BAALIM** a false god

BAALISM   *n* pl. **-S** the worship of a baal

BAAS   *n* pl. **-ES** master; boss

BAASKAAP   *n* pl. **-S** baaskap

BAASKAP   *n* pl. **-S** the policy of domination by white people in South Africa

BAASSKAP   *n* pl. **-S** baaskap

BABA   *n* pl. **-S** a rum cake

BABACU   *n* pl. **-S** babassu

BABASSU   *n* pl. **-S** a palm tree

BABBITRY   *n* pl. **-RIES** conventional middle-class attitudes and behavior stressing respectability and material success

BABBITT   *v* **-ED, -ING, -S** to line with babbitt (an alloy of tin, copper, and antimony)

BABBLE   *v* **-BLED, -BLING, -BLES** to talk idly or excessively

BABBLER   *n* pl. **-S** one that babbles

BABBLING   *n* pl. **-S** idle talk

BABE   *n* pl. **-S** a baby

BABEL   *n* pl. **-S** confusion

BABESIA   *n* pl. **-SIAS** or **-SIAE** a parasitic protozoan

BABICHE   *n* pl. **-S** rawhide thongs

BABIED   past tense of baby

BABIER   comparative of baby

BABIES   present 3d person sing. of baby

BABIEST   superlative of baby

BABIRUSA   *n* pl. **-S** a wild pig

BABKA   *n* pl. **-S** a coffee cake

BABOO   *n* pl. **-BOOS** a Hindu gentleman

BABOOL   *n* pl. **-S** babul

BABOON   *n* pl. **-S** a large ape

BABOUCHE   *n* pl. **-S** a heelless slipper

BABU   *n* pl. **-S** baboo

BABUL   *n* pl. **-S** a North African tree

BABUSHKA   *n* pl. **-S** a woman's scarf

BABY   *adj* **BABIER, BABIEST** resembling a baby (an infant)

BABY   *v* **-BIED, -BYING, -BIES** to coddle

BABYDOLL   *n* pl. **-S** short, sheer pajamas for women

BABYHOOD   *n* pl. **-S** the state of being a baby

BABYISH   *adj* resembling a baby

BABYLIKE   *adj* resembling a baby

BABYSIT   *v* **-SAT, -SITTING, -SITS** to care for a child temporarily

BACALAO   *n* pl. **-LAOS** baccala

BACALHAU   *n* pl. **-S** baccala

BACCA   *n* pl. **-CAE** a berry

BACCALA   *n* pl. **-S** a codfish

BACCARA   *n* pl. **-S** baccarat

BACCARAT   *n* pl. **-S** a card game

BACCATE   *adj* pulpy like a berry

BACCATED   *adj* baccate

BACCHANT   *n* pl. **-S** or **-ES** a carouser

BACCHIC   *adj* riotous

BACCHIUS   *n* pl. **-CHII** a type of metrical foot

BACCY   *n* pl. **BACCIES** tobacco

BACH   *v* **-ED, -ING, -ES** to live as a bachelor

BACHELOR   *n* pl. **-S** an unmarried man

BACILLAR   *adj* rod-shaped

BACILLUS   *n* pl. **-LI** any of a class of rod-shaped bacteria

BACK   *v* **-ED, -ING, -S** to support

BACKACHE   *n* pl. **-S** a pain in the back

BACKBAR *n* pl. **-S** the space behind a bar with shelves for bottles

BACKBEAT *n* pl. **-S** a type of rhythm in music

BACKBEND *n* pl. **-S** an acrobatic feat

BACKBITE *v* **-BIT, -BITTEN, -BITING, -BITES** to slander

BACKBONE *n* pl. **-S** the spine

BACKCAST *n* pl. **-S** a backward movement in casting a fishing line

BACKCHAT *n* pl. **-S** repartee

BACKCOMB *v* **-ED, -ING, -S** to comb the hair from the ends to the scalp

BACKDATE *v* **-DATED, -DATING, -DATES** to predate

BACKDOOR *adj* secretive

BACKDOWN *n* pl. **-S** the act of backing down

BACKDROP *v* **-DROPPED** or **-DROPT, -DROPPING, -DROPS** to provide with a scenic background

BACKER *n* pl. **-S** a supporter

BACKFAT *n* pl. **-S** a layer of fat between the skin and muscle in animals

BACKFILL *v* **-ED, -ING, -S** to refill

BACKFIRE *v* **-FIRED, -FIRING, -FIRES** to produce undesirable effects

BACKFIT *v* **-FITTED, -FITTING, -FITS** to retrofit

BACKFLIP *v* **-FLIPPED, -FLIPPING, -FLIPS** to perform a backward somersault

BACKFLOW *n* pl. **-S** a flowing back toward a source

BACKHAND *v* **-ED, -ING, -S** to strike with the back of the hand

BACKHAUL *v* **-ED, -ING, -S** to return after delivering a load

BACKHOE *v* **-HOED, -HOEING, -HOES** to use a backhoe (a type of excavating machine)

BACKING *n* pl. **-S** support

BACKLAND *n* pl. **-S** a region remote from cities

BACKLASH *v* **-ED, -ING, -ES** to cause a reaction

BACKLESS *adj* having no back

BACKLIST *v* **-ED, -ING, -S** to include in a publisher's list of older book titles

BACKLIT *adj* illuminated from behind

BACKLOAD *v* **-ED, -ING, -S** to defer a financial obligation

BACKLOG *v* **-LOGGED, -LOGGING, -LOGS** to accumulate

BACKLOT *n* pl. **-S** an outdoor area in a movie studio

BACKMOST *adj* hindmost

BACKOUT *n* pl. **-S** a reversal of launching procedures

BACKPACK *v* **-ED, -ING, -S** to hike with a pack on one's back

BACKREST *n* pl. **-S** a back support

BACKROOM *n* pl. **-S** a place for meeting inconspicuously

BACKRUSH *n* pl. **-ES** the seaward return of water from a wave

BACKSAW *n* pl. **-S** a type of saw

BACKSEAT *n* pl. **-S** a rear seat

BACKSET *n* pl. **-S** a setback

BACKSIDE *n* pl. **-S** the hind part

BACKSLAP *v* **-SLAPPED, -SLAPPING, -SLAPS** to show much approval

BACKSLID past tense of backslide (to revert to sin)

BACKSPIN *n* pl. **-S** a backward rotation

BACKSTAB *v* **-STABBED, -STABBING, -STABS** to attack or betray behind one's back

BACKSTAY *n* pl. **-STAYS** a support for a mast

BACKSTOP *v* **-STOPPED, -STOPPING, -STOPS** to bolster

BACKTALK *n* pl. **-S** an impudent reply

BACKUP *n* pl. **-S** a substitute

BACKWARD *adv* toward the back

BACKWASH *v* **-ED, -ING, -ES** to spray water backward

BACKWIND *v* **-ED, -ING, -S** to deflect airflow into the back of a sail

BACKWOOD *adj* uncouth

BACKWRAP *n* pl. **-S** a wraparound garment that fastens in the back

BACKYARD *n* pl. **-S** an area at the rear of a house

BACLOFEN *n* pl. **-S** a muscle relaxant

BACON *n* pl. **-S** a side of a pig cured and smoked

BACTERIA *n* pl. **-S** a group of microscopic organisms

BACTERIN *n* pl. **-S** a vaccine prepared from dead bacteria

BACULINE *adj* pertaining to a rod

BACULUM *n* pl. **-LUMS** or **-LA** a bone in the penis of many mammals

BAD	*adj* **BADDER, BADDEST** very good
BAD	*adj* **WORSE, WORST** not good
BAD	*n* pl. **-S** something that is bad **BADDISH** *adj*
BADDIE	*n* pl. **-S** a bad person
BADDY	*n* pl. **-DIES** baddie
BADE	past tense of bid
BADGE	*v* **BADGED, BADGING, BADGES** to supply with an insignia
BADGER	*v* **-ED, -ING, -S** to harass
BADGERLY	*adj* bothersome
BADINAGE	*v* **-NAGED, -NAGING, -NAGES** to banter
BADLAND	*n* pl. **-S** a barren, hilly area
BADLY	*adv* in a bad manner
BADMAN	*n* pl. **-MEN** an outlaw
BADMOUTH	*v* **-ED, -ING, -S** to criticize
BADNESS	*n* pl. **-ES** the state of being bad
BAFF	*v* **-ED, -ING, -S** to strike under a golf ball
BAFFIES	pl. of baffy
BAFFLE	*v* **-FLED, -FLING, -FLES** to confuse
BAFFLER	*n* pl. **-S** one that baffles
BAFFY	*n* pl. **-FIES** a wooden golf club
BAG	*v* **BAGGED, BAGGING, BAGS** to put into a bag (a flexible container)
BAGASS	*n* pl. **-ES** bagasse
BAGASSE	*n* pl. **-S** crushed sugarcane
BAGEL	*n* pl. **-S** a ring-shaped roll
BAGFUL	*n* pl. **BAGFULS** or **BAGSFUL** as much as a bag can hold
BAGGAGE	*n* pl. **-S** luggage
BAGGED	past tense of bag
BAGGER	*n* pl. **-S** one that bags
BAGGIE	*n* pl. **-S** the stomach
BAGGING	*n* pl. **-S** material for making bags
BAGGY	*adj* **-GIER, -GIEST** loose-fitting **BAGGILY** *adv*
BAGHOUSE	*n* pl. **-S** a facility for removing particulates from exhaust gases
BAGLIKE	*adj* resembling a bag
BAGMAN	*n* pl. **-MEN** a traveling salesman
BAGNIO	*n* pl. **-NIOS** a brothel
BAGPIPE	*v* **-PIPED, -PIPING, -PIPES** to play a bagpipe (a wind instrument)
BAGPIPER	*n* pl. **-S** one that plays bagpipes
BAGSFUL	a pl. of bagful
BAGUET	*n* pl. **-S** baguette
BAGUETTE	*n* pl. **-S** a rectangular gem
BAGWIG	*n* pl. **-S** a type of wig
BAGWORM	*n* pl. **-S** the larva of certain moths
BAH	*interj* — used to express disgust
BAHADUR	*n* pl. **-S** a Hindu title of respect
BAHT	*n* pl. **-S** a monetary unit of Thailand
BAIDAR	*n* pl. **-S** bidarka
BAIDARKA	*n* pl. **-S** bidarka
BAIL	*v* **-ED, -ING, -S** to transfer property temporarily **BAILABLE** *adj*
BAILEE	*n* pl. **-S** a person to whom property is bailed
BAILER	*n* pl. **-S** bailor
BAILEY	*n* pl. **-LEYS** an outer castle wall
BAILIE	*n* pl. **-S** a Scottish magistrate
BAILIFF	*n* pl. **-S** a court officer
BAILMENT	*n* pl. **-S** the act of bailing
BAILOR	*n* pl. **-S** a person who bails property to another
BAILOUT	*n* pl. **-S** the act of parachuting from an aircraft
BAILSMAN	*n* pl. **-MEN** one who provides security for another
BAIRN	*n* pl. **-S** a child **BAIRNISH** *adj*
BAIRNLY	*adj* **-LIER, -LIEST** childish
BAIT	*v* **-ED, -ING, -S** to lure
BAITER	*n* pl. **-S** one that baits
BAITFISH	*n* pl. **-ES** a fish used as bait
BAITH	*adj* both
BAIZA	*n* pl. **-S** a monetary unit of Oman
BAIZE	*n* pl. **-S** a green, woolen fabric
BAKE	*v* **BAKED, BAKING, BAKES** to prepare food in an oven
BAKEMEAT	*n* pl. **-S** a pastry
BAKER	*n* pl. **-S** one that bakes
BAKERY	*n* pl. **-ERIES** a place where baked goods are sold
BAKESHOP	*n* pl. **-S** a bakery
BAKEWARE	*n* pl. **-S** dishes used for baking
BAKING	*n* pl. **-S** a quantity baked
BAKLAVA	*n* pl. **-S** a Turkish pastry
BAKLAWA	*n* pl. **-S** baklava
BAKSHISH	*v* **-ED, -ING, -ES** to give a tip
BAL	*n* pl. **-S** a balmoral

BALAFON *n* pl. **-S** a musical instrument of Africa

BALANCE *v* **-ANCED, -ANCING, -ANCES** to weigh

BALANCER *n* pl. **-S** one that balances

BALAS *n* pl. **-ES** a red variety of spinel

BALATA *n* pl. **-S** a tropical tree

BALBOA *n* pl. **-S** a monetary unit of Panama

BALCONY *n* pl. **-NIES** an elevated platform

BALD *adj* **BALDER, BALDEST** lacking hair

BALD *v* **-ED, -ING, -S** to become bald

BALDHEAD *n* pl. **-S** a bald person

BALDISH *adj* somewhat bald

BALDLY *adv* in a plain and blunt manner

BALDNESS *n* pl. **-ES** the state of being bald

BALDPATE *n* pl. **-S** a baldhead

BALDRIC *n* pl. **-S** a shoulder belt

BALDRICK *n* pl. **-S** baldric

BALDY *n* pl. **BALDIES** a bald person

BALE *v* **BALED, BALING, BALES** to form into tightly compressed bundles

BALEEN *n* pl. **-S** whalebone

BALEFIRE *n* pl. **-S** a bonfire

BALEFUL *adj* menacing

BALER *n* pl. **-S** one that bales

BALING *n* pl. **-S** the forming of something into tight bundles

BALISAUR *n* pl. **-S** a long-tailed badger

BALK *v* **-ED, -ING, -S** to stop short and refuse to proceed

BALKER *n* pl. **-S** one that balks

BALKLINE *n* pl. **-S** the starting line in track events

BALKY *adj* **BALKIER, BALKIEST** stubborn **BALKILY** *adv*

BALL *v* **-ED, -ING, -S** to form into a ball (a spherical object)

BALLAD *n* pl. **-S** a narrative poem or song **BALLADIC** *adj*

BALLADE *n* pl. **-S** a type of poem

BALLADRY *n* pl. **-RIES** ballad poetry

BALLAST *v* **-ED, -ING, -S** to stabilize

BALLBOY *n* pl. **-BOYS** a boy who retrieves balls during games

BALLCOCK *n* pl. **-S** a type of valve

BALLER *n* pl. **-S** one that balls

BALLET *n* pl. **-S** a classical dance form **BALLETIC** *adj*

BALLGAME *n* pl. **-S** a game played with a ball

BALLGIRL *n* pl. **-S** a girl who retrieves balls during games

BALLHAWK *n* pl. **-S** a very good defensive ballplayer

BALLIES pl. of bally

BALLISTA *n* pl. **-TAE** or **-TAS** an ancient weapon

BALLON *n* pl. **-S** lightness of movement

BALLONET *n* pl. **-S** a small balloon

BALLONNE *n* pl. **-S** a ballet jump

BALLOON *v* **-ED, -ING, -S** to swell out

BALLOT *v* **-ED, -ING, -S** to vote

BALLOTER *n* pl. **-S** one that ballots

BALLPARK *n* pl. **-S** a facility in which ballgames are played

BALLROOM *n* pl. **-S** a large room for dancing

BALLS *v* **-ED, -ING, -ES** to make a mistake in doing something

BALLUTE *n* pl. **-S** a small inflatable parachute

BALLY *n* pl. **-LIES** a noisy uproar

BALLYARD *n* pl. **-S** a ballpark

BALLYHOO *v* **-ED, -ING, -S** to promote by uproar

BALLYRAG *v* **-RAGGED, -RAGGING, -RAGS** to bullyrag

BALM *n* pl. **-S** a fragrant resin **BALMLIKE** *adj*

BALMORAL *n* pl. **-S** a type of shoe

BALMY *adj* **BALMIER, BALMIEST** mild **BALMILY** *adv*

BALNEAL *adj* pertaining to baths

BALONEY *n* pl. **-NEYS** bologna

BALSA *n* pl. **-S** a tropical tree

BALSAM *v* **-ED, -ING, -S** to anoint with balsam (an aromatic, resinous substance)

BALSAMIC *adj* containing balsam

BALTI *n* pl. **-S** a type of Pakistani cuisine

BALUSTER *n* pl. **-S** a railing support

BAM *v* **BAMMED, BAMMING, BAMS** to strike with a dull resounding noise

BAMBINO *n* pl. **-NOS** or **-NI** a baby

BAMBOO *n* pl. **-BOOS** a tropical grass

BAN *n* pl. **BANI** a monetary unit of Romania

BAN	v **BANNED, BANNING, BANS** to prohibit
BANAL	adj ordinary **BANALLY** adv
BANALITY	n pl. **-TIES** something banal
BANALIZE	v **-IZED, -IZING, -IZES** to make banal
BANANA	n pl. **-S** an edible fruit
BANAUSIC	adj practical
BANC	n pl. **-S** a bench
BANCO	n pl. **-COS** a bet in certain gambling games
BAND	v **-ED, -ING, -S** to decorate with flexible strips of material
BANDA	n pl. **-S** a style of Mexican dance music
BANDAGE	v **-DAGED, -DAGING, -DAGES** to cover a wound with a strip of cloth
BANDAGER	n pl. **-S** one that bandages
BANDAID	adj providing superficial relief
BANDANA	n pl. **-S** bandanna
BANDANNA	n pl. **-S** a large, colored handkerchief
BANDBOX	n pl. **-ES** a lightweight box
BANDEAU	n pl. **-DEAUS** or **-DEAUX** a headband
BANDER	n pl. **-S** one that bands
BANDEROL	n pl. **-S** a streamer
BANDIED	past tense of bandy
BANDIES	present 3d person sing. of bandy
BANDING	n pl. **-S** the presence of stripes of contrasting colors
BANDIT	n pl. **-DITS** or **-DITTI** a robber
BANDITO	n pl. **-TOS** a bandit
BANDITRY	n pl. **-TRIES** robbery by bandits
BANDMATE	n pl. **-S** a fellow member of a band
BANDOG	n pl. **-S** a watchdog
BANDORA	n pl. **-S** bandore
BANDORE	n pl. **-S** an ancient lute
BANDPASS	n pl. **-ES** the range of frequencies transmitted through a filter
BANDSAW	v **-ED, -ING, -S** to saw with an electric cutting tool
BANDSMAN	n pl. **-MEN** a member of a musical band
BANDURA	n pl. **-S** a Ukrainian stringed instrument
BANDY	v **-DIED, -DYING, -DIES** to throw to and fro
BANDY	adj **-DIER, -DIEST** curved apart at the knees
BANE	v **BANED, BANING, BANES** to kill with poison
BANEFUL	adj poisonous
BANG	v **-ED, -ING, -S** to hit sharply
BANGER	n pl. **-S** a sausage
BANGKOK	n pl. **-S** a straw hat
BANGLE	n pl. **-S** a bracelet
BANGTAIL	n pl. **-S** a racehorse
BANI	pl. of ban
BANIAN	n pl. **-S** a Hindu merchant
BANING	present participle of bane
BANISH	v **-ED, -ING, -ES** to expel
BANISHER	n pl. **-S** one that banishes
BANISTER	n pl. **-S** a handrail
BANJAX	v **-ED, -ING, -ES** to damage or ruin
BANJO	n pl. **-JOS** or **-JOES** a musical instrument
BANJOIST	n pl. **-S** one who plays the banjo
BANK	v **-ED, -ING, -S** to keep money in a bank (an institution dealing in money matters) **BANKABLE** adj
BANKBOOK	n pl. **-S** a depositor's book
BANKCARD	n pl. **-S** a credit card issued by a bank
BANKER	n pl. **-S** one who works in a bank **BANKERLY** adj
BANKING	n pl. **-S** the business of a bank
BANKIT	n pl. **-S** a raised sidewalk
BANKNOTE	n pl. **-S** a promissory note
BANKROLL	v **-ED, -ING, -S** to fund
BANKRUPT	v **-ED, -ING, -S** to impoverish
BANKSIA	n pl. **-S** an Australian plant
BANKSIDE	n pl. **-S** the slope of a river bank
BANNABLE	adj liable to be banned
BANNED	past tense of ban
BANNER	v **-ED, -ING, -S** to furnish with a flag
BANNERET	n pl. **-S** a small flag
BANNEROL	n pl. **-S** a banderol
BANNET	n pl. **-S** a bonnet
BANNING	present participle of ban
BANNOCK	n pl. **-S** a type of cake
BANNS	n/pl a marriage notice
BANQUET	v **-ED, -ING, -S** to feast
BANSHEE	n pl. **-S** a female spirit

BANSHIE	*n* pl. **-S** banshee
BANTAM	*n* pl. **-S** a small fowl
BANTENG	*n* pl. **-S** a wild ox
BANTER	*v* **-ED, -ING, -S** to exchange mildly teasing remarks
BANTERER	*n* pl. **-S** one that banters
BANTLING	*n* pl. **-S** a very young child
BANTY	*n* pl. **-TIES** a bantam
BANYAN	*n* pl. **-S** an East Indian tree
BANZAI	*n* pl. **-S** a Japanese battle cry
BAOBAB	*n* pl. **-S** a tropical tree
BAP	*n* pl. **-S** a small bun or roll
BAPTISE	*v* **-TISED, -TISING, -TISES** to baptize
BAPTISIA	*n* pl. **-S** a flowering plant
BAPTISM	*n* pl. **-S** a Christian ceremony
BAPTIST	*n* pl. **-S** one who baptizes
BAPTIZE	*v* **-TIZED, -TIZING, -TIZES** to administer baptism to
BAPTIZER	*n* pl. **-S** a baptist
BAR	*v* **BARRED, BARRING, BARS** to exclude
BARATHEA	*n* pl. **-S** a silk fabric
BARB	*v* **-ED, -ING, -S** to furnish with a barb (a sharp projection)
BARBAL	*adj* pertaining to the beard
BARBARIC	*adj* uncivilized
BARBASCO	*n* pl. **-COS** or **-COES** a tropical tree
BARBATE	*adj* bearded
BARBE	*n* pl. **-S** a medieval cloth headdress
BARBECUE	*v* **-CUED, -CUING, -CUES** to cook over live coals or an open fire
BARBEL	*n* pl. **-S** an organ of a fish
BARBELL	*n* pl. **-S** an exercise apparatus
BARBEQUE	*v* **-QUED, -QUING, -QUES** to barbecue
BARBER	*v* **-ED, -ING, -S** to cut hair
BARBERRY	*n* pl. **-RIES** a shrub
BARBET	*n* pl. **-S** a tropical bird
BARBETTE	*n* pl. **-S** a platform
BARBICAN	*n* pl. **-S** an outer fortification
BARBICEL	*n* pl. **-S** a part of a feather
BARBIE	*n* pl. **-S** a portable fireplace for cooking
BARBITAL	*n* pl. **-S** a sedative
BARBLESS	*adj* having no barbs
BARBOT	*n* pl. **-S** barbotte
BARBOTTE	*n* pl. **-S** a large catfish
BARBULE	*n* pl. **-S** a small barb
BARBUT	*n* pl. **-S** a type of helmet
BARBWIRE	*n* pl. **-S** barbed wire
BARCA	*n* pl. **-S** a double-ended boat
BARCHAN	*n* pl. **-S** a type of sand dune
BARCODE	*n* pl. **-S** a group of thick and thin marks placed on a product
BARD	*v* **-ED, -ING, -S** to armor a horse
BARDE	*v* **BARDED, BARDING, BARDES** to bard
BARDIC	*adj* poetic
BARE	*adj* **BARER, BAREST** naked
BARE	*v* **BARED, BARING, BARES** to expose
BAREBACK	*adv* without a saddle
BAREBOAT	*n* pl. **-S** a pleasure boat rented without personnel
BAREFIT	*adj* barefoot
BAREFOOT	*adj* being without shoes
BAREGE	*n* pl. **-S** a sheer fabric
BAREHAND	*v* **-ED, -ING, -S** to catch with a bare hand
BAREHEAD	*adv* without a hat
BARELY	*adv* scarcely
BARENESS	*n* pl. **-ES** the state of being bare
BARER	comparative of bare
BARESARK	*n* pl. **-S** an ancient warrior
BAREST	superlative of bare
BARF	*v* **-ED, -ING, -S** to vomit
BARFI	*n* pl. **-S** burfi
BARFLY	*n* pl. **-FLIES** a drinker who frequents bars
BARGAIN	*v* **-ED, -ING, -S** to discuss terms for selling or buying
BARGE	*v* **BARGED, BARGING, BARGES** to move by barge (a long, large boat)
BARGEE	*n* pl. **-S** a bargeman
BARGELLO	*n* pl. **-LOS** a needlepoint stitch that makes a zigzag pattern
BARGEMAN	*n* pl. **-MEN** the master or a crew member of a barge
BARGHEST	*n* pl. **-S** a goblin
BARGING	present participle of barge
BARGOON	*n* pl. **-S** a bargain
BARGUEST	*n* pl. **-S** barghest

BARHOP *v* **-HOPPED, -HOPPING, -HOPS** to visit a number of bars during an evening

BARIC *adj* pertaining to barium

BARILLA *n* pl. **-S** a chemical compound

BARING present participle of bare

BARISTA *n* pl. **-S** one who makes and serves coffee to the public

BARITE *n* pl. **-S** a mineral

BARITONE *n* pl. **-S** a male singing voice

BARIUM *n* pl. **-S** a metallic element

BARK *v* **-ED, -ING, -S** to cry like a dog

BARKEEP *n* pl. **-S** a bartender

BARKER *n* pl. **-S** one that barks

BARKLESS *adj* having no bark; unable to bark

BARKY *adj* **BARKIER, BARKIEST** covered with bark (tough outer covering of a root or stem)

BARLEDUC *n* pl. **-S** a fruit jam

BARLESS *adj* having no restraints

BARLEY *n* pl. **-LEYS** a cereal grass

BARLOW *n* pl. **-S** a jackknife

BARM *n* pl. **-S** the foam on malt liquors

BARMAID *n* pl. **-S** a female bartender

BARMAN *n* pl. **-MEN** a male bartender

BARMIE *adj* barmy

BARMY *adj* **BARMIER, BARMIEST** full of barm; frothy **BARMILY** *adv*

BARN *v* **-ED, -ING, -S** to store in a barn (a large storage building)

BARNACLE *n* pl. **-S** a shellfish

BARNEY *n* pl. **-NEYS** a noisy argument

BARNLIKE *adj* resembling a barn

BARNWOOD *n* pl. **-S** wide wood for building barns

BARNY *adj* **BARNIER, BARNIEST** resembling a barn in size, shape, or smell

BARNYARD *n* pl. **-S** a yard near a barn

BAROGRAM *n* pl. **-S** a barometric reading

BARON *n* pl. **-S** a lower member of nobility

BARONAGE *n* pl. **-S** the rank of a baron

BARONESS *n* pl. **-ES** the wife of a baron

BARONET *n* pl. **-S** the holder of a rank below that of a baron

BARONG *n* pl. **-S** a broad knife

BARONIAL *adj* pertaining to a baron

BARONNE *n* pl. **-S** a baroness

BARONY *n* pl. **-ONIES** the domain of a baron

BAROQUE *n* pl. **-S** an ornate object

BAROSAUR *n* pl. **-S** a large dinosaur

BAROUCHE *n* pl. **-S** a type of carriage

BARQUE *n* pl. **-S** a sailing vessel

BARRABLE *adj* capable of being barred

BARRACK *v* **-ED, -ING, -S** to shout boisterously

BARRAGE *v* **-RAGED, -RAGING, -RAGES** to subject to a massive attack

BARRANCA *n* pl. **-S** a steep ravine

BARRANCO *n* pl. **-COS** barranca

BARRATER *n* pl. **-S** barrator

BARRATOR *n* pl. **-S** one who commits barratry

BARRATRY *n* pl. **-TRIES** fraud committed by a master or crew of a ship

BARRE *v* **BARRED, BARRING, BARRES** to play a type of guitar chord

BARRED past tense of bar

BARREL *v* **-RELED, -RELING, -RELS** or **-RELLED, -RELLING, -RELS** to move fast

BARREN *adj* **-RENER, -RENEST** unproductive **BARRENLY** *adv*

BARREN *n* pl. **-S** a tract of barren land

BARRET *n* pl. **-S** a flat cap

BARRETOR *n* pl. **-S** barrator

BARRETRY *n* pl. **-TRIES** barratry

BARRETTE *n* pl. **-S** a hair clip

BARRIER *n* pl. **-S** an obstacle

BARRING present participle of bar and barre

BARRIO *n* pl. **-RIOS** a district

BARRIQUE *n* pl. **-S** a wine barrel

BARROOM *n* pl. **-S** a room where liquor is sold

BARROW *n* pl. **-S** a type of cart

BARRY *adj* divided into horizontal bars

BARSTOOL *n* pl. **-S** a stool in a barroom

BARTEND *v* **-ED, -ING, -S** to tend a barroom

BARTER *v* **-ED, -ING, -S** to trade

BARTERER *n* pl. **-S** one that barters

BARTISAN *n* pl. **-S** bartizan

BARTIZAN *n* pl. **-S** a small turret

BARWARE *n* pl. **-S** barroom equipment

BARYE *n* pl. **-S** a unit of pressure

BARYON *n* pl. **-S** a type of subatomic particle **BARYONIC** *adj*

BARYTA	*n* pl. **-S** a compound of barium **BARYTIC** *adj*
BARYTE	*n* pl. **-S** barite
BARYTON	*n* pl. **-S** a stringed instrument
BARYTONE	*n* pl. **-S** baritone
BASAL	*adj* pertaining to the foundation **BASALLY** *adv*
BASALT	*n* pl. **-S** a volcanic rock **BASALTIC** *adj*
BASALTES	*n* pl. **BASALTES** unglazed stoneware
BASCINET	*n* pl. **-S** basinet
BASCULE	*n* pl. **-S** a type of seesaw
BASE	*adj* **BASER, BASEST** morally low
BASE	*v* **BASED, BASING, BASES** to found
BASEBALL	*n* pl. **-S** a type of ball
BASEBORN	*adj* of low birth
BASED	past tense of base
BASEHEAD	*n* pl. **-S** a person who freebases
BASELESS	*adj* having no foundation
BASELINE	*n* pl. **-S** a line at either end of a court in certain sports
BASELOAD	*n* pl. **-S** the permanent load on power supplies
BASELY	*adv* in a base manner
BASEMAN	*n* pl. **-MEN** a certain player in baseball
BASEMENT	*n* pl. **-S** the part of a building below ground level
BASENESS	*n* pl. **-ES** the state of being base
BASENJI	*n* pl. **-S** a barkless dog
BASEPATH	*n* pl. **-S** a base runner's path between bases
BASER	comparative of base
BASES	pl. of basis
BASEST	superlative of base
BASH	*v* **-ED, -ING, -ES** to smash
BASHAW	*n* pl. **-S** a pasha
BASHER	*n* pl. **-S** one that bashes
BASHFUL	*adj* shy; timid
BASHING	*n* pl. **-S** an act of beating
BASHLYK	*n* pl. **-S** a cloth hood
BASIC	*n* pl. **-S** a fundamental
BASICITY	*n* pl. **-TIES** the state of being alkaline
BASIDIUM	*n* pl. **-IA** a structure on a fungus **BASIDIAL** *adj*
BASIFIER	*n* pl. **-S** one that basifies
BASIFY	*v* **-FIED, -FYING, -FIES** to alkalize
BASIL	*n* pl. **-S** an aromatic herb
BASILAR	*adj* basal
BASILARY	*adj* basilar
BASILECT	*n* pl. **-S** the least prestigious language of an area
BASILIC	*adj* pertaining to a basilica
BASILICA	*n* pl. **-CAS** or **-CAE** an ancient Roman building
BASILISK	*n* pl. **-S** a fabled serpent
BASIN	*n* pl. **-S** a large bowl **BASINAL, BASINED** *adj*
BASINET	*n* pl. **-S** a medieval helmet
BASINFUL	*n* pl. **-S** as much as a basin can hold
BASING	present participle of base
BASION	*n* pl. **-S** a part of the skull
BASIS	*n* pl. **BASES** the foundation of something
BASK	*v* **-ED, -ING, -S** to lie in a pleasant warmth
BASKET	*n* pl. **-S** a wooden container
BASKETRY	*n* pl. **-RIES** basket weaving
BASMATI	*n* pl. **-S** a long-grain rice
BASOPHIL	*n* pl. **-S** a type of cell
BASQUE	*n* pl. **-S** a bodice
BASS	*n* pl. **-ES** an edible fish
BASS	*adj* **BASSER, BASSEST** deep-sounding
BASSET	*v* **-SETED, -SETING, -SETS** or **-SETTED, -SETTING, -SETS** to outcrop
BASSI	a pl. of basso
BASSINET	*n* pl. **-S** a basket used as a baby's crib
BASSIST	*n* pl. **-S** a person who plays a double bass
BASSLY	*adv* in a low-pitched manner
BASSNESS	*n* pl. **-ES** lowness in pitch
BASSO	*n* pl. **-SOS** or **-SI** a low-pitched singer
BASSOON	*n* pl. **-S** a low-pitched instrument
BASSWOOD	*n* pl. **-S** a linden tree
BASSY	*adj* low in pitch
BAST	*n* pl. **-S** a woody fiber
BASTARD	*n* pl. **-S** an illegitimate child

BASTARDY *n* pl. **-TARDIES** the state of being a bastard

BASTE *v* **BASTED, BASTING, BASTES** to sew loosely together

BASTER *n* pl. **-S** one that bastes

BASTILE *n* pl. **-S** bastille

BASTILLE *n* pl. **-S** a prison

BASTING *n* pl. **-S** the thread used by a baster

BASTION *n* pl. **-S** a fortified place

BAT *v* **BATTED, BATTING, BATS** to hit a baseball

BATARD *n* pl. **-S** a birchbark canoe

BATATA *n* pl. **-S** a sweet potato

BATBOY *n* pl. **-BOYS** a boy who minds baseball equipment

BATCH *v* **-ED, -ING, -ES** to bring together

BATCHER *n* pl. **-S** one that batches

BATE *v* **BATED, BATING, BATES** to reduce the force of

BATEAU *n* pl. **-TEAUX** a flat-bottomed boat

BATFISH *n* pl. **-ES** a batlike fish

BATFOWL *v* **-ED, -ING, -S** to catch birds at night

BATGIRL *n* pl. **-S** a girl who minds baseball equipment

BATH *n* pl. **-S** a washing

BATHE *v* **BATHED, BATHING, BATHES** to wash

BATHER *n* pl. **-S** one that bathes

BATHETIC *adj* trite

BATHING *n* pl. **-S** the act of one that bathes

BATHLESS *adj* not having had a bath

BATHMAT *n* pl. **-S** a mat used in a bathroom

BATHOS *n* pl. **-ES** triteness

BATHROBE *n* pl. **-S** a housecoat

BATHROOM *n* pl. **-S** a room in which to bathe

BATHTUB *n* pl. **-S** a tub in which to bathe

BATHYAL *adj* pertaining to deep water

BATIK *v* **-ED, -ING, -S** to dye fabric by a particular process

BATING present participle of bate

BATISTE *n* pl. **-S** a sheer fabric

BATLIKE *adj* resembling a bat (a flying mammal)

BATMAN *n* pl. **-MEN** an orderly

BATON *n* pl. **-S** a short rod

BATSMAN *n* pl. **-MEN** one who bats

BATT *n* pl. **-S** a sheet of cotton

BATTALIA *n* pl. **-S** a military unit

BATTEAU *n* pl. **-TEAUX** bateau

BATTED past tense of bat

BATTEN *v* **-ED, -ING, -S** to fasten with strips of wood

BATTENER *n* pl. **-S** one that battens

BATTER *v* **-ED, -ING, -S** to beat repeatedly

BATTERER *n* pl. **-S** one that batters

BATTERIE *n* pl. **-S** a ballet movement

BATTERY *n* pl. **-TERIES** a device for generating an electric current

BATTIER comparative of batty

BATTIEST superlative of batty

BATTIK *n* pl. **-S** a fabric dyed by batiking

BATTILY *adv* in a batty manner

BATTING *n* pl. **-S** a batt

BATTLE *v* **-TLED, -TLING, -TLES** to fight

BATTLER *n* pl. **-S** one that battles

BATTU *adj* pertaining to a ballet movement

BATTUE *n* pl. **-S** a type of hunt

BATTY *adj* **-TIER, -TIEST** crazy

BATWING *adj* shaped like a bat's wing

BAUBEE *n* pl. **-S** bawbee

BAUBLE *n* pl. **-S** a cheap trinket

BAUD *n* pl. **-S** a unit of data transmission speed

BAUDEKIN *n* pl. **-S** a brocaded fabric

BAUDRONS *n* pl. **-ES** a cat

BAUHINIA *n* pl. **-S** a small tropical tree

BAULK *v* **-ED, -ING, -S** to balk

BAULKER *n* pl. **-S** balker

BAULKY *adj* **BAULKIER, BAULKIEST** balky

BAUSOND *adj* having white marks

BAUXITE *n* pl. **-S** an ore of aluminum **BAUXITIC** *adj*

BAWBEE *n* pl. **-S** a Scottish coin

BAWCOCK *n* pl. **-S** a fine fellow

BAWD *n* pl. **-S** a madam

BAWDIER comparative of bawdy

BAWDIES pl. of bawdy

BAWDIEST superlative of bawdy

BAWDILY *adv* in a bawdy manner

BAWDRIC *n* pl. **-S** baldric

BAWDRY   *n* pl. **-RIES** obscenity

BAWDY   *adj* **BAWDIER, BAWDIEST** obscene

BAWDY   *n* pl. **BAWDIES** obscene language

BAWK   *n* pl. **-S** an Atlantic seabird

BAWL   *v* **-ED, -ING, -S** to cry loudly

BAWLER   *n* pl. **-S** one that bawls

BAWN   *n* pl. **-S** a meadow for cows

BAWSUNT   *adj* bausond

BAWTIE   *n* pl. **-S** a dog

BAWTY   *n* pl. **-TIES** bawtie

BAY   *v* **-ED, -ING, -S** to howl

BAY   *adj* **BAYER, BAYEST** dark reddish-brown

BAYADEER   *n* pl. **-S** bayadere

BAYADERE   *n* pl. **-S** a dancing girl

BAYAMO   *n* pl. **-MOS** a strong wind

BAYARD   *n* pl. **-S** a horse

BAYBERRY   *n* pl. **-RIES** a berry tree

BAYFRONT   *n* pl. **-S** the shoreline of a bay (an inlet of the sea)

BAYMAN   *n* pl. **-MEN** a person who fishes on a bay

BAYNODDY   *n* pl. **-DIES** a bayman

BAYONET   *v* **-NETED, -NETING, -NETS** or **-NETTED, -NETTING, -NETS** to stab with a dagger-like weapon

BAYOU   *n* pl. **-S** a marshy body of water

BAYSIDE   *n* pl. **-S** the shore of a bay (an inlet of the sea)

BAYWOOD   *n* pl. **-S** a coarse mahogany

BAZAAR   *n* pl. **-S** a marketplace

BAZAR   *n* pl. **-S** bazaar

BAZOO   *n* pl. **-ZOOS** the mouth

BAZOOKA   *n* pl. **-S** a small rocket launcher

BAZZ   *v* **-ED, -ING, -ES** to throw (as a stone)

BDELLIUM   *n* pl. **-S** a gum resin

BE   *v* present sing. 1st person **AM**, 2d **ARE** or **ART**, 3d **IS**, past sing. 1st and 3d persons **WAS**, 2d **WERE** or **WAST** or **WERT**, past participle **BEEN**, present participle **BEING** to have actuality

BEACH   *v* **-ED, -ING, -ES** to drive ashore

BEACHBOY   *n* pl. **-BOYS** a male beach attendant

BEACHY   *adj* **BEACHIER, BEACHIEST** sandy or pebbly

BEACON   *v* **-ED, -ING, -S** to warn or guide

BEAD   *v* **-ED, -ING, -S** to adorn with beads (round pieces of glass)

BEADER   *n* pl. **-S** one that beads

BEADIER   comparative of beady

BEADIEST   superlative of beady

BEADILY   *adv* in a beady manner

BEADING   *n* pl. **-S** beaded material

BEADLE   *n* pl. **-S** a parish official

BEADLIKE   *adj* beady

BEADMAN   *n* pl. **-MEN** beadsman

BEADROLL   *n* pl. **-S** a list of names

BEADSMAN   *n* pl. **-MEN** one who prays for another

BEADWORK   *n* pl. **-S** beading

BEADY   *adj* **BEADIER, BEADIEST** resembling beads

BEAGLE   *v* **-GLED, -GLING, -GLES** to hunt with beagles (small hounds)

BEAGLER   *n* pl. **-S** one that hunts game with beagles

BEAGLING   *n* pl. **-S** the activity of hunting with beagles

BEAK   *n* pl. **-S** a bird's bill **BEAKED, BEAKLESS, BEAKLIKE** *adj*

BEAKER   *n* pl. **-S** a large cup

BEAKY   *adj* **BEAKIER, BEAKIEST** resembling a beak

BEAL   *n* pl. **-S** an infected sore (a painful place on the body)

BEALING   *n* pl. **-S** a beal

BEAM   *v* **-ED, -ING, -S** to emit in beams (rays of light)

BEAMIER   comparative of beamy

BEAMIEST   superlative of beamy

BEAMILY   *adv* in a beamy manner

BEAMISH   *adj* cheerful

BEAMLESS   *adj* having no beam

BEAMLIKE   *adj* resembling a beam

BEAMY   *adj* **BEAMIER, BEAMIEST** beaming

BEAN   *v* **-ED, -ING, -S** to hit on the head

BEANBAG   *n* pl. **-S** a small cloth bag

BEANBALL   *n* pl. **-S** a baseball thrown at the head

BEANERY   *n* pl. **-ERIES** a cheap restaurant

BEANIE   *n* pl. **-S** a small cap

BEANLIKE   *adj* resembling a bean

BEANO *n* pl. **BEANOS** a form of bingo

BEANPOLE *n* pl. **-S** a thin pole

BEAR *v* **BORE, BORNE** or **BORN, BEARING, BEARS** to endure **BEARABLE** *adj* **BEARABLY** *adv*

BEARCAT *n* pl. **-S** a small mammal

BEARD *v* **-ED, -ING, -S** to oppose boldly

BEARER *n* pl. **-S** one that bears

BEARHUG *n* pl. **-S** a rough tight embrace

BEARING *n* pl. **-S** demeanor

BEARISH *adj* resembling a bear (a large mammal)

BEARLIKE *adj* bearish

BEARPAW *n* pl. **-S** the paw of a bear

BEARSKIN *n* pl. **-S** the skin of a bear

BEARWOOD *n* pl. **-S** a small tree of the buckthorn family

BEAST *n* pl. **-S** an animal

BEASTIE *n* pl. **-S** a tiny animal

BEASTLY *adj* **-LIER, -LIEST** resembling a beast

BEAT *v* **BEAT, BEATEN, BEATING, BEATS** to strike repeatedly **BEATABLE** *adj*

BEATBOX *v* **-ED, -ING, -ES** to sing to the rhythm of rap music

BEATDOWN *n* pl. **-S** an overwhelming defeat

BEATER *n* pl. **-S** one that beats

BEATIFIC *adj* blissful

BEATIFY *v* **-FIED, -FYING, -FIES** to make happy

BEATING *n* pl. **-S** a defeat

BEATLESS *adj* having no rhythm

BEATNIK *n* pl. **-S** a nonconformist

BEAU *n* pl. **BEAUS** or **BEAUX** a boyfriend **BEAUISH** *adj*

BEAUCOUP *n* pl. **-S** an abundance

BEAUT *n* pl. **-S** something beautiful

BEAUT *adj* **BEAUTER, BEAUTEST** beautiful

BEAUTIFY *v* **-FIED, -FYING, -FIES** to make beautiful

BEAUTY *n* pl. **-TIES** one that is lovely

BEAUX a pl. of beau

BEAVER *v* **-ED, -ING, -S** to work hard

BEBEERU *n* pl. **-S** a tropical tree

BEBLOOD *v* **-ED, -ING, -S** to cover with blood

BEBOP *n* pl. **-S** a type of jazz

BEBOPPER *n* pl. **-S** one that likes bebop

BECALM *v* **-ED, -ING, -S** to make calm

BECAME past tense of become

BECAP *v* **-CAPPED, -CAPPING, -CAPS** to put a cap on

BECARPET *v* **-ED, -ING, -S** to cover with a carpet

BECAUSE *conj* for the reason that

BECHALK *v* **-ED, -ING, -S** to cover with chalk

BECHAMEL *n* pl. **-S** a white sauce

BECHANCE *v* **-CHANCED, -CHANCING, -CHANCES** to befall

BECHARM *v* **-ED, -ING, -S** to hold under a spell

BECK *v* **-ED, -ING, -S** to beckon

BECKET *n* pl. **-S** a securing rope

BECKON *v* **-ED, -ING, -S** to signal by sign or gesture

BECKONER *n* pl. **-S** one that beckons

BECLAMOR *v* **-ED, -ING, -S** to clamor loudly

BECLASP *v* **-ED, -ING, -S** to embrace

BECLOAK *v* **-ED, -ING, -S** to place a cloak on

BECLOG *v* **-CLOGGED, -CLOGGING, -CLOGS** to clog thoroughly

BECLOTHE *v* **-CLOTHED, -CLOTHING, -CLOTHES** to clothe

BECLOUD *v* **-ED, -ING, -S** to make cloudy

BECLOWN *v* **-ED, -ING, -S** to cause to appear ridiculous

BECOME *v* **-CAME, -COMING, -COMES** to come to be

BECOMING *n* pl. **-S** a process of change

BECOWARD *v* **-ED, -ING, -S** to accuse of cowardice

BECRAWL *v* **-ED, -ING, -S** to crawl over

BECRIME *v* **-CRIMED, -CRIMING, -CRIMES** to make guilty of a crime

BECROWD *v* **-ED, -ING, -S** to crowd closely

BECRUST *v* **-ED, -ING, -S** to cover with a crust

BECUDGEL *v* **-GELLED, -GELLING, -GELS** or **-GELED, -GELING, -GELS** to cudgel thoroughly

BECURSE *v* **-CURSED** or **-CURST, -CURSING, -CURSES** to curse severely

BED *v* **BEDDED, BEDDING, BEDS** to provide with a bed (a piece of furniture used for sleeping)

BEDABBLE *v* **-BLED, -BLING, -BLES** to soil

BEDAD	*interj* — used as a mild oath
BEDAMN	*v* **-ED, -ING, -S** to swear at
BEDARKEN	*v* **-ED, -ING, -S** to darken
BEDAUB	*v* **-ED, -ING, -S** to besmear
BEDAZZLE	*v* **-ZLED, -ZLING, -ZLES** to confuse
BEDBOARD	*n* pl. **-S** a board placed between a mattress and bedspring
BEDBUG	*n* pl. **-S** a bloodsucking insect
BEDCHAIR	*n* pl. **-S** a chair near a bed
BEDCOVER	*n* pl. **-S** a cover for a bed
BEDDABLE	*adj* suitable for taking to bed
BEDDED	past tense of bed
BEDDER	*n* pl. **-S** one that makes up beds
BEDDING	*n* pl. **-S** material for making up a bed
BEDEAFEN	*v* **-ED, -ING, -S** to deafen
BEDECK	*v* **-ED, -ING, -S** to clothe with finery
BEDEL	*n* pl. **-S** an English university officer
BEDELL	*n* pl. **-S** bedel
BEDEMAN	*n* pl. **-MEN** beadsman
BEDESMAN	*n* pl. **-MEN** beadsman
BEDEVIL	*v* **-ILED, -ILING, -ILS** or **-ILLED, -ILLING, -ILS** to harass
BEDEW	*v* **-ED, -ING, -S** to wet with dew
BEDFAST	*adj* confined to bed
BEDFRAME	*n* pl. **-S** the frame of a bed
BEDGOWN	*n* pl. **-S** a dressing gown
BEDHEAD	*n* pl. **-S** an upright board at the head of a bed
BEDIAPER	*v* **-ED, -ING, -S** to ornament with a kind of design
BEDIGHT	*v* **-ED, -ING, -S** to bedeck
BEDIM	*v* **-DIMMED, -DIMMING, -DIMS** to make dim
BEDIMPLE	*v* **-PLED, -PLING, -PLES** to dimple
BEDIRTY	*v* **-DIRTIED, -DIRTYING, -DIRTIES** to make dirty
BEDIZEN	*v* **-ED, -ING, -S** to dress gaudily
BEDLAM	*n* pl. **-S** confusion
BEDLAMER	*n* pl. **-S** a young harp seal (an aquatic mammal)
BEDLAMP	*n* pl. **-S** a lamp near a bed
BEDLESS	*adj* having no bed
BEDLIKE	*adj* resembling a bed
BEDLINER	*n* pl. **-S** a protective covering for the bed of a truck
BEDMAKER	*n* pl. **-S** one that makes beds
BEDMATE	*n* pl. **-S** a bed companion
BEDOTTED	*adj* covered with dots
BEDOUIN	*n* pl. **-S** a nomadic Arab
BEDPAN	*n* pl. **-S** a toilet pan
BEDPLATE	*n* pl. **-S** a frame support
BEDPOST	*n* pl. **-S** a post of a bed
BEDQUILT	*n* pl. **-S** a quilt for a bed
BEDRAIL	*n* pl. **-S** a board at bedside
BEDRAPE	*v* **-DRAPED, -DRAPING, -DRAPES** to drape
BEDRENCH	*v* **-ED, -ING, -ES** to drench thoroughly
BEDREST	*n* pl. **-S** confinement to bed
BEDRID	*adj* bedfast
BEDRIVEL	*v* **-ELLED, -ELLING, -ELS** or **-ELED, -ELING, -ELS** to cover with saliva
BEDROCK	*n* pl. **-S** the rock under soil
BEDROLL	*n* pl. **-S** a portable roll of bedding
BEDROOM	*n* pl. **-S** a room for sleeping
BEDRUG	*v* **-DRUGGED, -DRUGGING, -DRUGS** to make sleepy
BEDSHEET	*n* pl. **-S** a sheet for a bed
BEDSIDE	*n* pl. **-S** the side of a bed
BEDSIT	*n* pl. **-S** a one-room apartment
BEDSKIRT	*n* pl. **-S** drapery attached to a bed frame
BEDSOCK	*n* pl. **-S** a sock for wear in a bed
BEDSONIA	*n* pl. **-S** a virus
BEDSORE	*n* pl. **-S** a type of sore
BEDSTAND	*n* pl. **-S** a table next to a bed
BEDSTEAD	*n* pl. **-S** a support for a bed
BEDSTRAW	*n* pl. **-S** a woody herb
BEDTICK	*n* pl. **-S** the cloth case of a mattress
BEDTIME	*n* pl. **-S** a time for going to bed
BEDU	*n* pl. **BEDU** a bedouin
BEDUIN	*n* pl. **-S** bedouin
BEDUMB	*v* **-ED, -ING, -S** to render speechless
BEDUNCE	*v* **-DUNCED, -DUNCING, -DUNCES** to make a dunce of
BEDWARD	*adv* toward bed
BEDWARDS	*adv* bedward
BEDWARF	*v* **-ED, -ING, -S** to cause to appear small by comparison

BEE	*n* pl. **-S** a winged insect
BEEBEE	*n* pl. **-S** a pellet
BEEBREAD	*n* pl. **-S** a pollen mixture
BEECH	*n* pl. **-ES** a type of tree **BEECHEN** *adj*
BEECHNUT	*n* pl. **-S** the nut of a beech
BEECHY	*adj* **BEECHIER, BEECHIEST** abounding in beeches
BEEDI	*n* pl. **-DIES** bidi
BEEF	*n* pl. **BEEFS** or **BEEVES** a steer or cow fattened for food
BEEF	*v* **-ED, -ING, -S** to add bulk to
BEEFALO	*n* pl. **-LOS** or **-LOES** the offspring of an American buffalo and domestic cattle
BEEFCAKE	*n* pl. **-S** pictures of male physiques
BEEFIER	comparative of beefy
BEEFIEST	superlative of beefy
BEEFILY	*adv* in a beefy manner
BEEFLESS	*adj* being without beef
BEEFWOOD	*n* pl. **-S** a hardwood tree
BEEFY	*adj* **BEEFIER, BEEFIEST** brawny
BEEHIVE	*n* pl. **-S** a hive for bees
BEEHIVED	*adj* having a hairdo shaped like a beehive
BEELIKE	*adj* resembling a bee
BEELINE	*v* **-LINED, -LINING, -LINES** to go in a straight direct course
BEEN	past participle of be
BEEP	*v* **-ED, -ING, -S** to honk a horn
BEEPER	*n* pl. **-S** a signaling device
BEER	*n* pl. **-S** an alcoholic beverage
BEERNUT	*n* pl. **-S** a peanut with a sweet coating
BEERY	*adj* **BEERIER, BEERIEST** affected by beer **BEERILY** *adv*
BEESWAX	*v* **-ED, -ING, -ES** to polish furniture with a type of wax
BEESWING	*n* pl. **-S** a crust that forms on wines
BEET	*n* pl. **-S** a garden plant
BEETLE	*v* **-TLED, -TLING, -TLES** to jut out
BEETLER	*n* pl. **-S** one that operates a cloth-finishing machine
BEETROOT	*n* pl. **-S** the root of the beet
BEEVES	a pl. of beef
BEEYARD	*n* pl. **-S** an apiary
BEEZER	*n* pl. **-S** the nose

BEFALL	*v* **-FELL, -FALLEN, -FALLING, -FALLS** to happen to
BEFINGER	*v* **-ED, -ING, -S** to touch all over
BEFIT	*v* **-FITTED, -FITTING, -FITS** to be suitable to
BEFLAG	*v* **-FLAGGED, -FLAGGING, -FLAGS** to deck with flags
BEFLEA	*v* **-ED, -ING, -S** to infest with fleas
BEFLECK	*v* **-ED, -ING, -S** to fleck
BEFLOWER	*v* **-ED, -ING, -S** to cover with flowers
BEFOG	*v* **-FOGGED, -FOGGING, -FOGS** to envelop in fog
BEFOOL	*v* **-ED, -ING, -S** to deceive
BEFORE	*adv* previously
BEFOUL	*v* **-ED, -ING, -S** to foul
BEFOULER	*n* pl. **-S** one that befouls
BEFRET	*v* **-FRETTED, -FRETTING, -FRETS** to gnaw
BEFRIEND	*v* **-ED, -ING, -S** to act as a friend to
BEFRINGE	*v* **-FRINGED, -FRINGING, -FRINGES** to border with a fringe
BEFUDDLE	*v* **-DLED, -DLING, -DLES** to confuse
BEG	*v* **BEGGED, BEGGING, BEGS** to plead
BEGAD	*interj* — used as a mild oath
BEGALL	*v* **-ED, -ING, -S** to make sore by rubbing
BEGAN	past tense of begin
BEGAZE	*v* **-GAZED, -GAZING, -GAZES** to gaze at
BEGEM	*v* **-GEMMED, -GEMMING, -GEMS** to gem
BEGET	*v* **-GOT** or **-GAT, -GOTTEN, -GETTING, -GETS** to cause to exist
BEGETTER	*n* pl. **-S** one that begets
BEGGAR	*v* **-ED, -ING, -S** to impoverish
BEGGARLY	*adj* very poor
BEGGARY	*n* pl. **-GARIES** extreme poverty
BEGGED	past tense of beg
BEGGING	present participle of beg
BEGIN	*v* **-GAN, -GUN, -GINNING, -GINS** to start
BEGINNER	*n* pl. **-S** one that begins
BEGIRD	*v* **-GIRDED** or **-GIRT, -GIRDING, -GIRDS** to surround
BEGIRDLE	*v* **-DLED, -DLING, -DLES** to surround

BEGLAD	*v* **-GLADDED, -GLADDING, -GLADS** to gladden
BEGLAMOR	*v* **-ED, -ING, -S** to dazzle with glamor
BEGLOOM	*v* **-ED, -ING, -S** to make gloomy
BEGONE	*v* to go away —this is the only form in use
BEGONIA	*n* pl. **-S** a tropical herb
BEGORAH	*interj* begorra
BEGORRA	*interj* — used as a mild oath
BEGORRAH	*interj* begorra
BEGOT	a past tense of beget
BEGOTTEN	past participle of beget
BEGRIM	*v* **-GRIMMED, -GRIMMING, -GRIMS** to begrime
BEGRIME	*v* **-GRIMED, -GRIMING, -GRIMES** to dirty
BEGROAN	*v* **-ED, -ING, -S** to groan at
BEGRUDGE	*v* **-GRUDGED, -GRUDGING, -GRUDGES** to concede reluctantly
BEGUILE	*v* **-GUILED, -GUILING, -GUILES** to deceive
BEGUILER	*n* pl. **-S** one that beguiles
BEGUINE	*n* pl. **-S** a lively dance
BEGULF	*v* **-ED, -ING, -S** to engulf
BEGUM	*n* pl. **-S** a Muslim lady of high rank
BEGUN	past participle of begin
BEHALF	*n* pl. **-HALVES** interest, support, or benefit
BEHAVE	*v* **-HAVED, -HAVING, -HAVES** to act properly
BEHAVER	*n* pl. **-S** one that behaves
BEHAVIOR	*n* pl. **-S** demeanor
BEHEAD	*v* **-ED, -ING, -S** to cut off the head of
BEHEADAL	*n* pl. **-S** the act of beheading
BEHEADER	*n* pl. **-S** one that beheads
BEHELD	past tense of behold
BEHEMOTH	*n* pl. **-S** a large beast
BEHEST	*n* pl. **-S** a command
BEHIND	*n* pl. **-S** the buttocks
BEHOLD	*v* **-HELD, -HOLDING, -HOLDS** to view
BEHOLDEN	*adj* indebted
BEHOLDER	*n* pl. **-S** one that beholds
BEHOOF	*n* pl. **-HOOVES** or **-HOOFS** use, advantage, or benefit
BEHOOVE	*v* **-HOOVED, -HOOVING, -HOOVES** to be proper for
BEHOVE	*v* **-HOVED, -HOVING, -HOVES** to behoove
BEHOWL	*v* **-ED, -ING, -S** to howl at
BEIGE	*n* pl. **-S** a tan color
BEIGE	*adj* **BEIGER, BEIGEST** of a tan color
BEIGNE	*n* pl. **-S** beignet
BEIGNET	*n* pl. **-S** a type of fritter or doughnut
BEIGY	*adj* of the color beige
BEING	*n* pl. **-S** something that exists
BEJABERS	*n* pl. **-ES** bejesus
BEJASUS	*n* pl. **-ES** bejesus
BEJEEZUS	*n* pl. **-ES** bejesus
BEJESUS	*n* pl. **-ES** an exclamation used as a mild oath
BEJEWEL	*v* **-ELED, -ELING, -ELS** or **-ELLED, -ELLING, -ELS** to adorn with jewels
BEJUMBLE	*v* **-BLED, -BLING, -BLES** to jumble
BEKISS	*v* **-ED, -ING, -ES** to cover with kisses
BEKNIGHT	*v* **-ED, -ING, -S** to raise to knighthood
BEKNOT	*v* **-KNOTTED, -KNOTTING, -KNOTS** to tie in knots
BEL	*n* pl. **-S** a unit of power
BELABOR	*v* **-ED, -ING, -S** to discuss for an absurd amount of time
BELABOUR	*v* **-ED, -ING, -S** to belabor
BELACED	*adj* adorned with lace
BELADY	*v* **-DIED, -DYING, -DIES** to apply the title of lady to
BELATED	*adj* late or too late
BELAUD	*v* **-ED, -ING, -S** to praise
BELAY	*v* **-ED, -ING, -S** to fasten a rope
BELAYER	*n* pl. **-S** one that belays
BELCH	*v* **-ED, -ING, -ES** to expel gas through the mouth
BELCHER	*n* pl. **-S** one that belches
BELDAM	*n* pl. **-S** an old woman
BELDAME	*n* pl. **-S** beldam
BELEAP	*v* **-LEAPED** or **-LEAPT, -LEAPING, -LEAPS** to leap upon
BELFRY	*n* pl. **-FRIES** a bell tower **BELFRIED** *adj*
BELGA	*n* pl. **-S** a former Belgian monetary unit

BELIE *v* **-LIED, -LYING, -LIES** to misrepresent

BELIEF *n* pl. **-S** acceptance of the truth or actuality of something

BELIER *n* pl. **-S** one that belies

BELIEVE *v* **-LIEVED, -LIEVING, -LIEVES** to accept as true or real

BELIEVER *n* pl. **-S** one that believes

BELIKE *adv* perhaps

BELIQUOR *v* **-ED, -ING, -S** to soak with liquor

BELITTLE *v* **-TLED, -TLING, -TLES** to disparage

BELIVE *adv* in due time

BELL *v* **-ED, -ING, -S** to provide with a bell (a ringing device)

BELLBIRD *n* pl. **-S** a tropical bird

BELLBOY *n* pl. **-BOYS** a hotel's errand boy

BELLBUOY *n* pl. **-BUOYS** a buoy (a warning float) having a bell

BELLCAST *adj* designating a style of roof architecture

BELLE *n* pl. **-S** an attractive woman

BELLEEK *n* pl. **-S** a very thin translucent porcelain

BELLHOP *n* pl. **-S** a bellboy

BELLIED past tense of belly

BELLIES present 3d person sing. of belly

BELLING *n* pl. **-S** a mock serenade for newlyweds

BELLMAN *n* pl. **-MEN** a town crier

BELLOW *v* **-ED, -ING, -S** to shout in a deep voice

BELLOWER *n* pl. **-S** one that bellows

BELLPULL *n* pl. **-S** a cord pulled to ring a bell

BELLWORT *n* pl. **-S** a flowering plant

BELLY *v* **-LIED, -LYING, -LIES** to swell out

BELLYFUL *n* pl. **-S** an excessive amount

BELON *n* pl. **-S** a flat oyster

BELONG *v* **-ED, -ING, -S** to be a member of

BELOVED *n* pl. **-S** one who is loved

BELOW *n* pl. **-S** something that is beneath

BELT *v* **-ED, -ING, -S** to fasten with a belt (a strap or band worn around the waist)

BELTER *n* pl. **-S** one that belts

BELTING *n* pl. **-S** material for belts

BELTLESS *adj* having no belt

BELTLINE *n* pl. **-S** the waistline

BELTWAY *n* pl. **-WAYS** a highway around an urban area

BELUGA *n* pl. **-S** a white sturgeon

BELYING present participle of belie

BEMA *n* pl. **-MAS** or **-MATA** a platform in a synagogue

BEMADAM *v* **-ED, -ING, -S** to call by the title of madam

BEMADDEN *v* **-ED, -ING, -S** to madden

BEMEAN *v* **-ED, -ING, -S** to debase

BEMINGLE *v* **-GLED, -GLING, -GLES** to mix together

BEMIRE *v* **-MIRED, -MIRING, -MIRES** to soil with mud

BEMIST *v* **-ED, -ING, -S** to envelop in a mist

BEMIX *v* **-MIXED** or **-MIXT, -MIXING, -MIXES** to mix thoroughly

BEMOAN *v* **-ED, -ING, -S** to lament

BEMOCK *v* **-ED, -ING, -S** to mock

BEMUDDLE *v* **-DLED, -DLING, -DLES** to confuse completely

BEMURMUR *v* **-ED, -ING, -S** to murmur at

BEMUSE *v* **-MUSED, -MUSING, -MUSES** to confuse

BEMUZZLE *v* **-ZLED, -ZLING, -ZLES** to muzzle

BEN *n* pl. **-S** an inner room

BENAME *v* **-NAMED, -NEMPT** or **-NEMPTED, -NAMING, -NAMES** to name

BENCH *v* **-ED, -ING, -ES** to take a player out of a game (a team competition)

BENCHER *n* pl. **-S** a magistrate

BENCHTOP *adj* suitable for use on a workbench

BEND *v* **BENDED** or **BENT, BENDING, BENDS** to curve **BENDABLE** *adj*

BENDAY *v* **-ED, -ING, -S** to reproduce using a certain process

BENDEE *n* pl. **-S** bendy

BENDER *n* pl. **-S** one that bends

BENDWAYS *adv* bendwise

BENDWISE *adv* diagonally

BENDY *n* pl. **-DYS** okra

BENDY *adj* **BENDIER, BENDIEST** flexible

BENE *n* pl. **-S** benne

BENEATH *prep* under

BENEDICK *n* pl. **-S** benedict

BENEDICT *n* pl. **-S** a newly married man

BENEFIC *adj* kindly

BENEFICE	*v* **-FICED, -FICING, -FICES** to endow with land	**BERASCAL**	*v* **-ED, -ING, -S** to accuse of being a rascal
BENEFIT	*v* **-FITED, -FITING, -FITS** or **-FITTED, -FITTING, -FITS** to be helpful or useful to	**BERATE**	*v* **-RATED, -RATING, -RATES** to scold severely
BENEMPT	a past participle of bename	**BERBER**	*n* pl. **-S** a type of carpet
BENEMPTED	a past participle of bename	**BERBERIN**	*n* pl. **-S** a medicinal alkaloid
BENIGN	*adj* kind **BENIGNLY** *adv*	**BERBERIS**	*n* pl. **-ES** a barberry
BENISON	*n* pl. **-S** a blessing	**BERCEUSE**	*n* pl. **-S** a lullaby
BENJAMIN	*n* pl. **-S** benzoin	**BERDACHE**	*n* pl. **-S** a Native American male transvestite
BENNE	*n* pl. **-S** the sesame plant	**BERDASH**	*n* pl. **-ES** berdache
BENNET	*n* pl. **-S** a perennial herb	**BEREAVE**	*v* **-REAVED** or **-REFT, -REAVING, -REAVES** to deprive
BENNI	*n* pl. **-S** benne		
BENNY	*n* pl. **-NIES** an amphetamine tablet	**BEREAVER**	*n* pl. **-S** one that bereaves
BENOMYL	*n* pl. **-S** a chemical compound	**BERET**	*n* pl. **-S** a soft, flat cap
BENT	*n* pl. **-S** an inclination	**BERETTA**	*n* pl. **-S** biretta
BENTHAL	*adj* benthic	**BERG**	*n* pl. **-S** an iceberg
BENTHIC	*adj* pertaining to oceanic depths	**BERGAMOT**	*n* pl. **-S** a citrus tree
BENTHON	*n* pl. **-S** the organisms living in the benthos	**BERGENIA**	*n* pl. **-S** a flowering plant
		BERGERE	*n* pl. **-S** an upholstered armchair
BENTHOS	*n* pl. **-ES** the bottom of the sea	**BERHYME**	*v* **-RHYMED, -RHYMING, -RHYMES** to compose in rhyme
BENTO	*n* pl. **-TOS** obento		
BENTWOOD	*n* pl. **-S** wood bent for use in furniture	**BERIBERI**	*n* pl. **-S** a thiamine deficiency disease
BENUMB	*v* **-ED, -ING, -S** to make numb	**BERIMBAU**	*n* pl. **-S** a Brazilian musical instrument
BENZAL	*adj* pertaining to a certain chemical group	**BERIME**	*v* **-RIMED, -RIMING, -RIMES** to berhyme
BENZENE	*n* pl. **-S** a volatile liquid	**BERINGED**	*adj* adorned with rings
BENZIDIN	*n* pl. **-S** a hydrocarbon	**BERK**	*n* pl. **-S** a foolish person
BENZIN	*n* pl. **-S** benzine	**BERLIN**	*n* pl. **-S** a type of carriage
BENZINE	*n* pl. **-S** a volatile liquid	**BERLINE**	*n* pl. **-S** a limousine
BENZOATE	*n* pl. **-S** a chemical salt	**BERM**	*v* **-ED, -ING, -S** to provide with a berm (a ledge)
BENZOIN	*n* pl. **-S** a gum resin **BENZOIC** *adj*	**BERME**	*n* pl. **-S** berm
BENZOL	*n* pl. **-S** a benzene	**BERMUDAS**	*n/pl* knee-length walking shorts
BENZOLE	*n* pl. **-S** benzol	**BERNICLE**	*n* pl. **-S** a wild goose
BENZOYL	*n* pl. **-S** a univalent chemical radical	**BEROBED**	*adj* wearing a robe
BENZYL	*n* pl. **-S** a univalent chemical radical **BENZYLIC** *adj*	**BEROUGED**	*adj* obviously or thickly rouged
		BERRETTA	*n* pl. **-S** biretta
BEPAINT	*v* **-ED, -ING, -S** to tinge	**BERRY**	*v* **-RIED, -RYING, -RIES** to produce berries (fleshy fruits)
BEPIMPLE	*v* **-PLED, -PLING, -PLES** to cover with pimples	**BERRYING**	*n* pl. **-S** the activity of gathering berries
BEQUEATH	*v* **-ED, -ING, -S** to grant by testament	**BERSEEM**	*n* pl. **-S** a clover
BEQUEST	*n* pl. **-S** a legacy	**BERSERK**	*n* pl. **-S** a fierce warrior
BERAKE	*v* **-RAKED, -RAKING, -RAKES** to rake all over	**BERTH**	*v* **-ED, -ING, -S** to provide with a mooring

BERTHA *n* pl. **-S** a wide collar

BERTHING *n* pl. **-S** the action of mooring a ship

BERYL *n* pl. **-S** a green mineral **BERYLINE** *adj*

BES *n* pl. **BESES** beth

BESCORCH *v* **-ED, -ING, -ES** to scorch

BESCOUR *v* **-ED, -ING, -S** to scour thoroughly

BESCREEN *v* **-ED, -ING, -S** to screen

BESEECH *v* **-SEECHED** or **-SOUGHT, -SEECHING, -SEECHES** to implore

BESEEM *v* **-ED, -ING, -S** to be suitable

BESET *v* **-SET, -SETTING, -SETS** to assail

BESETTER *n* pl. **-S** one that besets

BESHADOW *v* **-ED, -ING, -S** to cast a shadow on

BESHAME *v* **-SHAMED, -SHAMING, -SHAMES** to put to shame

BESHIVER *v* **-ED, -ING, -S** to break into small pieces

BESHOUT *v* **-ED, -ING, -S** to shout at

BESHREW *v* **-ED, -ING, -S** to curse

BESHROUD *v* **-ED, -ING, -S** to cover

BESIDE *prep* next to

BESIDES *adv* in addition

BESIEGE *v* **-SIEGED, -SIEGING, -SIEGES** to surround

BESIEGER *n* pl. **-S** one that besieges

BESLAVED *adj* filled with slaves

BESLIME *v* **-SLIMED, -SLIMING, -SLIMES** to cover with slime

BESMEAR *v* **-ED, -ING, -S** to smear over

BESMILE *v* **-SMILED, -SMILING, -SMILES** to smile on

BESMIRCH *v* **-ED, -ING, -ES** to dirty

BESMOKE *v* **-SMOKED, -SMOKING, -SMOKES** to soil with smoke

BESMOOTH *v* **-ED, -ING, -S** to smooth

BESMUDGE *v* **-SMUDGED, -SMUDGING, -SMUDGES** to smudge

BESMUT *v* **-SMUTTED, -SMUTTING, -SMUTS** to blacken with smut

BESNOW *v* **-ED, -ING, -S** to cover with snow

BESOM *n* pl. **-S** a broom

BESOOTHE *v* **-SOOTHED, -SOOTHING, -SOOTHES** to soothe

BESOT *v* **-SOTTED, -SOTTING, -SOTS** to stupefy

BESOUGHT a past tense of beseech

BESPEAK *v* **-SPOKE** or **-SPAKE, -SPOKEN, -SPEAKING, -SPEAKS** to claim in advance

BESPOUSE *v* **-SPOUSED, -SPOUSING, -SPOUSES** to marry

BESPREAD *v* **-SPREAD, -SPREADING, -SPREADS** to spread over

BESPRENT *adj* sprinkled over

BEST *v* **-ED, -ING, -S** to outdo

BESTEAD *v* **-ED, -ING, -S** to help

BESTIAL *adj* pertaining to beasts

BESTIARY *n* pl. **-ARIES** a collection of animal fables

BESTIE *n* pl. **-S** a person who someone likes very much

BESTIR *v* **-STIRRED, -STIRRING, -STIRS** to rouse

BESTOW *v* **-ED, -ING, -S** to present as a gift

BESTOWAL *n* pl. **-S** a gift

BESTOWER *n* pl. **-S** one that bestows

BESTREW *v* **-STREWED, -STREWN, -STREWING, -STREWS** to scatter

BESTRIDE *v* **-STRODE** or **-STRID, -STRIDDEN, -STRIDING, -STRIDES** to straddle

BESTROW *v* **-STROWED, -STROWN, -STROWING, -STROWS** to bestrew

BESTUD *v* **-STUDDED, -STUDDING, -STUDS** to dot

BESUITED *adj* wearing a suit

BESWARM *v* **-ED, -ING, -S** to swarm all over

BET *v* **BET** or **BETTED, BETTING, BETS** to wager

BETA *n* pl. **-S** a Greek letter

BETAINE *n* pl. **-S** an alkaloid

BETAKE *v* **-TOOK, -TAKEN, -TAKING, -TAKES** to cause to go

BETATRON *n* pl. **-S** an electron accelerator

BETATTER *v* **-ED, -ING, -S** to tatter

BETAXED *adj* burdened with taxes

BETEL *n* pl. **-S** a climbing plant

BETELNUT *n* pl. **-S** a seed chewed as a stimulant

BETH *n* pl. **-S** a Hebrew letter

BETHANK *v* **-ED, -ING, -S** to thank

BETHEL *n* pl. **-S** a holy place

BETHESDA *n* pl. **-S** a chapel

BETHINK	v **-THOUGHT, -THINKING, -THINKS** to consider
BETHORN	v **-ED, -ING, -S** to fill with thorns
BETHUMP	v **-ED, -ING, -S** to thump soundly
BETIDE	v **-TIDED, -TIDING, -TIDES** to befall
BETIME	adv betimes
BETIMES	adv soon
BETISE	n pl. **-S** stupidity
BETOKEN	v **-ED, -ING, -S** to indicate
BETON	n pl. **-S** a type of concrete
BETONY	n pl. **-NIES** a European herb
BETOOK	past tense of betake
BETRAY	v **-ED, -ING, -S** to aid an enemy of
BETRAYAL	n pl. **-S** the act of betraying
BETRAYER	n pl. **-S** one that betrays
BETROTH	v **-ED, -ING, -S** to engage to marry
BETTA	n pl. **-S** a freshwater fish
BETTED	a past tense of bet
BETTER	v **-ED, -ING, -S** to improve
BETTING	n pl. **-S** the act of gambling on the outcome of a race
BETTOR	n pl. **-S** one that bets
BETWEEN	prep in the space that separates
BETWIXT	prep between
BEUNCLED	adj having many uncles
BEVATRON	n pl. **-S** a proton accelerator
BEVEL	v **-ELED, -ELING, -ELS** or **-ELLED, -ELLING, -ELS** to cut at an angle
BEVELER	n pl. **-S** one that bevels
BEVELLER	n pl. **-S** beveler
BEVERAGE	n pl. **-S** a liquid for drinking
BEVIES	pl. of bevy
BEVOMIT	v **-ED, -ING, -S** to vomit all over
BEVOR	n pl. **-S** a piece of armor for the lower face
BEVVY	n pl. **BEVVIES** an alcoholic drink
BEVY	n pl. **BEVIES** a group
BEWAIL	v **-ED, -ING, -S** to lament
BEWAILER	n pl. **-S** one that bewails
BEWARE	v **-WARED, -WARING, -WARES** to be careful
BEWEARY	v **-WEARIED, -WEARYING, -WEARIES** to make weary
BEWEEP	v **-WEPT, -WEEPING, -WEEPS** to lament
BEWIG	v **-WIGGED, -WIGGING, -WIGS** to adorn with a wig
BEWILDER	v **-ED, -ING, -S** to confuse
BEWINGED	adj having wings
BEWITCH	v **-ED, -ING, -ES** to affect by witchcraft or magic
BEWORM	v **-ED, -ING, -S** to infest with worms
BEWORRY	v **-RIED, -RYING, -RIES** to worry
BEWRAP	v **-WRAPPED** or **-WRAPT, -WRAPPING, -WRAPS** to wrap completely
BEWRAY	v **-ED, -ING, -S** to divulge
BEWRAYER	n pl. **-S** one that bewrays
BEY	n pl. **BEYS** a Turkish ruler
BEYLIC	n pl. **-S** the domain of a bey
BEYLIK	n pl. **-S** beylic
BEYOND	n pl. **-S** something that lies farther ahead
BEZANT	n pl. **-S** a coin of ancient Rome
BEZAZZ	n pl. **-ES** pizazz
BEZEL	n pl. **-S** a slanted surface
BEZIL	n pl. **-S** bezel
BEZIQUE	n pl. **-S** a card game
BEZOAR	n pl. **-S** a gastric mass
BEZZANT	n pl. **-S** bezant
BHAJI	n pl. **-S** an Indian dish of fried vegetables
BHAKTA	n pl. **-S** one who practices bhakti
BHAKTI	n pl. **-S** a selfless devotion to a deity in Hinduism
BHANG	n pl. **-S** the hemp plant
BHANGRA	n pl. **-S** a form of popular Punjabi dance music
BHARAL	n pl. **-S** a goatlike Asian mammal
BHEESTIE	n pl. **-S** bheesty
BHEESTY	n pl. **-TIES** a water carrier
BHELPURI	n pl. **-S** a dish of rice, spices, and chutney
BHISTIE	n pl. **-S** bheesty
BHOOT	n pl. **-S** bhut
BHUT	n pl. **-S** a small whirlwind
BI	n pl. **-S** a bisexual
BIACETYL	n pl. **-S** a chemical flavor enhancer
BIALI	n pl. **-S** bialy
BIALY	n pl. **-ALYS** or **-ALIES** an onion roll
BIANNUAL	adj occurring twice a year

BIAS	v **-ASED, -ASING, -ASES** or **-ASSED, -ASSING, -ASSES** to prejudice **BIASEDLY** adv	**BICYCLER**	n pl. **-S** one that bicycles
		BICYCLIC	adj having two cycles
BIASNESS	n pl. **-ES** the state of being slanted	**BID**	v **BADE, BIDDEN, BIDDING, BIDS** to make a bid (an offer of a price)
BIATHLON	n pl. **-S** an athletic contest	**BIDARKA**	n pl. **-S** an Inuit canoe
BIAXAL	adj biaxial	**BIDARKEE**	n pl. **-S** bidarka
BIAXIAL	adj having two axes	**BIDDABLE**	adj obedient **BIDDABLY** adv
BIB	v **BIBBED, BIBBING, BIBS** to tipple	**BIDDEN**	past participle of bid
BIBASIC	adj dibasic	**BIDDER**	n pl. **-S** one that bids
BIBB	n pl. **-S** a mast support	**BIDDING**	n pl. **-S** a command
BIBBED	past tense of bib	**BIDDY**	n pl. **-DIES** a hen
BIBBER	n pl. **-S** a tippler	**BIDE**	v **BIDED** or **BODE, BIDING, BIDES** to wait
BIBBERY	n pl. **-BERIES** the act of tippling	**BIDENTAL**	adj having two teeth
BIBBING	n pl. **-S** the act of tippling	**BIDER**	n pl. **-S** one that bides
BIBCOCK	n pl. **-S** a type of faucet	**BIDET**	n pl. **-S** a low basin used for washing
BIBE	n pl. **-S** a creature whose crying is an omen of death	**BIDI**	n pl. **-S** a cigarette of India
BIBELOT	n pl. **-S** a trinket	**BIDING**	present participle of bide
BIBIMBAP	n pl. **-S** a dish of cooked rice and vegetables	**BIELD**	v **-ED, -ING, -S** to shelter
		BIENNALE	n pl. **-S** a biennial show
BIBLE	n pl. **-S** an authoritative publication **BIBLICAL** adj	**BIENNIAL**	n pl. **-S** an event that occurs every two years
BIBLESS	adj having no bib (a cloth covering)	**BIENNIUM**	n pl. **-NIUMS** or **-NIA** a period of two years
BIBLIKE	adj resembling a bib	**BIER**	n pl. **-S** a coffin stand
BIBLIST	n pl. **-S** one who takes the words of the Bible literally	**BIFACE**	n pl. **-S** a stone tool having a cutting edge
BIBULOUS	adj given to drinking	**BIFACIAL**	adj having two faces
BICARB	n pl. **-S** sodium bicarbonate	**BIFF**	v **-ED, -ING, -S** to hit
BICAUDAL	adj having two tails	**BIFFIN**	n pl. **-S** a cooking apple
BICE	n pl. **-S** a blue or green pigment	**BIFFY**	n pl. **-FIES** a toilet
BICEP	n pl. **-S** biceps	**BIFID**	adj divided into two parts **BIFIDLY** adv
BICEPS	n pl. **-ES** an arm muscle		
BICHROME	adj two-colored	**BIFIDITY**	n pl. **-TIES** the state of being bifid
BICKER	v **-ED, -ING, -S** to argue	**BIFILAR**	adj having two threads
BICKERER	n pl. **-S** one that bickers	**BIFLEX**	adj bent in two places
BICOLOR	n pl. **-S** something having two colors	**BIFOCAL**	n pl. **-S** a type of lens
		BIFOLD	n pl. **-S** a two-piece door
BICOLOUR	n pl. **-S** bicolor	**BIFORATE**	adj having two perforations
BICONVEX	adj convex on both sides	**BIFORKED**	adj divided into two branches
BICORN	n pl. **-S** bicorne	**BIFORM**	adj having two forms
BICORNE	n pl. **-S** a type of hat	**BIFORMED**	adj biform
BICRON	n pl. **-S** one billionth of a meter	**BIG**	adj **BIGGER, BIGGEST** of considerable size
BICUSPID	n pl. **-S** a tooth		
BICYCLE	v **-CLED, -CLING, -CLES** to ride a bicycle (a two-wheeled vehicle)	**BIG**	n pl. **-S** one of great importance
		BIGAMIES	pl. of bigamy

BIGAMIST	*n* pl. **-S** one who commits bigamy	**BIKE**	*v* **BIKED, BIKING, BIKES** to bicycle
BIGAMOUS	*adj* guilty of bigamy	**BIKER**	*n* pl. **-S** one that bikes
BIGAMY	*n* pl. **-MIES** the crime of being married to two people at once	**BIKEWAY**	*n* pl. **-WAYS** a route for bikes
BIGARADE	*n* pl. **-S** a citrus tree	**BIKIE**	*n* pl. **-S** biker
BIGAROON	*n* pl. **-S** a type of cherry	**BIKING**	present participle of bike
BIGEMINY	*n* pl. **-NIES** the state of having a double pulse	**BIKINI**	*n* pl. **-S** a type of two-piece bathing suit **BIKINIED** *adj*
BIGEYE	*n* pl. **-S** a marine fish	**BILABIAL**	*n* pl. **-S** a sound articulated with both lips
BIGFOOT	*n* pl. **-FOOTS** or **-FEET** an influential person	**BILANDER**	*n* pl. **-S** a small ship
BIGFOOT	*v* **-ED, -ING, -S** to apply one's influence as a bigfoot	**BILAYER**	*n* pl. **-S** a film with two molecular layers
BIGGER	comparative of big	**BILBERRY**	*n* pl. **-RIES** an edible berry
BIGGEST	superlative of big	**BILBO**	*n* pl. **-BOS** or **-BOES** a finely tempered sword
BIGGETY	*adj* biggity	**BILBOA**	*n* pl. **-S** bilbo
BIGGIE	*n* pl. **-S** one that is big	**BILBY**	*n* pl. **-BIES** a small nocturnal mammal
BIGGIES	pl. of biggy		
BIGGIN	*n* pl. **-S** a house	**BILE**	*n* pl. **-S** a fluid secreted by the liver
BIGGING	*n* pl. **-S** biggin	**BILEVEL**	*n* pl. **-S** a house having two levels
BIGGISH	*adj* somewhat big	**BILGE**	*v* **BILGED, BILGING, BILGES** to spring a leak
BIGGITY	*adj* conceited		
BIGGY	*n* pl. **-GIES** biggie	**BILGY**	*adj* **BILGIER, BILGIEST** smelling like seepage
BIGHEAD	*n* pl. **-S** a disease of animals	**BILIARY**	*adj* pertaining to bile
BIGHORN	*n* pl. **-S** a wild sheep	**BILINEAR**	*adj* pertaining to two lines
BIGHT	*v* **-ED, -ING, -S** to fasten with a loop of rope	**BILIOUS**	*adj* pertaining to bile
BIGLY	*adv* in a big manner	**BILK**	*v* **-ED, -ING, -S** to cheat
BIGMOUTH	*n* pl. **-S** a talkative person	**BILKER**	*n* pl. **-S** one that bilks
BIGNESS	*n* pl. **-ES** the state of being big	**BILL**	*v* **-ED, -ING, -S** to present a statement of costs to **BILLABLE** *adj*
BIGNONIA	*n* pl. **-S** a climbing plant		
BIGOS	*n* pl. **-ES** a Polish stew	**BILLBUG**	*n* pl. **-S** a weevil
BIGOT	*n* pl. **-S** a prejudiced person	**BILLER**	*n* pl. **-S** one that bills
BIGOTED	*adj* intolerant	**BILLET**	*v* **-ED, -ING, -S** to lodge soldiers
BIGOTRY	*n* pl. **-RIES** prejudice	**BILLETEE**	*n* pl. **-S** one that is billeted
BIGSTICK	*adj* threatening military force	**BILLETER**	*n* pl. **-S** one that billets
BIGTIME	*adj* pertaining to the highest level	**BILLFISH**	*n* pl. **-ES** a fish with long, slender jaws
BIGUINE	*n* pl. **-S** beguine		
BIGWIG	*n* pl. **-S** an important person	**BILLFOLD**	*n* pl. **-S** a wallet
BIHOURLY	*adj* occurring every two hours	**BILLHEAD**	*n* pl. **-S** a letterhead
BIJOU	*n* pl. **-JOUS** or **-JOUX** a jewel	**BILLHOOK**	*n* pl. **-S** a cutting tool
BIJUGATE	*adj* two-paired	**BILLIARD**	*n* pl. **-S** a carom shot in billiards (a table game)
BIJUGOUS	*adj* bijugate		
BIJURAL	*adj* pertaining to a single jurisdiction with two legal systems	**BILLIE**	*n* pl. **-S** a comrade
		BILLIES	pl. of billy

BILLING   *n* pl. **-S** the relative position in which a performer is listed

BILLION   *n* pl. **-S** a number

BILLON   *n* pl. **-S** an alloy of silver and copper

BILLOW   *v* **-ED, -ING, -S** to swell

BILLOWY   *adj* **-LOWIER, -LOWIEST** swelling; surging

BILLY   *n* pl. **-LIES** a short club

BILLYCAN   *n* pl. **-S** a pot for heating water

BILOBATE   *adj* having two lobes

BILOBED   *adj* bilobate

BILSTED   *n* pl. **-S** a hardwood tree

BILTONG   *n* pl. **-S** dried and cured meat

BIMA   *n* pl. **-S** bema

BIMAH   *n* pl. **-S** bema

BIMANOUS   *adj* two-handed

BIMANUAL   *adj* done with two hands

BIMBETTE   *n* pl. **-S** an attractive but empty-headed young woman

BIMBO   *n* pl. **-BOS** or **-BOES** a disreputable person

BIMENSAL   *adj* occurring every two months

BIMESTER   *n* pl. **-S** a two-month period

BIMETAL   *n* pl. **-S** something composed of two metals

BIMETHYL   *n* pl. **-S** ethane

BIMINI   *n* pl. **-S** a type of awning for a yacht

BIMODAL   *adj* having two statistical modes

BIMORPH   *n* pl. **-S** a device consisting of two crystals cemented together

BIN   *v* **BINNED, BINNING, BINS** to store in a large receptacle

BINAL   *adj* twofold

BINARISM   *n* pl. **-S** a mode of thought based on oppositions

BINARY   *n* pl. **-RIES** a combination of two things

BINATE   *adj* growing in pairs **BINATELY** *adv*

BINAURAL   *adj* hearing with both ears

BIND   *v* **BOUND, BINDING, BINDS** to tie or secure **BINDABLE** *adj*

BINDER   *n* pl. **-S** one that binds

BINDERY   *n* pl. **-ERIES** a place where books are bound

BINDI   *n* pl. **-S** a dot worn on the forehead by women in India

BINDING   *n* pl. **-S** the cover and fastenings of a book

BINDLE   *n* pl. **-S** a bundle

BINDWEED   *n* pl. **-S** a twining plant

BINE   *n* pl. **-S** a twining plant stem

BINER   *n* pl. **-S** a soldier armed with a carbine

BING   *interj* — used to indicate a sudden action

BINGE   *v* **BINGED, BINGEING** or **BINGING, BINGES** to indulge in something to excess

BINGEING   *n* pl. **-S** the act of indulging in something to excess

BINGER   *n* pl. **-S** one that binges

BINGING   *n* pl. **-S** bingeing

BINGO   *n* pl. **-GOS** or **-GOES** a game of chance

BINIT   *n* pl. **-S** a unit of computer information

BINMAN   *n* pl. **-MEN** a garbage collector

BINNACLE   *n* pl. **-S** a compass stand

BINNED   past tense of bin

BINNING   present participle of bin

BINOCLE   *n* pl. **-S** a binocular

BINOCS   *n/pl* binoculars

BINOMIAL   *n* pl. **-S** an algebraic expression

BINT   *n* pl. **-S** a woman

BIO   *n* pl. **BIOS** a biography

BIOASSAY   *v* **-ED, -ING, -S** to test a substance (as a drug) in order to determine its strength

BIOCHIP   *n* pl. **-S** a hypothetical computer component that uses proteins to store or process data

BIOCIDE   *n* pl. **-S** a substance destructive to living organisms **BIOCIDAL** *adj*

BIOCLEAN   *adj* free of harmful organisms

BIOCYCLE   *n* pl. **-S** a life-supporting region

BIOETHIC   *adj* pertaining to ethical questions arising from advances in biology

BIOFILM   *n* pl. **-S** a thin layer of microorganisms

BIOFUEL   *n* pl. **-S** fuel composed of biological raw materials

BIOG   *n* pl. **-S** a biography

BIOGAS   *n* pl. **-GASES** or **-GASSES** fuel gas produced by organic waste

BIOGEN   *n* pl. **-S** a hypothetical protein molecule

BIOGENIC   *adj* produced by living organisms

BIOGENY   *n* pl. **-NIES** the development of life from preexisting life

BIOHERM   *n* pl. **-S** a mass of marine fossils

BIOLOGIC   *n* pl. **-S** a drug obtained from an organic source

BIOLOGY   *n* pl. **-GIES** the science of life

BIOLYSIS   *n* pl. **-YSES** death **BIOLYTIC** *adj*

BIOMASS   *n* pl. **-ES** an amount of living matter

BIOME   *n* pl. **-S** an ecological community

BIOMETER   *n* pl. **-S** a device for measuring carbon dioxide given off by living matter

BIOMETRY   *n* pl. **-TRIES** the statistical study of biological data

BIOMORPH   *n* pl. **-S** an art form resembling a living organism in shape

BIONICS   *n/pl* a science joining biology and electronics **BIONIC** *adj*

BIONOMY   *n* pl. **-MIES** ecology **BIONOMIC** *adj*

BIONT   *n* pl. **-S** a living organism **BIONTIC** *adj*

BIOPIC   *n* pl. **-S** a biographical movie

BIOPLASM   *n* pl. **-S** living matter

BIOPSIC   *adj* pertaining to the examination of living tissue

BIOPSY   *v* **-SIED, -SYING, -SIES** to examine living tissue

BIOPTIC   *adj* biopsic

BIOSCOPE   *n* pl. **-S** an early movie projector

BIOSCOPY   *n* pl. **-PIES** a type of medical examination

BIOSOLID   *n* pl. **-S** solid organic matter obtained from treated sewage

BIOTA   *n* pl. **-S** flora and fauna

BIOTECH   *n* pl. **-S** applied biology

BIOTIC   *adj* pertaining to life

BIOTICAL   *adj* biotic

BIOTICS   *n/pl* a life science

BIOTIN   *n* pl. **-S** a B vitamin

BIOTITE   *n* pl. **-S** a form of mica **BIOTITIC** *adj*

BIOTOPE   *n* pl. **-S** a stable habitat

BIOTOXIN   *n* pl. **-S** poison made by a plant or animal

BIOTRON   *n* pl. **-S** a climate control chamber

BIOTYPE   *n* pl. **-S** a group of genetically similar organisms **BIOTYPIC** *adj*

BIOVULAR   *adj* derived from two ova

BIOWASTE   *n* pl. **-S** waste composed chiefly of organic matter

BIPACK   *n* pl. **-S** a pair of films

BIPAROUS   *adj* producing offspring in pairs

BIPARTED   *adj* having two parts

BIPARTY   *adj* of two parties

BIPED   *n* pl. **-S** a two-footed animal **BIPEDAL** *adj*

BIPHASIC   *adj* having two phases

BIPHENYL   *n* pl. **-S** a hydrocarbon

BIPLANE   *n* pl. **-S** a type of airplane

BIPOD   *n* pl. **-S** a two-legged support

BIPOLAR   *adj* having two poles

BIRACIAL   *adj* having members of two races

BIRADIAL   *adj* having dual symmetry

BIRAMOSE   *adj* biramous

BIRAMOUS   *adj* divided into two branches

BIRCH   *v* **-ED, -ING, -ES** to whip

BIRCHEN   *adj* made of birch wood

BIRD   *v* **-ED, -ING, -S** to hunt birds (winged, warm-blooded vertebrates)

BIRDBATH   *n* pl. **-S** a bath for birds

BIRDCAGE   *n* pl. **-S** a cage for birds

BIRDCALL   *n* pl. **-S** the call of a bird

BIRDDOG   *v* **-DOGGED, -DOGGING, -DOGS** to follow closely

BIRDER   *n* pl. **-S** a bird hunter

BIRDFARM   *n* pl. **-S** an aircraft carrier

BIRDFEED   *n* pl. **-S** birdseed

BIRDIE   *v* **BIRDIED, BIRDIEING, BIRDIES** to shoot in one stroke under par in golf

BIRDING   *n* pl. **-S** bird-watching

BIRDLIFE   *n* pl. **BIRDLIFE** avifauna

BIRDLIKE   *adj* resembling a bird

BIRDLIME   *v* **-LIMED, -LIMING, -LIMES** to trap small birds

BIRDMAN   *n* pl. **-MEN** one who keeps birds

BIRDSEED   *n* pl. **-S** a mixture of seeds used for feeding birds

BIRDSEYE   *n* pl. **-S** a flowering plant

BIRDSHOT   *n* pl. **-S** small shot for shooting birds

BIRDSONG   *n* pl. **-S** the song of a bird

BIREME   *n* pl. **-S** an ancient galley

BIRETTA	*n* pl. **-S** a cap worn by clergymen	**BISTOURY**	*n* pl. **-RIES** a surgical knife
BIRIANI	*n* pl. **-S** biryani	**BISTRE**	*n* pl. **-S** bister **BISTRED** *adj*
BIRK	*n* pl. **-S** a birch tree	**BISTRO**	*n* pl. **-TROS** a small tavern **BISTROIC** *adj*
BIRKIE	*n* pl. **-S** a lively person		
BIRL	*v* **-ED, -ING, -S** to rotate a floating log	**BIT**	*v* **BITTED, BITTING, BITS** to restrain
BIRLE	*v* **BIRLED, BIRLING, BIRLES** to carouse	**BITABLE**	*adj* capable of being bitten
		BITCH	*v* **-ED, -ING, -ES** to complain
BIRLER	*n* pl. **-S** one that birls	**BITCHEN**	*adj* excellent
BIRLING	*n* pl. **-S** a lumberjack's game	**BITCHERY**	*n* pl. **-ERIES** bitchy behavior
BIRR	*n* pl. **BIRROTCH** a monetary unit of Ethiopia	**BITCHY**	*adj* **BITCHIER, BITCHIEST** malicious **BITCHILY** *adv*
BIRR	*v* **-ED, -ING, -S** to make a whirring noise	**BITCOIN**	*n* pl. **-S** a digital currency
BIRRETTA	*n* pl. **-S** biretta	**BITE**	*v* **BIT, BITTEN, BITING, BITES** to seize with the teeth **BITEABLE** *adj*
BIRSE	*n* pl. **-S** a bristle	**BITER**	*n* pl. **-S** one that bites
BIRTH	*v* **-ED, -ING, -S** to originate	**BITEWING**	*n* pl. **-S** a dental X-ray film
BIRTHDAY	*n* pl. **-DAYS** an anniversary of a birth	**BITING**	present participle of bite
BIRTHING	*n* pl. **-S** the act of giving birth	**BITINGLY**	*adv* sarcastically
BIRYANI	*n* pl. **-S** an Indian dish of meat, fish, or vegetables and rice	**BITMAP**	*n* pl. **-S** an array of binary data
		BITRATE	*n* pl. **-S** the speed of data processing
BIS	*adv* twice		
BISCOTTO	*n* pl. **-COTTI** a crisp, anise-flavored cookie	**BITSTOCK**	*n* pl. **-S** a brace on a drill
		BITSY	*adj* **-SIER, -SIEST** tiny
BISCUIT	*n* pl. **-S** a small cake of shortened bread **BISCUITY** *adj*	**BITT**	*v* **-ED, -ING, -S** to secure a cable around a post
BISE	*n* pl. **-S** a cold wind	**BITTED**	past tense of bit
BISECT	*v* **-ED, -ING, -S** to cut into two parts	**BITTEN**	a past participle of bite
BISECTOR	*n* pl. **-S** something that bisects	**BITTER**	*adj* **-TERER, -TEREST** having a disagreeable taste **BITTERLY** *adv*
BISEXUAL	*n* pl. **-S** one who is attracted to both sexes	**BITTER**	*v* **-ED, -ING, -S** to make bitter
BISH	*n* pl. **-ES** a bishop	**BITTERN**	*n* pl. **-S** a wading bird
BISHOP	*v* **-ED, -ING, -S** to appoint as a bishop (the head of a diocese)	**BITTIER**	comparative of bitty
		BITTIEST	superlative of bitty
BISK	*n* pl. **-S** bisque	**BITTING**	*n* pl. **-S** an indentation in a key
BISMARCK	*n* pl. **-S** a type of pastry	**BITTOCK**	*n* pl. **-S** a small amount
BISMUTH	*n* pl. **-S** a metallic element	**BITTY**	*adj* **-TIER, -TIEST** tiny **BITTILY** *adv*
BISNAGA	*n* pl. **-S** a type of cactus		
BISON	*n* pl. **-S** an ox-like animal	**BITUMEN**	*n* pl. **-S** an asphalt
BISQUE	*n* pl. **-S** a thick soup	**BITURBO**	*n* pl. **-S** an engine with two turbos
BISTABLE	*n* pl. **-S** an electronic circuit that has two stable states	**BITWISE**	*adj* denoting an operator in a computer program that deals with bits
BISTATE	*adj* pertaining to two states	**BIUNIQUE**	*adj* being a type of correspondence between two sets
BISTER	*n* pl. **-S** a brown pigment **BISTERED** *adj*	**BIVALENT**	*n* pl. **-S** a pair of chromosomes
		BIVALVE	*n* pl. **-S** a bivalved mollusk
BISTORT	*n* pl. **-S** a perennial herb with roots used as astringents	**BIVALVED**	*adj* having a two-valved shell

BIVINYL _n_ pl. **-S** a flammable gas used in making synthetic rubber

BIVOUAC _v_ **-OUACKED, -OUACKING, -OUACKS** or **-OUACS** to make a camp

BIWEEKLY _n_ pl. **-LIES** a publication issued every two weeks

BIYEARLY _adj_ occurring every two years

BIZ _n_ pl. **BIZZES** business

BIZARRE _n_ pl. **-S** a strangely striped flower

BIZARRO _n_ pl. **-ROS** one that is strikingly unusual

BIZE _n_ pl. **-S** bise

BIZJET _n_ pl. **-S** a small airplane used for business

BIZNAGA _n_ pl. **-S** bisnaga

BIZONE _n_ pl. **-S** two combined zones **BIZONAL** _adj_

BLAB _v_ **BLABBED, BLABBING, BLABS** to talk idly

BLABBER _v_ **-ED, -ING, -S** to blab

BLABBY _adj_ **-BIER, -BIEST** talkative

BLACK _adj_ **BLACKER, BLACKEST** being of the darkest color

BLACK _v_ **-ED, -ING, -S** to make black

BLACKBOY _n_ pl. **-BOYS** an Australian plant

BLACKCAP _n_ pl. **-S** a small European bird

BLACKEN _v_ **-ED, -ING, -S** to make black

BLACKFIN _n_ pl. **-S** a food fish

BLACKFLY _n_ pl. **-FLIES** a biting fly

BLACKGUM _n_ pl. **-S** a tupelo

BLACKING _n_ pl. **-S** black shoe polish

BLACKISH _adj_ somewhat black

BLACKLEG _n_ pl. **-S** a cattle disease

BLACKLY _adv_ in a black manner

BLACKOUT _n_ pl. **-S** a power failure

BLACKTIP _n_ pl. **-S** a small shark

BLACKTOP _v_ **-TOPPED, -TOPPING, -TOPS** to pave with asphalt

BLADDER _n_ pl. **-S** a saclike receptacle **BLADDERY** _adj_

BLADE _v_ **BLADED, BLADING, BLADES** to skate on in-line skates

BLADER _n_ pl. **-S** one that blades

BLADING _n_ pl. **-S** the act of skating on in-line skates

BLAE _adj_ bluish-black

BLAFF _n_ pl. **-S** a West Indian stew

BLAG _v_ **BLAGGED, BLAGGING, BLAGS** to rob with violence

BLAGGER _n_ pl. **-S** one that blags

BLAGGING _n_ pl. **-S** informal talk in public

BLAGUE _n_ pl. **-S** pretentious nonsense

BLAH _n_ pl. **-S** nonsense

BLAH _adj_ **BLAHER, BLAHEST** dull, unexciting

BLAIN _n_ pl. **-S** a blister

BLAM _v_ **BLAMMED, BLAMMING, BLAMS** to make a loud sound like that of a gunshot

BLAMABLE _adj_ being at fault **BLAMABLY** _adv_

BLAME _v_ **BLAMED, BLAMING, BLAMES** to find fault with

BLAMEFUL _adj_ blamable

BLAMER _n_ pl. **-S** one that blames

BLAMING present participle of blame

BLANCH _v_ **-ED, -ING, -ES** to whiten

BLANCHER _n_ pl. **-S** a whitener

BLAND _adj_ **BLANDER, BLANDEST** soothing **BLANDLY** _adv_

BLANDISH _v_ **-ED, -ING, -ES** to coax by flattery

BLANK _adj_ **BLANKER, BLANKEST** empty

BLANK _v_ **-ED, -ING, -S** to delete

BLANKET _v_ **-ED, -ING, -S** to cover uniformly

BLANKETY _n_ pl. **-TIES** a euphemism for an unmentionable word

BLANKIE _n_ pl. **-S** a child's blanket (a piece of fabric used as a cover)

BLANKLY _adv_ in a blank manner

BLARE _v_ **BLARED, BLARING, BLARES** to sound loudly

BLARNEY _v_ **-NEYED, -NEYING, -NEYS** to beguile with flattery

BLASE _adj_ indifferent

BLAST _v_ **-ED, -ING, -S** to use an explosive

BLASTEMA _n_ pl. **-MAS** or **-MATA** a region of embryonic cells

BLASTER _n_ pl. **-S** one that blasts

BLASTIE _n_ pl. **-S** a dwarf

BLASTIER comparative of blasty

BLASTIEST superlative of blasty

BLASTING _n_ pl. **-S** the act of one that blasts

BLASTOFF _n_ pl. **-S** the launching of a rocket

BLASTOMA _n_ pl. **-MAS** or **-MATA** a type of tumor

BLASTULA   *n* pl. **-LAS** or **-LAE** an early embryo

BLASTY   *adj* **BLASTIER, BLASTIEST** gusty

BLAT   *v* **BLATTED, BLATTING, BLATS** to bleat

BLATANCY   *n* pl. **-CIES** something blatant

BLATANT   *adj* obvious

BLATE   *adj* timid

BLATHER   *v* **-ED, -ING, -S** to talk foolishly

BLATTED   past tense of blat

BLATTER   *v* **-ED, -ING, -S** to chatter

BLATTING   present participle of blat

BLAUBOK   *n* pl. **-S** an extinct antelope

BLAW   *v* **BLAWED, BLAWN, BLAWING, BLAWS** to blow

BLAZE   *v* **BLAZED, BLAZING, BLAZES** to burn brightly

BLAZER   *n* pl. **-S** a lightweight jacket **BLAZERED** *adj*

BLAZON   *v* **-ED, -ING, -S** to proclaim

BLAZONER   *n* pl. **-S** one that blazons

BLAZONRY   *n* pl. **-RIES** a great display

BLEACH   *v* **-ED, -ING, -ES** to whiten

BLEACHER   *n* pl. **-S** one that bleaches

BLEAK   *adj* **BLEAKER, BLEAKEST** dreary

BLEAK   *n* pl. **-S** a freshwater fish

BLEAKISH   *adj* somewhat bleak

BLEAKLY   *adv* in a bleak manner

BLEAR   *v* **-ED, -ING, -S** to dim

BLEAR   *adj* **BLEARER, BLEAREST** dim

BLEARY   *adj* **BLEARIER, BLEARIEST** dimmed **BLEARILY** *adv*

BLEAT   *v* **-ED, -ING, -S** to utter the cry of a sheep

BLEATER   *n* pl. **-S** one that bleats

BLEB   *n* pl. **-S** a blister **BLEBBY** *adj*

BLEBBING   *n* pl. **-S** the forming of a blister

BLECH   *interj* — used to express disgust

BLEED   *v* **BLED, BLEEDING, BLEEDS** to lose blood

BLEEDER   *n* pl. **-S** one that bleeds

BLEEDING   *n* pl. **-S** the act of losing blood

BLEEP   *v* **-ED, -ING, -S** to blip

BLEEPER   *n* pl. **-S** one that bleeps

BLELLUM   *n* pl. **-S** a babbler

BLEMISH   *v* **-ED, -ING, -ES** to mar

BLENCH   *v* **-ED, -ING, -ES** to flinch

BLENCHER   *n* pl. **-S** one that blenches

BLEND   *v* **BLENDED** or **BLENT, BLENDING, BLENDS** to mix smoothly and inseparably together

BLENDE   *n* pl. **-S** a shiny mineral

BLENDER   *n* pl. **-S** one that blends

BLENDING   *n* pl. **-S** the action of mixing together

BLENNY   *n* pl. **-NIES** a marine fish

BLENT   a past tense of blend

BLESBOK   *n* pl. **-S** a large antelope

BLESBUCK   *n* pl. **-S** blesbok

BLESS   *v* **BLESSED** or **BLEST, BLESSING, BLESSES** to sanctify

BLESSED   *adj* **-EDER, -EDEST** holy

BLESSER   *n* pl. **-S** one that blesses

BLESSING   *n* pl. **-S** a prayer

BLEST   a past tense of bless

BLET   *n* pl. **-S** a decay of fruit

BLETHER   *v* **-ED, -ING, -S** to blather

BLEW   past tense of blow

BLEWIT   *n* pl. **-S** blewits

BLEWITS   *n* pl. **-ES** a pale lilac mushroom

BLIGHT   *v* **-ED, -ING, -S** to cause decay

BLIGHTER   *n* pl. **-S** one that blights

BLIGHTY   *n* pl. **BLIGHTIES** a wound causing one to be sent home to England

BLIMEY   *interj* — used as an expression of surprise

BLIMP   *n* pl. **-S** a nonrigid aircraft **BLIMPISH** *adj*

BLIMPERY   *n* pl. **-ERIES** pompous behavior

BLIMY   *interj* blimey

BLIN   *n* pl. **BLINI** or **BLINIS** or **BLINY** a blintze

BLIND   *adj* **BLINDER, BLINDEST** sightless

BLIND   *v* **-ED, -ING, -S** to make sightless

BLINDAGE   *n* pl. **-S** a protective screen

BLINDER   *n* pl. **-S** an obstruction to sight

BLINDGUT   *n* pl. **-S** a cecum

BLINDING   *n* pl. **-S** the act of causing blindness

BLINDLY   *adv* in a blind manner

BLING   *v* **-ED, -ING, -S** to adopt a flamboyant appearance

BLINI   a pl. of blin

BLINIS   a pl. of blin

BLINK   *v* **-ED, -ING, -S** to open and shut the eyes

BLINKARD   *n* pl. **-S** one who habitually blinks

BLINKER   *v* **-ED, -ING, -S** to put blinders on

BLINTZ   *n* pl. **-ES** blintze

BLINTZE   *n* pl. **-S** a thin pancake

BLINY   a pl. of blin

BLIP   *v* **BLIPPED, BLIPPING, BLIPS** to remove sound from a recording

BLISS   *v* **-ED, -ING, -ES** to experience or produce ecstasy

BLISSFUL   *adj* very happy

BLISTER   *v* **-ED, -ING, -S** to cause blisters (skin swellings)

BLISTERY   *adj* having blisters

BLITE   *n* pl. **-S** an annual herb

BLITHE   *adj* **BLITHER, BLITHEST** merry **BLITHELY** *adv*

BLITHER   *v* **-ED, -ING, -S** to blather

BLITZ   *v* **-ED, -ING, -ES** to subject to a sudden attack

BLITZER   *n* pl. **-S** one that blitzes

BLIZZARD   *n* pl. **-S** a heavy snowstorm

BLOAT   *v* **-ED, -ING, -S** to swell

BLOATER   *n* pl. **-S** a smoked herring

BLOATING   *n* pl. **-S** the state of being swollen

BLOB   *v* **BLOBBED, BLOBBING, BLOBS** to splotch

BLOBBY   *adj* **-BIER, -BIEST** splotchy

BLOC   *n* pl. **-S** a coalition

BLOCK   *v* **-ED, -ING, -S** to obstruct

BLOCKADE   *v* **-ADED, -ADING, -ADES** to block

BLOCKAGE   *n* pl. **-S** the act of blocking

BLOCKER   *n* pl. **-S** one that blocks

BLOCKING   *n* pl. **-S** the act of obstructing

BLOCKISH   *adj* blocky

BLOCKY   *adj* **BLOCKIER, BLOCKIEST** short and stout

BLOG   *v* **BLOGGED, BLOGGING, BLOGS** to record personal comments on a website

BLOGGER   *n* pl. **-S** one who blogs

BLOGGING   *n* pl. **-S** the act or practice of recording personal comments on a website

BLOGGY   *adj* **-GIER, -GIEST** characteristic of blogging

BLOKE   *n* pl. **-S** a fellow

BLOKEISH   *adj* resembling the typical behavior of a bloke

BLOKEY   *adj* **BLOKIER, BLOKIEST** blokeish

BLOND   *adj* **BLONDER, BLONDEST** light-colored

BLOND   *n* pl. **-S** a person with blond hair

BLONDE   *n* pl. **-S** blond

BLONDINE   *v* **-INED, -INING, -INES** to bleach hair blond

BLONDISH   *adj* somewhat blond

BLOOD   *v* **-ED, -ING, -S** to stain with blood (the fluid circulated by the heart)

BLOODFIN   *n* pl. **-S** a freshwater fish

BLOODIED   past tense of bloody

BLOODIER   comparative of bloody

BLOODIES   present 3d person sing. of bloody

BLOODIEST   superlative of bloody

BLOODILY   *adv* in a bloody manner

BLOODING   *n* pl. **-S** a fox hunting ceremony

BLOODRED   *adj* of the color of blood

BLOODY   *adj* **BLOODIER, BLOODIEST** stained with blood

BLOODY   *v* **BLOODIED, BLOODYING, BLOODIES** to make bloody

BLOOEY   *adj* being out of order

BLOOIE   *adj* blooey

BLOOM   *v* **-ED, -ING, -S** to bear flowers

BLOOMER   *n* pl. **-S** a blooming plant

BLOOMERY   *n* pl. **-ERIES** a furnace for smelting iron

BLOOMING   *n* pl. **-S** a process for smelting iron

BLOOMY   *adj* **BLOOMIER, BLOOMIEST** covered with flowers

BLOOP   *v* **-ED, -ING, -S** to hit a short fly ball

BLOOPER   *n* pl. **-S** a public blunder

BLOOPY   *adj* **BLOOPIER, BLOOPIEST** being a hit that is a short fly ball

BLOSSOM   *v* **-ED, -ING, -S** to bloom

BLOSSOMY   *adj* having blossoms

BLOT   *v* **BLOTTED, BLOTTING, BLOTS** to spot or stain

BLOTCH   *v* **-ED, -ING, -ES** to mark with large spots

BLOTCHY   *adj* **BLOTCHIER, BLOTCHIEST** blotched

BLOTLESS   *adj* spotless

BLOTTED   past tense of blot

BLOTTER *n* pl. **-S** a piece of ink-absorbing paper

BLOTTIER comparative of blotty

BLOTTIEST superlative of blotty

BLOTTING present participle of blot

BLOTTO *adj* drunk

BLOTTY *adj* **-TIER, -TIEST** spotty

BLOUSE *v* **BLOUSED, BLOUSING, BLOUSES** to hang loosely

BLOUSON *n* pl. **-S** a woman's garment

BLOUSY *adj* **BLOUSIER, BLOUSIEST** blowsy **BLOUSILY** *adv*

BLOVIATE *v* **-ATED, -ATING, -ATES** to speak pompously

BLOW *v* **BLEW, BLOWED, BLOWING, BLOWS** to damn

BLOW *v* **BLEW, BLOWN, BLOWING, BLOWS** to drive or impel by a current of air

BLOWBACK *n* pl. **-S** an escape of gases

BLOWBALL *n* pl. **-S** a fluffy seed ball

BLOWBY *n* pl. **-BYS** leakage of exhaust fumes

BLOWDART *n* pl. **-S** a dart shot from a blowpipe

BLOWDOWN *n* pl. **-S** a tree blown down by the wind

BLOWER *n* pl. **-S** one that blows

BLOWFISH *n* pl. **-ES** a marine fish

BLOWFLY *n* pl. **-FLIES** a type of fly

BLOWGUN *n* pl. **-S** a tube through which darts may be blown

BLOWHARD *n* pl. **-S** a braggart

BLOWHOLE *n* pl. **-S** an air or gas vent

BLOWIER comparative of blowy

BLOWIEST superlative of blowy

BLOWLAMP *n* pl. **-S** a blowtorch

BLOWN past participle of blow

BLOWOFF *n* pl. **-S** the expelling of gas

BLOWOUT *n* pl. **-S** a sudden rupture

BLOWPIPE *n* pl. **-S** a blowgun

BLOWSED *adj* blowsy

BLOWSY *adj* **-SIER, -SIEST** slovenly **BLOWSILY** *adv*

BLOWTUBE *n* pl. **-S** a blowgun

BLOWUP *n* pl. **-S** an explosion

BLOWY *adj* **BLOWIER, BLOWIEST** windy

BLOWZED *adj* blowzy

BLOWZY *adj* **-ZIER, -ZIEST** blowsy **BLOWZILY** *adv*

BLUB *v* **BLUBBED, BLUBBING, BLUBS** to blubber

BLUBBER *v* **-ED, -ING, -S** to weep noisily

BLUBBERY *adj* fat; swollen

BLUCHER *n* pl. **-S** a half boot

BLUDGE *v* **BLUDGED, BLUDGING, BLUDGES** to avoid work

BLUDGEON *v* **-ED, -ING, -S** to hit with a club

BLUDGER *n* pl. **-S** a loafer or shirker

BLUE *adj* **BLUER, BLUEST** having the color of the clear sky

BLUE *v* **BLUED, BLUEING** or **BLUING, BLUES** to make blue

BLUEBACK *n* pl. **-S** a bird or fish having a bluish back

BLUEBALL *n* pl. **-S** a medicinal herb

BLUEBEAT *n* pl. **-S** ska

BLUEBELL *n* pl. **-S** a flowering plant

BLUEBILL *n* pl. **-S** the scaup duck

BLUEBIRD *n* pl. **-S** a songbird

BLUEBOOK *n* pl. **-S** an examination booklet

BLUECAP *n* pl. **-S** a flowering plant

BLUECOAT *n* pl. **-S** a police officer

BLUED past tense of blue

BLUEFIN *n* pl. **-S** a large tuna

BLUEFISH *n* pl. **-ES** a marine fish

BLUEGILL *n* pl. **-S** an edible sunfish

BLUEGUM *n* pl. **-S** a timber tree

BLUEHEAD *n* pl. **-S** a marine fish

BLUEING *n* pl. **-S** bluing

BLUEISH *adj* bluish

BLUEJACK *n* pl. **-S** an oak tree

BLUEJAY *n* pl. **-JAYS** a corvine bird

BLUELINE *n* pl. **-S** a line that divides a hockey rink

BLUELY *adv* in a blue manner

BLUENESS *n* pl. **-ES** the state of being blue

BLUENOSE *n* pl. **-S** a puritanical person

BLUER comparative of blue

BLUESIER comparative of bluesy

BLUESIEST superlative of bluesy

BLUESMAN *n* pl. **-MEN** one who plays the blues

BLUEST superlative of blue

BLUESTEM *n* pl. **-S** a prairie grass

BLUESY	*adj* **BLUESIER, BLUESIEST** resembling the blues (a musical form)
BLUET	*n* pl. **-S** a meadow flower
BLUETICK	*n* pl. **-S** a hunting dog
BLUEWEED	*n* pl. **-S** a bristly weed
BLUEWOOD	*n* pl. **-S** a shrub
BLUEY	*n* pl. **BLUEYS** a bag of clothing carried in travel
BLUFF	*adj* **BLUFFER, BLUFFEST** having a broad front **BLUFFLY** *adv*
BLUFF	*v* **-ED, -ING, -S** to mislead
BLUFFER	*n* pl. **-S** one that bluffs
BLUING	*n* pl. **-S** a fabric coloring
BLUISH	*adj* somewhat blue
BLUME	*v* **BLUMED, BLUMING, BLUMES** to blossom
BLUNDER	*v* **-ED, -ING, -S** to make a mistake
BLUNGE	*v* **BLUNGED, BLUNGING, BLUNGES** to mix clay with water
BLUNGER	*n* pl. **-S** one that blunges
BLUNT	*adj* **BLUNTER, BLUNTEST** not sharp or pointed **BLUNTLY** *adv*
BLUNT	*v* **-ED, -ING, -S** to make blunt
BLUR	*v* **BLURRED, BLURRING, BLURS** to make unclear
BLURB	*v* **-ED, -ING, -S** to praise in a publicity notice
BLURBIST	*n* pl. **-S** one that blurbs
BLURRY	*adj* **-RIER, -RIEST** unclear **BLURRILY** *adv*
BLURT	*v* **-ED, -ING, -S** to speak abruptly
BLURTER	*n* pl. **-S** one that blurts
BLUSH	*v* **-ED, -ING, -ES** to become red
BLUSHER	*n* pl. **-S** one that blushes
BLUSHFUL	*adj* of a red color
BLUSTER	*v* **-ED, -ING, -S** to blow violently
BLUSTERY	*adj* windy
BLYPE	*n* pl. **-S** a shred
BO	*n* pl. **BOS** a pal
BOA	*n* pl. **-S** a large snake
BOAR	*n* pl. **-S** a male pig
BOARD	*v* **-ED, -ING, -S** to take meals for a fixed price
BOARDER	*n* pl. **-S** one that boards
BOARDING	*n* pl. **-S** a surface of wooden boards
BOARDMAN	*n* pl. **-MEN** a board member
BOARFISH	*n* pl. **-ES** a marine fish
BOARISH	*adj* swinish; coarse
BOART	*n* pl. **-S** bort
BOAST	*v* **-ED, -ING, -S** to brag
BOASTER	*n* pl. **-S** one that boasts
BOASTFUL	*adj* given to boasting
BOAT	*v* **-ED, -ING, -S** to travel by boat (watercraft) **BOATABLE** *adj*
BOATBILL	*n* pl. **-S** a wading bird
BOATEL	*n* pl. **-S** a waterside hotel
BOATER	*n* pl. **-S** one that boats
BOATFUL	*n* pl. **-S** as much as a boat can hold
BOATHOOK	*n* pl. **-S** a pole with a metal hook for use aboard a boat
BOATING	*n* pl. **-S** the sport of traveling by boat
BOATLIFT	*v* **-ED, -ING, -S** to transport by boats
BOATLIKE	*adj* resembling a boat
BOATLOAD	*n* pl. **-S** the amount that a boat holds
BOATMAN	*n* pl. **-MEN** one who works on boats
BOATNECK	*n* pl. **-S** a wide neckline
BOATPORT	*n* pl. **-S** an enclosure for boats
BOATSMAN	*n* pl. **-MEN** boatman
BOATYARD	*n* pl. **-S** a marina
BOB	*v* **BOBBED, BOBBING, BOBS** to move up and down
BOBBER	*n* pl. **-S** one that bobs
BOBBERY	*n* pl. **-BERIES** a disturbance
BOBBIES	pl. of bobby
BOBBIN	*n* pl. **-S** a thread holder
BOBBINET	*n* pl. **-S** a machine-made net
BOBBING	present participle of bob
BOBBLE	*v* **-BLED, -BLING, -BLES** to fumble
BOBBLY	*adj* **-BLIER, -BLIEST** resembling a small ball of wool
BOBBY	*n* pl. **-BIES** a police officer
BOBBYSOX	*n/pl* girls' socks that reach above the ankle
BOBCAT	*n* pl. **-S** a lynx
BOBECHE	*n* pl. **-S** a glass collar on a candle holder
BOBO	*n* pl. **-BOS** a well-to-do person who holds bohemian values and leads a bourgeois life

BOBOLINK *n* pl. **-S** a songbird

BOBSKATE *n* pl. **-S** a child's skate having two parallel blades

BOBSLED *v* **-SLEDDED, -SLEDDING, -SLEDS** to ride on a bobsled (a racing sled)

BOBSTAY *n* pl. **-STAYS** a steadying rope

BOBTAIL *v* **-ED, -ING, -S** to cut short

BOBWHITE *n* pl. **-S** a game bird

BOCACCIO *n* pl. **-CIOS** a rockfish

BOCCE *n* pl. **-S** boccie

BOCCI *n* pl. **-S** boccie

BOCCIA *n* pl. **-S** boccie

BOCCIE *n* pl. **-S** an Italian bowling game

BOCK *n* pl. **-S** a dark beer

BOD *n* pl. **-S** a body

BODE *v* **BODED, BODING, BODES** to be an omen of

BODEGA *n* pl. **-S** a grocery store

BODEMENT *n* pl. **-S** an omen

BODHRAN *n* pl. **-S** an Irish drum

BODICE *n* pl. **-S** a corset

BODIED past tense of body

BODIES present 3d person sing. of body

BODILESS *adj* lacking material form

BODILY *adj* of the body

BODING *n* pl. **-S** an omen

BODINGLY *adv* ominously

BODKIN *n* pl. **-S** a sharp instrument

BODY *v* **BODIED, BODYING, BODIES** to give form to

BODYMAN *n* pl. **-MEN** one who repairs auto bodies

BODYSIDE *n* pl. **-S** the side of the body of a vehicle

BODYSUIT *n* pl. **-S** a one-piece garment for the torso

BODYSURF *v* **-ED, -ING, -S** to ride a wave without a surfboard

BODYWASH *n* pl. **-ES** a liquid product for cleansing the body

BODYWORK *n* pl. **-S** a vehicle body

BOEHMITE *n* pl. **-S** a mineral

BOEUF *n* pl. **-S** beef

BOFF *n* pl. **-S** a hearty laugh

BOFFIN *n* pl. **-S** a scientific expert **BOFFINY** *adj*

BOFFO *n* pl. **-FOS** a boff

BOFFOLA *n* pl. **-S** a boff

BOG *v* **BOGGED, BOGGING, BOGS** to impede

BOGAN *n* pl. **-S** a backwater or tributary

BOGART *v* **-ED, -ING, -S** to use without sharing

BOGBEAN *n* pl. **-S** a marsh plant

BOGEY *v* **-GEYED, -GEYING, -GEYS** to shoot in one stroke over par in golf

BOGEYMAN *n* pl. **-MEN** a terrifying creature

BOGGED past tense of bog

BOGGIER comparative of boggy

BOGGIEST superlative of boggy

BOGGING present participle of bog

BOGGISH *adj* boggy

BOGGLE *v* **-GLED, -GLING, -GLES** to hesitate

BOGGLER *n* pl. **-S** one that causes another to boggle

BOGGY *adj* **-GIER, -GIEST** marshy

BOGHOLE *n* pl. **-S** a natural hole in the ground with a swampy bottom

BOGIE *n* pl. **-S** bogy

BOGIES pl. of bogy

BOGLAND *n* pl. **-S** an area of boggy land

BOGLE *n* pl. **-S** a bogy

BOGUS *adj* not genuine; fake **BOGUSLY** *adv*

BOGWOOD *n* pl. **-S** preserved tree wood

BOGY *n* pl. **-GIES** a goblin

BOGYISM *n* pl. **-S** behavior characteristic of a bogy

BOGYMAN *n* pl. **-MEN** bogeyman

BOHEA *n* pl. **-S** a black tea

BOHEMIA *n* pl. **-S** a community of bohemians

BOHEMIAN *n* pl. **-S** an unconventional person

BOHO *n* pl. **-HOS** a bohemian

BOHRIUM *n* pl. **-S** a radioactive element

BOIL *v* **-ED, -ING, -S** to vaporize liquid **BOILABLE** *adj*

BOILER *n* pl. **-S** a vessel for boiling

BOILOFF *n* pl. **-S** the vaporization of liquid

BOILOVER *n* pl. **-S** an overflowing while boiling

BOING *v* **-ED, -ING, -S** to make the sound of reverberation or vibration

BOISERIE *n* pl. **-S** wood paneling on a wall

BOITE *n* pl. **-S** a nightclub

BOKEH   *n* pl. **-S** the blurred quality of a photograph

BOKKEN   *n* pl. **-S** a wooden sword used for training

BOLA   *n* pl. **-S** a throwing weapon

BOLAR   *adj* pertaining to bole

BOLAS   *n* pl. **-ES** bola

BOLD   *adj* **BOLDER, BOLDEST** daring **BOLDLY** *adv*

BOLD   *v* **-ED, -ING, -S** to boldface

BOLDFACE   *v* **-FACED, -FACING, -FACES** to print in thick type

BOLDNESS   *n* pl. **-ES** the quality of being bold

BOLE   *n* pl. **-S** a fine clay

BOLERO   *n* pl. **-ROS** a Spanish dance

BOLETE   *n* pl. **-S** boletus

BOLETUS   *n* pl. **-TUSES** or **-TI** a fungus

BOLIDE   *n* pl. **-S** an exploding meteor

BOLIVAR   *n* pl. **-S** or **-ES** a monetary unit of Venezuela

BOLIVIA   *n* pl. **-S** a soft fabric

BOLL   *v* **-ED, -ING, -S** to form pods

BOLLARD   *n* pl. **-S** a thick post on a ship or wharf

BOLLIX   *v* **-ED, -ING, -ES** to bungle

BOLLOX   *v* **-ED, -ING, -ES** to bollix

BOLLWORM   *n* pl. **-S** the larva of a certain moth

BOLO   *n* pl. **-LOS** a machete

BOLOGNA   *n* pl. **-S** a seasoned sausage

BOLONEY   *n* pl. **-NEYS** bologna

BOLSHIE   *n* pl. **-S** a Bolshevik

BOLSHY   *n* pl. **-SHIES** bolshie

BOLSON   *n* pl. **-S** a flat arid valley

BOLSTER   *v* **-ED, -ING, -S** to support

BOLT   *v* **-ED, -ING, -S** to sift

BOLTER   *n* pl. **-S** a sifting machine

BOLTHEAD   *n* pl. **-S** a matrass

BOLTHOLE   *n* pl. **-S** a place or way of escape

BOLTLESS   *adj* having no bolt (a type of metal fastener)

BOLTLIKE   *adj* resembling a bolt

BOLTONIA   *n* pl. **-S** a perennial herb

BOLTROPE   *n* pl. **-S** a rope sewn to a sail

BOLUS   *n* pl. **-ES** a large pill

BOMB   *v* **-ED, -ING, -S** to attack with bombs (explosive projectiles) **BOMBABLE** *adj*

BOMBARD   *v* **-ED, -ING, -S** to bomb

BOMBARDE   *n* pl. **-S** a medieval shawm

BOMBAST   *n* pl. **-S** pompous language

BOMBAX   *adj* pertaining to a family of tropical trees

BOMBE   *n* pl. **-S** a frozen dessert

BOMBER   *n* pl. **-S** one that bombs

BOMBESIN   *n* pl. **-S** a combination of amino acids

BOMBING   *n* pl. **-S** an attack with bombs

BOMBLET   *n* pl. **-S** a small bomb

BOMBLOAD   *n* pl. **-S** the quantity of bombs being carried

BOMBORA   *n* pl. **-S** a sea area over a ridge of rock

BOMBYCID   *n* pl. **-S** a moth

BOMBYX   *n* pl. **-ES** a silkworm

BONACI   *n* pl. **-S** an edible fish

BONANZA   *n* pl. **-S** a rich mine

BONBON   *n* pl. **-S** a sugared candy

BONCE   *n* pl. **-S** a person's head

BOND   *v* **-ED, -ING, -S** to join together **BONDABLE** *adj*

BONDAGE   *n* pl. **-S** slavery

BONDER   *n* pl. **-S** one that bonds

BONDING   *n* pl. **-S** the formation of a close personal relationship

BONDLESS   *adj* having no bond

BONDMAID   *n* pl. **-S** a female slave

BONDMAN   *n* pl. **-MEN** a male slave

BONDSMAN   *n* pl. **-MEN** bondman

BONDUC   *n* pl. **-S** a prickly seed

BONE   *v* **BONED, BONING, BONES** to debone

BONEBED   *n* pl. **-S** an area containing dinosaur fossils

BONEFISH   *n* pl. **-ES** a slender marine fish

BONEHEAD   *n* pl. **-S** a stupid person

BONELESS   *adj* having no bones (hard connective tissue)

BONEMEAL   *n* pl. **-S** fertilizer or feed made from crushed bone

BONER   *n* pl. **-S** a blunder

BONESET   *n* pl. **-S** a perennial herb

BONEY   *adj* **BONEYER, BONEYEST** bony

BONEYARD   *n* pl. **-S** a junkyard

BONFIRE   *n* pl. **-S** an open fire

BONG   *v* **-ED, -ING, -S** to make a deep, ringing sound

BONGO   *n* pl. **-GOS** or **-GOES** a small drum

BONGOIST   *n* pl. **-S** a bongo player

BONHOMIE   *n* pl. **-S** friendliness

BONIATO   *n* pl. **-TOS** a sweet potato

BONIER   comparative of bony

BONIEST   superlative of bony

BONIFACE   *n* pl. **-S** an innkeeper

BONINESS   *n* pl. **-ES** the state of being bony

BONING   present participle of bone

BONITA   *n* pl. **-S** bonito

BONITO   *n* pl. **-TOS** or **-TOES** a marine food fish

BONK   *v* **-ED, -ING, -S** to hit on the head with a hollow blow

BONKERS   *adj* crazy

BONNE   *n* pl. **-S** a housemaid

BONNET   *v* **-ED, -ING, -S** to provide with a bonnet (a type of hat)

BONNIE   *adj* bonny

BONNOCK   *n* pl. **-S** bannock

BONNY   *adj* **-NIER, -NIEST** pretty
BONNILY *adv*

BONNY   *n* pl. **-NIES** a person that one loves

BONOBO   *n* pl. **-BOS** an anthropoid ape

BONSAI   *n* pl. **BONSAI** a potted shrub that has been dwarfed

BONSPELL   *n* pl. **-S** bonspiel

BONSPIEL   *n* pl. **-S** a curling match or tournament

BONTBOK   *n* pl. **-S** bontebok

BONTEBOK   *n* pl. **-S** an antelope

BONUS   *n* pl. **-ES** an additional payment

BONUSING   *n* pl. **-S** the act of subsidizing something

BONY   *adj* **BONIER, BONIEST** full of bones

BONZE   *n* pl. **-S** a Buddhist monk

BONZER   *adj* very good

BOO   *v* **-ED, -ING, -S** to cry "boo" to express disapproval or to startle

BOOB   *v* **-ED, -ING, -S** to make a foolish mistake

BOOBIRD   *n* pl. **-S** a fan who boos players of the home team

BOOBISH   *adj* doltish

BOOBOO   *n* pl. **-BOOS** a mistake

BOOBY   *n* pl. **-BIES** a dolt

BOOCOO   *n* pl. **-COOS** beaucoup

BOODLE   *v* **-DLED, -DLING, -DLES** to take bribes

BOODLER   *n* pl. **-S** one that boodles

BOOGALOO   *v* **-ED, -ING, -S** to dance to rock music

BOOGER   *n* pl. **-S** a bogeyman

BOOGEY   *v* **-GEYED, -GEYING, -GEYS** to boogie

BOOGIE   *v* **-GIED, -GIEING, -GIES** to dance to rock music

BOOGY   *v* **-GIED, -GYING, -GIES** to boogie

BOOGYMAN   *n* pl. **-MEN** bogeyman

BOOHOO   *v* **-ED, -ING, -S** to weep noisily

BOOJUM   *n* pl. **-S** a spiny desert tree

BOOK   *v* **-ED, -ING, -S** to engage services
BOOKABLE *adj*

BOOKBAG   *n* pl. **-S** a bag for carrying books

BOOKCASE   *n* pl. **-S** a case which holds books (literary volumes)

BOOKEND   *v* **-ED, -ING, -S** to place something at either end of

BOOKER   *n* pl. **-S** one that books

BOOKFUL   *n* pl. **-S** as much as a book can hold

BOOKIE   *n* pl. **-S** a bet taker

BOOKING   *n* pl. **-S** an engagement

BOOKISH   *adj* pertaining to books

BOOKLET   *n* pl. **-S** a small book

BOOKLICE   *n/pl* wingless insects that damage books

BOOKLORE   *n* pl. **-S** book learning

BOOKMAN   *n* pl. **-MEN** a scholar

BOOKMARK   *v* **-ED, -ING, -S** to create a shortcut to a previously viewed website

BOOKOO   *n* pl. **-KOOS** beaucoup

BOOKRACK   *n* pl. **-S** a support for an open book

BOOKREST   *n* pl. **-S** a bookrack

BOOKSHOP   *n* pl. **-S** a store where books are sold

BOOKWORK   *n* pl. **-S** the keeping of records of accounts

BOOKWORM   *n* pl. **-S** an avid book reader

BOOM   *v* **-ED, -ING, -S** to make a deep, resonant sound

BOOMBOX   *n* pl. **-ES** a portable radio and tape or compact disc player

BOOMER   *n* pl. **-S** one that booms

BOOMIER	comparative of boomy
BOOMIEST	superlative of boomy
BOOMKIN	*n* pl. **-S** a bumkin
BOOMLET	*n* pl. **-S** a small increase in prosperity
BOOMTOWN	*n* pl. **-S** a prospering town
BOOMY	*adj* **BOOMIER, BOOMIEST** prospering
BOON	*n* pl. **-S** a timely benefit
BOONDOCK	*adj* pertaining to a backwoods area
BOONIES	*n/pl* a backwoods area
BOONLESS	*adj* having no boon
BOOR	*n* pl. **-S** a rude person
BOORISH	*adj* rude
BOOST	*v* **-ED, -ING, -S** to support
BOOSTER	*n* pl. **-S** one that boosts
BOOT	*v* **-ED, -ING, -S** to load a program into a computer **BOOTABLE** *adj*
BOOTEE	*n* pl. **-S** a baby's sock
BOOTERY	*n* pl. **-ERIES** a shoe store
BOOTH	*n* pl. **-S** a small enclosure
BOOTIE	*n* pl. **-S** bootee
BOOTIES	pl. of booty
BOOTJACK	*n* pl. **-S** a device for pulling off boots
BOOTLACE	*n* pl. **-S** a shoelace
BOOTLEG	*v* **-LEGGED, -LEGGING, -LEGS** to smuggle
BOOTLESS	*adj* useless
BOOTLICK	*v* **-ED, -ING, -S** to flatter servilely
BOOTY	*n* pl. **-TIES** a rich gain or prize
BOOZE	*v* **BOOZED, BOOZING, BOOZES** to drink liquor excessively
BOOZER	*n* pl. **-S** one that boozes
BOOZING	*n* pl. **-S** the act of drinking liquor excessively
BOOZY	*adj* **BOOZIER, BOOZIEST** drunken **BOOZILY** *adv*
BOP	*v* **BOPPED, BOPPING, BOPS** to hit or strike
BOPEEP	*n* pl. **-S** a game of peekaboo
BOPPER	*n* pl. **-S** a bebopper
BOPPISH	*adj* boppy
BOPPY	*adj* **-PIER, -PIEST** suggestive of bebop
BORA	*n* pl. **-S** a cold wind
BORACES	a pl. of borax
BORACIC	*adj* boric
BORACITE	*n* pl. **-S** a mineral
BORAGE	*n* pl. **-S** a medicinal herb
BORAL	*n* pl. **-S** a mixture of boron carbide and aluminum
BORANE	*n* pl. **-S** a chemical compound
BORATE	*v* **-RATED, -RATING, -RATES** to mix with borax or boric acid
BORAX	*n* pl. **-RAXES** or **-RACES** a white crystalline compound
BORAZON	*n* pl. **-S** a hard form of boron nitride
BORDEAUX	*n* pl. **BORDEAUX** a red or white wine
BORDEL	*n* pl. **-S** a brothel
BORDELLO	*n* pl. **-LOS** a brothel
BORDER	*v* **-ED, -ING, -S** to put a border (an edge) on
BORDERER	*n* pl. **-S** one that borders
BORDURE	*n* pl. **-S** a border around a shield
BORE	*v* **BORED, BORING, BORES** to pierce with a rotary tool
BOREAL	*adj* pertaining to the north
BOREAS	*n* pl. **-ES** the north wind
BORECOLE	*n* pl. **-S** kale
BORED	past tense of bore
BOREDOM	*n* pl. **-S** tedium
BOREEN	*n* pl. **-S** a lane in Ireland
BOREHOLE	*n* pl. **-S** a hole bored in the earth
BORER	*n* pl. **-S** one that bores
BORESOME	*adj* tedious
BORIC	*adj* pertaining to boron
BORIDE	*n* pl. **-S** a boron compound
BORING	*n* pl. **-S** an inner cavity
BORINGLY	*adv* tediously
BORK	*v* **-ED, -ING, -S** to attack a candidate in the media
BORKING	*n* pl. **-S** the act of attacking a candidate in the media
BORN	*adj* having particular qualities from birth
BORNE	a past participle of bear
BORNEOL	*n* pl. **-S** an alcohol
BORNITE	*n* pl. **-S** an ore of copper **BORNITIC** *adj*
BORON	*n* pl. **-S** a nonmetallic element **BORONIC** *adj*
BORONIA	*n* pl. **-S** an Australian shrub
BOROUGH	*n* pl. **-S** an incorporated town

BORRELIA	*n* pl. **-S** a coiled spirochete
BORROW	*v* **-ED, -ING, -S** to take on loan
BORROWER	*n* pl. **-S** one that borrows
BORSCH	*n* pl. **-ES** borscht
BORSCHT	*n* pl. **-S** a beet soup
BORSHT	*n* pl. **-S** borscht
BORSTAL	*n* pl. **-S** a reformatory
BORT	*n* pl. **-S** a low-quality diamond **BORTY** *adj*
BORTZ	*n* pl. **-ES** bort
BORZOI	*n* pl. **-S** a Russian hound
BOSCAGE	*n* pl. **-S** a thicket
BOSCHBOK	*n* pl. **-S** bushbuck
BOSH	*n* pl. **-ES** nonsense
BOSHBOK	*n* pl. **-S** bushbuck
BOSHVARK	*n* pl. **-S** a wild hog
BOSK	*n* pl. **-S** a small wooded area
BOSKAGE	*n* pl. **-S** boscage
BOSKER	*adj* fine; very good
BOSKET	*n* pl. **-S** a thicket
BOSKY	*adj* **BOSKIER, BOSKIEST** wooded; bushy
BOSOM	*v* **-ED, -ING, -S** to embrace
BOSOMY	*adj* swelling outward
BOSON	*n* pl. **-S** a subatomic particle **BOSONIC** *adj*
BOSQUE	*n* pl. **-S** bosk
BOSQUET	*n* pl. **-S** bosket
BOSS	*v* **-ED, -ING, -ES** to supervise
BOSS	*adj* **BOSSER, BOSSEST** first-rate, excellent
BOSSDOM	*n* pl. **-S** the domain of a political boss
BOSSIES	pl. of bossy
BOSSISM	*n* pl. **-S** control by political bosses
BOSSY	*adj* **BOSSIER, BOSSIEST** domineering **BOSSILY** *adv*
BOSSY	*n* pl. **BOSSIES** a cow
BOSTON	*n* pl. **-S** a card game
BOSUN	*n* pl. **-S** a boatswain
BOT	*n* pl. **-S** the larva of a botfly
BOTA	*n* pl. **-S** a leather bottle
BOTANIC	*adj* pertaining to botany
BOTANICA	*n* pl. **-S** a shop that sells herbs and magic charms
BOTANIES	pl. of botany
BOTANISE	*v* **-NISED, -NISING, -NISES** to botanize
BOTANIST	*n* pl. **-S** one skilled in botany
BOTANIZE	*v* **-NIZED, -NIZING, -NIZES** to study plants
BOTANY	*n* pl. **-NIES** the science of plants
BOTCH	*v* **-ED, -ING, -ES** to bungle
BOTCHER	*n* pl. **-S** one that botches
BOTCHERY	*n* pl. **-ERIES** something botched
BOTCHY	*adj* **BOTCHIER, BOTCHIEST** badly done **BOTCHILY** *adv*
BOTEL	*n* pl. **-S** boatel
BOTFLY	*n* pl. **-FLIES** a type of fly
BOTH	*adj* being the two
BOTHER	*v* **-ED, -ING, -S** to annoy
BOTHIE	*n* pl. **-S** bothy
BOTHRIUM	*n* pl. **-RIUMS** or **-RIA** a groove on a tapeworm
BOTHY	*n* pl. **BOTHIES** a hut in Scotland
BOTNET	*n* pl. **-S** a group of computers linked by malware
BOTONEE	*adj* having arms ending in a trefoil — used of a heraldic cross
BOTONNEE	*adj* botonee
BOTRYOID	*adj* resembling a cluster of grapes
BOTRYOSE	*adj* botryoid
BOTRYTIS	*n* pl. **-TISES** a plant disease
BOTT	*n* pl. **-S** bot
BOTTLE	*v* **-TLED, -TLING, -TLES** to put into a bottle (a rigid container)
BOTTLER	*n* pl. **-S** one that bottles
BOTTLING	*n* pl. **-S** a bottled beverage
BOTTOM	*v* **-ED, -ING, -S** to comprehend
BOTTOMER	*n* pl. **-S** one that bottoms
BOTTOMRY	*n* pl. **-RIES** a maritime contract
BOTULIN	*n* pl. **-S** a nerve poison
BOTULISM	*n* pl. **-S** botulin poisoning
BOUBOU	*n* pl. **-S** a long flowing garment
BOUCHEE	*n* pl. **-S** a small patty shell
BOUCLE	*n* pl. **-S** a knitted fabric
BOUDIN	*n* pl. **-S** a spicy Cajun sausage
BOUDOIR	*n* pl. **-S** a woman's bedroom
BOUFFANT	*n* pl. **-S** a woman's hairdo
BOUFFE	*n* pl. **-S** a comic opera
BOUGH	*n* pl. **-S** a tree branch **BOUGHED** *adj*
BOUGHPOT	*n* pl. **-S** a large vase

BOX
77

BOUGHT	past tense of buy
BOUGHTEN	*adj* purchased
BOUGIE	*n* pl. **-S** a wax candle
BOUILLON	*n* pl. **-S** a clear broth
BOULDER	*v* **-ED, -ING, -S** to climb up large rocks
BOULDERY	*adj* characterized by large rocks
BOULE	*n* pl. **-S** buhl
BOULLE	*n* pl. **-S** buhl
BOULT	*v* **-ED, -ING, -S** to bolt (sift)
BOUNCE	*v* **BOUNCED, BOUNCING, BOUNCES** to spring back
BOUNCER	*n* pl. **-S** one that bounces
BOUNCY	*adj* **BOUNCIER, BOUNCIEST** tending to bounce **BOUNCILY** *adv*
BOUND	*v* **-ED, -ING, -S** to leap
BOUNDARY	*n* pl. **-ARIES** a dividing line
BOUNDEN	*adj* obliged
BOUNDER	*n* pl. **-S** one that bounds
BOUNTY	*n* pl. **-TIES** a reward **BOUNTIED** *adj*
BOUQUET	*n* pl. **-S** a bunch of flowers
BOURBON	*n* pl. **-S** a whiskey
BOURDON	*n* pl. **-S** a part of a bagpipe
BOURG	*n* pl. **-S** a medieval town
BOURGEON	*v* **-ED, -ING, -S** to burgeon
BOURN	*n* pl. **-S** a stream
BOURNE	*n* pl. **-S** bourn
BOURREE	*n* pl. **-S** an old French dance
BOURRIDE	*n* pl. **-S** a fish stew
BOURSE	*n* pl. **-S** a stock exchange
BOURTREE	*n* pl. **-S** a European tree
BOUSE	*v* **BOUSED, BOUSING, BOUSES** to haul by means of a tackle
BOUSOUKI	*n* pl. **-KIS** or **-KIA** bouzouki
BOUSY	*adj* boozy
BOUT	*n* pl. **-S** a contest
BOUTADE	*n* pl. **-S** a sudden outburst
BOUTIQUE	*n* pl. **-S** a small shop
BOUTON	*n* pl. **-S** an enlarged end of a nerve fiber
BOUVIER	*n* pl. **-S** a large dog
BOUZOUKI	*n* pl. **-KIS** or **-KIA** a stringed musical instrument
BOVID	*n* pl. **-S** a bovine
BOVINE	*n* pl. **-S** an ox-like animal

BOVINELY	*adv* stolidly
BOVINITY	*n* pl. **-TIES** the state of being a bovine
BOVVER	*n* pl. **-S** rowdy behavior
BOW	*v* **-ED, -ING, -S** to bend forward
BOWEL	*v* **-ELED, -ELING, -ELS** or **-ELLED, -ELLING, -ELS** to disbowel
BOWER	*v* **-ED, -ING, -S** to embower
BOWERY	*n* pl. **-ERIES** a colonial Dutch farm
BOWFIN	*n* pl. **-S** a freshwater fish
BOWFRONT	*adj* having a curved front
BOWHEAD	*n* pl. **-S** an arctic whale
BOWHUNT	*v* **-ED, -ING, -S** to hunt with a bow and arrow
BOWING	*n* pl. **-S** the technique of managing the bow of a stringed instrument
BOWINGLY	*adv* in a bowing manner
BOWKNOT	*n* pl. **-S** a type of knot
BOWL	*v* **-ED, -ING, -S** to play at bowling
BOWLDER	*n* pl. **-S** boulder
BOWLEG	*n* pl. **-S** an outwardly curved leg
BOWLER	*n* pl. **-S** one that bowls
BOWLESS	*adj* being without an archery bow
BOWLFUL	*n* pl. **-S** as much as a bowl can hold
BOWLIKE	*adj* curved
BOWLINE	*n* pl. **-S** a type of knot
BOWLING	*n* pl. **-S** a game in which balls are rolled at objects
BOWLLIKE	*adj* concave
BOWMAN	*n* pl. **-MEN** an archer
BOWPOT	*n* pl. **-S** boughpot
BOWSAW	*n* pl. **-S** a saw having a blade in a bow-shaped frame
BOWSE	*v* **BOWSED, BOWSING, BOWSES** to bouse
BOWSER	*n* pl. **-S** a truck having a tank for fuel or water
BOWSHOT	*n* pl. **-S** the distance an arrow is shot
BOWSMAN	*n* pl. **-MEN** a bowman
BOWSPRIT	*n* pl. **-S** a ship's spar
BOWWOOD	*n* pl. **-S** a deciduous tree
BOWWOW	*v* **-ED, -ING, -S** to bark like a dog
BOWYER	*n* pl. **-S** a maker of archery bows
BOX	*v* **-ED, -ING, -ES** to put in a box (a rectangular container)

BOXBALL	*n* pl. **-S** a form of handball
BOXBERRY	*n* pl. **-RIES** an evergreen plant
BOXBOARD	*n* pl. **-S** stiff paperboard
BOXCAR	*n* pl. **-S** a roofed freight car
BOXER	*n* pl. **-S** one that packs boxes
BOXFISH	*n* pl. **-ES** a marine fish
BOXFUL	*n* pl. **-S** as much as a box can hold
BOXHAUL	*v* **-ED, -ING, -S** to veer a ship around
BOXIER	comparative of boxy
BOXIEST	superlative of boxy
BOXINESS	*n* pl. **-ES** the state of being boxy
BOXING	*n* pl. **-S** a casing
BOXLA	*n* pl. **-S** a form of lacrosse played in an enclosed area
BOXLIKE	*adj* resembling a box
BOXTHORN	*n* pl. **-S** a thorny shrub
BOXWOOD	*n* pl. **-S** an evergreen shrub
BOXY	*adj* **BOXIER, BOXIEST** resembling a box **BOXILY** *adv*
BOY	*n* pl. **BOYS** a male child
BOYAR	*n* pl. **-S** a former Russian aristocrat
BOYARD	*n* pl. **-S** boyar
BOYARISM	*n* pl. **-S** the rule of boyars
BOYCHICK	*n* pl. **-S** boychik
BOYCHIK	*n* pl. **-S** a young man
BOYCOTT	*v* **-ED, -ING, -S** to refuse to buy
BOYHOOD	*n* pl. **-S** the state of being a boy
BOYISH	*adj* resembling a boy **BOYISHLY** *adv*
BOYLA	*n* pl. **-S** a witch doctor
BOYO	*n* pl. **BOYOS** a boy
BOZO	*n* pl. **-ZOS** a fellow
BRA	*n* pl. **-S** a brassiere
BRABBLE	*v* **-BLED, -BLING, -BLES** to quarrel noisily
BRABBLER	*n* pl. **-S** one that brabbles
BRACE	*v* **BRACED, BRACING, BRACES** to support
BRACELET	*n* pl. **-S** a wrist ornament
BRACER	*n* pl. **-S** one that braces
BRACERO	*n* pl. **-ROS** a Mexican laborer
BRACH	*n* pl. **-S** or **-ES** a hound bitch
BRACHET	*n* pl. **-S** a brach
BRACHIAL	*n* pl. **-S** a part of the arm
BRACHIUM	*n* pl. **-IA** the upper part of the arm
BRACING	*n* pl. **-S** a brace or reinforcement
BRACIOLA	*n* pl. **-S** a thin slice of meat
BRACIOLE	*n* pl. **-S** braciola
BRACKEN	*n* pl. **-S** a large fern
BRACKET	*v* **-ED, -ING, -S** to classify
BRACKISH	*adj* salty
BRACONID	*n* pl. **-S** any of a family of flies
BRACT	*n* pl. **-S** a leaflike plant part **BRACTEAL, BRACTED** *adj*
BRACTLET	*n* pl. **-S** a small bract
BRAD	*v* **BRADDED, BRADDING, BRADS** to fasten with thin nails
BRADAWL	*n* pl. **-S** a type of awl
BRADOON	*n* pl. **-S** bridoon
BRAE	*n* pl. **-S** a hillside
BRAG	*adj* **BRAGGER, BRAGGEST** first-rate
BRAG	*v* **BRAGGED, BRAGGING, BRAGS** to speak vainly of one's deeds
BRAGGART	*n* pl. **-S** one who brags
BRAGGER	*n* pl. **-S** a braggart
BRAGGY	*adj* **-GIER, -GIEST** tending to brag
BRAHMA	*n* pl. **-S** a large domestic fowl
BRAHMAN	*n* pl. **-S** a member of the highest Hindu caste
BRAID	*v* **-ED, -ING, -S** to weave together
BRAIDER	*n* pl. **-S** one that braids
BRAIDING	*n* pl. **-S** something made of braided material
BRAIL	*v* **-ED, -ING, -S** to haul in a sail
BRAILLE	*v* **BRAILLED, BRAILLING, BRAILLES** to write in braille (raised writing for the blind)
BRAILLER	*n* pl. **-S** a machine for printing in braille
BRAIN	*v* **-ED, -ING, -S** to hit on the head
BRAINIAC	*n* pl. **-S** a very intelligent person
BRAINIER	comparative of brainy
BRAINIEST	superlative of brainy
BRAINILY	*adv* in a brainy manner
BRAINISH	*adj* impetuous
BRAINPAN	*n* pl. **-S** the skull
BRAINY	*adj* **BRAINIER, BRAINIEST** smart
BRAISE	*v* **BRAISED, BRAISING, BRAISES** to cook in fat
BRAIZE	*n* pl. **-S** a marine fish

BRAKE	*v* **BRAKED, BRAKING, BRAKES** to slow down or stop
BRAKEAGE	*n* pl. **-S** the act of braking
BRAKEMAN	*n* pl. **-MEN** a trainman
BRAKING	present participle of brake
BRAKY	*adj* **BRAKIER, BRAKIEST** abounding in shrubs or ferns
BRALESS	*adj* wearing no bra
BRAMBLE	*v* **-BLED, -BLING, -BLES** to gather berries
BRAMBLY	*adj* **-BLIER, -BLIEST** prickly
BRAN	*v* **BRANNED, BRANNING, BRANS** to soak in water mixed with bran (the outer coat of cereals)
BRANCH	*v* **-ED, -ING, -ES** to form branches (offshoots)
BRANCHIA	*n* pl. **-CHIAE** a respiratory organ of aquatic animals
BRANCHY	*adj* **BRANCHIER, BRANCHIEST** having many branches
BRAND	*v* **-ED, -ING, -S** to mark with a hot iron
BRANDADE	*n* pl. **-S** a dish of cod mixed with olive oil and milk
BRANDER	*n* pl. **-S** one that brands
BRANDING	*n* pl. **-S** the promoting of a product by associating it with a brand name
BRANDISH	*v* **-ED, -ING, -ES** to wave menacingly
BRANDY	*v* **-DIED, -DYING, -DIES** to mix with brandy (a liquor)
BRANK	*n* pl. **-S** a device used to restrain the tongue
BRANNED	past tense of bran
BRANNER	*n* pl. **-S** one that brans
BRANNING	present participle of bran
BRANNY	*adj* **-NIER, -NIEST** containing bran
BRANT	*n* pl. **-S** a wild goose
BRANTAIL	*n* pl. **-S** a singing bird
BRASH	*adj* **BRASHER, BRASHEST** rash; hasty **BRASHLY** *adv*
BRASH	*n* pl. **-ES** a mass of fragments
BRASHY	*adj* **BRASHIER, BRASHIEST** brash
BRASIER	*n* pl. **-S** brazier
BRASIL	*n* pl. **-S** brazil
BRASILIN	*n* pl. **-S** brazilin
BRASS	*v* **-ED, -ING, -ES** to coat with brass (an alloy of copper and zinc)
BRASSAGE	*n* pl. **-S** a fee for coining money
BRASSARD	*n* pl. **-S** an insignia
BRASSART	*n* pl. **-S** brassard
BRASSICA	*n* pl. **-S** a tall herb
BRASSIE	*n* pl. **-S** a golf club
BRASSISH	*adj* resembling brass
BRASSY	*adj* **BRASSIER, BRASSIEST** resembling brass **BRASSILY** *adv*
BRAT	*n* pl. **-S** a spoiled child **BRATTISH** *adj*
BRATTICE	*v* **-TICED, -TICING, -TICES** to partition
BRATTLE	*v* **-TLED, -TLING, -TLES** to clatter
BRATTY	*adj* **-TIER, -TIEST** resembling a brat
BRAUNITE	*n* pl. **-S** a mineral
BRAVA	*n* pl. **-S** a shout of approval
BRAVADO	*n* pl. **-DOS** or **-DOES** false bravery
BRAVE	*adj* **BRAVER, BRAVEST** showing courage **BRAVELY** *adv*
BRAVE	*v* **BRAVED, BRAVING, BRAVES** to face with courage
BRAVER	*n* pl. **-S** one that braves
BRAVERY	*n* pl. **-ERIES** courage
BRAVEST	superlative of brave
BRAVI	a pl. of bravo
BRAVING	present participle of brave
BRAVO	*n* pl. **-VOS** or **-VOES** or **-VI** a hired killer
BRAVO	*v* **-ED, -ING, -ES** to applaud by shouting "bravo"
BRAVURA	*n* pl. **-RAS** or **-RE** fine musical technique
BRAW	*adj* **BRAWER, BRAWEST** splendid
BRAWL	*v* **-ED, -ING, -S** to fight
BRAWLER	*n* pl. **-S** a fighter
BRAWLIE	*adv* splendidly
BRAWLY	*adj* **BRAWLIER, BRAWLIEST** inclined to brawl
BRAWN	*n* pl. **-S** muscular strength
BRAWNY	*adj* **BRAWNIER, BRAWNIEST** muscular **BRAWNILY** *adv*
BRAWS	*n/pl* fine clothes
BRAXY	*n* pl. **BRAXIES** a fever of sheep
BRAY	*v* **BRAYED, BRAYING, BRAYS** to utter a harsh cry

BRAYER	*n* pl. **-S** a roller used to spread ink	**BREED**	*v* **BRED, BREEDING, BREEDS** to cause to give birth
BRAZA	*n* pl. **-S** a Spanish unit of length		
BRAZE	*v* **BRAZED, BRAZING, BRAZES** to solder together	**BREEDER**	*n* pl. **-S** one that breeds
		BREEDING	*n* pl. **-S** upbringing
BRAZEN	*v* **-ED, -ING, -S** to face boldly	**BREEKS**	*n/pl* breeches
BRAZENLY	*adv* boldly	**BREEZE**	*v* **BREEZED, BREEZING, BREEZES** to move swiftly
BRAZER	*n* pl. **-S** one that brazes		
BRAZIER	*n* pl. **-S** one who works in brass	**BREEZY**	*adj* **BREEZIER, BREEZIEST** windy **BREEZILY** *adv*
BRAZIL	*n* pl. **-S** a dyewood		
BRAZILIN	*n* pl. **-S** a chemical compound	**BREGMA**	*n* pl. **-MATA** or **-MAS** a junction point of the skull **BREGMATE** *adj*
BRAZING	present participle of braze		
BREACH	*v* **-ED, -ING, -ES** to break through	**BREKKIE**	*n* pl. **-S** breakfast
		BREN	*n* pl. **-S** a light machine gun
BREACHER	*n* pl. **-S** one that breaches	**BRENT**	*n* pl. **-S** brant
BREAD	*v* **-ED, -ING, -S** to cover with crumbs of bread (a baked foodstuff made from flour)	**BRESAOLA**	*n* pl. **-S** a dish of sliced dried beef
		BRETHREN	a pl. of brother
BREADBOX	*n* pl. **-ES** a container for bread	**BREVE**	*n* pl. **-S** a symbol used to indicate a short vowel
BREADNUT	*n* pl. **-S** a tropical fruit		
BREADTH	*n* pl. **-S** width	**BREVET**	*v* **-VETED, -VETING, -VETS** or **-VETTED, -VETTING, -VETS** to confer an honorary rank upon
BREADY	*adj* resembling or characteristic of bread		
		BREVETCY	*n* pl. **-CIES** an honorary rank
BREAK	*v* **BROKE, BROKEN, BREAKING, BREAKS** to reduce to fragments	**BREVIARY**	*n* pl. **-RIES** a prayer book
		BREVIER	*n* pl. **-S** a size of type
BREAKAGE	*n* pl. **-S** the act of breaking	**BREVITY**	*n* pl. **-TIES** shortness of duration
BREAKER	*n* pl. **-S** one that breaks	**BREW**	*v* **-ED, -ING, -S** to make beer or the like
BREAKING	*n* pl. **-S** the change of a pure vowel to a diphthong		
		BREWAGE	*n* pl. **-S** a brewed beverage
BREAKOUT	*n* pl. **-S** an escape	**BREWER**	*n* pl. **-S** one that brews
BREAKUP	*n* pl. **-S** the act of breaking up	**BREWERY**	*n* pl. **-ERIES** a place for brewing
BREAM	*v* **-ED, -ING, -S** to clean a ship's bottom	**BREWING**	*n* pl. **-S** a quantity brewed at one time
BREAST	*v* **-ED, -ING, -S** to confront boldly	**BREWIS**	*n* pl. **BREWISES** broth
BREATH	*n* pl. **-S** air inhaled and exhaled	**BREWPUB**	*n* pl. **-S** a restaurant that sells beverages brewed on the premises
BREATHE	*v* **BREATHED, BREATHING, BREATHES** to inhale and exhale air		
		BREWSKI	*n* pl. **-SKIES** or **-SKIS** a serving of beer
BREATHER	*n* pl. **-S** one that breathes		
BREATHY	*adj* **BREATHIER, BREATHIEST** marked by loud breathing	**BRIAR**	*n* pl. **-S** brier **BRIARY** *adj*
		BRIARD	*n* pl. **-S** a large dog
BRECCIA	*n* pl. **-S** a type of rock **BRECCIAL** *adj*	**BRIBE**	*v* **BRIBED, BRIBING, BRIBES** to practice bribery **BRIBABLE** *adj*
BRECHAM	*n* pl. **-S** a collar for a horse	**BRIBEE**	*n* pl. **-S** one that is bribed
BRECHAN	*n* pl. **-S** brecham	**BRIBER**	*n* pl. **-S** one that bribes
BRED	past tense of breed	**BRIBERY**	*n* pl. **-ERIES** an act of influencing corruptly
BREDE	*n* pl. **-S** a braid		
BREE	*n* pl. **-S** broth	**BRIBING**	present participle of bribe
BREECH	*v* **-ED, -ING, -ES** to clothe with breeches (trousers)	**BRICK**	*v* **-ED, -ING, -S** to build with bricks (blocks of clay)

BRICKBAT	*n* pl. **-S** a piece of brick
BRICKLE	*n* pl. **-S** a brittle candy
BRICKY	*adj* **BRICKIER, BRICKIEST** made of bricks
BRICOLE	*n* pl. **-S** a cushion shot in billiards
BRIDAL	*n* pl. **-S** a wedding
BRIDALLY	*adv* in a manner befitting a bride
BRIDE	*n* pl. **-S** a woman just married or about to be married
BRIDGE	*v* **BRIDGED, BRIDGING, BRIDGES** to connect
BRIDGING	*n* pl. **-S** a bracing
BRIDIE	*n* pl. **-S** a pastry filled with meat and onions
BRIDLE	*v* **-DLED, -DLING, -DLES** to control with a restraint
BRIDLER	*n* pl. **-S** one that bridles
BRIDOON	*n* pl. **-S** a device used to control a horse
BRIE	*n* pl. **-S** bree
BRIEF	*adj* **BRIEFER, BRIEFEST** short
BRIEF	*v* **-ED, -ING, -S** to summarize
BRIEFER	*n* pl. **-S** one that briefs
BRIEFING	*n* pl. **-S** a short lecture
BRIEFLY	*adv* in a brief manner
BRIER	*n* pl. **-S** a thorny shrub **BRIERY** *adj*
BRIG	*n* pl. **-S** a two-masted ship
BRIGADE	*v* **-GADED, -GADING, -GADES** to group together
BRIGAND	*n* pl. **-S** a bandit
BRIGHT	*adj* **BRIGHTER, BRIGHTEST** emitting much light **BRIGHTLY** *adv*
BRIGHT	*n* pl. **-S** a light-hued tobacco
BRIGHTEN	*v* **-ED, -ING, -S** to make bright
BRILL	*n* pl. **-S** an edible flatfish
BRIM	*v* **BRIMMED, BRIMMING, BRIMS** to fill to the top
BRIMFUL	*adj* ready to overflow
BRIMFULL	*adj* brimful
BRIMLESS	*adj* having no brim (an upper edge)
BRIMMED	past tense of brim
BRIMMER	*n* pl. **-S** a brimming cup or glass
BRIMMING	present participle of brim
BRIN	*n* pl. **-S** a rib of a fan
BRINDED	*adj* brindled
BRINDLE	*n* pl. **-S** a brindled color
BRINDLED	*adj* streaked
BRINE	*v* **BRINED, BRINING, BRINES** to treat with brine (salted water)
BRINER	*n* pl. **-S** one that brines
BRING	*v* **BROUGHT** or **BRUNG, BRINGING, BRINGS** to take with oneself to a place
BRINGER	*n* pl. **-S** one that brings
BRINIER	comparative of briny
BRINIES	pl. of briny
BRINIEST	superlative of briny
BRINING	present participle of brine
BRINISH	*adj* resembling brine
BRINK	*n* pl. **-S** an extreme edge
BRINY	*adj* **BRINIER, BRINIEST** salty
BRINY	*n* pl. **BRINIES** the sea
BRIO	*n* pl. **BRIOS** liveliness
BRIOCHE	*n* pl. **-S** a rich roll
BRIONY	*n* pl. **-NIES** bryony
BRIQUET	*v* **-QUETTED, -QUETTING, -QUETS** to mold into small bricks
BRIS	*n* pl. **-ES** a Jewish circumcision rite
BRISANCE	*n* pl. **-S** the shattering effect of an explosive **BRISANT** *adj*
BRISK	*adj* **BRISKER, BRISKEST** lively
BRISK	*v* **-ED, -ING, -S** to make brisk
BRISKET	*n* pl. **-S** the breast of an animal
BRISKLY	*adv* in a brisk manner
BRISLING	*n* pl. **-S** a small herring
BRISS	*n* pl. **-ES** bris
BRISTLE	*v* **-TLED, -TLING, -TLES** to rise stiffly
BRISTLY	*adj* **-TLIER, -TLIEST** stiffly erect
BRISTOL	*n* pl. **-S** a smooth cardboard
BRIT	*n* pl. **-S** a young herring
BRITCHES	*n/pl* breeches; trousers
BRITH	*n* pl. **-S** bris
BRITSKA	*n* pl. **-S** an open carriage
BRITT	*n* pl. **-S** brit
BRITTLE	*adj* **-TLER, -TLEST** likely to break
BRITTLE	*v* **-TLED, -TLING, -TLES** to become brittle
BRITTLY	*adv* in a brittle manner
BRITZKA	*n* pl. **-S** britska
BRITZSKA	*n* pl. **-S** britska
BRO	*n* pl. **BROS** a brother

BROACH	*v* **-ED, -ING, -ES** to pierce so as to withdraw a liquid	**BROMANCE**	*n* pl. **-S** a close nonsexual relationship between men
BROACHER	*n* pl. **-S** one that broaches	**BROMATE**	*v* **-MATED, -MATING, -MATES** to combine with bromine
BROAD	*adj* **BROADER, BROADEST** wide	**BROME**	*n* pl. **-S** a tall grass
BROAD	*n* pl. **-S** an expansion of a river	**BROMELIA**	*n* pl. **-S** a tropical plant with stiff leaves
BROADAX	*n* pl. **-ES** a broad-edged ax		
BROADAXE	*n* pl. **-S** broadax	**BROMELIN**	*n* pl. **-S** an enzyme
BROADEN	*v* **-ED, -ING, -S** to make broad	**BROMIC**	*adj* containing bromine
BROADISH	*adj* somewhat broad	**BROMID**	*n* pl. **-S** bromide
BROADLY	*adv* in a broad manner	**BROMIDE**	*n* pl. **-S** a bromine compound
BROADWAY	*n* pl. **-WAYS** a large main road	**BROMIDIC**	*adj* commonplace; trite
BROAST	*v* **-ED, -ING, -S** to broil and roast food	**BROMIN**	*n* pl. **-S** bromine
		BROMINE	*n* pl. **-S** a volatile liquid element
BROCADE	*v* **-CADED, -CADING, -CADES** to weave with a raised design	**BROMISM**	*n* pl. **-S** a diseased condition of the skin
BROCATEL	*n* pl. **-S** a heavy fabric	**BROMIZE**	*v* **-MIZED, -MIZING, -MIZES** to treat with bromine or a bromide
BROCCOLI	*n* pl. **-S** a vegetable related to the cabbage	**BROMO**	*n* pl. **-MOS** a medicinal compound
BROCH	*n* pl. **-S** a prehistoric stone tower	**BRONC**	*n* pl. **-S** bronco
BROCHE	*adj* brocaded	**BRONCHI**	pl. of bronchus
BROCHURE	*n* pl. **-S** a pamphlet	**BRONCHIA**	*n/pl* the main air passages of the lungs
BROCK	*n* pl. **-S** a badger		
BROCKAGE	*n* pl. **-S** an imperfectly minted coin	**BRONCHO**	*n* pl. **-CHOS** bronco
BROCKET	*n* pl. **-S** a small, red deer	**BRONCHUS**	*n* pl. **-CHI** a tracheal branch
BROCOLI	*n* pl. **-S** broccoli	**BRONCO**	*n* pl. **-COS** a wild horse
BROGAN	*n* pl. **-S** a heavy shoe	**BRONZE**	*v* **BRONZED, BRONZING, BRONZES** to make brown or tan
BROGUE	*n* pl. **-S** an Irish accent		
BROGUERY	*n* pl. **-ERIES** the use of an Irish accent	**BRONZER**	*n* pl. **-S** one that bronzes
		BRONZING	*n* pl. **-S** a brownish coloring
BROGUISH	*adj* resembling a brogue	**BRONZY**	*adj* **BRONZIER, BRONZIEST** of a brownish color
BROIDER	*v* **-ED, -ING, -S** to adorn with needlework		
		BROO	*n* pl. **BROOS** a bree
BROIDERY	*n* pl. **-DERIES** the act of broidering	**BROOCH**	*n* pl. **-ES** a decorative pin
BROIL	*v* **-ED, -ING, -S** to cook by direct heat	**BROOD**	*v* **-ED, -ING, -S** to ponder deeply
		BROODER	*n* pl. **-S** one that broods
BROILER	*n* pl. **-S** a device for broiling	**BROODY**	*adj* **BROODIER, BROODIEST** tending to brood **BROODILY** *adv*
BROKAGE	*n* pl. **-S** the business of a broker		
BROKE	past tense of break	**BROOK**	*v* **-ED, -ING, -S** to tolerate
BROKEN	*adj* shattered **BROKENLY** *adv*	**BROOKIE**	*n* pl. **-S** a brook trout
BROKER	*v* **-ED, -ING, -S** to act as a broker (an agent who buys and sells stocks)	**BROOKITE**	*n* pl. **-S** a mineral
		BROOKLET	*n* pl. **-S** a small brook or creek
		BROOM	*v* **-ED, -ING, -S** to sweep
BROKING	*n* pl. **-S** the business of a broker	**BROOMY**	*adj* **BROOMIER, BROOMIEST** abounding in broom (a type of shrub)
BROLGA	*n* pl. **-S** a large Australian bird		
BROLLY	*n* pl. **-LIES** an umbrella	**BROS**	pl. of bro
BROMAL	*n* pl. **-S** a medicinal liquid	**BROSE**	*n* pl. **-S** a porridge

BROSY *adj* smeared with brose

BROTH *n* pl. **-S** a thin clear soup

BROTHEL *n* pl. **-S** a house of prostitution

BROTHER *n* pl. **BROTHERS** or **BRETHREN** a male sibling

BROTHER *v* **-ED, -ING, -S** to treat like a brother

BROTHY *adj* resembling broth

BROUGHAM *n* pl. **-S** a type of carriage

BROUGHT past tense of bring

BROUHAHA *n* pl. **-S** an uproar

BROW *n* pl. **-S** the forehead **BROWED** *adj*

BROWBAND *n* pl. **-S** a band designed to cross the forehead

BROWBEAT *v* **-BEAT, -BEATEN, -BEATING, -BEATS** to intimidate

BROWBONE *n* pl. **-S** the ridge of bone above the eye

BROWLESS *adj* lacking eyebrows

BROWN *adj* **BROWNER, BROWNEST** of a dark color

BROWN *v* **-ED, -ING, -S** to make brown

BROWNER *n* pl. **-S** a fawning person

BROWNIE *n* pl. **-S** a small sprite

BROWNIER comparative of browny

BROWNIEST superlative of browny

BROWNING *n* pl. **-S** brown flour used for coloring gravy

BROWNISH *adj* somewhat brown

BROWNOUT *n* pl. **-S** a power reduction

BROWNY *adj* **BROWNIER, BROWNIEST** somewhat brown

BROWSE *v* **BROWSED, BROWSING, BROWSES** to look at casually

BROWSER *n* pl. **-S** one that browses

BRR *interj* brrr

BRRR *interj* — used to indicate that one feels cold

BRUCELLA *n* pl. **-LAS** or **-LAE** any of a genus of harmful bacteria

BRUCIN *n* pl. **-S** brucine

BRUCINE *n* pl. **-S** a poisonous alkaloid

BRUCITE *n* pl. **-S** a form of magnesium hydroxide

BRUGH *n* pl. **-S** a borough

BRUIN *n* pl. **-S** a bear

BRUISE *v* **BRUISED, BRUISING, BRUISES** to injure without breaking the surface of the skin

BRUISER *n* pl. **-S** a big, husky man

BRUISING *n* pl. **-S** an injury that does not break the surface of the skin

BRUIT *v* **-ED, -ING, -S** to spread news of

BRUITER *n* pl. **-S** one that bruits

BRULOT *n* pl. **-S** a biting fly

BRULYIE *n* pl. **-S** a noisy quarrel

BRULZIE *n* pl. **-S** brulyie

BRUMAL *adj* wintry

BRUMBY *n* pl. **-BIES** a wild horse

BRUME *n* pl. **-S** fog **BRUMOUS** *adj*

BRUNCH *v* **-ED, -ING, -ES** to eat a late morning meal

BRUNCHER *n* pl. **-S** one that brunches

BRUNET *n* pl. **-S** a dark-haired male

BRUNETTE *n* pl. **-S** a dark-haired female

BRUNG a past tense of bring

BRUNIZEM *n* pl. **-S** a prairie soil

BRUNT *n* pl. **-S** the main impact

BRUSH *v* **-ED, -ING, -ES** to touch lightly

BRUSHER *n* pl. **-S** one that brushes

BRUSHIER comparative of brushy

BRUSHIEST superlative of brushy

BRUSHOFF *n* pl. **-S** an abrupt dismissal

BRUSHUP *n* pl. **-S** a quick review

BRUSHY *adj* **BRUSHIER, BRUSHIEST** shaggy; rough

BRUSK *adj* **BRUSKER, BRUSKEST** brusque

BRUSQUE *adj* **BRUSQUER, BRUSQUEST** abrupt in manner

BRUT *n* pl. **-S** a very dry champagne

BRUTAL *adj* cruel; savage **BRUTALLY** *adv*

BRUTE *v* **BRUTED, BRUTING, BRUTES** to shape a diamond by rubbing it with another diamond

BRUTE *adj* **BRUTER, BRUTEST** resembling an animal; cruel

BRUTELY *adv* in a brutal manner

BRUTIFY *v* **-FIED, -FYING, -FIES** to make brutal

BRUTISH *adj* brutal

BRUTISM *n* pl. **-S** the state of being brutal

BRUX *v* **-ED, -ING, -ES** to grind the teeth

BRUXISM *n* pl. **-S** a nervous grinding of the teeth

BRYOLOGY *n* pl. **-GIES** the study of mosses

BRYONY	*n* pl. **-NIES** a climbing plant	**BUCKTAIL**	*n* pl. **-S** a fishing lure
BRYOZOAN	*n* pl. **-S** a type of small aquatic animal	**BUCOLIC**	*n* pl. **-S** a pastoral poem
BUB	*n* pl. **-S** young fellow	**BUD**	*v* **BUDDED, BUDDING, BUDS** to put forth buds (undeveloped plant parts)
BUBAL	*n* pl. **-S** a large antelope		
BUBALE	*n* pl. **-S** bubal	**BUDDER**	*n* pl. **-S** one that buds
BUBALINE	*adj* pertaining to the bubal	**BUDDIED**	past tense of buddy
BUBALIS	*n* pl. **-LISES** bubal	**BUDDIES**	present 3d person sing. of buddy
BUBBE	*n* pl. **-S** a Jewish grandmother	**BUDDING**	*n* pl. **-S** a type of asexual reproduction
BUBBIE	*n* pl. **-S** bubbe		
BUBBLE	*v* **-BLED, -BLING, -BLES** to form bubbles (bodies of gas contained within a liquid)	**BUDDLE**	*n* pl. **-S** an apparatus on which crushed ore is washed
		BUDDLEIA	*n* pl. **-S** a tropical shrub
BUBBLER	*n* pl. **-S** a drinking fountain	**BUDDY**	*v* **-DIED, -DYING, -DIES** to become close friends
BUBBLY	*adj* **-BLIER, -BLIEST** full of bubbles		
		BUDGE	*v* **BUDGED, BUDGING, BUDGES** to move slightly
BUBBLY	*n* pl. **-BLIES** champagne		
BUBINGA	*n* pl. **-S** an African tree	**BUDGER**	*n* pl. **-S** one that budges
BUBKES	*n/pl* the least amount	**BUDGET**	*v* **-ED, -ING, -S** to estimate expenditures
BUBO	*n* pl. **-BOES** a swelling of a lymph gland **BUBOED** *adj*		
		BUDGETER	*n* pl. **-S** one that budgets
BUBONIC	*adj* pertaining to a bubo	**BUDGIE**	*n* pl. **-S** a small parrot
BUBU	*n* pl. **-S** boubou	**BUDGING**	present participle of budge
BUCCAL	*adj* pertaining to the cheek **BUCCALLY** *adv*	**BUDLESS**	*adj* being without buds
		BUDLIKE	*adj* resembling a bud
BUCK	*v* **-ED, -ING, -S** to leap forward and upward suddenly	**BUDWOOD**	*n* pl. **-S** a branch having buds that is used for grafting
BUCKAROO	*n* pl. **-ROOS** a cowboy	**BUDWORM**	*n* pl. **-S** a caterpillar that eats buds
BUCKAYRO	*n* pl. **-ROS** buckaroo		
BUCKBEAN	*n* pl. **-S** a marsh plant	**BUFF**	*adj* **BUFFER, BUFFEST** having a muscular physique
BUCKEEN	*n* pl. **-S** a poor man who acts as if wealthy		
		BUFF	*v* **-ED, -ING, -S** to polish **BUFFABLE** *adj*
BUCKER	*n* pl. **-S** a bucking horse		
BUCKEROO	*n* pl. **-ROOS** buckaroo	**BUFFALO**	*n* pl. **-LOS** or **-LOES** an ox-like animal
BUCKET	*v* **-ED, -ING, -S** to hurry		
BUCKEYE	*n* pl. **-S** a nut-bearing tree	**BUFFALO**	*v* **-ED, -ING, -ES** to intimidate
BUCKISH	*adj* foppish	**BUFFER**	*v* **-ED, -ING, -S** to cushion
BUCKLE	*v* **-LED, -LING, -LES** to bend under pressure	**BUFFET**	*v* **-ED, -ING, -S** to hit sharply
		BUFFETER	*n* pl. **-S** one that buffets
BUCKLER	*v* **-ED, -ING, -S** to shield	**BUFFI**	a pl. of buffo
BUCKO	*n* pl. **BUCKOS** or **BUCKOES** a bully	**BUFFIER**	comparative of buffy
		BUFFIEST	superlative of buffy
BUCKRAM	*v* **-ED, -ING, -S** to stiffen	**BUFFO**	*n* pl. **-FOS** or **-FI** an operatic clown
BUCKSAW	*n* pl. **-S** a wood-cutting saw	**BUFFOON**	*n* pl. **-S** a clown
BUCKSHEE	*n* pl. **-S** something extra obtained free	**BUFFY**	*adj* **BUFFIER, BUFFIEST** of a yellowish-brown color
		BUG	*v* **BUGGED, BUGGING, BUGS** to annoy
BUCKSHOT	*n* pl. **-S** a large lead shot		
BUCKSKIN	*n* pl. **-S** the skin of a male deer	**BUGABOO**	*n* pl. **-BOOS** a bugbear

BUGBANE	*n* pl. **-S** a perennial herb
BUGBEAR	*n* pl. **-S** an object or source of dread
BUGEYE	*n* pl. **-S** a small boat
BUGGED	past tense of bug
BUGGER	*v* **-ED, -ING, -S** to damn
BUGGERY	*n* pl. **-GERIES** sodomy
BUGGING	present participle of bug
BUGGY	*adj* **-GIER, -GIEST** infested with bugs
BUGGY	*n* pl. **-GIES** a light carriage
BUGHOUSE	*n* pl. **-S** an insane asylum
BUGLE	*v* **-GLED, -GLING, -GLES** to play a bugle (a brass wind instrument)
BUGLER	*n* pl. **-S** one that plays a bugle
BUGLOSS	*n* pl. **-ES** a coarse plant
BUGOUT	*n* pl. **-S** one that leaves hurriedly
BUGSEED	*n* pl. **-S** an annual herb
BUGSHA	*n* pl. **-S** buqsha
BUHL	*n* pl. **-S** a style of furniture decoration
BUHLWORK	*n* pl. **-S** buhl
BUHR	*n* pl. **-S** a heavy stone
BUILD	*v* **BUILT** or **BUILDED, BUILDING, BUILDS** to construct
BUILDER	*n* pl. **-S** one that builds
BUILDING	*n* pl. **-S** something that is built
BUILDOUT	*n* pl. **-S** work done to expand a system
BUILDUP	*n* pl. **-S** an accumulation
BUILT	a past tense of build
BUIRDLY	*adj* burly
BULB	*n* pl. **-S** an underground bud **BULBAR, BULBED** *adj*
BULBEL	*n* pl. **-S** bulbil
BULBIL	*n* pl. **-S** a small bulb
BULBLET	*n* pl. **-S** a small bulb
BULBOUS	*adj* bulb-shaped; bulging
BULBUL	*n* pl. **-S** a songbird
BULGAR	*n* pl. **-S** bulgur
BULGE	*v* **BULGED, BULGING, BULGES** to swell out
BULGER	*n* pl. **-S** a golf club
BULGHUR	*n* pl. **-S** bulgur
BULGUR	*n* pl. **-S** crushed wheat
BULGY	*adj* **BULGIER, BULGIEST** bulging
BULIMIA	*n* pl. **-S** insatiable appetite **BULIMIAC** *adj*
BULIMIC	*n* pl. **-S** one who is affected with bulimia
BULK	*v* **-ED, -ING, -S** to gather into a mass
BULKAGE	*n* pl. **-S** a peristaltic stimulant
BULKER	*n* pl. **-S** a ship that carries cargo in bulk (a mass)
BULKHEAD	*n* pl. **-S** a partition in a ship
BULKY	*adj* **BULKIER, BULKIEST** massive **BULKILY** *adv*
BULL	*v* **-ED, -ING, -S** to push ahead
BULLA	*n* pl. **-LAE** a large blister
BULLACE	*n* pl. **-S** a purple plum
BULLATE	*adj* blistered in appearance
BULLBAT	*n* pl. **-S** a nocturnal bird
BULLCOOK	*n* pl. **-S** a worker in a logging camp
BULLDOG	*v* **-DOGGED, -DOGGING, -DOGS** to throw a steer
BULLDOZE	*v* **-DOZED, -DOZING, -DOZES** to bully
BULLET	*v* **-ED, -ING, -S** to move swiftly
BULLETIN	*v* **-ED, -ING, -S** to issue a news item
BULLEY	*n* pl. **-LEYS** a two-masted fishing boat
BULLFROG	*n* pl. **-S** a large frog
BULLHEAD	*n* pl. **-S** a freshwater catfish
BULLHORN	*n* pl. **-S** an electric megaphone
BULLIED	past tense of bully
BULLIER	comparative of bully
BULLIES	present 3d person sing. of bully
BULLIEST	superlative of bully
BULLION	*n* pl. **-S** uncoined gold or silver
BULLISH	*adj* stubborn
BULLNECK	*n* pl. **-S** a thick neck
BULLNOSE	*n* pl. **-S** a disease of swine
BULLOCK	*n* pl. **-S** a castrated bull **BULLOCKY** *adj*
BULLOUS	*adj* resembling bullae
BULLPEN	*n* pl. **-S** an enclosure for bulls
BULLPOUT	*n* pl. **-S** a bullhead
BULLRING	*n* pl. **-S** a bullfight arena
BULLRUSH	*n* pl. **-ES** bulrush
BULLSEYE	*n* pl. **-S** the center of a target
BULLSHOT	*n* pl. **-S** a drink made of vodka and bouillon

BULLWEED   *n* pl. **-S** knapweed

BULLWHIP   *v* **-WHIPPED, -WHIPPING, -WHIPS** to strike with a long whip

BULLY   *adj* **-LIER, -LIEST** wonderful

BULLY   *v* **-LIED, -LYING, -LIES** to treat abusively

BULLYBOY   *n* pl. **-BOYS** a ruffian

BULLYRAG   *v* **-RAGGED, -RAGGING, -RAGS** to bully

BULRUSH   *n* pl. **-ES** a tall marsh plant

BULWARK   *v* **-ED, -ING, -S** to fortify with a defensive wall

BUM   *adj* **BUMMER, BUMMEST** of little value; worthless

BUM   *v* **BUMMED, BUMMING, BUMS** to live idly

BUMBAG   *n* pl. **-S** a pack that straps to the waist

BUMBLE   *v* **-BLED, -BLING, -BLES** to bungle

BUMBLER   *n* pl. **-S** one that bumbles

BUMBLING   *n* pl. **-S** an instance of clumsiness

BUMBOAT   *n* pl. **-S** a boat used to peddle wares to larger ships

BUMELIA   *n* pl. **-S** a thorny tree

BUMF   *n* pl. **-S** paperwork

BUMKIN   *n* pl. **-S** a ship's spar

BUMMALO   *n* pl. **-LOS** a small Asian fish

BUMMED   past tense of bum

BUMMER   *n* pl. **-S** one that bums

BUMMEST   superlative of bum

BUMMING   present participle of bum

BUMP   *v* **-ED, -ING, -S** to knock against

BUMPER   *v* **-ED, -ING, -S** to fill to the brim

BUMPH   *n* pl. **-S** bumf

BUMPKIN   *n* pl. **-S** an unsophisticated rustic

BUMPY   *adj* **BUMPIER, BUMPIEST** of uneven surface **BUMPILY** *adv*

BUN   *n* pl. **-S** a small bread roll

BUNA   *n* pl. **-S** a synthetic rubber

BUNCH   *v* **-ED, -ING, -ES** to group together

BUNCHER   *n* pl. **-S** one that gathers things together

BUNCHY   *adj* **BUNCHIER, BUNCHIEST** clustered **BUNCHILY** *adv*

BUNCO   *v* **-ED, -ING, -S** or **-ES** to swindle

BUNCOMBE   *n* pl. **-S** nonsense

BUND   *n* pl. **-S** a political association

BUNDIST   *n* pl. **-S** a member of a bund

BUNDLE   *v* **-DLED, -DLING, -DLES** to fasten a group of objects together

BUNDLER   *n* pl. **-S** one that bundles

BUNDLING   *n* pl. **-S** a former courtship custom

BUNDT   *n* pl. **-S** a type of cake pan

BUNFIGHT   *n* pl. **-S** a crowded boisterous party

BUNG   *v* **-ED, -ING, -S** to plug with a cork or stopper

BUNGALOW   *n* pl. **-S** a small cottage

BUNGEE   *n* pl. **-S** an elasticized cord

BUNGHOLE   *n* pl. **-S** a hole in a keg or barrel

BUNGLE   *v* **-GLED, -GLING, -GLES** to work, make, or do clumsily

BUNGLER   *n* pl. **-S** one that bungles

BUNGLING   *n* pl. **-S** something done clumsily

BUNHEAD   *n* pl. **-S** a female ballet dancer

BUNION   *n* pl. **-S** a painful swelling of the foot

BUNK   *v* **-ED, -ING, -S** to go to bed

BUNKER   *v* **-ED, -ING, -S** to store in a large bin

BUNKIE   *n* pl. **-S** a small separate building for guests

BUNKMATE   *n* pl. **-S** a person with whom sleeping quarters are shared

BUNKO   *v* **-ED, -ING, -S** to bunco

BUNKUM   *n* pl. **-S** nonsense

BUNN   *n* pl. **-S** bun

BUNNY   *n* pl. **-NIES** a rabbit

BUNRAKU   *n* pl. **-S** a Japanese puppet show

BUNT   *v* **-ED, -ING, -S** to butt

BUNTER   *n* pl. **-S** one that bunts

BUNTING   *n* pl. **-S** a fabric used for flags

BUNTLINE   *n* pl. **-S** a rope used to haul up a sail

BUNYA   *n* pl. **-S** an evergreen tree

BUNYIP   *n* pl. **-S** a fabulous monster of swamps

BUOY   *v* **-ED, -ING, -S** to mark with a buoy (a warning float)

BUOYAGE   *n* pl. **-S** a group of buoys

BUOYANCE   *n* pl. **-S** buoyancy

BUOYANCY   *n* pl. **-CIES** the tendency to float

BUOYANT   *adj* having buoyancy

BUPKES   *n/pl* bubkes

BUPKIS   *n/pl* bubkes

BUPKUS	*n/pl* bubkes
BUPPIE	*n* pl. **-S** a black professional person working in a city
BUPPY	*n* pl. **-PIES** buppie
BUQSHA	*n* pl. **-S** a monetary unit of Yemen
BUR	*v* **BURRED, BURRING, BURS** to burr
BURA	*n* pl. **-S** buran
BURAN	*n* pl. **-S** a violent windstorm
BURB	*n* pl. **-S** a suburb
BURBLE	*v* **-BLED, -BLING, -BLES** to speak quickly and excitedly
BURBLER	*n* pl. **-S** one that burbles
BURBLING	*n* pl. **-S** the breaking up of an airflow into turbulence
BURBLY	*adj* **-BLIER, -BLIEST** burbling
BURBOT	*n* pl. **-S** a freshwater fish
BURD	*n* pl. **-S** a maiden
BURDEN	*v* **-ED, -ING, -S** to load heavily
BURDENER	*n* pl. **-S** one that burdens
BURDIE	*n* pl. **-S** burd
BURDOCK	*n* pl. **-S** a coarse weed
BUREAU	*n* pl. **-REAUS** or **-REAUX** a chest of drawers
BURET	*n* pl. **-S** burette
BURETTE	*n* pl. **-S** a measuring tube
BURFI	*n* pl. **-S** a dessert made from milk solids and sugar
BURG	*n* pl. **-S** a city or town
BURGAGE	*n* pl. **-S** a feudal tenure
BURGEE	*n* pl. **-S** a small flag
BURGEON	*v* **-ED, -ING, -S** to develop rapidly
BURGER	*n* pl. **-S** a hamburger
BURGESS	*n* pl. **-ES** a citizen of an English borough
BURGH	*n* pl. **-S** a Scottish borough **BURGHAL** *adj*
BURGHER	*n* pl. **-S** a citizen of a borough
BURGLAR	*n* pl. **-S** one who commits burglary
BURGLARY	*n* pl. **-GLARIES** a felonious theft
BURGLE	*v* **-GLED, -GLING, -GLES** to commit burglary
BURGONET	*n* pl. **-S** an open helmet
BURGOO	*n* pl. **-GOOS** a thick oatmeal
BURGOUT	*n* pl. **-S** burgoo
BURGRAVE	*n* pl. **-S** a German nobleman
BURGUNDY	*n* pl. **-DIES** a red wine
BURIAL	*n* pl. **-S** the act of burying
BURIED	past tense of bury
BURIER	*n* pl. **-S** one that buries
BURIES	present 3d person sing. of bury
BURIN	*n* pl. **-S** an engraving tool
BURK	*n* pl. **-S** berk
BURKA	*n* pl. **-S** a long loose outer garment worn by some Muslim women
BURKE	*v* **BURKED, BURKING, BURKES** to murder by suffocation
BURKER	*n* pl. **-S** one that burkes
BURKHA	*n* pl. **-S** burka
BURKITE	*n* pl. **-S** a burker
BURL	*v* **-ED, -ING, -S** to finish cloth by removing lumps
BURLAP	*n* pl. **-S** a coarse fabric
BURLER	*n* pl. **-S** one that burls
BURLESK	*n* pl. **-S** a type of stage show
BURLEY	*n* pl. **-LEYS** a light tobacco
BURLY	*adj* **-LIER, -LIEST** heavy and muscular **BURLILY** *adv*
BURN	*v* **BURNED** or **BURNT, BURNING, BURNS** to destroy by fire
BURNABLE	*n* pl. **-S** something that can be burned
BURNER	*n* pl. **-S** one that burns
BURNET	*n* pl. **-S** a perennial herb
BURNIE	*n* pl. **-S** a brooklet
BURNING	*n* pl. **-S** the firing of ceramic materials
BURNISH	*v* **-ED, -ING, -ES** to polish
BURNOOSE	*n* pl. **-S** a hooded cloak
BURNOUS	*n* pl. **-ES** burnoose
BURNOUT	*n* pl. **-S** a destructive fire
BURNSIDE	*n* pl. **-S** a mustache and side whiskers on the cheeks
BURNT	a past tense of burn
BURP	*v* **-ED, -ING, -S** to belch
BURPEE	*n* pl. **-S** a physical exercise
BURQA	*n* pl. **-S** burka
BURR	*v* **-ED, -ING, -S** to remove a rough edge from
BURRED	past tense of bur
BURRER	*n* pl. **-S** one that burrs
BURRFISH	*n* pl. **-ES** a fish with erect spines
BURRIER	comparative of burry
BURRIEST	superlative of burry

BURRING	present participle of bur
BURRITO	*n* pl. **-TOS** a tortilla rolled around a filling
BURRO	*n* pl. **-ROS** a small donkey
BURROW	*v* **-ED, -ING, -S** to dig a hole or tunnel in the ground
BURROWER	*n* pl. **-S** one that burrows
BURRY	*adj* **-RIER, -RIEST** prickly
BURSA	*n* pl. **-SAS** or **-SAE** a bodily pouch **BURSAL** *adj*
BURSAR	*n* pl. **-S** a college treasurer
BURSARY	*n* pl. **-RIES** a college treasury
BURSATE	*adj* pertaining to a bursa
BURSE	*n* pl. **-S** a small bag or pouch
BURSEED	*n* pl. **-S** a coarse weed
BURSERA	*adj* designating a family of shrubs and trees
BURSITIS	*n* pl. **-TISES** inflammation of a bursa
BURST	*v* **BURSTED** or **BURST, BURSTING, BURSTS** to break open suddenly or violently
BURSTER	*n* pl. **-S** one that bursts
BURSTONE	*n* pl. **-S** a heavy stone
BURSTY	*adj* **BURSTIER, BURSTIEST** occurring in short sudden episodes or groups
BURTHEN	*v* **-ED, -ING, -S** to burden
BURTON	*n* pl. **-S** a hoisting tackle
BURWEED	*n* pl. **-S** a coarse weed
BURY	*v* **BURIED, BURYING, BURIES** to put in the ground and cover with earth
BUS	*v* **BUSED, BUSING, BUSES** or **BUSSED, BUSSING, BUSSES** to transport by bus (a large motor vehicle)
BUSBAR	*n* pl. **-S** a type of electrical conductor
BUSBOY	*n* pl. **-BOYS** a boy or man who is a server's assistant in a restaurant
BUSBY	*n* pl. **-BIES** a tall fur hat
BUSGIRL	*n* pl. **-S** a girl or woman who is a server's assistant in a restaurant
BUSH	*v* **-ED, -ING, -ES** to cover with bushes (shrubs)
BUSHBABY	*n* pl. **-BIES** a small tree-dwelling primate
BUSHBUCK	*n* pl. **-S** a small antelope

BUSHEL	*v* **-ELED, -ELING, -ELS** or **-ELLED, -ELLING, -ELS** to mend clothing
BUSHELER	*n* pl. **-S** one that bushels
BUSHER	*n* pl. **-S** a minor league baseball player
BUSHFIRE	*n* pl. **-S** a fire in a wooded area
BUSHGOAT	*n* pl. **-S** a bushbuck
BUSHIDO	*n* pl. **-DOS** the code of the samurai
BUSHIER	comparative of bushy
BUSHIES	pl. of bushy
BUSHIEST	superlative of bushy
BUSHILY	*adv* in a bushy manner
BUSHING	*n* pl. **-S** a lining for a hole
BUSHLAND	*n* pl. **-S** unsettled forest land
BUSHLESS	*adj* having no bushes
BUSHLIKE	*adj* resembling a bush
BUSHLOT	*n* pl. **-S** a woodlot
BUSHMAN	*n* pl. **-MEN** a woodsman
BUSHPIG	*n* pl. **-S** a wild African pig
BUSHTIT	*n* pl. **-S** a titmouse
BUSHVELD	*n* pl. **-S** a veld with shrubby vegetation
BUSHWA	*n* pl. **-S** nonsense
BUSHWAH	*n* pl. **-S** bushwa
BUSHY	*adj* **BUSHIER, BUSHIEST** covered with bushes
BUSHY	*n* pl. **BUSHIES** a person who lives in the bush (the wilderness)
BUSIED	past tense of busy
BUSIER	comparative of busy
BUSIES	present 3d person sing. of busy
BUSIEST	superlative of busy
BUSILY	*adv* in a busy manner
BUSINESS	*n* pl. **-ES** an occupation, profession, or trade
BUSING	*n* pl. **-S** the act of transporting by bus
BUSK	*v* **-ED, -ING, -S** to prepare
BUSKER	*n* pl. **-S** a roaming entertainer
BUSKIN	*n* pl. **-S** a high shoe **BUSKINED** *adj*
BUSKING	*n* pl. **-S** the act of performing as a busker
BUSLOAD	*n* pl. **-S** a load that fills a bus
BUSMAN	*n* pl. **-MEN** a bus operator
BUSS	*v* **-ED, -ING, -ES** to kiss

BUSSED	a past tense of bus
BUSSES	a present 3d person sing. of bus
BUSSING	*n* pl. **-S** busing
BUST	*v* **-ED, -ING, -S** to burst
BUSTARD	*n* pl. **-S** a game bird
BUSTEE	*n* pl. **-S** a slum in India
BUSTER	*n* pl. **-S** one that breaks up something
BUSTIC	*n* pl. **-S** a tropical tree
BUSTIER	*n* pl. **-S** a woman's undergarment
BUSTLE	*v* **-TLED, -TLING, -TLES** to move energetically
BUSTLER	*n* pl. **-S** one that bustles
BUSTLINE	*n* pl. **-S** the distance around the bust (the upper torso of a woman)
BUSTY	*adj* **BUSTIER, BUSTIEST** full-bosomed
BUSULFAN	*n* pl. **-S** a medicine
BUSY	*adj* **BUSIER, BUSIEST** occupied
BUSY	*v* **BUSIED, BUSYING, BUSIES** to make busy
BUSYBODY	*n* pl. **-BODIES** a nosy person
BUSYNESS	*n* pl. **-ES** the state of being busy
BUSYWORK	*n* pl. **-S** active but valueless work
BUT	*n* pl. **-S** a flatfish
BUTANE	*n* pl. **-S** a flammable gas
BUTANOL	*n* pl. **-S** a flammable alcohol
BUTANONE	*n* pl. **-S** a flammable ketone
BUTCH	*adj* **-ER, -EST** notably masculine in appearance or manner
BUTCHER	*v* **-ED, -ING, -S** to slaughter
BUTCHERY	*n* pl. **-ERIES** wanton or cruel killing
BUTE	*n* pl. **-S** a drug for treating arthritis
BUTENE	*n* pl. **-S** butylene
BUTEO	*n* pl. **-TEOS** a hawk
BUTLE	*v* **-LED, -LING, -LES** to buttle
BUTLER	*n* pl. **-S** a male servant
BUTLERY	*n* pl. **-LERIES** a storage room
BUTLES	present 3d person sing. of butle
BUTLING	present participle of butle
BUTOH	*n* pl. **-S** a style of modern Japanese dance
BUTT	*v* **-ED, -ING, -S** to hit with the head
BUTTALS	*n/pl* boundary lines
BUTTE	*n* pl. **-S** an isolated hill
BUTTER	*v* **-ED, -ING, -S** to spread with butter (a milk product)
BUTTERY	*adj* **-TERIER, -TERIEST** containing butter
BUTTERY	*n* pl. **-TERIES** a wine cellar
BUTTHEAD	*n* pl. **-S** a stupid person
BUTTIES	pl. of butty
BUTTLE	*v* **-TLED, -TLING, -TLES** to serve as a butler
BUTTOCK	*n* pl. **-S** either of the two rounded parts of the rump
BUTTON	*v* **-ED, -ING, -S** to fasten with a button (a small disk)
BUTTONER	*n* pl. **-S** one that buttons
BUTTONY	*adj* resembling a button
BUTTRESS	*v* **-ED, -ING, -ES** to prop up
BUTTY	*n* pl. **-TIES** a fellow workman
BUTUT	*n* pl. **-S** a monetary unit of Gambia
BUTYL	*n* pl. **-S** a hydrocarbon radical
BUTYLATE	*v* **-ATED, -ATING, -ATES** to add a butyl to
BUTYLENE	*n* pl. **-S** a gaseous hydrocarbon
BUTYRAL	*n* pl. **-S** a chemical compound
BUTYRATE	*n* pl. **-S** a chemical salt
BUTYRIC	*adj* derived from butter
BUTYRIN	*n* pl. **-S** a chemical compound
BUTYROUS	*adj* resembling butter
BUTYRYL	*n* pl. **-S** a radical of butyric acid
BUXOM	*adj* **-OMER, -OMEST** healthily plump **BUXOMLY** *adv*
BUY	*v* **BOUGHT, BUYING, BUYS** to purchase **BUYABLE** *adj*
BUYBACK	*n* pl. **-S** the repurchase by a corporation of its own stock
BUYER	*n* pl. **-S** one that buys
BUYOFF	*n* pl. **-S** a payment for a consideration
BUYOUT	*n* pl. **-S** the purchase of a business
BUZUKI	*n* pl. **-KIS** or **-KIA** bouzouki
BUZZ	*v* **-ED, -ING, -ES** to make a vibrating sound
BUZZARD	*n* pl. **-S** a large bird of prey
BUZZBAIT	*n* pl. **-S** a vibrating fishing lure
BUZZCUT	*n* pl. **-S** a very short haircut
BUZZER	*n* pl. **-S** a signaling device
BUZZIER	comparative of buzzy
BUZZIEST	superlative of buzzy
BUZZING	*n* pl. **-S** a vibrating sound
BUZZKILL	*n* pl. **-S** one that has a depressing or negative effect

BUZZWIG *n* pl. **-S** a large, thick wig

BUZZWORD *n* pl. **-S** a word used to impress someone

BUZZY *adj* **BUZZIER, BUZZIEST** having a vibrating sound

BWANA *n* pl. **-S** master; boss

BY *n* pl. **BYS** a pass in certain card games

BYCATCH *n* pl. **-ES** marine animals caught unintentionally

BYE *n* pl. **-S** a side issue

BYELAW *n* pl. **-S** bylaw

BYGONE *n* pl. **-S** a past occurrence

BYLAW *n* pl. **-S** a secondary law

BYLINE *v* **-LINED, -LINING, -LINES** to write under a byline (a line giving the author's name)

BYLINER *n* pl. **-S** one that writes under a byline

BYNAME *n* pl. **-S** a secondary name

BYPASS *v* **-ED, -ING, -ES** to avoid by going around

BYPAST *adj* past; gone by

BYPATH *n* pl. **-S** an indirect road

BYPLAY *n* pl. **-PLAYS** secondary action

BYRE *n* pl. **-S** a cowshed

BYRL *v* **-ED, -ING, -S** to birle

BYRNIE *n* pl. **-S** an armored shirt

BYROAD *n* pl. **-S** a side road

BYSSUS *n* pl. **BYSSUSES** or **BYSSI** a fine linen **BYSSAL** *adj*

BYSTREET *n* pl. **-S** a side street

BYTALK *n* pl. **-S** small talk

BYTE *n* pl. **-S** a group of adjacent binary digits

BYWAY *n* pl. **-WAYS** a side road

BYWORD *n* pl. **-S** a well-known saying

BYWORK *n* pl. **-S** work done during leisure time

BYZANT *n* pl. **-S** bezant

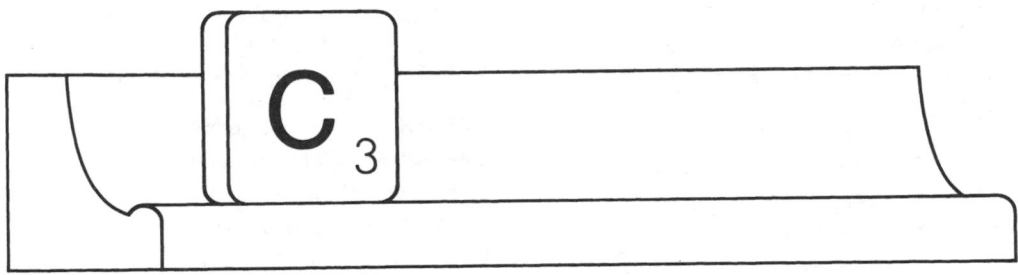

CAB   *v* **CABBED, CABBING, CABS** to take or drive a taxicab

CABAL   *v* **-BALLED, -BALLING, -BALS** to conspire

CABALA   *n* pl. **-S** an occult or secret doctrine

CABALISM   *n* pl. **-S** adherence to a cabala

CABALIST   *n* pl. **-S** one who practices cabalism

CABALLED   past tense of cabal

CABALLING   present participle of cabal

CABANA   *n* pl. **-S** a small cabin

CABARET   *n* pl. **-S** a music hall

CABBAGE   *v* **-BAGED, -BAGING, -BAGES** to steal

CABBAGEY   *adj* resembling a cabbage (a leafy vegetable)

CABBAGY   *adj* cabbagey

CABBALA   *n* pl. **-S** cabala

CABBALAH   *n* pl. **-S** cabala

CABBED   past tense of cab

CABBIE   *n* pl. **-S** cabby

CABBING   present participle of cab

CABBY   *n* pl. **-BIES** a driver of a cab

CABER   *n* pl. **-S** a heavy pole thrown as a trial of strength

CABERNET   *n* pl. **-S** a dry red wine

CABESTRO   *n* pl. **-TROS** a lasso

CABEZON   *n* pl. **-S** a large, edible fish

CABEZONE   *n* pl. **-S** cabezon

CABILDO   *n* pl. **-DOS** a town council

CABIN   *v* **-ED, -ING, -S** to live in a cabin (a roughly built house)

CABINET   *n* pl. **-S** a piece of furniture with shelves and drawers

CABLE   *v* **-BLED, -BLING, -BLES** to fasten with a cable (a heavy rope)

CABLER   *n* pl. **-S** one that supplies a cable

CABLET   *n* pl. **-S** a small cable

CABLEWAY   *n* pl. **-WAYS** a suspended cable

CABLING   *n* pl. **-S** a cable or cables used for fastening something

CABMAN   *n* pl. **-MEN** a driver of a cab

CABOB   *n* pl. **-S** kabob

CABOCHED   *adj* full-faced — used of an animal's head in heraldry

CABOCHON   *n* pl. **-S** a precious stone

CABOMBA   *n* pl. **-S** an aquatic plant

CABOODLE   *n* pl. **-S** a collection

CABOOSE   *n* pl. **-S** the last car of a freight train

CABOSHED   *adj* caboched

CABOTAGE   *n* pl. **-S** coastal trade

CABOVER   *n* pl. **-S** a truck having the driver's compartment over the engine

CABRESTA   *n* pl. **-S** cabestro

CABRESTO   *n* pl. **-TOS** cabestro

CABRETTA   *n* pl. **-S** a soft leather

CABRILLA   *n* pl. **-S** a sea bass

CABRIOLE   *n* pl. **-S** a curved furniture leg

CABSTAND   *n* pl. **-S** a place where cabs await hire

CACA   *n* pl. **-S** excrement

CACAO   *n* pl. **-CAOS** a tropical tree

CACHACA   *n* pl. **-S** a Brazilian liquor

CACHALOT   *n* pl. **-S** a large whale

CACHE   *v* **CACHED, CACHING, CACHES** to store in a hiding place

CACHEPOT   *n* pl. **-S** an ornamental container for a flowerpot

CACHET   *v* **-ED, -ING, -S** to print a design on an envelope

CACHEXIA   *n* pl. **-S** general ill health **CACHEXIC** *adj*

CACHEXY   *n* pl. **-CHEXIES** cachexia

CACHING   present participle of cache

CACHOU	*n* pl. **-S** catechu
CACHUCHA	*n* pl. **-S** a Spanish dance
CACIQUE	*n* pl. **-S** a tropical oriole
CACKLE	*v* **-LED, -LING, -LES** to make the sound of a hen
CACKLER	*n* pl. **-S** one that cackles
CACODYL	*n* pl. **-S** a poisonous liquid
CACOMIXL	*n* pl. **-S** a raccoon-like mammal
CACONYM	*n* pl. **-S** an erroneous name
CACONYMY	*n* pl. **-MIES** the state of having an erroneous name
CACTUS	*n* pl. **-TUSES** or **-TI** a plant native to arid regions **CACTOID** *adj*
CAD	*n* pl. **-S** an ungentlemanly man
CADASTER	*n* pl. **-S** a public record of land ownership
CADASTRE	*n* pl. **-S** cadaster
CADAVER	*n* pl. **-S** a corpse
CADDICE	*n* pl. **-S** caddis
CADDIE	*v* **-DIED, -DYING, -DIES** to serve as a golfer's assistant
CADDIS	*n* pl. **-DISES** a coarse woolen fabric **CADDISED** *adj*
CADDISH	*adj* resembling a cad
CADDY	*v* **-DIED, -DYING, -DIES** to caddie
CADE	*n* pl. **-S** a European shrub
CADELLE	*n* pl. **-S** a small, black beetle
CADENCE	*v* **-DENCED, -DENCING, -DENCES** to make rhythmic
CADENCY	*n* pl. **-CIES** a rhythm
CADENT	*adj* having rhythm
CADENZA	*n* pl. **-S** an elaborate musical passage
CADET	*n* pl. **-S** a student at a military school
CADGE	*v* **CADGED, CADGING, CADGES** to get by begging
CADGER	*n* pl. **-S** one that cadges
CADGY	*adj* cheerful
CADI	*n* pl. **-S** a Muslim judge
CADMIUM	*n* pl. **-S** a metallic element **CADMIC** *adj*
CADRE	*n* pl. **-S** a nucleus of trained personnel
CADUCEUS	*n* pl. **-CEI** a heraldic wand or staff **CADUCEAN** *adj*
CADUCITY	*n* pl. **-TIES** senility
CADUCOUS	*adj* transitory; perishable

CAECUM	*n* pl. **-CA** cecum **CAECAL** *adj* **CAECALLY** *adv*
CAEOMA	*n* pl. **-S** a spore-forming organ of a fungus
CAESAR	*n* pl. **-S** an emperor
CAESIOUS	*adj* bluish green
CAESIUM	*n* pl. **-S** cesium
CAESTUS	*n* pl. **-ES** cestus
CAESURA	*n* pl. **-RAS** or **-RAE** a pause in a line of verse **CAESURAL, CAESURIC** *adj*
CAF	*n* pl. **-S** a cafeteria or cafe
CAFARD	*n* pl. **-S** a state of depression
CAFE	*n* pl. **-S** a small restaurant
CAFF	*n* pl. **-S** a caf
CAFFEIN	*n* pl. **-S** caffeine
CAFFEINE	*n* pl. **-S** a bitter alkaloid used as a stimulant
CAFTAN	*n* pl. **-S** a full-length tunic **CAFTANED** *adj*
CAGE	*v* **CAGED, CAGING, CAGES** to confine
CAGEFUL	*n* pl. **-S** the number held in a cage (an enclosure)
CAGELIKE	*adj* resembling a cage (an enclosure)
CAGELING	*n* pl. **-S** a caged bird
CAGER	*n* pl. **-S** a basketball player
CAGEY	*adj* **CAGIER, CAGIEST** shrewd
CAGIER	comparative of cagy
CAGIEST	superlative of cagy
CAGILY	*adv* in a cagey manner
CAGINESS	*n* pl. **-ES** the quality of being cagey
CAGING	present participle of cage
CAGOULE	*n* pl. **-S** a hooded waterproof garment
CAGY	*adj* **CAGIER, CAGIEST** cagey
CAHIER	*n* pl. **-S** a notebook
CAHOOT	*n* pl. **-S** partnership
CAHOUN	*n* pl. **-S** cohune
CAHOW	*n* pl. **-S** a sea bird
CAID	*n* pl. **-S** a Muslim leader
CAIMAN	*n* pl. **-S** a tropical reptile
CAIN	*n* pl. **-S** kain
CAIQUE	*n* pl. **-S** a long, narrow rowboat
CAIRD	*n* pl. **-S** a gypsy

CAIRN	n pl. **-S** a mound of stones set up as a memorial **CAIRNED, CAIRNY** adj
CAISSON	n pl. **-S** a watertight chamber
CAITIFF	n pl. **-S** a despicable person
CAJAPUT	n pl. **-S** cajeput
CAJEPUT	n pl. **-S** an Australian tree
CAJOLE	v **-JOLED, -JOLING, -JOLES** to persuade by flattery
CAJOLER	n pl. **-S** one that cajoles
CAJOLERY	n pl. **-ERIES** persuasion by flattery
CAJON	n pl. **-ES** a steep-sided canyon
CAJUPUT	n pl. **-S** cajeput
CAKE	v **CAKED, CAKING, CAKES** to form into a hardened mass
CAKEBOX	n pl. **-ES** a container for a cake (a sweet baked food)
CAKEHOLE	n pl. **-S** a person's mouth
CAKEWALK	v **-ED, -ING, -S** to step stylishly
CAKEY	adj **CAKIER, CAKIEST** tending to form lumps
CAKINESS	n pl. **-ES** the state of being cakey
CAKY	adj **CAKIER, CAKIEST** cakey
CALABASH	n pl. **-ES** a gourd
CALABAZA	n pl. **-S** a large winter squash
CALADIUM	n pl. **-S** a tropical plant
CALAMAR	n pl. **-S** calamary
CALAMARI	n pl. **-S** squid used as food
CALAMARY	n pl. **-MARIES** a squid
CALAMATA	n pl. **-S** kalamata
CALAMI	pl. of calamus
CALAMINE	v **-MINED, -MINING, -MINES** to apply an ointment for skin ailments
CALAMINT	n pl. **-S** a perennial herb
CALAMITE	n pl. **-S** an extinct treelike plant
CALAMITY	n pl. **-TIES** a grievous misfortune
CALAMUS	n pl. **-MI** a marsh plant
CALANDO	adj gradually diminishing
CALASH	n pl. **-ES** a light carriage
CALATHEA	n pl. **-S** a plant with colorful leaves
CALATHOS	n pl. **-THI** a fruit basket
CALATHUS	n pl. **-THI** calathos
CALCANEA	n/pl calcanei
CALCANEI	n/pl bones of the heel
CALCAR	n pl. **-CARIA** an anatomical projection
CALCAR	n pl. **-S** a type of oven

CALCEATE	adj wearing shoes
CALCES	a pl. of calx
CALCIC	adj pertaining to lime or calcium
CALCIFIC	adj containing salts of calcium
CALCIFY	v **-FIED, -FYING, -FIES** to harden
CALCINE	v **-CINED, -CINING, -CINES** to reduce to a calx by heat
CALCITE	n pl. **-S** a mineral **CALCITIC** adj
CALCIUM	n pl. **-S** a metallic element
CALCRETE	n pl. **-S** a type of concrete made with calcium carbonate
CALCSPAR	n pl. **-S** a calcite
CALCTUFA	n pl. **-S** a mineral deposit
CALCTUFF	n pl. **-S** calctufa
CALCULUS	n pl. **-LUSES** or **-LI** a branch of mathematics
CALDARIA	n/pl rooms for taking hot baths
CALDERA	n pl. **-S** a large crater
CALDRON	n pl. **-S** a large kettle or boiler
CALECHE	n pl. **-S** calash
CALENDAL	adj pertaining to calends
CALENDAR	v **-ED, -ING, -S** to schedule
CALENDER	v **-ED, -ING, -S** to smooth by pressing between rollers
CALENDS	n pl. **CALENDS** the first day of the Roman month
CALESA	n pl. **-S** a calash
CALF	n pl. **CALVES** or **CALFS** a young cow or bull **CALFLIKE** adj
CALFHOOD	n pl. **-S** the state or time of being a calf
CALFSKIN	n pl. **-S** the skin of a calf
CALIBER	n pl. **-S** the diameter of a gun barrel
CALIBRE	n pl. **-S** caliber **CALIBRED** adj
CALICES	pl. of calix
CALICHE	n pl. **-S** a mineral deposit
CALICLE	n pl. **-S** a cup-shaped anatomical structure
CALICO	n pl. **-COS** or **-COES** a cotton fabric
CALIF	n pl. **-S** caliph
CALIFATE	n pl. **-S** the domain of a calif
CALIPASH	n pl. **-ES** an edible part of a turtle
CALIPEE	n pl. **-S** an edible part of a turtle
CALIPER	v **-ED, -ING, -S** to use a type of measuring device

CALIPH *n* pl. **-S** a Muslim leader **CALIPHAL** *adj*

CALISAYA *n* pl. **-S** the medicinal bark of the cinchona

CALIX *n* pl. **-LICES** or **-LIXES** a cup

CALK *v* **-ED, -ING, -S** to caulk

CALKER *n* pl. **-S** one that calks

CALKIN *n* pl. **-S** a gripping projection on a horseshoe

CALKING *n* pl. **-S** material used to calk

CALL *v* **-ED, -ING, -S** to summon **CALLABLE** *adj*

CALLA *n* pl. **-S** a tropical plant

CALLALOO *n* pl. **-LOOS** a crabmeat soup

CALLALOU *n* pl. **-S** callaloo

CALLAN *n* pl. **-S** callant

CALLANT *n* pl. **-S** a lad

CALLBACK *n* pl. **-S** a recall of a defective product

CALLBOY *n* pl. **-BOYS** a bellboy

CALLEE *n* pl. **-S** one that is called

CALLER *n* pl. **-S** one that calls

CALLET *n* pl. **-S** a prostitute

CALLING *n* pl. **-S** a vocation or profession

CALLIOPE *n* pl. **-S** a keyboard musical instrument

CALLIPEE *n* pl. **-S** calipee

CALLIPER *v* **-ED, -ING, -S** to caliper

CALLOSE *n* pl. **-S** a part of a plant cell wall

CALLOUS *v* **-ED, -ING, -ES** to make or become hard

CALLOUT *n* pl. **-S** an inset in a printed article

CALLOW *adj* **-LOWER, -LOWEST** immature **CALLOWLY** *adv*

CALLUNA *n* pl. **-S** an evergreen shrub

CALLUS *v* **-ED, -ING, -ES** to form a hard growth

CALM *adj* **CALMER, CALMEST** free from agitation **CALMLY** *adv*

CALM *v* **-ED, -ING, -S** to make calm

CALMNESS *n* pl. **-ES** the state of being calm

CALO *n* pl. **-LOS** a Spanish argot used by Chicano youths

CALOMEL *n* pl. **-S** a chemical compound used as a purgative

CALORIC *n* pl. **-S** heat

CALORIE *n* pl. **-S** a unit of heat

CALORIZE *v* **-RIZED, -RIZING, -RIZES** to coat steel with aluminum

CALORY *n* pl. **-RIES** calorie

CALOTTE *n* pl. **-S** a skullcap

CALOTYPE *n* pl. **-S** a kind of photograph

CALOYER *n* pl. **-S** a monk of the Eastern Church

CALPAC *n* pl. **-S** a sheepskin hat

CALPACK *n* pl. **-S** calpac

CALPAIN *n* pl. **-S** an enzyme for digesting proteins

CALQUE *v* **CALQUED, CALQUING, CALQUES** to model a word's meaning upon that of an analogous word in another language

CALTHROP *n* pl. **-S** caltrop

CALTRAP *n* pl. **-S** caltrop

CALTROP *n* pl. **-S** a spiny plant

CALUMET *n* pl. **-S** a ceremonial pipe

CALUMNY *v* **-NIED, -NYING, -NIES** to make a false and malicious accusation

CALUTRON *n* pl. **-S** a device used for separating isotopes

CALVADOS *n* pl. **-ES** a dry apple brandy

CALVARIA *n* pl. **-IAE** or **-IAS** the dome of the skull

CALVARY *n* pl. **-RIES** a representation of the Crucifixion

CALVE *v* **CALVED, CALVING, CALVES** to give birth to a calf

CALVES a pl. of calf

CALX *n* pl. **CALXES** or **CALCES** a mineral residue

CALYCATE *adj* calycine

CALYCEAL *adj* calycine

CALYCES a pl. of calyx

CALYCINE *adj* pertaining to a calyx

CALYCLE *n* pl. **-S** an outer calyx

CALYCULI *n/pl* small, cup-shaped structures

CALYPSO *n* pl. **-SOS** or **-SOES** an improvised song

CALYPTER *n* pl. **-S** calyptra

CALYPTRA *n* pl. **-S** a hood-shaped organ of flowers

CALYX *n* pl. **-LYXES** or **-LYCES** the outer protective covering of a flower

CALZONE *n* pl. **-NES** or **-NI** a turnover with a savory filling

CAM *n* pl. **-S** a rotating or sliding piece of machinery

CAMAIL *n* pl. **-S** a piece of armor for the neck **CAMAILED** *adj*

CAMAS *n* pl. **-ES** camass

CAMASS *n* pl. **-ES** a perennial herb

CAMBER *v* **-ED, -ING, -S** to arch slightly

CAMBIA a pl. of cambium

CAMBIAL *adj* pertaining to cambium

CAMBISM *n* pl. **-S** the theory and practice of exchange in commerce

CAMBIST *n* pl. **-S** a dealer in bills of exchange

CAMBIUM *n* pl. **-BIUMS** or **-BIA** a layer of plant tissue

CAMBOGIA *n* pl. **-S** a gum resin

CAMBOOSE *n* pl. **-S** a large cabin at a logging camp

CAMBRIC *n* pl. **-S** a fine linen

CAMCORD *v* **-ED, -ING, -S** to videotape with a portable camera

CAME *n* pl. **-S** a leaden window rod

CAMEL *n* pl. **-S** a large, humped mammal

CAMELEER *n* pl. **-S** a camel driver

CAMELIA *n* pl. **-S** camellia

CAMELID *n* pl. **-S** any of a family of 2-toed ruminant mammals

CAMELLIA *n* pl. **-S** a tropical shrub

CAMEO *v* **-ED, -ING, -S** to portray in sharp, delicate relief

CAMERA *n* pl. **-ERAS** or **-ERAE** a judge's chamber **CAMERAL** *adj*

CAMI *n* pl. **-S** a camisole

CAMION *n* pl. **-S** a military truck

CAMISA *n* pl. **-S** a shirt or chemise

CAMISADE *n* pl. **-S** camisado

CAMISADO *n* pl. **-DOS** or **-DOES** an attack made at night

CAMISE *n* pl. **-S** a loose shirt or gown

CAMISIA *n* pl. **-S** camise

CAMISOLE *n* pl. **-S** a brief negligee

CAMLET *n* pl. **-S** a durable fabric

CAMMIE *n* pl. **-S** camouflage

CAMO *n* pl. **CAMOS** a camouflage pattern

CAMOMILE *n* pl. **-S** a medicinal herb

CAMORRA *n* pl. **-S** an unscrupulous secret society

CAMP *v* **-ED, -ING, -S** to live in the open

CAMPAGNA *n* pl. **-PAGNE** a flat, open plain

CAMPAIGN *v* **-ED, -ING, -S** to conduct a series of operations to reach a specific goal

CAMPER *n* pl. **-S** one that camps

CAMPFIRE *n* pl. **-S** an outdoor fire

CAMPHENE *n* pl. **-S** camphine

CAMPHINE *n* pl. **-S** an explosive liquid

CAMPHIRE *n* pl. **-S** a flowering plant

CAMPHOL *n* pl. **-S** borneol

CAMPHOR *n* pl. **-S** a volatile compound

CAMPI pl. of campo

CAMPIER comparative of campy

CAMPIEST superlative of campy

CAMPILY *adv* in a campy manner

CAMPING *n* pl. **-S** the act of living outdoors

CAMPION *n* pl. **-S** an herb

CAMPO *n* pl. **-PI** an open space in a town

CAMPO *n* pl. **-POS** a level, grassy plain

CAMPONG *n* pl. **-S** kampong

CAMPOREE *n* pl. **-S** a gathering of Boy Scouts

CAMPOUT *n* pl. **-S** a camping out by a group

CAMPSITE *n* pl. **-S** an area suitable for camping

CAMPUS *v* **-ED, -ING, -ES** to restrict a student to the school grounds

CAMPY *adj* **CAMPIER, CAMPIEST** comically exaggerated

CAMSHAFT *n* pl. **-S** a shaft fitted with cams

CAMWOOD *n* pl. **-S** an African hardwood tree

CAN *v* **CANNED, CANNING, CANS** to put in a can (a cylindrical container)

CAN *v* present sing. 2d person **CAN** or **CANST**, past sing. 2d person **COULD** or **COULDEST** or **COULDST** — used as an auxiliary to express ability

CANAILLE *n* pl. **-S** the common people

CANAKIN *n* pl. **-S** cannikin

CANAL *v* **-NALLED, -NALLING, -NALS** or **-NALED, -NALING, -NALS** to dig an artificial waterway through

CANALISE *v* **-ISED, -ISING, -ISES** to canalize

CANALIZE *v* **-IZED, -IZING, -IZES** to canal

CANALLER *n* pl. **-S** a freight boat

CANALLING a present participle of canal

CANAPE *n* pl. **-S** a food served before a meal

CANARD *n* pl. **-S** a false story

CANARY *n* pl. **-NARIES** a songbird

CANASTA *n* pl. **-S** a card game

CANCAN *n* pl. **-S** a dance marked by high kicking

CANCEL *v* **-CELED, -CELING, -CELS** or **-CELLED, -CELLING, -CELS** to annul

CANCELER *n* pl. **-S** one that cancels

CANCER *n* pl. **-S** a malignant growth **CANCERED** *adj*

CANCHA *n* pl. **-S** a jai alai court

CANCROID *n* pl. **-S** a skin cancer

CANDELA *n* pl. **-S** a unit of light intensity

CANDENT *adj* glowing

CANDID *adj* **-DIDER, -DIDEST** frank and sincere

CANDID *n* pl. **-S** an unposed photograph

CANDIDA *n* pl. **-S** a parasitic fungus **CANDIDAL** *adj*

CANDIDLY *adv* in a candid manner

CANDIED past tense of candy

CANDIES present 3d person sing. of candy

CANDLE *v* **-DLED, -DLING, -DLES** to examine eggs in front of a light

CANDLER *n* pl. **-S** one that candles

CANDOR *n* pl. **-S** frankness; sincerity

CANDOUR *n* pl. **-S** candor

CANDY *v* **-DIED, -DYING, -DIES** to coat with sugar

CANDYMAN *n* pl. **-MEN** one who sells illegal drugs

CANE *v* **CANED, CANING, CANES** to weave or furnish with cane (hollow woody stems)

CANELLA *n* pl. **-S** a medicinal tree bark

CANEPHOR *n* pl. **-S** a Greek maiden bearing a basket on her head

CANER *n* pl. **-S** one that canes

CANEWARE *n* pl. **-S** a yellowish stoneware

CANFIELD *n* pl. **-S** a card game

CANFUL *n* pl. **CANFULS** or **CANSFUL** as much as a can holds

CANGUE *n* pl. **-S** an ancient Chinese punishing device

CANID *n* pl. **-S** any member of the dog family Canidae

CANIKIN *n* pl. **-S** cannikin

CANINE *n* pl. **-S** a dog

CANING *n* pl. **-S** punishment with a cane

CANINITY *n* pl. **-TIES** the state of being a canine

CANISTEL *n* pl. **-S** a tropical tree

CANISTER *n* pl. **-S** a small, metal box

CANITIES *n* pl. **CANITIES** the turning gray of the hair

CANKER *v* **-ED, -ING, -S** to affect with ulcerous sores

CANKLE *n* pl. **-S** a thick ankle

CANNA *n* pl. **-S** a tropical plant

CANNABIC *adj* pertaining to cannabis

CANNABIN *n* pl. **-S** a resin extracted from cannabis

CANNABIS *n* pl. **-BISES** hemp

CANNED past tense of can

CANNEL *n* pl. **-S** an oily, compact coal

CANNELON *n* pl. **-S** a stuffed roll

CANNER *n* pl. **-S** one that cans food

CANNERY *n* pl. **-NERIES** a place where food is canned

CANNIBAL *n* pl. **-S** one that eats its own kind

CANNIE *adj* **-NIER, -NIEST** canny

CANNIER comparative of canny

CANNIEST superlative of canny

CANNIKIN *n* pl. **-S** a small can or cup

CANNILY *adv* in a canny manner

CANNING *n* pl. **-S** the business of preserving food in airtight containers

CANNOLI *n* pl. **-S** a tube of pastry with a sweet filling

CANNON *v* **-ED, -ING, -S** to fire a cannon (a heavy firearm)

CANNONRY *n* pl. **-RIES** artillery

CANNOT the negative form of can

CANNULA *n* pl. **-LAS** or **-LAE** a tube inserted into a bodily cavity **CANNULAR** *adj*

CANNY *adj* **-NIER, -NIEST** prudent

CANOE *v* **-NOED, -NOEING, -NOES** to paddle a canoe (a light, slender boat)

CANOEING *n* pl. **-S** the action or sport of paddling a canoe

CANOEIST *n* pl. **-S** one who canoes

CANOEMAN *n* pl. **-MEN** a canoeist

CANOER	*n* pl. **-S** one who canoes
CANOLA	*n* pl. **-S** an oil from the seeds of a kind of herb
CANON	*n* pl. **-S** a law decreed by a church council **CANONIC** *adj*
CANONESS	*n* pl. **-ES** a woman who lives according to a canon
CANONISE	*v* **-ISED, -ISING, -ISES** to canonize
CANONIST	*n* pl. **-S** a specialist in canon law
CANONIZE	*v* **-IZED, -IZING, -IZES** to declare to be a saint
CANONRY	*n* pl. **-RIES** a clerical office
CANOODLE	*v* **-DLED, -DLING, -DLES** to caress
CANOPIC	*adj* pertaining to an Egyptian jar
CANOPY	*v* **-PIED, -PYING, -PIES** to cover from above
CANOROUS	*adj* melodic
CANSFUL	a pl. of canful
CANSO	*n* pl. **-SOS** a love song
CANST	a present 2d person sing. of can
CANT	*v* **-ED, -ING, -S** to tilt or slant
CANTAL	*n* pl. **-S** a hard cheese of France
CANTALA	*n* pl. **-S** a tropical plant
CANTATA	*n* pl. **-S** a vocal composition
CANTDOG	*n* pl. **-S** a device used to move logs
CANTEEN	*n* pl. **-S** a small container for carrying water
CANTER	*v* **-ED, -ING, -S** to ride a horse at a moderate pace
CANTHARI	*n/pl* two-handled drinking cups
CANTHUS	*n* pl. **-THI** a corner of the eye **CANTHAL, CANTHIC** *adj*
CANTIC	*adj* slanted
CANTICLE	*n* pl. **-S** a hymn
CANTINA	*n* pl. **-S** a saloon
CANTLE	*n* pl. **-S** the rear part of a saddle
CANTO	*n* pl. **-TOS** a division of a long poem
CANTON	*v* **-ED, -ING, -S** to divide into cantons (districts)
CANTONAL	*adj* pertaining to a canton
CANTOR	*n* pl. **-S** a religious singer
CANTORIS	*adj* to be sung by the north side of the choir in a church
CANTRAIP	*n* pl. **-S** cantrip
CANTRAP	*n* pl. **-S** cantrip
CANTRIP	*n* pl. **-S** a magic spell

CANTUS	*n* pl. **CANTUS** a style of church music
CANTY	*adj* cheerful
CANULA	*n* pl. **-LAS** or **-LAE** cannula **CANULAR** *adj*
CANULATE	*v* **-LATED, -LATING, -LATES** to insert a canula into
CANVAS	*v* **-ED, -ING, -ES** to canvass
CANVASER	*n* pl. **-S** one that canvases
CANVASS	*v* **-ED, -ING, -ES** to examine thoroughly
CANYON	*n* pl. **-S** a deep valley with steep sides
CANZONA	*n* pl. **-S** canzone
CANZONE	*n* pl. **-NES** or **-NI** a form of lyric poetry
CANZONET	*n* pl. **-S** a short song
CAP	*v* **CAPPED, CAPPING, CAPS** to provide with a cap (a type of head covering)
CAPABLE	*adj* **-BLER, -BLEST** having ability **CAPABLY** *adv*
CAPACITY	*n* pl. **-TIES** the ability to receive or contain
CAPCOM	*n* pl. **-S** a person who assists a space mission
CAPE	*v* **CAPED, CAPING, CAPES** to skin the head and neck of an animal
CAPEESH	*v* to capisce — used interrogatively without inflection
CAPELAN	*n* pl. **-S** capelin
CAPELET	*n* pl. **-S** a small cape
CAPELIN	*n* pl. **-S** a small, edible fish
CAPER	*v* **-ED, -ING, -S** to frolic
CAPERER	*n* pl. **-S** one that capers
CAPESKIN	*n* pl. **-S** a soft leather
CAPEWORK	*n* pl. **-S** a bullfighting technique
CAPFUL	*n* pl. **-S** as much as a cap can hold
CAPH	*n* pl. **-S** kaph
CAPIAS	*n* pl. **-ES** a judicial writ
CAPICHE	*v* to capisce — used interrogatively without inflection
CAPING	present participle of cape
CAPISCE	*v* to understand — used interrogatively without inflection
CAPISH	*v* to capisce — used interrogatively without inflection
CAPITA	pl. of caput
CAPITAL	*n* pl. **-S** the upper part of a column

CAPITATE *n* pl. **-S** a bone of the wrist of primates

CAPITOL *n* pl. **-S** a building occupied by a state legislature

CAPITULA *n/pl* flower clusters

CAPIZ *n* pl. **-ES** a bivalve mollusk

CAPLESS *adj* being without a cap

CAPLET *n* pl. **-S** a coated tablet

CAPLIN *n* pl. **-S** capelin

CAPMAKER *n* pl. **-S** one that makes caps

CAPO *n* pl. **-POS** a pitch-raising device for fretted instruments

CAPOEIRA *n* pl. **-S** a Brazilian dance

CAPON *n* pl. **-S** a gelded rooster

CAPONATA *n* pl. **-S** a relish made with eggplant

CAPONIER *n* pl. **-S** a type of defense

CAPONISE *v* **-ISED, -ISING, -ISES** to caponize

CAPONIZE *v* **-IZED, -IZING, -IZES** to geld a rooster

CAPORAL *n* pl. **-S** a coarse tobacco

CAPOT *n* pl. **-S** a capote

CAPOTE *n* pl. **-S** a hooded cloak or overcoat

CAPOUCH *n* pl. **-ES** capuche

CAPPED past tense of cap

CAPPER *n* pl. **-S** a capmaker

CAPPING *n* pl. **-S** a wax covering in a honeycomb

CAPRESE *n* pl. **-S** a salad containing mozzarella, tomatoes, basil, and olive oil

CAPRI *n* pl. **-S** a woman's tapered pants

CAPRIC *adj* pertaining to a goat

CAPRICCI *n/pl* caprices

CAPRICE *n* pl. **-S** a whim

CAPRIFIG *n* pl. **-S** a European tree

CAPRINE *adj* capric

CAPRIOLE *v* **-OLED, -OLING, -OLES** to leap

CAPRIS *n/pl* pants for women

CAPROCK *n* pl. **-S** an overlying rock layer

CAPSICIN *n* pl. **-S** a liquid used as a flavoring

CAPSICUM *n* pl. **-S** a tropical herb

CAPSID *n* pl. **-S** the outer shell of a virus particle **CAPSIDAL** *adj*

CAPSIZE *v* **-SIZED, -SIZING, -SIZES** to overturn

CAPSOMER *n* pl. **-S** a protein forming the capsid

CAPSTAN *n* pl. **-S** a machine used to hoist weights

CAPSTONE *n* pl. **-S** the top stone of a structure

CAPSULAR *adj* enclosed and compact

CAPSULE *v* **-SULED, -SULING, -SULES** to condense into a brief form

CAPTAIN *v* **-ED, -ING, -S** to lead or command

CAPTAN *n* pl. **-S** a fungicide

CAPTCHA *n* pl. **-S** a test that must be done to access a website

CAPTION *v* **-ED, -ING, -S** to provide with a title

CAPTIOUS *adj* tending to find fault

CAPTIVE *n* pl. **-S** a prisoner

CAPTOR *n* pl. **-S** one who takes or holds a captive

CAPTURE *v* **-TURED, -TURING, -TURES** to take by force or cunning

CAPTURER *n* pl. **-S** one that captures

CAPUCHE *n* pl. **-S** a hood or cowl **CAPUCHED** *adj*

CAPUCHIN *n* pl. **-S** a long-tailed monkey

CAPUT *n* pl. **CAPITA** a head or head-like part

CAPYBARA *n* pl. **-S** a large rodent

CAR *n* pl. **-S** an automobile

CARABAO *n* pl. **-BAOS** a water buffalo

CARABID *n* pl. **-S** a predatory beetle

CARABIN *n* pl. **-S** carbine

CARABINE *n* pl. **-S** carbine

CARACAL *n* pl. **-S** an African lynx

CARACARA *n* pl. **-S** a large hawk

CARACK *n* pl. **-S** carrack

CARACOL *v* **-COLLED, -COLLING, -COLS** to caracole

CARACOLE *v* **-COLED, -COLING, -COLES** to perform a half turn on a horse

CARACUL *n* pl. **-S** karakul

CARAFE *n* pl. **-S** a glass bottle

CARAGANA *n* pl. **-S** an Asian shrub

CARAGEEN *n* pl. **-S** an edible seaweed

CARAMBA *interj* — used to express surprise or dismay

CARAMEL *n* pl. **-S** a chewy candy

CARANGID *n* pl. **-S** a marine fish

CARAPACE *n* pl. **-S** a hard, protective outer covering

CARAPAX *n pl.* **-ES** carapace

CARASSOW *n pl.* **-S** curassow

CARAT *n pl.* **-S** a unit of weight for gems

CARATE *n pl.* **-S** a tropical skin disease

CARAVAN *v* **-VANED, -VANING, -VANS** or **-VANNED, -VANNING, -VANS** to travel in a group

CARAVEL *n pl.* **-S** a small sailing ship

CARAWAY *n pl.* **-WAYS** an herb used in cooking

CARB *n pl.* **-S** a carburetor

CARBAMIC *adj* pertaining to a type of acid

CARBAMYL *n pl.* **-S** a chemical radical

CARBARN *n pl.* **-S** a garage for buses

CARBARYL *n pl.* **-S** an insecticide

CARBIDE *n pl.* **-S** a carbon compound

CARBINE *n pl.* **-S** a light rifle

CARBINOL *n pl.* **-S** an alcohol

CARBO *n pl.* **-BOS** a carbohydrate

CARBOLIC *n pl.* **-S** an acidic compound

CARBON *n pl.* **-S** a nonmetallic element **CARBONIC** *adj*

CARBONYL *n pl.* **-S** a chemical compound

CARBORA *n pl.* **-S** a wood-boring worm

CARBOXYL *n pl.* **-S** a univalent acid radical

CARBOY *n pl.* **-BOYS** a large bottle **CARBOYED** *adj*

CARBURET *v* **-RETED, -RETING, -RETS** or **-RETTED, -RETTING, -RETS** to combine chemically with carbon

CARCAJOU *n pl.* **-S** a carnivorous mammal

CARCANET *n pl.* **-S** a jeweled necklace

CARCASE *n pl.* **-S** carcass

CARCASS *n pl.* **-ES** the body of a dead animal

CARCEL *n pl.* **-S** a unit of illumination

CARCERAL *adj* pertaining to a prison

CARD *v* **-ED, -ING, -S** to provide with a card (a stiff piece of paper)

CARDAMOM *n pl.* **-S** a tropical herb

CARDAMON *n pl.* **-S** cardamom

CARDAMUM *n pl.* **-S** cardamom

CARDCASE *n pl.* **-S** a case for holding cards

CARDER *n pl.* **-S** one that does carding

CARDIA *n pl.* **-DIAS** or **-DIAE** an opening of the esophagus

CARDIAC *n pl.* **-S** a person with a heart disorder

CARDIGAN *n pl.* **-S** a type of sweater

CARDINAL *n pl.* **-S** a bright red bird

CARDING *n pl.* **-S** the process of combing and cleaning cotton fibers; cleaned and combed fibers

CARDIO *n pl.* **-DIOS** an exercise involving the heart and blood vessels

CARDIOID *n pl.* **-S** a heart-shaped curve

CARDITIS *n pl.* **-TISES** inflammation of the heart **CARDITIC** *adj*

CARDON *n pl.* **-S** cardoon

CARDOON *n pl.* **-S** a perennial plant

CARE *v* **CARED, CARING, CARES** to be concerned or interested

CAREEN *v* **-ED, -ING, -S** to lurch while moving

CAREENER *n pl.* **-S** one that careens

CAREER *v* **-ED, -ING, -S** to go at full speed

CAREERER *n pl.* **-S** one that careers

CAREFREE *adj* being without worry or anxiety

CAREFUL *adj* **-FULLER, -FULLEST** cautious

CARELESS *adj* inattentive; negligent

CARER *n pl.* **-S** one that cares

CARESS *v* **-ED, -ING, -ES** to touch lovingly

CARESSER *n pl.* **-S** one that caresses

CARET *n pl.* **-S** a proofreaders' symbol

CARETAKE *v* **-TOOK, -TAKEN, -TAKING, -TAKES** to take care of someone else's house or land

CAREWORN *adj* haggard

CAREX *n pl.* **CARICES** a marsh plant

CARFARE *n pl.* **-S** payment for a bus or car ride

CARFUL *n pl.* **-S** as much as a car can hold

CARGO *n pl.* **-GOS** or **-GOES** conveyed merchandise

CARHOP *v* **-HOPPED, -HOPPING, -HOPS** to serve customers at a drive-in restaurant

CARIBE *n pl.* **-S** the piranha

CARIBOO *n pl.* **-BOOS** a caribou

CARIBOU *n pl.* **-S** a large deer

CARICES pl. of carex

CARIES *n pl.* **CARIES** tooth decay **CARIED** *adj*

CARILLON *v* **-LONNED, -LONNING, -LONS** to play a set of bells

CARINA *n pl.* **-NAS** or **-NAE** a carinate anatomical part **CARINAL** *adj*

CARINATE *adj* shaped like the keel of a ship

CARING *n* pl. **-S** the work of looking after someone

CARINGLY *adv* in a caring manner

CARIOCA *n* pl. **-S** a South American dance

CARIOLE *n* pl. **-S** a small, open carriage

CARIOUS *adj* decayed

CARITAS *n* pl. **-ES** love for all people

CARJACK *v* **-ED, -ING, -S** to steal a vehicle from its driver by force

CARK *v* **-ED, -ING, -S** to worry

CARL *n* pl. **-S** a peasant

CARLE *n* pl. **-S** carl

CARLESS *adj* being without a car

CARLIN *n* pl. **-S** an old woman

CARLINE *n* pl. **-S** carling

CARLING *n* pl. **-S** a beam supporting a ship's deck

CARLISH *adj* resembling a carl

CARLOAD *n* pl. **-S** as much as a car can hold

CARMAKER *n* pl. **-S** an automobile manufacturer

CARMAN *n* pl. **-MEN** a streetcar driver

CARMINE *n* pl. **-S** a vivid red color

CARN *n* pl. **-S** cairn

CARNAGE *n* pl. **-S** great and bloody slaughter

CARNAL *adj* pertaining to bodily appetites **CARNALLY** *adv*

CARNAUBA *n* pl. **-S** a palm tree

CARNET *n* pl. **-S** an official permit

CARNEY *n* pl. **-NEYS** carny

CARNIE *n* pl. **-S** carny

CARNIES pl. of carny

CARNIFY *v* **-FIED, -FYING, -FIES** to form into flesh

CARNIVAL *n* pl. **-S** a traveling amusement show

CARNY *n* pl. **-NIES** a carnival

CAROACH *n* pl. **-ES** caroche

CAROB *n* pl. **-S** an evergreen tree

CAROCH *n* pl. **-ES** caroche

CAROCHE *n* pl. **-S** a stately carriage

CAROL *v* **-OLED, -OLING, -OLS** or **-OLLED, -OLLING, -OLS** to sing joyously

CAROLER *n* pl. **-S** one that carols

CAROLI a pl. of carolus

CAROLING *n* pl. **-S** the act of singing joyously

CAROLLER *n* pl. **-S** caroler

CAROLLING a present participle of carol

CAROLUS *n* pl. **-LUSES** or **-LI** an old English coin

CAROM *v* **-ED, -ING, -S** to collide with and rebound

CAROTENE *n* pl. **-S** a plant pigment

CAROTID *n* pl. **-S** an artery in the neck

CAROTIN *n* pl. **-S** carotene

CAROUSAL *n* pl. **-S** a boisterous drinking party

CAROUSE *v* **-ROUSED, -ROUSING, -ROUSES** to engage in a carousal

CAROUSEL *n* pl. **-S** an amusement park ride

CAROUSER *n* pl. **-S** one that carouses

CAROUSING present participle of carouse

CARP *v* **-ED, -ING, -S** to find fault unreasonably

CARPAL *n* pl. **-S** carpale

CARPALE *n* pl. **-LIA** a bone of the wrist

CARPEL *n* pl. **-S** a simple pistil

CARPER *n* pl. **-S** one that carps

CARPET *v* **-ED, -ING, -S** to cover a floor with a heavy fabric

CARPI pl. of carpus

CARPING *n* pl. **-S** the act of one who carps

CARPOOL *v* **-ED, -ING, -S** to take turns driving a group of commuters

CARPORT *n* pl. **-S** a shelter for a car

CARPUS *n* pl. **-PI** the wrist

CARR *n* pl. **-S** a marsh

CARRACK *n* pl. **-S** a type of merchant ship

CARREL *n* pl. **-S** a desk in a library stack for solitary study

CARRELL *n* pl. **-S** carrel

CARRIAGE *n* pl. **-S** a wheeled, horse-drawn vehicle

CARRIED past tense of carry

CARRIER *n* pl. **-S** one that carries

CARRIES present 3d person sing. of carry

CARRIOLE *n* pl. **-S** cariole

CARRION *n* pl. **-S** dead and putrefying flesh

CARRITCH *n* pl. **-ES** a religious handbook

CARROCH *n* pl. **-ES** caroche

CARROM *v* **-ED, -ING, -S** to carom

CARROT *n* pl. **-S** an edible orange root

CARROTIN *n* pl. **-S** carotene

CARROTY *adj* **-ROTIER, -ROTIEST** resembling a carrot in color

CARRY *v* **-RIED, -RYING, -RIES** to convey from one place to another

CARRYALL *n* pl. **-S** a light covered carriage

CARRYCOT *n* pl. **-S** a portable baby's cot

CARRYON *n* pl. **-S** a small piece of luggage

CARRYOUT *n* pl. **-S** a take-out order of food

CARSE *n* pl. **-S** low, fertile land along a river

CARSICK *adj* nauseated from riding in a car

CARSPIEL *n* pl. **-S** a curling match in which curlers compete for a car

CART *v* **-ED, -ING, -S** to convey in a cart (a two-wheeled vehicle) **CARTABLE** *adj*

CARTAGE *n* pl. **-S** the act of carting

CARTE *n* pl. **-S** a menu

CARTEL *n* pl. **-S** a business organization

CARTER *n* pl. **-S** one that carts

CARTFUL *n* pl. **-S** a cartload

CARTLOAD *n* pl. **-S** as much as a cart can hold

CARTON *v* **-ED, -ING, -S** to pack in a cardboard box

CARTOON *v* **-ED, -ING, -S** to sketch a cartoon (a humorous representation) of

CARTOONY *adj* resembling a cartoon

CARTOP *adj* able to fit on top of a car

CARTOUCH *n* pl. **-ES** a scroll-like tablet

CARUNCLE *n* pl. **-S** a fleshy outgrowth

CARVE *v* **CARVED, CARVING, CARVES** to form by cutting

CARVEL *n* pl. **-S** caravel

CARVEN *adj* carved

CARVER *n* pl. **-S** one that carves

CARVERY *n* pl. **-ERIES** a buffet restaurant serving roast beef

CARVING *n* pl. **-S** a carved figure or design

CARWASH *n* pl. **-ES** an establishment equipped to wash automobiles

CARYATIC *adj* resembling a caryatid

CARYATID *n* pl. **-S** or **-ES** a sculptured female figure used as a column

CARYOTIN *n* pl. **-S** karyotin

CASA *n* pl. **-S** a dwelling

CASABA *n* pl. **-S** a variety of melon

CASAVA *n* pl. **-S** cassava

CASBAH *n* pl. **-S** the old section of a North African city

CASCABEL *n* pl. **-S** the rear part of a cannon

CASCABLE *n* pl. **-S** cascabel

CASCADE *v* **-CADED, -CADING, -CADES** to fall like a waterfall

CASCARA *n* pl. **-S** a medicinal tree bark

CASE *v* **CASED, CASING, CASES** to put in a case (a container or receptacle)

CASEASE *n* pl. **-S** an enzyme

CASEATE *v* **-ATED, -ATING, -ATES** to become cheesy

CASEBOOK *n* pl. **-S** a law textbook

CASED past tense of case

CASEFY *v* **-FIED, -FYING, -FIES** to caseate

CASEIN *n* pl. **-S** a milk protein **CASEIC** *adj*

CASELAW *n* pl. **-S** a law established by previous cases

CASELOAD *n* pl. **-S** the number of cases being handled

CASEMATE *n* pl. **-S** a bombproof shelter

CASEMENT *n* pl. **-S** a type of window

CASEOSE *n* pl. **-S** a proteose

CASEOUS *adj* cheesy

CASERN *n* pl. **-S** a barracks for soldiers

CASERNE *n* pl. **-S** casern

CASETTE *n* pl. **-S** cassette

CASEWORK *n* pl. **-S** a form of social work

CASEWORM *n* pl. **-S** an insect larva

CASH *v* **-ED, -ING, -ES** to convert into cash (ready money) **CASHABLE** *adj*

CASHAW *n* pl. **-S** cushaw

CASHBACK *n* pl. **-S** an incentive of cash given back to a purchaser

CASHBOOK *n* pl. **-S** a book of monetary records

CASHBOX *n* pl. **-ES** a container for money

CASHEW *n* pl. **-S** a nut-bearing tree

CASHIER *v* **-ED, -ING, -S** to dismiss in disgrace

CASHLESS *adj* having no cash

CASHMERE *n* pl. **-S** a fine wool

CASHOO *n* pl. **-SHOOS** catechu

CASIMERE *n* pl. **-S** a woolen fabric

CASIMIRE *n* pl. **-S** casimere

CASING *n* pl. **-S** a protective outer covering

CASINO   *n* pl. **-NOS** or **-NI** a gambling room

CASITA   *n* pl. **-S** a small house

CASK   *v* **-ED, -ING, -S** to store in a cask (a strong barrel)

CASKET   *v* **-ED, -ING, -S** to place in a casket (a burial case)

CASKY   *adj* resembling a cask

CASQUE   *n* pl. **-S** a helmet **CASQUED** *adj*

CASSABA   *n* pl. **-S** casaba

CASSATA   *n* pl. **-S** an Italian ice cream

CASSAVA   *n* pl. **-S** a tropical plant

CASSENA   *n* pl. **-S** cassina

CASSENE   *n* pl. **-S** cassina

CASSETTE   *n* pl. **-S** a small case containing audiotape or videotape

CASSIA   *n* pl. **-S** a variety of cinnamon

CASSINA   *n* pl. **-S** an evergreen tree

CASSINE   *n* pl. **-S** cassina

CASSINO   *n* pl. **-NOS** a card game

CASSIOPE   *n* pl. **-S** an evergreen shrub

CASSIS   *n* pl. **-SISES** a European bush

CASSOCK   *n* pl. **-S** a long garment worn by clergymen

CAST   *v* **CAST, CASTING, CASTS** to throw with force **CASTABLE** *adj*

CASTANET   *n* pl. **-S** a rhythm instrument

CASTAWAY   *n* pl. **-AWAYS** an outcast

CASTE   *n* pl. **-S** a system of distinct social classes

CASTEISM   *n* pl. **-S** the use of a caste system

CASTER   *n* pl. **-S** a small, swiveling wheel **CASTERED** *adj*

CASTING   *n* pl. **-S** something made in a mold

CASTLE   *v* **-TLED, -TLING, -TLES** to make a certain move in chess

CASTLING   *n* pl. **-S** a certain move in chess

CASTOFF   *n* pl. **-S** a discarded person or thing

CASTOR   *n* pl. **-S** caster

CASTRATE   *v* **-TRATED, -TRATING, -TRATES** to remove the testes of

CASTRATO   *n* pl. **-TOS** or **-TI** a singer castrated in boyhood

CASUAL   *n* pl. **-S** one who works occasionally

CASUALLY   *adv* informally

CASUALTY   *n* pl. **-TIES** a victim of war or disaster

CASUIST   *n* pl. **-S** one who resolves ethical problems

CASUS   *n* pl. **CASUS** a legal occurrence or event

CAT   *v* **CATTED, CATTING, CATS** to hoist an anchor to the cathead

CATACOMB   *n* pl. **-S** an underground cemetery

CATAGEN   *n* pl. **-S** a period of hair growth

CATALASE   *n* pl. **-S** an enzyme

CATALO   *n* pl. **-LOS** or **-LOES** a hybrid between a buffalo and a cow

CATALOG   *v* **-ED, -ING, -S** to classify information descriptively

CATALPA   *n* pl. **-S** a tree

CATALYSE   *v* **-LYSED, -LYSING, -LYSES** to catalyze

CATALYST   *n* pl. **-S** a substance that accelerates a chemical reaction

CATALYZE   *v* **-LYZED, -LYZING, -LYZES** to act as a catalyst

CATAMITE   *n* pl. **-S** a boy used in sodomy

CATAPULT   *v* **-ED, -ING, -S** to hurl through the air

CATARACT   *n* pl. **-S** a tremendous waterfall

CATARRH   *n* pl. **-S** inflammation of a mucous membrane

CATAWBA   *n* pl. **-S** a variety of fox grape

CATBIRD   *n* pl. **-S** a songbird

CATBOAT   *n* pl. **-S** a small sailboat

CATBRIAR   *n* pl. **-S** catbrier

CATBRIER   *n* pl. **-S** a thorny vine

CATCALL   *v* **-ED, -ING, -S** to deride by making shrill sounds

CATCH   *v* **CAUGHT, CATCHING, CATCHES** to capture after pursuit

CATCHALL   *n* pl. **-S** a container for odds and ends

CATCHER   *n* pl. **-S** one that catches

CATCHFLY   *n* pl. **-FLIES** an insect-catching plant

CATCHUP   *n* pl. **-S** ketchup

CATCHY   *adj* **CATCHIER, CATCHIEST** pleasing and easily remembered **CATCHILY** *adv*

CATCLAW   *n* pl. **-S** a flowering shrub

CATE   *n* pl. **-S** a choice food

CATECHIN   *n* pl. **-S** a chemical used in dyeing

CATECHOL   *n* pl. **-S** a chemical used in photography

CATECHU   *n* pl. **-S** a resin used in tanning

CATEGORY *n* pl. **-RIES** a division in any system of classification

CATENA *n* pl. **-NAS** or **-NAE** a closely linked series

CATENARY *n* pl. **-NARIES** a mathematical curve

CATENATE *v* **-NATED, -NATING, -NATES** to link together

CATENOID *n* pl. **-S** a geometric surface

CATER *v* **-ED, -ING, -S** to provide food and service for

CATERAN *n* pl. **-S** a brigand

CATERER *n* pl. **-S** one that caters

CATERESS *n* pl. **-ES** a woman who caters

CATERING *n* pl. **-S** the work of a caterer

CATFACE *n* pl. **-S** a deformity of fruit

CATFALL *n* pl. **-S** an anchor line

CATFIGHT *n* pl. **-S** a fight between two women

CATFISH *n* pl. **-ES** a scaleless, large-headed fish

CATGUT *n* pl. **-S** a strong cord

CATHEAD *n* pl. **-S** a beam projecting from a ship's bow

CATHECT *v* **-ED, -ING, -S** to invest with psychic energy

CATHEDRA *n* pl. **-DRAS** or **-DRAE** a bishop's throne

CATHETER *n* pl. **-S** a medical instrument

CATHEXIS *n* pl. **-THEXES** the concentration of psychic energy on a person or idea

CATHODE *n* pl. **-S** a negatively charged electrode **CATHODAL, CATHODIC** *adj*

CATHOLIC *n* pl. **-S** a member of the universal Christian church

CATHOUSE *n* pl. **-S** a brothel

CATION *n* pl. **-S** a positively charged ion **CATIONIC** *adj*

CATJANG *n* pl. **-S** an African shrub

CATKIN *n* pl. **-S** a flower cluster

CATLIKE *adj* resembling a cat; stealthy; silent

CATLIN *n* pl. **-S** catling

CATLING *n* pl. **-S** a surgical knife

CATMINT *n* pl. **-S** catnip

CATNAP *v* **-NAPPED, -NAPPING, -NAPS** to doze

CATNAPER *n* pl. **-S** one that steals cats

CATNIP *n* pl. **-S** an aromatic herb

CATSPAW *n* pl. **-S** a light wind

CATSUIT *n* pl. **-S** a close-fitting one-piece garment

CATSUP *n* pl. **-S** ketchup

CATTAIL *n* pl. **-S** a marsh plant

CATTALO *n* pl. **-LOS** or **-LOES** catalo

CATTED past tense of cat

CATTERY *n* pl. **-TERIES** an establishment for breeding cats

CATTIE *n* pl. **-S** an Asian unit of weight

CATTIER comparative of catty

CATTIEST superlative of catty

CATTILY *adv* in a catty manner

CATTING present participle of cat

CATTISH *adj* catty

CATTLE *n/pl* domesticated bovines

CATTLEYA *n* pl. **-S** a tropical orchid

CATTY *adj* **-TIER, -TIEST** catlike; spiteful

CATWALK *n* pl. **-S** a narrow walkway

CAUCUS *v* **-CUSED, -CUSING, -CUSES** or **-CUSSED, -CUSSING, -CUSSES** to hold a political meeting

CAUDAD *adv* toward the tail

CAUDAL *adj* taillike **CAUDALLY** *adv*

CAUDATE *n* pl. **-S** a basal ganglion of the brain

CAUDATED *adj* having a tail

CAUDEX *n* pl. **-DEXES** or **-DICES** the woody base of some plants

CAUDILLO *n* pl. **-DILLOS** a military dictator

CAUDLE *n* pl. **-S** a warm beverage

CAUGHT past tense of catch

CAUL *n* pl. **-S** a fetal membrane

CAULD *n* pl. **-S** cold

CAULDRON *n* pl. **-S** caldron

CAULES pl. of caulis

CAULICLE *n* pl. **-S** a small stem

CAULINE *adj* pertaining to a stem

CAULIS *n* pl. **-LES** a plant stem

CAULK *v* **-ED, -ING, -S** to make the seams of a ship watertight

CAULKER *n* pl. **-S** one that caulks

CAULKING *n* pl. **-S** the material used to caulk

CAURI *n* pl. **-S** a former monetary unit of Guinea

CAUSABLE *adj* capable of being caused

CAUSAL *n* pl. **-S** a word expressing cause or reason

CAUSALLY *adv* by way of causing

CAUSE *v* **CAUSED, CAUSING, CAUSES** to bring about

CAUSER *n* pl. **-S** one that causes

CAUSERIE *n* pl. **-S** an informal conversation

CAUSEWAY *v* **-ED, -ING, -S** to build a causeway (a raised roadway) over

CAUSEY *n* pl. **-SEYS** a paved road

CAUSING present participle of cause

CAUSTIC *n* pl. **-S** a corrosive substance

CAUTERY *n* pl. **-TERIES** something used to destroy tissue

CAUTION *v* **-ED, -ING, -S** to warn

CAUTIOUS *adj* exercising prudence to avoid danger

CAVA *n* pl. **-S** a sparkling Spanish wine

CAVALERO *n* pl. **-ROS** a horseman

CAVALIER *v* **-ED, -ING, -S** to behave haughtily

CAVALLA *n* pl. **-S** a large food fish

CAVALLY *n* pl. **-LIES** cavalla

CAVALRY *n* pl. **-RIES** a mobile army unit

CAVATINA *n* pl. **-NAS** or **-NE** a simple song

CAVE *v* **CAVED, CAVING, CAVES** to hollow out

CAVEAT *v* **-ED, -ING, -S** to enter a type of legal notice

CAVEATOR *n* pl. **-S** one that files a caveat

CAVED past tense of cave

CAVEFISH *n* pl. **-ES** a sightless fish

CAVELIKE *adj* resembling a cave (an underground chamber)

CAVEMAN *n* pl. **-MEN** a cave dweller

CAVEOLA *n* pl. **-LAE** a tiny pit in a cell membrane **CAVEOLAR** *adj*

CAVER *n* pl. **-S** one that caves

CAVERN *v* **-ED, -ING, -S** to hollow out

CAVETTO *n* pl. **-TOS** or **-TI** a concave molding

CAVIAR *n* pl. **-S** the roe of sturgeon

CAVIARE *n* pl. **-S** caviar

CAVICORN *adj* having hollow horns

CAVIE *n* pl. **-S** a hencoop

CAVIES pl. of cavy

CAVIL *v* **-ILED, -ILING, -ILS** or **-ILLED, -ILLING, -ILS** to carp

CAVILER *n* pl. **-S** one that cavils

CAVILLER *n* pl. **-S** caviler

CAVILLING a present participle of cavil

CAVING *n* pl. **-S** the sport of exploring caves

CAVITARY *adj* pertaining to the formation of cavities in tissue

CAVITATE *v* **-TATED, -TATING, -TATES** to form cavities

CAVITY *n* pl. **-TIES** an unfilled space within a mass **CAVITIED** *adj*

CAVORT *v* **-ED, -ING, -S** to frolic

CAVORTER *n* pl. **-S** one that cavorts

CAVY *n* pl. **-VIES** a short-tailed rodent

CAW *v* **-ED, -ING, -S** to utter the sound of a crow

CAY *n* pl. **CAYS** a small low island

CAYENNE *n* pl. **-S** a hot seasoning **CAYENNED** *adj*

CAYMAN *n* pl. **-S** caiman

CAYUSE *n* pl. **-S** an Indian pony

CAZH *adj* casual

CAZIQUE *n* pl. **-S** cacique

CEASE *v* **CEASED, CEASING, CEASES** to stop

CEBID *n* pl. **-S** ceboid

CEBOID *n* pl. **-S** one of a family of monkeys

CECITY *n* pl. **-TIES** blindness

CECROPIA *n* pl. **-S** a large North American moth

CECUM *n* pl. **CECA** a bodily cavity with one opening **CECAL** *adj* **CECALLY** *adv*

CEDAR *n* pl. **-S** an evergreen tree **CEDARN, CEDARY** *adj*

CEDE *v* **CEDED, CEDING, CEDES** to yield

CEDER *n* pl. **-S** one that cedes

CEDI *n* pl. **-S** a monetary unit of Ghana

CEDILLA *n* pl. **-S** a pronunciation mark

CEDING present participle of cede

CEDULA *n* pl. **-S** a Philippine tax

CEE *n* pl. **-S** the letter C

CEIBA *n* pl. **-S** a tropical tree

CEIL *v* **-ED, -ING, -S** to furnish with a ceiling

CEILER *n* pl. **-S** one that ceils

CEILI *n* pl. **-S** ceilidh

CEILIDH *n* pl. **-S** an Irish or Scottish party

CEILING *n* pl. **-S** the overhead lining of a room

CEINTURE *n* pl. **-S** a belt for the waist

CEL *n* pl. **-S** a sheet of celluloid used in animation

CELADON *n* pl. **-S** a pale green color

CELEB *n* pl. **-S** a celebrity; a famous person

CELERIAC *n* pl. **-S** a variety of celery

CELERITY *n* pl. **-TIES** swiftness

CELERY *n* pl. **-ERIES** a plant with edible stalks

CELESTA *n* pl. **-S** a keyboard instrument

CELESTE *n* pl. **-S** celesta

CELIAC *n* pl. **-S** one that has a chronic nutritional disturbance

CELIBACY *n* pl. **-CIES** abstention from sexual intercourse

CELIBATE *n* pl. **-S** one who lives a life of celibacy

CELL *v* **-ED, -ING, -S** to store in a honeycomb

CELLA *n* pl. **-LAE** the interior of an ancient temple

CELLAR *v* **-ED, -ING, -S** to store in an underground room

CELLARER *n* pl. **-S** the steward of a monastery

CELLARET *n* pl. **-S** a cabinet for wine bottles

CELLIST *n* pl. **-S** one who plays the cello

CELLMATE *n* pl. **-S** one of two or more prisoners sharing a cell

CELLO *n* pl. **-LOS** or **-LI** a stringed musical instrument

CELLULAR *n* pl. **-S** a cell phone

CELLULE *n* pl. **-S** a small cell

CELOM *n* pl. **-LOMS** or **-LOMATA** coelom

CELOSIA *n* pl. **-S** a flowering plant

CELT *n* pl. **-S** a primitive ax

CEMBALO *n* pl. **-LOS** or **-LI** a harpsichord

CEMENT *v* **-ED, -ING, -S** to bind firmly

CEMENTER *n* pl. **-S** one that cements

CEMENTUM *n* pl. **-TUMS** or **-TA** the hard tissue covering the roots of the teeth

CEMETERY *n* pl. **-TERIES** a burial ground

CENACLE *n* pl. **-S** a small dining room

CENOBITE *n* pl. **-S** a member of a religious order

CENOTAPH *n* pl. **-S** an empty tomb

CENOTE *n* pl. **-S** a sinkhole in limestone

CENSE *v* **CENSED, CENSING, CENSES** to perfume with incense

CENSER *n* pl. **-S** a vessel for burning incense

CENSOR *v* **-ED, -ING, -S** to delete an objectionable word or passage

CENSUAL *adj* pertaining to the act of censusing

CENSURE *v* **-SURED, -SURING, -SURES** to criticize severely

CENSURER *n* pl. **-S** one that censures

CENSUS *v* **-ED, -ING, -ES** to take an official count of

CENT *n* pl. **-S** the 100th part of a dollar

CENTAL *n* pl. **-S** a unit of weight

CENTARE *n* pl. **-S** a measure of land area

CENTAS *n* pl. **CENTAI** or **CENTU** a monetary unit of Lithuania

CENTAUR *n* pl. **-S** a mythological creature

CENTAURY *n* pl. **-RIES** a medicinal herb

CENTAVO *n* pl. **-VOS** a coin of various Spanish-American nations

CENTER *v* **-ED, -ING, -S** to place at the center (the midpoint)

CENTESIS *n* pl. **-TESES** a surgical puncture

CENTIARE *n* pl. **-S** centare

CENTILE *n* pl. **-S** a value of a statistical variable

CENTIME *n* pl. **-S** the 100th part of a franc

CENTIMO *n* pl. **-MOS** any of various small coins

CENTNER *n* pl. **-S** a unit of weight

CENTO *n* pl. **-TOS** or **-TONES** a literary work made up of parts from other works

CENTRA a pl. of centrum

CENTRAL *adj* **-TRALER, -TRALEST** situated at, in, or near the center

CENTRAL *n* pl. **-S** a telephone exchange

CENTRE *v* **-TRED, -TRING, -TRES** to center

CENTRIC *adj* situated at the center

CENTRING *n* pl. **-S** a temporary framework for an arch

CENTRISM *n* pl. **-S** a moderate political philosophy

CENTRIST *n* pl. **-S** an advocate of centrism

CENTROID *n* pl. **-S** the center of mass of an object

CENTRUM *n* pl. **-TRUMS** or **-TRA** the body of a vertebra

CENTU	a pl. of centas
CENTUM	*n* pl. **-S** one hundred
CENTUPLE	*v* **-PLED, -PLING, -PLES** to increase a hundredfold
CENTURY	*n* pl. **-RIES** a period of 100 years
CEORL	*n* pl. **-S** a freeman of low birth **CEORLISH** *adj*
CEP	*n* pl. **-S** cepe
CEPE	*n* pl. **-S** a large mushroom
CEPHALAD	*adv* toward the head
CEPHALIC	*adj* pertaining to the head
CEPHALIN	*n* pl. **-S** a bodily chemical
CEPHEID	*n* pl. **-S** a giant star
CERAMAL	*n* pl. **-S** a heat-resistant alloy
CERAMIC	*n* pl. **-S** an item made of baked clay
CERAMIDE	*n* pl. **-S** any of various lipids
CERAMIST	*n* pl. **-S** one who makes ceramics
CERASTES	*n* pl. **CERASTES** a venomous snake
CERATE	*n* pl. **-S** a medicated ointment
CERATED	*adj* covered with wax
CERATIN	*n* pl. **-S** keratin
CERATOID	*adj* hornlike
CERCARIA	*n* pl. **-IAS** or **-IAE** a parasitic worm
CERCIS	*n* pl. **-CISES** a shrub
CERCUS	*n* pl. **CERCI** a sensory appendage of an insect **CERCAL** *adj*
CERE	*v* **CERED, CERING, CERES** to wrap in a waxy cloth
CEREAL	*n* pl. **-S** a food made from grain
CEREBRAL	*n* pl. **-S** a kind of consonant
CEREBRUM	*n* pl. **-BRUMS** or **-BRA** a part of the brain **CEREBRIC** *adj*
CERED	past tense of cere
CEREMENT	*n* pl. **-S** a waxy cloth
CEREMONY	*n* pl. **-NIES** a formal observance
CERESIN	*n* pl. **-S** a hard whitish wax
CEREUS	*n* pl. **-ES** a tall cactus
CERIA	*n* pl. **-S** a chemical compound
CERIC	*adj* containing cerium
CERING	present participle of cere
CERIPH	*n* pl. **-S** serif
CERISE	*n* pl. **-S** a red color
CERITE	*n* pl. **-S** a mineral
CERIUM	*n* pl. **-S** a metallic element
CERMET	*n* pl. **-S** ceramal
CERNUOUS	*adj* drooping or nodding
CERO	*n* pl. **CEROS** a large food fish
CEROTIC	*adj* pertaining to beeswax
CEROTYPE	*n* pl. **-S** a process of engraving using wax
CEROUS	*adj* pertaining to cerium
CERT	*n* pl. **-S** an event considered certain to happen
CERTAIN	*adj* **-TAINER, -TAINEST** absolutely confident
CERTES	*adv* in truth
CERTIFY	*v* **-FIED, -FYING, -FIES** to confirm
CERULEAN	*n* pl. **-S** a blue color
CERUMEN	*n* pl. **-S** a waxy secretion of the ear
CERUSE	*n* pl. **-S** a lead compound
CERUSITE	*n* pl. **-S** a lead ore
CERVELAS	*n* pl. **-ES** cervelat
CERVELAT	*n* pl. **-S** a smoked sausage
CERVEZA	*n* pl. **-S** beer
CERVICAL	*adj* pertaining to the cervix
CERVID	*n* pl. **-S** a mammal of the deer family
CERVINE	*adj* pertaining to deer
CERVIX	*n* pl. **-VIXES** or **-VICES** the neck
CESAREAN	*n* pl. **-S** a method of child delivery
CESARIAN	*n* pl. **-S** cesarean
CESIUM	*n* pl. **-S** a metallic element
CESS	*v* **-ED, -ING, -ES** to tax or assess
CESSION	*n* pl. **-S** the act of ceding
CESSPIT	*n* pl. **-S** a cesspool
CESSPOOL	*n* pl. **-S** a covered well or pit for sewage
CESTA	*n* pl. **-S** a basket used in jai alai (a game played with a small hard ball)
CESTI	pl. of cestus
CESTODE	*n* pl. **-S** a tapeworm
CESTOID	*n* pl. **-S** cestode
CESTOS	*n* pl. **-TOI** cestus
CESTUS	*n* pl. **-ES** a hand covering for ancient Roman boxers
CESTUS	*n* pl. **-TI** a belt or girdle
CESURA	*n* pl. **-RAS** or **-RAE** caesura
CETACEAN	*n* pl. **-S** an aquatic mammal
CETANE	*n* pl. **-S** a diesel fuel
CETE	*n* pl. **-S** a group of badgers

CETOLOGY	*n* pl. **-GIES** the study of whales
CEVICHE	*n* pl. **-S** seviche
CHABLIS	*n* pl. **CHABLIS** a dry white wine
CHABOUK	*n* pl. **-S** a type of whip
CHABUK	*n* pl. **-S** chabouk
CHACHKA	*n* pl. **-S** chatchka
CHACMA	*n* pl. **-S** a large baboon
CHACONNE	*n* pl. **-S** an ancient dance
CHAD	*n* pl. **-S** a scrap of paper **CHADLESS** *adj*
CHADAR	*n* pl. **-DARS** or **-DRI** chador
CHADARIM	a pl. of cheder
CHADOR	*n* pl. **-DORS** or **-DRI** a large shawl
CHAEBOL	*n* pl. **-S** a group of businesses in Korea owned by one family
CHAETA	*n* pl. **-TAE** a bristle or seta **CHAETAL** *adj*
CHAFE	*v* **CHAFED, CHAFING, CHAFES** to warm by rubbing
CHAFER	*n* pl. **-S** a large beetle
CHAFF	*v* **-ED, -ING, -S** to poke fun at
CHAFFER	*v* **-ED, -ING, -S** to bargain or haggle
CHAFFY	*adj* **CHAFFIER, CHAFFIEST** worthless
CHAFING	present participle of chafe
CHAGRIN	*v* **-GRINED, -GRINING, -GRINS** or **-GRINNED, -GRINNING, -GRINS** to humiliate
CHAI	*n* pl. **-S** spiced tea with honey and milk
CHAIN	*v* **-ED, -ING, -S** to bind with a chain (a series of connected rings)
CHAINE	*n* pl. **-S** a series of ballet turns
CHAINER	*n* pl. **-S** a chainman
CHAINMAN	*n* pl. **-MEN** a surveyor's assistant who uses a measuring chain
CHAINSAW	*v* **-SAWED, -SAWING, -SAWS** to cut with a chain saw
CHAIR	*v* **-ED, -ING, -S** to install in office
CHAIRMAN	*n* pl. **-MEN** the presiding officer of a meeting
CHAIRMAN	*v* **-MANED, -MANING, -MANS** or **-MANNED, -MANNING, -MANS** to act as chairman of
CHAISE	*n* pl. **-S** a light carriage
CHAKRA	*n* pl. **-S** a body center in yoga
CHALAH	*n* pl. **-LAHS** or **-LOTH** or **-LOT** challah

CHALAZA	*n* pl. **-ZAS** or **-ZAE** a band of tissue in an egg **CHALAZAL** *adj*
CHALAZIA	*n/pl* tumors of the eyelid
CHALCID	*n* pl. **-S** a tiny fly
CHALDRON	*n* pl. **-S** a unit of dry measure
CHALEH	*n* pl. **-S** challah
CHALET	*n* pl. **-S** a Swiss cottage
CHALICE	*n* pl. **-S** a drinking cup **CHALICED** *adj*
CHALK	*v* **-ED, -ING, -S** to mark with chalk (a soft limestone)
CHALKY	*adj* **CHALKIER, CHALKIEST** resembling chalk
CHALLA	*n* pl. **-S** challah
CHALLAH	*n* pl. **-LAHS** or **-LOTH** or **-LOT** a kind of bread
CHALLIE	*n* pl. **-S** challis
CHALLIES	pl. of chally
CHALLIS	*n* pl. **-LISES** a light fabric
CHALLOT	a pl. of challah
CHALLOTH	a pl. of challah
CHALLY	*n* pl. **-LIES** challis
CHALONE	*n* pl. **-S** a hormone
CHALOT	a pl. of chalah
CHALOTH	a pl. of chalah
CHALUPA	*n* pl. **-S** a fried corn tortilla spread with a savory mixture
CHALUTZ	*n* pl. **-LUTZIM** halutz
CHAM	*n* pl. **-S** a khan
CHAMADE	*n* pl. **-S** a signal made with a drum
CHAMBER	*v* **-ED, -ING, -S** to put in a chamber (a room)
CHAMBRAY	*n* pl. **-BRAYS** a fine fabric
CHAMBRE	*adj* brought (as wine) to room temperature
CHAMFER	*v* **-ED, -ING, -S** to groove
CHAMFRON	*n* pl. **-S** armor for a horse's head
CHAMISA	*n* pl. **-S** a saltbush of the Southwest
CHAMISE	*n* pl. **-S** chamiso
CHAMISO	*n* pl. **-SOS** a flowering shrub
CHAMMY	*v* **-MIED, -MYING, -MIES** to chamois
CHAMOIS	*n* pl. **-OIX** a soft leather
CHAMOIS	*v* **-ED, -ING, -ES** to prepare leather like chamois
CHAMP	*v* **-ED, -ING, -S** to chew noisily
CHAMPAC	*n* pl. **-S** champak

CHAMPACA	*n* pl. **-S** champak
CHAMPAK	*n* pl. **-S** an East Indian tree
CHAMPER	*n* pl. **-S** one that champs
CHAMPION	*v* **-ED, -ING, -S** to defend or support
CHAMPY	*adj* broken up by the trampling of beasts
CHANA	*n* pl. **-S** a snack of chick peas
CHANCE	*v* **CHANCED, CHANCING, CHANCES** to risk
CHANCEL	*n* pl. **-S** an area around a church altar
CHANCER	*n* pl. **-S** an opportunist
CHANCERY	*n* pl. **-CERIES** a court of public record
CHANCIER	comparative of chancy
CHANCIEST	superlative of chancy
CHANCILY	*adv* in a chancy manner
CHANCING	present participle of chance
CHANCRE	*n* pl. **-S** a hard-based sore
CHANCY	*adj* **CHANCIER, CHANCIEST** risky
CHANDLER	*n* pl. **-S** a dealer in provisions
CHANFRON	*n* pl. **-S** chamfron
CHANG	*n* pl. **-S** a cattie
CHANGE	*v* **CHANGED, CHANGING, CHANGES** to make different
CHANGER	*n* pl. **-S** one that changes
CHANGEUP	*n* pl. **-S** a slow pitch thrown like a fastball
CHANNEL	*v* **-NELED, -NELING, -NELS** or **-NELLED, -NELLING, -NELS** to direct along some desired course
CHANOYU	*n* pl. **-S** a Japanese tea ritual
CHANSON	*n* pl. **-S** a song
CHANT	*v* **-ED, -ING, -S** to sing
CHANTAGE	*n* pl. **-S** blackmail
CHANTER	*n* pl. **-S** one that chants
CHANTEY	*n* pl. **-TEYS** a sailor's song
CHANTIES	pl. of chanty
CHANTOR	*n* pl. **-S** chanter
CHANTRY	*n* pl. **-TRIES** an endowment given to a church
CHANTY	*n* pl. **-TIES** chantey
CHAO	*n* pl. **CHAO** a monetary unit of Vietnam
CHAOS	*n* pl. **-ES** a state of total disorder; a confused mass **CHAOTIC** *adj*
CHAP	*v* **CHAPPED** or **CHAPT, CHAPPING, CHAPS** to split, crack, or redden
CHAPATI	*n* pl. **-S** an unleavened bread of India
CHAPATTI	*n* pl. **-S** chapati
CHAPBOOK	*n* pl. **-S** a small book of popular tales
CHAPE	*n* pl. **-S** a part of a scabbard
CHAPEAU	*n* pl. **-PEAUS** or **-PEAUX** a hat
CHAPEL	*n* pl. **-S** a place of worship
CHAPERON	*v* **-ED, -ING, -S** to accompany
CHAPITER	*n* pl. **-S** the capital of a column
CHAPLAIN	*n* pl. **-S** a clergyman for a chapel
CHAPLET	*n* pl. **-S** a wreath for the head
CHAPMAN	*n* pl. **-MEN** a peddler
CHAPPAL	*n* pl. **-S** a sandal worn in India
CHAPPATI	*n* pl. **-S** chapati
CHAPPED	a past tense of chap
CHAPPIE	*n* pl. **-S** a fellow
CHAPPING	present participle of chap
CHAPT	a past tense of chap
CHAPTER	*v* **-ED, -ING, -S** to divide a book into chapters (main sections)
CHAQUETA	*n* pl. **-S** a jacket worn by cowboys
CHAR	*v* **CHARRED, CHARRING, CHARS** to burn slightly
CHARACID	*n* pl. **-S** characin
CHARACIN	*n* pl. **-S** a tropical fish
CHARADE	*n* pl. **-S** a word represented by pantomime
CHARAS	*n* pl. **-ES** hashish
CHARCOAL	*v* **-ED, -ING, -S** to blacken with charcoal (a dark, porous carbon)
CHARD	*n* pl. **-S** a variety of beet
CHARE	*v* **CHARED, CHARING, CHARES** to do small jobs
CHARETTE	*n* pl. **-S** a meeting for brainstorming
CHARGE	*v* **CHARGED, CHARGING, CHARGES** to accuse formally
CHARGER	*n* pl. **-S** one that charges
CHARGING	*n* pl. **-S** an illegal play in hockey
CHARIER	comparative of chary
CHARIEST	superlative of chary
CHARILY	*adv* in a chary manner
CHARING	present participle of chare

CHARIOT	*v* **-ED, -ING, -S** to ride in a chariot (a type of cart)	**CHASSEUR**	*n* pl. **-S** a cavalry soldier
CHARISM	*n* pl. **-S** charisma	**CHASSIS**	*n* pl. **CHASSIS** the frame of a car
CHARISMA	*n* pl. **-MAS** or **-MATA** a special magnetic appeal	**CHASTE**	*adj* **CHASTER, CHASTEST** morally pure **CHASTELY** *adv*
CHARITY	*n* pl. **-TIES** something given to the needy	**CHASTEN**	*v* **-ED, -ING, -S** to chastise
CHARK	*v* **-ED, -ING, -S** to char	**CHASTISE**	*v* **-TISED, -TISING, -TISES** to discipline by punishment
CHARKA	*n* pl. **-S** charkha	**CHASTITY**	*n* pl. **-TIES** moral purity
CHARKHA	*n* pl. **-S** a spinning wheel	**CHASUBLE**	*n* pl. **-S** a sleeveless vestment
CHARLADY	*n* pl. **-DIES** a cleaning woman	**CHAT**	*v* **CHATTED, CHATTING, CHATS** to converse informally
CHARLEY	*n* pl. **-LEYS** charlie		
CHARLIE	*n* pl. **-LIES** a fool	**CHATCHKA**	*n* pl. **-S** a knickknack
CHARLOCK	*n* pl. **-S** a troublesome weed	**CHATCHKE**	*n* pl. **-S** chatchka
CHARM	*v* **-ED, -ING, -S** to attract irresistibly	**CHATEAU**	*n* pl. **-TEAUS** or **-TEAUX** a large country house
CHARMER	*n* pl. **-S** one that charms	**CHATLINE**	*n* pl. **-S** a telephone service that allows conversation among several callers
CHARMING	*adj* **-INGER, -INGEST** pleasing		
CHARNEL	*n* pl. **-S** a room where corpses are placed	**CHATROOM**	*n* pl. **-S** a real-time online discussion group
CHARPAI	*n* pl. **-S** charpoy	**CHATTED**	past tense of chat
CHARPOY	*n* pl. **-POYS** a bed used in India	**CHATTEL**	*n* pl. **-S** a slave
CHARQUI	*n* pl. **-S** a type of meat **CHARQUID** *adj*	**CHATTER**	*v* **-ED, -ING, -S** to talk rapidly and trivially **CHATTERY** *adj*
CHARR	*n* pl. **-S** a small-scaled trout	**CHATTING**	present participle of chat
CHARRED	past tense of char	**CHATTY**	*adj* **-TIER, -TIEST** talkative **CHATTILY** *adv*
CHARRIER	comparative of charry		
CHARRIEST	superlative of charry	**CHAUFER**	*n* pl. **-S** chauffer
CHARRING	present participle of char	**CHAUFFER**	*n* pl. **-S** a small furnace
CHARRO	*n* pl. **-ROS** a cowboy	**CHAUNT**	*v* **-ED, -ING, -S** to chant
CHARRY	*adj* **-RIER, -RIEST** resembling charcoal	**CHAUNTER**	*n* pl. **-S** one that chaunts
		CHAUSSES	*n/pl* medieval armor
CHART	*v* **-ED, -ING, -S** to map out	**CHAW**	*v* **-ED, -ING, -S** to chew
CHARTER	*v* **-ED, -ING, -S** to lease or hire	**CHAWER**	*n* pl. **-S** one that chaws
CHARTISM	*n* pl. **-S** the use of financial charts to predict future trends	**CHAY**	*n* pl. **CHAYS** the root of an East Indian herb
CHARTIST	*n* pl. **-S** a stock market specialist	**CHAYOTE**	*n* pl. **-S** a tropical vine
CHARY	*adj* **CHARIER, CHARIEST** cautious	**CHAZAN**	*n* pl. **-ZANS** or **-ZANIM** a cantor
		CHAZZAN	*n* pl. **-ZANS** or **-ZANIM** chazan
CHASE	*v* **CHASED, CHASING, CHASES** to pursue	**CHAZZEN**	*n* pl. **-ZENS** or **-ZENIM** chazan
CHASER	*n* pl. **-S** one that chases	**CHEAP**	*adj* **CHEAPER, CHEAPEST** inexpensive
CHASING	*n* pl. **-S** a design engraved on metal	**CHEAP**	*n* pl. **-S** a market
CHASM	*n* pl. **-S** a deep cleft in the earth **CHASMAL, CHASMED, CHASMIC, CHASMY** *adj*	**CHEAPEN**	*v* **-ED, -ING, -S** to make cheap
		CHEAPIE	*n* pl. **-S** one that is cheap
		CHEAPISH	*adj* somewhat cheap
CHASSE	*v* **CHASSED, CHASSEING, CHASSES** to perform a dance movement	**CHEAPLY**	*adv* in a cheap manner
		CHEAPO	*n* pl. **CHEAPOS** a cheapie

CHEAT	v **-ED, -ING, -S** to defraud
CHEATER	n pl. **-S** one that cheats
CHEBEC	n pl. **-S** a small bird
CHECHAKO	n pl. **-KOS** a newcomer
CHECK	v **-ED, -ING, -S** to inspect
CHECKBOX	n pl. **-ES** a small box on a computer screen to be clicked on to select a feature
CHECKER	v **-ED, -ING, -S** to mark with squares
CHECKOFF	n pl. **-S** a method of collecting union dues
CHECKOUT	n pl. **-S** a test of a machine
CHECKROW	v **-ED, -ING, -S** to plant in rows which divide the land into squares
CHECKSUM	n pl. **-S** a sum derived from bits of computer data
CHECKUP	n pl. **-S** an examination
CHEDDAR	n pl. **-S** a type of cheese **CHEDDARY** adj
CHEDDITE	n pl. **-S** chedite
CHEDER	n pl. **CHEDERS** or **CHADARIM** or **CHEDARIM** heder
CHEDITE	n pl. **-S** an explosive
CHEEK	v **-ED, -ING, -S** to speak impudently to
CHEEKFUL	n pl. **-S** the amount held in one's cheek
CHEEKY	adj **CHEEKIER, CHEEKIEST** impudent **CHEEKILY** adv
CHEEP	v **-ED, -ING, -S** to chirp
CHEEPER	n pl. **-S** one that cheeps
CHEER	v **-ED, -ING, -S** to applaud with shouts of approval
CHEERER	n pl. **-S** one that cheers
CHEERFUL	adj **-FULLER, -FULLEST** full of spirits
CHEERIER	comparative of cheery
CHEERIEST	superlative of cheery
CHEERILY	adv in a cheery manner
CHEERIO	n pl. **-IOS** a greeting
CHEERLED	past tense of cheerlead
CHEERLY	adv cheerily
CHEERO	n pl. **CHEEROS** cheerio
CHEERY	adj **CHEERIER, CHEERIEST** cheerful
CHEESE	v **CHEESED, CHEESING, CHEESES** to stop

CHEESY	adj **CHEESIER, CHEESIEST** resembling cheese (a food made from milk curds) **CHEESILY** adv
CHEETAH	n pl. **-S** a swift-running wildcat
CHEF	v **CHEFFED, CHEFFING, CHEFS** or **CHEFED, CHEFING, CHEFS** to work as a chef (a chief cook)
CHEFDOM	n pl. **-S** the status of a chef
CHEGOE	n pl. **-S** chigoe
CHELA	n pl. **-LAE** a pincerlike claw
CHELA	n pl. **-S** a pupil of a guru
CHELATE	v **-LATED, -LATING, -LATES** to combine a metal ion with a compound
CHELATOR	n pl. **-S** one that chelates
CHELIPED	n pl. **-S** a claw-bearing leg
CHELOID	n pl. **-S** keloid
CHEM	n pl. **-S** a chemistry class or course
CHEMIC	n pl. **-S** a chemist
CHEMICAL	n pl. **-S** a substance obtained by a process of chemistry
CHEMISE	n pl. **-S** a loose dress
CHEMISM	n pl. **-S** chemical attraction
CHEMIST	n pl. **-S** one versed in chemistry
CHEMO	n pl. **-S** treatment (as of disease) with chemical agents
CHEMURGY	n pl. **-GIES** a branch of applied chemistry
CHENILLE	n pl. **-S** a soft fabric
CHENOPOD	n pl. **-S** a flowering plant
CHEQUE	n pl. **-S** a written order directing a bank to pay money
CHEQUER	v **-ED, -ING, -S** to checker
CHERISH	v **-ED, -ING, -ES** to hold dear
CHEROOT	n pl. **-S** a square-cut cigar
CHERRY	n pl. **-RIES** a fruit
CHERRY	adj **-RIER, -RIEST** of a light red color
CHERT	n pl. **-S** a compact rock
CHERTY	adj **CHERTIER, CHERTIEST** resembling chert
CHERUB	n pl. **-UBS** or **-UBIM** or **-UBIMS** an angel **CHERUBIC** adj
CHERVIL	n pl. **-S** an aromatic herb
CHESHIRE	n pl. **-S** a hard English cheese
CHESS	n pl. **-ES** a weed

CHESSMAN   *n* pl. **-MEN** one of the pieces used in chess (a board game for two players)

CHEST   *n* pl. **-S** a part of the body **CHESTED** *adj*

CHESTFUL   *n* pl. **-S** as much as a chest or box can hold

CHESTNUT   *n* pl. **-S** an edible nut

CHESTY   *adj* **CHESTIER, CHESTIEST** proud **CHESTILY** *adv*

CHETAH   *n* pl. **-S** cheetah

CHETH   *n* pl. **-S** heth

CHETRUM   *n* pl. **CHETRUMS** or **CHHERTUM** a monetary unit of Bhutan

CHEVALET   *n* pl. **-S** a part of a stringed instrument

CHEVERON   *n* pl. **-S** chevron

CHEVET   *n* pl. **-S** the apsidal end of a church

CHEVIED   past tense of chevy

CHEVIES   present 3d person sing. of chevy

CHEVIOT   *n* pl. **-S** a coarse fabric

CHEVRE   *n* pl. **-S** a cheese made from goat's milk

CHEVRET   *n* pl. **-S** chevre

CHEVRON   *n* pl. **-S** a V-shaped pattern

CHEVY   *v* **CHEVIED, CHEVYING, CHEVIES** to chase about

CHEW   *v* **-ED, -ING, -S** to crush or grind with the teeth **CHEWABLE** *adj*

CHEWER   *n* pl. **-S** one that chews

CHEWINK   *n* pl. **-S** a common finch

CHEWY   *adj* **CHEWIER, CHEWIEST** not easily chewed

CHEZ   *prep* at the home of

CHHERTUM   pl. of chetrum

CHI   *n* pl. **-S** a Greek letter

CHIA   *n* pl. **-S** a Mexican herb

CHIANTI   *n* pl. **-S** a dry red wine

CHIAO   *n* pl. **CHIAO** a monetary unit of China

CHIASM   *n* pl. **-S** chiasma

CHIASMA   *n* pl. **-MAS** or **-MATA** an anatomical junction **CHIASMAL, CHIASMIC** *adj*

CHIASMUS   *n* pl. **-MI** a reversal of word order between parallel phrases **CHIASTIC** *adj*

CHIAUS   *n* pl. **-ES** a Turkish messenger

CHIBOUK   *n* pl. **-S** a Turkish tobacco pipe

CHIC   *adj* **CHICER, CHICEST** smartly stylish

CHIC   *n* pl. **-S** elegance of dress or manner

CHICA   *n* pl. **-S** a girl or young woman

CHICANE   *v* **-CANED, -CANING, -CANES** to trick by a clever ruse

CHICANER   *n* pl. **-S** one that chicanes

CHICANO   *n* pl. **-NOS** an American of Mexican descent

CHICCORY   *n* pl. **-RIES** chicory

CHICHI   *adj* **CHICHIER, CHICHIEST** showily stylish

CHICHI   *n* pl. **-S** elaborate ornamentation

CHICK   *n* pl. **-S** a young bird

CHICKEE   *n* pl. **-S** a stilt house of the Seminole Indians

CHICKEN   *v* **-ED, -ING, -S** to lose one's nerve

CHICKORY   *n* pl. **-RIES** chicory

CHICKPEA   *n* pl. **-S** an Asian herb

CHICLE   *n* pl. **-S** a tree gum

CHICLY   *adv* in an elegant manner

CHICNESS   *n* pl. **-ES** elegance

CHICO   *n* pl. **-COS** a prickly shrub

CHICORY   *n* pl. **-RIES** a perennial herb

CHICOT   *n* pl. **-S** a dead tree

CHIDE   *v* **CHIDED** or **CHID, CHIDDEN, CHIDING, CHIDES** to scold

CHIDER   *n* pl. **-S** one that chides

CHIEF   *adj* **CHIEFER, CHIEFEST** highest in authority

CHIEF   *n* pl. **-S** the person highest in authority

CHIEFDOM   *n* pl. **-S** the domain of a chief

CHIEFLY   *adv* above all

CHIEL   *n* pl. **-S** chield

CHIELD   *n* pl. **-S** a young man

CHIFFON   *n* pl. **-S** a sheer fabric

CHIGETAI   *n* pl. **-S** a wild ass

CHIGGER   *n* pl. **-S** a parasitic mite

CHIGNON   *n* pl. **-S** a woman's hairdo

CHIGOE   *n* pl. **-S** a tropical flea

CHILD   *n* pl. **CHILDREN** a young person

CHILDBED   *n* pl. **-S** the state of a woman giving birth

CHILDE   *n* pl. **-S** a youth of noble birth

CHILDING   *adj* pregnant

CHILDISH   *adj* resembling a child

CHILDLY   *adj* **-LIER, -LIEST** resembling a child

CHILDREN   pl. of child

CHILE   *n* pl. **-S** chili

CHILI   *n* pl. **-S** or **-ES** a hot pepper

CHILIAD   *n* pl. **-S** a group of one thousand

CHILIASM   *n* pl. **-S** a religious doctrine

CHILIAST   *n* pl. **-S** a supporter of chiliasm

CHILIDOG   *n* pl. **-S** a hot dog topped with chili

CHILL   *adj* **CHILLER, CHILLEST** cool

CHILL   *v* **-ED, -ING, -S** to make cold

CHILLAX   *v* **-ED, -ING, -ES** to calm down

CHILLER   *n* pl. **-S** one that chills

CHILLI   *n* pl. **-ES** or **-S** chili

CHILLUM   *n* pl. **-S** a part of a water pipe

CHILLY   *adj* **CHILLIER, CHILLIEST** cool **CHILLILY** *adv*

CHILOPOD   *n* pl. **-S** a multi-legged insect

CHIMAERA   *n* pl. **-S** a marine fish

CHIMAR   *n* pl. **-S** chimere

CHIMB   *n* pl. **-S** the rim of a cask

CHIMBLEY   *n* pl. **-BLEYS** chimley

CHIMBLY   *n* pl. **-BLIES** chimley

CHIME   *v* **CHIMED, CHIMING, CHIMES** to ring harmoniously

CHIMENEA   *n* pl. **-S** an outdoor fireplace shaped like a lightbulb

CHIMER   *n* pl. **-S** one that chimes

CHIMERA   *n* pl. **-S** an imaginary monster

CHIMERE   *n* pl. **-S** a bishop's robe

CHIMERIC   *adj* imaginary; unreal

CHIMINEA   *n* pl. **-S** chimenea

CHIMING   present participle of chime

CHIMLA   *n* pl. **-S** chimley

CHIMLEY   *n* pl. **-LEYS** a chimney

CHIMNEY   *n* pl. **-NEYS** a flue

CHIMP   *n* pl. **-S** a chimpanzee

CHIN   *v* **CHINNED, CHINNING, CHINS** to hold with the chin (the lower part of the face)

CHINA   *n* pl. **-S** fine porcelain ware

CHINBONE   *n* pl. **-S** the lower jaw

CHINCH   *v* **-ED, -ING, -ES** to chinse

CHINCHY   *adj* **CHINCHIER, CHINCHIEST** stingy

CHINE   *v* **CHINED, CHINING, CHINES** to cut through the backbone of

CHING   *n* pl. **-S** a high-pitched ringing sound

CHINK   *v* **-ED, -ING, -S** to fill cracks or fissures in

CHINKY   *adj* **CHINKIER, CHINKIEST** full of cracks

CHINLESS   *adj* lacking a chin

CHINNED   past tense of chin

CHINNING   present participle of chin

CHINO   *n* pl. **-NOS** a strong fabric

CHINOIS   *n* pl. **-NOISES** a cone-shaped sieve

CHINONE   *n* pl. **-S** quinone

CHINOOK   *n* pl. **-S** a warm wind

CHINSE   *v* **CHINSED, CHINSING, CHINSES** to fill the seams in a boat or cabin

CHINTS   *n* pl. **-ES** chintz

CHINTZ   *n* pl. **-ES** a cotton fabric

CHINTZY   *adj* **CHINTZIER, CHINTZIEST** gaudy; cheap

CHINWAG   *v* **-WAGGED, -WAGGING, -WAGS** to gossip

CHIP   *v* **CHIPPED, CHIPPING, CHIPS** to break a small piece from

CHIPMUCK   *n* pl. **-S** a chipmunk

CHIPMUNK   *n* pl. **-S** a small rodent

CHIPOTLE   *n* pl. **-S** a smoked and dried jalapeno pepper

CHIPPED   past tense of chip

CHIPPER   *v* **-ED, -ING, -S** to chirp

CHIPPIE   *n* pl. **-S** chippy

CHIPPING   present participle of chip

CHIPPY   *adj* **-PIER, -PIEST** belligerent

CHIPPY   *n* pl. **-PIES** a prostitute

CHIPSET   *n* pl. **-S** a set of integrated circuits

CHIRAL   *adj* pertaining to an asymmetrical molecule

CHIRK   *adj* **CHIRKER, CHIRKEST** cheerful

CHIRK   *v* **-ED, -ING, -S** to make a shrill noise

CHIRM   *v* **-ED, -ING, -S** to chirp

CHIRO   *n* pl. **-ROS** a marine fish

CHIRP   *v* **-ED, -ING, -S** to utter a short, shrill sound

CHIRPER   *n* pl. **-S** one that chirps

CHIRPY	*adj* **CHIRPIER, CHIRPIEST** cheerful **CHIRPILY** *adv*	**CHLORIN**	*n* pl. **-S** chlorine
CHIRR	*v* **-ED, -ING, -S** to make a harsh, vibrant sound	**CHLORINE**	*n* pl. **-S** a gaseous element
		CHLORITE	*n* pl. **-S** a mineral group
CHIRRE	*v* **CHIRRED, CHIRRING, CHIRRES** to chirr	**CHLOROUS**	*adj* pertaining to chlorine
		CHOANA	*n* pl. **-NAE** a funnel-shaped opening
CHIRREN	*n/pl* children		
CHIRRUP	*v* **-ED, -ING, -S** to chirp repeatedly **CHIRRUPY** *adj*	**CHOC**	*n* pl. **-S** a chocolate
		CHOCK	*v* **-ED, -ING, -S** to secure with a wedge of wood or metal
CHIRU	*n* pl. **-S** a Tibetan antelope		
CHISEL	*v* **-ELED, -ELING, -ELS** or **-ELLED, -ELLING, -ELS** to use a chisel (a cutting tool)	**CHOCKFUL**	*adj* full to the limit
		CHOICE	*adj* **CHOICER, CHOICEST** of fine quality **CHOICELY** *adv*
CHISELER	*n* pl. **-S** one that chisels	**CHOICE**	*n* pl. **-S** one that is chosen
CHIT	*n* pl. **-S** a short letter	**CHOIL**	*n* pl. **-S** the end of a knife blade nearer the handle
CHITAL	*n* pl. **-S** an Asian deer		
CHITCHAT	*v* **-CHATTED, -CHATTING, -CHATS** to indulge in small talk	**CHOIR**	*v* **-ED, -ING, -S** to sing in unison
		CHOIRBOY	*n* pl. **-BOYS** a boy who sings in a choir (a body of church singers)
CHITIN	*n* pl. **-S** the main component of insect shells		
		CHOKE	*v* **CHOKED, CHOKING, CHOKES** to impede the breathing of
CHITLIN	*n* pl. **-S** chitling		
CHITLING	*n* pl. **-S** a part of the small intestine of swine	**CHOKER**	*n* pl. **-S** one that chokes
		CHOKEY	*adj* **CHOKIER, CHOKIEST** choky
CHITON	*n* pl. **-S** a tunic worn in ancient Greece	**CHOKEY**	*n* pl. **CHOKEYS** choky
		CHOKY	*adj* **CHOKIER, CHOKIEST** tending to cause choking
CHITOSAN	*n* pl. **-S** a compound derived from chitin		
		CHOKY	*n* pl. **CHOKIES** a prison
CHITTER	*v* **-ED, -ING, -S** to twitter	**CHOLATE**	*n* pl. **-S** a chemical salt
CHITTY	*n* pl. **-TIES** a chit	**CHOLENT**	*n* pl. **-S** a traditional Jewish stew
CHIVALRY	*n* pl. **-RIES** knightly behavior and skill	**CHOLER**	*n* pl. **-S** anger
		CHOLERA	*n* pl. **-S** an acute disease
CHIVAREE	*v* **-REED, -REEING, -REES** to perform a mock serenade	**CHOLERIC**	*adj* bad-tempered
		CHOLI	*n* pl. **-S** a bodice worn by some Hindu women
CHIVARI	*v* **-RIED, -RIING, -RIES** to chivaree		
CHIVE	*n* pl. **-S** an herb used as a seasoning	**CHOLIAMB**	*n* pl. **-S** a type of poetic meter
		CHOLINE	*n* pl. **-S** a B vitamin
CHIVVY	*v* **-VIED, -VYING, -VIES** to chevy	**CHOLLA**	*n* pl. **-S** a treelike cactus
CHIVY	*v* **CHIVIED, CHIVYING, CHIVIES** to chevy	**CHOMP**	*v* **-ED, -ING, -S** to champ
		CHOMPER	*n* pl. **-S** one that chomps
CHLAMYS	*n* pl. **-MYSES** or **-MYDES** a garment worn in ancient Greece	**CHON**	*n* pl. **CHON** a monetary unit of North and South Korea
CHLOASMA	*n* pl. **-MAS** or **-MATA** a skin discoloration		
		CHOOK	*n* pl. **-S** a chicken
CHLORAL	*n* pl. **-S** a chemical compound	**CHOOSE**	*v* **CHOSE, CHOSEN, CHOOSING, CHOOSES** to take by preference
CHLORATE	*n* pl. **-S** a chemical salt		
CHLORDAN	*n* pl. **-S** a toxic compound of chlorine	**CHOOSER**	*n* pl. **-S** one that chooses
		CHOOSEY	*adj* **CHOOSIER, CHOOSIEST** choosy
CHLORIC	*adj* pertaining to chlorine		
CHLORID	*n* pl. **-S** chloride	**CHOOSY**	*adj* **CHOOSIER, CHOOSIEST** hard to please **CHOOSILY** *adv*
CHLORIDE	*n* pl. **-S** a chlorine compound		

CHOP	*v* **CHOPPED, CHOPPING, CHOPS** to sever with a sharp tool
CHOPIN	*n* pl. **-S** chopine
CHOPINE	*n* pl. **-S** a type of shoe
CHOPPED	past tense of chop
CHOPPER	*v* **-ED, -ING, -S** to travel by helicopter
CHOPPING	present participle of chop
CHOPPY	*adj* **CHOPPIER, CHOPPIEST** full of short, rough waves **CHOPPILY** *adv*
CHORAGUS	*n* pl. **-GUSES** or **-GI** the leader of a chorus or choir **CHORAGIC** *adj*
CHORAL	*n* pl. **-S** chorale
CHORALE	*n* pl. **-S** a hymn that is sung in unison
CHORALLY	*adv* harmoniously
CHORD	*v* **-ED, -ING, -S** to play a chord (a combination of three or more musical tones)
CHORDAL	*adj* pertaining to a chord
CHORDATE	*n* pl. **-S** any of a large phylum of animals
CHORDING	*n* pl. **-S** the act of playing a chord
CHORE	*v* **CHORED, CHORING, CHORES** to do small jobs
CHOREA	*n* pl. **-S** a nervous disorder **CHOREAL, CHOREIC** *adj*
CHOREBOY	*n* pl. **-BOYS** a boy employed to do odd jobs
CHOREGUS	*n* pl. **-GUSES** or **-GI** choragus
CHOREMAN	*n* pl. **-MEN** a menial worker
CHOREOID	*adj* resembling chorea
CHORIAL	*adj* pertaining to the chorion
CHORIAMB	*n* pl. **-S** a type of metrical foot
CHORIC	*adj* pertaining to a chorus
CHORINE	*n* pl. **-S** a chorus girl
CHORING	present participle of chore
CHORIOID	*n* pl. **-S** choroid
CHORION	*n* pl. **-S** an embryonic membrane
CHORIZO	*n* pl. **-ZOS** a highly seasoned sausage
CHOROID	*n* pl. **-S** a membrane of the eye
CHORTEN	*n* pl. **-S** a Tibetan shrine
CHORTLE	*v* **-TLED, -TLING, -TLES** to chuckle with glee
CHORTLER	*n* pl. **-S** one that chortles
CHORUS	*v* **-RUSED, -RUSING, -RUSES** or **-RUSSED, -RUSSING, -RUSSES** to sing in unison
CHOSE	*n* pl. **-S** an item of personal property
CHOSEN	past participle of choose
CHOTT	*n* pl. **-S** a saline lake
CHOUGH	*n* pl. **-S** a crow-like bird
CHOUSE	*v* **CHOUSED, CHOUSING, CHOUSES** to swindle
CHOUSER	*n* pl. **-S** one that chouses
CHOUSH	*n* pl. **-ES** chiaus
CHOW	*v* **-ED, -ING, -S** to eat
CHOWCHOW	*n* pl. **-S** a relish of mixed pickles in mustard
CHOWDER	*v* **-ED, -ING, -S** to make a thick soup of
CHOWSE	*v* **CHOWSED, CHOWSING, CHOWSES** to chouse
CHOWTIME	*n* pl. **-S** mealtime
CHRESARD	*n* pl. **-S** the available water of the soil
CHRISM	*n* pl. **-S** a consecrated oil **CHRISMAL** *adj*
CHRISMON	*n* pl. **-MONS** or **-MA** a Christian monogram
CHRISOM	*n* pl. **-S** chrism
CHRISTEN	*v* **-ED, -ING, -S** to baptize
CHRISTIE	*n* pl. **-S** christy
CHRISTY	*n* pl. **-TIES** a skiing turn
CHROMA	*n* pl. **-S** the purity of a color
CHROMATE	*n* pl. **-S** a chemical salt
CHROME	*v* **CHROMED, CHROMING, CHROMES** to plate with chromium
CHROMIC	*adj* pertaining to chromium
CHROMIDE	*n* pl. **-S** a tropical fish
CHROMING	*n* pl. **-S** a chromium ore
CHROMITE	*n* pl. **-S** a chromium ore
CHROMIUM	*n* pl. **-S** a metallic element
CHROMIZE	*v* **-MIZED, -MIZING, -MIZES** to chrome
CHROMO	*n* pl. **-MOS** a type of color picture
CHROMOLY	*n* pl. **-LIES** a steel alloy made of chromium and molybdenum
CHROMOUS	*adj* pertaining to chromium
CHROMY	*adj* **CHROMIER, CHROMIEST** decorated with chrome
CHROMYL	*n* pl. **-S** a bivalent radical

CHRONAXY *n pl.* **-AXIES** the time required to excite a nerve cell electrically

CHRONIC *n pl.* **-S** one that suffers from a long-lasting disease

CHRONON *n pl.* **-S** a hypothetical unit of time

CHTHONIC *adj* pertaining to the gods of the underworld

CHUB *n pl.* **-S** a freshwater fish

CHUBASCO *n pl.* **-COS** a violent thunderstorm

CHUBBY *adj* **-BIER, -BIEST** plump **CHUBBILY** *adv*

CHUCK *v* **-ED, -ING, -S** to throw

CHUCKER *n pl.* **-S** one that chucks

CHUCKIES pl. of chucky

CHUCKLE *v* **-LED, -LING, -LES** to laugh quietly

CHUCKLER *n pl.* **-S** one that chuckles

CHUCKY *n pl.* **CHUCKIES** a little chick

CHUDDAH *n pl.* **-S** chuddar

CHUDDAR *n pl.* **-S** a large, square shawl

CHUDDER *n pl.* **-S** chuddar

CHUFA *n pl.* **-S** a European sedge

CHUFF *adj* **CHUFFER, CHUFFEST** gruff

CHUFF *v* **-ED, -ING, -S** to chug

CHUFFY *adj* **-FIER, -FIEST** plump

CHUG *v* **CHUGGED, CHUGGING, CHUGS** to move with a dull explosive sound

CHUGALUG *v* **-LUGGED, -LUGGING, -LUGS** to drink without pause

CHUGGER *n pl.* **-S** one that chugs

CHUKAR *n pl.* **-S** a game bird

CHUKKA *n pl.* **-S** a type of boot

CHUKKAR *n pl.* **-S** a chukker

CHUKKER *n pl.* **-S** a period of play in polo

CHUM *v* **CHUMMED, CHUMMING, CHUMS** to be close friends with someone

CHUMMY *adj* **-MIER, -MIEST** friendly **CHUMMILY** *adv*

CHUMP *v* **-ED, -ING, -S** to munch

CHUMSHIP *n pl.* **-S** friendship

CHUNDER *v* **-ED, -ING, -S** to vomit

CHUNK *v* **-ED, -ING, -S** to make a dull explosive sound

CHUNKY *adj* **CHUNKIER, CHUNKIEST** stocky **CHUNKILY** *adv*

CHUNNEL *n pl.* **-S** a tunnel under the English Channel

CHUNTER *v* **-ED, -ING, -S** to mutter

CHUPPA *n pl.* **CHUPPAS** or **CHUPPOT** chuppah

CHUPPAH *n pl.* **CHUPPAHS** or **CHUPPOT** a canopy used at a Jewish wedding

CHURCH *v* **-ED, -ING, -ES** to bring to church (a building for Christian worship)

CHURCHLY *adj* **-LIER, -LIEST** pertaining to a church

CHURCHY *adj* **CHURCHIER, CHURCHIEST** churchly

CHURINGA *n pl.* **-S** a sacred object of Australian Aboriginals

CHURL *n pl.* **-S** a rude person **CHURLISH** *adj*

CHURN *v* **-ED, -ING, -S** to stir briskly in order to make butter

CHURNER *n pl.* **-S** one that churns

CHURNING *n pl.* **-S** the butter churned at one time

CHURR *v* **-ED, -ING, -S** to make a vibrant sound

CHURRO *n pl.* **-ROS** a Spanish and Mexican pastry

CHUSE *v* **CHUSED, CHUSING, CHUSES** to choose

CHUTE *v* **CHUTED, CHUTING, CHUTES** to convey by chute (a vertical passage)

CHUTIST *n pl.* **-S** a parachutist

CHUTNEE *n pl.* **-S** chutney

CHUTNEY *n pl.* **-NEYS** a sweet and sour sauce

CHUTZPA *n pl.* **-S** chutzpah

CHUTZPAH *n pl.* **-S** supreme self-confidence

CHYLE *n pl.* **-S** a digestive fluid **CHYLOUS** *adj*

CHYME *n pl.* **-S** semi-digested food

CHYMIC *n pl.* **-S** chemic

CHYMIST *n pl.* **-S** chemist

CHYMOSIN *n pl.* **-S** rennin

CHYMOUS *adj* pertaining to chyme

CHYRON *n pl.* **-S** a group of words that appears on a television screen

CHYTRID *n pl.* **-S** an aquatic or soil fungus

CIABATTA *n pl.* **-S** a type of Italian bread

CIAO *interj* — used as an expression of greeting and farewell

CIBOL *n pl.* **-S** a variety of onion

CIBORIUM   *n* pl. **-RIA** a vessel for holding holy bread

CIBOULE   *n* pl. **-S** cibol

CICADA   *n* pl. **-DAS** or **-DAE** a winged insect

CICALA   *n* pl. **-LAS** or **-LE** cicada

CICATRIX   *n* pl. **-TRIXES** or **-TRICES** scar tissue

CICELY   *n* pl. **-LIES** a fragrant herb

CICERO   *n* pl. **-ROS** a unit of measure in printing

CICERONE   *n* pl. **-NES** or **-NI** a tour guide

CICHLID   *n* pl. **-LIDS** or **-LIDAE** a tropical fish

CICISBEO   *n* pl. **-BEOS** or **-BEI** a lover of a married woman

CICOREE   *n* pl. **-S** a perennial herb

CIDER   *n* pl. **-S** the juice pressed from apples

CIG   *n* pl. **-S** a cigarette

CIGAR   *n* pl. **-S** a roll of tobacco leaf for smoking

CIGARET   *n* pl. **-S** a cigarette

CIGGIE   *n* pl. **-S** a cigarette

CIGGY   *n* pl. **CIGGIES** ciggie

CILANTRO   *n* pl. **-TROS** an herb used in cooking

CILIA   pl. of cilium

CILIARY   *adj* pertaining to cilia

CILIATE   *n* pl. **-S** one of a class of ciliated protozoans

CILIATED   *adj* having cilia

CILICE   *n* pl. **-S** a coarse cloth

CILIUM   *n* pl. **CILIA** a short, hairlike projection

CIMBALOM   *n* pl. **-S** a Hungarian dulcimer

CIMEX   *n* pl. **-MICES** a bedbug

CINCH   *v* **-ED, -ING, -ES** to girth

CINCHONA   *n* pl. **-S** a Peruvian tree

CINCTURE   *v* **-TURED, -TURING, -TURES** to gird or encircle

CINDER   *v* **-ED, -ING, -S** to reduce to cinders (ashes)

CINDERY   *adj* containing cinders

CINE   *n* pl. **-S** a motion picture

CINEAST   *n* pl. **-S** a devotee of motion pictures

CINEASTE   *n* pl. **-S** cineast

CINEMA   *n* pl. **-S** a motion-picture theater

CINEOL   *n* pl. **-S** a liquid used as an antiseptic

CINEOLE   *n* pl. **-S** cineol

CINERARY   *adj* used for cremated ashes

CINERIN   *n* pl. **-S** a compound used in insecticides

CINGULUM   *n* pl. **-LA** an anatomical band or girdle **CINGULAR** *adj*

CINNABAR   *n* pl. **-S** the principal ore of mercury

CINNAMON   *n* pl. **-S** a spice obtained from tree bark **CINNAMIC** *adj*

CINNAMYL   *n* pl. **-S** a chemical used to make soap

CINQ   *n* pl. **-S** cinque

CINQUAIN   *n* pl. **-S** a stanza of five lines

CINQUE   *n* pl. **-S** the number five

CION   *n* pl. **-S** a cutting from a plant or tree

CIOPPINO   *n* pl. **-NOS** a spicy fish stew

CIPAILLE   *n* pl. **-S** a pie with layers of meat and pastry

CIPHER   *v* **-ED, -ING, -S** to solve problems in arithmetic

CIPHERER   *n* pl. **-S** one that ciphers

CIPHONY   *n* pl. **-NIES** the electronic scrambling of voice transmissions

CIPOLIN   *n* pl. **-S** a type of marble

CIRCA   *prep* about; around

CIRCLE   *v* **-CLED, -CLING, -CLES** to move or revolve around

CIRCLER   *n* pl. **-S** one that circles

CIRCLET   *n* pl. **-S** a small ring or ring-shaped object

CIRCS   *n/pl* circumstances

CIRCUIT   *v* **-ED, -ING, -S** to move around

CIRCUITY   *n* pl. **-ITIES** lack of straightforwardness

CIRCULAR   *n* pl. **-S** a leaflet intended for wide distribution

CIRCUS   *n* pl. **-ES** a public entertainment **CIRCUSY** *adj*

CIRE   *n* pl. **-S** a highly glazed finish for fabrics

CIRQUE   *n* pl. **-S** a deep, steep-walled basin on a mountain

CIRRATE   *adj* having cirri

CIRRI   pl. of cirrus

CIRRIPED   *n* pl. **-S** any of an order of crustaceans

CIRROSE	*adj* cirrous	**CITRON**	*n* pl. **-S** a lemonlike fruit
CIRROUS	*adj* having cirri	**CITROUS**	*adj* pertaining to a citrus tree
CIRRUS	*n* pl. **-RI** a tendril or similar part	**CITRUS**	*n* pl. **-ES** any of a genus of tropical, fruit-bearing trees **CITRUSY** *adj*
CIRSOID	*adj* varicose		
CIS	*adj* having certain atoms on the same side of the molecule	**CITTERN**	*n* pl. **-S** a pear-shaped guitar
		CITY	*n* pl. **CITIES** a large town
CISCO	*n* pl. **-COS** or **-COES** a freshwater fish	**CITYFIED**	*adj* having the customs and manners of city people
CISLUNAR	*adj* situated between the earth and the moon	**CITYWARD**	*adv* toward the city
		CITYWIDE	*adj* including all parts of a city
CISSOID	*n* pl. **-S** a type of geometric curve	**CIVET**	*n* pl. **-S** a catlike mammal
CISSY	*n* pl. **-SIES** sissy	**CIVIC**	*adj* pertaining to a city
CIST	*n* pl. **-S** a prehistoric stone coffin **CISTED** *adj*	**CIVICISM**	*n* pl. **-S** a system of government based upon individual rights
CISTERN	*n* pl. **-S** a water tank	**CIVICS**	*n/pl* the science of civic affairs
CISTERNA	*n* pl. **-NAE** a fluid-containing sac	**CIVIE**	*n* pl. **-S** civvy
CISTRON	*n* pl. **-S** a segment of DNA	**CIVIL**	*adj* pertaining to citizens
CISTUS	*n* pl. **-ES** a flowering shrub	**CIVILIAN**	*n* pl. **-S** a nonmilitary person
CITABLE	*adj* citeable	**CIVILISE**	*v* **-LISED, -LISING, -LISES** to civilize
CITADEL	*n* pl. **-S** a fortress or stronghold		
CITATION	*n* pl. **-S** the act of citing **CITATORY** *adj*	**CIVILITY**	*n* pl. **-TIES** courtesy; politeness
		CIVILIZE	*v* **-LIZED, -LIZING, -LIZES** to bring out of savagery
CITATOR	*n* pl. **-S** one that cites		
CITE	*v* **CITED, CITING, CITES** to quote as an authority or example	**CIVILLY**	*adv* politely
		CIVISM	*n* pl. **-S** good citizenship
CITEABLE	*adj* suitable for citation	**CIVVY**	*n* pl. **-VIES** a civilian
CITER	*n* pl. **-S** one that cites	**CLABBER**	*v* **-ED, -ING, -S** to curdle
CITHARA	*n* pl. **-S** an ancient stringed instrument	**CLACH**	*n* pl. **-S** clachan
		CLACHAN	*n* pl. **-S** a hamlet
CITHER	*n* pl. **-S** cittern	**CLACK**	*v* **-ED, -ING, -S** to make an abrupt, dry sound
CITHERN	*n* pl. **-S** cittern		
CITHREN	*n* pl. **-S** cittern	**CLACKER**	*n* pl. **-S** one that clacks
CITIED	*adj* having cities	**CLAD**	*v* **CLADDED, CLADDING, CLADS** to coat one metal over another
CITIES	pl. of city		
CITIFY	*v* **-FIED, -FYING, -FIES** to urbanize	**CLADDAGH**	*n* pl. **-S** a ring designed with two hands clasping
CITING	present participle of cite		
CITIZEN	*n* pl. **-S** a resident of a city or town	**CLADDING**	*n* pl. **-S** something that overlays
CITOLA	*n* pl. **-S** a cittern	**CLADE**	*n* pl. **-S** a group of biological taxa
CITOLE	*n* pl. **-S** citola	**CLADISM**	*n* pl. **-S** the method of a cladist
CITRAL	*n* pl. **-S** a lemon flavoring	**CLADIST**	*n* pl. **-S** a taxonomist who uses clades in classifying life-forms
CITRATE	*n* pl. **-S** a salt of citric acid **CITRATED** *adj*		
		CLADODE	*n* pl. **-S** a leaflike part of a stem
CITREOUS	*adj* having a lemonlike color	**CLAFOUTI**	*n* pl. **-S** a dessert consisting of a layer of fruit topped with batter and baked
CITRIC	*adj* derived from citrus fruits		
CITRIN	*n* pl. **-S** a citric vitamin		
CITRINE	*n* pl. **-S** a variety of quartz	**CLAG**	*v* **CLAGGED, CLAGGING, CLAGS** to clog
CITRININ	*n* pl. **-S** an antibiotic		

CLAIM   *v* **-ED, -ING, -S** to demand as one's due

CLAIMANT   *n* pl. **-S** one that asserts a right or title

CLAIMER   *n* pl. **-S** one that claims

CLAM   *v* **CLAMMED, CLAMMING, CLAMS** to dig for clams (bivalve mollusks)

CLAMANT   *adj* noisy

CLAMBAKE   *n* pl. **-S** a beach picnic

CLAMBER   *v* **-ED, -ING, -S** to climb awkwardly

CLAMLIKE   *adj* resembling a clam

CLAMMED   past tense of clam

CLAMMER   *n* pl. **-S** one that clams

CLAMMING   present participle of clam

CLAMMY   *adj* **-MIER, -MIEST** cold and damp **CLAMMILY** *adv*

CLAMOR   *v* **-ED, -ING, -S** to make loud outcries

CLAMORER   *n* pl. **-S** one that clamors

CLAMOUR   *v* **-ED, -ING, -S** to clamor

CLAMP   *v* **-ED, -ING, -S** to fasten with a clamp (a securing device)

CLAMPER   *n* pl. **-S** a device worn on shoes to prevent slipping on ice

CLAMWORM   *n* pl. **-S** a marine worm

CLAN   *n* pl. **-S** a united group of families

CLANG   *v* **-ED, -ING, -S** to ring loudly

CLANGER   *n* pl. **-S** a blunder

CLANGOR   *v* **-ED, -ING, -S** to clang repeatedly

CLANGOUR   *v* **-ED, -ING, -S** to clangor

CLANK   *v* **-ED, -ING, -S** to make a sharp, metallic sound

CLANKY   *adj* **CLANKIER, CLANKIEST** making a sharp, metallic sound

CLANNISH   *adj* characteristic of a clan

CLANSMAN   *n* pl. **-MEN** a member of a clan

CLAP   *v* **CLAPPED** or **CLAPT, CLAPPING, CLAPS** to strike one palm against the other

CLAPPER   *n* pl. **-S** one that claps

CLAPTRAP   *n* pl. **-S** pretentious language

CLAQUE   *n* pl. **-S** a group of hired applauders

CLAQUER   *n* pl. **-S** claqueur

CLAQUEUR   *n* pl. **-S** a member of a claque

CLARENCE   *n* pl. **-S** a closed carriage

CLARET   *n* pl. **-S** a dry red wine

CLARIES   pl. of clary

CLARIFY   *v* **-FIED, -FYING, -FIES** to make clear

CLARINET   *n* pl. **-S** a woodwind instrument

CLARION   *v* **-ED, -ING, -S** to proclaim by blowing a medieval trumpet

CLARITY   *n* pl. **-TIES** the state of being clear

CLARKIA   *n* pl. **-S** an annual herb

CLARO   *n* pl. **-ROS** or **-ROES** a mild cigar

CLARY   *n* pl. **CLARIES** an aromatic herb

CLASH   *v* **-ED, -ING, -ES** to conflict or disagree

CLASHER   *n* pl. **-S** one that clashes

CLASP   *v* **CLASPED** or **CLASPT, CLASPING, CLASPS** to embrace tightly

CLASPER   *n* pl. **-S** one that clasps

CLASS   *v* **-ED, -ING, -ES** to classify

CLASSER   *n* pl. **-S** one that classes

CLASSES   pl. of classis

CLASSIC   *n* pl. **-S** a work of enduring excellence

CLASSICO   *adj* made from grapes grown in a certain part of Italy

CLASSIER   comparative of classy

CLASSIEST   superlative of classy

CLASSIFY   *v* **-FIED, -FYING, -FIES** to arrange according to characteristics

CLASSILY   *adv* in a classy manner

CLASSIS   *n* pl. **CLASSES** a governing body in certain churches

CLASSISM   *n* pl. **-S** discrimination based on social class

CLASSIST   *n* pl. **-S** an advocate of classism

CLASSON   *n* pl. **-S** a subatomic particle

CLASSY   *adj* **CLASSIER, CLASSIEST** stylish; elegant

CLAST   *n* pl. **-S** a fragment of rock

CLASTIC   *n* pl. **-S** a rock made up of other rocks

CLATTER   *v* **-ED, -ING, -S** to move with a rattling noise

CLATTERY   *adj* having a rattling noise

CLAUCHT   a past tense of cleek

CLAUGHT   *v* **-ED, -ING, -S** to clutch

CLAUSE   *n* pl. **-S** a distinct part of a composition **CLAUSAL** *adj*

CLAUSTRA   *n/pl* basal ganglia in the brain

CLAVATE   *adj* shaped like a club

CLAVE	*n* pl. **-S** one of a pair of percussion sticks		**CLEAROUT**	*n* pl. **-S** the action of removing unwanted material from a place
CLAVER	*v* **-ED, -ING, -S** to gossip		**CLEARWAY**	*n* pl. **-WAYS** a road on which stopping is not permitted
CLAVI	pl. of clavus		**CLEAT**	*v* **-ED, -ING, -S** to strengthen with a strip of wood or iron
CLAVICLE	*n* pl. **-S** a bone of the shoulder			
CLAVIER	*n* pl. **-S** a keyboard instrument		**CLEAVAGE**	*n* pl. **-S** the act of cleaving
CLAVUS	*n* pl. **-VI** a horny thickening of the skin		**CLEAVE**	*v* **CLEAVED** or **CLEFT** or **CLOVE** or **CLAVE, CLOVEN, CLEAVING, CLEAVES** to split or divide
CLAW	*v* **-ED, -ING, -S** to scratch with claws (sharp, curved toenails)		**CLEAVER**	*n* pl. **-S** a heavy knife
CLAWBACK	*n* pl. **-S** money taken back by taxation		**CLEEK**	*v* **CLAUCHT** or **CLEEKED, CLEEKING, CLEEKS** to clutch
CLAWER	*n* pl. **-S** one that claws		**CLEF**	*n* pl. **-S** a musical symbol
CLAWLESS	*adj* having no claws		**CLEFT**	*v* **-ED, -ING, -S** to insert a scion into the stock of a plant
CLAWLIKE	*adj* resembling a claw			
CLAXON	*n* pl. **-S** klaxon		**CLEG**	*n* pl. **-S** a horsefly
CLAY	*v* **-ED, -ING, -S** to treat with clay (a fine-grained, earthy material)		**CLEIDOIC**	*adj* enclosed in a shell
			CLEMATIS	*n* pl. **-TISES** a flowering vine
CLAYBANK	*n* pl. **-S** a yellow-brown color		**CLEMENCY**	*n* pl. **-CIES** mercy
CLAYEY	*adj* **CLAYIER, CLAYIEST** resembling clay		**CLEMENT**	*adj* merciful
CLAYISH	*adj* resembling or containing clay		**CLENCH**	*v* **-ED, -ING, -ES** to grasp firmly
CLAYLIKE	*adj* resembling clay		**CLENCHER**	*n* pl. **-S** one that clenches
CLAYMORE	*n* pl. **-S** a type of sword		**CLEOME**	*n* pl. **-S** a tropical plant
CLAYPAN	*n* pl. **-S** a shallow natural depression		**CLEPE**	*v* **CLEPED** or **CLEPT, CLEPING, CLEPES** to call by name
CLAYWARE	*n* pl. **-S** pottery		**CLERGY**	*n* pl. **-GIES** the body of persons ordained for religious service
CLEAN	*adj* **CLEANER, CLEANEST** free from dirt or stain **CLEANISH** *adj*			
CLEAN	*v* **-ED, -ING, -S** to rid of dirt or stain		**CLERIC**	*n* pl. **-S** a member of the clergy
CLEANER	*n* pl. **-S** one that cleans		**CLERICAL**	*n* pl. **-S** a cleric
CLEANING	*n* pl. **-S** the act of ridding of dirt or stain		**CLERID**	*n* pl. **-S** a predatory beetle
			CLERIHEW	*n* pl. **-S** a humorous poem
CLEANLY	*adj* **-LIER, -LIEST** habitually clean		**CLERISY**	*n* pl. **-SIES** the well-educated class
CLEANOUT	*n* pl. **-S** the act of cleaning something out		**CLERK**	*v* **-ED, -ING, -S** to serve as a clerk (an office worker)
CLEANSE	*v* **CLEANSED, CLEANSING, CLEANSES** to clean		**CLERKDOM**	*n* pl. **-S** the status or function of a clerk
CLEANSER	*n* pl. **-S** one that cleanses		**CLERKISH**	*adj* resembling or suitable to a clerk
CLEANUP	*n* pl. **-S** an act of cleaning			
CLEAR	*adj* **CLEARER, CLEAREST** clean and pure		**CLERKLY**	*adj* **-LIER, -LIEST** pertaining to a clerk
CLEAR	*v* **-ED, -ING, -S** to remove obstructions		**CLEVEITE**	*n* pl. **-S** a radioactive mineral
			CLEVER	*adj* **-ERER, -EREST** mentally keen **CLEVERLY** *adv*
CLEARCUT	*v* **-CUT, -CUTTING, -CUTS** to cut a forest completely		**CLEVIS**	*n* pl. **-ISES** a metal fastening device
CLEARER	*n* pl. **-S** one that clears		**CLEW**	*v* **-ED, -ING, -S** to roll into a ball
CLEARING	*n* pl. **-S** an open space		**CLICHE**	*n* pl. **-S** a trite expression **CLICHED** *adj*
CLEARLY	*adv* in a clear manner			

CLICK | *v* **-ED, -ING, -S** to make a short, sharp sound
CLICKER | *n* pl. **-S** one that clicks
CLIENT | *n* pl. **-S** a customer **CLIENTAL** *adj*
CLIFF | *n* pl. **-S** a high, steep face of rock
CLIFFTOP | *n* pl. **-S** the top of a cliff
CLIFFY | *adj* **CLIFFIER, CLIFFIEST** abounding in cliffs
CLIFT | *n* pl. **-S** cliff
CLIMATE | *n* pl. **-S** the weather conditions characteristic of an area **CLIMATAL, CLIMATIC** *adj*
CLIMAX | *v* **-ED, -ING, -ES** to reach a high or dramatic point
CLIMB | *v* **CLIMBED** or **CLOMB, CLIMBING, CLIMBS** to ascend
CLIMBER | *n* pl. **-S** one that climbs
CLIMBING | *n* pl. **-S** the sport or activity of ascending mountains
CLIME | *n* pl. **-S** climate
CLINAL | *adj* pertaining to a cline
CLINALLY | *adv* in a clinal manner
CLINCH | *v* **-ED, -ING, -ES** to settle a matter decisively
CLINCHER | *n* pl. **-S** a decisive fact or remark
CLINE | *n* pl. **-S** a series of changes within a species
CLING | *v* **-ED, -ING, -S** to make a high-pitched ringing sound
CLING | *v* **CLUNG, CLINGING, CLINGS** to adhere closely
CLINGER | *n* pl. **-S** one that clings
CLINGY | *adj* **CLINGIER, CLINGIEST** adhesive
CLINIC | *n* pl. **-S** a medical facility **CLINICAL** *adj*
CLINK | *v* **-ED, -ING, -S** to make a soft, sharp, ringing sound
CLINKER | *v* **-ED, -ING, -S** to form fused residue in burning
CLIP | *v* **CLIPPED** or **CLIPT, CLIPPING, CLIPS** to trim by cutting
CLIPPER | *n* pl. **-S** one that clips
CLIPPING | *n* pl. **-S** something that is clipped out or off
CLIPT | a past participle of clip
CLIQUE | *v* **CLIQUED, CLIQUING, CLIQUES** to form a clique (an exclusive group of persons)
CLIQUEY | *adj* **CLIQUIER, CLIQUIEST** inclined to form cliques

CLIQUISH | *adj* cliquey
CLIQUY | *adj* **CLIQUIER, CLIQUIEST** cliquey
CLITELLA | *n/pl* regions in the body walls of certain annelids
CLITIC | *n* pl. **-S** a word pronounced as part of a neighboring word
CLITORIS | *n* pl. **-RISES** or **-RIDES** a sex organ **CLITORAL, CLITORIC** *adj*
CLITTER | *v* **-ED, -ING, -S** to make a thin rattling sound
CLIVERS | *n* pl. **CLIVERS** an annual herb
CLIVIA | *n* pl. **-S** a flowering plant
CLOACA | *n* pl. **-ACAS** or **-ACAE** a sewer **CLOACAL** *adj*
CLOAK | *v* **-ED, -ING, -S** to conceal
CLOBBER | *v* **-ED, -ING, -S** to trounce
CLOCHARD | *n* pl. **-S** a vagrant
CLOCHE | *n* pl. **-S** a bell-shaped hat
CLOCK | *v* **-ED, -ING, -S** to time with a stopwatch
CLOCKER | *n* pl. **-S** one that clocks
CLOD | *n* pl. **-S** a dolt **CLODDISH** *adj*
CLODDY | *adj* **-DIER, -DIEST** lumpy
CLODPATE | *n* pl. **-S** a stupid person
CLODPOLE | *n* pl. **-S** clodpate
CLODPOLL | *n* pl. **-S** clodpate
CLOG | *v* **CLOGGED, CLOGGING, CLOGS** to block up or obstruct
CLOGGER | *n* pl. **-S** one that clogs
CLOGGING | *n* pl. **-S** the act of dancing while wearing shoes with thick wooden soles
CLOGGY | *adj* **-GIER, -GIEST** clogging or able to clog **CLOGGILY** *adv*
CLOISTER | *v* **-ED, -ING, -S** to seclude
CLOMB | a past tense of climb
CLOMP | *v* **-ED, -ING, -S** to walk heavily and clumsily
CLON | *n* pl. **-S** a group of asexually derived organisms **CLONAL** *adj* **CLONALLY** *adv*
CLONE | *v* **CLONED, CLONING, CLONES** to reproduce by asexual means
CLONER | *n* pl. **-S** one that clones
CLONIC | *adj* pertaining to clonus
CLONING | *n* pl. **-S** a technique for reproducing by asexual means
CLONISM | *n* pl. **-S** the condition of having clonus

CLONK	*v* **-ED, -ING, -S** to make a dull thumping sound	**CLOUT**	*v* **-ED, -ING, -S** to hit with the hand
CLONKY	*adj* **CLONKIER, CLONKIEST** making a dull thumping sound	**CLOUTER**	*n* pl. **-S** one that clouts
		CLOVE	*n* pl. **-S** a spice
CLONUS	*n* pl. **-ES** a form of muscular spasm	**CLOVEN**	a past participle of cleave
CLOOT	*n* pl. **-S** a cloven hoof	**CLOVER**	*n* pl. **-S** a plant **CLOVERED, CLOVERY** *adj*
CLOP	*v* **CLOPPED, CLOPPING, CLOPS** to make the sound of a hoof striking pavement	**CLOWDER**	*n* pl. **-S** a group of cats
		CLOWN	*v* **-ED, -ING, -S** to act like a clown (a humorous performer)
CLOQUE	*n* pl. **-S** a fabric with an embossed design	**CLOWNERY**	*n* pl. **-ERIES** clownish behavior
		CLOWNISH	*adj* resembling or befitting a clown
CLOSE	*adj* **CLOSER, CLOSEST** near **CLOSELY** *adv*	**CLOY**	*v* **-ED, -ING, -S** to gratify beyond desire
CLOSE	*v* **CLOSED, CLOSING, CLOSES** to block against entry or passage **CLOSABLE** *adj*	**CLOZE**	*n* pl. **-S** a test of reading comprehension
CLOSEOUT	*n* pl. **-S** a clearance sale	**CLUB**	*v* **CLUBBED, CLUBBING, CLUBS** to form a club (an organized group of persons)
CLOSER	*n* pl. **-S** one that closes		
CLOSEST	superlative of close	**CLUBABLE**	*adj* sociable
CLOSET	*v* **-ED, -ING, -S** to enclose in a private room	**CLUBBER**	*n* pl. **-S** a member of a club
		CLUBBING	*n* pl. **-S** the practice of frequenting nightclubs
CLOSEUP	*n* pl. **-S** a photograph taken at close range		
		CLUBBISH	*adj* clubby
CLOSING	*n* pl. **-S** a concluding part	**CLUBBY**	*adj* **-BIER, -BIEST** characteristic of a club
CLOSURE	*v* **-SURED, -SURING, -SURES** to cloture		
		CLUBFACE	*n* pl. **-S** the striking surface of a clubhead
CLOT	*v* **CLOTTED, CLOTTING, CLOTS** to form into a clot (a thick mass)		
		CLUBFOOT	*n* pl. **-FEET** a deformed foot
CLOTBUR	*n* pl. **-S** a type of plant with prickly seeds	**CLUBHAND**	*n* pl. **-S** a deformed hand
		CLUBHAUL	*v* **-ED, -ING, -S** to put a vessel about
CLOTH	*n* pl. **-S** fabric		
CLOTHE	*v* **CLOTHED** or **CLAD, CLOTHING, CLOTHES** to provide with clothing	**CLUBHEAD**	*n* pl. **-S** the part of a golf club that strikes the ball
		CLUBLAND	*n* pl. **-S** an area having many nightclubs
CLOTHIER	*n* pl. **-S** one who makes or sells clothing		
		CLUBMAN	*n* pl. **-MEN** a male member of a club
CLOTHING	*n* pl. **-S** wearing apparel		
CLOTTED	past tense of clot	**CLUBMATE**	*n* pl. **-S** a fellow member of a club
CLOTTING	present participle of clot	**CLUBMOSS**	*n* pl. **-ES** a green plant resembling a large moss
CLOTTY	*adj* tending to clot		
CLOTURE	*v* **-TURED, -TURING, -TURES** to end a debate by calling for a vote	**CLUBROOM**	*n* pl. **-S** a room for a club's meetings
		CLUBROOT	*n* pl. **-S** a plant disease
CLOUD	*v* **-ED, -ING, -S** to cover with clouds (masses of visible vapor)	**CLUCK**	*v* **-ED, -ING, -S** to make the sound of a hen
CLOUDLET	*n* pl. **-S** a small cloud		
CLOUDY	*adj* **CLOUDIER, CLOUDIEST** overcast with clouds **CLOUDILY** *adv*	**CLUCKER**	*n* pl. **-S** a chicken
		CLUE	*v* **CLUED, CLUEING** or **CLUING, CLUES** to give guiding information
CLOUGH	*n* pl. **-S** a ravine		
CLOUR	*v* **-ED, -ING, -S** to knock or bump	**CLUELESS**	*adj* hopelessly confused or ignorant

CLUMBER	*n* pl. **-S** a stocky spaniel	**COAEVAL**	*n* pl. **-S** coeval
CLUMP	*v* **-ED, -ING, -S** to form into a thick mass	**COAGENCY**	*n* pl. **-CIES** a joint agency
CLUMPER	*n* pl. **-S** a large floating chunk of ice	**COAGENT**	*n* pl. **-S** a person, force, or other agent working together with another
CLUMPET	*n* pl. **-S** a clumper	**COAGULUM**	*n* pl. **-LUMS** or **-LA** a clot
CLUMPISH	*adj* resembling a clump (a thick mass)	**COAL**	*v* **-ED, -ING, -S** to supply with coal (a carbon fuel)
CLUMPY	*adj* **CLUMPIER, CLUMPIEST** lumpy	**COALA**	*n* pl. **-S** koala
CLUMSY	*adj* **-SIER, -SIEST** awkward **CLUMSILY** *adv*	**COALBIN**	*n* pl. **-S** a bin for storing coal
		COALBOX	*n* pl. **-ES** a box for storing coal
CLUNG	past tense of cling	**COALER**	*n* pl. **-S** one that supplies coal
CLUNK	*v* **-ED, -ING, -S** to thump	**COALESCE**	*v* **-ALESCED, -ALESCING, -ALESCES** to blend
CLUNKER	*n* pl. **-S** a jalopy		
CLUNKY	*adj* **CLUNKIER, CLUNKIEST** clumsy in style	**COALFACE**	*n* pl. **-S** the place where coal is cut out of the rock
CLUPEID	*n* pl. **-S** a fish of the herring family	**COALFISH**	*n* pl. **-ES** a blackish fish
CLUPEOID	*n* pl. **-S** a clupeid	**COALHOLE**	*n* pl. **-S** a compartment for storing coal
CLUSTER	*v* **-ED, -ING, -S** to form into a cluster (a group of similar objects)	**COALIER**	comparative of coaly
CLUSTERY	*adj* pertaining to a cluster	**COALIEST**	superlative of coaly
CLUTCH	*v* **-ED, -ING, -ES** to grasp and hold tightly	**COALIFY**	*v* **-FIED, -FYING, -FIES** to convert into coal
CLUTCHY	*adj* tending to clutch	**COALLESS**	*adj* lacking coal
CLUTTER	*v* **-ED, -ING, -S** to pile in a disorderly state	**COALPIT**	*n* pl. **-S** a pit from which coal is obtained
CLUTTERY	*adj* characterized by disorder	**COALSACK**	*n* pl. **-S** a dark region of the Milky Way
CLYPEUS	*n* pl. **CLYPEI** a shield-like structure **CLYPEAL, CLYPEATE** *adj*	**COALSHED**	*n* pl. **-S** a shed for storing coal
CLYSTER	*n* pl. **-S** an enema	**COALY**	*adj* **COALIER, COALIEST** containing coal
CNIDA	*n* pl. **-DAE** a stinging organ in a jellyfish	**COALYARD**	*n* pl. **-S** a yard for storing coal
COACH	*v* **-ED, -ING, -ES** to tutor or train	**COAMING**	*n* pl. **-S** a raised border
COACHER	*n* pl. **-S** one that coaches	**COANCHOR**	*v* **-ED, -ING, -S** to present televised news reports jointly
COACHING	*n* pl. **-S** the work of one that coaches	**COANNEX**	*v* **-ED, -ING, -ES** to annex jointly
COACHMAN	*n* pl. **-MEN** one who drives a coach or carriage	**COAPPEAR**	*v* **-ED, -ING, -S** to appear together or at the same time
COACT	*v* **-ED, -ING, -S** to act together	**COAPT**	*v* **-ED, -ING, -S** to fit together and make fast
COACTION	*n* pl. **-S** joint action		
COACTIVE	*adj* mutually active	**COARSE**	*adj* **COARSER, COARSEST** rough **COARSELY** *adv* **COARSISH** *adj*
COACTOR	*n* pl. **-S** a fellow actor in a production	**COARSEN**	*v* **-ED, -ING, -S** to make coarse
COADMIRE	*v* **-MIRED, -MIRING, -MIRES** to admire together	**COASSIST**	*v* **-ED, -ING, -S** to assist jointly
COADMIT	*v* **-MITTED, -MITTING, -MITS** to admit several things equally	**COASSUME**	*v* **-SUMED, -SUMING, -SUMES** to assume together
		COAST	*v* **-ED, -ING, -S** to slide down a hill
COADY	*n* pl. **-DIES** a sauce made from molasses	**COASTAL**	*adj* pertaining to or located near a seashore

COASTER	*n* pl. **-S** a sled
COASTING	*n* pl. **-S** coastal trade
COAT	*v* **-ED, -ING, -S** to cover with a coat (an outer garment)
COATEE	*n* pl. **-S** a small coat
COATER	*n* pl. **-S** one that coats
COATI	*n* pl. **-S** a tropical mammal
COATING	*n* pl. **-S** a covering layer
COATLESS	*adj* lacking a coat
COATRACK	*n* pl. **-S** a rack or stand for coats
COATROOM	*n* pl. **-S** a room for storing coats
COATTAIL	*n* pl. **-S** the back lower portion of a coat
COATTEND	*v* **-ED, -ING, -S** to attend together
COATTEST	*v* **-ED, -ING, -S** to attest jointly
COAUTHOR	*v* **-ED, -ING, -S** to write together
COAX	*v* **-ED, -ING, -ES** to cajole
COAXAL	*adj* coaxial
COAXER	*n* pl. **-S** one that coaxes
COAXIAL	*adj* having a common axis
COAXING	*n* pl. **-S** an act of cajoling
COB	*n* pl. **-S** a corncob
COBALT	*n* pl. **-S** a metallic element **COBALTIC** *adj*
COBB	*n* pl. **-S** a seagull
COBBER	*n* pl. **-S** a comrade
COBBIER	comparative of cobby
COBBIEST	superlative of cobby
COBBLE	*v* **-BLED, -BLING, -BLES** to mend
COBBLER	*n* pl. **-S** a mender of shoes
COBBY	*adj* **-BIER, -BIEST** stocky
COBIA	*n* pl. **-S** a large game fish
COBLE	*n* pl. **-S** a small fishing boat
COBNUT	*n* pl. **-S** an edible nut
COBRA	*n* pl. **-S** a venomous snake
COBWEB	*v* **-WEBBED, -WEBBING, -WEBS** to cover with cobwebs (spider webs)
COBWEBBY	*adj* **-BIER, -BIEST** covered with cobwebs
COCA	*n* pl. **-S** a South American shrub
COCAIN	*n* pl. **-S** cocaine
COCAINE	*n* pl. **-S** a narcotic alkaloid
COCCAL	*adj* pertaining to a coccus
COCCI	pl. of coccus
COCCIC	*adj* coccal

COCCID	*n* pl. **-S** an insect
COCCIDIA	*n/pl* parasitic protozoans
COCCOID	*n* pl. **-S** a spherical cell or body
COCCUS	*n* pl. **COCCI** a spherical bacterium **COCCOUS** *adj*
COCCYX	*n* pl. **-CYXES** or **-CYGES** a bone of the spine
COCHAIR	*v* **-ED, -ING, -S** to serve jointly as chairman of
COCHIN	*n* pl. **-S** a large domestic chicken
COCHLEA	*n* pl. **-CHLEAS** or **-CHLEAE** a part of the ear **COCHLEAR** *adj*
COCINERA	*n* pl. **-S** a cook
COCK	*v* **-ED, -ING, -S** to tilt to one side
COCKADE	*n* pl. **-S** an ornament worn on a hat **COCKADED** *adj*
COCKAPOO	*n* pl. **-POOS** a hybrid between a cocker spaniel and a poodle
COCKATOO	*n* pl. **-TOOS** a parrot
COCKBILL	*v* **-ED, -ING, -S** to raise the yardarm on a ship
COCKBOAT	*n* pl. **-S** a small boat
COCKCROW	*n* pl. **-S** daybreak
COCKER	*v* **-ED, -ING, -S** to pamper
COCKEREL	*n* pl. **-S** a young rooster
COCKEYE	*n* pl. **-S** a squinting eye **COCKEYED** *adj*
COCKIER	comparative of cocky
COCKIES	pl. of cocky
COCKIEST	superlative of cocky
COCKILY	*adv* in a cocky manner
COCKISH	*adj* cocky
COCKLE	*v* **-LED, -LING, -LES** to wrinkle or pucker
COCKLIKE	*adj* resembling a rooster
COCKLOFT	*n* pl. **-S** a small attic
COCKNEY	*n* pl. **-NEYS** a resident of the East End of London
COCKPIT	*n* pl. **-S** a pilot's compartment in certain airplanes
COCKSHUT	*n* pl. **-S** the close of day
COCKSHY	*n* pl. **-SHIES** a target in a throwing contest
COCKSPUR	*n* pl. **-S** a thorny plant
COCKSURE	*adj* certain
COCKTAIL	*v* **-ED, -ING, -S** to drink alcoholic beverages
COCKUP	*n* pl. **-S** a turned-up part of something

COCKY	*adj* **COCKIER, COCKIEST** arrogantly self-confident
COCKY	*n* pl. **COCKIES** a cockatoo
COCO	*n* pl. **-COS** a tall palm tree
COCOA	*n* pl. **-S** chocolate
COCOANUT	*n* pl. **-S** coconut
COCOBOLA	*n* pl. **-S** cocobolo
COCOBOLO	*n* pl. **-LOS** a tropical tree
COCOMAT	*n* pl. **-S** a matting made from coir
COCONUT	*n* pl. **-S** the fruit of the coco
COCOON	*v* **-ED, -ING, -S** to wrap or envelop tightly
COCOONER	*n* pl. **-S** one who retreats to the private world of the family
COCOPLUM	*n* pl. **-S** an evergreen shrub
COCOTTE	*n* pl. **-S** a prostitute
COCOYAM	*n* pl. **-S** a tropical plant having edible rootstocks
COCREATE	*v* **-ATED, -ATING, -ATES** to create together
COCURATE	*v* **-RATED, -RATING, -RATES** to curate jointly
COD	*v* **CODDED, CODDING, CODS** to fool
CODA	*n* pl. **-S** a passage at the end of a musical composition
CODABLE	*adj* capable of being coded
CODDER	*n* pl. **-S** a cod fisherman
CODDING	present participle of cod
CODDLE	*v* **-DLED, -DLING, -DLES** to pamper
CODDLER	*n* pl. **-S** one that coddles
CODE	*v* **CODED, CODING, CODES** to convert into symbols
CODEBOOK	*n* pl. **-S** a book listing words and their coded equivalents
CODEBTOR	*n* pl. **-S** one that shares a debt
CODEC	*n* pl. **-S** an integrated circuit
CODED	past tense of code
CODEIA	*n* pl. **-S** codeine
CODEIN	*n* pl. **-S** codeine
CODEINA	*n* pl. **-S** codeine
CODEINE	*n* pl. **-S** a narcotic alkaloid
CODELESS	*adj* being without a set of laws
CODEN	*n* pl. **-S** a coding classification
CODER	*n* pl. **-S** one that codes
CODERIVE	*v* **-RIVED, -RIVING, -RIVES** to derive jointly
CODESIGN	*v* **-ED, -ING, -S** to design jointly
CODEX	*n* pl. **-DICES** or **-DEXES** an ancient manuscript
CODFISH	*n* pl. **-ES** a marine food fish
CODGER	*n* pl. **-S** an old man
CODICES	pl. of codex
CODICIL	*n* pl. **-S** a supplement to a will
CODIFIER	*n* pl. **-S** one that codifies
CODIFY	*v* **-FIED, -FYING, -FIES** to arrange or systematize
CODING	*n* pl. **-S** the process of converting into symbols
CODIRECT	*v* **-ED, -ING, -S** to direct jointly
CODLIN	*n* pl. **-S** codling
CODLING	*n* pl. **-S** an unripe apple
CODOMAIN	*n* pl. **-S** a mathematical set
CODON	*n* pl. **-S** a triplet of nucleotides (basic components of DNA)
CODPIECE	*n* pl. **-S** a cover for the crotch in men's breeches
CODRIVE	*v* **-DROVE, -DRIVEN, -DRIVING, -DRIVES** to work as a codriver
CODRIVER	*n* pl. **-S** one who takes turns driving a vehicle
COED	*n* pl. **-S** a female student
COEDIT	*v* **-ED, -ING, -S** to edit with another person
COEDITOR	*n* pl. **-S** one that coedits
COEFFECT	*n* pl. **-S** an accompanying effect
COELIAC	*n* pl. **-S** celiac
COELOM	*n* pl. **-LOMS** or **-LOMATA** a body cavity in some animals **COELOMIC** *adj*
COELOME	*n* pl. **-S** coelom
COEMBODY	*v* **-BODIED, -BODYING, -BODIES** to embody jointly
COEMPLOY	*v* **-ED, -ING, -S** to employ together
COEMPT	*v* **-ED, -ING, -S** to buy up the entire supply of a product
COENACT	*v* **-ED, -ING, -S** to enact jointly or at the same time
COENAMOR	*v* **-ED, -ING, -S** to inflame with mutual love
COENDURE	*v* **-DURED, -DURING, -DURES** to endure together
COENURE	*n* pl. **-S** coenurus
COENURUS	*n* pl. **-RI** a tapeworm larva
COENZYME	*n* pl. **-S** a substance necessary for the functioning of certain enzymes

COEQUAL	*n* pl. **-S** one who is equal with another
COEQUATE	*v* **-QUATED, -QUATING, -QUATES** to equate with something else
COERCE	*v* **-ERCED, -ERCING, -ERCES** to compel by force or threat
COERCER	*n* pl. **-S** one that coerces
COERCION	*n* pl. **-S** the act of coercing
COERCIVE	*adj* serving to coerce
COERECT	*v* **-ED, -ING, -S** to erect together
COESITE	*n* pl. **-S** a type of silica
COEVAL	*n* pl. **-S** one of the same era or period as another
COEVALLY	*adv* contemporarily
COEVOLVE	*v* **-VOLVED, -VOLVING, -VOLVES** to evolve together
COEXERT	*v* **-ED, -ING, -S** to exert jointly
COEXIST	*v* **-ED, -ING, -S** to exist together
COEXTEND	*v* **-ED, -ING, -S** to extend through the same space or time as another
COFACTOR	*n* pl. **-S** a coenzyme
COFF	*v* **COFT, COFFING, COFFS** to buy
COFFEE	*n* pl. **-S** an aromatic, mildly stimulating beverage
COFFER	*v* **-ED, -ING, -S** to put in a strongbox
COFFIN	*v* **-ED, -ING, -S** to put in a coffin (a burial case)
COFFING	present participle of coff
COFFLE	*v* **-FLED, -FLING, -FLES** to chain slaves together
COFFRET	*n* pl. **-S** a small strongbox
COFOUND	*v* **-ED, -ING, -S** to found jointly
COFT	past tense of coff
COG	*v* **COGGED, COGGING, COGS** to cheat at dice
COGENCY	*n* pl. **-CIES** the state of being cogent
COGENT	*adj* convincing **COGENTLY** *adv*
COGITATE	*v* **-TATED, -TATING, -TATES** to ponder
COGITO	*n* pl. **-TOS** a philosophical principle
COGNAC	*n* pl. **-S** a brandy
COGNATE	*n* pl. **-S** one that is related to another
COGNISE	*v* **-NISED, -NISING, -NISES** to cognize
COGNIZE	*v* **-NIZED, -NIZING, -NIZES** to become aware of in one's mind
COGNIZER	*n* pl. **-S** one that cognizes
COGNOMEN	*n* pl. **-MENS** or **-MINA** a family name
COGNOVIT	*n* pl. **-S** a written admission of liability
COGON	*n* pl. **-S** a tall tropical grass
COGWAY	*n* pl. **-WAYS** a railway operating on steep slopes
COGWHEEL	*n* pl. **-S** a toothed wheel
COHABIT	*v* **-ED, -ING, -S** to live or exist together
COHEAD	*v* **-ED, -ING, -S** to head jointly
COHEIR	*n* pl. **-S** a joint heir
COHERE	*v* **-HERED, -HERING, -HERES** to stick together
COHERENT	*adj* sticking together
COHERER	*n* pl. **-S** a device used to detect radio waves
COHESION	*n* pl. **-S** the act or state of cohering **COHESIVE** *adj*
COHO	*n* pl. **-HOS** a small salmon
COHOBATE	*v* **-BATED, -BATING, -BATES** to distill again
COHOE	*n* pl. **-S** coho
COHOG	*n* pl. **-S** a quahog
COHOLDER	*n* pl. **-S** an athlete who holds a record with another
COHORT	*n* pl. **-S** a companion or associate
COHOSH	*n* pl. **-ES** a medicinal plant
COHOST	*v* **-ED, -ING, -S** to host jointly
COHUNE	*n* pl. **-S** a palm tree
COIF	*v* **-ED, -ING, -S** to style the hair
COIFFE	*v* **COIFFED, COIFFING, COIFFES** to coif
COIFFEUR	*n* pl. **-S** a male hairdresser
COIFFURE	*v* **-FURED, -FURING, -FURES** to coif
COIGN	*v* **-ED, -ING, -S** to quoin
COIGNE	*v* **COIGNED, COIGNING, COIGNES** to quoin
COIL	*v* **-ED, -ING, -S** to wind in even rings
COILER	*n* pl. **-S** one who coils
COIN	*v* **-ED, -ING, -S** to make coins (metal currency) **COINABLE** *adj*
COINAGE	*n* pl. **-S** the act of making coins

COINCIDE	*v* **-CIDED, -CIDING, -CIDES** to be in the same place	**COLEAD**	*v* **-LED, -LEADING, -LEADS** to lead jointly
COINER	*n* pl. **-S** one that coins	**COLEADER**	*n* pl. **-S** one that coleads
COINFECT	*v* **-ED, -ING, -S** to infect with two organisms	**COLESEED**	*n* pl. **-S** colza
		COLESLAW	*n* pl. **-S** a salad made of shredded raw cabbage
COINFER	*v* **-FERRED, -FERRING, -FERS** to infer jointly	**COLESSEE**	*n* pl. **-S** a joint lessee
COINHERE	*v* **-HERED, -HERING, -HERES** to inhere jointly	**COLESSOR**	*n* pl. **-S** a joint lessor
COINMATE	*n* pl. **-S** a fellow inmate	**COLEUS**	*n* pl. **-ES** a tropical plant
COINSURE	*v* **-SURED, -SURING, -SURES** to insure with another	**COLEWORT**	*n* pl. **-S** cole
		COLIC	*n* pl. **-S** acute abdominal pain
COINTER	*v* **-TERRED, -TERRING, -TERS** to bury together	**COLICIN**	*n* pl. **-S** an antibacterial substance
		COLICINE	*n* pl. **-S** colicin
COINVENT	*v* **-ED, -ING, -S** to invent together	**COLICKY**	*adj* pertaining to or associated with colic
COINVEST	*v* **-ED, -ING, -S** to invest jointly		
COIR	*n* pl. **-S** a fiber obtained from coconut husks	**COLIES**	pl. of coly
		COLIFORM	*n* pl. **-S** a bacillus of the colon
COISTREL	*n* pl. **-S** a knave	**COLIN**	*n* pl. **-S** the bobwhite
COISTRIL	*n* pl. **-S** coistrel	**COLINEAR**	*adj* lying in the same straight line
COITION	*n* pl. **-S** coitus	**COLISEUM**	*n* pl. **-S** a large structure for public entertainment
COITUS	*n* pl. **-ES** sexual intercourse **COITAL** *adj* **COITALLY** *adv*		
		COLISTIN	*n* pl. **-S** an antibiotic
COJOIN	*v* **-ED, -ING, -S** to join together	**COLITIS**	*n* pl. **-TISES** inflammation of the colon **COLITIC** *adj*
COKE	*v* **COKED, COKING, COKES** to change into a carbon fuel		
		COLLAGE	*v* **-LAGED, -LAGING, -LAGES** to arrange materials in a collage (a kind of artistic composition)
COKEHEAD	*n* pl. **-S** a cocaine addict		
COKELIKE	*adj* resembling coke (a carbon fuel)	**COLLAGEN**	*n* pl. **-S** a protein
		COLLAPSE	*v* **-LAPSED, -LAPSING, -LAPSES** to crumble suddenly
COKING	*n* pl. **-S** the process of converting coal into coke (a carbon fuel)	**COLLAR**	*v* **-ED, -ING, -S** to provide with a collar (something worn around the neck)
COKY	*adj* cokelike		
COL	*n* pl. **-S** a depression between two mountains		
		COLLARD	*n* pl. **-S** a variety of kale
COLA	*n* pl. **-S** a carbonated beverage	**COLLARET**	*n* pl. **-S** a small collar
COLANDER	*n* pl. **-S** a kitchen utensil for draining off liquids	**COLLATE**	*v* **-LATED, -LATING, -LATES** to compare critically
COLBY	*n* pl. **-BYS** a mild cheese	**COLLATOR**	*n* pl. **-S** one that collates
COLD	*adj* **COLDER, COLDEST** having little or no warmth	**COLLECT**	*v* **-ED, -ING, -S** to bring together in a group
COLD	*n* pl. **-S** the relative lack of heat; a chill	**COLLEEN**	*n* pl. **-S** an Irish girl
		COLLEGE	*n* pl. **-S** a school of higher learning
COLDCOCK	*v* **-ED, -ING, -S** to knock unconscious	**COLLEGER**	*n* pl. **-S** a student supported by funds from his or her college
COLDISH	*adj* somewhat cold		
COLDLY	*adv* in a cold manner	**COLLEGIA**	*n/pl* soviet executive councils
COLDNESS	*n* pl. **-ES** the state of being cold	**COLLET**	*v* **-ED, -ING, -S** to set a gem in a rim or ring
COLE	*n* pl. **-S** a plant of the cabbage family	**COLLIDE**	*v* **-LIDED, -LIDING, -LIDES** to come together with violent impact

COLLIDER *n pl.* **-S** a type of particle accelerator

COLLIE *n pl.* **-S** a large dog

COLLIED past tense of colly

COLLIER *n pl.* **-S** a coal miner

COLLIERY *n pl.* **-LIERIES** a coal mine

COLLIES present 3d person sing. of colly

COLLINS *n pl.* **-ES** an alcoholic beverage

COLLOGUE *v* **-LOGUED, -LOGUING, -LOGUES** to conspire

COLLOID *n pl.* **-S** a type of chemical suspension

COLLOP *n pl.* **-S** a small portion of meat

COLLOQUY *n pl.* **-QUIES** a conversation

COLLUDE *v* **-LUDED, -LUDING, -LUDES** to conspire

COLLUDER *n pl.* **-S** one that colludes

COLLUVIA *n/pl* rock debris

COLLY *v* **-LIED, -LYING, -LIES** to blacken with coal dust

COLLYRIA *n/pl* medicinal lotions

COLOBOMA *n pl.* **-MATA** or **-MAS** a lesion of the eye

COLOBUS *n pl.* **-BUSES** or **-BI** a large African monkey

COLOCATE *v* **-CATED, -CATING, -CATES** to place two or more housing units in close proximity

COLOG *n pl.* **-S** the logarithm of the reciprocal of a number

COLOGNE *n pl.* **-S** a scented liquid **COLOGNED** *adj*

COLON *n pl.* **-ES** a monetary unit of Costa Rica

COLON *n pl.* **-S** a section of the large intestine

COLONE *n pl.* **-S** colon

COLONEL *n pl.* **-S** a military officer

COLONI pl. of colonus

COLONIAL *n pl.* **-S** a citizen of a colony

COLONIC *n pl.* **-S** irrigation of the colon

COLONIES pl. of colony

COLONISE *v* **-NISED, -NISING, -NISES** to colonize

COLONIST *n pl.* **-S** one who settles a colony

COLONIZE *v* **-NIZED, -NIZING, -NIZES** to establish a colony

COLONUS *n pl.* **-NI** a freeborn serf

COLONY *n pl.* **-NIES** a group of emigrants living in a new land

COLOPHON *n pl.* **-S** an inscription placed at the end of a book

COLOR *v* **-ED, -ING, -S** to give color (a visual attribute of objects) to

COLORADO *adj* of medium strength and color — used of cigars

COLORANT *n pl.* **-S** a pigment or dye

COLORED *adj* having color

COLORER *n pl.* **-S** one that colors

COLORFUL *adj* full of color

COLORING *n pl.* **-S** appearance in regard to color

COLORISE *v* **-ISED, -ISING, -ISES** to colorize

COLORISM *n pl.* **-S** coloring

COLORIST *n pl.* **-S** a person skilled in the use of color

COLORIZE *v* **-IZED, -IZING, -IZES** to give color to a black-and-white film

COLORMAN *n pl.* **-MEN** a sportscaster who provides commentary during a game

COLORWAY *n pl.* **-WAYS** an arrangement of colors

COLOSSAL *adj* gigantic

COLOSSUS *n pl.* **-LOSSUSES** or **-LOSSI** a gigantic statue

COLOTOMY *n pl.* **-MIES** a surgical incision of the colon

COLOUR *v* **-ED, -ING, -S** to color

COLOURER *n pl.* **-S** colorer

COLPITIS *n pl.* **-TISES** a vaginal inflammation

COLT *n pl.* **-S** a young male horse **COLTISH** *adj*

COLTAN *n pl.* **-S** a black ore containing columbite and tantalite

COLTER *n pl.* **-S** a blade on a plow

COLTHOOD *n pl.* **-S** the state or time of being a colt

COLUBRID *n pl.* **-S** any of a large family of snakes

COLUGO *n pl.* **-GOS** a small mammal

COLUMBIC *adj* pertaining to niobium

COLUMEL *n pl.* **-S** a small column-like anatomical part

COLUMN *n pl.* **-S** a vertical cylindrical support **COLUMNAL, COLUMNAR, COLUMNED** *adj*

COLUMNEA *n pl.* **-S** a bushy tropical plant

COLURE   *n* pl. **-S** an astronomical circle

COLY   *n* pl. **COLIES** an African bird

COLZA   *n* pl. **-S** a plant of the cabbage family

COMA   *n* pl. **-MAE** a tuft of silky hairs

COMA   *n* pl. **-S** a condition of prolonged unconsciousness

COMAKE   *v* **-MADE, -MAKING, -MAKES** to serve as comaker for another's loan

COMAKER   *n* pl. **-S** one who assumes financial responsibility for another's default

COMAL   *adj* comose

COMANAGE   *v* **-AGED, -AGING, -AGES** to manage jointly

COMATE   *n* pl. **-S** a companion

COMATIC   *adj* having blurred vision as a result of coma

COMATIK   *n* pl. **-S** komatik

COMATOSE   *adj* affected with coma

COMATULA   *n* pl. **-LAE** a marine animal

COMB   *v* **-ED, -ING, -S** to arrange or clean with a comb (a toothed instrument)

COMBAT   *v* **-BATED, -BATING, -BATS** or **-BATTED, -BATTING, -BATS** to fight against

COMBATER   *n* pl. **-S** one that combats

COMBE   *n* pl. **-S** a narrow valley

COMBER   *n* pl. **-S** one that combs

COMBI   *n* pl. **-S** a machine having a combined function

COMBINE   *v* **-BINED, -BINING, -BINES** to blend

COMBINED   *n* pl. **-S** a skiing competition combining two events

COMBINER   *n* pl. **-S** one that combines

COMBINGS   *n/pl* hair removed by a comb

COMBINING   present participle of combine

COMBLIKE   *adj* resembling a comb

COMBO   *n* pl. **-BOS** a small jazz band

COMBOVER   *n* pl. **-S** hair that is combed over a bald spot

COMBUST   *v* **-ED, -ING, -S** to burn

COME   *v* **CAME, COMING, COMES** or **COMETH** to move toward something or someone

COMEBACK   *n* pl. **-S** a return to former prosperity

COMEDIAN   *n* pl. **-S** a humorous entertainer

COMEDIC   *adj* pertaining to comedy

COMEDIES   pl. of comedy

COMEDIST   *n* pl. **-S** a writer of comedies

COMEDO   *n* pl. **-DOS** or **-DONES** a skin blemish

COMEDOWN   *n* pl. **-S** a drop in status

COMEDY   *n* pl. **-DIES** a humorous play, movie, or other work

COMELY   *adj* **-LIER, -LIEST** pleasing to look at **COMELILY** *adv*

COMEMBER   *n* pl. **-S** one that shares membership

COMER   *n* pl. **-S** one showing great promise

COMET   *n* pl. **-S** a celestial body **COMETARY** *adj*

COMETH   a present 3d person sing. of come

COMETHER   *n* pl. **-S** an affair or matter

COMETIC   *adj* pertaining to a comet

COMFIER   comparative of comfy

COMFIEST   superlative of comfy

COMFIT   *n* pl. **-S** a candy

COMFORT   *v* **-ED, -ING, -S** to soothe in time of grief

COMFREY   *n* pl. **-FREYS** a coarse herb

COMFY   *adj* **-FIER, -FIEST** comfortable **COMFILY** *adv*

COMIC   *n* pl. **-S** a comedian

COMICAL   *adj* funny

COMING   *n* pl. **-S** arrival

COMINGLE   *v* **-GLED, -GLING, -GLES** to blend thoroughly

COMITIA   *n* pl. **COMITIA** a public assembly in ancient Rome **COMITIAL** *adj*

COMITY   *n* pl. **-TIES** civility

COMIX   *n/pl* comic books or strips

COMM   *n* pl. **-S** communication

COMMA   *n* pl. **-MAS** or **-MATA** a fragment of a few words or feet in ancient prosody

COMMAND   *v* **-ED, -ING, -S** to direct with authority

COMMANDO   *n* pl. **-DOS** or **-DOES** a military unit

COMMATA   a pl. of comma

COMMENCE   *v* **-MENCED, -MENCING, -MENCES** to begin

COMMEND   *v* **-ED, -ING, -S** to praise

COMMENT   *v* **-ED, -ING, -S** to remark

COMMERCE   *v* **-MERCED, -MERCING, -MERCES** to commune

COMMIE   *n* pl. **-S** a Communist

COMMIES   pl. of commy

COMMIS   n pl. **COMMIS** a junior chef

COMMISH   n pl. **-ES** a commissioner

COMMIT   v **-MITTED, -MITTING, -MITS** to do, perform, or perpetrate

COMMIX   v **-MIXED** or **-MIXT, -MIXING, -MIXES** to mix together

COMMO   n pl. **-MOS** communication

COMMODE   n pl. **-S** a cabinet

COMMON   adj **-MONER, -MONEST** ordinary

COMMON   n pl. **-S** a tract of publicly used land

COMMONER   n pl. **-S** one of the common people

COMMONLY   adv in a common manner

COMMOVE   v **-MOVED, -MOVING, -MOVES** to move violently

COMMUNAL   adj belonging to a community; public

COMMUNE   v **-MUNED, -MUNING, -MUNES** to converse intimately

COMMUNER   n pl. **-S** one that communes

COMMUTE   v **-MUTED, -MUTING, -MUTES** to exchange

COMMUTER   n pl. **-S** one that commutes

COMMY   n pl. **-MIES** commie

COMORBID   adj existing simultaneously with another medical condition

COMOSE   adj bearing a tuft of silky hairs

COMOUS   adj comose

COMP   v **-ED, -ING, -S** to play a jazz accompaniment

COMPACT   adj **-PACTER, -PACTEST** closely and firmly united

COMPACT   v **-ED, -ING, -S** to pack closely together

COMPADRE   n pl. **-S** a close friend

COMPANY   v **-NIED, -NYING, -NIES** to associate with

COMPARE   v **-PARED, -PARING, -PARES** to represent as similar

COMPARER   n pl. **-S** one that compares

COMPART   v **-ED, -ING** to divide into parts

COMPAS   n a popular music of Haiti

COMPASS   v **-ED, -ING, -ES** to go around

COMPEER   v **-ED, -ING, -S** to equal or match

COMPEL   v **-PELLED, -PELLING, -PELS** to urge forcefully

COMPEND   n pl. **-S** a brief summary

COMPERE   v **-PERED, -PERING, -PERES** to act as master of ceremonies

COMPETE   v **-PETED, -PETING, -PETES** to vie

COMPILE   v **-PILED, -PILING, -PILES** to collect into a volume

COMPILER   n pl. **-S** one that compiles

COMPING   n pl. **-S** the playing of a jazz accompaniment

COMPLAIN   v **-ED, -ING, -S** to express discontent

COMPLEAT   v **-ED, -ING, -S** to complete

COMPLECT   v **-ED, -ING, -S** to weave together

COMPLETE   adj **-PLETER, -PLETEST** having all necessary parts

COMPLETE   v **-PLETED, -PLETING, -PLETES** to bring to an end

COMPLEX   adj **-PLEXER, -PLEXEST** complicated

COMPLEX   v **-ED, -ING, -ES** to make complex

COMPLICE   n pl. **-S** an associate

COMPLIED   past tense of comply

COMPLIER   n pl. **-S** one that complies

COMPLIES   present 3d person sing. of comply

COMPLIN   n pl. **-S** compline

COMPLINE   n pl. **-S** the last liturgical prayer of the day

COMPLOT   v **-PLOTTED, -PLOTTING, -PLOTS** to conspire

COMPLY   v **-PLIED, -PLYING, -PLIES** to obey

COMPO   n pl. **-POS** a mixed substance

COMPONE   adj compony

COMPONY   adj composed of squares of alternating colors

COMPORT   v **-ED, -ING, -S** to conduct oneself in a certain way

COMPOSE   v **-POSED, -POSING, -POSES** to form the substance of

COMPOSER   n pl. **-S** one that writes music

COMPOST   v **-ED, -ING, -S** to fertilize

COMPOTE   n pl. **-S** fruit stewed in syrup

COMPOUND   v **-ED, -ING, -S** to add to

COMPRESS   v **-ED, -ING, -ES** to compact

COMPRISE   v **-PRISED, -PRISING, -PRISES** to include or contain

COMPRIZE   v **-PRIZED, -PRIZING, -PRIZES** to comprise

COMPT   v **-ED, -ING, -S** to count

COMPUTE *v* **-PUTED, -PUTING, -PUTES** to calculate

COMPUTER *n* pl. **-S** a machine that computes automatically

COMRADE *n* pl. **-S** a close friend

COMTE *n* pl. **-S** a French nobleman

CON *v* **CONNED, CONNING, CONS** to study carefully

CONATION *n* pl. **-S** the inclination to act purposefully **CONATIVE** *adj*

CONATUS *n* pl. **CONATUS** an effort

CONCAVE *v* **-CAVED, -CAVING, -CAVES** to make concave (curving inward)

CONCEAL *v* **-ED, -ING, -S** to keep from sight or discovery

CONCEDE *v* **-CEDED, -CEDING, -CEDES** to acknowledge as true

CONCEDER *n* pl. **-S** one that concedes

CONCEIT *v* **-ED, -ING, -S** to imagine

CONCEIVE *v* **-CEIVED, -CEIVING, -CEIVES** to understand

CONCENT *n* pl. **-S** harmony

CONCEPT *n* pl. **-S** a general idea

CONCEPTI *n/pl* fertilized eggs

CONCERN *v* **-ED, -ING, -S** to be of interest to

CONCERT *v* **-ED, -ING, -S** to plan

CONCERTO *n* pl. **-TOS** or **-TI** a musical composition

CONCH *n* pl. **-S** or **-ES** a marine mollusk

CONCHA *n* pl. **-S** an ornamental disk

CONCHA *n* pl. **-CHAE** an anatomical shell-like structure **CONCHAL** *adj*

CONCHIE *n* pl. **-S** conchy

CONCHO *n* pl. **-CHOS** concha (ornamental disk)

CONCHOID *n* pl. **-S** a type of geometric curve

CONCHY *n* pl. **-CHIES** a conscientious objector

CONCISE *adj* **-CISER, -CISEST** succinct

CONCLAVE *n* pl. **-S** a secret meeting

CONCLUDE *v* **-CLUDED, -CLUDING, -CLUDES** to finish

CONCOCT *v* **-ED, -ING, -S** to prepare by combining ingredients

CONCORD *n* pl. **-S** a state of agreement

CONCOURS *n* pl. **CONCOURS** a public competition

CONCRETE *v* **-CRETED, -CRETING, -CRETES** to solidify

CONCUR *v* **-CURRED, -CURRING, -CURS** to agree

CONCUSS *v* **-ED, -ING, -ES** to injure the brain by a violent blow

CONDEMN *v* **-ED, -ING, -S** to criticize severely

CONDENSE *v* **-DENSED, -DENSING, -DENSES** to compress

CONDIGN *adj* deserved; appropriate

CONDO *n* pl. **-DOS** or **-DOES** an individually owned unit in a multiunit structure

CONDOLE *v* **-DOLED, -DOLING, -DOLES** to mourn

CONDOLER *n* pl. **-S** one that condoles

CONDOM *n* pl. **-S** a prophylactic

CONDONE *v* **-DONED, -DONING, -DONES** to forgive or overlook

CONDONER *n* pl. **-S** one that condones

CONDOR *n* pl. **-S** or **-ES** a coin of Chile

CONDUCE *v* **-DUCED, -DUCING, -DUCES** to contribute to a result

CONDUCER *n* pl. **-S** one that conduces

CONDUCT *v* **-ED, -ING, -S** to lead or guide

CONDUIT *n* pl. **-S** a channel or pipe for conveying fluids

CONDYLE *n* pl. **-S** a protuberance on a bone **CONDYLAR** *adj*

CONE *v* **CONED, CONING, CONES** to shape like a cone (a geometric solid)

CONELRAD *n* pl. **-S** a system of defense in the event of air attack

CONENOSE *n* pl. **-S** a bloodsucking insect

CONEPATE *n* pl. **-S** a skunk

CONEPATL *n* pl. **-S** conepate

CONEY *n* pl. **-NEYS** cony

CONFAB *v* **-FABBED, -FABBING, -FABS** to chat

CONFECT *v* **-ED, -ING, -S** to prepare from various ingredients

CONFER *v* **-FERRED, -FERRING, -FERS** to bestow

CONFEREE *n* pl. **-S** one upon whom something is conferred

CONFERVA *n* pl. **-VAS** or **-VAE** a freshwater alga

CONFESS *v* **-ED, -ING, -ES** to acknowledge or disclose

CONFETTO *n* pl. **-TI** a bonbon

CONFIDE *v* **-FIDED, -FIDING, -FIDES** to reveal in trust or confidence

CONFIDER *n* pl. **-S** one that confides

CONFINE *v* **-FINED, -FINING, -FINES** to shut within an enclosure

CONFINER *n* pl. **-S** one that confines

CONFIRM *v* **-ED, -ING, -S** to assure the validity of

CONFIT *n* pl. **-S** meat cooked and preserved in its own fat

CONFLATE *v* **-FLATED, -FLATING, -FLATES** to blend

CONFLICT *v* **-ED, -ING, -S** to come into opposition

CONFLUX *n* pl. **-ES** a flowing together of streams

CONFOCAL *adj* having the same focus or foci

CONFORM *v* **-ED, -ING, -S** to become the same or similar

CONFOUND *v* **-ED, -ING, -S** to confuse

CONFRERE *n* pl. **-S** a colleague

CONFRONT *v* **-ED, -ING, -S** to face defiantly

CONFUSE *v* **-FUSED, -FUSING, -FUSES** to mix up mentally

CONFUTE *v* **-FUTED, -FUTING, -FUTES** to disprove

CONFUTER *n* pl. **-S** one that confutes

CONGA *v* **-ED, -ING, -S** to perform a conga (Latin-American dance)

CONGE *n* pl. **-S** permission to depart

CONGEAL *v* **-ED, -ING, -S** to change from a fluid to a solid

CONGEE *v* **-GEED, -GEEING, -GEES** to bow politely

CONGENER *n* pl. **-S** one of the same kind or class

CONGER *n* pl. **-S** a marine eel

CONGEST *v* **-ED, -ING, -S** to fill to excess

CONGIUS *n* pl. **-GII** an ancient unit of measure

CONGLOBE *v* **-GLOBED, -GLOBING, -GLOBES** to become a globule

CONGO *n* pl. **-GOES** an eellike amphibian

CONGO *n* pl. **-GOS** congou

CONGOU *n* pl. **-S** a Chinese tea

CONGRATS *n/pl* congratulations

CONGRESS *v* **-ED, -ING, -ES** to assemble together

CONI pl. of conus

CONIC *n* pl. **-S** a geometric curve

CONICAL *adj* shaped like a cone

CONICITY *n* pl. **-TIES** the state of being conical

CONIDIUM *n* pl. **-NIDIA** a fungus spore **CONIDIAL, CONIDIAN** *adj*

CONIES pl. of cony

CONIFER *n* pl. **-S** an evergreen tree

CONIINE *n* pl. **-S** a poisonous alkaloid

CONIN *n* pl. **-S** coniine

CONINE *n* pl. **-S** coniine

CONING present participle of cone

CONIOSIS *n* pl. **-OSES** an infection caused by the inhalation of dust

CONIUM *n* pl. **-S** a poisonous herb

CONJOIN *v* **-ED, -ING, -S** to join together **CONJOINT** *adj*

CONJUGAL *adj* pertaining to marriage

CONJUNCT *n* pl. **-S** one that is joined with another

CONJUNTO *n* pl. **-TOS** a style of dance music along the Mexican border

CONJURE *v* **-JURED, -JURING, -JURES** to summon a spirit

CONJURER *n* pl. **-S** a sorcerer

CONJUROR *n* pl. **-S** conjurer

CONK *v* **-ED, -ING, -S** to hit on the head

CONKER *n* pl. **-S** a chestnut used in a British game

CONKY *adj* full of a tree fungus

CONLANG *n* pl. **-S** an invented language

CONN *v* **-ED, -ING, -S** to direct the steering of a ship

CONNATE *adj* innate

CONNECT *v* **-ED, -ING, -S** to join together

CONNED past tense of con

CONNER *n* pl. **-S** one that cons

CONNING present participle of con

CONNIVE *v* **-NIVED, -NIVING, -NIVES** to feign ignorance of wrongdoing

CONNIVER *n* pl. **-S** one that connives

CONNOR *n* pl. **-S** a saltwater fish

CONNOTE *v* **-NOTED, -NOTING, -NOTES** to imply another meaning besides the literal one

CONODONT *n* pl. **-S** a fossil

CONOID *n* pl. **-S** a geometric solid **CONOIDAL** *adj*

CONQUER *v* **-ED, -ING, -S** to overcome by force

CONQUEST *n* pl. **-S** the act of conquering

CONQUIAN	*n* pl. **-S** a card game
CONSENT	*v* **-ED, -ING, -S** to permit or approve
CONSERVE	*v* **-SERVED, -SERVING, -SERVES** to protect from loss or depletion
CONSIDER	*v* **-ED, -ING, -S** to think about
CONSIGN	*v* **-ED, -ING, -S** to give over to another's care
CONSIST	*v* **-ED, -ING, -S** to be made up or composed
CONSOL	*n* pl. **-S** a government bond
CONSOLE	*v* **-SOLED, -SOLING, -SOLES** to comfort
CONSOLER	*n* pl. **-S** one that consoles
CONSOMME	*n* pl. **-S** a clear soup
CONSORT	*v* **-ED, -ING, -S** to keep company
CONSPIRE	*v* **-SPIRED, -SPIRING, -SPIRES** to plan secretly with another
CONSTANT	*n* pl. **-S** something that does not vary
CONSTRUE	*v* **-STRUED, -STRUING, -STRUES** to interpret
CONSUL	*n* pl. **-S** an official serving abroad **CONSULAR** *adj*
CONSULT	*v* **-ED, -ING, -S** to ask an opinion of
CONSUME	*v* **-SUMED, -SUMING, -SUMES** to use up
CONSUMER	*n* pl. **-S** one that consumes
CONTACT	*v* **-ED, -ING, -S** to communicate with
CONTAGIA	*n/pl* causative agents of infectious diseases
CONTAIN	*v* **-ED, -ING, -S** to hold within
CONTANGO	*n* pl. **-GOS** postponement of the transfer of stock
CONTE	*n* pl. **-S** a short story
CONTEMN	*v* **-ED, -ING, -S** to scorn
CONTEMPO	*adj* contemporary
CONTEMPT	*n* pl. **-S** the feeling of one who views something as mean, vile, or worthless
CONTEND	*v* **-ED, -ING, -S** to vie
CONTENT	*v* **-ED, -ING, -S** to satisfy
CONTESSA	*n* pl. **-S** an Italian countess
CONTEST	*v* **-ED, -ING, -S** to compete for
CONTEXT	*n* pl. **-S** the part of a discourse in which a particular word or phrase appears
CONTINUA	*n/pl* mathematical sets
CONTINUE	*v* **-UED, -UING, -UES** to go on with
CONTINUO	*n* pl. **-UOS** a type of instrumental part
CONTO	*n* pl. **-TOS** a Portuguese money of account
CONTORT	*v* **-ED, -ING, -S** to twist out of shape
CONTOUR	*v* **-ED, -ING, -S** to make the outline of
CONTRA	*n* pl. **-S** a Nicaraguan revolutionary
CONTRACT	*v* **-ED, -ING, -S** to decrease in size or volume
CONTRAIL	*n* pl. **-S** a visible trail of water vapor from an aircraft
CONTRARY	*n* pl. **-TRARIES** an opposite
CONTRAST	*v* **-ED, -ING, -S** to place in opposition to set off differences
CONTRITE	*adj* deeply sorry for one's sins
CONTRIVE	*v* **-TRIVED, -TRIVING, -TRIVES** to devise
CONTROL	*v* **-TROLLED, -TROLLING, -TROLS** to exercise authority over
CONTUSE	*v* **-TUSED, -TUSING, -TUSES** to bruise
CONURE	*n* pl. **-S** a tropical American parakeet
CONUS	*n* pl. **CONI** an anatomical part in mammals
CONVECT	*v* **-ED, -ING, -S** to transfer heat by a process of circulation
CONVENE	*v* **-VENED, -VENING, -VENES** to assemble
CONVENER	*n* pl. **-S** one that convenes
CONVENOR	*n* pl. **-S** convener
CONVENT	*v* **-ED, -ING, -S** to convene
CONVERGE	*v* **-VERGED, -VERGING, -VERGES** to come together
CONVERSE	*v* **-VERSED, -VERSING, -VERSES** to speak together
CONVERSO	*n* pl. **-SOS** a Jew who converted to Christianity
CONVERT	*v* **-ED, -ING, -S** to change into another form
CONVEX	*n* pl. **-ES** a surface or body that is convex (curving outward)
CONVEXLY	*adv* in a convex manner
CONVEY	*v* **-ED, -ING, -S** to transport
CONVEYER	*n* pl. **-S** one that conveys
CONVEYOR	*n* pl. **-S** conveyer
CONVICT	*v* **-ED, -ING, -S** to prove guilty
CONVINCE	*v* **-VINCED, -VINCING, -VINCES** to cause to believe something

CONVOKE	v -**VOKED, -VOKING, -VOKES** to cause to assemble	**COOLIBAH**	n pl. -**S** coolabah
CONVOKER	n pl. -**S** one that convokes	**COOLIE**	n pl. -**S** a laborer in or from the Far East
CONVOLVE	v -**VOLVED, -VOLVING, -VOLVES** to roll together	**COOLIES**	pl. of cooly
CONVOY	v -**ED, -ING, -S** to escort	**COOLISH**	adj somewhat cool
CONVULSE	v -**VULSED, -VULSING, -VULSES** to shake violently	**COOLLY**	adv in a cool manner
		COOLNESS	n pl. -**ES** the state of being cool
CONY	n pl. **CONIES** a rabbit	**COOLTH**	n pl. -**S** coolness
COO	v -**ED, -ING, -S** to make the sound of a dove	**COOLY**	n pl. **COOLIES** coolie
		COOMB	n pl. -**S** combe
COOCH	n pl. -**ES** a sinuous dance	**COOMBE**	n pl. -**S** combe
COOCOO	adj crazy	**COON**	n pl. -**S** a raccoon
COOEE	v **COOEED, COOEEING, COOEES** to cry out shrilly	**COONCAN**	n pl. -**S** conquian
		COONSKIN	n pl. -**S** the pelt of a raccoon
COOER	n pl. -**S** one that coos	**COONTIE**	n pl. -**S** a tropical plant
COOEY	v -**EYED, -EYING, -EYS** to cooee	**COOP**	v -**ED, -ING, -S** to confine
COOF	n pl. -**S** a dolt	**COOPER**	v -**ED, -ING, -S** to make or mend barrels
COOING	present participle of coo		
COOINGLY	adv in the manner of cooing doves; affectionately	**COOPERY**	n pl. -**ERIES** the trade of coopering
		COOPT	v -**ED, -ING, -S** to elect or appoint
COOK	v -**ED, -ING, -S** to prepare food by heating **COOKABLE** adj	**COOPTION**	n pl. -**S** the act of coopting
		COOT	n pl. -**S** an aquatic bird
COOKBOOK	n pl. -**S** a book of recipes	**COOTER**	n pl. -**S** a turtle
COOKER	n pl. -**S** one that cooks	**COOTIE**	n pl. -**S** a body louse
COOKERY	n pl. -**ERIES** the art of cooking	**COP**	v **COPPED, COPPING, COPS** to steal
COOKEY	n pl. -**EYS** cookie		
COOKIE	n pl. -**S** a small, flat cake	**COPAIBA**	n pl. -**S** a resin
COOKING	n pl. -**S** the act of one that cooks	**COPAL**	n pl. -**S** a resin
COOKLESS	adj having no person that cooks	**COPALM**	n pl. -**S** a hardwood tree
COOKOFF	n pl. -**S** a cooking contest	**COPARENT**	v -**ED, -ING, -S** to share in the custody of one's child
COOKOUT	n pl. -**S** a meal eaten and prepared outdoors	**COPASTOR**	n pl. -**S** one that shares the duties of a pastor
COOKSHOP	n pl. -**S** a shop that sells cooked food	**COPATRON**	n pl. -**S** a fellow patron
COOKTOP	n pl. -**S** a counter-top cooking apparatus	**COPAY**	n pl. -**PAYS** a fee required by a health insurer to be paid by the patient
COOKWARE	n pl. -**S** utensils used in cooking		
COOKY	n pl. **COOKIES** cookie	**COPE**	v **COPED, COPING, COPES** to contend or strive
COOL	adj **COOLER, COOLEST** moderately cold	**COPECK**	n pl. -**S** kopeck
COOL	v -**ED, -ING, -S** to make less warm	**COPEMATE**	n pl. -**S** an antagonist
COOLABAH	n pl. -**S** an Australian gum tree	**COPEN**	n pl. -**S** a blue color
COOLANT	n pl. -**S** a fluid used to cool engines	**COPEPOD**	n pl. -**S** a minute crustacean
		COPER	n pl. -**S** a horse dealer
COOLDOWN	n pl. -**S** a gradual return of physiological functions to normal levels after strenuous exercise	**COPIABLE**	adj capable of being copied
		COPIED	past tense of copy
COOLER	n pl. -**S** something that cools	**COPIER**	n pl. -**S** one that copies

COPIES present 3d person sing. of copy

COPIHUE *n* pl. **-S** a climbing vine

COPILOT *v* **-ED, -ING, -S** to act as an assistant pilot

COPING *n* pl. **-S** the top part of a wall

COPIOUS *adj* abundant

COPLANAR *adj* lying in the same plane

COPLOT *v* **-PLOTTED, -PLOTTING, -PLOTS** to plot together

COPOUT *n* pl. **-S** a backing out of a responsibility

COPPED past tense of cop

COPPER *v* **-ED, -ING, -S** to cover with copper (a metallic element)

COPPERAH *n* pl. **-S** copra

COPPERAS *n* pl. **-ES** a compound used in making inks

COPPERY *adj* resembling copper

COPPICE *v* **-PICED, -PICING, -PICES** to cause to grow in the form of a coppice (a thicket)

COPPING present participle of cop

COPPRA *n* pl. **-S** copra

COPRA *n* pl. **-S** dried coconut meat

COPRAH *n* pl. **-S** copra

COPREMIA *n* pl. **-S** a form of blood poisoning **COPREMIC** *adj*

COPRINCE *n* pl. **-S** one of two princes ruling jointly

COPSE *n* pl. **-S** a coppice **COPSY** *adj*

COPTER *n* pl. **-S** a helicopter

COPULA *n* pl. **-LAS** or **-LAE** something that links **COPULAR** *adj*

COPULATE *v* **-LATED, -LATING, -LATES** to engage in coitus

COPURIFY *v* **-FIED, -FYING, -FIES** to become purified with another substance

COPY *v* **COPIED, COPYING, COPIES** to imitate **COPYABLE** *adj*

COPYBOOK *n* pl. **-S** a book used in teaching penmanship

COPYBOY *n* pl. **-BOYS** a boy who runs errands in a newspaper office

COPYCAT *v* **-CATTED, -CATTING, -CATS** to imitate

COPYDESK *n* pl. **-S** an editor's desk in a newspaper office

COPYEDIT *v* **-ED, -ING, -S** to prepare copy for the printer

COPYGIRL *n* pl. **-S** a girl who runs errands in a newspaper office

COPYHOLD *n* pl. **-S** a type of ownership of land

COPYIST *n* pl. **-S** an imitator

COPYLEFT *n* pl. **-S** a license that allows free use of copyrighted software

COPYREAD *v* **-READ, -READING, -READS** to copyedit

COQUET *v* **-QUETTED, -QUETTING, -QUETS** to flirt

COQUETRY *n* pl. **-TRIES** flirtatious behavior

COQUETTE *v* **-QUETTED, -QUETTING, -QUETTES** to coquet

COQUI *n* pl. **-S** a small arboreal frog

COQUILLE *n* pl. **-S** a cooking utensil

COQUINA *n* pl. **-S** a small marine clam

COQUITO *n* pl. **-TOS** a palm tree

COR *n* pl. **-S** an ancient unit of measure

CORACLE *n* pl. **-S** a small boat

CORACOID *n* pl. **-S** a bone of the shoulder girdle

CORAL *n* pl. **-S** a mass of marine animal skeletons

CORANTO *n* pl. **-TOS** or **-TOES** courante

CORBAN *n* pl. **-S** an offering to God

CORBEIL *n* pl. **-S** a sculptured fruit basket

CORBEL *v* **-BELED, -BELING, -BELS** or **-BELLED, -BELLING, -BELS** to provide a wall with a bracket

CORBIE *n* pl. **-S** a raven or crow

CORBINA *n* pl. **-S** a food and game fish

CORBY *n* pl. **CORBIES** corbie

CORD *v* **-ED, -ING, -S** to fasten with a cord (a thin rope)

CORDAGE *n* pl. **-S** the amount of wood in an area

CORDATE *adj* heart-shaped

CORDELLE *v* **-DELLED, -DELLING, -DELLES** to tow a boat with a cordelle (a towrope)

CORDER *n* pl. **-S** one that cords

CORDIAL *n* pl. **-S** a liqueur

CORDING *n* pl. **-S** the ribbed surface of cloth

CORDITE *n* pl. **-S** an explosive powder

CORDLESS *n* pl. **-ES** an electrical device with its own power supply

CORDLIKE *adj* resembling a cord

CORDOBA *n* pl. **-S** a monetary unit of Nicaragua

CORDON _v_ **-ED, -ING, -S** to form a barrier around

CORDOVAN _n_ pl. **-S** a fine leather

CORDUROY _v_ **-ED, -ING, -S** to build a type of road

CORDWAIN _n_ pl. **-S** cordovan

CORDWOOD _n_ pl. **-S** wood used for fuel

CORE _v_ **CORED, CORING, CORES** to remove the core (the central part) of

COREDEEM _v_ **-ED, -ING, -S** to redeem jointly

COREIGN _n_ pl. **-S** a joint reign

CORELATE _v_ **-LATED, -LATING, -LATES** to place into mutual or reciprocal relation

CORELESS _adj_ having no core

CORELLA _n_ pl. **-S** a small cockatoo

COREMIUM _n_ pl. **-MIA** an organ of certain fungi

CORER _n_ pl. **-S** a utensil for coring apples

CORF _n_ pl. **CORVES** a wagon used in a mine

CORGI _n_ pl. **-S** a short-legged dog

CORING present participle of core

CORIUM _n_ pl. **-RIA** a skin layer

CORK _v_ **-ED, -ING, -S** to stop up

CORKAGE _n_ pl. **-S** a charge for wine in a restaurant

CORKER _n_ pl. **-S** one that corks

CORKIER comparative of corky

CORKIEST superlative of corky

CORKLIKE _adj_ resembling cork (a porous tree bark)

CORKWOOD _n_ pl. **-S** a small tree

CORKY _adj_ **CORKIER, CORKIEST** corklike

CORM _n_ pl. **-S** a stem of certain plants **CORMLIKE, CORMOID, CORMOUS** _adj_

CORMEL _n_ pl. **-S** a small corm

CORMLET _n_ pl. **-S** a small corm

CORN _v_ **-ED, -ING, -S** to preserve with salt

CORNBALL _n_ pl. **-S** a hick

CORNCAKE _n_ pl. **-S** a cake made of cornmeal

CORNCOB _n_ pl. **-S** the woody core of an ear of corn

CORNCRIB _n_ pl. **-S** a building in which corn is stored

CORNEA _n_ pl. **-S** a part of the eye **CORNEAL** _adj_

CORNEL _n_ pl. **-S** a hardwood tree or shrub

CORNEOUS _adj_ of a hornlike texture

CORNER _v_ **-ED, -ING, -S** to gain control of

CORNET _n_ pl. **-S** a trumpetlike instrument

CORNETCY _n_ **-CIES** a rank in the British cavalry

CORNETT _n_ pl. **-S** cornetto

CORNETTO _n_ pl. **-TOS** or **-TI** a musical wind instrument

CORNFED _adj_ fed on corn

CORNHUSK _n_ pl. **-S** the husk covering an ear of corn

CORNICE _v_ **-NICED, -NICING, -NICES** to decorate with a molding

CORNICHE _n_ pl. **-S** a road built along a cliff

CORNICLE _n_ pl. **-S** a part of an aphid

CORNIER comparative of corny

CORNIEST superlative of corny

CORNIFY _v_ **-FIED, -FYING, -FIES** to form keratin

CORNILY _adv_ in a corny manner

CORNMEAL _n_ pl. **-S** meal made from corn

CORNPONE _n_ pl. **-S** a bread made with cornmeal

CORNROW _v_ **-ED, -ING, -S** to braid hair tightly in rows close to the scalp

CORNSILK _n_ pl. **-S** a silky thread on an ear of corn

CORNU _n_ pl. **-NUA** a hornlike bone formation **CORNUAL** _adj_

CORNUS _n_ pl. **-ES** a cornel

CORNUTE _adj_ horn-shaped

CORNUTED _adj_ cornute

CORNUTO _n_ pl. **-TOS** the husband of an unfaithful wife

CORNY _adj_ **CORNIER, CORNIEST** trite

CORODY _n_ pl. **-DIES** an allowance of food or clothes

COROLLA _n_ pl. **-S** a protective covering of a flower

CORONA _n_ pl. **-NAS** or **-NAE** a luminous circle around a celestial body

CORONACH _n_ pl. **-S** a dirge

CORONAL _n_ pl. **-S** a wreath worn on the head

CORONARY _n_ pl. **-NARIES** an artery supplying blood to the heart

CORONATE _v_ **-NATED, -NATING, -NATES** to crown

CORONEL _n_ pl. **-S** coronal

CORONER *n* pl. **-S** an officer who investigates questionable deaths

CORONET *n* pl. **-S** a small crown

CORONOID *adj* crown-shaped

COROTATE *v* **-TATED, -TATING, -TATES** to rotate together

COROZO *n* pl. **-ZOS** a tropical palm tree

CORPORA a pl. of corpus

CORPORAL *n* pl. **-S** a military rank

CORPS *n* pl. **CORPS** a military unit

CORPSE *n* pl. **-S** a dead body

CORPSMAN *n* pl. **-MEN** an enlisted man trained in first aid

CORPUS *n* pl. **-PORA** or **-PUSES** a human or animal body

CORRADE *v* **-RADED, -RADING, -RADES** to erode

CORRAL *v* **-RALLED, -RALLING, -RALS** to place livestock in a corral (an enclosure)

CORRECT *adj* **-RECTER, -RECTEST** free from error

CORRECT *v* **-ED, -ING, -S** to make free from error

CORRETTO *n* pl. **-TOS** espresso mixed with brandy or liqueur

CORRIDA *n* pl. **-S** a bullfight

CORRIDOR *n* pl. **-S** a narrow hallway

CORRIE *n* pl. **-S** a cirque

CORRIVAL *n* pl. **-S** a rival or opponent

CORRODE *v* **-RODED, -RODING, -RODES** to eat away gradually

CORRODY *n* pl. **-DIES** corody

CORRUPT *adj* **-RUPTER, -RUPTEST** dishonest and venal

CORRUPT *v* **-ED, -ING, -S** to subvert the honesty or integrity of

CORSAC *n* pl. **-S** an Asian fox

CORSAGE *n* pl. **-S** a small bouquet of flowers

CORSAIR *n* pl. **-S** a pirate

CORSE *n* pl. **-S** a corpse

CORSELET *n* pl. **-S** a piece of body armor

CORSET *v* **-ED, -ING, -S** to fit with a corset (a supporting undergarment)

CORSETRY *n* pl. **-RIES** the work of making corsets

CORSLET *n* pl. **-S** corselet

CORTEGE *n* pl. **-S** a retinue

CORTEX *n* pl. **-TEXES** or **-TICES** the outer layer of an organ **CORTICAL** *adj*

CORTIN *n* pl. **-S** a hormone

CORTINA *n* pl. **-S** a membrane on some mushrooms

CORTISOL *n* pl. **-S** a hormone

CORULER *n* pl. **-S** one that rules jointly

CORUNDUM *n* pl. **-S** a hard mineral

CORVEE *n* pl. **-S** an obligation to perform feudal service

CORVES pl. of corf

CORVET *n* pl. **-S** corvette

CORVETTE *n* pl. **-S** a small, swift warship

CORVID *n* pl. **-S** any of a family of passerine birds

CORVINA *n* pl. **-S** corbina

CORVINE *adj* pertaining or belonging to the crow family of birds

CORY *n* pl. **CORY** a former monetary unit of Guinea

CORYBANT *n* pl. **-BANTS** or **-BANTES** a reveler

CORYMB *n* pl. **-S** a flower cluster **CORYMBED** *adj*

CORYPHEE *n* pl. **-S** a ballet dancer

CORYZA *n* pl. **-S** a head cold **CORYZAL** *adj*

COS *n* pl. **-ES** a variety of lettuce

COSCRIPT *v* **-ED, -ING, -S** to collaborate in preparing a script for

COSEC *n* pl. **-S** cosecant

COSECANT *n* pl. **-S** a trigonometric function of an angle

COSET *n* pl. **-S** a mathematical subset

COSEY *n* pl. **-SEYS** a covering for a teapot

COSH *v* **-ED, -ING, -ES** to bludgeon

COSHER *v* **-ED, -ING, -S** to coddle

COSIE *n* pl. **-S** cosey

COSIED past tense of cosy

COSIER comparative of cosy

COSIES present 3d person sing. of cosy

COSIEST superlative of cosy

COSIGN *v* **-ED, -ING, -S** to sign jointly

COSIGNER *n* pl. **-S** one that cosigns

COSILY *adv* in a cosy manner

COSINE *n* pl. **-S** a trigonometric function of an angle

COSINESS *n* pl. **-ES** coziness

COSMETIC *n* pl. **-S** a beauty preparation

COSMIC	*adj* pertaining to the cosmos
COSMICAL	*adj* cosmic
COSMID	*n* pl. **-S** a hybrid vector used in cloning
COSMISM	*n* pl. **-S** a philosophical theory
COSMIST	*n* pl. **-S** a supporter of cosmism
COSMOS	*n* pl. **-ES** the universe regarded as an orderly system
COSS	*n* pl. **COSS** kos
COSSACK	*n* pl. **-S** a Russian cavalryman
COSSET	*v* **-ED, -ING, -S** to fondle
COST	*v* **COST** or **COSTED, COSTING, COSTS** to estimate a price for production of
COSTA	*n* pl. **-TAE** a rib **COSTAL** *adj* **COSTALLY** *adv*
COSTAR	*v* **-STARRED, -STARRING, -STARS** to star with another actor
COSTARD	*n* pl. **-S** a large cooking apple
COSTATE	*adj* having a rib or ribs
COSTER	*n* pl. **-S** a hawker of fruit or vegetables
COSTING	*n* pl. **-S** an estimation of the price of the production of something
COSTIVE	*adj* constipated
COSTLESS	*adj* free of charge
COSTLY	*adj* **-LIER, -LIEST** expensive
COSTMARY	*n* pl. **-MARIES** an herb used in salads
COSTREL	*n* pl. **-S** a flask
COSTUME	*v* **-TUMED, -TUMING, -TUMES** to supply with a costume (a style of dress)
COSTUMER	*n* pl. **-S** one that costumes
COSTUMEY	*adj* of or pertaining to a costume
COSY	*adj* **COSIER, COSIEST** cozy
COSY	*v* **COSIED, COSYING, COSIES** to cozy
COT	*n* pl. **-S** a light, narrow bed
COTAN	*n* pl. **-S** a trigonometric function of an angle
COTE	*v* **COTED, COTING, COTES** to pass by
COTEAU	*n* pl. **-TEAUX** or **-TEAUS** the higher ground of a region
COTENANT	*n* pl. **-S** one who is a tenant with another in the same place
COTERIE	*n* pl. **-S** a clique
COTHURN	*n* pl. **-S** a buskin worn by ancient Roman actors
COTHURNI	*n/pl* cothurns
COTIDAL	*adj* indicating coincidence of the tides
COTIJA	*n* a Mexican cheese
COTILLON	*n* pl. **-S** a ballroom dance
COTING	present participle of cote
COTINGA	*n* pl. **-S** a tropical bird
COTININE	*n* pl. **-S** an alkaloid produced by nicotine in the body
COTQUEAN	*n* pl. **-S** a vulgar woman
COTTA	*n* pl. **-TAS** or **-TAE** a short surplice
COTTAGE	*v* **-TAGED, -TAGING, -TAGES** to vacation at a small house
COTTAGER	*n* pl. **-S** one that lives in a small house
COTTAGEY	*adj* resembling a small house
COTTAR	*n* pl. **-S** a tenant farmer
COTTER	*n* pl. **-S** a pin or wedge used for fastening parts together **COTTERED** *adj*
COTTIER	*n* pl. **-S** cottar
COTTON	*v* **-ED, -ING, -S** to take a liking
COTTONY	*adj* resembling cotton (a soft, fibrous material)
COTURNIX	*n* pl. **-ES** a small quail
COTYLOID	*adj* cup-shaped
COTYPE	*n* pl. **-S** a taxonomic type
COUCH	*v* **-ED, -ING, -ES** to put into words
COUCHANT	*adj* lying down
COUCHER	*n* pl. **-S** one that couches
COUCHING	*n* pl. **-S** a form of embroidery
COUDE	*n* pl. **-S** a type of telescope
COUGAR	*n* pl. **-S** a mountain lion
COUGH	*v* **-ED, -ING, -S** to expel air from the lungs noisily
COUGHER	*n* pl. **-S** one that coughs
COULD	past tense of can
COULDEST	a past 2d person sing. of can
COULDST	a past 2d person sing. of can
COULEE	*n* pl. **-S** a small ravine
COULIS	*n* pl. **COULIS** a thick sauce of pureed vegetable or fruit
COULISSE	*n* pl. **-S** a side scene of a theatre stage
COULOIR	*n* pl. **-S** a deep gorge or gully
COULOMB	*n* pl. **-S** an electrical measure
COULTER	*n* pl. **-S** colter

COUMARIN *n* pl. **-S** a chemical compound **COUMARIC** *adj*

COUMAROU *n* pl. **-S** the seed of a tropical tree

COUNCIL *n* pl. **-S** a group of persons appointed for a certain function

COUNSEL *v* **-SELED, -SELING, -SELS** or **-SELLED, -SELLING, -SELS** to advise

COUNT *v* **-ED, -ING, -S** to list or mention the units of one by one to ascertain the total

COUNTER *v* **-ED, -ING, -S** to oppose

COUNTESS *n* pl. **-ES** a noblewoman

COUNTIAN *n* pl. **-S** a resident of a county

COUNTRY *n* pl. **-TRIES** the territory of a nation

COUNTY *n* pl. **-TIES** an administrative division of a state

COUP *v* **-ED, -ING, -S** to overturn

COUPE *n* pl. **-S** an automobile with two doors

COUPLE *v* **-PLED, -PLING, -PLES** to unite in pairs

COUPLER *n* pl. **-S** one that couples

COUPLET *n* pl. **-S** a pair of successive lines of verse

COUPLING *n* pl. **-S** a joining device

COUPON *n* pl. **-S** a certificate entitling the holder to certain benefits

COURAGE *n* pl. **-S** the quality that enables one to face danger fearlessly; spirit

COURANT *n* pl. **-S** courante

COURANTE *n* pl. **-S** an old, lively dance

COURANTO *n* pl. **-TOS** or **-TOES** courante

COURIER *v* **-ED, -ING, -S** to send or transport by a messenger

COURLAN *n* pl. **-S** a wading bird

COURSE *v* **COURSED, COURSING, COURSES** to cause hounds to chase game

COURSER *n* pl. **-S** one that courses

COURSING *n* pl. **-S** the pursuit of game by hounds

COURT *v* **-ED, -ING, -S** to woo

COURTER *n* pl. **-S** one that courts

COURTESY *v* **-SIED, -SYING, -SIES** to curtsy

COURTIER *n* pl. **-S** one who attends a royal court

COURTLY *adj* **-LIER, -LIEST** stately

COUSCOUS *n* pl. **-ES** a North African cereal

COUSIN *n* pl. **-S** a child of one's aunt or uncle **COUSINLY** *adj*

COUSINRY *n* pl. **-RIES** cousins collectively

COUTEAU *n* pl. **-TEAUX** a knife

COUTER *n* pl. **-S** a piece of armor for the elbow

COUTH *adj* **COUTHER, COUTHEST** sophisticated

COUTH *n* pl. **-S** refinement

COUTHIE *adj* **COUTHIER, COUTHIEST** friendly

COUTURE *n* pl. **-S** the business of dressmaking

COUVADE *n* pl. **-S** a primitive birth ritual

COVALENT *adj* sharing electron pairs

COVARY *v* **-VARIED, -VARYING, -VARIES** to exhibit variation of two or more variables

COVE *v* **COVED, COVING, COVES** to curve over or inward

COVEN *n* pl. **-S** a group of witches

COVENANT *v* **-ED, -ING, -S** to enter into a binding agreement

COVER *v* **-ED, -ING, -S** to place something over or upon

COVERAGE *n* pl. **-S** the extent to which something is covered

COVERALL *n* pl. **-S** a one-piece work garment

COVERER *n* pl. **-S** one that covers

COVERING *n* pl. **-S** something that covers

COVERLET *n* pl. **-S** a bed covering

COVERLID *n* pl. **-S** a coverlet

COVERT *n* pl. **-S** a hiding place

COVERTLY *adv* secretly

COVERUP *n* pl. **-S** something used to conceal improper activity

COVET *v* **-ED, -ING, -S** to desire greatly

COVETER *n* pl. **-S** one that covets

COVETOUS *adj* excessively desirous

COVEY *n* pl. **-EYS** a flock of birds

COVIN *n* pl. **-S** a conspiracy to defraud

COVINE *n* pl. **-S** covin

COVING *n* pl. **-S** a concave molding

COW *v* **-ED, -ING, -S** to intimidate

COWAGE *n* pl. **-S** a tropical vine

COWARD *n* pl. **-S** one who lacks courage

COWARDLY *adj* lacking courage

COWBANE *n* pl. **-S** a poisonous plant

COWBELL	*n* pl. **-S** a bell around a cow's neck
COWBERRY	*n* pl. **-RIES** a pasture shrub
COWBIND	*n* pl. **-S** a species of bryony
COWBIRD	*n* pl. **-S** a blackbird
COWBOY	*v* **-BOYED, -BOYING, -BOYS** to tend cattle or horses
COWEDLY	*adv* in a cowed manner
COWER	*v* **-ED, -ING, -S** to cringe
COWFISH	*n* pl. **-ES** an aquatic mammal
COWFLAP	*n* pl. **-S** cowflop
COWFLOP	*n* pl. **-S** a cowpat
COWGIRL	*n* pl. **-S** a female ranch worker
COWHAGE	*n* pl. **-S** cowage
COWHAND	*n* pl. **-S** a ranch worker
COWHERB	*n* pl. **-S** an annual herb
COWHERD	*n* pl. **-S** one who tends cattle
COWHIDE	*v* **-HIDED, -HIDING, -HIDES** to flog with a leather whip
COWIER	comparative of cowy
COWIEST	superlative of cowy
COWINNER	*n* pl. **-S** one of two or more winners
COWL	*v* **-ED, -ING, -S** to cover with a hood
COWLICK	*n* pl. **-S** a lock of unruly hair
COWLIKE	*adj* resembling a cow
COWLING	*n* pl. **-S** a covering for an aircraft engine
COWMAN	*n* pl. **-MEN** one who owns cattle
COWORKER	*n* pl. **-S** a fellow worker
COWPAT	*n* pl. **-S** a dropping of cow dung
COWPEA	*n* pl. **-S** a black-eyed pea
COWPIE	*n* pl. **-S** a cowpat
COWPLOP	*n* pl. **-S** a cowpat
COWPOKE	*n* pl. **-S** a cowhand
COWPOX	*n* pl. **-ES** a cattle disease
COWPUNK	*n* pl. **-S** music combining country and western styles with punk rock
COWRIE	*n* pl. **-S** cowry
COWRITE	*v* **-WROTE, -WRITTEN, -WRITING, -WRITES** to collaborate in writing
COWRITER	*n* pl. **-S** one that cowrites
COWRY	*n* pl. **-RIES** a glossy seashell
COWSHED	*n* pl. **-S** a shelter for cows
COWSKIN	*n* pl. **-S** the hide of a cow
COWSLIP	*n* pl. **-S** a flowering plant
COWTOWN	*n* pl. **-S** a town or city in a cattle-raising area
COWY	*adj* **COWIER, COWIEST** suggestive of a cow
COX	*v* **-ED, -ING, -ES** to coxswain
COXA	*n* pl. **COXAE** the hip or hip joint **COXAL** *adj*
COXALGIA	*n* pl. **-S** pain in the hip **COXALGIC** *adj*
COXALGY	*n* pl. **-GIES** coxalgia
COXCOMB	*n* pl. **-S** a conceited dandy
COXITIS	*n* pl. **COXITIDES** inflammation of the hip joint
COXLESS	*adj* having no coxswain (the director of the crew of a racing rowboat)
COXSWAIN	*v* **-ED, -ING, -S** to direct (a crew) as coxswain
COY	*adj* **COYER, COYEST** shy
COY	*v* **-ED, -ING, -S** to caress
COYAU	*n* pl. **-S** a steep roof design
COYDOG	*n* pl. **-S** a hybrid between a coyote and a wild dog
COYISH	*adj* somewhat coy
COYLY	*adv* in a coy manner
COYNESS	*n* pl. **-ES** the state of being coy
COYOTE	*n* pl. **-S** a small wolf
COYPOU	*n* pl. **-S** a coypu
COYPU	*n* pl. **-S** an aquatic rodent
COZ	*n* pl. **COZES** or **COZZES** a cousin
COZEN	*v* **-ED, -ING, -S** to deceive
COZENAGE	*n* pl. **-S** the practice of cozening
COZENER	*n* pl. **-S** one that cozens
COZEY	*n* pl. **-ZEYS** a cover for a teapot
COZIE	*n* pl. **-S** a cozey
COZIED	past tense of cozy
COZIER	comparative of cozy
COZIES	present 3d person sing. of cozy
COZINESS	*n* pl. **-ES** the state of being cozy
COZY	*adj* **COZIER, COZIEST** snug and comfortable **COZILY** *adv*
COZY	*v* **COZIED, COZYING, COZIES** to attempt to get on friendly terms
COZZES	a pl. of coz
CRAAL	*v* **-ED, -ING, -S** to kraal
CRAB	*v* **CRABBED, CRABBING, CRABS** to complain
CRABBER	*n* pl. **-S** one that crabs

CRABBY *adj* **-BIER, -BIEST** grumpy **CRABBILY** *adv*

CRABLIKE *adj* resembling a crab

CRABMEAT *n* pl. **-S** the edible part of a crab

CRABWISE *adv* sideways

CRACK *v* **-ED, -ING, -S** to break without dividing into parts

CRACKER *n* pl. **-S** a thin, crisp biscuit

CRACKIE *n* pl. **-S** a small dog of mixed breed

CRACKING *n* pl. **-S** a chemical process

CRACKLE *v* **-LED, -LING, -LES** to make a succession of snapping sounds

CRACKLY *adj* **-LIER, -LIEST** brittle

CRACKNEL *n* pl. **-S** a hard, crisp biscuit

CRACKPOT *n* pl. **-S** an eccentric person

CRACKUP *n* pl. **-S** a collision

CRACKY *adj* **CRACKIER, CRACKIEST** having cracks

CRADLE *v* **-DLED, -DLING, -DLES** to nurture during infancy

CRADLER *n* pl. **-S** one that cradles

CRADLING *n* pl. **-S** a framework in a ceiling

CRAFT *v* **-ED, -ING, -S** to make by hand

CRAFTER *n* pl. **-S** one that crafts

CRAFTY *adj* **CRAFTIER, CRAFTIEST** skillful in deceiving **CRAFTILY** *adv*

CRAG *n* pl. **-S** a large jagged rock **CRAGGED** *adj*

CRAGGY *adj* **-GIER, -GIEST** full of crags **CRAGGILY** *adv*

CRAGSMAN *n* pl. **-MEN** one who climbs crags

CRAKE *n* pl. **-S** a small, harsh-voiced bird

CRAM *v* **CRAMMED, CRAMMING, CRAMS** to fill or pack tightly

CRAMBE *n* pl. **-S** an annual herb

CRAMBO *n* pl. **-BOS** or **-BOES** a word game

CRAMMER *n* pl. **-S** one that crams

CRAMMING *n* pl. **-S** the fraudulent adding to the charges of a phone bill

CRAMOISY *n* pl. **-SIES** crimson cloth

CRAMP *v* **-ED, -ING, -S** to restrain or confine

CRAMPIT *n* pl. **-S** a piece of equipment used in curling

CRAMPON *n* pl. **-S** a device for raising heavy objects

CRAMPOON *n* pl. **-S** crampon

CRAMPY *adj* **CRAMPIER, CRAMPIEST** affected with a cramp

CRANCH *v* **-ED, -ING, -ES** to craunch

CRANE *v* **CRANED, CRANING, CRANES** to stretch out one's neck

CRANIA a pl. of cranium

CRANIAL *adj* pertaining to the skull

CRANIATE *n* pl. **-S** one that has a skull

CRANING present participle of crane

CRANIUM *n* pl. **-NIUMS** or **-NIA** the skull

CRANK *adj* **CRANKER, CRANKEST** lively

CRANK *v* **-ED, -ING, -S** to start manually

CRANKIER comparative of cranky

CRANKIEST superlative of cranky

CRANKILY *adv* in a cranky manner

CRANKISH *adj* eccentric

CRANKLE *v* **-KLED, -KLING, -KLES** to crinkle

CRANKLY *adv* in a crank manner

CRANKOUS *adj* cranky

CRANKPIN *n* pl. **-S** the handle of a crank

CRANKY *adj* **CRANKIER, CRANKIEST** grumpy

CRANNIES pl. of cranny

CRANNOG *n* pl. **-S** an artificial island

CRANNOGE *n* pl. **-S** crannog

CRANNY *n* pl. **-NIES** a crevice **CRANNIED** *adj*

CRAP *v* **CRAPPED, CRAPPING, CRAPS** to throw a 2, 3, or 12 in a dice game

CRAPE *v* **CRAPED, CRAPING, CRAPES** to crepe

CRAPOLA *n* pl. **-S** nonsense, drivel

CRAPPIE *n* pl. **-S** an edible fish

CRAPPY *adj* **-PIER, -PIEST** markedly inferior in quality

CRASH *v* **-ED, -ING, -ES** to collide noisily

CRASHER *n* pl. **-S** one that crashes

CRASIS *n* pl. **CRASES** a vowel contraction

CRASS *adj* **CRASSER, CRASSEST** grossly vulgar or stupid **CRASSLY** *adv*

CRATCH *n* pl. **-ES** a manger

CRATE *v* **CRATED, CRATING, CRATES** to put in a packing box

CRATEFUL *n* pl. **-S** as much as a crate can hold

CRATER *v* **-ED, -ING, -S** to form cavities in a surface

CRATON *n* pl. **-S** a part of the earth's crust **CRATONIC** *adj*

CRAUNCH *v* **-ED, -ING, -ES** to crunch

CRAVAT *n* pl. **-S** a necktie

CRAVE *v* **CRAVED, CRAVING, CRAVES** to desire greatly

CRAVEN *v* **-ED, -ING, -S** to make cowardly

CRAVENLY *adv* in a cowardly manner

CRAVER *n* pl. **-S** one that craves

CRAVING *n* pl. **-S** a great desire

CRAW *n* pl. **-S** the stomach of an animal

CRAWDAD *n* pl. **-S** a crayfish

CRAWFISH *v* **-ED, -ING, -ES** to back out or retreat

CRAWL *v* **-ED, -ING, -S** to move with the body on or near the ground

CRAWLER *n* pl. **-S** one that crawls

CRAWLWAY *n* pl. **-WAYS** a small, low tunnel

CRAWLY *adj* **CRAWLIER, CRAWLIEST** creepy

CRAYFISH *n* pl. **-ES** a crustacean

CRAYON *v* **-ED, -ING, -S** to use a drawing implement

CRAYONER *n* pl. **-S** one that crayons

CRAZE *v* **CRAZED, CRAZING, CRAZES** to make insane

CRAZING *n* pl. **-S** a fine surface crack on pottery

CRAZY *adj* **-ZIER, -ZIEST** insane **CRAZILY** *adv*

CRAZY *n* pl. **-ZIES** a crazy person

CREAK *v* **-ED, -ING, -S** to squeak

CREAKY *adj* **CREAKIER, CREAKIEST** creaking **CREAKILY** *adv*

CREAM *v* **-ED, -ING, -S** to form cream (a part of milk)

CREAMER *n* pl. **-S** a cream pitcher

CREAMERY *n* pl. **-ERIES** a dairy

CREAMY *adj* **CREAMIER, CREAMIEST** rich in cream **CREAMILY** *adv*

CREASE *v* **CREASED, CREASING, CREASES** to make a fold or wrinkle in

CREASER *n* pl. **-S** one that creases

CREASY *adj* **CREASIER, CREASIEST** having folds or wrinkles

CREATE *v* **-ATED, -ATING, -ATES** to cause to exist

CREATIN *n* pl. **-S** creatine

CREATINE *n* pl. **-S** a chemical compound

CREATION *n* pl. **-S** something created

CREATIVE *n* pl. **-S** one who has the ability to create

CREATOR *n* pl. **-S** one that creates

CREATURE *n* pl. **-S** a living being

CRECHE *n* pl. **-S** a day nursery

CRED *n* pl. **-S** credibility

CREDAL *adj* pertaining to a creed

CREDENCE *n* pl. **-S** belief

CREDENDA *n/pl* articles of faith

CREDENT *adj* believing

CREDENZA *n* pl. **-S** a piece of furniture

CREDIBLE *adj* believable **CREDIBLY** *adv*

CREDIT *v* **-ED, -ING, -S** to accept as true

CREDITOR *n* pl. **-S** one to whom money is owed

CREDO *n* pl. **-DOS** a creed

CREED *n* pl. **-S** a statement of belief **CREEDAL** *adj*

CREEK *n* pl. **-S** a watercourse smaller than a river

CREEL *v* **-ED, -ING, -S** to put fish in a creel (a fish basket)

CREEP *v* **CREPT** or **CREEPED, CREEPING, CREEPS** to crawl

CREEPAGE *n* pl. **-S** gradual movement

CREEPER *n* pl. **-S** one that creeps

CREEPIE *n* pl. **-S** a low stool

CREEPING present participle of creep

CREEPY *adj* **CREEPIER, CREEPIEST** repugnant **CREEPILY** *adv*

CREESE *n* pl. **-S** kris

CREESH *v* **-ED, -ING, -ES** to grease

CREMAINS *n/pl* the ashes of a cremated body

CREMATE *v* **-MATED, -MATING, -MATES** to reduce to ashes by burning

CREMATOR *n* pl. **-S** one that cremates

CREME *n* pl. **-S** cream

CREMINI *n* pl. **-S** a brown mushroom

CRENATE *adj* having an edge with rounded projections

CRENATED *adj* crenate

CRENEL *v* **-ELED, -ELING, -ELS** or **-ELLED, -ELLING, -ELS** to provide with crenelles

CRENELLE *n* pl. **-S** a rounded projection

CRENSHAW *n* pl. **-S** a variety of honeydew melon

CREODONT *n* pl. **-S** an extinct carnivore

CREOLE *n* pl. **-S** a type of mixed language

CREOLISE *v* **-ISED, -ISING, -ISES** to creolize

CREOLIZE *v* **-IZED, -IZING, -IZES** to cause a language to become a creole

CREOSOL *n* pl. **-S** a chemical compound

CREOSOTE *v* **-SOTED, -SOTING, -SOTES** to treat with a wood preservative

CREPE *v* **CREPED, CREPING, CREPES** to frizz the hair

CREPERIE *n* pl. **-S** a restaurant that serves crepes (thin pancakes)

CREPEY *adj* **CREPIER, CREPIEST** crinkly

CREPITUS *n* pl. **CREPITUS** a grating sound made in breathing

CREPON *n* pl. **-S** a crinkled fabric

CREPT past tense of creep

CREPY *adj* **CREPIER, CREPIEST** crepey

CRESCENT *n* pl. **-S** the figure of the moon in its first or last quarter

CRESCIVE *adj* increasing

CRESOL *n* pl. **-S** a chemical disinfectant

CRESS *n* pl. **-ES** a plant used in salads **CRESSY** *adj*

CRESSET *n* pl. **-S** a metal cup for burning oil

CREST *v* **-ED, -ING, -S** to reach a crest (a peak)

CRESTAL *adj* pertaining to a crest

CRESTING *n* pl. **-S** a decorative coping

CRESYL *n* pl. **-S** tolyl

CRESYLIC *adj* pertaining to cresol

CRETIC *n* pl. **-S** a type of metrical foot

CRETIN *n* pl. **-S** an idiot

CRETONNE *n* pl. **-S** a heavy fabric

CRETONS *n/pl* a spread of shredded pork and onions

CREVALLE *n* pl. **-S** a food and game fish

CREVASSE *v* **-VASSED, -VASSING, -VASSES** to fissure

CREVICE *n* pl. **-S** a cleft **CREVICED** *adj*

CREW *v* **-ED, -ING, -S** to serve aboard a ship

CREWCUT *n* pl. **-S** a short haircut

CREWEL *n* pl. **-S** a woolen yarn

CREWLESS *adj* being without any crewmen

CREWMAN *n* pl. **-MEN** one who serves on a ship

CREWMATE *n* pl. **-S** a fellow crewman

CREWNECK *n* pl. **-S** a sweater with a collarless neckline

CRIB *v* **CRIBBED, CRIBBING, CRIBS** to confine closely

CRIBBAGE *n* pl. **-S** a card game

CRIBBER *n* pl. **-S** one that cribs

CRIBBING *n* pl. **-S** a supporting framework

CRIBBLED *adj* covered with dots

CRIBROUS *adj* pierced with small holes

CRIBWORK *n* pl. **-S** a framework of logs

CRICETID *n* pl. **-S** a small rodent

CRICK *v* **-ED, -ING, -S** to cause a spasm of the neck

CRICKET *v* **-ED, -ING, -S** to play cricket (a ball game)

CRICKEY *interj* — used as a mild oath

CRICOID *n* pl. **-S** a cartilage of the larynx

CRIED past tense of cry

CRIER *n* pl. **-S** one that cries

CRIES present 3d person sing. of cry

CRIKEY *interj* — used as a mild oath

CRIME *n* pl. **-S** a violation of the law

CRIMINAL *n* pl. **-S** one who has committed a crime

CRIMINE *interj* — used to express surprise or anger

CRIMINI *n* pl. **-S** cremini

CRIMINY *interj* crimine

CRIMMER *n* pl. **-S** krimmer

CRIMP *v* **-ED, -ING, -S** to pleat

CRIMPER *n* pl. **-S** one that crimps

CRIMPLE *v* **-PLED, -PLING, -PLES** to wrinkle

CRIMPY *adj* **CRIMPIER, CRIMPIEST** wavy

CRIMSON *v* **-ED, -ING, -S** to make crimson (a red color)

CRINGE *v* **CRINGED, CRINGING, CRINGES** to shrink in fear

CRINGER *n* pl. **-S** one that cringes

CRINGLE *n* pl. **-S** a small loop of rope

CRINITE *n* pl. **-S** a fossil crinoid

CRINKLE *v* **-KLED, -KLING, -KLES** to wrinkle

CRINKLY *adj* **-KLIER, -KLIEST** crinkled

CRINOID *n* pl. **-S** a marine animal

CRINUM	*n* pl. **-S** a tropical herb
CRIOLLO	*n* pl. **-LOS** a person of Spanish ancestry
CRIPE	*interj* — used as a mild oath
CRIPES	*interj* — used as a mild oath
CRIPPLE	*v* **-PLED, -PLING, -PLES** to disable or impair
CRIPPLER	*n* pl. **-S** one that cripples
CRIS	*n* pl. **-ES** kris
CRISIS	*n* pl. **CRISES** a crucial turning point **CRISIC** *adj*
CRISP	*adj* **CRISPER, CRISPEST** brittle
CRISP	*v* **-ED, -ING, -S** to make crisp
CRISPATE	*adj* curled
CRISPEN	*v* **-ED, -ING, -S** to make crisp
CRISPER	*n* pl. **-S** one that crisps
CRISPLY	*adv* in a crisp manner
CRISPY	*adj* **CRISPIER, CRISPIEST** crisp **CRISPILY** *adv*
CRISSUM	*n* pl. **CRISSA** a region of feathers on a bird **CRISSAL** *adj*
CRISTA	*n* pl. **-TAE** a part of a cell
CRISTATE	*adj* having a projection on the head
CRIT	*n* pl. **-S** criticism
CRITERIA	*n/pl* standards of judgment
CRITIC	*n* pl. **-S** one who judges the merits of something **CRITICAL** *adj*
CRITIQUE	*v* **-TIQUED, -TIQUING, -TIQUES** to judge as a critic
CRITTER	*n* pl. **-S** a creature
CRITTUR	*n* pl. **-S** critter
CROAK	*v* **-ED, -ING, -S** to utter a low, hoarse sound
CROAKER	*n* pl. **-S** one that croaks
CROAKY	*adj* **CROAKIER, CROAKIEST** low and hoarse **CROAKILY** *adv*
CROC	*n* pl. **-S** a crocodile
CROCEIN	*n* pl. **-S** a red dye
CROCEINE	*n* pl. **-S** crocein
CROCHET	*v* **-ED, -ING, -S** to do a type of needlework
CROCI	a pl. of crocus
CROCINE	*adj* pertaining to the crocus
CROCK	*v* **-ED, -ING, -S** to soil
CROCKERY	*n* pl. **-ERIES** pottery
CROCKET	*n* pl. **-S** an architectural ornament
CROCKPOT	*n* pl. **-S** an electric cooking pot

CROCOITE	*n* pl. **-S** a mineral
CROCUS	*n* pl. **-CUSES** or **-CI** a flowering plant
CROFT	*v* **-ED, -ING, -S** to farm on a small tenant farm
CROFTER	*n* pl. **-S** a tenant farmer
CROJIK	*n* pl. **-S** a triangular sail
CROMLECH	*n* pl. **-S** a dolmen
CRONE	*n* pl. **-S** a withered old woman **CRONISH** *adj*
CRONY	*n* pl. **CRONIES** a close friend
CRONYISM	*n* pl. **-S** a kind of political favoritism
CROOK	*adj* **CROOKER, CROOKEST** sick
CROOK	*v* **-ED, -ING, -S** to bend
CROOKED	*adj* **-EDER, -EDEST** dishonest
CROOKERY	*n* pl. **-ERIES** crooked activity
CROON	*v* **-ED, -ING, -S** to sing softly
CROONER	*n* pl. **-S** one that croons
CROONY	*adj* **-NIER, -NIEST** having or being a soft singing style
CROP	*v* **CROPPED, CROPPING, CROPS** to cut off short
CROPLAND	*n* pl. **-S** farmland
CROPLESS	*adj* being without crops (agricultural produce)
CROPPER	*n* pl. **-S** one that crops
CROPPIE	*n* pl. **-S** crappie
CROPPING	present participle of crop
CROQUET	*v* **-ED, -ING, -S** to drive a ball away in a certain game
CROQUIS	*n* pl. **CROQUIS** a sketch
CRORE	*n* pl. **-S** a monetary unit of India
CROSIER	*n* pl. **-S** a bishop's staff
CROSS	*adj* **CROSSER, CROSSEST** ill-tempered
CROSS	*v* **-ED, -ING, -ES** to intersect
CROSSARM	*n* pl. **-S** a horizontal bar
CROSSBAR	*v* **-BARRED, -BARRING, -BARS** to fasten with crossarms
CROSSBOW	*n* pl. **-S** a kind of weapon
CROSSCUT	*v* **-CUT, -CUTTING, -CUTS** to cut across
CROSSE	*n* pl. **-S** a lacrosse stick
CROSSER	*n* pl. **-S** one that crosses
CROSSING	*n* pl. **-S** an intersection
CROSSLET	*n* pl. **-S** a heraldic symbol
CROSSLY	*adv* in a cross manner

CROSSPLY	*adj* having layers of fabric with cords lying crosswise in a tire
CROSSTIE	*n* pl. **-S** a transverse beam
CROSSWAY	*n* pl. **-WAYS** a road that crosses another road
CROSTATA	*n* pl. **-S** a type of fruit tart
CROSTINO	*n* pl. **-NI** a small piece of toast topped with a spread
CROTALE	*n* pl. **-S** a small cymbal
CROTCH	*n* pl. **-ES** an angle formed by two diverging parts **CROTCHED** *adj*
CROTCHET	*n* pl. **-S** a small hook
CROTON	*n* pl. **-S** a tropical plant
CROUCH	*v* **-ED, -ING, -ES** to stoop
CROUP	*n* pl. **-S** a disease of the throat
CROUPE	*n* pl. **-S** the rump of certain animals
CROUPIER	*n* pl. **-S** an attendant in a casino
CROUPOUS	*adj* pertaining to croup
CROUPY	*adj* **CROUPIER, CROUPIEST** affected with croup **CROUPILY** *adv*
CROUSE	*adj* lively **CROUSELY** *adv*
CROUTE	*n* pl. **-S** a pastry case
CROUTON	*n* pl. **-S** a small cube of toasted bread
CROW	*v* **-ED, -ING, -S** to boast
CROWBAIT	*n* pl. **-S** an old horse
CROWBAR	*v* **-BARRED, -BARRING, -BARS** to use a steel bar as a lever
CROWD	*v* **-ED, -ING, -S** to press into an insufficient space
CROWDER	*n* pl. **-S** one that crowds
CROWDIE	*n* pl. **-S** crowdy
CROWDY	*n* pl. **-DIES** porridge
CROWER	*n* pl. **-S** one that crows
CROWFOOT	*n* pl. **-FOOTS** or **-FEET** a flowering plant
CROWN	*v* **-ED, -ING, -S** to supply with a crown (a royal headpiece)
CROWNER	*n* pl. **-S** a coroner
CROWNET	*n* pl. **-S** a coronet
CROWSTEP	*n* pl. **-S** a step on top of a wall
CROZE	*n* pl. **-S** a tool used in barrel-making
CROZER	*n* pl. **-S** a croze
CROZIER	*n* pl. **-S** crosier
CRU	*n* pl. **-S** a grade or class of wine
CRUCES	a pl. of crux
CRUCIAL	*adj* of supreme importance
CRUCIAN	*n* pl. **-S** a European fish
CRUCIATE	*adj* cross-shaped
CRUCIBLE	*n* pl. **-S** a heat-resistant vessel
CRUCIFER	*n* pl. **-S** one who carries a cross
CRUCIFIX	*n* pl. **-ES** a cross bearing an image of Christ
CRUCIFY	*v* **-FIED, -FYING, -FIES** to put to death on a cross
CRUCK	*n* pl. **-S** a curved roof timber
CRUD	*v* **CRUDDED, CRUDDING, CRUDS** to curd
CRUDDY	*adj* **-DIER, -DIEST** filthy; contemptible
CRUDE	*adj* **CRUDER, CRUDEST** unrefined **CRUDELY** *adv*
CRUDE	*n* pl. **-S** unrefined petroleum
CRUDITES	*n/pl* pieces of raw vegetables served with a dip
CRUDITY	*n* pl. **-TIES** the state of being crude
CRUDO	*n* pl. **CRUDOS** sliced, uncooked seafood often served with a sauce
CRUEL	*adj* **CRUELER, CRUELEST** or **CRUELLER, CRUELLEST** indifferent to the pain of others **CRUELLY** *adv*
CRUELTY	*n* pl. **-TIES** a cruel act
CRUET	*n* pl. **-S** a glass bottle
CRUFT	*n* pl. **-S** technical material that is redundant, old, or inferior
CRUISE	*v* **CRUISED, CRUISING, CRUISES** to sail about touching at several ports
CRUISER	*n* pl. **-S** a boat that cruises
CRUISEY	*adj* **CRUISIER, CRUISIEST** cruisy
CRUISING	*n* pl. **-S** the act of driving around in search of fun
CRUISY	*adj* **CRUISIER, CRUISIEST** frequented by homosexuals seeking partners
CRULLER	*n* pl. **-S** a small sweet cake
CRUMB	*v* **-ED, -ING, -S** to break into crumbs (small pieces)
CRUMBER	*n* pl. **-S** one that crumbs
CRUMBIER	comparative of crumby
CRUMBIEST	superlative of crumby
CRUMBLE	*v* **-BLED, -BLING, -BLES** to break into small pieces
CRUMBLY	*adj* **-BLIER, -BLIEST** easily crumbled

CRUMBUM   *n* pl. **-S** a despicable person

CRUMBY   *adj* **CRUMBIER, CRUMBIEST** full of crumbs

CRUMHORN   *n* pl. **-S** a double-reed woodwind instrument

CRUMMIE   *n* pl. **-S** a cow with crooked horns

CRUMMY   *adj* **-MIER, -MIEST** of little or no value **CRUMMILY** *adv*

CRUMP   *v* **-ED, -ING, -S** to crunch

CRUMPET   *n* pl. **-S** a small cake cooked on a griddle

CRUMPLE   *v* **-PLED, -PLING, -PLES** to wrinkle

CRUMPLY   *adj* **-PLIER, -PLIEST** easily wrinkled

CRUNCH   *v* **-ED, -ING, -ES** to chew with a crackling sound

CRUNCHER   *n* pl. **-S** one that crunches

CRUNCHY   *adj* **CRUNCHIER, CRUNCHIEST** crisp

CRUNCHY   *n* pl. **CRUNCHIES** something that makes a crackling sound when eaten

CRUNK   *n* pl. **-S** a type of rap music

CRUNODE   *n* pl. **-S** a point at which a curve crosses itself **CRUNODAL** *adj*

CRUOR   *n* pl. **-S** clotted blood

CRUPPER   *n* pl. **-S** the rump of a horse

CRURAL   *adj* pertaining to the thigh or leg

CRUS   *n* pl. **CRURA** a part of the leg

CRUSADE   *v* **-SADED, -SADING, -SADES** to engage in a holy war

CRUSADER   *n* pl. **-S** one that crusades

CRUSADO   *n* pl. **-DOS** or **-DOES** an old Portuguese coin

CRUSE   *n* pl. **-S** a small bottle

CRUSET   *n* pl. **-S** a melting pot

CRUSH   *v* **-ED, -ING, -ES** to press or squeeze out of shape

CRUSHER   *n* pl. **-S** one that crushes

CRUSILY   *adj* covered with crosslets

CRUST   *v* **-ED, -ING, -S** to form a crust (a hardened outer surface)

CRUSTAL   *adj* pertaining to the earth's crust

CRUSTOSE   *adj* forming a thin, brittle crust

CRUSTY   *adj* **CRUSTIER, CRUSTIEST** surly **CRUSTILY** *adv*

CRUTCH   *v* **-ED, -ING, -ES** to prop up or support

CRUX   *n* pl. **CRUXES** or **CRUCES** a basic or decisive point

CRUZADO   *n* pl. **-DOS** or **-DOES** crusado

CRUZEIRO   *n* pl. **-ROS** a former monetary unit of Brazil

CRWTH   *n* pl. **-S** an ancient stringed musical instrument

CRY   *v* **CRIED, CRYING, CRIES** to weep **CRYINGLY** *adv*

CRYBABY   *n* pl. **-BIES** a person who cries easily

CRYER   *n* pl. **-S** crier

CRYOBANK   *n* pl. **-S** a place for storing human tissue at very low temperatures

CRYOGEN   *n* pl. **-S** a substance for producing low temperatures

CRYOGENY   *n* pl. **-NIES** a branch of physics

CRYOLITE   *n* pl. **-S** a mineral

CRYONICS   *n/pl* the practice of freezing dead bodies for future revival **CRYONIC** *adj*

CRYOSTAT   *n* pl. **-S** a refrigerating device

CRYOTRON   *n* pl. **-S** an electronic device

CRYPT   *n* pl. **-S** a burial vault **CRYPTAL** *adj*

CRYPTIC   *adj* mysterious

CRYPTO   *n* pl. **-TOS** one who belongs secretly to a group

CRYSTAL   *n* pl. **-S** a transparent mineral

CSARDAS   *n* pl. **-ES** czardas

CTENIDIA   *n/pl* comblike anatomical structures

CTENOID   *adj* comblike

CUATRO   *n* pl. **-ROS** a small guitar of Latin America

CUB   *v* **CUBBED, CUBBING, CUBS** to give birth to the young of certain animals

CUBAGE   *n* pl. **-S** cubature

CUBATURE   *n* pl. **-S** cubical content

CUBBISH   *adj* resembling a cub

CUBBY   *n* pl. **-BIES** a small, enclosed space

CUBE   *v* **CUBED, CUBING, CUBES** to form into a cube (a regular solid)

CUBEB   *n* pl. **-S** a woody vine

CUBER   *n* pl. **-S** one that cubes

CUBIC   *n* pl. **-S** a mathematical equation or expression

CUBICAL   *adj* shaped like a cube

CUBICITY   *n* pl. **-TIES** the state of being cubical

CUBICLE   *n* pl. **-S** a small chamber

CUBICLY   *adv* in the form of a cube

CUBICULA   *n/pl* burial chambers

CUBIFORM   *adj* shaped like a cube

CUBING   present participle of cube

CUBISM   *n* pl. **-S** a style of art **CUBISTIC** *adj*

CUBIST   *n* pl. **-S** an adherent of cubism

CUBIT   *n* pl. **-S** an ancient measure of length **CUBITAL** *adj*

CUBITUS   *n* pl. **-TI** the forearm

CUBOID   *n* pl. **-S** a bone of the foot **CUBOIDAL** *adj*

CUCKOLD   *v* **-ED, -ING, -S** to make a cuckold (a cornuto) of

CUCKOO   *v* **-ED, -ING, -S** to repeat monotonously

CUCUMBER   *n* pl. **-S** a garden vegetable

CUCURBIT   *n* pl. **-S** a gourd

CUD   *n* pl. **-S** a portion of food to be chewed again

CUDBEAR   *n* pl. **-S** a red dye

CUDDIE   *n* pl. **-S** cuddy

CUDDIES   pl. of cuddy

CUDDLE   *v* **-DLED, -DLING, -DLES** to hug tenderly

CUDDLER   *n* pl. **-S** one that cuddles

CUDDLY   *adj* **-DLIER, -DLIEST** fit for cuddling

CUDDY   *n* pl. **-DIES** a donkey

CUDGEL   *v* **-ELED, -ELING, -ELS** or **-ELLED, -ELLING, -ELS** to beat with a heavy club

CUDGELER   *n* pl. **-S** one that cudgels

CUDWEED   *n* pl. **-S** a perennial herb

CUE   *v* **CUED, CUING** or **CUEING, CUES** to give a signal to an actor

CUEIST   *n* pl. **-S** one that uses a cue (a straight tapering rod) in billiards

CUESTA   *n* pl. **-S** a type of land elevation

CUFF   *v* **-ED, -ING, -S** to furnish with a cuff (a part of a sleeve)

CUFFABLE   *adj* intended to be folded down to the ankle — used of a sock

CUFFLESS   *adj* having no cuff

CUFFLINK   *n* pl. **-S** a fastening for a shirt cuff

CUIF   *n* pl. **-S** coof

CUING   a present participle of cue

CUIRASS   *v* **-ED, -ING, -ES** to cover with a type of armor

CUISH   *n* pl. **-ES** cuisse

CUISINE   *n* pl. **-S** a style of cooking

CUISSE   *n* pl. **-S** a piece of armor for the thigh

CUITTLE   *v* **-TLED, -TLING, -TLES** to coax

CUKE   *n* pl. **-S** a cucumber

CULCH   *n* pl. **-ES** an oyster bed

CULET   *n* pl. **-S** a piece of armor for the lower back

CULEX   *n* pl. **CULEXES** or **CULICES** a mosquito

CULICID   *n* pl. **-S** a culicine

CULICINE   *n* pl. **-S** a mosquito

CULINARY   *adj* pertaining to cookery

CULL   *v* **-ED, -ING, -S** to select from others

CULLAY   *n* pl. **-LAYS** quillai

CULLER   *n* pl. **-S** one that culls

CULLET   *n* pl. **-S** broken glass gathered for remelting

CULLIED   past tense of cully

CULLION   *n* pl. **-S** a vile fellow

CULLIS   *n* pl. **-LISES** a gutter in a roof

CULLY   *v* **-LIED, -LYING, -LIES** to trick

CULM   *v* **-ED, -ING, -S** to form a hollow stem

CULMEN   *n* pl. **-MINA** the upper ridge of a bird's beak

CULOTTE   *n* pl. **-S** a divided skirt

CULPA   *n* pl. **-PAE** negligence for which one is liable

CULPABLE   *adj* deserving blame or censure **CULPABLY** *adv*

CULPRIT   *n* pl. **-S** one that is guilty

CULT   *n* pl. **-S** a group of zealous devotees

CULTCH   *n* pl. **-ES** culch

CULTI   a pl. of cultus

CULTIC   *adj* pertaining to a cult

CULTIGEN   *n* pl. **-S** a cultivar

CULTISH   *adj* pertaining to a cult

CULTISM   *n* pl. **-S** devotion to a cult

CULTIST   *n* pl. **-S** a member of a cult

CULTIVAR   *n* pl. **-S** a variety of plant originating under cultivation

CULTLIKE   *adj* resembling a cult

CULTRATE   *adj* sharp-edged and pointed

CULTURAL   *adj* produced by breeding

CULTURE	*v* **-TURED, -TURING, -TURES** to make fit for raising crops
CULTUS	*n* pl. **-TUSES** or **-TI** a cult
CULVER	*n* pl. **-S** a pigeon
CULVERIN	*n* pl. **-S** a medieval musket
CULVERT	*v* **-ED, -ING, -S** to channel a stream through a conduit
CUM	*prep* together with
CUMARIN	*n* pl. **-S** coumarin
CUMBER	*v* **-ED, -ING, -S** to hinder
CUMBERER	*n* pl. **-S** one that cumbers
CUMBIA	*n* pl. **-S** a Latin-American dance
CUMBROUS	*adj* unwieldy
CUMIN	*n* pl. **-S** a plant used in cooking
CUMMER	*n* pl. **-S** a godmother
CUMMIN	*n* pl. **-S** cumin
CUMQUAT	*n* pl. **-S** kumquat
CUMSHAW	*n* pl. **-S** a gift
CUMULATE	*v* **-LATED, -LATING, -LATES** to heap
CUMULUS	*n* pl. **-LI** a type of cloud **CUMULOUS** *adj*
CUNDUM	*n* pl. **-S** condom
CUNEAL	*adj* cuneate
CUNEATE	*adj* wedge-shaped; triangular
CUNEATED	*adj* cuneate
CUNEATIC	*adj* cuneate
CUNIFORM	*n* pl. **-S** wedge-shaped writing characters
CUNIT	*n* pl. **-S** 100 cubic feet (2.83 cubic meters) of wood
CUNNER	*n* pl. **-S** a marine fish
CUNNING	*adj* **-NINGER, -NINGEST** crafty
CUNNING	*n* pl. **-S** skill in deception
CUP	*v* **CUPPED, CUPPING, CUPS** to place in a cup (a small, open container)
CUPBOARD	*n* pl. **-S** a cabinet
CUPCAKE	*n* pl. **-S** a small cake
CUPEL	*v* **-PELED, -PELING, -PELS** or **-PELLED, -PELLING, -PELS** to refine gold or silver in a cuplike vessel
CUPELER	*n* pl. **-S** cupeller
CUPELLER	*n* pl. **-S** one that cupels
CUPFUL	*n* pl. **CUPFULS** or **CUPSFUL** as much as a cup can hold
CUPID	*n* pl. **-S** a naked, winged representation of the Roman god of love
CUPIDITY	*n* pl. **-TIES** greed; lust
CUPLIKE	*adj* resembling a cup
CUPOLA	*v* **-ED, -ING, -S** to shape like a dome
CUPPA	*n* pl. **-S** a cup of tea
CUPPED	past tense of cup
CUPPER	*n* pl. **-S** one that performs cupping
CUPPING	*n* pl. **-S** an archaic medical process
CUPPY	*adj* **-PIER, -PIEST** cuplike
CUPREOUS	*adj* containing copper
CUPRIC	*adj* containing copper
CUPRITE	*n* pl. **-S** an ore of copper
CUPROUS	*adj* containing copper
CUPRUM	*n* pl. **-S** copper
CUPSFUL	a pl. of cupful
CUPULA	*n* pl. **-LAE** cupule
CUPULAR	*adj* cupulate
CUPULATE	*adj* cup-shaped
CUPULE	*n* pl. **-S** a cup-shaped anatomical structure
CUR	*n* pl. **-S** a mongrel dog
CURABLE	*adj* capable of being cured **CURABLY** *adv*
CURACAO	*n* pl. **-S** a type of liqueur
CURACOA	*n* pl. **-S** curacao
CURACY	*n* pl. **-CIES** the office of a curate
CURAGH	*n* pl. **-S** currach
CURARA	*n* pl. **-S** curare
CURARE	*n* pl. **-S** an arrow poison
CURARI	*n* pl. **-S** curare
CURARINE	*n* pl. **-S** a poisonous alkaloid
CURARIZE	*v* **-RIZED, -RIZING, -RIZES** to poison with curare
CURASSOW	*n* pl. **-S** a turkey-like bird
CURATE	*v* **-RATED, -RATING, -RATES** to act as curator of
CURATION	*n* pl. **-S** the work of a curator
CURATIVE	*n* pl. **-S** something that cures
CURATOR	*n* pl. **-S** a museum manager
CURB	*v* **-ED, -ING, -S** to restrain **CURBABLE** *adj*
CURBER	*n* pl. **-S** one that curbs

CURBING	*n* pl. **-S** a concrete border along a street
CURBSIDE	*n* pl. **-S** the side of a pavement bordered by a curbing
CURCH	*n* pl. **-ES** a kerchief
CURCULIO	*n* pl. **-LIOS** a weevil
CURCUMA	*n* pl. **-S** a tropical plant
CURCUMIN	*n* pl. **-S** the coloring ingredient of the spice turmeric
CURD	*v* **-ED, -ING, -S** to curdle
CURDLE	*v* **-DLED, -DLING, -DLES** to congeal
CURDLER	*n* pl. **-S** one that curdles
CURDY	*adj* **CURDIER, CURDIEST** curdled
CURE	*v* **CURED, CURING, CURES** to restore to health
CURELESS	*adj* not curable
CURER	*n* pl. **-S** one that cures
CURET	*n* pl. **-S** a surgical instrument
CURETTE	*v* **-RETTED, -RETTING, -RETTES** to treat with a curet
CURF	*n* pl. **-S** an incision made by a cutting tool
CURFEW	*n* pl. **-S** a regulation concerning the hours which one may keep
CURIA	*n* pl. **-RIAE** a court of justice **CURIAL** *adj*
CURIE	*n* pl. **-S** a unit of radioactivity
CURING	present participle of cure
CURIO	*n* pl. **-RIOS** an unusual art object
CURIOSA	*n/pl* pornographic books
CURIOUS	*adj* **-OUSER, -OUSEST** eager for information
CURITE	*n* pl. **-S** a radioactive mineral
CURIUM	*n* pl. **-S** a radioactive element
CURL	*v* **-ED, -ING, -S** to form into ringlets
CURLER	*n* pl. **-S** one that curls
CURLEW	*n* pl. **-S** a shore bird
CURLICUE	*v* **-CUED, -CUING, -CUES** to decorate with curlicues (fancy spiral figures)
CURLING	*n* pl. **-S** a game played on ice
CURLY	*adj* **CURLIER, CURLIEST** tending to curl **CURLILY** *adv*
CURLYCUE	*n* pl. **-S** curlicue
CURN	*n* pl. **-S** grain
CURR	*v* **-ED, -ING, -S** to purr
CURRACH	*n* pl. **-S** a coracle
CURRAGH	*n* pl. **-S** currach
CURRAN	*n* pl. **-S** curn
CURRANT	*n* pl. **-S** an edible berry
CURRENCY	*n* pl. **-CIES** money
CURRENT	*n* pl. **-S** a continuous flow
CURRICLE	*n* pl. **-S** a light carriage
CURRIE	*v* **-RIED, -RYING, -RIES** to prepare food a certain way
CURRIED	past tense of curry
CURRIER	*n* pl. **-S** one that curries leather
CURRIERY	*n* pl. **-ERIES** the shop of a currier
CURRISH	*adj* resembling a cur
CURRY	*v* **-RIED, -RYING, -RIES** to prepare leather for use or sale
CURRYING	present participle of currie
CURSE	*v* **CURSED** or **CURST, CURSING, CURSES** to wish evil upon
CURSED	*adj* **CURSEDER, CURSEDEST** wicked **CURSEDLY** *adv*
CURSER	*n* pl. **-S** one that curses
CURSILLO	*n* pl. **-LOS** a type of spiritual retreat (seclusion with a group)
CURSING	present participle of curse
CURSIVE	*n* pl. **-S** a style of print
CURSOR	*n* pl. **-S** a light indicator on a computer display
CURSORY	*adj* hasty and superficial
CURST	a past tense of curse
CURT	*adj* **CURTER, CURTEST** abrupt
CURTAIL	*v* **-ED, -ING, -S** to cut short
CURTAIN	*v* **-ED, -ING, -S** to provide with a hanging piece of fabric
CURTAL	*n* pl. **-S** an animal with a clipped tail
CURTALAX	*n* pl. **-ES** a cutlass
CURTANA	*n* pl. **-S** a type of English sword
CURTATE	*adj* shortened
CURTESY	*n* pl. **-SIES** a type of legal tenure
CURTLY	*adv* in a curt manner
CURTNESS	*n* pl. **-ES** the quality of being curt
CURTSEY	*v* **-ED, -ING, -S** to curtsy
CURTSY	*v* **-SIED, -SYING, -SIES** to bow politely
CURULE	*adj* of the highest rank
CURVE	*v* **CURVED, CURVING, CURVES** to deviate from straightness **CURVEDLY** *adv*

CURVET	*v* **-VETED, -VETING, -VETS** or **-VETTED, -VETTING, -VETS** to prance
CURVEY	*adj* **CURVIER, CURVIEST** curvy
CURVING	present participle of curve
CURVY	*adj* **CURVIER, CURVIEST** curved
CUSCUS	*n* pl. **-ES** an arboreal mammal
CUSEC	*n* pl. **-S** a volumetric unit of flow of liquids
CUSHAT	*n* pl. **-S** a pigeon
CUSHAW	*n* pl. **-S** a variety of squash
CUSHIER	comparative of cushy
CUSHIEST	superlative of cushy
CUSHILY	*adv* in a cushy manner
CUSHION	*v* **-ED, -ING, -S** to pad with soft material
CUSHIONY	*adj* soft
CUSHY	*adj* **CUSHIER, CUSHIEST** easy
CUSK	*n* pl. **-S** a marine food fish
CUSP	*n* pl. **-S** a pointed end **CUSPAL, CUSPATE, CUSPATED, CUSPED** *adj*
CUSPID	*n* pl. **-S** a pointed tooth
CUSPIDAL	*adj* having a cusp
CUSPIDOR	*n* pl. **-S** a spittoon
CUSPIS	*n* pl. **-PIDES** a cusp
CUSS	*v* **-ED, -ING, -ES** to curse
CUSSEDLY	*adv* in a cranky manner
CUSSER	*n* pl. **-S** one that cusses
CUSSO	*n* pl. **-SOS** an Ethiopian tree
CUSSWORD	*n* pl. **-S** a profane or obscene word
CUSTARD	*n* pl. **-S** a thick, soft dessert **CUSTARDY** *adj*
CUSTODES	pl. of custos
CUSTODY	*n* pl. **-DIES** guardianship
CUSTOM	*n* pl. **-S** a habitual practice
CUSTOMER	*n* pl. **-S** one who buys something
CUSTOS	*n* pl. **-TODES** a guardian or keeper
CUSTUMAL	*n* pl. **-S** a written record of laws and customs
CUT	*v* **CUT, CUTTING, CUTS** to divide into parts with a sharp-edged instrument
CUTAWAY	*n* pl. **-AWAYS** a type of coat
CUTBACK	*n* pl. **-S** a reduction
CUTBANK	*n* pl. **-S** a steep stream bank
CUTBLOCK	*n* pl. **-S** a limited area authorized for logging

CUTCH	*n* pl. **-ES** catechu
CUTCHERY	*n* pl. **-CHERIES** a judicial office in India
CUTDOWN	*n* pl. **-S** a reduction
CUTE	*adj* **CUTER, CUTEST** pleasingly attractive **CUTELY** *adv*
CUTENESS	*n* pl. **-ES** the quality of being cute
CUTES	a pl. of cutis
CUTESIE	*adj* **-SIER, -SIEST** cutesy
CUTEST	superlative of cute
CUTESY	*adj* **-SIER, -SIEST** self-consciously cute
CUTEY	*n* pl. **-TEYS** cutie
CUTGRASS	*n* pl. **-ES** a swamp grass
CUTICLE	*n* pl. **-S** the epidermis
CUTICULA	*n* pl. **-LAE** the outer hard covering of an insect
CUTIE	*n* pl. **-S** a cute person
CUTIN	*n* pl. **-S** a waxy substance found on plants
CUTINISE	*v* **-ISED, -ISING, -ISES** to cutinize
CUTINIZE	*v* **-IZED, -IZING, -IZES** to become coated with cutin
CUTIS	*n* pl. **-TISES** or **-TES** the corium
CUTLAS	*n* pl. **-ES** cutlass
CUTLASS	*n* pl. **-ES** a short sword
CUTLER	*n* pl. **-S** one who sells and repairs cutting tools
CUTLERY	*n* pl. **-LERIES** the occupation of a cutler
CUTLET	*n* pl. **-S** a slice of meat
CUTLETTE	*n* pl. **-S** a breaded patty of chopped meat
CUTLINE	*n* pl. **-S** a caption
CUTOFF	*n* pl. **-S** the point at which something terminates
CUTOUT	*n* pl. **-S** something cut out
CUTOVER	*n* pl. **-S** land cleared of trees
CUTPURSE	*n* pl. **-S** a pickpocket
CUTSCENE	*n* pl. **-S** a type of scene in computer games
CUTTABLE	*adj* capable of being cut
CUTTAGE	*n* pl. **-S** a means of plant propagation
CUTTER	*n* pl. **-S** one that cuts
CUTTIES	pl. of cutty
CUTTING	*n* pl. **-S** a section cut from a plant

CUTTLE   v **-TLED, -TLING, -TLES** to fold cloth in a particular fashion

CUTTY   n pl. **-TIES** a thickset girl

CUTUP   n pl. **-S** a mischievous person

CUTWATER   n pl. **-S** the front part of a ship's prow

CUTWORK   n pl. **-S** a type of embroidery

CUTWORM   n pl. **-S** a caterpillar

CUVEE   n pl. **-S** wine blended in casks

CUVETTE   n pl. **-S** a small tube or vessel

CUZ   n pl. **CUZZES** or **CUZES** a cousin

CWM   n pl. **-S** a cirque

CYAN   n pl. **-S** a blue color

CYANAMID   n pl. **-S** a chemical compound

CYANATE   n pl. **-S** a chemical salt

CYANIC   adj blue or bluish

CYANID   n pl. **-S** a compound of cyanogen

CYANIDE   v **-NIDED, -NIDING, -NIDES** to treat an ore with cyanid

CYANIN   n pl. **-S** cyanine

CYANINE   n pl. **-S** a blue dye

CYANITE   n pl. **-S** a mineral **CYANITIC** adj

CYANO   adj pertaining to cyanogen

CYANOGEN   n pl. **-S** a reactive compound of carbon and nitrogen

CYANOSIS   n pl. **-NOSES** bluish discoloration of the skin **CYANOSED, CYANOTIC** adj

CYATHIUM   n pl. **-ATHIA** the flower head of certain plants

CYBER   adj pertaining to computers

CYBERSEX   n pl. **-ES** an online sex-oriented conversation

CYBERWAR   n pl. **-S** a conflict in which enemies try to gain access to each other's computer systems

CYBORG   n pl. **-S** a human linked to a mechanical device for life support

CYCAD   n pl. **-S** a tropical plant

CYCAS   n pl. **-ES** a tropical plant

CYCASIN   n pl. **-S** a sugar derivative

CYCLAMEN   n pl. **-S** a flowering plant

CYCLASE   n pl. **-S** an enzyme

CYCLE   v **-CLED, -CLING, -CLES** to ride a bicycle

CYCLECAR   n pl. **-S** a type of motor vehicle

CYCLER   n pl. **-S** a cyclist

CYCLERY   n pl. **-RIES** a bicycle shop

CYCLEWAY   n pl. **-WAYS** a bikeway

CYCLIC   adj moving in complete circles **CYCLICLY** adv

CYCLICAL   n pl. **-S** a stock whose earnings fluctuate widely with variations in the economy

CYCLIN   n pl. **-S** any of a group of proteins that control the cell cycle

CYCLING   n pl. **-S** the act of riding a bicycle

CYCLIST   n pl. **-S** one who rides a bicycle

CYCLITOL   n pl. **-S** a chemical compound

CYCLIZE   v **-CLIZED, -CLIZING, -CLIZES** to form one or more rings in a chemical compound

CYCLO   n pl. **-CLOS** a three-wheeled motor vehicle

CYCLOID   n pl. **-S** a geometric curve

CYCLONE   n pl. **-S** a rotating system of winds **CYCLONAL, CYCLONIC** adj

CYCLOPS   n pl. **CYCLOPS** a minute one-eyed crustacean

CYCLOSIS   n pl. **-CLOSES** the circulation of protoplasm within a cell

CYDER   n pl. **-S** cider

CYESIS   n pl. **CYESES** pregnancy

CYGNET   n pl. **-S** a young swan

CYLINDER   v **-ED, -ING, -S** to furnish with a cylinder (a chamber in an engine)

CYLIX   n pl. **CYLICES** kylix

CYMA   n pl. **-MAS** or **-MAE** a curved molding

CYMAR   n pl. **-S** simar

CYMATIUM   n pl. **-TIA** a cyma

CYMBAL   n pl. **-S** a percussion instrument

CYMBALER   n pl. **-S** one that plays the cymbals

CYMBALOM   n pl. **-S** cimbalom

CYMBIDIA   n/pl tropical orchids

CYMBLING   n pl. **-S** cymling

CYME   n pl. **-S** a flower cluster

CYMENE   n pl. **-S** a hydrocarbon

CYMLIN   n pl. **-S** cymling

CYMLING   n pl. **-S** a variety of squash

CYMOGENE   n pl. **-S** a volatile compound

CYMOID   adj resembling a cyma

CYMOL   n pl. **-S** cymene

CYMOSE   adj resembling a cyme **CYMOSELY** adv

CYMOUS   adj cymose

CYNIC	*n* pl. **-S** a cynical person
CYNICAL	*adj* distrusting the motives of others
CYNICISM	*n* pl. **-S** cynical quality
CYNODONT	*n* pl. **-S** a type of fossil reptile
CYNOSURE	*n* pl. **-S** a center of attraction
CYPHER	*v* **-ED, -ING, -S** to cipher
CYPRES	*n* pl. **-ES** a legal doctrine
CYPRESS	*n* pl. **-ES** a thin fabric
CYPRIAN	*n* pl. **-S** a prostitute
CYPRINID	*n* pl. **-S** a small freshwater fish
CYPRUS	*n* pl. **-ES** cypress
CYPSELA	*n* pl. **-LAE** an achene in certain plants
CYST	*n* pl. **-S** a sac
CYSTEIN	*n* pl. **-S** cysteine
CYSTEINE	*n* pl. **-S** an amino acid
CYSTIC	*adj* pertaining to a cyst
CYSTINE	*n* pl. **-S** an amino acid
CYSTITIS	*n* pl. **-TITIDES** inflammation of the urinary bladder
CYSTOID	*n* pl. **-S** a cyst-like structure
CYTASTER	*n* pl. **-S** a structure formed in a cell during mitosis
CYTIDINE	*n* pl. **-S** a compound containing cytosine
CYTOGENY	*n* pl. **-NIES** the formation of cells
CYTOKINE	*n* pl. **-S** a kind of substance secreted by cells of the immune system
CYTOLOGY	*n* pl. **-GIES** a study of cells
CYTON	*n* pl. **-S** the body of a nerve cell
CYTOSINE	*n* pl. **-S** a component of DNA and RNA
CYTOSOL	*n* pl. **-S** the fluid portion of cell material
CZAR	*n* pl. **-S** an emperor or king
CZARDAS	*n* pl. **-ES** a Hungarian dance
CZARDOM	*n* pl. **-S** the domain of a czar
CZAREVNA	*n* pl. **-S** the daughter of a czar
CZARINA	*n* pl. **-S** the wife of a czar
CZARISM	*n* pl. **-S** autocratic government
CZARIST	*n* pl. **-S** a supporter of czarism
CZARITZA	*n* pl. **-S** a czarina

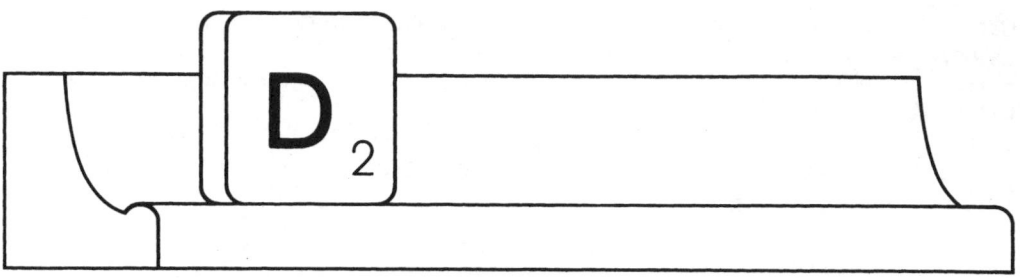

DA   *n* **-S** dad

DAB   *v* **DABBED, DABBING, DABS** to touch lightly

DABBER   *n* pl. **-S** one that dabs

DABBLE   *v* **-BLED, -BLING, -BLES** to involve oneself in a superficial interest

DABBLER   *n* pl. **-S** one that dabbles

DABBLING   *n* pl. **-S** a superficial interest

DABCHICK   *n* pl. **-S** a small grebe

DABSTER   *n* pl. **-S** a dabbler

DACE   *n* pl. **-S** a freshwater fish

DACHA   *n* pl. **-S** a Russian cottage

DACITE   *n* pl. **-S** a light gray rock

DACKER   *v* **-ED, -ING, -S** to waver

DACOIT   *n* pl. **-S** a bandit in India

DACOITY   *n* pl. **-COITIES** robbery by dacoits

DACTYL   *n* pl. **-S** a type of metrical foot

DACTYLIC   *n* pl. **-S** a verse consisting of dactyls

DACTYLUS   *n* pl. **-LI** a leg joint of certain insects

DAD   *n* pl. **-S** father

DADA   *n* pl. **-S** an artistic and literary movement

DADAISM   *n* pl. **-S** the dada movement

DADAIST   *n* pl. **-S** a follower of dadaism

DADDLE   *v* **-DLED, -DLING, -DLES** to diddle

DADDY   *n* pl. **-DIES** father

DADGUM   *adj* — used as an intensive

DADO   *v* **-ED, -ING, -S** or **-ES** to set into a groove

DAEDAL   *adj* skillful

DAEMON   *n* pl. **-S** demon **DAEMONIC** *adj*

DAEMON   *n* pl. **-S** or **-ES** daimon

DAFF   *v* **-ED, -ING, -S** to thrust aside

DAFFODIL   *n* pl. **-S** a flowering plant

DAFFY   *adj* **-FIER, -FIEST** silly **DAFFILY** *adv*

DAFT   *adj* **DAFTER, DAFTEST** insane **DAFTLY** *adv*

DAFTNESS   *n* pl. **-ES** the quality of being daft

DAG   *n* pl. **-S** a hanging end or shred

DAGGA   *n* pl. **-S** marijuana

DAGGER   *v* **-ED, -ING, -S** to stab with a small knife

DAGGLE   *v* **-GLED, -GLING, -GLES** to drag in mud

DAGLOCK   *n* pl. **-S** a dirty or tangled lock of wool

DAGOBA   *n* pl. **-S** a Buddhist shrine

DAGWOOD   *n* pl. **-S** a large sandwich

DAH   *n* pl. **-S** a dash in Morse code

DAHABEAH   *n* pl. **-S** a large passenger boat

DAHABIAH   *n* pl. **-S** dahabeah

DAHABIEH   *n* pl. **-S** dahabeah

DAHABIYA   *n* pl. **-S** dahabeah

DAHL   *n* pl. **-S** dal

DAHLIA   *n* pl. **-S** a flowering plant

DAHOON   *n* pl. **-S** an evergreen tree

DAIDZEIN   *n* pl. **-S** a chemical found chiefly in soybeans

DAIKER   *v* **-ED, -ING, -S** to dacker

DAIKON   *n* pl. **-S** a Japanese radish

DAILY   *n* pl. **-LIES** a newspaper published every weekday

DAIMEN   *adj* occasional

DAIMIO   *n* pl. **-MIOS** a former Japanese nobleman

DAIMON   *n* pl. **-S** or **-ES** an attendant spirit **DAIMONIC** *adj*

DAIMYO   *n* pl. **-MYOS** daimio

DAINTY   *adj* **-TIER, -TIEST** delicately pretty **DAINTILY** *adv*

DAINTY   *n* pl. **-TIES** something delicious

DAIQUIRI	*n* pl. **-S** a cocktail
DAIRY	*n* pl. **DAIRIES** an establishment dealing in milk products
DAIRYING	*n* pl. **-S** the business of a dairy
DAIRYMAN	*n* pl. **-MEN** a man who works in or owns a dairy
DAIS	*n* pl. **-ISES** a raised platform
DAISHIKI	*n* pl. **-S** dashiki
DAISY	*n* pl. **-SIES** a flowering plant **DAISIED** *adj*
DAK	*n* pl. **-S** transportation by relays of men and horses
DAKERHEN	*n* pl. **-S** a European bird
DAKOIT	*n* pl. **-S** dacoit
DAKOITY	*n* pl. **-TIES** dacoity
DAL	*n* pl. **-S** a dish of lentils and spices in India
DALAPON	*n* pl. **-S** an herbicide used on unwanted grasses
DALASI	*n* pl. **-S** a unit of Gambian currency
DALE	*n* pl. **-S** a valley
DALEDH	*n* pl. **-S** daleth
DALESMAN	*n* pl. **-MEN** one living in a dale
DALETH	*n* pl. **-S** a Hebrew letter
DALLES	*n/pl* rapids
DALLIER	*n* pl. **-S** one that dallies
DALLY	*v* **-LIED, -LYING, -LIES** to waste time
DALMATIC	*n* pl. **-S** a wide-sleeved vestment
DALTON	*n* pl. **-S** a unit of atomic mass
DALTONIC	*adj* pertaining to a form of color blindness
DAM	*v* **DAMMED, DAMMING, DAMS** to build a barrier to obstruct the flow of water
DAMAGE	*v* **-AGED, -AGING, -AGES** to injure
DAMAGER	*n* pl. **-S** one that damages
DAMAN	*n* pl. **-S** a small mammal
DAMAR	*n* pl. **-S** dammar
DAMASK	*v* **-ED, -ING, -S** to weave with elaborate design
DAME	*n* pl. **-S** a matron
DAMEWORT	*n* pl. **-S** a flowering plant
DAMFOOL	*n* pl. **-S** a stupid or foolish person
DAMIANA	*n* pl. **-S** a tropical American shrub
DAMMAR	*n* pl. **-S** a hard resin
DAMMED	past tense of dam
DAMMER	*n* pl. **-S** dammar
DAMMING	present participle of dam
DAMMIT	*interj* — used to express anger
DAMN	*v* **-ED, -ING, -S** to curse
DAMNABLE	*adj* detestable **DAMNABLY** *adv*
DAMNDEST	*n* pl. **-S** utmost
DAMNED	*adj* **DAMNEDER, DAMNEDEST** or **DAMNDEST** damnable
DAMNER	*n* pl. **-S** one that damns
DAMNEST	*n* pl. **-S** damndest
DAMNIFY	*v* **-FIED, -FYING, -FIES** to cause loss or damage to
DAMOSEL	*n* pl. **-S** damsel
DAMOZEL	*n* pl. **-S** damsel
DAMP	*adj* **DAMPER, DAMPEST** moist
DAMP	*v* **-ED, -ING, -S** to lessen in intensity
DAMPEN	*v* **-ED, -ING, -S** to moisten
DAMPENER	*n* pl. **-S** one that dampens
DAMPER	*n* pl. **-S** one that damps
DAMPING	*n* pl. **-S** the ability of a device to prevent instability
DAMPISH	*adj* somewhat damp
DAMPLY	*adv* in a damp manner
DAMPNESS	*n* pl. **-ES** the state of being damp
DAMSEL	*n* pl. **-S** a maiden
DAMSON	*n* pl. **-S** a small purple plum
DAN	*n* pl. **-S** a level of skill in martial arts
DANAZOL	*n* pl. **-S** a synthetic androgen
DANCE	*v* **DANCED, DANCING, DANCES** to move rhythmically to music
DANCER	*n* pl. **-S** one that dances
DANCEY	*adj* **DANCIER, DANCIEST** suitable for dancing
DANDER	*v* **-ED, -ING, -S** to stroll
DANDIER	comparative of dandy
DANDIES	pl. of dandy
DANDIEST	superlative of dandy
DANDIFY	*v* **-FIED, -FYING, -FIES** to cause to resemble a dandy
DANDILY	*adv* in a dandy manner
DANDLE	*v* **-DLED, -DLING, -DLES** to fondle
DANDLER	*n* pl. **-S** one that dandles
DANDRIFF	*n* pl. **-S** dandruff
DANDRUFF	*n* pl. **-S** a scurf that forms on the scalp
DANDY	*adj* **-DIER, -DIEST** fine

DANDY *n pl.* **-DIES** a man who is overly concerned about his appearance

DANDYISH *adj* suggestive of a dandy

DANDYISM *n pl.* **-S** the style or conduct of a dandy

DANEGELD *n pl.* **-S** an annual tax in medieval England

DANEGELT *n pl.* **-S** danegeld

DANEWEED *n pl.* **-S** a danewort

DANEWORT *n pl.* **-S** a flowering plant

DANG *v* **-ED, -ING, -S** to damn

DANG *adj* **DANGER, DANGEST** damned

DANGER *v* **-ED, -ING, -S** to endanger

DANGLE *v* **-GLED, -GLING, -GLES** to hang loosely

DANGLER *n pl.* **-S** one that dangles

DANGLY *adj* **-GLIER, -GLIEST** dangling

DANIO *n pl.* **-NIOS** an aquarium fish

DANISH *n pl.* **-ES** a pastry of raised dough

DANK *adj* **DANKER, DANKEST** unpleasantly damp **DANKLY** *adv*

DANKNESS *n pl.* **-ES** the state of being dank

DANSAK *n pl.* **-S** dhansak

DANSEUR *n pl.* **-S** a male ballet dancer

DANSEUSE *n pl.* **-S** a female ballet dancer

DAP *v* **DAPPED, DAPPING, DAPS** to dip lightly or quickly into water

DAPHNE *n pl.* **-S** a flowering shrub

DAPHNIA *n pl.* **-S** a minute crustacean

DAPPER *adj* **-PERER, -PEREST** looking neat and trim **DAPPERLY** *adv*

DAPPING present participle of dap

DAPPLE *v* **-PLED, -PLING, -PLES** to mark with spots

DAPSONE *n pl.* **-S** a medicinal substance

DARB *n pl.* **-S** something considered extraordinary

DARBAR *n pl.* **-S** durbar

DARBIES *n/pl* handcuffs

DARE *v* **DARED** or **DURST, DARING, DARES** to have the necessary courage

DAREFUL *adj* brave

DARER *n pl.* **-S** one that dares

DARESAY *v* to venture to say — DARESAY is the only form of this verb; it is not conjugated

DARIC *n pl.* **-S** an ancient Persian coin

DARING *n pl.* **-S** bravery

DARINGLY *adv* in a brave manner

DARIOLE *n pl.* **-S** a type of pastry filled with cream, custard, or jelly

DARK *adj* **DARKER, DARKEST** having little or no light

DARK *v* **-ED, -ING, -S** to darken

DARKEN *v* **-ED, -ING, -S** to make dark

DARKENER *n pl.* **-S** one that darkens

DARKISH *adj* somewhat dark

DARKLE *v* **-KLED, -KLING, -KLES** to become dark

DARKLING *n pl.* **-S** the dark

DARKLY *adv* **-LIER, -LIEST** in a dark manner

DARKNESS *n pl.* **-ES** the state of being dark

DARKROOM *n pl.* **-S** a room in which film is processed

DARKSOME *adj* dark

DARLING *n pl.* **-S** a much-loved person

DARN *v* **-ED, -ING, -S** to mend with interlacing stitches

DARNDEST *n pl.* **-S** damndest

DARNED *adj* **DARNEDER, DARNEDEST** or **DARNDEST** damned

DARNEL *n pl.* **-S** an annual grass

DARNER *n pl.* **-S** one that darns

DARNEST *n pl.* **-S** damndest

DARNING *n pl.* **-S** things to be darned

DARSHAN *n pl.* **-S** a Hindu blessing

DART *v* **-ED, -ING, -S** to move suddenly or swiftly

DARTER *n pl.* **-S** one that darts

DARTLE *v* **-TLED, -TLING, -TLES** to dart repeatedly

DASH *v* **-ED, -ING, -ES** to strike violently

DASHEEN *n pl.* **-S** a tropical plant

DASHER *n pl.* **-S** one that dashes

DASHI *n pl.* **-S** a fish broth

DASHIER comparative of dashy

DASHIEST superlative of dashy

DASHIKI *n pl.* **-S** an African tunic

DASHPOT *n pl.* **-S** a shock absorber

DASHY *adj* **DASHIER, DASHIEST** stylish

DASSIE *n pl.* **-S** a hyrax

DASTARD *n pl.* **-S** a base coward

DASYURE *n pl.* **-S** a flesh-eating mammal

DATA	a pl. of datum
DATABANK	*n* pl. **-S** a database
DATABASE	*v* **-BASED, -BASING, -BASES** to put data into a database (a collection of data in a computer)
DATABLE	*adj* capable of being dated
DATARY	*n* pl. **-RIES** a cardinal in the Roman Catholic Church
DATCHA	*n* pl. **-S** dacha
DATE	*v* **DATED, DATING, DATES** to determine or record the date of **DATEABLE** *adj*
DATEBOOK	*n* pl. **-S** a notebook for listing appointments
DATEDLY	*adv* in an old-fashioned manner
DATELESS	*adj* having no date
DATELINE	*v* **-LINED, -LINING, -LINES** to provide a news story with its date and place of origin
DATER	*n* pl. **-S** one that dates
DATING	*n* pl. **-S** the act of one that dates
DATIVE	*n* pl. **-S** a grammatical case **DATIVAL** *adj* **DATIVELY** *adv*
DATO	*n* pl. **-TOS** datto
DATTO	*n* pl. **-TOS** a Philippine tribal chief
DATUM	*n* pl. **-TUMS** or **-TA** something used as a basis for calculating
DATURA	*n* pl. **-S** a flowering plant **DATURIC** *adj*
DAUB	*v* **-ED, -ING, -S** to smear
DAUBE	*n* pl. **-S** a braised meat stew
DAUBER	*n* pl. **-S** one that daubs
DAUBERY	*n* pl. **-ERIES** a bad or inexpert painting
DAUBRY	*n* pl. **-RIES** daubery
DAUBY	*adj* **DAUBIER, DAUBIEST** smeary
DAUGHTER	*n* pl. **-S** a female child
DAUNDER	*v* **-ED, -ING, -S** to dander
DAUNT	*v* **-ED, -ING, -S** to intimidate
DAUNTER	*n* pl. **-S** one that daunts
DAUPHIN	*n* pl. **-S** the eldest son of a French king
DAUPHINE	*n* pl. **-S** the wife of a dauphin
DAUT	*v* **-ED, -ING, -S** to fondle
DAUTIE	*n* pl. **-S** a small pet
DAVEN	*v* **-ED, -ING, -S** to utter Jewish prayers
DAVIT	*n* pl. **-S** a hoisting device on a ship
DAVY	*n* pl. **-VIES** a safety lamp
DAW	*v* **DAWED, DAWEN, DAWING, DAWS** to dawn
DAWDLE	*v* **-DLED, -DLING, -DLES** to waste time
DAWDLER	*n* pl. **-S** one that dawdles
DAWK	*n* pl. **-S** dak
DAWN	*v* **-ED, -ING, -S** to begin to grow light in the morning
DAWNING	*n* pl. **-S** daybreak
DAWNLIKE	*adj* suggestive of daybreak
DAWT	*v* **-ED, -ING, -S** to daut
DAWTIE	*n* pl. **-S** dautie
DAY	*n* pl. **DAYS** the time between sunrise and sunset
DAYBED	*n* pl. **-S** a couch that can be converted into a bed
DAYBOOK	*n* pl. **-S** a diary
DAYBREAK	*n* pl. **-S** the first appearance of light in the morning
DAYCARE	*n* pl. **-S** care for children and disabled adults during the day
DAYDREAM	*v* **-DREAMED** or **-DREAMT, -DREAMING, -DREAMS** to fantasize
DAYFLY	*n* pl. **-FLIES** a mayfly
DAYGLOW	*n* pl. **-S** airglow seen during the day
DAYLIGHT	*v* **-LIGHTED** or **-LIT, -LIGHTING, -LIGHTS** to illuminate with the light of day
DAYLILY	*n* pl. **-LILIES** a flowering plant
DAYLONG	*adj* lasting all day
DAYMARE	*n* pl. **-S** a nightmarish fantasy experienced while awake
DAYPACK	*n* pl. **-S** a bag carrying things that is strapped on one's back
DAYROOM	*n* pl. **-S** a room for reading and recreation
DAYSAIL	*v* **-ED, -ING, -S** to sail a yacht for a day
DAYSIDE	*n* pl. **-S** the sun side of a planet or the moon
DAYSMAN	*n* pl. **-MEN** an arbiter
DAYSTAR	*n* pl. **-S** a planet visible in the east just before sunrise
DAYTIME	*n* pl. **-S** day
DAYWEAR	*n* pl. **DAYWEAR** clothing suitable for informal occasions
DAYWORK	*n* pl. **-S** work done on a daily basis
DAZE	*v* **DAZED, DAZING, DAZES** to stun **DAZEDLY** *adv*

DAZZLE   *v* **-ZLED, -ZLING, -ZLES** to blind by bright light

DAZZLER   *n* pl. **-S** one that dazzles

DE   *prep* of; from — used in names

DEACON   *v* **-ED, -ING, -S** to read a hymn aloud

DEACONRY   *n* pl. **-RIES** a clerical office

DEAD   *adj* **DEADER, DEADEST** deprived of life

DEAD   *n* pl. **-S** the period of greatest intensity

DEADBEAT   *n* pl. **-S** a loafer

DEADBOLT   *n* pl. **-S** a lock for a door

DEADEN   *v* **-ED, -ING, -S** to diminish the sensitivity or vigor of

DEADENER   *n* pl. **-S** one that deadens

DEADEYE   *n* pl. **-S** an expert marksman

DEADFALL   *n* pl. **-S** a type of animal trap

DEADHEAD   *v* **-ED, -ING, -S** to travel without freight

DEADLIER   comparative of deadly

DEADLIEST   superlative of deadly

DEADLIFT   *v* **-ED, -ING, -S** to execute a type of lift in weight lifting

DEADLINE   *v* **-LINED, -LINING, -LINES** to set a time limit on something

DEADLOCK   *v* **-ED, -ING, -S** to come to a standstill

DEADLY   *adj* **-LIER, -LIEST** fatal

DEADMAN   *n* pl. **-MEN** an anchor for securing a rope in mountain climbing

DEADNESS   *n* pl. **-ES** the state of being dead

DEADPAN   *v* **-PANNED, -PANNING, -PANS** to act without emotion

DEADWOOD   *n* pl. **-S** a reinforcement in a ship's keel

DEAERATE   *v* **-ATED, -ATING, -ATES** to remove air or gas from

DEAF   *adj* **DEAFER, DEAFEST** lacking the sense of hearing

DEAFEN   *v* **-ED, -ING, -S** to make deaf

DEAFISH   *adj* somewhat deaf

DEAFLY   *adv* in a deaf manner

DEAFNESS   *n* pl. **-ES** the state of being deaf

DEAIR   *v* **-ED, -ING, -S** to remove air from

DEAL   *v* **DEALT, DEALING, DEALS** to trade or do business

DEALATE   *n* pl. **-S** an insect divested of its wings **DEALATED** *adj*

DEALER   *n* pl. **-S** one that deals

DEALFISH   *n* pl. **-ES** a marine fish

DEALIGN   *v* **-ED, -ING, -S** to withdraw allegiance to a political party

DEALING   *n* pl. **-S** a business transaction

DEALT   past tense of deal

DEAN   *v* **-ED, -ING, -S** to serve as dean (the head of a faculty)

DEANERY   *n* pl. **-ERIES** the office of a dean

DEANSHIP   *n* pl. **-S** deanery

DEAR   *adj* **DEARER, DEAREST** greatly loved

DEAR   *n* pl. **-S** a loved one

DEAREST   *n* pl. **-S** a much-loved person

DEARIE   *n* pl. **-S** deary

DEARIES   pl. of deary

DEARLY   *adv* in a dear manner

DEARNESS   *n* pl. **-ES** the state of being dear

DEARTH   *n* pl. **-S** scarcity

DEARY   *n* pl. **DEARIES** darling

DEASH   *v* **-ED, -ING, -ES** to remove ash from

DEASIL   *adv* clockwise

DEATH   *n* pl. **-S** the end of life

DEATHBED   *n* pl. **-S** the bed on which a person dies

DEATHCUP   *n* pl. **-S** a poisonous mushroom

DEATHFUL   *adj* fatal

DEATHLY   *adj* **-LIER, -LIEST** resembling or suggestive of death

DEATHY   *adj* deathly

DEAVE   *v* **DEAVED, DEAVING, DEAVES** to deafen

DEB   *n* pl. **-S** a debutante

DEBACLE   *n* pl. **-S** a sudden collapse

DEBAG   *v* **-BAGGED, -BAGGING, -BAGS** to remove the pants from someone

DEBAR   *v* **-BARRED, -BARRING, -BARS** to exclude

DEBARK   *v* **-ED, -ING, -S** to unload from a ship

DEBARKER   *n* pl. **-S** one that removes bark (the outer covering of woody plants)

DEBASE   *v* **-BASED, -BASING, -BASES** to lower in character, quality, or value

DEBASER   *n* pl. **-S** one that debases

DEBATE   *v* **-BATED, -BATING, -BATES** to argue about

DEBATER	*n pl.* **-S** one that debates
DEBAUCH	*v* **-ED, -ING, -ES** to corrupt
DEBEAK	*v* **-ED, -ING, -S** to remove the tip of the upper beak of
DEBEARD	*v* **-ED, -ING, -S** to remove filaments from a mussel
DEBILITY	*n pl.* **-TIES** weakness
DEBIT	*v* **-ED, -ING, -S** to charge with a debt
DEBONAIR	*adj* suave
DEBONE	*v* **-BONED, -BONING, -BONES** to remove the bones from
DEBONER	*n pl.* **-S** a bone remover
DEBOUCH	*v* **-ED, -ING, -ES** to march into the open
DEBOUCHE	*n pl.* **-S** an opening for the passage of troops
DEBRIDE	*v* **-BRIDED, -BRIDING, -BRIDES** to remove dead tissue surgically
DEBRIEF	*v* **-ED, -ING, -S** to question after a mission
DEBRIS	*n pl.* **DEBRIS** fragments or scattered remains
DEBRUISE	*v* **-BRUISED, -BRUISING, -BRUISES** to cross a coat of arms
DEBT	*n pl.* **-S** something that is owed **DEBTLESS** *adj*
DEBTOR	*n pl.* **-S** one who owes something to another
DEBUG	*v* **-BUGGED, -BUGGING, -BUGS** to remove bugs from
DEBUGGER	*n pl.* **-S** one that debugs
DEBUNK	*v* **-ED, -ING, -S** to expose the sham or falseness of
DEBUNKER	*n pl.* **-S** one that debunks
DEBUR	*v* **-BURRED, -BURRING, -BURS** deburr
DEBURR	*v* **-BURRED, -BURRING, -BURRS** to remove rough edges from
DEBUT	*v* **-ED, -ING, -S** to make one's first public appearance
DEBUTANT	*n pl.* **-S** one who is debuting
DEBYE	*n pl.* **-S** a unit of measure for electric dipole moments
DECADE	*n pl.* **-S** a period of ten years **DECADAL** *adj*
DECADENT	*n pl.* **-S** one in a state of mental or moral decay
DECAF	*n pl.* **-S** decaffeinated coffee
DECAGON	*n pl.* **-S** a ten-sided polygon
DECAGRAM	*n pl.* **-S** dekagram

DECAL	*n pl.* **-S** a picture or design made to be transferred from specially prepared paper
DECALOG	*n pl.* **-S** the Ten Commandments
DECAMP	*v* **-ED, -ING, -S** to depart from a camping ground
DECAN	*n pl.* **-S** one of three equal 10-degree divisions of a sign of the zodiac
DECANAL	*adj* pertaining to a dean
DECANE	*n pl.* **-S** a hydrocarbon
DECANI	*adj* to be sung by the right side of the choir
DECANT	*v* **-ED, -ING, -S** to pour from one container into another
DECANTER	*n pl.* **-S** a decorative bottle
DECAPOD	*n pl.* **-S** a ten-legged crustacean
DECARE	*n pl.* **-S** dekare
DECAY	*v* **-ED, -ING, -S** to decompose
DECAYER	*n pl.* **-S** one that decays
DECEASE	*v* **-CEASED, -CEASING, -CEASES** to die
DECEASED	*n pl.* **-S** a deceased person
DECEDENT	*n pl.* **-S** a deceased person
DECEIT	*n pl.* **-S** the act of deceiving
DECEIVE	*v* **-CEIVED, -CEIVING, -CEIVES** to mislead by falsehood
DECEIVER	*n pl.* **-S** one that deceives
DECEMVIR	*n pl.* **-VIRS** or **-VIRI** one of a body of ten Roman magistrates
DECENARY	*n pl.* **-RIES** a tithing
DECENCY	*n pl.* **-CIES** the state of being decent
DECENNIA	*n/pl* decades
DECENT	*adj* **-CENTER, -CENTEST** conforming to recognized standards of propriety **DECENTLY** *adv*
DECENTER	*v* **-ED, -ING, -S** to put out of center
DECENTRE	*v* **-TRED, -TRING, -TRES** to decenter
DECERN	*v* **-ED, -ING, -S** to decree by judicial sentence
DECIARE	*n pl.* **-S** a metric unit of area
DECIBEL	*n pl.* **-S** a unit of sound intensity
DECIDE	*v* **-CIDED, -CIDING, -CIDES** to make a choice or judgment
DECIDER	*n pl.* **-S** one that decides

DECIDUA   *n* pl. **-UAS** or **-UAE** a mucous membrane of the uterus **DECIDUAL** *adj*

DECIGRAM   *n* pl. **-S** one tenth of a gram

DECILE   *n* pl. **-S** a statistical interval

DECIMAL   *n* pl. **-S** a fraction whose denominator is some power of ten

DECIMATE   *v* **-MATED, -MATING, -MATES** to destroy a large part of

DECIPHER   *v* **-ED, -ING, -S** to decode

DECISION   *v* **-ED, -ING, -S** to win a victory over a boxing opponent on points

DECISIVE   *adj* conclusive

DECK   *v* **-ED, -ING, -S** to adorn

DECKEL   *n* pl. **-S** deckle

DECKER   *n* pl. **-S** something having a specified number of levels, floors, or layers

DECKHAND   *n* pl. **-S** a seaman who performs manual duties

DECKING   *n* pl. **-S** material for a ship's deck (the platform serving as a floor)

DECKLE   *n* pl. **-S** a frame used in making paper by hand

DECKLESS   *adj* lacking a deck

DECLAIM   *v* **-ED, -ING, -S** to speak formally

DECLARE   *v* **-CLARED, -CLARING, -CLARES** to make known clearly

DECLARER   *n* pl. **-S** one that declares

DECLASS   *v* **-ED, -ING, -ES** to lower in status

DECLASSE   *adj* lowered in status

DECLAW   *v* **-CLAWED, -CLAWING, -CLAWS** to surgically remove the claws of

DECLINE   *v* **-CLINED, -CLINING, -CLINES** to refuse

DECLINER   *n* pl. **-S** one that declines

DECLUTCH   *v* **-ED, -ING, -ES** to disengage the clutch (a coupling mechanism) of a motor vehicle

DECO   *n* pl. **DECOS** a decorative style

DECOCT   *v* **-ED, -ING, -S** to extract the flavor of by boiling

DECODE   *v* **-CODED, -CODING, -CODES** to convert a coded message into plain language

DECODER   *n* pl. **-S** one that decodes

DECOLOR   *v* **-ED, -ING, -S** to deprive of color

DECOLOUR   *v* **-ED, -ING, -S** to decolor

DECOR   *n* pl. **-S** style or mode of decoration

DECORATE   *v* **-RATED, -RATING, -RATES** to adorn

DECOROUS   *adj* proper

DECORUM   *n* pl. **-S** conformity to social conventions

DECOUPLE   *v* **-PLED, -PLING, -PLES** to disconnect

DECOY   *v* **-ED, -ING, -S** to lure into a trap

DECOYER   *n* pl. **-S** one that decoys

DECREASE   *v* **-CREASED, -CREASING, -CREASES** to diminish

DECREE   *v* **-CREED, -CREEING, -CREES** to order or establish by law or edict

DECREER   *n* pl. **-S** one that decrees

DECREPIT   *adj* worn out by long use

DECRETAL   *n* pl. **-S** a papal edict

DECRIAL   *n* pl. **-S** the act of decrying

DECRIED   past tense of decry

DECRIER   *n* pl. **-S** one that decries

DECROWN   *v* **-ED, -ING, -S** to deprive of a crown; depose

DECRY   *v* **-CRIED, -CRYING, -CRIES** to denounce

DECRYPT   *v* **-ED, -ING, -S** to decode

DECUMAN   *adj* extremely large

DECUPLE   *v* **-PLED, -PLING, -PLES** to increase tenfold

DECURIES   pl. of decury

DECURION   *n* pl. **-S** a commander of a decury

DECURVE   *v* **-CURVED, -CURVING, -CURVES** to curve downward

DECURY   *n* pl. **-RIES** a group of ten soldiers in ancient Rome

DEDAL   *adj* daedal

DEDANS   *n* pl. **DEDANS** a gallery for tennis spectators

DEDENDUM   *n* pl. **-DUMS** or **-DA** the root of a gear tooth

DEDICATE   *v* **-CATED, -CATING, -CATES** to set apart for some special use

DEDUCE   *v* **-DUCED, -DUCING, -DUCES** to infer

DEDUCT   *v* **-ED, -ING, -S** to subtract

DEE   *n* pl. **-S** the letter D

DEED   *v* **-ED, -ING, -S** to transfer by deed (a legal document)

DEEDLESS   *adj* being without deeds

DEEDY   *adj* **DEEDIER, DEEDIEST** industrious

DEEJAY	v **-JAYED, -JAYING, -JAYS** to work as a disc jockey
DEEM	v **-ED, -ING, -S** to hold as an opinion
DEEMSTER	n pl. **-S** a judicial officer of the Isle of Man
DEEP	adj **DEEPER, DEEPEST** extending far down from a surface
DEEP	n pl. **-S** a place or thing of great depth
DEEPEN	v **-ED, -ING, -S** to make deep
DEEPENER	n pl. **-S** one that deepens
DEEPLY	adv at or to a great depth
DEEPNESS	n pl. **-ES** the quality of being deep
DEER	n pl. **-S** a ruminant mammal **DEERLIKE** adj
DEERFLY	n pl. **-FLIES** a bloodsucking fly
DEERSKIN	n pl. **-S** the skin of a deer
DEERWEED	n pl. **-S** a bushlike herb
DEERYARD	n pl. **-S** an area where deer herd in winter
DEET	n pl. **-S** an insect repellent
DEEWAN	n pl. **-S** dewan
DEF	adj **DEFFER, DEFFEST** excellent
DEFACE	v **-FACED, -FACING, -FACES** to mar the appearance of
DEFACER	n pl. **-S** one that defaces
DEFAME	v **-FAMED, -FAMING, -FAMES** to attack the good name of
DEFAMER	n pl. **-S** one that defames
DEFANG	v **-ED, -ING, -S** to make harmless
DEFAT	v **-FATTED, -FATTING, -FATS** to remove fat from
DEFAULT	v **-ED, -ING, -S** to fail to do something required
DEFEAT	v **-ED, -ING, -S** to win victory over
DEFEATER	n pl. **-S** one that defeats
DEFECATE	v **-CATED, -CATING, -CATES** to discharge feces
DEFECT	v **-ED, -ING, -S** to desert an allegiance
DEFECTOR	n pl. **-S** one that defects
DEFENCE	v **-FENCED, -FENCING, -FENCES** to defense
DEFEND	v **-ED, -ING, -S** to protect
DEFENDER	n pl. **-S** one that defends
DEFENSE	v **-FENSED, -FENSING, -FENSES** to guard against a specific attack

DEFER	v **-FERRED, -FERRING, -FERS** to postpone
DEFERENT	n pl. **-S** an imaginary circle around the earth
DEFERRAL	n pl. **-S** the act of deferring
DEFERRER	n pl. **-S** one that defers
DEFERRING	present participle of defer
DEFFER	comparative of def
DEFFEST	superlative of def
DEFI	n pl. **-S** a challenge
DEFIANCE	n pl. **-S** bold opposition
DEFIANT	adj showing defiance
DEFICIT	n pl. **-S** a shortage
DEFIED	past tense of defy
DEFIER	n pl. **-S** one that defies
DEFIES	present 3d person sing. of defy
DEFILADE	v **-LADED, -LADING, -LADES** to shield from enemy fire
DEFILE	v **-FILED, -FILING, -FILES** to make dirty
DEFILER	n pl. **-S** one that defiles
DEFINE	v **-FINED, -FINING, -FINES** to state the meaning of
DEFINER	n pl. **-S** one that defines
DEFINITE	n pl. **-S** something that is known for certain
DEFLATE	v **-FLATED, -FLATING, -FLATES** to release the air or gas from
DEFLATER	n pl. **-S** one that deflates
DEFLATOR	n pl. **-S** one that deflates
DEFLEA	v **-ED, -ING, -S** to rid of fleas
DEFLECT	v **-ED, -ING, -S** to turn aside
DEFLEXED	adj bent downward
DEFLOWER	v **-ED, -ING, -S** to deprive of flowers
DEFOAM	v **-ED, -ING, -S** to remove foam from
DEFOAMER	n pl. **-S** one that defoams
DEFOCUS	v **-CUSED, -CUSING, -CUSES** or **-CUSSED, -CUSSING, -CUSSES** to cause to go out of focus
DEFOG	v **-FOGGED, -FOGGING, -FOGS** to remove fog from
DEFOGGER	n pl. **-S** one that defogs
DEFORCE	v **-FORCED, -FORCING, -FORCES** to withhold by force
DEFORCER	n pl. **-S** one that deforces
DEFOREST	v **-ED, -ING, -S** to clear of forests

DEFORM	v **-ED, -ING, -S** to spoil the form of	**DEGREE**	n pl. **-S** one of a series of stages **DEGREED** adj
DEFORMER	n pl. **-S** one that deforms	**DEGUM**	v **-GUMMED, -GUMMING, -GUMS** to free from gum
DEFRAG	v **-FRAGGED, -FRAGGING, -FRAGS** to eliminate fragmentation in a computer file	**DEGUST**	v **-ED, -ING, -S** to taste with pleasure
DEFRAUD	v **-ED, -ING, -S** to swindle	**DEHAIR**	v **-ED, -ING, -S** to remove the hair from
DEFRAY	v **-ED, -ING, -S** to pay		
DEFRAYAL	n pl. **-S** the act of defraying	**DEHISCE**	v **-HISCED, -HISCING, -HISCES** to split open
DEFRAYER	n pl. **-S** one that defrays		
DEFRIEND	v **-ED, -ING, -S** to remove (a person's name) from a list of friends	**DEHORN**	v **-ED, -ING, -S** to deprive of horns
		DEHORNER	n pl. **-S** one that dehorns
DEFROCK	v **-ED, -ING, -S** to unfrock	**DEHORS**	prep other than
DEFROST	v **-ED, -ING, -S** to remove frost from	**DEHORT**	v **-ED, -ING, -S** to try to dissuade
		DEICE	v **-ICED, -ICING, -ICES** to free from ice
DEFT	adj **DEFTER, DEFTEST** skillful **DEFTLY** adv		
		DEICER	n pl. **-S** one that deices
DEFTNESS	n pl. **-ES** the quality of being deft	**DEICIDE**	n pl. **-S** the killing of a god **DEICIDAL** adj
DEFUEL	v **-ELED, -ELING, -ELS** or **-ELLED, -ELLING, -ELS** to remove fuel from	**DEICTIC**	n pl. **-S** a word or phrase that specifies identity or location
DEFUNCT	adj deceased	**DEIFIC**	adj godlike
DEFUND	v **-ED, -ING, -S** to withdraw funding from	**DEIFICAL**	adj deific
		DEIFIED	past tense of deify
DEFUSE	v **-FUSED, -FUSING, -FUSES** to remove the fuse from	**DEIFIER**	n pl. **-S** one that deifies
		DEIFORM	adj having the form of a god
DEFUSER	n pl. **-S** one that defuses	**DEIFY**	v **-FIED, -FYING, -FIES** to make a god of
DEFUZE	v **-FUZED, -FUZING, -FUZES** to defuse		
		DEIGN	v **-ED, -ING, -S** to lower oneself to do something
DEFY	v **-FIED, -FYING, -FIES** to resist openly and boldly		
		DEIL	n pl. **-S** the devil
DEGAGE	adj free and relaxed in manner	**DEIONISE**	v **-ISED, -ISING, -ISES** to deionize
DEGAME	n pl. **-S** a tropical tree	**DEIONISER**	n pl. **-S** deionizer
DEGAMI	n pl. **-S** degame	**DEIONIZE**	v **-IZED, -IZING, -IZES** to remove ions from
DEGAS	v **-GASSED, -GASSING, -GASES** or **-GASSES** to remove gas from		
		DEIONIZER	n pl. **-S** one that deionizes
DEGASSER	n pl. **-S** one that degasses	**DEISM**	n pl. **-S** a religious philosophy
DEGAUSS	v **-ED, -ING, -ES** to demagnetize	**DEIST**	n pl. **-S** an adherent of deism **DEISTIC** adj
DEGENDER	v **-ED, -ING, -S** to remove references to a person's gender		
		DEITY	n pl. **-TIES** a god or goddess
DEGERM	v **-ED, -ING, -S** to remove germs from	**DEIXIS**	n pl. **DEIXISES** the specifying function of some words
DEGLAZE	v **-GLAZED, -GLAZING, -GLAZES** to remove the glaze from	**DEJECT**	v **-ED, -ING, -S** to depress
		DEJECTA	n/pl excrements
DEGRADE	v **-GRADED, -GRADING, -GRADES** to debase	**DEJEUNER**	n pl. **-S** a late breakfast
		DEKAGRAM	n pl. **-S** a measure equal to ten grams
DEGRADER	n pl. **-S** one that degrades		
DEGREASE	v **-GREASED, -GREASING, -GREASES** to remove the grease from	**DEKARE**	n pl. **-S** a measure equal to ten ares

DEKE *v* **DEKED, DEKING** or **DEKEING, DEKES** to fake an opponent out of position

DEKKO *n* pl. **-KOS** a look

DEL *n* pl. **-S** an operator in differential calculus

DELAINE *n* pl. **-S** a wool fabric

DELATE *v* **-LATED, -LATING, -LATES** to accuse

DELATION *n* pl. **-S** the act of delating

DELATOR *n* pl. **-S** one that delates

DELAY *v* **-ED, -ING, -S** to put off to a later time

DELAYER *n* pl. **-S** one that delays

DELE *v* **DELED, DELEING, DELES** to delete

DELEAD *v* **-ED, -ING, -S** to remove lead from

DELEAVE *v* **-LEAVED, -LEAVING, -LEAVES** to separate the copies of

DELEGACY *n* pl. **-CIES** the act of delegating

DELEGATE *v* **-GATED, -GATING, -GATES** to appoint as one's representative

DELETE *v* **-LETED, -LETING, -LETES** to remove written or printed matter

DELETION *n* pl. **-S** the act of deleting

DELF *n* pl. **-S** delft

DELFT *n* pl. **-S** an earthenware

DELI *n* pl. **DELIS** a delicatessen

DELICACY *n* pl. **-CIES** a choice food

DELICATE *n* pl. **-S** a delicacy

DELICT *n* pl. **-S** an offense against civil law

DELIGHT *v* **-ED, -ING, -S** to give great pleasure to

DELIME *v* **-LIMED, -LIMING, -LIMES** to free from lime

DELIMIT *v* **-ED, -ING, -S** to mark the boundaries of

DELINK *v* **-ED, -ING, -S** to break a connection between

DELIRIUM *n* pl. **-IUMS** or **-IA** wild frenzy

DELISH *adj* delicious

DELIST *v* **-ED, -ING, -S** to remove from a list

DELIVER *v* **-ED, -ING, -S** to take to the intended recipient

DELIVERY *n* pl. **-ERIES** the act of delivering

DELL *n* pl. **-S** a small, wooded valley

DELLY *n* pl. **DELLIES** deli

DELOUSE *v* **-LOUSED, -LOUSING, -LOUSES** to remove lice from

DELOUSER *n* pl. **-S** one that gets rid of lice

DELPHIC *adj* ambiguous

DELT *n* pl. **-S** a deltoid

DELTA *n* pl. **-S** an alluvial deposit at the mouth of a river **DELTAIC, DELTIC** *adj*

DELTOID *n* pl. **-S** a shoulder muscle

DELUDE *v* **-LUDED, -LUDING, -LUDES** to mislead the mind or judgment of

DELUDER *n* pl. **-S** one that deludes

DELUGE *v* **-UGED, -UGING, -UGES** to flood

DELUSION *n* pl. **-S** the act of deluding

DELUSIVE *adj* tending to delude

DELUSORY *adj* delusive

DELUSTER *v* **-ED, -ING, -S** to lessen the sheen of

DELUXE *adj* of special elegance or luxury

DELVE *v* **DELVED, DELVING, DELVES** to search in depth

DELVER *n* pl. **-S** one that delves

DEMAGOG *v* **-ED, -ING, -S** to behave like a demagog (a leader who appeals to emotions and prejudices)

DEMAGOGY *n* pl. **-GOGIES** the rule of a demagog

DEMAND *v* **-ED, -ING, -S** to ask for with authority

DEMANDER *n* pl. **-S** one that demands

DEMARCHE *n* pl. **-S** a procedure

DEMARK *v* **-ED, -ING, -S** to delimit

DEMAST *v* **-ED, -ING, -S** to strip masts from

DEME *n* pl. **-S** a Greek district

DEMEAN *v* **-ED, -ING, -S** to conduct oneself in a particular manner

DEMEANOR *n* pl. **-S** the manner in which one conducts oneself

DEMENT *v* **-ED, -ING, -S** to make insane

DEMENTI *n* pl. **-S** an official denial of a published statement

DEMENTIA *n* pl. **-S** mental illness

DEMERARA *n* pl. **-S** a coarse light-brown sugar

DEMERGE *v* **-MERGED, -MERGING, -MERGES** to remove a division from a corporation

DEMERGER *v* **-ED, -ING, -S** to demerge

DEMERIT *v* **-ED, -ING, -S** to lower in rank or status

DEMERSAL *adj* found at the bottom of the sea

DEMESNE *n* pl. **-S** the legal possession of land as one's own

DEMETON *n* pl. **-S** an insecticide

DEMIC *adj* pertaining to a deme

DEMIES pl. of demy

DEMIGOD *n* pl. **-S** a lesser god

DEMIJOHN *n* pl. **-S** a narrow-necked jug

DEMILUNE *n* pl. **-S** a half-moon

DEMINER *n* pl. **-S** one that removes mines (explosive devices)

DEMINING *n* pl. **-S** the removal of mines

DEMIREP *n* pl. **-S** a prostitute

DEMISE *v* **-MISED, -MISING, -MISES** to bequeath

DEMIST *v* **-ED, -ING, -S** to defog

DEMISTER *n* pl. **-S** one that defogs

DEMIT *v* **-MITTED, -MITTING, -MITS** to resign

DEMIURGE *n* pl. **-S** a magistrate of ancient Greece

DEMIVOLT *n* pl. **-S** a half turn made by a horse

DEMO *v* **-ED, -ING, -S** to demonstrate

DEMOB *v* **-MOBBED, -MOBBING, -MOBS** to discharge from military service

DEMOCRAT *n* pl. **-S** one who believes in political and social equality

DEMODE *adj* demoded

DEMODED *adj* out-of-date

DEMOI *n* pl. of demos

DEMOLISH *v* **-ED, -ING, -ES** to destroy

DEMON *n* pl. **-S** an evil spirit

DEMONESS *n* pl. **-ES** a female demon

DEMONIAC *n* pl. **-S** one regarded as possessed by a demon

DEMONIAN *adj* demonic

DEMONIC *adj* characteristic of a demon

DEMONISE *v* **-ISED, -ISING, -ISES** to demonize

DEMONISM *n* pl. **-S** belief in demons

DEMONIST *n* pl. **-S** one who believes in demons

DEMONIZE *v* **-IZED, -IZING, -IZES** to make a demon of

DEMOS *n* pl. **-MOI** the people of an ancient Greek state

DEMOTE *v* **-MOTED, -MOTING, -MOTES** to lower in rank or grade

DEMOTIC *adj* pertaining to a simplified form of ancient Egyptian writing

DEMOTICS *n/pl* the study of people in society

DEMOTION *n* pl. **-S** the act of demoting

DEMOTIST *n* pl. **-S** a student of demotic writings

DEMOUNT *v* **-ED, -ING, -S** to remove from a mounting

DEMPSTER *n* pl. **-S** a deemster

DEMUR *v* **-MURRED, -MURRING, -MURS** to object

DEMURE *adj* **-MURER, -MUREST** shy and modest **DEMURELY** *adv*

DEMURRAL *n* pl. **-S** the act of demurring

DEMURRER *n* pl. **-S** one that demurs

DEMURRING present participle of demur

DEMY *n* pl. **-MIES** a size of paper

DEN *v* **DENNED, DENNING, DENS** to live in a lair

DENAR *n* pl. **-NARS** or **-NARI** a monetary unit of Macedonia

DENARIUS *n* pl. **DENARII** a coin of ancient Rome

DENARY *adj* containing ten

DENATURE *v* **-TURED, -TURING, -TURES** to deprive of natural qualities

DENAZIFY *v* **-FIED, -FYING, -FIES** to rid of Nazism

DENDRITE *n* pl. **-S** a branched part of a nerve cell

DENDROID *n* pl. **-S** a fossil marine invertebrate

DENDRON *n* pl. **-S** a dendrite

DENE *n* pl. **-S** a valley

DENGUE *n* pl. **-S** a tropical disease

DENI *n* pl. **DENI** a monetary unit of Macedonia

DENIABLE *adj* capable of being denied **DENIABLY** *adv*

DENIAL *n* pl. **-S** the act of denying

DENIED past tense of deny

DENIER *n* pl. **-S** one that denies

DENIES present 3d person sing. of deny

DENIM *n* pl. **-S** a durable fabric **DENIMED** *adj*

DENIZEN *v* **-ED, -ING, -S** to make a citizen of

DENNED past tense of den

DENNING present participle of den

DENOTE *v* **-NOTED, -NOTING, -NOTES** to indicate **DENOTIVE** *adj*

DENOUNCE	*v* **-NOUNCED, -NOUNCING, -NOUNCES** to condemn openly	**DEPART**	*v* **-ED, -ING, -S** to go away
		DEPARTED	*n* pl. **-S** one that has died
DENSE	*adj* **DENSER, DENSEST** compact **DENSELY** *adv*	**DEPARTEE**	*n* pl. **-S** one that departs
		DEPEND	*v* **-ED, -ING, -S** to rely
DENSIFY	*v* **-FIED, -FYING, -FIES** to make denser	**DEPEOPLE**	*v* **-PLED, -PLING, -PLES** to reduce the population of
DENSITY	*n* pl. **-TIES** the state of being dense	**DEPERM**	*v* **-ED, -ING, -S** to demagnetize
DENT	*v* **-ED, -ING, -S** to make a depression in	**DEPICT**	*v* **-ED, -ING, -S** to portray
		DEPICTER	*n* pl. **-S** one that depicts
DENTAL	*n* pl. **-S** a dentally produced sound	**DEPICTOR**	*n* pl. **-S** depicter
DENTALIA	*n/pl* mollusks with long, tapering shells	**DEPILATE**	*v* **-LATED, -LATING, -LATES** to remove hair from
DENTALLY	*adv* with the tip of the tongue against the upper front teeth	**DEPLANE**	*v* **-PLANED, -PLANING, -PLANES** to get off an airplane
DENTARY	*n* pl. **-RIES** the lower jaw in mammals	**DEPLETE**	*v* **-PLETED, -PLETING, -PLETES** to lessen or exhaust the supply of
DENTATE	*adj* having teeth	**DEPLETER**	*n* pl. **-S** one that depletes
DENTATED	*adj* dentate	**DEPLORE**	*v* **-PLORED, -PLORING, -PLORES** to regret strongly
DENTELLE	*n* pl. **-S** a lacy style of book-cover decoration	**DEPLORER**	*n* pl. **-S** one that deplores
DENTICLE	*n* pl. **-S** a small tooth	**DEPLOY**	*v* **-ED, -ING, -S** to position troops for battle
DENTIL	*n* pl. **-S** a small rectangular block **DENTILED** *adj*	**DEPLOYER**	*n* pl. **-S** one that deploys
DENTIN	*n* pl. **-S** the hard substance forming the body of a tooth **DENTINAL** *adj*	**DEPLUME**	*v* **-PLUMED, -PLUMING, -PLUMES** to deprive of feathers
		DEPOLISH	*v* **-ED, -ING, -ES** to remove the gloss or polish of
DENTINE	*n* pl. **-S** dentin	**DEPONE**	*v* **-PONED, -PONING, -PONES** to testify under oath
DENTIST	*n* pl. **-S** one who treats the teeth		
DENTOID	*adj* resembling a tooth	**DEPONENT**	*n* pl. **-S** one that depones
DENTURE	*n* pl. **-S** a set of teeth **DENTURAL** *adj*	**DEPORT**	*v* **-ED, -ING, -S** to expel from a country
DENUDATE	*v* **-DATED, -DATING, -DATES** to denude	**DEPORTEE**	*n* pl. **-S** one who is deported
		DEPORTER	*n* pl. **-S** one that deports
DENUDE	*v* **-NUDED, -NUDING, -NUDES** to strip of all covering	**DEPOSAL**	*n* pl. **-S** the act of deposing
DENUDER	*n* pl. **-S** one that denudes	**DEPOSE**	*v* **-POSED, -POSING, -POSES** to remove from office
DENY	*v* **-NIED, -NYING, -NIES** to declare to be untrue	**DEPOSER**	*n* pl. **-S** one that deposes
DEODAND	*n* pl. **-S** property forfeited to the crown under a former English law	**DEPOSIT**	*v* **-ED, -ING, -S** to place
		DEPOT	*n* pl. **-S** a railroad or bus station
DEODAR	*n* pl. **-S** an East Indian cedar	**DEPRAVE**	*v* **-PRAVED, -PRAVING, -PRAVES** to corrupt in morals
DEODARA	*n* pl. **-S** deodar		
DEONTIC	*adj* pertaining to moral obligation	**DEPRAVER**	*n* pl. **-S** one that depraves
DEORBIT	*v* **-ED, -ING, -S** to come out of an orbit	**DEPRENYL**	*n* pl. **-S** a drug for treating Parkinson's disease
DEOXY	*adj* having less oxygen than the compound from which it is derived	**DEPRESS**	*v* **-ED, -ING, -ES** to make sad
		DEPRIVAL	*n* pl. **-S** the act of depriving
DEP	*n* pl. **-S** a convenience store	**DEPRIVE**	*v* **-PRIVED, -PRIVING, -PRIVES** to take something away from
DEPAINT	*v* **-ED, -ING, -S** to depict		

DEPRIVER *n* pl. **-S** one that deprives

DEPSIDE *n* pl. **-S** an aromatic compound

DEPTH *n* pl. **-S** deepness

DEPURATE *v* **-RATED, -RATING, -RATES** to free from impurities

DEPUTE *v* **-PUTED, -PUTING, -PUTES** to delegate

DEPUTISE *v* **-TISED, -TISING, -TISES** to deputize

DEPUTIZE *v* **-TIZED, -TIZING, -TIZES** to appoint as a deputy

DEPUTY *n* pl. **-TIES** one appointed to act for another

DERACINE *n* pl. **-S** a displaced person

DERAIGN *v* **-ED, -ING, -S** to dispute a claim

DERAIL *v* **-ED, -ING, -S** to run off the rails of a track

DERANGE *v* **-RANGED, -RANGING, -RANGES** to disorder

DERANGER *n* pl. **-S** one that deranges

DERAT *v* **-RATTED, -RATTING, -RATS** to rid of rats

DERATE *v* **-RATED, -RATING, -RATES** to lower the rated capability of

DERATION *v* **-ED, -ING, -S** to free (as food) from rationing

DERAY *n* pl. **-RAYS** disorderly revelry

DERBY *n* pl. **-BIES** a type of hat

DERE *adj* dire

DERECHO *n* pl. **-CHOS** a line of intense widespread windstorms

DERELICT *n* pl. **-S** something abandoned

DERIDE *v* **-RIDED, -RIDING, -RIDES** to ridicule

DERIDER *n* pl. **-S** one that derides

DERINGER *n* pl. **-S** a short-barreled pistol

DERISION *n* pl. **-S** the act of deriding

DERISIVE *adj* expressing derision

DERISORY *adj* derisive

DERIVATE *n* pl. **-S** something derived

DERIVE *v* **-RIVED, -RIVING, -RIVES** to obtain or receive from a source

DERIVER *n* pl. **-S** one that derives

DERM *n* pl. **-S** derma

DERMA *n* pl. **-S** a layer of the skin **DERMAL** *adj*

DERMIS *n* pl. **-MISES** derma **DERMIC** *adj*

DERMOID *n* pl. **-S** a cystic tumor

DERNIER *adj* last

DEROGATE *v* **-GATED, -GATING, -GATES** to detract

DERRICK *n* pl. **-S** a hoisting apparatus

DERRIERE *n* pl. **-S** the buttocks

DERRIS *n* pl. **-RISES** a climbing plant

DERRY *n* pl. **-RIES** a meaningless word used in the chorus of old songs

DERVISH *n* pl. **-ES** a member of a Muslim religious order

DESALT *v* **-ED, -ING, -S** to remove the salt from

DESALTER *n* pl. **-S** one that desalts

DESAND *v* **-ED, -ING, -S** to remove sand from

DESCALE *v* **-SCALED, -SCALING, -SCALES** to remove the scales from

DESCANT *v* **-ED, -ING, -S** to sing a counterpoint to a melody

DESCEND *v* **-ED, -ING, -S** to come or go down

DESCENT *n* pl. **-S** the act of descending

DESCRIBE *v* **-SCRIBED, -SCRIBING, -SCRIBES** to give a verbal account of

DESCRIER *n* pl. **-S** one that descries

DESCRY *v* **-SCRIED, -SCRYING, -SCRIES** to discern

DESEED *v* **-ED, -ING, -S** to remove the seeds from

DESEEDER *n* pl. **-S** one that deseeds

DESELECT *v* **-ED, -ING, -S** to dismiss from a training program

DESERT *v* **-ED, -ING, -S** to abandon

DESERTER *n* pl. **-S** one that deserts

DESERTIC *adj* arid and barren

DESERVE *v* **-SERVED, -SERVING, -SERVES** to be entitled to or worthy of

DESERVER *n* pl. **-S** one that deserves

DESEX *v* **-ED, -ING, -ES** to castrate or spay

DESHI *n* pl. **-S** desi

DESI *n* pl. **-S** a person of Indian, Pakistani, or Bangladeshi birth who lives abroad

DESIGN *v* **-ED, -ING, -S** to conceive and plan out

DESIGNEE *n* pl. **-S** one who is designated

DESIGNER *n* pl. **-S** one that designs

DESILVER *v* **-ED, -ING, -S** to remove the silver from

DESINENT *adj* terminating

DESIRE *v* **-SIRED, -SIRING, -SIRES** to wish for

DESIRER *n* pl. **-S** one that desires

DESIROUS *adj* desiring

DESIST *v* **-ED, -ING, -S** to cease doing something

DESK *n* pl. **-S** a writing table

DESKILL *v* **-ED, -ING, -S** to reduce the level of skill required

DESKMAN *n* pl. **-MEN** one who works at a desk

DESKTOP *n* pl. **-S** the top of a desk

DESMAN *n* pl. **-S** an aquatic mammal

DESMID *n* pl. **-S** a freshwater alga

DESMOID *n* pl. **-S** a very hard tumor

DESOLATE *v* **-LATED, -LATING, -LATES** to lay waste

DESORB *v* **-ED, -ING, -S** to remove by the reverse of absorption

DESORBER *n* pl. **-S** one that desorbs

DESOXY *adj* deoxy

DESPAIR *v* **-ED, -ING, -S** to lose all hope

DESPATCH *v* **-ED, -ING, -ES** to dispatch

DESPISAL *n* pl. **-S** intense dislike

DESPISE *v* **-SPISED, -SPISING, -SPISES** to loathe

DESPISER *n* pl. **-S** one that despises

DESPITE *v* **-SPITED, -SPITING, -SPITES** to treat with contempt

DESPOIL *v* **-ED, -ING, -S** to plunder

DESPOND *v* **-ED, -ING, -S** to lose spirit or hope

DESPOT *n* pl. **-S** a tyrant **DESPOTIC** *adj*

DESSERT *n* pl. **-S** something served as the last course of a meal

DESTAIN *v* **-ED, -ING, -S** to remove stain from

DESTINE *v* **-TINED, -TINING, -TINES** to determine beforehand

DESTINY *n* pl. **-NIES** the fate or fortune to which one is destined

DESTREAM *v* **-ED, -ING, -S** to reverse the categorizing of students

DESTRESS *v* **-ED, -ING, -ES** to remove stress from

DESTRIER *n* pl. **-S** a warhorse

DESTROY *v* **-ED, -ING, -S** to damage beyond repair or renewal

DESTRUCT *v* **-ED, -ING, -S** to destroy

DESUGAR *v* **-ED, -ING, -S** to remove sugar from

DESULFUR *v* **-ED, -ING, -S** to free from sulfur

DETACH *v* **-ED, -ING, -ES** to unfasten and separate

DETACHER *n* pl. **-S** one that detaches

DETAIL *v* **-ED, -ING, -S** to report with complete particulars

DETAILER *n* pl. **-S** one that details

DETAIN *v* **-ED, -ING, -S** to hold in custody

DETAINEE *n* pl. **-S** one who is detained

DETAINER *n* pl. **-S** the unlawful withholding of another's property

DETANGLE *v* **-GLED, -GLING, -GLES** to remove knots from

DETANGLER *n* pl. **-S** one that detangles

DETASSEL *v* **-SELED, -SELING, -SELS** or **-SELLED, -SELLING, -SELS** to remove tassels from

DETECT *v* **-ED, -ING, -S** to discover or perceive

DETECTER *n* pl. **-S** detector

DETECTOR *n* pl. **-S** one that detects

DETENT *n* pl. **-S** a locking or unlocking mechanism

DETENTE *n* pl. **-S** an easing of international tension

DETER *v* **-TERRED, -TERRING, -TERS** to stop from proceeding

DETERGE *v* **-TERGED, -TERGING, -TERGES** to cleanse

DETERGER *n* pl. **-S** one that deterges

DETERRER *n* pl. **-S** one that deters

DETERRING present participle of deter

DETEST *v* **-ED, -ING, -S** to dislike intensely

DETESTER *n* pl. **-S** one that detests

DETHATCH *v* **-ED, -ING, -ES** to remove thatch from

DETHRONE *v* **-THRONED, -THRONING, -THRONES** to remove from a throne

DETICK *v* **-ED, -ING, -S** to remove ticks from

DETICKER *n* pl. **-S** one that deticks

DETINUE *n* pl. **-S** an action to recover property wrongfully detained

DETONATE *v* **-NATED, -NATING, -NATES** to cause to explode

DETOUR	*v* **-ED, -ING, -S** to take an indirect route
DETOX	*v* **-ED, -ING, -ES** to detoxify
DETOXIFY	*v* **-FIED, -FYING, -FIES** to remove a toxin from
DETRACT	*v* **-ED, -ING, -S** to take away
DETRAIN	*v* **-ED, -ING, -S** to get off a railroad train
DETRITUS	*n* pl. **DETRITUS** particles of rock **DETRITAL** *adj*
DETRUDE	*v* **-TRUDED, -TRUDING, -TRUDES** to thrust out
DETUNE	*v* **-TUNED, -TUNING, -TUNES** to adjust (an instrument) so that it is no longer in tune
DEUCE	*v* **DEUCED, DEUCING, DEUCES** to bring a tennis score to a tie
DEUCEDLY	*adv* extremely
DEUTERIC	*adj* pertaining to heavy hydrogen
DEUTERON	*n* pl. **-S** an atomic particle
DEUTZIA	*n* pl. **-S** an ornamental shrub
DEV	*n* pl. **-S** deva
DEVA	*n* pl. **-S** a Hindu god
DEVALUE	*v* **-UED, -UING, -UES** to lessen the worth of
DEVEIN	*v* **-ED, -ING, -S** to remove the dorsal vein from
DEVEL	*v* **-ED, -ING, -S** to strike forcibly
DEVELOP	*v* **-ED, -ING, -S** to bring to a more advanced or effective state
DEVELOPE	*v* **-OPED, -OPING, -OPES** to develop
DEVERBAL	*n* pl. **-S** a word derived from a verb
DEVEST	*v* **-ED, -ING, -S** to divest
DEVI	*n* pl. **-S** a Hindu goddess
DEVIANCE	*n* pl. **-S** the behavior of a deviant
DEVIANCY	*n* pl. **-CIES** deviance
DEVIANT	*n* pl. **-S** one that deviates from a norm
DEVIATE	*v* **-ATED, -ATING, -ATES** to turn aside from a course or norm
DEVIATOR	*n* pl. **-S** one that deviates
DEVICE	*n* pl. **-S** something devised or constructed for a specific purpose
DEVIL	*v* **-ILED, -ILING, -ILS** or **-ILLED, -ILLING, -ILS** to prepare food with pungent seasoning
DEVILISH	*adj* fiendish
DEVILKIN	*n* pl. **-S** a small demon
DEVILRY	*n* pl. **-RIES** deviltry
DEVILTRY	*n* pl. **-TRIES** mischief
DEVIOUS	*adj* indirect
DEVISAL	*n* pl. **-S** the act of devising
DEVISE	*v* **-VISED, -VISING, -VISES** to form in the mind
DEVISEE	*n* pl. **-S** one to whom a will is made
DEVISER	*n* pl. **-S** one that devises
DEVISOR	*n* pl. **-S** one who makes a will
DEVOICE	*v* **-VOICED, -VOICING, -VOICES** to unvoice
DEVOID	*adj* completely lacking
DEVOIR	*n* pl. **-S** an act of civility or respect
DEVOLVE	*v* **-VOLVED, -VOLVING, -VOLVES** to transfer from one person to another
DEVON	*n* pl. **-S** one of a breed of small, hardy cattle
DEVOTE	*v* **-VOTED, -VOTING, -VOTES** to give oneself wholly to
DEVOTEE	*n* pl. **-S** an ardent follower or supporter
DEVOTION	*n* pl. **-S** the act of devoting
DEVOUR	*v* **-ED, -ING, -S** to eat up voraciously
DEVOURER	*n* pl. **-S** one that devours
DEVOUT	*adj* **-VOUTER, -VOUTEST** pious **DEVOUTLY** *adv*
DEW	*v* **-ED, -ING, -S** to wet with dew (condensed moisture)
DEWAN	*n* pl. **-S** an official in India
DEWAR	*n* pl. **-S** a double-walled flask
DEWATER	*v* **-ED, -ING, -S** to remove water from
DEWAX	*v* **-ED, -ING, -ES** to remove wax from
DEWBERRY	*n* pl. **-RIES** an edible berry
DEWCLAW	*n* pl. **-S** a vestigial toe
DEWDROP	*n* pl. **-S** a drop of dew
DEWFALL	*n* pl. **-S** the formation of dew
DEWIER	comparative of dewy
DEWIEST	superlative of dewy
DEWILY	*adv* in a dewy manner
DEWINESS	*n* pl. **-ES** the state of being dewy
DEWLAP	*n* pl. **-S** a fold of loose skin under the neck
DEWLESS	*adj* having no dew
DEWOOL	*v* **-ED, -ING, -S** to remove the wool from
DEWORM	*v* **-ED, -ING, -S** to rid of worms

DEWORMER	*n* pl. **-S** one that deworms
DEWY	*adj* **DEWIER, DEWIEST** moist with dew
DEX	*n* pl. **-ES** a sulfate used as a central nervous system stimulant
DEXIE	*n* pl. **-S** a tablet of dex
DEXIES	pl. of dexy
DEXTER	*n* pl. **-S** an animal of a breed of Irish cattle
DEXTRAL	*n* pl. **-S** a right-handed person
DEXTRAN	*n* pl. **-S** a substance used as a blood plasma substitute
DEXTRIN	*n* pl. **-S** a substance used as an adhesive
DEXTRINE	*n* pl. **-S** dextrin
DEXTRO	*adj* turning to the right
DEXTROSE	*n* pl. **-S** a form of glucose
DEXTROUS	*adj* adroit
DEXY	*n* pl. **DEXIES** dexie
DEY	*n* pl. **DEYS** a former North African ruler
DEZINC	*v* **-ZINCKED, -ZINCKING, -ZINCS** or **-ZINCED, -ZINCING, -ZINCS** to remove zinc from
DHAK	*n* pl. **-S** an Asian tree
DHAL	*n* pl. **-S** dal
DHANSAK	*n* pl. **-S** a casserole of meats and vegetables
DHARMA	*n* pl. **-S** conformity to Hindu law **DHARMIC** *adj*
DHARNA	*n* pl. **-S** a form of protest in India
DHIKR	*n* pl. **-S** a Sufi religious ceremony
DHOBI	*n* pl. **-S** a person who does laundry in India
DHOLAK	*n* pl. **-S** a two-headed drum
DHOLE	*n* pl. **-S** a wild dog of India
DHOLL	*n* pl. **-S** dal
DHOOLY	*n* pl. **-LIES** doolee
DHOORA	*n* pl. **-S** durra
DHOOTI	*n* pl. **-S** dhoti
DHOOTIE	*n* pl. **-S** dhoti
DHOTI	*n* pl. **-S** a loincloth worn by Hindu men
DHOURRA	*n* pl. **-S** durra
DHOW	*n* pl. **-S** an Arabian sailing vessel
DHURNA	*n* pl. **-S** dharna
DHURRA	*n* pl. **-S** durra
DHURRIE	*n* pl. **-S** a cotton rug made in India
DHUTI	*n* pl. **-S** dhoti
DHYANA	*n* pl. **-S** profound meditation in Hinduism
DIABASE	*n* pl. **-S** an igneous rock **DIABASIC** *adj*
DIABETES	*n* pl. **DIABETES** a metabolic disorder
DIABETIC	*n* pl. **-S** one who has diabetes
DIABLERY	*n* pl. **-RIES** sorcery
DIABOLIC	*adj* devilish
DIABOLO	*n* pl. **-LOS** a game requiring manual dexterity
DIACETYL	*n* pl. **-S** biacetyl
DIACID	*n* pl. **-S** a type of acid **DIACIDIC** *adj*
DIACONAL	*adj* pertaining to a deacon
DIADEM	*v* **-ED, -ING, -S** to adorn with a crown
DIAGNOSE	*v* **-NOSED, -NOSING, -NOSES** to recognize a disease by its signs and symptoms
DIAGONAL	*n* pl. **-S** an oblique line
DIAGRAM	*v* **-GRAMED, -GRAMING, -GRAMS** or **-GRAMMED, -GRAMMING, -GRAMS** to illustrate by a diagram (a graphic design)
DIAGRAPH	*n* pl. **-S** a drawing device
DIAL	*v* **DIALED, DIALING, DIALS** or **DIALLED, DIALLING, DIALS** to manipulate a calibrated disk
DIALECT	*n* pl. **-S** a regional variety of a language
DIALER	*n* pl. **-S** one that dials
DIALING	*n* pl. **-S** the measurement of time by sundials
DIALIST	*n* pl. **-S** a dialer
DIALLAGE	*n* pl. **-S** a mineral
DIALLED	a past tense of dial
DIALLEL	*adj* pertaining to a genetic crossing
DIALLER	*n* pl. **-S** dialer
DIALLING	*n* pl. **-S** dialing
DIALLIST	*n* pl. **-S** dialist
DIALOG	*v* **-ED, -ING, -S** to dialogue
DIALOGER	*n* pl. **-S** one that dialogs
DIALOGIC	*adj* conversational
DIALOGUE	*v* **-LOGUED, -LOGUING, -LOGUES** to carry on a conversation

DIALYSE	v **-LYSED, -LYSING, -LYSES** to dialyze	**DIASTOLE**	n pl. **-S** the normal rhythmical dilation of the heart
DIALYSER	n pl. **-S** dialyzer	**DIATOM**	n pl. **-S** any of a class of algae
DIALYSIS	n pl. **-YSES** the separation of substances in a solution by diffusion through a membrane	**DIATOMIC**	adj composed of two atoms
		DIATONIC	adj pertaining to a type of musical scale
DIALYTIC	adj pertaining to dialysis	**DIATREME**	n pl. **-S** a volcanic vent produced by gaseous explosions
DIALYZE	v **-LYZED, -LYZING, -LYZES** to subject to dialysis	**DIATRIBE**	n pl. **-S** a bitter and abusive criticism
DIALYZER	n pl. **-S** an apparatus used for dialysis	**DIATRON**	n pl. **-S** a circuitry design that uses diodes
DIAMANTE	n pl. **-S** a sparkling decoration	**DIAZEPAM**	n pl. **-S** a tranquilizer
DIAMETER	n pl. **-S** a straight line passing through the center of a circle and ending at the periphery	**DIAZIN**	n pl. **-S** diazine
		DIAZINE	n pl. **-S** a chemical compound
DIAMIDE	n pl. **-S** a chemical compound	**DIAZINON**	n pl. **-S** an insecticide
DIAMIN	n pl. **-S** diamine	**DIAZO**	n pl. **-AZOS** a type of coloring or copying process
DIAMINE	n pl. **-S** a chemical compound		
DIAMOND	v **-ED, -ING, -S** to adorn with diamonds (precious gems)	**DIAZOLE**	n pl. **-S** a chemical compound
DIANTHUS	n pl. **-ES** an ornamental herb	**DIB**	v **DIBBED, DIBBING, DIBS** to fish by letting the bait bob lightly on the water
DIAPASON	n pl. **-S** a burst of harmonious sound		
DIAPAUSE	v **-PAUSED, -PAUSING, -PAUSES** to undergo dormancy	**DIBASIC**	adj having two replaceable hydrogen atoms
		DIBBER	n pl. **-S** a planting implement
DIAPER	v **-ED, -ING, -S** to put a diaper (a baby's breechcloth) on	**DIBBLE**	v **-BLED, -BLING, -BLES** to dib
		DIBBLER	n pl. **-S** one that dibbles
DIAPHONE	n pl. **-S** a low-pitched foghorn	**DIBBUK**	n pl. **-BUKS** or **-BUKIM** dybbuk
DIAPHONY	n pl. **-NIES** organum	**DICAMBA**	n pl. **-S** an herbicide
DIAPIR	n pl. **-S** a bend in a layer of rock **DIAPIRIC** adj	**DICAST**	n pl. **-S** a judge of ancient Athens **DICASTIC** adj
DIAPSID	n pl. **-S** a reptile with two pairs of temporal openings in the skull	**DICE**	v **DICED, DICING, DICES** to cut into small cubes
DIARCHY	n pl. **-CHIES** a government with two rulers **DIARCHIC** adj **DIARCHAL** adj	**DICENTRA**	n pl. **-S** a perennial herb
		DICER	n pl. **-S** a device that dices food
DIARIES	pl. of diary	**DICEY**	adj **DICIER, DICIEST** dangerous
DIARIST	n pl. **-S** one who keeps a diary	**DICHASIA**	n/pl flower clusters
DIARRHEA	n pl. **-S** an intestinal disorder	**DICHOTIC**	adj affecting the two ears differently
DIARY	n pl. **-RIES** a personal journal	**DICHROIC**	adj having two colors
DIASPORA	n pl. **-S** migration	**DICIER**	comparative of dicey
DIASPORE	n pl. **-S** a mineral	**DICIEST**	superlative of dicey
DIASTASE	n pl. **-S** an enzyme	**DICING**	present participle of dice
DIASTEM	n pl. **-S** an interruption in the deposition of sediment	**DICK**	n pl. **-S** a detective
		DICKENS	n pl. **-ES** devil
DIASTEMA	n pl. **-MAS** or **-MATA** a space between teeth	**DICKER**	v **-ED, -ING, -S** to bargain
		DICKERER	n pl. **-S** one who dickers
DIASTER	n pl. **-S** a stage in mitosis **DIASTRAL** adj	**DICKEY**	n pl. **-EYS** a blouse front

DICKIE *n* pl. **-S** dickey

DICKY *adj* **DICKIER, DICKIEST** poor in condition

DICKY *n* pl. **DICKIES** dickey

DICLINY *n* pl. **-NIES** the state of having stamens and pistils in separate flowers

DICOT *n* pl. **-S** a plant with two seed leaves

DICOTYL *n* pl. **-S** dicot

DICROTAL *adj* dicrotic

DICROTIC *adj* having a double pulse beat

DICTA a pl. of dictum

DICTATE *v* **-TATED, -TATING, -TATES** to read aloud for recording

DICTATOR *n* pl. **-S** one that dictates

DICTION *n* pl. **-S** choice and use of words in speech or writing

DICTUM *n* pl. **-TUMS** or **-TA** an authoritative statement

DICTY *adj* **-TIER, -TIEST** snobbish

DICYCLIC *adj* having two maxima of population each year

DICYCLY *n* pl. **-CLIES** the state of being dicyclic

DID a past tense of do

DIDACT *n* pl. **-S** a didactic person

DIDACTIC *adj* instructive

DIDACTYL *adj* having two digits at the end of each limb

DIDAPPER *n* pl. **-S** a dabchick

DIDDLE *v* **-DLED, -DLING, -DLES** to swindle

DIDDLER *n* pl. **-S** one that diddles

DIDDLEY *n* pl. **-DLEYS** diddly

DIDDLY *n* pl. **-DLIES** the least amount

DIDDUMS *interj* — used to express sympathy to a child

DIDIE *n* pl. **-S** didy

DIDIES pl. of didy

DIDO *n* pl. **-DOS** or **-DOES** a mischievous act

DIDST a past tense of do

DIDY *n* pl. **-DIES** a diaper

DIDYMIUM *n* pl. **-S** a mixture of rare-earth elements

DIDYMO *n* pl. **-S** a class of algae

DIDYMOUS *adj* occurring in pairs

DIDYNAMY *n* pl. **-MIES** the state of having four stamens in pairs of unequal length

DIE *v* **DIED, DIEING, DIES** to cut with a die (a device for shaping material)

DIE *v* **DIED, DYING, DIES** to cease living

DIEBACK *n* pl. **-S** a gradual dying of plant shoots

DIECIOUS *adj* dioicous

DIED past tense of die

DIEHARD *n* pl. **-S** a stubborn person

DIEL *adj* involving a full day

DIELDRIN *n* pl. **-S** an insecticide

DIEMAKER *n* pl. **-S** one that makes dies

DIENE *n* pl. **-S** a chemical compound

DIEOFF *n* pl. **-S** a sudden decline in a population

DIERESIS *n* pl. **DIERESES** the separation of two vowels into two syllables **DIERETIC** *adj*

DIESEL *v* **-ED, -ING, -S** to continue running after the ignition is turned off

DIESIS *n* pl. **DIESES** a reference mark in printing

DIESTER *n* pl. **-S** a type of chemical compound

DIESTOCK *n* pl. **-S** a frame for holding dies

DIESTRUM *n* pl. **-S** diestrus

DIESTRUS *n* pl. **-ES** a period of sexual inactivity

DIET *v* **-ED, -ING, -S** to regulate one's daily sustenance

DIETARY *n* pl. **-ETARIES** a system of dieting

DIETER *n* pl. **-S** one that diets

DIETETIC *adj* pertaining to diet

DIETHER *n* pl. **-S** a chemical compound

DIF *n* pl. **-S** diff

DIFF *n* pl. **-S** a difference

DIFFER *v* **-ED, -ING, -S** to be unlike

DIFFRACT *v* **-ED, -ING, -S** to separate into parts

DIFFUSE *v* **-FUSED, -FUSING, -FUSES** to spread widely or thinly

DIFFUSER *n* pl. **-S** one that diffuses

DIFFUSOR *n* pl. **-S** diffuser

DIG *v* **DUG** or **DIGGED, DIGGING, DIGS** to break up, turn over, or remove earth

DIGAMIES pl. of digamy

DIGAMIST *n* pl. **-S** one who practices digamy

DIGAMMA *n* pl. **-S** a Greek letter

DIGAMY *n* pl. **-MIES** a second legal marriage **DIGAMOUS** *adj*

DIGERATI *n/pl* persons skilled in the use of computers

DIGEST *v* **-ED, -ING, -S** to render food usable for the body

DIGESTER *n* pl. **-S** an apparatus in which substances are softened or decomposed

DIGESTIF *n* pl. **-S** an alcoholic drink taken after a meal

DIGESTOR *n* pl. **-S** digester

DIGGED a past tense of dig

DIGGER *n* pl. **-S** one that digs

DIGGING present participle of dig

DIGGINGS *n/pl* an excavation site

DIGHT *v* **-ED, -ING, -S** to adorn

DIGICAM *n* pl. **-S** a digital camera

DIGIT *n* pl. **-S** a finger or toe

DIGITAL *n* pl. **-S** a piano key

DIGITATE *adj* having digits

DIGITISE *v* **-TISED, -TISING, -TISES** to digitize

DIGITIZE *v* **-TIZED, -TIZING, -TIZES** to put data into digital notation

DIGLOT *n* pl. **-S** a bilingual book or edition

DIGNIFY *v* **-FIED, -FYING, -FIES** to add dignity to

DIGNITY *n* pl. **-TIES** stateliness and nobility of manner

DIGOXIN *n* pl. **-S** a drug to improve heart function

DIGRAPH *n* pl. **-S** a pair of letters representing a single speech sound

DIGRESS *v* **-ED, -ING, -ES** to stray from the main topic

DIHEDRAL *n* pl. **-S** a dihedron

DIHEDRON *n* pl. **-S** a figure formed by two intersecting planes

DIHYBRID *n* pl. **-S** an offspring of parents differing in two pairs of genes

DIHYDRIC *adj* containing two hydroxyl radicals

DIKDIK *n* pl. **-S** a small antelope

DIKE *v* **DIKED, DIKING, DIKES** to furnish with an embankment

DIKER *n* pl. **-S** one that dikes

DIKTAT *n* pl. **-S** a harsh settlement imposed on a defeated nation

DILATANT *n* pl. **-S** a dilator

DILATATE *adj* dilated

DILATE *v* **-LATED, -LATING, -LATES** to make wider or larger

DILATER *n* pl. **-S** dilator

DILATION *n* pl. **-S** the act of dilating

DILATIVE *adj* tending to dilate

DILATOR *n* pl. **-S** one that dilates

DILATORY *adj* tending to delay

DILDO *n* pl. **-DOS** an object used as a penis substitute

DILDOE *n* pl. **-S** dildo

DILEMMA *n* pl. **-S** a perplexing situation **DILEMMIC** *adj*

DILIGENT *adj* persevering

DILL *n* pl. **-S** an annual herb

DILLED *adj* flavored with dill

DILLWEED *n* pl. **-S** the leaves of the dill plant

DILLY *n* pl. **DILLIES** something remarkable

DILUENT *n* pl. **-S** a diluting substance

DILUTE *v* **-LUTED, -LUTING, -LUTES** to thin or reduce the concentration of

DILUTER *n* pl. **-S** one that dilutes

DILUTION *n* pl. **-S** the act of diluting

DILUTIVE *adj* tending to dilute

DILUTOR *n* pl. **-S** diluter

DILUVIA a pl. of diluvium

DILUVIAL *adj* pertaining to a flood

DILUVIAN *adj* diluvial

DILUVION *n* pl. **-S** diluvium

DILUVIUM *n* pl. **-VIUMS** or **-VIA** coarse rock material deposited by glaciers

DIM *adj* **DIMMER, DIMMEST** obscure **DIMMISH** *adj*

DIM *v* **DIMMED, DIMMING, DIMS** to make dim

DIME *n* pl. **-S** a coin of the United States

DIMER *n* pl. **-S** a molecule composed of two identical molecules

DIMERIC *adj* dimerous

DIMERISM *n* pl. **-S** the state of being dimerous

DIMERIZE *v* **-IZED, -IZING, -IZES** to form a dimer

DIMEROUS *adj* composed of two parts

DIMETER *n* pl. **-S** a verse of two metrical feet

DIMETHYL	*n* pl. **-S** ethane
DIMETRIC	*adj* pertaining to a type of crystal system
DIMINISH	*v* **-ED, -ING, -ES** to lessen
DIMITY	*n* pl. **-TIES** a cotton fabric
DIMLY	*adv* in a dim manner
DIMMABLE	*adj* capable of being dimmed
DIMMED	past tense of dim
DIMMER	*n* pl. **-S** a device for varying the intensity of illumination
DIMMEST	superlative of dim
DIMMING	present participle of dim
DIMMISH	*adj* somewhat dim
DIMNESS	*n* pl. **-ES** the state of being dim
DIMORPH	*n* pl. **-S** either of two distinct forms
DIMOUT	*n* pl. **-S** a condition of partial darkness
DIMPLE	*v* **-PLED, -PLING, -PLES** to mark with indentations
DIMPLY	*adj* **-PLIER, -PLIEST** dimpled
DIMWIT	*n* pl. **-S** a dunce
DIN	*v* **DINNED, DINNING, DINS** to make a loud noise
DINAR	*n* pl. **-S** an ancient gold coin of Muslim areas
DINDLE	*v* **-DLED, -DLING, -DLES** to tingle
DINE	*v* **DINED, DINING, DINES** to eat dinner
DINER	*n* pl. **-S** one that dines
DINERIC	*adj* pertaining to the interface between two immiscible liquids
DINERO	*n* pl. **-ROS** a former silver coin of Peru
DINETTE	*n* pl. **-S** a small dining room
DING	*v* **-ED, -ING, -S** to ring
DINGBAT	*n* pl. **-S** a typographical ornament
DINGDONG	*v* **-ED, -ING, -S** to make a ringing sound
DINGE	*n* pl. **-S** the condition of being dingy
DINGER	*n* pl. **-S** a home run
DINGEY	*n* pl. **-GEYS** dinghy
DINGHY	*n* pl. **-GHIES** a small boat
DINGIER	comparative of dingy
DINGIES	pl. of dingy
DINGIEST	superlative of dingy
DINGILY	*adv* in a dingy manner
DINGLE	*n* pl. **-S** a dell

DINGO	*n* pl. **-GOES** or **-GOS** a wild dog of Australia
DINGUS	*n* pl. **-ES** a doodad
DINGY	*adj* **-GIER, -GIEST** grimy
DINGY	*n* pl. **-GIES** dinghy
DINING	*n* pl. **-S** the activity of eating dinner
DINITRO	*adj* containing two nitro groups
DINK	*v* **-ED, -ING, -S** to adorn
DINKEY	*n* pl. **-KEYS** a small locomotive
DINKIER	comparative of dinky
DINKIES	pl. of dinky
DINKIEST	superlative of dinky
DINKLY	*adv* neatly
DINKUM	*n* pl. **-S** the truth
DINKY	*adj* **-KIER, -KIEST** small
DINKY	*n* pl. **-KIES** dinkey
DINNED	past tense of din
DINNER	*n* pl. **-S** the main meal of the day
DINNING	present participle of din
DINO	*n* pl. **-NOS** a dinosaur
DINOSAUR	*n* pl. **-S** one of a group of extinct reptiles
DINT	*v* **-ED, -ING, -S** to dent
DIOBOL	*n* pl. **-S** a coin of ancient Greece
DIOBOLON	*n* pl. **-S** diobol
DIOCESAN	*n* pl. **-S** a bishop
DIOCESE	*n* pl. **-S** an ecclesiastical district
DIODE	*n* pl. **-S** a type of electron tube
DIOECISM	*n* pl. **-S** the state of being dioicous
DIOECY	*n* pl. **DIOECIES** dioecism
DIOICOUS	*adj* unisexual
DIOL	*n* pl. **-S** a chemical compound
DIOLEFIN	*n* pl. **-S** a hydrocarbon
DIOPSIDE	*n* pl. **-S** a mineral
DIOPTASE	*n* pl. **-S** a mineral
DIOPTER	*n* pl. **-S** a measure of refractive power **DIOPTRAL** *adj*
DIOPTRE	*n* pl. **-S** diopter
DIOPTRIC	*adj* aiding the vision by refraction
DIORAMA	*n* pl. **-S** a three-dimensional exhibit **DIORAMIC** *adj*
DIORITE	*n* pl. **-S** an igneous rock **DIORITIC** *adj*
DIOXAN	*n* pl. **-S** dioxane
DIOXANE	*n* pl. **-S** a flammable liquid
DIOXID	*n* pl. **-S** dioxide

DIOXIDE   *n* pl. **-S** a type of oxide

DIOXIN   *n* pl. **-S** a toxic solid hydrocarbon

DIP   *v* **DIPPED** or **DIPT, DIPPING, DIPS** to immerse briefly

DIPHASE   *adj* having two phases

DIPHASIC   *adj* diphase

DIPHENYL   *n* pl. **-S** biphenyl

DIPLEGIA   *n* pl. **-S** paralysis of the same part on both sides of the body **DIPLEGIC** *adj*

DIPLEX   *adj* pertaining to the simultaneous transmission or reception of two radio signals

DIPLEXER   *n* pl. **-S** a coupling device

DIPLOE   *n* pl. **-S** a bony tissue of the cranium **DIPLOIC** *adj*

DIPLOID   *n* pl. **-S** a cell having the basic chromosome number doubled

DIPLOIDY   *n* pl. **-DIES** the condition of being a diploid

DIPLOMA   *n* pl. **-MAS** or **-MATA** a certificate of an academic degree

DIPLOMA   *v* **-ED, -ING, -S** to furnish with a diploma

DIPLOMAT   *n* pl. **-S** a governmental official

DIPLONT   *n* pl. **-S** an organism having a particular chromosomal structure

DIPLOPIA   *n* pl. **-S** double vision **DIPLOPIC** *adj*

DIPLOPOD   *n* pl. **-S** a multi-legged insect

DIPLOSIS   *n* pl. **-LOSES** a method of chromosome formation

DIPNET   *v* **-NETTED, -NETTING, -NETS** to scoop fish with a type of net

DIPNOAN   *n* pl. **-S** a lungfish

DIPODY   *n* pl. **-DIES** a dimeter **DIPODIC** *adj*

DIPOLE   *n* pl. **-S** a pair of equal and opposite electric charges **DIPOLAR** *adj*

DIPPABLE   *adj* capable of being dipped

DIPPED   a past tense of dip

DIPPER   *n* pl. **-S** one that dips

DIPPING   present participle of dip

DIPPY   *adj* **-PIER, -PIEST** foolish

DIPROTIC   *adj* having two hydrogen ions to donate to bases

DIPSAS   *n* pl. **DIPSADES** a fabled serpent

DIPSO   *n* pl. **-SOS** a person who craves alcoholic liquors

DIPSTICK   *n* pl. **-S** a measuring rod

DIPT   a past tense of dip

DIPTERA   pl. of dipteron

DIPTERAL   *adj* having two rows or columns

DIPTERAN   *n* pl. **-S** a two-winged fly

DIPTERON   *n* pl. **-TERA** dipteran

DIPTYCA   *n* pl. **-S** diptych

DIPTYCH   *n* pl. **-S** an ancient writing tablet

DIQUAT   *n* pl. **-S** an herbicide

DIRAM   *n* pl. **-S** a monetary unit of Tajikistan

DIRDUM   *n* pl. **-S** blame

DIRE   *adj* **DIRER, DIREST** disastrous

DIRECT   *adj* **-RECTER, -RECTEST** straightforward **DIRECTLY** *adv*

DIRECT   *v* **-ED, -ING, -S** to control or conduct the affairs of

DIRECTOR   *n* pl. **-S** one that directs

DIREFUL   *adj* dreadful

DIRELY   *adv* in a dire manner

DIRENESS   *n* pl. **-ES** the state of being dire

DIRER   comparative of dire

DIREST   superlative of dire

DIRGE   *n* pl. **-S** a funeral song **DIRGEFUL** *adj*

DIRHAM   *n* pl. **-S** a monetary unit of Morocco

DIRIMENT   *adj* nullifying

DIRK   *v* **-ED, -ING, -S** to stab with a small knife

DIRL   *v* **-ED, -ING, -S** to tremble

DIRNDL   *n* pl. **-S** a woman's dress

DIRT   *n* pl. **-S** earth or soil

DIRTBAG   *n* pl. **-S** a dirty or contemptible person

DIRTBALL   *n* pl. **-S** a dirty or contemptible person

DIRTY   *adj* **DIRTIER, DIRTIEST** unclean **DIRTILY** *adv*

DIRTY   *v* **DIRTIED, DIRTYING, DIRTIES** to make dirty

DIS   *v* **DISSED, DISSING, DISSES** to insult or criticize

DISABLE   *v* **-ABLED, -ABLING, -ABLES** to render incapable or unable

DISABLER   *n* pl. **-S** one that disables

DISABUSE   *v* **-ABUSED, -ABUSING, -ABUSES** to free from false or mistaken ideas

DISAGREE   *v* **-AGREED, -AGREEING, -AGREES** to differ in opinion

DISALLOW   *v* **-ED, -ING, -S** to refuse to allow

DISANNUL   *v* **-NULLED, -NULLING, -NULS** to annul

DISARM   *v* **-ED, -ING, -S** to deprive of weapons

DISARMER   *n* pl. **-S** one that disarms

DISARRAY   *v* **-ED, -ING, -S** to disorder

DISASTER   *n* pl. **-S** a calamity

DISAVOW   *v* **-ED, -ING, -S** to disclaim responsibility for

DISBAND   *v* **-ED, -ING, -S** to break up

DISBAR   *v* **-BARRED, -BARRING, -BARS** to expel from the legal profession

DISBOSOM   *v* **-ED, -ING, -S** to confess

DISBOUND   *adj* not having a binding

DISBOWEL   *v* **-ELED, -ELING, -ELS** or **-ELLED, -ELLING, -ELS** to remove the intestines of

DISBUD   *v* **-BUDDED, -BUDDING, -BUDS** to remove buds from

DISBURSE   *v* **-BURSED, -BURSING, -BURSES** to pay out

DISC   *v* **-ED, -ING, -S** to disk

DISCANT   *v* **-ED, -ING, -S** to descant

DISCARD   *v* **-ED, -ING, -S** to throw away

DISCASE   *v* **-CASED, -CASING, -CASES** to remove the case of

DISCEPT   *v* **-ED, -ING, -S** to debate

DISCERN   *v* **-ED, -ING, -S** to perceive

DISCI   a pl. of discus

DISCIPLE   *v* **-PLED, -PLING, -PLES** to cause to become a follower

DISCLAIM   *v* **-ED, -ING, -S** to renounce any claim to or connection with

DISCLESS   *adj* diskless

DISCLIKE   *adj* disklike

DISCLOSE   *v* **-CLOSED, -CLOSING, -CLOSES** to reveal

DISCO   *v* **-ED, -ING, -S** or **-ES** to dance at a discotheque

DISCOID   *n* pl. **-S** a disk

DISCOLOR   *v* **-ED, -ING, -S** to alter the color of

DISCORD   *v* **-ED, -ING, -S** to disagree

DISCOUNT   *v* **-ED, -ING, -S** to reduce the price of

DISCOVER   *v* **-ED, -ING, -S** to gain sight or knowledge of

DISCREET   *adj* **-CREETER, -CREETEST** tactful

DISCRETE   *adj* separate

DISCROWN   *v* **-ED, -ING, -S** to deprive of a crown

DISCUS   *n* pl. **-CUSES** or **-CI** a disk hurled in athletic competition

DISCUSS   *v* **-ED, -ING, -ES** to talk over or write about

DISDAIN   *v* **-ED, -ING, -S** to scorn

DISEASE   *v* **-EASED, -EASING, -EASES** to make unhealthy

DISENDOW   *v* **-ED, -ING, -S** to deprive of endowment

DISEUR   *n* pl. **-S** a skilled reciter

DISEUSE   *n* pl. **-S** a female entertainer

DISFAVOR   *v* **-ED, -ING, -S** to regard with disapproval

DISFROCK   *v* **-ED, -ING, -S** to unfrock

DISGORGE   *v* **-GORGED, -GORGING, -GORGES** to vomit

DISGRACE   *v* **-GRACED, -GRACING, -GRACES** to bring shame or discredit upon

DISGUISE   *v* **-GUISED, -GUISING, -GUISES** to alter the appearance of

DISGUST   *v* **-ED, -ING, -S** to cause nausea or loathing in

DISH   *v* **-ED, -ING, -ES** to put into a dish (a concave vessel)

DISHELM   *v* **-ED, -ING, -S** to deprive of a helmet

DISHERIT   *v* **-ED, -ING, -S** to deprive of an inheritance

DISHEVEL   *v* **-ELED, -ELING, -ELS** or **-ELLED, -ELLING, -ELS** to make messy

DISHFUL   *n* pl. **-S** as much as a dish can hold

DISHIER   comparative of dishy

DISHIEST   superlative of dishy

DISHLIKE   *adj* resembling a dish

DISHONOR   *v* **-ED, -ING, -S** to deprive of honor

DISHPAN   *n* pl. **-S** a pan for washing dishes

DISHRAG   *n* pl. **-S** a cloth for washing dishes

DISHWARE   *n* pl. **-S** tableware used in serving food

DISHY   *adj* **DISHIER, DISHIEST** attractive

DISINTER   *v* **-TERRED, -TERRING, -TERS** to exhume

DISJECT   *v* **-ED, -ING, -S** to disperse

DISJOIN   *v* **-ED, -ING, -S** to separate

DISJOINT	*v* **-ED, -ING, -S** to put out of order
DISJUNCT	*n* pl. **-S** an alternative in a logical disjunction
DISK	*v* **-ED, -ING, -S** to break up land with a type of farm implement
DISKER	*n* pl. **-S** one that disks
DISKETTE	*n* pl. **-S** a floppy disk for a computer
DISKLESS	*adj* having no disk (a round, flat storage device for a computer)
DISKLIKE	*adj* resembling a disk (a flat, circular plate)
DISLIKE	*v* **-LIKED, -LIKING, -LIKES** to regard with aversion
DISLIKER	*n* pl. **-S** one that dislikes
DISLIMN	*v* **-ED, -ING, -S** to make dim
DISLODGE	*v* **-LODGED, -LODGING, -LODGES** to remove from a firm position
DISLOYAL	*adj* not loyal
DISMAL	*adj* **-MALER, -MALEST** cheerless and depressing **DISMALLY** *adv*
DISMAL	*n* pl. **-S** a track of swampy land
DISMAST	*v* **-ED, -ING, -S** to remove the mast of
DISMAY	*v* **-ED, -ING, -S** to deprive of courage or resolution
DISME	*n* pl. **-S** a former coin of the United States
DISMISS	*v* **-ED, -ING, -ES** to permit or cause to leave
DISMOUNT	*v* **-ED, -ING, -S** to get down from an elevated position
DISOBEY	*v* **-ED, -ING, -S** to fail to obey
DISODIUM	*adj* containing two atoms of sodium
DISOMIC	*adj* having a number of chromosomes duplicated
DISOMY	*n* pl. **-MIES** the condition of being disomic
DISORDER	*v* **-ED, -ING, -S** to put out of order
DISOWN	*v* **-ED, -ING, -S** to deny the ownership of
DISOWNER	*n* pl. **-S** one that disowns
DISPART	*v* **-ED, -ING, -S** to separate
DISPATCH	*v* **-ED, -ING, -ES** to send off with speed
DISPEL	*v* **-PELLED, -PELLING, -PELS** to drive off in various directions
DISPEND	*v* **-ED, -ING, -S** to squander
DISPENSE	*v* **-PENSED, -PENSING, -PENSES** to distribute
DISPERSE	*v* **-PERSED, -PERSING, -PERSES** to scatter
DISPIRIT	*v* **-ED, -ING, -S** to lower in spirit
DISPLACE	*v* **-PLACED, -PLACING, -PLACES** to remove from the usual or proper place
DISPLANT	*v* **-ED, -ING, -S** to dislodge
DISPLAY	*v* **-ED, -ING, -S** to make evident or obvious
DISPLODE	*v* **-PLODED, -PLODING, -PLODES** to explode
DISPLUME	*v* **-PLUMED, -PLUMING, -PLUMES** to deplume
DISPORT	*v* **-ED, -ING, -S** to amuse oneself
DISPOSAL	*n* pl. **-S** the act of disposing
DISPOSE	*v* **-POSED, -POSING, -POSES** to put in place
DISPOSER	*n* pl. **-S** one that disposes
DISPREAD	*v* **-SPREAD, -SPREADING, -SPREADS** to spread out
DISPRIZE	*v* **-PRIZED, -PRIZING, -PRIZES** to disdain
DISPROOF	*n* pl. **-S** the act of disproving
DISPROVE	*v* **-PROVED, -PROVEN, -PROVING, -PROVES** to refute
DISPUTE	*v* **-PUTED, -PUTING, -PUTES** to argue about
DISPUTER	*n* pl. **-S** one that disputes
DISQUIET	*v* **-ED, -ING, -S** to deprive of quiet, rest, or peace
DISRATE	*v* **-RATED, -RATING, -RATES** to lower in rating or rank
DISROBE	*v* **-ROBED, -ROBING, -ROBES** to undress
DISROBER	*n* pl. **-S** one that disrobes
DISROOT	*v* **-ED, -ING, -S** to uproot
DISRUPT	*v* **-ED, -ING, -S** to throw into confusion
DISS	*v* **-ED, -ING, -ES** to dis
DISSAVE	*v* **-SAVED, -SAVING, -SAVES** to use savings for current expenses
DISSAVER	*n* pl. **-S** one that dissaves
DISSEAT	*v* **-ED, -ING, -S** to unseat
DISSECT	*v* **-ED, -ING, -S** to cut apart for scientific examination
DISSED	past tense of dis
DISSEISE	*v* **-SEISED, -SEISING, -SEISES** to deprive

DISSEIZE   *v* **-SEIZED, -SEIZING, -SEIZES** to disseise

DISSENT   *v* **-ED, -ING, -S** to disagree

DISSERT   *v* **-ED, -ING, -S** to discuss in a learned or formal manner

DISSERVE   *v* **-SERVED, -SERVING, -SERVES** to treat badly

DISSES   present 3d person sing. of dis

DISSEVER   *v* **-ED, -ING, -S** to sever

DISSING   present participle of dis

DISSOLVE   *v* **-SOLVED, -SOLVING, -SOLVES** to make into a solution

DISSUADE   *v* **-SUADED, -SUADING, -SUADES** to persuade not to do something

DISTAFF   *n* pl. **-TAFFS** or **-TAVES** a type of staff

DISTAIN   *v* **-ED, -ING, -S** to stain

DISTAL   *adj* located far from the point of origin **DISTALLY** *adv*

DISTANCE   *v* **-TANCED, -TANCING, -TANCES** to leave behind

DISTANT   *adj* far off or apart

DISTASTE   *v* **-TASTED, -TASTING, -TASTES** to dislike

DISTAVES   a pl. of distaff

DISTEND   *v* **-ED, -ING, -S** to swell

DISTENT   *adj* distended

DISTICH   *n* pl. **-S** a couplet

DISTIL   *v* **-TILLED, -TILLING, -TILS** to distill

DISTILL   *v* **-ED, -ING, -S** to extract by vaporization and condensation

DISTINCT   *adj* **-TINCTER, -TINCTEST** clearly different

DISTOME   *n* pl. **-S** a parasitic flatworm

DISTORT   *v* **-ED, -ING, -S** to put out of shape

DISTRACT   *v* **-ED, -ING, -S** to divert the attention of

DISTRAIN   *v* **-ED, -ING, -S** to seize and hold property as security

DISTRAIT   *adj* absentminded

DISTRESS   *v* **-ED, -ING, -ES** to cause anxiety or suffering to

DISTRICT   *v* **-ED, -ING, -S** to divide into localities

DISTRUST   *v* **-ED, -ING, -S** to have no trust in

DISTURB   *v* **-ED, -ING, -S** to interrupt the quiet, rest, or peace of

DISULFID   *n* pl. **-S** a chemical compound

DISUNION   *n* pl. **-S** the state of being disunited

DISUNITE   *v* **-UNITED, -UNITING, -UNITES** to separate

DISUNITY   *n* pl. **-TIES** lack of unity

DISUSE   *v* **-USED, -USING, -USES** to stop using

DISVALUE   *v* **-UED, -UING, -UES** to treat as of little value

DISYOKE   *v* **-YOKED, -YOKING, -YOKES** to free from a yoke

DIT   *n* pl. **-S** a dot in Morse code

DITA   *n* pl. **-S** a Philippine tree

DITCH   *v* **-ED, -ING, -ES** to dig a long, narrow excavation in the ground

DITCHER   *n* pl. **-S** one that ditches

DITE   *n* pl. **-S** a small amount

DITHEISM   *n* pl. **-S** belief in two coequal gods

DITHEIST   *n* pl. **-S** an adherent of ditheism

DITHER   *v* **-ED, -ING, -S** to act nervously or indecisively

DITHERER   *n* pl. **-S** one that dithers

DITHERY   *adj* nervously excited

DITHIOL   *adj* containing two chemical groups both of which include sulfur and hydrogen

DITSY   *adj* **-SIER, -SIEST** silly, eccentric

DITTANY   *n* pl. **-NIES** a perennial herb

DITTO   *v* **-ED, -ING, -S** to repeat

DITTY   *n* pl. **-TIES** a short, simple song

DITZ   *n* pl. **-ES** a ditsy person

DITZY   *adj* **-ZIER, -ZIEST** ditsy

DIURESIS   *n* pl. **DIURESES** excessive discharge of urine

DIURETIC   *n* pl. **-S** a drug which increases urinary discharge

DIURNAL   *n* pl. **-S** a diary

DIURON   *n* pl. **-S** an herbicide

DIVA   *n* pl. **-S** a distinguished female operatic singer

DIVAGATE   *v* **-GATED, -GATING, -GATES** to wander

DIVALENT   *adj* having a valence of two

DIVAN   *n* pl. **-S** a sofa or couch

DIVE   *v* **DIVED** or **DOVE, DIVING, DIVES** to plunge headfirst into water

DIVEBOMB   *v* **-ED, -ING, -S** to drop bombs on a target from a diving airplane

DIVER   *n* pl. **-S** one that dives

DIVERGE	*v* **-VERGED, -VERGING, -VERGES** to move in different directions from a common point
DIVERSE	*adj* different
DIVERT	*v* **-ED, -ING, -S** to turn aside
DIVERTER	*n* pl. **-S** one that diverts
DIVEST	*v* **-ED, -ING, -S** to strip or deprive of anything
DIVIDE	*v* **-VIDED, -VIDING, -VIDES** to separate into parts, areas, or groups
DIVIDEND	*n* pl. **-S** a quantity to be divided
DIVIDER	*n* pl. **-S** one that divides
DIVIDING	present participle of divide
DIVIDUAL	*adj* capable of being divided
DIVINE	*adj* **-VINER, -VINEST** pertaining to or characteristic of a god **DIVINELY** *adv*
DIVINE	*v* **-VINED, -VINING, -VINES** to foretell by occult means
DIVINER	*n* pl. **-S** one that divines
DIVING	*n* pl. **-S** the act or sport of plunging headfirst into water
DIVINING	present participle of divine
DIVINISE	*v* **-NISED, -NISING, -NISES** to divinize
DIVINITY	*n* pl. **-TIES** the state of being divine
DIVINIZE	*v* **-NIZED, -NIZING, -NIZES** to make divine
DIVISION	*n* pl. **-S** the act of dividing
DIVISIVE	*adj* causing disunity or dissension
DIVISOR	*n* pl. **-S** a number by which a dividend is divided
DIVORCE	*v* **-VORCED, -VORCING, -VORCES** to terminate the marriage contract between
DIVORCEE	*n* pl. **-S** a divorced woman
DIVORCER	*n* pl. **-S** one that divorces
DIVOT	*n* pl. **-S** a piece of turf
DIVULGE	*v* **-VULGED, -VULGING, -VULGES** to reveal
DIVULGER	*n* pl. **-S** one that divulges
DIVULSE	*v* **-VULSED, -VULSING, -VULSES** to tear away
DIVVY	*v* **-VIED, -VYING, -VIES** to divide
DIWAN	*n* pl. **-S** dewan
DIXIT	*n* pl. **-S** a statement
DIZEN	*v* **-ED, -ING, -S** to dress in fine clothes
DIZYGOUS	*adj* developed from two fertilized ova
DIZZY	*adj* **-ZIER, -ZIEST** having a sensation of whirling **DIZZILY** *adv*
DIZZY	*v* **-ZIED, -ZYING, -ZIES** to make dizzy
DJEBEL	*n* pl. **-S** jebel
DJELLABA	*n* pl. **-S** a long hooded garment
DJEMBE	*n* pl. **-S** a type of African hand drum
DJIBBA	*n* pl. **-S** jibba
DJIBBAH	*n* pl. **-S** jibba
DJIN	*n* pl. **-S** jinni
DJINN	*n* pl. **-S** jinni
DJINNI	*n* pl. **DJINN** jinni
DJINNY	*n* pl. **DJINN** jinni
DO	*n* pl. **DOS** the first tone of the diatonic musical scale
DO	*v* **DID** or **DIDST, DONE, DOING,** present sing. 2d person **DO** or **DOEST** or **DOST,** 3d person **DOES** or **DOETH** or **DOTH** to begin and carry through to completion
DOABLE	*adj* able to be done
DOAT	*v* **-ED, -ING, -S** to dote
DOBBER	*n* pl. **-S** a float for a fishing line
DOBBIN	*n* pl. **-S** a farm horse
DOBBY	*n* pl. **-BIES** a fool
DOBE	*n* pl. **-S** adobe
DOBIE	*n* pl. **-S** adobe
DOBIES	pl. of doby
DOBLA	*n* pl. **-S** a former gold coin of Spain
DOBLON	*n* pl. **-S** or **-ES** a former gold coin of Spain and Spanish America
DOBRA	*n* pl. **-S** a former gold coin of Portugal
DOBSON	*n* pl. **-S** an aquatic insect larva
DOBY	*n* pl. **-BIES** dobie
DOC	*n* pl. **-S** doctor
DOCENT	*n* pl. **-S** a college or university lecturer
DOCETIC	*adj* pertaining to a religious doctrine
DOCILE	*adj* easily trained **DOCILELY** *adv*
DOCILITY	*n* pl. **-TIES** the quality of being docile
DOCK	*v* **-ED, -ING, -S** to bring into a dock (a wharf)

DOCKAGE	*n* pl. **-S** a charge for the use of a dock
DOCKER	*n* pl. **-S** a dock worker
DOCKET	*v* **-ED, -ING, -S** to supply with an identifying statement
DOCKHAND	*n* pl. **-S** a docker
DOCKLAND	*n* pl. **-S** the part of a port occupied by docks
DOCKSIDE	*n* pl. **-S** the area adjacent to a dock
DOCKYARD	*n* pl. **-S** a shipyard
DOCTOR	*v* **-ED, -ING, -S** to treat medically **DOCTORLY** *adj*
DOCTORAL	*adj* pertaining to a doctor
DOCTRINE	*n* pl. **-S** a belief or set of beliefs taught or advocated
DOCUMENT	*v* **-ED, -ING, -S** to support by conclusive information or evidence
DOCUSOAP	*n* pl. **-S** a television series about the activities of real people
DODDER	*v* **-ED, -ING, -S** to totter
DODDERER	*n* pl. **-S** one that dodders
DODDERY	*adj* feeble
DODDLE	*n* pl. **-S** an easy task
DODGE	*v* **DODGED, DODGING, DODGES** to evade
DODGEM	*n* pl. **-S** an amusement park ride
DODGER	*n* pl. **-S** one that dodges
DODGERY	*n* pl. **-ERIES** evasion
DODGING	present participle of dodge
DODGY	*adj* **DODGIER, DODGIEST** evasive
DODO	*n* pl. **-DOS** or **-DOES** an extinct flightless bird
DODOISM	*n* pl. **-S** a stupid remark
DOE	*n* pl. **-S** a female deer
DOER	*n* pl. **-S** one that does something
DOES	a present 3d person sing. of do
DOESKIN	*n* pl. **-S** the skin of a doe
DOEST	a present 2d person sing. of do
DOETH	a present 3d person sing. of do
DOFF	*v* **-ED, -ING, -S** to take off
DOFFER	*n* pl. **-S** one that doffs
DOG	*v* **DOGGED, DOGGING, DOGS** to follow after like a dog (a domesticated, carnivorous mammal)
DOGBANE	*n* pl. **-S** a perennial herb
DOGBERRY	*n* pl. **-RIES** a wild berry
DOGCART	*n* pl. **-S** a one-horse carriage

DOGDOM	*n* pl. **-S** the world of dogs
DOGE	*n* pl. **-S** the chief magistrate in the former republics of Venice and Genoa
DOGEAR	*v* **-ED, -ING, -S** to turn down a corner of a page
DOGEDOM	*n* pl. **-S** the domain of a doge
DOGESHIP	*n* pl. **-S** the office of a doge
DOGEY	*n* pl. **-GEYS** dogie
DOGFACE	*n* pl. **-S** a soldier in the U.S. Army
DOGFIGHT	*v* **-FOUGHT, -FIGHTING, -FIGHTS** to engage in an aerial battle
DOGFISH	*n* pl. **-ES** a small shark
DOGGED	past tense of dog
DOGGEDLY	*adv* stubbornly
DOGGER	*n* pl. **-S** a fishing vessel
DOGGEREL	*n* pl. **-S** trivial, awkwardly written verse
DOGGERY	*n* pl. **-GERIES** surly behavior
DOGGIE	*n* pl. **-S** doggy
DOGGIER	comparative of doggy
DOGGIES	pl. of doggy
DOGGIEST	superlative of doggy
DOGGING	present participle of dog
DOGGISH	*adj* doglike
DOGGO	*adv* in hiding
DOGGONE	*adj* **-GONER, -GONEST** damned
DOGGONE	*v* **-GONED, -GONING, -GONES** to damn
DOGGONED	*adj* **-GONEDER, -GONEDEST** damned
DOGGREL	*n* pl. **-S** doggerel
DOGGY	*adj* **-GIER, -GIEST** resembling or suggestive of a dog
DOGGY	*n* pl. **-GIES** a small dog
DOGHOUSE	*n* pl. **-S** a shelter for a dog
DOGIE	*n* pl. **-S** a stray calf
DOGIES	pl. of dogy
DOGLEG	*v* **-LEGGED, -LEGGING, -LEGS** to move along a bent course
DOGLIKE	*adj* resembling a dog
DOGMA	*n* pl. **-MAS** or **-MATA** a principle or belief put forth as authoritative **DOGMATIC** *adj*
DOGNAP	*v* **-NAPED, -NAPING, -NAPS** or **-NAPPED, -NAPPING, -NAPS** to steal a dog
DOGNAPER	*n* pl. **-S** one that dognaps

DOGSBODY *n* pl. **-BODIES** a menial worker

DOGSKIN *n* pl. **-S** leather made from the skin of a dog

DOGSLED *v* **-SLEDDED, -SLEDDING, -SLEDS** to move on a sled drawn by dogs

DOGSTAIL *n* pl. **-S** a grass with spiky flower heads

DOGTAIL *n* pl. **-S** a type of grass

DOGTOOTH *n* pl. **-TEETH** a cuspid

DOGTROT *v* **-TROTTED, -TROTTING, -TROTS** to move at a steady trot

DOGVANE *n* pl. **-S** a small vane

DOGWATCH *n* pl. **-ES** a short period of watch duty on a ship

DOGWOOD *n* pl. **-S** a tree

DOGY *n* pl. **-GIES** dogie

DOH *n* pl. **-S** the first tone of the diatonic scale

DOILED *adj* dazed

DOILY *n* pl. **-LIES** a small napkin

DOING *n* pl. **-S** an action

DOIT *n* pl. **-S** a former Dutch coin

DOITED *adj* old and feeble

DOJO *n* pl. **-JOS** a school that teaches judo or karate

DOL *n* pl. **-S** a unit of pain intensity

DOLCE *n* pl. **-CI** a soft-toned organ stop

DOLCETTO *n* pl. **-TOS** a red wine of Italy

DOLDRUMS *n/pl* a slump or slack period

DOLE *v* **DOLED, DOLING, DOLES** to distribute in small portions

DOLEFUL *adj* **-FULLER, -FULLEST** mournful

DOLERITE *n* pl. **-S** a variety of basalt

DOLESOME *adj* doleful

DOLING present participle of dole

DOLL *v* **-ED, -ING, -S** to dress stylishly

DOLLAR *n* pl. **-S** a monetary unit of the United States

DOLLIED past tense of dolly

DOLLIES present 3d person sing. of dolly

DOLLISH *adj* pretty

DOLLOP *v* **-ED, -ING, -S** to dispense in small amounts

DOLLY *v* **-LIED, -LYING, -LIES** to move on a wheeled platform

DOLMA *n* pl. **-MAS** or **-MADES** a stuffed grape leaf

DOLMAN *n* pl. **-S** a Turkish robe

DOLMEN *n* pl. **-S** a prehistoric monument **DOLMENIC** *adj*

DOLOMITE *n* pl. **-S** a mineral

DOLOR *n* pl. **-S** grief

DOLOROSO *adj* having a mournful musical quality

DOLOROUS *adj* mournful

DOLOUR *n* pl. **-S** dolor

DOLPHIN *n* pl. **-S** a marine mammal

DOLT *n* pl. **-S** a stupid person **DOLTISH** *adj*

DOM *n* pl. **-S** a title given to certain monks

DOMAIN *n* pl. **-S** an area of control

DOMAINE *n* pl. **-S** a vineyard in Burgundy

DOMAL *adj* domical

DOME *v* **DOMED, DOMING, DOMES** to cover with a dome (a rounded roof)

DOMELIKE *adj* resembling a dome

DOMESDAY *n* pl. **-DAYS** doomsday

DOMESTIC *n* pl. **-S** a household servant

DOMIC *adj* domical

DOMICAL *adj* shaped like a dome

DOMICIL *v* **-ED, -ING, -S** to domicile

DOMICILE *v* **-CILED, -CILING, -CILES** to establish in a residence

DOMINANT *n* pl. **-S** a controlling genetic character

DOMINATE *v* **-NATED, -NATING, -NATES** to control

DOMINE *n* pl. **-S** master

DOMINEER *v* **-ED, -ING, -S** to tyrannize

DOMING present participle of dome

DOMINICK *n* pl. **-S** one of an American breed of chickens

DOMINIE *n* pl. **-S** a clergyman

DOMINION *n* pl. **-S** supreme authority

DOMINIUM *n* pl. **-S** the right of ownership and control of property

DOMINO *n* pl. **-NOS** or **-NOES** a small mask

DON *v* **DONNED, DONNING, DONS** to put on

DONA *n* pl. **-S** a Spanish lady

DONAIR *n* pl. **-S** sliced lamb rolled in pita bread

DONATE *v* **-NATED, -NATING, -NATES** to contribute

DONATION *n* pl. **-S** something donated

DONATIVE *n* pl. **-S** a donation

DONATOR *n* pl. **-S** a donor

DONE past participle of do

DONEE *n* pl. **-S** a recipient of a gift

DONEGAL *n* pl. **-S** a type of tweed

DONENESS *n* pl. **-ES** the state of being cooked enough

DONG *v* **-ED, -ING, -S** to make a deep sound like that of a large bell

DONGA *n* pl. **-S** a gully in a veldt

DONGLE *n* pl. **-S** a device for a computer

DONGOLA *n* pl. **-S** a type of leather

DONJON *n* pl. **-S** the main tower of a castle

DONKEY *n* pl. **-KEYS** the domestic ass

DONNA *n* pl. **DONNAS** or **DONNE** an Italian lady

DONNED past tense of don

DONNEE *n* pl. **-S** the set of assumptions upon which a story proceeds

DONNERD *adj* donnered

DONNERED *adj* dazed

DONNERT *adj* donnered

DONNIKER *n* pl. **-S** a bathroom or privy

DONNING present participle of don

DONNISH *adj* scholarly

DONOR *n* pl. **-S** one that donates

DONSHIP *n* pl. **-S** the position of a don (a senior member of a British university)

DONSIE *adj* unlucky

DONSY *adj* donsie

DONUT *n* pl. **-S** doughnut

DONZEL *n* pl. **-S** a young squire

DOOB *n* pl. **-S** a doobie

DOOBIE *n* pl. **-S** a marijuana cigarette

DOODAD *n* pl. **-S** an article whose name is unknown or forgotten

DOODAH *n* pl. **-S** a small useful device

DOODLE *v* **-DLED, -DLING, -DLES** to draw or scribble aimlessly

DOODLER *n* pl. **-S** one that doodles

DOODOO *n* pl. **-DOOS** feces

DOODY *n* pl. **-DIES** feces

DOOFUS *n* pl. **-ES** a stupid or foolish person

DOOLEE *n* pl. **-S** a stretcher for the sick or wounded

DOOLIE *n* pl. **-S** doolee

DOOLY *n* pl. **-LIES** doolee

DOOM *v* **-ED, -ING, -S** to destine to an unhappy fate

DOOMFUL *adj* ominous

DOOMSDAY *n* pl. **-DAYS** judgment day

DOOMSTER *n* pl. **-S** a judge

DOOMY *adj* **DOOMIER, DOOMIEST** doomful **DOOMILY** *adv*

DOOR *n* pl. **-S** a movable barrier at an entranceway **DOORED** *adj*

DOORBELL *n* pl. **-S** a bell at a door

DOORCASE *n* pl. **-S** the frame for a door

DOORJAMB *n* pl. **-S** a vertical piece at the side of a doorway

DOORKNOB *n* pl. **-S** a handle for opening a door

DOORLESS *adj* having no door

DOORMAN *n* pl. **-MEN** the door attendant of a building

DOORMAT *n* pl. **-S** a mat placed in front of a door

DOORNAIL *n* pl. **-S** a large-headed nail

DOORPOST *n* pl. **-S** a doorjamb

DOORSILL *n* pl. **-S** the sill of a door

DOORSTEP *n* pl. **-S** a step leading to a door

DOORSTOP *n* pl. **-S** an object used for holding a door open

DOORWAY *n* pl. **-WAYS** the entranceway to a room or building

DOORYARD *n* pl. **-S** a yard in front of a house

DOOWOP *n* pl. **-S** a singing style

DOOZER *n* pl. **-S** doozy

DOOZIE *n* pl. **-S** doozy

DOOZY *n* pl. **-ZIES** an extraordinary one of its kind

DOPA *n* pl. **-S** a drug to treat Parkinson's disease

DOPAMINE *n* pl. **-S** a form of dopa used to stimulate the heart

DOPANT *n* pl. **-S** an impurity added to a pure substance

DOPE *v* **DOPED, DOPING, DOPES** to give a narcotic to

DOPE *adj* **DOPER, DOPEST** excellent, outstanding

DOPEHEAD *n* pl. **-S** a drug addict

DOPER *n* pl. **-S** one that dopes

DOPESTER *n* pl. **-S** one who predicts the outcomes of contests

DOPEY *adj* **DOPIER, DOPIEST** lethargic; stupid **DOPILY** *adv*

DOPIER comparative of dopy

DOPIEST superlative of dopy

DOPINESS *n* pl. **-ES** the state of being dopey

DOPING *n* pl. **-S** the use of drugs by athletes

DOPY *adj* **DOPIER, DOPIEST** dopey

DOR *n* pl. **-S** a black European beetle

DORADO *n* pl. **-DOS** a marine fish

DORBUG *n* pl. **-S** a dor

DORE *n* pl. **-S** a large freshwater fish

DORHAWK *n* pl. **-S** a nocturnal bird

DORIES pl. of dory

DORK *n* pl. **-S** a stupid or foolish person

DORKY *adj* **DORKIER, DORKIEST** stupid, foolish

DORM *n* pl. **-S** a dormitory

DORMANCY *n* pl. **-CIES** the state of being dormant

DORMANT *adj* lying asleep

DORMER *n* pl. **-S** a type of window **DORMERED** *adj*

DORMICE pl. of dormouse

DORMIE *adj* being ahead by as many holes in golf as remain to be played

DORMIENT *adj* dormant

DORMIN *n* pl. **-S** a plant hormone

DORMOUSE *n* pl. **-MICE** a small rodent

DORMY *adj* dormie

DORNECK *n* pl. **-S** dornick

DORNICK *n* pl. **-S** a heavy linen fabric

DORNOCK *n* pl. **-S** dornick

DORP *n* pl. **-S** a village

DORPER *n* pl. **-S** one of a breed of mutton-producing sheep

DORR *n* pl. **-S** dor

DORSA pl. of dorsum

DORSAD *adv* dorsally

DORSAL *n* pl. **-S** a dorsally located anatomical part

DORSALLY *adv* toward the back

DORSEL *n* pl. **-S** a dossal

DORSER *n* pl. **-S** dosser

DORSUM *n* pl. **-SA** the back

DORTY *adj* sullen

DORY *n* pl. **-RIES** a flat-bottomed boat

DORYMAN *n* pl. **-MEN** one that fishes from a dory

DOSA *n* pl. **DOSAS** or **DOSAI** a pancake made from rice flour

DOSAGE *n* pl. **-S** the amount of medicine to be given

DOSE *v* **DOSED, DOSING, DOSES** to give a specified quantity of medicine to

DOSER *n* pl. **-S** one that doses

DOSH *n* money

DOSHA *n* pl. **-S** each of three energies believed to circulate in the body

DOSS *v* **-ED, -ING, -ES** to sleep in any convenient place

DOSSAL *n* pl. **-S** an ornamental cloth hung behind an altar

DOSSEL *n* pl. **-S** dossal

DOSSER *n* pl. **-S** a basket carried on the back

DOSSERET *n* pl. **-S** a block resting on the capital of a column

DOSSIER *n* pl. **-S** a file of papers on a single subject

DOSSIL *n* pl. **-S** a cloth roll for wiping ink

DOST a present 2d person sing. of do

DOT *v* **DOTTED, DOTTING, DOTS** to cover with dots (tiny round marks)

DOTAGE *n* pl. **-S** a state of senility

DOTAL *adj* pertaining to a dowry

DOTARD *n* pl. **-S** a senile person **DOTARDLY** *adj*

DOTATION *n* pl. **-S** an endowment

DOTE *v* **DOTED, DOTING, DOTES** to show excessive affection

DOTER *n* pl. **-S** one that dotes

DOTH a present 3d person sing. of do

DOTIER comparative of doty

DOTIEST superlative of doty

DOTING present participle of dote

DOTINGLY *adv* in an excessively affectionate manner

DOTTED past tense of dot

DOTTEL *n* pl. **-S** dottle

DOTTER *n* pl. **-S** one that dots

DOTTEREL *n* pl. **-S** a shorebird

DOTTIER comparative of dotty

DOTTIEST	superlative of dotty
DOTTILY	*adv* in a dotty manner
DOTTING	present participle of dot
DOTTLE	*n* pl. **-S** a mass of half-burnt pipe tobacco
DOTTREL	*n* pl. **-S** dotterel
DOTTY	*adj* **-TIER, -TIEST** crazy
DOTY	*adj* **DOTIER, DOTIEST** stained by decay
DOUBLE	*v* **-BLED, -BLING, -BLES** to make twice as great
DOUBLER	*n* pl. **-S** one that doubles
DOUBLET	*n* pl. **-S** a close-fitting jacket
DOUBLING	present participle of double
DOUBLOON	*n* pl. **-S** a former Spanish gold coin
DOUBLURE	*n* pl. **-S** the lining of a book cover
DOUBLY	*adv* to twice the degree
DOUBT	*v* **-ED, -ING, -S** to be uncertain about
DOUBTER	*n* pl. **-S** one that doubts
DOUBTFUL	*adj* uncertain
DOUCE	*adj* **DOUCER, DOUCEST** sober, sedate **DOUCELY** *adv*
DOUCEUR	*n* pl. **-S** a gratuity
DOUCHE	*v* **DOUCHED, DOUCHING, DOUCHES** to cleanse with a jet of water
DOUCHING	*n* pl. **-S** a cleansing with a jet of water
DOUGH	*n* pl. **-S** a flour mixture
DOUGHBOY	*n* pl. **-BOYS** an infantryman
DOUGHIER	comparative of doughy
DOUGHIEST	superlative of doughy
DOUGHNUT	*n* pl. **-S** a ring-shaped cake
DOUGHT	a past tense of dow
DOUGHTY	*adj* **-TIER, -TIEST** courageous
DOUGHY	*adj* **DOUGHIER, DOUGHIEST** resembling dough
DOULA	*n* pl. **-S** a woman who assists another woman during childbirth
DOUM	*n* pl. **-S** an African palm tree
DOUMA	*n* pl. **-S** duma
DOUPIONI	*n* pl. **-S** a silk yarn
DOUR	*adj* **DOURER, DOUREST** sullen
DOURA	*n* pl. **-S** durra
DOURAH	*n* pl. **-S** durra
DOURINE	*n* pl. **-S** a disease of horses
DOURLY	*adv* in a dour manner
DOURNESS	*n* pl. **-ES** the state of being dour
DOUSE	*v* **DOUSED, DOUSING, DOUSES** to plunge into water
DOUSER	*n* pl. **-S** one that douses
DOUT	*v* **-ED, -ING, -S** to extinguish (as a fire)
DOUX	*adj* very sweet — used of champagne
DOUZEPER	*n* pl. **-S** one of twelve legendary knights
DOVE	*n* pl. **-S** a bird of the pigeon family
DOVECOT	*n* pl. **-S** dovecote
DOVECOTE	*n* pl. **-S** a roost for domesticated pigeons
DOVEKEY	*n* pl. **-KEYS** dovekie
DOVEKIE	*n* pl. **-S** a seabird
DOVELIKE	*adj* resembling or suggestive of a dove
DOVEN	*v* **-ED, -ING, -S** to daven
DOVETAIL	*v* **-ED, -ING, -S** to fit together closely
DOVISH	*adj* not warlike
DOW	*v* **DOWED** or **DOUGHT, DOWING, DOWS** to prosper
DOWABLE	*adj* entitled to an endowment
DOWAGER	*n* pl. **-S** a dignified elderly woman
DOWDY	*adj* **DOWDIER, DOWDIEST** lacking in stylishness or neatness **DOWDILY** *adv* **DOWDYISH** *adj*
DOWDY	*n* pl. **DOWDIES** a dowdy woman
DOWEL	*v* **-ELED, -ELING, -ELS** or **-ELLED, -ELLING, -ELS** to fasten with wooden pins
DOWELING	*n* pl. **-S** a cylindrical rod
DOWER	*v* **-ED, -ING, -S** to provide with a dowry
DOWERY	*n* pl. **-ERIES** dowry
DOWIE	*adj* dreary
DOWN	*v* **-ED, -ING, -S** to cause to fall
DOWNBEAT	*n* pl. **-S** the first beat of a musical measure
DOWNBOW	*n* pl. **-S** a type of stroke in playing a bowed instrument
DOWNCAST	*n* pl. **-S** an overthrow or ruin
DOWNCOME	*n* pl. **-S** downfall
DOWNER	*n* pl. **-S** a depressant drug
DOWNFALL	*n* pl. **-S** a sudden fall

DOWNHAUL	*n* pl. **-S** a rope for hauling down sails
DOWNHILL	*n* pl. **-S** a downward slope
DOWNHOLE	*adj* used down or in an oil well
DOWNIER	comparative of downy
DOWNIEST	superlative of downy
DOWNILY	*adv* in a downy manner
DOWNLAND	*n* pl. **-S** a rolling treeless upland
DOWNLESS	*adj* having no down (soft furry feathers)
DOWNLIKE	*adj* resembling down
DOWNLINK	*v* **-ED, -ING, -S** to transmit data from a satellite to earth
DOWNLOAD	*v* **-ED, -ING, -S** to transfer data from a large computer to a smaller one
DOWNPIPE	*n* pl. **-S** a pipe for draining water from a roof
DOWNPLAY	*v* **-ED, -ING, -S** to de-emphasize
DOWNPOUR	*n* pl. **-S** a heavy rain
DOWNRATE	*v* **-RATED, -RATING, -RATES** to make lower in value
DOWNSIDE	*n* pl. **-S** a negative aspect
DOWNSIZE	*v* **-SIZED, -SIZING, -SIZES** to produce in a smaller size
DOWNSPIN	*n* pl. **-S** a spinning motion
DOWNTICK	*n* pl. **-S** a stock market transaction
DOWNTIME	*n* pl. **-S** the time when a machine or factory is inactive
DOWNTOWN	*n* pl. **-S** the business district of a city
DOWNTROD	*adj* oppressed
DOWNTURN	*n* pl. **-S** a downward turn
DOWNWARD	*adv* from a higher to a lower place
DOWNWARP	*n* pl. **-S** a broad surface depression
DOWNWASH	*n* pl. **-ES** a downward deflection of air
DOWNWIND	*adv* in the direction that the wind blows
DOWNY	*adj* **DOWNIER, DOWNIEST** soft
DOWNZONE	*v* **-ZONED, -ZONING, -ZONES** to reduce or limit the number of buildings permitted
DOWRY	*n* pl. **-RIES** the money or property a wife brings to her husband at marriage
DOWSABEL	*n* pl. **-S** a sweetheart
DOWSE	*v* **DOWSED, DOWSING, DOWSES** to search for underground water with a divining rod
DOWSER	*n* pl. **-S** one that dowses
DOWSING	*n* pl. **-S** a technique for searching for underground water
DOXIE	*n* pl. **-S** doxy
DOXOLOGY	*n* pl. **-GIES** a hymn or verse of praise to God
DOXY	*n* pl. **DOXIES** a doctrine
DOYEN	*n* pl. **-S** the senior member of a group
DOYENNE	*n* pl. **-S** a female doyen
DOYLEY	*n* pl. **-LEYS** doily
DOYLY	*n* pl. **-LIES** doily
DOZE	*v* **DOZED, DOZING, DOZES** to sleep lightly
DOZEN	*v* **-ED, -ING, -S** to stun
DOZENTH	*n* pl. **-S** twelfth
DOZER	*n* pl. **-S** one that dozes
DOZIER	comparative of dozy
DOZIEST	superlative of dozy
DOZILY	*adv* in a dozy manner
DOZINESS	*n* pl. **-ES** the state of being dozy
DOZING	present participle of doze
DOZY	*adj* **DOZIER, DOZIEST** drowsy
DRAB	*adj* **DRABBER, DRABBEST** cheerless
DRAB	*v* **DRABBED, DRABBING, DRABS** to consort with prostitutes
DRABBET	*n* pl. **-S** a coarse linen fabric
DRABBLE	*v* **-BLED, -BLING, -BLES** to draggle
DRABLY	*adv* in a drab manner
DRABNESS	*n* pl. **-ES** the quality of being drab
DRACAENA	*n* pl. **-S** a tropical plant
DRACENA	*n* pl. **-S** dracaena
DRACHM	*n* pl. **-S** a unit of weight
DRACHMA	*n* pl. **-MAS, -MAE** or **-MAI** a former monetary unit of Greece
DRACONIC	*adj* pertaining to a dragon
DRAFF	*n* pl. **-S** the damp remains of malt after brewing
DRAFFISH	*adj* draffy
DRAFFY	*adj* **DRAFFIER, DRAFFIEST** worthless
DRAFT	*v* **-ED, -ING, -S** to conscript for military service

DRAFTEE	*n* pl. **-S** one that is drafted
DRAFTER	*n* pl. **-S** one that drafts
DRAFTING	*n* pl. **-S** mechanical drawing
DRAFTY	*adj* **DRAFTIER, DRAFTIEST** having or exposed to currents of air **DRAFTILY** *adv*
DRAG	*v* **DRAGGED, DRAGGING, DRAGS** to pull along the ground
DRAGEE	*n* pl. **-S** a sugarcoated candy
DRAGGER	*n* pl. **-S** one that drags
DRAGGIER	comparative of draggy
DRAGGIEST	superlative of draggy
DRAGGING	present participle of drag
DRAGGLE	*v* **-GLED, -GLING, -GLES** to make wet and dirty
DRAGGY	*adj* **-GIER, -GIEST** sluggish
DRAGLINE	*n* pl. **-S** a line used for dragging
DRAGNET	*n* pl. **-S** a net for trawling
DRAGOMAN	*n* pl. **-MANS** or **-MEN** an interpreter in Near Eastern countries
DRAGON	*n* pl. **-S** a mythical monster resembling a serpent
DRAGONET	*n* pl. **-S** a marine fish
DRAGOON	*v* **-ED, -ING, -S** to harass by the use of troops
DRAGROPE	*n* pl. **-S** a rope used for dragging
DRAGSTER	*n* pl. **-S** a vehicle used in drag racing
DRAIL	*n* pl. **-S** a heavy fishhook
DRAIN	*v* **-ED, -ING, -S** to draw off a liquid
DRAINAGE	*n* pl. **-S** the act of draining
DRAINER	*n* pl. **-S** one that drains
DRAKE	*n* pl. **-S** a male duck
DRAM	*v* **DRAMMED, DRAMMING, DRAMS** to tipple
DRAMA	*n* pl. **-S** a composition written for theatrical performance
DRAMADY	*n* pl. **-DIES** dramedy
DRAMATIC	*adj* pertaining to drama
DRAMEDY	*n* pl. **-DIES** a sitcom having dramatic scenes
DRAMMED	past tense of dram
DRAMMING	present participle of dram
DRAMMOCK	*n* pl. **-S** raw oatmeal mixed with cold water
DRAMSHOP	*n* pl. **-S** a barroom
DRANK	past tense of drink

DRAPE	*v* **DRAPED, DRAPING, DRAPES** to arrange in graceful folds **DRAPABLE** *adj*
DRAPER	*n* pl. **-S** a dealer in cloth
DRAPERY	*n* pl. **-ERIES** cloth arranged in graceful folds
DRAPEY	*adj* characterized by graceful folds
DRAPING	present participle of drape
DRASTIC	*adj* extremely severe
DRAT	*v* **DRATTED, DRATTING, DRATS** to damn
DRAUGHT	*v* **-ED, -ING, -S** to draft
DRAUGHTY	*adj* **DRAUGHTIER, DRAUGHTIEST** drafty
DRAVE	a past tense of drive
DRAW	*v* **DREW, DRAWN, DRAWING, DRAWS** to move by pulling **DRAWABLE** *adj*
DRAWBACK	*n* pl. **-S** a hindrance
DRAWBAR	*n* pl. **-S** a railroad coupler
DRAWBORE	*n* pl. **-S** a hole for joining a mortise and tenon
DRAWCORD	*n* pl. **-S** a cord for drawing a garment tight
DRAWDOWN	*n* pl. **-S** a lowering of a water level
DRAWEE	*n* pl. **-S** the person on whom a bill of exchange is drawn
DRAWER	*n* pl. **-S** one that draws
DRAWING	*n* pl. **-S** a portrayal in lines of a form or figure
DRAWL	*v* **-ED, -ING, -S** to speak slowly with vowels greatly prolonged
DRAWLER	*n* pl. **-S** one that drawls
DRAWLY	*adj* **DRAWLIER, DRAWLIEST** marked by drawling
DRAWN	past participle of draw
DRAWTUBE	*n* pl. **-S** a tube that slides within another tube
DRAY	*v* **-ED, -ING, -S** to transport by dray (a low, strong cart)
DRAYAGE	*n* pl. **-S** transportation by dray
DRAYMAN	*n* pl. **-MEN** one who drives a dray
DREAD	*v* **-ED, -ING, -S** to fear greatly
DREAD	*adj* **DREADER, DREADEST** frightening
DREADFUL	*n* pl. **-S** a publication containing sensational material
DREAM	*v* **DREAMED** or **DREAMT, DREAMING, DREAMS** to have a dream (a series of images occurring during sleep)

DREAMER	*n* pl. **-S** one that dreams
DREAMFUL	*adj* dreamy
DREAMY	*adj* **DREAMIER, DREAMIEST** full of dreams **DREAMILY** *adv*
DREAR	*n* pl. **-S** the state of being dreary
DREAR	*adj* **DREARER, DREAREST** dreary
DREARY	*adj* **DREARIER, DREARIEST** dismal **DREARILY** *adv*
DREARY	*n* pl. **DREARIES** a dismal person
DRECK	*n* pl. **-S** rubbish **DRECKISH** *adj*
DRECKY	*adj* **DRECKIER, DRECKIEST** trashy
DREDGE	*v* **DREDGED, DREDGING, DREDGES** to clear with a dredge (a machine for scooping mud)
DREDGER	*n* pl. **-S** one that dredges
DREDGING	*n* pl. **-S** matter that is dredged up
DREE	*v* **DREED, DREEING, DREES** to suffer
DREG	*n* pl. **-S** the sediment of liquors **DREGGISH** *adj*
DREGGY	*adj* **-GIER, -GIEST** full of dregs
DREICH	*adj* dreary
DREIDEL	*n* pl. **-S** a spinning toy
DREIDL	*n* pl. **-S** dreidel
DREIGH	*adj* dreich
DREK	*n* pl. **-S** dreck
DREKKY	*adj* **DREKKIER, DREKKIEST** drecky
DRENCH	*v* **-ED, -ING, -ES** to wet thoroughly
DRENCHER	*n* pl. **-S** one that drenches
DRESS	*v* **DRESSED** or **DREST, DRESSING, DRESSES** to put clothes on
DRESSAGE	*n* pl. **-S** the training of a horse in obedience and deportment
DRESSER	*n* pl. **-S** one that dresses
DRESSING	*n* pl. **-S** material applied to cover a wound
DRESSY	*adj* **DRESSIER, DRESSIEST** stylish **DRESSILY** *adv*
DREST	a past tense of dress
DREW	past tense of draw
DRIB	*v* **DRIBBED, DRIBBING, DRIBS** to drip
DRIBBLE	*v* **-BLED, -BLING, -BLES** to drivel
DRIBBLER	*n* pl. **-S** one that dribbles
DRIBBLET	*n* pl. **-S** driblet
DRIBBLING	present participle of dribble
DRIBBLY	*adj* tending to dribble
DRIBLET	*n* pl. **-S** a small drop of liquid
DRIED	past tense of dry
DRIEGH	*adj* dreary
DRIER	*n* pl. **-S** one that dries
DRIES	present 3d person sing. of dry
DRIEST	a superlative of dry
DRIFT	*v* **-ED, -ING, -S** to move along in a current
DRIFTAGE	*n* pl. **-S** the act of drifting
DRIFTER	*n* pl. **-S** one that drifts
DRIFTNET	*n* pl. **-S** a large fishnet arranged to drift with the tide or current
DRIFTPIN	*n* pl. **-S** a metal rod for securing timbers
DRIFTY	*adj* **DRIFTIER, DRIFTIEST** full of drifts (masses of wind-driven snow)
DRILL	*v* **-ED, -ING, -S** to bore a hole in
DRILLER	*n* pl. **-S** one that drills
DRILLING	*n* pl. **-S** a heavy twilled cotton fabric
DRILY	*adv* dryly
DRINK	*v* **DRANK, DRUNK, DRINKING, DRINKS** to swallow liquid
DRINKER	*n* pl. **-S** one that drinks
DRINKING	*n* pl. **-S** a habit of drinking alcoholic beverages
DRIP	*v* **DRIPPED** or **DRIPT, DRIPPING, DRIPS** to fall in drops
DRIPLESS	*adj* designed not to drip
DRIPPER	*n* pl. **-S** something from which a liquid drips
DRIPPING	*n* pl. **-S** juice drawn from meat during cooking
DRIPPY	*adj* **-PIER, -PIEST** very wet **DRIPPILY** *adv*
DRIPT	a past tense of drip
DRIVE	*v* **DROVE** or **DRAVE, DRIVEN, DRIVING, DRIVES** to urge or propel forward **DRIVABLE** *adj*
DRIVEL	*v* **-ELED, -ELING, -ELS** or **-ELLED, -ELLING, -ELS** to let saliva flow from the mouth
DRIVELER	*n* pl. **-S** one that drivels
DRIVER	*n* pl. **-S** one that drives
DRIVEWAY	*n* pl. **-WAYS** a private road providing access to a building

DRIVING *n* pl. **-S** management of a motor vehicle

DRIZZLE *v* **-ZLED, -ZLING, -ZLES** to rain lightly

DRIZZLY *adj* **-ZLIER, -ZLIEST** characterized by light rain

DROGUE *n* pl. **-S** a sea anchor

DROID *n* pl. **-S** an android

DROIT *n* pl. **-S** a legal right

DROKE *n* pl. **-S** a grove of trees

DROLL *adj* **DROLLER, DROLLEST** comical

DROLL *v* **-ED, -ING, -S** to jest

DROLLERY *n* pl. **-ERIES** something droll

DROLLY *adv* in a droll manner

DROMON *n* pl. **-S** dromond

DROMOND *n* pl. **-S** a large fast-sailing medieval galley

DRONE *v* **DRONED, DRONING, DRONES** to make a continuous low sound

DRONER *n* pl. **-S** one that drones

DRONGO *n* pl. **-GOS** or **-GOES** a tropical bird

DRONISH *adj* habitually lazy

DROOL *v* **-ED, -ING, -S** to drivel

DROOLY *adj* **DROOLIER, DROOLIEST** drooling

DROOP *v* **-ED, -ING, -S** to hang downward

DROOPY *adj* **DROOPIER, DROOPIEST** drooping **DROOPILY** *adv*

DROP *v* **DROPPED** or **DROPT, DROPPING, DROPS** to fall in drops (globules)

DROPDOWN *n* pl. **-S** a menu that appears on a computer screen below a selected item

DROPHEAD *n* pl. **-S** a convertible car

DROPKICK *n* pl. **-S** a type of kick in football

DROPLET *n* pl. **-S** a tiny drop

DROPOUT *n* pl. **-S** one who quits school prematurely

DROPPED a past tense of drop

DROPPER *n* pl. **-S** a tube for dispensing liquid in drops

DROPPING *n* pl. **-S** something that has been dropped

DROPSEED *n* pl. **-S** a type of grass

DROPSHOT *n* pl. **-S** a type of shot in tennis

DROPSY *n* pl. **-SIES** an excessive accumulation of serous fluid **DROPSIED** *adj*

DROPT a past tense of drop

DROPTOP *n* pl. **-S** a convertible automobile

DROPWORT *n* pl. **-S** a perennial herb

DROSERA *n* pl. **-S** a sundew

DROSHKY *n* pl. **-KIES** an open carriage

DROSKY *n* pl. **-KIES** droshky

DROSS *n* pl. **-ES** waste matter

DROSSY *adj* **DROSSIER, DROSSIEST** worthless

DROUGHT *n* pl. **-S** a dry period

DROUGHTY *adj* **DROUGHTIER, DROUGHTIEST** dry

DROUK *v* **-ED, -ING, -S** to drench

DROUTH *n* pl. **-S** drought

DROUTHY *adj* **DROUTHIER, DROUTHIEST** droughty

DROVE *v* **DROVED, DROVING, DROVES** to drive cattle or sheep

DROVER *n* pl. **-S** a driver of cattle or sheep

DROVING *n* pl. **-S** the work of a drover

DROWN *v* **-ED, -ING, -S** to suffocate in water

DROWND *v* **-ED, -ING, -S** to drown

DROWNER *n* pl. **-S** one that drowns

DROWSE *v* **DROWSED, DROWSING, DROWSES** to doze

DROWSY *adj* **DROWSIER, DROWSIEST** sleepy **DROWSILY** *adv*

DRUB *v* **DRUBBED, DRUBBING, DRUBS** to beat severely

DRUBBER *n* pl. **-S** one that drubs

DRUBBING *n* pl. **-S** a severe beating

DRUDGE *v* **DRUDGED, DRUDGING, DRUDGES** to do hard, menial, or tedious work

DRUDGER *n* pl. **-S** one that drudges

DRUDGERY *n* pl. **-ERIES** hard, menial, or tedious work

DRUG *v* **DRUGGED, DRUGGING, DRUGS** to affect with a drug (a medicinal substance)

DRUGGET *n* pl. **-S** a coarse woolen fabric

DRUGGIE *n* pl. **-S** a drug addict

DRUGGIST *n* pl. **-S** a pharmacist

DRUGGY *adj* **-GIER, -GIEST** affected by drugs

DRUGLESS	*adj* being without drugs
DRUID	*n* pl. **-S** one of an ancient Celtic order of priests **DRUIDIC** *adj*
DRUIDESS	*n* pl. **-ES** a female druid
DRUIDISM	*n* pl. **-S** the religious system of the druids
DRUM	*v* **DRUMMED, DRUMMING, DRUMS** to beat a drum (a percussion instrument)
DRUMBEAT	*n* pl. **-S** the sound of a drum
DRUMBLE	*v* **-BLED, -BLING, -BLES** to move slowly
DRUMFIRE	*n* pl. **-S** heavy, continuous gunfire
DRUMFISH	*n* pl. **-ES** a fish that makes a drumming sound
DRUMHEAD	*n* pl. **-S** the material stretched over the end of a drum
DRUMLIKE	*adj* resembling the head of a drum
DRUMLIN	*n* pl. **-S** a long hill of glacial drift
DRUMLY	*adj* **-LIER, -LIEST** dark and gloomy
DRUMMED	past tense of drum
DRUMMER	*n* pl. **-S** one that drums
DRUMMING	*n* pl. **-S** the act of beating a drum
DRUMROLL	*n* pl. **-S** a roll played on a drum
DRUNK	*adj* **DRUNKER, DRUNKEST** intoxicated
DRUNK	*n* pl. **-S** a drunken person
DRUNKARD	*n* pl. **-S** one who is habitually drunk
DRUNKEN	*adj* drunk
DRUNKISH	*adj* somewhat drunk
DRUPE	*n* pl. **-S** a fleshy fruit
DRUPEL	*n* pl. **-S** drupelet
DRUPELET	*n* pl. **-S** a small drupe
DRUSE	*n* pl. **-S** a crust of small crystals lining a rock cavity
DRUTHER	*n* pl. **-S** one's preference
DRY	*adj* **DRIER, DRIEST** or **DRYER, DRYEST** having no moisture
DRY	*n* pl. **DRYS** a prohibitionist
DRY	*v* **DRIED, DRYING, DRIES** to make dry **DRYABLE** *adj*
DRYAD	*n* pl. **-S** or **-ES** a nymph of the woods **DRYADIC** *adj*
DRYAS	*n* pl. **DRYAS** a flowering alpine plant
DRYER	*n* pl. **-S** drier
DRYISH	*adj* somewhat dry
DRYLAND	*n* pl. **-S** an arid region
DRYLOT	*n* pl. **-S** an enclosure for livestock
DRYLY	*adv* in a dry manner
DRYNESS	*n* pl. **-ES** the state of being dry
DRYPOINT	*n* pl. **-S** a method of engraving
DRYSTONE	*adj* constructed of stone without mortar
DRYSUIT	*n* pl. **-S** a waterproof rubber suit worn by divers
DRYWALL	*v* **-ED, -ING, -S** to cover a wall with plasterboard
DRYWELL	*n* pl. **-S** a hole for receiving drainage from a roof
DUAD	*n* pl. **-S** a pair
DUAL	*n* pl. **-S** a linguistic form
DUALISE	*v* **-ISED, -ISING, -ISES** to dualize
DUALISM	*n* pl. **-S** a philosophical theory
DUALIST	*n* pl. **-S** an adherent of dualism
DUALITY	*n* pl. **-TIES** the state of being twofold
DUALIZE	*v* **-IZED, -IZING, -IZES** to make twofold
DUALLIE	*n* pl. **-S** dually
DUALLY	*n* pl. **-LIES** a pickup truck with double rear wheels
DUATHLON	*n* pl. **-S** a long-distance race involving running and bicycling
DUB	*v* **DUBBED, DUBBING, DUBS** to confer knighthood on
DUBBER	*n* pl. **-S** one that dubs
DUBBIN	*v* **-ED, -ING, -S** to apply dubbing to leather
DUBBING	*n* pl. **-S** material for softening and waterproofing leather
DUBIETY	*n* pl. **-ETIES** the state of being dubious
DUBIOUS	*adj* doubtful
DUBNIUM	*n* pl. **-S** a radioactive element
DUBONNET	*n* pl. **-S** a red color
DUBSTEP	*n* pl. **-S** a type of electronic dance music
DUCAL	*adj* pertaining to a duke (a high-ranking nobleman) **DUCALLY** *adv*
DUCAT	*n* pl. **-S** any of several gold coins formerly used in Europe
DUCE	*n* pl. **DUCES** or **DUCI** a leader
DUCHESS	*n* pl. **-ES** the wife or widow of a duke
DUCHY	*n* pl. **DUCHIES** the domain of a duke
DUCI	a pl. of duce

DUCK	v **-ED, -ING, -S** to lower quickly	**DUELIST**	n pl. **-S** a dueler
DUCKBILL	n pl. **-S** a platypus	**DUELLER**	n pl. **-S** dueler
DUCKER	n pl. **-S** one that ducks	**DUELLI**	a pl. of duello
DUCKIE	adj ducky	**DUELLING**	n pl. **-S** dueling
DUCKIER	comparative of ducky	**DUELLIST**	n pl. **-S** duelist
DUCKIES	pl. of ducky	**DUELLO**	n pl. **-LOS** or **-LI** the art of dueling; a duel
DUCKIEST	superlative of ducky		
DUCKISH	n pl. **-ES** dusk	**DUENDE**	n pl. **-S** charisma
DUCKLING	n pl. **-S** a young duck	**DUENESS**	n pl. **-ES** the state of being owed
DUCKPIN	n pl. **-S** a type of bowling pin	**DUENNA**	n pl. **-S** a governess
DUCKTAIL	n pl. **-S** a style of haircut	**DUET**	v **DUETED, DUETING, DUETS** or **DUETTED, DUETTING, DUETS** to perform a duet (a musical composition for two)
DUCKWALK	v **-ED, -ING, -S** to walk in a squatting position		
DUCKWEED	n pl. **-S** an aquatic plant	**DUETTIST**	n pl. **-S** a participant in a duet
DUCKY	adj **DUCKIER, DUCKIEST** excellent	**DUFF**	v **-ED, -ING, -S** to mishit a ball in golf
DUCKY	n pl. **DUCKIES** a darling	**DUFF**	adj **DUFFER, DUFFEST** worthless, useless
DUCT	v **-ED, -ING, -S** to convey through a duct (a tubular passage)	**DUFFEL**	n pl. **-S** a coarse woolen fabric
DUCTAL	adj made up of ducts	**DUFFER**	n pl. **-S** a clumsy person
DUCTILE	adj easily molded or shaped	**DUFFLE**	n pl. **-S** duffel
DUCTING	n pl. **-S** a system of ducts	**DUFUS**	n pl. **-ES** doofus
DUCTLESS	adj being without a duct	**DUG**	n pl. **-S** the teat or udder of a female mammal
DUCTULE	n pl. **-S** a small duct		
DUCTWORK	n pl. **-S** a system of ducts	**DUGONG**	n pl. **-S** an aquatic mammal
DUD	n pl. **-S** a bomb that fails to explode	**DUGOUT**	n pl. **-S** a canoe made by hollowing out a log
DUDDIE	adj ragged	**DUH**	interj — used to indicate that something just stated is too obvious
DUDDY	adj duddie		
DUDE	v **DUDED, DUDING, DUDES** to dress up in flashy clothes	**DUI**	a pl. of duo
		DUIKER	n pl. **-S** a small antelope
DUDEEN	n pl. **-S** a short tobacco pipe	**DUIT**	n pl. **-S** doit
DUDENESS	n pl. **-ES** the state of being a dude (a dandy)	**DUKE**	v **DUKED, DUKING, DUKES** to fight
DUDETTE	n pl. **-S** a dudish female	**DUKEDOM**	n pl. **-S** a duchy
DUDGEON	n pl. **-S** a feeling of resentment	**DULCE**	n pl. **-S** a sweet food or drink
DUDING	present participle of dude	**DULCET**	n pl. **-S** a soft-toned organ stop
DUDISH	adj resembling a dude (a dandy)	**DULCETLY**	adv melodiously
DUDISHLY	adv in the manner of a dude	**DULCIAN**	n pl. **-S** an early type of bassoon
DUE	n pl. **-S** something that is owed	**DULCIANA**	n pl. **-S** a soft-toned organ stop
DUECENTO	n pl. **-TOS** the thirteenth century	**DULCIFY**	v **-FIED, -FYING, -FIES** to sweeten
DUEL	v **DUELED, DUELING, DUELS** or **DUELLED, DUELLING, DUELS** to fight formally	**DULCIMER**	n pl. **-S** a stringed instrument
		DULCINEA	n pl. **-S** a sweetheart
DUELER	n pl. **-S** one that duels	**DULIA**	n pl. **-S** veneration of saints
DUELING	n pl. **-S** a contest between two persons with deadly weapons	**DULL**	adj **DULLER, DULLEST** mentally slow

DULL	*v* **-ED, -ING, -S** to make less sharp
DULLARD	*n* pl. **-S** a dolt
DULLISH	*adj* somewhat dull
DULLNESS	*n* pl. **-ES** the state of being dull
DULLY	*adv* in a dull manner
DULNESS	*n* pl. **-ES** dullness
DULSE	*n* pl. **-S** an edible seaweed
DULY	*adv* rightfully
DUM	*adj* cooked with steam
DUMA	*n* pl. **-S** a Russian council
DUMB	*adj* **DUMBER, DUMBEST** incapable of speech
DUMB	*v* **-ED, -ING, -S** to make silent
DUMBBELL	*n* pl. **-S** a weight lifted for muscular exercise
DUMBCANE	*n* pl. **-S** a tropical plant
DUMBHEAD	*n* pl. **-S** a stupid person
DUMBLY	*adv* in a dumb manner
DUMBNESS	*n* pl. **-ES** the state of being dumb
DUMBO	*n* pl. **-BOS** a stupid person
DUMBSHOW	*n* pl. **-S** a presentation in which communication is solely by signs and gestures
DUMBSIZE	*v* **-SIZED, -SIZING, -SIZES** to reduce the workforce so low that work cannot be done effectively
DUMDUM	*n* pl. **-S** a type of bullet
DUMFOUND	*v* **-ED, -ING, -S** to astonish
DUMKA	*n* pl. **-KAS** or **-KY** a Slavic folk ballad
DUMMKOPF	*n* pl. **-S** a dolt
DUMMY	*v* **-MIED, -MYING, -MIES** to make a representation of
DUMP	*v* **-ED, -ING, -S** to let fall heavily
DUMPCART	*n* pl. **-S** a type of cart
DUMPER	*n* pl. **-S** one that dumps
DUMPIER	comparative of dumpy
DUMPIEST	superlative of dumpy
DUMPILY	*adv* in a dumpy manner
DUMPING	*n* pl. **-S** the selling of large quantities of goods at below the market price
DUMPISH	*adj* sad
DUMPLING	*n* pl. **-S** a ball of dough cooked with stew or soup
DUMPSITE	*n* pl. **-S** a place for dumping rubbish

DUMPY	*adj* **DUMPIER, DUMPIEST** short and thick
DUN	*adj* **DUNNER, DUNNEST** of a dull brown color
DUN	*v* **DUNNED, DUNNING, DUNS** to make demands upon for payment of a debt
DUNAM	*n* pl. **-S** a unit of land measure in Israel
DUNCE	*n* pl. **-S** a stupid person **DUNCICAL, DUNCISH** *adj*
DUNCH	*n* pl. **-ES** a push
DUNE	*n* pl. **-S** a hill of sand **DUNELIKE** *adj*
DUNELAND	*n* pl. **-S** an area having many dunes
DUNG	*v* **-ED, -ING, -S** to fertilize with manure
DUNGAREE	*n* pl. **-S** a coarse cotton fabric
DUNGEON	*v* **-ED, -ING, -S** to confine in a dungeon (an underground prison)
DUNGHEAP	*n* pl. **-S** a dunghill
DUNGHILL	*n* pl. **-S** a heap of manure
DUNGY	*adj* **DUNGIER, DUNGIEST** filthy
DUNITE	*n* pl. **-S** an igneous rock **DUNITIC** *adj*
DUNK	*v* **-ED, -ING, -S** to dip into liquid
DUNKER	*n* pl. **-S** one that dunks
DUNKING	*n* pl. **-S** the act of dipping something into liquid
DUNLIN	*n* pl. **-S** a wading bird
DUNNAGE	*n* pl. **-S** packing material used to protect cargo
DUNNED	past tense of dun
DUNNER	comparative of dun
DUNNESS	*n* pl. **-ES** the state of being dun
DUNNEST	superlative of dun
DUNNING	present participle of dun
DUNNITE	*n* pl. **-S** an explosive
DUNT	*v* **-ED, -ING, -S** to strike with a heavy blow
DUO	*n* pl. **DUOS** or **DUI** an instrumental duet
DUODENUM	*n* pl. **-DENUMS** or **-DENA** the first portion of the small intestine **DUODENAL** *adj*
DUOLOG	*n* pl. **-S** duologue
DUOLOGUE	*n* pl. **-S** a conversation between two persons
DUOMO	*n* pl. **-MOS** or **-MI** a cathedral

DUOPOLY *n pl.* **-LIES** the market condition existing when there are two sellers only

DUOPSONY *n pl.* **-NIES** the market condition existing when there are two buyers only

DUOTONE *n pl.* **-S** an illustration in two tones

DUP *v* **DUPPED, DUPPING, DUPS** to open

DUPATTA *n pl.* **-S** a scarf or headdress worn by some Muslim women

DUPE *v* **DUPED, DUPING, DUPES** to deceive **DUPABLE** *adj*

DUPER *n pl.* **-S** one that dupes

DUPERY *n pl.* **-ERIES** the act of duping

DUPING *n pl.* **-S** the act of duplicating something

DUPION *n pl.* **-S** a type of silk fabric

DUPLE *adj* having two parts or elements

DUPLET *n pl.* **-S** a set of two of one kind

DUPLEX *v* **-ED, -ING, -ES** to make duple

DUPLEXER *n pl.* **-S** an electronic switching device

DUPPED past tense of dup

DUPPING present participle of dup

DURA *n pl.* **-S** durra

DURABLE *adj* able to withstand wear or decay **DURABLY** *adv*

DURABLES *n/pl* durable goods

DURAL *adj* of the dura mater (a brain membrane)

DURAMEN *n pl.* **-S** the central wood of a tree

DURANCE *n pl.* **-S** restraint by or as if by physical force

DURATION *n pl.* **-S** continuance in time

DURATIVE *n pl.* **-S** a type of verb

DURBAR *n pl.* **-S** the court of a native ruler in India

DURE *v* **DURED, DURING, DURES** to endure

DURESS *n pl.* **-ES** compulsion by threat

DURIAN *n pl.* **-S** an East Indian tree

DURION *n pl.* **-S** durian

DURMAST *n pl.* **-S** a European oak

DURN *v* **-ED, -ING, -S** to damn

DURNED *adj* **DURNEDER, DURNEDEST** or **DURNDEST** damned

DURO *n pl.* **-ROS** a Spanish silver dollar

DUROC *n pl.* **-S** a large red hog

DURR *n pl.* **-S** durra

DURRA *n pl.* **-S** a cereal grain

DURRIE *n pl.* **-S** dhurrie

DURST a past tense of dare

DURUM *n pl.* **-S** a kind of wheat

DUSK *v* **-ED, -ING, -S** to become dark

DUSKISH *adj* dusky

DUSKY *adj* **DUSKIER, DUSKIEST** somewhat dark **DUSKILY** *adv*

DUST *v* **-ED, -ING, -S** to make free of dust (minute particles of matter)

DUSTBALL *n pl.* **-S** a ball of dust

DUSTBIN *n pl.* **-S** a trash can

DUSTCART *n pl.* **-S** a garbage truck

DUSTER *n pl.* **-S** one that dusts

DUSTHEAP *n pl.* **-S** a pile of trash

DUSTIER comparative of dusty

DUSTIEST superlative of dusty

DUSTILY *adv* in a dusty manner

DUSTING *n pl.* **-S** a light sprinkling

DUSTLESS *adj* being without dust

DUSTLIKE *adj* resembling dust

DUSTMAN *n pl.* **-MEN** a trashman

DUSTOFF *n pl.* **-S** a military helicopter for evacuating the wounded

DUSTPAN *n pl.* **-S** a pan for holding swept dust

DUSTRAG *n pl.* **-S** a rag used for dusting

DUSTUP *n pl.* **-S** an argument

DUSTY *adj* **DUSTIER, DUSTIEST** full of dust

DUTCH *adv* with each person paying for himself or herself

DUTCHMAN *n pl.* **-MEN** something used to hide structural defects

DUTEOUS *adj* dutiful

DUTIABLE *adj* subject to import tax

DUTIFUL *adj* obedient

DUTY *n pl.* **-TIES** a moral or legal obligation

DUUMVIR *n pl.* **-VIRS** or **-VIRI** a magistrate of ancient Rome

DUVET *n pl.* **-S** a down-filled bed covering

DUVETINE *n pl.* **-S** duvetyn

DUVETYN *n pl.* **-S** a soft fabric

DUVETYNE *n pl.* **-S** duvetyn

DUXELLES   *n* pl. **DUXELLES** a garnish or sauce with minced mushrooms

DUYKER   *n* pl. **-S** duiker

DWALE   *n* pl. **-S** a poisonous plant with purple flowers

DWARF   *adj* **DWARFER, DWARFEST** extremely small

DWARF   *n* pl. **DWARFS** or **DWARVES** an extremely small person

DWARF   *v* **-ED, -ING, -S** to cause to appear small

DWARFISH   *adj* resembling a dwarf

DWARFISM   *n* pl. **-S** a condition of stunted growth

DWARVES   a pl. of dwarf

DWEEB   *n* pl. **-S** an unattractive or inept person **DWEEBISH** *adj*

DWEEBY   *adj* **DWEEBIER, DWEEBIEST** socially inept

DWELL   *v* **DWELT** or **DWELLED, DWELLING, DWELLS** to reside

DWELLER   *n* pl. **-S** one that dwells

DWELLING   *n* pl. **-S** a place of residence

DWINDLE   *v* **-DLED, -DLING, -DLES** to decrease steadily

DWINE   *v* **DWINED, DWINING, DWINES** to pine or waste away

DYABLE   *adj* dyeable

DYAD   *n* pl. **-S** a pair of units

DYADIC   *n* pl. **-S** a sum of mathematical dyads

DYARCHY   *n* pl. **-CHIES** diarchy **DYARCHAL, DYARCHIC** *adj*

DYBBUK   *n* pl. **-BUKS** or **-BUKIM** a wandering soul in Jewish folklore

DYE   *v* **DYED, DYEING, DYES** to treat with a dye (a coloring matter)

DYEABLE   *adj* capable of being dyed

DYEING   *n* pl. **-S** something colored with a dye

DYER   *n* pl. **-S** one that dyes

DYESTUFF   *n* pl. **-S** a dye

DYEWEED   *n* pl. **-S** a shrub that yields a yellow dye

DYEWOOD   *n* pl. **-S** a wood from which a dye is extracted

DYING   *n* pl. **-S** a passing out of existence

DYKE   *v* **DYKED, DYKING, DYKES** to dike

DYNAMIC   *n* pl. **-S** a physical force

DYNAMISM   *n* pl. **-S** a theory that explains the universe in terms of force or energy

DYNAMIST   *n* pl. **-S** an adherent of dynamism

DYNAMITE   *v* **-MITED, -MITING, -MITES** to blow up with a powerful explosive

DYNAMO   *n* pl. **-MOS** a generator

DYNAST   *n* pl. **-S** a ruler

DYNASTY   *n* pl. **-TIES** a succession of rulers from the same line of descent **DYNASTIC** *adj*

DYNATRON   *n* pl. **-S** a type of electron tube

DYNE   *n* pl. **-S** a unit of force

DYNEIN   *n* pl. **-S** an enzyme involved in cell movement

DYNEL   *n* pl. **-S** a synthetic fiber

DYNODE   *n* pl. **-S** a type of electrode

DYSGENIC   *adj* causing the deterioration of hereditary qualities

DYSLALIA   *n* pl. **-S** the inability to articulate speech

DYSLEXIA   *n* pl. **-S** impairment of the ability to read

DYSLEXIC   *n* pl. **-S** one who is affected with dyslexia

DYSPEPSY   *n* pl. **-SIES** indigestion

DYSPNEA   *n* pl. **-S** labored breathing **DYSPNEAL, DYSPNEIC** *adj*

DYSPNOEA   *n* pl. **-S** dyspnea **DYSPNOIC** *adj*

DYSTAXIA   *n* pl. **-S** a form of muscular tremor

DYSTOCIA   *n* pl. **-S** difficult labor and delivery in childbirth

DYSTONIA   *n* pl. **-S** a condition of disordered tonicity of muscle tissue **DYSTONIC** *adj*

DYSTOPIA   *n* pl. **-S** a wretched place

DYSURIA   *n* pl. **-S** painful urination **DYSURIC** *adj*

DYVOUR   *n* pl. **-S** one who is bankrupt

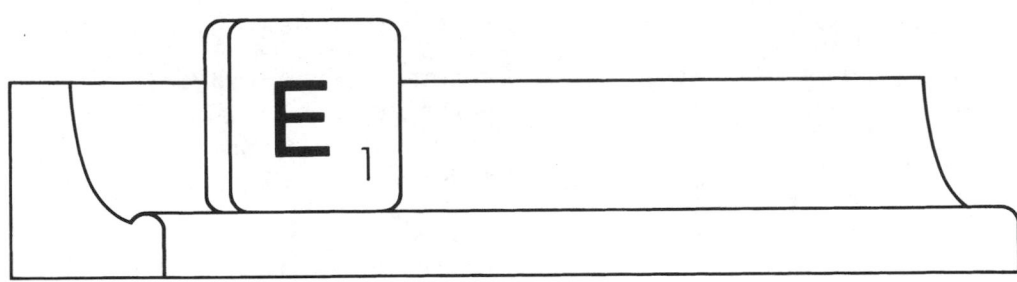

EACH *adj* being one of two or more distinct individuals

EAGER *adj* **-GERER, -GEREST** impatiently longing **EAGERLY** *adv*

EAGER *n* pl. **-S** eagre

EAGLE *v* **EAGLED, EAGLING, EAGLES** to score an eagle (two strokes under par) on a hole in golf

EAGLET *n* pl. **-S** a young eagle

EAGRE *n* pl. **-S** a tidal flood

EANLING *n* pl. **-S** yeanling

EAR *v* **-ED, -ING, -S** to form the fruiting head of a cereal

EARACHE *n* pl. **-S** a pain in the ear (an organ of hearing)

EARBUD *n* pl. **-S** a small earphone

EARDROP *n* pl. **-S** an earring

EARDRUM *n* pl. **-S** the tympanic membrane

EARED *adj* having ears

EARFLAP *n* pl. **-S** a part of a cap designed to cover the ears

EARFUL *n* pl. **-S** a flow of information

EARHOLE *n* pl. **-S** the external opening of the ear

EARING *n* pl. **-S** a line on a ship

EARL *n* pl. **-S** a British nobleman

EARLAP *n* pl. **-S** an earflap

EARLDOM *n* pl. **-S** the rank of an earl

EARLESS *adj* lacking ears

EARLIER comparative of early

EARLIEST superlative of early

EARLOBE *n* pl. **-S** a part of the ear

EARLOCK *n* pl. **-S** a curl of hair by the ear

EARLSHIP *n* pl. **-S** earldom

EARLY *adv* **-LIER, -LIEST** near the beginning of a period of time or a series of events

EARMARK *v* **-ED, -ING, -S** to designate for a specific use

EARMUFF *n* pl. **-S** one of a pair of ear coverings

EARN *v* **-ED, -ING, -S** to gain or deserve for one's labor or service

EARNER *n* pl. **-S** one that earns

EARNEST *n* pl. **-S** a down payment

EARNINGS *n/pl* something earned

EARPHONE *n* pl. **-S** a listening device worn over the ear

EARPIECE *n* pl. **-S** an earphone

EARPLUG *n* pl. **-S** a plug for the ear

EARRING *n* pl. **-S** an ornament for the earlobe

EARSHOT *n* pl. **-S** the range within which sound can be heard

EARSTONE *n* pl. **-S** an otolith

EARTH *v* **-ED, -ING, -S** to cover with earth (soil)

EARTHEN *adj* made of earth

EARTHIER comparative of earthy

EARTHIEST superlative of earthy

EARTHILY *adv* in an earthy manner

EARTHLY *adj* **-LIER, -LIEST** worldly

EARTHMAN *n* pl. **-MEN** a person from the planet earth

EARTHNUT *n* pl. **-S** a European herb

EARTHPEA *n* pl. **-S** a twining plant

EARTHSET *n* pl. **-S** the setting of the earth as seen from the moon

EARTHY *adj* **EARTHIER, EARTHIEST** composed of, resembling, or suggestive of earth

EARWAX *n* pl. **-ES** cerumen

EARWIG *v* **-WIGGED, -WIGGING, -WIGS** to insinuate against in secret

EARWORM *n* pl. **-S** a bollworm

EASE	*v* **EASED, EASING, EASES** to give rest or relief to
EASEFUL	*adj* restful
EASEL	*n* pl. **-S** a three-legged frame **EASELED** *adj*
EASEMENT	*n* pl. **-S** relief
EASER	*v* pl. **-S** one that eases
EASIER	comparative of easy
EASIES	pl. of easy
EASIEST	superlative of easy
EASILY	*adv* without difficulty
EASINESS	*n* pl. **-ES** the state of being easy
EASING	present participle of ease
EAST	*n* pl. **-S** a cardinal point of the compass
EASTER	*n* pl. **-S** a wind or storm from the east
EASTERLY	*n* pl. **-LIES** a wind from the east
EASTERN	*adj* being to, toward, or in the east
EASTING	*n* pl. **-S** a movement toward the east
EASTWARD	*n* pl. **-S** a direction toward the east
EASY	*adj* **EASIER, EASIEST** not difficult
EASY	*n* pl. **EASIES** a communications code word for the letter E
EAT	*v* **ATE** or **ET, EATEN, EATING, EATS** to consume food
EATABLE	*n* pl. **-S** an edible
EATER	*n* pl. **-S** one that eats
EATERY	*n* pl. **-ERIES** a lunchroom
EATH	*adj* easy
EATING	*n* pl. **-S** the act of consuming food
EAU	*n* pl. **EAUX** water (a transparent, tasteless, odorless liquid)
EAVE	*n* pl. **-S** the lower projecting edge of a roof **EAVED** *adj*
EBB	*v* **-ED, -ING, -S** to recede
EBBET	*n* pl. **-S** a common green newt
EBON	*n* pl. **-S** ebony
EBONICS	*n/pl* a dialect of English spoken by some African-Americans
EBONIES	pl. of ebony
EBONISE	*v* **-ISED, -ISING, -ISES** to ebonize
EBONITE	*n* pl. **-S** a hard rubber
EBONIZE	*v* **-IZED, -IZING, -IZES** to stain black in imitation of ebony
EBONY	*n* pl. **-NIES** a hard, heavy wood
EBOOK	*n* pl. **-S** a device for reading books in electronic format
ECARTE	*n* pl. **-S** a card game
ECAUDATE	*adj* having no tail
ECBOLIC	*n* pl. **-S** a type of drug
ECCLESIA	*n* pl. **-SIAE** an assembly in ancient Greece
ECCRINE	*adj* producing secretions externally
ECDYSIS	*n* pl. **-DYSES** the shedding of an outer layer of skin **ECDYSIAL** *adj*
ECDYSON	*n* pl. **-S** ecdysone
ECDYSONE	*n* pl. **-S** an insect hormone
ECESIS	*n* pl. **-SISES** the establishment of a plant or animal in a new environment **ECESIC** *adj*
ECHAPPE	*adj* moving from a closed to an open position of the feet in ballet
ECHARD	*n* pl. **-S** the water in the soil not available to plants
ECHE	*v* **ECHED, ECHING, ECHES** to increase
ECHELLE	*n* pl. **-S** a device for spreading light into its component colors
ECHELON	*v* **-ED, -ING, -S** to group in a particular formation
ECHIDNA	*n* pl. **-NAS** or **-NAE** a spiny anteater
ECHINATE	*adj* spiny
ECHING	present participle of eche
ECHINOID	*n* pl. **-S** a spiny marine animal
ECHINUS	*n* pl. **-NI** an echinoid
ECHO	*n* pl. **ECHOS** or **ECHOES** a repetition of sound by reflection of sound waves
ECHO	*v* **-ED, -ING, -ES** to produce an echo
ECHOER	*n* pl. **-S** one that echoes
ECHOEY	*adj* full of echoes
ECHOGRAM	*n* pl. **-S** a record produced by a device that uses ultrasonic waves
ECHOIC	*adj* resembling an echo
ECHOISM	*n* pl. **-S** the formation of words in imitation of sounds
ECHOLESS	*adj* producing no echo
ECHT	*adj* genuine
ECLAIR	*n* pl. **-S** a type of pastry
ECLAT	*n* pl. **-S** brilliance
ECLECTIC	*n* pl. **-S** one who draws his or her beliefs from various sources

ECLIPSE	*v* **ECLIPSED, ECLIPSING, ECLIPSES** to obscure
ECLIPSER	*n* pl. **-S** one that eclipses
ECLIPSIS	*n* pl. **ECLIPSISES** or **ECLIPSES** an ellipsis
ECLIPTIC	*n* pl. **-S** an astronomical plane
ECLOGITE	*n* pl. **-S** a type of rock
ECLOGUE	*n* pl. **-S** a pastoral poem
ECLOSE	*v* **ECLOSED, ECLOSING, ECLOSES** to emerge as a larva from an egg
ECLOSION	*n* pl. **-S** the emergence of an insect larva from an egg
ECO	*n* pl. **-S** ecology
ECOCIDE	*n* pl. **-S** the destruction of the natural environment **ECOCIDAL** *adj*
ECOFREAK	*n* pl. **-S** a zealous environmentalist
ECOGIFT	*n* pl. **-S** a donation of land to a government for ecological purposes
ECOLOGY	*n* pl. **-GIES** an environmental science **ECOLOGIC** *adj*
ECONOBOX	*n* pl. **-ES** a small economical car
ECONOMIC	*adj* pertaining to financial matters
ECONOMY	*n* pl. **-MIES** thrift
ECORCHE	*n* pl. **-S** an anatomical figure with the skin removed to show the musculature
ECOTAGE	*n* pl. **-S** obstructive action in defense of the natural environment
ECOTONE	*n* pl. **-S** a type of ecological zone **ECOTONAL** *adj*
ECOTOPIA	*n* pl. **-S** an ecologically ideal region or form of society
ECOTOUR	*n* pl. **-S** a tour of a natural habitat
ECOTYPE	*n* pl. **-S** a subspecies adapted to specific environmental conditions **ECOTYPIC** *adj*
ECOZONE	*n* pl. **-S** a regional ecosystem
ECRASEUR	*n* pl. **-S** a surgical instrument
ECRU	*n* pl. **-S** a yellowish brown color
ECSTASY	*n* pl. **-SIES** a state of exaltation
ECSTATIC	*n* pl. **-S** one that is subject to ecstasies
ECTASIS	*n* pl. **-TASES** the lengthening of a usually short syllable **ECTATIC** *adj*
ECTHYMA	*n* pl. **-MATA** a virus disease
ECTODERM	*n* pl. **-S** the outermost germ layer of an embryo
ECTOGENE	*n* pl. **-S** a gene involved in the development of an embryo in artificial conditions
ECTOMERE	*n* pl. **-S** a cell that develops into ectoderm
ECTOPIA	*n* pl. **-S** congenital displacement of parts or organs **ECTOPIC** *adj*
ECTOSARC	*n* pl. **-S** the outermost layer of protoplasm of certain protozoans
ECTOZOAN	*n* pl. **-S** ectozoon
ECTOZOON	*n* pl. **-ZOA** a parasite on the body of an animal
ECTYPE	*n* pl. **-S** a copy **ECTYPAL** *adj*
ECU	*n* pl. **-S** an old French coin
ECUMENE	*n* pl. **-S** an inhabited area
ECUMENIC	*adj* universal
ECZEMA	*n* pl. **-S** a skin disease
ED	*n* pl. **-S** education
EDACIOUS	*adj* voracious
EDACITY	*n* pl. **-TIES** gluttony
EDAMAME	*n* pl. **-S** green soybeans in a pod
EDAPHIC	*adj* pertaining to the soil
EDDO	*n* pl. **-DOES** a tropical plant
EDDY	*v* **-DIED, -DYING, -DIES** to move against the main current
EDEMA	*n* pl. **-MAS** or **-MATA** an excessive accumulation of serous fluid
EDENIC	*adj* pertaining to a paradise
EDENTATE	*n* pl. **-S** a toothless mammal
EDGE	*v* **EDGED, EDGING, EDGES** to provide with an edge (a bounding or dividing line)
EDGELESS	*adj* lacking an edge
EDGER	*n* pl. **-S** a tool used to trim a lawn's edge
EDGEWAYS	*adv* edgewise
EDGEWISE	*adv* sideways
EDGIER	comparative of edgy
EDGIEST	superlative of edgy
EDGILY	*adv* in an edgy manner
EDGINESS	*n* pl. **-ES** the state of being edgy
EDGING	*n* pl. **-S** something that forms or serves as an edge
EDGY	*adj* **EDGIER, EDGIEST** tense, nervous, or irritable
EDH	*n* pl. **-S** an Old English letter
EDIBLE	*n* pl. **-S** something fit to be eaten

EDICT   *n* pl. **-S** an authoritative order having the force of law **EDICTAL** *adj*

EDIFICE   *n* pl. **-S** a building

EDIFIER   *n* pl. **-S** one that edifies

EDIFY   *v* **-FIED, -FYING, -FIES** to enlighten

EDILE   *n* pl. **-S** aedile

EDIT   *v* **-ED, -ING, -S** to correct and prepare for publication **EDITABLE** *adj*

EDITION   *n* pl. **-S** a particular series of printed material

EDITOR   *n* pl. **-S** one that edits

EDITRESS   *n* pl. **-ES** a female editor

EDITRIX   *n* pl. **-TRIXES** or **-TRICES** a female editor

EDUCABLE   *n* pl. **-S** a mildly retarded person

EDUCATE   *v* **-CATED, -CATING, -CATES** to teach

EDUCATOR   *n* pl. **-S** one that educates

EDUCE   *v* **EDUCED, EDUCING, EDUCES** to draw forth or bring out **EDUCIBLE** *adj*

EDUCT   *n* pl. **-S** something educed

EDUCTION   *n* pl. **-S** the act of educing **EDUCTIVE** *adj*

EDUCTOR   *n* pl. **-S** one that educes

EEEW   *interj* — used to express disgust

EEJIT   *n* pl. **-S** an idiot

EEK   *interj* — used to express sudden fright

EEL   *n* pl. **-S** a snakelike fish

EELGRASS   *n* pl. **-ES** an aquatic plant

EELIER   comparative of eely

EELIEST   superlative of eely

EELING   *n* the activity of catching eels

EELLIKE   *adj* resembling an eel

EELPOUT   *n* pl. **-S** a marine fish

EELWORM   *n* pl. **-S** a small roundworm

EELY   *adj* **EELIER, EELIEST** resembling an eel

EENSY   *adj* **-SIER, -SIEST** tiny

EERIE   *adj* **-RIER, -RIEST** weird **EERILY** *adv*

EERINESS   *n* pl. **-ES** the state of being eerie

EERY   *adj* **-RIER, -RIEST** eerie

EEW   *interj* eeew

EF   *n* pl. **-S** the letter F

EFF   *n* pl. **-S** ef

EFFABLE   *adj* capable of being uttered or expressed

EFFACE   *v* **-FACED, -FACING, -FACES** to rub or wipe out

EFFACER   *n* pl. **-S** one that effaces

EFFECT   *v* **-ED, -ING, -S** to bring about

EFFECTER   *n* pl. **-S** effector

EFFECTOR   *n* pl. **-S** a bodily organ that responds to a nerve impulse

EFFENDI   *n* pl. **-S** a Turkish title of respect

EFFERENT   *n* pl. **-S** an organ or part conveying nervous impulses to an effector

EFFETE   *adj* exhausted of vigor or energy **EFFETELY** *adv*

EFFICACY   *n* pl. **-CIES** effectiveness

EFFIGIAL   *adj* resembling an effigy

EFFIGY   *n* pl. **-GIES** a likeness or representation

EFFLUENT   *n* pl. **-S** an outflow

EFFLUVIA   *n/pl* byproducts in the form of waste

EFFLUX   *n* pl. **-ES** an outflow

EFFORT   *n* pl. **-S** a deliberate exertion

EFFULGE   *v* **-FULGED, -FULGING, -FULGES** to shine forth

EFFUSE   *v* **-FUSED, -FUSING, -FUSES** to pour forth

EFFUSION   *n* pl. **-S** an outpouring of emotion

EFFUSIVE   *adj* pouring forth

EFT   *n* pl. **-S** a newt

EFTSOON   *adv* soon afterward

EFTSOONS   *adv* eftsoon

EGAD   *interj* — used as a mild oath

EGADS   *interj* egad

EGAL   *adj* equal

EGALITE   *n* pl. **-S** equality

EGER   *n* pl. **-S** eagre

EGEST   *v* **-ED, -ING, -S** to discharge from the body

EGESTA   *n/pl* egested matter

EGESTION   *n* pl. **-S** the act of egesting **EGESTIVE** *adj*

EGG   *v* **-ED, -ING, -S** to incite or urge

EGGAR   *n* pl. **-S** egger

EGGCUP   *n* pl. **-S** a cup from which an egg is eaten

EGGER   *n* pl. **-S** a kind of moth

EGGFRUIT	*n* pl. **-S** a tropical tree
EGGHEAD	*n* pl. **-S** an intellectual
EGGIER	comparative of eggy
EGGIEST	superlative of eggy
EGGLESS	*adj* lacking eggs
EGGNOG	*n* pl. **-S** a beverage
EGGPLANT	*n* pl. **-S** a perennial herb yielding edible fruit
EGGSHELL	*n* pl. **-S** the hard exterior of a bird's egg
EGGY	*adj* **EGGIER, EGGIEST** tasting or smelling of egg
EGIS	*n* pl. **EGISES** aegis
EGLATERE	*n* pl. **-S** a wild rose
EGLOMISE	*adj* made of glass with a painted picture on the back
EGO	*n* pl. **EGOS** the conscious self
EGOISM	*n* pl. **-S** extreme devotion to self-interest
EGOIST	*n* pl. **-S** one who practices egoism **EGOISTIC** *adj*
EGOLESS	*adj* not characterized by egoism
EGOMANIA	*n* pl. **-S** extreme egotism
EGOTISM	*n* pl. **-S** self-conceit
EGOTIST	*n* pl. **-S** a conceited person
EGOTIZE	*v* **-TIZED, -TIZING, -TIZES** to talk and think about oneself excessively
EGRESS	*v* **-ED, -ING, -ES** to go out
EGRET	*n* pl. **-S** a wading bird
EGYPTIAN	*n* pl. **-S** a typeface with squared serifs
EH	*interj* — used to express doubt or surprise
EIDE	pl. of eidos
EIDER	*n* pl. **-S** a large sea duck
EIDETIC	*n* pl. **-S** a person able to recall vivid images
EIDOLIC	*adj* pertaining to an eidolon
EIDOLON	*n* pl. **-LONS** or **-LA** a phantom
EIDOS	*n* pl. **EIDE** an essence
EIGHT	*n* pl. **-S** a number
EIGHTEEN	*n* pl. **-S** a number
EIGHTH	*n* pl. **-S** one of eight equal parts
EIGHTHLY	*adv* in the eighth place
EIGHTVO	*n* pl. **-VOS** octavo
EIGHTY	*n* pl. **EIGHTIES** a number
EIKON	*n* pl. **-S** or **-ES** icon
EINKORN	*n* pl. **-S** a variety of wheat
EINSTEIN	*n* pl. **-S** a very intelligent person
EIRENIC	*adj* irenic
EIRENICS	*n/pl* irenics
EISWEIN	*n* pl. **-S** a sweet German wine
EITHER	*adj* being one or the other
EJECT	*v* **-ED, -ING, -S** to throw out forcibly
EJECTA	*n/pl* ejected material
EJECTION	*n* pl. **-S** the act of ejecting
EJECTIVE	*n* pl. **-S** a sound produced with air compressed above the closed glottis
EJECTOR	*n* pl. **-S** one that ejects
EJIDO	*n* pl. **-DOS** a piece of land farmed communally in Mexico
EKE	*v* **EKED, EKING, EKES** to supplement with great effort
EKISTICS	*n/pl* a science dealing with human habitats **EKISTIC** *adj*
EKKA	*n* pl. **-S** a one-horse vehicle of India
EKPWELE	*n* pl. **-S** a former monetary unit of Equatorial Guinea
EKTEXINE	*n* pl. **-S** an outer layer of the exine
EKUELE	*n* pl. **EKUELE** ekpwele
EL	*n* pl. **-S** an elevated railroad or train
ELAIN	*n* pl. **-S** olein
ELAN	*n* pl. **-S** enthusiasm
ELAND	*n* pl. **-S** a large antelope
ELAPHINE	*adj* pertaining to a genus of deer
ELAPID	*n* pl. **-S** a venomous snake
ELAPINE	*adj* pertaining to a family of snakes
ELAPSE	*v* **ELAPSED, ELAPSING, ELAPSES** to pass away
ELASTANE	*n* pl. **-S** spandex
ELASTASE	*n* pl. **-S** an enzyme
ELASTIC	*n* pl. **-S** a stretchable material
ELASTIN	*n* pl. **-S** a bodily protein
ELATE	*v* **ELATED, ELATING, ELATES** to raise the spirits of **ELATEDLY** *adv*
ELATER	*n* pl. **-S** a click beetle
ELATERID	*n* pl. **-S** an elater
ELATERIN	*n* pl. **-S** a chemical compound
ELATING	present participle of elate
ELATION	*n* pl. **-S** a feeling of great joy
ELATIVE	*n* pl. **-S** an adjective form in some languages

ELBOW   *v* **-ED, -ING, -S** to jostle

ELBOWING   *n* pl. **-S** the act of fouling an opponent with an elbow (a joint of the arm)

ELD   *n* pl. **-S** old age

ELDER   *n* pl. **-S** an older person

ELDERLY   *n* pl. **-LIES** a rather old person

ELDEST   *n* pl. **-S** the oldest one of three or more

ELDORADO   *n* pl. **-DOS** a place of great abundance

ELDRESS   *n* pl. **-ES** a female elder (a church officer)

ELDRICH   *adj* eldritch

ELDRITCH   *adj* weird

ELECT   *v* **-ED, -ING, -S** to select by vote for an office

ELECTEE   *n* pl. **-S** a person who has been elected

ELECTION   *n* pl. **-S** the act of electing

ELECTIVE   *n* pl. **-S** an optional course of study

ELECTOR   *n* pl. **-S** one that elects

ELECTRET   *n* pl. **-S** a type of nonconductor

ELECTRIC   *n* pl. **-S** something run by electricity

ELECTRO   *v* **-ED, -ING, -S** to make a metallic copy of a page of type for printing

ELECTRON   *n* pl. **-S** an elementary particle

ELECTRUM   *n* pl. **-S** an alloy of gold and silver

ELEGANCE   *n* pl. **-S** tasteful opulence

ELEGANCY   *n* pl. **-CIES** elegance

ELEGANT   *adj* tastefully opulent

ELEGIAC   *n* pl. **-S** a type of verse

ELEGIES   pl. of elegy

ELEGISE   *v* **-GISED, -GISING, -GISES** to elegize

ELEGIST   *n* pl. **-S** one that writes elegies

ELEGIT   *n* pl. **-S** a type of judicial writ

ELEGIZE   *v* **-GIZED, -GIZING, -GIZES** to write an elegy

ELEGY   *n* pl. **-GIES** a mournful poem for one who is dead

ELEMENT   *n* pl. **-S** a substance that cannot be separated into simpler substances by chemical means

ELEMI   *n* pl. **-S** a fragrant resin

ELENCHUS   *n* pl. **-CHI** a logical refutation **ELENCHIC, ELENCTIC** *adj*

ELEPHANT   *n* pl. **-S** a large mammal

ELEVATE   *v* **-VATED, -VATING, -VATES** to raise

ELEVATED   *n* pl. **-S** a railway that operates on a raised structure

ELEVATOR   *n* pl. **-S** one that elevates

ELEVEN   *n* pl. **-S** a number

ELEVENTH   *n* pl. **-S** one of eleven equal parts

ELEVON   *n* pl. **-S** a type of airplane control surface

ELF   *n* pl. **ELVES** a small, often mischievous fairy **ELFLIKE** *adj*

ELFIN   *n* pl. **-S** an elf

ELFISH   *adj* resembling an elf **ELFISHLY** *adv*

ELFLOCK   *n* pl. **-S** a lock of tangled hair

ELHI   *adj* pertaining to school grades 1 through 12

ELICIT   *v* **-ED, -ING, -S** to educe

ELICITOR   *n* pl. **-S** one that elicits

ELIDE   *v* **ELIDED, ELIDING, ELIDES** to omit **ELIDIBLE** *adj*

ELIGIBLE   *n* pl. **-S** one that is qualified to be chosen

ELIGIBLY   *adv* in a qualified manner

ELINT   *n* pl. **-S** the gathering of intelligence by electronic devices

ELISION   *n* pl. **-S** the act of eliding

ELITE   *n* pl. **-S** a socially superior group

ELITISM   *n* pl. **-S** belief in rule by an elite

ELITIST   *n* pl. **-S** an adherent of elitism

ELIXIR   *n* pl. **-S** a medicinal beverage

ELK   *n* pl. **-S** a large deer

ELKHOUND   *n* pl. **-S** a hunting dog

ELL   *n* pl. **-S** the letter L

ELLIPSE   *n* pl. **-S** a type of plane curve

ELLIPSIS   *n* pl. **-LIPSES** an omission of a word or words in a sentence

ELLIPTIC   *adj* having the shape of an ellipse

ELM   *n* pl. **-S** a deciduous tree

ELMWOOD   *n* pl. **-S** the wood of an elm

ELMY   *adj* **-MIER, -MIEST** abounding in elms

ELODEA   *n* pl. **-S** an aquatic herb

ELOIGN   *v* **-ED, -ING, -S** to remove to a distant place

ELOIGNER   *n* pl. **-S** one that eloigns

ELOIN   *v* **-ED, -ING, -S** to eloign

ELOINER   *n* pl. **-S** one that eloins

ELONGATE	*v* **-GATED, -GATING, -GATES** to lengthen
ELOPE	*v* **ELOPED, ELOPING, ELOPES** to run off secretly to be married
ELOPER	*n* pl. **-S** one that elopes
ELOQUENT	*adj* fluent and convincing in speech
ELSE	*adv* in a different place, time, or way
ELUANT	*n* pl. **-S** a solvent
ELUATE	*n* pl. **-S** the material obtained by eluting
ELUDE	*v* **ELUDED, ELUDING, ELUDES** to evade
ELUDER	*n* pl. **-S** one that eludes
ELUENT	*n* pl. **-S** eluant
ELUSION	*n* pl. **-S** the act of eluding
ELUSIVE	*adj* tending to elude
ELUSORY	*adj* elusive
ELUTE	*v* **ELUTED, ELUTING, ELUTES** to remove by means of a solvent
ELUTION	*n* pl. **-S** the act of eluting
ELUVIA	a pl. of eluvium
ELUVIAL	*adj* pertaining to an eluvium
ELUVIATE	*v* **-ATED, -ATING, -ATES** to undergo a transfer of materials in the soil
ELUVIUM	*n* pl. **-VIUMS** or **-VIA** a soil deposit
ELVEN	*adj* resembling an elf
ELVER	*n* pl. **-S** a young eel
ELVES	pl. of elf
ELVISH	*adj* elfish **ELVISHLY** *adv*
ELYSIAN	*adj* delightful
ELYTRON	*n* pl. **-TRA** a hardened forewing of certain insects **ELYTROID, ELYTROUS** *adj*
ELYTRUM	*n* pl. **-TRA** elytron
EM	*n* pl. **-S** the letter M
EMACIATE	*v* **-ATED, -ATING, -ATES** to make thin
EMAIL	*v* **-ED, -ING, -S** to send a message to by computer
EMANANT	*adj* issuing from a source
EMANATE	*v* **-NATED, -NATING, -NATES** to send forth
EMANATOR	*n* pl. **-S** one that emanates
EMBALM	*v* **-ED, -ING, -S** to treat so as to protect from decay
EMBALMER	*n* pl. **-S** one that embalms

EMBANK	*v* **-ED, -ING, -S** to confine or protect with a raised structure
EMBAR	*v* **-BARRED, -BARRING, -BARS** to imprison
EMBARGO	*v* **-ED, -ING, -ES** to restrain trade by a governmental order
EMBARK	*v* **-ED, -ING, -S** to make a start
EMBASSY	*n* pl. **-SIES** the headquarters of an ambassador
EMBATTLE	*v* **-TLED, -TLING, -TLES** to prepare for battle
EMBAY	*v* **-ED, -ING, -S** to enclose in a bay
EMBED	*v* **-BEDDED, -BEDDING, -BEDS** to fix firmly into a surrounding mass
EMBER	*n* pl. **-S** a glowing fragment from a fire
EMBEZZLE	*v* **-ZLED, -ZLING, -ZLES** to appropriate fraudulently to one's own use
EMBITTER	*v* **-ED, -ING, -S** to make bitter
EMBLAZE	*v* **-BLAZED, -BLAZING, -BLAZES** to set on fire
EMBLAZER	*n* pl. **-S** one that emblazes
EMBLAZON	*v* **-ED, -ING, -S** to decorate with brilliant colors
EMBLEM	*v* **-ED, -ING, -S** to represent with an emblem (a graphical symbol)
EMBODIER	*n* pl. **-S** one that embodies
EMBODY	*v* **-BODIED, -BODYING, -BODIES** to provide with a body
EMBOLDEN	*v* **-ED, -ING, -S** to instill with courage
EMBOLI	pl. of embolus
EMBOLIES	pl. of emboly
EMBOLISM	*n* pl. **-S** the obstruction of a blood vessel by an embolus **EMBOLIC** *adj*
EMBOLUS	*n* pl. **-LI** an abnormal particle circulating in the blood
EMBOLY	*n* pl. **-LIES** a phase of embryonic growth
EMBORDER	*v* **-ED, -ING, -S** to provide with a border
EMBOSK	*v* **-ED, -ING, -S** to conceal with foliage
EMBOSOM	*v* **-ED, -ING, -S** to embrace
EMBOSS	*v* **-ED, -ING, -ES** to decorate with raised designs
EMBOSSER	*n* pl. **-S** one that embosses
EMBOW	*v* **-ED, -ING, -S** to arch

EMBOWEL *v* **-ELED, -ELING, -ELS** or **-ELLED, -ELLING, -ELS** to disbowel

EMBOWER *v* **-ED, -ING, -S** to surround with foliage

EMBRACE *v* **-BRACED, -BRACING, -BRACES** to hug

EMBRACER *n* pl. **-S** one that embraces

EMBROIL *v* **-ED, -ING, -S** to involve in conflict

EMBROWN *v* **-ED, -ING, -S** to make brown

EMBRUE *v* **-BRUED, -BRUING, -BRUES** to imbrue

EMBRUTE *v* **-BRUTED, -BRUTING, -BRUTES** to imbrute

EMBRYO *n* pl. **-BRYOS** an organism in its early stages of development

EMBRYOID *n* pl. **-S** a mass of tissue that resembles an embryo

EMBRYON *n* pl. **-S** an embryo

EMCEE *v* **-CEED, -CEEING, -CEES** to serve as master of ceremonies

EMDASH *n* pl. **-ES** a mark in writing that indicates a break in thought or structure

EME *n* pl. **-S** an uncle

EMEER *n* pl. **-S** emir

EMEERATE *n* pl. **-S** emirate

EMEND *v* **-ED, -ING, -S** to correct

EMENDATE *v* **-DATED, -DATING, -DATES** to emend

EMENDER *n* pl. **-S** one that emends

EMERALD *n* pl. **-S** a green gem

EMERG *n* pl. **-S** the section of a hospital that deals with emergencies

EMERGE *v* **EMERGED, EMERGING, EMERGES** to come out into view

EMERGENT *n* pl. **-S** a type of aquatic plant

EMERIES pl. of emery

EMERITA *n* pl. **-TAS** or **-TAE** a retired woman who retains an honorary title

EMERITUS *n* pl. **-TI** a retired person who retains an honorary title

EMEROD *n* pl. **-S** a tumor

EMEROID *n* pl. **-S** emerod

EMERSED *adj* standing out of water

EMERSION *n* pl. **-S** the act of emerging

EMERY *n* pl. **-ERIES** a granular corundum

EMESIS *n* pl. **EMESES** the act of vomiting

EMETIC *n* pl. **-S** a substance which induces vomiting

EMETIN *n* pl. **-S** emetine

EMETINE *n* pl. **-S** an alkaloid

EMEU *n* pl. **-S** emu

EMEUTE *n* pl. **-S** a riot

EMICS *n/pl* a type of linguistic analysis **EMIC** *adj*

EMIGRANT *n* pl. **-S** one that emigrates

EMIGRATE *v* **-GRATED, -GRATING, -GRATES** to leave one country or region to settle in another

EMIGRE *n* pl. **-S** an emigrant

EMINENCE *n* pl. **-S** high station or rank

EMINENCY *n* pl. **-CIES** eminence

EMINENT *adj* of high station or rank

EMIR *n* pl. **-S** an Arab chieftain or prince

EMIRATE *n* pl. **-S** the rank of an emir

EMISSARY *n* pl. **-SARIES** a person sent on a mission

EMISSION *n* pl. **-S** the act of emitting **EMISSIVE** *adj*

EMIT *v* **EMITTED, EMITTING, EMITS** to send forth

EMITTER *n* pl. **-S** one that emits

EMMER *n* pl. **-S** a type of wheat

EMMET *n* pl. **-S** an ant

EMO *n* pl. **EMOS** a style of rock music with emotional lyrics

EMOCORE *n* pl. **-S** emo

EMODIN *n* pl. **-S** a chemical compound

EMOJI *n* pl. **-S** a small computer symbol used to express emotion

EMOTE *v* **EMOTED, EMOTING, EMOTES** to express emotion in an exaggerated manner

EMOTER *n* pl. **-S** one that emotes

EMOTICON *n* pl. **-S** a group of keyboard characters used to suggest a facial expression or an emotion

EMOTION *n* pl. **-S** an affective state of consciousness

EMOTIVE *adj* pertaining to emotion

EMPALE *v* **-PALED, -PALING, -PALES** to impale

EMPALER *n* pl. **-S** one that empales

EMPANADA *n* pl. **-S** a pastry turnover

EMPANEL *v* **-ELED, -ELING, -ELS** or **-ELLED, -ELLING, -ELS** to impanel

EMPATHY	*n* pl. **-THIES** imaginative identification with another's thoughts and feelings **EMPATHIC** *adj*
EMPEROR	*n* pl. **-S** the ruler of an empire
EMPERY	*n* pl. **-PERIES** absolute dominion
EMPHASIS	*n* pl. **-PHASES** special significance imparted to something
EMPHATIC	*adj* strongly expressive
EMPIRE	*n* pl. **-S** a major political unit
EMPIRIC	*n* pl. **-S** one who relies on practical experience
EMPLACE	*v* **-PLACED, -PLACING, -PLACES** to position
EMPLANE	*v* **-PLANED, -PLANING, -PLANES** to enplane
EMPLOY	*v* **-ED, -ING, -S** to hire
EMPLOYE	*n* pl. **-S** employee
EMPLOYEE	*n* pl. **-S** a person who is employed
EMPLOYER	*n* pl. **-S** one that employs
EMPOISON	*v* **-ED, -ING, -S** to embitter
EMPORIUM	*n* pl. **-RIUMS** or **-RIA** a trading or market center
EMPOWER	*v* **-ED, -ING, -S** to give legal power to
EMPRESS	*n* pl. **-ES** a female ruler of an empire
EMPRISE	*n* pl. **-S** an adventurous undertaking
EMPRIZE	*n* pl. **-S** emprise
EMPTIED	past tense of empty
EMPTIER	*n* pl. **-S** one that empties
EMPTIES	present 3d person sing. of empty
EMPTIEST	superlative of empty
EMPTILY	*adv* in an empty manner
EMPTINGS	*n/pl* emptins
EMPTINS	*n/pl* a liquid leavening
EMPTY	*adj* **-TIER, -TIEST** containing nothing
EMPTY	*v* **-TIED, -TYING, -TIES** to remove the contents of
EMPURPLE	*v* **-PLED, -PLING, -PLES** to tinge with purple
EMPYEMA	*n* pl. **-EMAS** or **-EMATA** a collection of pus in a body cavity **EMPYEMIC** *adj*
EMPYREAL	*adj* pertaining to the sky
EMPYREAN	*n* pl. **-S** the highest heaven
EMU	*n* pl. **-S** a large, flightless bird
EMULATE	*v* **-LATED, -LATING, -LATES** to try to equal or surpass
EMULATOR	*n* pl. **-S** one that emulates
EMULOUS	*adj* eager to equal or surpass another
EMULSIFY	*v* **-FIED, -FYING, -FIES** to make into an emulsion
EMULSION	*n* pl. **-S** a type of liquid mixture **EMULSIVE** *adj*
EMULSOID	*n* pl. **-S** a liquid dispersed in another liquid
EMYD	*n* pl. **-S** a freshwater tortoise
EMYDE	*n* pl. **-S** emyd
EN	*n* pl. **-S** the letter N
ENABLE	*v* **-BLED, -BLING, -BLES** to make possible
ENABLER	*n* pl. **-S** one that enables
ENACT	*v* **-ED, -ING, -S** to make into a law
ENACTION	*n* pl. **-S** the action of enacting
ENACTIVE	*adj* having the power to enact
ENACTOR	*n* pl. **-S** one that enacts
ENACTORY	*adj* pertaining to the enactment of law
ENAMEL	*v* **-ELED, -ELING, -ELS** or **-ELLED, -ELLING, -ELS** to cover with a hard, glossy surface
ENAMELER	*n* pl. **-S** one that enamels
ENAMINE	*n* pl. **-S** a type of amine
ENAMOR	*v* **-ED, -ING, -S** to inspire with love
ENAMOUR	*v* **-ED, -ING, -S** to enamor
ENATE	*n* pl. **-S** a relative on the mother's side **ENATIC** *adj*
ENATION	*n* pl. **-S** an outgrowth from the surface of an organ
ENCAENIA	*n/pl* annual university ceremonies
ENCAGE	*v* **-CAGED, -CAGING, -CAGES** to confine in a cage
ENCAMP	*v* **-ED, -ING, -S** to set up a camp
ENCASE	*v* **-CASED, -CASING, -CASES** to enclose in a case
ENCASH	*v* **-ED, -ING, -ES** to cash
ENCEINTE	*n* pl. **-S** an encircling fortification
ENCHAIN	*v* **-ED, -ING, -S** to bind with chains
ENCHANT	*v* **-ED, -ING, -S** to delight
ENCHASE	*v* **-CHASED, -CHASING, -CHASES** to place in an ornamental setting
ENCHASER	*n* pl. **-S** one that enchases

ENCHORIC *adj* belonging to a particular country

ENCINA *n* pl. **-S** an evergreen oak **ENCINAL** *adj*

ENCIPHER *v* **-ED, -ING, -S** to write in characters of hidden meaning

ENCIRCLE *v* **-CLED, -CLING, -CLES** to form a circle around

ENCLASP *v* **-ED, -ING, -S** to embrace

ENCLAVE *v* **-CLAVED, -CLAVING, -CLAVES** to enclose within a foreign territory

ENCLITIC *n* pl. **-S** a word pronounced as part of the preceding word

ENCLOSE *v* **-CLOSED, -CLOSING, -CLOSES** to close in on all sides

ENCLOSER *n* pl. **-S** one that encloses

ENCODE *v* **-CODED, -CODING, -CODES** to put into code

ENCODER *n* pl. **-S** one that encodes

ENCOMIUM *n* pl. **-MIUMS** or **-MIA** a eulogy

ENCORE *v* **-CORED, -CORING, -CORES** to call for the reappearance of a performer

ENCROACH *v* **-ED, -ING, -ES** to advance beyond the proper limits

ENCRUST *v* **-ED, -ING, -S** to cover with a crust

ENCRYPT *v* **-ED, -ING, -S** to encipher

ENCUMBER *v* **-ED, -ING, -S** to hinder in action or movement

ENCYCLIC *n* pl. **-S** a letter addressed by the pope to the bishops of the world

ENCYST *v* **-ED, -ING, -S** to enclose in a cyst

END *v* **-ED, -ING, -S** to terminate

ENDAMAGE *v* **-AGED, -AGING, -AGES** to damage

ENDAMEBA *n* pl. **-BAS** or **-BAE** a parasitic ameba

ENDANGER *v* **-ED, -ING, -S** to imperil

ENDARCH *adj* formed from the center outward

ENDARCHY *n* pl. **-CHIES** the condition of being endarch

ENDASH *n* pl. **-ES** a mark in writing used to connect elements of a compound

ENDBRAIN *n* pl. **-S** a part of the brain

ENDCAP *n* pl. **-S** a display of products at the end of an aisle in a store

ENDEAR *v* **-ED, -ING, -S** to make dear or beloved

ENDEAVOR *v* **-ED, -ING, -S** to make an effort

ENDEMIAL *adj* peculiar to a country or people

ENDEMIC *n* pl. **-S** an endemial disease

ENDEMISM *n* pl. **-S** the state of being endemial

ENDER *n* pl. **-S** one that ends something

ENDERMIC *adj* acting by absorption through the skin

ENDEXINE *n* pl. **-S** an inner layer of the exine

ENDGAME *n* pl. **-S** the last stage of a chess game

ENDING *n* pl. **-S** a termination

ENDITE *v* **-DITED, -DITING, -DITES** to indite

ENDIVE *n* pl. **-S** an herb cultivated as a salad plant

ENDLEAF *n* pl. **-LEAVES** or **-LEAFS** an endpaper

ENDLESS *adj* enduring forever

ENDLONG *adv* lengthwise

ENDMOST *adj* farthest

ENDNOTE *n* pl. **-S** a note placed at the end of the text

ENDOCARP *n* pl. **-S** the inner layer of a pericarp

ENDOCAST *n* pl. **-S** a cast of the cranial cavity

ENDODERM *n* pl. **-S** the innermost germ layer of an embryo

ENDOGAMY *n* pl. **-MIES** marriage within a particular group

ENDOGEN *n* pl. **-S** a type of plant

ENDOGENY *n* pl. **-NIES** growth from within

ENDOPOD *n* pl. **-S** a branch of a crustacean limb

ENDORSE *v* **-DORSED, -DORSING, -DORSES** to sign the back of a negotiable document

ENDORSEE *n* pl. **-S** one to whom a document is transferred by endorsement

ENDORSER *n* pl. **-S** one that endorses

ENDORSOR *n* pl. **-S** endorser

ENDOSARC *n* pl. **-S** a portion of a cell

ENDOSMOS *n* pl. **-ES** a form of osmosis

ENDOSOME *n* pl. **-S** a cellular particle

ENDOSTEA *n/pl* bone membranes

ENDOW *v* **-ED, -ING, -S** to provide with something

ENDOWER *n* pl. **-S** one that endows

ENDOZOIC *adj* involving passage through an animal

ENDPAPER *n* pl. **-S** a sheet of paper used in bookbinding

ENDPLATE *n* pl. **-S** a type of nerve terminal

ENDPLAY *v* **-ED, -ING, -S** to force (an opponent in bridge) to lead

ENDPOINT *n* pl. **-S** either of two points that mark the end of a line segment

ENDRIN *n* pl. **-S** an insecticide

ENDUE *v* **-DUED, -DUING, -DUES** to provide with some quality or gift

ENDURE *v* **-DURED, -DURING, -DURES** to last

ENDURER *n* pl. **-S** one that endures

ENDURO *n* pl. **-DUROS** a long race

ENDWAYS *adv* endwise

ENDWISE *adv* lengthwise

ENEMA *n* pl. **-MAS** or **-MATA** a liquid injected into the rectum

ENEMY *n* pl. **-MIES** one that is antagonistic toward another

ENERGID *n* pl. **-S** a nucleus and the body of cytoplasm with which it interacts

ENERGIES pl. of energy

ENERGISE *v* **-GISED, -GISING, -GISES** to energize

ENERGIZE *v* **-GIZED, -GIZING, -GIZES** to give energy to

ENERGY *n* **-GIES** the capacity for vigorous activity

ENERVATE *v* **-VATED, -VATING, -VATES** to deprive of strength or vitality

ENFACE *v* **-FACED, -FACING, -FACES** to write on the front of

ENFEEBLE *v* **-BLED, -BLING, -BLES** to make feeble

ENFEOFF *v* **-ED, -ING, -S** to invest with a feudal estate

ENFETTER *v* **-ED, -ING, -S** to enchain

ENFEVER *v* **-ED, -ING, -S** to fever

ENFILADE *v* **-LADED, -LADING, -LADES** to direct heavy gunfire along the length of

ENFLAME *v* **-FLAMED, -FLAMING, -FLAMES** to inflame

ENFOLD *v* **-ED, -ING, -S** to envelop

ENFOLDER *n* pl. **-S** one that enfolds

ENFORCE *v* **-FORCED, -FORCING, -FORCES** to compel obedience to

ENFORCER *n* pl. **-S** one that enforces

ENFRAME *v* **-FRAMED, -FRAMING, -FRAMES** to frame

ENG *n* pl. **-S** a phonetic symbol

ENGAGE *v* **-GAGED, -GAGING, -GAGES** to employ

ENGAGER *n* pl. **-S** one that engages

ENGENDER *v* **-ED, -ING, -S** to bring into existence

ENGILD *v* **-ED, -ING, -S** to brighten

ENGINE *v* **-GINED, -GINING, -GINES** to equip with machinery

ENGINEER *v* **-ED, -ING, -S** to carry through or manage by contrivance

ENGINERY *n* pl. **-RIES** machinery

ENGINING present participle of engine

ENGINOUS *adj* ingenious

ENGIRD *v* **-GIRT** or **-GIRDED, -GIRDING, -GIRDS** to gird

ENGIRDLE *v* **-DLED, -DLING, -DLES** to engird

ENGLISH *v* **-ED, -ING, -ES** to cause a billiard ball to spin around its vertical axis

ENGLUT *v* **-GLUTTED, -GLUTTING, -GLUTS** to gulp down

ENGORGE *v* **-GORGED, -GORGING, -GORGES** to fill with blood

ENGRAFT *v* **-ED, -ING, -S** to graft for propagation

ENGRAIL *v* **-ED, -ING, -S** to ornament the edge of with curved indentations

ENGRAIN *v* **-ED, -ING, -S** to ingrain

ENGRAM *n* pl. **-S** the durable mark caused by a stimulus upon protoplasm

ENGRAMME *n* pl. **-S** engram

ENGRAVE *v* **-GRAVED, -GRAVING, -GRAVES** to form by incision

ENGRAVER *n* pl. **-S** one that engraves

ENGROSS *v* **-ED, -ING, -ES** to occupy completely

ENGULF *v* **-ED, -ING, -S** to surround completely

ENHALO *v* **-ED, -ING, -S** or **-ES** to surround with a halo

ENHANCE *v* **-HANCED, -HANCING, -HANCES** to raise to a higher degree

ENHANCER *n* pl. **-S** one that enhances

ENIGMA *n* pl. **-MAS** or **-MATA** something that is hard to understand or explain

ENISLE *v* **-ISLED, -ISLING, -ISLES** to isolate

ENJAMB *v* **-ED, -ING, -S** to continue a sentence from one line of a poem to the next

ENJOIN *v* **-ED, -ING, -S** to command

ENJOINER *n* pl. **-S** one that enjoins

ENJOY *v* **-ED, -ING, -S** to receive pleasure from

ENJOYER *n* pl. **-S** one that enjoys

ENKINDLE *v* **-DLED, -DLING, -DLES** to set on fire

ENLACE *v* **-LACED, -LACING, -LACES** to bind with laces

ENLARGE *v* **-LARGED, -LARGING, -LARGES** to make or become larger

ENLARGER *n* pl. **-S** a device used to enlarge photographs

ENLIST *v* **-ED, -ING, -S** to engage for military service

ENLISTEE *n* pl. **-S** one that is enlisted

ENLISTER *n* pl. **-S** one that enlists

ENLIVEN *v* **-ED, -ING, -S** to make lively

ENMESH *v* **-ED, -ING, -ES** to ensnare or entangle in a net

ENMITY *n* pl. **-TIES** hostility

ENNEAD *n* pl. **-S** a group of nine **ENNEADIC** *adj*

ENNEAGON *n* pl. **-S** a nonagon

ENNOBLE *v* **-BLED, -BLING, -BLES** to make noble

ENNOBLER *n* pl. **-S** one that ennobles

ENNUI *n* pl. **-S** a feeling of weariness and discontent

ENNUYE *adj* oppressed with ennui

ENNUYEE *adj* ennuye

ENOKI *n* pl. **-S** a small mushroom

ENOL *n* pl. **-S** a chemical compound **ENOLIC** *adj*

ENOLASE *n* pl. **-S** an enzyme

ENOLOGY *n* pl. **-GIES** oenology

ENOPHILE *n* pl. **-S** oenophile

ENORM *adj* enormous

ENORMITY *n* pl. **-TIES** great wickedness

ENORMOUS *adj* huge

ENOSIS *n* pl. **-SISES** union

ENOUGH *n* pl. **-S** a sufficient supply

ENOUNCE *v* **ENOUNCED, ENOUNCING, ENOUNCES** to announce

ENOW *n* pl. **-S** enough

ENPLANE *v* **-PLANED, -PLANING, -PLANES** to board an airplane

ENQUIRE *v* **-QUIRED, -QUIRING, -QUIRES** to inquire

ENQUIRER *n* pl. **-S** one that inquires

ENQUIRY *n* pl. **-RIES** inquiry

ENRAGE *v* **-RAGED, -RAGING, -RAGES** to make very angry

ENRAPT *adj* rapt

ENRAVISH *v* **-ED, -ING, -ES** to delight greatly

ENRICH *v* **-ED, -ING, -ES** to add desirable elements to

ENRICHER *n* pl. **-S** one that enriches

ENROBE *v* **-ROBED, -ROBING, -ROBES** to dress

ENROBER *n* pl. **-S** one that enrobes

ENROL *v* **-ROLLED, -ROLLING, -ROLS** to enroll

ENROLL *v* **-ED, -ING, -S** to enter the name of in a register, record, or roll

ENROLLEE *n* pl. **-S** one that is enrolled

ENROLLER *n* pl. **-S** one that enrolls

ENROLLING present participle of enrol

ENROOT *v* **-ED, -ING, -S** to implant

ENS *n* pl. **ENTIA** an entity

ENSAMPLE *n* pl. **-S** an example

ENSCONCE *v* **-SCONCED, -SCONCING, -SCONCES** to settle securely or comfortably

ENSCROLL *v* **-ED, -ING, -S** to write on a scroll

ENSEMBLE *n* pl. **-S** a group of complementary parts

ENSERF *v* **-ED, -ING, -S** to make a serf of

ENSHEATH *v* **-ED, -ING, -S** to enclose in a sheath

ENSHRINE *v* **-SHRINED, -SHRINING, -SHRINES** to place in a shrine

ENSHROUD *v* **-ED, -ING, -S** to conceal

ENSIFORM *adj* sword-shaped

ENSIGN *n* pl. **-S** a navy officer

ENSIGNCY *n* pl. **-CIES** the rank of an ensign

ENSILAGE *v* **-LAGED, -LAGING, -LAGES** to ensile

ENSILE *v* **-SILED, -SILING, -SILES** to store in a silo

ENSKY *v* **-SKIED** or **-SKYED, -SKYING, -SKIES** to raise to the skies

ENSLAVE *v* **-SLAVED, -SLAVING, -SLAVES** to make a slave of

ENSLAVER *n* pl. **-S** one that enslaves

ENSNARE *v* **-SNARED, -SNARING, -SNARES** to trap

ENSNARER *n* pl. **-S** one that ensnares

ENSNARL *v* **-ED, -ING, -S** to tangle

ENSORCEL *v* **-ED, -ING, -S** to bewitch

ENSOUL *v* **-ED, -ING, -S** to endow with a soul

ENSPHERE *v* **-SPHERED, -SPHERING, -SPHERES** to enclose in a sphere

ENSUE *v* **-SUED, -SUING, -SUES** to occur afterward or as a result

ENSUITE *n* pl. **-S** a room (as a bathroom) adjoining another room

ENSURE *v* **-SURED, -SURING, -SURES** to make certain

ENSURER *n* pl. **-S** one that ensures

ENSWATHE *v* **-SWATHED, -SWATHING, -SWATHES** to swathe

ENTAIL *v* **-ED, -ING, -S** to restrict the inheritance of to a specified line of heirs

ENTAILER *n* pl. **-S** one that entails

ENTAMEBA *n* pl. **-BAS** or **-BAE** endameba

ENTANGLE *v* **-TANGLED, -TANGLING, -TANGLES** to tangle

ENTASIA *n* pl. **-S** spasmodic contraction of a muscle

ENTASIS *n* pl. **-TASES** a slight convexity in a column **ENTASTIC** *adj*

ENTELLUS *n* pl. **-ES** a hanuman

ENTENTE *n* pl. **-S** an agreement between nations

ENTER *v* **-ED, -ING, -S** to come or go into

ENTERA a pl. of enteron

ENTERAL *adj* enteric

ENTERER *n* pl. **-S** one that enters

ENTERIC *adj* pertaining to the enteron

ENTERICS *n/pl* a family of bacteria

ENTERON *n* pl. **-TERONS** or **-TERA** the alimentary canal

ENTHALPY *n* pl. **-PIES** a thermodynamic measure of heat

ENTHETIC *adj* introduced from outside

ENTHRAL *v* **-THRALLED, -THRALLING, -THRALS** to enthrall

ENTHRALL *v* **-ED, -ING, -S** to charm

ENTHRONE *v* **-THRONED, -THRONING, -THRONES** to place on a throne

ENTHUSE *v* **-THUSED, -THUSING, -THUSES** to show enthusiasm

ENTIA pl. of ens

ENTICE *v* **-TICED, -TICING, -TICES** to allure

ENTICER *n* pl. **-S** one that entices

ENTIRE *n* pl. **-S** the whole of something

ENTIRELY *adv* completely

ENTIRETY *n* pl. **-TIES** completeness

ENTITLE *v* **-TLED, -TLING, -TLES** to give a title to

ENTITY *n* pl. **-TIES** something that has a real existence

ENTODERM *n* pl. **-S** endoderm

ENTOIL *v* **-ED, -ING, -S** to entrap

ENTOMB *v* **-ED, -ING, -S** to place in a tomb

ENTOPIC *adj* situated in the normal place

ENTOZOA pl. of entozoon

ENTOZOAL *adj* entozoic

ENTOZOAN *n* pl. **-S** an entozoic parasite

ENTOZOIC *adj* living within an animal

ENTOZOON *n* pl. **-ZOA** entozoan

ENTRAILS *n/pl* the internal organs

ENTRAIN *v* **-ED, -ING, -S** to board a train

ENTRANCE *v* **-TRANCED, -TRANCING, -TRANCES** to fill with delight or wonder

ENTRANT *n* pl. **-S** one that enters

ENTRAP *v* **-TRAPPED, -TRAPPING, -TRAPS** to trap

ENTREAT *v* **-ED, -ING, -S** to ask for earnestly

ENTREATY *n* pl. **-TREATIES** an earnest request

ENTREE *n* pl. **-S** the principal dish of a meal

ENTRENCH *v* **-ED, -ING, -ES** to establish firmly

ENTREPOT *n* pl. **-S** a warehouse

ENTRESOL *n* pl. **-S** a mezzanine

ENTRIES pl. of entry

ENTROPY *n* pl. **-PIES** a thermodynamic measure of disorder **ENTROPIC** *adj*

ENTRUST *v* **-ED, -ING, -S** to give over for safekeeping

ENTRY *n* pl. **-TRIES** a place of entrance

ENTRYWAY *n* pl. **-WAYS** a passage serving as an entrance

ENTWINE *v* **-TWINED, -TWINING, -TWINES** to twine around

ENTWIST *v* **-ED, -ING, -S** to twist together

ENURE *v* **-URED, -URING, -URES** to inure

ENURESIS *n* pl. **-RESES** involuntary urination

ENURETIC *n* pl. **-S** one who is affected with enuresis

ENVELOP *v* **-ED, -ING, -S** to cover completely

ENVELOPE *n* pl. **-S** a paper container

ENVENOM *v* **-ED, -ING, -S** to put venom into

ENVIABLE *adj* desirable **ENVIABLY** *adv*

ENVIED past tense of envy

ENVIER *n* pl. **-S** one that envies

ENVIES present 3d person sing. of envy

ENVIOUS *adj* resentful and desirous of another's possessions or qualities

ENVIRO *n* pl. **-ROS** an advocate for the preservation of the natural environment

ENVIRON *v* **-ED, -ING, -S** to encircle

ENVISAGE *v* **-AGED, -AGING, -AGES** to form a mental image of

ENVISION *v* **-ED, -ING, -S** to envisage

ENVOI *n* pl. **-S** the closing of a poem or prose work

ENVOY *n* pl. **-VOYS** a representative

ENVY *v* **-VIED, -VYING, -VIES** to be envious of

ENWHEEL *v* **-ED, -ING, -S** to encircle

ENWIND *v* **-WOUND, -WINDING, -WINDS** to wind around

ENWOMB *v* **-ED, -ING, -S** to enclose as if in a womb

ENWRAP *v* **-WRAPPED, -WRAPPING, -WRAPS** to envelop

ENZOOTIC *n* pl. **-S** a type of animal disease

ENZYM *n* pl. **-S** enzyme

ENZYME *n* pl. **-S** a complex protein **ENZYMIC** *adj*

EOBIONT *n* pl. **-S** a type of basic organism

EOHIPPUS *n* pl. **-ES** an extinct horse

EOLIAN *adj* pertaining to the wind

EOLIPILE *n* pl. **-S** a type of engine

EOLITH *n* pl. **-S** a prehistoric stone tool **EOLITHIC** *adj*

EOLOPILE *n* pl. **-S** eolipile

EON *n* pl. **-S** an indefinitely long period of time

EONIAN *adj* everlasting

EONISM *n* pl. **-S** adoption of the dress and mannerisms of the opposite sex

EOSIN *n* pl. **-S** a red dye **EOSINIC** *adj*

EOSINE *n* pl. **-S** eosin

EPACT *n* pl. **-S** the difference between the lengths of the solar and lunar years

EPARCH *n* pl. **-S** the head of an eparchy

EPARCHY *n* pl. **-CHIES** a district of modern Greece

EPATER *v* **-ED, -ING, -S** to shock complacent people

EPAULET *n* pl. **-S** a shoulder ornament

EPAZOTE *n* pl. **-S** an herb of the goosefoot family

EPEE *n* pl. **-S** a type of sword

EPEEIST *n* pl. **-S** one who fences with an epee

EPEIRIC *adj* pertaining to vertical movement of the earth's crust

EPENDYMA *n* pl. **-S** a membrane lining certain body cavities

EPERGNE *n* pl. **-S** an ornamental dish

EPHA *n* pl. **-S** ephah

EPHAH *n* pl. **-S** a Hebrew unit of dry measure

EPHEBE *n* pl. **-S** ephebus **EPHEBIC** *adj*

EPHEBOS *n* pl. **-BOI** ephebus

EPHEBUS *n* pl. **-BI** a young man of ancient Greece

EPHEDRA *n* pl. **-S** a desert shrub

EPHEDRIN *n* pl. **-S** an alkaloid used to treat allergies

EPHEMERA *n* pl. **-ERAS** or **-ERAE** something of very short life or duration

EPHOD *n* pl. **-S** an ancient Hebrew vestment

EPHOR *n* pl. **-ORS** or **-ORI** a magistrate of ancient Greece **EPHORAL** *adj*

EPHORATE *n* pl. **-S** the office of ephor

EPIBLAST *n* pl. **-S** the ectoderm

EPIBOLY *n* pl. **-LIES** the growth of one part around another **EPIBOLIC** *adj*

EPIC *n* pl. **-S** a long narrative poem **EPICAL** *adj* **EPICALLY** *adv*

EPICALYX *n* pl. **-LYXES** or **-LYCES** a set of bracts close to and resembling a calyx

EPICARP *n* pl. **-S** the outer layer of a pericarp

EPICEDIA *n/pl* funeral songs

EPICENE *n* pl. **-S** one having both male and female characteristics

EPICLIKE *adj* resembling an epic

EPICOTYL *n* pl. **-S** a part of a plant embryo

EPICURE   *n* pl. **-S** a gourmet

EPICYCLE   *n* pl. **-S** a circle that rolls on the circumference of another circle

EPIDEMIC   *n* pl. **-S** a rapid spread of a disease

EPIDERM   *n* pl. **-S** the outer layer of skin

EPIDOTE   *n* pl. **-S** a mineral **EPIDOTIC** *adj*

EPIDURAL   *n* pl. **-S** an injection to produce loss of sensation

EPIFAUNA   *n* pl. **-FAUNAS** or **-FAUNAE** fauna living on a hard sea floor

EPIFOCAL   *adj* pertaining to the point of origin of an earthquake

EPIGEAL   *adj* epigeous

EPIGEAN   *adj* epigeous

EPIGEIC   *adj* epigeous

EPIGENE   *adj* occurring near the surface of the earth

EPIGENIC   *adj* pertaining to change in the mineral character of a rock

EPIGEOUS   *adj* growing on or close to the ground

EPIGON   *n* pl. **-S** epigone

EPIGONE   *n* pl. **-S** an inferior imitator **EPIGONIC** *adj*

EPIGONUS   *n* pl. **-NI** epigone

EPIGRAM   *n* pl. **-S** a brief, witty remark

EPIGRAPH   *n* pl. **-S** an engraved inscription

EPIGYNY   *n* pl. **-NIES** the state of having floral organs near the top of the ovary

EPILATE   *v* **-LATED, -LATING, -LATES** to remove hair from

EPILATOR   *n* pl. **-S** an agent for removing hair

EPILEPSY   *n* pl. **-SIES** a disorder of the nervous system

EPILOG   *n* pl. **-S** a concluding section

EPILOGUE   *v* **-LOGUED, -LOGUING, -LOGUES** to provide with a concluding section

EPIMER   *n* pl. **-S** a type of sugar compound **EPIMERIC** *adj*

EPIMERE   *n* pl. **-S** a part of an embryo

EPIMYSIA   *n/pl* muscle sheaths

EPINAOS   *n* pl. **-NAOI** a rear vestibule

EPINASTY   *n* pl. **-TIES** a downward bending of plant parts

EPIPHANY   *n* pl. **-NIES** an appearance of a deity

EPIPHYTE   *n* pl. **-S** a plant growing upon another plant

EPISCIA   *n* pl. **-S** a tropical herb

EPISCOPE   *n* pl. **-S** a type of projector

EPISODE   *n* pl. **-S** an incident in the course of a continuous experience **EPISODIC** *adj*

EPISOME   *n* pl. **-S** a genetic determinant **EPISOMAL** *adj*

EPISTASY   *n* pl. **-SIES** a suppression of genetic effect

EPISTLE   *n* pl. **-S** a long or formal letter

EPISTLER   *n* pl. **-S** one that writes epistles

EPISTOME   *n* pl. **-S** a structure covering the mouth of various invertebrates

EPISTYLE   *n* pl. **-S** a part of a classical building

EPITAPH   *n* pl. **-S** an inscription on a tomb

EPITASIS   *n* pl. **-ASES** the main part of a classical drama

EPITAXY   *n* pl. **-TAXIES** a type of crystalline growth **EPITAXIC** *adj*

EPITHET   *n* pl. **-S** a term used to characterize a person or thing

EPITOME   *n* pl. **-S** a typical or ideal example **EPITOMIC** *adj*

EPITOPE   *n* pl. **-S** a region on the surface of an antigen

EPIZOA   pl. of epizoon

EPIZOIC   *adj* living on the body of an animal

EPIZOISM   *n* pl. **-S** the state of being epizoic

EPIZOITE   *n* pl. **-S** an epizoic organism

EPIZOON   *n* pl. **-ZOA** an epizoic parasite

EPIZOOTY   *n* pl. **-TIES** a type of animal disease

EPOCH   *n* pl. **-S** a particular period of time **EPOCHAL** *adj*

EPODE   *n* pl. **-S** a type of poem

EPONYM   *n* pl. **-S** the person for whom something is named **EPONYMIC** *adj*

EPONYMY   *n* pl. **-MIES** the derivation of an eponymic name

EPOPEE   *n* pl. **-S** an epic poem

EPOPOEIA   *n* pl. **-S** epopee

EPOS   *n* pl. **-ES** an epic poem

EPOXIDE   *n* pl. **-S** an epoxy compound

EPOXY   *v* **EPOXIED** or **EPOXYED, EPOXYING, EPOXIES** to glue with epoxy (a type of resin)

EPSILON	*n* pl. **-S** a Greek letter
EQUABLE	*adj* not changing or varying greatly **EQUABLY** *adv*
EQUAL	*adj* having the same capability, quantity, or effect as another
EQUAL	*v* **EQUALED, EQUALING, EQUALS** or **EQUALLED, EQUALLING, EQUALS** to be equal to
EQUALISE	*v* **-ISED, -ISING, -ISES** to equalize
EQUALITY	*n* pl. **-TIES** the state of being equal
EQUALIZE	*v* **-IZED, -IZING, -IZES** to make equal
EQUALLED	a past tense of equal
EQUALLING	a present participle of equal
EQUALLY	*adv* in an equal manner
EQUATE	*v* **EQUATED, EQUATING, EQUATES** to make equal
EQUATION	*n* pl. **-S** the act of equating
EQUATIVE	*adj* denoting a sentence in which one term is identified with another
EQUATOR	*n* pl. **-S** a great circle of spherical celestial bodies
EQUERRY	*n* pl. **-RIES** an officer in charge of the care of horses
EQUES	*n* pl. **EQUITES** a member of a privileged military class of ancient Rome
EQUID	*n* pl. **-S** an animal of the horse family
EQUINE	*n* pl. **-S** a horse
EQUINELY	*adv* in a horselike manner
EQUINITY	*n* pl. **-TIES** the state of being like a horse
EQUINOX	*n* pl. **-ES** a point on the celestial sphere
EQUIP	*v* **EQUIPPED, EQUIPPING, EQUIPS** to provide with whatever is needed
EQUIPAGE	*n* pl. **-S** a carriage
EQUIPPER	*n* pl. **-S** one that equips
EQUISETA	*n/pl* rushlike plants
EQUITANT	*adj* overlapping
EQUITES	pl. of eques
EQUITY	*n* pl. **-TIES** fairness or impartiality
EQUIVOKE	*n* pl. **-S** a play on words
ER	*interj* — used to express hesitation
ERA	*n* pl. **-S** an epoch
ERADIATE	*v* **-ATED, -ATING, -ATES** to radiate

ERASE	*v* **ERASED, ERASING, ERASES** to rub or scrape out **ERASABLE** *adj*
ERASER	*n* pl. **-S** one that erases
ERASION	*n* pl. **-S** an erasure
ERASURE	*n* pl. **-S** the act of erasing
ERBIUM	*n* pl. **-S** a metallic element
ERE	*prep* previous to; before
ERECT	*v* **-ED, -ING, -S** to build
ERECTER	*n* pl. **-S** erector
ERECTILE	*adj* capable of being raised upright
ERECTION	*n* pl. **-S** the act of erecting
ERECTIVE	*adj* tending to erect
ERECTLY	*adv* in an upright manner
ERECTOR	*n* pl. **-S** one that erects
ERELONG	*adv* soon
EREMITE	*n* pl. **-S** a hermit **EREMITIC** *adj*
EREMURUS	*n* pl. **-URUSES** or **-URI** a perennial herb
ERENOW	*adv* before this time
EREPSIN	*n* pl. **-S** a mixture of enzymes in the small intestine
ERETHISM	*n* pl. **-S** abnormal irritability **ERETHIC** *adj*
EREWHILE	*adv* some time ago
ERG	*n* pl. **-S** a unit of work or energy
ERGASTIC	*adj* constituting the nonliving by-products of protoplasmic activity
ERGATE	*n* pl. **-S** a worker ant
ERGATIVE	*n* pl. **-S** a type of verb
ERGO	*conj* therefore
ERGODIC	*adj* pertaining to the probability that any state will recur
ERGOT	*n* pl. **-S** a fungus **ERGOTIC** *adj*
ERGOTISM	*n* pl. **-S** poisoning produced by eating ergot-infected grain
ERICA	*n* pl. **-S** a shrub of the heath family
ERICOID	*adj* resembling heath
ERIGERON	*n* pl. **-S** an herb
ERINGO	*n* pl. **-GOS** or **-GOES** eryngo
ERISTIC	*n* pl. **-S** an expert in debate
ERLKING	*n* pl. **-S** an evil spirit of Germanic folklore
ERMINE	*n* pl. **-S** the fur of certain weasels **ERMINED** *adj*
ERN	*n* pl. **-S** erne
ERNE	*n* pl. **-S** a sea eagle

ERODABLE	*adj* erosible
ERODE	*v* **ERODED, ERODING, ERODES** to wear away by constant friction
ERODENT	*adj* erosive
ERODIBLE	*adj* erosible
EROGENIC	*adj* arousing sexual desire
EROS	*n* pl. **-ES** sexual desire
EROSE	*adj* uneven **EROSELY** *adv*
EROSIBLE	*adj* capable of being eroded
EROSION	*n* pl. **-S** the act of eroding
EROSIVE	*adj* causing erosion
EROTIC	*n* pl. **-S** an amatory poem **EROTICAL** *adj*
EROTICA	*n/pl* literature or art dealing with sexual love
EROTISM	*n* pl. **-S** sexual excitement
EROTIZE	*v* **-TIZED, -TIZING, -TIZES** to give a sexual meaning to
ERR	*v* **-ED, -ING, -S** to make a mistake **ERRABLE** *adj*
ERRANCY	*n* pl. **-CIES** an instance of erring
ERRAND	*n* pl. **-S** a short trip made for a particular purpose
ERRANT	*n* pl. **-S** a wanderer
ERRANTLY	*adv* in a wandering manner
ERRANTRY	*n* pl. **-RIES** the state of wandering
ERRATA	*n* pl. **-S** a list of printing errors
ERRATIC	*n* pl. **-S** an eccentric person
ERRATUM	*n* pl. **-TA** a printing error
ERRHINE	*n* pl. **-S** a substance that promotes nasal discharge
ERRINGLY	*adv* in a mistaken manner
ERROR	*n* pl. **-S** a mistake
ERS	*n* pl. **-ES** ervil
ERSATZ	*n* pl. **-ES** a substitute
ERST	*adv* formerly
ERUCT	*v* **-ED, -ING, -S** to belch
ERUCTATE	*v* **-TATED, -TATING, -TATES** to eruct
ERUDITE	*adj* scholarly
ERUGO	*n* pl. **-GOS** aerugo
ERUMPENT	*adj* bursting forth
ERUPT	*v* **-ED, -ING, -S** to burst forth
ERUPTION	*n* pl. **-S** the act of erupting
ERUPTIVE	*n* pl. **-S** a type of rock
ERUV	*n* pl. **ERUVIM** or **ERUVS** an enclosed area in which Jews are permitted to carry on activities normally forbidden on the Sabbath
ERVIL	*n* pl. **-S** a European vetch
ERYNGIUM	*n* pl. **-S** a plant of the parsley family
ERYNGO	*n* pl. **-GOS** or **-GOES** a medicinal herb
ERYTHEMA	*n* pl. **-S** a redness of the skin
ERYTHRON	*n* pl. **-S** a bodily organ consisting of the red blood cells
ES	*n* pl. **ESES** ess
ESCALADE	*v* **-LADED, -LADING, -LADES** to enter by means of ladders
ESCALATE	*v* **-LATED, -LATING, -LATES** to increase
ESCALLOP	*v* **-ED, -ING, -S** to scallop
ESCALOP	*v* **-ED, -ING, -S** to escallop
ESCALOPE	*n* pl. **-S** a thin slice of meat or fish
ESCAPADE	*n* pl. **-S** a reckless adventure
ESCAPE	*v* **-CAPED, -CAPING, -CAPES** to get away
ESCAPEE	*n* pl. **-S** one that has escaped
ESCAPER	*n* pl. **-S** one that escapes
ESCAPISM	*n* pl. **-S** the avoidance of reality by diversion of the mind
ESCAPIST	*n* pl. **-S** one given to escapism
ESCAR	*n* pl. **-S** esker
ESCARGOT	*n* pl. **-S** an edible snail
ESCAROLE	*n* pl. **-S** a variety of endive
ESCARP	*v* **-ED, -ING, -S** to cause to slope steeply
ESCHALOT	*n* pl. **-S** a shallot
ESCHAR	*n* pl. **-S** a hard, dry scab
ESCHEAT	*v* **-ED, -ING, -S** to confiscate
ESCHEW	*v* **-ED, -ING, -S** to avoid
ESCHEWAL	*n* pl. **-S** the act of eschewing
ESCHEWER	*n* pl. **-S** one that avoids something
ESCOLAR	*n* pl. **-S** a food fish
ESCORT	*v* **-ED, -ING, -S** to accompany
ESCOT	*v* **-ED, -ING, -S** to provide support for
ESCROW	*v* **-ED, -ING, -S** to place in the custody of a third party
ESCUAGE	*n* pl. **-S** scutage
ESCUDO	*n* pl. **-DOS** a former monetary unit of Portugal
ESCULENT	*n* pl. **-S** something that is edible

ESERINE	*n* pl. **-S** a toxic alkaloid
ESKAR	*n* pl. **-S** esker
ESKER	*n* pl. **-S** a narrow ridge of gravel and sand
ESNE	*n* pl. **-S** a laborer in Anglo-Saxon England
ESOPHAGI	*n/pl* tubes connecting the mouth to the stomach
ESOTERIC	*adj* designed for a select few
ESPALIER	*v* **-ED, -ING, -S** to furnish with a trellis
ESPANOL	*n* pl. **-ES** a native of Spain
ESPARTO	*n* pl. **-TOS** a perennial grass
ESPECIAL	*adj* special
ESPIAL	*n* pl. **-S** the act of espying
ESPIED	past tense of espy
ESPIEGLE	*adj* playful
ESPIES	present 3d person sing. of espy
ESPOIR	*n* pl. **-S** a category of wrestlers
ESPOUSAL	*n* pl. **-S** a marriage ceremony
ESPOUSE	*v* **-POUSED, -POUSING, -POUSES** to marry
ESPOUSER	*n* pl. **-S** one that espouses
ESPRESSO	*n* pl. **-SOS** a strong coffee
ESPRIT	*n* pl. **-S** spirit
ESPY	*v* **-PIED, -PYING, -PIES** to catch sight of
ESQUIRE	*v* **-QUIRED, -QUIRING, -QUIRES** to escort
ESS	*n* pl. **-ES** the letter S
ESSAY	*v* **-ED, -ING, -S** to try
ESSAYER	*n* pl. **-S** one that essays
ESSAYIST	*n* pl. **-S** a writer of essays (prose compositions)
ESSE	*n* pl. **-S** essential nature
ESSENCE	*n* pl. **-S** a fundamental nature or quality
ESSOIN	*n* pl. **-S** an excuse
ESSONITE	*n* pl. **-S** a variety of garnet
EST	*n* pl. **-S** a group technique for raising self-awareness
ESTANCIA	*n* pl. **-S** a cattle ranch
ESTATE	*v* **-TATED, -TATING, -TATES** to provide with landed property
ESTEEM	*v* **-ED, -ING, -S** to have a high opinion of
ESTER	*n* pl. **-S** a type of chemical compound
ESTERASE	*n* pl. **-S** a type of enzyme
ESTERIFY	*v* **-FIED, -FYING, -FIES** to convert into an ester
ESTHESIA	*n* pl. **-S** the ability to receive sensation
ESTHESIS	*n* pl. **-THESISES** or **-THESES** esthesia
ESTHETE	*n* pl. **-S** an esthetic person
ESTHETIC	*n* pl. **-S** a conception of beauty
ESTIMATE	*v* **-MATED, -MATING, -MATES** to make an approximate judgment of
ESTIVAL	*adj* pertaining to summer
ESTIVATE	*v* **-VATED, -VATING, -VATES** to spend the summer
ESTOP	*v* **-TOPPED, -TOPPING, -TOPS** to impede by estoppel
ESTOPPEL	*n* pl. **-S** a legal restraint preventing a person from contradicting his or her own previous statement
ESTOVERS	*n/pl* necessities allowed by law
ESTRAGON	*n* pl. **-S** tarragon
ESTRAL	*adj* estrous
ESTRANGE	*v* **-TRANGED, -TRANGING, -TRANGES** to alienate
ESTRAY	*v* **-ED, -ING, -S** to stray
ESTREAT	*v* **-ED, -ING, -S** to copy from court records for use in prosecution
ESTRIN	*n* pl. **-S** estrone
ESTRIOL	*n* pl. **-S** an estrogen
ESTROGEN	*n* pl. **-S** a female sex hormone promoting or producing estrus
ESTRONE	*n* pl. **-S** an estrogen
ESTROUS	*adj* pertaining to estrus
ESTRUAL	*adj* estrous
ESTRUM	*n* pl. **-S** estrus
ESTRUS	*n* pl. **-ES** the period of heat in female mammals
ESTUARY	*n* pl. **-ARIES** an inlet of the sea at a river's lower end
ESURIENT	*adj* greedy
ET	a past tense of eat
ETA	*n* pl. **-S** a Greek letter
ETAGERE	*n* pl. **-S** an ornamental stand
ETALON	*n* pl. **-S** an optical instrument
ETAMIN	*n* pl. **-S** etamine
ETAMINE	*n* pl. **-S** a loosely woven fabric
ETAPE	*n* pl. **-S** a warehouse
ETATISM	*n* pl. **-S** state socialism **ETATIST** *adj*

ETCETERA n pl. **-S** a number of additional items

ETCH v **-ED, -ING, -ES** to engrave with acid

ETCHANT n pl. **-S** a substance used in etching

ETCHER n pl. **-S** one that etches

ETCHING n pl. **-S** an etched design

ETERNAL n pl. **-S** something lasting forever

ETERNE adj everlasting

ETERNISE v **-NISED, -NISING, -NISES** to eternize

ETERNITY n pl. **-TIES** infinite time

ETERNIZE v **-NIZED, -NIZING, -NIZES** to make everlasting

ETESIAN n pl. **-S** an annually recurring wind

ETH n pl. **-S** edh

ETHANAL n pl. **-S** a volatile liquid compound

ETHANE n pl. **-S** a gaseous hydrocarbon

ETHANOL n pl. **-S** an alcohol

ETHENE n pl. **-S** ethylene

ETHEPHON n pl. **-S** a synthetic plant growth regulator

ETHER n pl. **-S** a volatile liquid used as an anesthetic **ETHERIC** adj

ETHEREAL adj airy

ETHERIFY v **-FIED, -FYING, -FIES** to convert into ether

ETHERISE v **-ISED, -ISING, -ISES** to etherize

ETHERISH adj resembling ether

ETHERIZE v **-IZED, -IZING, -IZES** to treat with ether

ETHIC n pl. **-S** a body of moral principles

ETHICAL n pl. **-S** a drug sold by prescription only

ETHICIAN n pl. **-S** an ethicist

ETHICIST n pl. **-S** a specialist in ethics

ETHICIZE v **-CIZED, -CIZING, -CIZES** to make ethical

ETHINYL n pl. **-S** ethynyl

ETHION n pl. **-S** a pesticide

ETHMOID n pl. **-S** a bone of the nasal cavity

ETHNARCH n pl. **-S** the ruler of a people or province

ETHNIC n pl. **-S** a member of a particular ethnos **ETHNICAL** adj

ETHNONYM n pl. **-S** the name of an ethnic group

ETHNOS n pl. **-ES** a group of people who share a common and distinctive culture

ETHOGRAM n pl. **-S** a list of the behavior patterns of a species

ETHOLOGY n pl. **-GIES** the study of animal behavior

ETHOS n pl. **-ES** the fundamental character of a culture

ETHOXY n pl. **-OXIES** ethoxyl

ETHOXYL n pl. **-S** a univalent chemical radical

ETHYL n pl. **-S** a univalent chemical radical

ETHYLATE v **-ATED, -ATING, -ATES** to introduce the ethyl group into

ETHYLENE n pl. **-S** a flammable gas

ETHYLIC adj pertaining to ethyl

ETHYNE n pl. **-S** a flammable gas

ETHYNYL n pl. **-S** a univalent chemical radical

ETICS n/pl a type of linguistic analysis **ETIC** adj

ETIOLATE v **-LATED, -LATING, -LATES** to whiten

ETIOLOGY n pl. **-GIES** the study of the causes of diseases

ETNA n pl. **-S** a container for heating liquids

ETOILE n pl. **-S** a star

ETOUFFEE n pl. **-S** a Cajun stew

ETRIER n pl. **-S** a short rope ladder

ETUDE n pl. **-S** a piece of music for the practice of a point of technique

ETUI n pl. **-S** a case for holding small articles

ETWEE n pl. **-S** etui

ETYMON n pl. **-MONS** or **-MA** the earliest known form of a word

EUCAINE n pl. **-S** an anesthetic

EUCALYPT n pl. **-S** an evergreen tree

EUCHARIS n pl. **-RISES** a flowering plant

EUCHRE v **-CHRED, -CHRING, -CHRES** to prevent from winning three tricks in euchre (a card game)

EUCLASE n pl. **-S** a mineral

EUCRITE n pl. **-S** a type of meteorite **EUCRITIC** adj

EUDAEMON n pl. **-S** eudemon

EUDAIMON n pl. **-S** eudemon

EUDEMON   *n* pl. **-S** a good spirit

EUGENIA   *n* pl. **-S** a tropical evergreen tree

EUGENICS   *n/pl* the science of hereditary improvement **EUGENIC** *adj*

EUGENIST   *n* pl. **-S** a student of eugenics

EUGENOL   *n* pl. **-S** an aromatic liquid

EUGLENA   *n* pl. **-S** a freshwater protozoan

EUGLENID   *n* pl. **-S** a euglena

EULACHAN   *n* pl. **-S** eulachon

EULACHON   *n* pl. **-S** a marine food fish

EULOGIA   *n* pl. **-GIAE** holy bread

EULOGIA   *n* pl. **-S** a blessing

EULOGIES   pl. of eulogy

EULOGISE   *v* **-GISED, -GISING, -GISES** to eulogize

EULOGIST   *n* pl. **-S** one that eulogizes

EULOGIUM   *n* pl. **-GIUMS** or **-GIA** a eulogy

EULOGIZE   *v* **-GIZED, -GIZING, -GIZES** to praise highly

EULOGY   *n* pl. **-GIES** a formal expression of high praise

EUNUCH   *n* pl. **-S** a castrated man

EUONYMUS   *n* pl. **-ES** any of a genus of shrubs or small trees

EUPATRID   *n* pl. **-RIDS** or **-RIDAE** an aristocrat of ancient Athens

EUPEPSIA   *n* pl. **-S** good digestion **EUPEPTIC** *adj*

EUPEPSY   *n* pl. **-SIES** eupepsia

EUPHENIC   *adj* dealing with biological improvement

EUPHONY   *n* pl. **-NIES** pleasant sound **EUPHONIC** *adj*

EUPHORIA   *n* pl. **-S** a feeling of well-being **EUPHORIC** *adj*

EUPHOTIC   *adj* pertaining to the upper layer of a body of water

EUPHRASY   *n* pl. **-SIES** an annual herb

EUPHROE   *n* pl. **-S** a device used to adjust a shipboard awning

EUPHUISM   *n* pl. **-S** an artificially elegant style of speech or writing

EUPHUIST   *n* pl. **-S** one given to euphuism

EUPLOID   *n* pl. **-S** a cell having three or more identical genomes

EUPLOIDY   *n* pl. **-DIES** the state of being a euploid

EUPNEA   *n* pl. **-S** normal breathing **EUPNEIC** *adj*

EUPNOEA   *n* pl. **-S** eupnea **EUPNOEIC** *adj*

EUREKA   *n* pl. **-S** a fortunate discovery

EURIPUS   *n* pl. **-PI** a swift sea channel

EURO   *n* pl. **EUROS** the unit of currency used by most European countries

EUROKY   *n* pl. **-KIES** the ability of an organism to live under variable conditions **EUROKOUS** *adj*

EUROLAND   *n* pl. **-S** the eurozone

EUROPIUM   *n* pl. **-S** a metallic element

EUROZONE   *n* pl. **-S** the area formed by the countries using the euro

EURYBATH   *n* pl. **-S** an organism that can live in a wide range of water depths

EURYOKY   *n* pl. **-KIES** euroky

EURYTHMY   *n* pl. **-MIES** harmony of movement or structure

EUSOCIAL   *adj* pertaining to an animal society marked by specialization of tasks

EUSTACY   *n* pl. **-CIES** a worldwide change in sea level **EUSTATIC** *adj*

EUSTASY   *n* pl. **-SIES** eustacy

EUSTELE   *n* pl. **-S** a plant part

EUSTRESS   *n* pl. **-ES** a form of stress that is beneficial to one's health or well-being

EUTAXY   *n* pl. **-TAXIES** good order

EUTECTIC   *n* pl. **-S** an alloy that has the lowest possible melting point

EUTROPHY   *n* pl. **-PHIES** healthful nutrition

EUXENITE   *n* pl. **-S** a mineral

EVACUANT   *n* pl. **-S** a cathartic medicine

EVACUATE   *v* **-ATED, -ATING, -ATES** to remove from a dangerous area

EVACUEE   *n* pl. **-S** one that is evacuated

EVADE   *v* **EVADED, EVADING, EVADES** to escape or avoid by cleverness or deceit **EVADABLE, EVADIBLE** *adj*

EVADER   *n* pl. **-S** one that evades

EVALUATE   *v* **-ATED, -ATING, -ATES** to determine the value of

EVANESCE   *v* **-NESCED, -NESCING, -NESCES** to fade away

EVANGEL   *n* pl. **-S** a preacher of the gospel

EVANISH   *v* **-ED, -ING, -ES** to vanish

EVASION   *n* pl. **-S** the act of evading

EVASIVE   *adj* tending to evade

EVE   *n* pl. **-S** evening

EVECTION   *n* pl. **-S** irregularity in the moon's motion

EVEN   *adj* **EVENER, EVENEST** flat and smooth

EVEN   *v* **-ED, -ING, -S** to make even

EVENER   *n* pl. **-S** one that evens

EVENFALL   *n* pl. **-S** twilight

EVENING   *n* pl. **-S** the latter part of the day and early part of the night

EVENLY   *adv* in an even manner

EVENNESS   *n* pl. **-ES** the state of being even

EVENSONG   *n* pl. **-S** an evening prayer service

EVENT   *n* pl. **-S** something that occurs

EVENTER   *n* pl. **-S** a horse or rider competing in eventing

EVENTFUL   *adj* momentous

EVENTIDE   *n* pl. **-S** evening

EVENTING   *n* pl. **-S** an equestrian competition

EVENTIVE   *adj* denoting an event

EVENTUAL   *adj* occurring at a later time

EVER   *adv* at all times

EVERMORE   *adv* forever

EVERSION   *n* pl. **-S** the act of everting

EVERT   *v* **-ED, -ING, -S** to turn outward or inside out

EVERTOR   *n* pl. **-S** a muscle that turns a part outward

EVERY   *adj* each without exception

EVERYDAY   *n* pl. **-S** the routine day

EVERYMAN   *n* pl. **-MEN** the typical or ordinary man

EVERYONE   *pron* every person

EVERYWAY   *adv* in every way

EVICT   *v* **-ED, -ING, -S** to expel by legal process

EVICTEE   *n* pl. **-S** one that is evicted

EVICTION   *n* pl. **-S** the act of evicting

EVICTOR   *n* pl. **-S** one that evicts

EVIDENCE   *v* **-DENCED, -DENCING, -DENCES** to indicate clearly

EVIDENT   *adj* clear to the vision or understanding

EVIL   *adj* **EVILER, EVILEST** or **EVILLER, EVILLEST** morally bad

EVIL   *n* pl. **-S** something that is evil

EVILDOER   *n* pl. **-S** one that does evil

EVILLY   *adv* in an evil manner

EVILNESS   *n* pl. **-ES** the quality of being evil

EVINCE   *v* **EVINCED, EVINCING, EVINCES** to show clearly **EVINCIVE** *adj*

EVITE   *v* **EVITED, EVITING, EVITES** to avoid **EVITABLE** *adj*

EVOCABLE   *adj* capable of being evoked

EVOCATOR   *n* pl. **-S** one that evokes

EVOKE   *v* **EVOKED, EVOKING, EVOKES** to call forth

EVOKER   *n* pl. **-S** an evocator

EVOLUTE   *n* pl. **-S** a type of geometric curve

EVOLVE   *v* **EVOLVED, EVOLVING, EVOLVES** to develop

EVOLVER   *n* pl. **-S** one that evolves

EVONYMUS   *n* pl. **-ES** euonymus

EVULSE   *v* **EVULSED, EVULSING, EVULSES** to extract forcibly

EVULSION   *n* pl. **-S** the act of pulling out

EVZONE   *n* pl. **-S** a Greek soldier

EW   *interj* — used to express disgust

EWE   *n* pl. **-S** a female sheep

EWER   *n* pl. **-S** a large pitcher

EX   *v* **-ED, -ING, -ES** to cross out

EXABYTE   *n* pl. **-S** one quintillion bytes

EXACT   *adj* **-ACTER, -ACTEST** precise

EXACT   *v* **-ED, -ING, -S** to force the payment or yielding of

EXACTA   *n* pl. **-S** a type of horse racing bet

EXACTER   *n* pl. **-S** one that exacts

EXACTION   *n* pl. **-S** the act of exacting

EXACTLY   *adv* in an exact manner

EXACTOR   *n* pl. **-S** exacter

EXAHERTZ   *n* pl. **EXAHERTZ** one quintillion hertz

EXALT   *v* **-ED, -ING, -S** to raise

EXALTER   *n* pl. **-S** one that exalts

EXAM   *n* pl. **-S** an examination

EXAMEN   *n* pl. **-S** a critical study

EXAMINE   *v* **-INED, -INING, -INES** to inspect

EXAMINEE   *n* pl. **-S** one that is taking an examination

EXAMINER   *n* pl. **-S** one that examines

EXAMPLE   *v* **-PLED, -PLING, -PLES** to show by representation

EXANTHEM   *n* pl. **-S** a skin eruption

EXAPTED   *adj* utilized for a function other than the one developed through natural selection

EXAPTIVE   *adj* pertaining to an exapted function

EXARCH   *n* pl. **-S** the ruler of a province in the Byzantine Empire **EXARCHAL** *adj*

EXARCHY   *n* pl. **-CHIES** the domain of an exarch

EXCAVATE   *v* **-VATED, -VATING, -VATES** to dig out

EXCEED   *v* **-ED, -ING, -S** to go beyond

EXCEEDER   *n* pl. **-S** one that exceeds

EXCEL   *v* **-CELLED, -CELLING, -CELS** to surpass others

EXCEPT   *v* **-ED, -ING, -S** to leave out

EXCERPT   *v* **-ED, -ING, -S** to pick out a passage from for quoting

EXCESS   *v* **-ED, -ING, -ES** to eliminate the position of

EXCHANGE   *v* **-CHANGED, -CHANGING, -CHANGES** to give and receive reciprocally

EXCIDE   *v* **-CIDED, -CIDING, -CIDES** to excise

EXCIMER   *n* pl. **-S** a dimer that exists in an excited state

EXCIPLE   *n* pl. **-S** a rim around the hymenium of various lichens

EXCISE   *v* **-CISED, -CISING, -CISES** to remove by cutting out

EXCISION   *n* pl. **-S** the act of excising

EXCITANT   *n* pl. **-S** a stimulant

EXCITE   *v* **-CITED, -CITING, -CITES** to arouse the emotions of

EXCITER   *n* pl. **-S** one that excites

EXCITON   *n* pl. **-S** a phenomenon occurring in an excited crystal

EXCITOR   *n* pl. **-S** exciter

EXCLAIM   *v* **-ED, -ING, -S** to cry out suddenly

EXCLAVE   *n* pl. **-S** a portion of a country which is isolated in foreign territory

EXCLUDE   *v* **-CLUDED, -CLUDING, -CLUDES** to shut out

EXCLUDER   *n* pl. **-S** one that excludes

EXCRETA   *n/pl* excreted matter **EXCRETAL** *adj*

EXCRETE   *v* **-CRETED, -CRETING, -CRETES** to separate and eliminate from an organic body

EXCRETER   *n* pl. **-S** one that excretes

EXCURSUS   *n* pl. **-ES** a long appended exposition of a topic

EXCUSE   *v* **-CUSED, -CUSING, -CUSES** to apologize for

EXCUSER   *n* pl. **-S** one that excuses

EXEC   *n* pl. **-S** an executive officer

EXECRATE   *v* **-CRATED, -CRATING, -CRATES** to curse

EXECUTE   *v* **-CUTED, -CUTING, -CUTES** to carry out

EXECUTER   *n* pl. **-S** executor

EXECUTOR   *n* pl. **-S** one that executes

EXEDRA   *n* pl. **-DRAS** or **-DRAE** a curved outdoor bench

EXEGESIS   *n* pl. **-GESES** critical explanation or analysis **EXEGETIC** *adj*

EXEGETE   *n* pl. **-S** one skilled in exegesis

EXEMPLAR   *n* pl. **-S** one that is worthy of being copied

EXEMPLUM   *n* pl. **-PLA** an example

EXEMPT   *v* **-ED, -ING, -S** to free from an obligation required of others

EXEQUY   *n* pl. **-QUIES** a funeral procession **EXEQUIAL** *adj*

EXERCISE   *v* **-CISED, -CISING, -CISES** to make use of

EXERGUE   *n* pl. **-S** a space on a coin **EXERGUAL** *adj*

EXERT   *v* **-ED, -ING, -S** to put into action

EXERTION   *n* pl. **-S** the act of exerting

EXERTIVE   *adj* tending to exert

EXEUNT   *v* they leave the stage — used as a stage direction

EXHALANT   *n* pl. **-S** something that exhales

EXHALE   *v* **-HALED, -HALING, -HALES** to expel air or vapor

EXHALENT   *n* pl. **-S** exhalant

EXHAUST   *v* **-ED, -ING, -S** to use up

EXHEDRA   *n* pl. **-DRAE** exedra

EXHIBIT   *v* **-ED, -ING, -S** to present for public viewing

EXHORT   *v* **-ED, -ING, -S** to advise urgently

EXHORTER   *n* pl. **-S** one that exhorts

EXHUME   *v* **-HUMED, -HUMING, -HUMES** to dig out of the earth

EXHUMER   *n* pl. **-S** one that exhumes

EXIGENCE   *n* pl. **-S** exigency

EXIGENCY   *n* pl. **-CIES** urgency

EXIGENT   *adj* urgent

EXIGIBLE   *adj* liable to be demanded

EXIGUITY   *n* pl. **-ITIES** the state of being exiguous

EXIGUOUS   *adj* meager

EXILE   *v* **-ILED, -ILING, -ILES** to banish from one's own country **EXILABLE** *adj*

EXILER   *n* pl. **-S** one that exiles

EXILIAN   *adj* exilic

EXILIC   *adj* pertaining to exile (banishment from one's own country)

EXILING   present participle of exile

EXIMIOUS   *adj* excellent

EXINE   *n* pl. **-S** the outer layer of certain spores

EXIST   *v* **-ED, -ING, -S** to be

EXISTENT   *n* pl. **-S** something that exists

EXIT   *v* **-ED, -ING, -S** to go out

EXITLESS   *adj* lacking a way out

EXOCARP   *n* pl. **-S** the epicarp

EXOCRINE   *n* pl. **-S** an external secretion

EXOCYTIC   *adj* pertaining to cellular excretion

EXODERM   *n* pl. **-S** the ectoderm

EXODOS   *n* pl. **-DOI** a concluding dramatic scene

EXODUS   *n* pl. **-ES** a movement away

EXOERGIC   *adj* releasing energy

EXOGAMY   *n* pl. **-MIES** marriage outside of a particular group **EXOGAMIC** *adj*

EXOGEN   *n* pl. **-S** a type of plant

EXOGENIC   *adj* formed or occurring on the surface of the earth

EXOME   *n* pl. **-S** a part of the genome consisting of exons

EXON   *n* pl. **-S** a sequence in the genetic code **EXONIC** *adj*

EXONEREE   *n* pl. **-S** a person who is proven not guilty of a crime

EXONUMIA   *n/pl* collectible items other than coins or paper money

EXONYM   *n* pl. **-S** a name for a people used by outsiders and not by the people themselves

EXORABLE   *adj* persuadable

EXORCISE   *v* **-CISED, -CISING, -CISES** to free of an evil spirit

EXORCISM   *n* pl. **-S** the act of exorcising

EXORCIST   *n* pl. **-S** one who practices exorcism

EXORCIZE   *v* **-CIZED, -CIZING, -CIZES** to exorcise

EXORDIUM   *n* pl. **-DIUMS** or **-DIA** a beginning **EXORDIAL** *adj*

EXOSMOSE   *n* pl. **-S** a form of osmosis **EXOSMIC** *adj*

EXOSPORE   *n* pl. **-S** the outer coat of a spore

EXOTERIC   *adj* suitable for the public

EXOTIC   *n* pl. **-S** something from another part of the world

EXOTICA   *n/pl* things excitingly different or unusual

EXOTISM   *n* pl. **-S** an exotic

EXOTOXIN   *n* pl. **-S** an excreted toxin **EXOTOXIC** *adj*

EXPAND   *v* **-ED, -ING, -S** to increase in size or volume

EXPANDER   *n* pl. **-S** one that expands

EXPANDOR   *n* pl. **-S** a type of transducer

EXPANSE   *n* pl. **-S** a wide, continuous area

EXPAT   *n* pl. **-S** an expatriate person

EXPECT   *v* **-ED, -ING, -S** to anticipate

EXPECTER   *n* pl. **-S** one that expects

EXPEDITE   *v* **-DITED, -DITING, -DITES** to speed up the progress of

EXPEL   *v* **-PELLED, -PELLING, -PELS** to force out

EXPELLEE   *n* pl. **-S** a deportee

EXPELLER   *n* pl. **-S** one that expels

EXPEND   *v* **-ED, -ING, -S** to use up

EXPENDER   *n* pl. **-S** one that expends

EXPENSE   *v* **-PENSED, -PENSING, -PENSES** to charge with costs

EXPERT   *v* **-ED, -ING, -S** to serve as an authority

EXPERTLY   *adv* skillfully

EXPIABLE   *adj* capable of being expiated

EXPIATE   *v* **-ATED, -ATING, -ATES** to atone for

EXPIATOR   *n* pl. **-S** one that expiates

EXPIRE   *v* **-PIRED, -PIRING, -PIRES** to come to an end

EXPIRER   *n* pl. **-S** one that expires

EXPIRY   *n* pl. **-RIES** a termination

EXPLAIN   *v* **-ED, -ING, -S** to make plain or understandable

EXPLANT   *v* **-ED, -ING, -S** to remove from the natural site of growth and place in a medium

EXPLICIT   *n* pl. **-S** a statement formerly used at the close of a book

EXPLODE *v* **-PLODED, -PLODING, -PLODES** to blow up

EXPLODER *n* pl. **-S** one that explodes

EXPLOIT *v* **-ED, -ING, -S** to take advantage of

EXPLORE *v* **-PLORED, -PLORING, -PLORES** to travel through for the purpose of discovery

EXPLORER *n* pl. **-S** one that explores

EXPO *n* pl. **-POS** a public exhibition

EXPONENT *n* pl. **-S** one who expounds

EXPORT *v* **-ED, -ING, -S** to send to other countries for commercial purposes

EXPORTER *n* pl. **-S** one that exports

EXPOSAL *n* pl. **-S** an exposure

EXPOSE *v* **-POSED, -POSING, -POSES** to lay open to view

EXPOSER *n* pl. **-S** one that exposes

EXPOSIT *v* **-ED, -ING, -S** to expound

EXPOSURE *n* pl. **-S** the act of exposing

EXPOUND *v* **-ED, -ING, -S** to explain in detail

EXPRESS *v* **-ED, -ING, -ES** to set forth in words

EXPRESSO *n* pl. **-SOS** espresso

EXPULSE *v* **-PULSED, -PULSING, -PULSES** to expel

EXPUNGE *v* **-PUNGED, -PUNGING, -PUNGES** to delete

EXPUNGER *n* pl. **-S** one that expunges

EXSCIND *v* **-ED, -ING, -S** to cut out

EXSECANT *n* pl. **-S** a trigonometric function of an angle

EXSECT *v* **-ED, -ING, -S** to cut out

EXSERT *v* **-ED, -ING, -S** to thrust out

EXTANT *adj* still in existence

EXTEND *v* **-ED, -ING, -S** to stretch out to full length

EXTENDER *n* pl. **-S** a substance added to another substance

EXTENSOR *n* pl. **-S** a muscle that extends a limb

EXTENT *n* pl. **-S** the range over which something extends

EXTERIOR *n* pl. **-S** a part or surface that is outside

EXTERN *n* pl. **-S** a nonresident of an institution

EXTERNAL *n* pl. **-S** an exterior

EXTERNE *n* pl. **-S** extern

EXTINCT *v* **-ED, -ING, -S** to extinguish

EXTOL *v* **-TOLLED, -TOLLING, -TOLS** to praise highly

EXTOLL *v* **-ED, -ING, -S** to extol

EXTOLLER *n* pl. **-S** one that extols

EXTORT *v* **-ED, -ING, -S** to obtain from a person by violence or intimidation

EXTORTER *n* pl. **-S** one that extorts

EXTRA *n* pl. **-S** something additional

EXTRACT *v* **-ED, -ING, -S** to pull or draw out

EXTRADOS *n* pl. **-ES** the outer curve of an arch

EXTRANET *n* pl. **-S** an intranet that permits limited access by outsiders

EXTREMA pl. of extremum

EXTREME *adj* **-TREMER, -TREMEST** existing in a very high degree

EXTREME *n* pl. **-S** the highest degree

EXTREMUM *n* pl. **-MA** a maximum or a minimum of a mathematical function

EXTROPY *n* pl. **-PIES** the prediction that human intelligence will enable life to expand throughout the universe

EXTRORSE *adj* facing outward

EXTRUDE *v* **-TRUDED, -TRUDING, -TRUDES** to force, thrust, or push out

EXTRUDER *n* pl. **-S** one that extrudes

EXTUBATE *v* **-BATED, -BATING, -BATES** to remove a tube from

EXUDATE *n* pl. **-S** an exuded substance

EXUDE *v* **-UDED, -UDING, -UDES** to ooze forth

EXULT *v* **-ED, -ING, -S** to rejoice greatly

EXULTANT *adj* exulting

EXURB *n* pl. **-S** a residential area lying beyond the suburbs of a city **EXURBAN** *adj*

EXURBIA *n* pl. **-S** an exurb

EXUVIATE *v* **-ATED, -ATING, -ATES** to molt

EXUVIUM *n* pl. **-VIAE** or **-VIA** the molted covering of an animal **EXUVIAL** *adj*

EYAS *n* pl. **-ES** a young hawk

EYASS *n* pl. **-ES** eyas

EYE *n* pl. **EYES** or **EYEN** or **EYNE** the organ of sight

EYE *v* **EYED, EYING** or **EYEING, EYES** to watch closely **EYEABLE** *adj*

EYEBALL *v* **-ED, -ING, -S** to eye

EYEBAR   *n* pl. **-S** a metal bar with a loop at one or both ends

EYEBEAM   *n* pl. **-S** a glance

EYEBLACK   *n* pl. **-S** a dark pigment applied under the eyes

EYEBLINK   *n* pl. **-S** an instant

EYEBOLT   *n* pl. **-S** a type of bolt or screw

EYEBROW   *n* pl. **-S** the ridge over the eye

EYECUP   *n* pl. **-S** a cup used for applying lotions to the eyes

EYED   past tense of eye

EYEDNESS   *n* pl. **-ES** preference for the use of one eye over the other

EYEDROPS   *n/pl* a medicated solution for the eyes applied in drops

EYEFOLD   *n* pl. **-S** a fold of skin of the upper eyelid

EYEFUL   *n* pl. **-S** a complete view

EYEGLASS   *n* pl. **-ES** a lens used to aid vision

EYEHOLE   *n* pl. **-S** a small opening

EYEHOOK   *n* pl. **-S** a type of hook

EYELASH   *n* pl. **-ES** a hair growing on the edge of an eyelid

EYELESS   *adj* lacking eyes

EYELET   *v* **-LETTED, -LETTING, -LETS** or **-LETED, -LETING, -LETS** to make a small hole in

EYELID   *n* pl. **-S** the lid of skin that can be closed over an eyeball

EYELIFT   *n* pl. **-S** plastic surgery of the eyelid

EYELIKE   *adj* resembling an eye

EYELINER   *n* pl. **-S** makeup for the eyes

EYEN   a pl. of eye

EYEPATCH   *n* pl. **-ES** a patch worn to protect an injured eye

EYEPIECE   *n* pl. **-S** the lens or lens group nearest the eye in an optical instrument

EYEPOINT   *n* pl. **-S** the point at which an eye is placed in using an optical instrument

EYER   *n* pl. **-S** one that eyes

EYESHADE   *n* pl. **-S** a visor for shading the eyes

EYESHINE   *n* pl. **-S** a reflection from the eyes of some animals

EYESHOT   *n* pl. **-S** the range of vision

EYESIGHT   *n* pl. **-S** the ability to see

EYESOME   *adj* pleasant to look at

EYESORE   *n* pl. **-S** something offensive to the sight

EYESPOT   *n* pl. **-S** a simple visual organ of lower animals

EYESTALK   *n* pl. **-S** a stalklike structure with an eye at its tip

EYESTONE   *n* pl. **-S** a disk used to remove foreign matter from the eye

EYETOOTH   *n* pl. **-TEETH** a cuspid

EYEWASH   *n* pl. **-ES** an eye lotion

EYEWATER   *n* pl. **-S** an eyewash

EYEWEAR   *n* pl. **EYEWEAR** a device worn on or over the eyes

EYEWINK   *n* pl. **-S** a wink of the eye

EYING   a present participle of eye

EYNE   a pl. of eye

EYRA   *n* pl. **-S** a wild cat of tropical America

EYRE   *n* pl. **-S** a journey

EYRIE   *n* pl. **-S** aerie

EYRIR   *n* pl. **AURAR** a monetary unit of Iceland

EYRY   *n* pl. **-RIES** aerie

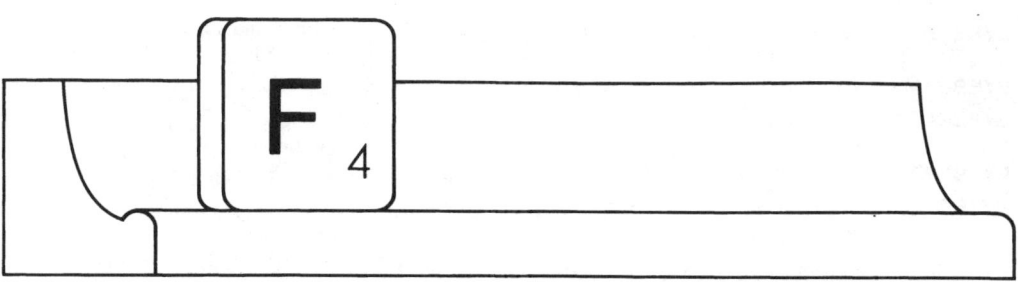

FA	*n* pl. **-S** the fourth tone of the diatonic musical scale
FAB	*n* pl. **-S** something created or constructed
FAB	*adj* **FABBER, FABBEST** fabulous
FABLE	*v* **-BLED, -BLING, -BLES** to compose or tell fictitious tales
FABLER	*n* pl. **-S** one that fables
FABLIAU	*n* pl. **-AUX** a short metrical tale popular in medieval France
FABLING	present participle of fable
FABRIC	*n* pl. **-S** a woven, felted, or knitted material
FABRIQUE	*n* pl. **-S** a parish group that deals with church property
FABULAR	*adj* legendary
FABULATE	*v* **-LATED, -LATING, -LATES** to compose fables
FABULISM	*n* pl. **-S** the placing of fantastical elements into everyday settings
FABULIST	*n* pl. **-S** a liar
FABULOUS	*adj* almost unbelievable
FACADE	*n* pl. **-S** the front of a building
FACE	*v* **FACED, FACING, FACES** to oppose or meet defiantly **FACEABLE** *adj*
FACEDOWN	*n* pl. **-S** a confrontation between opponents
FACELESS	*adj* lacking personal distinction or identity
FACELIFT	*v* **-ED, -ING, -S** to perform plastic surgery on the face
FACEMASK	*n* pl. **-S** a device to shield the face
FACEOFF	*n* pl. **-S** the action that starts a hockey game
FACEPALM	*v* **-ED, -ING, -S** to cover the face with the hand
FACER	*n* pl. **-S** one that faces
FACET	*v* **-ETED, -ETING, -ETS** or **-ETTED, -ETTING, -ETS** to cut small plane surfaces on
FACETE	*adj* witty **FACETELY** *adv*
FACETIAE	*n/pl* witty sayings or writings
FACETING	*n* pl. **-S** a surface of a cut gemstone
FACEUP	*adv* with the front part up
FACIA	*n* pl. **-CIAE** or **-CIAS** fascia
FACIAL	*n* pl. **-S** a treatment for the face
FACIALLY	*adv* with respect to the face
FACIEND	*n* pl. **-S** a number to be multiplied by another
FACIES	*n* pl. **FACIES** general appearance
FACILE	*adj* easily achieved or performed **FACILELY** *adv*
FACILITY	*n* pl. **-TIES** the quality of being facile
FACING	*n* pl. **-S** a lining at the edge of a garment
FACT	*n* pl. **-S** something known with certainty **FACTFUL** *adj*
FACTICE	*n* pl. **-S** a rubber-like material
FACTION	*n* pl. **-S** a clique within a larger group
FACTIOUS	*adj* promoting dissension
FACTOID	*n* pl. **-S** a brief news item
FACTOR	*v* **-ED, -ING, -S** to express as a product of two or more quantities
FACTORY	*n* pl. **-RIES** a building or group of buildings in which goods are manufactured
FACTOTUM	*n* pl. **-S** a person employed to do many kinds of work
FACTUAL	*adj* pertaining to facts
FACTUM	*n* pl. **-TUMS** or **-TA** a statement of the facts of a case being appealed
FACTURE	*n* pl. **-S** the act of making something

FACULA	*n* pl. **-LAE** an unusually bright spot on the sun's surface **FACULAR** *adj*
FACULTY	*n* pl. **-TIES** an inherent power or ability
FAD	*n* pl. **-S** a practice or interest that enjoys brief popularity
FADABLE	*adj* capable of fading
FADDIER	comparative of faddy
FADDIEST	superlative of faddy
FADDISH	*adj* inclined to take up fads
FADDISM	*n* pl. **-S** inclination to take up fads
FADDIST	*n* pl. **-S** a faddish person
FADDY	*adj* **-DIER, -DIEST** faddish
FADE	*v* **FADED, FADING, FADES** to lose color or brightness **FADEDLY** *adv*
FADEAWAY	*n* pl. **-AWAYS** a type of pitch in baseball
FADEIN	*n* pl. **-S** a gradual increase in the brightness of an image
FADELESS	*adj* not fading
FADEOUT	*n* pl. **-S** a gradual disappearance of an image
FADER	*n* pl. **-S** one that fades
FADGE	*v* **FADGED, FADGING, FADGES** to succeed
FADING	*n* pl. **-S** an Irish dance
FADLIKE	*adj* resembling a fad
FADO	*n* pl. **-DOS** a Portuguese folk song
FAECES	*n/pl* feces **FAECAL** *adj*
FAENA	*n* pl. **-S** a series of passes made by a matador in a bullfight
FAERIE	*n* pl. **-S** a fairy
FAERY	*n* pl. **-ERIES** faerie
FAFF	*v* **-ED, -ING, -S** to make a fuss
FAG	*v* **FAGGED, FAGGING, FAGS** to make weary by hard work
FAGGOT	*v* **-ED, -ING, -S** to fagot
FAGIN	*n* pl. **-S** a person who instructs others in crime
FAGOT	*v* **-ED, -ING, -S** to bind together into a bundle
FAGOTER	*n* pl. **-S** one that fagots
FAGOTING	*n* pl. **-S** a type of embroidery
FAH	*n* pl. **-S** fa
FAHLBAND	*n* pl. **-S** a band or stratum of rock impregnated with metallic sulfides
FAIENCE	*n* pl. **-S** a variety of glazed pottery

FAIL	*v* **-ED, -ING, -S** to be unsuccessful in an attempt
FAILING	*n* pl. **-S** a minor fault or weakness
FAILLE	*n* pl. **-S** a woven fabric
FAILURE	*n* pl. **-S** the act of failing
FAIN	*adj* **FAINER, FAINEST** glad
FAINEANT	*n* pl. **-S** a lazy person
FAINT	*adj* **FAINTER, FAINTEST** lacking strength or vigor
FAINT	*v* **-ED, -ING, -S** to lose consciousness
FAINTER	*n* pl. **-S** one that faints
FAINTISH	*adj* somewhat faint
FAINTLY	*adv* in a faint manner
FAIR	*adj* **FAIRER, FAIREST** free from bias, dishonesty, or injustice
FAIR	*v* **-ED, -ING, -S** to make smooth
FAIRGOER	*n* pl. **-S** one who attends a fair
FAIRIES	pl. of fairy
FAIRING	*n* pl. **-S** a structure on an aircraft serving to reduce drag
FAIRISH	*adj* moderately good
FAIRLEAD	*n* pl. **-S** a device used to hold a ship's rigging in place
FAIRLY	*adv* in a fair manner
FAIRNESS	*n* pl. **-ES** the quality of being fair
FAIRWAY	*n* pl. **-WAYS** the mowed part of a golf course between tee and green
FAIRY	*n* pl. **FAIRIES** an imaginary supernatural being
FAIRY	*adj* **FAIRIER, FAIRIEST** pertaining to or resembling a fairy
FAIRYISM	*n* pl. **-S** the quality of being like a fairy
FAITH	*v* **-ED, -ING, -S** to believe or trust
FAITHFUL	*n* pl. **-S** a loyal follower or member
FAITOUR	*n* pl. **-S** an impostor
FAJITA	*n* pl. **-S** marinated and grilled beef, chicken, or shrimp served with a flour tortilla
FAKE	*v* **FAKED, FAKING, FAKES** to contrive and present as genuine
FAKEER	*n* pl. **-S** fakir
FAKER	*n* pl. **-S** one that fakes
FAKERY	*n* pl. **-ERIES** the practice of faking
FAKEY	*adj* not genuine; phony
FAKIE	*n* pl. **-S** a movement in skateboarding and snowboarding
FAKING	present participle of fake

FAKIR   *n* pl. **-S** a Hindu ascetic

FALAFEL   *n* pl. **-S** ground spiced vegetables formed into patties

FALBALA   *n* pl. **-S** a trimming for a woman's garment

FALCATE   *adj* curved and tapering to a point

FALCATED   *adj* falcate

FALCES   pl. of falx

FALCHION   *n* pl. **-S** a broad-bladed sword

FALCON   *n* pl. **-S** a bird of prey

FALCONER   *n* pl. **-S** one that hunts with hawks

FALCONET   *n* pl. **-S** a small falcon

FALCONRY   *n* pl. **-RIES** the sport of hunting with falcons

FALDERAL   *n* pl. **-S** nonsense

FALDEROL   *n* pl. **-S** falderal

FALL   *v* **FELL, FALLEN, FALLING, FALLS** to descend under the force of gravity

FALLACY   *n* pl. **-CIES** a false idea

FALLAL   *n* pl. **-S** a showy article of dress

FALLAWAY   *n* pl. **-AWAYS** a shot in basketball

FALLBACK   *n* pl. **-S** an act of retreating

FALLEN   past participle of fall

FALLER   *n* pl. **-S** one that falls

FALLFISH   *n* pl. **-ES** a freshwater fish

FALLIBLE   *adj* capable of erring **FALLIBLY** *adv*

FALLING   *n* pl. **-S** the felling of trees for timber

FALLOFF   *n* pl. **-S** a decline in quantity or quality

FALLOUT   *n* pl. **-S** radioactive debris resulting from a nuclear explosion

FALLOW   *v* **-ED, -ING, -S** to plow and leave unseeded

FALSE   *adj* **FALSER, FALSEST** contrary to truth or fact **FALSELY** *adv*

FALSETTO   *n* pl. **-TOS** an artificially high voice

FALSIE   *n* pl. **-S** a pad worn within a brassiere

FALSIFY   *v* **-FIED, -FYING, -FIES** to represent falsely

FALSITY   *n* pl. **-TIES** something false

FALTBOAT   *n* pl. **-S** a collapsible boat resembling a kayak

FALTER   *v* **-ED, -ING, -S** to hesitate

FALTERER   *n* pl. **-S** one that falters

FALX   *n* pl. **FALCES** a sickle-shaped structure

FAME   *v* **FAMED, FAMING, FAMES** to make famous

FAMELESS   *adj* not famous

FAMILIAL   *adj* pertaining to a family

FAMILIAR   *n* pl. **-S** a close friend or associate

FAMILISM   *n* pl. **-S** a social structure in which the family takes precedence over the individual **FAMILIST** *adj*

FAMILY   *n* pl. **-LIES** a group of persons related by blood or marriage

FAMINE   *n* pl. **-S** a widespread scarcity of food

FAMING   present participle of fame

FAMISH   *v* **-ED, -ING, -ES** to suffer extreme hunger

FAMOUS   *adj* well-known **FAMOUSLY** *adv*

FAMULUS   *n* pl. **-LI** a servant or attendant

FAN   *v* **FANNED, FANNING, FANS** to cool or refresh with a fan (a device for putting air into motion)

FANATIC   *n* pl. **-S** a zealot

FANBOY   *n* pl. **-BOYS** a male who is an enthusiastic devotee of something

FANCIED   past tense of fancy

FANCIER   *n* pl. **-S** one that has a special liking for something

FANCIES   present 3d person sing. of fancy

FANCIFUL   *adj* unrealistic

FANCIFY   *v* **-FIED, -FYING, -FIES** to make fancy

FANCY   *adj* **-CIER, -CIEST** ornamental **FANCILY** *adv*

FANCY   *v* **-CIED, -CYING, -CIES** to take a liking to

FANDANGO   *n* pl. **-GOS** or **-GOES** a lively Spanish dance

FANDOM   *n* pl. **-S** an aggregate of enthusiastic devotees

FANE   *n* pl. **-S** a temple

FANEGA   *n* pl. **-S** a Spanish unit of dry measure

FANEGADA   *n* pl. **-S** a Spanish unit of area

FANFARE   *n* pl. **-S** a short, lively musical flourish

FANFARON   *n* pl. **-S** a braggart

FANFIC   *n* pl. **-S** fiction written by fans of an admired work

FANFOLD   *v* **-ED, -ING, -S** to fold paper like a fan

FANG — *n* pl. **-S** a long, pointed tooth **FANGED, FANGLESS, FANGLIKE** *adj*

FANGA — *n* pl. **-S** fanega

FANGIRL — *n* pl. **-S** a female who is an enthusiastic devotee of something

FANION — *n* pl. **-S** a small flag

FANJET — *n* pl. **-S** a type of jet engine

FANLIGHT — *n* pl. **-S** a type of window

FANLIKE — *adj* resembling a fan

FANNED — past tense of fan

FANNER — *n* pl. **-S** one that fans

FANNING — present participle of fan

FANNY — *n* pl. **-NIES** the buttocks

FANO — *n* pl. **FANOS** a fanon

FANON — *n* pl. **-S** a cape worn by the pope

FANTAIL — *n* pl. **-S** a fan-shaped tail or end

FANTASIA — *n* pl. **-S** a free-form musical composition

FANTASIE — *n* pl. **-S** a fantasia

FANTASIED — past tense of fantasy

FANTASM — *n* pl. **-S** phantasm

FANTAST — *n* pl. **-S** an impractical person

FANTASY — *v* **-SIED, -SYING, -SIES** to imagine

FANTOD — *n* pl. **-S** an emotional outburst

FANTOM — *n* pl. **-S** phantom

FANUM — *n* pl. **-S** fanon

FANWISE — *adj* spread out like an open fan

FANWORT — *n* pl. **-S** an aquatic plant

FANZINE — *n* pl. **-S** a magazine written by and for enthusiastic devotees

FAQIR — *n* pl. **-S** fakir

FAQUIR — *n* pl. **-S** fakir

FAR — *adv* **FARTHER, FARTHEST** or **FURTHER, FURTHEST** at or to a great distance

FARAD — *n* pl. **-S** a unit of electrical capacitance

FARADAIC — *adj* faradic

FARADAY — *n* pl. **-DAYS** a unit of electricity

FARADIC — *adj* pertaining to a type of electric current

FARADISE — *v* **-DISED, -DISING, -DISES** to faradize

FARADISM — *n* pl. **-S** the use of faradic current for therapeutic purposes

FARADIZE — *v* **-DIZED, -DIZING, -DIZES** to treat by faradism

FARAWAY — *adj* distant

FARCE — *v* **FARCED, FARCING, FARCES** to fill out with witty material

FARCER — *n* pl. **-S** farceur

FARCEUR — *n* pl. **-S** a joker

FARCI — *adj* stuffed with finely chopped meat

FARCICAL — *adj* absurd

FARCIE — *adj* farci

FARCING — present participle of farce

FARCY — *n* pl. **-CIES** a disease of horses

FARD — *v* **-ED, -ING, -S** to apply cosmetics to

FARDEL — *n* pl. **-S** a bundle

FARE — *v* **FARED, FARING, FARES** to get along

FAREBOX — *n* pl. **-ES** a receptacle for fares on a bus

FARER — *n* pl. **-S** a traveler

FAREWELL — *v* **-ED, -ING, -S** to say goodby

FARFAL — *n* pl. **-S** farfel

FARFALLE — *n* pl. **-S** pasta in the shape of bow ties

FARFEL — *n* pl. **-S** noodles in the form of small pellets or granules

FARINA — *n* pl. **-S** a fine meal made from cereal grain

FARING — present participle of fare

FARINHA — *n* pl. **-S** a meal made from the root of the cassava

FARINOSE — *adj* resembling farina

FARL — *n* pl. **-S** a thin oatmeal cake

FARLE — *n* pl. **-S** farl

FARM — *v* **-ED, -ING, -S** to manage and cultivate as a farm (a tract of land devoted to agriculture) **FARMABLE** *adj*

FARMER — *n* pl. **-S** one that farms

FARMHAND — *n* pl. **-S** a farm laborer

FARMING — *n* pl. **-S** the business of operating a farm

FARMLAND — *n* pl. **-S** cultivated land

FARMWIFE — *n* pl. **-WIVES** a farmer's wife

FARMWORK — *n* pl. **-S** labor done on a farm

FARMYARD — *n* pl. **-S** an area surrounded by farm buildings

FARNESOL — *n* pl. **-S** an alcohol used in perfumes

FARNESS	*n* pl. **-ES** the state of being far off or apart	**FAT**	*adj* **FATTER, FATTEST** having an abundance of flesh
FARO	*n* pl. **FAROS** a card game	**FAT**	*v* **FATTED, FATTING, FATS** to make fat
FAROLITO	*n* pl. **-TOS** a candle in a paper bag weighted with sand	**FATAL**	*adj* causing or capable of causing death
FAROUCHE	*adj* sullenly shy	**FATALISM**	*n* pl. **-S** the doctrine that all events are predetermined
FARRAGO	*n* pl. **-GOES** or **-GOS** a confused mixture	**FATALIST**	*n* pl. **-S** a believer in fatalism
FARRIER	*n* pl. **-S** one that shoes horses	**FATALITY**	*n* pl. **-TIES** a death resulting from an unexpected occurrence
FARRIERY	*n* pl. **-ERIES** the trade of a farrier	**FATALLY**	*adv* in a fatal manner
FARRO	*n* pl. **-ROS** a variety of wheat	**FATBACK**	*n* pl. **-S** a marine fish
FARROW	*v* **-ED, -ING, -S** to give birth to a litter of pigs	**FATBIRD**	*n* pl. **-S** a wading bird
FARSIDE	*n* pl. **-S** the farther side	**FATE**	*v* **FATED, FATING, FATES** to destine
FARTHER	a comparative of far	**FATEFUL**	*adj* decisively important
FARTHEST	a superlative of far	**FATHEAD**	*n* pl. **-S** a dolt
FARTHING	*n* pl. **-S** a former British coin	**FATHER**	*v* **-ED, -ING, -S** to cause to exist
FARTLEK	*n* pl. **-S** an athletic training technique	**FATHERLY**	*adj* paternal
FASCES	*n* pl. **FASCES** an ancient Roman symbol of power	**FATHOM**	*v* **-ED, -ING, -S** to understand
		FATHOMER	*n* pl. **-S** one that fathoms
FASCIA	*n* pl. **-CIAS** or **-CIAE** a broad and distinct band of color **FASCIAL, FASCIATE** *adj*	**FATIDIC**	*adj* pertaining to prophecy
		FATIGUE	*v* **-TIGUED, -TIGUING, -TIGUES** to weary
FASCICLE	*n* pl. **-S** a small bundle	**FATING**	present participle of fate
FASCINE	*n* pl. **-S** a bundle of sticks used in building fortifications	**FATLESS**	*adj* having no fat
		FATLIKE	*adj* resembling fat
FASCISM	*n* pl. **-S** an oppressive political system	**FATLING**	*n* pl. **-S** a young animal fattened for slaughter
FASCIST	*n* pl. **-S** an advocate of fascism	**FATLY**	*adv* in the manner of one that is fat
FASCITIS	*n* pl. **-TISES** inflammation of a connective tissue	**FATNESS**	*n* pl. **-ES** the state of being fat
FASH	*v* **-ED, -ING, -ES** to annoy	**FATSTOCK**	*n* pl. **-S** livestock that is fat and ready for market
FASHION	*v* **-ED, -ING, -S** to give a particular shape or form to	**FATTED**	past tense of fat
FASHIONY	*adj* fashionable, trendy	**FATTEN**	*v* **-ED, -ING, -S** to make fat
FASHIOUS	*adj* annoying	**FATTENER**	*n* pl. **-S** one that fattens
FAST	*adj* **FASTER, FASTEST** moving or able to move quickly	**FATTER**	comparative of fat
		FATTEST	superlative of fat
FAST	*v* **-ED, -ING, -S** to abstain from eating	**FATTIER**	comparative of fatty
FASTBACK	*n* pl. **-S** a type of automobile roof	**FATTIES**	pl. of fatty
FASTBALL	*n* pl. **-S** a type of pitch in baseball	**FATTIEST**	superlative of fatty
FASTEN	*v* **-ED, -ING, -S** to secure	**FATTILY**	*adv* in a fatty manner
FASTENER	*n* pl. **-S** one that fastens	**FATTING**	present participle of fat
FASTING	*n* pl. **-S** abstention from eating	**FATTISH**	*adj* somewhat fat
FASTNESS	*n* pl. **-ES** the quality of being fast	**FATTY**	*adj* **-TIER, -TIEST** greasy; oily
FASTUOUS	*adj* arrogant	**FATTY**	*n* pl. **-TIES** one that is fat

FATUITY *n* pl. **-ITIES** something foolish or stupid

FATUOUS *adj* smugly stupid

FATWA *n* pl. **-S** an Islamic legal decree

FATWOOD *n* pl. **-S** wood used for kindling

FAUBOURG *n* pl. **-S** a suburb

FAUCAL *n* pl. **-S** a sound produced in the fauces

FAUCES *n/pl* the passage from the mouth to the pharynx

FAUCET *n* pl. **-S** a device for controlling the flow of liquid from a pipe

FAUCETRY *n* pl. **-TRIES** an array of faucets

FAUCIAL *adj* pertaining to the fauces

FAUGH *interj* — used to express disgust

FAULD *n* pl. **-S** a piece of armor below the breastplate

FAULT *v* **-ED, -ING, -S** to criticize

FAULTY *adj* **FAULTIER, FAULTIEST** imperfect **FAULTILY** *adv*

FAUN *n* pl. **-S** a woodland deity of Roman mythology **FAUNLIKE** *adj*

FAUNA *n* pl. **-NAS** or **-NAE** the animal life of a particular region **FAUNAL** *adj* **FAUNALLY** *adv*

FAUNIST *n* pl. **-S** a specialist on faunas

FAUTEUIL *n* pl. **-S** an armchair

FAUVE *n* pl. **-S** a fauvist

FAUVISM *n* pl. **-S** a movement in painting

FAUVIST *n* pl. **-S** an advocate of fauvism

FAUX *adj* not genuine; fake

FAVA *n* pl. **-S** the edible seed of a climbing vine

FAVE *n* pl. **-S** a favorite

FAVELA *n* pl. **-S** a slum area

FAVELLA *n* pl. **-S** favela

FAVISM *n* pl. **-S** an acute anemia

FAVONIAN *adj* pertaining to the west wind

FAVOR *v* **-ED, -ING, -S** to regard with approval

FAVORER *n* pl. **-S** one that favors

FAVORITE *n* pl. **-S** a person or thing preferred above all others

FAVOUR *v* **-ED, -ING, -S** to favor

FAVOURER *n* pl. **-S** favorer

FAVUS *n* pl. **-ES** a skin disease

FAWN *v* **-ED, -ING, -S** to seek notice or favor by servile demeanor

FAWNER *n* pl. **-S** one that fawns

FAWNLIKE *adj* resembling a young deer

FAWNY *adj* **FAWNIER, FAWNIEST** of a yellowish-brown color

FAX *v* **-ED, -ING, -ES** to transmit and reproduce by electronic means **FAXABLE** *adj*

FAY *v* **-ED, -ING, -S** to join closely

FAYALITE *n* pl. **-S** a mineral

FAZE *v* **FAZED, FAZING, FAZES** to disturb the composure of

FAZENDA *n* pl. **-S** a Brazilian plantation

FE *n* pl. **-S** a Hebrew letter

FEAL *adj* loyal

FEALTY *n* pl. **-TIES** loyalty

FEAR *v* **-ED, -ING, -S** to be afraid of

FEARER *n* pl. **-S** one that fears

FEARFUL *adj* **-FULLER, -FULLEST** afraid

FEARLESS *adj* unafraid

FEARSOME *adj* frightening

FEASANCE *n* pl. **-S** the performance of a condition, obligation, or duty

FEASE *v* **FEASED, FEASING, FEASES** to faze

FEASIBLE *adj* capable of being done **FEASIBLY** *adv*

FEAST *v* **-ED, -ING, -S** to eat sumptuously

FEASTER *n* pl. **-S** one that feasts

FEASTFUL *adj* festive

FEAT *adj* **FEATER, FEATEST** skillful

FEAT *n* pl. **-S** a notable act or achievement

FEATHER *v* **-ED, -ING, -S** to cover with feathers (horny structures that form the principal covering of birds)

FEATHERY *adj* **-ERIER, -ERIEST** resembling feathers

FEATLY *adj* **-LIER, -LIEST** graceful

FEATURE *v* **-TURED, -TURING, -TURES** to give special prominence to

FEAZE *v* **FEAZED, FEAZING, FEAZES** to faze

FEBRIFIC *adj* feverish

FEBRILE *adj* feverish

FECAL *adj* pertaining to feces

FECES *n/pl* bodily waste discharged through the anus

FECIAL *n* pl. **-S** fetial

FECK *n* pl. **-S** value

FECKLESS	*adj* worthless
FECKLY	*adv* almost
FECULA	*n* pl. **-LAE** fecal matter
FECULENT	*adj* foul with impurities
FECUND	*adj* fruitful
FED	*n* pl. **-S** a federal agent
FEDAYEE	*n* pl. **-YEEN** an Arab commando
FEDERACY	*n* pl. **-CIES** an alliance
FEDERAL	*n* pl. **-S** a supporter of a type of central government
FEDERATE	*v* **-ATED, -ATING, -ATES** to unite in an alliance
FEDEX	*v* **-ED, -ING, -ES** to send by Federal Express
FEDORA	*n* pl. **-S** a type of hat
FEE	*v* **FEED, FEEING, FEES** to pay a fee (a fixed charge) to
FEEB	*n* pl. **-S** a wimp (a weak or ineffective person)
FEEBLE	*adj* **-BLER, -BLEST** weak **FEEBLY** *adv*
FEEBLISH	*adj* somewhat feeble
FEED	*v* **FED, FEEDING, FEEDS** to give food to **FEEDABLE** *adj*
FEEDBACK	*n* pl. **-S** the return of a portion of the output to the input
FEEDBAG	*n* pl. **-S** a bag for feeding horses
FEEDBOX	*n* pl. **-ES** a box for animal feed
FEEDER	*n* pl. **-S** one that feeds
FEEDHOLE	*n* pl. **-S** one of a series of holes in paper tape
FEEDING	*n* pl. **-S** the act of giving food to a person or animal
FEEDLOT	*n* pl. **-S** a plot of land on which livestock is fattened
FEEDYARD	*n* pl. **-S** a feedlot
FEEL	*v* **FELT, FEELING, FEELS** to perceive through the sense of touch
FEELER	*n* pl. **-S** a tactile organ
FEELESS	*adj* requiring no fee
FEELING	*n* pl. **-S** the function or power of perceiving by touch
FEET	pl. of foot
FEETLESS	*adj* having no feet
FEEZE	*v* **FEEZED, FEEZING, FEEZES** to faze
FEH	*n* pl. **-S** peh
FEIGN	*v* **-ED, -ING, -S** to pretend

FEIGNER	*n* pl. **-S** one that feigns
FEIJOA	*n* pl. **-S** a green edible fruit
FEINT	*v* **-ED, -ING, -S** to make a deceptive movement
FEIRIE	*adj* nimble
FEIST	*n* pl. **-S** a small dog of mixed breed
FEISTY	*adj* **FEISTIER, FEISTIEST** full of nervous energy **FEISTILY** *adv*
FELAFEL	*n* pl. **-S** falafel
FELDSHER	*n* pl. **-S** a medical worker in Russia
FELDSPAR	*n* pl. **-S** a mineral
FELICITY	*n* pl. **-TIES** happiness
FELID	*n* pl. **-S** a feline
FELINE	*n* pl. **-S** an animal of the cat family
FELINELY	*adv* in a catlike manner
FELINITY	*n* pl. **-TIES** the quality of being catlike
FELL	*adj* **FELLER, FELLEST** cruel
FELL	*v* **-ED, -ING, -S** to cause to fall
FELLA	*n* pl. **-S** a man or boy
FELLABLE	*adj* capable of being felled
FELLAH	*n* pl. **-LAHS, -LAHIN** or **-LAHEEN** a peasant or laborer in Arab countries
FELLATE	*v* **-LATED, -LATING, -LATES** to perform fellatio
FELLATIO	*n* pl. **-TIOS** oral stimulation of the penis
FELLATOR	*n* pl. **-S** one that fellates
FELLER	*n* pl. **-S** one that fells
FELLIES	pl. of felly
FELLNESS	*n* pl. **-ES** extreme cruelty
FELLOE	*n* pl. **-S** the rim of a wheel
FELLOW	*v* **-ED, -ING, -S** to produce an equal to
FELLOWLY	*adj* friendly
FELLY	*n* pl. **-LIES** a felloe
FELON	*n* pl. **-S** a person who has committed a felony
FELONRY	*n* pl. **-RIES** the whole class of felons
FELONY	*n* pl. **-NIES** a grave crime
FELSIC	*adj* consisting of feldspar and silicates
FELSITE	*n* pl. **-S** an igneous rock **FELSITIC** *adj*
FELSPAR	*n* pl. **-S** feldspar
FELSTONE	*n* pl. **-S** felsite

FELT	*v* **-ED, -ING, -S** to mat together
FELTING	*n* pl. **-S** felted material
FELTLIKE	*adj* like a cloth made from wool
FELTY	*adj* **FELTIER, FELTIEST** resembling a cloth made from wool
FELUCCA	*n* pl. **-S** a swift sailing vessel
FELWORT	*n* pl. **-S** a flowering plant
FEM	*n* pl. **-S** a passive homosexual
FEMALE	*n* pl. **-S** an individual that bears young or produces ova
FEME	*n* pl. **-S** a wife
FEMINACY	*n* pl. **-CIES** the state of being a female
FEMINIE	*n/pl* women collectively
FEMININE	*n* pl. **-S** a word or form having feminine gender
FEMINISE	*v* **-NISED, -NISING, -NISES** to feminize
FEMINISM	*n* pl. **-S** a doctrine advocating rights for women equal to those of men
FEMINIST	*n* pl. **-S** a supporter of feminism
FEMINITY	*n* pl. **-TIES** the quality of being womanly
FEMINIZE	*v* **-NIZED, -NIZING, -NIZES** to make womanly
FEMME	*n* pl. **-S** a woman
FEMORAL	*adj* pertaining to the femur
FEMUR	*n* pl. **-MURS** or **-MORA** a bone of the leg
FEN	*n* pl. **-S** a marsh
FENAGLE	*v* **-GLED, -GLING, -GLES** to finagle
FENCE	*v* **FENCED, FENCING, FENCES** to practice the art of fencing
FENCER	*n* pl. **-S** one that fences
FENCEROW	*n* pl. **-S** the land occupied by a fence
FENCIBLE	*n* pl. **-S** a soldier enlisted for home service only
FENCING	*n* pl. **-S** the art of using a sword in attack and defense
FEND	*v* **-ED, -ING, -S** to ward off
FENDER	*n* pl. **-S** a metal guard over the wheel of a motor vehicle **FENDERED** *adj*
FENESTRA	*n* pl. **-TRAE** a small anatomical opening
FENING	*n* pl. **-INGA** or **-INGS** a monetary unit of Bosnia and Herzegovina

FENLAND	*n* pl. **-S** marshy ground
FENNEC	*n* pl. **-S** an African fox
FENNEL	*n* pl. **-S** a perennial herb
FENNY	*adj* **-NIER, -NIEST** marshy
FENTANYL	*n* pl. **-S** a narcotic opioid
FENTHION	*n* pl. **-S** an insecticide
FENURON	*n* pl. **-S** an herbicide
FEOD	*n* pl. **-S** a fief
FEODARY	*n* pl. **-RIES** a vassal
FEOFF	*v* **-ED, -ING, -S** to grant a fief to
FEOFFEE	*n* pl. **-S** one to whom a fief is granted
FEOFFER	*n* pl. **-S** one that grants a fief to another
FEOFFOR	*n* pl. **-S** feoffer
FER	*prep* for
FERACITY	*n* pl. **-TIES** the state of being fruitful
FERAL	*n* pl. **-S** a wild beast
FERBAM	*n* pl. **-S** a fungicide
FERE	*n* pl. **-S** a companion
FERETORY	*n* pl. **-RIES** a receptacle in which sacred relics are kept
FERIA	*n* pl. **-RIAS** or **-RIAE** a weekday of a church calendar on which no feast is celebrated **FERIAL** *adj*
FERINE	*adj* feral
FERITY	*n* pl. **-TIES** wildness
FERLIE	*n* pl. **-S** a strange sight
FERLY	*n* pl. **-LIES** ferlie
FERMATA	*n* pl. **-TAS** or **-TE** the sustaining of a musical note, chord, or rest beyond its written time value
FERMENT	*v* **-ED, -ING, -S** to undergo a type of chemical reaction
FERMI	*n* pl. **-S** a unit of length
FERMION	*n* pl. **-S** a type of atomic particle
FERMIUM	*n* pl. **-S** a radioactive element
FERN	*n* pl. **-S** a flowerless vascular plant **FERNLESS, FERNLIKE** *adj*
FERNERY	*n* pl. **-ERIES** a place in which ferns are grown
FERNINST	*prep* near to
FERNY	*adj* **FERNIER, FERNIEST** abounding in ferns
FEROCITY	*n* pl. **-TIES** fierceness
FERRATE	*n* pl. **-S** a chemical salt

FERREL	*v* **-RELED, -RELING, -RELS** or **-RELLED, -RELLING, -RELS** to ferrule
FERREOUS	*adj* containing iron
FERRET	*v* **-ED, -ING, -S** to search out by careful investigation
FERRETER	*n* pl. **-S** one that ferrets
FERRETY	*adj* suggestive of a ferret (a polecat)
FERRIAGE	*n* pl. **-S** transportation by ferry
FERRIC	*adj* pertaining to iron
FERRIED	past tense of ferry
FERRIES	present 3d person sing. of ferry
FERRITE	*n* pl. **-S** a magnetic substance **FERRITIC** *adj*
FERRITIN	*n* pl. **-S** a protein that contains iron
FERROUS	*adj* pertaining to iron
FERRULE	*v* **-RULED, -RULING, -RULES** to furnish with a metal ring or cap to prevent splitting
FERRUM	*n* pl. **-S** iron
FERRY	*v* **-RIED, -RYING, -RIES** to transport by ferry (a type of boat)
FERRYMAN	*n* pl. **-MEN** one who operates a ferry
FERTILE	*adj* capable of reproducing
FERULA	*n* pl. **-LAS** or **-LAE** a flat piece of wood
FERULE	*v* **-ULED, -ULING, -ULES** to ferrule
FERVENCY	*n* pl. **-CIES** fervor
FERVENT	*adj* marked by fervor
FERVID	*adj* fervent **FERVIDLY** *adv*
FERVOR	*n* pl. **-S** great warmth or intensity
FERVOUR	*n* pl. **-S** fervor
FESCUE	*n* pl. **-S** a perennial grass
FESS	*v* **-ED, -ING, -ES** to confess
FESSE	*n* pl. **-S** a horizontal band across the middle of a heraldic shield
FESSWISE	*adv* horizontally
FEST	*n* pl. **-S** a gathering for an activity
FESTA	*n* pl. **-S** a religious festival
FESTAL	*adj* festive **FESTALLY** *adv*
FESTER	*v* **-ED, -ING, -S** to generate pus
FESTIVAL	*n* pl. **-S** a day or time of celebration
FESTIVE	*adj* of or befitting a festival
FESTOON	*v* **-ED, -ING, -S** to hang decorative chains or strips on

FET	*v* **FETTED, FETTING, FETS** to fetch
FETA	*n* pl. **-S** a Greek cheese
FETAL	*adj* pertaining to a fetus
FETATION	*n* pl. **-S** the development of a fetus
FETCH	*v* **-ED, -ING, -ES** to go after and bring back
FETCHER	*n* pl. **-S** one that fetches
FETE	*v* **FETED, FETING, FETES** to honor with a celebration
FETERITA	*n* pl. **-S** a cereal grass
FETIAL	*n* pl. **-S** a priest of ancient Rome
FETIALIS	*n* pl. **-LES** fetial
FETICH	*n* pl. **-ES** fetish
FETICIDE	*n* pl. **-S** the killing of a fetus
FETID	*adj* having an offensive odor **FETIDLY** *adv*
FETIDITY	*n* pl. **-TIES** the state of being fetid
FETING	present participle of fete
FETISH	*n* pl. **-ES** an object believed to have magical power
FETLOCK	*n* pl. **-S** a joint of a horse's leg
FETOLOGY	*n* pl. **-GIES** the branch of medicine dealing with the fetus
FETOR	*n* pl. **-S** an offensive odor
FETTED	past tense of fet
FETTER	*v* **-ED, -ING, -S** to shackle
FETTERER	*n* pl. **-S** one that fetters
FETTING	present participle of fet
FETTLE	*v* **-TLED, -TLING, -TLES** to cover the hearth of with fettling
FETTLER	*n* pl. **-S** one who fettles
FETTLING	*n* pl. **-S** loose material thrown on the hearth of a furnace to protect it
FETUS	*n* pl. **-ES** the unborn organism carried within the womb in the later stages of its development
FEU	*v* **-ED, -ING, -S** to grant land to under Scottish feudal law
FEUAR	*n* pl. **-S** one granted land under Scottish feudal law
FEUD	*v* **-ED, -ING, -S** to engage in a feud (a bitter, continuous hostility)
FEUDAL	*adj* pertaining to a political and economic system of medieval Europe **FEUDALLY** *adv*
FEUDARY	*n* pl. **-RIES** a vassal
FEUDIST	*n* pl. **-S** one that feuds

FEVER   v **-ED, -ING, -S** to affect with fever (abnormal elevation of the body temperature)

FEVERFEW   n pl. **-S** a perennial herb

FEVERISH   adj having a fever

FEVEROUS   adj feverish

FEW   adj **FEWER, FEWEST** amounting to or consisting of a small number

FEWNESS   n pl. **-ES** the state of being few

FEWTRILS   n/pl things of little value

FEY   adj **FEYER, FEYEST** crazy **FEYLY** adv

FEYNESS   n pl. **-ES** the state of being fey

FEZ   n pl. **FEZES** or **FEZZES** a brimless cap worn by men in the Near East **FEZZED, FEZZY** adj

FIACRE   n pl. **-S** a small carriage

FIANCE   n pl. **-S** a man engaged to be married

FIANCEE   n pl. **-S** a woman engaged to be married

FIAR   n pl. **-S** the holder of a type of absolute ownership of land under Scottish law

FIASCO   n pl. **-COES** or **-CHI** a wine bottle

FIASCO   n pl. **-COS** or **-COES** a complete failure

FIAT   n pl. **-S** an authoritative order

FIB   v **FIBBED, FIBBING, FIBS** to tell a trivial lie

FIBBER   n pl. **-S** one that fibs

FIBER   n pl. **-S** a thread or threadlike object or structure **FIBERED** adj

FIBERIZE   v **-IZED, -IZING, -IZES** to break into fibers

FIBRANNE   n pl. **-S** a fabric made of spun-rayon yarn

FIBRATE   n pl. **-S** a drug that regulates lipids

FIBRE   n pl. **-S** fiber **FIBRED** adj

FIBRIL   n pl. **-S** a small fiber

FIBRILLA   n pl. **-LAE** a fibril

FIBRIN   n pl. **-S** an insoluble protein

FIBROID   n pl. **-S** a fibroma

FIBROIN   n pl. **-S** an insoluble protein

FIBROMA   n pl. **-MAS** or **-MATA** a benign tumor composed of fibrous tissue

FIBROSIS   n pl. **-BROSES** the development of excess fibrous tissue in a bodily organ **FIBROTIC** adj

FIBROUS   adj containing, consisting of, or resembling fibers

FIBSTER   n pl. **-S** one that fibs

FIBULA   n pl. **-LAS** or **-LAE** a bone of the leg **FIBULAR** adj

FICE   n pl. **-S** a feist

FICHE   n pl. **-S** a sheet of microfilm

FICHU   n pl. **-S** a woman's scarf

FICIN   n pl. **-S** an enzyme

FICKLE   adj **-LER, -LEST** not constant or loyal **FICKLY** adv

FICO   n pl. **-COES** something of little worth

FICTILE   adj moldable

FICTION   n pl. **-S** a literary work whose content is produced by the imagination

FICTIVE   adj imaginary

FICUS   n pl. **-ES** a tropical tree

FID   n pl. **-S** a square bar used as a support for a topmast

FIDDLE   v **-DLED, -DLING, -DLES** to play a violin

FIDDLER   n pl. **-S** one that fiddles

FIDDLING   n pl. **-S** the action of playing a violin

FIDDLY   adj **FIDDLIER, FIDDLIEST** intricately difficult to handle

FIDEISM   n pl. **-S** reliance on faith rather than reason

FIDEIST   n pl. **-S** a believer in fideism

FIDELITY   n pl. **-TIES** loyalty

FIDGE   v **FIDGED, FIDGING, FIDGES** to fidget

FIDGET   v **-ED, -ING, -S** to move nervously or restlessly

FIDGETER   n pl. **-S** one that fidgets

FIDGETY   adj nervously restless

FIDGING   present participle of fidge

FIDO   n pl. **-DOS** a defective coin

FIDUCIAL   adj based on faith or trust

FIE   interj — used to express disapproval

FIEF   n pl. **-S** a feudal estate

FIEFDOM   n pl. **-S** a fief

FIELD   v **-ED, -ING, -S** to play as a fielder

FIELDER   n pl. **-S** one that catches or picks up a ball in play

FIEND   n pl. **-S** a demon

FIENDISH *adj* extremely wicked or cruel

FIERCE *adj* **FIERCER, FIERCEST** violently hostile or aggressive **FIERCELY** *adv*

FIERY *adj* **-ERIER, -ERIEST** intensely hot **FIERILY** *adv*

FIESTA *n* pl. **-S** a festival

FIFE *v* **FIFED, FIFING, FIFES** to play a fife (a high-pitched flute)

FIFER *n* pl. **-S** one that plays a fife

FIFTEEN *n* pl. **-S** a number

FIFTH *n* pl. **-S** one of five equal parts

FIFTHLY *adv* in the fifth place

FIFTIETH *n* pl. **-S** one of fifty equal parts

FIFTY *n* pl. **-TIES** a number

FIFTYISH *adj* being about fifty years old

FIG *v* **FIGGED, FIGGING, FIGS** to adorn

FIGEATER *n* pl. **-S** a large beetle

FIGHT *v* **FOUGHT, FIGHTING, FIGHTS** to attempt to defeat an adversary

FIGHTER *n* pl. **-S** one that fights

FIGHTING *n* pl. **-S** the act of one that fights

FIGMENT *n* pl. **-S** a product of mental invention

FIGTREE *n* pl. **-S** a tree that bears figs (soft, sweet dark fruits)

FIGULINE *n* pl. **-S** a piece of pottery

FIGURAL *adj* consisting of human or animal form

FIGURANT *n* pl. **-S** a ballet dancer who dances only in groups

FIGURATE *adj* having a definite shape

FIGURE *v* **-URED, -URING, -URES** to compute

FIGURER *n* pl. **-S** one that figures

FIGURINE *n* pl. **-S** a small statue

FIGWORT *n* pl. **-S** a flowering plant

FIL *n* pl. **-S** a coin of Iraq and Jordan

FILA pl. of filum

FILAGREE *v* **-GREED, -GREEING, -GREES** to filigree

FILAMENT *n* pl. **-S** a very thin thread or threadlike structure

FILAR *adj* pertaining to a thread

FILAREE *n* pl. **-S** a European weed

FILARIA *n* pl. **-IAE** a parasitic worm **FILARIAL, FILARIAN** *adj*

FILARIID *n* pl. **-S** filaria

FILATURE *n* pl. **-S** the reeling of silk from cocoons

FILBERT *n* pl. **-S** the edible nut of a European shrub

FILCH *v* **-ED, -ING, -ES** to steal

FILCHER *n* pl. **-S** one that filches

FILE *v* **FILED, FILING, FILES** to arrange in order for future reference **FILEABLE** *adj*

FILEFISH *n* pl. **-ES** a marine fish

FILEMOT *adj* of a brownish yellow color

FILENAME *n* pl. **-S** the name of a computer file

FILER *n* pl. **-S** one that files

FILET *v* **-ED, -ING, -S** to fillet

FILIAL *adj* pertaining to a son or daughter **FILIALLY** *adv*

FILIATE *v* **-ATED, -ATING, -ATES** to bring into close association

FILIBEG *n* pl. **-S** a pleated skirt worn by Scottish Highlanders

FILICIDE *n* pl. **-S** the killing of one's child

FILIFORM *adj* shaped like a filament

FILIGREE *v* **-GREED, -GREEING, -GREES** to adorn with intricate ornamental work

FILING *n* pl. **-S** a particle removed by a file

FILISTER *n* pl. **-S** a groove on a window frame

FILK *n* pl. **-S** a type of popular music that parodies folk songs

FILL *v* **-ED, -ING, -S** to put as much as can be held into **FILLABLE** *adj*

FILLE *n* pl. **-S** a girl

FILLER *n* pl. **-S** one that fills

FILLET *v* **-ED, -ING, -S** to cut boneless slices from

FILLETER *n* pl. **-S** one who fillets

FILLIES pl. of filly

FILLING *n* pl. **-S** that which is used to fill something

FILLIP *v* **-ED, -ING, -S** to strike sharply

FILLO *n* pl. **-LOS** phyllo

FILLY *n* pl. **-LIES** a young female horse

FILM *v* **-ED, -ING, -S** to make a motion picture **FILMABLE** *adj*

FILMCARD *n* pl. **-S** a fiche

FILMDOM *n* pl. **-S** the motion-picture industry

FILMER *n* pl. **-S** one that films

FILMFEST *n* pl. **-S** a festival at which many films are shown

FILMGOER *n* pl. **-S** one that goes to see motion pictures

FILMI *n* pl. **-S** music composed for Indian films

FILMIC *adj* pertaining to motion pictures

FILMIER comparative of filmy

FILMIEST superlative of filmy

FILMILY *adv* in a filmy manner

FILMLAND *n* pl. **-S** filmdom

FILMLESS *adj* having no film

FILMLIKE *adj* resembling film

FILMSET *v* **-SET, -SETTING, -SETS** to photoset

FILMY *adj* **FILMIER, FILMIEST** resembling or covered with film; hazy

FILO *n* pl. **-LOS** phyllo

FILOSE *adj* resembling a thread

FILTER *v* **-ED, -ING, -S** to pass through a filter (a device for removing suspended matter)

FILTERER *n* pl. **-S** one that filters

FILTH *n* pl. **-S** foul or dirty matter

FILTHY *adj* **FILTHIER, FILTHIEST** offensively dirty **FILTHILY** *adv*

FILTRATE *v* **-TRATED, -TRATING, -TRATES** to filter

FILUM *n* pl. **-LA** a threadlike anatomical structure

FIMBLE *n* pl. **-S** the male hemp plant

FIMBRIA *n* pl. **-BRIAE** a fringe or fringe-like structure **FIMBRIAL** *adj*

FIN *v* **FINNED, FINNING, FINS** to equip with fins (external paddle-like structures)

FINABLE *adj* subject to the payment of a fine

FINAGLE *v* **-GLED, -GLING, -GLES** to obtain by trickery

FINAGLER *n* pl. **-S** one that finagles

FINAL *n* pl. **-S** the last examination of an academic course

FINALE *n* pl. **-S** a close or termination of something

FINALIS *n* pl. **-LES** a type of tone in medieval music

FINALISE *v* **-ISED, -ISING, -ISES** finalize

FINALISM *n* pl. **-S** the doctrine that all events are determined by ultimate purposes

FINALIST *n* pl. **-S** a contestant who reaches the last part of a competition

FINALITY *n* pl. **-TIES** the state of being conclusive

FINALIZE *v* **-IZED, -IZING, -IZES** to put into finished form

FINALLY *adv* at the end

FINANCE *v* **-NANCED, -NANCING, -NANCES** to supply the money for

FINBACK *n* pl. **-S** the rorqual

FINCA *n* pl. **-S** an estate in Spanish America

FINCH *n* pl. **-ES** a small bird

FIND *v* **FOUND, FINDING, FINDS** to come upon after a search **FINDABLE** *adj*

FINDER *n* pl. **-S** one that finds

FINDING *n* pl. **-S** something that is found

FINE *adj* **FINER, FINEST** excellent

FINE *v* **FINED, FINING, FINES** to subject to a fine (a monetary penalty)

FINEABLE *adj* finable

FINELY *adv* in a fine manner

FINENESS *n* pl. **-ES** the quality of being fine

FINER comparative of fine

FINERY *n* pl. **-ERIES** elaborate adornment

FINESPUN *adj* developed with extreme care

FINESSE *v* **-NESSED, -NESSING, -NESSES** to bring about by adroit maneuvering

FINEST *n* pl. **-S** the police of a specified city

FINFISH *n* pl. **-ES** a true fish

FINFOOT *n* pl. **-S** an aquatic bird

FINGER *v* **-ED, -ING, -S** to touch with the fingers (the terminating members of the hand)

FINGERER *n* pl. **-S** one that fingers

FINIAL *n* pl. **-S** a crowning ornament **FINIALED** *adj*

FINICAL *adj* finicky

FINICKIN *adj* finicky

FINICKY *adj* **-ICKIER, -ICKIEST** difficult to please

FINIKIN *adj* finicky

FINIKING *adj* finicky

FINING *n* pl. **-S** the clarifying of wines

FINIS *n* pl. **-NISES** the end

FINISH	*v* **-ED, -ING, -ES** to bring to an end
FINISHER	*n* pl. **-S** one that finishes
FINITE	*n* pl. **-S** something that is finite (having definite limits)
FINITELY	*adv* to a finite extent
FINITISM	*n* pl. **-S** the belief that a particular entity is finite
FINITIST	*n* pl. **-S** an advocate of finitism
FINITO	*adj* finished
FINITUDE	*n* pl. **-S** the state of being finite
FINK	*v* **-ED, -ING, -S** to inform to the police
FINLESS	*adj* having no fins
FINLIKE	*adj* resembling a fin
FINMARK	*n* pl. **-S** a former monetary unit of Finland
FINNAN	*n* pl. **-S** smoked haddock
FINNED	past tense of fin
FINNICKY	*adj* **-NICKIER, -NICKIEST** finicky
FINNIER	comparative of finny
FINNIEST	superlative of finny
FINNING	present participle of fin
FINNMARK	*n* pl. **-S** finmark
FINNY	*adj* **-NIER, -NIEST** having or characterized by fins
FINO	*n* pl. **-NOS** a very dry sherry
FINOCHIO	*n* pl. **-CHIOS** a perennial herb
FIORD	*n* pl. **-S** fjord
FIPPLE	*n* pl. **-S** a plug of wood at the mouth of certain wind instruments
FIQUE	*n* pl. **-S** a tropical plant
FIR	*n* pl. **-S** an evergreen tree
FIRE	*v* **FIRED, FIRING, FIRES** to project by discharging from a gun **FIREABLE** *adj*
FIREARM	*n* pl. **-S** a weapon from which a shot is discharged by gunpowder
FIREBACK	*n* pl. **-S** a cast-iron plate along the back of a fireplace
FIREBALL	*n* pl. **-S** a luminous meteor
FIREBASE	*n* pl. **-S** a military base from which fire is directed against the enemy
FIREBIRD	*n* pl. **-S** a brightly colored bird
FIREBOAT	*n* pl. **-S** a boat equipped with firefighting apparatus
FIREBOMB	*v* **-ED, -ING, -S** to attack with incendiary bombs
FIREBOX	*n* pl. **-ES** a chamber in which fuel is burned

FIREBRAT	*n* pl. **-S** a small, wingless insect
FIREBUG	*n* pl. **-S** an arsonist
FIRECLAY	*n* pl. **-CLAYS** a heat-resistant clay
FIRED	past tense of fire
FIREDAMP	*n* pl. **-S** a combustible gas
FIREDOG	*n* pl. **-S** an andiron
FIREFANG	*v* **-ED, -ING, -S** to decompose by oxidation
FIREFLY	*n* pl. **-FLIES** a luminous insect
FIREHALL	*n* pl. **-S** a fire station
FIREHOSE	*n* pl. **-S** a hose used by firefighters
FIRELESS	*adj* having no fire
FIRELIT	*adj* lighted by firelight
FIRELOCK	*n* pl. **-S** a type of gun
FIREMAN	*n* pl. **-MEN** a man employed to extinguish fires
FIREPAN	*n* pl. **-S** an open pan for holding live coals
FIREPINK	*n* pl. **-S** a flowering plant
FIREPIT	*n* pl. **-S** a depression dug in the ground in which a fire is made
FIREPLUG	*n* pl. **-S** a hydrant
FIREPOT	*n* pl. **-S** a clay pot filled with burning items
FIRER	*n* pl. **-S** one that fires
FIREREEL	*n* pl. **-S** a fire engine
FIREROOM	*n* pl. **-S** a room containing a ship's boilers
FIRESHIP	*n* pl. **-S** a burning ship sent among the enemy's ships
FIRESIDE	*n* pl. **-S** the area immediately surrounding a fireplace
FIRETRAP	*n* pl. **-S** a building that is likely to catch on fire
FIREWALL	*n* pl. **-S** a computer component that prevents unauthorized access to data
FIREWEED	*n* pl. **-S** a perennial herb
FIREWOOD	*n* pl. **-S** wood used as fuel
FIREWORK	*n* pl. **-S** a device for producing a striking display of light or a loud noise
FIREWORM	*n* pl. **-S** a glowworm
FIRING	*n* pl. **-S** the process of maturing ceramic products by heat
FIRKIN	*n* pl. **-S** a British unit of capacity
FIRM	*adj* **FIRMER, FIRMEST** unyielding to pressure
FIRM	*v* **-ED, -ING, -S** to make firm

FIRMAN	*n* pl. **-S** an edict issued by a Middle Eastern sovereign		**FISHPOND**	*n* pl. **-S** a pond abounding in edible fish
FIRMER	*n* pl. **-S** a woodworking tool		**FISHTAIL**	*v* **-ED, -ING, -S** to have the rear end of a moving vehicle slide from side to side
FIRMLY	*adv* in a firm manner			
FIRMNESS	*n* pl. **-ES** the state of being firm		**FISHWAY**	*n* pl. **-WAYS** a device for enabling fish to pass around a dam
FIRMWARE	*n* pl. **-S** computer programs permanently stored on a microchip		**FISHWIFE**	*n* pl. **-WIVES** a woman who sells fish
FIRN	*n* pl. **-S** neve		**FISHWORM**	*n* pl. **-S** a worm used as bait
FIRRY	*adj* **-RIER, -RIEST** abounding in firs		**FISHY**	*adj* **FISHIER, FISHIEST** of or resembling fish
FIRST	*n* pl. **-S** something that precedes all others		**FISSATE**	*adj* deeply split
			FISSILE	*adj* capable of being split
FIRSTLY	*adv* before all others		**FISSION**	*v* **-ED, -ING, -S** to split into parts
FIRTH	*n* pl. **-S** an inlet of the sea		**FISSIPED**	*n* pl. **-S** a mammal that has separated toes
FISC	*n* pl. **-S** a state or royal treasury			
FISCAL	*n* pl. **-S** a public prosecutor		**FISSURAL**	*adj* pertaining to a long narrow opening
FISCALLY	*adv* with regard to financial matters		**FISSURE**	*v* **-SURED, -SURING, -SURES** to split
FISH	*v* **-ED, -ING, -ES** to catch or try to catch fish (cold-blooded aquatic vertebrates)		**FIST**	*v* **-ED, -ING, -S** to strike with the fist (the hand closed tightly)
FISHABLE	*adj* suitable for fishing		**FISTFUL**	*n* pl. **-S** a handful
FISHBOAT	*n* pl. **-S** a watercraft used for fishing		**FISTIC**	*adj* pertaining to pugilism
FISHBOLT	*n* pl. **-S** a type of bolt		**FISTNOTE**	*n* pl. **-S** a part of a text to which attention is drawn by an index mark
FISHBONE	*n* pl. **-S** a bone of a fish			
FISHBOWL	*n* pl. **-S** a bowl in which live fish are kept		**FISTULA**	*n* pl. **-LAS** or **-LAE** a duct formed by the imperfect closing of a wound **FISTULAR** *adj*
FISHER	*n* pl. **-S** one that fishes			
FISHERY	*n* pl. **-ERIES** a place for catching fish		**FIT**	*adj* **FITTER, FITTEST** healthy
			FIT	*v* **FITTED, FITTING, FITS** to bring to a required form and size
FISHEYE	*n* pl. **-S** a suspicious stare			
FISHGIG	*n* pl. **-S** a pronged implement for spearing fish		**FITCH**	*n* pl. **-ES** a polecat
FISHHOOK	*n* pl. **-S** a barbed hook for catching fish		**FITCHEE**	*adj* fitchy
			FITCHET	*n* pl. **-S** a fitch
FISHIER	comparative of fishy		**FITCHEW**	*n* pl. **-S** a fitch
FISHIEST	superlative of fishy		**FITCHY**	*adj* having the arms ending in a point — used of a heraldic cross
FISHILY	*adv* in a fishy manner			
FISHING	*n* pl. **-S** the occupation or pastime of catching fish		**FITFUL**	*adj* recurring irregularly **FITFULLY** *adv*
FISHKILL	*n* pl. **-S** the sudden destruction of large numbers of fish		**FITLY**	*adv* in a fit manner
FISHLESS	*adj* having no fish		**FITMENT**	*n* pl. **-S** equipment
FISHLIKE	*adj* resembling a fish		**FITNESS**	*n* pl. **-ES** the state of being fit
FISHLINE	*n* pl. **-S** a line used in fishing		**FITTABLE**	*adj* capable of being fitted
FISHMEAL	*n* pl. **-S** ground dried fish		**FITTED**	past tense of fit
FISHNET	*n* pl. **-S** a net for catching fish		**FITTER**	*n* pl. **-S** one that fits
FISHPOLE	*n* pl. **-S** a fishing rod		**FITTEST**	superlative of fit

FITTING	*n* pl. **-S** a small often standardized accessory part
FIVE	*n* pl. **-S** a number
FIVEFOLD	*adj* five times as great
FIVEPINS	*n/pl* a bowling game
FIVER	*n* pl. **-S** a five-dollar bill
FIX	*v* **FIXED** or **FIXT, FIXING, FIXES** to repair **FIXABLE** *adj*
FIXATE	*v* **-ATED, -ATING, -ATES** to make stable or stationary
FIXATIF	*n* pl. **-S** fixative
FIXATION	*n* pl. **-S** the act of fixating
FIXATIVE	*n* pl. **-S** a substance for preserving paintings or drawings
FIXEDLY	*adv* firmly
FIXER	*n* pl. **-S** one that fixes
FIXINGS	*n/pl* accompaniments to the main dish of a meal
FIXIT	*n* pl. **-S** a person known for fixing things
FIXITY	*n* pl. **-TIES** stability
FIXT	a past tense of fix
FIXTURE	*n* pl. **-S** a permanent part or appendage of a house
FIXURE	*n* pl. **-S** firmness
FIZ	*n* pl. **FIZZES** a hissing or sputtering sound
FIZGIG	*n* pl. **-S** fishgig
FIZZ	*v* **-ED, -ING, -ES** to make a hissing or sputtering sound
FIZZER	*n* pl. **-S** one that fizzes
FIZZES	pl. of fiz
FIZZLE	*v* **-ZLED, -ZLING, -ZLES** to fizz
FIZZY	*adj* **FIZZIER, FIZZIEST** fizzing **FIZZILY** *adv*
FJELD	*n* pl. **-S** a high, barren plateau
FJORD	*n* pl. **-S** a narrow inlet of the sea between steep cliffs **FJORDIC** *adj*
FLAB	*n* pl. **-S** flabby body tissue
FLABBY	*adj* **-BIER, -BIEST** flaccid **FLABBILY** *adv*
FLABELLA	*n/pl* fan-shaped anatomical structures
FLACCID	*adj* lacking firmness
FLACK	*v* **-ED, -ING, -S** to work as a press agent
FLACKERY	*n* pl. **-ERIES** publicity
FLACON	*n* pl. **-S** a small stoppered bottle
FLAG	*v* **FLAGGED, FLAGGING, FLAGS** to mark with a flag (a piece of cloth used as a symbol)
FLAGELLA	*n/pl* long, slender plant shoots
FLAGGER	*n* pl. **-S** one that flags
FLAGGING	*n* pl. **-S** a type of pavement
FLAGGY	*adj* **-GIER, -GIEST** drooping
FLAGLESS	*adj* having no flag
FLAGMAN	*n* pl. **-MEN** one who carries a flag
FLAGON	*n* pl. **-S** a large bulging bottle
FLAGPOLE	*n* pl. **-S** a pole on which a flag is displayed
FLAGRANT	*adj* extremely conspicuous
FLAGSHIP	*n* pl. **-S** a ship bearing the flag of a fleet
FLAIL	*v* **-ED, -ING, -S** to swing freely
FLAIR	*n* pl. **-S** a natural aptitude
FLAK	*n* pl. **FLAK** antiaircraft fire
FLAKE	*v* **FLAKED, FLAKING, FLAKES** to peel off in flakes (flat, thin pieces)
FLAKER	*n* pl. **-S** one that flakes
FLAKEY	*adj* **FLAKIER, FLAKIEST** flaky
FLAKY	*adj* **FLAKIER, FLAKIEST** resembling flakes **FLAKILY** *adv*
FLAM	*v* **FLAMMED, FLAMMING, FLAMS** to deceive
FLAMBE	*v* **-BEED, -BEING, -BES** to douse with a liqueur and ignite
FLAMBEAU	*n* pl. **-BEAUS** or **-BEAUX** a flaming torch
FLAMBEE	*adj* flaming
FLAME	*v* **FLAMED, FLAMING, FLAMES** to burn brightly
FLAMEN	*n* pl. **-MENS** or **-MINES** a priest of ancient Rome
FLAMENCO	*n* pl. **-COS** a strongly rhythmic style of dancing
FLAMEOUT	*n* pl. **-S** a failure of a jet engine in flight
FLAMER	*n* pl. **-S** one that flames
FLAMIER	comparative of flamy
FLAMIEST	superlative of flamy
FLAMINES	a pl. of flamen
FLAMING	present participle of flame
FLAMINGO	*n* pl. **-GOS** or **-GOES** a wading bird
FLAMMED	past tense of flam
FLAMMING	present participle of flam
FLAMY	*adj* **FLAMIER, FLAMIEST** flaming

FLAN   *n* pl. **-S** or **-ES** a type of custard

FLANCARD   *n* pl. **-S** a piece of armor for the side of a horse

FLANERIE   *n* pl. **-S** idleness

FLANEUR   *n* pl. **-S** an idler

FLANGE   *v* **FLANGED, FLANGING, FLANGES** to provide with a protecting rim

FLANGER   *n* pl. **-S** one that flanges

FLANGING   *n* pl. **-S** the providing of a protecting rim on an object

FLANK   *v* **-ED, -ING, -S** to be located at the side of

FLANKEN   *n/pl* beef cut from the sides that is boiled with vegetables

FLANKER   *n* pl. **-S** one that flanks

FLANNEL   *v* **-NELED, -NELING, -NELS** or **-NELLED, -NELLING, -NELS** to cover with flannel (a soft fabric)

FLAP   *v* **FLAPPED, FLAPPING, FLAPS** to wave up and down

FLAPERON   *n* pl. **-S** an airfoil that functions as a flap and an aileron

FLAPJACK   *n* pl. **-S** a pancake

FLAPLESS   *adj* having no flap (a flat appendage)

FLAPPED   past tense of flap

FLAPPER   *n* pl. **-S** one that flaps

FLAPPING   present participle of flap

FLAPPY   *adj* **-PIER, -PIEST** flapping

FLARE   *v* **FLARED, FLARING, FLARES** to burn with a bright, wavering light

FLAREUP   *n* pl. **-S** a sudden outbreak

FLASH   *v* **-ED, -ING, -ES** to send forth a sudden burst of light

FLASHER   *n* pl. **-S** one that flashes

FLASHGUN   *n* pl. **-S** a photographic apparatus

FLASHING   *n* pl. **-S** sheet metal used in waterproofing a roof

FLASHY   *adj* **FLASHIER, FLASHIEST** gaudy **FLASHILY** *adv*

FLASK   *n* pl. **-S** a narrow-necked container

FLASKET   *n* pl. **-S** a small flask

FLAT   *adj* **FLATTER, FLATTEST** having a smooth or even surface

FLAT   *v* **FLATTED, FLATTING, FLATS** to flatten

FLATBED   *n* pl. **-S** a type of truck or trailer

FLATBOAT   *n* pl. **-S** a flat-bottomed boat

FLATBROD   *n* pl. **-S** a wafer made of rye

FLATCAP   *n* pl. **-S** a type of hat

FLATCAR   *n* pl. **-S** a railroad car without sides or roof

FLATFISH   *n* pl. **-ES** any of an order of marine fishes

FLATFOOT   *n* pl. **-FEET** a foot condition

FLATFOOT   *v* **-ED, -ING, -S** to walk with a dragging gait

FLATHEAD   *n* pl. **-S** a marine food fish

FLATIRON   *n* pl. **-S** a device for pressing clothes

FLATLAND   *n* pl. **-S** land lacking significant variation in elevation

FLATLET   *n* pl. **-S** a type of apartment

FLATLINE   *v* **-LINED, -LINING, -LINES** to register as having no brain waves or heartbeat

FLATLING   *adv* with a flat side or edge

FLATLONG   *adv* flatling

FLATLY   *adv* in a flat manner

FLATMATE   *n* pl. **-S** one with whom an apartment is shared

FLATNESS   *n* pl. **-ES** the state of being flat

FLATPACK   *n* pl. **-S** a package for an integrated circuit

FLATTED   past tense of flat

FLATTEN   *v* **-ED, -ING, -S** to make or become flat

FLATTER   *v* **-ED, -ING, -S** to praise excessively

FLATTERY   *n* pl. **-TERIES** the act of flattering

FLATTEST   superlative of flat

FLATTIE   *n* pl. **-S** a flat-heeled shoe

FLATTING   present participle of flat

FLATTISH   *adj* somewhat flat

FLATTOP   *n* pl. **-S** an aircraft carrier

FLATUS   *n* pl. **-ES** intestinal gas

FLATWARE   *n* pl. **-S** tableware that is fairly flat

FLATWASH   *n* pl. **-ES** flatwork

FLATWAYS   *adv* flatwise

FLATWISE   *adv* with the flat side in a particular position

FLATWORK   *n* pl. **-S** laundry that can be ironed mechanically

FLATWORM   *n* pl. **-S** a flat-bodied worm

FLAUNT   *v* **-ED, -ING, -S** to exhibit in a gaudy manner

FLAUNTER   *n* pl. **-S** one that flaunts

FLAUNTY	*adj* **FLAUNTIER, FLAUNTIEST** gaudy	**FLEE**	*v* **FLED, FLEEING, FLEES** to run away
FLAUTA	*n* pl. **-S** a tortilla rolled around a filling and fried	**FLEECE**	*v* **FLEECED, FLEECING, FLEECES** to remove the coat of wool from
FLAUTIST	*n* pl. **-S** flutist		
FLAVA	*n* pl. **-S** a style of hip-hop music	**FLEECER**	*n* pl. **-S** one that fleeces
FLAVANOL	*n* pl. **-S** flavonol	**FLEECH**	*v* **-ED, -ING, -ES** to coax
FLAVIN	*n* pl. **-S** a yellow pigment	**FLEECY**	*adj* **FLEECIER, FLEECIEST** woolly **FLEECILY** *adv*
FLAVINE	*n* pl. **-S** flavin		
FLAVONE	*n* pl. **-S** a chemical compound	**FLEER**	*v* **-ED, -ING, -S** to deride
FLAVONOL	*n* pl. **-S** a derivative of flavone	**FLEET**	*adj* **FLEETER, FLEETEST** swift **FLEETLY** *adv*
FLAVOR	*v* **-ED, -ING, -S** to give flavor (distinctive taste) to	**FLEET**	*v* **-ED, -ING, -S** to move swiftly
FLAVORER	*n* pl. **-S** one that flavors	**FLEHMEN**	*v* **-ED, -ING, -S** to inhale with the mouth open and upper lip curled
FLAVORY	*adj* full of flavor		
FLAVOUR	*v* **-ED, -ING, -S** to flavor	**FLEISHIG**	*adj* made of meat or meat products
FLAVOURY	*adj* flavory	**FLEMISH**	*v* **-ED, -ING, -ES** to coil rope in a certain manner
FLAW	*v* **-ED, -ING, -S** to produce a flaw (an imperfection) in		
FLAWLESS	*adj* having no flaw	**FLENCH**	*v* **-ED, -ING, -ES** to flense
FLAWY	*adj* **FLAWIER, FLAWIEST** full of flaws	**FLENSE**	*v* **FLENSED, FLENSING, FLENSES** to strip the blubber or skin from
FLAX	*n* pl. **-ES** an annual herb	**FLENSER**	*n* pl. **-S** one that flenses
FLAXEN	*adj* of a pale yellow color	**FLESH**	*v* **-ED, -ING, -ES** to plunge into the flesh (soft body tissue)
FLAXSEED	*n* pl. **-S** the seed of flax		
FLAXY	*adj* **FLAXIER, FLAXIEST** flaxen	**FLESHER**	*n* pl. **-S** one that removes flesh from animal hides
FLAY	*v* **-ED, -ING, -S** to strip off the skin of		
		FLESHIER	comparative of fleshy
		FLESHIEST	superlative of fleshy
FLAYER	*n* pl. **-S** one that flays	**FLESHING**	*n* pl. **-S** the distribution of the lean and fat on an animal
FLEA	*n* pl. **-S** a parasitic insect		
FLEABAG	*n* pl. **-S** an inferior hotel	**FLESHLY**	*adj* **-LIER, -LIEST** pertaining to the body
FLEABANE	*n* pl. **-S** a flowering plant		
FLEABITE	*n* pl. **-S** the bite of a flea	**FLESHPOT**	*n* pl. **-S** a pot for cooking meat
FLEAM	*n* pl. **-S** a surgical instrument	**FLESHY**	*adj* **FLESHIER, FLESHIEST** having much flesh **FLESHILY** *adv*
FLEAPIT	*n* pl. **-S** a run-down movie theater		
FLEAWORT	*n* pl. **-S** a European herb	**FLETCH**	*v* **-ED, -ING, -ES** to fledge
FLECHE	*n* pl. **-S** a steeple	**FLETCHER**	*n* pl. **-S** one that makes arrows
FLECK	*v* **-ED, -ING, -S** to mark with flecks (tiny streaks or spots)	**FLEURON**	*n* pl. **-S** a floral ornament
		FLEURY	*adj* having the arms terminating in three leaves — used of a heraldic cross
FLECKY	*adj* flecked		
FLECTION	*n* pl. **-S** the act of bending	**FLEW**	*n* pl. **-S** a fishing net
FLED	past tense of flee	**FLEX**	*v* **-ED, -ING, -ES** to bend
FLEDGE	*v* **FLEDGED, FLEDGING, FLEDGES** to furnish with feathers	**FLEXAGON**	*n* pl. **-S** a folded paper construction
		FLEXIBLE	*adj* capable of being bent **FLEXIBLY** *adv*
FLEDGY	*adj* **FLEDGIER, FLEDGIEST** covered with feathers	**FLEXILE**	*adj* flexible
		FLEXION	*n* pl. **-S** flection

FLEXOR   *n* pl. **-S** a muscle that serves to bend a bodily part

FLEXTIME   *n* pl. **-S** a system that allows flexible working hours

FLEXUOSE   *adj* flexuous

FLEXUOUS   *adj* winding

FLEXURE   *n* pl. **-S** the act of bending **FLEXURAL** *adj*

FLEXWING   *n* pl. **-S** a collapsible fabric wing used in hang gliders

FLEY   *v* **-ED, -ING, -S** to frighten

FLIC   *n* pl. **-S** a Parisian policeman

FLICHTER   *v* **-ED, -ING, -S** to flicker

FLICK   *v* **-ED, -ING, -S** to strike with a quick, light blow

FLICKER   *v* **-ED, -ING, -S** to move waveringly

FLICKERY   *adj* flickering

FLIED   a past tense of fly

FLIER   *n* pl. **-S** one that flies

FLIES   present 3d person sing. of fly

FLIEST   superlative of fly

FLIGHT   *v* **-ED, -ING, -S** to fly in a flock

FLIGHTY   *adj* **FLIGHTIER, FLIGHTIEST** fickle

FLIMFLAM   *v* **-FLAMMED, -FLAMMING, -FLAMS** to swindle

FLIMSY   *adj* **-SIER, -SIEST** lacking solidity or strength **FLIMSILY** *adv*

FLIMSY   *n* pl. **-SIES** a thin paper

FLINCH   *v* **-ED, -ING, -ES** to shrink back involuntarily

FLINCHER   *n* pl. **-S** one that flinches

FLINDER   *n* pl. **-S** a small fragment

FLING   *v* **FLUNG, FLINGING, FLINGS** to throw with force

FLINGER   *n* pl. **-S** one that flings

FLINKITE   *n* pl. **-S** a mineral

FLINT   *v* **-ED, -ING, -S** to provide with flint (a spark-producing rock)

FLINTY   *adj* **FLINTIER, FLINTIEST** resembling flint **FLINTILY** *adv*

FLIP   *adj* **FLIPPER, FLIPPEST** flippant

FLIP   *v* **FLIPPED, FLIPPING, FLIPS** to throw with a brisk motion

FLIPBOOK   *n* pl. **-S** a book of a series of images that when flipped give the illusion of movement

FLIPFLOP   *v* **-FLOPPED, -FLOPPING, -FLOPS** to perform a backward somersault

FLIPPANT   *adj* impudent

FLIPPED   past tense of flip

FLIPPER   *n* pl. **-S** a broad, flat limb adapted for swimming

FLIPPEST   superlative of flip

FLIPPING   present participle of flip

FLIPPY   *adj* **FLIPPIER, FLIPPIEST** flaring at the bottom

FLIR   *n* pl. **-S** an electronic heat sensor

FLIRT   *v* **-ED, -ING, -S** to behave amorously without serious intent

FLIRTER   *n* pl. **-S** one that flirts

FLIRTY   *adj* **FLIRTIER, FLIRTIEST** given to flirting

FLIT   *v* **FLITTED, FLITTING, FLITS** to move lightly and swiftly

FLITCH   *v* **-ED, -ING, -ES** to cut into strips

FLITE   *v* **FLITED, FLITING, FLITES** to quarrel

FLITTED   past tense of flit

FLITTER   *v* **-ED, -ING, -S** to flutter

FLITTING   present participle of flit

FLIVVER   *n* pl. **-S** an old, battered car

FLIXWEED   *n* pl. **-S** a plant of the mustard family

FLOAT   *v* **-ED, -ING, -S** to rest or remain on the surface of a liquid

FLOATAGE   *n* pl. **-S** flotage

FLOATEL   *n* pl. **-S** a houseboat used as a hotel

FLOATER   *n* pl. **-S** one that floats

FLOATY   *adj* **FLOATIER, FLOATIEST** tending to float

FLOC   *v* **FLOCCED, FLOCCING, FLOCS** to aggregate into floccules

FLOCCI   pl. of floccus

FLOCCOSE   *adj* having woolly tufts

FLOCCULE   *n* pl. **-S** a tuft-like mass

FLOCCULI   *n/pl* small, loosely aggregated masses

FLOCCUS   *n* pl. **FLOCCI** a floccule

FLOCK   *v* **-ED, -ING, -S** to gather or move in a crowd

FLOCKING   *n* pl. **-S** a velvety design in short fibers on cloth or paper

FLOCKY   *adj* **FLOCKIER, FLOCKIEST** woolly

FLOE   *n* pl. **-S** a large mass of floating ice

FLOG	*v* **FLOGGED, FLOGGING, FLOGS** to beat with a whip or rod
FLOGGER	*n* pl. **-S** one that flogs
FLOGGING	*n* pl. **-S** a whipping
FLOKATI	*n* pl. **-S** a Greek handwoven rug
FLONG	*n* pl. **-S** a sheet of a certain type of paper
FLOOD	*v* **-ED, -ING, -S** to inundate
FLOODER	*n* pl. **-S** one that floods
FLOODING	*n* pl. **-S** a filling with fluid to excess
FLOODLIT	*adj* illuminated by floodlights
FLOODWAY	*n* pl. **-WAYS** an overflow channel
FLOOEY	*adj* awry
FLOOIE	*adj* flooey
FLOOR	*v* **-ED, -ING, -S** to provide with a floor (the level base of a room)
FLOORAGE	*n* pl. **-S** floor space
FLOORER	*n* pl. **-S** one that floors
FLOORING	*n* pl. **-S** a floor
FLOORPAN	*n* pl. **-S** the bottom part of the interior of a motor vehicle
FLOOSIE	*n* pl. **-S** floozy
FLOOSY	*n* pl. **-SIES** floozy
FLOOZIE	*n* pl. **-S** floozy
FLOOZY	*n* pl. **-ZIES** a prostitute
FLOP	*v* **FLOPPED, FLOPPING, FLOPS** to fall heavily and noisily
FLOPOVER	*n* pl. **-S** a defect in television reception
FLOPPER	*n* pl. **-S** one that flops
FLOPPING	present participle of flop
FLOPPY	*adj* **-PIER, -PIEST** soft and flexible **FLOPPILY** *adv*
FLOPPY	*n* pl. **-PIES** a type of computer disk
FLOPS	*n* pl. **FLOPS** a measure of computer speed
FLORA	*n* pl. **-RAS** or **-RAE** the plant life of a particular region
FLORAL	*n* pl. **-S** a design having flowers
FLORALLY	*adv* in a manner like that of a flower
FLOREAT	*v* may he/she/it flourish
FLORENCE	*n* pl. **-S** florin
FLORET	*n* pl. **-S** a small flower
FLORID	*adj* ruddy **FLORIDLY** *adv*
FLORIGEN	*n* pl. **-S** a plant hormone
FLORIN	*n* pl. **-S** a former gold coin of Europe
FLORIST	*n* pl. **-S** a grower or seller of flowers
FLORUIT	*n* pl. **-S** a period of flourishing
FLOSS	*v* **-ED, -ING, -ES** to clean between the teeth with a thread
FLOSSER	*n* pl. **-S** one that flosses
FLOSSIE	*n* pl. **-S** a floozy
FLOSSING	*n* pl. **-S** the act of one that flosses
FLOSSY	*adj* **FLOSSIER, FLOSSIEST** resembling floss (a soft, light fiber) **FLOSSILY** *adv*
FLOTA	*n* pl. **-S** a fleet of Spanish ships
FLOTAGE	*n* pl. **-S** the act of floating
FLOTEL	*n* pl. **-S** floatel
FLOTILLA	*n* pl. **-S** a fleet of ships
FLOTSAM	*n* pl. **-S** floating wreckage of a ship or its cargo
FLOUNCE	*v* **FLOUNCED, FLOUNCING, FLOUNCES** to move with exaggerated motions
FLOUNCY	*adj* **FLOUNCIER, FLOUNCIEST** flouncing
FLOUNDER	*v* **-ED, -ING, -S** to struggle clumsily
FLOUR	*v* **-ED, -ING, -S** to cover with flour (a finely ground meal of grain)
FLOURISH	*v* **-ED, -ING, -ES** to thrive
FLOURY	*adj* **FLOURIER, FLOURIEST** resembling flour
FLOUT	*v* **-ED, -ING, -S** to treat with contempt
FLOUTER	*n* pl. **-S** one that flouts
FLOW	*v* **-ED, -ING, -S** to move steadily and smoothly along **FLOWABLE** *adj*
FLOWAGE	*n* pl. **-S** the act of flowing
FLOWER	*v* **-ED, -ING, -S** to put forth flowers (reproductive structures of seed-bearing plants)
FLOWERER	*n* pl. **-S** a plant that flowers at a certain time
FLOWERET	*n* pl. **-S** a floret
FLOWERY	*adj* **-ERIER, -ERIEST** abounding in flowers
FLOWN	a past participle of fly
FLU	*n* pl. **-S** a virus disease
FLUB	*v* **FLUBBED, FLUBBING, FLUBS** to bungle
FLUBBER	*n* pl. **-S** one that flubs
FLUBDUB	*n* pl. **-S** pretentious nonsense

FLUE	*n* pl. **-S** an enclosed passageway for directing a current **FLUED** *adj*
FLUENCY	*n* pl. **-CIES** the quality of being fluent
FLUENT	*adj* spoken or written with effortless ease **FLUENTLY** *adv*
FLUERICS	*n/pl* fluidics **FLUERIC** *adj*
FLUFF	*v* **-ED, -ING, -S** to make fluffy
FLUFFER	*n* pl. **-S** one that fluffs
FLUFFY	*adj* **FLUFFIER, FLUFFIEST** light and soft **FLUFFILY** *adv*
FLUID	*n* pl. **-S** a substance that tends to flow **FLUIDAL** *adj*
FLUIDICS	*n/pl* a branch of mechanical engineering **FLUIDIC** *adj*
FLUIDISE	*v* **-ISED, -ISING, -ISES** to fluidize
FLUIDITY	*n* pl. **-TIES** the quality of being able to flow
FLUIDIZE	*v* **-IZED, -IZING, -IZES** to cause to flow like a fluid
FLUIDLY	*adv* with fluidity
FLUIDRAM	*n* pl. **-S** a unit of liquid capacity
FLUISH	*adj* having symptoms like those of the flu
FLUKE	*v* **FLUKED, FLUKING, FLUKES** to obtain by chance
FLUKEY	*adj* **FLUKIER, FLUKIEST** fluky
FLUKY	*adj* **FLUKIER, FLUKIEST** happening by or depending on chance **FLUKILY** *adv*
FLUME	*v* **FLUMED, FLUMING, FLUMES** to convey by means of an artificial water channel
FLUMMERY	*n* pl. **-MERIES** a sweet dessert
FLUMMOX	*v* **-ED, -ING, -ES** to confuse
FLUMP	*v* **-ED, -ING, -S** to fall heavily
FLUNG	past tense of fling
FLUNK	*v* **-ED, -ING, -S** to fail an examination or course
FLUNKER	*n* pl. **-S** one that flunks
FLUNKEY	*n* pl. **-KEYS** flunky
FLUNKIE	*n* pl. **-S** flunky
FLUNKY	*n* pl. **-KIES** a servile follower
FLUOR	*n* pl. **-S** fluorite **FLUORIC** *adj*
FLUORENE	*n* pl. **-S** a chemical compound
FLUORID	*n* pl. **-S** fluoride
FLUORIDE	*n* pl. **-S** a compound of fluorine
FLUORIN	*n* pl. **-S** fluorine
FLUORINE	*n* pl. **-S** a gaseous element
FLUORITE	*n* pl. **-S** a mineral
FLURRY	*v* **-RIED, -RYING, -RIES** to confuse
FLUSH	*adj* **FLUSHER, FLUSHEST** ruddy
FLUSH	*v* **-ED, -ING, -ES** to blush
FLUSHER	*n* pl. **-S** one that flushes
FLUSHING	*n* pl. **-S** the act of blushing
FLUSTER	*v* **-ED, -ING, -S** to put into a state of nervous confusion
FLUTE	*v* **FLUTED, FLUTING, FLUTES** to play on a flute (a woodwind instrument)
FLUTER	*n* pl. **-S** a flutist
FLUTEY	*adj* **FLUTEYER, FLUTEYEST** or **FLUTIER, FLUTIEST** fluty
FLUTING	*n* pl. **-S** a series of parallel grooves
FLUTIST	*n* pl. **-S** one who plays the flute
FLUTTER	*v* **-ED, -ING, -S** to wave rapidly and irregularly
FLUTTERY	*adj* marked by fluttering
FLUTY	*adj* **FLUTIER, FLUTIEST** resembling a flute in sound
FLUVIAL	*adj* pertaining to a river
FLUX	*v* **-ED, -ING, -ES** to melt
FLUXGATE	*n* pl. **-S** a device to measure a magnetic field
FLUXION	*n* pl. **-S** the act of flowing
FLUYT	*n* pl. **-S** a type of ship
FLY	*adj* **FLIER, FLIEST** clever
FLY	*v* **FLEW, FLOWN, FLYING, FLIES** to move through the air
FLY	*v* **FLIED, FLYING, FLIES** to hit a ball high into the air in baseball
FLYABLE	*adj* suitable for flying
FLYAWAY	*n* pl. **-AWAYS** one that is elusive
FLYBELT	*n* pl. **-S** an area infested with tsetse flies
FLYBLOW	*v* **-BLEW, -BLOWN, -BLOWING, -BLOWS** to taint
FLYBOAT	*n* pl. **-S** a small, fast boat
FLYBOY	*n* pl. **-BOYS** a pilot in an air force
FLYBY	*n* pl. **-BYS** a flight of aircraft close to a specified place
FLYER	*n* pl. **-S** flier
FLYING	*n* pl. **-S** the operation of an aircraft
FLYLEAF	*n* pl. **-LEAVES** a blank leaf at the beginning or end of a book
FLYLESS	*adj* free of flies (winged insects)
FLYLINE	*n* pl. **-S** a type of line used in fly fishing

FLYMAN   *n* pl. **-MEN** a stage worker in a theater

FLYOFF   *n* pl. **-S** a competitive testing of model aircraft

FLYOVER   *n* pl. **-S** a flight of aircraft over a specific location

FLYPAPER   *n* pl. **-S** paper designed to catch or kill flies

FLYPAST   *n* pl. **-S** a flyby

FLYSCH   *n* pl. **-ES** a sandstone deposit

FLYSHEET   *n* pl. **-S** a circular

FLYSPECK   *v* **-ED, -ING, -S** to mark with minute spots

FLYTE   *v* **FLYTED, FLYTING, FLYTES** to flite

FLYTIER   *n* pl. **-S** a maker of fishing flies

FLYTING   *n* pl. **-S** a dispute in verse form

FLYTRAP   *n* pl. **-S** a trap for catching flies

FLYWAY   *n* pl. **-WAYS** an established air route of migratory birds

FLYWHEEL   *n* pl. **-S** a heavy disk used in machinery

FOAL   *v* **-ED, -ING, -S** to give birth to a horse

FOALING   *n* pl. **-S** the act of giving birth to a horse

FOAM   *v* **-ED, -ING, -S** to form foam (a light, bubbly, gas and liquid mass) **FOAMABLE** *adj*

FOAMER   *n* pl. **-S** one that foams

FOAMIER   comparative of foamy

FOAMIEST   superlative of foamy

FOAMILY   *adv* in a foamy manner

FOAMLESS   *adj* being without foam

FOAMLIKE   *adj* resembling foam

FOAMY   *adj* **FOAMIER, FOAMIEST** covered with foam

FOB   *v* **FOBBED, FOBBING, FOBS** to deceive

FOCACCIA   *n* pl. **-S** a flat Italian bread

FOCAL   *adj* pertaining to a focus

FOCALISE   *v* **-ISED, -ISING, -ISES** to focalize

FOCALIZE   *v* **-IZED, -IZING, -IZES** to focus

FOCALLY   *adv* with regard to focus

FOCUS   *n* pl. **-CUSES** or **-CI** a point at which rays converge or from which they diverge

FOCUS   *v* **-CUSED, -CUSING, -CUSES** or **-CUSSED, -CUSSING, -CUSSES** to bring to a focus

FOCUSER   *n* pl. **-S** one that focuses

FODDER   *v* **-ED, -ING, -S** to feed with coarse food

FODGEL   *adj* plump

FOE   *n* pl. **-S** an enemy

FOEHN   *n* pl. **-S** a warm, dry wind

FOEMAN   *n* pl. **-MEN** an enemy in war

FOETAL   *adj* fetal

FOETID   *adj* fetid **FOETIDLY** *adv*

FOETOR   *n* pl. **-S** fetor

FOETUS   *n* pl. **-ES** fetus

FOG   *v* **FOGGED, FOGGING, FOGS** to cover with fog (condensed water vapor near the earth's surface)

FOGBOUND   *adj* surrounded by fog

FOGBOW   *n* pl. **-S** a nebulous arc of light sometimes seen in a fog

FOGDOG   *n* pl. **-S** a fogbow

FOGEY   *n* pl. **-GEYS** fogy **FOGEYISH** *adj*

FOGEYDOM   *n* pl. **-S** fogydom

FOGEYISM   *n* pl. **-S** fogyism

FOGFRUIT   *n* pl. **-S** a flowering plant

FOGGAGE   *n* pl. **-S** a second growth of grass

FOGGED   past tense of fog

FOGGER   *n* pl. **-S** one that fogs

FOGGING   *n* pl. **-S** the covering with fog

FOGGY   *adj* **-GIER, -GIEST** filled with fog **FOGGILY** *adv*

FOGHORN   *n* pl. **-S** a horn sounded in a fog

FOGIE   *n* pl. **-S** fogy

FOGLESS   *adj* having no fog

FOGLIGHT   *n* pl. **-S** a motor-vehicle light used in foggy conditions

FOGY   *n* pl. **-GIES** an old-fashioned person **FOGYISH** *adj*

FOGYDOM   *n* pl. **-S** all the fogies

FOGYISM   *n* pl. **-S** old-fashioned behavior

FOH   *interj* faugh

FOHN   *n* pl. **-S** foehn

FOIBLE   *n* pl. **-S** a minor weakness

FOIL   *v* **-ED, -ING, -S** to prevent the success of **FOILABLE** *adj*

FOILIST   *n* pl. **-S** one who fences with a foil (a sword without cutting edges)

FOILSMAN   *n* pl. **-MEN** a fencer

FOIN   *v* **-ED, -ING, -S** to thrust with a pointed weapon

FOISON	*n* pl. **-S** strength
FOIST	*v* **-ED, -ING, -S** to force upon slyly
FOLACIN	*n* pl. **-S** a B vitamin
FOLATE	*n* pl. **-S** folacin
FOLD	*v* **-ED, -ING, -S** to lay one part over another part of **FOLDABLE** *adj*
FOLDAWAY	*n* pl. **-S** an object designed to be folded out of the way
FOLDAWAY	*adj* designed to fold out of the way
FOLDBOAT	*n* pl. **-S** a faltboat
FOLDER	*n* pl. **-S** one that folds
FOLDEROL	*n* pl. **-S** falderal
FOLDOUT	*n* pl. **-S** a gatefold
FOLDUP	*n* pl. **-S** an object that folds up
FOLEY	*n* pl. **-LEYS** a process for creating sounds for films
FOLIA	a pl. of folium
FOLIAGE	*n* pl. **-S** the growth of leaves of a plant **FOLIAGED** *adj*
FOLIAR	*adj* pertaining to a leaf
FOLIATE	*v* **-ATED, -ATING, -ATES** to hammer into thin plates
FOLIC	*adj* derived from folic acid
FOLIO	*v* **-ED, -ING, -S** to number the pages of
FOLIOSE	*adj* having leaves
FOLIOUS	*adj* foliose
FOLIUM	*n* pl. **-LIUMS** or **-LIA** a thin layer
FOLK	*n* pl. **-S** a people or tribe
FOLKIE	*adj* **FOLKIER, FOLKIEST** being in the style of folk music
FOLKIE	*n* pl. **-S** a performer of folk music
FOLKISH	*adj* characteristic of the common people
FOLKLIFE	*n* pl. **-LIVES** the traditions, skills, and products of a people
FOLKLIKE	*adj* folkish
FOLKLORE	*n* pl. **-S** the lore of a people
FOLKMOOT	*n* pl. **-S** a general assembly of the people in early England
FOLKMOT	*n* pl. **-S** folkmoot
FOLKMOTE	*n* pl. **-S** folkmoot
FOLKSONG	*n* pl. **-S** a song of the folk music of an area
FOLKSY	*adj* **FOLKSIER, FOLKSIEST** friendly **FOLKSILY** *adv*
FOLKTALE	*n* pl. **-S** a tale forming part of the oral tradition of a people
FOLKWAY	*n* pl. **-WAYS** a traditional custom of a people
FOLKY	*adj* **FOLKIER, FOLKIEST** folkie
FOLKY	*n* pl. **FOLKIES** folkie
FOLLES	pl. of follis
FOLLICLE	*n* pl. **-S** a small bodily cavity
FOLLIES	pl. of folly
FOLLIS	*n* pl. **-LES** a coin of ancient Rome
FOLLOW	*v* **-ED, -ING, -S** to come or go after
FOLLOWER	*n* pl. **-S** one that follows
FOLLOWUP	*n* pl. **-S** a news article that adds information to a previous article
FOLLY	*n* pl. **-LIES** a foolish idea or action
FOMENT	*v* **-ED, -ING, -S** to promote the development of
FOMENTER	*n* pl. **-S** one that foments
FOMITE	*n* pl. **-S** an inanimate object that serves to transmit infectious organisms
FON	*n* pl. **-S** foehn
FOND	*adj* **FONDER, FONDEST** having an affection
FOND	*v* **-ED, -ING, -S** to display affection
FONDANT	*n* pl. **-S** a soft, creamy candy
FONDLE	*v* **-DLED, -DLING, -DLES** to caress
FONDLER	*n* pl. **-S** one that fondles
FONDLING	*n* pl. **-S** one that is fondled
FONDLY	*adv* in a fond manner
FONDNESS	*n* pl. **-ES** affection
FONDU	*n* pl. **-S** a dish of melted cheese
FONDUE	*v* **-DUED, -DUING** or **-DUEING, -DUES** to cook in a pot of melted cheese
FONT	*n* pl. **-S** a receptacle for the water used in baptism **FONTAL** *adj*
FONTANEL	*n* pl. **-S** a space in the fetal and infantile skull
FONTINA	*n* pl. **-S** an Italian cheese
FOO	*n* pl. **FOOS** a name for temporary computer variables or files
FOOD	*n* pl. **-S** a substance taken into the body to maintain life and growth **FOODLESS** *adj*
FOODERY	*n* pl. **-ERIES** a restaurant
FOODIE	*n* pl. **-S** an enthusiast of foods and their preparation
FOODLAND	*n* pl. **-S** land for the production of food
FOODWAYS	*n/pl* the eating habits of a people

FOOFARAW	*n* pl. **-S** excessive ornamentation
FOOL	*v* **-ED, -ING, -S** to deceive
FOOLERY	*n* pl. **-ERIES** foolish behavior or speech
FOOLFISH	*n* pl. **-ES** a marine fish
FOOLISH	*adj* **-ISHER, -ISHEST** lacking good sense or judgment
FOOLSCAP	*n* pl. **-S** a paper size
FOOSBALL	*n* pl. **-S** a table game resembling soccer
FOOT	*n* pl. **FEET** the terminal part of the leg on which the body stands and moves
FOOT	*v* **-ED, -ING, -S** to walk
FOOTAGE	*n* pl. **-S** a length or quantity expressed in feet
FOOTBAG	*n* pl. **-S** a small bag filled with pellets that is kept aloft with the feet
FOOTBALL	*n* pl. **-S** a type of ball
FOOTBATH	*n* pl. **-S** a bath for the feet
FOOTBED	*n* pl. **-S** an insole in a boot or shoe
FOOTBOY	*n* pl. **-BOYS** a serving boy
FOOTER	*n* pl. **-S** one that walks
FOOTFALL	*n* pl. **-S** the sound of a footstep
FOOTGEAR	*n* pl. **FOOTGEAR** footwear
FOOTHILL	*n* pl. **-S** a low hill at the foot of higher hills
FOOTHOLD	*n* pl. **-S** a secure support for the feet
FOOTIE	*n* pl. **-S** footsie
FOOTIER	comparative of footy
FOOTIEST	superlative of footy
FOOTING	*n* pl. **-S** a foothold
FOOTLE	*v* **-TLED, -TLING, -TLES** to waste time
FOOTLER	*n* pl. **-S** one that footles
FOOTLESS	*adj* having no feet
FOOTLIKE	*adj* resembling a foot
FOOTLING	present participle of footle
FOOTLONG	*n* pl. **-S** a hot dog one foot long
FOOTMAN	*n* pl. **-MEN** a male servant
FOOTMARK	*n* pl. **-S** a mark left by the foot on a surface
FOOTNOTE	*v* **-NOTED, -NOTING, -NOTES** to furnish with explanatory notes
FOOTPACE	*n* pl. **-S** a walking pace
FOOTPAD	*n* pl. **-S** one who robs a pedestrian
FOOTPATH	*n* pl. **-S** a path for pedestrians
FOOTRACE	*n* pl. **-S** a race run on foot
FOOTREST	*n* pl. **-S** a support for the feet
FOOTROPE	*n* pl. **-S** a rope used in sailing
FOOTSIE	*n* pl. **-S** a flirting game played with the feet
FOOTSLOG	*v* **-SLOGGED, -SLOGGING, -SLOGS** to march through mud
FOOTSORE	*adj* having sore or tired feet
FOOTSTEP	*n* pl. **-S** a step with the foot
FOOTSY	*n* pl. **-SIES** footsie
FOOTWALL	*n* pl. **-S** the layer of rock beneath a vein of ore
FOOTWAY	*n* pl. **-WAYS** a footpath
FOOTWEAR	*n* pl. **FOOTWEAR** wearing apparel for the feet
FOOTWELL	*n* pl. **-S** a space for the feet in a motor vehicle
FOOTWORK	*n* pl. **-S** the use of the feet
FOOTWORN	*adj* footsore
FOOTY	*adj* **-TIER, -TIEST** paltry
FOOZLE	*v* **-ZLED, -ZLING, -ZLES** to bungle
FOOZLER	*n* pl. **-S** one that foozles
FOP	*v* **FOPPED, FOPPING, FOPS** to deceive
FOPPERY	*n* pl. **-PERIES** foppish behavior
FOPPISH	*adj* characteristic of a dandy
FOR	*prep* directed or sent to
FORA	a pl. of forum
FORAGE	*v* **-AGED, -AGING, -AGES** to search about
FORAGER	*n* pl. **-S** one that forages
FORAM	*n* pl. **-S** a marine rhizopod
FORAMEN	*n* pl. **-MENS** or **-MINA** a small anatomical opening
FORAY	*v* **-ED, -ING, -S** to raid
FORAYER	*n* pl. **-S** one that forays
FORB	*n* pl. **-S** an herb other than grass
FORBEAR	*v* **-BORE** or **-BARE, -BORNE, -BEARING, -BEARS** to refrain from
FORBID	*v* **-BADE** or **-BAD, -BIDDEN, -BIDDING, -BIDS** to command not to do something
FORBIDAL	*n* pl. **-S** the act of forbidding
FORBODE	*v* **-BODED, -BODING, -BODES** to forebode
FORBORE	past tense of forbear

FORBORNE   past participle of forbear

FORBY   *prep* close by

FORBYE   *prep* forby

FORCE   *v* **FORCED, FORCING, FORCES** to overcome resistance by the exertion of strength **FORCEDLY** *adv*

FORCEFUL   *adj* strong

FORCEOUT   *n* pl. **-S** a play by which a runner in baseball is put out

FORCEPS   *n* pl. **-CIPES** an instrument for seizing and holding objects

FORCER   *n* pl. **-S** one that forces

FORCIBLE   *adj* effected by force **FORCIBLY** *adv*

FORCING   present participle of force

FORCIPES   pl. of forceps

FORD   *v* **-ED, -ING, -S** to cross by wading **FORDABLE** *adj*

FORDLESS   *adj* unable to be forded

FORDO   *v* **-DID, -DONE, -DOING, -DOES** to destroy

FORE   *n* pl. **-S** the front part of something

FOREARM   *v* **-ED, -ING, -S** to arm in advance

FOREBAY   *n* pl. **-BAYS** a reservoir from which water is taken to run equipment

FOREBEAR   *n* pl. **-S** an ancestor

FOREBODE   *v* **-BODED, -BODING, -BODES** to indicate in advance

FOREBODY   *n* pl. **-BODIES** the forward part of a ship

FOREBOOM   *n* pl. **-S** the boom of a ship's foremast

FOREBY   *prep* forby

FOREBYE   *prep* forby

FORECAST   *v* **-ED, -ING, -S** to estimate or calculate in advance

FOREDATE   *v* **-DATED, -DATING, -DATES** to antedate

FOREDECK   *n* pl. **-S** the forward part of a ship's deck

FOREDO   *v* **-DID, -DONE, -DOING, -DOES** to fordo

FOREDOOM   *v* **-ED, -ING, -S** to doom in advance

FOREFACE   *n* pl. **-S** the front part of the head of a quadruped

FOREFEEL   *v* **-FELT, -FEELING, -FEELS** to have a premonition of

FOREFEND   *v* **-ED, -ING, -S** to forfend

FOREFOOT   *n* pl. **-FEET** one of the front feet of an animal

FOREGO   *v* **-WENT, -GONE, -GOING, -GOES** to go before

FOREGOER   *n* pl. **-S** one that foregoes

FOREGUT   *n* pl. **-S** the front part of the embryonic alimentary canal

FOREHAND   *n* pl. **-S** a type of tennis stroke

FOREHEAD   *n* pl. **-S** the part of the face above the eyes

FOREHOOF   *n* pl. **-HOOFS** or **-HOOVES** the hoof of a forefoot

FOREIGN   *adj* situated outside a place or country

FOREKNOW   *v* **-KNEW, -KNOWN, -KNOWING, -KNOWS** to know in advance

FORELADY   *n* pl. **-DIES** a woman who supervises workers

FORELAND   *n* pl. **-S** a projecting mass of land

FORELEG   *n* pl. **-S** one of the front legs of an animal

FORELIMB   *n* pl. **-S** a foreleg

FORELOCK   *v* **-ED, -ING, -S** to fasten with a linchpin

FOREMAN   *n* pl. **-MEN** a man who supervises workers

FOREMAST   *n* pl. **-S** the forward mast of a ship

FOREMILK   *n* pl. **-S** the milk secreted immediately after childbirth

FOREMOST   *adj* first in position

FORENAME   *n* pl. **-S** a first name

FORENOON   *n* pl. **-S** the period of daylight before noon

FORENSIC   *n* pl. **-S** an argumentative exercise

FOREPART   *n* pl. **-S** the front part

FOREPAST   *adj* already in the past

FOREPAW   *n* pl. **-S** the paw of a foreleg

FOREPEAK   *n* pl. **-S** the forward part of a ship's hold

FOREPLAY   *n* pl. **-PLAYS** erotic stimulation preceding sexual intercourse

FORERANK   *n* pl. **-S** the first rank

FORERUN   *v* **-RAN, -RUNNING, -RUNS** to run in advance of

FORESAID   *adj* previously said

FORESAIL   *n* pl. **-S** the lowest sail on a foremast

FORESEE   *v* **-SAW, -SEEN, -SEEING, -SEES** to see in advance

FORESEER   *n* pl. **-S** one that foresees

FORESHOW *v* **-SHOWED, -SHOWN, -SHOWING, -SHOWS** to show in advance

FORESIDE *n* pl. **-S** the front side

FORESKIN *n* pl. **-S** the prepuce

FOREST *v* **-ED, -ING, -S** to convert into a forest (a densely wooded area)

FORESTAL *adj* of or pertaining to a forest

FORESTAY *n* pl. **-STAYS** a wire or rope used to support a foremast

FORESTER *n* pl. **-S** one skilled in forestry

FORESTRY *n* pl. **-RIES** the science of planting and managing forests

FORETELL *v* **-TOLD, -TELLING, -TELLS** to tell of or about in advance

FORETIME *n* pl. **-S** the past

FORETOP *n* pl. **-S** the platform at the head of a ship's foremast

FOREVER *n* pl. **-S** an indefinite length of time

FOREWARN *v* **-ED, -ING, -S** to warn in advance

FOREWENT past tense of forego

FOREWING *n* pl. **-S** an anterior wing of an insect

FOREWORD *n* pl. **-S** an introductory statement

FOREWORN *adj* forworn

FOREX *n* pl. **-ES** a foreign exchange

FOREYARD *n* pl. **-S** the lowest yard on a foremast

FORFEIT *v* **-ED, -ING, -S** to lose as a penalty

FORFEND *v* **-ED, -ING, -S** to protect

FORGAT a past tense of forget

FORGAVE past tense of forgive

FORGE *v* **FORGED, FORGING, FORGES** to fashion or reproduce for fraudulent purposes

FORGER *n* pl. **-S** one that forges

FORGERY *n* pl. **-ERIES** the act of forging

FORGET *v* **-GOT** or **-GAT, -GOTTEN, -GETTING, -GETS** to fail to remember

FORGING *n* pl. **-S** a forgery

FORGIVE *v* **-GAVE, -GIVEN, -GIVING, -GIVES** to pardon

FORGIVER *n* pl. **-S** one that forgives

FORGO *v* **-WENT, -GONE, -GOING, -GOES** to refrain from

FORGOER *n* pl. **-S** one that forgoes

FORGOT a past tense of forget

FORGOTTEN past participle of forget

FORINT *n* pl. **-S** a monetary unit of Hungary

FORJUDGE *v* **-JUDGED, -JUDGING, -JUDGES** to deprive by judgment of a court

FORK *v* **-ED, -ING, -S** to work with a fork (a pronged implement) **FORKEDLY** *adv*

FORKBALL *n* pl. **-S** a breaking pitch in baseball

FORKER *n* pl. **-S** one that forks

FORKFUL *n* pl. **FORKFULS** or **FORKSFUL** as much as a fork will hold

FORKIER comparative of forky

FORKIEST superlative of forky

FORKLESS *adj* having no fork

FORKLIFT *v* **-ED, -ING, -S** to raise or transport by means of a forklift (a machine with projecting prongs)

FORKLIKE *adj* resembling a fork

FORKSFUL a pl. of forkful

FORKY *adj* **FORKIER, FORKIEST** resembling a fork

FORLORN *adj* **-LORNER, -LORNEST** dreary

FORM *v* **-ED, -ING, -S** to produce **FORMABLE** *adj* **FORMABLY** *adv*

FORMAL *n* pl. **-S** a social event that requires evening dress

FORMALIN *n* pl. **-S** an aqueous solution of formaldehyde

FORMALLY *adv* in a prescribed or customary manner

FORMANT *n* pl. **-S** a characteristic component of the quality of a speech sound

FORMAT *v* **-MATTED, -MATTING, -MATS** to produce in a specified style

FORMATE *n* pl. **-S** a chemical salt

FORME *n* pl. **-S** an assemblage of printing type secured in a metal frame

FORMEE *adj* having the arms narrow at the center and expanding toward the ends — used of a heraldic cross

FORMER *n* pl. **-S** one that forms

FORMERLY *adv* previously

FORMFUL *adj* exhibiting good form

FORMIC *adj* pertaining to ants

FORMLESS *adj* lacking structure

FORMOL *n* pl. **-S** formalin

FORMULA *n* pl. **-LAS** or **-LAE** an exact method for doing something

FORMWORK *n* pl. **-S** a set of forms to hold concrete until it sets

FORMYL	*n* pl. **-S** a univalent chemical radical
FORNENT	*prep* near to
FORNIX	*n* pl. **-NICES** an arched anatomical structure **FORNICAL** *adj*
FORRADER	*adv* further ahead
FORRIT	*adv* toward the front
FORSAKE	*v* **-SOOK, -SAKEN, -SAKING, -SAKES** to quit or leave entirely
FORSAKER	*n* pl. **-S** one that forsakes
FORSOOTH	*adv* in truth
FORSPENT	*adj* worn out
FORSWEAR	*v* **-SWORE, -SWORN, -SWEARING, -SWEARS** to deny under oath
FORT	*n* pl. **-S** a fortified enclosure or structure
FORTE	*n* pl. **-S** a strong point
FORTES	pl. of fortis
FORTH	*adv* onward in time, place, or order
FORTIES	pl. of forty
FORTIETH	*n* pl. **-S** one of forty equal parts
FORTIFY	*v* **-FIED, -FYING, -FIES** to strengthen against attack
FORTIS	*n* pl. **-TES** a consonant pronounced with relatively strong release of breath
FORTRESS	*v* **-ED, -ING, -ES** to fortify
FORTUITY	*n* pl. **-ITIES** an accidental occurrence
FORTUNE	*v* **-TUNED, -TUNING, -TUNES** to endow with wealth
FORTY	*n* pl. **-TIES** a number
FORTYISH	*adj* being about forty years old
FORUM	*n* pl. **-RUMS** or **-RA** a public meeting place
FORWARD	*adj* **-WARDER, -WARDEST** being at a point in advance
FORWARD	*v* **-ED, -ING, -S** to help onward
FORWENT	past tense of forgo
FORWHY	*adv* for what reason
FORWORN	*adj* worn out
FORZANDO	*n* pl. **-DOS** or **-DI** sforzato
FOSS	*n* pl. **-ES** fosse
FOSSA	*n* pl. **-S** a catlike mammal
FOSSA	*n* pl. **-SAE** an anatomical depression **FOSSATE** *adj*
FOSSE	*n* pl. **-S** a ditch
FOSSETTE	*n* pl. **-S** a small fossa

FOSSICK	*v* **-ED, -ING, -S** to search for gold
FOSSIL	*n* pl. **-S** the remains of an animal or plant preserved in the earth's crust
FOSTER	*v* **-ED, -ING, -S** to promote the growth of
FOSTERER	*n* pl. **-S** one that fosters
FOU	*adj* drunk
FOUETTE	*n* pl. **-S** a movement in ballet
FOUGHT	past tense of fight
FOUGHTEN	*adj* exhausted especially from fighting
FOUL	*adj* **FOULER, FOULEST** offensive to the senses
FOUL	*v* **-ED, -ING, -S** to make foul
FOULARD	*n* pl. **-S** a soft fabric
FOULING	*n* pl. **-S** a deposit or crust
FOULLY	*adv* in a foul manner
FOULNESS	*n* pl. **-ES** the state of being foul
FOUND	*v* **-ED, -ING, -S** to establish
FOUNDER	*v* **-ED, -ING, -S** to become disabled
FOUNDRY	*n* pl. **-RIES** an establishment in which metal is cast
FOUNT	*n* pl. **-S** a fountain
FOUNTAIN	*v* **-ED, -ING, -S** to flow like a fountain (a spring of water)
FOUR	*n* pl. **-S** a number
FOURCHEE	*adj* having the end of each arm forked — used of a heraldic cross
FOUREYED	*adj* wearing eyeglasses
FOURFOLD	*adj* four times as great
FOURGON	*n* pl. **-S** a wagon for carrying baggage
FOURPLEX	*n* pl. **-ES** quadplex
FOURSOME	*n* pl. **-S** a group of four
FOURTEEN	*n* pl. **-S** a number
FOURTH	*n* pl. **-S** one of four equal parts
FOURTHLY	*adv* in the fourth place
FOUSTY	*adj* **FOUSTIER, FOUSTIEST** moldy
FOVEA	*n* pl. **-VEAS** or **-VEAE** a shallow anatomical depression **FOVEAL, FOVEATE, FOVEATED** *adj*
FOVEOLA	*n* pl. **-LAS** or **-LAE** a small fovea **FOVEOLAR** *adj*
FOVEOLE	*n* pl. **-S** a foveola
FOVEOLET	*n* pl. **-S** a foveola
FOWL	*v* **-ED, -ING, -S** to hunt birds

FOWLER *n* pl. **-S** one that fowls

FOWLING *n* pl. **-S** the hunting of birds

FOWLPOX *n* pl. **-ES** a virus disease of poultry

FOX *v* **-ED, -ING, -ES** to outwit

FOXBERRY *n* pl. **-RIES** a cowberry

FOXFIRE *n* pl. **-S** a glow produced by certain fungi on decaying wood

FOXFISH *n* pl. **-ES** a large shark

FOXGLOVE *n* pl. **-S** a flowering plant

FOXHOLE *n* pl. **-S** a small pit used for cover in a battle area

FOXHOUND *n* pl. **-S** a hunting dog

FOXHUNT *v* **-ED, -ING, -S** to hunt with hounds for a fox

FOXIER comparative of foxy

FOXIEST superlative of foxy

FOXILY *adv* in a foxy manner

FOXINESS *n* pl. **-ES** the state of being foxy

FOXING *n* pl. **-S** a piece of material used to cover the upper portion of a shoe

FOXLIKE *adj* resembling a fox (a carnivorous mammal)

FOXSKIN *n* pl. **-S** the skin of a fox

FOXTAIL *n* pl. **-S** the tail of a fox

FOXTROT *v* **-TROTTED, -TROTTING, -TROTS** to dance the fox trot (a dance for couples)

FOXY *adj* **FOXIER, FOXIEST** crafty

FOY *n* pl. **FOYS** a farewell feast or gift

FOYER *n* pl. **-S** an entrance room or hall

FOZINESS *n* pl. **-ES** the state of being fozy

FOZY *adj* **-ZIER, -ZIEST** too ripe

FRABJOUS *adj* splendid

FRACAS *n* pl. **-ES** a brawl

FRACK *v* **-ED, -ING, -S** to engage in fracking

FRACKING *n* pl. **-S** the injection of fluid into shale beds in order to free up petroleum reserves

FRACTAL *n* pl. **-S** a complex geometric curve

FRACTED *adj* broken

FRACTI pl. of fractus

FRACTION *v* **-ED, -ING, -S** to divide into portions

FRACTUR *n* pl. **-S** fraktur

FRACTURE *v* **-TURED, -TURING, -TURES** to break

FRACTUS *n* pl. **-TI** a ragged cloud

FRAE *prep* from

FRAENUM *n* pl. **-NUMS** or **-NA** frenum

FRAG *v* **FRAGGED, FRAGGING, FRAGS** to injure with a type of grenade

FRAGGING *n* pl. **-S** the act of one that frags

FRAGILE *adj* easily broken or damaged

FRAGMENT *v* **-ED, -ING, -S** to break into pieces

FRAGRANT *adj* having a pleasant odor

FRAIL *adj* **FRAILER, FRAILEST** fragile **FRAILLY** *adv*

FRAIL *n* pl. **-S** a basket for holding dried fruits

FRAILTY *n* pl. **-TIES** a weakness of character

FRAISE *n* pl. **-S** a barrier of pointed stakes

FRAKTUR *n* pl. **-S** a style of type

FRAME *v* **FRAMED, FRAMING, FRAMES** to construct by putting together the various parts **FRAMABLE** *adj*

FRAMER *n* pl. **-S** one that frames

FRAMING *n* pl. **-S** framework

FRANC *n* pl. **-S** a former monetary unit of France

FRANCISE *v* **-CISED, -CISING, -CISES** to francize

FRANCIUM *n* pl. **-S** a radioactive element

FRANCIZE *v* **-CIZED, -CIZING, -CIZES** to force to adopt French customs and language

FRANK *adj* **FRANKER, FRANKEST** honest and unreserved in speech

FRANK *v* **-ED, -ING, -S** to mark (a piece of mail) for free delivery

FRANKER *n* pl. **-S** one that franks

FRANKLIN *n* pl. **-S** a medieval English landowner

FRANKLY *adv* in a frank manner

FRANKUM *n* pl. **-S** the hardened resin of a spruce tree

FRANTIC *adj* wildly excited

FRAP *v* **FRAPPED, FRAPPING, FRAPS** to bind firmly

FRAPPE *n* pl. **-S** a partly frozen drink

FRASCATI *n* pl. **-S** an Italian white wine

FRASS *n* pl. **-ES** debris made by insects

FRAT *n* pl. **-S** a college fraternity

FRATER *n* pl. **-S** a comrade

FRAUD *n* pl. **-S** trickery

FRAUGHT	*v* **-ED, -ING, -S** to load down
FRAULEIN	*n* pl. **-S** a German governess
FRAY	*v* **-ED, -ING, -S** to wear off by rubbing
FRAYING	*n* pl. **-S** something worn off by rubbing
FRAZIL	*n* pl. **-S** tiny ice crystals formed in supercooled waters
FRAZZLE	*v* **-ZLED, -ZLING, -ZLES** to fray
FREAK	*v* **-ED, -ING, -S** to streak with color
FREAKIER	comparative of freaky
FREAKIEST	superlative of freaky
FREAKILY	*adv* in a freaky manner
FREAKISH	*adj* unusual
FREAKOUT	*n* pl. **-S** an event marked by wild excitement
FREAKY	*adj* **FREAKIER, FREAKIEST** freakish
FRECKLE	*v* **-LED, -LING, -LES** to mark with freckles (small, brownish spots)
FRECKLY	*adj* **-LIER, -LIEST** marked with freckles
FREE	*adj* **FREER, FREEST** not subject to restriction or control
FREE	*v* **FREED, FREEING, FREES** to make free
FREEBASE	*v* **-BASED, -BASING, -BASES** to use a form of cocaine that is inhaled
FREEBEE	*n* pl. **-S** freebie
FREEBIE	*n* pl. **-S** something given or received without charge
FREEBOOT	*v* **-ED, -ING, -S** to plunder
FREEBORN	*adj* born free
FREED	past tense of free
FREEDMAN	*n* pl. **-MEN** a man who has been freed from slavery
FREEDOM	*n* pl. **-S** the state of being free
FREEFORM	*adj* having a free-flowing design or shape
FREEGAN	*n* pl. **-S** an activist who scavenges for free food to reduce consumption of resources
FREEHAND	*adj* drawn by hand without mechanical aids
FREEHOLD	*n* pl. **-S** a form of tenure of real property
FREELOAD	*v* **-ED, -ING, -S** to live at the expense of others
FREELY	*adv* in a free manner
FREEMAN	*n* pl. **-MEN** one who is free
FREENESS	*n* pl. **-ES** freedom
FREER	*n* pl. **-S** one that frees
FREERIDE	*n* pl. **-S** a type of snowboard
FREESIA	*n* pl. **-S** an African herb
FREEST	superlative of free
FREEWARE	*n* pl. **-S** software distributed without charge
FREEWAY	*n* pl. **-WAYS** an express highway
FREEWILL	*adj* voluntary
FREEZE	*v* **FROZE, FROZEN, FREEZING, FREEZES** to become hardened into a solid body by loss of heat
FREEZER	*n* pl. **-S** an apparatus for freezing food
FREEZING	*n* pl. **-S** the method by which foods are frozen to preserve them
FREIGHT	*v* **-ED, -ING, -S** to load with goods for transportation
FREMD	*adj* strange
FREMITUS	*n* pl. **-ES** a palpable vibration
FRENA	a pl. of frenum
FRENCH	*v* **-ED, -ING, -ES** to cut into thin strips before cooking
FRENEMY	*n* pl. **-MIES** one who pretends to be a friend but is actually an enemy
FRENETIC	*n* pl. **-S** a frantic person
FRENULUM	*n* pl. **-LUMS** or **-LA** a frenum **FRENULAR** *adj*
FRENUM	*n* pl. **-NUMS** or **-NA** a connecting fold of membrane
FRENZILY	*adv* in a frantic manner
FRENZY	*v* **-ZIED, -ZYING, -ZIES** to make frantic
FREQUENT	*adj* **-QUENTER, -QUENTEST** occurring again and again
FREQUENT	*v* **-ED, -ING, -S** to be in or at often
FRERE	*n* pl. **-S** brother
FRESCO	*v* **-ED, -ING, -S** or **-ES** to paint on a surface of plaster
FRESCOER	*n* pl. **-S** one that frescoes
FRESH	*adj* **FRESHER, FRESHEST** new
FRESH	*v* **-ED, -ING, -ES** to freshen
FRESHEN	*v* **-ED, -ING, -S** to make or become fresh
FRESHER	*n* pl. **-S** a freshman
FRESHET	*n* pl. **-S** a sudden overflow of a stream

FRESHLY *adv* in a fresh manner

FRESHMAN *n* pl. **-MEN** a first-year student at a high school, university, or college

FRESNEL *n* pl. **-S** a type of lens used in lights

FRET *v* **FRETTED, FRETTING, FRETS** to worry

FRETFUL *adj* inclined to fret

FRETLESS *adj* having no fretwork

FRETSAW *n* pl. **-S** a narrow-bladed saw

FRETSOME *adj* fretful

FRETTED past tense of fret

FRETTER *n* pl. **-S** one that frets

FRETTING present participle of fret

FRETTY *adj* **-TIER, -TIEST** fretful

FRETWORK *n* pl. **-S** ornamental work consisting of interlacing parts

FRIABLE *adj* easily crumbled

FRIAR *n* pl. **-S** a member of a religious order **FRIARLY** *adj*

FRIARY *n* pl. **-ARIES** a monastery of friars

FRIBBLE *v* **-BLED, -BLING, -BLES** to act foolishly

FRIBBLER *n* pl. **-S** one that fribbles

FRICANDO *n* pl. **-DOES** a roasted loin of veal

FRICOT *n* pl. **-S** a stew with potatoes and meat or fish

FRICTION *n* pl. **-S** the rubbing of one body against another

FRIDGE *n* pl. **-S** a refrigerator

FRIED past tense of fry

FRIEND *v* **-ED, -ING, -S** to enter into a warm association with

FRIENDLY *adj* **-LIER, -LIEST** inclined to approve, help, or support

FRIENDLY *n* pl. **-LIES** one who is friendly

FRIER *n* pl. **-S** fryer

FRIES present 3d person sing. of fry

FRIEZE *n* pl. **-S** a coarse woolen fabric

FRIG *n* pl. **-ES** a refrigerator

FRIG *v* **FRIGGED, FRIGGING, FRIGS** to cheat or trick

FRIGATE *n* pl. **-S** a sailing vessel

FRIGHT *v* **-ED, -ING, -S** to frighten

FRIGHTEN *v* **-ED, -ING, -S** to make afraid

FRIGID *adj* very cold **FRIGIDLY** *adv*

FRIJOL *n* pl. **-ES** a bean used as food

FRIJOLE *n* pl. **-S** frijol

FRILL *v* **-ED, -ING, -S** to provide with a frill (an ornamental ruffled edge)

FRILLER *n* pl. **-S** one that frills

FRILLERY *n* pl. **-ERIES** an arrangement of frills

FRILLIES *n/pl* an item of women's underwear

FRILLING *n* pl. **-S** an arrangement of frills

FRILLY *adj* **FRILLIER, FRILLIEST** having frills

FRINGE *v* **FRINGED, FRINGING, FRINGES** to provide with a fringe (an ornamental border)

FRINGING *n* pl. **-S** an ornamental border of loose short strips

FRINGY *adj* **FRINGIER, FRINGIEST** resembling a fringe

FRIPPERY *n* pl. **-PERIES** excessive ornamentation

FRISE *n* pl. **-S** frieze

FRISEE *n* pl. **-S** curly leaves of endive

FRISETTE *n* pl. **-S** frizette

FRISEUR *n* pl. **-S** a hairdresser

FRISK *v* **-ED, -ING, -S** to move or leap about playfully

FRISKER *n* pl. **-S** one that frisks

FRISKET *n* pl. **-S** a frame used to protect paper in a printing press

FRISKY *adj* **FRISKIER, FRISKIEST** lively and playful **FRISKILY** *adv*

FRISSON *n* pl. **-S** a shudder

FRIT *v* **FRITTED, FRITTING, FRITS** to fuse into a vitreous substance

FRITES *n/pl* french fries

FRITH *n* pl. **-S** firth

FRITT *v* **-ED, -ING, -S** to frit

FRITTATA *n* pl. **-S** an unfolded omelet with chopped vegetables or meat

FRITTED past tense of frit

FRITTER *v* **-ED, -ING, -S** to squander little by little

FRITTING present participle of frit

FRITZ *n* pl. **-ES** a nonfunctioning state

FRIULANO *n* pl. **-NOS** a mild Italian cheese

FRIVOL *v* **-OLED, -OLING, -OLS** or **-OLLED, -OLLING, -OLS** to behave playfully

FRIVOLER *n* pl. **-S** one that frivols

FRIZ *v* **-ED, -ING, -ES** to frizz

FRIZER *n* pl. **-S** frizzer

FRIZETTE	*n* pl. **-S** a frizzed fringe of hair
FRIZZ	*v* **-ED, -ING, -ES** to form into small, tight curls
FRIZZER	*n* pl. **-S** one that frizzes
FRIZZIER	comparative of frizzy
FRIZZIES	*n/pl* frizzy hair
FRIZZIEST	superlative of frizzy
FRIZZILY	*adv* in a frizzy manner
FRIZZLE	*v* **-ZLED, -ZLING, -ZLES** to frizz
FRIZZLER	*n* pl. **-S** one that frizzles
FRIZZLY	*adj* **-ZLIER, -ZLIEST** frizzy
FRIZZY	*adj* **FRIZZIER, FRIZZIEST** tightly curled
FRO	*adv* away
FROCK	*v* **-ED, -ING, -S** to clothe in a long, loose outer garment
FROE	*n* pl. **-S** a cleaving tool
FROG	*v* **FROGGED, FROGGING, FROGS** to hunt frogs (web-footed, tailless amphibians)
FROGEYE	*n* pl. **-S** a plant disease **FROGEYED** *adj*
FROGFISH	*n* pl. **-ES** a marine fish
FROGGED	past tense of frog
FROGGING	*n* pl. **-S** a type of ornamental coat fastener
FROGGY	*adj* **-GIER, -GIEST** abounding in frogs
FROGLET	*n* pl. **-S** a young frog
FROGLIKE	*adj* resembling a frog
FROGMAN	*n* pl. **-MEN** a person equipped for extended periods of underwater swimming
FROIDEUR	*n* pl. **-S** an aloof manner
FROLIC	*v* **-ICKED, -ICKING, -ICS** to play and run about merrily **FROLICKY** *adj*
FROM	*prep* starting at
FROMAGE	*n* pl. **-S** cheese
FROMENTY	*n* pl. **-TIES** frumenty
FROND	*n* pl. **-S** a type of leaf **FRONDED, FRONDOSE** *adj*
FRONDEUR	*n* pl. **-S** a rebel
FRONS	*n* pl. **FRONTES** the upper anterior portion of an insect's head
FRONT	*adj* **FRONTER, FRONTEST** pertaining to or situated at the forward part of a surface
FRONT	*v* **-ED, -ING, -S** to provide with a front (a forward part)
FRONTAGE	*n* pl. **-S** the front of a building or lot
FRONTAL	*n* pl. **-S** a bone of the skull
FRONTES	pl. of frons
FRONTIER	*n* pl. **-S** a border between two countries
FRONTLET	*n* pl. **-S** a decorative band worn across the forehead
FRONTMAN	*n* pl. **-MEN** the most prominent member of a group of musicians
FRONTON	*n* pl. **-S** a jai alai arena
FRORE	*adj* frozen
FROSH	*n* pl. **-ES** a freshman
FROST	*v* **-ED, -ING, -S** to cover with frost (a deposit of minute ice crystals)
FROSTBIT	*adj* injured by extreme cold
FROSTED	*n* pl. **-S** a type of milk shake
FROSTING	*n* pl. **-S** icing
FROSTNIP	*n* pl. **-S** the freezing of outer skin layers
FROSTY	*adj* **FROSTIER, FROSTIEST** covered with frost **FROSTILY** *adv*
FROTH	*v* **-ED, -ING, -S** to foam
FROTHER	*n* pl. **-S** one that froths
FROTHING	*n* pl. **-S** a layer of foam in a liquid or solid
FROTHY	*adj* **FROTHIER, FROTHIEST** foamy **FROTHILY** *adv*
FROTTAGE	*n* pl. **-S** masturbation by rubbing against another person
FROTTEUR	*n* pl. **-S** one who practices frottage
FROUFROU	*n* pl. **-S** a rustling sound
FROUNCE	*v* **FROUNCED, FROUNCING, FROUNCES** to pleat
FROUZY	*adj* **-ZIER, -ZIEST** frowzy
FROW	*n* pl. **-S** froe
FROWARD	*adj* disobedient
FROWN	*v* **-ED, -ING, -S** to contract the brow in displeasure
FROWNER	*n* pl. **-S** one that frowns
FROWNY	*adj* **FROWNIER, FROWNIEST** showing a frown
FROWST	*v* **-ED, -ING, -S** to lounge in a stuffy room
FROWSTY	*adj* **-TIER, -TIEST** musty
FROWSY	*adj* **-SIER, -SIEST** frowzy
FROWZY	*adj* **-ZIER, -ZIEST** unkempt **FROWZILY** *adv*
FROZE	past tense of freeze
FROZEN	*adj* very cold **FROZENLY** *adv*

FRUCTIFY   *v* **-FIED, -FYING, -FIES** to bear fruit

FRUCTOSE   *n* pl. **-S** a sugar found in various fruits

FRUG   *v* **FRUGGED, FRUGGING, FRUGS** to perform a type of vigorous dance

FRUGAL   *adj* thrifty **FRUGALLY** *adv*

FRUIT   *v* **-ED, -ING, -S** to bear fruit (usually edible reproductive bodies of a seed plant)

FRUITAGE   *n* pl. **-S** the process of bearing fruit

FRUITER   *n* pl. **-S** one that grows or sells fruit

FRUITFUL   *adj* **-FULLER, -FULLEST** producing abundantly

FRUITIER   comparative of fruity

FRUITIEST   superlative of fruity

FRUITING   *n* pl. **-S** the production of fruit on a tree

FRUITION   *n* pl. **-S** the accomplishment of something desired

FRUITLET   *n* pl. **-S** a small fruit

FRUITY   *adj* **FRUITIER, FRUITIEST** suggestive of fruit **FRUITILY** *adv*

FRUMENTY   *n* pl. **-TIES** a dish of wheat boiled in milk and sweetened with sugar

FRUMP   *n* pl. **-S** a dowdy woman **FRUMPISH** *adj*

FRUMPY   *adj* **FRUMPIER, FRUMPIEST** dowdy **FRUMPILY** *adv*

FRUSTULE   *n* pl. **-S** the shell of a diatom

FRUSTUM   *n* pl. **-TUMS** or **-TA** a part of a conical solid

FRY   *v* **FRIED, FRYING, FRIES** to cook over direct heat in hot fat or oil **FRYABLE** *adj*

FRYBREAD   *n* pl. **-S** a fried bread

FRYER   *n* pl. **-S** one that fries

FRYPAN   *n* pl. **-S** a pan for frying food

FUB   *v* **FUBBED, FUBBING, FUBS** to fob

FUBSY   *adj* **FUBSIER, FUBSIEST** chubby and somewhat squat

FUCHSIA   *n* pl. **-S** a flowering shrub

FUCHSIN   *n* pl. **-S** a red dye

FUCHSINE   *n* pl. **-S** fuchsin

FUCI   a pl. of fucus

FUCOID   *n* pl. **-S** a brown seaweed **FUCOIDAL** *adj*

FUCOSE   *n* pl. **-S** a type of sugar

FUCOUS   *adj* of or pertaining to fucoids

FUCUS   *n* pl. **-CUSES** or **-CI** any of a genus of brown algae

FUD   *n* pl. **-S** an old-fashioned person

FUDDLE   *v* **-DLED, -DLING, -DLES** to confuse

FUDDY   *n* pl. **-DIES** a fussy person

FUDGE   *v* **FUDGED, FUDGING, FUDGES** to falsify

FUDGY   *adj* **-GIER, -GIEST** resembling fudge (a soft, sweet candy)

FUEHRER   *n* pl. **-S** fuhrer

FUEL   *v* **-ELED, -ELING, -ELS** or **-ELLED, -ELLING, -ELS** to provide with fuel (material used to produce energy)

FUELER   *n* pl. **-S** one that fuels

FUELLER   *n* pl. **-S** fueler

FUELWOOD   *n* pl. **-S** firewood

FUG   *v* **FUGGED, FUGGING, FUGS** to make stuffy and odorous

FUGACITY   *n* pl. **-TIES** lack of enduring qualities

FUGAL   *adj* being in the style of a fugue **FUGALLY** *adv*

FUGATO   *n* pl. **-TOS** a fugal composition

FUGGED   past tense of fug

FUGGING   present participle of fug

FUGGY   *adj* **-GIER, -GIEST** stuffy and odorous **FUGGILY** *adv*

FUGIO   *n* pl. **-GIOS** a former coin of the United States

FUGITIVE   *n* pl. **-S** one who flees

FUGLE   *v* **-GLED, -GLING, -GLES** to lead by setting an example

FUGLEMAN   *n* pl. **-MEN** a leader

FUGU   *n* pl. **-S** a toxin-containing fish

FUGUE   *v* **FUGUED, FUGUING, FUGUES** to compose a fugue (a type of musical composition)

FUGUIST   *n* pl. **-S** one who composes fugues

FUHRER   *n* pl. **-S** a leader

FUJI   *n* pl. **-S** a silk fabric

FULCRUM   *n* pl. **-CRUMS** or **-CRA** a support for a lever

FULFIL   *v* **-FILLED, -FILLING, -FILS** to fulfill

FULFILL   *v* **-ED, -ING, -S** to bring about the accomplishment of

FULGENT   *adj* shining brightly

FULGID   *adj* fulgent

FULHAM   *n* pl. **-S** a loaded die

FULL   *adj* **FULLER, FULLEST** filled completely

FULL   *v* **-ED, -ING, -S** to shrink and thicken, as cloth

FULLAM   *n* pl. **-S** fulham

FULLBACK   *n* pl. **-S** an offensive back in football

FULLER   *v* **-ED, -ING, -S** to groove with a type of hammer

FULLERY   *n* pl. **-ERIES** a place for fulling cloth

FULLFACE   *n* pl. **-S** a heavy-faced type

FULLNESS   *n* pl. **-ES** the state of being full

FULLY   *adv* in a full manner

FULMAR   *n* pl. **-S** an arctic seabird

FULMINE   *v* **-MINED, -MINING, -MINES** to explode loudly

FULMINIC   *adj* highly explosive

FULNESS   *n* pl. **-ES** fullness

FULSOME   *adj* repulsive

FULVOUS   *adj* of a brownish yellow color

FUMARASE   *n* pl. **-S** an enzyme

FUMARATE   *n* pl. **-S** a chemical salt

FUMARIC   *adj* pertaining to a certain acid

FUMAROLE   *n* pl. **-S** a hole from which volcanic vapors issue

FUMATORY   *n* pl. **-RIES** a fumigation chamber

FUMBLE   *v* **-BLED, -BLING, -BLES** to handle clumsily

FUMBLER   *n* pl. **-S** one that fumbles

FUME   *v* **FUMED, FUMING, FUMES** to give off fumes (gaseous exhalations)

FUMELESS   *adj* having no fumes

FUMELIKE   *adj* resembling fumes

FUMER   *n* pl. **-S** one that fumes

FUMET   *n* pl. **-S** the odor of meat while cooking

FUMETTE   *n* pl. **-S** fumet

FUMIER   comparative of fumy

FUMIEST   superlative of fumy

FUMIGANT   *n* pl. **-S** a substance used in fumigating

FUMIGATE   *v* **-GATED, -GATING, -GATES** to subject to fumes in order to destroy pests

FUMING   present participle of fume

FUMINGLY   *adv* angrily

FUMITORY   *n* pl. **-RIES** a climbing plant

FUMULUS   *n* pl. **-LI** a thin cloud

FUMY   *adj* **FUMIER, FUMIEST** producing or full of fumes

FUN   *adj* **FUNNER, FUNNEST** providing enjoyment

FUN   *v* **FUNNED, FUNNING, FUNS** to act playfully

FUNCTION   *v* **-ED, -ING, -S** to be in action

FUNCTOR   *n* pl. **-S** one that functions

FUND   *v* **-ED, -ING, -S** to provide money for **FUNDABLE** *adj*

FUNDER   *n* pl. **-S** a provider of money

FUNDING   *n* pl. **-S** money provided for a particular purpose

FUNDUS   *n* pl. **-DI** the inner basal surface of a bodily organ **FUNDIC** *adj*

FUNERAL   *n* pl. **-S** a ceremony held for a dead person

FUNERARY   *adj* pertaining to a funeral

FUNEREAL   *adj* funerary

FUNEST   *adj* portending death or evil

FUNFAIR   *n* pl. **-S** an amusement park

FUNFEST   *n* pl. **-S** a party for fun

FUNGAL   *n* pl. **-S** a fungus

FUNGI   a pl. of fungus

FUNGIBLE   *n* pl. **-S** something that may be exchanged for an equivalent unit of the same class

FUNGIC   *adj* fungous

FUNGO   *n* pl. **-GOES** or **-GOS** a fly ball hit to a fielder for practice in baseball

FUNGOID   *n* pl. **-S** a growth resembling a fungus

FUNGOUS   *adj* pertaining to a fungus

FUNGUS   *n* pl. **-GUSES** or **-GI** any of a major group of lower plants

FUNHOUSE   *n* pl. **-S** an amusement park attraction

FUNICLE   *n* pl. **-S** a cordlike anatomical structure

FUNICULI   *n/pl* funicles

FUNK   *v* **-ED, -ING, -S** to shrink back in fear

FUNKER   *n* pl. **-S** one that funks

FUNKIA   *n* pl. **-S** a flowering plant

FUNKSTER   *n* pl. **-S** a fan or performer of earthy, bluesy music

FUNKY	*adj* **FUNKIER, FUNKIEST** having an offensive odor **FUNKILY** *adv*
FUNNED	past tense of fun
FUNNEL	*v* **-NELED, -NELING, -NELS** or **-NELLED, -NELLING, -NELS** to pass through a funnel (a cone-shaped utensil)
FUNNER	comparative of fun
FUNNEST	superlative of fun
FUNNING	present participle of fun
FUNNY	*adj* **-NIER, -NIEST** causing laughter or amusement **FUNNILY** *adv*
FUNNY	*n* pl. **-NIES** a comic strip
FUNNYMAN	*n* pl. **-MEN** a comedian
FUNPLEX	*n* pl. **-ES** a building with facilities for sports and games
FUNSTER	*n* pl. **-S** one that makes fun; a comedian
FUR	*v* **FURRED, FURRING, FURS** to cover with fur (a dressed animal pelt)
FURAN	*n* pl. **-S** a flammable liquid
FURANE	*n* pl. **-S** furan
FURANOSE	*n* pl. **-S** a type of sugar
FURBALL	*n* pl. **-S** a ball of fur regurgitated by a cat
FURBELOW	*v* **-ED, -ING, -S** to decorate with ruffles
FURBISH	*v* **-ED, -ING, -ES** to polish
FURCATE	*v* **-CATED, -CATING, -CATES** to divide into branches
FURCRAEA	*n* pl. **-S** a tropical plant
FURCULA	*n* pl. **-LAE** a forked bone **FURCULAR** *adj*
FURCULUM	*n* pl. **-LA** a furcula
FURFUR	*n* pl. **-ES** dandruff
FURFURAL	*n* pl. **-S** a chemical compound
FURFURAN	*n* pl. **-S** furan
FURIBUND	*adj* furious
FURIES	pl. of fury
FURIOSO	*adv* with great force — used as a musical direction
FURIOUS	*adj* extremely angry
FURL	*v* **-ED, -ING, -S** to roll up **FURLABLE** *adj*
FURLER	*n* pl. **-S** one that furls
FURLESS	*adj* having no fur
FURLONG	*n* pl. **-S** a unit of distance
FURLOUGH	*v* **-ED, -ING, -S** to grant a leave of absence to
FURMENTY	*n* pl. **-TIES** frumenty
FURMETY	*n* pl. **-TIES** frumenty
FURMITY	*n* pl. **-TIES** frumenty
FURNACE	*v* **-NACED, -NACING, -NACES** to subject to heat
FURNISH	*v* **-ED, -ING, -ES** to equip
FUROR	*n* pl. **-S** an uproar
FURORE	*n* pl. **-S** furor
FURPIECE	*n* pl. **-S** an item of clothing made out of fur
FURRED	past tense of fur
FURRIER	*n* pl. **-S** one that deals in furs
FURRIERY	*n* pl. **-ERIES** the business of a furrier
FURRIEST	superlative of furry
FURRILY	*adv* in a furry manner
FURRINER	*n* pl. **-S** a foreigner
FURRING	*n* pl. **-S** a trimming or lining of fur
FURROW	*v* **-ED, -ING, -S** to make furrows (narrow depressions) in
FURROWER	*n* pl. **-S** one that furrows
FURROWY	*adj* marked by furrows
FURRY	*adj* **-RIER, -RIEST** covered with fur
FURTHER	*v* **-ED, -ING, -S** to help forward
FURTHEST	a superlative of far
FURTIVE	*adj* stealthy
FURUNCLE	*n* pl. **-S** a painful swelling of the skin
FURY	*n* pl. **-RIES** violent anger
FURZE	*n* pl. **-S** a spiny shrub
FURZY	*adj* **FURZIER, FURZIEST** abounding in furze
FUSAIN	*n* pl. **-S** a fine charcoal used in drawing
FUSARIUM	*n* pl. **-SARIUMS** or **-SARIA** a disease-causing fungus
FUSCOUS	*adj* of a dusky color
FUSE	*v* **FUSED, FUSING, FUSES** to equip with a fuse (a detonating device)
FUSEE	*n* pl. **-S** a large-headed friction match
FUSEL	*n* pl. **-S** an oily liquid
FUSELAGE	*n* pl. **-S** the body of an airplane
FUSELESS	*adj* lacking a fuse
FUSELIKE	*adj* resembling a fuse

FUSIBLE   *adj* capable of being melted **FUSIBLY** *adv*

FUSIFORM   *adj* tapering toward each end

FUSIL   *n* pl. **-S** a type of musket

FUSILE   *adj* formed by melting

FUSILEER   *n* pl. **-S** fusilier

FUSILIER   *n* pl. **-S** a soldier armed with a fusil

FUSILLI   *n* pl. **-S** spiral-shaped pasta

FUSING   present participle of fuse

FUSION   *n* pl. **-S** the act of melting together **FUSIONAL** *adj*

FUSS   *v* **-ED, -ING, -ES** to be overly concerned with small details

FUSSER   *n* pl. **-S** one that fusses

FUSSPOT   *n* pl. **-S** a fusser

FUSSY   *adj* **FUSSIER, FUSSIEST** overly concerned with small details **FUSSILY** *adv*

FUSTIAN   *n* pl. **-S** a cotton fabric

FUSTIC   *n* pl. **-S** a tropical tree

FUSTY   *adj* **-TIER, -TIEST** musty **FUSTILY** *adv*

FUSUMA   *n* pl. **FUSUMA** a sliding partitiion in a Japanese house

FUTHARC   *n* pl. **-S** futhark

FUTHARK   *n* pl. **-S** an ancient alphabet

FUTHORC   *n* pl. **-S** futhark

FUTHORK   *n* pl. **-S** futhark

FUTILE   *adj* having no useful result **FUTILELY** *adv*

FUTILITY   *n* pl. **-TIES** the quality of being futile

FUTON   *n* pl. **-S** a cotton filled mattress for use as a bed

FUTTOCK   *n* pl. **-S** a curved timber in the frame of a wooden ship

FUTURE   *n* pl. **-S** the time yet to come **FUTURAL** *adj*

FUTURISM   *n* pl. **-S** an artistic and literary movement

FUTURIST   *n* pl. **-S** an advocate of futurism

FUTURITY   *n* pl. **-TIES** the future

FUTZ   *v* **-ED, -ING, -ES** to spend time aimlessly

FUZE   *v* **FUZED, FUZING, FUZES** to fuse

FUZEE   *n* pl. **-S** fusee

FUZELESS   *adj* fuseless

FUZIL   *n* pl. **-S** fusil

FUZING   present participle of fuze

FUZZ   *v* **-ED, -ING, -ES** to become fuzzy

FUZZBALL   *n* pl. **-S** a ball of fuzz (a fluffy mass of hair or fiber)

FUZZTONE   *n* pl. **-S** a blurred audio effect

FUZZY   *adj* **FUZZIER, FUZZIEST** blurry **FUZZILY** *adv*

FYCE   *n* pl. **-S** feist

FYKE   *n* pl. **-S** a bag-shaped fishnet

FYLFOT   *n* pl. **-S** a swastika

FYNBOS   *n* pl. **FYNBOS** a type of biome in South Africa

FYTTE   *n* pl. **-S** a division of a poem or song

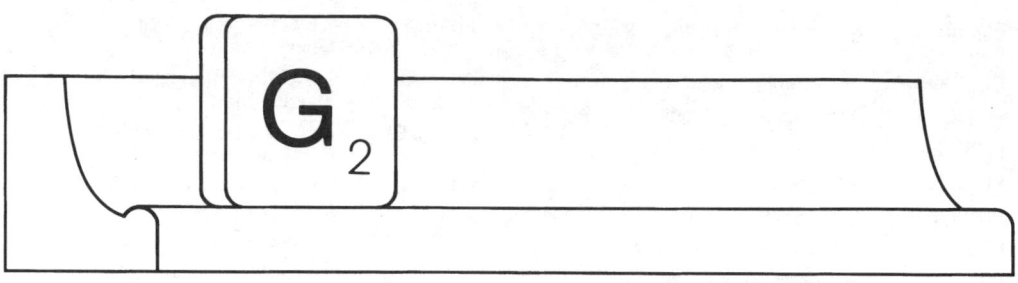

GAB	*v* **GABBED, GABBING, GABS** to chatter	**GADGET**	*n* pl. **-S** a mechanical device **GADGETY** *adj*
GABBA	*n* pl. **-S** aggressive sounding music with a very fast beat	**GADGETRY**	*n* pl. **-RIES** the devising or constructing of gadgets
GABBARD	*n* pl. **-S** a barge	**GADI**	*n* pl. **-S** gaddi
GABBART	*n* pl. **-S** gabbard	**GADID**	*n* pl. **-S** gadoid
GABBED	past tense of gab	**GADOID**	*n* pl. **-S** a type of fish
GABBER	*n* pl. **-S** one that gabs	**GADROON**	*v* **-ED, -ING, -S** to decorate with bands of fluted or reeded molding
GABBIER	comparative of gabby		
GABBIEST	superlative of gabby	**GADWALL**	*n* pl. **-S** a wild duck
GABBING	present participle of gab	**GADZOOKS**	*interj* — used as a mild oath
GABBLE	*v* **-BLED, -BLING, -BLES** to jabber	**GAE**	*v* **GAED, GANE** or **GAEN, GAEING** or **GAUN, GAES** to go
GABBLER	*n* pl. **-S** one that gabbles	**GAFF**	*v* **-ED, -ING, -S** to catch a fish with a sharp hook
GABBRO	*n* pl. **-BROS** a type of rock **GABBROIC, GABBROID** *adj*		
		GAFFE	*n* pl. **-S** a social blunder
GABBY	*adj* **-BIER, -BIEST** talkative	**GAFFER**	*n* pl. **-S** an old man
GABELLE	*n* pl. **-S** a tax on salt **GABELLED** *adj*	**GAG**	*v* **GAGGED, GAGGING, GAGS** to stop up the mouth
GABFEST	*n* pl. **-S** an informal gathering for general talk	**GAGA**	*adj* crazy
		GAGAKU	*n* pl. **-S** ancient court music of Japan
GABIES	pl. of gaby		
GABION	*n* pl. **-S** a type of basket	**GAGE**	*v* **GAGED, GAGING, GAGES** to pledge as security **GAGEABLE** *adj*
GABLE	*v* **-BLED, -BLING, -BLES** to form a triangular section of a wall		
GABOON	*n* pl. **-S** a spittoon	**GAGER**	*n* pl. **-S** gauger
GABY	*n* pl. **-BIES** a dolt	**GAGGED**	past tense of gag
GACH	*v* **-ED, -ING, -ES** to gatch	**GAGGER**	*n* pl. **-S** one that gags
GACHER	*n* pl. **-S** gatcher	**GAGGING**	present participle of gag
GAD	*v* **GADDED, GADDING, GADS** to roam about restlessly	**GAGGLE**	*v* **-GLED, -GLING, -GLES** to cackle
GADABOUT	*n* pl. **-S** one that gads about	**GAGING**	present participle of gage
GADARENE	*adj* headlong	**GAGMAN**	*n* pl. **-MEN** one who writes jokes
GADDED	past tense of gad	**GAGSTER**	*n* pl. **-S** a gagman
GADDER	*n* pl. **-S** one that gads about	**GAHNITE**	*n* pl. **-S** a mineral
GADDI	*n* pl. **-S** a hassock	**GAIETY**	*n* pl. **-ETIES** festive activity
GADDING	present participle of gad	**GAIJIN**	*n* pl. **GAIJIN** a foreigner in Japan
GADFLY	*n* pl. **-FLIES** a biting fly	**GAILY**	*adv* in a gay manner

GAIN	*v* **-ED, -ING, -S** to acquire **GAINABLE** *adj*
GAINER	*n* pl. **-S** one that gains
GAINFUL	*adj* profitable
GAINLESS	*adj* profitless
GAINLY	*adj* **-LIER, -LIEST** graceful
GAINSAY	*v* **-SAID, -SAYING, -SAYS** to deny
GAINST	*prep* against
GAIT	*v* **-ED, -ING, -S** to train a horse to move in a particular way
GAITER	*n* pl. **-S** a covering for the lower leg **GAITERED** *adj*
GAL	*n* pl. **-S** a girl
GALA	*n* pl. **-S** a celebration
GALABIA	*n* pl. **-S** djellaba
GALABIEH	*n* pl. **-S** djellaba
GALABIYA	*n* pl. **-S** djellaba
GALACTIC	*adj* pertaining to a galaxy
GALAGO	*n* pl. **-GOS** a small primate
GALAH	*n* pl. **-S** a cockatoo
GALANGA	*n* pl. **-S** galangal
GALANGAL	*n* pl. **-S** a medicinal plant
GALATEA	*n* pl. **-S** a strong cotton fabric
GALAVANT	*v* **-ED, -ING, -S** to gad about
GALAX	*n* pl. **-ES** an evergreen herb
GALAXY	*n* pl. **-AXIES** a large system of celestial bodies
GALBANUM	*n* pl. **-S** a gum resin
GALE	*v* **GALED, GALING, GALES** to frolic playfully
GALEA	*n* pl. **-LEAS** or **-LEAE** a helmet-shaped anatomical part **GALEATE, GALEATED** *adj*
GALENA	*n* pl. **-S** the principal ore of lead **GALENIC** *adj*
GALENITE	*n* pl. **-S** galena
GALERE	*n* pl. **-S** a group of people having a common quality
GALETTE	*n* pl. **-S** a flat round cake
GALILEE	*n* pl. **-S** a type of porch
GALING	present participle of gale
GALIOT	*n* pl. **-S** galliot
GALIPOT	*n* pl. **-S** a type of turpentine
GALIVANT	*v* **-ED, -ING, -S** to gad about
GALL	*v* **-ED, -ING, -S** to vex or irritate
GALLANT	*v* **-ED, -ING, -S** to court a woman
GALLATE	*n* pl. **-S** a chemical salt

GALLEASS	*n* pl. **-ES** a large war galley
GALLEIN	*n* pl. **-S** a green dye
GALLEON	*n* pl. **-S** a large sailing vessel
GALLERIA	*n* pl. **-S** a roofed promenade or court
GALLERY	*v* **-LERIED, -LERYING, -LERIES** to provide with a long covered area
GALLET	*v* **-ED, -ING, -S** to fill in mortar joints with stone chips
GALLETA	*n* pl. **-S** a perennial grass
GALLEY	*n* pl. **-LEYS** a long, low medieval ship
GALLFLY	*n* pl. **-FLIES** a small insect
GALLIARD	*n* pl. **-S** a lively dance
GALLIASS	*n* pl. **-ES** galleass
GALLIC	*adj* containing gallium
GALLICA	*n* pl. **-S** a European rose
GALLICAN	*adj* pertaining to a French religious movement
GALLIED	past tense of gally
GALLIES	present 3d person sing. of gally
GALLIOT	*n* pl. **-S** a small galley
GALLIPOT	*n* pl. **-S** a small earthen jar
GALLIUM	*n* pl. **-S** a metallic element
GALLNUT	*n* pl. **-S** an abnormal swelling of plant tissue
GALLON	*n* pl. **-S** a unit of liquid measure
GALLOON	*n* pl. **-S** an ornamental braid
GALLOOT	*n* pl. **-S** galoot
GALLOP	*v* **-ED, -ING, -S** to ride a horse at full speed
GALLOPER	*n* pl. **-S** one that gallops
GALLOUS	*adj* containing gallium
GALLOWAY	*n* pl. **-WAYS** a breed of hornless cattle
GALLOWS	*n* pl. **-ES** a structure used for hanging a condemned person
GALLUS	*n* pl. **-ES** a suspender for trousers **GALLUSED** *adj*
GALLY	*v* **-LIED, -LYING, -LIES** to frighten
GALOOT	*n* pl. **-S** an awkward or uncouth person
GALOP	*v* **-ED, -ING, -S** to dance a galop (a lively round dance)
GALOPADE	*n* pl. **-S** a lively round dance
GALORE	*n* pl. **-S** abundance
GALOSH	*n* pl. **-ES** an overshoe **GALOSHED** *adj*

GALOSHE	*n* pl. **-S** galosh	**GAMEPLAY**	*n* pl. **-S** the way a computer or video game is played
GALUMPH	*v* **-ED, -ING, -S** to move clumsily		
GALVANIC	*adj* pertaining to a direct electric current	**GAMER**	*n* pl. **-S** an avid game player
		GAMESMAN	*n* pl. **-MEN** one who plays games
GALYAC	*n* pl. **-S** galyak	**GAMESOME**	*adj* playful
GALYAK	*n* pl. **-S** a fur made from lambskin	**GAMEST**	superlative of game
GAM	*v* **GAMMED, GAMMING, GAMS** to visit socially	**GAMESTER**	*n* pl. **-S** a gambler
		GAMETE	*n* pl. **-S** a mature reproductive cell **GAMETAL, GAMETIC** *adj*
GAMA	*n* pl. **-S** a pasture grass		
GAMASHES	*n/pl* boots worn by horseback riders	**GAMEY**	*adj* **GAMIER, GAMIEST** gamy
		GAMIC	*adj* requiring fertilization
GAMAY	*n* pl. **-MAYS** a red grape	**GAMIER**	comparative of gamy
GAMB	*n* pl. **-S** a leg	**GAMIEST**	superlative of gamy
GAMBA	*n* pl. **-S** a bass viol	**GAMIFY**	*v* **-FIED, -FYING, -FIES** to add games to
GAMBADE	*n* pl. **-S** a gambado		
GAMBADO	*n* pl. **-DOS** or **-DOES** a leap made by a horse	**GAMILY**	*adv* in a game manner
		GAMIN	*n* pl. **-S** an urchin
GAMBE	*n* pl. **-S** gamb	**GAMINE**	*n* pl. **-S** a tomboy
GAMBESON	*n* pl. **-S** a medieval coat	**GAMINESS**	*n* pl. **-ES** the quality of being gamy
GAMBIA	*n* pl. **-S** gambier	**GAMING**	*n* pl. **-S** the practice of gambling
GAMBIER	*n* pl. **-S** an extract obtained from an Asian vine	**GAMMA**	*n* pl. **-S** a Greek letter
		GAMMADIA	*n/pl* Greek ornamental designs
GAMBIR	*n* pl. **-S** gambier	**GAMMED**	past tense of gam
GAMBIT	*n* pl. **-S** a type of chess opening	**GAMMER**	*n* pl. **-S** an old woman
GAMBLE	*v* **-BLED, -BLING, -BLES** to play a game of chance for money or valuables	**GAMMIER**	comparative of gammy
		GAMMIEST	superlative of gammy
		GAMMING	present participle of gam
GAMBLER	*n* pl. **-S** one that gambles	**GAMMON**	*v* **-ED, -ING, -S** to mislead by deceptive talk
GAMBOGE	*n* pl. **-S** a gum resin		
GAMBOL	*v* **-BOLED, -BOLING, -BOLS** or **-BOLLED, -BOLLING, -BOLS** to leap about playfully	**GAMMONER**	*n* pl. **-S** one that gammons
		GAMMY	*adj* **-MIER, -MIEST** lame
		GAMODEME	*n* pl. **-S** a somewhat isolated breeding community of organisms
GAMBREL	*n* pl. **-S** a part of a horse's leg		
GAMBUSIA	*n* pl. **-S** a small fish	**GAMP**	*n* pl. **-S** a large umbrella
GAME	*adj* **GAMER, GAMEST** plucky	**GAMUT**	*n* pl. **-S** an entire range
GAME	*v* **GAMED, GAMING, GAMES** to gamble	**GAMY**	*adj* **GAMIER, GAMIEST** plucky
		GAN	past tense of gin
GAMEBOOK	*n* pl. **-S** a book of strategies used by a sports team	**GANACHE**	*n* pl. **-S** creamy chocolate mixture
		GANDER	*v* **-ED, -ING, -S** to wander
GAMECOCK	*n* pl. **-S** a rooster trained for fighting	**GANE**	a past participle of gae
		GANEF	*n* pl. **-S** a thief
GAMEFISH	*n* pl. **-ES** a fish caught for sport	**GANEV**	*n* pl. **-S** ganef
GAMEFOWL	*n* pl. **-S** a gamecock	**GANG**	*v* **-ED, -ING, -S** to form into a gang (a group)
GAMELAN	*n* pl. **-S** a type of orchestra		
GAMELIKE	*adj* similar to a game (a contest governed by a set of rules)	**GANGBANG**	*v* **-ED, -ING, -S** to participate in gang-related activities
GAMELY	*adv* in a game manner		
GAMENESS	*n* pl. **-ES** the quality of being game		

GANGER *n* pl. **-S** a foreman of a gang of laborers

GANGLAND *n* pl. **-S** the criminal underworld

GANGLE *v* **-GLED, -GLING, -GLES** to move awkwardly

GANGLIA a pl. of ganglion

GANGLIAL *adj* gangliar

GANGLIAR *adj* pertaining to a ganglion

GANGLIER comparative of gangly

GANGLIEST superlative of gangly

GANGLING *adj* awkwardly tall and lanky

GANGLION *n* pl. **-GLIONS** or **-GLIA** a group of nerve cells

GANGLY *adj* **-GLIER, -GLIEST** gangling

GANGPLOW *n* pl. **-S** an agricultural implement

GANGREL *n* pl. **-S** a vagabond

GANGRENE *v* **-GRENED, -GRENING, -GRENES** to suffer the loss of tissue in part of the body

GANGSTA *n* pl. **-S** a member of a street gang

GANGSTER *n* pl. **-S** a member of a criminal gang

GANGUE *n* pl. **-S** the worthless rock in which valuable minerals are found

GANGWAY *n* pl. **-WAYS** a passageway

GANISTER *n* pl. **-S** a type of rock

GANJA *n* pl. **-S** cannabis used for smoking

GANJAH *n* pl. **-S** ganja

GANNET *n* pl. **-S** a large seabird

GANNETRY *n* pl. **-RIES** a place where gannets breed

GANOF *n* pl. **-S** ganef

GANOID *n* pl. **-S** a type of fish

GANTLET *v* **-ED, -ING, -S** to overlap railroad tracks

GANTLINE *n* pl. **-S** a rope on a ship

GANTLOPE *n* pl. **-S** a former military punishment

GANTRY *n* pl. **-TRIES** a structure for supporting railroad signals

GANYMEDE *n* pl. **-S** a youth who serves liquors

GANZFELD *n* pl. **-S** a technique of controlled sensory input used in parapsychology

GAOL *v* **-ED, -ING, -S** to jail

GAOLBIRD *n* pl. **-S** jailbird

GAOLER *n* pl. **-S** jailer

GAP *v* **GAPPED, GAPPING, GAPS** to make an opening in

GAPE *v* **GAPED, GAPING, GAPES** to stare with open mouth

GAPER *n* pl. **-S** one that gapes

GAPESEED *n* pl. **-S** something that causes wonder

GAPEWORM *n* pl. **-S** a worm that causes a disease of young birds

GAPING present participle of gape

GAPINGLY *adv* in a gaping manner

GAPLESS *adj* having no gap

GAPOSIS *n* pl. **-SISES** a gap in a row of buttons or snaps

GAPPED past tense of gap

GAPPING present participle of gap

GAPPY *adj* **-PIER, -PIEST** having openings

GAPY *adj* infested with gapeworms

GAR *v* **GARRED, GARRING, GARS** to cause or compel

GARAGE *v* **-RAGED, -RAGING, -RAGES** to put in a garage (a car shelter)

GARB *v* **-ED, -ING, -S** to clothe

GARBAGE *n* pl. **-S** food waste **GARBAGEY, GARBAGY** *adj*

GARBANZO *n* pl. **-ZOS** a chickpea

GARBLE *v* **-BLED, -BLING, -BLES** to distort the meaning of

GARBLER *n* pl. **-S** one that garbles

GARBLESS *adj* being without clothing

GARBOARD *n* pl. **-S** a plank on a ship's bottom

GARBOIL *n* pl. **-S** turmoil

GARCON *n* pl. **-S** a waiter

GARDA *n* pl. **-DAI** a police officer in Ireland

GARDANT *adj* turned directly toward the observer — used of a heraldic animal

GARDEN *v* **-ED, -ING, -S** to cultivate a plot of ground

GARDENER *n* pl. **-S** one that gardens

GARDENIA *n* pl. **-S** a tropical shrub or tree

GARDYLOO *interj* — used as a warning cry

GARFISH *n* pl. **-ES** a freshwater fish

GARGANEY *n* pl. **-NEYS** a small duck

GARGET *n* pl. **-S** mastitis of domestic animals **GARGETY** *adj*

GARGLE *v* **-GLED, -GLING, -GLES** to rinse the mouth or throat

GARGLER *n* pl. **-S** one that gargles

GARGOYLE *n* pl. **-S** an ornamental figure

GARIGUE *n* pl. **-S** a low scrubland

GARISH *adj* gaudy **GARISHLY** *adv*

GARLAND *v* **-ED, -ING, -S** to deck with wreaths of flowers

GARLIC *v* **-LICKED, -LICKING, -LICS** to season with garlic (an herb used in cooking)

GARLICKY *adj* **-LICKIER, -LICKIEST** smelling or tasting of garlic

GARMENT *v* **-ED, -ING, -S** to clothe

GARNER *v* **-ED, -ING, -S** to gather and store

GARNET *n* pl. **-S** a mineral

GARNI *adj* garnished

GARNISH *v* **-ED, -ING, -ES** to decorate

GAROTE *v* **-ROTED, -ROTING, -ROTES** to garrote

GAROTTE *v* **-ROTTED, -ROTTING, -ROTTES** to garrote

GAROTTER *n* pl. **-S** one that garottes

GARPIKE *n* pl. **-S** a garfish

GARRED past tense of gar

GARRET *n* pl. **-S** an attic **GARRETED** *adj*

GARRING present participle of gar

GARRISON *v* **-ED, -ING, -S** to assign to a military post

GARRON *n* pl. **-S** a small, sturdy horse

GARROTE *v* **-ROTED, -ROTING, -ROTES** to execute by strangling

GARROTER *n* pl. **-S** one that garrotes

GARROTTE *v* **-ROTTED, -ROTTING, -ROTTES** to garrote

GARTER *v* **-ED, -ING, -S** to fasten with an elastic band

GARTH *n* pl. **-S** a yard or garden

GARVEY *n* pl. **-VEYS** a small scow

GAS *v* **GASSED, GASSING, GASES** or **GASSES** to supply with gas (a substance capable of indefinite expansion)

GASALIER *n* pl. **-S** gaselier

GASBAG *n* pl. **-S** a bag for holding gas

GASCON *n* pl. **-S** a boaster

GASEITY *n* pl. **-TIES** the state of being a gas

GASELIER *n* pl. **-S** a gaslight chandelier

GASEOUS *adj* pertaining to gas

GASH *adj* **GASHER, GASHEST** knowing

GASH *v* **-ED, -ING, -ES** to make a long deep cut in

GASHOUSE *n* pl. **-S** a gasworks

GASIFIED past tense of gasify

GASIFIER *n* pl. **-S** one that gasifies

GASIFORM *adj* having the form of gas

GASIFY *v* **-IFIED, -IFYING, -IFIES** to convert into gas

GASKET *n* pl. **-S** packing for making something fluid-tight **GASKETED** *adj*

GASKIN *n* pl. **-S** a part of a horse's leg

GASKING *n* pl. **-S** a gasket

GASLESS *adj* having no gas

GASLIGHT *v* **-ED, -ING, -S** to make a person believe he or she is going insane

GASLIT *adj* illuminated by gaslight

GASMAN *n* pl. **-MEN** an employee of a gas company

GASOGENE *n* pl. **-S** gazogene

GASOHOL *n* pl. **-S** a fuel mixture of gasoline and ethyl alcohol

GASOLENE *n* pl. **-S** gasoline

GASOLIER *n* pl. **-S** gaselier

GASOLINE *n* pl. **-S** a liquid fuel

GASP *v* **-ED, -ING, -S** to breathe convulsively

GASPER *n* pl. **-S** a cigarette

GASSED past tense of gas

GASSER *n* pl. **-S** one that gasses

GASSES a present 3d person sing. of gas

GASSING *n* pl. **-S** a poisoning by noxious gas

GASSY *adj* **-SIER, -SIEST** containing gas **GASSILY** *adv*

GAST *v* **-ED, -ING, -S** to scare

GASTER *n* pl. **-S** the enlarged part of the abdomen in some insects

GASTHAUS *n* pl. **-ES** or **-ER** a small hotel in Germany

GASTIGHT *adj* not allowing gas to escape or enter

GASTNESS *n* pl. **-ES** fright

GASTRAEA *n* pl. **-S** a type of metazoan

GASTRAL *adj* pertaining to the stomach

GASTREA *n* pl. **-S** gastraea

GASTRIC *adj* pertaining to the stomach

GASTRIN *n* pl. **-S** a hormone

GASTRULA *n* pl. **-LAS** or **-LAE** a metazoan embryo

GASWORKS *n* pl. **GASWORKS** a factory where gas is produced

GAT	*n* pl. **-S** a pistol
GATCH	*v* **-ED, -ING, -ES** to behave boastfully
GATCHER	*n* pl. **-S** one that gatches
GATE	*v* **GATED, GATING, GATES** to supply with a gate (a movable barrier)
GATEAU	*n* pl. **-TEAUS** or **-TEAUX** a fancy cake
GATEFOLD	*n* pl. **-S** a folded insert in a book or magazine
GATELEG	*n* pl. **-S** a table with extensions supported by movable legs
GATELESS	*adj* lacking a gate
GATELIKE	*adj* resembling a gate
GATEMAN	*n* pl. **-MEN** a person in charge of a gate
GATEPOST	*n* pl. **-S** a post from which a gate is hung
GATER	*n* pl. **-S** gator
GATEWAY	*n* pl. **-WAYS** a passage that may be closed by a gate
GATHER	*v* **-ED, -ING, -S** to bring together into one place or group
GATHERER	*n* pl. **-S** one that gathers
GATING	*n* pl. **-S** the process of opening and closing a channel
GATOR	*n* pl. **-S** an alligator
GAUCH	*v* **-ED, -ING, -ES** to gatch
GAUCHE	*adj* **GAUCHER, GAUCHEST** lacking social grace **GAUCHELY** *adv*
GAUCHER	*n* pl. **-S** gatcher
GAUCHO	*n* pl. **-CHOS** a cowboy of the South American pampas
GAUD	*n* pl. **-S** a showy ornament
GAUDERY	*n* pl. **-ERIES** finery
GAUDY	*adj* **GAUDIER, GAUDIEST** tastelessly showy **GAUDILY** *adv*
GAUDY	*n* pl. **-DIES** a festival
GAUFFER	*v* **-ED, -ING, -S** to goffer
GAUGE	*v* **GAUGED, GAUGING, GAUGES** to measure precisely
GAUGER	*n* pl. **-S** one that gauges
GAULT	*n* pl. **-S** a heavy, thick clay soil
GAUM	*v* **-ED, -ING, -S** to smear
GAUN	present participle of gae
GAUNCH	*n* pl. **-ES** underpants
GAUNT	*adj* **GAUNTER, GAUNTEST** emaciated **GAUNTLY** *adv*
GAUNTLET	*v* **-ED, -ING, -S** to gantlet
GAUNTRY	*n* pl. **-TRIES** gantry
GAUR	*n* pl. **-S** a wild ox
GAUSS	*n* pl. **-ES** a unit of magnetic induction
GAUZE	*n* pl. **-S** a transparent fabric
GAUZY	*adj* **GAUZIER, GAUZIEST** resembling gauze **GAUZILY** *adv*
GAVAGE	*n* pl. **-S** introduction of material into the stomach by a tube
GAVE	past tense of give
GAVEL	*v* **-ELED, -ELING, -ELS** or **-ELLED, -ELLING, -ELS** to signal for attention or order by use of a gavel (a small mallet)
GAVELOCK	*n* pl. **-S** a crowbar
GAVIAL	*n* pl. **-S** a large reptile
GAVOT	*n* pl. **-S** a French dance
GAVOTTE	*v* **-VOTTED, -VOTTING, -VOTTES** to dance a gavot
GAWK	*v* **-ED, -ING, -S** to stare stupidly
GAWKER	*n* pl. **-S** one that gawks
GAWKIER	comparative of gawky
GAWKIES	pl. of gawky
GAWKISH	*adj* gawky
GAWKY	*adj* **GAWKIER, GAWKIEST** awkward **GAWKILY** *adv*
GAWKY	*n* pl. **GAWKIES** an awkward person
GAWMOGE	*n* pl. **-S** a clownish person
GAWP	*v* **-ED, -ING, -S** to stare stupidly
GAWPER	*n* pl. **-S** one that gawps
GAWSIE	*adj* well-fed and healthy looking
GAWSY	*adj* gawsie
GAY	*adj* **GAYER, GAYEST** 1. merry 2. homosexual
GAY	*n* pl. **GAYS** a homosexual
GAYAL	*n* pl. **-S** a domesticated ox
GAYDAR	*n* pl. **-S** the ability to recognize that a person is homosexual
GAYETY	*n* pl. **-ETIES** gaiety
GAYLY	*adv* in a gay manner
GAYNESS	*n* pl. **-ES** the state of being gay
GAYWINGS	*n* pl. **GAYWINGS** a perennial herb
GAZABO	*n* pl. **-BOS** or **-BOES** a fellow
GAZANIA	*n* pl. **-S** a South African herb
GAZAR	*n* pl. **-S** silky sheer fabric

GAZE	*v* **GAZED, GAZING, GAZES** to look intently
GAZEBO	*n* pl. **-BOS** or **-BOES** a roofed structure open on the sides
GAZELLE	*n* pl. **-S** a small antelope
GAZER	*n* pl. **-S** one that gazes
GAZETTE	*v* **-ZETTED, -ZETTING, -ZETTES** to announce in an official journal
GAZING	present participle of gaze
GAZOGENE	*n* pl. **-S** an apparatus for carbonating liquids
GAZPACHO	*n* pl. **-CHOS** a cold, spicy soup
GAZUMP	*v* **-ED, -ING, -S** to cheat by raising the price originally agreed upon
GAZUMPER	*n* pl. **-S** one that gazumps
GAZUNDER	*v* **-ED, -ING, -S** to lower the buyer's offer to a seller of a property
GEAN	*n* pl. **-S** a wild sweet cherry
GEAR	*v* **-ED, -ING, -S** to provide with gears (toothed machine parts)
GEARBOX	*n* pl. **-ES** an automotive transmission
GEARCASE	*n* pl. **-S** a casing for gears
GEARHEAD	*n* pl. **-S** a mechanically inclined person
GEARING	*n* pl. **-S** a system of gears
GEARLESS	*adj* being without gears
GECK	*v* **-ED, -ING, -S** to mock
GECKO	*n* pl. **GECKOS** or **GECKOES** a small lizard
GED	*n* pl. **-S** a food fish
GEE	*v* **GEED, GEEING, GEES** to turn to the right
GEEGAW	*n* pl. **-S** gewgaw
GEEK	*n* pl. **-S** a single-minded enthusiast or expert
GEEKDOM	*n* pl. **-S** the world of geeks
GEEKED	*adj* filled with enthusiasm
GEEKISH	*adj* geeky
GEEKY	*adj* **GEEKIER, GEEKIEST** socially awkward or unappealing
GEEPOUND	*n* pl. **-S** a unit of mass
GEESE	pl. of goose
GEEST	*n* pl. **-S** old alluvial matter
GEEZ	*interj* jeez
GEEZER	*n* pl. **-S** an eccentric man
GEISHA	*n* pl. **-S** a Japanese girl trained to entertain

GEL	*v* **GELLED, GELLING, GELS** to become like jelly **GELABLE** *adj*
GELADA	*n* pl. **-S** a baboon
GELANT	*n* pl. **-S** gellant
GELATE	*v* **-ATED, -ATING, -ATES** to gel
GELATI	*n* pl. **-S** gelato
GELATIN	*n* pl. **-S** a glutinous substance
GELATINE	*n* pl. **-S** gelatin
GELATING	present participle of gelate
GELATION	*n* pl. **-S** the process of gelling
GELATO	*n* pl. **-TOS** or **-TI** Italian ice cream
GELCAP	*n* pl. **-S** a tablet coated with gelatin
GELCOAT	*n* pl. **-S** a surface layer of polyester resin
GELD	*v* **-ED, -ING, -S** to castrate
GELDER	*n* pl. **-S** one that gelds
GELDING	*n* pl. **-S** a castrated animal
GELEE	*n* pl. **-S** a cosmetic gel
GELID	*adj* icy **GELIDLY** *adv*
GELIDITY	*n* pl. **-TIES** iciness
GELLANT	*n* pl. **-S** a substance used to produce gelling
GELLED	past tense of gel
GELLING	present participle of gel
GELLY	*n* pl. **GELLIES** gelignite (a high explosive)
GELSEMIA	*n/pl* medicinal plant roots
GELT	*n* pl. **-S** money
GEM	*v* **GEMMED, GEMMING, GEMS** to adorn with gems (precious stones)
GEMATRIA	*n* pl. **-S** a cabalistic method of interpreting the Scriptures
GEMINAL	*adj* of or pertaining to two substituents on the same atom
GEMINATE	*v* **-NATED, -NATING, -NATES** to arrange in pairs
GEMLIKE	*adj* resembling a gem
GEMMA	*n* pl. **-MAE** an asexual reproductive structure
GEMMATE	*v* **-MATED, -MATING, -MATES** to produce gemmae
GEMMED	past tense of gem
GEMMIER	comparative of gemmy
GEMMIEST	superlative of gemmy
GEMMILY	*adv* in a manner suggesting a gem
GEMMING	present participle of gem
GEMMULE	*n* pl. **-S** a small gemma

GEMMY *adj* **-MIER, -MIEST** resembling a gem

GEMOLOGY *n* pl. **-GIES** the science of gems

GEMOT *n* pl. **-S** a public meeting in Anglo-Saxon England

GEMOTE *n* pl. **-S** gemot

GEMSBOK *n* pl. **-S** a large antelope

GEMSBUCK *n* pl. **-S** gemsbok

GEMSTONE *n* pl. **-S** a precious stone

GEN *v* **GENNED, GENNING, GENS** to provide or obtain information

GENDARME *n* pl. **-S** a policeman

GENDER *v* **-ED, -ING, -S** to engender

GENE *n* pl. **-S** a hereditary unit

GENERA a pl. of genus

GENERAL *n* pl. **-S** a military officer

GENERATE *v* **-ATED, -ATING, -ATES** to bring into existence

GENERIC *n* pl. **-S** a type of drug

GENEROUS *adj* willing to give

GENESIS *n* pl. **GENESES** an origin

GENET *n* pl. **-S** a carnivorous mammal

GENETIC *adj* pertaining to genetics

GENETICS *n/pl* the science of heredity

GENETTE *n* pl. **-S** genet

GENEVA *n* pl. **-S** a liquor

GENIAL *adj* having a pleasant or friendly manner **GENIALLY** *adv*

GENIC *adj* pertaining to genes

GENIE *n* pl. **-S** jinni

GENII a pl. of genius

GENIP *n* pl. **-S** a tropical tree

GENIPAP *n* pl. **-S** a tropical tree

GENIPAPO *n* pl. **-POS** genipap

GENISTA *n* pl. **-S** a shrub with yellow flowers

GENITAL *adj* pertaining to reproduction

GENITALS *n/pl* the sexual organs

GENITIVE *n* pl. **-S** a grammatical case

GENITOR *n* pl. **-S** a male parent

GENITURE *n* pl. **-S** birth

GENIUS *n* pl. **GENIUSES** or **GENII** an exceptional natural aptitude

GENLOCK *n* pl. **-S** a device for synchronizing different video signals

GENNAKER *n* pl. **-S** a spinnaker sail

GENNED past tense of gen

GENNING present participle of gen

GENOA *n* pl. **-S** a triangular sail

GENOCIDE *n* pl. **-S** the deliberate extermination of a national or racial group

GENOGRAM *n* pl. **-S** a diagram of the history of behavior patterns of a family

GENOISE *n* pl. **-S** a rich sponge cake

GENOM *n* pl. **-S** genome

GENOME *n* pl. **-S** a haploid set of chromosomes **GENOMIC** *adj*

GENOMICS *n/pl* the study of genomes

GENOTYPE *n* pl. **-S** the genetic constitution of an organism

GENRE *n* pl. **-S** a type or kind

GENRO *n* pl. **-ROS** a group of elder statesmen in Japan

GENS *n* pl. **GENTES** a type of clan

GENSENG *n* pl. **-S** ginseng

GENT *n* pl. **-S** a gentleman

GENTEEL *adj* **-TEELER, -TEELEST** well-bred or refined

GENTES pl. of gens

GENTIAN *n* pl. **-S** a flowering plant

GENTIL *adj* kind

GENTILE *n* pl. **-S** a non-Jewish person

GENTLE *adj* **-TLER, -TLEST** mild **GENTLY** *adv*

GENTLE *v* **-TLED, -TLING, -TLES** to tame

GENTOO *n* pl. **-TOOS** a gray-backed penguin

GENTRICE *n* pl. **-S** good breeding

GENTRIFY *v* **-FIED, -FYING, -FIES** to renew a decayed urban area so as to attract middle-class residents

GENTRY *n* pl. **-TRIES** people of high social class

GENTS *n/pl* a public men's room

GENU *n* pl. **GENUA** the knee

GENUINE *adj* authentic

GENUS *n* pl. **GENUSES** or **GENERA** a kind, sort, or class

GEOCACHE *v* **-CACHED, -CACHING, -CACHES** to search for hidden items by using a Global Positioning System device as part of a game

GEODE *n* pl. **-S** a type of rock

GEODESIC *n* pl. **-S** a geometric line

GEODESY *n* pl. **-SIES** geographical surveying

GEODETIC	*adj* pertaining to geodesy	**GERMINA**	a pl. of germen
GEODIC	*adj* of or pertaining to a geode	**GERMINAL**	*adj* being in the earliest stage of development
GEODUCK	*n* pl. **-S** a large, edible clam	**GERMLIKE**	*adj* resembling a germ
GEOGNOSY	*n* pl. **-SIES** a branch of geology	**GERMY**	*adj* **GERMIER, GERMIEST** full of germs
GEOID	*n* pl. **-S** a hypothetical surface of the earth **GEOIDAL** *adj*	**GERONTIC**	*adj* pertaining to old age
GEOLOGER	*n* pl. **-S** a specialist in geology	**GERUND**	*n* pl. **-S** a verbal noun
GEOLOGY	*n* pl. **-GIES** the science that deals with the origin and structure of the earth **GEOLOGIC** *adj*	**GESNERIA**	*adj* designating a type of flowering plant
GEOMANCY	*n* pl. **-CIES** a method of foretelling the future by geographical features	**GESSO**	*n* pl. **-SOES** a plaster mixture
GEOMETER	*n* pl. **-S** a specialist in geometry	**GESSOED**	*adj* having gesso as a coating
GEOMETRY	*n* pl. **-TRIES** a branch of mathematics	**GEST**	*n* pl. **-S** a feat
		GESTALT	*n* pl. **-STALTS** or **-STALTEN** a unified whole
GEOPHAGY	*n* pl. **-GIES** the practice of eating earthy substances	**GESTAPO**	*n* pl. **-POS** a secret-police organization
GEOPHONE	*n* pl. **-S** a device that detects vibrations in the earth	**GESTATE**	*v* **-TATED, -TATING, -TATES** to carry in the uterus during pregnancy
GEOPHYTE	*n* pl. **-S** a plant having underground buds		
GEOPONIC	*adj* pertaining to farming	**GESTE**	*n* pl. **-S** gest
GEOPROBE	*n* pl. **-S** a spacecraft for exploring space near the earth	**GESTIC**	*adj* pertaining to bodily motion
		GESTICAL	*adj* gestic
GEORGIC	*n* pl. **-S** a poem about farming	**GESTURAL**	*adj* pertaining to or consisting of gestures (expressive bodily motions)
GEOTAXIS	*n* pl. **-TAXES** the movement of an organism in response to gravity		
GERAH	*n* pl. **-S** a Hebrew unit of weight	**GESTURE**	*v* **-TURED, -TURING, -TURES** to express by bodily motion
GERANIAL	*n* pl. **-S** citral	**GESTURER**	*n* pl. **-S** one that gestures
GERANIOL	*n* pl. **-S** an alcohol used in perfumes	**GET**	*n* pl. **GITTIN** a divorce by Jewish law
GERANIUM	*n* pl. **-S** a flowering plant	**GET**	*v* **GOT, GOTTEN, GETTING, GETS** to obtain or acquire **GETABLE, GETTABLE** *adj*
GERARDIA	*n* pl. **-S** an herb		
GERBERA	*n* pl. **-S** an herb	**GETA**	*n* pl. **-S** a Japanese wooden clog
GERBIL	*n* pl. **-S** a burrowing rodent	**GETAWAY**	*n* pl. **-AWAYS** an escape
GERBILLE	*n* pl. **-S** gerbil	**GETOUT**	*n* pl. **-S** an excuse to avoid doing something
GERENT	*n* pl. **-S** a ruler or manager		
GERENUK	*n* pl. **-S** a long-necked antelope	**GETTER**	*v* **-ED, -ING, -S** to purify with a chemically active substance
GERM	*n* pl. **-S** a microorganism that causes disease	**GETTING**	present participle of get
GERMAN	*n* pl. **-S** an elaborate dance	**GETUP**	*n* pl. **-S** a costume
GERMANE	*adj* relevant	**GEUM**	*n* pl. **-S** a perennial herb
GERMANIC	*adj* containing germanium (a metallic element)	**GEWGAW**	*n* pl. **-S** a showy trinket **GEWGAWED** *adj*
GERMEN	*n* pl. **-MENS** or **-MINA** something that serves as an origin	**GEY**	*adv* very
		GEYSER	*v* **-ED, -ING, -S** to eject jets of hot water and steam
GERMFREE	*adj* free from germs	**GHARIAL**	*n* pl. **-S** a large reptile
GERMIER	comparative of germy	**GHARRI**	*n* pl. **-S** gharry
GERMIEST	superlative of germy		

GHARRY *n* pl. **-RIES** a carriage used in India

GHAST *adj* ghastly

GHASTFUL *adj* frightful

GHASTLY *adj* **-LIER, -LIEST** terrifying

GHAT *n* pl. **-S** a passage to a river

GHAUT *n* pl. **-S** ghat

GHAZAL *n* pl. **-S** an amatory lyric poem

GHAZI *n* pl. **-S** or **-ES** a Muslim war hero

GHEE *n* pl. **-S** a kind of liquid butter

GHERAO *v* **-ED, -ING, -S** or **-ES** to coerce by physical means

GHERKIN *n* pl. **-S** a small cucumber

GHETTO *v* **-ED, -ING, -S** or **-ES** to isolate in a slum

GHI *n* pl. **-S** ghee

GHIBLI *n* pl. **-S** a hot desert wind

GHILLIE *n* pl. **-S** a type of shoe

GHOST *v* **-ED, -ING, -S** to haunt

GHOSTING *n* pl. **-S** a false image on a television screen

GHOSTLY *adj* **-LIER, -LIEST** spectral

GHOSTY *adj* **GHOSTIER, GHOSTIEST** ghostly

GHOUL *n* pl. **-S** a demon **GHOULISH** *adj*

GHOULIE *n* pl. **-S** a ghoul

GHYLL *n* pl. **-S** a ravine

GI *n* pl. **-S** a white garment worn in martial arts

GIANT *n* pl. **-S** a person or thing of great size

GIANTESS *n* pl. **-ES** a female giant

GIANTISM *n* pl. **-S** the condition of being a giant

GIAOUR *n* pl. **-S** a non-Muslim

GIARDIA *n* pl. **-S** a protozoan inhabiting the intestines

GIB *v* **GIBBED, GIBBING, GIBS** to fasten with a wedge of wood or metal

GIBBER *v* **-ED, -ING, -S** to jabber

GIBBET *v* **-BETED, -BETING, -BETS** or **-BETTED, -BETTING, -BETS** to execute by hanging

GIBBON *n* pl. **-S** an arboreal ape

GIBBOSE *adj* gibbous

GIBBOUS *adj* irregularly rounded

GIBBSITE *n* pl. **-S** a mineral

GIBE *v* **GIBED, GIBING, GIBES** to jeer **GIBINGLY** *adv*

GIBER *n* pl. **-S** one that gibes

GIBLET *n* pl. **-S** an edible part of a fowl

GIBSON *n* pl. **-S** a martini served with a tiny onion

GID *n* pl. **-S** a disease of sheep

GIDDAP *interj* — used as a command to a horse to go faster

GIDDY *adj* **-DIER, -DIEST** dizzy **GIDDILY** *adv*

GIDDY *v* **-DIED, -DYING, -DIES** to make giddy

GIDDYAP *interj* giddap

GIDDYUP *interj* giddap

GIE *v* **GIED, GIEN, GIEING, GIES** to give

GIF *n* pl. **-S** a computer file in a format for images

GIFT *v* **-ED, -ING, -S** to present with a gift (something given without charge)

GIFTABLE *n* pl. **-S** something appropriate for a gift

GIFTEDLY *adv* in a talented manner

GIFTEE *n* pl. **-S** one that receives a gift

GIFTING *n* pl. **-S** the act of presenting with a gift

GIFTLESS *adj* being without a gift

GIFTWARE *n* pl. **-S** wares suitable for gifts

GIFTWRAP *v* **-WRAPPED, -WRAPPING, -WRAPS** to wrap with decorative paper

GIG *v* **GIGGED, GIGGING, GIGS** to catch fish with a pronged spear

GIGA *n* pl. **GIGHE** a gigue

GIGABIT *n* pl. **-S** a unit of information

GIGABYTE *n* pl. **-S** 1,073,741,824 bytes

GIGAFLOP *n* pl. **-S** a measure of computing speed

GIGANTIC *adj* huge

GIGAS *adj* pertaining to variations in plant development

GIGATON *n* pl. **-S** a unit of weight

GIGAWATT *n* pl. **-S** a unit of power

GIGGED past tense of gig

GIGGING present participle of gig

GIGGLE *v* **-GLED, -GLING, -GLES** to laugh in a silly manner

GIGGLER *n* pl. **-S** one that giggles

GIGGLY	adj **-GLIER, -GLIEST** tending to giggle	**GIN**	v **GINNED, GINNING, GINS** to remove seeds from cotton
GIGHE	pl. of giga	**GINCH**	n pl. **-ES** gotch
GIGLET	n pl. **-S** a playful girl	**GINGAL**	n pl. **-S** jingal
GIGLOT	n pl. **-S** giglet	**GINGALL**	n pl. **-S** jingal
GIGOLO	n pl. **-LOS** a man supported financially by a woman	**GINGELEY**	n pl. **-LEYS** gingelly
		GINGELI	n pl. **-S** gingelly
GIGOT	n pl. **-S** a leg of lamb	**GINGELIES**	pl. of gingely
GIGUE	n pl. **-S** a lively dance	**GINGELLI**	n pl. **-S** gingelly
GILBERT	n pl. **-S** a unit of magnetomotive force	**GINGELLY**	n pl. **-LIES** the sesame seed or its oil
GILD	v **GILDED** or **GILT, GILDING, GILDS** to cover with a thin layer of gold	**GINGELY**	n pl. **-LIES** gingelly
		GINGER	v **-ED, -ING, -S** to flavor with ginger (a pungent spice)
GILDER	n pl. **-S** one that gilds	**GINGERLY**	adv in a careful manner
GILDHALL	n pl. **-S** a town hall	**GINGERY**	adj having the characteristics of ginger
GILDING	n pl. **-S** the application of gilt		
GILL	v **-ED, -ING, -S** to catch fish with a type of net	**GINGHAM**	n pl. **-S** a cotton fabric
GILLER	n pl. **-S** one that gills	**GINGILI**	n pl. **-LIS** gingelly
GILLIE	n pl. **-S** ghillie	**GINGILLI**	n pl. **-S** gingelly
GILLNET	v **-NETTED, -NETTING, -NETS** to gill	**GINGIVA**	n pl. **-VAE** the fleshy tissue that surrounds the teeth **GINGIVAL** adj
GILLY	v **-LIED, -LYING, -LIES** to transport on a type of wagon	**GINGKO**	n pl. **-KOS** or **-KOES** ginkgo
		GINK	n pl. **-S** a fellow
GILT	n pl. **-S** the gold with which something is gilded	**GINKGO**	n pl. **-GOS** or **-GOES** an ornamental tree
GILTHEAD	n pl. **-S** a marine fish	**GINNED**	past tense of gin
GIMBAL	v **-BALED, -BALING, -BALS** or **-BALLED, -BALLING, -BALS** to support on a set of rings	**GINNER**	n pl. **-S** one that gins cotton
		GINNING	n pl. **-S** cotton as it comes from a gin
GIMCRACK	n pl. **-S** a gewgaw	**GINNY**	adj **GINNIER, GINNIEST** affected with gin (a strong liquor)
GIMEL	n pl. **-S** a Hebrew letter		
GIMLET	v **-ED, -ING, -S** to pierce with a boring tool	**GINSENG**	n pl. **-S** a perennial herb
GIMMAL	n pl. **-S** a pair of interlocked rings	**GIP**	v **GIPPED, GIPPING, GIPS** to gyp
		GIPON	n pl. **-S** jupon
GIMME	n pl. **-S** something easily won	**GIPPER**	n pl. **-S** one that gips
GIMMICK	v **-ED, -ING, -S** to provide with a gimmick (a novel or tricky feature)	**GIPSY**	v **-SIED, -SYING, -SIES** to gypsy
GIMMICKY	adj having or being like a gimmick	**GIPSYDOM**	n pl. **-S** gypsydom
GIMMIE	n pl. **-MIES** an easy golf putt conceded to an opponent	**GIPSYISH**	adj gypsyish
		GIPSYISM	n pl. **-S** gypsyism
GIMP	v **-ED, -ING, -S** to limp	**GIRAFFE**	n pl. **-S** a long-necked mammal
GIMPIER	comparative of gimpy	**GIRASOL**	n pl. **-S** a variety of opal
GIMPIEST	superlative of gimpy	**GIRASOLE**	n pl. **-S** girasol
GIMPY	adj **GIMPIER, GIMPIEST** limping	**GIRD**	v **GIRDED** or **GIRT, GIRDING, GIRDS** to surround
GIN	v **GAN, GUNNEN, GINNING, GINS** to begin		
		GIRDER	n pl. **-S** a horizontal support

GIRDLE	*v* **-DLED, -DLING, -DLES** to encircle with a belt	**GLACE**	*v* **-CEED** or **-CED, -CEING, -CES** to cover with icing
GIRDLER	*n* pl. **-S** one that girdles	**GLACIAL**	*adj* of or pertaining to glaciers
GIRL	*n* pl. **-S** a female child	**GLACIATE**	*v* **-ATED, -ATING, -ATES** to cover with glaciers
GIRLHOOD	*n* pl. **-S** the state of being a girl	**GLACIER**	*n* pl. **-S** a huge mass of ice
GIRLIE	*adj* **GIRLIER, GIRLIEST** girlish	**GLACIS**	*n* pl. **-CISES** a slope
GIRLISH	*adj* of, pertaining to, or having the characteristics of a girl	**GLAD**	*adj* **GLADDER, GLADDEST** feeling pleasure
GIRLY	*adj* **GIRLIER, GIRLIEST** girlie	**GLAD**	*v* **GLADDED, GLADDING, GLADS** to gladden
GIRN	*v* **-ED, -ING, -S** to snarl		
GIRO	*n* pl. **-ROS** an autogiro	**GLADDEN**	*v* **-ED, -ING, -S** to make glad
GIROLLE	*n* pl. **-S** an edible mushroom	**GLADDER**	comparative of glad
GIRON	*n* pl. **-S** gyron	**GLADDEST**	superlative of glad
GIROSOL	*n* pl. **-S** girasol	**GLADDING**	present participle of glad
GIRSH	*n* pl. **-ES** qursh	**GLADE**	*n* pl. **-S** an open space in a forest
GIRT	*v* **-ED, -ING, -S** to gird	**GLADIATE**	*adj* shaped like a sword
GIRTH	*v* **-ED, -ING, -S** to encircle	**GLADIER**	comparative of glady
GISARME	*n* pl. **-S** a medieval weapon	**GLADIEST**	superlative of glady
GISMO	*n* pl. **-MOS** a gadget	**GLADIOLA**	*n* pl. **-S** a flowering plant
GIST	*n* pl. **-S** the main point	**GLADIOLI**	*n/pl* segments of the sternum
GIT	*v* **GITTED, GITTING, GITS** to get	**GLADLY**	*adv* **-LIER, -LIEST** in a glad manner
GITANO	*n* pl. **-NOS** a Spanish gypsy	**GLADNESS**	*n* pl. **-ES** the state of being glad
GITCH	*n* pl. **-ES** gotch	**GLADSOME**	*adj* **-SOMER, -SOMEST** glad
GITE	*n* pl. **-S** a vacation retreat in France	**GLADY**	*adj* **GLADIER, GLADIEST** having glades
GITTED	past tense of git		
GITTERN	*n* pl. **-S** a medieval guitar	**GLAIKET**	*adj* glaikit
GITTIN	pl. of get	**GLAIKIT**	*adj* foolish
GITTING	present participle of git	**GLAIR**	*v* **-ED, -ING, -S** to coat with egg white
GIVE	*v* **GAVE, GIVEN, GIVING, GIVES** to transfer freely to another's possession **GIVEABLE** *adj*	**GLAIRE**	*v* **GLAIRED, GLAIRING, GLAIRES** to glair
GIVEAWAY	*n* pl. **-AWAYS** something given away free of charge	**GLAIRY**	*adj* **GLAIRIER, GLAIRIEST** resembling egg white
GIVEBACK	*n* pl. **-S** a worker's benefit given back to management	**GLAIVE**	*n* pl. **-S** a sword **GLAIVED** *adj*
GIVEN	*n* pl. **-S** something assigned as a basis for a calculation	**GLAM**	*v* **GLAMMED, GLAMMING, GLAMS** to make oneself look alluringly attractive
GIVER	*n* pl. **-S** one that gives	**GLAM**	*adj* **GLAMMER, GLAMMEST** characterized by extravagant glamor
GIVING	present participle of give		
GIZMO	*n* pl. **-MOS** gismo	**GLAMMY**	*adj* **GLAMMIER, GLAMMIEST** alluringly attractive
GIZZARD	*n* pl. **-S** a digestive organ		
GJETOST	*n* pl. **-S** a hard brown cheese	**GLAMOR**	*n* pl. **-S** alluring attractiveness
GLABELLA	*n* pl. **-BELLAE** the smooth area between the eyebrows	**GLAMOUR**	*v* **-ED, -ING, -S** to bewitch
		GLANCE	*v* **GLANCED, GLANCING, GLANCES** to look quickly
GLABRATE	*adj* glabrous		
GLABROUS	*adj* smooth	**GLANCER**	*n* pl. **-S** one that glances

GLAND   *n* pl. **-S** a secreting organ

GLANDERS   *n/pl* a disease of horses

GLANDULE   *n* pl. **-S** a small gland

GLANS   *n* pl. **GLANDES** the tip of the penis or clitoris

GLARE   *v* **GLARED, GLARING, GLARES** to shine with a harshly brilliant light

GLARY   *adj* **GLARIER, GLARIEST** glaring

GLASNOST   *n* pl. **-S** a Soviet policy of open political discussion

GLASS   *v* **-ED, -ING, -ES** to encase in glass (a transparent substance)

GLASSFUL   *n* pl. **-FULS** as much as a drinking glass will hold

GLASSIE   *n* pl. **-S** a type of playing marble

GLASSIER   comparative of glassy

GLASSIEST   superlative of glassy

GLASSILY   *adv* in a glassy manner

GLASSINE   *n* pl. **-S** a type of paper

GLASSMAN   *n* pl. **-MEN** a glazier

GLASSY   *adj* **GLASSIER, GLASSIEST** resembling glass

GLAUCOMA   *n* pl. **-S** a disease of the eye

GLAUCOUS   *adj* bluish green

GLAZE   *v* **GLAZED, GLAZING, GLAZES** to fit windows with glass panes

GLAZER   *n* pl. **-S** a glazier

GLAZIER   *n* pl. **-S** one that glazes

GLAZIERY   *n* pl. **-ZIERIES** the work of a glazier

GLAZING   *n* pl. **-S** glaziery

GLAZY   *adj* **GLAZIER, GLAZIEST** covered with a smooth, glossy coating **GLAZILY** *adv*

GLEAM   *v* **-ED, -ING, -S** to shine with a soft radiance

GLEAMER   *n* pl. **-S** one that gleams

GLEAMY   *adj* **GLEAMIER, GLEAMIEST** gleaming

GLEAN   *v* **-ED, -ING, -S** to gather little by little

GLEANER   *n* pl. **-S** one that gleans

GLEANING   *n* pl. **-S** something that is gleaned

GLEBA   *n* pl. **-BAE** a spore-bearing mass of some fungi

GLEBE   *n* pl. **-S** the soil or earth

GLED   *n* pl. **-S** glede

GLEDE   *n* pl. **-S** a bird of prey

GLEE   *n* pl. **-S** an unaccompanied song

GLEED   *n* pl. **-S** a glowing coal

GLEEFUL   *adj* merry

GLEEK   *v* **-ED, -ING, -S** to gibe

GLEEMAN   *n* pl. **-MEN** a minstrel

GLEESOME   *adj* gleeful

GLEET   *v* **-ED, -ING, -S** to discharge mucus from the urethra

GLEETY   *adj* **GLEETIER, GLEETIEST** resembling mucus

GLEG   *adj* alert **GLEGLY** *adv*

GLEGNESS   *n* pl. **-ES** alertness

GLEN   *n* pl. **-S** a small valley **GLENLIKE** *adj*

GLENOID   *adj* having the shallow or slightly cupped form of a bone socket

GLEY   *n* pl. **GLEYS** a clay soil layer **GLEYED** *adj*

GLEYING   *n* pl. **-S** development of gley

GLIA   *n* pl. **-S** supporting tissue that binds nerve tissue

GLIADIN   *n* pl. **-S** a simple protein

GLIADINE   *n* pl. **-S** gliadin

GLIAL   *adj* pertaining to the supporting tissue of the central nervous system

GLIB   *adj* **GLIBBER, GLIBBEST** fluent **GLIBLY** *adv*

GLIBNESS   *n* pl. **-ES** the quality of being glib

GLIDE   *v* **GLIDED, GLIDING, GLIDES** to move effortlessly

GLIDER   *n* pl. **-S** a type of aircraft

GLIFF   *n* pl. **-S** a brief moment

GLIM   *n* pl. **-S** a light or lamp

GLIME   *v* **GLIMED, GLIMING, GLIMES** to glance slyly

GLIMMER   *v* **-ED, -ING, -S** to shine faintly or unsteadily

GLIMPSE   *v* **GLIMPSED, GLIMPSING, GLIMPSES** to see for an instant

GLIMPSER   *n* pl. **-S** one that glimpses

GLINT   *v* **-ED, -ING, -S** to glitter

GLINTY   *adj* **GLINTIER, GLINTIEST** glittering

GLIOMA   *n* pl. **-MAS** or **-MATA** a type of tumor

GLIOSIS   *n* pl. **-OSES** pathological proliferation of glial cells

GLISSADE   *v* **-SADED, -SADING, -SADES** to perform a gliding dance step

GLISSE   *n* pl. **-S** a dance step

GLISTEN _v_ **-ED, -ING, -S** to shine by reflection

GLISTER _v_ **-ED, -ING, -S** to glisten

GLITCH _n_ pl. **-ES** a malfunction

GLITCHY _adj_ **GLITCHIER, GLITCHIEST** characterized by glitches

GLITTER _v_ **-ED, -ING, -S** to sparkle

GLITTERY _adj_ glittering

GLITZ _v_ **-ED, -ING, -ES** to make flashy in appearance

GLITZY _adj_ **GLITZIER, GLITZIEST** showy **GLITZILY** _adv_

GLOAM _n_ pl. **-S** twilight

GLOAMING _n_ pl. **-S** twilight

GLOAT _v_ **-ED, -ING, -S** to regard with great or excessive satisfaction

GLOATER _n_ pl. **-S** one that gloats

GLOB _n_ pl. **-S** a rounded mass

GLOBAL _adj_ spherical **GLOBALLY** _adv_

GLOBATE _adj_ spherical

GLOBATED _adj_ spherical

GLOBBY _adj_ **-BIER, -BIEST** full of globs

GLOBE _v_ **GLOBED, GLOBING, GLOBES** to form into a perfectly round body

GLOBIN _n_ pl. **-S** a simple protein

GLOBOID _n_ pl. **-S** a spheroid

GLOBOSE _adj_ spherical

GLOBOUS _adj_ spherical

GLOBULAR _n_ pl. **-S** a spherical cluster of stars

GLOBULE _n_ pl. **-S** a small spherical mass

GLOBULIN _n_ pl. **-S** a simple protein

GLOCHID _n_ pl. **-S** a barbed hair on some plants

GLOGG _n_ pl. **-S** an alcoholic beverage

GLOM _v_ **GLOMMED, GLOMMING, GLOMS** to steal

GLOMUS _n_ pl. **-MERA** a type of vascular tuft

GLONOIN _n_ pl. **-S** nitroglycerin

GLOOM _v_ **-ED, -ING, -S** to become dark

GLOOMFUL _adj_ gloomy

GLOOMING _n_ pl. **-S** gloaming

GLOOMY _adj_ **GLOOMIER, GLOOMIEST** dismally dark **GLOOMILY** _adv_

GLOOP _n_ pl. **-S** sticky material

GLOOPY _adj_ **GLOOPIER, GLOOPIEST** resembling gloop

GLOP _v_ **GLOPPED, GLOPPING, GLOPS** to cover with glop (a messy mass or mixture)

GLOPPY _adj_ **-PIER, -PIEST** resembling glop

GLORIA _n_ pl. **-S** a halo

GLORIED past tense of glory

GLORIES present 3d person sing. of glory

GLORIFY _v_ **-FIED, -FYING, -FIES** to bestow honor or praise on

GLORIOLE _n_ pl. **-S** a halo

GLORIOUS _adj_ magnificent

GLORY _v_ **-RIED, -RYING, -RIES** to rejoice proudly

GLOSS _v_ **-ED, -ING, -ES** to make lustrous

GLOSSA _n_ pl. **-SAS** or **-SAE** the tongue **GLOSSAL** _adj_

GLOSSARY _n_ pl. **-RIES** a list of terms and their definitions

GLOSSEME _n_ pl. **-S** the smallest linguistic unit that signals a meaning

GLOSSER _n_ pl. **-S** one that glosses

GLOSSIES pl. of glossy

GLOSSINA _n_ pl. **-S** a tsetse fly

GLOSSY _adj_ **GLOSSIER, GLOSSIEST** lustrous **GLOSSILY** _adv_

GLOSSY _n_ pl. **GLOSSIES** a type of photograph

GLOST _n_ pl. **-S** pottery that has been coated with a glassy surface

GLOTTIS _n_ pl. **-TISES** or **-TIDES** the opening between the vocal cords **GLOTTAL, GLOTTIC** _adj_

GLOUT _v_ **-ED, -ING, -S** to scowl

GLOVE _v_ **GLOVED, GLOVING, GLOVES** to furnish with gloves (hand coverings)

GLOVEBOX _n_ pl. **-ES** a small compartment in the dashboard of a vehicle

GLOVER _n_ pl. **-S** a maker or seller of gloves

GLOW _v_ **-ED, -ING, -S** to emit light and heat

GLOWER _v_ **-ED, -ING, -S** to scowl

GLOWFLY _n_ pl. **-FLIES** a firefly

GLOWWORM _n_ pl. **-S** a luminous insect

GLOXINIA _n_ pl. **-S** a tropical plant

GLOZE _v_ **GLOZED, GLOZING, GLOZES** to explain away

GLUCAGON _n_ pl. **-S** a hormone

GLUCAN _n_ pl. **-S** a polymer of glucose

GLUCINUM *n* pl. **-S** a metallic element **GLUCINIC** *adj*

GLUCOSE *n* pl. **-S** a sugar **GLUCOSIC** *adj*

GLUE *v* **GLUED, GLUING** or **GLUEING, GLUES** to fasten with glue (an adhesive substance)

GLUELIKE *adj* resembling glue

GLUEPOT *n* pl. **-S** a pot for melting glue

GLUER *n* pl. **-S** one that glues

GLUEY *adj* **GLUIER, GLUIEST** resembling glue **GLUILY** *adv*

GLUG *v* **GLUGGED, GLUGGING, GLUGS** to make a gurgling sound

GLUHWEIN *n* pl. **-S** wine flavored with spices

GLUINESS *n* pl. **-ES** the state of being gluey

GLUING present participle of glue

GLUM *n* pl. **-S** glumness

GLUM *adj* **GLUMMER, GLUMMEST** being in low spirits **GLUMLY** *adv*

GLUME *n* pl. **-S** a bract on grassy plants

GLUMNESS *n* pl. **-ES** the state of being glum

GLUMPY *adj* **GLUMPIER, GLUMPIEST** glum **GLUMPILY** *adv*

GLUNCH *v* **-ED, -ING, -ES** to frown

GLUON *n* pl. **-S** a hypothetical massless particle binding quarks together

GLUT *v* **GLUTTED, GLUTTING, GLUTS** to feed or fill to excess

GLUTCH *v* **-ED, -ING, -ES** to gulp or swallow

GLUTE *n* pl. **-S** a gluteus

GLUTEAL *adj* of or pertaining to the buttock muscles

GLUTEI pl. of gluteus

GLUTELIN *n* pl. **-S** any of a group of proteins occurring in cereal grains

GLUTEN *n* pl. **-S** a sticky component of grain flours that contains glutenin

GLUTENIN *n* pl. **-S** a protein of cereal grains that gives adhesiveness to bread dough

GLUTEUS *n* pl. **-TEI** a buttock muscle

GLUTTED past tense of glut

GLUTTING present participle of glut

GLUTTON *n* pl. **-S** a person who eats to excess

GLUTTONY *n* pl. **-TONIES** excessive eating

GLYCAN *n* pl. **-S** a carbohydrate

GLYCEMIA *n* pl. **-S** the presence of glucose in the blood **GLYCEMIC** *adj*

GLYCERIN *n* pl. **-S** a glycerol **GLYCERIC** *adj*

GLYCEROL *n* pl. **-S** a syrupy alcohol

GLYCERYL *n* pl. **-S** a radical derived from glycerol

GLYCIN *n* pl. **-S** a compound used in photography

GLYCINE *n* pl. **-S** an amino acid

GLYCOGEN *n* pl. **-S** a carbohydrate

GLYCOL *n* pl. **-S** an alcohol **GLYCOLIC** *adj*

GLYCONIC *n* pl. **-S** a type of verse line

GLYCOSYL *n* pl. **-S** a radical derived from glucose

GLYCYL *n* pl. **-S** a radical derived from glycine

GLYPH *n* pl. **-S** an ornamental groove **GLYPHIC** *adj*

GLYPTIC *n* pl. **-S** the art or process of engraving on gems

GNAR *v* **GNARRED, GNARRING, GNARS** to snarl

GNARL *v* **-ED, -ING, -S** to twist into a state of deformity

GNARLY *adj* **GNARLIER, GNARLIEST** gnarled

GNARR *v* **-ED, -ING, -S** to gnar

GNARRED past tense of gnar

GNARRING present participle of gnar

GNASH *v* **-ED, -ING, -ES** to grind the teeth together

GNAT *n* pl. **-S** a small winged insect

GNATHAL *adj* gnathic

GNATHIC *adj* of or pertaining to the jaw

GNATHION *n* pl. **-S** the tip of the chin

GNATHITE *n* pl. **-S** a jawlike appendage of an insect

GNATLIKE *adj* resembling a gnat

GNATTY *adj* **-TIER, -TIEST** infested with gnats

GNAW *v* **GNAWED, GNAWN, GNAWING, GNAWS** to wear away by persistent biting **GNAWABLE** *adj*

GNAWER *n* pl. **-S** one that gnaws

GNAWING *n* pl. **-S** a persistent dull pain

GNEISS *n* pl. **-ES** a type of rock **GNEISSIC** *adj*

GNOCCHI *n/pl* dumplings made of pasta

GNOME *n* pl. **-S** a dwarf

GNOMIC *adj* resembling or containing aphorisms

GNOMICAL	*adj* gnomic
GNOMISH	*adj* resembling a gnome
GNOMIST	*n* pl. **-S** a writer of aphorisms
GNOMON	*n* pl. **-S** a part of a sundial **GNOMONIC** *adj*
GNOSIS	*n* pl. **GNOSES** mystical knowledge
GNOSTIC	*n* pl. **-S** an adherent of gnosticism
GNU	*n* pl. **-S** a large antelope
GO	*v* **WENT, GONE, GOING** or **GWINE, GOES** to move along
GO	*n* pl. **GOS** a Japanese board game
GOA	*n* pl. **-S** an Asian gazelle
GOAD	*v* **-ED, -ING, -S** to drive animals with a goad (a pointed stick)
GOADLIKE	*adj* resembling a goad
GOAL	*v* **-ED, -ING, -S** to score a goal (a point-scoring play in some games)
GOALBALL	*n* pl. **-S** a ball thrown at a goal to score
GOALIE	*n* pl. **-S** a player who defends against goals
GOALLESS	*adj* having no goal
GOALPOST	*n* pl. **-S** a post that marks a boundary of the scoring area in some games
GOALWARD	*adv* toward a goal (a point-scoring area)
GOANNA	*n* pl. **-S** a large monitor lizard
GOAT	*n* pl. **-S** a horned mammal
GOATEE	*n* pl. **-S** a small pointed beard **GOATEED** *adj*
GOATFISH	*n* pl. **-ES** a tropical fish
GOATHERD	*n* pl. **-S** one who tends goats
GOATIER	comparative of goaty
GOATIEST	superlative of goaty
GOATISH	*adj* resembling a goat
GOATLIKE	*adj* goatish
GOATSKIN	*n* pl. **-S** the hide of a goat
GOATY	*adj* **GOATIER, GOATIEST** suggestive of a goat
GOB	*v* **GOBBED, GOBBING, GOBS** to fill a mine pit with waste material
GOBAN	*n* pl. **-S** gobang
GOBANG	*n* pl. **-S** a Japanese game
GOBBED	past tense of gob
GOBBET	*n* pl. **-S** a piece of raw meat
GOBBING	present participle of gob

GOBBLE	*v* **-BLED, -BLING, -BLES** to eat hastily
GOBBLER	*n* pl. **-S** a male turkey
GOBIES	pl. of goby
GOBIOID	*n* pl. **-S** a fish of the goby family
GOBLET	*n* pl. **-S** a drinking vessel
GOBLIN	*n* pl. **-S** an evil or mischievous creature
GOBO	*n* pl. **-BOS** or **-BOES** a device used to shield a microphone from extraneous sounds
GOBONEE	*adj* gobony
GOBONY	*adj* compony
GOBY	*n* pl. **GOBIES** a small fish
GOD	*v* **GODDED, GODDING, GODS** to treat as a god (a supernatural being)
GODAWFUL	*adj* extremely unpleasant
GODCHILD	*n* pl. **-CHILDREN** one whom a person sponsors at baptism
GODDED	past tense of god
GODDESS	*n* pl. **-ES** a female god
GODDING	present participle of god
GODET	*n* pl. **-S** insert of cloth in a seam
GODETIA	*n* pl. **-S** a showy annual herb
GODHEAD	*n* pl. **-S** godhood
GODHOOD	*n* pl. **-S** the state of being a god
GODLESS	*adj* worshiping no god
GODLIKE	*adj* divine
GODLING	*n* pl. **-S** a lesser god
GODLY	*adj* **-LIER, -LIEST** pious **GODLILY** *adv*
GODOWN	*n* pl. **-S** an Asian warehouse
GODROON	*n* pl. **-S** gadroon
GODSEND	*n* pl. **-S** an unexpected boon
GODSHIP	*n* pl. **-S** the rank of a god
GODSON	*n* pl. **-S** a male godchild
GODWARD	*adv* toward God
GODWARDS	*adv* Godward
GODWIT	*n* pl. **-S** a wading bird
GOER	*n* pl. **-S** one that goes
GOEST	*v* a 2d person sing. of go
GOETH	*v* a 3d person sing. of go
GOETHITE	*n* pl. **-S** an ore of iron
GOFER	*n* pl. **-S** an employee who runs errands

GOFFER   *v* **-ED, -ING, -S** to press ridges or pleats into

GOGGLE   *v* **-GLED, -GLING, -GLES** to stare with wide eyes

GOGGLER   *n* pl. **-S** one that goggles

GOGGLY   *adj* **-GLIER, -GLIEST** wide-eyed

GOGLET   *n* pl. **-S** a long-necked jar

GOGO   *n* pl. **-GOS** a discotheque

GOING   *n* pl. **-S** an advance toward an objective

GOITER   *n* pl. **-S** an enlargement of the thyroid gland **GOITERED** *adj* **GOITROUS** *adj*

GOITRE   *n* pl. **-S** goiter **GOITRED** *adj*

GOJI   *n* pl. **-S** the red berry of an Asian shrub

GOLCONDA   *n* pl. **-S** a source of great wealth

GOLD   *adj* **GOLDER, GOLDEST** golden

GOLD   *n* pl. **-S** a gold medal

GOLDARN   *n* pl. **-S** an expression of anger

GOLDBUG   *n* pl. **-S** a gold beetle

GOLDEN   *adj* **-ENER, -ENEST** of the color of gold **GOLDENLY** *adv*

GOLDEYE   *n* pl. **-S** a freshwater fish

GOLDFISH   *n* pl. **-ES** a freshwater fish

GOLDTONE   *adj* made to resemble gold

GOLDURN   *n* pl. **-S** goldarn

GOLEM   *n* pl. **-S** a legendary creature

GOLF   *v* **-ED, -ING, -S** to play golf (a type of ball game)

GOLFER   *n* pl. **-S** one that golfs

GOLFING   *n* pl. **-S** the game of golf

GOLGOTHA   *n* pl. **-S** a place of burial

GOLIARD   *n* pl. **-S** a wandering student

GOLIATH   *n* pl. **-S** a person considered to be a giant

GOLLIWOG   *n* pl. **-S** a grotesque doll

GOLLY   *interj* — used as a mild oath

GOLLYWOG   *n* pl. **-S** golliwog

GOLOSH   *n* pl. **-ES** galosh

GOLOSHE   *n* pl. **-S** galosh

GOMBEEN   *n* pl. **-S** usury

GOMBO   *n* pl. **-BOS** gumbo

GOMBROON   *n* pl. **-S** a kind of Persian pottery

GOMER   *n* pl. **-S** an undesirable hospital patient

GOMERAL   *n* pl. **-S** a fool

GOMEREL   *n* pl. **-S** gomeral

GOMERIL   *n* pl. **-S** gomeral

GOMUTI   *n* pl. **-S** a palm tree

GONAD   *n* pl. **-S** a sex gland **GONADAL, GONADIAL, GONADIC** *adj*

GONCH   *n* pl. **-ES** gaunch

GONDOLA   *n* pl. **-S** a long, narrow boat

GONE   *adj* departed

GONEF   *n* pl. **-S** ganef

GONENESS   *n* pl. **-ES** a state of exhaustion

GONER   *n* pl. **-S** one who is in a hopeless situation

GONFALON   *n* pl. **-S** a banner

GONFANON   *n* pl. **-S** gonfalon

GONG   *v* **-ED, -ING, -S** to make the sound of a gong (a disk-shaped percussion instrument)

GONGLIKE   *adj* resembling a gong

GONIA   pl. of gonion and of gonium

GONIDIUM   *n* pl. **-IA** an asexual reproductive cell **GONIDIAL, GONIDIC** *adj*

GONIF   *n* pl. **-S** ganef

GONIFF   *n* pl. **-S** ganef

GONION   *n* pl. **-NIA** a part of the lower jaw

GONIUM   *n* pl. **-NIA** an immature reproductive cell

GONOCYTE   *n* pl. **-S** a cell that produces gametes

GONOF   *n* pl. **-S** ganef

GONOPH   *n* pl. **-S** ganef

GONOPORE   *n* pl. **-S** a genital pore

GONZO   *adj* bizarre

GOO   *n* pl. **GOOS** a sticky or viscid substance

GOOBER   *n* pl. **-S** a peanut

GOOD   *adj* **BETTER, BEST** having positive or desirable qualities

GOOD   *n* pl. **-S** something that is good

GOODBY   *n* pl. **-BYS** goodbye

GOODBYE   *n* pl. **-S** a concluding remark or gesture at parting

GOODIE   *n* pl. **-S** goody

GOODIES   pl. of goody

GOODISH   *adj* somewhat good

GOODLY   *adj* **-LIER, -LIEST** of pleasing appearance

GOODMAN   *n* pl. **-MEN** the master of a household

GOODNESS *n* pl. **-ES** the state of being good

GOODWIFE *n* pl. **-WIVES** the mistress of a household

GOODWILL *n* pl. **-S** an attitude of friendliness

GOODY *n* pl. **GOODIES** a desirable food

GOOEY *adj* **GOOIER, GOOIEST** sticky or viscid

GOOF *v* **-ED, -ING, -S** to blunder

GOOFBALL *n* pl. **-S** a sleeping pill

GOOFUS *n* pl. **-ES** a foolish or stupid person

GOOFY *adj* **GOOFIER, GOOFIEST** silly **GOOFILY** *adv*

GOOGLE *v* **-GLED, -GLING, -GLES** to use an Internet search engine

GOOGLY *n* pl. **-GLIES** a type of bowled ball in cricket

GOOGOL *n* pl. **-S** an enormous number

GOOIER comparative of gooey

GOOIEST superlative of gooey

GOOK *n* pl. **-S** goo **GOOKY** *adj*

GOOMBAH *n* pl. **-S** an older man who is a friend

GOOMBAY *n* pl. **-BAYS** calypso music of the Bahamas

GOON *n* pl. **-S** a hired thug

GOONDA *n* pl. **-S** a hired thug

GOONERY *n* pl. **-ERIES** thuggish behavior

GOONEY *n* pl. **-NEYS** an albatross

GOONIE *n* pl. **-S** gooney

GOONY *n* pl. **-NIES** gooney

GOONY *adj* **GOONIER, GOONIEST** stupid

GOOP *n* pl. **-S** goo, gunk

GOOPY *adj* **GOOPIER, GOOPIEST** sticky, gooey

GOORAL *n* pl. **-S** goral

GOOSE *n* pl. **GEESE** a swimming bird

GOOSE *v* **GOOSED, GOOSING, GOOSES** to poke between the buttocks

GOOSEY *adj* **GOOSIER, GOOSIEST** goosy

GOOSY *adj* **GOOSIER, GOOSIEST** resembling a goose

GOPHER *n* pl. **-S** a burrowing rodent

GOPIK *n* pl. **-S** a monetary unit of Azerbaijan

GOR *interj* — used as a mild oath

GORAL *n* pl. **-S** a goat antelope

GORBELLY *n* pl. **-LIES** a potbelly

GORBLIMY *interj* blimey

GORCOCK *n* pl. **-S** the male red grouse

GORDITA *n* pl. **-S** a stuffed and fried pocket of cornmeal dough

GORE *v* **GORED, GORING, GORES** to pierce with a horn or tusk

GOREFEST *n* pl. **-S** a movie featuring much bloodshed

GORGE *v* **GORGED, GORGING, GORGES** to stuff with food **GORGEDLY** *adv*

GORGEOUS *adj* beautiful

GORGER *n* pl. **-S** one that gorges

GORGERIN *n* pl. **-S** a part of a column

GORGET *n* pl. **-S** a piece of armor for the throat **GORGETED** *adj*

GORGING present participle of gorge

GORGON *n* pl. **-S** an ugly woman

GORHEN *n* pl. **-S** the female red grouse

GORIER comparative of gory

GORIEST superlative of gory

GORILLA *n* pl. **-S** a large ape

GORILY *adv* in a gory manner

GORINESS *n* pl. **-ES** the state of being gory

GORING present participle of gore

GORM *v* **-ED, -ING, -S** to gaum

GORMAND *n* pl. **-S** gourmand

GORMLESS *adj* stupid

GORP *n* pl. **-S** a snack for quick energy

GORSE *n* pl. **-S** furze

GORSY *adj* **GORSIER, GORSIEST** abounding in gorse

GORY *adj* **GORIER, GORIEST** bloody

GOSH *interj* — used as an exclamation of surprise

GOSHAWK *n* pl. **-S** a large hawk

GOSLING *n* pl. **-S** a young goose

GOSPEL *n* pl. **-S** the message concerning Christ, the kingdom of God, and salvation

GOSPELER *n* pl. **-S** one that teaches the gospel

GOSPELLY *adj* having characteristics of gospel music

GOSPORT *n* pl. **-S** a communication device in an airplane

GOSSAMER *n* pl. **-S** a fine film of cobwebs

GOSSAN *n* pl. **-S** a type of decomposed rock

GOSSIP   *v* **-SIPED, -SIPING, -SIPS** or **-SIPPED, -SIPPING, -SIPS** to talk idly about the affairs of others

GOSSIPER   *n* pl. **-S** one that gossips

GOSSIPRY   *n* pl. **-RIES** the practice of gossiping

GOSSIPY   *adj* inclined to gossip

GOSSOON   *n* pl. **-S** a boy

GOSSYPOL   *n* pl. **-S** a toxic pigment

GOT   past tense of get

GOTCH   *n* pl. **-ES** underpants

GOTCHA   *n* pl. **-S** an instance of catching a person out in a deceit or wrongdoing

GOTCHIES   *n/pl* underpants

GOTH   *n* pl. **-S** a morbid style of rock music

GOTHIC   *n* pl. **-S** a style of printing

GOTHITE   *n* pl. **-S** goethite

GOTTEN   past participle of get

GOUACHE   *n* pl. **-S** a method of painting

GOUGE   *v* **GOUGED, GOUGING, GOUGES** to cut or scoop out

GOUGER   *n* pl. **-S** one that gouges

GOULASH   *n* pl. **-ES** a beef stew

GOURAMI   *n* pl. **-S** or **-ES** a food fish

GOURD   *n* pl. **-S** a hard-shelled fruit

GOURDE   *n* pl. **-S** a monetary unit of Haiti

GOURDFUL   *n* pl. **-S** as much as a hollowed gourd can hold

GOURMAND   *n* pl. **-S** one who loves to eat

GOURMET   *n* pl. **-S** a connoisseur of fine food and drink

GOUT   *n* pl. **-S** a metabolic disease

GOUTWEED   *n* pl. **-S** a plant with white flowers

GOUTY   *adj* **GOUTIER, GOUTIEST** affected with gout **GOUTILY** *adv*

GOVERN   *v* **-ED, -ING, -S** to rule or direct

GOVERNOR   *n* pl. **-S** one that governs

GOWAN   *n* pl. **-S** a daisy **GOWANED, GOWANY** *adj*

GOWD   *n* pl. **-S** gold

GOWK   *n* pl. **-S** a fool

GOWN   *v* **-ED, -ING, -S** to dress in a gown (a long, loose outer garment)

GOWNSMAN   *n* pl. **-MEN** a professional or academic person

GOX   *n* pl. **-ES** gaseous oxygen

GRAAL   *n* pl. **-S** grail

GRAB   *v* **GRABBED, GRABBING, GRABS** to grasp suddenly

GRABBER   *n* pl. **-S** one that grabs

GRABBIER   comparative of grabby

GRABBIEST   superlative of grabby

GRABBING   present participle of grab

GRABBLE   *v* **-BLED, -BLING, -BLES** to grope

GRABBLER   *n* pl. **-S** one that grabbles

GRABBY   *adj* **-BIER, -BIEST** tending to grab

GRABEN   *n* pl. **-S** a depression of the earth's crust

GRACE   *v* **GRACED, GRACING, GRACES** to give beauty to

GRACEFUL   *adj* **-FULLER, -FULLEST** having beauty of form or movement

GRACILE   *adj* gracefully slender

GRACILIS   *n* pl. **-LES** a thigh muscle

GRACING   present participle of grace

GRACIOSO   *n* pl. **-SOS** a clown in Spanish comedy

GRACIOUS   *adj* marked by kindness and courtesy

GRACKLE   *n* pl. **-S** a blackbird

GRAD   *n* pl. **-S** a graduate

GRADATE   *v* **-DATED, -DATING, -DATES** to change by degrees

GRADE   *v* **GRADED, GRADING, GRADES** to arrange in steps or degrees **GRADABLE** *adj*

GRADER   *n* pl. **-S** one that grades

GRADIENT   *n* pl. **-S** a rate of inclination

GRADIN   *n* pl. **-S** gradine

GRADINE   *n* pl. **-S** one of a series of steps

GRADING   present participle of grade

GRADUAL   *n* pl. **-S** a hymn sung in alternate parts

GRADUAND   *n* pl. **-S** one who is about to graduate

GRADUATE   *v* **-ATED, -ATING, -ATES** to receive an academic degree or diploma

GRADUS   *n* pl. **-ES** a dictionary of prosody

GRAECIZE   *v* **-CIZED, -CIZING, -CIZES** to grecize

GRAFFITI   *v* **-TIED, -TIING** or **-TING, -TIS** to draw graffiti on

GRAFFITO   *n* pl. **-TI** an inscription or drawing made on a rock or wall

GRAFT	*v* **-ED, -ING, -S** to unite with a growing plant by insertion	**GRANGE**	*n* pl. **-S** a farm
		GRANGER	*n* pl. **-S** a farmer
GRAFTAGE	*n* pl. **-S** the process of grafting	**GRANITA**	*n* pl. **-S** an iced dessert
GRAFTER	*n* pl. **-S** one that grafts	**GRANITE**	*n* pl. **-S** a type of rock **GRANITIC** *adj*
GRAHAM	*n* pl. **-S** whole-wheat flour		
GRAIL	*n* pl. **-S** the object of a long quest	**GRANNIE**	*n* pl. **-S** granny
GRAIN	*v* **-ED, -ING, -S** to form into small particles	**GRANNY**	*n* pl. **-NIES** a grandmother
		GRANOLA	*n* pl. **-S** a breakfast cereal
GRAINER	*n* pl. **-S** one that grains	**GRANT**	*v* **-ED, -ING, -S** to bestow upon
GRAINY	*adj* **GRAINIER, GRAINIEST** granular	**GRANTEE**	*n* pl. **-S** one to whom something is granted
GRAM	*n* pl. **-S** a unit of mass and weight	**GRANTER**	*n* pl. **-S** one that grants
GRAMA	*n* pl. **-S** a pasture grass	**GRANTOR**	*n* pl. **-S** granter
GRAMARY	*n* pl. **-RIES** gramarye	**GRANULAR**	*adj* composed of granules
GRAMARYE	*n* pl. **-S** occult learning; magic	**GRANULE**	*n* pl. **-S** a small particle
GRAMERCY	*n* pl. **-CIES** an expression of gratitude	**GRANUM**	*n* pl. **GRANA** a part of a plant chloroplast
GRAMMA	*n* pl. **-S** grama	**GRAPE**	*n* pl. **-S** an edible berry
GRAMMAR	*n* pl. **-S** the study of the formal features of a language	**GRAPERY**	*n* pl. **-ERIES** a vinery
		GRAPEY	*adj* **GRAPIER, GRAPIEST** grapy
GRAMME	*n* pl. **-S** gram	**GRAPH**	*v* **-ED, -ING, -S** to represent by means of a diagram
GRAMP	*n* pl. **-S** grandfather		
GRAMPA	*n* pl. **-S** a grandfather	**GRAPHEME**	*n* pl. **-S** a unit of a writing system
GRAMPUS	*n* pl. **-ES** a marine mammal	**GRAPHENE**	*n* pl. **-S** a carbon capable of transmitting electricity
GRAMPY	*n* pl. **-PIES** grampa		
GRAN	*n* pl. **-S** a grandmother	**GRAPHIC**	*n* pl. **-S** a product of the art of representation
GRANA	pl. of granum		
GRANARY	*n* pl. **-RIES** a storehouse for grain	**GRAPHITE**	*n* pl. **-S** a variety of carbon
GRAND	*adj* **GRANDER, GRANDEST** large and impressive	**GRAPIER**	comparative of grapy
		GRAPIEST	superlative of grapy
GRAND	*n* pl. **-S** a type of piano	**GRAPLIN**	*n* pl. **-S** a grapnel
GRANDAD	*n* pl. **-S** granddad	**GRAPLINE**	*n* pl. **-S** graplin
GRANDAM	*n* pl. **-S** a grandmother	**GRAPNEL**	*n* pl. **-S** a type of anchor
GRANDAME	*n* pl. **-S** grandam	**GRAPPA**	*n* pl. **-S** an Italian brandy
GRANDDAD	*n* pl. **-S** a grandfather	**GRAPPLE**	*v* **-PLED, -PLING, -PLES** to struggle or contend
GRANDDAM	*n* pl. **-S** the female parent of an animal with offspring		
		GRAPPLER	*n* pl. **-S** one that grapples
GRANDEE	*n* pl. **-S** man of high social position	**GRAPY**	*adj* **GRAPIER, GRAPIEST** resembling grapes
GRANDEUR	*n* pl. **-S** the state of being grand		
GRANDKID	*n* pl. **-S** the child of one's son or daughter	**GRASP**	*v* **-ED, -ING, -S** to seize firmly with the hand
		GRASPER	*n* pl. **-S** one that grasps
GRANDLY	*adv* in a grand manner	**GRASS**	*v* **-ED, -ING, -ES** to cover with grass (herbaceous plants)
GRANDMA	*n* pl. **-S** a grandmother		
GRANDPA	*n* pl. **-S** a grandfather	**GRASSY**	*adj* **GRASSIER, GRASSIEST** of, resembling, or pertaining to grass **GRASSILY** *adv*
GRANDSIR	*n* pl. **-S** a grandfather		
GRANDSON	*n* pl. **-S** a son of one's son or daughter	**GRAT**	past tense of greet (to weep)

GRATE	v **GRATED, GRATING, GRATES** to reduce to shreds by rubbing	**GRAYBACK**	n pl. **-S** a gray bird
		GRAYFISH	n pl. **-ES** a dogfish
GRATEFUL	adj **-FULLER, -FULLEST** deeply thankful	**GRAYISH**	adj somewhat gray
GRATER	n pl. **-S** one that grates	**GRAYLAG**	n pl. **-S** a wild goose
GRATIFY	v **-FIED, -FYING, -FIES** to satisfy	**GRAYLING**	n pl. **-S** a food fish
GRATIN	n pl. **-S** a type of food crust	**GRAYLY**	adv in a gray manner
GRATINE	adj covered with a crust	**GRAYMAIL**	n pl. **-S** pressure on an official to reveal sensitive information
GRATINEE	v **-NEED, -NEEING, -NEES** to cook food that is covered with a crust	**GRAYNESS**	n pl. **-ES** the state of being gray
		GRAYOUT	n pl. **-S** a temporary blurring of vision
GRATING	n pl. **-S** a network of bars covering an opening	**GRAZE**	v **GRAZED, GRAZING, GRAZES** to feed on growing grass **GRAZABLE** adj
GRATIS	adj free of charge		
GRATUITY	n pl. **-ITIES** a gift of money	**GRAZER**	n pl. **-S** one that grazes
GRAUPEL	n pl. **-S** granular snow pellets	**GRAZIER**	n pl. **-S** one that grazes cattle
GRAVAMEN	n pl. **-MENS** or **-MINA** the most serious part of an accusation	**GRAZING**	n pl. **-S** land used for the feeding of animals
GRAVE	adj **GRAVER, GRAVEST** extremely serious	**GRAZIOSO**	adj graceful in style
GRAVE	v **GRAVED, GRAVEN, GRAVING, GRAVES** to engrave	**GREASE**	v **GREASED, GREASING, GREASES** to smear with grease (a lubricating substance)
GRAVEL	v **-ELED, -ELING, -ELS** or **-ELLED, -ELLING, -ELS** to pave with gravel (a mixture of rock fragments)	**GREASER**	n pl. **-S** one that greases
		GREASY	adj **GREASIER, GREASIEST** containing or resembling grease **GREASILY** adv
GRAVELLY	adj containing gravel		
GRAVELY	adv in a grave manner	**GREAT**	adj **GREATER, GREATEST** large
GRAVEN	past participle of grave	**GREAT**	n pl. **-S** a distinguished or outstanding person
GRAVER	n pl. **-S** an engraver		
GRAVEST	superlative of grave	**GREATEN**	v **-ED, -ING, -S** to make greater
GRAVID	adj pregnant **GRAVIDLY** adv	**GREATLY**	adv in a great manner
GRAVIDA	n pl. **-DAS** or **-DAE** a pregnant woman	**GREAVE**	n pl. **-S** a piece of armor for the leg **GREAVED** adj
GRAVIES	pl. of gravy	**GREBE**	n pl. **-S** a diving bird
GRAVING	present participle of grave	**GRECIZE**	v **-CIZED, -CIZING, -CIZES** to provide with a Greek style
GRAVITAS	n pl. **-ES** reserved, dignified behavior		
GRAVITON	n pl. **-S** a hypothetical particle	**GREE**	v **GREED, GREEING, GREES** to agree
GRAVITY	n pl. **-TIES** the force of attraction toward the earth's center	**GREED**	n pl. **-S** excessive desire for gain or wealth
GRAVLAKS	n pl. **GRAVLAKS** gravlax	**GREEDY**	adj **GREEDIER, GREEDIEST** marked by greed **GREEDILY** adv
GRAVLAX	n pl. **GRAVLAX** cured salmon		
GRAVURE	n pl. **-S** a printing process	**GREEGREE**	n pl. **-S** grigri
GRAVY	n pl. **-VIES** a sauce of the fat and juices from cooked meat	**GREEK**	n pl. **GREEK** something unintelligible
GRAY	adj **GRAYER, GRAYEST** of a color between white and black	**GREEN**	adj **GREENER, GREENEST** of the color of growing foliage
GRAY	v **-ED, -ING, -S** to make gray	**GREEN**	v **-ED, -ING, -S** to become green
		GREENBUG	n pl. **-S** a green aphid
		GREENERY	n pl. **-ERIES** green vegetation

GREENFLY	*n* pl. **-FLIES** a green aphid
GREENIE	*n* pl. **-S** an amphetamine pill
GREENIER	comparative of greeny
GREENIEST	superlative of greeny
GREENING	*n* pl. **-S** a variety of apple
GREENISH	*adj* somewhat green
GREENLET	*n* pl. **-S** a vireo
GREENLIT	a past tense of greenlight (to give approval for)
GREENLY	*adv* in a green manner
GREENTH	*n* pl. **-S** verdure
GREENWAY	*n* pl. **-WAYS** piece of undeveloped land in a city
GREENY	*adj* **GREENIER, GREENIEST** somewhat green
GREET	*v* **-ED, -ING, -S** to address in a friendly and courteous way
GREET	*v* **GRAT, GRUTTEN, GREETING, GREETS** to weep
GREETER	*n* pl. **-S** one that greets
GREETING	*n* pl. **-S** a salutation
GREGO	*n* pl. **-GOS** a hooded coat
GREIGE	*n* pl. **-S** fabric in a gray state
GREISEN	*n* pl. **-S** a type of rock
GREMIAL	*n* pl. **-S** a lap cloth used by a bishop during a service
GREMLIN	*n* pl. **-S** a mischievous creature
GREMMIE	*n* pl. **-S** an inexperienced surfer
GREMMY	*n* pl. **-MIES** gremmie
GRENADE	*n* pl. **-S** an explosive device
GREW	past tense of grow
GREWSOME	*adj* **-SOMER, -SOMEST** gruesome
GREY	*adj* **GREYER, GREYEST** gray
GREY	*v* **-ED, -ING, -S** to gray
GREYHEN	*n* pl. **-S** the female black grouse
GREYISH	*adj* grayish
GREYLAG	*n* pl. **-S** graylag
GREYLY	*adv* grayly
GREYNESS	*n* pl. **-ES** grayness
GRIBBLE	*n* pl. **-S** a marine isopod
GRID	*v* **GRIDDED, GRIDDING, GRIDS** to put into or set out as a framework of bars or lines
GRIDDER	*n* pl. **-S** a football player
GRIDDLE	*v* **-DLED, -DLING, -DLES** to cook on a flat pan
GRIDE	*v* **GRIDED, GRIDING, GRIDES** to scrape harshly
GRIDIRON	*v* **-ED, -ING, -S** to mark off into squares
GRIDLOCK	*v* **-ED, -ING, -S** to bring to a standstill
GRIEF	*n* pl. **-S** intense mental distress
GRIEVANT	*n* pl. **-S** one that submits a complaint for arbitration
GRIEVE	*v* **GRIEVED, GRIEVING, GRIEVES** to feel grief
GRIEVER	*n* pl. **-S** one that grieves
GRIEVOUS	*adj* causing grief
GRIFF	*n* pl. **-S** griffe
GRIFFE	*n* pl. **-S** a person of mixed ancestry
GRIFFIN	*n* pl. **-S** a mythological creature
GRIFFON	*n* pl. **-S** griffin
GRIFT	*v* **-ED, -ING, -S** to swindle
GRIFTER	*n* pl. **-S** a swindler
GRIG	*n* pl. **-S** a lively person
GRIGRI	*n* pl. **-S** a fetish or amulet
GRILL	*v* **-ED, -ING, -S** to broil on a gridiron
GRILLADE	*n* pl. **-S** a dish of grilled meat
GRILLAGE	*n* pl. **-S** a framework of timber
GRILLE	*n* pl. **-S** a grating
GRILLER	*n* pl. **-S** one that grills
GRILLERY	*n* pl. **-ERIES** a place where grilled foods are served
GRILSE	*n* pl. **-S** a young salmon
GRIM	*adj* **GRIMMER, GRIMMEST** stern and unrelenting
GRIMACE	*v* **-MACED, -MACING, -MACES** to contort the facial features
GRIMACER	*n* pl. **-S** one that grimaces
GRIME	*v* **GRIMED, GRIMING, GRIMES** to make dirty
GRIMIER	comparative of grimy
GRIMIEST	superlative of grimy
GRIMILY	*adv* in a grimy manner
GRIMING	present participle of grime
GRIMLY	*adv* in a grim manner
GRIMMER	comparative of grim
GRIMMEST	superlative of grim
GRIMNESS	*n* pl. **-ES** the quality of being grim
GRIMOIRE	*n* pl. **-S** a book of magic spells
GRIMY	*adj* **GRIMIER, GRIMIEST** dirty

GRIN	v **GRINNED, GRINNING, GRINS** to smile broadly
GRINCH	n pl. **-ES** one who spoils the fun of others
GRIND	v **GROUND** or **GRINDED, GRINDING, GRINDS** to wear, smooth, or sharpen by friction
GRINDER	n pl. **-S** one that grinds
GRINDERY	n pl. **-ERIES** a place where tools are ground
GRINNED	past tense of grin
GRINNER	n pl. **-S** one that grins
GRINNING	present participle of grin
GRIOT	n pl. **-S** a tribal entertainer in West Africa
GRIP	v **GRIPPED** or **GRIPT, GRIPPING, GRIPS** to grasp
GRIPE	v **GRIPED, GRIPING, GRIPES** to complain peevishly
GRIPER	n pl. **-S** one that gripes
GRIPEY	adj **GRIPIER, GRIPIEST** gripy
GRIPIER	comparative of gripy
GRIPIEST	superlative of gripy
GRIPING	present participle of gripe
GRIPINGLY	adv in a complaining manner
GRIPMAN	n pl. **-MEN** a cable car operator
GRIPPE	n pl. **-S** a virus disease
GRIPPED	a past tense of grip
GRIPPER	n pl. **-S** one that grips
GRIPPING	present participle of grip
GRIPPLE	adj greedy
GRIPPY	adj **GRIPPIER, GRIPPIEST** affected with the grippe
GRIPSACK	n pl. **-S** a valise
GRIPT	a past tense of grip
GRIPY	adj **GRIPIER, GRIPIEST** causing sharp pains in the bowels
GRISEOUS	adj grayish
GRISETTE	n pl. **-S** a young French working-class girl
GRISKIN	n pl. **-S** the lean part of a loin of pork
GRISLY	adj **-LIER, -LIEST** horrifying
GRISON	n pl. **-S** a carnivorous mammal
GRIST	n pl. **-S** grain for grinding
GRISTER	n pl. **-S** one that grinds grain
GRISTLE	n pl. **-S** the tough part of meat
GRISTLY	adj **-TLIER, -TLIEST** containing gristle
GRIT	v **GRITTED, GRITTING, GRITS** to press the teeth together
GRITH	n pl. **-S** sanctuary for a limited period of time
GRITTER	n pl. **-S** one that grits
GRITTY	adj **-TIER, -TIEST** plucky **GRITTILY** adv
GRIVET	n pl. **-S** a small monkey
GRIZ	n pl. **GRIZ** or **GRIZZES** a grizzly
GRIZZLE	v **-ZLED, -ZLING, -ZLES** to complain
GRIZZLER	n pl. **-S** one that grizzles
GRIZZLY	adj **-ZLIER, -ZLIEST** grayish
GRIZZLY	n pl. **-ZLIES** a large bear
GROAN	v **-ED, -ING, -S** to utter a low, mournful sound
GROANER	n pl. **-S** one that groans
GROAT	n pl. **-S** an old English coin
GROCER	n pl. **-S** a dealer in foodstuffs and household supplies
GROCERY	n pl. **-CERIES** a grocer's store
GRODY	adj **GRODIER, GRODIEST** sleazy
GROG	n pl. **-S** a mixture of liquor and water
GROGGERY	n pl. **-GERIES** a barroom
GROGGY	adj **-GIER, -GIEST** dazed **GROGGILY** adv
GROGRAM	n pl. **-S** a coarse silk fabric
GROGSHOP	n pl. **-S** a groggery
GROIN	v **-ED, -ING, -S** to build with intersecting arches
GROK	v **GROKKED, GROKKING, GROKS** to understand intuitively
GROMMET	v **-ED, -ING, -S** to fasten with a reinforcing ring of metal
GROMWELL	n pl. **-S** an herb
GROOM	v **-ED, -ING, -S** to clean and care for
GROOMER	n pl. **-S** one that grooms
GROOVE	v **GROOVED, GROOVING, GROOVES** to form a groove (a long, narrow depression)
GROOVER	n pl. **-S** one that grooves
GROOVY	adj **GROOVIER, GROOVIEST** marvelous **GROOVILY** adv
GROPE	v **GROPED, GROPING, GROPES** to feel about with the hands
GROPER	n pl. **-S** one that gropes

GROSBEAK *n* pl. **-S** a finch

GROSCHEN *n* pl. **GROSCHEN** a formerly used Austrian coin

GROSS *adj* **GROSSER, GROSSEST** flagrant

GROSS *v* **-ED, -ING, -ES** to earn exclusive of deductions

GROSSER *n* pl. **-S** a product yielding a large volume of business

GROSSLY *adv* in a gross manner

GROSZ *n* pl. **GROSZY** a Polish coin

GROSZE *n* pl. **GROSZY** grosz

GROT *n* pl. **-S** a grotto

GROTTO *n* pl. **-TOS** or **-TOES** a cave **GROTTOED** *adj*

GROTTY *adj* **-TIER, -TIEST** wretched

GROUCH *v* **-ED, -ING, -ES** to complain

GROUCHY *adj* **GROUCHIER, GROUCHIEST** ill-tempered

GROUND *v* **-ED, -ING, -S** to place on a foundation

GROUNDER *n* pl. **-S** a type of batted baseball

GROUP *v* **-ED, -ING, -S** to arrange in a group (an assemblage of persons or things)

GROUPAGE *n* pl. **-S** the arranging of persons or things into groups

GROUPER *n* pl. **-S** a food fish

GROUPIE *n* pl. **-S** a follower of rock groups

GROUPING *n* pl. **-S** a set of objects

GROUPOID *n* pl. **-S** a type of mathematical set

GROUSE *v* **GROUSED, GROUSING, GROUSES** to complain

GROUSER *n* pl. **-S** one that grouses

GROUT *v* **-ED, -ING, -S** to fill with a thin mortar

GROUTER *n* pl. **-S** one that grouts

GROUTY *adj* **GROUTIER, GROUTIEST** surly

GROVE *n* pl. **-S** a small forested area **GROVED** *adj*

GROVEL *v* **-ELED, -ELING, -ELS** or **-ELLED, -ELLING, -ELS** to crawl in an abject manner

GROVELER *n* pl. **-S** one that grovels

GROVY *adj* **GROVIER, GROVIEST** resembling or suggestive of a grove

GROW *v* **GREW, GROWN, GROWING, GROWS** to cultivate **GROWABLE** *adj*

GROWER *n* pl. **-S** one that grows

GROWL *v* **-ED, -ING, -S** to utter a deep, harsh sound

GROWLER *n* pl. **-S** one that growls

GROWLY *adj* **GROWLIER, GROWLIEST** deep and harsh in speech

GROWN *adj* mature

GROWNUP *n* pl. **-S** a mature person

GROWTH *n* pl. **-S** development

GROWTHY *adj* **GROWTHIER, GROWTHIEST** fast-growing

GROYNE *n* pl. **-S** a structure built to protect a shore from erosion

GRR *interj* — used to express anger or annoyance

GRRRL *n* pl. **-S** a young woman who resists the exploitation of women

GRUB *v* **GRUBBED, GRUBBING, GRUBS** to dig

GRUBBER *n* pl. **-S** one that grubs

GRUBBY *adj* **-BIER, -BIEST** dirty **GRUBBILY** *adv*

GRUBWORM *n* pl. **-S** the larva of some insects

GRUDGE *v* **GRUDGED, GRUDGING, GRUDGES** to be unwilling to give or admit

GRUDGER *n* pl. **-S** one that grudges

GRUE *n* pl. **-S** a shudder of fear

GRUEL *v* **-ELED, -ELING, -ELS** or **-ELLED, -ELLING, -ELS** to disable by hard work

GRUELER *n* pl. **-S** one that gruels

GRUELING *n* pl. **-S** an exhausting experience

GRUELLED a past tense of gruel

GRUELLER *n* pl. **-S** grueler

GRUELLING present participle of gruel

GRUESOME *adj* **-SOMER, -SOMEST** repugnant

GRUFF *adj* **GRUFFER, GRUFFEST** low and harsh in speech

GRUFF *v* **-ED, -ING, -S** to utter in a gruff voice

GRUFFIER comparative of gruffy

GRUFFIEST superlative of gruffy

GRUFFILY *adv* in a gruffy manner

GRUFFISH *adj* somewhat gruff

GRUFFLY *adv* in a gruff manner

GRUFFY *adj* **GRUFFIER, GRUFFIEST** gruff

GRUGRU *n* pl. **-S** a palm tree

GRUIFORM *adj* designating an order of birds

GRUM	*adj* **GRUMMER, GRUMMEST** morose
GRUMBLE	*v* **-BLED, -BLING, -BLES** to mutter in discontent
GRUMBLER	*n* pl. **-S** one that grumbles
GRUMBLY	*adj* **-BLIER, -BLIEST** given to grumbling
GRUME	*n* pl. **-S** a thick, viscid substance
GRUMMER	comparative of grum
GRUMMEST	superlative of grum
GRUMMET	*v* **-ED, -ING, -S** to grommet
GRUMOSE	*adj* grumous
GRUMOUS	*adj* consisting of clustered grains
GRUMP	*v* **-ED, -ING, -S** to complain
GRUMPHIE	*n* pl. **-S** a pig
GRUMPHY	*n* pl. **GRUMPHIES** grumphie
GRUMPISH	*adj* grumpy
GRUMPY	*adj* **GRUMPIER, GRUMPIEST** ill-tempered **GRUMPILY** *adv*
GRUNGE	*n* pl. **-S** dirt
GRUNGER	*n* pl. **-S** a fan of a style of rock music and associated fashions
GRUNGY	*adj* **-GIER, -GIEST** dirty
GRUNION	*n* pl. **-S** a small food fish
GRUNT	*v* **-ED, -ING, -S** to utter a deep, guttural sound
GRUNTER	*n* pl. **-S** one that grunts
GRUNTLE	*v* **-TLED, -TLING, -TLES** to put in a good humor
GRUSHIE	*adj* thriving
GRUTCH	*v* **-ED, -ING, -ES** to grudge
GRUTTEN	past participle of greet (to weep)
GRUYERE	*n* pl. **-S** a Swiss cheese
GRYPHON	*n* pl. **-S** griffin
GUACHARO	*n* pl. **-ROS** or **-ROES** a tropical bird
GUACO	*n* pl. **-COS** a tropical plant
GUAIAC	*n* pl. **-S** guaiacum
GUAIACOL	*n* pl. **-S** a chemical compound
GUAIACUM	*n* pl. **-S** a medicinal resin
GUAIOCUM	*n* pl. **-S** guaiacum
GUAN	*n* pl. **-S** a large bird
GUANACO	*n* pl. **-COS** a South American mammal
GUANASE	*n* pl. **-S** an enzyme
GUANAY	*n* pl. **-NAYS** a Peruvian cormorant
GUANIDIN	*n* pl. **-S** a chemical compound
GUANIN	*n* pl. **-S** guanine
GUANINE	*n* pl. **-S** a chemical compound
GUANO	*n* pl. **-NOS** the accumulated excrement of seabirds
GUAR	*n* pl. **-S** a drought-tolerant legume
GUARACHE	*n* pl. **-S** huarache
GUARANA	*n* pl. **-S** a South American shrub
GUARANI	*n* pl. **-NIS** or **-NIES** a monetary unit of Paraguay
GUARANTY	*v* **-TIED, -TYING, -TIES** to assume responsibility for the quality of
GUARD	*v* **-ED, -ING, -S** to protect
GUARDANT	*n* pl. **-S** a guardian
GUARDDOG	*n* pl. **-S** a dog trained to guard persons or property
GUARDER	*n* pl. **-S** one that guards
GUARDIAN	*n* pl. **-S** one that guards
GUAVA	*n* pl. **-S** a tropical shrub
GUAYULE	*n* pl. **-S** a shrub that is a source of rubber
GUBBINS	*n* pl. **GUBBINSES** a trivial object
GUCK	*n* pl. **-S** a messy substance
GUDE	*n* pl. **-S** good
GUDGEON	*v* **-ED, -ING, -S** to dupe
GUENON	*n* pl. **-S** a long-tailed monkey
GUERDON	*v* **-ED, -ING, -S** to reward
GUERIDON	*n* pl. **-S** a small stand or table
GUERILLA	*n* pl. **-S** a member of a small independent band of soldiers
GUERNSEY	*n* pl. **-SEYS** a woolen shirt
GUESS	*v* **-ED, -ING, -ES** to form an opinion from little or no evidence
GUESSER	*n* pl. **-S** one that guesses
GUEST	*v* **-ED, -ING, -S** to appear as a visitor
GUFF	*n* pl. **-S** foolish talk
GUFFAW	*v* **-ED, -ING, -S** to laugh loudly
GUGGLE	*v* **-GLED, -GLING, -GLES** to gurgle
GUGLET	*n* pl. **-S** goglet
GUID	*n* pl. **-S** good
GUIDANCE	*n* pl. **-S** advice
GUIDE	*v* **GUIDED, GUIDING, GUIDES** to show the way to **GUIDABLE** *adj*
GUIDER	*n* pl. **-S** one that guides
GUIDEWAY	*n* pl. **-WAYS** a track for controlling the line of motion of something
GUIDON	*n* pl. **-S** a small flag

GUILD *n* pl. **-S** an association of people of the same trade

GUILDER *n* pl. **-S** a former monetary unit of the Netherlands

GUILE *v* **GUILED, GUILING, GUILES** to beguile

GUILEFUL *adj* cunning

GUILT *v* **-ED, -ING, -S** to cause (someone) to feel guilty

GUILTY *adj* **GUILTIER, GUILTIEST** worthy of blame for an offense **GUILTILY** *adv*

GUIMPE *n* pl. **-S** a short blouse

GUINEA *n* pl. **-S** a formerly used British coin

GUINEP *n* pl. **-S** genip

GUIPURE *n* pl. **-S** a type of lace

GUIRO *n* pl. **-ROS** a percussion instrument

GUISARD *n* pl. **-S** a masker

GUISE *v* **GUISED, GUISING, GUISES** to disguise

GUITAR *n* pl. **-S** a stringed musical instrument

GUITGUIT *n* pl. **-S** a tropical American bird

GUL *n* pl. **-S** a design in oriental carpets

GULAG *n* pl. **-S** a forced-labor camp

GULAR *n* pl. **-S** a scale on the throat of a reptile or fish

GULCH *n* pl. **-ES** a deep, narrow ravine

GULDEN *n* pl. **-S** a guilder

GULES *n* pl. **GULES** the color red

GULF *v* **-ED, -ING, -S** to swallow up

GULFIER comparative of gulfy

GULFIEST superlative of gulfy

GULFLIKE *adj* resembling a deep chasm

GULFWEED *n* pl. **-S** a brownish seaweed

GULFY *adj* **GULFIER, GULFIEST** full of whirlpools

GULL *v* **-ED, -ING, -S** to deceive

GULLABLE *adj* gullible **GULLABLY** *adv*

GULLERY *n* pl. **-ERIES** a place where gulls (web-footed seabirds) breed

GULLET *n* pl. **-S** the throat

GULLEY *n* pl. **-LEYS** a ravine

GULLIBLE *adj* easily deceived **GULLIBLY** *adv*

GULLWING *adj* hinged at the top to swing upward

GULLY *v* **-LIED, -LYING, -LIES** to form ravines by the action of water

GULOSITY *n* pl. **-TIES** gluttony

GULP *v* **-ED, -ING, -S** to swallow rapidly

GULPER *n* pl. **-S** one that gulps

GULPY *adj* **GULPIER, GULPIEST** marked by gulping

GUM *v* **GUMMED, GUMMING, GUMS** to smear, seal, or clog with gum (a sticky, viscid substance)

GUMBALL *n* pl. **-S** a small ball of chewing gum

GUMBO *n* pl. **-BOS** the okra plant

GUMBOIL *n* pl. **-S** an abscess in the gum

GUMBOOT *n* pl. **-S** a rubber boot

GUMBOTIL *n* pl. **-S** a sticky clay

GUMDROP *n* pl. **-S** a chewy candy

GUMLESS *adj* having no gum

GUMLIKE *adj* resembling gum

GUMLINE *n* pl. **-S** the edge of the gums meeting the teeth

GUMMA *n* pl. **-MAS** or **-MATA** a soft tumor

GUMMED past tense of gum

GUMMER *n* pl. **-S** one that gums

GUMMI *n* pl. **-S** a rubbery, flavored candy

GUMMIER comparative of gummy

GUMMIEST superlative of gummy

GUMMILY *adv* in a toothless manner

GUMMING present participle of gum

GUMMITE *n* pl. **-S** a mixture of various minerals

GUMMOSE *adj* gummy

GUMMOSIS *n* pl. **-MOSES** a disease of plants

GUMMOUS *adj* gummy

GUMMY *adj* **-MIER, -MIEST** resembling gum

GUMPTION *n* pl. **-S** shrewdness

GUMSHOE *v* **-SHOED, -SHOEING, -SHOES** to investigate stealthily

GUMTREE *n* pl. **-S** a tree that yields gum

GUMWEED *n* pl. **-S** a plant covered with a gummy substance

GUMWOOD *n* pl. **-S** the wood of a gumtree

GUN *v* **GUNNED, GUNNING, GUNS** to shoot with a gun (a portable firearm)

GUNBOAT *n* pl. **-S** an armed vessel

GUNDOG *n* pl. **-S** a hunting dog

GUNFIGHT *v* **-FOUGHT, -FIGHTING, -FIGHTS** to fight with guns

GUNFIRE	*n* pl. **-S** the firing of guns
GUNFLINT	*n* pl. **-S** the flint in a flintlock
GUNGE	*v* **GUNGED, GUNGING, GUNGES** to obstruct with gunky material
GUNGY	*adj* **GUNGIER, GUNGIEST** gunky
GUNITE	*n* pl. **-S** a mixture of cement, sand, and water
GUNK	*v* **-ED, -ING, -S** to cause something to be gunky
GUNKHOLE	*v* **-HOLED, -HOLING, -HOLES** to make a series of short boat trips
GUNKY	*adj* **GUNKIER, GUNKIEST** filthy, sticky, or greasy
GUNLESS	*adj* having no gun
GUNLOCK	*n* pl. **-S** the mechanism which ignites the charge of a gun
GUNMAN	*n* pl. **-MEN** one who is armed with a gun
GUNMETAL	*n* pl. **-S** a dark gray color
GUNNED	past tense of gun
GUNNEL	*n* pl. **-S** a marine fish
GUNNEN	past participle of gin
GUNNER	*n* pl. **-S** one that operates a gun
GUNNERA	*n* pl. **-S** a plant with large leaves
GUNNERY	*n* pl. **-NERIES** the use of guns
GUNNING	*n* pl. **-S** the sport of hunting with a gun
GUNNY	*n* pl. **-NIES** a coarse fabric
GUNNYBAG	*n* pl. **-S** a bag made of gunny
GUNPAPER	*n* pl. **-S** a type of explosive paper
GUNPLAY	*n* pl. **-PLAYS** the shooting of guns
GUNPOINT	*n* pl. **-S** the point or aim of a gun
GUNPORT	*n* pl. **-S** an opening in a ship or airplane for a gun
GUNROOM	*n* pl. **-S** a room on a British warship
GUNSEL	*n* pl. **-S** a gunman
GUNSHIP	*n* pl. **-S** an armed helicopter
GUNSHOT	*n* pl. **-S** a projectile fired from a gun
GUNSIGHT	*n* pl. **-S** a device on a gun for aiming
GUNSMITH	*n* pl. **-S** one who makes or repairs firearms
GUNSTOCK	*n* pl. **-S** the rear wooden part of a rifle
GUNTER	*n* pl. **-S** a type of sail
GUNWALE	*n* pl. **-S** the upper edge of a ship's side
GUPPY	*n* pl. **-PIES** a small, tropical fish
GURDWARA	*n* pl. **-S** a Sikh temple
GURDY	*n* pl. **-DIES** a winch on a fishing boat
GURGE	*v* **GURGED, GURGING, GURGES** to swirl
GURGLE	*v* **-GLED, -GLING, -GLES** to flow with bubbling sounds
GURGLET	*n* pl. **-S** goglet
GURGLY	*adj* **-GLIER, -GLIEST** making bubbling sounds
GURNARD	*n* pl. **-S** a marine fish
GURNET	*n* pl. **-S** a gurnard
GURNEY	*n* pl. **-NEYS** a wheeled cot
GURRY	*n* pl. **-RIES** fish offal
GURSH	*n* pl. **-ES** qursh
GURU	*n* pl. **-S** a Hindu spiritual teacher
GURUSHIP	*n* pl. **-S** the office of a guru
GUSH	*v* **-ED, -ING, -ES** to flow forth forcefully
GUSHER	*n* pl. **-S** a gushing oil well
GUSHY	*adj* **GUSHIER, GUSHIEST** overly sentimental **GUSHILY** *adv*
GUSSET	*v* **-ED, -ING, -S** to furnish with a reinforcing piece of material
GUSSIE	*v* **-SIED, -SYING, -SIES** to gussy
GUSSY	*v* **-SIED, -SYING, -SIES** to dress up in fine or showy clothes
GUST	*v* **-ED, -ING, -S** to blow in gusts (sudden blasts of wind)
GUSTABLE	*n* pl. **-S** a savory food
GUSTIER	comparative of gusty
GUSTIEST	superlative of gusty
GUSTILY	*adv* in a gusty manner
GUSTLESS	*adj* having no gusts
GUSTO	*n* pl. **-TOES** or **-TOS** vigorous enjoyment
GUSTY	*adj* **GUSTIER, GUSTIEST** blowing in gusts
GUT	*v* **GUTTED, GUTTING, GUTS** to remove the guts (intestines) of
GUTFUL	*n* pl. **-S** an excessive amount
GUTLESS	*adj* lacking courage
GUTLIKE	*adj* resembling guts
GUTSILY	*adv* in a gutsy manner
GUTSY	*adj* **GUTSIER, GUTSIEST** brave
GUTTA	*n* pl. **-TAE** a drop of liquid
GUTTATE	*adj* resembling a drop
GUTTATED	*adj* guttate

GUTTED   past tense of gut

GUTTER   *v* **-ED, -ING, -S** to form channels for draining off water

GUTTERY   *adj* marked by extreme vulgarity or indecency

GUTTIER   comparative of gutty

GUTTIEST   superlative of gutty

GUTTING   present participle of gut

GUTTLE   *v* **-TLED, -TLING, -TLES** to eat rapidly

GUTTLER   *n* pl. **-S** one that guttles

GUTTURAL   *n* pl. **-S** a throaty sound

GUTTY   *adj* **-TIER, -TIEST** marked by courage

GUV   *n* pl. **-S** a governor

GUY   *v* **-ED, -ING, -S** to ridicule

GUYLINE   *n* pl. **-S** a rope, chain, or wire used as a brace

GUYOT   *n* pl. **-S** a flat-topped seamount

GUZZLE   *v* **-ZLED, -ZLING, -ZLES** to drink rapidly

GUZZLER   *n* pl. **-S** one that guzzles

GWEDUC   *n* pl. **-S** geoduck

GWEDUCK   *n* pl. **-S** geoduck

GWINE   a present participle of go

GYBE   *v* **GYBED, GYBING, GYBES** to shift from side to side while sailing

GYM   *n* pl. **-S** a room for athletic activities

GYMKHANA   *n* pl. **-S** an athletic meet

GYMNASIA   *n/pl* gyms

GYMNAST   *n* pl. **-S** one who is skilled in physical exercises

GYMSLIP   *n* pl. **-S** a sleeveless tunic often worn by schoolgirls

GYNAECEA   *n/pl* gynecia

GYNAECIA   *n/pl* gynecia

GYNANDRY   *n* pl. **-DRIES** the condition of having both male and female sexual organs

GYNARCHY   *n* pl. **-CHIES** government by women

GYNECIC   *adj* pertaining to women

GYNECIUM   *n* pl. **-CIA** the pistil of a flower

GYNECOID   *adj* resembling a woman

GYNIATRY   *n* pl. **-TRIES** the treatment of women's diseases

GYNIE   *n* pl. **-S** a gynecologist

GYNO   *n* pl. **GYNOS** a gynecologist

GYNOECIA   *n/pl* gynecia

GYOZA   *n* pl. **-S** a stuffed and fried pocket of dough

GYP   *v* **GYPPED, GYPPING, GYPS** to swindle

GYPLURE   *n* pl. **-S** a synthetic attractant to trap gypsy moths

GYPO   *n* pl. **GYPOS** a small-time logging operator

GYPPER   *n* pl. **-S** one that gyps

GYPPO   *n* pl. **GYPPOS** gypo

GYPSEIAN   *adj* of or pertaining to gypsies

GYPSEOUS   *adj* containing gypsum

GYPSTER   *n* pl. **-S** one that gyps

GYPSUM   *n* pl. **-S** a mineral

GYPSY   *v* **-SIED, -SYING, -SIES** to live like a gypsy (a wanderer)

GYPSYDOM   *n* pl. **-S** the realm of gypsies

GYPSYISH   *adj* resembling a gypsy

GYPSYISM   *n* pl. **-S** the mode of life of gypsies

GYRAL   *adj* gyratory **GYRALLY** *adv*

GYRASE   *n* pl. **-S** an enzyme

GYRATE   *v* **-RATED, -RATING, -RATES** to revolve or rotate

GYRATION   *n* pl. **-S** the act of gyrating

GYRATOR   *n* pl. **-S** one that gyrates

GYRATORY   *adj* moving in a circle or spiral

GYRE   *v* **GYRED, GYRING, GYRES** to move in a circle or spiral

GYRENE   *n* pl. **-S** a marine

GYRI   pl. of gyrus

GYRO   *n* pl. **-ROS** a gyroscope

GYROIDAL   *adj* spiral in arrangement

GYRON   *n* pl. **-S** a heraldic design

GYROSE   *adj* marked with wavy lines

GYROSTAT   *n* pl. **-S** a type of stabilizing device

GYRUS   *n* pl. **-RI** a ridge in the brain

GYTTJA   *n* pl. **-S** an organically rich mud

GYVE   *v* **GYVED, GYVING, GYVES** to shackle

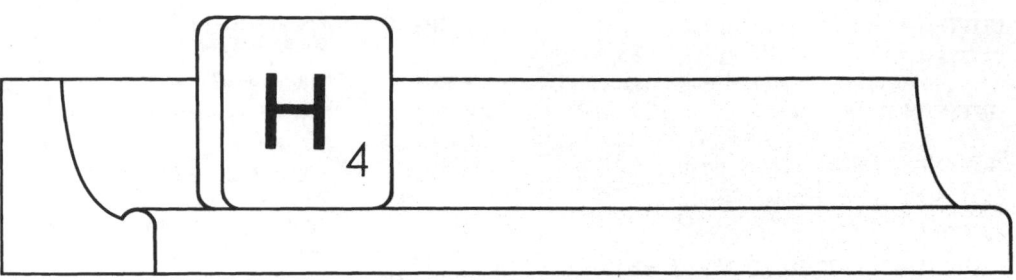

HA	n pl. **-S** a sound of surprise	**HACKLE**	v **-LED, -LING, -LES** to hack
HAAF	n pl. **-S** a deep-sea fishing ground	**HACKLER**	n pl. **-S** one that hackles
HAAR	n pl. **-S** a fog	**HACKLY**	adj **-LIER, -LIEST** jagged
HABANERA	n pl. **-S** a Cuban dance	**HACKMAN**	n pl. **-MEN** a hackie
HABANERO	n pl. **-ROS** a hot chili pepper	**HACKNEY**	v **-NEYED, -NEYING, -NEYS** to make common
HABDALAH	n pl. **-S** a Jewish ceremony		
HABENDUM	n pl. **-S** the part of a deed that limits the extent of ownership	**HACKSAW**	v **-SAWED, -SAWN, -SAWING, -SAWS** to use a saw having a fine-toothed blade
HABILE	adj skillful	**HACKWORK**	n pl. **-S** artistic work done according to formula
HABIT	v **-ED, -ING, -S** to clothe or dress		
HABITAN	n pl. **-S** a French settler	**HAD**	a past tense of have
HABITANT	n pl. **-S** an inhabitant	**HADAL**	adj pertaining to deep parts of the ocean
HABITAT	n pl. **-S** the natural environment of an organism	**HADARIM**	a pl. of heder
HABITUAL	adj occurring frequently or constantly	**HADDEST**	a past 2d person sing. of have
		HADDOCK	n pl. **-S** a food fish
HABITUDE	n pl. **-S** a usual course of action	**HADE**	v **HADED, HADING, HADES** to incline
HABITUE	n pl. **-S** a frequent customer		
HABITUS	n pl. **HABITUS** bodily build and constitution	**HADITH**	n pl. **HADITH** or **HADITHS** a record of the sayings of Muhammed
HABOOB	n pl. **-S** a violent sandstorm	**HADJ**	n pl. **-ES** a pilgrimage to Mecca
HABU	n pl. **-S** a poisonous snake	**HADJEE**	n pl. **-S** hadji
HACEK	n pl. **-S** a mark placed over a letter to modify it	**HADJI**	n pl. **-S** one who has made a hadj
HACHURE	v **-CHURED, -CHURING, -CHURES** to make a hatching on a map	**HADRON**	n pl. **-S** an elementary particle **HADRONIC** adj
		HADST	a past 2d person sing. of have
HACIENDA	n pl. **-S** an estate	**HAE**	v **HAED, HAEN, HAEING, HAES** to have
HACK	v **-ED, -ING, -S** to cut or chop roughly **HACKABLE** adj	**HAEM**	n pl. **-S** heme
HACKBUT	n pl. **-S** a type of gun	**HAEMAL**	adj hemal
HACKEE	n pl. **-S** a chipmunk	**HAEMATAL**	adj hemal
HACKER	n pl. **-S** one that hacks	**HAEMATIC**	n pl. **-S** hematic
HACKERY	n pl. **-ERIES** dull, unoriginal writing	**HAEMATIN**	n pl. **-S** hematin
HACKIE	n pl. **-S** a taxicab driver	**HAEMIC**	adj hemic
HACKING	n pl. **-S** the activity of riding a horse for pleasure	**HAEMIN**	n pl. **-S** hemin
		HAEMOID	adj hemoid

HAEN	past participle of hae
HAERES	*n* pl. **-REDES** heres
HAET	*n* pl. **-S** a small amount
HAFFET	*n* pl. **-S** the cheekbone and temple
HAFFIT	*n* pl. **-S** haffet
HAFIZ	*n* pl. **-ES** a Muslim who knows the Koran by heart
HAFNIUM	*n* pl. **-S** a metallic element
HAFT	*v* **-ED, -ING, -S** to supply with a handle
HAFTARA	*n* pl. **-RAS** or **-ROT** or **-ROTH** haphtara
HAFTARAH	*n* pl. **-RAHS** or **-ROS** or **-ROT** or **-ROTH** haphtara
HAFTER	*n* pl. **-S** one that hafts
HAFTORAH	*n* pl. **-RAHS** or **-ROT** or **-ROTH** haphtara
HAG	*v* **HAGGED, HAGGING, HAGS** to hack
HAGADIC	*adj* haggadic
HAGADIST	*n* pl. **-S** a haggadic scholar
HAGBERRY	*n* pl. **-RIES** a small cherry
HAGBORN	*adj* born of a witch
HAGBUSH	*n* pl. **-ES** a large tree
HAGBUT	*n* pl. **-S** hackbut
HAGDON	*n* pl. **-S** a seabird
HAGFISH	*n* pl. **-ES** an eellike fish
HAGGADA	*n* pl. **-DAS, -DOT** or **-DOTH** haggadah
HAGGADAH	*n* pl. **-DAHS** or **-DOT** or **-DOTH** a biblical narrative **HAGGADIC** *adj*
HAGGARD	*n* pl. **-S** an adult hawk
HAGGED	past tense of hag
HAGGING	present participle of hag
HAGGIS	*n* pl. **-GISES** a Scottish dish made of a sheep's inner organs, which are cut up, spiced, and cooked in a bag
HAGGISH	*adj* resembling a hag
HAGGLE	*v* **-GLED, -GLING, -GLES** to bargain
HAGGLER	*n* pl. **-S** one that haggles
HAGGLING	*n* pl. **-S** a bargaining about a price
HAGRIDE	*v* **-RODE, -RIDDEN, -RIDING, -RIDES** to harass
HAGRIDER	*n* pl. **-S** one that hagrides
HAH	*n* pl. **-S** ha
HAHA	*n* pl. **-S** a fence set in a ditch
HAHNIUM	*n* pl. **-S** a radioactive element
HAICK	*n* pl. **-S** haik
HAIK	*n* pl. **HAIKS** or **HAIKA** an outer garment worn by Arabs
HAIKU	*n* pl. **-S** a Japanese poem
HAIL	*v* **-ED, -ING, -S** to welcome
HAILER	*n* pl. **-S** one that hails
HAIMISH	*adj* homey, unpretentious
HAINT	*n* pl. **-S** a ghost
HAIR	*n* pl. **-S** a threadlike growth
HAIRBALL	*n* pl. **-S** a ball of hair
HAIRBAND	*n* pl. **-S** a headband
HAIRCAP	*n* pl. **-S** a hat
HAIRCUT	*n* pl. **-S** a cutting of the hair
HAIRDO	*n* pl. **-DOS** a style of wearing the hair
HAIRED	*adj* having hair
HAIRGRIP	*n* pl. **-S** a bobby pin
HAIRIER	comparative of hairy
HAIRIEST	superlative of hairy
HAIRILY	*adv* in a hairy manner
HAIRLESS	*adj* having no hair
HAIRLIKE	*adj* resembling a hair
HAIRLINE	*n* pl. **-S** a very thin line
HAIRLOCK	*n* pl. **-S** a lock of hair
HAIRNET	*n* pl. **-S** a net worn to keep the hair in place
HAIRPIN	*n* pl. **-S** a hair fastener
HAIRWING	*n* pl. **-S** a fishing lure tied with hair
HAIRWORK	*n* pl. **-S** the making of articles from hair
HAIRWORM	*n* pl. **-S** a parasitic worm
HAIRY	*adj* **HAIRIER, HAIRIEST** covered with hair
HAJ	*n* pl. **-ES** hadj
HAJI	*n* pl. **-S** hadji
HAJJ	*n* pl. **-ES** hadj
HAJJI	*n* pl. **-S** hadji
HAKE	*n* pl. **-S** a marine fish
HAKEEM	*n* pl. **-S** hakim
HAKIM	*n* pl. **-S** a Muslim physician
HAKU	*n* pl. **-S** a crown of flowers
HALACHA	*n* pl. **-CHAS** or **-CHOT** or **-CHOTH** the legal part of the Talmud **HALACHIC** *adj*
HALAKAH	*n* pl. **-KAHS** or **-KOTH** halacha **HALAKIC** *adj*

HALAKHA	*n* pl. **-KHAS** or **-KHOT** halacha **HALAKHIC** *adj*
HALAKHAH	*n* pl. **-KHAHS** or **-KHOTH** or **-KHOT** halacha **HALAKHIC** *adj*
HALAKIST	*n* pl. **-S** a halakic writer
HALAKOTH	a pl. of halakah
HALAL	*n* pl. **-S** meat prepared in accordance with Islamic law
HALALA	*n* pl. **-S** a Saudi Arabian coin
HALALAH	*n* pl. **-S** halala
HALATION	*n* pl. **-S** a blurring of light in photographs
HALAVAH	*n* pl. **-S** halvah
HALAZONE	*n* pl. **-S** a disinfectant for drinking water
HALBERD	*n* pl. **-S** an axlike weapon of the 15th and 16th centuries
HALBERT	*n* pl. **-S** halberd
HALCYON	*n* pl. **-S** a mythical bird
HALE	*adj* **HALER, HALEST** healthy
HALE	*v* **HALED, HALING, HALES** to compel to go
HALENESS	*n* pl. **-ES** the state of being hale
HALER	*n* pl. **-LERS** or **-LERU** a coin of the Czech Republic
HALEST	superlative of hale
HALF	*n* pl. **HALVES** one of two equal parts
HALFBACK	*n* pl. **-S** a football player
HALFBEAK	*n* pl. **-S** a marine fish
HALFLIFE	*n* pl. **-LIVES** a measure of radioactive decay
HALFNESS	*n* pl. **-ES** the state of being half
HALFPIPE	*n* pl. **-S** a U-shaped course used for skateboarding
HALFTIME	*n* pl. **-S** an intermission in a football game
HALFTONE	*n* pl. **-S** a shade between light and dark
HALFWAY	*adj* being in the middle
HALFWIT	*n* pl. **-S** a foolish or stupid person
HALIBUT	*n* pl. **-S** a flatfish
HALID	*n* pl. **-S** halide
HALIDE	*n* pl. **-S** a chemical compound
HALIDOM	*n* pl. **-S** something holy
HALIDOME	*n* pl. **-S** halidom
HALIER	*n* pl. **HALIERS** or **HALIEROV** a former monetary unit of Slovakia
HALING	present participle of hale
HALIOTIS	*n* pl. **HALIOTIS** a mollusk with an ear-shaped shell
HALITE	*n* pl. **-S** a mineral
HALITUS	*n* pl. **-ES** an exhalation
HALL	*n* pl. **-S** a large room for assembly
HALLAH	*n* pl. **-LAHS** or **-LOTH** or **-LOT** challah
HALLAL	*adj* prepared according to Islamic law
HALLEL	*n* pl. **-S** a chant of praise
HALLIARD	*n* pl. **-S** halyard
HALLMARK	*v* **-ED, -ING, -S** to mark with an official stamp
HALLO	*v* **-ED, -ING, -S** or **-ES** to shout
HALLOA	*v* **-ED, -ING, -S** to hallo
HALLOO	*v* **-ED, -ING, -S** to hallo
HALLOT	a pl. of hallah
HALLOTH	a pl. of hallah
HALLOW	*v* **-ED, -ING, -S** to make holy
HALLOWER	*n* pl. **-S** one that hallows
HALLUX	*n* pl. **-LUCES** the big toe **HALLUCAL** *adj*
HALLWAY	*n* pl. **-WAYS** a hall
HALM	*n* pl. **-S** haulm
HALMA	*n* pl. **-S** a board game
HALO	*v* **-ED, -ING, -S** or **-ES** to form a halo (a ring of light)
HALOGEN	*n* pl. **-S** a nonmetallic element
HALOID	*n* pl. **-S** a chemical salt
HALOLIKE	*adj* resembling a halo
HALON	*n* pl. **-S** a compound of carbon and bromine
HALT	*v* **-ED, -ING, -S** to stop
HALTER	*v* **-ED, -ING, -S** to put restraint upon
HALTERE	*n* pl. **-S** a pair of wings of an insect
HALTLESS	*adj* not hesitant
HALUTZ	*n* pl. **-LUTZIM** an Israeli farmer
HALVA	*n* pl. **-S** halvah
HALVAH	*n* pl. **-S** a Turkish confection
HALVE	*v* **HALVED, HALVING, HALVES** to divide into two equal parts
HALVERS	*n* pl. **HALVERS** half shares
HALVES	pl. of half
HALVING	*n* pl. **-S** the act of fitting timbers together by cutting out half the thickness of each
HALWA	*n* pl. **-S** a sweet Indian dish

HALYARD	*n* pl. **-S** a line used to hoist a sail	**HANDBOOK**	*n* pl. **-S** a manual
HAM	*v* **HAMMED, HAMMING, HAMS** to overact	**HANDCAR**	*n* pl. **-S** a hand-operated railroad car
HAMADA	*n* pl. **-S** hammada	**HANDCART**	*n* pl. **-S** a cart pushed by hand
HAMAL	*n* pl. **-S** a porter in eastern countries	**HANDCLAP**	*n* pl. **-S** a striking together of the palms of the hands
HAMARTIA	*n* pl. **-S** a defect of character	**HANDCUFF**	*v* **-ED, -ING, -S** to fetter with restraining cuffs
HAMATE	*n* pl. **-S** a wrist bone		
HAMATSA	*n* pl. **-S** a dance inspired by the spirit of a man-eating monster	**HANDER**	*n* pl. **-S** one that hands
		HANDFAST	*v* **-ED, -ING, -S** to grip securely
HAMAUL	*n* pl. **-S** hamal	**HANDFUL**	*n* pl. **HANDFULS** or **HANDSFUL** as much as the hand can hold
HAMBONE	*v* **-BONED, -BONING, -BONES** to overact	**HANDGRIP**	*n* pl. **-S** a grip by the hand or hands
HAMBURG	*n* pl. **-S** a patty of ground beef		
HAME	*n* pl. **-S** a part of a horse collar	**HANDGUN**	*n* pl. **-S** a small firearm
HAMFAT	*n* pl. **-S** an amateurish performer	**HANDHELD**	*n* pl. **-S** something held in the hand
HAMLET	*n* pl. **-S** a small town	**HANDHOLD**	*n* pl. **-S** a handgrip
HAMMADA	*n* pl. **-S** a desert plateau of bedrock	**HANDICAP**	*v* **-CAPPED, -CAPPING, -CAPS** to hinder
HAMMAL	*n* pl. **-S** hamal	**HANDIER**	comparative of handy
HAMMAM	*n* pl. **-S** a Turkish bath	**HANDIEST**	superlative of handy
HAMMED	past tense of ham	**HANDILY**	*adv* in a handy manner
HAMMER	*v* **-ED, -ING, -S** to strike repeatedly	**HANDLE**	*v* **-DLED, -DLING, -DLES** to touch with the hands
HAMMERER	*n* pl. **-S** one that hammers	**HANDLER**	*n* pl. **-S** one that handles
HAMMIER	comparative of hammy	**HANDLESS**	*adj* having no hands
HAMMIEST	superlative of hammy	**HANDLIKE**	*adj* resembling a hand
HAMMILY	*adv* in a hammy manner	**HANDLINE**	*n* pl. **-S** a fishing line worked by hand
HAMMING	present participle of ham		
HAMMOCK	*n* pl. **-S** a hanging cot	**HANDLING**	*n* pl. **-S** the manner in which something is handled
HAMMY	*adj* **-MIER, -MIEST** overly theatrical		
HAMPER	*v* **-ED, -ING, -S** to hinder	**HANDLIST**	*n* pl. **-S** a reference list
HAMPERER	*n* pl. **-S** one that hampers	**HANDLOOM**	*n* pl. **-S** a manually operated loom
HAMSTER	*n* pl. **-S** a burrowing rodent	**HANDMADE**	*adj* made by hand
HAMULUS	*n* pl. **-LI** a small hook **HAMULAR, HAMULATE, HAMULOSE, HAMULOUS** *adj*	**HANDMAID**	*n* pl. **-S** a female servant
		HANDOFF	*n* pl. **-S** a play in football
		HANDOUT	*n* pl. **-S** something given out free
HAMZA	*n* pl. **-S** an Arabic diacritical mark	**HANDOVER**	*n* pl. **-S** an instance of giving up control
HAMZAH	*n* pl. **-S** hamza		
HANAPER	*n* pl. **-S** a wicker receptacle	**HANDPICK**	*v* **-ED, -ING, -S** to choose carefully
HANCE	*n* pl. **-S** a side of an arch	**HANDRAIL**	*n* pl. **-S** a railing used for support
HAND	*v* **-ED, -ING, -S** to present with the hand (the end of the forearm)	**HANDSAW**	*n* pl. **-S** a saw used manually
		HANDSEL	*v* **-SELED, -SELING, -SELS** or **-SELLED, -SELLING, -SELS** to give a gift to
HANDAX	*n* pl. **-ES** a short-handled ax		
HANDBAG	*n* pl. **-S** a small carrying bag	**HANDSET**	*n* pl. **-S** a type of telephone
HANDBALL	*n* pl. **-S** a small rubber ball	**HANDSEWN**	*adj* sewn by hand
HANDBELL	*n* pl. **-S** a small bell with a handle	**HANDSFUL**	a pl. of handful
HANDBILL	*n* pl. **-S** a circular		

HANDSOME	*adj* **-SOMER, -SOMEST** attractive
HANDWORK	*n* pl. **-S** manual labor
HANDWRIT	*adj* written by hand
HANDY	*adj* **HANDIER, HANDIEST** convenient for handling
HANDYMAN	*n* pl. **-MEN** a man who does odd jobs
HANG	*v* **HUNG** or **HANGED, HANGING, HANGS** to attach from above only **HANGABLE** *adj*
HANGAR	*v* **-ED, -ING, -S** to place in an aircraft shelter
HANGBIRD	*n* pl. **-S** a type of bird
HANGDOG	*n* pl. **-S** a sneaky person
HANGER	*n* pl. **-S** one that hangs
HANGFIRE	*n* pl. **-S** a delay in detonation
HANGING	*n* pl. **-S** an execution by strangling with a suspended noose
HANGMAN	*n* pl. **-MEN** an executioner
HANGNAIL	*n* pl. **-S** an agnail
HANGNEST	*n* pl. **-S** a hangbird
HANGOUT	*n* pl. **-S** a place often visited
HANGOVER	*n* pl. **-S** the physical effects following a drinking binge
HANGTAG	*n* pl. **-S** a type of tag used commercially
HANGUL	*n* the Korean alphabetic script
HANGUP	*n* pl. **-S** an inhibition or obsession
HANIWA	*n/pl* Japanese clay sculptures
HANK	*v* **-ED, -ING, -S** to fasten a sail
HANKER	*v* **-ED, -ING, -S** to long for
HANKERER	*n* pl. **-S** one that hankers
HANKIE	*n* pl. **-S** hanky
HANKY	*n* pl. **-KIES** a handkerchief
HANSA	*n* pl. **-S** hanse
HANSE	*n* pl. **-S** a guild of merchants
HANSEL	*v* **-SELED, -SELING, -SELS** or **-SELLED, -SELLING, -SELS** to handsel
HANSOM	*n* pl. **-S** a light carriage
HANT	*v* **-ED, -ING, -S** to haunt
HANTLE	*n* pl. **-S** a large amount
HANUMAN	*n* pl. **-S** an East Indian monkey
HAO	*n* pl. **HAO** a monetary unit of Vietnam
HAP	*v* **HAPPED, HAPPING, HAPS** to happen
HAPAX	*n* pl. **-ES** a word that occurs only once
HAPHTARA	*n* pl. **-RAS** or **-ROT** or **-ROTH** a biblical selection
HAPKIDO	*n* pl. **-DOS** a Korean martial art
HAPLESS	*adj* luckless
HAPLITE	*n* pl. **-S** aplite
HAPLOID	*n* pl. **-S** a cell having only one set of chromosomes
HAPLOIDY	*n* pl. **-DIES** the state of being a haploid
HAPLONT	*n* pl. **-S** an organism having a particular chromosomal structure
HAPLOPIA	*n* pl. **-S** normal vision
HAPLOSIS	*n* pl. **-LOSES** the halving of the chromosome number
HAPLY	*adv* by chance
HAPPED	past tense of hap
HAPPEN	*v* **-ED, -ING, -S** to occur
HAPPI	*n* pl. **-S** a loose Japanese coat
HAPPING	present participle of hap
HAPPY	*adj* **-PIER, -PIEST** marked by joy **HAPPILY** *adv*
HAPTEN	*n* pl. **-S** a substance similar to an antigen **HAPTENIC** *adj*
HAPTENE	*n* pl. **-S** hapten
HAPTIC	*adj* pertaining to the sense of touch
HAPTICAL	*adj* haptic
HARAM	*adj* forbidden by Islamic law
HARANGUE	*v* **-RANGUED, -RANGUING, -RANGUES** to deliver a tirade to
HARASS	*v* **-ED, -ING, -ES** to bother persistently
HARASSER	*n* pl. **-S** one that harasses
HARBOR	*v* **-ED, -ING, -S** to shelter
HARBORER	*n* pl. **-S** one that harbors
HARBOUR	*v* **-ED, -ING, -S** to harbor
HARD	*adj* **HARDER, HARDEST** firm and unyielding
HARDBACK	*n* pl. **-S** a hardcover book
HARDBALL	*n* pl. **-S** baseball
HARDBODY	*n* pl. **-DIES** an attractive person with a muscular body
HARDBOOT	*n* pl. **-S** a horseman
HARDCASE	*n* pl. **-S** a tough or obstinate person
HARDCORE	*n* pl. **-S** hard material used in foundations

HARDEDGE *n* pl. **-S** a geometric painting

HARDEN *v* **-ED, -ING, -S** to make hard

HARDENER *n* pl. **-S** one that hardens

HARDHACK *n* pl. **-S** a woody plant

HARDHAT *n* pl. **-S** a conservative

HARDHEAD *n* pl. **-S** a practical person

HARDIER comparative of hardy

HARDIES pl. of hardy

HARDIEST superlative of hardy

HARDILY *adv* in a hardy manner

HARDISH *adj* somewhat hard

HARDLINE *adj* unyielding

HARDLY *adv* scarcely

HARDNESS *n* pl. **-ES** the state of being hard

HARDNOSE *n* pl. **-S** a stubborn person

HARDPACK *n* pl. **-S** compacted snow

HARDPAN *n* pl. **-S** a layer of hard subsoil

HARDS *n/pl* the coarse refuse of flax

HARDSET *adj* rigid

HARDSHIP *n* pl. **-S** a difficult, painful condition

HARDTACK *n* pl. **-S** a hard biscuit

HARDTOP *n* pl. **-S** a type of car

HARDWARE *n* pl. **-S** metal goods

HARDWIRE *v* **-WIRED, -WIRING, -WIRES** to permanently connect electronic components

HARDWOOD *n* pl. **-S** the hard, compact wood of various trees

HARDY *adj* **-DIER, -DIEST** very sturdy

HARDY *n* pl. **-DIES** a blacksmith's chisel

HARE *v* **HARED, HARING, HARES** to run

HAREBELL *n* pl. **-S** a perennial herb

HAREEM *n* pl. **-S** harem

HARELIKE *adj* resembling a hare (a long-eared mammal)

HARELIP *n* pl. **-S** a deformity of the upper lip

HAREM *n* pl. **-S** the section of a Muslim household reserved for women

HAREWOOD *n* pl. **-S** sycamore wood used for furniture

HARIANA *n* pl. **-S** a breed of cattle

HARICOT *n* pl. **-S** the seed of various string beans

HARIJAN *n* pl. **-S** an outcaste in India

HARING present participle of hare

HARISSA *n* pl. **-S** a spicy North African sauce

HARK *v* **-ED, -ING, -S** to listen to

HARKEN *v* **-ED, -ING, -S** to hearken

HARKENER *n* pl. **-S** one that harkens

HARL *n* pl. **-S** a herl

HARLOT *n* pl. **-S** a prostitute

HARLOTRY *n* pl. **-RIES** prostitution

HARM *v* **-ED, -ING, -S** to injure

HARMER *n* pl. **-S** one that harms

HARMFUL *adj* capable of harming

HARMIN *n* pl. **-S** harmine

HARMINE *n* pl. **-S** an alkaloid used as a stimulant

HARMLESS *adj* not harmful

HARMONIC *n* pl. **-S** an overtone

HARMONY *n* pl. **-NIES** agreement

HARNESS *v* **-ED, -ING, -ES** to put tackle on a draft animal

HARP *v* **-ED, -ING, -S** to play on a harp (a type of stringed musical instrument)

HARPER *n* pl. **-S** a harpist

HARPIES pl. of harpy

HARPIN *n* pl. **-S** harping

HARPING *n* pl. **-S** a wooden plank used in shipbuilding

HARPIST *n* pl. **-S** one that plays the harp

HARPOON *v* **-ED, -ING, -S** to strike with a barbed spear

HARPY *n* pl. **-PIES** a shrewish person

HARRIDAN *n* pl. **-S** a haggard woman

HARRIED past tense of harry

HARRIER *n* pl. **-S** a hunting dog

HARRIES present 3d person sing. of harry

HARROW *v* **-ED, -ING, -S** to break up and level soil

HARROWER *n* pl. **-S** one that harrows

HARRUMPH *v* **-ED, -ING, -S** to make a guttural sound

HARRY *v* **-RIED, -RYING, -RIES** to pillage

HARSH *adj* **HARSHER, HARSHEST** severe **HARSHLY** *adv*

HARSHEN *v* **-ED, -ING, -S** to make harsh

HARSLET *n* pl. **-S** haslet

HART *n* pl. **-S** a male deer

HARTAL *n* pl. **-S** a stoppage of work

HARUMPH *v* **-ED, -ING, -S** to harumph

HARUSPEX *n* pl. **-PICES** a soothsayer of ancient Rome

HARVEST *v* **-ED, -ING, -S** to gather a crop

HAS a present 3d person sing. of have

HASH *v* **-ED, -ING, -ES** to mince

HASHEESH *n* pl. **-ES** hashish

HASHHEAD *n* pl. **-S** a hashish addict

HASHISH *n* pl. **-ES** a mild narcotic

HASHTAG *n* pl. **-S** a word or phrase preceded by the symbol # that categorizes the accompanying text

HASLET *n* pl. **-S** the edible viscera of an animal

HASP *v* **-ED, -ING, -S** to fasten with a clasp

HASSEL *n* pl. **-S** an argument

HASSIUM *n* pl. **-S** a radioactive element

HASSLE *v* **-SLED, -SLING, -SLES** to argue

HASSOCK *n* pl. **-S** a footstool

HAST a present 2d person sing. of have

HASTATE *adj* triangular

HASTE *v* **HASTED, HASTING, HASTES** to hasten

HASTEFUL *adj* hasty

HASTEN *v* **-ED, -ING, -S** to hurry

HASTENER *n* pl. **-S** one that hastens

HASTING present participle of haste

HASTY *adj* **HASTIER, HASTIEST** speedy **HASTILY** *adv*

HAT *v* **HATTED, HATTING, HATS** to provide with a hat (a covering for the head)

HATABLE *adj* hateable

HATBAND *n* pl. **-S** a band worn on a hat

HATBOX *n* pl. **-ES** a box for a hat

HATCH *v* **-ED, -ING, -ES** to bring forth young from an egg

HATCHECK *n* pl. **-S** a room for the temporary keeping of hats

HATCHEL *v* **-ELED, -ELING, -ELS** or **-ELLED, -ELLING, -ELS** to separate flax fibers with a comb

HATCHER *n* pl. **-S** one that hatches

HATCHERY *n* pl. **-ERIES** a place for hatching eggs

HATCHET *n* pl. **-S** a small ax

HATCHING *n* pl. **-S** a series of lines used to show shading

HATCHWAY *n* pl. **-WAYS** an opening in the deck of a ship

HATE *v* **HATED, HATING, HATES** to despise

HATEABLE *adj* meriting hatred

HATEFUL *adj* detestable

HATER *n* pl. **-S** one that hates

HATFUL *n* pl. **HATFULS** or **HATSFUL** as much as a hat can hold

HATH a present 3d person sing. of have

HATING present participle of hate

HATLESS *adj* lacking a hat

HATLIKE *adj* resembling a hat

HATMAKER *n* pl. **-S** one that makes hats

HATPIN *n* pl. **-S** a pin for securing a hat

HATRACK *n* pl. **-S** a rack for hats

HATRED *n* pl. **-S** intense dislike or aversion

HATSFUL a pl. of hatful

HATTED past tense of hat

HATTER *n* pl. **-S** a hatmaker

HATTERIA *n* pl. **-S** a reptile

HATTING present participle of hat

HAUBERK *n* pl. **-S** a coat of armor

HAUGH *n* pl. **-S** a low-lying meadow

HAUGHTY *adj* **-TIER, -TIEST** arrogant

HAUL *v* **-ED, -ING, -S** to pull with force

HAULAGE *n* pl. **-S** the act of hauling

HAULBACK *n* pl. **-S** a line for drawing a cable back

HAULER *n* pl. **-S** one that hauls

HAULIER *n* pl. **-S** hauler

HAULING *n* pl. **-S** the action of transporting logs

HAULM *n* pl. **-S** a plant stem

HAULMY *adj* **HAULMIER, HAULMIEST** having haulms

HAULOUT *n* pl. **-S** the action of hauling a boat out of water

HAULYARD *n* pl. **-S** halyard

HAUNCH *n* pl. **-ES** the hindquarter **HAUNCHED** *adj*

HAUNT *v* **-ED, -ING, -S** to visit frequently

HAUNTER *n* pl. **-S** one that haunts

HAUNTING *n* pl. **-S** a visitation by a ghost

HAUSEN *n* pl. **-S** a Russian sturgeon

HAUSFRAU *n* pl. **-FRAUS** or **-FRAUEN** a housewife

HAUT	*adj* haute
HAUTBOIS	*n* pl. **HAUTBOIS** hautboy
HAUTBOY	*n* pl. **-BOYS** an oboe
HAUTE	*adj* **HAUTER, HAUTEST** high-class
HAUTEUR	*n* pl. **-S** haughty manner or spirit
HAVARTI	*n* pl. **-S** a Danish cheese
HAVDALAH	*n* pl. **-S** habdalah
HAVE	*v* **HAD, HAVING, HAS** to hold as a possession, privilege, or entitlement
HAVE	*n* pl. **-S** a wealthy person
HAVELOCK	*n* pl. **-S** a covering for a cap
HAVEN	*v* **-ED, -ING, -S** to shelter
HAVER	*v* **-ED, -ING, -S** to hem and haw
HAVEREL	*n* pl. **-S** a fool
HAVING	present participle of have
HAVIOR	*n* pl. **-S** behavior
HAVIOUR	*n* pl. **-S** havior
HAVOC	*v* **-OCKED, -OCKING, -OCS** to destroy
HAVOCKER	*n* pl. **-S** one that havocs
HAW	*v* **-ED, -ING, -S** to turn left
HAWALA	*n* pl. **-S** a type of financial arrangement in Islamic societies
HAWEATER	*n* pl. **-S** a resident of Manitoulin Island, Ontario
HAWFINCH	*n* pl. **-ES** a Eurasian finch
HAWK	*v* **-ED, -ING, -S** to peddle
HAWKBILL	*n* pl. **-S** a sea turtle
HAWKER	*n* pl. **-S** one that hawks
HAWKEY	*n* pl. **-EYS** a hawkie
HAWKEYED	*adj* having keen sight
HAWKIE	*n* pl. **-S** a white-faced cow
HAWKING	*n* pl. **-S** falconry
HAWKISH	*adj* warlike
HAWKLIKE	*adj* resembling a hawk (a bird of prey)
HAWKMOTH	*n* pl. **-S** a large moth
HAWKNOSE	*n* pl. **-S** a large, curved nose
HAWKSHAW	*n* pl. **-S** a detective
HAWKWEED	*n* pl. **-S** a weedlike herb
HAWSE	*n* pl. **-S** a part of a ship's bow
HAWSER	*n* pl. **-S** a mooring rope
HAWTHORN	*n* pl. **-S** a thorny shrub
HAY	*v* **-ED, -ING, -S** to convert into hay (grass, cut and dried for fodder)
HAYCOCK	*n* pl. **-S** a pile of hay
HAYER	*n* pl. **-S** one that hays
HAYEY	*adj* resembling hay
HAYFIELD	*n* pl. **-S** a field where grasses for hay are grown
HAYFORK	*n* pl. **-S** a tool for pitching hay
HAYING	*n* pl. **-S** the season for harvesting hay
HAYLAGE	*n* pl. **-S** a type of hay
HAYLOFT	*n* pl. **-S** a loft for hay storage
HAYMAKER	*n* pl. **-S** one that makes hay
HAYMOW	*n* pl. **-S** a hayloft
HAYRACK	*n* pl. **-S** a frame used in hauling hay
HAYRICK	*n* pl. **-S** a haystack
HAYRIDE	*n* pl. **-S** a wagon ride
HAYSEED	*n* pl. **-S** a bumpkin
HAYSTACK	*n* pl. **-S** a pile of hay
HAYWARD	*n* pl. **-S** an officer who tends cattle
HAYWIRE	*n* pl. **-S** wire used in baling hay
HAZAN	*n* pl. **-ZANS** or **-ZANIM** a cantor
HAZARD	*v* **-ED, -ING, -S** to venture
HAZARDER	*n* pl. **-S** one that hazards
HAZE	*v* **HAZED, HAZING, HAZES** to subject to a humiliating initiation
HAZEL	*n* pl. **-S** a shrub
HAZELHEN	*n* pl. **-S** a European grouse
HAZELLY	*adj* yellowish brown
HAZELNUT	*n* pl. **-S** an edible nut
HAZER	*n* pl. **-S** one that hazes
HAZIER	comparative of hazy
HAZIEST	superlative of hazy
HAZILY	*adv* in a hazy manner
HAZINESS	*n* pl. **-ES** the state of being hazy
HAZING	*n* pl. **-S** an attempt to embarrass or ridicule
HAZMAT	*n* pl. **-S** hazardous material
HAZY	*adj* **HAZIER, HAZIEST** unclear
HAZZAN	*n* pl. **HAZZANS** or **HAZZANIM** hazan
HE	*n* pl. **-S** a male person
HEAD	*v* **-ED, -ING, -S** to be chief of
HEADACHE	*n* pl. **-S** a pain inside the head
HEADACHY	*adj* **-ACHIER, -ACHIEST** having a headache
HEADBAND	*n* pl. **-S** a band worn on the head

HEADEND *n* pl. **-S** a facility that receives and distributes communications signals

HEADER *n* pl. **-S** a grain harvester

HEADFISH *n* pl. **-ES** a marine fish

HEADFUL *n* pl. **-S** a great amount of knowledge

HEADGATE *n* pl. **-S** a gate to control the flow of water

HEADGEAR *n* pl. **HEADGEAR** a covering for the head

HEADHUNT *v* **-ED, -ING, -S** to seek out, decapitate, and preserve the heads of enemies

HEADIER comparative of heady

HEADIEST superlative of heady

HEADILY *adv* in a heady manner

HEADING *n* pl. **-S** a title

HEADLAMP *n* pl. **-S** a light on the front of a car

HEADLAND *n* pl. **-S** a cliff

HEADLESS *adj* lacking a head

HEADLINE *v* **-LINED, -LINING, -LINES** to provide with a title

HEADLOCK *n* pl. **-S** a wrestling hold

HEADLONG *adj* rash; impetuous

HEADMAN *n* pl. **-MEN** a foreman

HEADMOST *adj* foremost

HEADNOTE *n* pl. **-S** a prefixed note

HEADPIN *n* pl. **-S** a bowling pin

HEADPOND *n* pl. **-S** a pond created behind a dam

HEADRACE *n* pl. **-S** a water channel

HEADRAIL *n* pl. **-S** a horizontal rail at the top of something

HEADREST *n* pl. **-S** a support for the head

HEADROOM *n* pl. **-S** clear vertical space

HEADSAIL *n* pl. **-S** a type of sail

HEADSET *n* pl. **-S** a pair of earphones

HEADSHIP *n* pl. **-S** the position of a leader

HEADSHOT *n* pl. **-S** a photograph of a person from the neck up

HEADSMAN *n* pl. **-MEN** an executioner

HEADSTAY *n* pl. **-STAYS** a support for a ship's foremast

HEADWARD *adv* toward the head

HEADWAY *n* pl. **-WAYS** forward movement

HEADWIND *n* pl. **-S** an oncoming wind

HEADWORD *n* pl. **-S** a word put at the beginning

HEADWORK *n* pl. **-S** mental work

HEADY *adj* **HEADIER, HEADIEST** intoxicating

HEAL *v* **-ED, -ING, -S** to make sound or whole **HEALABLE** *adj*

HEALER *n* pl. **-S** one that heals

HEALING *n* pl. **-S** the process of becoming healthy again

HEALTH *n* pl. **-S** the physical condition of an organism

HEALTHY *adj* **HEALTHIER, HEALTHIEST** having good health

HEAP *v* **-ED, -ING, -S** to pile up

HEAPER *n* pl. **-S** one that heaps

HEAPY *adj* resembling a heap (a group of things piled one on another)

HEAR *v* **HEARD, HEARING, HEARS** to perceive by the ear **HEARABLE** *adj*

HEARER *n* pl. **-S** one that hears

HEARING *n* pl. **-S** a preliminary examination

HEARKEN *v* **-ED, -ING, -S** to listen to

HEARSAY *n* pl. **-SAYS** secondhand information

HEARSE *v* **HEARSED, HEARSING, HEARSES** to transport in a hearse (a vehicle for conveying corpses)

HEART *v* **-ED, -ING, -S** to hearten

HEARTEN *v* **-ED, -ING, -S** to give courage to

HEARTH *n* pl. **-S** the floor of a fireplace

HEARTY *adj* **HEARTIER, HEARTIEST** very friendly **HEARTILY** *adv*

HEARTY *n* pl. **HEARTIES** a comrade

HEAT *v* **HEATED** or **HET, HEATING, HEATS** to make hot **HEATABLE** *adj*

HEATEDLY *adv* in an inflamed or excited manner

HEATER *n* pl. **-S** an apparatus for heating

HEATH *n* pl. **-S** an evergreen shrub

HEATHEN *n* pl. **-S** an uncivilized person

HEATHER *n* pl. **-S** an evergreen shrub **HEATHERY** *adj*

HEATHY *adj* **HEATHIER, HEATHIEST** abounding in heath

HEATING *n* pl. **-S** the act of making something hot

HEATLESS *adj* having no warmth

HEAUME *n* pl. **-S** a medieval helmet

HEAVE	*v* **HEAVED** or **HOVE, HEAVING, HEAVES** to lift forcefully	**HEDGY**	*adj* **HEDGIER, HEDGIEST** abounding in hedges
HEAVEN	*n* pl. **-S** the sky	**HEDONIC**	*adj* pertaining to pleasure
HEAVENLY	*adj* **-LIER, -LIEST** full of beauty and peace	**HEDONICS**	*n/pl* a branch of psychology
HEAVER	*n* pl. **-S** one that heaves	**HEDONISM**	*n* pl. **-S** the pursuit of pleasure
HEAVIER	comparative of heavy	**HEDONIST**	*n* pl. **-S** a follower of hedonism
HEAVIES	pl. of heavy	**HEED**	*v* **-ED, -ING, -S** to pay attention to
HEAVING	present participle of heave	**HEEDER**	*n* pl. **-S** one that heeds
HEAVY	*adj* **HEAVIER, HEAVIEST** having much weight **HEAVILY** *adv*	**HEEDFUL**	*adj* paying close attention
		HEEDLESS	*adj* paying little or no attention
HEAVY	*n* pl. **HEAVIES** a villain	**HEEHAW**	*v* **-ED, -ING, -S** to guffaw
HEAVYISH	*adj* somewhat heavy	**HEEL**	*v* **-ED, -ING, -S** to supply with a heel (the raised part of a shoe)
HEAVYSET	*adj* solidly built; stocky		
HEBDOMAD	*n* pl. **-S** the number seven	**HEELBALL**	*n* pl. **-S** a composition used for polishing
HEBETATE	*v* **-TATED, -TATING, -TATES** to make dull	**HEELER**	*n* pl. **-S** one that puts heels on shoes
HEBETIC	*adj* pertaining to puberty	**HEELING**	*n* pl. **-S** the act of inclining laterally
HEBETUDE	*n* pl. **-S** mental dullness	**HEELLESS**	*adj* lacking heels
HEBRAIZE	*v* **-IZED, -IZING, -IZES** to make Hebrew	**HEELPOST**	*n* pl. **-S** a post fitted to the end of something
HECATOMB	*n* pl. **-S** a great sacrifice or slaughter	**HEELTAP**	*n* pl. **-S** material put on the heel of a shoe
HECK	*n* pl. **-S** hell (a place or state of misery)	**HEEZE**	*v* **HEEZED, HEEZING, HEEZES** to hoist
HECKLE	*v* **-LED, -LING, -LES** to harass a speaker	**HEFT**	*v* **-ED, -ING, -S** to lift up
		HEFTER	*n* pl. **-S** one that hefts
HECKLER	*n* pl. **-S** one that heckles	**HEFTY**	*adj* **HEFTIER, HEFTIEST** heavy **HEFTILY** *adv*
HECTARE	*n* pl. **-S** a unit of area		
HECTIC	*adj* filled with turmoil **HECTICLY** *adv*	**HEGARI**	*n* pl. **-S** a grain
		HEGEMON	*n* pl. **-S** a political state having hegemony
HECTIC	*n* pl. **-S** a fever accompanied by flushed cheeks		
		HEGEMONY	*n* pl. **-NIES** great authority
HECTICAL	*adj* hectic	**HEGIRA**	*n* pl. **-S** an exodus
HECTOR	*v* **-ED, -ING, -S** to bully	**HEGUMEN**	*n* pl. **-S** the head of a monastery
HEDDLE	*n* pl. **-S** a part of a loom	**HEGUMENE**	*n* pl. **-S** the head of a nunnery
HEDER	*n* pl. **HEDERS** or **HADARIM** or **HEDARIM** a Jewish school	**HEGUMENY**	*n* pl. **-NIES** the office of a hegumen
		HEH	*n* pl. **-S** a Hebrew letter
HEDGE	*v* **HEDGED, HEDGING, HEDGES** to surround with a hedge (a dense row of shrubs)	**HEIFER**	*n* pl. **-S** a young cow
		HEIGH	*interj* — used to attract attention
HEDGEHOG	*n* pl. **-S** a small mammal	**HEIGHT**	*n* pl. **-S** the highest point
HEDGEHOP	*v* **-HOPPED, -HOPPING, -HOPS** to fly near the ground	**HEIGHTEN**	*v* **-ED, -ING, -S** to raise
		HEIGHTH	*n* pl. **-S** height
HEDGEPIG	*n* pl. **-S** a hedgehog	**HEIL**	*v* **-ED, -ING, -S** to salute
HEDGER	*n* pl. **-S** one that hedges	**HEIMISH**	*adj* haimish
HEDGEROW	*n* pl. **-S** a row of bushes	**HEINIE**	*n* pl. **-S** the buttocks
HEDGING	present participle of hedge	**HEINOUS**	*adj* very wicked

HEIR	v **-ED, -ING, -S** to inherit
HEIRDOM	n pl. **-S** heirship
HEIRESS	n pl. **-ES** a female inheritor
HEIRLESS	adj having no inheritors
HEIRLOOM	n pl. **-S** an inherited possession
HEIRSHIP	n pl. **-S** the right to inheritance
HEISHI	n/pl tiny beads made from shells
HEIST	v **-ED, -ING, -S** to steal
HEISTER	n pl. **-S** one that heists
HEJIRA	n pl. **-S** hegira
HEKTARE	n pl. **-S** hectare
HELD	past tense of hold
HELENIUM	n pl. **-S** a plant with daisylike flowers
HELIAC	adj heliacal
HELIACAL	adj pertaining to the sun
HELIAST	n pl. **-S** an Athenian judge
HELICAL	adj shaped like a helix
HELICES	a pl. of helix
HELICITY	n pl. **-TIES** a component of a particle's spin
HELICOID	n pl. **-S** a type of geometrical surface
HELICON	n pl. **-S** a large bass tuba
HELICOPT	v **-ED, -ING, -S** to travel by helicopter
HELILIFT	v **-ED, -ING, -S** to transport by helicopter
HELIO	n pl. **-LIOS** a signaling mirror
HELIPAD	n pl. **-S** a heliport
HELIPORT	n pl. **-S** an airport for helicopters
HELISKI	v **-ED, -ING, -S** to ski downhill on mountains reached by helicopter
HELISTOP	n pl. **-S** a heliport
HELITACK	n pl. **-S** the use of helicopters to fight forest fires
HELIUM	n pl. **-S** a gaseous element
HELIX	n pl. **-LIXES** or **-LICES** something spiral in form
HELL	v **-ED, -ING, -S** to behave raucously
HELLBENT	adj stubbornly determined
HELLBOX	n pl. **-ES** a printer's receptacle
HELLCAT	n pl. **-S** a shrewish person
HELLER	n pl. **-S** a hellion
HELLERI	n pl. **-S** or **-ES** a tropical fish
HELLERY	n pl. **-LERIES** rough play
HELLFIRE	n pl. **-S** the torment of hell (a place of great suffering)
HELLHOLE	n pl. **-S** a horrible place
HELLION	n pl. **-S** a troublesome person
HELLISH	adj horrible
HELLKITE	n pl. **-S** a cruel person
HELLO	v **-ED, -ING, -S** or **-ES** to greet
HELLUVA	adj disagreeable
HELLWARD	adv toward hell (a place of great suffering)
HELM	v **-ED, -ING, -S** to steer a ship
HELMET	v **-ED, -ING, -S** to supply with a helmet (a protective covering for the head)
HELMINTH	n pl. **-S** a worm
HELMLESS	adj lacking a helm (a steering system)
HELMSMAN	n pl. **-MEN** one that steers a ship
HELO	n pl. **HELOS** a helicopter
HELOT	n pl. **-S** a slave or serf
HELOTAGE	n pl. **-S** helotism
HELOTISM	n pl. **-S** slavery or serfdom
HELOTRY	n pl. **-RIES** helotism
HELP	v **HELPED** or **HOLP, HELPED** or **HOLPEN, HELPING, HELPS** to give assistance to **HELPABLE** adj
HELPDESK	n pl. **-S** a service that helps customers with problems
HELPER	n pl. **-S** one that helps
HELPFUL	adj being of service or assistance
HELPING	n pl. **-S** a portion of food
HELPLESS	adj defenseless
HELPLINE	n pl. **-S** a telephone service that provides advice
HELPMATE	n pl. **-S** a helpful companion
HELPMEET	n pl. **-S** a helpmate
HELVE	v **HELVED, HELVING, HELVES** to provide with a handle
HEM	v **HEMMED, HEMMING, HEMS** to provide with an edge
HEMAGOG	n pl. **-S** an agent that promotes blood flow
HEMAL	adj pertaining to the blood
HEMATAL	adj hemal
HEMATEIN	n pl. **-S** a chemical compound
HEMATIC	n pl. **-S** a medicine for a blood disease
HEMATIN	n pl. **-S** heme

HEMATINE *n* pl. **-S** hematin

HEMATITE *n* pl. **-S** an ore of iron

HEMATOID *adj* resembling blood

HEMATOMA *n* pl. **-MAS** or **-MATA** a swelling filled with blood

HEME *n* pl. **-S** a component of hemoglobin

HEMIC *adj* hemal

HEMIN *n* pl. **-S** a chloride of heme

HEMIOLA *n* pl. **-S** a rhythmic alteration in music

HEMIOLIA *n* pl. **-S** hemiola

HEMIPTER *n* pl. **-S** an insect

HEMLINE *n* pl. **-S** the bottom edge of a garment

HEMLOCK *n* pl. **-S** a poisonous herb

HEMMED past tense of hem

HEMMER *n* pl. **-S** one that hems

HEMMING present participle of hem

HEMOCOEL *n* pl. **-S** a body cavity

HEMOCYTE *n* pl. **-S** a blood cell

HEMOID *adj* hemal

HEMOLYZE *v* **-LYZED, -LYZING, -LYZES** to break down red blood cells

HEMOSTAT *n* pl. **-S** an instrument for reducing bleeding

HEMP *n* pl. **-S** a tall herb

HEMPEN *adj* made of hemp

HEMPIE *adj* **HEMPIER, HEMPIEST** hempy

HEMPIER comparative of hempy

HEMPIEST superlative of hempy

HEMPLIKE *adj* resembling hemp

HEMPSEED *n* pl. **-S** the seed of hemp

HEMPWEED *n* pl. **-S** a climbing plant

HEMPY *adj* **HEMPIER, HEMPIEST** mischievous

HEN *n* pl. **-S** a female chicken

HENBANE *n* pl. **-S** a poisonous herb

HENBIT *n* pl. **-S** a perennial herb

HENCE *adv* consequently

HENCHMAN *n* pl. **-MEN** an unscrupulous supporter

HENCOOP *n* pl. **-S** a cage for hens

HENEQUEN *n* pl. **-S** a fiber used to make ropes

HENEQUIN *n* pl. **-S** henequen

HENGE *n* pl. **-S** a circular Bronze Age structure in England

HENHOUSE *n* pl. **-S** a shelter for poultry

HENIQUEN *n* pl. **-S** henequen

HENLEY *n* pl. **-LEYS** a type of knit shirt

HENLIKE *adj* resembling a hen

HENNA *v* **-ED, -ING, -S** to dye with a reddish coloring

HENNERY *n* pl. **-NERIES** a poultry farm

HENNISH *adj* resembling a hen

HENPECK *v* **-ED, -ING, -S** to dominate by nagging

HENRY *n* pl. **-RYS** or **-RIES** a unit of inductance

HENT *v* **-ED, -ING, -S** to grasp

HEP *adj* **HEPPER, HEPPEST** hip

HEP *n* pl. **-S** hepatitis (inflammation of the liver)

HEPARIN *n* pl. **-S** a biochemical

HEPATIC *n* pl. **-S** a drug acting on the liver

HEPATICA *n* pl. **-CAS** or **-CAE** a perennial herb

HEPATIZE *v* **-TIZED, -TIZING, -TIZES** to convert tissue into a firm mass

HEPATOMA *n* pl. **-MAS** or **-MATA** a tumor of the liver

HEPCAT *n* pl. **-S** a jazz enthusiast

HEPTAD *n* pl. **-S** a group of seven

HEPTAGON *n* pl. **-S** a seven-sided polygon

HEPTANE *n* pl. **-S** a hydrocarbon used as a solvent

HEPTARCH *n* pl. **-S** one of a group of seven rulers

HEPTOSE *n* pl. **-S** a chemical compound

HER *pron* the objective or possessive case of the pronoun she

HERALD *v* **-ED, -ING, -S** to proclaim

HERALDIC *adj* pertaining to heraldry

HERALDRY *n* pl. **-RIES** the art or science of armorial bearings

HERB *n* pl. **-S** a flowering plant with a nonwoody stem

HERBAGE *n* pl. **-S** nonwoody plant life **HERBAGED** *adj*

HERBAL *n* pl. **-S** a book about herbs and plants

HERBARIA *n/pl* collections of dried plants

HERBED *adj* flavored with herbs

HERBLESS *adj* lacking herbs

HERBLIKE *adj* resembling an herb

HERBY *adj* **HERBIER, HERBIEST** abounding in herbs

HERCULES *n* pl. **-LESES** any man of great size and strength

HERD *v* **-ED, -ING, -S** to bring together in a herd (a group of animals)

HERDER *n* pl. **-S** one who tends a herd

HERDIC *n* pl. **-S** a type of carriage

HERDING *n* pl. **-S** the work of tending or moving livestock

HERDLIKE *adj* resembling a herd

HERDMAN *n* pl. **-MEN** herdsman

HERDSMAN *n* pl. **-MEN** a herder

HERE *n* pl. **-S** this place

HEREAT *adv* at this time

HEREAWAY *adv* in this vicinity

HEREBY *adv* by this means

HEREDES pl. of heres

HEREDITY *n* pl. **-TIES** the genetic transmission of characteristics

HEREIN *adv* in this

HEREINTO *adv* into this place

HEREOF *adv* of this

HEREON *adv* on this

HERES *n* pl. **HEREDES** an heir

HERESY *n* pl. **-SIES** a belief contrary to a church doctrine

HERETIC *n* pl. **-S** one that upholds heresy

HERETO *adv* to this matter

HERETRIX *n* pl. **-TRIXES** or **-TRICES** heritrix

HEREUNTO *adv* hereto

HEREUPON *adv* immediately following this

HEREWITH *adv* along with this

HERIOT *n* pl. **-S** a feudal tribute or payment

HERITAGE *n* pl. **-S** something that is inherited

HERITOR *n* pl. **-S** one that inherits

HERITRIX *n* pl. **-TRIXES** or **-TRICES** a female heritor

HERL *n* pl. **-S** a feathered fishing lure

HERM *n* pl. **-S** a type of statue

HERMA *n* pl. **-MAE** or **-MAI** a herm **HERMAEAN** *adj*

HERMETIC *adj* airtight

HERMIT *n* pl. **-S** a recluse **HERMITIC** *adj*

HERMITRY *n* pl. **-RIES** the state of being a hermit

HERN *n* pl. **-S** a heron

HERNIA *n* pl. **-NIAS** or **-NIAE** the protrusion of an organ through its surrounding wall **HERNIAL** *adj*

HERNIATE *v* **-ATED, -ATING, -ATES** to protrude through an abnormal bodily opening

HERO *n* pl. **-ROS** or **-ROES** a hoagie

HEROIC *n* pl. **-S** an epic verse

HEROICAL *adj* courageous; noble

HEROIN *n* pl. **-S** an addictive narcotic

HEROINE *n* pl. **-S** a brave woman

HEROISM *n* pl. **-S** heroic behavior

HEROIZE *v* **-IZED, -IZING, -IZES** to make heroic

HERON *n* pl. **-S** a wading bird

HERONRY *n* pl. **-RIES** a place where herons breed

HERPES *n* pl. **HERPES** a skin infection **HERPETIC** *adj*

HERRING *n* pl. **-S** a food fish

HERRY *v* **-RIED, -RYING, -RIES** to harry

HERS *pron* the possessive case of the pronoun she

HERSELF *pron* a form of the 3d person sing. feminine pronoun

HERSTORY *n* pl. **-RIES** history with a feminist viewpoint

HERTZ *n* pl. **HERTZ** a unit of frequency

HESITANT *adj* tending to hesitate

HESITATE *v* **-TATED, -TATING, -TATES** to hold back in uncertainty

HESSIAN *n* pl. **-S** a coarse cloth

HESSITE *n* pl. **-S** a mineral

HEST *n* pl. **-S** a command

HET *n* pl. **-S** heth

HETAERA *n* pl. **-RAS** or **-RAE** a concubine **HETAERIC** *adj*

HETAIRA *n* pl. **-RAS** or **-RAI** hetaera

HETERO *n* pl. **-EROS** a heterosexual

HETH *n* pl. **-S** a Hebrew letter

HETMAN *n* pl. **-MANS** or **-MEN** a cossack leader

HEUCH *n* pl. **-S** heugh

HEUCHERA *n* pl. **-S** a North American plant

HEUGH *n* pl. **-S** a steep cliff

HEVEA *n* pl. **-S** a tree yielding sap used for rubber

HEW	*v* **HEWED, HEWN, HEWING, HEWS** to cut with an ax **HEWABLE** *adj*
HEWER	*n* pl. **-S** one that hews
HEX	*v* **-ED, -ING, -ES** to cast an evil spell upon
HEXAD	*n* pl. **-S** a group of six **HEXADIC** *adj*
HEXADE	*n* pl. **-S** hexad
HEXAGON	*n* pl. **-S** a polygon having six sides
HEXAGRAM	*n* pl. **-S** a six-pointed star
HEXAMINE	*n* pl. **-S** a chemical compound
HEXANE	*n* pl. **-S** a volatile liquid
HEXAPLA	*n* pl. **-S** an edition in which six texts are set in parallel columns **HEXAPLAR** *adj*
HEXAPOD	*n* pl. **-S** a six-legged insect
HEXAPODY	*n* pl. **-DIES** a line of verse with six feet
HEXARCHY	*n* pl. **-CHIES** a group of six separate states
HEXER	*n* pl. **-S** one that hexes
HEXEREI	*n* pl. **-S** witchcraft
HEXONE	*n* pl. **-S** a hydrocarbon solvent
HEXOSAN	*n* pl. **-S** a carbohydrate
HEXOSE	*n* pl. **-S** a simple sugar
HEXYL	*n* pl. **-S** a hydrocarbon radical **HEXYLIC** *adj*
HEY	*interj* — used to attract attention
HEYDAY	*n* pl. **-DAYS** the period of one's greatest success
HEYDEY	*n* pl. **-DEYS** heyday
HI	*interj* — used as a greeting
HIATUS	*n* pl. **-ES** a gap or missing section **HIATAL** *adj*
HIBACHI	*n* pl. **-S** a cooking device
HIBERNAL	*adj* pertaining to winter
HIBISCUS	*n* pl. **-ES** a tropical plant
HIC	*interj* — used to represent a hiccup
HICCOUGH	*v* **-ED, -ING, -S** to hiccup
HICCUP	*v* **-CUPED, -CUPING, -CUPS** or **-CUPPED, -CUPPING, -CUPS** to make a peculiar-sounding, spasmodic inhalation
HICCUPY	*adj* having hiccups (spasmodic inhalations)
HICK	*n* pl. **-S** a rural person **HICKISH** *adj*
HICK	*adj* **HICKER, HICKEST** characteristic of rural people

HICKEY	*n* pl. **HICKEYS** or **HICKIES** a gadget
HICKIE	*n* pl. **-S** hickey
HICKORY	*n* pl. **-RIES** a hardwood tree
HID	a past tense of hide
HIDABLE	*adj* able to be hidden
HIDALGO	*n* pl. **-GOS** a minor Spanish nobleman
HIDDEN	*adj* concealed; obscure **HIDDENLY** *adv*
HIDE	*v* **HID, HIDDEN, HIDING, HIDES** to conceal
HIDE	*v* **HIDED, HIDING, HIDES** to flog
HIDEAWAY	*n* pl. **-AWAYS** a hideout
HIDELESS	*adj* lacking a skin
HIDEOUS	*adj* very ugly
HIDEOUT	*n* pl. **-S** a place of refuge
HIDER	*n* pl. **-S** one that hides
HIDING	*n* pl. **-S** a beating
HIDROSIS	*n* pl. **-DROSES** abnormal perspiration
HIDROTIC	*n* pl. **-S** a drug that induces perspiration
HIE	*v* **HIED, HIEING** or **HYING, HIES** to hurry
HIEMAL	*adj* pertaining to winter
HIERARCH	*n* pl. **-S** a religious leader
HIERATIC	*adj* pertaining to priests
HIERURGY	*n* pl. **-GIES** a rite of worship
HIGGLE	*v* **-GLED, -GLING, -GLES** to haggle
HIGGLER	*n* pl. **-S** one that higgles
HIGH	*adj* **HIGHER, HIGHEST** reaching far upward
HIGH	*n* pl. **-S** a high level
HIGHBALL	*v* **-ED, -ING, -S** to go at full speed
HIGHBORN	*adj* of noble birth
HIGHBOY	*n* pl. **-BOYS** a tall chest of drawers
HIGHBRED	*adj* highborn
HIGHBROW	*n* pl. **-S** a person who has superior tastes
HIGHBUSH	*adj* forming a tall bush
HIGHJACK	*v* **-ED, -ING, -S** to hijack
HIGHLAND	*n* pl. **-S** an elevated region
HIGHLIFE	*n* pl. **-S** the lifestyle of fashionable society
HIGHLY	*adv* to a high degree
HIGHNESS	*n* pl. **-ES** the state of being high

HIGHRISE	*n* pl. **-S** a building with many stories (horizontal divisions)
HIGHROAD	*n* pl. **-S** a highway
HIGHSPOT	*n* pl. **-S** an event of major importance
HIGHT	*v* **-ED, -ING, -S** to command
HIGHTAIL	*v* **-ED, -ING, -S** to retreat rapidly
HIGHTH	*n* pl. **-S** height
HIGHTOP	*n* pl. **-S** a sports shoe extending over the ankle
HIGHWAY	*n* pl. **-WAYS** a main road
HIJAB	*n* pl. **-S** a head covering worn by Muslim women
HIJACK	*v* **-ED, -ING, -S** to seize a vehicle while in transit
HIJACKER	*n* pl. **-S** one that hijacks
HIJINKS	*n/pl* mischievous fun
HIJRA	*n* pl. **-S** hegira
HIJRAH	*n* pl. **-S** hegira
HIKE	*v* **HIKED, HIKING, HIKES** to walk a long distance
HIKER	*n* pl. **-S** one that hikes
HILA	pl. of hilum
HILAR	*adj* pertaining to a hilum
HILARITY	*n* pl. **-TIES** noisy merriment
HILDING	*n* pl. **-S** a vile person
HILI	pl. of hilus
HILL	*v* **-ED, -ING, -S** to form into a hill (a rounded elevation)
HILLER	*n* pl. **-S** one that hills
HILLIER	comparative of hilly
HILLIEST	superlative of hilly
HILLO	*v* **-ED, -ING, -S** or **-ES** to hallo
HILLOA	*v* **-ED, -ING, -S** to hallo
HILLOCK	*n* pl. **-S** a small hill **HILLOCKY** *adj*
HILLSIDE	*n* pl. **-S** the side of a hill
HILLTOP	*n* pl. **-S** the top of a hill
HILLY	*adj* **HILLIER, HILLIEST** abounding in hills
HILT	*v* **-ED, -ING, -S** to provide with a hilt (a handle for a weapon)
HILTLESS	*adj* having no hilt
HILUM	*n* pl. **HILA** a small opening in a bodily organ
HILUS	*n* pl. **HILI** hilum
HIM	*n* pl. **-S** a male
HIMATION	*n* pl. **-MATIONS** or **-MATIA** a loose outer garment
HIMBO	*n* pl. **-BOS** an attractive but unintelligent man
HIMSELF	*pron* a form of the 3d person sing. masculine pronoun
HIN	*n* pl. **-S** a Hebrew unit of liquid measure
HIND	*n* pl. **-S** a female red deer
HINDER	*v* **-ED, -ING, -S** to impede
HINDERER	*n* pl. **-S** one that hinders
HINDGUT	*n* pl. **-S** the rear part of the alimentary canal
HINDMILK	*n* pl. **-S** breast milk exuded after the first part of a feeding
HINDMOST	*adj* farthest to the rear
HINDWING	*n* pl. **-S** a posterior wing of an insect
HINGE	*v* **HINGED, HINGING, HINGES** to attach a jointed device
HINGER	*n* pl. **-S** one that hinges
HINKY	*adj* **HINKIER, HINKIEST** suspicious
HINNIE	*n* pl. **-S** darling, sweetheart
HINNY	*v* **-NIED, -NYING, -NIES** to whinny
HINT	*v* **-ED, -ING, -S** to suggest indirectly
HINTER	*n* pl. **-S** one that hints
HIP	*adj* **HIPPER, HIPPEST** aware of the most current styles and trends
HIP	*v* **HIPPED, HIPPING, HIPS** to build a type of roof
HIPBONE	*n* pl. **-S** a pelvic bone
HIPLESS	*adj* lacking a hip (the pelvic joint)
HIPLIKE	*adj* suggestive of a hip
HIPLINE	*n* pl. **-S** the distance around the hips
HIPLY	*adv* in a hip manner
HIPNESS	*n* pl. **-ES** the state of being hip
HIPPARCH	*n* pl. **-S** a cavalry commander in ancient Greece
HIPPED	past tense of hip
HIPPER	comparative of hip
HIPPEST	superlative of hip
HIPPIE	*n* pl. **-S** a nonconformist
HIPPIER	comparative of hippy
HIPPIEST	superlative of hippy
HIPPING	present participle of hip
HIPPISH	*adj* depressed; sad
HIPPO	*n* pl. **-POS** a hippopotamus

HIPPY	adj **-PIER, -PIEST** having big hips	**HITCHER**	n pl. **-S** one that hitches
HIPPYISH	adj relating to or resembling a hippie	**HITHER**	adv toward this place
		HITHERTO	adv up to now
HIPSHOT	adj lame; awkward	**HITLESS**	adj being without a hit
HIPSTER	n pl. **-S** one that is hip	**HITMAKER**	n pl. **-S** a musician who produces best-selling records
HIRABLE	adj available for hire		
HIRAGANA	n pl. **-S** a Japanese cursive script	**HITMAN**	n pl. **-MEN** a professional killer
HIRCINE	adj pertaining to a goat	**HITTABLE**	adj capable of being hit
HIRE	v **HIRED, HIRING, HIRES** to engage the services of for payment **HIREABLE** adj	**HITTER**	n pl. **-S** one that hits
		HITTING	present participle of hit
		HIVE	v **HIVED, HIVING, HIVES** to cause to enter a hive (a bee's nest)
HIREE	n pl. **-S** one that is hired		
HIRELING	n pl. **-S** one that works for money only	**HIVELESS**	adj lacking a hive
		HIVEMIND	n pl. **-S** the shared ideas of a group
HIRER	n pl. **-S** one that hires		
HIRPLE	v **-PLED, -PLING, -PLES** to limp	**HIYA**	interj — used as an informal greeting
HIRSEL	v **-SELED, -SELING, -SELS** or **-SELLED, -SELLING, -SELS** to herd sheep		
		HIZZONER	n pl. **-S** — used as a title for a mayor
HIRSLE	v **-SLED, -SLING, -SLES** to slide along		
		HM	interj hmm
HIRSUTE	adj hairy	**HMM**	interj — used to express thoughtful consideration
HIRUDIN	n pl. **-S** an anticoagulant		
HIS	pron the possessive form of the pronoun he	**HMMM**	interj hmm
		HO	interj — used to express surprise
HISN	pron his	**HOACTZIN**	n pl. **-S** or **-ES** hoatzin
HISPID	adj covered with stiff hairs	**HOAGIE**	n pl. **-S** a long sandwich
HISS	v **-ED, -ING, -ES** to make a sibilant sound	**HOAGY**	n pl. **-GIES** hoagie
		HOAR	n pl. **-S** a white coating
HISSELF	pron himself	**HOARD**	v **-ED, -ING, -S** to gather and store away
HISSER	n pl. **-S** one that hisses		
HISSING	n pl. **-S** an object of scorn	**HOARDER**	n pl. **-S** one that hoards
HISSY	adj **HISSIER, HISSIEST** characterized by a hissing sound	**HOARDING**	n pl. **-S** something hoarded
		HOARIER	comparative of hoary
HISSY	n pl. **HISSIES** a tantrum	**HOARIEST**	superlative of hoary
HIST	v **-ED, -ING, -S** to hoist	**HOARILY**	adv in a hoary manner
HISTAMIN	n pl. **-S** an amine released in allergic reactions	**HOARSE**	adj **HOARSER, HOARSEST** low and rough in sound **HOARSELY** adv
HISTIDIN	n pl. **-S** an amino acid		
HISTOGEN	n pl. **-S** interior plant tissue	**HOARSEN**	v **-ED, -ING, -S** to make hoarse
HISTOID	adj pertaining to connective tissue	**HOARY**	adj **HOARIER, HOARIEST** white with age
HISTONE	n pl. **-S** a simple protein	**HOATZIN**	n pl. **-S** or **-ES** a tropical bird
HISTORIC	adj important in history	**HOAX**	v **-ED, -ING, -ES** to deceive
HISTORY	n pl. **-RIES** a chronological record of past events	**HOAXER**	n pl. **-S** one that hoaxes
		HOB	v **HOBBED, HOBBING, HOBS** to furnish with hobnails
HIT	v **HIT, HITTING, HITS** to strike forcibly		
		HOBBER	n pl. **-S** one that hobs
HITCH	v **-ED, -ING, -ES** to fasten with a knot or hook	**HOBBIES**	pl. of hobby

HOBBIT	*n* pl. **-S** a fictitious creature that lives underground	**HOGMANE**	*n* pl. **-S** hogmanay
HOBBLE	*v* **-BLED, -BLING, -BLES** to limp	**HOGMENAY**	*n* pl. **-NAYS** hogmanay
HOBBLER	*n* pl. **-S** one that hobbles	**HOGNOSE**	*n* pl. **-S** a nonvenomous snake
HOBBY	*n* pl. **-BIES** a recreational pastime	**HOGNUT**	*n* pl. **-S** a hickory nut
HOBBYIST	*n* pl. **-S** one that pursues a hobby	**HOGSHEAD**	*n* pl. **-S** a large cask
HOBLIKE	*adj* suggestive of an elf	**HOGTIE**	*v* **-TIED, -TIEING** or **-TYING, -TIES** to tie together the legs of
HOBNAIL	*v* **-ED, -ING, -S** to put hobnails (short nails with a broad head) on a shoe sole	**HOGWASH**	*n* pl. **-ES** meaningless talk
		HOGWEED	*n* pl. **-S** a coarse plant
HOBNOB	*v* **-NOBBED, -NOBBING, -NOBS** to associate in a friendly way	**HOICK**	*v* **-ED, -ING, -S** to change directions abruptly
HOBO	*v* **-ED, -ING, -S** or **-ES** to live like a hobo (a vagrant or tramp)	**HOIDEN**	*v* **-ED, -ING, -S** to hoyden
		HOISE	*v* **HOISED, HOISING, HOISES** to hoist
HOBOISM	*n* pl. **-S** the state of being a hobo	**HOISIN**	*n* pl. **-S** a spicy brown sauce
HOCK	*v* **-ED, -ING, -S** to pawn	**HOIST**	*v* **-ED, -ING, -S** to haul up by some mechanical means
HOCKER	*n* pl. **-S** one that hocks		
HOCKEY	*n* pl. **-EYS** a game played on ice	**HOISTER**	*n* pl. **-S** one that hoists
HOCKSHOP	*n* pl. **-S** a pawnshop	**HOKE**	*v* **HOKED, HOKING, HOKES** to give false value to
HOCUS	*v* **-CUSED, -CUSING, -CUSES** or **-CUSSED, -CUSSING, -CUSSES** to deceive or cheat	**HOKEY**	*adj* **HOKIER, HOKIEST** false; contrived **HOKILY** *adv*
HOD	*n* pl. **-S** a portable trough	**HOKINESS**	*n* pl. **-ES** the state of being hokey
HODAD	*n* pl. **-S** one who is not a surfer	**HOKKU**	*n* pl. **HOKKU** haiku
HODADDY	*n* pl. **-DIES** hodad	**HOKUM**	*n* pl. **-S** nonsense
HODDEN	*n* pl. **-S** a coarse cloth	**HOKYPOKY**	*n* pl. **-KIES** trickery
HODDIN	*n* pl. **-S** hodden	**HOLARD**	*n* pl. **-S** the total quantity of water in the soil
HOE	*v* **HOED, HOEING, HOES** to use a hoe (a gardening tool)	**HOLD**	*v* **HELD, HOLDEN, HOLDING, HOLDS** to maintain possession of **HOLDABLE** *adj*
HOECAKE	*n* pl. **-S** a cornmeal cake		
HOEDOWN	*n* pl. **-S** a square dance	**HOLDALL**	*n* pl. **-S** a carrying case
HOELIKE	*adj* resembling a hoe	**HOLDBACK**	*n* pl. **-S** a restraining device
HOER	*n* pl. **-S** one that hoes	**HOLDDOWN**	*n* pl. **-S** a clamp for holding an object in place
HOG	*v* **HOGGED, HOGGING, HOGS** to take more than one's share	**HOLDEN**	a past participle of hold
HOGAN	*n* pl. **-S** a Navaho Indian dwelling	**HOLDER**	*n* pl. **-S** one that holds
HOGBACK	*n* pl. **-S** a sharp ridge	**HOLDFAST**	*n* pl. **-S** a fastening device
HOGFISH	*n* pl. **-ES** a tropical fish	**HOLDING**	*n* pl. **-S** something held
HOGG	*n* pl. **-S** a young sheep	**HOLDOUT**	*n* pl. **-S** one who delays signing a contract
HOGGED	past tense of hog		
HOGGER	*n* pl. **-S** one that hogs	**HOLDOVER**	*n* pl. **-S** something left over
HOGGERY	*n* pl. **-GERIES** a pigpen	**HOLDUP**	*n* pl. **-S** a delay
HOGGET	*n* pl. **-S** a young unshorn sheep	**HOLE**	*v* **HOLED, HOLING, HOLES** to make a hole (a cavity in a solid)
HOGGING	present participle of hog		
HOGGISH	*adj* coarsely selfish	**HOLELESS**	*adj* lacking a hole
HOGLIKE	*adj* hoggish	**HOLEY**	*adj* full of holes
HOGMANAY	*n* pl. **-NAYS** a Scottish celebration	**HOLIBUT**	*n* pl. **-S** halibut

HOLIDAY	*v* **-ED, -ING, -S** to take a vacation
HOLIER	comparative of holy
HOLIES	pl. of holy
HOLIEST	superlative of holy
HOLILY	*adv* in a holy manner
HOLINESS	*n* pl. **-ES** the state of being holy
HOLING	present participle of hole
HOLISM	*n* pl. **-S** a philosophical theory
HOLIST	*n* pl. **-S** one who adheres to the theory of holism **HOLISTIC** *adj*
HOLK	*v* **-ED, -ING, -S** to howk
HOLLA	*v* **-ED, -ING, -S** to hallo
HOLLAND	*n* pl. **-S** a cotton fabric
HOLLER	*v* **-ED, -ING, -S** to yell
HOLLIES	pl. of holly
HOLLO	*v* **-ED, -ING, -S** or **-ES** to hallo
HOLLOA	*v* **-ED, -ING, -S** to hallo
HOLLOO	*v* **-ED, -ING, -S** to hallo
HOLLOW	*adj* **-LOWER, -LOWEST** not solid **HOLLOWLY** *adv*
HOLLOW	*v* **-ED, -ING, -S** to make hollow
HOLLY	*n* pl. **-LIES** a tree
HOLM	*n* pl. **-S** an island in a river
HOLME	*n* pl. **-S** holm
HOLMIUM	*n* pl. **-S** a metallic element **HOLMIC** *adj*
HOLO	*n* pl. **-S** a hologram
HOLOGAMY	*n* pl. **-MIES** the state of having gametes of the same size and form as other cells
HOLOGRAM	*n* pl. **-S** a three-dimensional photograph
HOLOGYNY	*n* pl. **-NIES** a trait transmitted solely in the female line
HOLOTYPE	*n* pl. **-S** an animal or plant specimen
HOLOZOIC	*adj* eating solid foods
HOLP	a past tense of help
HOLPEN	a past participle of help
HOLS	*n/pl* a vacation
HOLSTEIN	*n* pl. **-S** a breed of cattle
HOLSTER	*v* **-ED, -ING, -S** to put in a holster (a case for a pistol)
HOLT	*n* pl. **-S** a grove
HOLUBTSI	*n/pl* cabbage rolls
HOLY	*adj* **-LIER, -LIEST** having a divine nature or origin
HOLY	*n* pl. **-LIES** a holy place
HOLYDAY	*n* pl. **-DAYS** a religious holiday
HOLYTIDE	*n* pl. **-S** a time of religious observance
HOM	*n* pl. **-S** a sacred plant of the ancient Persians
HOMA	*n* pl. **-S** a hom
HOMAGE	*v* **-AGED, -AGING, -AGES** to pay tribute to
HOMAGER	*n* pl. **-S** a feudal vassal
HOMBRE	*n* pl. **-S** a fellow
HOMBURG	*n* pl. **-S** a felt hat
HOME	*v* **HOMED, HOMING, HOMES** to return to one's home (place of residence)
HOMEBODY	*n* pl. **-BODIES** one who likes to stay at home
HOMEBOY	*n* pl. **-BOYS** a boy or man from one's neighborhood
HOMEBRED	*n* pl. **-S** a native athlete
HOMEBREW	*n* pl. **-S** an alcoholic beverage made at home
HOMED	past tense of home
HOMEGIRL	*n* pl. **-S** a girl or woman from one's neighborhood
HOMELAND	*n* pl. **-S** one's native land
HOMELESS	*adj* lacking a home
HOMELIKE	*adj* suggestive of a home
HOMELY	*adj* **-LIER, -LIEST** unattractive
HOMEMADE	*adj* made at home
HOMEOBOX	*n* pl. **-ES** a short DNA sequence
HOMEOTIC	*adj* being a gene producing a shift in development
HOMEPAGE	*n* pl. **-S** the main page of a website
HOMEPORT	*v* **-ED, -ING, -S** to assign a ship to a port
HOMER	*v* **-ED, -ING, -S** to hit a home run
HOMERIC	*adj* having a large or grand quality
HOMEROOM	*n* pl. **-S** the classroom where pupils report before classes begin
HOMESICK	*adj* longing for home
HOMESITE	*n* pl. **-S** a location for a house
HOMESPUN	*n* pl. **-S** a loosely woven fabric
HOMESTAY	*n* pl. **-STAYS** a period during which a visitor in a foreign country lives with a local family
HOMETOWN	*n* pl. **-S** the town of one's birth or residence
HOMEWARD	*adv* toward home

HOMEWORK *n* pl. **-S** work done at home

HOMEY *adj* **HOMIER, HOMIEST** homelike

HOMEY *n* pl. **HOMEYS** a person from one's neighborhood

HOMICIDE *n* pl. **-S** the killing of one person by another

HOMIE *n* pl. **-S** homey

HOMIER comparative of homy

HOMIEST superlative of homy

HOMILIST *n* pl. **-S** one that delivers a homily

HOMILY *n* pl. **-LIES** a sermon

HOMINES a pl. of homo

HOMINESS *n* pl. **-ES** the quality of being homey

HOMING present participle of home

HOMINIAN *n* pl. **-S** a hominid

HOMINID *n* pl. **-S** a manlike creature

HOMINIES pl. of hominy

HOMININ *n* pl. **-S** a hominid of a tribe that includes recent humans and extinct related forms

HOMININE *adj* characteristic of man

HOMINIZE *v* **-NIZED, -NIZING, -NIZES** to alter the environment to conform with evolving man

HOMINOID *n* pl. **-S** a manlike animal

HOMINY *n* pl. **-NIES** hulled, dried corn

HOMMOCK *n* pl. **-S** a ridge in an ice field

HOMMOS *n* pl. **-ES** hummus

HOMO *n* pl. **HOMOS** or **HOMINES** a member of the genus that includes modern man

HOMOGAMY *n* pl. **-MIES** the bearing of sexually similar flowers

HOMOGENY *n* pl. **-NIES** correspondence in form or structure

HOMOGONY *n* pl. **-NIES** the condition of having flowers with uniform stamens and pistils

HOMOLOG *n* pl. **-S** something that exhibits homology

HOMOLOGY *n* pl. **-GIES** similarity in structure

HOMONYM *n* pl. **-S** a namesake

HOMONYMY *n* pl. **-MIES** the condition of having the same name

HOMOSEX *n* pl. **-ES** homosexuality

HOMY *adj* **HOMIER, HOMIEST** homey

HON *n* pl. **-S** a honeybun

HONAN *n* pl. **-S** a fine silk

HONCHO *v* **-ED, -ING, -S** or **-ES** to take charge of

HONDA *n* pl. **-S** a part of a lariat

HONDLE *v* **-DLED, -DLING, -DLES** to haggle

HONE *v* **HONED, HONING, HONES** to sharpen

HONER *n* pl. **-S** one that hones

HONEST *adj* **-ESTER, -ESTEST** truthful **HONESTLY** *adv*

HONESTY *n* pl. **-TIES** truthfulness

HONEWORT *n* pl. **-S** a perennial herb

HONEY *v* **HONEYED** or **HONIED, HONEYING, HONEYS** to sweeten with honey (a sweet, viscid fluid)

HONEYBEE *n* pl. **-S** a type of bee

HONEYBUN *n* pl. **-S** a sweetheart

HONEYDEW *n* pl. **-S** a sweet fluid

HONEYFUL *adj* containing much honey

HONEYPOT *n* pl. **-S** one that is attractive or desirable

HONG *n* pl. **-S** a Chinese factory

HONGI *v* **-GIED, -GIING, -GIES** to greet another by pressing noses together

HONIED a past tense of honey

HONING present participle of hone

HONK *v* **-ED, -ING, -S** to emit a cry like that of a goose

HONKER *n* pl. **-S** one that honks

HONOR *v* **-ED, -ING, -S** to respect

HONORAND *n* pl. **-S** an honoree

HONORARY *n* pl. **-ARIES** an honor society

HONOREE *n* pl. **-S** one that receives an honor

HONORER *n* pl. **-S** one that honors

HONOUR *v* **-ED, -ING, -S** to honor

HONOUREE *n* pl. **-S** honoree

HONOURER *n* pl. **-S** honorer

HOO *interj* — used to express surprise or apprehension

HOOCH *n* pl. **-ES** cheap whiskey

HOOCHIE *n* pl. **-S** a promiscuous young woman

HOOD *v* **-ED, -ING, -S** to furnish with a hood (a covering for the head)

HOODIE *n* pl. **-S** a gray crow of Europe

HOODIER comparative of hoody

HOODIEST superlative of hoody

HOODLESS	*adj* lacking a hood
HOODLIKE	*adj* resembling a hood
HOODLUM	*n* pl. **-S** a thug
HOODMOLD	*n* pl. **-S** a protective projection on a cornice
HOODOO	*v* **-ED, -ING, -S** to jinx
HOODWINK	*v* **-ED, -ING, -S** to trick
HOODY	*adj* **HOODIER, HOODIEST** resembling a hoodlum
HOOEY	*n* pl. **-EYS** nonsense
HOOF	*n* pl. **HOOVES** or **HOOFS** the hard covering on the feet of certain animals
HOOF	*v* **-ED, -ING, -S** to dance
HOOFBEAT	*n* pl. **-S** the sound of hooves striking the ground
HOOFER	*n* pl. **-S** a professional dancer
HOOFLESS	*adj* lacking hooves
HOOFLIKE	*adj* resembling a hoof
HOOK	*v* **-ED, -ING, -S** to catch with a hook (a bent piece of metal)
HOOKA	*n* pl. **-S** hookah
HOOKAH	*n* pl. **-S** a water pipe
HOOKER	*n* pl. **-S** a prostitute
HOOKEY	*n* pl. **-EYS** hooky
HOOKIER	comparative of hooky
HOOKIES	pl. of hooky
HOOKIEST	superlative of hooky
HOOKING	*n* pl. **-S** an illegal move in hockey involving the blade of the stick
HOOKLESS	*adj* lacking a hook
HOOKLET	*n* pl. **-S** a small hook
HOOKLIKE	*adj* resembling a hook
HOOKNOSE	*n* pl. **-S** an aquiline nose
HOOKUP	*n* pl. **-S** an electrical assemblage
HOOKWORM	*n* pl. **-S** a parasitic worm
HOOKY	*adj* **HOOKIER, HOOKIEST** full of hooks
HOOKY	*n* pl. **HOOKIES** truancy
HOOLIE	*adj* easy; slow
HOOLIGAN	*n* pl. **-S** a hoodlum
HOOLY	*adj* hoolie
HOOP	*v* **-ED, -ING, -S** to fasten with a hoop (a circular band of metal)
HOOPER	*n* pl. **-S** one that hoops
HOOPLA	*n* pl. **-S** commotion
HOOPLESS	*adj* lacking a hoop
HOOPLIKE	*adj* suggestive of a hoop
HOOPOE	*n* pl. **-S** a European bird
HOOPOO	*n* pl. **-POOS** hoopoe
HOOPSTER	*n* pl. **-S** a basketball player
HOORAH	*v* **-ED, -ING, -S** to hurrah
HOORAY	*v* **-ED, -ING, -S** to hurrah
HOOSEGOW	*n* pl. **-S** a jail
HOOSGOW	*n* pl. **-S** hoosegow
HOOT	*v* **-ED, -ING, -S** to cry like an owl
HOOTCH	*n* pl. **-ES** hooch
HOOTER	*n* pl. **-S** one that hoots
HOOTY	*adj* **HOOTIER, HOOTIEST** sounding like the cry of an owl
HOOVED	*adj* having hooves
HOOVER	*v* **-ED, -ING, -S** to clean with a vacuum cleaner
HOOVES	a pl. of hoof
HOP	*v* **HOPPED, HOPPING, HOPS** to move by jumping on one foot
HOPAK	*n* pl. **-S** a Ukrainian dance
HOPE	*v* **HOPED, HOPING, HOPES** to have a desire or expectation
HOPEFUL	*n* pl. **-S** one that aspires
HOPELESS	*adj* despairing
HOPER	*n* pl. **-S** one that hopes
HOPHEAD	*n* pl. **-S** a drug addict
HOPING	present participle of hope
HOPINGLY	*adv* in a hopeful manner
HOPLITE	*n* pl. **-S** a foot soldier of ancient Greece **HOPLITIC** *adj*
HOPPED	past tense of hop
HOPPER	*n* pl. **-S** one that hops
HOPPING	*n* pl. **-S** a going from one place to another of the same kind
HOPPLE	*v* **-PLED, -PLING, -PLES** to hobble
HOPPY	*adj* **-PIER, -PIEST** having the taste of hops (catkins of a particular vine)
HOPSACK	*n* pl. **-S** a coarse fabric
HOPTOAD	*n* pl. **-S** a toad
HORA	*n* pl. **-S** an Israeli dance
HORAH	*n* pl. **-S** hora
HORAL	*adj* hourly
HORARY	*adj* hourly
HORDE	*v* **HORDED, HORDING, HORDES** to gather in a large group
HORDEIN	*n* pl. **-S** a simple protein

HORDEOLA	*n/pl* swellings of the eyelid
HORIZON	*n* pl. **-S** the line where the sky seems to meet the earth
HORK	*v* **-ED, -ING, -S** to spit
HORMONE	*n* pl. **-S** a secretion of the endocrine organs **HORMONAL, HORMONIC** *adj*
HORN	*v* **-ED, -ING, -S** to form a horn (a hard projection of the head)
HORNBEAM	*n* pl. **-S** a small tree
HORNBILL	*n* pl. **-S** a large-billed bird
HORNBOOK	*n* pl. **-S** a primer
HORNDOG	*n* pl. **-S** a sexually aggressive man
HORNET	*n* pl. **-S** a stinging insect
HORNFELS	*n* pl. **HORNFELS** a silicate rock
HORNIER	comparative of horny
HORNIEST	superlative of horny
HORNILY	*adv* in a horny manner
HORNING	*n* pl. **-S** a mock serenade for newlyweds
HORNIST	*n* pl. **-S** a French horn player
HORNITO	*n* pl. **-TOS** a mound of volcanic matter
HORNLESS	*adj* lacking a horn
HORNLIKE	*adj* resembling a horn
HORNPIPE	*n* pl. **-S** a musical instrument
HORNPOUT	*n* pl. **-S** a catfish
HORNTAIL	*n* pl. **-S** a wasplike insect
HORNWORM	*n* pl. **-S** the larva of a hawkmoth
HORNWORT	*n* pl. **-S** an aquatic herb
HORNY	*adj* **HORNIER, HORNIEST** hornlike in hardness
HOROLOGE	*n* pl. **-S** a timepiece
HOROLOGY	*n* pl. **-GIES** the science of measuring time
HORRENT	*adj* bristling; standing erect
HORRIBLE	*n* pl. **-S** something that causes horror
HORRIBLY	*adv* dreadfully
HORRID	*adj* **-RIDER, -RIDEST** repulsive **HORRIDLY** *adv*
HORRIFIC	*adj* causing horror
HORRIFY	*v* **-FIED, -FYING, -FIES** to cause to feel horror
HORROR	*n* pl. **-S** a feeling of intense fear or repugnance
HORSE	*v* **HORSED, HORSING, HORSES** to provide with a horse (a large, hoofed mammal)
HORSEBOX	*n* pl. **-ES** a closed vehicle for transporting horses
HORSECAR	*n* pl. **-S** a streetcar drawn by a horse
HORSEFLY	*n* pl. **-FLIES** a large fly
HORSEMAN	*n* pl. **-MEN** one who rides a horse
HORSEPOX	*n* pl. **-ES** a skin disease of horses
HORSEY	*adj* **HORSIER, HORSIEST** horsy
HORSIE	*n* pl. **-S** a child's name for a horse
HORSIER	comparative of horsy
HORSIEST	superlative of horsy
HORSILY	*adv* in a horsy manner
HORSING	present participle of horse
HORST	*n* pl. **-S** a portion of the earth's crust
HORSTE	*n* pl. **-S** horst
HORSY	*adj* **HORSIER, HORSIEST** resembling a horse
HOSANNA	*v* **-ED, -ING, -S** to praise
HOSANNAH	*n* pl. **-S** a shout of fervent praise
HOSE	*n* pl. **HOSEN** stockings or socks
HOSE	*v* **HOSED, HOSING, HOSES** to spray with water
HOSEL	*n* pl. **-S** a part of a golf club
HOSELIKE	*adj* resembling a hose
HOSEPIPE	*n* pl. **-S** a flexible tube for conveying fluids
HOSER	*n* pl. **-S** an uncouth man
HOSEY	*v* **-SEYED, -SEYING, -SEYS** to choose sides for a children's game
HOSIER	*n* pl. **-S** one that makes hose
HOSIERY	*n* pl. **-SIERIES** hose
HOSING	present participle of hose
HOSPICE	*n* pl. **-S** a shelter
HOSPITAL	*n* pl. **-S** a medical institution
HOSPITIA	*n/pl* places of shelter
HOSPODAR	*n* pl. **-S** a governor of a region under Turkish rule
HOST	*v* **-ED, -ING, -S** to entertain socially
HOSTA	*n* pl. **-S** a plantain lily
HOSTAGE	*n* pl. **-S** a person held as security
HOSTEL	*v* **-TELED, -TELING, -TELS** or **-TELLED, -TELLING, -TELS** to stay at inns overnight while traveling
HOSTELER	*n* pl. **-S** an innkeeper
HOSTELRY	*n* pl. **-RIES** an inn

HOSTESS   *v* **-ED, -ING, -ES** to act as a hostess (a woman who entertains socially)

HOSTILE   *n* pl. **-S** an unfriendly person

HOSTLER   *n* pl. **-S** a person who tends horses or mules

HOSTLY   *adj* pertaining to one who hosts

HOT   *adj* **HOTTER, HOTTEST** having a high temperature

HOT   *v* **HOTTED, HOTTING, HOTS** to heat

HOTBED   *n* pl. **-S** a bed of rich soil

HOTBLOOD   *n* pl. **-S** a thoroughbred horse

HOTBOX   *n* pl. **-ES** an overheated bearing of a railroad car

HOTCAKE   *n* pl. **-S** a pancake

HOTCH   *v* **-ED, -ING, -ES** to wiggle

HOTCHPOT   *n* pl. **-S** the combining of properties in order to divide them equally among heirs

HOTDOG   *v* **-DOGGED, -DOGGING, -DOGS** to perform showily

HOTEL   *n* pl. **-S** a public lodging

HOTELDOM   *n* pl. **-S** hotels and hotel workers

HOTELIER   *n* pl. **-S** a hotel manager

HOTELMAN   *n* pl. **-MEN** a hotelier

HOTFOOT   *v* **-FOOTED, -FOOTING, -FOOTS** to hurry

HOTHEAD   *n* pl. **-S** a quick-tempered person

HOTHOUSE   *v* **-HOUSED, -HOUSING, -HOUSES** to grow in a hothouse (a heated greenhouse)

HOTLINE   *n* pl. **-S** a direct communications system for immediate contact

HOTLINER   *n* pl. **-S** a person who runs a radio phone-in show

HOTLINK   *n* pl. **-S** a connection between two computer files

HOTLY   *adv* in a hot manner

HOTNESS   *n* pl. **-ES** the state of being hot

HOTPOT   *n* pl. **-S** a casserole of meat and vegetables

HOTPRESS   *v* **-ED, -ING, -ES** to subject to heat and pressure

HOTROD   *n* pl. **-S** a car modified for high speeds

HOTSHOT   *n* pl. **-S** a showily skillful person

HOTSPOT   *n* pl. **-S** an area known for violence or unrest

HOTSPUR   *n* pl. **-S** a hothead

HOTTED   past tense of hot

HOTTER   comparative of hot

HOTTEST   superlative of hot

HOTTIE   *n* pl. **-S** an attractive person

HOTTING   present participle of hot

HOTTISH   *adj* somewhat hot

HOTTY   *n* pl. **-TIES** a hottie

HOUDAH   *n* pl. **-S** howdah

HOUMMOS   *n* pl. **-ES** hummus

HOUND   *v* **-ED, -ING, -S** to pursue relentlessly

HOUNDER   *n* pl. **-S** one that hounds

HOUNGAN   *n* pl. **-S** a voodoo priest

HOUR   *n* pl. **-S** a period of sixty minutes

HOURI   *n* pl. **-S** a beautiful maiden in Muslim belief

HOURLONG   *adj* lasting an hour

HOURLY   *n* pl. **-LIES** a worker paid by the hour

HOUSE   *v* **HOUSED, HOUSING, HOUSES** to lodge in a house (a building in which people live)

HOUSEBOY   *n* pl. **-BOYS** a male servant

HOUSEFLY   *n* pl. **-FLIES** a common fly

HOUSEFUL   *n* pl. **-S** as much as a house will hold

HOUSEL   *v* **-SELED, -SELING, -SELS** or **-SELLED, -SELLING, -SELS** to administer the Eucharist to

HOUSEMAN   *n* pl. **-MEN** a male servant

HOUSER   *n* pl. **-S** one who organizes housing projects

HOUSESIT   *v* **-SAT, -SITTING, -SITS** to occupy a dwelling while the tenants are away

HOUSETOP   *n* pl. **-S** the roof of a house

HOUSEY   *adj* **HOUSIER, HOUSIEST** being in the style of house music

HOUSING   *n* pl. **-S** any dwelling place

HOVE   a past tense of heave

HOVEL   *v* **-ELED, -ELING, -ELS** or **-ELLED, -ELLING, -ELS** to live in a small, miserable dwelling

HOVER   *v* **-ED, -ING, -S** to hang suspended in the air

HOVERER   *n* pl. **-S** something that hovers

HOVERFLY   *n* pl. **-FLIES** a fly noted for hovering

HOW   *n* pl. **-S** a method of doing something

HOWBEIT	*adv* nevertheless
HOWDAH	*n* pl. **-S** a seat on an elephant or camel for riders
HOWDIE	*n* pl. **-S** a midwife
HOWDY	*v* **-DIED, -DYING, -DIES** to greet with the words ``how do you do''
HOWE	*n* pl. **-S** a valley
HOWEVER	*adv* nevertheless
HOWF	*n* pl. **-S** a place frequently visited
HOWFF	*n* pl. **-S** howf
HOWITZER	*n* pl. **-S** a short cannon
HOWK	*v* **-ED, -ING, -S** to dig
HOWL	*v* **-ED, -ING, -S** to cry like a dog
HOWLER	*n* pl. **-S** one that howls
HOWLET	*n* pl. **-S** an owl
HOY	*n* pl. **HOYS** a heavy barge or scow
HOYA	*n* pl. **-S** a flowering plant
HOYDEN	*v* **-ED, -ING, -S** to act like a tomboy
HOYLE	*n* pl. **-S** a rule book
HRYVNA	*n* pl. **-S** hryvnia
HRYVNIA	*n* pl. **-S** a monetary unit of Ukraine
HRYVNYA	*n* pl. **-S** hryvnia
HUARACHE	*n* pl. **-S** a flat-heeled sandal
HUARACHO	*n* pl. **-CHOS** huarache
HUB	*n* pl. **-S** the center of a wheel
HUBBLY	*adj* having an uneven surface
HUBBUB	*n* pl. **-S** an uproar
HUBBY	*n* pl. **-BIES** a husband
HUBCAP	*n* pl. **-S** a covering for the hub of a wheel
HUBLESS	*adj* lacking a hub
HUBRIS	*n* pl. **-BRISES** arrogance
HUCK	*n* pl. **-S** a durable fabric
HUCKLE	*n* pl. **-S** the hip
HUCKSTER	*v* **-ED, -ING, -S** to peddle
HUDDLE	*v* **-DLED, -DLING, -DLES** to crowd together
HUDDLER	*n* pl. **-S** one that huddles
HUE	*n* pl. **-S** color **HUED, HUELESS** *adj*
HUFF	*v* **-ED, -ING, -S** to breathe heavily
HUFFISH	*adj* sulky
HUFFY	*adj* **HUFFIER, HUFFIEST** easily offended **HUFFILY** *adv*
HUG	*v* **HUGGED, HUGGING, HUGS** to clasp tightly in the arms
HUGE	*adj* **HUGER, HUGEST** very large **HUGELY** *adv*
HUGENESS	*n* pl. **-ES** the quality of being huge
HUGEOUS	*adj* huge
HUGGABLE	*adj* cuddlesome
HUGGED	past tense of hug
HUGGER	*n* pl. **-S** one that hugs
HUGGING	present participle of hug
HUGGY	*adj* **HUGGIER, HUGGIEST** involving or given to hugging
HUH	*interj* — used to express surprise
HUIC	*interj* — used to encourage hunting hounds
HUIPIL	*n* pl. **-S** or **-ES** an embroidered blouse or dress of Mexico
HUISACHE	*n* pl. **-S** a flowering plant
HULA	*n* pl. **-S** a Hawaiian dance
HULK	*v* **-ED, -ING, -S** to appear impressively large
HULKY	*adj* **HULKIER, HULKIEST** massive
HULL	*v* **-ED, -ING, -S** to remove the shell from a seed
HULLER	*n* pl. **-S** one that hulls
HULLO	*v* **-ED, -ING, -S** or **-ES** to hallo
HULLOA	*v* **-ED, -ING, -S** to hallo
HULLOO	*v* **-ED, -ING, -S** to hallo
HUM	*v* **HUMMED, HUMMING, HUMS** to sing without opening the lips or saying words
HUMAN	*n* pl. **-S** a person
HUMANE	*adj* **-MANER, -MANEST** compassionate **HUMANELY** *adv*
HUMANISE	*v* **-ISED, -ISING, -ISES** to humanize
HUMANISM	*n* pl. **-S** the quality of being human
HUMANIST	*n* pl. **-S** one who studies human nature
HUMANITY	*n* pl. **-TIES** the human race
HUMANIZE	*v* **-IZED, -IZING, -IZES** to make human
HUMANLY	*adv* in a human manner
HUMANOID	*n* pl. **-S** something having human form
HUMATE	*n* pl. **-S** a chemical salt
HUMBLE	*adj* **-BLER, -BLEST** modest
HUMBLE	*v* **-BLED, -BLING, -BLES** to reduce the pride of
HUMBLER	*n* pl. **-S** one that humbles
HUMBLEST	superlative of humble

HUMBLING	present participle of humble
HUMBLY	*adv* in a humble manner
HUMBUG	*v* **-BUGGED, -BUGGING, -BUGS** to deceive
HUMDRUM	*n* pl. **-S** a dull, boring person
HUMERAL	*n* pl. **-S** a bone of the shoulder
HUMERUS	*n* pl. **-MERI** the large bone of the upper arm
HUMIC	*adj* derived from humus
HUMID	*adj* having much humidity
HUMIDEX	*n* pl. **-ES** an index of discomfort
HUMIDIFY	*v* **-FIED, -FYING, -FIES** to make humid
HUMIDITY	*n* pl. **-TIES** moisture of the air
HUMIDLY	*adv* in a humid manner
HUMIDOR	*n* pl. **-S** a cigar case
HUMIFIED	*adj* converted into humus
HUMILITY	*n* pl. **-TIES** the quality of being humble
HUMINT	*n* pl. **-S** secret intelligence-gathering by agents
HUMITURE	*n* pl. **-S** a combined measurement of temperature and humidity
HUMMABLE	*adj* capable of being hummed
HUMMED	past tense of hum
HUMMER	*n* pl. **-S** one that hums
HUMMING	present participle of hum
HUMMOCK	*v* **-ED, -ING, -S** to form into hummocks (small rounded hills)
HUMMOCKY	*adj* abounding in hummocks
HUMMUS	*n* pl. **-ES** a paste of pureed chickpeas and tahini
HUMOR	*v* **-ED, -ING, -S** to indulge
HUMORAL	*adj* pertaining to bodily fluids
HUMORFUL	*adj* humorous
HUMORIST	*n* pl. **-S** a humorous writer or entertainer
HUMOROUS	*adj* funny; witty
HUMOUR	*v* **-ED, -ING, -S** to humor
HUMOUS	*n* pl. **-ES** hummus
HUMP	*v* **-ED, -ING, -S** to arch into a hump (a rounded protuberance)
HUMPBACK	*n* pl. **-S** a humped back
HUMPER	*n* pl. **-S** one that humps
HUMPH	*v* **-ED, -ING, -S** to utter a grunt
HUMPLESS	*adj* lacking a hump
HUMPY	*adj* **HUMPIER, HUMPIEST** full of humps
HUMPY	*n* pl. **HUMPIES** a primitive hut in Australia
HUMUS	*n* pl. **-ES** decomposed organic matter
HUMUSY	*adj* resembling humus
HUMVEE	*n* pl. **-S** a type of motor vehicle
HUN	*n* pl. **-S** a barbarous, destructive person
HUNCH	*v* **-ED, -ING, -ES** to arch forward
HUNDRED	*n* pl. **-S** a number
HUNG	a past tense of hang
HUNGER	*v* **-ED, -ING, -S** to crave
HUNGOVER	*adj* suffering from a hangover
HUNGRY	*adj* **-GRIER, -GRIEST** wanting food **HUNGRILY** *adv*
HUNH	*interj* — used to ask for a repetition of an utterance
HUNK	*n* pl. **-S** a large piece
HUNKER	*v* **-ED, -ING, -S** to squat
HUNKY	*adj* **HUNKIER, HUNKIEST** muscular and attractive
HUNNISH	*adj* resembling a hun
HUNT	*v* **-ED, -ING, -S** to pursue for food or sport **HUNTABLE** *adj* **HUNTEDLY** *adv*
HUNTER	*n* pl. **-S** one that hunts
HUNTING	*n* pl. **-S** an instance of searching
HUNTRESS	*n* pl. **-ES** a female hunter
HUNTSMAN	*n* pl. **-MEN** a hunter
HUP	*interj* — used to mark a marching cadence
HUPPAH	*n* pl. **HUPPAHS** or **CHUPPOT** chuppah
HURDIES	*n/pl* the buttocks
HURDLE	*v* **-DLED, -DLING, -DLES** to jump over
HURDLER	*n* pl. **-S** one that hurdles
HURDS	*n/pl* hards
HURL	*v* **-ED, -ING, -S** to throw with great force
HURLER	*n* pl. **-S** one that hurls
HURLEY	*n* pl. **-LEYS** hurling
HURLING	*n* pl. **-S** an Irish game
HURLY	*n* pl. **-LIES** commotion
HURRAH	*v* **-ED, -ING, -S** to cheer
HURRAY	*v* **-ED, -ING, -S** to hurrah
HURRIER	*n* pl. **-S** one that hurries

HURRY   *v* **-RIED, -RYING, -RIES** to move swiftly

HURST   *n* pl. **-S** a small hill

HURT   *v* **HURT, HURTING, HURTS** to injure

HURTER   *n* pl. **-S** one that hurts

HURTFUL   *adj* causing injury

HURTLE   *v* **-TLED, -TLING, -TLES** to rush violently

HURTLESS   *adj* harmless

HUSBAND   *v* **-ED, -ING, -S** to spend wisely

HUSH   *v* **-ED, -ING, -ES** to quiet **HUSHEDLY** *adv*

HUSHABY   *v* go to sleep — used imperatively to soothe a child

HUSHABYE   *v* hushaby

HUSHFUL   *adj* quiet

HUSK   *v* **-ED, -ING, -S** to remove the husk (the outer covering) from

HUSKER   *n* pl. **-S** one that husks

HUSKIER   comparative of husky

HUSKIES   pl. of husky

HUSKIEST   superlative of husky

HUSKILY   *adv* in a husky manner

HUSKING   *n* pl. **-S** a gathering of families to husk corn

HUSKLIKE   *adj* resembling a husk

HUSKY   *adj* **-KIER, -KIEST** hoarse

HUSKY   *n* pl. **-KIES** a dog of the arctic region

HUSSAR   *n* pl. **-S** a cavalry soldier

HUSSY   *n* pl. **-SIES** a lewd woman

HUSTINGS   *n* pl. **HUSTINGS** a British court

HUSTLE   *v* **-TLED, -TLING, -TLES** to hurry

HUSTLER   *n* pl. **-S** one that hustles

HUSWIFE   *n* pl. **-WIVES** or **-WIFES** a sewing kit

HUT   *v* **HUTTED, HUTTING, HUTS** to live in a hut (a simple shelter)

HUTCH   *v* **-ED, -ING, -ES** to store away

HUTLIKE   *adj* resembling a hut

HUTMENT   *n* pl. **-S** a group of huts

HUTTED   past tense of hut

HUTTING   present participle of hut

HUTZPA   *n* pl. **-S** chutzpah

HUTZPAH   *n* pl. **-S** chutzpah

HUZZA   *v* **-ED, -ING, -S** to cheer

HUZZAH   *v* **-ED, -ING, -S** to huzza

HWAN   *n* pl. **HWAN** a monetary unit of South Korea

HWYL   *n* **-S** an emotion that inspires impassioned eloquence

HYACINTH   *n* pl. **-S** a flowering plant

HYAENA   *n* pl. **-S** hyena **HYAENIC** *adj*

HYALIN   *n* pl. **-S** hyaline

HYALINE   *n* pl. **-S** a transparent substance

HYALITE   *n* pl. **-S** a colorless opal

HYALOGEN   *n* pl. **-S** a substance found in animal cells

HYALOID   *n* pl. **-S** a membrane of the eye

HYBRID   *n* pl. **-S** the offspring of genetically dissimilar parents

HYBRIS   *n* pl. **-BRISES** hubris

HYDATID   *n* pl. **-S** a cyst caused by a tapeworm

HYDRA   *n* pl. **-DRAS** or **-DRAE** a freshwater polyp

HYDRACID   *n* pl. **-S** an acid

HYDRAGOG   *n* pl. **-S** a purgative causing watery discharges

HYDRANT   *n* pl. **-S** an outlet from a water main

HYDRANTH   *n* pl. **-S** the oral opening of a hydra

HYDRASE   *n* pl. **-S** an enzyme

HYDRATE   *v* **-DRATED, -DRATING, -DRATES** to combine with water

HYDRATOR   *n* pl. **-S** one that hydrates

HYDRIA   *n* pl. **-DRIAE** a water jar

HYDRIC   *adj* pertaining to moisture

HYDRID   *n* pl. **-S** hydride

HYDRIDE   *n* pl. **-S** a chemical compound

HYDRILLA   *n* pl. **-S** an aquatic Asian plant

HYDRO   *n* pl. **-DROS** electricity produced by waterpower

HYDROGEL   *n* pl. **-S** a colloid

HYDROGEN   *n* pl. **-S** a gaseous element

HYDROID   *n* pl. **-S** a polyp

HYDROMEL   *n* pl. **-S** a mixture of honey and water

HYDRONIC   *adj* pertaining to heating and cooling by water

HYDROPIC   *adj* affected with hydropsy

HYDROPS   *n* pl. **-ES** hydropsy

HYDROPSY   *n* pl. **-SIES** dropsy

HYDROSKI *n* pl. **-S** a plate attached to a seaplane to facilitate takeoffs and landings

HYDROSOL *n* pl. **-S** an aqueous solution of a colloid

HYDROUS *adj* containing water

HYDROXY *adj* containing hydroxyl

HYDROXYL *n* pl. **-S** the radical or group containing oxygen and hydrogen

HYENA *n* pl. **-S** a wolflike mammal **HYENIC, HYENINE, HYENOID** *adj*

HYETAL *adj* pertaining to rain

HYGEIST *n* pl. **-S** an expert in hygiene

HYGIEIST *n* pl. **-S** hygeist

HYGIENE *n* pl. **-S** the science of health **HYGIENIC** *adj*

HYING present participle of hie

HYLA *n* pl. **-S** a tree frog

HYLOZOIC *adj* pertaining to the doctrine that life and matter are inseparable

HYMEN *n* pl. **-S** a vaginal membrane **HYMENAL** *adj*

HYMENEAL *n* pl. **-S** a wedding song or poem

HYMENIUM *n* pl. **-NIUMS** or **-NIA** a layer in certain fungi **HYMENIAL** *adj*

HYMN *v* **-ED, -ING, -S** to sing a hymn (a song of praise to God)

HYMNAL *n* pl. **-S** a book of hymns

HYMNARY *n* pl. **-RIES** a hymnal

HYMNBOOK *n* pl. **-S** a hymnal

HYMNIC *adj* pertaining to a hymn

HYMNIST *n* pl. **-S** one who composes hymns

HYMNLESS *adj* lacking a hymn

HYMNLIKE *adj* resembling a hymn

HYMNODY *n* pl. **-DIES** the singing of hymns

HYOID *n* pl. **-S** a bone of the tongue **HYOIDAL, HYOIDEAN** *adj*

HYOSCINE *n* pl. **-S** a sedative

HYP *n* pl. **-S** hypochondria

HYPE *v* **HYPED, HYPING, HYPES** to promote extravagantly

HYPER *adj* **-PERER, -PEREST** very excited

HYPER *n* pl. **-S** one that hypes

HYPERGOL *n* pl. **-S** a rocket fuel

HYPERNYM *n* pl. **-S** a word that denotes a broad category that includes more specific words

HYPERON *n* pl. **-S** an atomic particle

HYPEROPE *n* pl. **-S** a farsighted person

HYPHA *n* pl. **-PHAE** a threadlike element of a fungus **HYPHAL** *adj*

HYPHEMIA *n* pl. **-S** deficiency of blood

HYPHEN *v* **-ED, -ING, -S** to connect words or syllables with a hyphen (a mark of punctuation) **HYPHENIC** *adj*

HYPING present participle of hype

HYPNIC *adj* pertaining to sleep

HYPNOID *adj* pertaining to hypnosis or sleep

HYPNOSIS *n* pl. **-NOSES** an artificially induced state resembling sleep

HYPNOTIC *n* pl. **-S** a sleep-inducing drug

HYPO *v* **-ED, -ING, -S** to inject with a hypodermic needle

HYPOACID *adj* having a lower than normal degree of acidity

HYPODERM *n* pl. **-S** a skin layer

HYPOGEA pl. of hypogeum

HYPOGEAL *adj* underground

HYPOGEAN *adj* hypogeal

HYPOGENE *adj* formed underground

HYPOGEUM *n* pl. **-GEA** an underground chamber

HYPOGYNY *n* pl. **-NIES** the condition of having flowers with organs situated below the ovary

HYPOID *n* pl. **-S** a type of toothed wheel

HYPONEA *n* pl. **-S** hyponoia

HYPONOIA *n* pl. **-S** dulled mental activity

HYPONYM *n* pl. **-S** a word that denotes a subcategory

HYPONYMY *n* pl. **-MIES** the state of being a hyponym

HYPOPNEA *n* pl. **-S** abnormally shallow breathing

HYPOPYON *n* pl. **-S** an accumulation of pus in the eye

HYPOTHEC *n* pl. **-S** a type of mortgage

HYPOXIA *n* pl. **-S** a deficiency of oxygen in body tissue **HYPOXIC** *adj*

HYRACOID *n* pl. **-S** a hyrax

HYRAX *n* pl. **-RAXES** or **-RACES** a small, harelike mammal

HYSON *n* pl. **-S** a Chinese tea

HYSSOP *n* pl. **-S** a medicinal herb

HYSTERIA *n* pl. **-S** uncontrollable excitement or fear

HYSTERIC *n* pl. **-S** one who is subject to fits of hysteria

HYTE *adj* insane

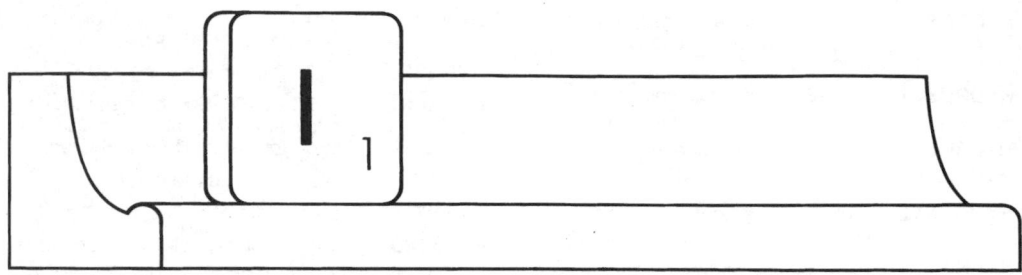

IAMB	*n* pl. **-S** a type of metrical foot
IAMBIC	*n* pl. **-S** an iamb
IAMBUS	*n* pl. **-BUSES** or **-BI** an iamb
IATRIC	*adj* pertaining to medicine
IATRICAL	*adj* iatric
IBEX	*n* pl. **IBEXES** or **IBICES** a wild goat
IBIDEM	*adv* in the same place
IBIS	*n* pl. **IBISES** a wading bird
IBOGAINE	*n* pl. **-S** an alkaloid used as an antidepressant
ICE	*v* **ICED, ICING, ICES** to cover with ice (frozen water)
ICEBERG	*n* pl. **-S** a large floating body of ice
ICEBLINK	*n* pl. **-S** a glare over an icefield
ICEBOAT	*v* **-ED, -ING, -S** to travel in a vehicle that sails on ice
ICEBOUND	*adj* surrounded by ice
ICEBOX	*n* pl. **-ES** a cabinet for cooling food
ICECAP	*n* pl. **-S** a covering of ice and snow
ICED	past tense of ice
ICEFALL	*n* pl. **-S** a kind of frozen waterfall
ICEFIELD	*n* pl. **-S** a large area of ice
ICEFISH	*v* **-ED, -ING, -ES** to fish through holes in the ice on a lake or river
ICEHOUSE	*n* pl. **-S** a building for storing ice
ICEKHANA	*n* pl. **-S** an automotive event held on a frozen lake
ICELESS	*adj* having no ice
ICELIKE	*adj* resembling ice
ICEMAKER	*n* pl. **-S** an appliance that makes ice
ICEMAN	*n* pl. **-MEN** a man who supplies ice
ICESCAPE	*n* pl. **-S** landscape covered with ice
ICEWINE	*n* pl. **-S** sweet wine made from grapes frozen on the vine
ICEWORM	*n* pl. **-S** a small worm found in glaciers
ICH	*n* pl. **ICHS** a disease of certain fishes
ICHNITE	*n* pl. **-S** a fossil footprint
ICHOR	*n* pl. **-S** a watery discharge from a wound **ICHOROUS** *adj*
ICHTHYIC	*adj* pertaining to fishes
ICICLE	*n* pl. **-S** a hanging spike of ice **ICICLED** *adj*
ICIER	comparative of icy
ICIEST	superlative of icy
ICILY	*adv* in an icy manner
ICINESS	*n* pl. **-ES** the state of being icy
ICING	*n* pl. **-S** a sweet mixture for covering cakes
ICK	*n* pl. **-S** something sticky or disgusting
ICKER	*n* pl. **-S** a head of grain
ICKINESS	*n* pl. **-ES** the state of being icky
ICKY	*adj* **ICKIER, ICKIEST** repulsive **ICKILY** *adv*
ICON	*n* pl. **-S** or **-ES** a representation **ICONIC, ICONICAL** *adj*
ICTERIC	*n* pl. **-S** a remedy for icterus
ICTERUS	*n* pl. **-ES** a diseased condition of the liver
ICTUS	*n* pl. **-ES** a recurring stress or beat in a poetical form **ICTIC** *adj*
ICY	*adj* **ICIER, ICIEST** covered with ice
ID	*n* pl. **-S** a part of the psyche
IDEA	*n* pl. **-S** a conception existing in the mind **IDEALESS** *adj*
IDEAL	*n* pl. **-S** a standard of perfection
IDEALISE	*v* **-ISED, -ISING, -ISES** to idealize
IDEALISM	*n* pl. **-S** the pursuit of noble goals
IDEALIST	*n* pl. **-S** an adherent of idealism

IDEALITY	*n* pl. **-TIES** the state of being perfect; something idealized
IDEALIZE	*v* **-IZED, -IZING, -IZES** to regard as perfect
IDEALLY	*adv* perfectly
IDEALOGY	*n* pl. **-GIES** ideology
IDEATE	*v* **-ATED, -ATING, -ATES** to form an idea
IDEATION	*n* pl. **-S** the act of ideating
IDEATIVE	*adj* pertaining to ideation
IDEM	*adj* the same
IDENT	*n* pl. **-S** identification
IDENTIC	*adj* identical
IDENTIFY	*v* **-FIED, -FYING, -FIES** to establish the identity of
IDENTITY	*n* pl. **-TIES** the essential character of a person or thing
IDEOGRAM	*n* pl. **-S** a type of written symbol
IDEOLOGY	*n* pl. **-GIES** a systematic body of ideas
IDES	*n* pl. **IDES** a certain day in the ancient Roman calendar
IDIOCY	*n* pl. **-CIES** the condition of being an idiot
IDIOLECT	*n* pl. **-S** one's speech pattern
IDIOM	*n* pl. **-S** an expression peculiar to a language
IDIOT	*n* pl. **-S** a mentally deficient person **IDIOTIC** *adj*
IDIOTISM	*n* pl. **-S** idiocy
IDIOTYPE	*n* pl. **-S** a structure of an antibody
IDLE	*adj* **IDLER, IDLEST** inactive
IDLE	*v* **IDLED, IDLING, IDLES** to pass time idly
IDLENESS	*n* pl. **-ES** the state of being idle
IDLER	*n* pl. **-S** one that idles
IDLESSE	*n* pl. **-S** idleness
IDLEST	superlative of idle
IDLING	present participle of idle
IDLY	*adv* in an idle manner
IDOCRASE	*n* pl. **-S** a mineral
IDOL	*n* pl. **-S** an object of worship
IDOLATER	*n* pl. **-S** one that worships idols
IDOLATOR	*n* pl. **-S** idolater
IDOLATRY	*n* pl. **-TRIES** the worship of idols
IDOLISE	*v* **-ISED, -ISING, -ISES** to idolize
IDOLISER	*n* pl. **-S** one that idolises
IDOLISM	*n* pl. **-S** idolatry
IDOLIZE	*v* **-IZED, -IZING, -IZES** to worship
IDOLIZER	*n* pl. **-S** one that idolizes
IDONEITY	*n* pl. **-TIES** the state of being idoneous
IDONEOUS	*adj* suitable
IDYL	*n* pl. **-S** a poem or prose work depicting scenes of rural simplicity
IDYLIST	*n* pl. **-S** a writer of idyls
IDYLL	*n* pl. **-S** idyl **IDYLLIC** *adj*
IDYLLIST	*n* pl. **-S** idylist
IF	*n* pl. **-S** a possibility
IFF	*conj* if and only if
IFFINESS	*n* pl. **-ES** the state of being iffy
IFFY	*adj* **IFFIER, IFFIEST** full of uncertainty **IFFILY** *adv*
IGG	*v* **-ED, -ING, -S** to ignore
IGLOO	*n* pl. **-LOOS** an Inuit dwelling
IGLU	*n* pl. **-S** igloo
IGNATIA	*n* pl. **-S** a medicinal seed
IGNEOUS	*adj* pertaining to fire
IGNIFY	*v* **-FIED, -FYING, -FIES** to burn
IGNITE	*v* **-NITED, -NITING, -NITES** to set on fire
IGNITER	*n* pl. **-S** one that ignites
IGNITION	*n* pl. **-S** the act of igniting
IGNITOR	*n* pl. **-S** igniter
IGNITRON	*n* pl. **-S** a type of rectifier tube
IGNOBLE	*adj* **-NOBLER, -NOBLEST** of low character **IGNOBLY** *adv*
IGNOMINY	*n* pl. **-NIES** disgrace or dishonor
IGNORAMI	*n/pl* utterly ignorant persons
IGNORANT	*adj* having no knowledge
IGNORE	*v* **-NORED, -NORING, -NORES** to refuse to notice
IGNORER	*n* pl. **-S** one that ignores
IGUANA	*n* pl. **-S** a tropical lizard
IGUANIAN	*n* pl. **-S** a lizard related to the iguana
IGUANID	*n* pl. **-S** a long-tailed lizard
IHRAM	*n* pl. **-S** the garb worn by Muslim pilgrims
IKAT	*n* pl. **-S** a fabric of tie-dyed yarns
IKEBANA	*n* pl. **-S** the Japanese art of flower arranging
IKON	*n* pl. **-S** icon
ILEA	pl. of ileum
ILEAC	*adj* pertaining to the ileum

ILEAL	*adj* ileac
ILEITIS	*n* pl. **ILEITIDES** or **ILEITISES** inflammation of the ileum
ILEUM	*n* pl. **ILEA** a part of the small intestine
ILEUS	*n* pl. **-ES** intestinal obstruction
ILEX	*n* pl. **-ES** a holly
ILIA	pl. of ilium
ILIAC	*adj* pertaining to the ilium
ILIAD	*n* pl. **-S** a long poem
ILIAL	*adj* iliac
ILIUM	*n* pl. **ILIA** a bone of the pelvis
ILK	*n* pl. **-S** a class or kind
ILKA	*adj* each
ILL	*adj* **ILLER, ILLEST** not well
ILL	*n* pl. **-S** an evil
ILLATION	*n* pl. **-S** the act of inferring
ILLATIVE	*n* pl. **-S** a word or phrase introducing an inference
ILLEGAL	*n* pl. **-S** a person who enters a country without authorization
ILLICIT	*adj* not permitted
ILLINIUM	*n* pl. **-S** a radioactive element
ILLIQUID	*adj* not being cash
ILLITE	*n* pl. **-S** a group of minerals **ILLITIC** *adj*
ILLNESS	*n* pl. **-ES** sickness
ILLOGIC	*n* pl. **-S** absence of logic
ILLUDE	*v* **-LUDED, -LUDING, -LUDES** to deceive
ILLUME	*v* **-LUMED, -LUMING, -LUMES** to illuminate
ILLUMINE	*v* **-MINED, -MINING, -MINES** to illuminate
ILLUSION	*n* pl. **-S** a false perception
ILLUSIVE	*adj* illusory
ILLUSORY	*adj* based on illusion
ILLUVIUM	*n* pl. **-VIUMS** or **-VIA** a type of material accumulated in soil **ILLUVIAL** *adj*
ILLY	*adv* badly
ILMENITE	*n* pl. **-S** a mineral
IMAGE	*v* **-AGED, -AGING, -AGES** to imagine
IMAGER	*n* pl. **-S** one that images
IMAGERY	*n* pl. **-ERIES** mental pictures
IMAGINAL	*adj* pertaining to an imago
IMAGINE	*v* **-INED, -INING, -INES** to form a mental picture of
IMAGINER	*n* pl. **-S** one that imagines
IMAGING	*n* pl. **-S** the action of producing a visible representation
IMAGINING	present participle of imagine
IMAGISM	*n* pl. **-S** a movement in poetry
IMAGIST	*n* pl. **-S** an adherent of imagism
IMAGO	*n* pl. **-GOS** or **-GOES** an adult insect
IMAM	*n* pl. **-S** a Muslim priest
IMAMATE	*n* pl. **-S** the office of an imam
IMARET	*n* pl. **-S** a Turkish inn
IMAUM	*n* pl. **-S** imam
IMBALM	*v* **-ED, -ING, -S** to embalm
IMBALMER	*n* pl. **-S** embalmer
IMBARK	*v* **-ED, -ING, -S** to embark
IMBECILE	*n* pl. **-S** a mentally deficient person
IMBED	*v* **-BEDDED, -BEDDING, -BEDS** to embed
IMBIBE	*v* **-BIBED, -BIBING, -BIBES** to drink
IMBIBER	*n* pl. **-S** one that imbibes
IMBITTER	*v* **-ED, -ING, -S** to embitter
IMBLAZE	*v* **-BLAZED, -BLAZING, -BLAZES** to emblaze
IMBODY	*v* **-BODIED, -BODYING, -BODIES** to embody
IMBOLDEN	*v* **-ED, -ING, -S** to embolden
IMBOSOM	*v* **-ED, -ING, -S** to embosom
IMBOWER	*v* **-ED, -ING, -S** to embower
IMBROWN	*v* **-ED, -ING, -S** to embrown
IMBRUE	*v* **-BRUED, -BRUING, -BRUES** to stain
IMBRUTE	*v* **-BRUTED, -BRUTING, -BRUTES** to make brutal
IMBUE	*v* **-BUED, -BUING, -BUES** to make thoroughly wet
IMID	*n* pl. **-S** imide
IMIDE	*n* pl. **-S** a chemical compound **IMIDIC** *adj*
IMIDO	*adj* containing an imide
IMINE	*n* pl. **-S** a chemical compound
IMINO	*adj* containing an imine
IMIPENEM	*n* pl. **-S** a drug that is used to kill bacteria
IMITABLE	*adj* capable of being imitated

IMITATE	*v* **-TATED, -TATING, -TATES** to behave in the same way as	**IMPALE**	*v* **-PALED, -PALING, -PALES** to pierce with a pointed object
IMITATOR	*n* pl. **-S** one that imitates	**IMPALER**	*n* pl. **-S** one that impales
IMMANE	*adj* great in size	**IMPANEL**	*v* **-ELED, -ELING, -ELS** or
IMMANENT	*adj* existing within		**-ELLED, -ELLING, -ELS** to enter on a list for jury duty
IMMATURE	*n* pl. **-S** an individual that is not fully grown or developed	**IMPARITY**	*n* pl. **-TIES** lack of equality
IMMENSE	*adj* **-MENSER, -MENSEST** great in size	**IMPARK**	*v* **-ED, -ING, -S** to confine in a park
		IMPART	*v* **-ED, -ING, -S** to make known
IMMERGE	*v* **-MERGED, -MERGING, -MERGES** to immerse	**IMPARTER**	*n* pl. **-S** one that imparts
IMMERSE	*v* **-MERSED, -MERSING, -MERSES** to plunge into a liquid	**IMPASSE**	*n* pl. **-S** a road or passage having no exit
IMMESH	*v* **-ED, -ING, -ES** to enmesh	**IMPASTE**	*v* **-PASTED, -PASTING, -PASTES** to make into a paste
IMMIES	pl. of immy	**IMPASTO**	*n* pl. **-TOS** a painting technique
IMMINENT	*adj* ready to take place	**IMPAVID**	*adj* brave
IMMINGLE	*v* **-GLED, -GLING, -GLES** to blend	**IMPAWN**	*v* **-ED, -ING, -S** to pawn
IMMIX	*v* **-ED, -ING, -ES** to mix in	**IMPEACH**	*v* **-ED, -ING, -ES** to charge with misconduct in office
IMMOBILE	*adj* incapable of being moved		
IMMODEST	*adj* not modest	**IMPEARL**	*v* **-ED, -ING, -S** to make pearly
IMMOLATE	*v* **-LATED, -LATING, -LATES** to kill as a sacrifice	**IMPEDE**	*v* **-PEDED, -PEDING, -PEDES** to obstruct the progress of
IMMORAL	*adj* contrary to established morality	**IMPEDER**	*n* pl. **-S** one that impedes
IMMORTAL	*n* pl. **-S** one who is not subject to death	**IMPEL**	*v* **-PELLED, -PELLING, -PELS** to force into action
IMMOTILE	*adj* lacking mobility	**IMPELLER**	*n* pl. **-S** one that impels
IMMUNE	*n* pl. **-S** one who is protected from a disease	**IMPELLOR**	*n* pl. **-S** impeller
		IMPEND	*v* **-ED, -ING, -S** to be imminent
IMMUNISE	*v* **-NISED, -NISING, -NISES** to immunize	**IMPERIA**	a pl. of imperium
IMMUNITY	*n* pl. **-TIES** the state of being protected from a disease	**IMPERIAL**	*n* pl. **-S** an emperor or empress
		IMPERIL	*v* **-ILED, -ILING, -ILS** or **-ILLED, -ILLING, -ILS** to place in jeopardy
IMMUNIZE	*v* **-NIZED, -NIZING, -NIZES** to protect from a disease	**IMPERIUM**	*n* pl. **-RIUMS** or **-RIA** absolute power
IMMURE	*v* **-MURED, -MURING, -MURES** to imprison	**IMPETIGO**	*n* pl. **-GOS** a skin disease
IMMY	*n* pl. **-MIES** a type of playing marble	**IMPETUS**	*n* pl. **-ES** an impelling force
		IMPHEE	*n* pl. **-S** an African grass
IMP	*v* **-ED, -ING, -S** to graft feathers onto a bird's wing	**IMPI**	*n* pl. **-S** a body of warriors
IMPACT	*v* **-ED, -ING, -S** to pack firmly together	**IMPIETY**	*n* pl. **-TIES** lack of piety
		IMPING	*n* pl. **-S** the process of grafting
IMPACTER	*n* pl. **-S** one that impacts	**IMPINGE**	*v* **-PINGED, -PINGING, -PINGES** to collide
IMPACTOR	*n* pl. **-S** impacter		
IMPAINT	*v* **-ED, -ING, -S** to paint or depict	**IMPINGER**	*n* pl. **-S** one that impinges
IMPAIR	*v* **-ED, -ING, -S** to make worse	**IMPIOUS**	*adj* not pious
IMPAIRER	*n* pl. **-S** one that impairs	**IMPISH**	*adj* mischievous **IMPISHLY** *adv*
IMPALA	*n* pl. **-S** an African antelope	**IMPLANT**	*v* **-ED, -ING, -S** to set securely

IMPLEAD	v **-PLEADED** or **-PLED**, **-PLEADING**, **-PLEADS** to sue in a court of law	**IMPROVE**	v **-PROVED**, **-PROVING**, **-PROVES** to make better
IMPLEDGE	v **-PLEDGED**, **-PLEDGING**, **-PLEDGES** to pawn	**IMPROVER**	n pl. **-S** one that improves
IMPLICIT	adj implied	**IMPUDENT**	adj offensively bold or disrespectful
IMPLIED	past tense of imply	**IMPUGN**	v **-ED**, **-ING**, **-S** to make insinuations against
IMPLIES	present 3d person sing. of imply	**IMPUGNER**	n pl. **-S** one that impugns
IMPLODE	v **-PLODED**, **-PLODING**, **-PLODES** to collapse inward	**IMPULSE**	v **-PULSED**, **-PULSING**, **-PULSES** to give impetus to
IMPLORE	v **-PLORED**, **-PLORING**, **-PLORES** to beg for urgently	**IMPUNITY**	n pl. **-TIES** exemption from penalty
IMPLORER	n pl. **-S** one that implores	**IMPURE**	adj **-PURER**, **-PUREST** not pure
IMPLY	v **-PLIED**, **-PLYING**, **-PLIES** to indicate or suggest indirectly	**IMPURE**	adj not pure **IMPURELY** adv
IMPOLICY	n pl. **-CIES** an unwise course of action	**IMPURITY**	n pl. **-TIES** something that is impure
IMPOLITE	adj not polite	**IMPUTE**	v **-PUTED**, **-PUTING**, **-PUTES** to credit to a person or a cause
IMPONE	v **-PONED**, **-PONING**, **-PONES** to wager	**IMPUTER**	n pl. **-S** one that imputes
IMPOROUS	adj extremely dense	**IN**	v **INNED**, **INNING**, **INS** to harvest
IMPORT	v **-ED**, **-ING**, **-S** to bring into a country from abroad	**INACTION**	n pl. **-S** lack of action
IMPORTER	n pl. **-S** one that imports	**INACTIVE**	adj not active
IMPOSE	v **-POSED**, **-POSING**, **-POSES** to establish as compulsory	**INANE**	adj **INANER**, **INANEST** nonsensical **INANELY** adv
IMPOSER	n pl. **-S** one that imposes	**INANE**	n pl. **-S** empty space
IMPOST	v **-ED**, **-ING**, **-S** to determine customs duties	**INANITY**	n pl. **-TIES** something that is inane
IMPOSTER	n pl. **-S** impostor	**INAPT**	adj not apt **INAPTLY** adv
IMPOSTOR	n pl. **-S** one that poses as another for deceptive purposes	**INARABLE**	adj not arable
IMPOTENT	n pl. **-S** one that is powerless	**INARCH**	v **-ED**, **-ING**, **-ES** to graft with in a certain way
IMPOUND	v **-ED**, **-ING**, **-S** to seize and retain in legal custody	**INARM**	v **-ED**, **-ING**, **-S** to encircle with the arms
IMPOWER	v **-ED**, **-ING**, **-S** to empower	**INASMUCH**	adv to the extent that
IMPREGN	v **-ED**, **-ING**, **-S** to make pregnant	**INBEING**	n pl. **-S** the state of being inherent
IMPRESA	n pl. **-S** a type of emblem	**INBOARD**	n pl. **-S** a type of boat motor
IMPRESE	n pl. **-S** impresa	**INBORN**	adj existing in one from birth
IMPRESS	v **-ED**, **-ING**, **-ES** to affect strongly	**INBOUND**	v **-ED**, **-ING**, **-S** to put a basketball in play from out of bounds
IMPREST	n pl. **-S** a loan or advance of money	**INBOUNDS**	adj being within certain boundaries
IMPRIMIS	adv in the first place	**INBOX**	n pl. **-ES** a window in which electronic mail is displayed
IMPRINT	v **-ED**, **-ING**, **-S** to produce a mark by pressure	**INBRED**	n pl. **-S** a product of inbreeding
IMPRISON	v **-ED**, **-ING**, **-S** to confine	**INBREED**	v **-BRED**, **-BREEDING**, **-BREEDS** to breed closely related stock
IMPRO	n pl. **IMPROS** improv	**INBUILT**	adj forming an integral part of a structure
IMPROPER	adj not proper	**INBURST**	n pl. **-S** the act of bursting inward
IMPROV	n pl. **-S** improvisation	**INBY**	adv inward
		INBYE	adv inby

INCAGE	v **-CAGED, -CAGING, -CAGES** to encage	**INCLUDE**	v **-CLUDED, -CLUDING, -CLUDES** to have as a part
INCANT	v **-ED, -ING, -S** to utter ritually	**INCOG**	n pl. **-S** a disguised person
INCASE	v **-CASED, -CASING, -CASES** to encase	**INCOME**	n pl. **-S** a sum of money earned regularly
INCENSE	v **-CENSED, -CENSING, -CENSES** to make angry	**INCOMER**	n pl. **-S** one that comes in
		INCOMING	n pl. **-S** an arrival
INCENT	v **-ED, -ING, -S** to provide with an incentive	**INCONNU**	n pl. **-S** a large food fish
		INCONY	adj pretty
INCENTER	n pl. **-S** the point where the three lines bisecting the angles of a triangle meet	**INCORPSE**	v **-CORPSED, -CORPSING, -CORPSES** to become combined with
INCEPT	v **-ED, -ING, -S** to take in	**INCREASE**	v **-CREASED, -CREASING, -CREASES** to make or become greater
INCEPTOR	n pl. **-S** one that incepts		
INCEST	n pl. **-S** sexual intercourse between closely related persons	**INCREATE**	adj not created
INCH	v **-ED, -ING, -ES** to move very slowly	**INCROSS**	v **-ED, -ING, -ES** to inbreed
		INCRUST	v **-ED, -ING, -S** to encrust
INCHER	n pl. **-S** something having a specified number of inches	**INCUBATE**	v **-BATED, -BATING, -BATES** to warm eggs for hatching
INCHMEAL	adv little by little		
INCHOATE	adj being in an early stage	**INCUBUS**	n pl. **-BUSES** or **-BI** a demon
INCHWORM	n pl. **-S** a type of worm	**INCUDAL**	adj pertaining to the incus
INCIDENT	n pl. **-S** an event	**INCUDATE**	adj incudal
INCIPIT	n pl. **-S** the opening words of a text	**INCUDES**	pl. of incus
INCISAL	adj being the cutting edge of a tooth	**INCULT**	adj uncultivated
		INCUMBER	v **-ED, -ING, -S** to encumber
INCISE	v **-CISED, -CISING, -CISES** to cut into	**INCUR**	v **-CURRED, -CURRING, -CURS** to bring upon oneself
INCISION	n pl. **-S** the act of incising	**INCURVE**	v **-CURVED, -CURVING, -CURVES** to curve inward
INCISIVE	adj penetrating		
INCISOR	n pl. **-S** a cutting tooth	**INCUS**	n pl. **INCUDES** a bone in the middle ear
INCISORY	adj adapted for cutting		
INCISURE	n pl. **-S** a notch or cleft of a body part	**INCUSE**	v **-CUSED, -CUSING, -CUSES** to mark by stamping
INCITANT	n pl. **-S** something that incites	**INDABA**	n pl. **-S** a meeting of South African tribes
INCITE	v **-CITED, -CITING, -CITES** to arouse to action	**INDAGATE**	v **-GATED, -GATING, -GATES** to investigate
INCITER	n pl. **-S** one that incites	**INDAMIN**	n pl. **-S** indamine
INCIVIL	adj discourteous	**INDAMINE**	n pl. **-S** a chemical compound
INCLASP	v **-ED, -ING, -S** to enclasp	**INDEBTED**	adj owing something to another
INCLINE	v **-CLINED, -CLINING, -CLINES** to slant	**INDECENT**	adj **-CENTER, -CENTEST** not decent
INCLINER	n pl. **-S** one that inclines	**INDEED**	adv in truth
INCLIP	v **-CLIPPED, -CLIPPING, -CLIPS** to clasp	**INDEEDY**	interj — used to emphasize an affirmative
INCLOSE	v **-CLOSED, -CLOSING, -CLOSES** to enclose	**INDENE**	n pl. **-S** a hydrocarbon
INCLOSER	n pl. **-S** one that incloses	**INDENT**	v **-ED, -ING, -S** to cut or tear irregularly

INDENTER *n* pl. **-S** one that indents

INDENTOR *n* pl. **-S** indenter

INDEVOUT *adj* not devout

INDEX *n* pl. **INDEXES** or **INDICES** a type of reference guide at the end of a book

INDEX *v* **-ED, -ING, -ES** to provide with an index

INDEXER *n* pl. **-S** one that indexes

INDEXING *n* pl. **-S** the linking of wages and prices to cost-of-living levels

INDICAN *n* pl. **-S** a chemical compound

INDICANT *n* pl. **-S** something that indicates

INDICATE *v* **-CATED, -CATING, -CATES** to point out

INDICES a pl. of index

INDICIA *n* pl. **-S** a distinctive mark

INDICIUM *n* pl. **-S** an indicia

INDICT *v* **-ED, -ING, -S** to charge with a crime

INDICTEE *n* pl. **-S** one that is indicted

INDICTER *n* pl. **-S** one that indicts

INDICTOR *n* pl. **-S** indicter

INDIE *n* pl. **-S** a person who is independent

INDIGEN *n* pl. **-S** indigene

INDIGENE *n* pl. **-S** a native

INDIGENT *n* pl. **-S** a needy person

INDIGN *adj* disgraceful **INDIGNLY** *adv*

INDIGO *n* pl. **-GOS** or **-GOES** a blue dye

INDIGOID *n* pl. **-S** a blue dye

INDIRECT *adj* not direct

INDITE *v* **-DITED, -DITING, -DITES** to write or compose

INDITER *n* pl. **-S** one that indites

INDIUM *n* pl. **-S** a metallic element

INDOCILE *adj* not docile

INDOL *n* pl. **-S** indole

INDOLE *n* pl. **-S** a chemical compound

INDOLENT *adj* lazy

INDOOR *adj* pertaining to the interior of a building

INDOORS *adv* in or into a house

INDORSE *v* **-DORSED, -DORSING, -DORSES** to endorse

INDORSEE *n* pl. **-S** endorsee

INDORSER *n* pl. **-S** endorser

INDORSING present participle of indorse

INDORSOR *n* pl. **-S** endorsor

INDOW *v* **-ED, -ING, -S** to endow

INDOXYL *n* pl. **-S** a chemical compound

INDRAFT *n* pl. **-S** an inward flow or current

INDRAWN *adj* drawn in

INDRI *n* pl. **-S** a short-tailed lemur

INDUCE *v* **-DUCED, -DUCING, -DUCES** to influence into doing something

INDUCER *n* pl. **-S** one that induces

INDUCT *v* **-ED, -ING, -S** to bring into military service

INDUCTEE *n* pl. **-S** one that is inducted

INDUCTOR *n* pl. **-S** one that inducts

INDUE *v* **-DUED, -DUING, -DUES** to endue

INDULGE *v* **-DULGED, -DULGING, -DULGES** to yield to the desire of

INDULGER *n* pl. **-S** one that indulges

INDULIN *n* pl. **-S** induline

INDULINE *n* pl. **-S** a blue dye

INDULT *n* pl. **-S** a privilege granted by the pope

INDUNA *n* pl. **-S** a tribal overseer in Africa

INDURATE *v* **-RATED, -RATING, -RATES** to make hard

INDUSIUM *n* pl. **-SIA** an enclosing membrane **INDUSIAL** *adj*

INDUSTRY *n* pl. **-TRIES** a group of productive enterprises

INDWELL *v* **-DWELT, -DWELLING, -DWELLS** to live within

INEARTH *v* **-ED, -ING, -S** to bury

INEDIBLE *adj* not fit to be eaten **INEDIBLY** *adv*

INEDITA *n/pl* unpublished literary works

INEDITED *adj* not published

INEPT *adj* **-ER, -EST** not suitable **INEPTLY** *adv*

INEQUITY *n* pl. **-TIES** unfairness

INERRANT *adj* free from error

INERT *n* pl. **-S** something that lacks active properties

INERTIA *n* pl. **-TIAS** or **-TIAE** the tendency of a body to resist acceleration **INERTIAL** *adj*

INERTLY *adv* inactively

INEXACT *adj* not exact

INEXPERT *n* pl. **-S** a novice

INFALL   *n* pl. **-S** movement under the influence of gravity toward a celestial object

INFAMOUS   *adj* having a vile reputation

INFAMY   *n* pl. **-MIES** the state of being infamous

INFANCY   *n* pl. **-CIES** the state of being an infant

INFANT   *n* pl. **-S** a child in the earliest stages of life

INFANTA   *n* pl. **-S** a daughter of a Spanish or Portuguese monarch

INFANTE   *n* pl. **-S** a younger son of a Spanish or Portuguese monarch

INFANTRY   *n* pl. **-TRIES** a branch of the army composed of foot soldiers

INFARCT   *n* pl. **-S** an area of dead or dying tissue

INFARE   *n* pl. **-S** a reception for newlyweds

INFAUNA   *n* pl. **-NAS** or **-NAE** fauna living on a soft sea floor **INFAUNAL** *adj*

INFECT   *v* **-ED, -ING, -S** to contaminate with disease-producing germs

INFECTER   *n* pl. **-S** one that infects

INFECTOR   *n* pl. **-S** infecter

INFECUND   *adj* barren

INFEED   *n* pl. **-S** the action of supplying material to a machine

INFEOFF   *v* **-ED, -ING, -S** to enfeoff

INFER   *v* **-FERRED, -FERRING, -FERS** to reach or derive by reasoning

INFERIOR   *n* pl. **-S** one of lesser rank

INFERNAL   *adj* pertaining to hell

INFERNO   *n* pl. **-NOS** a place that resembles or suggests hell

INFERRED   past tense of infer

INFERRER   *n* pl. **-S** one that infers

INFERRING   present participle of infer

INFEST   *v* **-ED, -ING, -S** to overrun in large numbers

INFESTER   *n* pl. **-S** one that infests

INFIDEL   *n* pl. **-S** one who has no religious faith

INFIELD   *n* pl. **-S** a part of a baseball field

INFIGHT   *v* **-FOUGHT, -FIGHTING, -FIGHTS** to contend with others within the same group

INFILL   *v* **-ED, -ING, -S** to fill in (a hole)

INFINITE   *n* pl. **-S** something that has no limits

INFINITY   *n* pl. **-TIES** the state of having no limits

INFIRM   *v* **-ED, -ING, -S** to weaken or destroy the validity of

INFIRMLY   *adv* in a feeble manner

INFIX   *v* **-ED, -ING, -ES** to implant

INFIXION   *n* pl. **-S** the act of infixing

INFLAME   *v* **-FLAMED, -FLAMING, -FLAMES** to set on fire

INFLAMER   *n* pl. **-S** one that inflames

INFLATE   *v* **-FLATED, -FLATING, -FLATES** to cause to expand by filling with gas or air

INFLATER   *n* pl. **-S** one that inflates

INFLATOR   *n* pl. **-S** inflater

INFLECT   *v* **-ED, -ING, -S** to bend

INFLEXED   *adj* bent inward

INFLICT   *v* **-ED, -ING, -S** to cause to be endured; impose

INFLIGHT   *adj* done during an air voyage

INFLOW   *n* pl. **-S** the act of flowing in

INFLUENT   *n* pl. **-S** a tributary

INFLUX   *n* pl. **-ES** a flowing in

INFO   *n* pl. **-FOS** information

INFOBAHN   *n* pl. **-S** an electronic communications network

INFOLD   *v* **-ED, -ING, -S** to fold inward

INFOLDER   *n* pl. **-S** one that infolds

INFORM   *v* **-ED, -ING, -S** to supply with information

INFORMAL   *adj* marked by the absence of formality or ceremony

INFORMER   *n* pl. **-S** one that informs

INFOTECH   *n* pl. **-S** computer technology for distributing data

INFOUGHT   past tense of infight

INFRA   *adv* below

INFRACT   *v* **-ED, -ING, -S** to break a legal rule

INFRARED   *n* pl. **-S** a part of the invisible spectrum

INFRINGE   *v* **-FRINGED, -FRINGING, -FRINGES** to violate an oath or a law

INFRUGAL   *adj* not frugal

INFULA   *n* pl. **INFULAE** either of the two ribbons on a bishop's miter

INFUSE   *v* **-FUSED, -FUSING, -FUSES** to permeate with something

INFUSER	*n* pl. **-S** one that infuses
INFUSION	*n* pl. **-S** the act of infusing
INFUSIVE	*adj* capable of infusing
INGATE	*n* pl. **-S** a channel by which molten metal enters a mold
INGATHER	*v* **-ED, -ING, -S** to gather in
INGENUE	*n* pl. **-S** a naive young woman
INGEST	*v* **-ED, -ING, -S** to take into the body
INGESTA	*n/pl* ingested material
INGLE	*n* pl. **-S** a fire
INGOING	*adj* entering
INGOT	*v* **-ED, -ING, -S** to shape into a convenient form for storage
INGRAFT	*v* **-ED, -ING, -S** to engraft
INGRAIN	*v* **-ED, -ING, -S** to impress firmly on the mind
INGRATE	*n* pl. **-S** an ungrateful person
INGRESS	*n* pl. **-ES** the act of entering
INGROUND	*adj* built into the ground
INGROUP	*n* pl. **-S** a group with which one feels a sense of solidarity
INGROWN	*adj* grown into the flesh
INGROWTH	*n* pl. **-S** growth inward
INGUINAL	*adj* pertaining to the groin
INGULF	*v* **-ED, -ING, -S** to engulf
INHABIT	*v* **-ED, -ING, -S** to live in
INHALANT	*n* pl. **-S** something that is inhaled
INHALE	*v* **-HALED, -HALING, -HALES** to take into the lungs
INHALER	*n* pl. **-S** one that inhales
INHAUL	*n* pl. **-S** a line for bringing in a sail
INHAULER	*n* pl. **-S** an inhaul
INHERE	*v* **-HERED, -HERING, -HERES** to be inherent
INHERENT	*adj* existing in something as an essential characteristic
INHERIT	*v* **-ED, -ING, -S** to receive by legal succession
INHESION	*n* pl. **-S** the state of inhering
INHIBIN	*n* pl. **-S** a human hormone
INHIBIT	*v* **-ED, -ING, -S** to restrain or hold back
INHOLDER	*n* pl. **-S** one that owns a tract of land within a national park
INHUMAN	*adj* lacking desirable human qualities
INHUMANE	*adj* not humane

INHUME	*v* **-HUMED, -HUMING, -HUMES** to bury
INHUMER	*n* pl. **-S** one that inhumes
INIMICAL	*adj* unfriendly
INION	*n* pl. **INIA** a part of the skull
INIQUITY	*n* pl. **-TIES** a gross injustice
INITIAL	*v* **-TIALED, -TIALING, -TIALS** or **-TIALLED, -TIALLING, -TIALS** to mark with the first letters of one's name
INITIATE	*v* **-ATED, -ATING, -ATES** to originate
INJECT	*v* **-ED, -ING, -S** to force a fluid into
INJECTOR	*n* pl. **-S** one that injects
INJERA	*n* pl. **-S** a type of Ethiopian bread
INJURE	*v* **-JURED, -JURING, -JURES** to do or cause injury to
INJURER	*n* pl. **-S** one that injures
INJURY	*n* pl. **-RIES** harm inflicted or suffered
INK	*v* **-ED, -ING, -S** to mark with ink (a colored fluid used for writing)
INKBERRY	*n* pl. **-RIES** a small shrub
INKBLOT	*n* pl. **-S** a blotted pattern of spilled ink
INKER	*n* pl. **-S** one that inks
INKHORN	*n* pl. **-S** a small container for ink
INKIER	comparative of inky
INKIEST	superlative of inky
INKINESS	*n* pl. **-ES** the state of being inky
INKJET	*n* pl. **-S** a printer that spurts ink to form letters
INKLE	*n* pl. **-S** a tape used for trimming
INKLESS	*adj* being without ink
INKLIKE	*adj* resembling ink
INKLING	*n* pl. **-S** a slight suggestion
INKPOT	*n* pl. **-S** an inkwell
INKSTAND	*n* pl. **-S** an inkwell
INKSTONE	*n* pl. **-S** a stone on which dry ink and water are mixed
INKWELL	*n* pl. **-S** a small container for ink
INKWOOD	*n* pl. **-S** an evergreen tree
INKY	*adj* **INKIER, INKIEST** resembling ink
INLACE	*v* **-LACED, -LACING, -LACES** to enlace
INLAID	past tense of inlay
INLAND	*n* pl. **-S** the interior of a region

INLANDER *n* pl. **-S** one living in the interior of a region

INLAY *v* **-LAID, -LAYING, -LAYS** to set into a surface

INLAYER *n* pl. **-S** one that inlays

INLET *v* **-LET, -LETTING, -LETS** to insert

INLIER *n* pl. **-S** a type of rock formation

INLY *adv* inwardly

INLYING *adj* located farther in

INMATE *n* pl. **-S** one who is confined to an institution

INMESH *v* **-ED, -ING, -ES** to enmesh

INMOST *adj* farthest within

INN *v* **-ED, -ING, -S** to put up at an inn (a public lodging house)

INNAGE *n* pl. **-S** the quantity of goods remaining in a container after shipment

INNARDS *n/pl* the internal organs

INNATE *adj* inborn **INNATELY** *adv*

INNED past tense of in

INNER *n* pl. **-S** something that is within

INNERLY *adv* inwardly

INNERVE *v* **-NERVED, -NERVING, -NERVES** to stimulate

INNING *n* pl. **-S** a division of a baseball game

INNINGS *n* pl. **-ES** a part of the game of cricket

INNLESS *adj* having no inns

INNOCENT *adj* **-CENTER, -CENTEST** free from guilt or sin

INNOCENT *n* pl. **-S** an innocent person

INNOVATE *v* **-VATED, -VATING, -VATES** to introduce something new

INNUENDO *v* **-ED, -ING, -S** or **-ES** to make a derogatory implication

INOCULUM *n* pl. **-LUMS** or **-LA** the material used in an inoculation

INOSINE *n* pl. **-S** a compound of hypoxanthine and ribose

INOSITE *n* pl. **-S** inositol

INOSITOL *n* pl. **-S** an alcohol found in plant and animal tissue

INOTROPE *n* pl. **-S** a drug for controlling the force of muscular contractions

INPHASE *adj* having matching electrical phases

INPOUR *v* **-ED, -ING, -S** to pour in

INPUT *v* **-PUTTED, -PUTTING, -PUTS** to enter data into a computer

INPUTTER *n* pl. **-S** one that inputs

INQUEST *n* pl. **-S** a legal inquiry

INQUIET *v* **-ED, -ING, -S** to disturb

INQUIRE *v* **-QUIRED, -QUIRING, -QUIRES** to ask about

INQUIRER *n* pl. **-S** one that inquires

INQUIRY *n* pl. **-RIES** a question

INRO *n* pl. **INRO** a Japanese ornamental container

INROAD *n* pl. **-S** a hostile invasion

INRUN *n* pl. **-S** the approach ramp of a ski jump

INRUSH *n* pl. **-ES** a rushing in

INSANE *adj* **-SANER, -SANEST** mentally unsound **INSANELY** *adv*

INSANITY *n* pl. **-TIES** the state of being insane; something utterly foolish

INSCAPE *n* pl. **-S** the inner essential quality of something

INSCRIBE *v* **-SCRIBED, -SCRIBING, -SCRIBES** to write or engrave as a lasting record

INSCROLL *v* **-ED, -ING, -S** to enscroll

INSCULP *v* **-ED, -ING, -S** to engrave

INSEAM *n* pl. **-S** an inner seam

INSECT *n* pl. **-S** any of a class of small invertebrate animals

INSECTAN *adj* pertaining to insects

INSECURE *adj* unsafe

INSERT *v* **-ED, -ING, -S** to put in

INSERTER *n* pl. **-S** one that inserts

INSET *v* **-SETTED, -SETTING, -SETS** to insert

INSETTER *n* pl. **-S** one that inserts

INSHEATH *v* **-ED, -ING, -S** to ensheath

INSHORE *adj* near the shore

INSHRINE *v* **-SHRINED, -SHRINING, -SHRINES** to enshrine

INSIDE *n* pl. **-S** something that lies within

INSIDER *n* pl. **-S** an accepted member of a clique

INSIGHT *n* pl. **-S** a perception of the inner nature of things

INSIGNE *n* pl. **INSIGNIA** an insignia

INSIGNIA *n* pl. **-S** an emblem of authority or honor

INSIPID *adj* dull and uninteresting

INSIST	*v* **-ED, -ING, -S** to be resolute on some matter
INSISTER	*n* pl. **-S** one that insists
INSNARE	*v* **-SNARED, -SNARING, -SNARES** to ensnare
INSNARER	*n* pl. **-S** ensnarer
INSOFAR	*adv* to such an extent
INSOLATE	*v* **-LATED, -LATING, -LATES** to expose to sunlight
INSOLE	*n* pl. **-S** the inner sole of a boot or shoe
INSOLENT	*n* pl. **-S** an extremely rude person
INSOMNIA	*n* pl. **-S** chronic inability to sleep
INSOMUCH	*adv* to such a degree
INSOUL	*v* **-ED, -ING, -S** to ensoul
INSOURCE	*v* **-SOURCED, -SOURCING, -SOURCES** to procure goods and services from within one's own country
INSPAN	*v* **-SPANNED, -SPANNING, -SPANS** to harness or yoke to a vehicle
INSPECT	*v* **-ED, -ING, -S** to look carefully at or over
INSPHERE	*v* **-SPHERED, -SPHERING, -SPHERES** to ensphere
INSPIRE	*v* **-SPIRED, -SPIRING, -SPIRES** to animate the mind or emotions of
INSPIRER	*n* pl. **-S** one that inspires
INSPIRIT	*v* **-ED, -ING, -S** to fill with spirit or life
INSTABLE	*adj* unstable
INSTAL	*v* **-STALLED, -STALLING, -STALS** to install
INSTALL	*v* **-ED, -ING, -S** to place in position for use
INSTANCE	*v* **-STANCED, -STANCING, -STANCES** to cite as an example
INSTANCY	*n* pl. **-CIES** urgency
INSTANT	*n* pl. **-S** a very short time
INSTAR	*v* **-STARRED, -STARRING, -STARS** to adorn with stars
INSTATE	*v* **-STATED, -STATING, -STATES** to place in office
INSTEAD	*adv* as a substitute or equivalent
INSTEP	*n* pl. **-S** a part of the foot
INSTIL	*v* **-STILLED, -STILLING, -STILS** to instill
INSTILL	*v* **-ED, -ING, -S** to infuse slowly
INSTINCT	*n* pl. **-S** an inborn behavioral pattern
INSTROKE	*n* pl. **-S** an inward stroke
INSTRUCT	*v* **-ED, -ING, -S** to supply with knowledge
INSULA	*n* pl. **-LAE** a region of the brain
INSULANT	*n* pl. **-S** an insulating material
INSULAR	*n* pl. **-S** an islander
INSULATE	*v* **-LATED, -LATING, -LATES** to separate with nonconducting material
INSULIN	*n* pl. **-S** a hormone
INSULT	*v* **-ED, -ING, -S** to treat offensively
INSULTER	*n* pl. **-S** one that insults
INSURANT	*n* pl. **-S** one who is insured
INSURE	*v* **-SURED, -SURING, -SURES** to guarantee against loss
INSURED	*n* pl. **-S** one who is insured
INSURER	*n* pl. **-S** one that insures
INSURING	present participle of insure
INSWATHE	*v* **-SWATHED, -SWATHING, -SWATHES** to enswathe
INSWEPT	*adj* narrowed in front
INTACT	*adj* not damaged in any way **INTACTLY** *adv*
INTAGLIO	*n* pl. **-GLIOS** or **-GLI** an incised or sunken design
INTAGLIO	*v* **-ED, -ING, -S** or **-ES** to engrave in intaglio
INTAKE	*n* pl. **-S** the act of taking in
INTARSIA	*n* pl. **-S** a decorative technique
INTEGER	*n* pl. **-S** a whole number
INTEGRAL	*n* pl. **-S** a total unit
INTEGRIN	*n* pl. **-S** a class of animal proteins
INTEND	*v* **-ED, -ING, -S** to have as a specific aim or purpose
INTENDED	*n* pl. **-S** one's spouse to-be
INTENDER	*n* pl. **-S** one that intends
INTENSE	*adj* **-TENSER, -TENSEST** existing in an extreme degree
INTENT	*n* pl. **-S** a purpose
INTENTLY	*adv* in an unwavering manner
INTER	*v* **-TERRED, -TERRING, -TERS** to bury
INTERACT	*v* **-ED, -ING, -S** to act on each other
INTERAGE	*adj* including persons of various ages
INTERBED	*v* **-BEDDED, -BEDDING, -BEDS** to insert between other layers

INTERCOM   *n* pl. **-S** a type of communication system

INTERCUT   *v* **-CUT, -CUTTING, -CUTS** to alternate camera shots

INTEREST   *v* **-ED, -ING, -S** to engage the attention of

INTERIM   *n* pl. **-S** an interval

INTERIOR   *n* pl. **-S** the inside

INTERLAP   *v* **-LAPPED, -LAPPING, -LAPS** to lap one over another

INTERLAY   *v* **-LAID, -LAYING, -LAYS** to place between

INTERMAT   *v* **-MATTED, -MATTING, -MATS** to mat fibers together

INTERMIT   *v* **-MITTED, -MITTING, -MITS** to stop temporarily

INTERMIX   *v* **-ED, -ING, -ES** to mix together

INTERN   *v* **-ED, -ING, -S** to confine during a war

INTERNAL   *n* pl. **-S** an inner attribute

INTERNE   *n* pl. **-S** a recent medical school graduate on a hospital staff

INTERNEE   *n* pl. **-S** one who has been interned

INTERNET   *n* pl. **-S** a system that connects computers around the world

INTERRED   past tense of inter

INTERREX   *n* pl. **-REGES** a type of sovereign

INTERRING   present participle of inter

INTERROW   *adj* existing between rows

INTERSEX   *n* pl. **-ES** a person having characteristics of both sexes

INTERTIE   *n* pl. **-S** a type of electrical connection

INTERVAL   *n* pl. **-S** a space of time between periods or events

INTERWAR   *adj* happening between wars

INTHRAL   *v* **-THRALLED, -THRALLING, -THRALS** to enthrall

INTHRALL   *v* **-ED, -ING, -S** to enthrall

INTHRONE   *v* **-THRONED, -THRONING, -THRONES** to enthrone

INTI   *n* pl. **-S** a former monetary unit of Peru

INTIFADA   *n* pl. **-S** an uprising of Palestinians against Israelis

INTIMA   *n* pl. **-MAS** or **-MAE** the innermost layer of an organ **INTIMAL** *adj*

INTIMACY   *n* pl. **-CIES** the state of being closely associated

INTIMATE   *v* **-MATED, -MATING, -MATES** to make known indirectly

INTIME   *adj* cozy

INTIMIST   *n* pl. **-S** a writer or artist who deals with deep personal experiences

INTINE   *n* pl. **-S** the inner wall of a spore

INTITLE   *v* **-TLED, -TLING, -TLES** to entitle

INTITULE   *v* **-ULED, -ULING, -ULES** to entitle

INTO   *prep* to the inside of

INTOMB   *v* **-ED, -ING, -S** to entomb

INTONATE   *v* **-NATED, -NATING, -NATES** to intone

INTONE   *v* **-TONED, -TONING, -TONES** to speak in a singing voice

INTONER   *n* pl. **-S** one that intones

INTORT   *v* **-ED, -ING, -S** to twist inward

INTOWN   *adj* located in the center of a city

INTRADAY   *adj* occurring within a single day

INTRADOS   *n* pl. **-ES** the inner curve of an arch

INTRANET   *n* pl. **-S** a computer network with restricted access

INTRANT   *n* pl. **-S** an entrant

INTREAT   *v* **-ED, -ING, -S** to entreat

INTRENCH   *v* **-ED, -ING, -ES** to entrench

INTREPID   *adj* fearless

INTRIGUE   *v* **-TRIGUED, -TRIGUING, -TRIGUES** to arouse the curiosity of

INTRO   *n* pl. **-TROS** an introduction

INTROFY   *v* **-FIED, -FYING, -FIES** to increase the wetting properties of

INTROIT   *n* pl. **-S** music sung at the beginning of a worship service

INTROMIT   *v* **-MITTED, -MITTING, -MITS** to put in

INTRON   *n* pl. **-S** an intervening sequence in the genetic code **INTRONIC** *adj*

INTRORSE   *adj* facing inward

INTRUDE   *v* **-TRUDED, -TRUDING, -TRUDES** to thrust or force oneself in

INTRUDER   *n* pl. **-S** one that intrudes

INTRUST   *v* **-ED, -ING, -S** to entrust

INTUBATE   *v* **-BATED, -BATING, -BATES** to insert a tube into

INTUIT   *v* **-ED, -ING, -S** to know without conscious reasoning

INTURN   *n* pl. **-S** a turning inward **INTURNED** *adj*

INTWINE   *v* **-TWINED, -TWINING, -TWINES** to entwine

INTWIST   *v* **-ED, -ING, -S** to entwist

INUKSHUK _n_ pl. **-S** a figure of a human made of stones

INUKSUK _n_ pl. **INUKSUKS** or **INUKSUIT** an inukshuk

INULASE _n_ pl. **-S** an enzyme

INULIN _n_ pl. **-S** a chemical compound

INUNDANT _adj_ inundating

INUNDATE _v_ **-DATED, -DATING, -DATES** to overwhelm with water

INURBANE _adj_ not urbane

INURE _v_ **-URED, -URING, -URES** to accustom to accept something undesirable

INURN _v_ **-ED, -ING, -S** to put in an urn

INUTILE _adj_ useless

INVADE _v_ **-VADED, -VADING, -VADES** to enter for conquest or plunder

INVADER _n_ pl. **-S** one that invades

INVALID _v_ **-ED, -ING, -S** to disable physically

INVAR _n_ pl. **-S** an iron-nickel alloy

INVASION _n_ pl. **-S** the act of invading **INVASIVE** _adj_

INVECTED _adj_ edged by convex curves

INVEIGH _v_ **-ED, -ING, -S** to protest angrily

INVEIGLE _v_ **-GLED, -GLING, -GLES** to induce by guile or flattery

INVENT _v_ **-ED, -ING, -S** to devise originally

INVENTER _n_ pl. **-S** inventor

INVENTOR _n_ pl. **-S** one that invents

INVERITY _n_ pl. **-TIES** lack of truth

INVERSE _v_ **-VERSED, -VERSING, -VERSES** to reverse

INVERT _v_ **-ED, -ING, -S** to turn upside down

INVERTER _n_ pl. **-S** one that inverts

INVERTIN _n_ pl. **-S** an enzyme

INVERTOR _n_ pl. **-S** a type of electrical device

INVEST _v_ **-ED, -ING, -S** to commit something of value for future profit

INVESTOR _n_ pl. **-S** one that invests

INVIABLE _adj_ not viable **INVIABLY** _adv_

INVIRILE _adj_ not virile

INVISCID _adj_ not viscid

INVITAL _adj_ not vital

INVITE _v_ **-VITED, -VITING, -VITES** to request the presence of

INVITEE _n_ pl. **-S** one that is invited

INVITER _n_ pl. **-S** one that invites

INVITING present participle of invite

INVOCATE _v_ **-CATED, -CATING, -CATES** to invoke

INVOICE _v_ **-VOICED, -VOICING, -VOICES** to bill

INVOKE _v_ **-VOKED, -VOKING, -VOKES** to appeal to for aid

INVOKER _n_ pl. **-S** one that invokes

INVOLUTE _v_ **-LUTED, -LUTING, -LUTES** to roll or curl up

INVOLVE _v_ **-VOLVED, -VOLVING, -VOLVES** to contain or include as a part

INVOLVER _n_ pl. **-S** one that involves

INWALL _v_ **-ED, -ING, -S** to surround with a wall

INWARD _adv_ toward the inside

INWARDLY _adv_ on the inside

INWARDS _adv_ inward

INWEAVE _v_ **-WOVE** or **-WEAVED, -WOVEN, -WEAVING, -WEAVES** to weave together

INWIND _v_ **-WOUND, -WINDING, -WINDS** to enwind

INWRAP _v_ **-WRAPPED, -WRAPPING, -WRAPS** to enwrap

IODATE _v_ **-DATED, -DATING, -DATES** to iodize

IODATION _n_ pl. **-S** the act of iodating

IODIC _adj_ pertaining to iodine

IODID _n_ pl. **-S** iodide

IODIDE _n_ pl. **-S** a compound of iodine

IODIN _n_ pl. **-S** iodine

IODINATE _v_ **-ATED, -ATING, -ATES** to iodize

IODINE _n_ pl. **-S** a nonmetallic element

IODISE _v_ **-DISED, -DISING, -DISES** to iodize

IODISM _n_ pl. **-S** iodine poisoning

IODIZE _v_ **-DIZED, -DIZING, -DIZES** to treat with iodine

IODIZER _n_ pl. **-S** one that iodizes

IODOFORM _n_ pl. **-S** an iodine compound

IODOPHOR _n_ pl. **-S** an iodine compound

IODOPSIN _n_ pl. **-S** a pigment in the retina

IODOUS _adj_ pertaining to iodine

IOLITE _n_ pl. **-S** a mineral

ION _n_ pl. **-S** an electrically charged atom

IONIC _n_ pl. **-S** a style of type

IONIC	*adj* pertaining to or using ions	**IRONER**	*n* pl. **-S** a machine for pressing clothes
IONICITY	*n* pl. **-TIES** the state of existing as or like an ion	**IRONIC**	*adj* pertaining to irony
IONISE	*v* **-ISED, -ISING, -ISES** to ionize	**IRONICAL**	*adj* ironic
IONISER	*n* pl. **-S** ionizer	**IRONIES**	pl. of irony
IONIUM	*n* pl. **-S** an isotope of thorium	**IRONING**	*n* pl. **-S** clothes pressed or to be pressed
IONIZE	*v* **-IZED, -IZING, -IZES** to convert into ions	**IRONISE**	*v* **-NISED, -NISING, -NISES** to ironize
IONIZER	*n* pl. **-S** one that ionizes	**IRONIST**	*n* pl. **-S** one who uses irony
IONOGEN	*n* pl. **-S** a compound capable of forming ions	**IRONIZE**	*v* **-NIZED, -NIZING, -NIZES** to mix with nutritional iron
IONOMER	*n* pl. **-S** a type of plastic	**IRONLESS**	*adj* having no iron
IONONE	*n* pl. **-S** a chemical compound	**IRONLIKE**	*adj* resembling iron
IOTA	*n* pl. **-S** a Greek letter	**IRONMAN**	*n* pl. **-MEN** a man of great strength and stamina
IOTACISM	*n* pl. **-S** excessive use of the letter iota	**IRONNESS**	*n* pl. **-ES** the state of being iron
IPECAC	*n* pl. **-S** a medicinal plant	**IRONSIDE**	*n* pl. **-S** a man of great strength
IPOMOEA	*n* pl. **-S** a flowering plant	**IRONWARE**	*n* pl. **-S** articles made of iron
IRACUND	*adj* easily angered	**IRONWEED**	*n* pl. **-S** a shrub
IRADE	*n* pl. **-S** a decree of a Muslim ruler	**IRONWOOD**	*n* pl. **-S** a hardwood tree
IRATE	*adj* **IRATER, IRATEST** angry **IRATELY** *adv*	**IRONWORK**	*n* pl. **-S** objects made of iron
IRE	*v* **IRED, IRING, IRES** to anger	**IRONY**	*n* pl. **-NIES** the use of words to express the opposite of what is literally said
IREFUL	*adj* angry **IREFULLY** *adv*		
IRELESS	*adj* not angry	**IRREAL**	*adj* not real
IRENIC	*adj* peaceful in purpose	**IRRIGATE**	*v* **-GATED, -GATING, -GATES** to supply with water by artificial means
IRENICAL	*adj* irenic		
IRENICS	*n/pl* a branch of theology	**IRRITANT**	*n* pl. **-S** something that irritates
IRID	*n* pl. **-S** a plant of the iris family	**IRRITATE**	*v* **-TATED, -TATING, -TATES** to excite to impatience or anger
IRIDES	a pl. of iris		
IRIDIC	*adj* pertaining to iridium	**IRRUPT**	*v* **-ED, -ING, -S** to rush in forcibly
IRIDIUM	*n* pl. **-S** a metallic element	**IS**	present 3d person sing. of be
IRING	present participle of ire	**ISAGOGE**	*n* pl. **-S** a type of introduction to a branch of study
IRIS	*n* pl. **IRISES** or **IRIDES** a part of the eye		
		ISAGOGIC	*n* pl. **-S** a branch of theology
IRIS	*v* **-ED, -ING, -ES** to give the form of a rainbow to	**ISARITHM**	*n* pl. **-S** an isopleth
		ISATIN	*n* pl. **-S** a chemical compound **ISATINIC** *adj*
IRITIS	*n* pl. **-TISES** inflammation of the iris **IRITIC** *adj*		
		ISATINE	*n* pl. **-S** isatin
IRK	*v* **-ED, -ING, -S** to annoy or weary	**ISBA**	*n* pl. **-S** a Russian log hut
IRKSOME	*adj* tending to irk	**ISCHEMIA**	*n* pl. **-S** a type of anemia **ISCHEMIC** *adj*
IROKO	*n* pl. **-KOS** a large African tree		
IRON	*v* **-ED, -ING, -S** to furnish with iron (a metallic element)	**ISCHIUM**	*n* pl. **-CHIA** a pelvic bone **ISCHIAL** *adj*
IRONBARK	*n* pl. **-S** a timber tree		
IRONCLAD	*n* pl. **-S** an armored warship	**ISLAND**	*v* **-ED, -ING, -S** to make into an island (a land area entirely surrounded by water)
IRONE	*n* pl. **-S** an aromatic oil		

ISLANDER *n pl.* **-S** one that lives on an island

ISLE *v* **ISLED, ISLING, ISLES** to place on an isle (a small island)

ISLELESS *adj* lacking an isle

ISLET *n pl.* **-S** a small island **ISLETED** *adj*

ISM *n pl.* **-S** a distinctive theory or doctrine

ISOBAR *n pl.* **-S** a type of atom **ISOBARIC** *adj*

ISOBARE *n pl.* **-S** isobar

ISOBATH *n pl.* **-S** a line on a map connecting points of equal water depth

ISOBUTYL *n pl.* **-S** a hydrocarbon radical

ISOCHEIM *n pl.* **-S** a type of isotherm

ISOCHIME *n pl.* **-S** isocheim

ISOCHOR *n pl.* **-S** isochore

ISOCHORE *n pl.* **-S** a curve used to show a relationship between pressure and temperature

ISOCHRON *n pl.* **-S** a line on a chart connecting points representing the same time

ISOCLINE *n pl.* **-S** a type of rock formation

ISOCRACY *n pl.* **-CIES** a form of government

ISODOSE *adj* pertaining to zones that receive equal doses of radiation

ISOFORM *n pl.* **-S** one of two or more proteins having a similar form

ISOGAMY *n pl.* **-MIES** the fusion of two similar gametes

ISOGENIC *adj* genetically similar

ISOGENY *n pl.* **-NIES** the state of being of similar origin

ISOGLOSS *n pl.* **-ES** a line on a map between linguistically varied areas

ISOGON *n pl.* **-S** a polygon having equal angles

ISOGONAL *n pl.* **-S** isogone

ISOGONE *n pl.* **-S** a line on a map used to show characteristics of the earth's magnetic field

ISOGONIC *n pl.* **-S** isogone

ISOGONY *n pl.* **-NIES** an equivalent relative growth of parts

ISOGRAFT *v* **-ED, -ING, -S** to transplant from one individual to another of the same species

ISOGRAM *n pl.* **-S** a line on a map connecting points of equal value

ISOGRAPH *n pl.* **-S** a line on a map indicating areas that are linguistically similar

ISOGRIV *n pl.* **-S** a line drawn on a map such that all points have equal grid variation

ISOHEL *n pl.* **-S** a line on a map connecting points receiving equal sunshine

ISOHYET *n pl.* **-S** a line on a map connecting points having equal rainfall

ISOLABLE *adj* capable of being isolated

ISOLATE *v* **-LATED, -LATING, -LATES** to set apart from others

ISOLATOR *n pl.* **-S** one that isolates

ISOLEAD *n pl.* **-S** a line on a ballistic graph

ISOLINE *n pl.* **-S** an isogram

ISOLOG *n pl.* **-S** isologue

ISOLOGUE *n pl.* **-S** a type of chemical compound

ISOMER *n pl.* **-S** a type of chemical compound **ISOMERIC** *adj*

ISOMETRY *n pl.* **-TRIES** equality of measure

ISOMORPH *n pl.* **-S** something similar to something else in form

ISONOMY *n pl.* **-MIES** equality of civil rights **ISONOMIC** *adj*

ISOPACH *n pl.* **-S** an isogram connecting points of equal thickness

ISOPHOTE *n pl.* **-S** a curve on a chart joining points of equal light intensity

ISOPLETH *n pl.* **-S** a type of isogram

ISOPOD *n pl.* **-S** a kind of crustacean

ISOPODAN *n pl.* **-S** an isopod

ISOPRENE *n pl.* **-S** a volatile liquid

ISOSPIN *n pl.* **-S** a type of quantum number

ISOSPORY *n pl.* **-RIES** the condition of producing sexual or asexual spores of but one kind

ISOSTACY *n pl.* **-CIES** isostasy

ISOSTASY *n pl.* **-SIES** the state of balance in the earth's crust

ISOTACH *n pl.* **-S** a line on a map connecting points of equal wind velocity

ISOTHERE *n pl.* **-S** a type of isotherm

ISOTHERM *n pl.* **-S** a line on a map connecting points of equal mean temperature

ISOTONE *n pl.* **-S** a type of atom

ISOTONIC *adj* of equal tension

ISOTOPE *n pl.* **-S** a form of an element **ISOTOPIC** *adj*

ISOTOPY	*n* pl. **-PIES** the state of being an isotope
ISOTROPY	*n* pl. **-PIES** the state of being identical in all directions
ISOTYPE	*n* pl. **-S** a type of diagram **ISOTYPIC** *adj*
ISOZYME	*n* pl. **-S** a type of enzyme **ISOZYMIC** *adj*
ISSEI	*n* pl. **-S** a Japanese immigrant to the United States
ISSUABLE	*adj* authorized for issuing **ISSUABLY** *adv*
ISSUANCE	*n* pl. **-S** the act of issuing
ISSUANT	*adj* coming forth
ISSUE	*v* **-SUED, -SUING, -SUES** to come forth
ISSUER	*n* pl. **-S** one that issues
ISTHMI	a pl. of isthmus
ISTHMIAN	*n* pl. **-S** a native of an isthmus
ISTHMIC	*adj* pertaining to an isthmus
ISTHMOID	*adj* isthmic
ISTHMUS	*n* pl. **-MUSES** or **-MI** a strip of land connecting two larger land masses
ISTLE	*n* pl. **-S** a strong fiber
IT	*pron* the 3d person sing. neuter pronoun
ITALIC	*n* pl. **-S** a style of print
ITCH	*v* **-ED, -ING, -ES** to have an uneasy or tingling skin sensation
ITCHING	*n* pl. **-S** an uneasy or tingling skin sensation
ITCHY	*adj* **ITCHIER, ITCHIEST** causing an itching sensation **ITCHILY** *adv*

ITEM	*v* **-ED, -ING, -S** to itemize
ITEMISE	*v* **-ISED, -ISING, -ISES** to itemize
ITEMISER	*n* **-S** itemizer
ITEMIZE	*v* **-IZED, -IZING, -IZES** to set down the particulars of
ITEMIZER	*n* pl. **-S** one that itemizes
ITERANCE	*n* pl. **-S** repetition
ITERANT	*adj* repeating
ITERATE	*v* **-ATED, -ATING, -ATES** to repeat
ITERUM	*adv* again; once more
ITHER	*adj* other
ITS	*pron* the possessive form of the pronoun it
ITSELF	*pron* a reflexive form of the pronoun it
IVORY	*n* pl. **-RIES** a hard white substance found in elephant tusks **IVORIED** *adj*
IVY	*n* pl. **IVIES** a climbing vine **IVYLIKE** *adj* **IVIED** *adj*
IWIS	*adv* certainly
IXIA	*n* pl. **-S** a flowering plant
IXNAY	*interj* no
IXODID	*n* pl. **-S** a bloodsucking insect
IXORA	*n* pl. **-S** a flowering plant
IXTLE	*n* pl. **-S** istle
IZAR	*n* pl. **-S** an outer garment worn by Muslim women
IZARD	*n* pl. **-S** a goatlike antelope
IZZARD	*n* pl. **-S** the letter Z

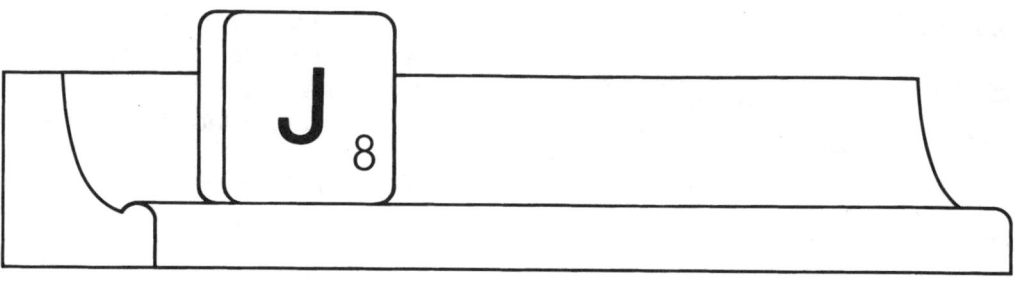

JAB	*v* **JABBED, JABBING, JABS** to poke sharply
JABBER	*v* **-ED, -ING, -S** to talk rapidly
JABBERER	*n* pl. **-S** one that jabbers
JABIRU	*n* pl. **-S** a wading bird
JABOT	*n* pl. **-S** a decoration on a shirt
JACAL	*n* pl. **-S** or **-ES** a hut
JACAMAR	*n* pl. **-S** a tropical bird
JACANA	*n* pl. **-S** a wading bird
JACINTH	*n* pl. **-S** a variety of zircon
JACINTHE	*n* pl. **-S** an orange color
JACK	*v* **-ED, -ING, -S** to raise with a type of lever
JACKAL	*n* pl. **-S** a doglike mammal
JACKAROO	*n* pl. **-ROOS** jackeroo
JACKASS	*n* pl. **-ES** a male donkey
JACKBOOT	*n* pl. **-S** a heavy boot
JACKDAW	*n* pl. **-S** a bird resembling a crow
JACKER	*n* pl. **-S** one that jacks
JACKEROO	*n* pl. **-ROOS** an inexperienced ranch hand
JACKET	*v* **-ED, -ING, -S** to provide with a jacket (a short coat)
JACKFISH	*n* pl. **-ES** a food fish
JACKIES	pl. of jacky
JACKLEG	*n* pl. **-S** an unskilled worker
JACKPOT	*n* pl. **-S** a top prize or reward
JACKROLL	*v* **-ED, -ING, -S** to rob a drunken or sleeping person
JACKSTAY	*n* pl. **-STAYS** a rope on a ship
JACKY	*n* pl. **JACKIES** a sailor
JACOBIN	*n* pl. **-S** a pigeon
JACOBUS	*n* pl. **-ES** an old English coin
JACONET	*n* pl. **-S** a cotton cloth
JACQUARD	*n* pl. **-S** a fabric of intricate weave
JACULATE	*v* **-LATED, -LATING, -LATES** to throw
JADE	*v* **JADED, JADING, JADES** to weary **JADEDLY** *adv*
JADEITE	*n* pl. **-S** a mineral **JADITIC** *adj*
JADELIKE	*adj* resembling jade (a green gemstone)
JADISH	*adj* worn-out **JADISHLY** *adv*
JAEGER	*n* pl. **-S** a hunter
JAG	*v* **JAGGED, JAGGING, JAGS** to cut unevenly
JAGER	*n* pl. **-S** jaeger
JAGG	*v* **-ED, -ING, -S** to jag
JAGGARY	*n* pl. **-RIES** jaggery
JAGGED	*adj* **-GEDER, -GEDEST** having a sharply uneven edge or surface **JAGGEDLY** *adv*
JAGGER	*n* pl. **-S** one that jags
JAGGERY	*n* pl. **-GERIES** a coarse, dark sugar
JAGGHERY	*n* pl. **-GHERIES** jaggery
JAGGIES	*n/pl* a jagged effect on a curved line
JAGGING	present participle of jag
JAGGY	*adj* **-GIER, -GIEST** jagged
JAGLESS	*adj* smooth and even
JAGRA	*n* pl. **-S** jaggery
JAGUAR	*n* pl. **-S** a large feline animal
JAIL	*v* **-ED, -ING, -S** to put in jail (a place of confinement) **JAILABLE** *adj*
JAILBIRD	*n* pl. **-S** a prisoner
JAILER	*n* pl. **-S** a keeper of a jail
JAILOR	*n* pl. **-S** jailer
JAKE	*adj* all right; fine
JAKES	*n/pl* an outhouse
JALAP	*n* pl. **-S** a Mexican plant **JALAPIC** *adj*

JALAPENO	*n* pl. **-NOS** a hot pepper
JALAPIN	*n* pl. **-S** a medicinal substance contained in jalap
JALOP	*n* pl. **-S** jalap
JALOPPY	*n* pl. **-PIES** jalopy
JALOPY	*n* pl. **-LOPIES** a decrepit car
JALOUSIE	*n* pl. **-S** a type of window
JAM	*v* **JAMMED, JAMMING, JAMS** to force together tightly **JAMMABLE** *adj*
JAMB	*v* **-ED, -ING, -S** to jam
JAMBE	*n* pl. **-S** a jambeau
JAMBEAU	*n* pl. **-BEAUX** or **-BEAUS** a piece of armor for the leg
JAMBOREE	*n* pl. **-S** a noisy celebration
JAMLIKE	*adj* resembling jam
JAMMED	past tense of jam
JAMMER	*n* pl. **-S** one that jams
JAMMIES	*n/pl* pajamas
JAMMING	present participle of jam
JAMMY	*adj* **-MIER, -MIEST** sticky with jam (boiled fruit and sugar)
JANE	*n* pl. **-S** a girl or woman
JANGLE	*v* **-GLED, -GLING, -GLES** to make a harsh, metallic sound
JANGLER	*n* pl. **-S** one that jangles
JANGLY	*adj* **-GLIER, -GLIEST** jangling
JANIFORM	*adj* hypocritical
JANISARY	*n* pl. **-SARIES** janizary
JANITOR	*n* pl. **-S** a maintenance man
JANIZARY	*n* pl. **-ZARIES** a Turkish soldier
JANNEY	*v* **-ED, -ING, -S** to janny
JANNY	*v* **-NIED, -NYING, -NIES** to act as a disguised merrymaker at Christmas
JANNYING	*n* pl. **-S** the action of one that jannies
JANTY	*adj* jaunty
JAPAN	*v* **-PANNED, -PANNING, -PANS** to coat with a glossy, black lacquer
JAPANIZE	*v* **-NIZED, -NIZING, -NIZES** to make Japanese
JAPANNER	*n* pl. **-S** one that japans
JAPE	*v* **JAPED, JAPING, JAPES** to mock
JAPER	*n* pl. **-S** one that japes
JAPERY	*n* pl. **-ERIES** mockery
JAPING	present participle of jape

JAPINGLY	*adv* in a japing manner
JAPONICA	*n* pl. **-S** an Asian shrub
JAR	*v* **JARRED, JARRING, JARS** to cause to shake
JARFUL	*n* pl. **JARFULS** or **JARSFUL** the quantity held by a jar (a cylindrical container)
JARGON	*v* **-ED, -ING, -S** to speak or write an obscure and often pretentious kind of language
JARGONEL	*n* pl. **-S** a variety of pear
JARGONY	*adj* characterized by the use of obscure language
JARGOON	*n* pl. **-S** a variety of zircon
JARHEAD	*n* pl. **-S** a marine soldier
JARINA	*n* pl. **-S** the hard seed of a palm tree
JARL	*n* pl. **-S** a Scandinavian nobleman
JARLDOM	*n* pl. **-S** the domain of a jarl
JAROSITE	*n* pl. **-S** a mineral
JAROVIZE	*v* **-VIZED, -VIZING, -VIZES** to hasten the flowering of a plant
JARRAH	*n* pl. **-S** an evergreen tree
JARRED	past tense of jar
JARRING	present participle of jar
JARSFUL	a pl. of jarful
JARVEY	*n* pl. **-VEYS** the driver of a carriage for hire
JASMIN	*n* pl. **-S** jasmine
JASMINE	*n* pl. **-S** a climbing shrub
JASPER	*n* pl. **-S** a variety of quartz **JASPERY** *adj*
JASSID	*n* pl. **-S** any of a family of plant pests
JATO	*n* pl. **-TOS** a takeoff aided by jet propulsion
JAUK	*v* **-ED, -ING, -S** to dawdle
JAUNCE	*v* **JAUNCED, JAUNCING, JAUNCES** to prance
JAUNDICE	*v* **-DICED, -DICING, -DICES** to prejudice unfavorably
JAUNT	*v* **-ED, -ING, -S** to make a pleasure trip
JAUNTY	*adj* **-TIER, -TIEST** having a lively and self-confident manner **JAUNTILY** *adv*
JAUP	*v* **-ED, -ING, -S** to splash
JAVA	*n* pl. **-S** coffee
JAVELIN	*v* **-ED, -ING, -S** to pierce with a javelin (a light spear)

JAVELINA	*n* pl. **-S** a peccary
JAW	*v* **-ED, -ING, -S** to jabber
JAWAN	*n* pl. **-S** a soldier of India
JAWBONE	*v* **-BONED, -BONING, -BONES** to attempt to convince
JAWBONER	*n* pl. **-S** one that jawbones
JAWLESS	*adj* having no jaw (a bony structure bordering the mouth)
JAWLIKE	*adj* resembling the jaw (the framework of the mouth)
JAWLINE	*n* pl. **-S** the outline of the lower jaw
JAY	*n* pl. **JAYS** a corvine bird
JAYBIRD	*n* pl. **-S** a jay
JAYGEE	*n* pl. **-S** a military officer
JAYVEE	*n* pl. **-S** a junior varsity player
JAYWALK	*v* **-ED, -ING, -S** to cross a street recklessly
JAZZ	*v* **-ED, -ING, -ES** to enliven
JAZZBO	*n* pl. **-BOS** a devotee of jazz (a style of lively syncopated music)
JAZZER	*n* pl. **-S** one that jazzes
JAZZLIKE	*adj* resembling a type of music
JAZZMAN	*n* pl. **-MEN** a type of musician
JAZZY	*adj* **JAZZIER, JAZZIEST** lively **JAZZILY** *adv*
JEALOUS	*adj* resentful of another's advantages
JEALOUSY	*n* pl. **-SIES** a jealous feeling
JEAN	*n* pl. **-S** a durable cotton fabric **JEANED** *adj*
JEBEL	*n* pl. **-S** a mountain
JEE	*v* **JEED, JEEING, JEES** to gee
JEEP	*v* **-ED, -ING, -S** to travel by a small type of motor vehicle
JEEPERS	*interj* — used as a mild oath
JEEPNEY	*n* pl. **-NEYS** a Philippine jitney
JEER	*v* **-ED, -ING, -S** to mock
JEERER	*n* pl. **-S** one that jeers
JEESLY	*adj* jeezly
JEEZ	*interj* — used as a mild oath
JEEZE	*interj* jeez
JEEZELY	*adj* jeezly
JEEZLY	*adj* used as an intensifier
JEFE	*n* pl. **-S** a chief
JEHAD	*n* pl. **-S** jihad
JEHADI	*n* pl. **-S** jihadi
JEHADIST	*n* pl. **-S** jihadist
JEHU	*n* pl. **-S** a fast driver
JEJUNA	pl. of jejunum
JEJUNAL	*adj* pertaining to the jejunum
JEJUNE	*adj* uninteresting; childish **JEJUNELY** *adv*
JEJUNITY	*n* pl. **-TIES** something that is jejune
JEJUNUM	*n* pl. **-NA** or **-NUMS** a part of the small intestine
JELL	*v* **-ED, -ING, -S** to congeal
JELLABA	*n* pl. **-S** djellaba
JELLIFY	*v* **-FIED, -FYING, -FIES** to jelly
JELLY	*v* **-LIED, -LYING, -LIES** to make into a jelly (a soft, semisolid substance)
JELUTONG	*n* pl. **-S** a tropical tree
JEMADAR	*n* pl. **-S** an officer in the army of India
JEMIDAR	*n* pl. **-S** jemadar
JEMMY	*v* **-MIED, -MYING, -MIES** to jimmy
JENNET	*n* pl. **-S** a small horse
JENNY	*n* pl. **-NIES** a female donkey
JEON	*n* pl. **JEON** a monetary unit of South Korea
JEOPARD	*v* **-ED, -ING, -S** to imperil
JEOPARDY	*n* pl. **-DIES** risk of loss or injury
JERBOA	*n* pl. **-S** a small rodent
JEREED	*n* pl. **-S** a wooden javelin
JEREMIAD	*n* pl. **-S** a tale of woe
JERID	*n* pl. **-S** jereed
JERK	*v* **-ED, -ING, -S** to move with a sharp, sudden motion
JERKER	*n* pl. **-S** one that jerks
JERKIN	*n* pl. **-S** a sleeveless jacket
JERKY	*adj* **JERKIER, JERKIEST** characterized by jerking movements **JERKILY** *adv*
JERKY	*n* pl. **-KIES** dried meat
JEROBOAM	*n* pl. **-S** a wine bottle
JERREED	*n* pl. **-S** jereed
JERRICAN	*n* pl. **-S** jerrycan
JERRID	*n* pl. **-S** jereed
JERRY	*n* pl. **-RIES** a German soldier
JERRYCAN	*n* pl. **-S** a fuel container
JERSEY	*n* pl. **-SEYS** a close-fitting knitted shirt **JERSEYED** *adj*
JESS	*v* **-ED, -ING, -ES** to fasten straps around the legs of a hawk
JESSANT	*adj* shooting forth

JESSE	*v* **JESSED, JESSING, JESSES** to jess
JEST	*v* **-ED, -ING, -S** to joke
JESTER	*n* pl. **-S** one that jests
JESTFUL	*adj* tending to jest
JESTING	*n* pl. **-S** the act of one who jests
JET	*v* **JETTED, JETTING, JETS** to spurt forth in a stream
JETBEAD	*n* pl. **-S** an ornamental shrub
JETE	*n* pl. **-S** a ballet leap
JETFOIL	*n* pl. **-S** a jet-powered hydrofoil (a boat with winglike structures for lifting the hull above the water)
JETLAG	*n* pl. **-S** the disruption of body rhythms after a flight through several time zones
JETLIKE	*adj* resembling a jet airplane
JETLINER	*n* pl. **-S** a type of aircraft
JETON	*n* pl. **-S** jetton
JETPACK	*n* pl. **-S** a backpack with jets to transport the wearer
JETPORT	*n* pl. **-S** a type of airport
JETSAM	*n* pl. **-S** goods cast overboard
JETSOM	*n* pl. **-S** jetsam
JETTED	past tense of jet
JETTIED	past tense of jetty
JETTIER	comparative of jetty
JETTIES	present 3d person sing. of jetty
JETTIEST	superlative of jetty
JETTING	present participle of jet
JETTISON	*v* **-ED, -ING, -S** to cast overboard
JETTON	*n* pl. **-S** a piece used in counting
JETTY	*adj* **-TIER, -TIEST** having the color jet black
JETTY	*v* **-TIED, -TYING, -TIES** to jut
JEU	*n* pl. **JEUX** a game
JEWEL	*v* **-ELED, -ELING, -ELS** or **-ELLED, -ELLING, -ELS** to adorn or equip with jewels (precious stones)
JEWELER	*n* pl. **-S** a dealer or maker of jewelry
JEWELLER	*n* pl. **-S** jeweler
JEWELRY	*n* pl. **-RIES** an article or articles for personal adornment
JEWFISH	*n* pl. **-ES** a large marine fish
JEZAIL	*n* pl. **-S** a type of firearm
JEZEBEL	*n* pl. **-S** a scheming, wicked woman
JIAO	*n* pl. **JIAO** chiao
JIB	*v* **JIBBED, JIBBING, JIBS** to refuse to proceed further
JIBB	*v* **-ED, -ING, -S** to shift from side to side while sailing
JIBBA	*n* pl. **-S** a long coat worn by Muslim men
JIBBAH	*n* pl. **-S** jibba
JIBBER	*n* pl. **-S** a horse that jibs
JIBBOOM	*n* pl. **-S** a ship's spar
JIBE	*v* **JIBED, JIBING, JIBES** to gibe **JIBINGLY** *adv*
JIBER	*n* pl. **-S** one that jibes
JICAMA	*n* pl. **-S** a tropical plant with edible roots
JIFF	*n* pl. **-S** jiffy
JIFFY	*n* pl. **-FIES** a short time
JIG	*v* **JIGGED, JIGGING, JIGS** to bob
JIGGER	*v* **-ED, -ING, -S** to jerk up and down
JIGGERED	*adj* damned
JIGGIER	comparative of jiggy
JIGGIEST	superlative of jiggy
JIGGISH	*adj* suitable for a jig (a lively dance)
JIGGLE	*v* **-GLED, -GLING, -GLES** to shake lightly
JIGGLY	*adj* **-GLIER, -GLIEST** unsteady
JIGGY	*adj* **-GIER, -GIEST** pleasurably excited
JIGLIKE	*adj* resembling a jig
JIGSAW	*v* **-SAWED, -SAWN, -SAWING, -SAWS** to cut with a type of saw
JIHAD	*n* pl. **-S** a Muslim holy war
JIHADI	*n* pl. **-S** a Muslim who participates in a jihad
JIHADIST	*n* pl. **-S** a jihadi
JILL	*n* pl. **-S** a unit of liquid measure
JILLION	*n* pl. **-S** a very large number
JILT	*v* **-ED, -ING, -S** to reject a lover
JILTER	*n* pl. **-S** one that jilts
JIMINY	*interj* — used to express surprise
JIMJAMS	*n/pl* violent delirium
JIMMIE	*n* pl. **-S** a tiny bit of candy for decorating ice cream
JIMMINY	*interj* jiminy
JIMMY	*v* **-MIED, -MYING, -MIES** to pry open with a crowbar

JIMP	*adj* **JIMPER, JIMPEST** natty **JIMPLY** *adv*
JIMPY	*adj* jimp
JIMSON	*n* pl. **-S** a tall poisonous weed
JIN	*n* pl. **-S** jinn
JINGAL	*n* pl. **-S** a heavy musket
JINGALL	*n* pl. **-S** jingal
JINGKO	*n* pl. **-KOES** ginkgo
JINGLE	*v* **-GLED, -GLING, -GLES** to make a tinkling sound
JINGLER	*n* pl. **-S** one that jingles
JINGLY	*adj* **-GLIER, -GLIEST** jingling
JINGO	*n* pl. **-GOES** a zealous patriot **JINGOISH** *adj*
JINGOISM	*n* pl. **-S** the spirit or policy of jingoes
JINGOIST	*n* pl. **-S** a jingo
JINK	*v* **-ED, -ING, -S** to move quickly out of the way
JINKER	*n* pl. **-S** one that jinks
JINN	*n* pl. **-S** a supernatural being in Muslim mythology
JINNEE	*n* pl. **JINN** jinn
JINNI	*n* pl. **-S** jinn
JINX	*v* **-ED, -ING, -ES** to bring bad luck to
JIPIJAPA	*n* pl. **-S** a tropical plant
JIRD	*n* pl. **-S** a long-tailed rodent
JITNEY	*n* pl. **-NEYS** a small bus
JITTER	*v* **-ED, -ING, -S** to fidget
JITTERY	*adj* **-TERIER, -TERIEST** extremely nervous
JIUJITSU	*n* pl. **-S** jujitsu
JIUJUTSU	*n* pl. **-S** jujitsu
JIVE	*v* **JIVED, JIVING, JIVES** to play jazz or swing music
JIVE	*adj* **JIVER, JIVEST** deceitful
JIVER	*n* pl. **-S** one that jives
JIVEY	*adj* **JIVIER, JIVIEST** jazzy, lively
JIVING	present participle of jive
JIVY	*adj* jivey
JNANA	*n* pl. **-S** knowledge acquired through meditation
JO	*n* pl. **JOES** a sweetheart
JOANNES	*n* pl. **JOANNES** johannes
JOB	*v* **JOBBED, JOBBING, JOBS** to work by the piece
JOBBER	*n* pl. **-S** a pieceworker
JOBBERY	*n* pl. **-BERIES** corruption in public office
JOBBIE	*n* pl. **-S** an example of its type
JOBLESS	*adj* having no job
JOBNAME	*n* pl. **-S** a computer code for a job instruction
JOCK	*n* pl. **-S** an athletic supporter
JOCKDOM	*n* pl. **-S** the world of athletes
JOCKETTE	*n* pl. **-S** a woman who rides horses in races
JOCKEY	*v* **-EYED, -EYING, -EYS** to maneuver for an advantage
JOCKISH	*adj* characteristic of an athlete
JOCKO	*n* pl. **JOCKOS** a monkey
JOCKY	*adj* **JOCKIER, JOCKIEST** resembling an athlete
JOCOSE	*adj* humorous **JOCOSELY** *adv*
JOCOSITY	*n* pl. **-TIES** the state of being jocose
JOCULAR	*adj* given to joking
JOCUND	*adj* cheerful **JOCUNDLY** *adv*
JODHPUR	*n* pl. **-S** a type of boot
JOE	*n* pl. **-S** a fellow
JOEY	*n* pl. **-EYS** a young kangaroo
JOG	*v* **JOGGED, JOGGING, JOGS** to run at a slow, steady pace
JOGGER	*n* pl. **-S** one that jogs
JOGGING	*n* pl. **-S** the practice of running at a slow, steady pace
JOGGLE	*v* **-GLED, -GLING, -GLES** to shake slightly
JOGGLER	*n* pl. **-S** one that joggles
JOGTROT	*n* pl. **-S** a slow regular way of walking or running
JOHANNES	*n* pl. **JOHANNES** a Portuguese coin
JOHN	*n* pl. **-S** a toilet
JOHNBOAT	*n* pl. **-S** a narrow square-ended boat
JOHNNIE	*n* pl. **-S** johnny
JOHNNY	*n* pl. **-NIES** a sleeveless hospital gown
JOIN	*v* **-ED, -ING, -S** to unite **JOINABLE** *adj*
JOINDER	*n* pl. **-S** a joining of parties in a lawsuit
JOINER	*n* pl. **-S** a carpenter
JOINERY	*n* pl. **-ERIES** the trade of a joiner
JOINING	*n* pl. **-S** a juncture

JOINT	v **-ED, -ING, -S** to fit together by means of a junction	**JORDAN**	n pl. **-S** a type of container
JOINTER	n pl. **-S** one that joints	**JORUM**	n pl. **-S** a large drinking bowl
JOINTLY	adv together	**JOSEPH**	n pl. **-S** a woman's long cloak
JOINTURE	v **-TURED, -TURING, -TURES** to set aside property as an inheritance	**JOSH**	v **-ED, -ING, -ES** to tease
		JOSHER	n pl. **-S** one that joshes
		JOSHING	n pl. **-S** the act of teasing
JOIST	v **-ED, -ING, -S** to support with horizontal beams	**JOSS**	n pl. **-ES** a Chinese idol
JOJOBA	n pl. **-S** a small tree	**JOSTLE**	v **-TLED, -TLING, -TLES** to bump or push roughly
JOKE	v **JOKED, JOKING, JOKES** to say something amusing	**JOSTLER**	n pl. **-S** one that jostles
		JOT	v **JOTTED, JOTTING, JOTS** to write down quickly
JOKER	n pl. **-S** one that jokes	**JOTA**	n pl. **-S** a Spanish dance
JOKESTER	n pl. **-S** a practical joker	**JOTTER**	n pl. **-S** one that jots
JOKEY	adj **JOKIER, JOKIEST** amusing **JOKILY** adv	**JOTTING**	n pl. **-S** a brief note
JOKIER	comparative of joky	**JOTTY**	adj written down quickly
JOKIEST	superlative of joky	**JOUAL**	n pl. **-S** a dialect of Canadian French
JOKINESS	n pl. **-ES** the state of being jokey		
JOKING	present participle of joke	**JOUK**	v **-ED, -ING, -S** to dodge
JOKINGLY	adv in a joking manner	**JOULE**	n pl. **-S** a unit of energy
JOKY	adj **JOKIER, JOKIEST** jokey	**JOUNCE**	v **JOUNCED, JOUNCING, JOUNCES** to move roughly up and down
JOLE	n pl. **-S** jowl		
JOLLIED	past tense of jolly	**JOUNCY**	adj **JOUNCIER, JOUNCIEST** marked by a jouncing motion
JOLLIER	n pl. **-S** one who puts others in good humor		
		JOURNAL	v **-ED, -ING, -S** to enter in a daily record
JOLLIES	present 3d person sing. of jolly		
JOLLIEST	superlative of jolly	**JOURNEY**	v **-ED, -ING, -S** to travel
JOLLIFY	v **-FIED, -FYING, -FIES** to make jolly	**JOURNO**	n pl. **-NOS** a writer for a news medium
JOLLITY	n pl. **-TIES** mirth	**JOUST**	v **-ED, -ING, -S** to engage in personal combat
JOLLY	adj **-LIER, -LIEST** cheerful **JOLLILY** adv		
		JOUSTER	n pl. **-S** one that jousts
JOLLY	v **-LIED, -LYING, -LIES** to put in a good humor for one's own purposes	**JOVIAL**	adj good-humored **JOVIALLY** adv
		JOVIALTY	n pl. **-TIES** the quality or state of being jovial
JOLT	v **-ED, -ING, -S** to jar or shake roughly	**JOW**	v **-ED, -ING, -S** to toll
JOLTER	n pl. **-S** one that jolts	**JOWAR**	n pl. **-S** a durra grown in India
JOLTY	adj **JOLTIER, JOLTIEST** marked by a jolting motion **JOLTILY** adv	**JOWL**	n pl. **-S** the fleshy part under the lower jaw **JOWLED** adj
JOMON	adj pertaining to a Japanese cultural period	**JOWLY**	adj **JOWLIER, JOWLIEST** having prominent jowls
JONES	v **-ED, -ING, -ES** to have a strong craving for something	**JOY**	v **-ED, -ING, -S** to rejoice
		JOYANCE	n pl. **-S** gladness
JONGLEUR	n pl. **-S** a minstrel	**JOYFUL**	adj **-FULLER, -FULLEST** happy **JOYFULLY** adv
JONQUIL	n pl. **-S** a perennial herb		
JOOK	n pl. **-S** a tavern that has a jukebox	**JOYLESS**	adj being without gladness
JORAM	n pl. **-S** jorum	**JOYOUS**	adj joyful **JOYOUSLY** adv

JOYPAD   *n* pl. **-S** a device with buttons to control computer images

JOYPOP   *v* **-POPPED, -POPPING, -POPS** to use habit-forming drugs occasionally

JOYRIDE   *v* **-RODE, -RIDDEN, -RIDING, -RIDES** to take an automobile ride for pleasure

JOYRIDER   *n* pl. **-S** one that joyrides

JOYSTICK   *n* pl. **-S** the control stick in an airplane

JUBA   *n* pl. **-S** a lively dance

JUBBAH   *n* pl. **-S** a loose outer garment

JUBE   *n* pl. **-S** a platform in a church

JUBHAH   *n* pl. **-S** jubbah

JUBILANT   *adj* exultant

JUBILATE   *v* **-LATED, -LATING, -LATES** to exult

JUBILE   *n* pl. **-S** jubilee

JUBILEE   *n* pl. **-S** a celebration

JUCO   *n* pl. **-COS** a junior college

JUDAS   *n* pl. **-ES** a peephole

JUDDER   *v* **-ED, -ING, -S** to vibrate

JUDDERY   *adj* vibrating

JUDGE   *v* **JUDGED, JUDGING, JUDGES** to decide on critically

JUDGER   *n* pl. **-S** one that judges

JUDGEY   *adj* judgy

JUDGMENT   *n* pl. **-S** an authoritative opinion

JUDGY   *adj* **JUDGIER, JUDGIEST** tending to judge others

JUDICARE   *n* pl. **-S** legal aid whereby lawyers are paid by the government for services to poor clients

JUDICIAL   *adj* pertaining to courts of law

JUDIES   pl. of judy

JUDO   *n* pl. **-DOS** a form of jujitsu

JUDOIST   *n* pl. **-S** one skilled in judo

JUDOKA   *n* pl. **-S** a judoist

JUDY   *n* pl. **JUDIES** a woman

JUG   *v* **JUGGED, JUGGING, JUGS** to put into a jug (a large, deep container with a narrow mouth and a handle)

JUGA   a pl. of jugum

JUGAL   *adj* pertaining to the cheek or cheekbone

JUGATE   *adj* occurring in pairs

JUGFUL   *n* pl. **JUGFULS** or **JUGSFUL** as much as a jug will hold

JUGGED   past tense of jug

JUGGING   present participle of jug

JUGGLE   *v* **-GLED, -GLING, -GLES** to perform feats of manual dexterity

JUGGLER   *n* pl. **-S** one that juggles

JUGGLERY   *n* pl. **-GLERIES** the art of a juggler

JUGGLING   *n* pl. **-S** jugglery

JUGHEAD   *n* pl. **-S** a dolt

JUGSFUL   a pl. of jugful

JUGULA   pl. of jugulum

JUGULAR   *n* pl. **-S** a vein of the neck

JUGULATE   *v* **-LATED, -LATING, -LATES** to suppress a disease by extreme measures

JUGULUM   *n* pl. **-LA** a part of a bird's neck

JUGUM   *n* pl. **-GUMS** or **-GA** a pair of the opposite leaflets of a pinnate leaf

JUICE   *v* **JUICED, JUICING, JUICES** to extract the juice (the liquid part of a fruit or vegetable) from

JUICER   *n* pl. **-S** a juice extractor

JUICY   *adj* **JUICIER, JUICIEST** full of juice **JUICILY** *adv*

JUJITSU   *n* pl. **-S** a Japanese art of self-defense

JUJU   *n* pl. **-S** an object regarded as having magical power

JUJUBE   *n* pl. **-S** a fruit-flavored candy

JUJUISM   *n* pl. **-S** the system of beliefs connected with jujus

JUJUIST   *n* pl. **-S** a follower of jujuism

JUJUTSU   *n* pl. **-S** jujitsu

JUKE   *v* **JUKED, JUKING, JUKES** to fake out of position

JUKEBOX   *n* pl. **-ES** a coin-operated phonograph

JUKU   *n* pl. **-S** an additional school in Japan for preparing students for college

JULEP   *n* pl. **-S** a sweet drink

JULIENNE   *v* **-ENNED, -ENNING, -ENNES** to cut food into long thin strips

JUMAR   *v* **-MARED, -MARING, -MARS** or **-MARRED, -MARRING, -MARS** to climb with ropes using a type of clamp

JUMBAL   *n* pl. **-S** a ring-shaped cookie

JUMBIE   *n* pl. **-S** a spirit of a dead person

JUMBLE   v **-BLED, -BLING, -BLES** to mix in a disordered manner

JUMBLER   n pl. **-S** one that jumbles

JUMBO   n pl. **-BOS** a very large specimen of its kind

JUMBUCK   n pl. **-S** a sheep

JUMP   v **-ED, -ING, -S** to spring off the ground **JUMPABLE** adj

JUMPER   n pl. **-S** one that jumps

JUMPING   n pl. **-S** the act of one that jumps

JUMPOFF   n pl. **-S** a starting point

JUMPROPE   n pl. **-S** a rope used in children's games for jumping

JUMPSHOT   n pl. **-S** a type of shot in basketball

JUMPSIES   n/pl a game involving jumping over a taut rope

JUMPSUIT   n pl. **-S** a one-piece garment

JUMPY   adj **JUMPIER, JUMPIEST** nervous **JUMPILY** adv

JUN   n pl. **JUN** a coin of North Korea

JUNCO   n pl. **-COS** or **-COES** a small finch

JUNCTION   n pl. **-S** a place where things join

JUNCTURE   n pl. **-S** the act of joining

JUNGLE   n pl. **-S** land covered with dense tropical vegetation **JUNGLED** adj

JUNGLIST   n pl. **-S** a performer of a style of fast dance music

JUNGLY   adj **-GLIER, -GLIEST** resembling a jungle

JUNIOR   n pl. **-S** a person who is younger than another

JUNIPER   n pl. **-S** an evergreen tree

JUNK   v **-ED, -ING, -S** to discard as trash

JUNKER   n pl. **-S** something ready for junking

JUNKET   v **-ED, -ING, -S** to banquet

JUNKETER   n pl. **-S** one that junkets

JUNKIE   n pl. **-S** a drug addict

JUNKMAN   n pl. **-MEN** one who buys and sells junk

JUNKY   adj **JUNKIER, JUNKIEST** worthless

JUNKYARD   n pl. **-S** a place where junk is stored

JUNTA   n pl. **-S** a political or governmental council

JUNTO   n pl. **-TOS** a political faction

JUPE   n pl. **-S** a woman's jacket

JUPON   n pl. **-S** a tunic

JURA   pl. of jus

JURAL   adj pertaining to law **JURALLY** adv

JURANT   n pl. **-S** one that takes an oath

JURAT   n pl. **-S** a statement on an affidavit

JURATORY   adj pertaining to an oath

JUREL   n pl. **-S** a food fish

JURIDIC   adj pertaining to the law

JURIST   n pl. **-S** one versed in the law **JURISTIC** adj

JUROR   n pl. **-S** a member of a jury (a committee for selecting material for exhibition)

JURY   v **-RIED, -RYING, -RIES** to select material for exhibition

JURYLESS   adj being without a jury

JURYMAN   n pl. **-MEN** a juror

JUS   n pl. **JURA** a legal right

JUSSIVE   n pl. **-S** a word used to express command

JUST   adj **JUSTER, JUSTEST** acting in conformity with what is morally good

JUST   v **-ED, -ING, -S** to joust

JUSTER   n pl. **-S** jouster

JUSTICE   n pl. **-S** a judge

JUSTIFY   v **-FIED, -FYING, -FIES** to show to be just, right, or valid

JUSTLE   v **-TLED, -TLING, -TLES** to jostle

JUSTLY   adv in a just manner

JUSTNESS   n pl. **-ES** the quality of being just

JUT   v **JUTTED, JUTTING, JUTS** to protrude

JUTE   n pl. **-S** a strong, coarse fiber

JUTELIKE   adj resembling jute

JUTTY   v **-TIED, -TYING, -TIES** to jut

JUVENAL   n pl. **-S** a young bird's plumage

JUVENILE   n pl. **-S** a young person

JUVIE   n pl. **-S** a juvenile delinquent

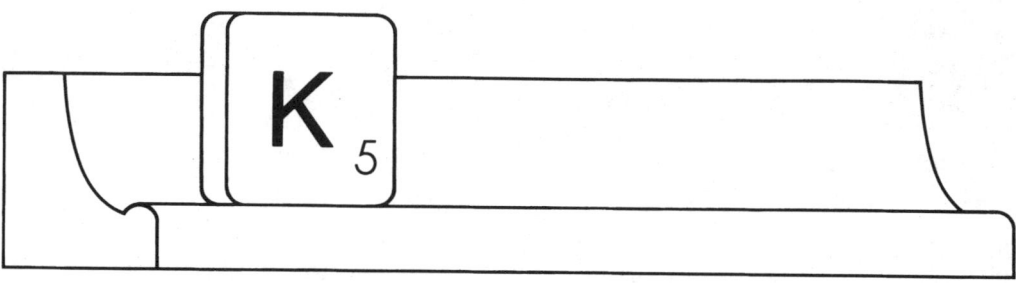

KA *n* pl. **-S** the spiritual self of a human being in Egyptian religion

KAAS *n* pl. **KAAS** kas

KAB *n* pl. **-S** an ancient Hebrew unit of measure

KABAB *n* pl. **-S** kabob

KABADDI *n* pl. **-S** a tackling sport of South Asia played by two teams

KABAKA *n* pl. **-S** a Ugandan emperor

KABALA *n* pl. **-S** cabala

KABALISM *n* pl. **-S** cabalism

KABALIST *n* pl. **-S** cabalist

KABAR *n* pl. **-S** caber

KABAYA *n* pl. **-S** a cotton jacket

KABBALA *n* pl. **-S** cabala

KABBALAH *n* pl. **-S** cabala

KABELJOU *n* pl. **-S** a large food fish

KABIKI *n* pl. **-S** a tropical tree

KABLOOEY *interj* — used to indicate an abrupt happening

KABLOOIE *interj* kablooey

KABLOONA *n* pl. **KABLOONAS** or **KABLOONAT** a person who is not an Inuit

KABOB *n* pl. **-S** cubes of meat cooked on a skewer

KABOCHA *n* pl. **-S** a type of Japanese pumpkin or squash

KABOODLE *n* pl. **-S** caboodle

KABOOM *n* pl. **-S** the sound of a loud explosion

KABUKI *n* pl. **-S** a form of Japanese theater

KACHINA *n* pl. **-S** an ancestral spirit

KADDISH *n* pl. **-DISHES** or **-DISHIM** a Jewish prayer

KADI *n* pl. **-S** cadi

KAE *n* pl. **-S** a bird resembling a crow

KAF *n* pl. **-S** kaph

KAFFIR *n* pl. **-S** kafir

KAFFIYAH *n* pl. **-S** kaffiyeh

KAFFIYEH *n* pl. **-S** a large, square kerchief

KAFIR *n* pl. **-S** a cereal grass

KAFTAN *n* pl. **-S** caftan

KAFUFFLE *n* pl. **-S** a disturbance or commotion

KAGU *n* pl. **-S** a flightless bird

KAHUNA *n* pl. **-S** a medicine man

KAIAK *n* pl. **-S** kayak

KAIF *n* pl. **-S** kef

KAIL *n* pl. **-S** kale

KAILYARD *n* pl. **-S** kaleyard

KAIN *n* pl. **-S** a tax paid in produce or livestock

KAINIT *n* pl. **-S** kainite

KAINITE *n* pl. **-S** a mineral salt

KAISER *n* pl. **-S** an emperor

KAISERIN *n* pl. **-S** a kaiser's wife

KAIZEN *n* pl. **-S** a Japanese business practice of continuous improvement

KAJEPUT *n* pl. **-S** cajuput

KAKA *n* pl. **-S** a parrot

KAKAPO *n* pl. **-POS** a flightless parrot

KAKEMONO *n* pl. **-NOS** a Japanese scroll

KAKI *n* pl. **-S** a Japanese tree

KAKIEMON *n* pl. **-S** a Japanese porcelain

KAKIVAK *n* pl. **-S** a fish spear used by the Inuits

KALAM *n* pl. **-S** a type of Muslim theology

KALAMATA *n* pl. **-S** a black olive grown in Greece

KALE *n* pl. **-S** a variety of cabbage

KALENDS *n* pl. **KALENDS** calends

KALEWIFE *n* pl. **-WIVES** a female vegetable vendor

KALEYARD	*n* pl. **-S** a kitchen garden
KALIAN	*n* pl. **-S** a hookah
KALIF	*n* pl. **-S** caliph
KALIFATE	*n* pl. **-S** califate
KALIMBA	*n* pl. **-S** an African musical instrument
KALIPH	*n* pl. **-S** caliph
KALIUM	*n* pl. **-S** potassium
KALLIDIN	*n* pl. **-S** a hormone
KALMIA	*n* pl. **-S** an evergreen shrub
KALONG	*n* pl. **-S** a fruit-eating bat
KALPA	*n* pl. **-S** a period of time in Hindu religion
KALPAC	*n* pl. **-S** calpac
KALPAK	*n* pl. **-S** calpac
KALYPTRA	*n* pl. **-S** a thin veil
KAMAAINA	*n* pl. **-S** a longtime resident of Hawaii
KAMACITE	*n* pl. **-S** an alloy of nickel and iron
KAMALA	*n* pl. **-S** an Asian tree
KAME	*n* pl. **-S** a mound of detrital material
KAMEEZ	*n* pl. **-ES** a long tunic worn by some people of India
KAMI	*n* pl. **KAMI** a sacred power or force
KAMIK	*n* pl. **-S** a type of boot
KAMIKAZE	*n* pl. **-S** a plane to be flown in a suicide crash on a target
KAMOTIK	*n* pl. **-S** komatik
KAMOTIQ	*n* pl. **-S** komatik
KAMPONG	*n* pl. **-S** a small village
KAMSEEN	*n* pl. **-S** khamsin
KAMSIN	*n* pl. **-S** khamsin
KANA	*n* pl. **-S** the Japanese syllabic script
KANBAN	*n* pl. **-S** a manufacturing strategy wherein parts are delivered only as needed
KANE	*n* pl. **-S** kain
KANGAROO	*n* pl. **-ROOS** an Australian mammal
KANJI	*n* pl. **-S** a system of Japanese writing
KANTAR	*n* pl. **-S** a unit of weight
KANTELE	*n* pl. **-S** a type of harp
KANZU	*n* pl. **-S** a long white garment worn in Africa
KAOLIANG	*n* pl. **-S** an Asian sorghum
KAOLIN	*n* pl. **-S** a fine white clay **KAOLINIC** *adj*
KAOLINE	*n* pl. **-S** kaolin
KAON	*n* pl. **-S** a type of meson **KAONIC** *adj*
KAPA	*n* pl. **-S** a coarse cloth
KAPEYKA	*n* pl. **KAPEEK** a monetary unit of Belarus
KAPH	*n* pl. **-S** a Hebrew letter
KAPOK	*n* pl. **-S** a mass of silky fibers
KAPOW	*n* pl. **-S** a sudden sharp sound
KAPPA	*n* pl. **-S** a Greek letter
KAPU	*n* pl. **-S** a Hawaiian set of rules for daily life
KAPUT	*adj* ruined
KAPUTT	*adj* kaput
KARAHI	*n* pl. **-S** a small frying pan used in India
KARAKUL	*n* pl. **-S** an Asian sheep
KARAOKE	*n* pl. **-S** a musical device to which a user sings along
KARAT	*n* pl. **-S** a unit of quality for gold
KARATE	*n* pl. **-S** a Japanese art of self-defense
KARMA	*n* pl. **-S** the force generated by a person's actions **KARMIC** *adj*
KARN	*n* pl. **-S** cairn
KAROO	*n* pl. **-ROOS** karroo
KAROSS	*n* pl. **-ES** an African garment
KARRI	*n* pl. **-S** an Australian eucalyptus
KARROO	*n* pl. **-ROOS** a dry plateau
KARST	*n* pl. **-S** a limestone region **KARSTIC** *adj*
KART	*n* pl. **-S** a small motor vehicle
KARTING	*n* pl. **-S** the sport of racing karts
KARYOTIN	*n* pl. **-S** the nuclear material of a cell
KAS	*n* pl. **KAS** a large cupboard
KASBAH	*n* pl. **-S** casbah
KASHA	*n* pl. **-S** a cooked cereal
KASHER	*v* **-ED, -ING, -S** to kosher
KASHMIR	*n* pl. **-S** cashmere
KASHRUT	*n* pl. **-S** kashruth
KASHRUTH	*n* pl. **-S** the Jewish dietary laws
KAT	*n* pl. **-S** an evergreen shrub
KATA	*n* pl. **-S** an exercise of set movements
KATAKANA	*n* pl. **-S** a Japanese syllabic symbol

KATANA *n* pl. **-S** a Japanese single-edged sword

KATCHINA *n* pl. **-S** kachina

KATCINA *n* pl. **-S** kachina

KATHODE *n* pl. **-S** cathode **KATHODAL, KATHODIC** *adj*

KATHUMP *n* pl. **-S** a loud thudding sound

KATION *n* pl. **-S** cation

KATSINA *n* pl. **-NAM** or **-NAS** kachina

KATSURA *n* pl. **-S** a deciduous tree of Japan and China

KATYDID *n* pl. **-S** a grasshopper

KAURI *n* pl. **-S** a timber tree

KAURY *n* pl. **-RIES** kauri

KAVA *n* pl. **-S** a tropical shrub

KAVAKAVA *n* pl. **-S** kava

KAVASS *n* pl. **-ES** a Turkish policeman

KAY *n* pl. **KAYS** the letter K

KAYAK *v* **-ED, -ING, -S** to travel in a kayak (an Inuit canoe)

KAYAKER *n* pl. **-S** one that rides in a kayak

KAYAKING *n* pl. **-S** the act or skill of managing a kayak

KAYLES *n/pl* a British game

KAYO *v* **-ED, -ING, -S** or **-ES** to knock out

KAZACHOC *n* pl. **-S** kazachok

KAZACHOK *n* pl. **-ZACHKI** a Russian folk dance

KAZATSKI *n* pl. **-ES** kazachok

KAZATSKY *n* pl. **-SKIES** kazachok

KAZOO *n* pl. **-ZOOS** a toy musical instrument

KBAR *n* pl. **-S** a kilobar

KEA *n* pl. **-S** a parrot

KEBAB *n* pl. **-S** kabob

KEBAR *n* pl. **-S** caber

KEBBIE *n* pl. **-S** a rough walking stick

KEBBOCK *n* pl. **-S** kebbuck

KEBBUCK *n* pl. **-S** a whole cheese

KEBLAH *n* pl. **-S** kiblah

KEBOB *n* pl. **-S** kabob

KECK *v* **-ED, -ING, -S** to retch

KECKLE *v* **-LED, -LING, -LES** to wind with rope to prevent chafing

KEDDAH *n* pl. **-S** an enclosure for elephants

KEDGE *v* **KEDGED, KEDGING, KEDGES** to move a vessel with the use of an anchor

KEDGEREE *n* pl. **-S** a food in India

KEEF *n* pl. **-S** kef

KEEK *v* **-ED, -ING, -S** to peep

KEEL *v* **-ED, -ING, -S** to capsize

KEELAGE *n* pl. **-S** the amount paid to keep a boat in a harbor

KEELBOAT *n* pl. **-S** a freight boat

KEELHALE *v* **-HALED, -HALING, -HALES** to keelhaul

KEELHAUL *v* **-ED, -ING, -S** to rebuke severely

KEELLESS *adj* having no keel (the main structural part of a ship)

KEELSON *n* pl. **-S** a beam in a ship

KEEN *adj* **KEENER, KEENEST** enthusiastic

KEEN *v* **-ED, -ING, -S** to wail loudly over the dead

KEENER *n* pl. **-S** one that keens

KEENING *n* pl. **-S** the act of wailing loudly over the dead

KEENLY *adv* in a keen manner

KEENNESS *n* pl. **-ES** sharpness

KEEP *v* **KEPT, KEEPING, KEEPS** to continue to possess **KEEPABLE** *adj*

KEEPER *n* pl. **-S** one that keeps

KEEPING *n* pl. **-S** custody

KEEPSAKE *n* pl. **-S** a memento

KEESHOND *n* pl. **-HONDS** or **-HONDEN** a small, heavy-coated dog

KEESTER *n* pl. **-S** keister

KEET *n* pl. **-S** a young guinea fowl

KEEVE *n* pl. **-S** a tub or vat

KEF *n* pl. **-S** hemp smoked to produce euphoria

KEFFIYAH *n* pl. **-S** kaffiyeh

KEFFIYEH *n* pl. **-S** kaffiyeh

KEFIR *n* pl. **-S** a fermented beverage made from cow's milk

KEG *v* **KEGGED, KEGGING, KEGS** to store in a keg (a small barrel)

KEGELER *n* pl. **-S** kegler

KEGGER *n* pl. **-S** a party having one or more kegs of beer

KEGLER *n* pl. **-S** a bowler

KEGLING *n* pl. **-S** bowling

KEIR	*n* pl. **-S** kier	**KEPT**	past tense of keep
KEIRETSU	*n* pl. **-S** a coalition of business groups in Japan	**KERAMIC**	*n* pl. **-S** ceramic
		KERATIN	*n* pl. **-S** a fibrous protein
KEISTER	*n* pl. **-S** the buttocks	**KERATOID**	*adj* horny
KEITLOA	*n* pl. **-S** a rhinoceros	**KERATOMA**	*n* pl. **-MAS** or **-MATA** a skin disease
KELEP	*n* pl. **-S** a stinging ant	
KELIM	*n* pl. **-S** kilim	**KERATOSE**	*adj* of or resembling horny tissue
KELLY	*n* pl. **-LIES** a bright green color	**KERB**	*v* **-ED, -ING, -S** to provide with curbing
KELOID	*n* pl. **-S** a scar caused by excessive growth of fibrous tissue **KELOIDAL** *adj*	
		KERBSIDE	*n* pl. **-S** curbside
KELP	*v* **-ED, -ING, -S** to burn a type of seaweed	**KERCHIEF**	*n* pl. **-CHIEFS** or **-CHIEVES** a cloth worn as a head covering
KELPFISH	*n* pl. **-ES** a fish that lives among seaweed	**KERCHOO**	*interj* ahchoo
		KERF	*v* **-ED, -ING, -S** to make an incision with a cutting tool
KELPIE	*n* pl. **-S** a water sprite	
KELPY	*n* pl. **-PIES** kelpie	**KERMES**	*n* pl. **KERMESES** a red dye
KELSON	*n* pl. **-S** keelson	**KERMESS**	*n* pl. **-ES** kermis
KELT	*n* pl. **-S** a salmon that has spawned	**KERMESSE**	*n* pl. **-S** kermis
KELTER	*n* pl. **-S** kilter	**KERMIS**	*n* pl. **-MISES** a festival
KELVIN	*n* pl. **-S** a unit of temperature	**KERMODE**	*n* pl. **-S** a type of black bear
KEMP	*n* pl. **-S** a champion	**KERN**	*v* **-ED, -ING, -S** to be formed with a projecting typeface
KEMPT	*adj* neatly kept	
KEMPY	*adj* **KEMPIER, KEMPIEST** having coarse hair or fibers	**KERNE**	*n* pl. **-S** a medieval foot soldier
		KERNEL	*v* **-NELED, -NELING, -NELS** or **-NELLED, -NELLING, -NELS** to envelop as a kernel (the inner part of a nut)
KEN	*v* **KENNED** or **KENT, KENNING, KENS** to know	
KENAF	*n* pl. **-S** an East Indian plant	**KERNELLY**	*adj* resembling kernels
KENCH	*n* pl. **-ES** a bin for salting fish	**KERNING**	*n* pl. **-S** the act of forming a projecting part of a typeface
KENDO	*n* pl. **-DOS** a Japanese sport	
KENDOIST	*n* pl. **-S** one skilled in kendo	**KERNITE**	*n* pl. **-S** a mineral
KENNED	a past tense of ken	**KEROGEN**	*n* pl. **-S** a substance found in shale
KENNEL	*v* **-NELED, -NELING, -NELS** or **-NELLED, -NELLING, -NELS** to keep in a shelter for dogs	**KEROSENE**	*n* pl. **-S** a fuel oil
		KEROSINE	*n* pl. **-S** kerosene
		KERPLUNK	*v* **-ED, -ING, -S** to fall or drop with a heavy sound
KENNING	*n* pl. **-S** a metaphorical compound word or phrase	
KENO	*n* pl. **-NOS** a game of chance	**KERRIA**	*n* pl. **-S** a Chinese shrub
KENOSIS	*n* pl. **-SISES** the incarnation of Christ **KENOTIC** *adj*	**KERRY**	*n* pl. **-RIES** one of an Irish breed of cattle
KENOTRON	*n* pl. **-S** a type of diode	**KERSEY**	*n* pl. **-SEYS** a woolen cloth
KENT	a past tense of ken	**KERYGMA**	*n* pl. **-MAS** or **-MATA** the preaching of the gospel
KENTE	*n* pl. **-S** a colorful fabric made in Ghana	
		KESTREL	*n* pl. **-S** a small falcon
KEP	*v* **KEPPED, KEPPEN** or **KIPPEN, KEPPING, KEPS** to catch	**KETA**	*n* pl. **-S** a type of salmon
		KETAINE	*adj* being in poor taste
KEPHALIN	*n* pl. **-S** cephalin	**KETAMINE**	*n* pl. **-S** a general anesthetic
KEPI	*n* pl. **-S** a type of cap	**KETCH**	*n* pl. **-ES** a sailing vessel

KETCHUP *n* pl. **-S** a spicy tomato sauce **KETCHUPY** *adj*

KETENE *n* pl. **-S** a toxic gas

KETO *adj* of or pertaining to ketone

KETOL *n* pl. **-S** a chemical compound

KETONE *n* pl. **-S** a type of chemical compound **KETONIC** *adj*

KETOSE *n* pl. **-S** a simple sugar

KETOSIS *n* pl. **-TOSES** a buildup of ketones in the body **KETOTIC** *adj*

KETTLE *n* pl. **-S** a vessel for boiling liquids

KEVEL *n* pl. **-S** a belaying cleat or peg

KEVIL *n* pl. **-S** kevel

KEX *n* pl. **-ES** a dry, hollow stalk

KEY *v* **-ED, -ING, -S** to provide with a key (a device used to turn the bolt in a lock)

KEYBOARD *v* **-ED, -ING, -S** to operate a machine by means of a keyset

KEYCARD *n* pl. **-S** a coded card for operating a device

KEYER *n* pl. **-S** a device that turns an electronic circuit on or off

KEYFRAME *n* pl. **-S** the frozen image in a sequence of animation

KEYHOLE *n* pl. **-S** a hole for a key

KEYLESS *adj* being without a key

KEYNOTE *v* **-NOTED, -NOTING, -NOTES** to deliver the main speech at a function

KEYNOTER *n* pl. **-S** one that keynotes

KEYPAD *n* pl. **-S** a small keyboard

KEYPAL *n* pl. **-S** a person with whom one corresponds by email

KEYPRESS *n* pl. **-ES** a single depression of a key on a keyset

KEYPUNCH *v* **-ED, -ING, -ES** to perforate with a machine

KEYSET *n* pl. **-S** a system of finger levers

KEYSTER *n* pl. **-S** keister

KEYSTONE *n* pl. **-S** the central stone of an arch

KEYWAY *n* pl. **-WAYS** a slot for a key

KEYWORD *n* pl. **-S** a significant word

KHADDAR *n* pl. **-S** a cotton cloth

KHADI *n* pl. **-S** khaddar

KHAF *n* pl. **-S** kaph

KHAKI *n* pl. **-S** a durable cloth

KHALIF *n* pl. **-S** caliph

KHALIFA *n* pl. **-S** caliph

KHAMSEEN *n* pl. **-S** khamsin

KHAMSIN *n* pl. **-S** a hot, dry wind

KHAN *n* pl. **-S** an Asian ruler

KHANATE *n* pl. **-S** the domain of a khan

KHAPH *n* pl. **-S** kaph

KHAT *n* pl. **-S** kat

KHAZEN *n* pl. **-ZENS** or **-ZENIM** hazzan

KHEDA *n* pl. **-S** keddah

KHEDAH *n* pl. **-S** keddah

KHEDIVE *n* pl. **-S** a Turkish viceroy **KHEDIVAL** *adj*

KHET *n* pl. **-S** heth

KHETH *n* pl. **-S** heth

KHI *n* pl. **-S** chi

KHIRKAH *n* pl. **-S** a patchwork garment

KHOUM *n* pl. **-S** a monetary unit of Mauritania

KI *n* pl. **KIS** qi

KIACK *n* pl. **-S** a fish of the herring family

KIANG *n* pl. **-S** a wild ass

KIAUGH *n* pl. **-S** trouble; worry

KIBBE *n* pl. **-S** a Near Eastern dish of ground lamb and bulgur

KIBBEH *n* pl. **-S** kibbe

KIBBI *n* pl. **-S** kibbe

KIBBITZ *v* **-ED, -ING, -ES** to kibitz

KIBBLE *v* **-BLED, -BLING, -BLES** to grind coarsely

KIBBUTZ *n* pl. **-BUTZIM** a collective farm in Israel

KIBE *n* pl. **-S** a sore caused by exposure to cold

KIBEI *n* pl. **-S** one born in America of immigrant Japanese parents and educated in Japan

KIBITKA *n* pl. **-S** a type of Russian sled or wagon

KIBITZ *v* **-ED, -ING, -ES** to meddle

KIBITZER *n* pl. **-S** one that kibitzes

KIBLA *n* pl. **-S** kiblah

KIBLAH *n* pl. **-S** the direction toward which Muslims face while praying

KIBOSH *v* **-ED, -ING, -ES** to stop

KICK *v* **-ED, -ING, -S** to strike out with the foot or feet **KICKABLE** *adj*

KICKBACK *n* pl. **-S** a strong reaction

KICKBALL *n* pl. **-S** baseball using an inflated ball that is kicked

KICKBOX   *v* **-ED, -ING, -ES** to box in a style that allows kicking

KICKER   *n* pl. **-S** one that kicks

KICKIER   comparative of kicky

KICKIEST   superlative of kicky

KICKING   *n* pl. **-S** the act of striking with the foot

KICKOFF   *n* pl. **-S** the kick that begins play in football

KICKSHAW   *n* pl. **-S** a trifle or trinket

KICKUP   *n* pl. **-S** a noisy argument

KICKY   *adj* **KICKIER, KICKIEST** exciting

KID   *v* **KIDDED, KIDDING, KIDS** to tease

KIDDER   *n* pl. **-S** one that kids

KIDDIE   *n* pl. **-S** a small child

KIDDIES   pl. of kiddy

KIDDING   present participle of kid

KIDDISH   *adj* childish

KIDDO   *n* pl. **-DOS** or **-DOES** — used as a form of familiar address

KIDDUSH   *n* pl. **-ES** a Jewish prayer

KIDDY   *n* pl. **-DIES** kiddie

KIDLIKE   *adj* resembling a child

KIDLIT   *n* pl. **-S** literature for children

KIDNAP   *v* **-NAPED, -NAPING, -NAPS** or **-NAPPED, -NAPPING, -NAPS** to take a person by force and often for ransom

KIDNAPEE   *n* pl. **-S** one that is kidnaped

KIDNAPER   *n* pl. **-S** one that kidnaps

KIDNAPPER   *n* pl. **-S** kidnaper

KIDNAPPING present participle of kidnap

KIDNEY   *n* pl. **-NEYS** a bodily organ

KIDSKIN   *n* pl. **-S** a type of leather

KIDVID   *n* pl. **-S** television programs for children

KIEF   *n* pl. **-S** kef

KIELBASA   *n* pl. **-BASAS, -BASI** or **-BASY** a smoked sausage

KIER   *n* pl. **-S** a vat for boiling and dyeing fabrics

KIESTER   *n* pl. **-S** keister

KIF   *n* pl. **-S** kef

KIKUYU   *n* pl. **-S** a type of grass

KILIM   *n* pl. **-S** an oriental tapestry

KILL   *v* **-ED, -ING, -S** to cause to die **KILLABLE** *adj*

KILLDEE   *n* pl. **-S** killdeer

KILLDEER   *n* pl. **-S** a wading bird

KILLER   *n* pl. **-S** one that kills

KILLICK   *n* pl. **-S** a small anchor

KILLIE   *n* pl. **-S** a freshwater fish

KILLING   *n* pl. **-S** a sudden notable success

KILLJOY   *n* pl. **-JOYS** one who spoils the fun of others

KILLOCK   *n* pl. **-S** killick

KILN   *v* **-ED, -ING, -S** to bake in a type of oven

KILO   *n* pl. **KILOS** a kilogram or kilometer

KILOBAR   *n* pl. **-S** a unit of atmospheric pressure

KILOBASE   *n* pl. **-S** unit of measure of a nucleic-acid chain

KILOBAUD   *n* pl. **-S** a unit of data transmission speed

KILOBIT   *n* pl. **-S** a unit of computer information

KILOBYTE   *n* pl. **-S** 1,024 bytes

KILOGRAM   *n* pl. **-S** a unit of mass and weight

KILOMOLE   *n* pl. **-S** one thousand moles

KILORAD   *n* pl. **-S** a unit of nuclear radiation

KILOTON   *n* pl. **-S** a unit of weight

KILOVOLT   *n* pl. **-S** a unit of electromotive force

KILOWATT   *n* pl. **-S** a unit of power

KILT   *v* **-ED, -ING, -S** to make creases or pleats in

KILTER   *n* pl. **-S** good condition

KILTIE   *n* pl. **-S** one who wears a kilt (a type of skirt)

KILTING   *n* pl. **-S** an arrangement of kilt pleats

KILTLIKE   *adj* resembling a kilt

KILTY   *n* pl. **KILTIES** kiltie

KIMCHEE   *n* pl. **-S** kimchi

KIMCHI   *n* pl. **-S** a spicy Korean dish of pickled cabbage

KIMONO   *n* pl. **-NOS** a loose robe **KIMONOED** *adj*

KIN   *n* pl. **-S** a group of persons of common ancestry

KINA   *n* pl. **-S** a monetary unit of Papua New Guinea

KINARA   *n* pl. **-S** a candelabra with seven candlesticks

KINASE   *n* pl. **-S** an enzyme

KIND   *adj* **KINDER, KINDEST** having a gentle, giving nature

KIND   *n* pl. **-S** a class of similar or related objects or individuals

KINDLE   *v* **-DLED, -DLING, -DLES** to cause to burn

KINDLER   *n* pl. **-S** one that kindles

KINDLESS   *adj* lacking kindness

KINDLING   *n* pl. **-S** material that is easily ignited

KINDLY   *adj* **-LIER, -LIEST** kind

KINDNESS   *n* pl. **-ES** the quality of being kind

KINDRED   *n* pl. **-S** a natural grouping

KINE   *n* pl. **-S** a type of television tube

KINEMA   *n* pl. **-S** cinema

KINESIC   *adj* pertaining to kinesics

KINESICS   *n/pl* the study of body motion in relation to communication

KINESIS   *n* pl. **-NESES** a type of movement

KINETIC   *adj* pertaining to motion

KINETICS   *n/pl* a branch of science dealing with motion

KINETIN   *n* pl. **-S** a substance that increases plant growth

KINFOLK   *n/pl* relatives

KINFOLKS   *n/pl* kinfolk

KING   *v* **-ED, -ING, -S** to reign as king (a male monarch)

KINGBIRD   *n* pl. **-S** an American bird

KINGBOLT   *n* pl. **-S** a kingpin

KINGCUP   *n* pl. **-S** a marsh plant

KINGDOM   *n* pl. **-S** the area ruled by a king

KINGFISH   *n* pl. **-ES** a marine food fish

KINGHOOD   *n* pl. **-S** the office of a king

KINGLESS   *adj* having no king

KINGLET   *n* pl. **-S** a king who rules over a small area

KINGLIKE   *adj* resembling a king

KINGLY   *adj* **-LIER, -LIEST** of or befitting a king

KINGPIN   *n* pl. **-S** a central bolt connecting an axle to a vehicle

KINGPOST   *n* pl. **-S** a supporting structure of a roof

KINGSHIP   *n* pl. **-S** the power or position of a king

KINGSIDE   *n* pl. **-S** a part of a chessboard

KINGWOOD   *n* pl. **-S** a hardwood tree

KININ   *n* pl. **-S** a hormone

KINK   *v* **-ED, -ING, -S** to form a tight curl or bend in

KINKAJOU   *n* pl. **-S** an arboreal mammal

KINKY   *adj* **KINKIER, KINKIEST** tightly curled **KINKILY** *adv*

KINLESS   *adj* having no kin

KINO   *n* pl. **-NOS** a gum resin

KINSFOLK   *n/pl* kinfolk

KINSHIP   *n* pl. **-S** relationship

KINSMAN   *n* pl. **-MEN** a male relative

KIOSK   *n* pl. **-S** an open booth

KIP   *v* **KIPPED, KIPPING, KIPS** to sleep

KIPPA   *n* pl. **-S** a yarmulke

KIPPAH   *n* pl. **-S** kippa

KIPPEN   a past participle of kep

KIPPER   *v* **-ED, -ING, -S** to cure fish by salting and smoking

KIPPERER   *n* pl. **-S** one that kippers

KIPPING   present participle of kip

KIPSKIN   *n* pl. **-S** an animal hide that has not been tanned

KIR   *n* pl. **-S** an alcoholic beverage

KIRIGAMI   *n* pl. **-S** the Japanese art of folding paper

KIRK   *n* pl. **-S** a church

KIRKMAN   *n* pl. **-MEN** a member of a church

KIRMESS   *n* pl. **-ES** kermis

KIRN   *v* **-ED, -ING, -S** to churn

KIRPAN   *n* pl. **-S** a dagger carried by Sikhs

KIRSCH   *n* pl. **-ES** a kind of brandy

KIRTLE   *n* pl. **-S** a man's tunic or coat **KIRTLED** *adj*

KISHKA   *n* pl. **-S** kishke

KISHKE   *n* pl. **-S** a sausage

KISKADEE   *n* pl. **-S** a large flycatcher

KISMAT   *n* pl. **-S** kismet

KISMET   *n* pl. **-S** destiny **KISMETIC** *adj*

KISS   *v* **-ED, -ING, -ES** to touch with the lips as a sign of affection **KISSABLE** *adj* **KISSABLY** *adv*

KISSER   *n* pl. **-S** one that kisses

KISSY   *adj* **KISSIER, KISSIEST** inclined to kiss

KIST   *n* pl. **-S** a chest, box, or coffin

KISTFUL   *n* pl. **-S** as much as a kist can hold

KIT	*v* **KITTED, KITTING, KITS** to equip
KITBAG	*n* pl. **-S** a knapsack
KITCHEN	*n* pl. **-S** a room where food is cooked
KITE	*v* **KITED, KITING, KITES** to obtain money or credit fraudulently
KITELIKE	*adj* resembling a kite (a light, covered frame flown in the wind)
KITER	*n* pl. **-S** one that kites
KITH	*n* pl. **-S** one's friends and neighbors
KITHARA	*n* pl. **-S** cithara
KITHE	*v* **KITHED, KITHING, KITHES** to make known
KITING	*n* pl. **-S** the act of flying a kite
KITLING	*n* pl. **-S** a young animal
KITSCH	*n* pl. **-ES** garish art or literature
KITSCHY	*adj* **KITSCHIER, KITSCHIEST** garish; gaudy
KITTED	past tense of kit
KITTEL	*n* pl. **KITTEL** a Jewish ceremonial robe
KITTEN	*v* **-ED, -ING, -S** to bear kittens (young cats)
KITTIES	pl. of kitty
KITTING	present participle of kit
KITTLE	*adj* **-TLER, -TLEST** ticklish
KITTLE	*v* **-TLED, -TLING, -TLES** to tickle
KITTY	*n* pl. **-TIES** a kitten or cat
KIVA	*n* pl. **-S** an underground ceremonial chamber
KIWI	*n* pl. **-S** a flightless bird
KLATCH	*n* pl. **-ES** a social gathering
KLATSCH	*n* pl. **-ES** klatch
KLAVERN	*n* pl. **-S** a local branch of the Ku Klux Klan
KLAXON	*n* pl. **-S** a low-pitched horn
KLEAGLE	*n* pl. **-S** an official in the Ku Klux Klan
KLEPHT	*n* pl. **-S** a Greek guerrilla **KLEPHTIC** *adj*
KLEPTO	*n* pl. **-TOS** one that steals impulsively
KLEZMER	*n* pl. **-MERS** or **-MORIM** a Jewish folk musician
KLICK	*n* pl. **-S** a kilometer
KLIEG	*n* pl. **-S** an electric lamp used in filming
KLIK	*n* pl. **-S** klick
KLISTER	*n* pl. **-S** a wax for skis
KLONDIKE	*n* pl. **-S** a card game
KLONG	*n* pl. **-S** a canal
KLOOF	*n* pl. **-S** a ravine
KLUDGE	*v* **KLUDGED, KLUDGING, KLUDGES** to put together from ill-fitting components
KLUDGEY	*adj* **KLUDGIER, KLUDGIEST** kludgy
KLUDGY	*adj* **KLUDGIER, KLUDGIEST** involving or put together with ill-fitting components
KLUGE	*v* **KLUGED, KLUGING, KLUGES** to kludge
KLUTZ	*n* pl. **-ES** a clumsy person
KLUTZY	*adj* **KLUTZIER, KLUTZIEST** clumsy
KLYSTRON	*n* pl. **-S** a type of electron tube
KNACK	*v* **-ED, -ING, -S** to strike sharply
KNACKER	*n* pl. **-S** one that buys old livestock
KNACKERY	*n* pl. **-ERIES** the place of business of a knacker
KNAIDEL	*n* pl. **KNAIDLACH** or **KNAIDELS** a type of dumpling
KNAP	*v* **KNAPPED, KNAPPING, KNAPS** to strike sharply
KNAPPER	*n* pl. **-S** one that knaps
KNAPSACK	*n* pl. **-S** a bag carried on the back
KNAPWEED	*n* pl. **-S** a meadow plant
KNAR	*n* pl. **-S** a bump on a tree **KNARRED, KNARRY** *adj*
KNAUR	*n* pl. **-S** knar
KNAVE	*n* pl. **-S** a dishonest person **KNAVISH** *adj*
KNAVERY	*n* pl. **-ERIES** trickery
KNAWE	*n* pl. **-S** knawel
KNAWEL	*n* pl. **-S** a Eurasian plant
KNEAD	*v* **-ED, -ING, -S** to work into a uniform mixture with the hands
KNEADER	*n* pl. **-S** one that kneads
KNEE	*v* **KNEED, KNEEING, KNEES** to strike with the knee (a joint of the leg)
KNEECAP	*v* **-CAPPED, -CAPPING, -CAPS** to maim by shooting in the kneecap (a bone at the front of the knee)
KNEEHOLE	*n* pl. **-S** a space for the knees
KNEEL	*v* **KNELT** or **KNEELED, KNEELING, KNEELS** to rest on the knees

KNEELER	*n* pl. **-S** one that kneels
KNEEPAD	*n* pl. **-S** a covering for a knee
KNEEPAN	*n* pl. **-S** the kneecap
KNEESIES	*n/pl* the pressing of one's knees against another person's knees
KNEESOCK	*n* pl. **-S** a sock reaching up to the knee
KNEIDEL	*n* pl. **KNEIDLACH** or **KNEIDELS** knaidel
KNELL	*v* **-ED, -ING, -S** to sound a bell
KNELT	a past tense of kneel
KNESSET	*n* pl. **-S** the Israeli parliament
KNEW	past tense of know
KNICKERS	*n/pl* loose-fitting pants gathered at the knee
KNIFE	*n* pl. **KNIVES** a sharp-edged instrument used for cutting
KNIFE	*v* **KNIFED, KNIFING, KNIFES** to cut with a knife
KNIFER	*n* pl. **-S** one that knifes
KNIFING	*n* pl. **-S** the act of stabbing with a knife
KNIGHT	*v* **-ED, -ING, -S** to make a knight (a medieval gentleman-soldier) of
KNIGHTLY	*adj* of or befitting a knight
KNISH	*n* pl. **-ES** dough stuffed with filling and fried
KNIT	*v* **KNITTED, KNITTING, KNITS** to make a fabric or garment by joining loops of yarn
KNITBONE	*n* pl. **-S** a comfrey
KNITTER	*n* pl. **-S** one that knits
KNITTING	*n* pl. **-S** work done by a knitter
KNITWEAR	*n* pl. **KNITWEAR** knitted clothing
KNIVES	pl. of knife
KNOB	*v* **KNOBBED, KNOBBING, KNOBS** to provide with a knob (a rounded protuberance)
KNOBBLY	*adj* **-BLIER, -BLIEST** having very small knobs
KNOBBY	*adj* **-BIER, -BIEST** full of knobs
KNOBLIKE	*adj* resembling a knob
KNOCK	*v* **-ED, -ING, -S** to strike sharply
KNOCKER	*n* pl. **-S** one that knocks
KNOCKOFF	*n* pl. **-S** a copy that sells for less than the original
KNOCKOUT	*n* pl. **-S** a blow that induces unconsciousness
KNOLL	*v* **-ED, -ING, -S** to knell

KNOLLER	*n* pl. **-S** one that knolls
KNOLLY	*adj* hilly
KNOP	*n* pl. **-S** a knob **KNOPPED** *adj*
KNOSP	*n* pl. **-S** a knob
KNOT	*v* **KNOTTED, KNOTTING, KNOTS** to tie in a knot (a closed loop)
KNOTHEAD	*n* pl. **-S** a stupid person
KNOTHOLE	*n* pl. **-S** a hole in a plank
KNOTLESS	*adj* having no knots
KNOTLIKE	*adj* resembling a knot
KNOTTED	past tense of knot
KNOTTER	*n* pl. **-S** one that knots
KNOTTING	*n* pl. **-S** a fringe made of knotted threads
KNOTTY	*adj* **-TIER, -TIEST** full of knots **KNOTTILY** *adv*
KNOTWEED	*n* pl. **-S** a common weed
KNOUT	*v* **-ED, -ING, -S** to flog with a leather whip
KNOW	*v* **KNEW, KNOWN, KNOWING, KNOWS** to have a true understanding of **KNOWABLE** *adj*
KNOWER	*n* pl. **-S** one that knows
KNOWING	*adj* **-INGER, -INGEST** astute
KNOWING	*n* pl. **-S** knowledge
KNOWN	*n* pl. **-S** a mathematical quantity whose value is given
KNUBBY	*adj* **-BIER, -BIEST** nubby
KNUCKLE	*v* **-LED, -LING, -LES** to hit with the knuckles (the joints of the fingers)
KNUCKLER	*n* pl. **-S** a type of baseball pitch
KNUCKLY	*adj* **-LIER, -LIEST** having prominent knuckles
KNUR	*n* pl. **-S** a bump on a tree
KNURL	*v* **-ED, -ING, -S** to make grooves or ridges in
KNURLY	*adj* **KNURLIER, KNURLIEST** gnarly
KNURR	*n* pl. **-S** knur
KOA	*n* pl. **-S** a timber tree
KOALA	*n* pl. **-S** an Australian mammal
KOAN	*n* pl. **-S** a paradox meditated on by Buddhist monks
KOB	*n* pl. **-S** a reddish brown antelope
KOBO	*n* pl. **-BOS** a monetary unit of Nigeria
KOBOLD	*n* pl. **-S** an elf
KOCHIA	*n* pl. **-S** a Eurasian plant

KOEL   *n* pl. **-S** an Australian bird

KOFTA   *n* pl. **-S** a spiced ball of meat or fish in Indian cooking

KOHL   *n* pl. **-S** a type of eye makeup

KOHLRABI   *n* pl. **-ES** a variety of cabbage

KOI   *n* pl. **-S** a large and colorful fish

KOINE   *n* pl. **-S** a type of dialect

KOJI   *n* pl. **-S** a fungus used to start fermentation

KOKAM   *n* pl. **-S** kokum

KOKANEE   *n* pl. **-S** a food fish

KOKUM   *n* pl. **-S** an East Indian tree

KOLA   *n* pl. **-S** cola

KOLACKY   *n* pl. **KOLACKY** a kind of pastry

KOLBASI   *n* pl. **-S** kielbasa

KOLBASSA   *n* pl. **-S** kielbasa

KOLBASSI   *n* pl. **-S** kielbasa

KOLHOZ   *n* pl. **-HOZES** or **-HOZY** kolkhoz

KOLINSKI   *n* pl. **-ES** kolinsky

KOLINSKY   *n* pl. **-SKIES** an Asian mink

KOLKHOS   *n* pl. **-KHOSES** or **-KHOSY** kolkhoz

KOLKHOZ   *n* pl. **-KHOZES** or **-KHOZY** a collective farm in Russia

KOLKOZ   *n* pl. **-KOZES** or **-KOZY** kolkhoz

KOLO   *n* pl. **-LOS** a European folk dance

KOMATIK   *n* pl. **-S** an Inuit sledge

KOMBU   *n* pl. **-S** kelp used in Japanese cooking

KOMONDOR   *n* pl. **-DORS** or **-DOROK** or **-DOROCK** a large, shaggy-coated dog

KONGONI   *n* pl. **KONGONI** an African antelope

KONK   *v* **-ED, -ING, -S** to conk

KOODOO   *n* pl. **-DOOS** kudu

KOOK   *n* pl. **-S** an eccentric person

KOOKIE   *adj* **KOOKIER, KOOKIEST** kooky

KOOKUM   *n* pl. **-S** kokum

KOOKY   *adj* **KOOKIER, KOOKIEST** eccentric **KOOKILY** *adv*

KOP   *n* pl. **-S** a hill

KOPECK   *n* pl. **-S** a Russian coin

KOPEK   *n* pl. **-S** kopeck

KOPH   *n* pl. **-S** a Hebrew letter

KOPIYKA   *n* pl. **-PIYKAS** or **-PIYKY** or **-PIYOK** a monetary unit of Ukraine

KOPJE   *n* pl. **-S** a small hill

KOPPA   *n* pl. **-S** a Greek letter

KOPPIE   *n* pl. **-S** kopje

KOR   *n* pl. **-S** a Hebrew unit of measure

KORA   *n* pl. **-S** a stringed African musical instrument

KORAT   *n* pl. **-S** a cat having a silver-blue coat

KORE   *n* pl. **-RAI** an ancient Greek statue of a young woman

KORMA   *n* pl. **-S** an Indian dish of meat or vegetables with spices

KORUNA   *n* pl. **KORUNAS** or **KORUNY** or **KORUN** a monetary unit of the Czech Republic

KOS   *n* pl. **KOS** a land measure in India

KOSHER   *v* **-ED, -ING, -S** to make fit to be eaten according to Jewish dietary laws

KOSS   *n* pl. **KOSS** kos

KOTO   *n* pl. **-TOS** a musical instrument

KOTOW   *v* **-ED, -ING, -S** to kowtow

KOTOWER   *n* pl. **-S** one that kotows

KOUMIS   *n* pl. **-MISES** koumiss

KOUMISS   *n* pl. **-ES** a beverage made from camel's milk

KOUMYS   *n* pl. **-ES** koumiss

KOUMYSS   *n* pl. **-ES** koumiss

KOUPREY   *n* pl. **-PREYS** a short-haired ox

KOUROS   *n* pl. **-ROI** an ancient Greek statue of a young man

KOUSSO   *n* pl. **-SOS** cusso

KOWTOW   *v* **-ED, -ING, -S** to behave in a servile manner

KOWTOWER   *n* pl. **-S** one that kowtows

KRAAL   *v* **-ED, -ING, -S** to pen in a type of enclosure

KRAFT   *n* pl. **-S** a strong paper

KRAI   *n* pl. **-S** an administrative territory of Russia

KRAIT   *n* pl. **-S** a venomous snake

KRAKEN   *n* pl. **-S** a legendary sea monster

KRATER   *n* pl. **-S** a type of vase

KRAUT   *n* pl. **-S** sauerkraut

KRAY   *n* pl. **KRAYS** krai

KREEP   *n* pl. **-S** a basaltic lunar rock

KREMLIN   *n* pl. **-S** a Russian citadel

KREPLACH   *n* pl. **KREPLACH** dumplings filled with ground meat or cheese

KREPLECH   *n* pl. **KREPLECH** kreplach

KREUTZER *n* pl. **-S** a former monetary unit of Austria

KREUZER *n* pl. **-S** kreutzer

KREWE *n* pl. **-S** a private group participating in the New Orleans Mardi Gras

KRILL *n* pl. **-S** an aggregate of small marine crustaceans

KRIMMER *n* pl. **-S** a kind of fur

KRIS *n* pl. **-ES** a short sword

KRONA *n* pl. **KRONOR** a monetary unit of Sweden

KRONA *n* pl. **KRONUR** a monetary unit of Iceland

KRONE *n* pl. **KRONEN** a former monetary unit of Austria

KRONE *n* pl. **KRONER** a monetary unit of Denmark

KRONOR pl. of krona

KRONUR pl. of krona

KROON *n* pl. **KROONS** or **KROONI** a former monetary unit of Estonia

KRUBI *n* pl. **-S** a tropical plant

KRUBUT *n* pl. **-S** krubi

KRULLER *n* pl. **-S** cruller

KRUMHORN *n* pl. **-S** crumhorn

KRUMKAKE *n* pl. **-S** a large thin cookie

KRYOLITE *n* pl. **-S** cryolite

KRYOLITH *n* pl. **-S** cryolite

KRYPTON *n* pl. **-S** a gaseous element

KUBASA *n* pl. **-S** a Ukrainian sausage

KUBIE *n* pl. **-S** a kubasa on a bun

KUCHEN *n* pl. **-S** a coffee cake

KUDLIK *n* pl. **-S** an Inuit oil lamp

KUDO *n* pl. **-DOS** award; honor

KUDU *n* pl. **-S** a large antelope

KUDZU *n* pl. **-S** an Asian vine

KUE *n* pl. **-S** the letter Q

KUFI *n* pl. **-S** a brimless hat

KUGEL *n* pl. **-S** a baked pudding of potatoes or noodles

KUKRI *n* pl. **-S** a long, curved knife of Nepal

KULAK *n* pl. **-LAKS** or **-LAKI** a rich Russian peasant

KULFI *n* pl. **-S** an Indian dessert resembling ice cream

KULTUR *n* pl. **-S** culture; civilization

KUMIS *n* pl. **-ES** koumiss

KUMISS *n* pl. **-ES** koumiss

KUMKUM *n* pl. **-S** a red powder used by Hindu women

KUMMEL *n* pl. **-S** a type of liqueur

KUMQUAT *n* pl. **-S** a citrus fruit

KUMYS *n* pl. **-ES** koumiss

KUNA *n* pl. **KUNE** a monetary unit of Croatia

KUNZITE *n* pl. **-S** a mineral

KURBASH *v* **-ED, -ING, -ES** to flog with a leather whip

KURGAN *n* pl. **-S** a mound of earth over a grave

KURTA *n* pl. **-S** a shirt worn in India

KURTOSIS *n* pl. **-TOSES** the relative degree of curvature in a statistical curve

KURU *n* pl. **-S** a disease of the nervous system

KURUSH *n* pl. **-ES** a monetary unit of Turkey

KUSSO *n* pl. **-SOS** cusso

KUVASZ *n* pl. **-VASZOK** a large dog having a white coat

KVAS *n* pl. **-ES** kvass

KVASS *n* pl. **-ES** a Russian beer

KVELL *v* **-ED, -ING, -S** to exclaim joyfully

KVETCH *v* **-ED, -ING, -ES** to complain

KVETCHER *n* pl. **-S** one that kvetches

KVETCHY *adj* **KVETCHIER, KVETCHIEST** habitually complaining

KWACHA *n* pl. **-S** a monetary unit of Malawi and Zambia

KWANZA *n* pl. **-S** a monetary unit of Angola

KYACK *n* pl. **-S** a packsack

KYAK *n* pl. **-S** a kayak (an Inuit canoe)

KYANISE *v* **-ISED, -ISING, -ISES** to kyanize

KYANITE *n* pl. **-S** cyanite **KYANITIC** *adj*

KYANIZE *v* **-IZED, -IZING, -IZES** to treat wood with a type of preservative

KYAR *n* pl. **-S** coir

KYAT *n* pl. **-S** a monetary unit of Myanmar (Burma)

KYBOSH *v* **-ED, -ING, -ES** to kibosh

KYE *n* pl. **-S** a private Korean-American banking club

KYLIN *n* pl. **-S** a composite mythical animal

KYLIX   *n* pl. **-LIKES** or **-LIXES** a drinking vessel

KYMOGRAM *n* pl. **-S** a record of fluid pressure

KYPHOSIS   *n* pl. **-PHOSES** abnormal curvature of the spine **KYPHOTIC** *adj*

KYRIE   *n* pl. **-S** a religious petition for mercy

KYTE   *n* pl. **-S** the stomach

KYTHE   *v* **KYTHED, KYTHING, KYTHES** to kithe

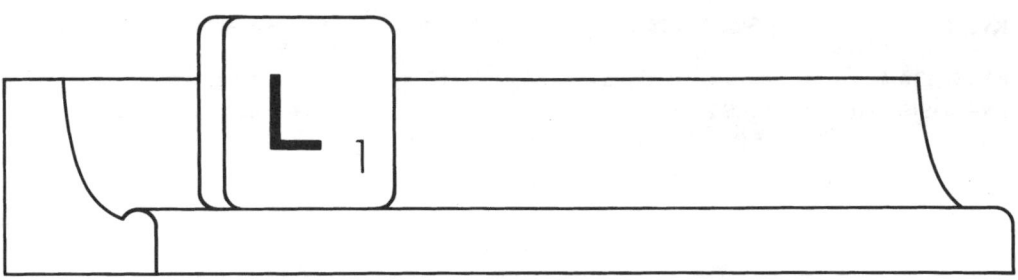

LA	*n* pl. **-S** the sixth tone of the diatonic musical scale	**LABROID**	*n* pl. **-S** a marine fish
LAAGER	*v* **-ED, -ING, -S** to form a defensive encampment	**LABRUM**	*n* pl. **-BRUMS** or **-BRA** a lip or liplike structure **LABRAL** *adj*
LAARI	*n* pl. **-S** a monetary unit of the Maldives	**LABRUSCA**	*n* pl. **-S** a fox grape
LAB	*n* pl. **-S** a laboratory	**LABURNUM**	*n* pl. **-S** an ornamental tree
LABARUM	*n* pl. **-RUMS** or **-RA** an ecclesiastical banner	**LAC**	*n* pl. **-S** a resinous substance secreted by certain insects
LABDANUM	*n* pl. **-S** a fragrant resin	**LACE**	*v* **LACED, LACING, LACES** to fasten by means of a lace (a cord for drawing together two edges)
LABEL	*v* **-BELED, -BELING, -BELS** or **-BELLED, -BELLING, -BELS** to describe or designate		
		LACELESS	*adj* lacking lace
LABELER	*n* pl. **-S** one that labels	**LACELIKE**	*adj* resembling lace
LABELLA	pl. of labellum	**LACER**	*n* pl. **-S** one that laces
LABELLER	*n* pl. **-S** labeler	**LACERATE**	*v* **-ATED, -ATING, -ATES** to tear roughly
LABELLING	a present participle of label		
LABELLUM	*n* pl. **-LA** the lower petal of an orchid	**LACERTID**	*n* pl. **-S** a type of lizard
		LACEWING	*n* pl. **-S** a winged insect
LABIA	pl. of labium	**LACEWOOD**	*n* pl. **-S** an Australian tree
LABIAL	*n* pl. **-S** a labially produced sound	**LACEWORK**	*n* pl. **-S** a delicate openwork fabric
LABIALLY	*adv* by means of the lips	**LACEY**	*adj* **LACIER, LACIEST** lacy
LABIATE	*n* pl. **-S** a labiated plant	**LACHES**	*n* pl. **LACHES** undue delay in asserting a legal right
LABIATED	*adj* having corollas that are divided into two liplike parts		
		LACIER	comparative of lacy
LABILE	*adj* likely to change	**LACIEST**	superlative of lacy
LABILITY	*n* pl. **-TIES** the state of being labile	**LACILY**	*adv* in a lacy manner
LABIUM	*n* pl. **-BIA** a fold of the vulva	**LACINESS**	*n* pl. **-ES** the quality of being lacy
LABOR	*v* **-ED, -ING, -S** to work	**LACING**	*n* pl. **-S** a contrasting marginal band of color
LABORER	*n* pl. **-S** one that labors		
LABORITE	*n* pl. **-S** a supporter of labor interests	**LACK**	*v* **-ED, -ING, -S** to be without
		LACKADAY	*interj* — used to express regret
LABOUR	*v* **-ED, -ING, -S** to labor	**LACKER**	*v* **-ED, -ING, -S** to lacquer
LABOURER	*n* pl. **-S** laborer	**LACKEY**	*v* **-ED, -ING, -S** to act in a servile manner
LABRA	a pl. of labrum		
LABRADOR	*n* pl. **-S** a hunting dog	**LACONIC**	*adj* using a minimum of words
LABRET	*n* pl. **-S** an ornament worn in a perforation of the lip	**LACONISM**	*n* pl. **-S** brevity of expression
		LACQUER	*v* **-ED, -ING, -S** to coat with a glossy substance

LACQUEY	*v* **-ED, -ING, -S** to lackey
LACRIMAL	*n* pl. **-S** a small bone of the eye socket
LACROSSE	*n* pl. **-S** a type of ball game
LACRYMAL	*n* pl. **-S** lacrimal
LACTAM	*n* pl. **-S** a chemical compound
LACTARY	*adj* pertaining to milk
LACTASE	*n* pl. **-S** an enzyme
LACTATE	*v* **-TATED, -TATING, -TATES** to secrete milk
LACTEAL	*n* pl. **-S** a lymphatic vessel
LACTEAN	*adj* lacteous
LACTEOUS	*adj* resembling milk
LACTIC	*adj* derived from milk
LACTITOL	*n* pl. **-S** an artificial sweetener
LACTONE	*n* pl. **-S** any of a group of esters **LACTONIC** *adj*
LACTOSE	*n* pl. **-S** a lactic sugar
LACUNA	*n* pl. **-NAS** or **-NAE** an empty space or missing part **LACUNAL, LACUNARY, LACUNATE** *adj*
LACUNAR	*n* pl. **-NARS** or **-NARIA** a ceiling with recessed panels
LACUNE	*n* pl. **-S** lacuna
LACUNOSE	*adj* marked by shallow depressions
LACY	*adj* **LACIER, LACIEST** resembling lacework
LAD	*n* pl. **-S** a boy or youth **LADDISH** *adj*
LADANUM	*n* pl. **-S** labdanum
LADDER	*v* **-ED, -ING, -S** to cause a run in a stocking
LADDIE	*n* pl. **-S** a lad
LADDISH	*adj* characteristic of boisterous lads
LADDISM	*n* pl. **-S** boisterous macho behavior by lads
LADDY	*adj* **LADDIER, LADDIEST** laddish in behavior
LADE	*v* **LADED, LADEN, LADING, LADES** to load with a cargo
LADEN	*v* **-ED, -ING, -S** to lade
LADER	*n* pl. **-S** one that lades
LADHOOD	*n* pl. **-S** the state of being a lad
LADIES	pl. of lady
LADING	*n* pl. **-S** cargo; freight
LADINO	*n* pl. **-NOS** a fast-growing clover

LADLE	*v* **-DLED, -DLING, -DLES** to lift out with a ladle (a type of spoon)
LADLEFUL	*n* pl. **-S** as much as a ladle will hold
LADLER	*n* pl. **-S** one that ladles
LADLING	present participle of ladle
LADRON	*n* pl. **-S** ladrone
LADRONE	*n* pl. **-S** a thief
LADY	*n* pl. **-DIES** a woman of refinement and gentle manners
LADYBIRD	*n* pl. **-S** a ladybug
LADYBUG	*n* pl. **-S** a small beetle
LADYFISH	*n* pl. **-ES** a bonefish
LADYHOOD	*n* pl. **-S** the state of being a lady
LADYISH	*adj* somewhat ladylike
LADYKIN	*n* pl. **-S** a small lady
LADYLIKE	*adj* resembling or suitable to a lady
LADYLOVE	*n* pl. **-S** a sweetheart
LADYNESS	*n* pl. **-ES** the quality or state of being a lady
LADYPALM	*n* pl. **-S** a palm tree
LADYSHIP	*n* pl. **-S** the condition of being a lady
LAETRILE	*n* pl. **-S** a drug derived from apricot pits
LAEVO	*adj* levo
LAG	*v* **LAGGED, LAGGING, LAGS** to stay or fall behind
LAGAN	*n* pl. **-S** goods thrown into the sea with a buoy attached to enable recovery
LAGEND	*n* pl. **-S** lagan
LAGER	*v* **-ED, -ING, -S** to laager
LAGGARD	*n* pl. **-S** one that lags
LAGGED	past tense of lag
LAGGER	*n* pl. **-S** a laggard
LAGGING	*n* pl. **-S** an insulating material
LAGNAPPE	*n* pl. **-S** a small gift given to a customer with a purchase
LAGOON	*n* pl. **-S** a shallow body of water **LAGOONAL** *adj*
LAGUNA	*n* pl. **-S** lagoon
LAGUNE	*n* pl. **-S** lagoon
LAH	*n* pl. **-S** la
LAHAL	*n* pl. **-S** a team game played by indigenous peoples of the Pacific Northwest
LAHAR	*n* pl. **-S** a flowing mass of volcanic debris

LAIC *n* pl. **-S** a layman **LAICAL** *adj* **LAICALLY** *adv*

LAICH *n* pl. **-S** laigh

LAICISE *v* **-ICISED, -ICISING, -ICISES** to laicize

LAICISM *n* pl. **-S** a political system free from clerical control

LAICIZE *v* **-ICIZED, -ICIZING, -ICIZES** to free from clerical control

LAID a past tense of lay

LAIGH *n* pl. **-S** a lowland

LAIN past participle of lie

LAIR *v* **-ED, -ING, -S** to live in a lair (a wild animal's resting or dwelling place)

LAIRAGE *n* pl. **-S** a place where cattle are housed at markets

LAIRD *n* pl. **-S** the owner of a landed estate **LAIRDLY** *adj*

LAIRY *adj* **-RIER, -RIEST** unpleasantly loud

LAITANCE *n* pl. **-S** a milky deposit on the surface of fresh concrete

LAITH *adj* loath **LAITHLY** *adv*

LAITY *n* pl. **-ITIES** the nonclerical membership of a religious faith

LAKE *n* pl. **-S** a sizable inland body of water **LAKELIKE** *adj*

LAKEBED *n* pl. **-S** the floor of a lake

LAKED *adj* subjected to the process of laking

LAKEFILL *n* pl. **-S** an area of land built by filling a lake

LAKEHEAD *n* pl. **-S** the shore of a lake farthest from the outlet

LAKELAND *n* pl. **-S** an area with many lakes

LAKEPORT *n* pl. **-S** a city located on the shore of a lake

LAKER *n* pl. **-S** a lake fish

LAKESIDE *n* pl. **-S** the land along the edge of a lake

LAKEVIEW *adj* overlooking a lake

LAKEWARD *adj* facing a lake

LAKH *n* pl. **-S** the sum of one hundred thousand

LAKING *n* pl. **-S** the reddening of blood plasma by the release of hemoglobin from the red corpuscles

LAKY *adj* **LAKIER, LAKIEST** of the color of blood

LALIQUE *n* pl. **-S** a style of cut glass or crystal

LALL *v* **-ED, -ING, -S** to articulate the letter *r* as *l*

LALLAN *n* pl. **-S** a lowland

LALLAND *n* pl. **-S** a lowland

LALLYGAG *v* **-GAGGED, -GAGGING, -GAGS** to dawdle

LAM *v* **LAMMED, LAMMING, LAMS** to flee hastily

LAMA *n* pl. **-S** a Buddhist monk

LAMASERY *n* pl. **-SERIES** a monastery of lamas

LAMB *v* **-ED, -ING, -S** to give birth to a lamb (a young sheep)

LAMBADA *n* pl. **-S** a Brazilian dance

LAMBAST *v* **-ED, -ING, -S** to lambaste

LAMBASTE *v* **-BASTED, -BASTING, -BASTES** to beat severely

LAMBDA *n* pl. **-S** a Greek letter **LAMBDOID** *adj*

LAMBENCY *n* pl. **-CIES** the quality or an instance of being lambent

LAMBENT *adj* flickering lightly and gently over a surface

LAMBER *n* pl. **-S** a ewe that is lambing

LAMBERT *n* pl. **-S** a unit of brightness

LAMBIE *n* pl. **-S** a lambkin

LAMBIER comparative of lamby

LAMBIEST superlative of lamby

LAMBING *n* pl. **-S** the birth of lambs on a farm

LAMBKILL *n* pl. **-S** an evergreen shrub

LAMBKIN *n* pl. **-S** a small lamb

LAMBLIKE *adj* resembling a lamb

LAMBSKIN *n* pl. **-S** the skin of a lamb

LAMBY *adj* **LAMBIER, LAMBIEST** resembling a lamb

LAME *adj* **LAMER, LAMEST** physically disabled

LAME *v* **LAMED, LAMING, LAMES** to make lame

LAMED *n* pl. **-S** a Hebrew letter

LAMEDH *n* pl. **-S** lamed

LAMELLA *n* pl. **-LAS** or **-LAE** a thin plate, scale, or membrane **LAMELLAR** *adj*

LAMELY *adv* in a lame manner

LAMENESS *n* pl. **-ES** the state of being lame

LAMENT   *v* **-ED, -ING, -S** to express sorrow or regret for

LAMENTER   *n* pl. **-S** one that laments

LAMER   comparative of lame

LAMEST   superlative of lame

LAMIA   *n* pl. **-MIAS** or **-MIAE** a female demon

LAMINA   *n* pl. **-NAS** or **-NAE** a thin plate, scale, or layer **LAMINAR, LAMINARY** *adj*

LAMINAL   *n* pl. **-S** a speech sound articulated with the blade of the tongue

LAMINATE   *v* **-NATED, -NATING, -NATES** to compress into a thin plate

LAMING   present participle of lame

LAMININ   *n* pl. **-S** a glycoprotein

LAMINOSE   *adj* composed of laminae

LAMINOUS   *adj* laminose

LAMISTER   *n* pl. **-S** lamster

LAMMED   past tense of lam

LAMMING   present participle of lam

LAMP   *v* **-ED, -ING, -S** to look at

LAMPAD   *n* pl. **-S** a candlestick

LAMPAS   *n* pl. **-ES** inflammation of the roof of a horse's mouth

LAMPERS   *n* pl. **-ES** lampas

LAMPION   *n* pl. **-S** a type of light-generating device

LAMPLESS   *adj* lacking a lamp (a device for giving light)

LAMPLIT   *adj* lighted by a lamp

LAMPOON   *v* **-ED, -ING, -S** to ridicule in a satirical composition

LAMPPOST   *n* pl. **-S** a post supporting a streetlight

LAMPREY   *n* pl. **-PREYS** an eellike fish

LAMPYRID   *n* pl. **-S** any of a family of beetles

LAMSTER   *n* pl. **-S** a fugitive

LANAI   *n* pl. **-S** a veranda

LANATE   *adj* covered with wool

LANATED   *adj* lanate

LANCE   *v* **LANCED, LANCING, LANCES** to pierce with a lance (a spearlike weapon)

LANCELET   *n* pl. **-S** a small marine organism

LANCER   *n* pl. **-S** a cavalryman armed with a lance

LANCET   *n* pl. **-S** a narrow, pointed arch **LANCETED** *adj*

LANCH   *v* **-ED, -ING, -ES** to haul a boat over ice

LANCIERS   *n* pl. **LANCIERS** a French dance

LANCING   present participle of lance

LAND   *v* **-ED, -ING, -S** to set down upon land (solid ground)

LANDAU   *n* pl. **-S** a type of carriage

LANDER   *n* pl. **-S** one that lands

LANDFALL   *n* pl. **-S** a sighting or approach to land

LANDFAST   *adj* attached to the shore — used of ice

LANDFILL   *v* **-ED, -ING, -S** to build up an area by burying refuse

LANDFORM   *n* pl. **-S** a natural feature of the earth's surface

LANDGRAB   *n* pl. **-S** a swift and often fraudulent seizure of land

LANDING   *n* pl. **-S** a place for discharging or taking on passengers or cargo

LANDLADY   *n* pl. **-DIES** a female landlord

LANDLER   *n* pl. **-S** a slow Austrian dance

LANDLESS   *adj* owning no land

LANDLINE   *n* pl. **-S** a line of communication on land

LANDLORD   *n* pl. **-S** one who owns and rents out real estate

LANDMAN   *n* pl. **-MEN** one who lives and works on land

LANDMARK   *v* **-ED, -ING, -S** to designate a building or site as a place of historical or aesthetic importance

LANDMASS   *n* pl. **-ES** a large area of land

LANDMEN   pl. of landman

LANDSIDE   *n* pl. **-S** a part of a plow

LANDSKIP   *n* pl. **-S** landscape

LANDSLID   past tense of landslide (to win an election by an overwhelming majority)

LANDSLIP   *n* pl. **-S** the fall of a mass of earth

LANDSMAN   *n* pl. **-MEN** landman

LANDSMAN   *n* pl. **LANDSLEIT** a fellow Jew coming from one's own section of Eastern Europe

LANDWARD   *adv* toward the land

LANDWASH   *n* pl. **-ES** the shore area between the high-water mark and the sea

LANE   *n* pl. **-S** a narrow passageway

LANELY   *adj* lonely

LANEWAY   *n* pl. **-WAYS** a lane

LANG	*adj* long
LANGLAUF	*n* pl. **-S** a cross-country ski run
LANGLEY	*n* pl. **-LEYS** a unit of illumination
LANGRAGE	*n* pl. **-S** a shot formerly used in naval warfare
LANGREL	*n* pl. **-S** langrage
LANGSHAN	*n* pl. **-S** any of a breed of large domestic fowl
LANGSYNE	*n* pl. **-S** time long past
LANGUAGE	*n* pl. **-S** a body of words and systems serving as a means of communication
LANGUE	*n* pl. **-S** a type of language
LANGUED	*adj* having the tongue of a specified color
LANGUET	*n* pl. **-S** a tonguelike part
LANGUID	*adj* lacking in vigor or vitality
LANGUISH	*v* **-ED, -ING, -ES** to lose vigor or vitality
LANGUOR	*n* pl. **-S** the state of being languid
LANGUR	*n* pl. **-S** an Asian monkey
LANIARD	*n* pl. **-S** lanyard
LANIARY	*n* pl. **-ARIES** a cuspid
LANITAL	*n* pl. **-S** a woollike fiber
LANK	*adj* **LANKER, LANKEST** long and slender **LANKLY** *adv*
LANKNESS	*n* pl. **-ES** the state of being lank
LANKY	*adj* **LANKIER, LANKIEST** ungracefully tall and thin **LANKILY** *adv*
LANNER	*n* pl. **-S** a falcon of Europe and Asia
LANNERET	*n* pl. **-S** a male lanner
LANOLIN	*n* pl. **-S** a fatty substance obtained from wool
LANOLINE	*n* pl. **-S** lanolin
LANOSE	*adj* lanate
LANOSITY	*n* pl. **-TIES** the state of being lanose
LANTANA	*n* pl. **-S** a tropical shrub
LANTERN	*n* pl. **-S** a protective case for a light
LANTHORN	*n* pl. **-S** a lantern
LANUGO	*n* pl. **-GOS** fine, soft hair
LANYARD	*n* pl. **-S** a fastening rope on a ship
LAOGAI	*n* pl. **-S** the system of forced-labor camps in China
LAP	*v* **LAPPED, LAPPING, LAPS** to fold over or around something
LAPBOARD	*n* pl. **-S** a flat board used as a table or desk
LAPDOG	*n* pl. **-S** a small dog
LAPEL	*n* pl. **-S** an extension of the collar of a garment **LAPELED, LAPELLED** *adj*
LAPFUL	*n* pl. **-S** as much as the lap can hold
LAPIDARY	*n* pl. **-DARIES** one who works with precious stones
LAPIDATE	*v* **-DATED, -DATING, -DATES** to hurl stones at
LAPIDIFY	*v* **-FIED, -FYING, -FIES** to turn to stone
LAPIDIST	*n* pl. **-S** a lapidary
LAPILLUS	*n* pl. **-LI** a small fragment of lava
LAPIN	*n* pl. **-S** a rabbit
LAPIS	*n* pl. **-PISES, -PIDES** a semiprecious stone
LAPPED	past tense of lap
LAPPER	*v* **-ED, -ING, -S** to lopper
LAPPET	*n* pl. **-S** a decorative flap on a garment **LAPPETED** *adj*
LAPPING	present participle of lap
LAPSE	*v* **LAPSED, LAPSING, LAPSES** to fall from a previous standard **LAPSABLE, LAPSIBLE** *adj*
LAPSER	*n* pl. **-S** one that lapses
LAPSUS	*n* pl. **LAPSUS** a mistake
LAPTOP	*n* pl. **-S** a small computer for use on one's lap
LAPWING	*n* pl. **-S** a shore bird
LAR	*n* pl. **-S** or **-ES** a tutelary god or spirit of an ancient Roman household
LARBOARD	*n* pl. **-S** the left-hand side of a ship
LARCENER	*n* pl. **-S** one that commits larceny
LARCENY	*n* pl. **-NIES** the felonious taking and removal of another's personal goods
LARCH	*n* pl. **-ES** a coniferous tree **LARCHEN** *adj*
LARD	*v* **-ED, -ING, -S** to coat with lard (the melted fat of hogs)
LARDER	*n* pl. **-S** a place where food is stored
LARDIER	comparative of lardy
LARDIEST	superlative of lardy
LARDLIKE	*adj* resembling lard
LARDON	*n* pl. **-S** a thin slice of bacon or pork

LARDOON *n* pl. **-S** lardon

LARDY *adj* **LARDIER, LARDIEST** resembling lard

LAREE *n* pl. **-S** lari

LARES a pl. of lar

LARGANDO *adj* becoming gradually slower — used as a musical direction

LARGE *adj* **LARGER, LARGEST** of considerable size or quantity **LARGELY** *adv*

LARGE *n* pl. **-S** generosity

LARGESS *n* pl. **-ES** generosity

LARGESSE *n* pl. **-S** largess

LARGEST superlative of large

LARGISH *adj* somewhat large

LARGO *n* pl. **-GOS** a slow musical movement

LARI *n* pl. **-S** a monetary unit of the Republic of Georgia

LARIAT *v* **-ED, -ING, -S** to lasso

LARIGAN *n* pl. **-S** a leather boot

LARINE *adj* resembling a gull

LARK *v* **-ED, -ING, -S** to behave playfully

LARKER *n* pl. **-S** one that larks

LARKIER comparative of larky

LARKIEST superlative of larky

LARKISH *adj* playful

LARKSOME *adj* playful

LARKSPUR *n* pl. **-S** a flowering plant

LARKY *adj* **LARKIER, LARKIEST** playful

LARN *v* **LARNED** or **LARNT, LARNING, LARNS** to learn

LARRIGAN *n* pl. **-S** larigan

LARRIKIN *n* pl. **-S** a rowdy

LARRUP *v* **-ED, -ING, -S** to beat or thrash

LARRUPER *n* pl. **-S** one that larrups

LARUM *n* pl. **-S** an alarm

LARVA *n* pl. **-VAS** or **-VAE** the immature form of various insects and animals when newly hatched **LARVAL** *adj*

LARYNGAL *n* pl. **-S** a speech sound articulated in the larynx

LARYNX *n* pl. **LARYNXES** or **LARYNGES** an organ of the respiratory tract

LASAGNA *n* pl. **-S** an Italian baked dish

LASAGNE *n* pl. **-S** lasagna

LASCAR *n* pl. **-S** an East Indian sailor

LASE *v* **LASED, LASING, LASES** to function as a laser

LASER *v* **-ED, -ING, -S** to treat with a laser (a device that amplifies light waves)

LASH *v* **-ED, -ING, -ES** to strike with a whip

LASHER *n* pl. **-S** one that lashes

LASHING *n* pl. **-S** a flogging

LASHINS *n/pl* an abundance

LASHKAR *n* pl. **-S** lascar

LASHLESS *adj* lacking a lash (a whip)

LASING present participle of lase

LASS *n* pl. **-ES** a young woman

LASSI *n* pl. **-S** a beverage of yogurt, water, and flavorings

LASSIE *n* pl. **-S** a lass

LASSO *v* **-ED, -ING, -S** or **-ES** to catch with a lasso (a long rope with a running noose)

LASSOER *n* pl. **-S** one that lassos

LASSY *n* pl. **LASSIES** molasses

LAST *v* **-ED, -ING, -S** to continue in existence

LASTBORN *n* pl. **-S** a child born last in a family

LASTER *n* pl. **-S** one that lasts

LASTING *n* pl. **-S** a durable fabric

LASTLY *adv* in conclusion

LAT *n* pl. **-S** a muscle of the back

LATAKIA *n* pl. **-S** a variety of Turkish tobacco

LATCH *v* **-ED, -ING, -ES** to close with a type of fastening device

LATCHET *n* pl. **-S** a thong used to fasten a shoe

LATCHKEY *n* pl. **-KEYS** a key for opening a latched door

LATE *adj* **LATER, LATEST** coming or occurring after the expected time

LATED *adj* belated

LATEEN *n* pl. **-S** a sailing vessel

LATEENER *n* pl. **-S** a lateen

LATELY *adv* not long ago

LATEN *v* **-ED, -ING, -S** to become late

LATENCY *n* pl. **-CIES** the state of being present but not manifest

LATENESS *n* pl. **-ES** the state of being late

LATENT *n* pl. **-S** a barely visible fingerprint that can be developed for study

LATENTLY *adv* in a dormant manner

LATER comparative of late

LATERAD *adv* toward the side

LATERAL *v* **-ALED, -ALING, -ALS** or **-ALLED, -ALLING, -ALS** to execute a type of pass in football

LATERITE *n* pl. **-S** a type of soil

LATERIZE *v* **-IZED, -IZING, -IZES** to convert to laterite

LATEST *n* pl. **-S** the most recent development

LATEWOOD *n* pl. **-S** a part of an annual ring of wood

LATEX *n* pl. **LATEXES** or **LATICES** a milky liquid of certain plants

LATH *v* **-ED, -ING, -S** to cover with laths (thin strips of wood)

LATHE *v* **LATHED, LATHING, LATHES** to cut or shape on a type of machine

LATHER *v* **-ED, -ING, -S** to cover with lather (a light foam)

LATHERER *n* pl. **-S** one that lathers

LATHERY *adj* covered with lather

LATHI *n* pl. **-S** a heavy stick of bamboo and iron in India

LATHING *n* pl. **-S** work made of or using laths

LATHWORK *n* pl. **-S** lathing

LATHY *adj* **LATHIER, LATHIEST** long and slender

LATI a pl. of lats

LATICES a pl. of latex

LATIGO *n* pl. **-GOS** or **-GOES** a strap used to fasten a saddle

LATILLA *n* pl. **-S** a peeled limb used in ceilings

LATINA *n* pl. **-S** a Latin-American woman or girl

LATINITY *n* pl. **-TIES** a manner of writing or speaking Latin

LATINIZE *v* **-IZED, -IZING, -IZES** to translate into Latin

LATINO *n* pl. **-NOS** a Latin American

LATISH *adj* somewhat late

LATITUDE *n* pl. **-S** freedom from narrow restrictions

LATKE *n* pl. **-S** a potato pancake

LATOSOL *n* pl. **-S** a tropical soil

LATRIA *n* pl. **-S** the supreme worship given to God only, in Roman Catholicism

LATRINE *n* pl. **-S** a type of toilet

LATS *n* pl. **LATI** or **LATU** a monetary unit of Latvia

LATTE *n* pl. **-S** espresso coffee with milk

LATTEN *n* pl. **-S** a brass-like alloy

LATTER *n* pl. **-S** the second mentioned person or thing of two

LATTERLY *adv* lately

LATTICE *v* **-TICED, -TICING, -TICES** to form a structure consisting of interlaced strips of material

LATTIN *n* pl. **-S** latten

LATU a pl. of lats

LAUAN *n* pl. **-S** a Philippine timber

LAUD *v* **-ED, -ING, -S** to praise

LAUDABLE *adj* worthy of praise **LAUDABLY** *adv*

LAUDANUM *n* pl. **-S** a type of opium preparation

LAUDATOR *n* pl. **-S** a lauder

LAUDER *n* pl. **-S** one that lauds

LAUGH *v* **-ED, -ING, -S** to express emotion, typically mirth, by a series of inarticulate sounds

LAUGHER *n* pl. **-S** one that laughs

LAUGHING *n* pl. **-S** laughter

LAUGHTER *n* pl. **-S** the act or sound of one that laughs

LAUNCE *n* pl. **-S** a marine fish

LAUNCH *v* **-ED, -ING, -ES** to set in motion

LAUNCHER *n* pl. **-S** a launching device

LAUNDER *v* **-ED, -ING, -S** to wash clothes

LAUNDRY *n* pl. **-DRIES** a collection of clothes to be washed

LAURA *n* pl. **-RAS** or **-RAE** a type of monastery

LAUREATE *v* **-ATED, -ATING, -ATES** to laurel

LAUREL *v* **-RELED, -RELING, -RELS** or **-RELLED, -RELLING, -RELS** to crown with a wreath of evergreen leaves

LAUWINE *n* pl. **-S** an avalanche

LAV *n* pl. **-S** a lavatory

LAVA *n* pl. **-S** molten rock that issues from a volcano

LAVABO *n* pl. **-BOS** or **-BOES** a ceremonial washing in certain Christian churches

LAVAGE *n* pl. **-S** a washing

LAVALAVA *n* pl. **-S** a Polynesian garment

LAVALIER   *n* pl. **-S** a pendant worn on a chain around the neck

LAVALIKE   *adj* resembling lava

LAVASH   *n* pl. **-ES** a thin flat bread of Armenian origin

LAVATERA   *n* pl. **-S** a plant of the mallow family

LAVATION   *n* pl. **-S** the acting of washing

LAVATORY   *n* pl. **-RIES** a room equipped with washing and toilet facilities

LAVE   *v* **LAVED, LAVING, LAVES** to wash

LAVEER   *v* **-ED, -ING, -S** to sail against the wind

LAVENDER   *v* **-ED, -ING, -S** to sprinkle with a type of perfume

LAVER   *n* pl. **-S** a vessel used for ancient Hebrew ceremonial washings

LAVEROCK   *n* pl. **-S** a songbird

LAVING   present participle of lave

LAVISH   *adj* **-ISHER, -ISHEST** expending or giving in great amounts **LAVISHLY** *adv*

LAVISH   *v* **-ED, -ING, -ES** to expend or give in great amounts

LAVISHER   *n* pl. **-S** one that lavishes

LAVROCK   *n* pl. **-S** laverock

LAW   *v* **-ED, -ING, -S** to take a complaint to court for settlement

LAWBOOK   *n* pl. **-S** a book containing or dealing with laws

LAWFUL   *adj* allowed by law (the body of rules governing the affairs of a community) **LAWFULLY** *adv*

LAWGIVER   *n* pl. **-S** one who institutes a legal system

LAWINE   *n* pl. **-S** lauwine

LAWING   *n* pl. **-S** a bill for food or drink in a tavern

LAWLESS   *adj* having no system of laws

LAWLIKE   *adj* being like the law

LAWMAKER   *n* pl. **-S** a legislator

LAWMAN   *n* pl. **-MEN** a law-enforcement officer

LAWN   *n* pl. **-S** an area of grass-covered land **LAWNY** *adj*

LAWNED   *adj* having a lawn

LAWSUIT   *n* pl. **-S** a legal action

LAWYER   *v* **-ED, -ING, -S** to work as a member of the legal profession

LAWYERLY   *adj* befitting a member of the legal profession

LAX   *adj* **LAXER, LAXEST** not strict or stringent

LAX   *n* pl. **-ES** a vowel articulated with relatively relaxed muscles

LAXATION   *n* pl. **-S** the act of relaxing

LAXATIVE   *n* pl. **-S** a drug that stimulates evacuation of the bowels

LAXITY   *n* pl. **-ITIES** the state of being lax

LAXLY   *adv* in a lax manner

LAXNESS   *n* pl. **-ES** laxity

LAY   *v* **LAID** or **LAYED, LAYING, LAYS** to deposit as a wager

LAYABOUT   *n* pl. **-S** a lazy person

LAYAWAY   *n* pl. **-AWAYS** an item that has been reserved with a down payment

LAYER   *v* **-ED, -ING, -S** to form a layer (a single thickness, coating, or covering)

LAYERAGE   *n* pl. **-S** a method of plant propagation

LAYERING   *n* pl. **-S** layerage

LAYETTE   *n* pl. **-S** an outfit of clothing and equipment for a newborn child

LAYIN   *n* pl. **-S** a type of shot in basketball

LAYMAN   *n* pl. **-MEN** a member of the laity

LAYOFF   *n* pl. **-S** the suspension or dismissal of employees

LAYOUT   *n* pl. **-S** an arrangement or plan

LAYOVER   *n* pl. **-S** a stopover

LAYUP   *n* pl. **-S** a shot in basketball

LAYWOMAN   *n* pl. **-WOMEN** a female member of the laity

LAZAR   *n* pl. **-S** a beggar afflicted with a loathsome disease

LAZARET   *n* pl. **-S** a hospital treating contagious diseases

LAZE   *v* **LAZED, LAZING, LAZES** to pass time lazily

LAZIED   past tense of lazy

LAZIER   comparative of lazy

LAZIES   present 3d person sing. of lazy

LAZIEST   superlative of lazy

LAZILY   *adv* in a lazy manner

LAZINESS   *n* pl. **-ES** the state of being lazy

LAZING   present participle of laze

LAZULI   *n* pl. **-S** a mineral

LAZULITE   *n* pl. **-S** a mineral

LAZURITE   *n* pl. **-S** a mineral

LAZY	*adj* **LAZIER, LAZIEST** disinclined toward work or exertion	**LEAFWORM**	*n* pl. **-S** a moth larva that feeds on leaves
LAZY	*v* **LAZIED, LAZYING, LAZIES** to move or lie lazily	**LEAFY**	*adj* **LEAFIER, LEAFIEST** covered with leaves
LAZYISH	*adj* somewhat lazy	**LEAGUE**	*v* **LEAGUED, LEAGUING, LEAGUES** to come together for a common purpose
LEA	*n* pl. **-S** a meadow		
LEACH	*v* **-ED, -ING, -ES** to subject to the filtering action of a liquid	**LEAGUER**	*v* **-ED, -ING, -S** to besiege
LEACHATE	*n* pl. **-S** a solution obtained by leaching	**LEAK**	*v* **-ED, -ING, -S** to permit the escape of something through a breach or flaw
LEACHER	*n* pl. **-S** one that leaches	**LEAKAGE**	*n* pl. **-S** the act or an instance of leaking
LEACHY	*adj* **LEACHIER, LEACHIEST** porous	**LEAKER**	*n* pl. **-S** one that leaks
LEAD	*v* **-ED, -ING, -S** to cover with lead (a heavy metallic element)	**LEAKLESS**	*adj* designed not to leak
		LEAKY	*adj* **LEAKIER, LEAKIEST** tending to leak **LEAKILY** *adv*
LEAD	*v* **LED, LEADING, LEADS** to show the way to by going in advance **LEADABLE** *adj*	**LEAL**	*adj* loyal **LEALLY** *adv*
		LEALTY	*n* pl. **-TIES** loyalty
LEADEN	*v* **-ED, -ING, -S** to make dull or sluggish **LEADENLY** *adv*	**LEAN**	*adj* **LEANER, LEANEST** having little fat **LEANLY** *adv*
LEADER	*n* pl. **-S** one that leads or guides	**LEAN**	*v* **LEANED** or **LEANT, LEANING, LEANS** to deviate from a vertical position
LEADIER	comparative of leady		
LEADIEST	superlative of leady		
LEADING	*n* pl. **-S** a covering or border of lead	**LEANER**	*n* pl. **-S** one that leans
		LEANING	*n* pl. **-S** a tendency
LEADLESS	*adj* having no lead	**LEANNESS**	*n* pl. **-ES** the state of being lean
LEADMAN	*n* pl. **-MEN** a worker in charge of other workers	**LEANT**	a past tense of lean
LEADOFF	*n* pl. **-S** an opening play or move	**LEAP**	*v* **LEAPED** or **LEAPT** or **LEPT, LEAPING, LEAPS** to spring off the ground
LEADSMAN	*n* pl. **-MEN** a seaman who measures the depth of water		
LEADWORK	*n* pl. **-S** something made of lead	**LEAPER**	*n* pl. **-S** one that leaps
LEADWORT	*n* pl. **-S** a tropical plant	**LEAPFROG**	*v* **-FROGGED, -FROGGING, -FROGS** to jump over with the legs wide apart
LEADY	*adj* **LEADIER, LEADIEST** resembling lead		
LEAF	*n* pl. **LEAVES** a usually green, flattened organ of vascular plants	**LEAR**	*n* pl. **-S** learning
		LEARIER	comparative of leary
LEAF	*v* **-ED, -ING, -S** to turn pages rapidly	**LEARIEST**	superlative of leary
		LEARN	*v* **LEARNED** or **LEARNT, LEARNING, LEARNS** to gain knowledge by experience, instruction, or study
LEAFAGE	*n* pl. **-S** foliage		
LEAFIER	comparative of leafy		
LEAFIEST	superlative of leafy	**LEARNER**	*n* pl. **-S** one that learns
LEAFLESS	*adj* having no leaves	**LEARNING**	*n* pl. **-S** acquired knowledge
LEAFLET	*v* **-LETED, -LETING, -LETS** or **-LETTED, -LETTING, -LETS** to distribute printed sheets of paper	**LEARY**	*adj* **LEARIER, LEARIEST** leery
		LEASE	*v* **LEASED, LEASING, LEASES** to grant temporary use of in exchange for rent **LEASABLE** *adj*
LEAFLIKE	*adj* resembling a leaf		
LEAFMOLD	*n* pl. **-S** soil composed mostly of decayed leaves	**LEASER**	*n* pl. **-S** one that leases
		LEASH	*v* **-ED, -ING, -ES** to restrain an animal with a line or thong
LEAFROLL	*n* pl. **-S** a virus disease of potatoes		

LEASING n pl. **-S** a falsehood

LEAST n pl. **-S** something that is smallest in size or degree

LEATHER v **-ED, -ING, -S** to cover with leather (the dressed or tanned hide of an animal)

LEATHERN adj made of leather

LEATHERY adj resembling leather

LEAVE v **LEFT, LEAVING, LEAVES** to go away from

LEAVED adj having a leaf or leaves

LEAVEN v **-ED, -ING, -S** to produce fermentation in

LEAVENER n pl. **-S** one that has a tempering influence

LEAVER n pl. **-S** one that leaves

LEAVES pl. of leaf

LEAVING n pl. **-S** a leftover

LEAVY adj **LEAVIER, LEAVIEST** leafy

LEBEN n pl. **-S** a type of liquid food

LECH v **-ED, -ING, -ES** to engage in lechery

LECHAYIM n pl. **-S** lehayim

LECHER v **-ED, -ING, -S** to engage in lechery

LECHERY n pl. **-ERIES** excessive sexual indulgence

LECHWE n pl. **-S** an African antelope

LECITHIN n pl. **-S** any of a group of fatty substances found in plant and animal tissues

LECTERN n pl. **-S** a reading desk

LECTIN n pl. **-S** a protein that binds to a sugar molecule

LECTION n pl. **-S** a portion of sacred writing read in a church service

LECTOR n pl. **-S** a reader of the lessons in a church service

LECTURE v **-TURED, -TURING, -TURES** to expound on a specific subject

LECTURER n pl. **-S** one that lectures

LECYTHIS adj designating a family of tropical shrubs

LECYTHUS n pl. **-THI** lekythos

LED past tense of lead

LEDE n pl. **-S** the introductory section of a news story

LEDGE n pl. **-S** a narrow, shelflike projection

LEDGED adj having ledges

LEDGER n pl. **-S** an account book of final entry

LEDGY adj **LEDGIER, LEDGIEST** abounding in ledges

LEE n pl. **-S** shelter from the wind

LEEBOARD n pl. **-S** a board attached to a sailing vessel to prevent leeway

LEECH v **-ED, -ING, -ES** to cling to and feed upon or drain

LEEK n pl. **-S** an herb used in cookery

LEER v **-ED, -ING, -S** to look with a sideways glance

LEERY adj **LEERIER, LEERIEST** suspicious **LEERILY** adv

LEET n pl. **-S** a former English court for petty offenses

LEEWARD n pl. **-S** the direction toward which the wind is blowing

LEEWAY n pl. **-WAYS** the lateral drift of a ship

LEFT adj **LEFTER, LEFTEST** pertaining to the side of the body to the north when one faces east

LEFT n pl. **-S** the left side or hand

LEFTIE n pl. **-S** lefty

LEFTISH adj inclined to be a leftist

LEFTISM n pl. **-S** a liberal political philosophy

LEFTIST n pl. **-S** an advocate of leftism

LEFTMOST adj farthest on the left

LEFTOVER n pl. **-S** an unused or unconsumed portion

LEFTWARD adv toward the left

LEFTWING adj favoring leftism

LEFTY n pl. **LEFTIES** a left-handed person

LEG v **LEGGED, LEGGING, LEGS** to move with the legs (appendages that serve as a means of support and locomotion)

LEGACY n pl. **-CIES** something bequeathed

LEGAL n pl. **-S** an authorized investment that may be made by investors such as savings banks

LEGALESE n pl. **-S** the specialized language of lawyers

LEGALISE v **-ISED, -ISING, -ISES** to legalize

LEGALISM n pl. **-S** strict conformity to the law

LEGALIST n pl. **-S** an adherent of legalism

LEGALITY n pl. **-TIES** the condition of being lawful

LEGALIZE   v **-IZED, -IZING, -IZES** to make lawful

LEGALLY   adv in a lawful manner

LEGATE   v **-GATED, -GATING, -GATES** to bequeath

LEGATEE   n pl. **-S** the inheritor of a legacy

LEGATINE   adj pertaining to an official envoy

LEGATING   present participle of legate

LEGATION   n pl. **-S** the sending of an official envoy

LEGATO   n pl. **-TOS** a smooth and flowing musical style

LEGATOR   n pl. **-S** one that legates

LEGEND   n pl. **-S** an unverified story from earlier times

LEGENDRY   n pl. **-RIES** a collection of legends

LEGER   n pl. **-S** fishing bait made to lie on the bottom

LEGERITY   n pl. **-TIES** quickness of the mind or body

LEGES   pl. of lex

LEGGED   past tense of leg

LEGGIER   comparative of leggy

LEGGIERO   adv in a light or graceful manner — used as a musical direction

LEGGIEST   superlative of leggy

LEGGIN   n pl. **-S** legging

LEGGING   n pl. **-S** a covering for the leg

LEGGY   adj **-GIER, -GIEST** having long legs

LEGHOLD   n pl. **-S** a trap that catches an animal by its leg

LEGHORN   n pl. **-S** a smooth, plaited straw

LEGIBLE   adj capable of being read **LEGIBLY** adv

LEGION   n pl. **-S** a large military force

LEGIST   n pl. **-S** one learned or skilled in the law

LEGIT   n pl. **-S** legitimate drama

LEGLESS   adj having no legs

LEGLIKE   adj resembling a leg

LEGMAN   n pl. **-MEN** a newspaperman assigned to gather information

LEGONG   n pl. **-S** a Balinese dance

LEGROOM   n pl. **-S** space in which to extend the legs

LEGUME   n pl. **-S** a type of plant

LEGUMIN   n pl. **-S** a plant protein

LEGWORK   n pl. **-S** work that involves extensive walking

LEHAYIM   n pl. **-S** a traditional Jewish toast

LEHR   n pl. **-S** a type of oven

LEHUA   n pl. **-S** a tropical tree

LEI   n pl. **-S** a wreath of flowers

LEISTER   v **-ED, -ING, -S** to spear with a three-pronged fishing implement

LEISURE   n pl. **-S** freedom from the demands of work or duty **LEISURED** adj

LEK   n pl. **LEKS** or **LEKE** or **LEKU** a monetary unit of Albania

LEK   v **LEKKED, LEKKING, LEKS** to assemble for competitive displays during the mating season

LEKVAR   n pl. **-S** a prune butter

LEKYTHOS   n pl. **-THOI** an oil jar used in ancient Greece

LEKYTHUS   n pl. **-THI** lekythos

LEMAN   n pl. **-S** a lover

LEMMA   n pl. **-MAS** or **-MATA** a type of proposition in logic

LEMMING   n pl. **-S** a mouselike rodent

LEMNISCI   n/pl bands of nerve fibers

LEMON   n pl. **-S** a citrus fruit **LEMONISH** adj

LEMONADE   n pl. **-S** a beverage

LEMONY   adj **-ONIER, -ONIEST** tasting like lemons

LEMPIRA   n pl. **-S** a monetary unit of Honduras

LEMUR   n pl. **-S** an arboreal mammal related to the monkeys

LEMURES   n/pl the ghosts of the dead in ancient Roman religion

LEMURINE   adj pertaining to a lemur

LEMUROID   n pl. **-S** a lemur

LEND   v **LENT, LENDING, LENDS** to give the temporary use of **LENDABLE** adj

LENDER   n pl. **-S** one that lends

LENDING   n pl. **-S** the act of giving something temporarily

LENES   pl. of lenis

LENGTH   n pl. **-S** the longer or longest dimension of an object

LENGTHEN   v **-ED, -ING, -S** to make or become longer

LENGTHY   adj **LENGTHIER, LENGTHIEST** very long

LENIENCE	*n* pl. **-S** leniency
LENIENCY	*n* pl. **-CIES** the quality of being lenient
LENIENT	*adj* gently tolerant
LENIS	*n* pl. **LENES** a speech sound pronounced with little or no aspiration
LENITE	*v* **-NITED, -NITING, -NITES** to articulate a lenis
LENITION	*n* pl. **-S** a change in articulation
LENITIVE	*n* pl. **-S** a soothing medicine
LENITY	*n* pl. **-TIES** leniency
LENO	*n* pl. **-NOS** a style of weaving
LENS	*n* pl. **-ES** a piece of transparent material used in changing the convergence of light rays **LENSLESS** *adj*
LENS	*v* **-ED, -ING, -ES** to make a film of
LENSE	*n* pl. **-S** lens
LENSING	*n* pl. **-S** the act or an instance of filming a motion picture
LENSMAN	*n* pl. **-MEN** a photographer
LENT	past tense of lend
LENTANDO	*adv* becoming slower — used as a musical direction
LENTEN	*adj* meager
LENTIC	*adj* pertaining to still water
LENTICEL	*n* pl. **-S** a mass of cells on a plant stem
LENTIGO	*n* pl. **-TIGINES** a freckle
LENTIL	*n* pl. **-S** a Eurasian annual plant
LENTISK	*n* pl. **-S** an evergreen tree
LENTO	*n* pl. **-TOS** a slow musical movement
LENTOID	*n* pl. **-S** an object shaped like a lens
LEONE	*n* pl. **-S** a monetary unit of Sierra Leone
LEONINE	*adj* pertaining to a lion
LEOPARD	*n* pl. **-S** a large, carnivorous feline mammal
LEOTARD	*n* pl. **-S** a close-fitting garment
LEPER	*n* pl. **-S** one affected with leprosy
LEPIDOTE	*n* pl. **-S** a flowering shrub
LEPORID	*n* pl. **-RIDS** or **-RIDAE** a gnawing mammal
LEPORINE	*adj* resembling a rabbit or hare
LEPROSE	*adj* leprous
LEPROSY	*n* pl. **-SIES** a chronic disease characterized by skin lesions and deformities
LEPROTIC	*adj* leprous
LEPROUS	*adj* affected with leprosy
LEPT	a past tense of leap
LEPTIN	*n* pl. **-S** a hormone released by fat cells
LEPTON	*n* pl. **-S** a subatomic particle **LEPTONIC** *adj*
LEPTON	*n* pl. **-TA** a former monetary unit of Greece
LESBIAN	*n* pl. **-S** a female homosexual
LESBIGAY	*n* pl. **-GAYS** a lesbian, bisexual, or male homosexual
LESION	*v* **-ED, -ING, -S** to cause an abnormal change in the structure of an organ
LESS	*adj* **LESSER, LEAST** not as great in quantity or degree
LESSEE	*n* pl. **-S** one to whom a lease is granted
LESSEN	*v* **-ED, -ING, -S** to make or become less
LESSER	*adj* not as large or important
LESSON	*v* **-ED, -ING, -S** to instruct
LESSOR	*n* pl. **-S** one that grants a lease
LEST	*conj* for fear that
LET	*v* **LETTED, LETTING, LETS** to hinder
LETCH	*v* **-ED, -ING, -ES** to lech
LETDOWN	*n* pl. **-S** a decrease
LETHAL	*n* pl. **-S** a death-causing genetic defect
LETHALLY	*adv* in a deadly manner
LETHARGY	*n* pl. **-GIES** drowsiness; sluggishness
LETHE	*n* pl. **-S** forgetfulness **LETHEAN** *adj*
LETOUT	*n* pl. **-S** something that makes it possible to avoid doing something
LETTED	past tense of let
LETTER	*v* **-ED, -ING, -S** to mark with letters (written symbols representing speech sounds)
LETTERER	*n* pl. **-S** one that letters
LETTING	present participle of let
LETTUCE	*n* pl. **-S** an herb cultivated as a salad plant
LETUP	*n* pl. **-S** a lessening or relaxation

LEU   *n* pl. **LEI** a monetary unit of Romania

LEUCEMIA   *n* pl. **-S** leukemia **LEUCEMIC** *adj*

LEUCIN   *n* pl. **-S** leucine

LEUCINE   *n* pl. **-S** an amino acid

LEUCISM   *n* pl. **-S** abnormal pale coloring of skin, feathers, or hair

LEUCITE   *n* pl. **-S** a mineral **LEUCITIC** *adj*

LEUCOMA   *n* pl. **-S** leukoma

LEUCON   *n* pl. **-S** a sponge of complex structure

LEUCOSIS   *n* pl. **-COSES** leukosis **LEUCOTIC** *adj*

LEUD   *n* pl. **-S** or **-ES** a feudal vassal

LEUKEMIA   *n* pl. **-S** a disease of the blood-forming organs

LEUKEMIC   *n* pl. **-S** one affected with leukemia

LEUKOMA   *n* pl. **-S** an opacity of the cornea

LEUKON   *n* pl. **-S** a bodily organ consisting of the white blood cells

LEUKOSIS   *n* pl. **-KOSES** leukemia **LEUKOTIC** *adj*

LEV   *n* pl. **LEVA** or **LEVAS** or **LEVS** a monetary unit of Bulgaria

LEVANT   *v* **-ED, -ING, -S** to avoid a debt

LEVANTER   *n* pl. **-S** an easterly Mediterranean wind

LEVATOR   *n* pl. **-S** or **-ES** a muscle that raises an organ or part

LEVEE   *v* **LEVEED, LEVEEING, LEVEES** to provide with an embankment

LEVEL   *v* **-ELED, -ELING, -ELS** or **-ELLED, -ELLING, -ELS** to make even

LEVELER   *n* pl. **-S** one that levels

LEVELLER   *n* pl. **-S** leveler

LEVELLING   a present participle of level

LEVELLY   *adv* in an even manner

LEVER   *v* **-ED, -ING, -S** to move with a lever (a rigid body used to lift weight)

LEVERAGE   *v* **-AGED, -AGING, -AGES** to provide with a type of economic advantage

LEVERET   *n* pl. **-S** a young hare

LEVIABLE   *adj* liable to be levied

LEVIED   past tense of levy

LEVIER   *n* pl. **-S** one that levies

LEVIES   present 3d person sing. of levy

LEVIGATE   *v* **-GATED, -GATING, -GATES** to reduce to a fine powder

LEVIN   *n* pl. **-S** lightning

LEVIRATE   *n* pl. **-S** the custom of marrying the widow of one's brother

LEVITATE   *v* **-TATED, -TATING, -TATES** to rise and float in the air

LEVITY   *n* pl. **-TIES** conduct characterized by a lack of seriousness

LEVO   *adj* turning toward the left

LEVODOPA   *n* pl. **-S** a form of dopa

LEVOGYRE   *adj* turning toward the left

LEVULIN   *n* pl. **-S** a chemical compound

LEVULOSE   *n* pl. **-S** a very sweet sugar

LEVY   *v* **LEVIED, LEVYING, LEVIES** to impose or collect by legal authority

LEWD   *adj* **LEWDER, LEWDEST** obscene **LEWDLY** *adv*

LEWDNESS   *n* pl. **-ES** the state of being lewd

LEWIS   *n* pl. **-ISES** a hoisting device

LEWISITE   *n* pl. **-S** a vesicant liquid

LEWISSON   *n* pl. **-S** lewis

LEX   *n* pl. **LEGES** law

LEXEME   *n* pl. **-S** a linguistic unit **LEXEMIC** *adj*

LEXICAL   *adj* pertaining to the words of a language

LEXICON   *n* pl. **-CONS** or **-CA** a dictionary

LEXIGRAM   *n* pl. **-S** a symbol representing a word

LEXIS   *n* pl. **LEXES** the vocabulary of a language, a group, or a subject field

LEY   *n* pl. **LEYS** lea

LI   *n* pl. **-S** a Chinese unit of distance

LIABLE   *adj* subject or susceptible to something possible or likely

LIAISE   *v* **LIAISED, LIAISING, LIAISES** to establish liaison

LIAISON   *n* pl. **-S** a means for maintaining communication

LIANA   *n* pl. **-S** a tropical vine

LIANE   *n* pl. **-S** liana

LIANG   *n* pl. **-S** a Chinese unit of weight

LIANOID   *adj* pertaining to a liana

LIAR   *n* pl. **-S** one that speaks falsely

LIARD   *n* pl. **-S** a former silver coin of France

LIAS _n_ pl. **LIASES** a blue limestone rock **LIASSIC** _adj_

LIATRIS _n_ pl. **-ATRISES** an herb with tubular flowers

LIB _n_ pl. **-S** liberation

LIBATION _n_ pl. **-S** a ceremonial pouring of a liquid

LIBECCIO _n_ pl. **-CIOS** a southwest wind

LIBEL _v_ **-BELED, -BELING, -BELS** or **-BELLED, -BELLING, -BELS** to make or publish a defamatory statement about

LIBELANT _n_ pl. **-S** a plaintiff in a type of lawsuit

LIBELEE _n_ pl. **-S** a defendant in a type of lawsuit

LIBELER _n_ pl. **-S** one that libels

LIBELIST _n_ pl. **-S** a libeler

LIBELLED a past tense of libel

LIBELLEE _n_ pl. **-S** libelee

LIBELLER _n_ pl. **-S** libeler

LIBELLING a present participle of libel

LIBELOUS _adj_ defamatory

LIBER _n_ pl. **LIBERS** or **LIBRI** a book of public records

LIBERAL _n_ pl. **-S** a person favorable to progress or reform

LIBERATE _v_ **-ATED, -ATING, -ATES** to set free

LIBERTY _n_ pl. **-TIES** the state of being free

LIBIDO _n_ pl. **-DOS** the energy derived from instinctual biological drives

LIBLAB _n_ pl. **-S** a person supporting a coalition of liberal and labor groups

LIBRA _n_ pl. **-BRAE** an ancient Roman unit of weight

LIBRA _n_ pl. **-S** a former gold coin of Peru

LIBRARY _n_ pl. **-BRARIES** a place where literary materials are kept for reading and reference

LIBRATE _v_ **-BRATED, -BRATING, -BRATES** to move from side to side

LIBRETTO _n_ pl. **-TOS** or **-TI** the text of an opera

LIBRI a pl. of liber

LICE pl. of louse

LICENCE _v_ **-CENCED, -CENCING, -CENCES** to license

LICENCEE _n_ pl. **-S** licensee

LICENCER _n_ pl. **-S** licenser

LICENSE _v_ **-CENSED, -CENSING, -CENSES** to issue or grant authoritative permission to

LICENSEE _n_ pl. **-S** one that is licensed

LICENSER _n_ pl. **-S** one that licenses

LICENSOR _n_ pl. **-S** licenser

LICENTE a pl. of sente

LICH _n_ pl. **-ES** a corpse

LICHEE _n_ pl. **-S** litchi

LICHEN _v_ **-ED, -ING, -S** to cover with lichens (flowerless plants)

LICHENIN _n_ pl. **-S** a chemical compound

LICHGATE _n_ pl. **-S** lychgate

LICHI _n_ pl. **-S** litchi

LICHT _v_ **-ED, -ING, -S** to light

LICHTLY _adv_ lightly

LICIT _adj_ lawful **LICITLY** _adv_

LICK _v_ **-ED, -ING, -S** to pass the tongue over the surface of

LICKER _n_ pl. **-S** one that licks

LICKING _n_ pl. **-S** a thrashing or beating

LICKSPIT _n_ pl. **-S** a fawning person

LICORICE _n_ pl. **-S** a perennial herb

LICTOR _n_ pl. **-S** a magistrate's attendant in ancient Rome

LID _v_ **LIDDED, LIDDING, LIDS** to provide with a lid (a movable cover)

LIDAR _n_ pl. **-S** an electronic locating device

LIDLESS _adj_ having no lid

LIDO _n_ pl. **-DOS** a fashionable beach resort

LIE _v_ **LAY, LAIN, LYING, LIES** to be in or get into a horizontal position

LIE _v_ **LIED, LYING, LIES** to speak falsely

LIED _n_ pl. **LIEDER** a German song

LIEF _adj_ **LIEFER, LIEFEST** willing **LIEFLY** _adv_

LIEGE _n_ pl. **-S** a feudal lord

LIEGEMAN _n_ pl. **-MEN** a feudal vassal

LIEN _n_ pl. **-S** a legal right to hold or sell a debtor's property

LIENABLE _adj_ capable of being subjected to a lien

LIENAL _adj_ pertaining to the spleen

LIENTERY _n_ pl. **-TERIES** a form of diarrhea

LIER _n_ pl. **-S** one that lies or reclines

LIERNE   *n* pl. **-S** a connecting part in Gothic vaulting

LIEU   *n* pl. **-S** place; stead

LIEVE   *adv* **LIEVER, LIEVEST** gladly

LIFE   *n* pl. **LIVES** the quality that distinguishes animals and plants from inanimate matter

LIFEBELT   *n* pl. **-S** a life preserver shaped like a belt

LIFEBOAT   *n* pl. **-S** a small rescue boat

LIFEBUOY   *n* pl. **-S** a life preserver shaped like a ring

LIFECARE   *n* pl. **-S** housing and health services for the elderly

LIFEFUL   *adj* full of life

LIFELESS   *adj* having no life

LIFELIKE   *adj* resembling a living thing

LIFELINE   *n* pl. **-S** a rope used to aid a person in distress

LIFELONG   *adj* lasting for a lifetime

LIFER   *n* pl. **-S** a prisoner serving a life sentence

LIFESPAN   *n* pl. **-S** a lifetime

LIFETIME   *n* pl. **-S** the period of living existence

LIFEWAY   *n* pl. **-WAYS** a way of living

LIFEWORK   *n* pl. **-S** the major work of one's lifetime

LIFT   *v* **-ED, -ING, -S** to move to a higher position **LIFTABLE** *adj*

LIFTER   *n* pl. **-S** one that lifts

LIFTGATE   *n* pl. **-S** a rear panel on a station wagon that opens upward

LIFTMAN   *n* pl. **-MEN** an elevator operator

LIFTOFF   *n* pl. **-S** the vertical takeoff of a rocket

LIGAMENT   *n* pl. **-S** a band of firm, fibrous tissue

LIGAN   *n* pl. **-S** lagan

LIGAND   *n* pl. **-S** a type of ion or molecule

LIGASE   *n* pl. **-S** an enzyme

LIGATE   *v* **-GATED, -GATING, -GATES** to bind

LIGATION   *n* pl. **-S** the act of ligating **LIGATIVE** *adj*

LIGATURE   *v* **-TURED, -TURING, -TURES** to ligate

LIGER   *n* pl. **-S** the offspring of a male lion and a female tiger

LIGHT   *adj* **LIGHTER, LIGHTEST** having little weight

LIGHT   *v* **LIGHTED** or **LIT, LIGHTING, LIGHTS** to illuminate

LIGHTEN   *v* **-ED, -ING, -S** to reduce the weight of

LIGHTER   *v* **-ED, -ING, -S** to convey in a type of barge

LIGHTFUL   *adj* brightly illuminated

LIGHTING   *n* pl. **-S** illumination

LIGHTISH   *adj* somewhat light

LIGHTLY   *adv* to a moderate degree

LIGNAN   *n* pl. **-S** a type of polymer

LIGNEOUS   *adj* of or resembling wood

LIGNIFY   *v* **-FIED, -FYING, -FIES** to convert into wood

LIGNIN   *n* pl. **-S** an essential part of woody tissue

LIGNITE   *n* pl. **-S** a type of coal **LIGNITIC** *adj*

LIGROIN   *n* pl. **-S** a flammable liquid

LIGROINE   *n* pl. **-S** ligroin

LIGULA   *n* pl. **-LAS** or **-LAE** a strap-shaped organ or part **LIGULAR, LIGULATE, LIGULOID** *adj*

LIGULE   *n* pl. **-S** a strap-shaped plant part

LIGURE   *n* pl. **-S** a precious stone

LIKABLE   *adj* pleasant **LIKABLY** *adv*

LIKE   *adj* **LIKER, LIKEST** possessing the same or almost the same characteristics

LIKE   *v* **LIKED, LIKING, LIKES** to find pleasant

LIKEABLE   *adj* likable **LIKEABLY** *adv*

LIKED   past tense of like

LIKELY   *adj* **-LIER, -LIEST** probable

LIKEN   *v* **-ED, -ING, -S** to represent as similar

LIKENESS   *n* pl. **-ES** a pictorial representation

LIKER   *n* pl. **-S** one that likes

LIKEST   superlative of like

LIKEWISE   *adv* in a similar manner

LIKING   *n* pl. **-S** a feeling of attraction or affection

LIKUTA   *n* pl. **MAKUTA** a former monetary unit of Zaire

LILAC   *n* pl. **-S** a flowering shrub

LILIED   *adj* covered with lilies

LILIES   pl. of lily

LILLIPUT	*n* pl. **-S** a very small person
LILT	*v* **-ED, -ING, -S** to sing or speak rhythmically
LILY	*n* pl. **LILIES** a flowering plant **LILYLIKE** *adj*
LIMA	*n* pl. **-S** the edible seed of a tropical American plant
LIMACINE	*adj* resembling a type of mollusk
LIMACON	*n* pl. **-S** a type of geometric curve
LIMAN	*n* pl. **-S** a lagoon
LIMB	*v* **-ED, -ING, -S** to cut off the arms or legs of
LIMBA	*n* pl. **-S** an African tree
LIMBATE	*adj* having an edge of a different color
LIMBECK	*n* pl. **-S** alembic
LIMBER	*adj* **-BERER, -BEREST** flexible **LIMBERLY** *adv*
LIMBER	*v* **-ED, -ING, -S** to make flexible
LIMBI	a pl. of limbus
LIMBIC	*adj* pertaining to a system of the brain
LIMBIER	comparative of limby
LIMBIEST	superlative of limby
LIMBLESS	*adj* having no arms or legs
LIMBO	*v* **-ED, -ING, -S** to perform a West Indian dance
LIMBUS	*n* pl. **-BUSES** or **-BI** a distinctive border
LIMBY	*adj* **LIMBIER, LIMBIEST** having many large branches
LIME	*v* **LIMED, LIMING, LIMES** to treat with lime (a calcium compound)
LIMEADE	*n* pl. **-S** a beverage
LIMEKILN	*n* pl. **-S** a furnace in which shells are burned to produce lime
LIMELESS	*adj* having no lime
LIMEN	*n* pl. **-MENS** or **-MINA** a sensory threshold
LIMERICK	*n* pl. **-S** a humorous verse
LIMES	*n* pl. **LIMITES** a fortified boundary
LIMEWASH	*n* pl. **-ES** a mixture of lime and water for coating walls
LIMEY	*n* pl. **-EYS** a British sailor
LIMIER	comparative of limy
LIMIEST	superlative of limy
LIMINA	a pl. of limen
LIMINAL	*adj* pertaining to the limen
LIMINESS	*n* pl. **-ES** the state of being limy

LIMING	present participle of lime
LIMIT	*v* **-ED, -ING, -S** to restrict
LIMITARY	*adj* limiting
LIMITED	*n* pl. **-S** a train or bus making few stops
LIMITER	*n* pl. **-S** one that limits
LIMITES	pl. of limes
LIMMER	*n* pl. **-S** a scoundrel
LIMN	*v* **-ED, -ING, -S** to depict by painting or drawing
LIMNER	*n* pl. **-S** one that limns
LIMNETIC	*adj* pertaining to the open water of a lake or pond
LIMNIC	*adj* limnetic
LIMO	*n* pl. **LIMOS** a limousine
LIMONENE	*n* pl. **-S** a chemical compound
LIMONITE	*n* pl. **-S** a major ore of iron
LIMONIUM	*n* pl. **-S** a sea plant of brightly colored funnel-like flowers
LIMP	*adj* **LIMPER, LIMPEST** lacking rigidity
LIMP	*v* **-ED, -ING, -S** to walk lamely
LIMPA	*n* pl. **-S** rye bread made with molasses
LIMPER	*n* pl. **-S** one that limps
LIMPET	*n* pl. **-S** a type of mollusk
LIMPID	*adj* transparent **LIMPIDLY** *adv*
LIMPKIN	*n* pl. **-S** a wading bird
LIMPLY	*adv* in a limp manner
LIMPNESS	*n* pl. **-ES** the state of being limp
LIMPSEY	*adj* **-SIER, -SIEST** limpsy
LIMPSY	*adj* **-SIER, -SIEST** lacking strength or vigor
LIMULOID	*n* pl. **-S** a horseshoe crab
LIMULUS	*n* pl. **-LI** a horseshoe crab
LIMY	*adj* **LIMIER, LIMIEST** resembling or containing lime
LIN	*n* pl. **-S** linn
LINABLE	*adj* lineable
LINAC	*n* pl. **-S** a device for imparting high velocities to charged particles
LINAGE	*n* pl. **-S** the number of lines of printed material
LINALOL	*n* pl. **-S** linalool
LINALOOL	*n* pl. **-S** a fragrant alcohol
LINCHPIN	*n* pl. **-S** a locking pin inserted in the end of a shaft
LINCTUS	*n* pl. **-TUSES** a syrupy medicine

LINDANE *n* pl. **-S** an insecticide

LINDEN *n* pl. **-S** a tall forest tree

LINDY *v* **-DIED, -DYING, -DIES** to perform a fast, lively dance

LINE *v* **LINED, LINING, LINES** to mark with lines (slender, continuous marks)

LINEABLE *adj* lying in a straight line

LINEAGE *n* pl. **-S** direct descent from an ancestor

LINEAL *adj* being directly descended from an ancestor **LINEALLY** *adv*

LINEAR *adj* of or resembling a straight line **LINEARLY** *adv*

LINEATE *adj* marked with lines

LINEATED *adj* lineate

LINEBRED *adj* produced by interbreeding within a particular line of descent

LINECUT *n* pl. **-S** a type of printing plate

LINED past tense of line

LINELESS *adj* having no lines

LINELIKE *adj* resembling a line

LINEMAN *n* pl. **-MEN** one who installs or repairs telephone wires

LINEMATE *n* pl. **-S** a hockey player on the same line as another

LINEN *n* pl. **-S** a fabric woven from the fibers of flax **LINENY** *adj*

LINER *n* pl. **-S** a commercial ship or airplane

LINESMAN *n* pl. **-MEN** a football official

LINEUP *n* pl. **-S** a row of persons

LINEY *adj* **LINIER, LINIEST** liny

LING *n* pl. **-S** a heath plant

LINGA *n* pl. **-S** lingam

LINGAM *n* pl. **-S** a Hindu phallic symbol

LINGCOD *n* pl. **-S** a marine food fish

LINGER *v* **-ED, -ING, -S** to delay leaving

LINGERER *n* pl. **-S** one that lingers

LINGERIE *n* pl. **-S** women's underwear

LINGIER comparative of lingy

LINGIEST superlative of lingy

LINGO *n* pl. **-GOES** or **-GOS** strange or incomprehensible language

LINGUA *n* pl. **-GUAE** the tongue or a tonguelike part

LINGUAL *n* pl. **-S** a sound articulated with the tongue

LINGUICA *n* pl. **-S** a spicy Portuguese sausage

LINGUINE *n* pl. **-S** linguini

LINGUINI *n* pl. **-S** a type of pasta

LINGUISA *n* pl. **-S** linguica

LINGUIST *n* pl. **-S** a person skilled in several languages

LINGULA *n* pl. **-LAE** an organ or process shaped like a tongue **LINGULAR** *adj*

LINGY *adj* **LINGIER, LINGIEST** covered with heaths

LINHAY *n* pl. **-HAYS** linny

LINIER comparative of liney and liny

LINIEST superlative of liney and liny

LINIMENT *n* pl. **-S** a medicinal liquid

LININ *n* pl. **-S** a substance in the nucleus of a cell

LINING *n* pl. **-S** an inner layer

LINK *v* **-ED, -ING, -S** to connect **LINKABLE** *adj*

LINKAGE *n* pl. **-S** the act of linking

LINKBOY *n* pl. **-BOYS** a man or boy hired to carry a torch to light the way along dark streets

LINKER *n* pl. **-S** one that links

LINKMAN *n* pl. **-MEN** a linkboy

LINKSMAN *n* pl. **-MEN** a golfer

LINKUP *n* pl. **-S** something that serves as a linking device

LINKWORK *n* pl. **-S** something composed of interlocking rings

LINKY *adj* full of interlocking rings

LINN *n* pl. **-S** a waterfall

LINNET *n* pl. **-S** a European songbird

LINNEY *n* pl. **-NEYS** linny

LINNY *n* pl. **-NIES** a row of rooms across the back of a house

LINO *n* pl. **-NOS** linoleum

LINOCUT *n* pl. **-S** a print made from a design cut into linoleum

LINOLEUM *n* pl. **-S** a durable material used as a floor covering

LINOTYPE *v* **-TYPED, -TYPING, -TYPES** to set type with a machine

LINSANG *n* pl. **-S** a carnivorous mammal

LINSEED *n* pl. **-S** flaxseed

LINSEY *n* pl. **-SEYS** a coarse fabric

LINSTOCK	*n* pl. **-S** a stick having one end divided to hold a match
LINT	*v* **-ED, -ING, -S** to give off lint (bits of fiber or fluff)
LINTEL	*n* pl. **-S** a horizontal supporting beam **LINTELED** *adj*
LINTER	*n* pl. **-S** a machine for removing fibers from cotton seeds
LINTIER	comparative of linty
LINTIEST	superlative of linty
LINTLESS	*adj* free from lint
LINTOL	*n* pl. **-S** lintel
LINTY	*adj* **LINTIER, LINTIEST** covered with lint
LINUM	*n* pl. **-S** a plant of the flax family
LINURON	*n* pl. **-S** an herbicide
LINY	*adj* **LINIER, LINIEST** resembling a line
LION	*n* pl. **-S** a large, carnivorous feline mammal
LIONESS	*n* pl. **-ES** a female lion
LIONFISH	*n* pl. **-ES** a tropical fish
LIONISE	*v* **-ISED, -ISING, -ISES** to lionize
LIONISER	*n* pl. **-S** one that lionises
LIONIZE	*v* **-IZED, -IZING, -IZES** to treat or regard as a celebrity
LIONIZER	*n* pl. **-S** one that lionizes
LIONLIKE	*adj* resembling a lion
LIP	*v* **LIPPED, LIPPING, LIPS** to touch with the lips (the folds of flesh around the mouth)
LIPA	*n* pl. **LIPE** or **LIPAS** a monetary unit of Croatia
LIPASE	*n* pl. **-S** an enzyme
LIPGLOSS	*n* pl. **-ES** a cosmetic for making lips glossy
LIPID	*n* pl. **-S** any of a class of fatty substances **LIPIDIC** *adj*
LIPIDE	*n* pl. **-S** lipid
LIPIN	*n* pl. **-S** a lipid
LIPLESS	*adj* having no lips
LIPLIKE	*adj* resembling a lip
LIPLINER	*n* pl. **-S** a cosmetic applied to outline the lips
LIPO	*n* pl. **-POS** liposuction
LIPOCYTE	*n* pl. **-S** a fat-producing cell
LIPOGRAM	*n* pl. **-S** a writing in which a certain letter of the alphabet is omitted
LIPOID	*n* pl. **-S** a lipid **LIPOIDAL** *adj*
LIPOMA	*n* pl. **-MAS** or **-MATA** a tumor of fatty tissue
LIPOSOME	*n* pl. **-S** a microscopic globule composed of lipids
LIPPED	past tense of lip
LIPPEN	*v* **-ED, -ING, -S** to trust
LIPPER	*v* **-ED, -ING, -S** to ripple
LIPPING	*n* pl. **-S** a liplike outgrowth of bone
LIPPY	*adj* **-PIER, -PIEST** impudent
LIPREAD	*v* **-READ, -READING, -READS** to understand spoken words by interpreting the lip movements of a speaker
LIPSTICK	*n* pl. **-S** a cosmetic used to color the lips
LIQUATE	*v* **-QUATED, -QUATING, -QUATES** to purify metal by heating
LIQUEFY	*v* **-FIED, -FYING, -FIES** to make or become liquid
LIQUEUR	*n* pl. **-S** a sweetened alcoholic beverage
LIQUID	*n* pl. **-S** a substance that flows freely **LIQUIDY** *adj*
LIQUIDLY	*adv* in a free-flowing manner
LIQUIFY	*v* **-FIED, -FYING, -FIES** to liquefy
LIQUOR	*v* **-ED, -ING, -S** to intoxicate with liquor (an alcoholic beverage)
LIRA	*n* pl. **LIRAS** or **LIRE** a former monetary unit of Italy
LIRA	*n* pl. **LIRI** a former monetary unit of Malta
LIRA	*n* pl. **LIROTH** or **LIROT** a former monetary unit of Israel
LIRIOPE	*n* pl. **-S** a stemless Asian herb
LIRIPIPE	*n* pl. **-S** a long scarf
LISENTE	a pl. of sente
LISLE	*n* pl. **-S** a fine, tightly twisted cotton thread
LISP	*v* **-ED, -ING, -S** to pronounce the letters *s* and *z* imperfectly
LISPER	*n* pl. **-S** one that lisps
LISPING	*n* pl. **-S** the act or an instance of pronouncing the letters *s* or *z* imperfectly
LISSOM	*adj* lissome **LISSOMLY** *adv*
LISSOME	*adj* lithe
LIST	*v* **-ED, -ING, -S** to write down in a particular order **LISTABLE** *adj*

LISTBOX	*n* pl. **-ES** a box on a computer screen that contains a list of options	**LITHOPS**	*n* pl. **LITHOPS** a succulent African plant
LISTEE	*n* pl. **-S** one that is on a list	**LITHOSOL**	*n* pl. **-S** a type of soil
LISTEL	*n* pl. **-S** a narrow molding	**LITIGANT**	*n* pl. **-S** one who is engaged in a lawsuit
LISTEN	*v* **-ED, -ING, -S** to make conscious use of the sense of hearing	**LITIGATE**	*v* **-GATED, -GATING, -GATES** to subject to legal proceedings
LISTENER	*n* pl. **-S** one that listens	**LITMUS**	*n* pl. **-ES** a blue coloring matter
LISTER	*n* pl. **-S** a type of plow	**LITORAL**	*adj* pertaining to a coastal region
LISTERIA	*n* pl. **-S** a rod-shaped bacterium	**LITOTES**	*n* pl. **LITOTES** a figure of speech in which an assertion is made by the negation of its opposite **LITOTIC** *adj*
LISTICLE	*n* pl. **-S** a list of items		
LISTING	*n* pl. **-S** something that is listed		
LISTLESS	*adj* languid	**LITRE**	*n* pl. **-S** liter
LISTSERV	*n* pl. **-S** an email system that automatically sends messages to all subscribers	**LITTEN**	*adj* lighted
		LITTER	*v* **-ED, -ING, -S** to scatter rubbish about
LIT	*n* pl. **-S** the litas	**LITTERER**	*n* pl. **-S** one that litters
LITANY	*n* pl. **-NIES** a ceremonial form of prayer	**LITTERY**	*adj* covered with rubbish
		LITTLE	*adj* **-TLER, -TLEST** small
LITAS	*n* pl. **LITAI** or **LITU** a monetary unit of Lithuania	**LITTLE**	*n* pl. **-S** a small amount
		LITTLISH	*adj* somewhat little
LITCHI	*n* pl. **-S** the edible fruit of a Chinese tree	**LITTORAL**	*n* pl. **-S** a coastal region
LITE	*n* pl. **-S** a beer having relatively few calories	**LITU**	a pl. of litas
		LITURGY	*n* pl. **-GIES** a prescribed system of public worship **LITURGIC** *adj*
LITENESS	*n* pl. **-ES** the state of being lite		
LITER	*n* pl. **-S** a unit of capacity	**LIVABLE**	*adj* suitable for living in
LITERACY	*n* pl. **-CIES** the ability to read and write	**LIVE**	*adj* **LIVER, LIVEST** having life
		LIVE	*v* **LIVED, LIVING, LIVES** to function as an animal or plant
LITERAL	*n* pl. **-S** a small error in printing or writing		
		LIVEABLE	*adj* livable
LITERARY	*adj* of, pertaining to, or having the characteristics of books and writings	**LIVELONG**	*adj* long in passing
		LIVELY	*adj* **-LIER, -LIEST** full of energy **LIVELILY** *adv*
LITERATE	*n* pl. **-S** one who can read and write	**LIVEN**	*v* **-ED, -ING, -S** to make lively
LITERATI	*n/pl* scholars collectively	**LIVENER**	*n* pl. **-S** one that livens
LITHARGE	*n* pl. **-S** a monoxide of lead	**LIVENESS**	*n* pl. **-ES** the state of being live
LITHE	*adj* **LITHER, LITHEST** bending easily **LITHELY** *adv*	**LIVER**	*v* **-ED, -ING, -S** to thicken or gel
		LIVERIED	*adj* wearing a livery
LITHEMIA	*n* pl. **-S** an excess of uric acid in the blood **LITHEMIC** *adj*	**LIVERISH**	*adj* having a disorder of the liver (a bodily organ)
LITHIA	*n* pl. **-S** an oxide of lithium	**LIVERY**	*n* pl. **-ERIES** a uniform worn by servants
LITHIC	*adj* pertaining to lithium		
LITHIFY	*v* **-FIED, -FYING, -FIES** to petrify	**LIVES**	pl. of life
LITHIUM	*n* pl. **-S** a metallic element	**LIVEST**	superlative of live
LITHO	*v* **-ED, -ING, -S** or **-ES** to make prints by lithography	**LIVETRAP**	*v* **-TRAPPED, -TRAPPING, -TRAPS** to capture in a type of animal trap
LITHOID	*adj* resembling stone	**LIVEWARE**	*n* pl. **-S** working personnel

LIVEWELL	*n* pl. **-S** a container of water in a boat for keeping fish alive	**LOATHER**	*n* pl. **-S** one that loathes
LIVEYER	*n* pl. **-S** livyer	**LOATHFUL**	*adj* repulsive
LIVID	*adj* having the skin abnormally discolored **LIVIDLY** *adv*	**LOATHING**	*n* pl. **-S** extreme dislike
		LOATHLY	*adj* repulsive
LIVIDITY	*n* pl. **-TIES** the state of being livid	**LOAVES**	pl. of loaf
LIVIER	*n* pl. **-S** livyer	**LOB**	*v* **LOBBED, LOBBING, LOBS** to throw or hit in a high arc
LIVING	*n* pl. **-S** a means of subsistence	**LOBAR**	*adj* pertaining to a lobe
LIVINGLY	*adv* realistically	**LOBATE**	*adj* having lobes **LOBATELY** *adv*
LIVRE	*n* pl. **-S** a former monetary unit of France	**LOBATED**	*adj* lobate
LIVYER	*n* pl. **-S** a permanent resident of Newfoundland	**LOBATION**	*n* pl. **-S** the formation of lobes
		LOBBED	past tense of lob
LIXIVIUM	*n* pl. **-IUMS** or **-IA** a solution obtained by leaching **LIXIVIAL** *adj*	**LOBBER**	*n* pl. **-S** one that lobs
		LOBBING	present participle of lob
LIZARD	*n* pl. **-S** any of a suborder of reptiles	**LOBBY**	*v* **-BIED, -BYING, -BIES** to attempt to influence legislators
LLAMA	*n* pl. **-S** a ruminant mammal	**LOBBYER**	*n* pl. **-S** a lobbyist
LLANO	*n* pl. **-NOS** an open, grassy plain	**LOBBYGOW**	*n* pl. **-S** an errand boy
LO	*interj* — used to attract attention or to express surprise	**LOBBYING**	*n* pl. **-S** the soliciting of support of an influential person
LOACH	*n* pl. **-ES** a freshwater fish	**LOBBYISM**	*n* pl. **-S** the practice of lobbying
LOAD	*v* **-ED, -ING, -S** to place in or on a means of conveyance **LOADABLE** *adj*	**LOBBYIST**	*n* pl. **-S** one who lobbies
		LOBE	*n* pl. **-S** a rounded, projecting anatomical part **LOBED** *adj*
LOADER	*n* pl. **-S** one that loads	**LOBEFIN**	*n* pl. **-S** a bony fish
LOADING	*n* pl. **-S** a burden	**LOBELESS**	*adj* lacking a lobe
LOADSTAR	*n* pl. **-S** lodestar	**LOBELIA**	*n* pl. **-S** a flowering plant
LOAF	*n* pl. **LOAVES** a shaped mass of bread	**LOBELINE**	*n* pl. **-S** a poisonous alkaloid
LOAF	*v* **-ED, -ING, -S** to pass time idly	**LOBLOLLY**	*n* pl. **-LIES** a pine tree
LOAFER	*n* pl. **-S** one that loafs	**LOBO**	*n* pl. **-BOS** the timber wolf
LOAFING	*n* pl. **-S** a place where cattle are allowed to roam freely	**LOBOTOMY**	*n* pl. **-MIES** a type of surgical operation
LOAM	*v* **-ED, -ING, -S** to cover with loam (a type of soil)	**LOBSTER**	*v* **-ED, -ING, -S** to fish for lobsters (marine crustaceans)
LOAMLESS	*adj* having no loam	**LOBSTICK**	*n* pl. **-S** a tree with its lower branches trimmed
LOAMY	*adj* **LOAMIER, LOAMIEST** resembling loam	**LOBTAIL**	*v* **-ED, -ING, -S** (of a whale) to slap its tail against the surface of the water
LOAN	*v* **-ED, -ING, -S** to lend **LOANABLE** *adj*		
LOANEE	*n* pl. **-S** one that receives a loan	**LOBULE**	*n* pl. **-S** a small lobe **LOBULAR, LOBULATE, LOBULOSE** *adj*
LOANER	*n* pl. **-S** one that loans		
LOANING	*n* pl. **-S** a lane	**LOBWORM**	*n* pl. **-S** a lugworm
LOANWORD	*n* pl. **-S** a word taken from another language	**LOCA**	a pl. of locus
		LOCAL	*n* pl. **-S** a train or bus making all stops
LOATH	*adj* unwilling		
LOATHE	*v* **LOATHED, LOATHING, LOATHES** to detest greatly	**LOCALE**	*n* pl. **-S** a locality
		LOCALISE	*v* **-ISED, -ISING, -ISES** to localize

LOCALISM *n* pl. **-S** a custom or mannerism peculiar to a locality

LOCALIST *n* pl. **-S** one who is strongly concerned with the matters of a locality

LOCALITE *n* pl. **-S** a resident of a locality

LOCALITY *n* pl. **-TIES** an area or neighborhood

LOCALIZE *v* **-IZED, -IZING, -IZES** to confine to a particular area

LOCALLY *adv* in a particular area

LOCATE *v* **-CATED, -CATING, -CATES** to determine the position of

LOCATER *n* pl. **-S** one that locates

LOCATION *n* pl. **-S** the place where something is at a given moment

LOCATIVE *n* pl. **-S** a type of grammatical case

LOCATOR *n* pl. **-S** locater

LOCAVORE *n* pl. **-S** one who eats foods grown locally when possible

LOCH *n* pl. **-S** a lake

LOCHAN *n* pl. **-S** a small lake

LOCHE *n* pl. **-S** a fish of the cod family

LOCHIA *n* pl. **-S** a vaginal discharge following childbirth **LOCHIAL** *adj*

LOCI *n* pl. **-S** an engine used in logging

LOCIE *n* pl. **-S** loci

LOCK *v* **-ED, -ING, -S** to secure by means of a mechanical fastening device **LOCKABLE** *adj*

LOCKAGE *n* pl. **-S** a toll on a ship passing through a canal

LOCKBOX *n* pl. **-ES** a box that locks

LOCKDOWN *n* pl. **-S** the confinement of prisoners to their cells

LOCKER *n* pl. **-S** an enclosure that may be locked

LOCKET *n* pl. **-S** a small ornamental case

LOCKJAW *n* pl. **-S** a form of tetanus

LOCKLESS *adj* lacking a lock (a mechanical fastening device)

LOCKNUT *n* pl. **-S** a nut which keeps another from loosening

LOCKOUT *n* pl. **-S** a closing of a business to coerce employees to agree to terms

LOCKRAM *n* pl. **-S** a coarse, linen fabric

LOCKSET *n* pl. **-S** a set of hardware for locking a door

LOCKSTEP *n* pl. **-S** a mode of marching in close file

LOCKUP *n* pl. **-S** a jail

LOCO *n* pl. **-COS** or **-COES** locoweed

LOCO *v* **-ED, -ING, -S** to poison with locoweed

LOCOFOCO *n* pl. **-COS** a type of friction match

LOCOISM *n* pl. **-S** a disease of livestock

LOCOMOTE *v* **-MOTED, -MOTING, -MOTES** to move about

LOCOWEED *n* pl. **-S** a plant that causes poisoning when eaten by livestock

LOCULAR *adj* having or divided into loculi

LOCULATE *adj* locular

LOCULE *n* pl. **-S** loculus **LOCULED** *adj*

LOCULUS *n* pl. **-LI** a small, cell-like chamber

LOCUM *n* pl. **-S** a temporary substitute

LOCUS *n* pl. **LOCI** or **LOCA** a place

LOCUST *n* pl. **-S** a migratory grasshopper

LOCUSTA *n* pl. **-TAE** a spikelet **LOCUSTAL** *adj*

LOCUTION *n* pl. **-S** a particular form of expression

LOCUTORY *n* pl. **-RIES** a room in a monastery

LODE *n* pl. **-S** a deposit of ore

LODEN *n* pl. **-S** a thick, woolen fabric

LODESTAR *n* pl. **-S** a star used as a point of reference

LODGE *v* **LODGED, LODGING, LODGES** to furnish with temporary quarters

LODGER *n* pl. **-S** one that resides in rented quarters

LODGING *n* pl. **-S** a temporary place to live

LODGMENT *n* pl. **-S** a lodging

LODICULE *n* pl. **-S** a scale at the base of the ovary of a grass

LOESS *n* pl. **-ES** a soil deposit **LOESSAL, LOESSIAL, LOESSIC** *adj*

LOFT *v* **-ED, -ING, -S** to store in a loft (an upper room)

LOFTER *n* pl. **-S** a type of golf club

LOFTIER comparative of lofty

LOFTIEST superlative of lofty

LOFTILY *adv* in a lofty manner

LOFTLESS *adj* having no loft

LOFTLIKE *adj* resembling a loft

LOFTY *adj* **LOFTIER, LOFTIEST** extending high in the air

LOG *v* **LOGGED, LOGGING, LOGS** to cut down trees for timber

LOGAN	*n* pl. **-S** a stone balanced to permit easy movement
LOGANIA	*adj* designating a family of flowering plants
LOGBOOK	*n* pl. **-S** a record book of a ship or aircraft
LOGE	*n* pl. **-S** a small compartment
LOGGATS	*n/pl* loggets
LOGGED	past tense of log
LOGGER	*n* pl. **-S** one that logs
LOGGETS	*n/pl* an old English throwing game
LOGGIA	*n* pl. **-GIAS** or **-GIE** an open gallery
LOGGING	*n* pl. **-S** the business of cutting down trees for timber
LOGGISH	*adj* resembling a log
LOGGY	*adj* **-GIER, -GIEST** logy
LOGIA	a pl. of logion
LOGIC	*n* pl. **-S** the science of reasoning
LOGICAL	*adj* pertaining to logic
LOGICIAN	*n* pl. **-S** one who is skilled in logic
LOGICISE	*v* **-CISED, -CISING, -CISES** to logicize
LOGICIZE	*v* **-CIZED, -CIZING, -CIZES** to reason
LOGIER	comparative of logy
LOGIEST	superlative of logy
LOGILY	*adv* in a logy manner
LOGIN	*n* pl. **-S** the process of identifying oneself to a computer
LOGINESS	*n* pl. **-ES** the state of being logy
LOGION	*n* pl. **-GIONS** or **-GIA** a saying attributed to Jesus
LOGISTIC	*n* pl. **-S** symbolic logic
LOGJAM	*v* **-JAMMED, -JAMMING, -JAMS** to cause to become tangled in a mass
LOGO	*n* pl. **LOGOS** an identifying symbol **LOGOED** *adj*
LOGOFF	*n* pl. **-S** a logout
LOGOGRAM	*n* pl. **-S** a symbol used to represent an entire word
LOGOMACH	*n* pl. **-S** one given to arguing about words
LOGON	*n* pl. **-S** login
LOGOS	*n* pl. **-GOI** the rational principle that governs the universe in ancient Greek philosophy
LOGOTYPE	*n* pl. **-S** a piece of type bearing a syllable, word, or words
LOGOTYPY	*n* pl. **-TYPIES** the use of logotypes
LOGOUT	*n* pl. **-S** the act of ending a connection with a computer system
LOGROLL	*v* **-ED, -ING, -S** to obtain passage of by exchanging political favors
LOGWAY	*n* pl. **-WAYS** a ramp used in logging
LOGWOOD	*n* pl. **-S** a tropical tree
LOGY	*adj* **-GIER, -GIEST** sluggish
LOIASIS	*n* pl. **-ASES** a tropical African disease
LOID	*v* **-ED, -ING, -S** to open a spring lock by using a piece of celluloid
LOIN	*n* pl. **-S** a part of the side and back between the ribs and the hipbone
LOITER	*v* **-ED, -ING, -S** to stand idly about
LOITERER	*n* pl. **-S** one that loiters
LOLL	*v* **-ED, -ING, -S** to lounge
LOLLER	*n* pl. **-S** one that lolls
LOLLIES	pl. of lolly
LOLLIPOP	*n* pl. **-S** a piece of candy on the end of a stick
LOLLOP	*v* **-ED, -ING, -S** to loll
LOLLOPY	*adj* characterized by a bobbing motion
LOLLY	*n* pl. **-LIES** a lollipop
LOLLYGAG	*v* **-GAGGED, -GAGGING, -GAGS** to lallygag
LOLLYPOP	*n* pl. **-S** lollipop
LOMEIN	*n* pl. **-S** a Chinese dish of noodles, meat, and vegetables
LOMENT	*n* pl. **-S** a type of plant pod
LOMENTUM	*n* pl. **-TUMS** or **-TA** loment
LONE	*adj* having no companions
LONELY	*adj* **-LIER, -LIEST** sad from lack of companionship **LONELILY** *adv*
LONENESS	*n* pl. **-ES** the state of being lone
LONER	*n* pl. **-S** one that avoids others
LONESOME	*n* pl. **-S** self
LONG	*adj* **LONGER, LONGEST** extending for a considerable distance
LONG	*v* **-ED, -ING, -S** to desire strongly
LONGAN	*n* pl. **-S** the edible fruit of a Chinese tree
LONGBOAT	*n* pl. **-S** the largest boat carried by a sailing vessel
LONGBOW	*n* pl. **-S** a type of archery bow

LONGE	*v* **LONGED, LONGEING, LONGES** to guide a horse by means of a long rope
LONGER	*n* pl. **-S** one that longs
LONGERON	*n* pl. **-S** a longitudinal support of an airplane
LONGFORM	*adj* unusually long in form
LONGHAIR	*n* pl. **-S** an intellectual
LONGHAND	*n* pl. **-S** ordinary handwriting
LONGHEAD	*n* pl. **-S** a person having a long skull
LONGHORN	*n* pl. **-S** one of a breed of long-horned cattle
LONGIES	*n/pl* long underwear
LONGING	*n* pl. **-S** a strong desire
LONGISH	*adj* somewhat long
LONGJUMP	*v* **-ED, -ING, -S** to jump for distance from a running start
LONGLEAF	*n* pl. **-LEAVES** an evergreen tree
LONGLINE	*n* pl. **-S** a type of fishing line
LONGLY	*adv* for a considerable distance
LONGNECK	*n* pl. **-S** a beer bottle with a long neck
LONGNESS	*n* pl. **-ES** the state of being long
LONGSHIP	*n* pl. **-S** a medieval ship
LONGSOME	*adj* tediously long
LONGSPUR	*n* pl. **-S** a long-clawed finch
LONGTIME	*adj* of long duration
LONGUEUR	*n* pl. **-S** a dull and tedious section
LONGWAYS	*adv* longwise
LONGWISE	*adv* lengthwise
LONICERA	*n* pl. **-S** a shrub with fragrant flowers
LOO	*v* **-ED, -ING, -S** to subject to a forfeit at loo (a card game)
LOOBY	*n* pl. **-BIES** a large, awkward person
LOOEY	*n* pl. **-EYS** looie
LOOF	*n* pl. **-S** the palm of the hand
LOOFA	*n* pl. **-S** loofah
LOOFAH	*n* pl. **-S** a tropical vine
LOOGIE	*n* pl. **-S** a mass of saliva and phlegm
LOOIE	*n* pl. **-S** a lieutenant of the armed forces
LOOK	*v* **-ED, -ING, -S** to use one's eyes in seeing
LOOKDOWN	*n* pl. **-S** a marine fish
LOOKER	*n* pl. **-S** one that looks
LOOKIE	*interj* looky
LOOKISM	*n* pl. **-S** discrimination based on physical appearance
LOOKIST	*n* pl. **-S** one that practices lookism
LOOKIT	*interj* — used to draw attention to something
LOOKOUT	*n* pl. **-S** one engaged in keeping watch
LOOKSISM	*n* pl. **-S** lookism
LOOKUP	*n* pl. **-S** the process of looking something up
LOOKY	*interj* — used to draw attention to something
LOOM	*v* **-ED, -ING, -S** to appear in an enlarged and indistinct form
LOON	*n* pl. **-S** a diving waterfowl
LOONEY	*adj* **-NIER, -NIEST** loony
LOONEY	*n* pl. **-EYS** loony
LOONIE	*n* pl. **-S** a coin worth one Canadian dollar
LOONY	*adj* **-NIER, -NIEST** crazy **LOONILY** *adv*
LOONY	*n* pl. **-NIES** a loony person
LOOP	*v* **-ED, -ING, -S** to form loops (circular or oval openings)
LOOPER	*n* pl. **-S** one that loops
LOOPHOLE	*v* **-HOLED, -HOLING, -HOLES** to make small openings in
LOOPY	*adj* **LOOPIER, LOOPIEST** full of loops **LOOPILY** *adv*
LOOSE	*adj* **LOOSER, LOOSEST** not firm, taut, or rigid **LOOSELY** *adv*
LOOSE	*v* **LOOSED, LOOSING, LOOSES** to set free
LOOSEN	*v* **-ED, -ING, -S** to make looser
LOOSENER	*n* pl. **-S** one that loosens
LOOSER	comparative of loose
LOOSEST	superlative of loose
LOOSING	present participle of loose
LOOT	*v* **-ED, -ING, -S** to plunder
LOOTER	*n* pl. **-S** one that loots
LOOTING	*n* pl. **-S** the act of stealing goods left unprotected
LOP	*v* **LOPPED, LOPPING, LOPS** to cut off branches or twigs from
LOPE	*v* **LOPED, LOPING, LOPES** to run with a steady, easy gait
LOPER	*n* pl. **-S** one that lopes

LOPINGLY *adv* in the manner of one that lopes

LOPPED past tense of lop

LOPPER *v* **-ED, -ING, -S** to curdle

LOPPET *n* pl. **-S** a long-distance cross-country ski race

LOPPING present participle of lop

LOPPY *adj* **-PIER, -PIEST** hanging limply

LOPSIDED *adj* leaning to one side

LOPSTICK *n* pl. **-S** lobstick

LOQUAT *n* pl. **-S** a small yellow fruit

LOQUITUR *v* he or she speaks

LOR *interj* — used to express surprise or dismay

LORAL *adj* pertaining to the space between the eye and bill of a bird

LORAN *n* pl. **-S** a type of navigational system

LORD *v* **-ED, -ING, -S** to invest with the power of a lord (a person having dominion over others)

LORDING *n* pl. **-S** a lordling

LORDLESS *adj* having no lord

LORDLIER comparative of lordly

LORDLIEST superlative of lordly

LORDLIKE *adj* lordly

LORDLING *n* pl. **-S** a young or unimportant lord

LORDLY *adj* **-LIER, -LIEST** of or befitting a lord

LORDOMA *n* pl. **-S** lordosis

LORDOSIS *n* pl. **-DOSES** a curvature of the spinal column **LORDOTIC** *adj*

LORDSHIP *n* pl. **-S** the power of a lord

LORE *n* pl. **-S** traditional knowledge or belief

LOREAL *adj* loral

LORGNON *n* pl. **-S** a pair of eyeglasses with a handle

LORICA *n* pl. **-CAE** or **-CAS** a protective covering or shell

LORICATE *n* pl. **-S** an animal having a lorica

LORIES pl. of lory

LORIKEET *n* pl. **-S** a small parrot

LORIMER *n* pl. **-S** a maker of implements for harnesses and saddles

LORINER *n* pl. **-S** lorimer

LORIS *n* pl. **-RISES** an Asian lemur

LORN *adj* abandoned

LORNNESS *n* pl. **-ES** the state of being lorn

LORRY *n* pl. **-RIES** a type of wagon or truck

LORY *n* pl. **-RIES** a small parrot

LOSE *v* **LOST, LOSING, LOSES** to come to be without and be unable to find **LOSABLE** *adj*

LOSEL *n* pl. **-S** a worthless person

LOSER *n* pl. **-S** one that loses

LOSING *n* pl. **-S** a loss

LOSINGLY *adv* in a manner characterized by defeat

LOSS *n* pl. **-ES** the act of one that loses

LOSSLESS *adj* done or being without loss

LOSSY *adj* causing dissipation of electrical energy

LOST *adj* not to be found or recovered

LOSTNESS *n* pl. **-ES** the state of being lost

LOT *v* **LOTTED, LOTTING, LOTS** to distribute proportionately

LOTA *n* pl. **-S** lotah

LOTAH *n* pl. **-S** a small water vessel used in India

LOTH *adj* loath

LOTHARIO *n* pl. **-IOS** a seducer of women

LOTHSOME *adj* repulsive

LOTI *n* pl. **MALOTI** a monetary unit of Lesotho

LOTIC *adj* pertaining to moving water

LOTION *n* pl. **-S** a liquid preparation for external application

LOTO *n* pl. **-S** lotto

LOTOS *n* pl. **-ES** lotus

LOTTE *n* pl. **-S** a monkfish

LOTTED past tense of lot

LOTTER *n* pl. **-S** one who assembles merchandise into salable lots

LOTTERY *n* pl. **-TERIES** a type of gambling game

LOTTING present participle of lot

LOTTO *n* pl. **-TOS** a game of chance

LOTUS *n* pl. **-ES** an aquatic plant

LOUCHE *adj* not reputable

LOUD *adj* **LOUDER, LOUDEST** strongly audible

LOUDEN *v* **-ED, -ING, -S** to make or become louder

LOUDISH *adj* somewhat loud

LOUDLY *adv* **-LIER, -LIEST** in a loud manner

LOUDNESS *n* pl. **-ES** the quality of being loud

LOUGH *n* pl. **-S** a lake

LOUIE *n* pl. **-S** looie

LOUIS *n* pl. **LOUIS** a former gold coin of France

LOUMA *n* pl. **-S** luma

LOUNGE *v* **LOUNGED, LOUNGING, LOUNGES** to recline or lean in a relaxed, lazy manner

LOUNGER *n* pl. **-S** one that lounges

LOUNGEY *adj* loungy

LOUNGY *adj* **LOUNGIER, LOUNGIEST** suitable for lounging

LOUP *v* **LOUPED, LOUPEN, LOUPING, LOUPS** to leap

LOUPE *n* pl. **-S** a small magnifying glass

LOUR *v* **-ED, -ING, -S** to lower

LOURY *adj* lowery

LOUSE *n* pl. **LICE** a parasitic insect

LOUSE *v* **LOUSED, LOUSING, LOUSES** to spoil or bungle

LOUSY *adj* **LOUSIER, LOUSIEST** mean or contemptible **LOUSILY** *adv*

LOUT *v* **-ED, -ING, -S** to bow in respect

LOUTISH *adj* clumsy

LOUVER *n* pl. **-S** a type of window **LOUVERED** *adj*

LOUVRE *n* pl. **-S** louver **LOUVRED** *adj*

LOVABLE *adj* having qualities that attract love **LOVABLY** *adv*

LOVAGE *n* pl. **-S** a perennial herb

LOVAT *n* pl. **-S** a chiefly green color mixture in fabrics

LOVE *v* **LOVED, LOVING, LOVES** to feel great affection for

LOVEABLE *adj* lovable **LOVEABLY** *adv*

LOVEBIRD *n* pl. **-S** a small parrot

LOVEBUG *n* pl. **-S** a small black fly that swarms along highways

LOVED past tense of love

LOVEFEST *n* pl. **-S** a gathering to promote good feeling

LOVELESS *adj* feeling no love

LOVELIER comparative of lovely

LOVELIES pl. of lovely

LOVELIEST superlative of lovely

LOVELILY *adv* in a lovely manner

LOVELOCK *n* pl. **-S** a lock of hair hanging separately

LOVELORN *adj* not loved

LOVELY *adj* **-LIER, -LIEST** beautiful

LOVELY *n* pl. **-LIES** a beautiful woman

LOVER *n* pl. **-S** one that loves another **LOVERLY** *adj*

LOVESEAT *n* pl. **-S** a small sofa for two persons

LOVESICK *adj* languishing with love

LOVESOME *adj* lovely

LOVEVINE *n* pl. **-S** a twining herb

LOVEY *n* pl. **LOVEYS** a sweetheart

LOVEY *adj* **LOVIER, LOVIEST** fondly affectionate

LOVING *n* pl. **-S** the act of expressing love

LOVINGLY *adv* in a loving manner

LOW *adj* **LOWER, LOWEST** having relatively little upward extension

LOW *v* **-ED, -ING, -S** to utter the sound characteristic of cattle

LOWBALL *v* **-ED, -ING, -S** to give a customer a deceptively low price

LOWBORN *adj* of humble birth

LOWBOY *n* pl. **-BOYS** a low chest of drawers

LOWBRED *adj* lowborn

LOWBROW *n* pl. **-S** an uncultivated person

LOWBUSH *n* pl. **-ES** a bush with sweet blueberries

LOWDOWN *n* pl. **-S** the whole truth

LOWE *v* **LOWED, LOWING, LOWES** to blaze

LOWER *v* **-ED, -ING, -S** to appear dark and threatening

LOWERY *adj* dark and threatening

LOWING *n* pl. **-S** the sound characteristic of cattle

LOWISH *adj* somewhat low

LOWLAND *n* pl. **-S** an area of land lying lower than the adjacent country

LOWLIFE *n* pl. **-LIFES** or **-LIVES** a despicable person

LOWLIFER *n* pl. **-S** a lowlife

LOWLIGHT *n* pl. **-S** an unpleasant event, detail, or part

LOWLY *adj* **-LIER, -LIEST** low in position or rank **LOWLILY** *adv*

LOWN *adj* peaceful

LOWNESS *n* pl. **-ES** the state of being low

LOWPASS   *adj* being a type of filter

LOWRIDER   *n* pl. **-S** a car having a lowered suspension

LOWSE   *adj* loose

LOX   *v* **-ED, -ING, -ES** to supply with lox (liquid oxygen)

LOYAL   *adj* **-ALER, -ALEST** faithful to one's allegiance

LOYALISM   *n* pl. **-S** loyalty

LOYALIST   *n* pl. **-S** one who is loyal

LOYALLY   *adv* in a loyal manner

LOYALTY   *n* pl. **-TIES** the state of being loyal

LOZENGE   *n* pl. **-S** a small, often medicated candy

LUAU   *n* pl. **-S** a Hawaiian feast

LUBBER   *n* pl. **-S** a clumsy person **LUBBERLY** *adj*

LUBE   *v* **LUBED, LUBING, LUBES** to lubricate

LUBRIC   *adj* slippery

LUBRICAL   *adj* lubric

LUCARNE   *n* pl. **-S** a type of window

LUCE   *n* pl. **-S** a freshwater fish

LUCENCE   *n* pl. **-S** lucency

LUCENCY   *n* pl. **-CIES** the quality of being lucent

LUCENT   *adj* giving off light **LUCENTLY** *adv*

LUCERN   *n* pl. **-S** lucerne

LUCERNE   *n* pl. **-S** alfalfa

LUCES   a pl. of lux

LUCID   *adj* **-ER, -EST** easily understood **LUCIDLY** *adv*

LUCIDITY   *n* pl. **-TIES** the quality of being lucid

LUCIFER   *n* pl. **-S** a friction match

LUCK   *v* **-ED, -ING, -S** to succeed by chance or good fortune

LUCKIE   *n* pl. **-S** an old woman

LUCKLESS   *adj* unlucky

LUCKY   *adj* **LUCKIER, LUCKIEST** having good fortune **LUCKILY** *adv*

LUCRE   *n* pl. **-S** monetary gain

LUCULENT   *adj* lucid

LUD   *n* pl. **-S** a form of address to a judge in a court

LUDE   *n* pl. **-S** a methaqualone pill

LUDIC   *adj* aimlessly playful

LUDO   *n* pl. **-DOS** a simple board game

LUES   *n* pl. **LUES** syphilis

LUETIC   *n* pl. **-S** one infected with syphilis

LUFF   *v* **-ED, -ING, -S** to steer a sailing vessel nearer into the wind

LUFFA   *n* pl. **-S** loofah

LUG   *v* **LUGGED, LUGGING, LUGS** to carry or pull with effort

LUGE   *v* **LUGED, LUGEING** or **LUGING, LUGES** to race on a luge (a small sled)

LUGER   *n* pl. **-S** one that luges

LUGGAGE   *n* pl. **-S** articles containing a traveler's belongings

LUGGED   past tense of lug

LUGGER   *n* pl. **-S** a small sailing vessel

LUGGIE   *n* pl. **-S** a small wooden dish or pail

LUGGING   present participle of lug

LUGSAIL   *n* pl. **-S** a type of sail

LUGWORM   *n* pl. **-S** a burrowing marine worm

LUKEWARM   *adj* moderately warm

LULL   *v* **-ED, -ING, -S** to cause to sleep or rest

LULLABY   *v* **-BIED, -BYING, -BIES** to lull with a soothing song

LULLER   *n* pl. **-S** one that lulls

LULU   *n* pl. **-S** something remarkable

LUM   *n* pl. **-S** a chimney

LUMA   *n* pl. **-S** a monetary unit of Armenia

LUMBAGO   *n* pl. **-GOS** pain in the lower back

LUMBAR   *n* pl. **-S** an anatomical part situated near the loins

LUMBER   *v* **-ED, -ING, -S** to cut down and prepare timber for market

LUMBERER   *n* pl. **-S** one that lumbers

LUMBERLY   *adj* moving slowly with a heavy gait

LUMEN   *n* pl. **-MENS** or **-MINA** the inner passage of a tubular organ **LUMENAL, LUMINAL** *adj*

LUMINARY   *n* pl. **-NARIES** a body that gives light

LUMINISM   *n* pl. **-S** a style of painting

LUMINIST   *n* pl. **-S** a painter who uses the effects of light

LUMINOUS   *adj* giving off light

LUMMOX   *n* pl. **-ES** a clumsy person

LUMP   *v* **-ED, -ING, -S** to make into lumps (shapeless masses)

LUMPEN   *n* pl. **-S** an uprooted individual

LUMPER *n* pl. **-S** a laborer employed to load and unload ships

LUMPFISH *n* pl. **-ES** a marine fish

LUMPIA *n* pl. **-S** an Indonesian spring roll

LUMPISH *adj* stupid

LUMPY *adj* **LUMPIER, LUMPIEST** full of lumps **LUMPILY** *adv*

LUN *n* pl. **-S** a lee

LUNA *n* pl. **-S** an alchemical designation for silver

LUNACY *n* pl. **-CIES** insanity

LUNAR *n* pl. **-S** an observation of the moon taken for navigational purposes

LUNARIAN *n* pl. **-S** a supposed inhabitant of the moon

LUNATE *adj* crescent-shaped **LUNATELY** *adv*

LUNATED *adj* lunate

LUNATIC *n* pl. **-S** an insane person

LUNATION *n* pl. **-S** the interval between two successive new moons

LUNCH *v* **-ED, -ING, -ES** to eat a noonday meal

LUNCHBOX *n* pl. **-ES** a container for carrying meals to school or work

LUNCHEON *n* pl. **-S** a noonday meal

LUNCHER *n* pl. **-S** one that lunches

LUNE *n* pl. **-S** a crescent-shaped figure

LUNET *n* pl. **-S** lunette

LUNETTE *n* pl. **-S** a crescent-shaped object

LUNG *n* pl. **-S** a respiratory organ

LUNGAN *n* pl. **-S** longan

LUNGE *v* **LUNGED, LUNGING** or **LUNGEING, LUNGES** to make a forceful forward movement

LUNGEE *n* pl. **-S** lungi

LUNGER *n* pl. **-S** one that lunges

LUNGFISH *n* pl. **-ES** a type of fish

LUNGFUL *n* pl. **-S** as much as the lungs can hold

LUNGI *n* pl. **-S** a loincloth worn by men in India

LUNGING a present participle of lunge

LUNGLESS *adj* having no lung

LUNGWORM *n* pl. **-S** a parasitic worm

LUNGWORT *n* pl. **-S** a European herb

LUNGYI *n* pl. **-S** lungi

LUNIER comparative of luny

LUNIES pl. of luny

LUNIEST superlative of luny

LUNK *n* pl. **-S** a lunkhead

LUNKER *n* pl. **-S** a large game fish

LUNKHEAD *n* pl. **-S** a stupid person

LUNT *v* **-ED, -ING, -S** to emit smoke

LUNULA *n* pl. **-LAE** a small crescent-shaped structure **LUNULAR, LUNULATE** *adj*

LUNULE *n* pl. **-S** lunula

LUNY *adj* **-NIER, -NIEST** loony

LUNY *n* pl. **-NIES** a loony

LUPANAR *n* pl. **-S** a brothel

LUPIN *n* pl. **-S** lupine

LUPINE *n* pl. **-S** a flowering plant

LUPULIN *n* pl. **-S** a medicinal powder obtained from the hop plant

LUPUS *n* pl. **-ES** a skin disease **LUPOID, LUPOUS** *adj*

LURCH *v* **-ED, -ING, -ES** to sway abruptly

LURCHER *n* pl. **-S** one that lurks or prowls

LURDAN *n* pl. **-S** a lazy or stupid person

LURDANE *n* pl. **-S** lurdan

LURE *v* **LURED, LURING, LURES** to attract with something desirable

LURER *n* pl. **-S** one that lures

LURID *adj* causing shock or horror **LURIDLY** *adv*

LURINGLY *adv* in an enticing manner

LURK *v* **-ED, -ING, -S** to wait in concealment

LURKER *n* pl. **-S** one that lurks

LUSCIOUS *adj* having a very pleasing taste or smell

LUSH *adj* **LUSHER, LUSHEST** abounding in vegetation **LUSHLY** *adv*

LUSH *v* **-ED, -ING, -ES** to drink to excess

LUSHNESS *n* pl. **-ES** the state of being lush

LUST *v* **-ED, -ING, -S** to have an intense desire

LUSTER *v* **-ED, -ING, -S** to make or become lustrous

LUSTFUL *adj* marked by excessive sexual desire

LUSTIER comparative of lusty

LUSTIEST superlative of lusty

LUSTILY *adv* in a lusty manner

LUSTRA	a pl. of lustrum
LUSTRAL	*adj* pertaining to a lustrum
LUSTRATE	*v* **-TRATED, -TRATING, -TRATES** to purify ceremonially
LUSTRE	*v* **-TRED, -TRING, -TRES** to luster
LUSTRINE	*n* pl. **-S** lustring
LUSTRING	*n* pl. **-S** a glossy silk fabric
LUSTROUS	*adj* reflecting light evenly and efficiently
LUSTRUM	*n* pl. **-TRUMS** or **-TRA** a ceremonial purification of the population in ancient Rome
LUSTY	*adj* **LUSTIER, LUSTIEST** full of vigor
LUSUS	*n* pl. **-ES** an abnormality
LUTANIST	*n* pl. **-S** one who plays the lute
LUTE	*v* **LUTED, LUTING, LUTES** to play a lute (a stringed musical instrument)
LUTEA	pl. of luteum
LUTEAL	*adj* pertaining to the luteum
LUTECIUM	*n* pl. **-S** lutetium
LUTED	past tense of lute
LUTEFISK	*n* pl. **-S** dried codfish
LUTEIN	*n* pl. **-S** a yellow pigment
LUTENIST	*n* pl. **-S** lutanist
LUTEOLIN	*n* pl. **-S** a yellow pigment
LUTEOUS	*adj* light to moderate greenish yellow in color
LUTETIUM	*n* pl. **-S** a metallic element
LUTEUM	*n* pl. **-TEA** a hormone-secreting body
LUTFISK	*n* pl. **-S** lutefisk
LUTHERN	*n* pl. **-S** a type of window
LUTHIER	*n* pl. **-S** one who makes stringed instruments
LUTING	*n* pl. **-S** a substance used as a sealant
LUTIST	*n* pl. **-S** a lutanist
LUTZ	*n* pl. **-ES** a jump in figure skating
LUV	*v* **LUVVED, LUVVING, LUVS** to love
LUVVIE	*n* pl. **-S** lovey
LUVVY	*n* pl. **LUVVIES** lovey
LUX	*n* pl. **LUXES** or **LUCES** a unit of illumination
LUXATE	*v* **-ATED, -ATING, -ATES** to put out of joint
LUXATION	*n* pl. **-S** the act of luxating
LUXE	*n* pl. **-S** luxury
LUXE	*adj* **LUXER, LUXEST** deluxe
LUXURY	*n* pl. **-RIES** free indulgence in that which affords pleasure or comfort
LWEI	*n* pl. **-S** a monetary unit of Angola
LYARD	*adj* streaked with gray
LYART	*adj* lyard
LYASE	*n* pl. **-S** an enzyme
LYCEE	*n* pl. **-S** a French secondary school
LYCEUM	*n* pl. **-CEUMS** or **-CEA** a hall for public lectures or discussions
LYCH	*n* pl. **-ES** lich
LYCHEE	*n* pl. **-S** litchi
LYCHGATE	*n* pl. **-S** a roofed gateway to a churchyard
LYCHNIS	*n* pl. **-NISES** a flowering plant
LYCOPENE	*n* pl. **-S** a red pigment
LYCOPOD	*n* pl. **-S** an evergreen plant
LYCOPSID	*n* pl. **-S** a type of club moss
LYDDITE	*n* pl. **-S** an explosive
LYE	*n* pl. **-S** a solution used in making soap
LYING	*n* pl. **-S** the act of telling lies
LYINGLY	*adv* falsely
LYMPH	*n* pl. **-S** a body fluid containing white blood cells **LYMPHOID, LYMPHOUS** *adj*
LYMPHOMA	*n* pl. **-MAS** or **-MATA** a type of tumor
LYNCEAN	*adj* of or resembling a lynx
LYNCH	*v* **-ED, -ING, -ES** to put to death without legal sanction
LYNCHER	*n* pl. **-S** one that lynches
LYNCHING	*n* pl. **-S** the act of one who lynches
LYNCHPIN	*n* pl. **-S** linchpin
LYNX	*n* pl. **-ES** a short-tailed wildcat
LYOPHILE	*adj* pertaining to a type of colloid
LYRATE	*adj* having the shape of a lyre **LYRATELY** *adv*
LYRATED	*adj* lyrate
LYRE	*n* pl. **-S** an ancient harp-like instrument
LYREBIRD	*n* pl. **-S** an Australian bird
LYRIC	*n* pl. **-S** a lyrical poem
LYRICAL	*adj* having the form of a song
LYRICISE	*v* **-CISED, -CISING, -CISES** to lyricize
LYRICISM	*n* pl. **-S** the quality of being lyrics

LYRICIST   *n* pl. **-S** one who writes the words for songs

LYRICIZE   *v* **-CIZED, -CIZING, -CIZES** to write lyrics

LYRICON   *n* pl. **-S** an electronic wind instrument

LYRIFORM   *adj* lyrate

LYRISM   *n* pl. **-S** lyricism

LYRIST   *n* pl. **-S** one who plays the lyre

LYSATE   *n* pl. **-S** a product of lysis

LYSE   *v* **LYSED, LYSING, LYSES** to cause to undergo lysis

LYSIN   *n* pl. **-S** a substance capable of disintegrating blood cells or bacteria

LYSINE   *n* pl. **-S** an amino acid

LYSING   present participle of lyse

LYSIS   *n* pl. **LYSES** the disintegration of cells by lysins

LYSOGEN   *n* pl. **-S** a type of antigen

LYSOGENY   *n* pl. **-NIES** the state of being like a lysogen

LYSOSOME   *n* pl. **-S** a saclike part of a cell

LYSOZYME   *n* pl. **-S** an enzyme

LYSSA   *n* pl. **-S** rabies

LYTIC   *adj* pertaining to lysis

LYTTA   *n* pl. **-TAS** or **-TAE** a fibrous band in the tongue of certain carnivorous mammals

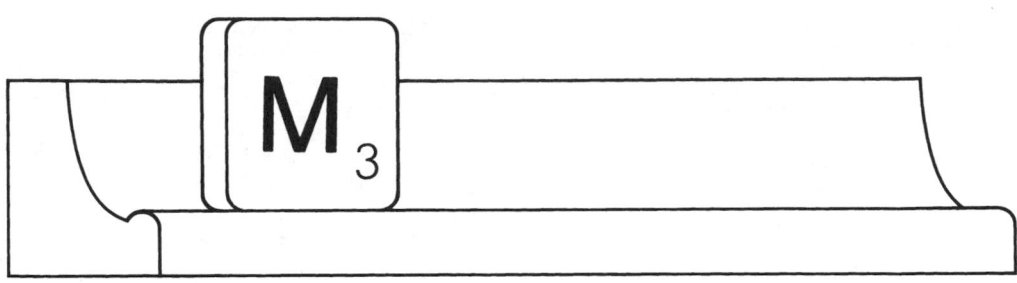

MA   *n* pl. **-S** mother

MAAR   *n* pl. **-S** a volcanic crater

MABE   *n* pl. **-S** a cultured pearl

MAC   *n* pl. **-S** a raincoat

MACABER   *adj* macabre

MACABRE   *adj* gruesome

MACACO   *n* pl. **-COS** a lemur

MACADAM   *n* pl. **-S** a type of pavement

MACAQUE   *n* pl. **-S** a short-tailed monkey

MACARON   *n* pl. **-S** a cookie with filling in the middle

MACARONI   *n* pl. **-NIS** or **-NIES** a tubular pasta

MACAROON   *n* pl. **-S** a type of cookie

MACAW   *n* pl. **-S** a large parrot

MACCABAW   *n* pl. **-S** maccaboy

MACCABOY   *n* pl. **-BOYS** a type of snuff

MACCHIA   *n* pl. **-CHIE** a dense growth of small trees and shrubs

MACCOBOY   *n* pl. **-BOYS** maccaboy

MACE   *v* **MACED, MACING, MACES** to attack with a weapon resembling a club (a heavy piece of wood)

MACER   *n* pl. **-S** an official who carries a ceremonial staff

MACERATE   *v* **-ATED, -ATING, -ATES** to soften by soaking in liquid

MACH   *n* pl. **-S** a number indicating the ratio of the speed of a body to the speed of sound

MACHACA   *n* pl. **-S** a Mexican dish featuring shredded meat fried with vegetables

MACHE   *n* pl. **-S** a European herb

MACHER   *n* pl. **-S** a person known for getting things done

MACHETE   *n* pl. **-S** a large, heavy knife

MACHINE   *v* **-CHINED, -CHINING, -CHINES** to process by machine (a mechanical device)

MACHISMO   *n* pl. **-MOS** strong masculinity

MACHO   *n* pl. **-CHOS** a person who exhibits machismo

MACHOISM   *n* pl. **-S** machismo

MACHREE   *n* pl. **-S** dear

MACHZOR   *n* pl. **-ZORS** or **-ZORIM** mahzor

MACING   present participle of mace

MACK   *n* pl. **-S** mac

MACKEREL   *n* pl. **-S** a marine food fish

MACKINAW   *n* pl. **-S** a woolen fabric

MACKLE   *v* **-LED, -LING, -LES** to blur in printing

MACLE   *n* pl. **-S** a spot or discoloration in a mineral **MACLED** *adj*

MACON   *n* pl. **-S** a red or white French wine

MACRAME   *n* pl. **-S** a trimming of knotted thread or cord

MACRO   *n* pl. **-ROS** a type of computer instruction

MACRON   *n* pl. **-S** a symbol placed over a vowel to show that it has a long sound

MACROPOD   *n* pl. **-S** a plant-eating marsupial mammal

MACRURAL   *adj* pertaining to macruran

MACRURAN   *n* pl. **-S** any of a suborder of crustaceans

MACULA   *n* pl. **-LAS** or **-LAE** a spot **MACULAR** *adj*

MACULATE   *v* **-LATED, -LATING, -LATES** to mark with spots

MACULE   *v* **-ULED, -ULING, -ULES** to mackle

MACUMBA   *n* pl. **-S** a religion practiced in Brazil

MAD   *adj* **MADDER, MADDEST** insane

MAD   *v* **MADDED, MADDING, MADS** to madden

MADAM	*n* pl. **-S** a woman who manages a brothel	
MADAME	*n* pl. **-S** madam	
MADAME	*n* pl. **MESDAMES** the French title of respect for a married woman	
MADCAP	*n* pl. **-S** an impulsive person	
MADDED	past tense of mad	
MADDEN	*v* **-ED, -ING, -S** to make or become mad	
MADDER	*n* pl. **-S** a perennial herb	
MADDEST	superlative of mad	
MADDING	present participle of mad	
MADDISH	*adj* somewhat mad	
MADE	past tense of make	
MADEIRA	*n* pl. **-S** a white wine	
MADERIZE	*v* **-IZED, -IZING, -IZES** to turn brown — used of white wine	
MADHOUSE	*n* pl. **-S** an insane asylum	
MADLY	*adv* in a mad manner	
MADMAN	*n* pl. **-MEN** a man who is insane	
MADNESS	*n* pl. **-ES** the state of being mad	
MADONNA	*n* pl. **-S** a former Italian title of respect for a woman	
MADRAS	*n* pl. **-ES** a cotton fabric	
MADRASA	*n* pl. **-S** madrassa	
MADRASAH	*n* pl. **-S** madrassa	
MADRASSA	*n* pl. **-S** a Muslim school	
MADRE	*n* pl. **-S** mother	
MADRIGAL	*n* pl. **-S** a short lyric poem	
MADRONA	*n* pl. **-S** an evergreen tree	
MADRONE	*n* pl. **-S** madrona	
MADRONO	*n* pl. **-NOS** madrona	
MADTOM	*n* pl. **-S** a North American catfish	
MADURO	*n* pl. **-ROS** a dark-colored, relatively strong cigar	
MADWOMAN	*n* pl. **-WOMEN** a woman who is insane	
MADWORT	*n* pl. **-S** a flowering plant	
MADZOON	*n* pl. **-S** matzoon	
MAE	*n* pl. **-S** more	
MAENAD	*n* pl. **-S** or **-ES** a female participant in ancient Greek orgies **MAENADIC** *adj*	
MAESTOSO	*n* pl. **-SOS** a stately musical passage	
MAESTRO	*n* pl. **-STROS** or **-STRI** a master of an art	
MAFFIA	*n* pl. **-S** mafia	

MAFFICK	*v* **-ED, -ING, -S** to celebrate boisterously
MAFIA	*n* pl. **-S** a secret criminal organization
MAFIC	*adj* pertaining to minerals rich in magnesium and iron
MAFIOSO	*n* pl. **-SOS** or **-SI** a member of the mafia
MAFTIR	*n* pl. **-S** the concluding section of a parashah
MAG	*n* pl. **-S** a magazine
MAGALOG	*n* pl. **-S** a sales catalog resembling a magazine
MAGAZINE	*n* pl. **-S** a type of periodical publication
MAGDALEN	*n* pl. **-S** a reformed prostitute
MAGE	*n* pl. **-S** a magician
MAGENTA	*n* pl. **-S** a purplish red dye
MAGGOT	*n* pl. **-S** the legless larva of certain insects **MAGGOTY** *adj*
MAGI	pl. of magus
MAGIAN	*n* pl. **-S** a magus
MAGIC	*v* **-ICKED, -ICKING, -ICS** to affect by magic (sorcery)
MAGICAL	*adj* resembling magic
MAGICIAN	*n* pl. **-S** one skilled in magic
MAGICKED	past tense of magic
MAGICKING	present participle of magic
MAGILP	*n* pl. **-S** megilp
MAGISTER	*n* pl. **-S** a master or teacher
MAGLEV	*n* pl. **-S** a train using magnets to move above the tracks
MAGMA	*n* pl. **-MAS** or **-MATA** the molten matter from which igneous rock is formed **MAGMATIC** *adj*
MAGNATE	*n* pl. **-S** a powerful or influential person
MAGNESIA	*n* pl. **-S** a medicinal compound **MAGNESIC** *adj*
MAGNET	*n* pl. **-S** a body that possesses the property of attracting iron
MAGNETIC	*n* pl. **-S** a magnet
MAGNETO	*n* pl. **-TOS** a type of electric generator
MAGNETON	*n* pl. **-S** a unit of magnetic moment
MAGNIFIC	*adj* magnificent
MAGNIFY	*v* **-FIED, -FYING, -FIES** to increase the perceived size of
MAGNOLIA	*n* pl. **-S** a flowering shrub or tree
MAGNOX	*n* pl. **-ES** a magnesium-based alloy

MAGNUM	*n* pl. **-S** a large wine bottle
MAGOT	*n* pl. **-S** a tailless ape
MAGPIE	*n* pl. **-S** a corvine bird
MAGUEY	*n* pl. **-GUEYS** a tropical plant
MAGUS	*n* pl. **-GI** a magician
MAHANT	*n* pl. **-S** a chief Hindu priest
MAHARAJA	*n* pl. **-S** a king or prince in India
MAHARANI	*n* pl. **-S** the wife of a maharaja
MAHATMA	*n* pl. **-S** a Hindu sage
MAHIMAHI	*n* pl. **-S** a food fish in Hawaii
MAHJONG	*n* pl. **-S** a game of Chinese origin
MAHJONGG	*n* pl. **-S** mahjong
MAHOE	*n* pl. **-S** a tropical tree
MAHOGANY	*n* pl. **-NIES** a tropical tree
MAHONIA	*n* pl. **-S** a flowering shrub
MAHOUT	*n* pl. **-S** the keeper and driver of an elephant
MAHUA	*n* pl. **-S** an Indian tree
MAHUANG	*n* pl. **-S** an Asian plant
MAHWA	*n* pl. **-S** mahua
MAHZOR	*n* pl. **-ZORS** or **-ZORIM** a Jewish prayer book
MAIASAUR	*n* pl. **-S** an herbivorous dinosaur
MAID	*n* pl. **-S** a maiden **MAIDISH** *adj*
MAIDAN	*n* pl. **-S** an open space in or near a town
MAIDEN	*n* pl. **-S** a young unmarried woman **MAIDENLY** *adj*
MAIDHOOD	*n* pl. **-S** the state of being a maiden
MAIEUTIC	*adj* pertaining to a method of eliciting knowledge
MAIGRE	*adj* containing neither flesh nor its juices
MAIHEM	*n* pl. **-S** mayhem
MAIL	*v* **-ED, -ING, -S** to send by a governmental postal system **MAILABLE** *adj*
MAILBAG	*n* pl. **-S** a bag for carrying mail (postal material)
MAILBOX	*n* pl. **-ES** a box for depositing mail
MAILE	*n* pl. **-S** a Pacific island vine
MAILER	*n* pl. **-S** one that mails
MAILING	*n* pl. **-S** a rented farm
MAILL	*n* pl. **-S** a payment
MAILLESS	*adj* having no armor
MAILLOT	*n* pl. **-S** a woman's one-piece bathing suit
MAILMAN	*n* pl. **-MEN** a man who carries and delivers mail
MAILROOM	*n* pl. **-S** a room for processing mail
MAILSHOT	*n* pl. **-S** something mailed to many people at one time
MAIM	*v* **-ED, -ING, -S** to injure so as to cause lasting damage
MAIMER	*n* pl. **-S** one that maims
MAIN	*n* pl. **-S** the principal part
MAINLAND	*n* pl. **-S** a principal land mass
MAINLINE	*v* **-LINED, -LINING, -LINES** to inject a narcotic into a major vein
MAINLY	*adv* for the most part
MAINMAST	*n* pl. **-S** the principal mast of a vessel
MAINSAIL	*n* pl. **-S** the principal sail of a vessel
MAINSTAY	*n* pl. **-STAYS** a principal support
MAINTAIN	*v* **-ED, -ING, -S** to keep in proper condition
MAINTOP	*n* pl. **-S** a platform at the head of a mainmast
MAIOLICA	*n* pl. **-S** majolica
MAIR	*n* pl. **-S** more
MAIST	*n* pl. **-S** most
MAIZE	*n* pl. **-S** an American cereal grass
MAJAGUA	*n* pl. **-S** a tropical tree
MAJESTIC	*adj* having majesty
MAJESTY	*n* pl. **-TIES** regal dignity
MAJLIS	*n* pl. **-ES** the parliament in various North African and Middle Eastern countries
MAJOLICA	*n* pl. **-S** a type of pottery
MAJOR	*v* **-ED, -ING, -S** to pursue a specific principal course of study
MAJORITY	*n* pl. **-TIES** the greater number or part
MAJORLY	*adv* mainly
MAKAR	*n* pl. **-S** a poet
MAKE	*v* **MADE, MAKING, MAKES** to cause to exist **MAKABLE, MAKEABLE** *adj*
MAKEBATE	*n* pl. **-S** one that encourages quarrels
MAKEFAST	*n* pl. **-S** an object to which a boat is tied
MAKEOVER	*n* pl. **-S** a changing of appearance
MAKER	*n* pl. **-S** one that makes

MAKEUP *n* pl. **-S** the way in which the parts or ingredients of something are put together

MAKI *n* pl. **-S** a dish of sushi and raw vegetables wrapped in seaweed

MAKIMONO *n* pl. **-NOS** a Japanese ornamental scroll

MAKING *n* pl. **-S** material from which something can be developed

MAKO *n* pl. **-KOS** a large shark

MAKUTA pl. of likuta

MALACCA *n* pl. **-S** the cane of an Asian rattan palm

MALADY *n* pl. **-DIES** an illness

MALAISE *n* pl. **-S** a feeling of vague discomfort

MALAMUTE *n* pl. **-S** an Alaskan sled dog

MALANGA *n* pl. **-S** a yautia

MALAPERT *n* pl. **-S** an impudent person

MALAPROP *n* pl. **-S** a humorous misuse of a word

MALAR *n* pl. **-S** the cheekbone

MALARIA *n* pl. **-S** an infectious disease **MALARIAL, MALARIAN** *adj*

MALARKEY *n* pl. **-KEYS** nonsense

MALARKY *n* pl. **-KIES** malarkey

MALAROMA *n* pl. **-S** a malodor

MALATE *n* pl. **-S** a chemical salt

MALE *n* pl. **-S** an individual that begets young by fertilizing the female

MALEATE *n* pl. **-S** a chemical salt

MALEDICT *v* **-ED, -ING, -S** to curse

MALEFIC *adj* producing or causing evil

MALEMIUT *n* pl. **-S** malamute

MALEMUTE *n* pl. **-S** malamute

MALENESS *n* pl. **-ES** the quality of being a male

MALFED *adj* badly fed

MALGRE *prep* in spite of

MALIC *adj* pertaining to apples

MALICE *n* pl. **-S** a desire to injure another

MALIGN *v* **-ED, -ING, -S** to speak evil of

MALIGNER *n* pl. **-S** one that maligns

MALIGNLY *adv* in an evil manner

MALIHINI *n* pl. **-S** a newcomer to Hawaii

MALINE *n* pl. **-S** a delicate net used for veils

MALINGER *v* **-ED, -ING, -S** to feign illness in order to avoid duty or work

MALISON *n* pl. **-S** a curse

MALKIN *n* pl. **-S** an untidy woman

MALL *v* **-ED, -ING, -S** to maul

MALLARD *n* pl. **-S** a wild duck

MALLEE *n* pl. **-S** an evergreen tree

MALLEI pl. of malleus

MALLEOLI *n/pl* bony protuberances of the ankle

MALLET *n* pl. **-S** a type of hammer

MALLEUS *n* pl. **-LEI** a bone of the middle ear

MALLING *n* pl. **-S** the practice of shopping at malls (large buildings with many shops)

MALLOW *n* pl. **-S** a flowering plant

MALM *n* pl. **-S** a soft, friable limestone

MALMSEY *n* pl. **-SEYS** a white wine

MALMY *adj* **MALMIER, MALMIEST** resembling malm

MALODOR *n* pl. **-S** an offensive odor

MALONATE *n* pl. **-S** a salt or ester of malonic acid

MALOTI pl. of loti

MALPOSED *adj* being in the wrong position

MALT *v* **-ED, -ING, -S** to treat or combine with malt (germinated grain)

MALTASE *n* pl. **-S** an enzyme

MALTED *n* pl. **-S** a sweet beverage

MALTHA *n* pl. **-S** a natural tar

MALTIER comparative of malty

MALTIEST superlative of malty

MALTING *n* pl. **-S** the process of preparing grain for brewing

MALTOL *n* pl. **-S** a chemical compound

MALTOSE *n* pl. **-S** a type of sugar

MALTREAT *v* **-ED, -ING, -S** to treat badly

MALTSTER *n* pl. **-S** one that makes malt

MALTY *adj* **MALTIER, MALTIEST** resembling malt

MALVASIA *n* pl. **-S** malmsey

MALWARE *n* pl. **-S** software designed to disable computers

MAM *n* pl. **-S** mother

MAMA *n* pl. **-S** mother

MAMALIGA *n* pl. **-S** a cornmeal porridge

MAMASAN *n* pl. **-S** a Japanese woman in a position of authority

MAMATEEK	*n* pl. **-S** a type of wigwam
MAMBA	*n* pl. **-S** a venomous snake
MAMBO	*v* **-ED, -ING, -ES** or **-S** to perform a ballroom dance
MAMEE	*n* pl. **-S** mamey
MAMELUKE	*n* pl. **-S** a slave in Muslim countries
MAMEY	*n* pl. **-MEYS** or **-MEYES** a tropical tree
MAMIE	*n* pl. **-S** mamey
MAMILLA	*n* pl. **-LAE** mammilla
MAMLUK	*n* pl. **-S** mameluke
MAMMA	*n* pl. **-MAE** a milk-secreting organ
MAMMA	*n* pl. **-S** mama
MAMMAL	*n* pl. **-S** any of a class of warm-blooded vertebrates
MAMMARY	*adj* pertaining to the mammae
MAMMATE	*adj* having mammae
MAMMATUS	*n* pl. **-TI** a type of cloud
MAMMEE	*n* pl. **-S** mamey
MAMMER	*v* **-ED, -ING, -S** to hesitate
MAMMET	*n* pl. **-S** maumet
MAMMEY	*n* pl. **-MEYS** mamey
MAMMIE	*n* pl. **-S** mammy
MAMMIES	pl. of mammy
MAMMILLA	*n* pl. **-LAE** a nipple
MAMMITIS	*n* pl. **-MITIDES** mastitis
MAMMOCK	*v* **-ED, -ING, -S** to shred
MAMMON	*n* pl. **-S** material wealth
MAMMOTH	*n* pl. **-S** an extinct elephant
MAMMY	*n* pl. **-MIES** mother
MAMZER	*n* pl. **-S** a bastard
MAN	*n* pl. **MEN** an adult human male
MAN	*v* **MANNED, MANNING, MANS** to supply with men
MANA	*n* pl. **-S** a supernatural force in certain Pacific island religions
MANACLE	*v* **-CLED, -CLING, -CLES** to handcuff
MANAGE	*v* **-AGED, -AGING, -AGES** to control or direct
MANAGER	*n* pl. **-S** one that manages
MANAKIN	*n* pl. **-S** a tropical bird
MANANA	*n* pl. **-S** tomorrow
MANAT	*n* pl. **-S** a monetary unit of Azerbaijan
MANATEE	*n* pl. **-S** an aquatic mammal **MANATOID** *adj*

MANCHE	*n* pl. **-S** a heraldic design
MANCHET	*n* pl. **-S** a small loaf of fine white bread
MANCIPLE	*n* pl. **-S** an officer authorized to purchase provisions
MANDALA	*n* pl. **-S** a Hindu or Buddhist graphic symbol of the universe **MANDALIC** *adj*
MANDAMUS	*v* **-ED, -ING, -ES** to command by means of writ issued by a superior court
MANDARIN	*n* pl. **-S** a citrus fruit
MANDATE	*v* **-DATED, -DATING, -DATES** to authorize or decree
MANDATOR	*n* pl. **-S** one that mandates
MANDIBLE	*n* pl. **-S** the bone of the lower jaw
MANDIOCA	*n* pl. **-S** manioc
MANDOLA	*n* pl. **-S** an ancient lute
MANDOLIN	*n* pl. **-S** a stringed musical instrument
MANDORA	*n* pl. **-S** a stringed musical instrument
MANDORLA	*n* pl. **-S** a pointed oval figure
MANDRAKE	*n* pl. **-S** a European herb
MANDREL	*n* pl. **-S** a shaft on which a tool is mounted
MANDRIL	*n* pl. **-S** mandrel
MANDRILL	*n* pl. **-S** a large baboon
MANE	*n* pl. **-S** the long hair growing on and about the neck of some animals **MANED, MANELESS** *adj*
MANEB	*n* pl. **-S** a powder for killing fungi
MANEGE	*n* pl. **-S** the art of training and riding horses
MANEUVER	*v* **-ED, -ING, -S** to change the position of for a specific purpose
MANFUL	*adj* courageous **MANFULLY** *adv*
MANGA	*n* pl. **-S** a Japanese graphic novel
MANGABEY	*n* pl. **-BEYS** a long-tailed monkey
MANGABY	*n* pl. **-BIES** mangabey
MANGANIC	*adj* containing manganese (a metallic element)
MANGANIN	*n* pl. **-S** an alloy of copper, manganese, and nickel
MANGE	*n* pl. **-S** a skin disease of domestic animals
MANGEL	*n* pl. **-S** a variety of beet
MANGER	*n* pl. **-S** a trough or box from which horses or cattle eat
MANGEY	*adj* **MANGIER, MANGIEST** mangy

MANGIER	comparative of mangy
MANGIEST	superlative of mangy
MANGILY	*adv* in a mangy manner
MANGLE	*v* **-GLED, -GLING, -GLES** to cut, slash, or crush so as to disfigure
MANGLER	*n* pl. **-S** one that mangles
MANGO	*n* pl. **-GOS** or **-GOES** an edible tropical fruit
MANGOLD	*n* pl. **-S** mangel
MANGONEL	*n* pl. **-S** a medieval military device for hurling stones
MANGROVE	*n* pl. **-S** a tropical tree or shrub
MANGY	*adj* **MANGIER, MANGIEST** affected with mange
MANHOLE	*n* pl. **-S** a hole providing entrance to an underground or enclosed structure
MANHOOD	*n* pl. **-S** the state of being a man
MANHUNT	*n* pl. **-S** an intensive search for a person
MANIA	*n* pl. **-S** an excessive interest or enthusiasm
MANIAC	*n* pl. **-S** an insane person **MANIACAL** *adj*
MANIC	*n* pl. **-S** one that is affected with mania
MANICURE	*v* **-CURED, -CURING, -CURES** to trim and polish the fingernails of
MANIFEST	*v* **-ED, -ING, -S** to show clearly
MANIFOLD	*v* **-ED, -ING, -S** to make several copies of
MANIHOT	*n* pl. **-S** a tropical plant
MANIKIN	*n* pl. **-S** an anatomical model of the human body
MANILA	*n* pl. **-S** a strong paper
MANILLA	*n* pl. **-S** manila
MANILLE	*n* pl. **-S** the second highest trump in certain card games
MANIOC	*n* pl. **-S** a tropical plant
MANIOCA	*n* pl. **-S** manioc
MANIPLE	*n* pl. **-S** a silk band worn on the left arm as a vestment
MANITO	*n* pl. **-TOS** manitou
MANITOU	*n* pl. **-S** an Algonquian Indian deity
MANITU	*n* pl. **-S** manitou
MANKIND	*n* pl. **MANKIND** the human race
MANKY	*adj* **MANKIER, MANKIEST** inferior, defective
MANLESS	*adj* having no men
MANLIKE	*adj* resembling a man
MANLY	*adj* **-LIER, -LIEST** having the qualities of a man **MANLILY** *adv*
MANMADE	*adj* made by man
MANNA	*n* pl. **-S** divinely supplied food
MANNAN	*n* pl. **-S** a type of sugar
MANNED	past tense of man
MANNER	*n* pl. **-S** a way of acting **MANNERED** *adj*
MANNERLY	*adj* polite
MANNIKIN	*n* pl. **-S** manikin
MANNING	present participle of man
MANNISH	*adj* resembling or characteristic of a man
MANNITE	*n* pl. **-S** mannitol **MANNITIC** *adj*
MANNITOL	*n* pl. **-S** an alcohol
MANNOSE	*n* pl. **-S** a type of sugar
MANO	*n* pl. **-NOS** a stone used for grinding foods
MANOR	*n* pl. **-S** a landed estate or territorial unit **MANORIAL** *adj*
MANPACK	*adj* designed to be carried by one person
MANPOWER	*n* pl. **-S** the number of men available for service
MANQUE	*adj* frustrated in the fulfillment of one's aspirations
MANROPE	*n* pl. **-S** a rope used as a handrail
MANSARD	*n* pl. **-S** a type of roof
MANSCAPE	*v* **-SCAPED, -SCAPING, -SCAPES** to trim or shave a man's body hair to enhance appearance
MANSE	*n* pl. **-S** a clergyman's house
MANSION	*n* pl. **-S** a large, impressive house
MANTA	*n* pl. **-S** a cotton fabric
MANTEAU	*n* pl. **-TEAUS** or **-TEAUX** a loose cloak
MANTEL	*n* pl. **-S** a shelf above a fireplace
MANTELET	*n* pl. **-S** a mobile screen used to protect soldiers
MANTES	a pl. of mantis
MANTIC	*adj* having powers of prophecy
MANTID	*n* pl. **-S** mantis
MANTILLA	*n* pl. **-S** a woman's scarf
MANTIS	*n* pl. **-TISES** or **-TES** a predatory insect
MANTISSA	*n* pl. **-S** the decimal part of a logarithm
MANTLE	*v* **-TLED, -TLING, -TLES** to cloak

MANTLET	*n* pl. **-S** mantelet
MANTLING	*n* pl. **-S** an ornamental cloth
MANTRA	*n* pl. **-S** a mystical formula of prayer or incantation in Hinduism **MANTRIC** *adj*
MANTRAM	*n* pl. **-S** mantra
MANTRAP	*n* pl. **-S** a trap for catching men
MANTUA	*n* pl. **-S** a woman's gown
MANUAL	*n* pl. **-S** a small reference book
MANUALLY	*adv* by means of the hands
MANUARY	*adj* involving the hands
MANUBRIA	*n/pl* handle-shaped anatomical parts
MANUCODE	*n* pl. **-S** a bird of paradise
MANUKA	*n* pl. **-S** a small tree of New Zealand
MANUMIT	*v* **-MITTED, -MITTING, -MITS** to free from slavery
MANURE	*v* **-NURED, -NURING, -NURES** to fertilize with manure (animal excrement)
MANURER	*n* pl. **-S** one that manures
MANURIAL	*adj* of or pertaining to manure
MANURING	present participle of manure
MANUS	*n* pl. **MANUS** the end of the forelimb in vertebrates
MANWARD	*adv* toward man
MANWARDS	*adv* manward
MANWISE	*adv* in a manner characteristic of man
MANY	*adj* **MORE, MOST** consisting of or amounting to a large number
MANYFOLD	*adv* by many times
MAP	*v* **MAPPED, MAPPING, MAPS** to delineate on a map (a representation of a region)
MAPLE	*n* pl. **-S** a hardwood tree
MAPLESS	*adj* lacking a map
MAPLIKE	*adj* resembling a map
MAPMAKER	*n* pl. **-S** one that makes maps
MAPPABLE	*adj* capable of being mapped
MAPPED	past tense of map
MAPPER	*n* pl. **-S** one that maps
MAPPING	*n* pl. **-S** a mathematical correspondence
MAQUETTE	*n* pl. **-S** a small preliminary model
MAQUI	*n* pl. **-S** maquis
MAQUILA	*n* pl. **-S** a foreign-owned assembly factory in Mexico

MAQUIS	*n* pl. **MAQUIS** a thick underbrush
MAR	*v* **MARRED, MARRING, MARS** to detract from the perfection or wholeness of
MARA	*n* pl. **-S** a cavy of Argentina
MARABOU	*n* pl. **-S** an African stork
MARABOUT	*n* pl. **-S** a marabou
MARACA	*n* pl. **-S** a percussion instrument
MARAKA	a pl. of marka
MARANTA	*n* pl. **-S** a tropical plant
MARASCA	*n* pl. **-S** a wild cherry
MARASMUS	*n* pl. **-ES** a wasting away of the body **MARASMIC** *adj*
MARATHON	*n* pl. **-S** a long-distance race
MARAUD	*v* **-ED, -ING, -S** to rove in search of booty
MARAUDER	*n* pl. **-S** one that marauds
MARAVEDI	*n* pl. **-S** a former coin of Spain
MARBLE	*v* **-BLED, -BLING, -BLES** to give a mottled appearance to
MARBLER	*n* pl. **-S** one that marbles
MARBLING	*n* pl. **-S** an intermixture of fat and lean in meat
MARBLY	*adj* **-BLIER, -BLIEST** mottled
MARC	*n* pl. **-S** the residue remaining after a fruit has been pressed
MARCATO	*n* pl. **-TOS** a musical passage played with strong accentuation
MARCEL	*v* **-CELLED, -CELLING, -CELS** to make a deep, soft wave in the hair
MARCH	*v* **-ED, -ING, -ES** to walk in a formal military manner
MARCHEN	*n* pl. **MARCHEN** a folktale
MARCHER	*n* pl. **-S** one that marches
MARCHESA	*n* pl. **-CHESE** the wife or widow of a marchese
MARCHESE	*n* pl. **-CHESI** an Italian nobleman
MARCONI	*n* pl. **-S** a two-way radio
MARE	*n* pl. **-RIA** a dark area on the surface of the moon or Mars
MARE	*n* pl. **-S** a mature female horse
MAREMMA	*n* pl. **-REMME** a marshy coastal region
MARENGO	*adj* served with a sauce of oil, mushrooms, tomatoes, and wine
MARGARIC	*adj* pearly
MARGARIN	*n* pl. **-S** a butter substitute
MARGATE	*n* pl. **-S** a tropical fish

MARGAY *n* pl. **-GAYS** a small American wildcat

MARGE *n* pl. **-S** a margin

MARGENT *v* **-ED, -ING, -S** to margin

MARGIN *v* **-ED, -ING, -S** to provide with a margin (a border)

MARGINAL *n* pl. **-S** one considered to be at a lower or outer limit

MARGRAVE *n* pl. **-S** the military governor of a medieval German border province

MARIA pl. of mare

MARIACHI *n* pl. **-S** a Mexican musical band

MARIGOLD *n* pl. **-S** a flowering plant

MARIMBA *n* pl. **-S** a percussion instrument

MARINA *n* pl. **-S** a docking area for small boats

MARINADE *v* **-NADED, -NADING, -NADES** to marinate

MARINARA *n* pl. **-S** a seasoned tomato sauce

MARINATE *v* **-NATED, -NATING, -NATES** to soak in a seasoned liquid before cooking

MARINE *n* pl. **-S** a soldier trained for service at sea and on land

MARINER *n* pl. **-S** a sailor

MARIPOSA *n* pl. **-S** a flowering plant

MARISH *n* pl. **-ES** a marsh

MARITAL *adj* pertaining to marriage

MARITIME *adj* pertaining to navigation or commerce on the sea

MARJORAM *n* pl. **-S** a fragrant herb

MARK *v* **-ED, -ING, -S** to make a visible impression on

MARKA *n* pl. **MARKAS** or **MARAKA** a monetary unit of Bosnia and Herzegovina

MARKDOWN *n* pl. **-S** a reduction in price

MARKEDLY *adv* in an evident manner

MARKER *n* pl. **-S** one that marks

MARKET *v* **-ED, -ING, -S** to offer for sale

MARKETER *n* pl. **-S** one that markets

MARKHOOR *n* pl. **-S** markhor

MARKHOR *n* pl. **-S** a wild goat

MARKING *n* pl. **-S** a pattern of marks

MARKKA *n* pl. **-KAS** or **-KAA** a former monetary unit of Finland

MARKSMAN *n* pl. **-MEN** a person skillful at hitting a target

MARKUP *n* pl. **-S** an increase in price

MARL *v* **-ED, -ING, -S** to fertilize with marl (an earthy deposit containing lime, clay, and sand)

MARLIER comparative of marly

MARLIEST superlative of marly

MARLIN *n* pl. **-S** a marine game fish

MARLINE *n* pl. **-S** a rope used on a ship

MARLING *n* pl. **-S** marline

MARLITE *n* pl. **-S** a type of marl **MARLITIC** *adj*

MARLY *adj* **MARLIER, MARLIEST** abounding with marl

MARMITE *n* pl. **-S** a large soup kettle

MARMOSET *n* pl. **-S** a small monkey

MARMOT *n* pl. **-S** a burrowing rodent

MAROCAIN *n* pl. **-S** a light crinkled fabric

MAROON *v* **-ED, -ING, -S** to abandon in an isolated place

MARPLOT *n* pl. **-S** one that ruins a plan by meddling

MARQUE *n* pl. **-S** reprisal

MARQUEE *n* pl. **-S** a rooflike structure projecting over an entrance

MARQUESS *n* pl. **-ES** marquis

MARQUIS *n* pl. **-ES** a European nobleman

MARQUISE *n* pl. **-S** the wife or widow of a marquis

MARRAM *n* pl. **-S** a beach grass

MARRANO *n* pl. **-NOS** a Jew in Spain who professed Christianity to avoid persecution

MARRED past tense of mar

MARRER *n* pl. **-S** one that mars

MARRIAGE *n* pl. **-S** the legal union of two persons of the opposite or same sex

MARRIED *n* pl. **-S** one who has entered into marriage

MARRIER *n* pl. **-S** one that marries

MARRIES present 3d person sing. of marry

MARRING present participle of mar

MARRON *n* pl. **-S** a variety of chestnut

MARROW *v* **-ED, -ING, -S** to marry

MARROWY *adj* pithy

MARRY *v* **-RIED, -RYING, -RIES** to enter into marriage

MARSALA *n* pl. **-S** a Sicilian wine

MARSE *n* pl. **-S** master

MARSH	*n* pl. **-ES** a tract of low, wet land **MARSHED** *adj*
MARSHAL	*v* **-ED, -ING, -S** to put in proper order
MARSHALL	*v* **-ED, -ING, -S** to marshal
MARSHY	*adj* **MARSHIER, MARSHIEST** resembling a marsh
MARSUPIA	*n/pl* abdominal pouches of certain mammals
MART	*v* **-ED, -ING, -S** to market
MARTAGON	*n* pl. **-S** a flowering plant
MARTELLO	*n* pl. **-LOS** a circular fort
MARTEN	*n* pl. **-S** a carnivorous mammal
MARTIAL	*adj* pertaining to war
MARTIAN	*n* pl. **-S** a supposed inhabitant of the planet Mars
MARTIN	*n* pl. **-S** a small bird
MARTINET	*n* pl. **-S** one who demands rigid adherence to rules
MARTINI	*n* pl. **-S** an alcoholic beverage
MARTLET	*n* pl. **-S** a martin
MARTYR	*v* **-ED, -ING, -S** to put to death for adhering to a belief
MARTYRLY	*adj* resembling a martyr
MARTYRY	*n* pl. **-TYRIES** a shrine erected in honor of a martyred person
MARVEL	*v* **-VELED, -VELING, -VELS** or **-VELLED, -VELLING, -VELS** to be filled with wonder or astonishment
MARVELER	*n* pl. **-S** one who marvels
MARVY	*adj* marvelous
MARYJANE	*n* pl. **-S** marijuana
MARZIPAN	*n* pl. **-S** an almond candy
MASA	*n* pl. **-S** dough made of dried corn
MASALA	*n* pl. **-S** a blend of spices used in Indian cooking
MASCARA	*v* **-ED, -ING, -S** to color the eyelashes or eyebrows with a cosmetic
MASCON	*n* pl. **-S** a concentration of dense mass beneath the moon's surface
MASCOT	*n* pl. **-S** a person, animal, or object believed to bring good luck
MASER	*n* pl. **-S** a device for amplifying electrical impulses
MASH	*v* **-ED, -ING, -ES** to reduce to a pulpy mass
MASHER	*n* pl. **-S** one that mashes
MASHGIAH	*n* pl. **-GIHIM** an inspector of kosher establishments
MASHIE	*n* pl. **-S** a golf club
MASHY	*n* pl. **MASHIES** mashie
MASJID	*n* pl. **-S** a mosque
MASK	*v* **-ED, -ING, -S** to cover with a mask (a covering used to disguise the face) **MASKABLE** *adj*
MASKEG	*n* pl. **-S** muskeg
MASKER	*n* pl. **-S** one that wears a mask
MASKING	*n* pl. **-S** a piece of scenery used to conceal parts of a stage from the audience
MASKLIKE	*adj* suggestive of a mask
MASON	*v* **-ED, -ING, -S** to build with stone or brick
MASONIC	*adj* pertaining to masonry
MASONRY	*n* pl. **-RIES** a structure built of stone or brick
MASQUE	*n* pl. **-S** a dramatic entertainment formerly popular in England
MASQUER	*n* pl. **-S** masker
MASS	*v* **-ED, -ING, -ES** to assemble in a mass (a body of coherent matter)
MASSA	*n* pl. **-S** master
MASSACRE	*v* **-CRED, -CRING, -CRES** to kill indiscriminately
MASSAGE	*v* **-SAGED, -SAGING, -SAGES** to manipulate parts of the body for remedial or hygienic purposes
MASSAGER	*n* pl. **-S** one that massages
MASSCULT	*n* pl. **-S** culture as popularized by the mass media
MASSE	*n* pl. **-S** a type of shot in billiards
MASSEDLY	*adv* in a massed manner
MASSETER	*n* pl. **-S** a muscle that raises the lower jaw
MASSEUR	*n* pl. **-S** a man who massages
MASSEUSE	*n* pl. **-S** a woman who massages
MASSICOT	*n* pl. **-S** a yellow pigment
MASSIER	comparative of massy
MASSIEST	superlative of massy
MASSIF	*n* pl. **-S** a principal mountain mass
MASSIVE	*adj* of considerable size
MASSLESS	*adj* having no mass
MASSY	*adj* **MASSIER, MASSIEST** massive
MAST	*v* **-ED, -ING, -S** to provide with a mast (a long pole on a ship that supports the sails and rigging)
MASTABA	*n* pl. **-S** an ancient Egyptian tomb

MASTABAH *n* pl. **-S** mastaba

MASTER *v* **-ED, -ING, -S** to become skilled in

MASTERLY *adj* very skillful

MASTERY *n* pl. **-TERIES** superior knowledge or skill

MASTHEAD *v* **-ED, -ING, -S** to raise to the top of a mast

MASTIC *n* pl. **-S** an aromatic resin

MASTICHE *n* pl. **-S** mastic

MASTIFF *n* pl. **-S** a large, short-haired dog

MASTITIS *n* pl. **-TITIDES** inflammation of the breast **MASTITIC** *adj*

MASTIX *n* pl. **-ES** mastic

MASTLESS *adj* having no mast

MASTLIKE *adj* resembling a mast

MASTODON *n* pl. **-S** an extinct elephant-like mammal

MASTOID *n* pl. **-S** the rear portion of the temporal bone

MASURIUM *n* pl. **-S** a metallic element

MAT *v* **MATTED, MATTING, MATS** to pack down into a dense mass

MATADOR *n* pl. **-S** the bullfighter who kills the bull in a bullfight

MATAMBALA a pl. of tambala

MATCH *v* **-ED, -ING, -ES** to set in competition or opposition

MATCHBOX *n* pl. **-ES** a small box

MATCHER *n* pl. **-S** one that matches

MATCHUP *n* pl. **-S** a setting of two players against each other

MATE *v* **MATED, MATING, MATES** to join as mates (partners in a union)

MATELESS *adj* having no mate

MATELOT *n* pl. **-S** a sailor

MATELOTE *n* pl. **-S** a fish stew

MATER *n* pl. **-TERS** or **-TRES** mother

MATERIAL *n* pl. **-S** the substance of which anything is or may be composed

MATERIEL *n* pl. **-S** the aggregate of equipment and supplies used by an organization

MATERNAL *adj* pertaining to or characteristic of a mother

MATESHIP *n* pl. **-S** the state of being a mate

MATEY *n* pl. **-EYS** a friend

MATEY *adj* **MATIER, MATIEST** companionable

MATH *n* pl. **-S** mathematics

MATILDA *n* pl. **-S** a hobo's bundle

MATIN *n* pl. **-S** a morning song, as of birds

MATINAL *adj* pertaining to the morning

MATINEE *n* pl. **-S** a daytime performance

MATINESS *n* pl. **-ES** friendliness

MATING *n* pl. **-S** the period during which a seasonal-breeding animal can mate

MATLESS *adj* having no mats (small floor coverings)

MATRASS *n* pl. **-ES** a long-necked glass vessel

MATRES a pl. of mater

MATRIC *n* pl. **-S** matriculation (admission into a university)

MATRIX *n* pl. **-TRIXES** or **-TRICES** something within which something else originates or develops

MATRON *n* pl. **-S** a married woman of established social position **MATRONAL, MATRONLY** *adj*

MATSAH *n* pl. **-S** matzo

MATT *v* **-ED, -ING, -S** to matte

MATTE *v* **MATTED, MATTING, MATTES** to produce a dull finish on

MATTED past tense of mat, matt, and matte

MATTEDLY *adv* in a tangled manner

MATTER *v* **-ED, -ING, -S** to be of importance

MATTERY *adj* producing pus

MATTIN *n* pl. **-S** matin

MATTING *n* pl. **-S** a woven fabric used as a floor covering

MATTOCK *n* pl. **-S** a digging tool

MATTOID *n* pl. **-S** a mentally unbalanced person

MATTRASS *n* pl. **-ES** matrass

MATTRESS *n* pl. **-ES** a large pad filled with resilient material used on or as a bed

MATURATE *v* **-RATED, -RATING, -RATES** to mature

MATURE *adj* **-TURER, -TUREST** fully developed **MATURELY** *adv*

MATURE *v* **-TURED, -TURING, -TURES** to make or become mature

MATURER *n* pl. **-S** one that brings something to maturity

MATURITY *n* pl. **-TIES** the state of being mature

MATZA	*n* pl. **-S** matzo
MATZAH	*n* pl. **-S** matzo
MATZO	*n* pl. **-ZOS** or **-ZOT** or **-ZOTH** an unleavened bread
MATZOH	*n* pl. **-S** matzo
MATZOON	*n* pl. **-S** a food made from milk
MAUD	*n* pl. **-S** a Scottish gray and black plaid
MAUDLIN	*adj* excessively emotional
MAUGER	*prep* maugre
MAUGRE	*prep* in spite of
MAUL	*v* **-ED, -ING, -S** to injure by beating
MAULER	*n* pl. **-S** one that mauls
MAULING	*n* pl. **-S** the act of injuring by beating
MAUMET	*n* pl. **-S** an idol
MAUMETRY	*n* pl. **-RIES** idolatry
MAUN	*v* must — MAUN is the only form of this verb; it cannot be conjugated
MAUND	*n* pl. **-S** an Asian unit of weight
MAUNDER	*v* **-ED, -ING, -S** to talk incoherently
MAUNDY	*n* pl. **-DIES** the religious ceremony of washing the feet of the poor
MAUSOLEA	*n/pl* large, stately tombs
MAUSY	*adj* **MAUSIER, MAUSIEST** mauzy
MAUT	*n* pl. **-S** malt
MAUVE	*n* pl. **-S** a purple color
MAUZY	*adj* **MAUZIER, MAUZIEST** foggy, misty
MAVEN	*n* pl. **-S** mavin
MAVERICK	*n* pl. **-S** an unbranded range animal
MAVIE	*n* pl. **-S** mavis
MAVIN	*n* pl. **-S** an expert
MAVIS	*n* pl. **-VISES** a songbird
MAW	*v* **MAWED, MAWN, MAWING, MAWS** to mow
MAWKISH	*adj* offensively sentimental
MAX	*v* **-ED, -ING, -ES** to reach the upper limit
MAXI	*n* pl. **-S** a long skirt or coat
MAXIBOAT	*n* pl. **-S** a large racing yacht
MAXICOAT	*n* pl. **-S** a long coat
MAXILLA	*n* pl. **-LAS** or **-LAE** the upper jaw or jawbone
MAXIM	*n* pl. **-S** a brief statement of a general truth or principle
MAXIMA	a pl. of maximum
MAXIMAL	*n* pl. **-S** an element of a mathematical set that is followed by no other
MAXIMAND	*n* pl. **-S** something that is to be maximized
MAXIMIN	*n* pl. **-S** the maximum of a set of minima
MAXIMISE	*v* **-MISED, -MISING, -MISES** to maximize
MAXIMITE	*n* pl. **-S** a powerful explosive
MAXIMIZE	*v* **-MIZED, -MIZING, -MIZES** to make as great as possible
MAXIMUM	*n* pl. **-MUMS** or **-MA** the greatest possible amount, quantity, or degree
MAXIXE	*n* pl. **-S** a Brazilian dance
MAXWELL	*n* pl. **-S** a unit of magnetic flux
MAY	*v* **-ED, -ING, -S** to gather flowers in the spring
MAYA	*n* pl. **-S** the power to produce illusions, in Hindu philosophy **MAYAN** *adj*
MAYAPPLE	*n* pl. **-S** a perennial herb
MAYBE	*n* pl. **-S** an uncertainty
MAYBIRD	*n* pl. **-S** a bobolink
MAYBUSH	*n* pl. **-ES** a flowering shrub
MAYDAY	*n* pl. **-DAYS** a radio distress call
MAYEST	a present 2d person sing. of may
MAYFLY	*n* pl. **-FLIES** a winged insect
MAYHAP	*adv* maybe
MAYHEM	*n* pl. **-S** the offense of willfully maiming a person
MAYING	*n* pl. **-S** the gathering of spring flowers
MAYO	*n* pl. **-YOS** mayonnaise
MAYOR	*n* pl. **-S** the chief executive official of a city or borough **MAYORAL** *adj*
MAYORESS	*n* pl. **-ES** a female mayor
MAYPOLE	*n* pl. **-S** a decorated pole used in a spring celebration
MAYPOP	*n* pl. **-S** a flowering vine
MAYST	a present 2d person sing. of may
MAYVIN	*n* pl. **-S** mavin
MAYWEED	*n* pl. **-S** a malodorous weed
MAZAEDIA	*n/pl* spore-producing organs of certain lichens
MAZARD	*n* pl. **-S** the head or face
MAZE	*v* **MAZED, MAZING, MAZES** to bewilder **MAZEDLY** *adv*
MAZELIKE	*adj* mazy

MAZELTOV *interj* — used to express congratulations

MAZER *n* pl. **-S** a large drinking bowl

MAZIER comparative of mazy

MAZIEST superlative of mazy

MAZILY *adv* in a mazy manner

MAZINESS *n* pl. **-ES** the quality of being mazy

MAZING present participle of maze

MAZOURKA *n* pl. **-S** mazurka

MAZUMA *n* pl. **-S** money

MAZURKA *n* pl. **-S** a Polish dance

MAZY *adj* **MAZIER, MAZIEST** full of confusing turns and passages

MAZZARD *n* pl. **-S** a wild cherry

MBAQANGA *n* pl. **-S** a South African dance music

MBIRA *n* pl. **-S** an African musical instrument

ME *n* pl. **-S** mi

MEAD *n* pl. **-S** an alcoholic beverage

MEADOW *n* pl. **-S** a tract of grassland **MEADOWY** *adj*

MEAGER *adj* **MEAGERER, MEAGEREST** deficient in quantity or quality **MEAGERLY** *adv*

MEAGRE *adj* **MEAGRER, MEAGREST** meager **MEAGRELY** *adv*

MEAL *n* pl. **-S** the food served and eaten in one sitting

MEALIE *n* pl. **-S** an ear of corn

MEALIER comparative of mealy

MEALIEST superlative of mealy

MEALLESS *adj* lacking a meal

MEALTIME *n* pl. **-S** the usual time for a meal

MEALWORM *n* pl. **-S** the destructive larva of certain beetles

MEALY *adj* **MEALIER, MEALIEST** soft, dry, and friable

MEALYBUG *n* pl. **-S** a destructive insect

MEAN *adj* **MEANER, MEANEST** inferior in grade, quality, or character

MEAN *v* **MEANT, MEANING, MEANS** to intend

MEANDER *v* **-ED, -ING, -S** to wander

MEANER *n* pl. **-S** one that means

MEANIE *n* pl. **-S** a nasty person

MEANIES pl. of meany

MEANING *n* pl. **-S** something that one intends to convey by language

MEANLY *adv* in a mean manner

MEANNESS *n* pl. **-ES** the state of being mean

MEANT past tense of mean

MEANTIME *n* pl. **-S** the intervening time

MEANY *n* pl. **MEANIES** meanie

MEASLE *n* pl. **-S** a tapeworm larva **MEASLED** *adj*

MEASLY *adj* **-SLIER, -SLIEST** meager

MEASURE *v* **-SURED, -SURING, -SURES** to ascertain the dimensions, quantity, or capacity of

MEASURER *n* pl. **-S** one that measures

MEAT *n* pl. **-S** animal flesh used as food **MEATED** *adj*

MEATAL *adj* pertaining to a meatus

MEATBALL *n* pl. **-S** a small ball of chopped meat

MEATHEAD *n* pl. **-S** a dolt

MEATHOOK *n* pl. **-S** a hook on which to hang meat

MEATIER comparative of meaty

MEATIEST superlative of meaty

MEATILY *adv* in a meaty manner

MEATLESS *adj* having no meat

MEATLOAF *n* pl. **-LOAVES** a baked loaf of ground meat

MEATMAN *n* pl. **-MEN** a vendor of meat

MEATUS *n* pl. **-ES** a natural body passage

MEATY *adj* **MEATIER, MEATIEST** full of meat

MECCA *n* pl. **-S** a place visited by many people

MECH *n* pl. **-S** a mechanic

MECHANIC *n* pl. **-S** a person who works with machines

MECHITZA *n* pl. **-TZAS** or **-TZOT** a partition separating men and women in a synagogue

MECHOUI *n* pl. **-S** a meal of meat roasted on a spit

MECONIUM *n* pl. **-S** the first fecal excretion of a newborn child

MED *n* pl. **-S** medication

MEDAKA *n* pl. **-S** a Japanese fish

MEDAL *v* **-ALED, -ALING, -ALS** or **-ALLED, -ALLING, -ALS** to honor with a medal (a commemorative piece of metal)

MEDALIST *n* pl. **-S** a person to whom a medal has been awarded

MEDALLIC   *adj* of or pertaining to a medal

MEDALLING   a present participle of medal

MEDDLE   *v* **-DLED, -DLING, -DLES** to interest oneself in what is not one's concern

MEDDLER   *n* pl. **-S** one that meddles

MEDEVAC   *v* **-VACED, -VACING, -VACS** or **-VACKED, -VACKING, -VACS** to evacuate the wounded from a battlefield by helicopter

MEDFLY   *n* pl. **-FLIES** a Mediterranean fruit fly

MEDIA   *n* pl. **-DIAE** the middle layer of a blood or lymph vessel

MEDIA   *n* pl. **-S** a channel of communication

MEDIACY   *n* pl. **-CIES** the act of mediating

MEDIAD   *adv* toward the middle of a body or part

MEDIAE   pl. of media

MEDIAL   *n* pl. **-S** a sound, syllable, or letter in the middle of a word

MEDIALLY   *adv* in a central manner

MEDIAN   *n* pl. **-S** a central part

MEDIANLY   *adv* medially

MEDIANT   *n* pl. **-S** a type of musical tone

MEDIATE   *v* **-ATED, -ATING, -ATES** to act between disputing parties in order to bring about a settlement

MEDIATOR   *n* pl. **-S** one that mediates

MEDIC   *n* pl. **-S** one engaged in medical work

MEDICAID   *n* pl. **-S** a type of governmental health program

MEDICAL   *n* pl. **-S** a physical examination

MEDICANT   *n* pl. **-S** a healing substance

MEDICARE   *n* pl. **-S** a type of governmental health program

MEDICATE   *v* **-CATED, -CATING, -CATES** to treat with medicine

MEDICIDE   *n* pl. **-S** a medically assisted suicide

MEDICINE   *v* **-CINED, -CINING, -CINES** to administer medicine (a substance used in the treatment of disease) to

MEDICK   *n* pl. **-S** a flowering plant

MEDICO   *n* pl. **-COS** a doctor or medical student

MEDIEVAL   *n* pl. **-S** a person belonging to the Middle Ages

MEDIGAP   *n* pl. **-S** a supplemental health insurance

MEDII   pl. of medius

MEDINA   *n* pl. **-S** the native quarter of a North African city

MEDIOCRE   *adj* neither good nor bad

MEDITATE   *v* **-TATED, -TATING, -TATES** to ponder

MEDIUM   *n* pl. **-DIUMS** or **-DIA** a surrounding environment in which something functions and thrives

MEDIUS   *n* pl. **-DII** the middle finger

MEDIVAC   *v* **-VACED, -VACING, -VACS** or **-VACKED, -VACKING, -VACS** medevac

MEDLAR   *n* pl. **-S** a Eurasian tree

MEDLEY   *n* pl. **-LEYS** a mixture

MEDRESE   *n* pl. **-S** madrassa

MEDULLA   *n* pl. **-LAS** or **-LAE** the central tissue in the stems of certain plants **MEDULLAR** *adj*

MEDUSA   *n* pl. **-SAS** or **-SAE** a jellyfish **MEDUSAL** *adj*

MEDUSAN   *n* pl. **-S** medusa

MEDUSOID   *n* pl. **-S** medusa

MEED   *n* pl. **-S** a deserved reward

MEEK   *adj* **MEEKER, MEEKEST** lacking in spirit and courage **MEEKLY** *adv*

MEEKNESS   *n* pl. **-ES** the quality of being meek

MEERKAT   *n* pl. **-S** an African mongoose

MEET   *v* **MET, MEETING, MEETS** to come into the company or presence of

MEETER   *n* pl. **-S** one that meets

MEETING   *n* pl. **-S** an assembly for a common purpose

MEETLY   *adv* suitably

MEETNESS   *n* pl. **-ES** suitability

MEG   *n* pl. **-S** a megabyte

MEGA   *adj* great in size or importance

MEGABAR   *n* pl. **-S** a unit of pressure

MEGABIT   *n* pl. **-S** a unit of computer information

MEGABUCK   *n* pl. **-S** one million dollars

MEGABYTE   *n* pl. **-S** 1,048,576 bytes

MEGACITY   *n* pl. **-CITIES** a very large city

MEGADEAL   *n* pl. **-S** a business deal involving a lot of money

MEGADOSE   *n* pl. **-S** an abnormally large dose

MEGADYNE *n* pl. **-S** a unit of force

MEGAFLOP *n* pl. **-S** a measure of computing speed

MEGAHIT *n* pl. **-S** something extremely successful

MEGALITH *n* pl. **-S** a huge stone used in prehistoric monuments

MEGALOPS *n* pl. **-LOPSES** a larval stage of most crabs

MEGAMALL *n* pl. **-S** a very large shopping mall

MEGAPLEX *n* pl. **-ES** a large building having many movie theaters

MEGAPOD *n* pl. **-S** megapode

MEGAPODE *n* pl. **-S** a large-footed bird

MEGARON *n* pl. **-ARA** the great central hall of an ancient Greek house

MEGASS *n* pl. **-ES** a bagasse

MEGASSE *n* pl. **-S** megass

MEGASTAR *n* pl. **-S** an extremely successful performer

MEGATON *n* pl. **-S** a unit of explosive force

MEGAVOLT *n* pl. **-S** a unit of electromotive force

MEGAWATT *n* pl. **-S** a unit of power

MEGILLA *n* pl. **-S** megillah

MEGILLAH *n* pl. **-S** a long, involved story

MEGILP *n* pl. **-S** a substance with which pigments are mixed in painting

MEGILPH *n* pl. **-S** megilp

MEGOHM *n* pl. **-S** a unit of electrical resistance

MEGRIM *n* pl. **-S** a migraine

MEH *adj* not impressive; boring

MEHNDI *n* pl. **-S** the art of painting patterns on the skin with henna

MEIKLE *adj* large

MEINIE *n* pl. **-S** meiny

MEINY *n* pl. **-NIES** a retinue

MEIOSIS *n* pl. **-OSES** a type of cell division **MEIOTIC** *adj*

MEISTER *n* pl. **-S** one who is knowledgeable about something specified

MEL *n* pl. **-S** honey

MELAENA *n* pl. **-S** melena

MELAMED *n* pl. **-LAMDIM** a teacher in a Jewish school

MELAMINE *n* pl. **-S** a chemical compound

MELANGE *n* pl. **-S** a mixture

MELANIAN *adj* pertaining to dark pigmentation

MELANIC *n* pl. **-S** one who is affected with melanism

MELANIN *n* pl. **-S** a dark pigment

MELANISM *n* pl. **-S** abnormally dark pigmentation of the skin

MELANIST *n* pl. **-S** a melanic

MELANITE *n* pl. **-S** a black variety of garnet

MELANIZE *v* **-NIZED, -NIZING, -NIZES** to make dark

MELANOID *n* pl. **-S** a dark pigment

MELANOMA *n* pl. **-MAS** or **-MATA** a darkly pigmented tumor

MELANOUS *adj* having dark skin and hair

MELD *v* **-ED, -ING, -S** to blend

MELDER *n* pl. **-S** the amount of grain ground at one time

MELEE *n* pl. **-S** a confused struggle

MELENA *n* pl. **-S** a condition marked by black tarry stool

MELIC *adj* pertaining to song

MELILITE *n* pl. **-S** a mineral group

MELILOT *n* pl. **-S** a flowering plant

MELINITE *n* pl. **-S** a powerful explosive

MELISMA *n* pl. **-MAS** or **-MATA** melodic embellishment

MELL *v* **-ED, -ING, -S** to mix

MELLIFIC *adj* producing honey

MELLOW *adj* **-LOWER, -LOWEST** soft and full-flavored from ripeness **MELLOWLY** *adv*

MELLOW *v* **-ED, -ING, -S** to make or become mellow

MELODEON *n* pl. **-S** a small accordion

MELODIA *n* pl. **-S** a type of organ stop

MELODIC *adj* pertaining to melody

MELODICA *n* pl. **-S** a harmonica with a small keyboard at one end

MELODIES pl. of melody

MELODION *n* pl. **-S** melodeon

MELODISE *v* **-DISED, -DISING, -DISES** to melodize

MELODIST *n* pl. **-S** a composer of melodies

MELODIZE *v* **-DIZED, -DIZING, -DIZES** to compose a melody

MELODY *n* pl. **-DIES** an agreeable succession of musical sounds

MELOID *n* pl. **-S** a type of beetle

MELON *n* pl. **-S** any of various gourds **MELONY** *adj*

MELT	*v* **-ED, -ING, -S** to change from a solid to a liquid state by heat **MELTABLE** *adj*	**MENDING**	*n* pl. **-S** an accumulation of articles to be mended
MELTAGE	*n* pl. **-S** the process of melting	**MENFOLK**	*n/pl* the men of a family or community
MELTDOWN	*n* pl. **-S** the melting of the core of a nuclear reactor	**MENFOLKS**	*n/pl* menfolk
MELTER	*n* pl. **-S** one that melts	**MENHADEN**	*n* pl. **-S** a marine fish
MELTON	*n* pl. **-S** a heavy woolen fabric	**MENHIR**	*n* pl. **-S** a prehistoric monument
MELTY	*adj* resembling a melted solid	**MENIAL**	*n* pl. **-S** a domestic servant
MEM	*n* pl. **-S** a Hebrew letter	**MENIALLY**	*adv* in a servile manner
MEMBER	*n* pl. **-S** a distinct part of a whole **MEMBERED** *adj*	**MENINX**	*n* pl. **-NINGES** any of the membranes enclosing the brain and spinal cord
MEMBRANE	*n* pl. **-S** a thin, pliable layer of tissue	**MENISCUS**	*n* pl. **-CUSES** or **-CI** a crescent-shaped body **MENISCAL** *adj*
MEME	*n* pl. **-S** an idea or practice that spreads from person to person **MEMETIC** *adj*	**MENO**	*adv* less — used as a musical direction
MEMENTO	*n* pl. **-TOS** or **-TOES** something that serves as a reminder of the past	**MENOLOGY**	*n* pl. **-GIES** an ecclesiastical calendar
MEMETICS	*n/pl* the study of memes and their effects	**MENORAH**	*n* pl. **-S** a candleholder used in Jewish worship
MEMO	*n* pl. **MEMOS** a note designating something to be remembered	**MENSA**	*n* pl. **-SAS** or **-SAE** the grinding surface of a tooth
MEMOIR	*n* pl. **-S** a biography	**MENSAL**	*adj* pertaining to or used at the table
MEMORIAL	*n* pl. **-S** something that serves as a remembrance of a person or event	**MENSCH**	*n* pl. **MENSCHES** or **MENSCHEN** an admirable person **MENSCHY** *adj*
MEMORISE	*v* **-RISED, -RISING, -RISES** to memorize	**MENSE**	*v* **MENSED, MENSING, MENSES** to do honor to
MEMORIZE	*v* **-RIZED, -RIZING, -RIZES** to commit to memory	**MENSEFUL**	*adj* proper
MEMORY	*n* pl. **-RIES** the mental faculty of retaining and recalling past experience	**MENSH**	*n* pl. **MENSHES** or **MENSHEN** mensch
MEMSAHIB	*n* pl. **-S** a European woman living in colonial India	**MENSTRUA**	*n/pl* solvents
		MENSURAL	*adj* pertaining to measure
		MENSWEAR	*n* pl. **MENSWEAR** clothing for men
MEN	pl. of man	**MENTA**	pl. of mentum
MENACE	*v* **-ACED, -ACING, -ACES** to threaten	**MENTAL**	*adj* pertaining to the mind **MENTALLY** *adv*
MENACER	*n* pl. **-S** one that menaces	**MENTEE**	*n* pl. **-S** one who is being mentored
MENAD	*n* pl. **-S** maenad	**MENTHENE**	*n* pl. **-S** a liquid hydrocarbon
MENAGE	*n* pl. **-S** a household	**MENTHOL**	*n* pl. **-S** an alcohol
MENARCHE	*n* pl. **-S** the first occurrence of menstruation	**MENTION**	*v* **-ED, -ING, -S** to refer to in a casual manner
MENAZON	*n* pl. **-S** an insecticide	**MENTO**	*n* pl. **-TOS** a style of Jamaican folk music
MEND	*v* **-ED, -ING, -S** to repair **MENDABLE** *adj*	**MENTOR**	*v* **-ED, -ING, -S** to serve as a friend and teacher to
MENDER	*n* pl. **-S** one that mends	**MENTUM**	*n* pl. **-TA** the chin
MENDIGO	*n* pl. **-GOS** a freshwater fish	**MENU**	*n* pl. **-S** a list of the dishes available in a restaurant

MENUDO *n pl.* **-DOS** a tripe stew with chili peppers

MEOU *v* **-ED, -ING, -S** to meow

MEOW *v* **-ED, -ING, -S** to make the crying sound of a cat

MEPHITIS *n pl.* **-TISES** an offensive odor **MEPHITIC** *adj*

MERC *n pl.* **-S** or **-ES** a mercenary

MERCADO *n pl.* **-DOS** a market

MERCAPTO *adj* containing a particular chemical group

MERCER *n pl.* **-S** a dealer in textiles

MERCERY *n pl.* **-CERIES** a mercer's shop

MERCH *n pl.* **-ES** merchandise

MERCHANT *v* **-ED, -ING, -S** to buy and sell goods for profit

MERCIES pl. of mercy

MERCIFUL *adj* full of mercy

MERCURY *n pl.* **-RIES** a metallic element **MERCURIC** *adj*

MERCY *n pl.* **-CIES** compassion shown to an offender or enemy

MERE *adj* **MERER, MEREST** being nothing more than **MERELY** *adv*

MERE *n pl.* **-S** a pond or lake

MERENGUE *n pl.* **-S** a ballroom dance

MERGE *v* **MERGED, MERGING, MERGES** to combine

MERGEE *n pl.* **-S** a company acquired by a merger

MERGENCE *n pl.* **-S** the act of merging

MERGER *n pl.* **-S** the union of two or more businesses into a single enterprise

MERGING *n pl.* **-S** the act of combining

MERGUEZ *n pl.* **MERGUEZ** a spicy beef and lamb sausage

MERIDIAN *n pl.* **-S** a circle around the earth passing through both poles

MERINGUE *n pl.* **-S** a topping for pastries

MERINO *n pl.* **-NOS** a fine wool

MERISIS *n pl.* **MERISES** growth

MERISTEM *n pl.* **-S** formative plant tissue

MERISTIC *adj* made up of segments

MERIT *v* **-ED, -ING, -S** to earn

MERK *n pl.* **-S** a former coin of Scotland

MERL *n pl.* **-S** merle

MERLE *n pl.* **-S** a blackbird

MERLIN *n pl.* **-S** a European falcon

MERLON *n pl.* **-S** the solid part of an indented parapet

MERLOT *n pl.* **-S** a dry red wine

MERMAID *n pl.* **-S** a legendary marine creature

MERMAN *n pl.* **-MEN** a legendary marine creature

MERONYM *n pl.* **-S** a term for a part of something that is used to denote the whole of it

MERONYMY *n pl.* **-MIES** the semantic relationship between a part and the whole

MEROPIA *n pl.* **-S** partial blindness **MEROPIC** *adj*

MERRY *adj* **-RIER, -RIEST** cheerful **MERRILY** *adv*

MESA *n pl.* **-S** a land formation having a flat top and steep sides

MESALLY *adv* medially

MESARCH *adj* originating in a mesic habitat

MESCAL *n pl.* **-S** a cactus used as a source of liquor

MESCALIN *n pl.* **-S** mescaline (a hallucinogenic compound)

MESCLUN *n pl.* **-S** a mixture of young tender green herbs

MESDAMES pl. of madame

MESEEMS *v* past tense **MESEEMED,** present 3d person sing. **MESEEMETH** it seems to me — MESEEMS is an impersonal verb and is used only in the 3d person sing.

MESH *v* **-ED, -ING, -ES** to entangle

MESHIER comparative of meshy

MESHIEST superlative of meshy

MESHING *n pl.* **-S** the act of fitting together

MESHUGA *adj* crazy

MESHUGAH *adj* meshuga

MESHUGGA *adj* meshuga

MESHUGGE *adj* meshuga

MESHWORK *n pl.* **-S** a network

MESHY *adj* **MESHIER, MESHIEST** netty

MESIAL *adj* situated in the middle **MESIALLY** *adv*

MESIAN *adj* mesial

MESIC *adj* characterized by a medium supply of moisture

MESMERIC *adj* pertaining to hypnotism

MESNALTY *n pl.* **-TIES** a type of feudal estate

MESNE *n* pl. **-S** a feudal lord holding land from a superior

MESOCARP *n* pl. **-S** the middle layer of a pericarp

MESODERM *n* pl. **-S** the middle germ layer of an embryo

MESOGLEA *n* pl. **-S** a gelatinous material in sponges

MESOMERE *n* pl. **-S** an embryonic segment

MESON *n* pl. **-S** a subatomic particle **MESONIC** *adj*

MESOPHYL *n* pl. **-S** the soft tissue of a leaf

MESOSAUR *n* pl. **-S** an extinct aquatic reptile

MESOSOME *n* pl. **-S** a specialized cellular part

MESOTRON *n* pl. **-S** a meson

MESOZOAN *n* pl. **-S** any of a phylum of wormlike organisms

MESQUIT *n* pl. **-S** mesquite

MESQUITE *n* pl. **-S** a spiny tree or shrub

MESS *v* **-ED, -ING, -ES** to make dirty or untidy

MESSAGE *v* **-SAGED, -SAGING, -SAGES** to send as a message (an oral, written, or signaled communication)

MESSAN *n* pl. **-S** a lapdog

MESSIAH *n* pl. **-S** an expected liberator

MESSIER comparative of messy

MESSIEST superlative of messy

MESSIEURS pl. of monsieur

MESSILY *adv* in a messy manner

MESSMAN *n* pl. **-MEN** a serviceman who works in a dining facility

MESSMATE *n* pl. **-S** a person with whom one eats regularly

MESSUAGE *n* pl. **-S** a dwelling house with its adjacent buildings and land

MESSY *adj* **MESSIER, MESSIEST** dirty or untidy

MESTEE *n* pl. **-S** mustee

MESTESO *n* pl. **-SOS** or **-SOES** mestizo

MESTINO *n* pl. **-NOS** or **-NOES** mestizo

MESTIZA *n* pl. **-S** a female mestizo

MESTIZO *n* pl. **-ZOS** or **-ZOES** a person of mixed ancestry

MET past tense of meet

META *adj* pertaining to positions in a benzene ring separated by one carbon atom

METADATA *n/pl* a set of data that gives information about other data

METAGE *n* pl. **-S** an official measurement of weight or contents

METAL *v* **-ALED, -ALING, -ALS** or **-ALLED, -ALLING, -ALS** to cover with metal (any of various ductile, fusible, and lustrous substances)

METALISE *v* **-ISED, -ISING, -ISES** to metalize

METALIST *n* pl. **-S** one who works with metals

METALIZE *v* **-IZED, -IZING, -IZES** to treat with metal

METALLED a past tense of metal

METALLIC *n* pl. **-S** a fabric or yarn made of or coated with metal

METALLING a present participle of metal

METAMER *n* pl. **-S** a type of chemical compound

METAMERE *n* pl. **-S** a somite

METANOIA *n* pl. **-S** a spiritual conversion

METAPHOR *n* pl. **-S** a type of figure of speech

METATAG *n* pl. **-S** an HTML tag having information about a webpage

METATE *n* pl. **-S** a stone used for grinding grains

METAZOAN *n* pl. **-S** any of a major division of multicellular animals **METAZOAL, METAZOIC** *adj*

METAZOON *n* pl. **-ZOA** a metazoan

METE *v* **METED, METING, METES** to distribute by measure

METEOR *n* pl. **-S** a small celestial body that enters the earth's atmosphere **METEORIC** *adj*

METEPA *n* pl. **-S** a chemical compound

METER *v* **-ED, -ING, -S** to measure by mechanical means

METERAGE *n* pl. **-S** the process of metering

METH *n* pl. **-S** a stimulant drug

METHADON *n* pl. **-S** a narcotic drug

METHANAL *n* pl. **-S** formaldehyde

METHANE *n* pl. **-S** a flammable gas

METHANOL *n* pl. **-S** a toxic alcohol

METHINKS *v* past tense **METHOUGHT** it seems to me — METHINKS is an impersonal verb and is used only in the 3d person sing.

METHOD *n* pl. **-S** a means of procedure

METHODIC *adj* systematic

METHOXY *adj* containing a certain chemical group

METHOXYL	*adj* methoxy
METHYL	*n* pl. **-S** a univalent radical **METHYLIC** *adj*
METHYLAL	*n* pl. **-S** a flammable liquid
METICA	*n* pl. **-S** metical
METICAL	*n* pl. **-CALS** or **-CAIS** a monetary unit of Mozambique
METIER	*n* pl. **-S** a vocation
METING	present participle of mete
METIS	*n* pl. **METIS** a person of mixed ancestry
METISSE	*n* pl. **-S** a female metis
METOL	*n* pl. **-S** a powder used as a photographic developer
METONYM	*n* pl. **-S** a word used in metonymy
METONYMY	*n* pl. **-MIES** a type of figure of speech
METOPE	*n* pl. **-PES** or **-PAE** a space between two triglyphs
METOPIC	*adj* pertaining to the forehead
METOPON	*n* pl. **-S** a narcotic drug
METRAZOL	*n* pl. **-S** a powder used as a stimulant
METRE	*v* **-TRED, -TRING, -TRES** to meter
METRIC	*n* pl. **-S** a standard of measurement
METRICAL	*adj* pertaining to or composed in a system of arranged and measured rhythm
METRIFY	*v* **-FIED, -FYING, -FIES** to compose in metrical form
METRING	present participle of metre
METRIST	*n* pl. **-S** one who metrifies
METRITIS	*n* pl. **-TISES** inflammation of the uterus
METRO	*n* pl. **-ROS** a subway
METTLE	*n* pl. **-S** quality of character **METTLED** *adj*
METUMP	*n* pl. **-S** a tumpline
MEUNIERE	*adj* cooked in browned butter
MEW	*v* **-ED, -ING, -S** to confine
MEWL	*v* **-ED, -ING, -S** to whimper
MEWLER	*n* pl. **-S** one that mewls
MEWS	*n* pl. **-ES** a street lined with houses that originally were stables
MEZCAL	*n* pl. **-S** mescal
MEZE	*n* pl. **-S** a Greek or Middle Eastern appetizer
MEZEREON	*n* pl. **-S** a flowering shrub
MEZEREUM	*n* pl. **-S** mezereon
MEZQUIT	*n* pl. **-S** mesquite
MEZQUITE	*n* pl. **-S** mesquite
MEZUZA	*n* pl. **-S** mezuzah
MEZUZAH	*n* pl. **-ZAHS** or **-ZOT** or **-ZOTH** a Judaic scroll
MEZZO	*n* pl. **-ZOS** a female voice of a full, deep quality
MHO	*n* pl. **MHOS** a unit of electrical conductance
MI	*n* pl. **-S** the third tone of the diatonic musical scale
MIAOU	*v* **-ED, -ING, -S** to meow
MIAOW	*v* **-ED, -ING, -S** to meow
MIASM	*n* pl. **-S** miasma
MIASMA	*n* pl. **-MAS** or **-MATA** a noxious vapor **MIASMAL, MIASMIC** *adj*
MIAUL	*v* **-ED, -ING, -S** to meow
MIB	*n* pl. **-S** a type of playing marble
MIC	*n* pl. **-S** a microphone
MICA	*n* pl. **-S** a mineral
MICAWBER	*n* pl. **-S** a person who remains hopeful despite adversity
MICE	pl. of mouse
MICELL	*n* pl. **-S** micelle
MICELLA	*n* pl. **-LAE** micelle
MICELLE	*n* pl. **-S** a coherent strand or structure in a fiber **MICELLAR** *adj*
MICHE	*v* **MICHED, MICHING, MICHES** to skulk
MICKEY	*n* pl. **-EYS** a drugged drink
MICKLE	*adj* **-LER, -LEST** large
MICKLE	*n* pl. **-S** a large amount
MICKY	*n* pl. **MICKIES** mickey
MICRA	a pl. of micron
MICRIFY	*v* **-FIED, -FYING, -FIES** to make small
MICRO	*n* pl. **-CROS** a very small computer
MICROBAR	*n* pl. **-S** a unit of atmospheric pressure
MICROBE	*n* pl. **-S** a minute life form **MICROBIC** *adj*
MICROBUS	*n* pl. **-BUSES** or **-BUSSES** a small bus
MICROCAP	*adj* of or pertaining to a company whose retained earnings are very small
MICROCAR	*n* pl. **-S** a very small car
MICRODOT	*n* pl. **-S** a copy of printed matter reduced to the size of a dot

MICROHM *n* pl. **-S** a unit of electrical resistance

MICROLUX *n* pl. **-LUXES** or **-LUCES** a unit of illumination

MICROMHO *n* pl. **-S** a unit of electrical conductance

MICRON *n* pl. **-CRONS** or **-CRA** a unit of length

MICRURGY *n* pl. **-GIES** the use of minute tools under high magnification

MID *n* pl. **-S** the middle

MIDAIR *n* pl. **-S** a region in the middle of the air

MIDBRAIN *n* pl. **-S** the middle region of the brain

MIDCAP *adj* of or pertaining to a corporation whose retained earnings are between those of a small company and a large corporation

MIDCULT *n* pl. **-S** middle-class culture

MIDDAY *n* pl. **-DAYS** the middle of the day

MIDDEN *n* pl. **-S** a dunghill

MIDDIES pl. of middy

MIDDLE *v* **-DLED, -DLING, -DLES** to place in the middle (the area or point equidistant from extremes or limits)

MIDDLER *n* pl. **-S** a student in an intermediate grade

MIDDLING *n* pl. **-S** a cut of pork

MIDDY *n* pl. **-DIES** a loosely fitting blouse

MIDFIELD *n* pl. **-S** the middle portion of a playing field

MIDGE *n* pl. **-S** a small winged insect

MIDGET *n* pl. **-S** a very small person

MIDGUT *n* pl. **-S** the middle part of the embryonic digestive tract

MIDI *n* pl. **-S** a skirt or coat that extends to the middle of the calf

MIDIRON *n* pl. **-S** a golf club

MIDLAND *n* pl. **-S** the middle part of a country

MIDLEG *n* pl. **-S** the middle of the leg

MIDLIFE *n* pl. **-LIVES** middle age

MIDLIFER *n* pl. **-S** a middle-aged person

MIDLINE *n* pl. **-S** a median line

MIDLIST *n* pl. **-S** a section of a publisher's list of current titles

MIDMONTH *n* pl. **-S** the middle of the month

MIDMOST *n* pl. **-S** a part exactly in the middle

MIDNIGHT *n* pl. **-S** the middle of the night

MIDNOON *n* pl. **-S** midday

MIDPOINT *n* pl. **-S** a point at the middle

MIDRANGE *n* pl. **-S** the middle of a range

MIDRASH *n* pl. **-RASHIM** or **-RASHOTH** or **-RASHOT** an early Jewish interpretation of a biblical text

MIDRIB *n* pl. **-S** the central vein of a leaf

MIDRIFF *n* pl. **-S** the middle part of the body

MIDSHIP *adj* pertaining to the middle of a ship

MIDSHIPS *adv* toward the middle of a ship

MIDSHORE *adj* designating a fishery that is between the inshore and offshore fisheries

MIDSIZE *adj* of intermediate size

MIDSIZED *adj* midsize

MIDSOLE *n* pl. **-S** a middle layer of the sole of a shoe

MIDSPACE *n* pl. **-S** the middle of a space

MIDST *n* pl. **-S** the middle

MIDSTORY *n* pl. **-RIES** the middle of a story

MIDTERM *n* pl. **-S** an examination given in the middle of an academic semester

MIDTOWN *n* pl. **-S** the central part of a city

MIDWATCH *n* pl. **-ES** a watch on a ship between midnight and 4 A.M.

MIDWATER *n* pl. **-S** the middle portion vertically of a body of water

MIDWAY *n* pl. **-WAYS** an avenue at a fair or carnival for concessions and amusements

MIDWEEK *n* pl. **-S** the middle of the week

MIDWIFE *v* **-WIFED, -WIFING, -WIFES** or **-WIVED, -WIVING, -WIVES** to assist a woman in childbirth

MIDYEAR *n* pl. **-S** the middle of the year

MIEN *n* pl. **-S** demeanor

MIFF *v* **-ED, -ING, -S** to annoy

MIFFY *adj* **MIFFIER, MIFFIEST** easily annoyed

MIG *n* pl. **-S** a type of playing marble

MIGAWD *interj* — used to express surprise

MIGG *n* pl. **-S** mig

MIGGLE *n* pl. **-S** a mig

MIGHT *n* pl. **-S** strength

MIGHTY *adj* **MIGHTIER, MIGHTIEST** strong **MIGHTILY** *adv*

MIGNON *n* pl. **-S** a cut of beef

MIGNONNE *adj* daintily small

MIGRAINE *n* pl. **-S** a severe headache

MIGRANT *n* pl. **-S** one that migrates

MIGRATE *v* **-GRATED, -GRATING, -GRATES** to move from one region to another

MIGRATOR *n* pl. **-S** a migrant

MIHRAB *n* pl. **-S** a niche in a mosque

MIJNHEER *n* pl. **-S** mynheer

MIKADO *n* pl. **-DOS** an emperor of Japan

MIKE *v* **MIKED, MIKING, MIKES** to amplify or record by use of a microphone

MIKRON *n* pl. **-KRONS** or **-KRA** micron

MIKVA *n* pl. **-S** mikvah

MIKVAH *n* pl. **-VAHS** or **-VOTH** or **-VOT** or **-VOS** a place for ritual bathing by Orthodox Jews

MIKVEH *n* pl. **-S** mikvah

MIL *n* pl. **-S** a unit of length

MILADI *n* pl. **-S** milady

MILADY *n* pl. **-DIES** an English gentlewoman

MILAGE *n* pl. **-S** mileage

MILCH *adj* giving milk

MILCHIG *adj* made of or derived from milk

MILD *v* **-ED, -ING, -S** to diminish

MILD *adj* **MILDER, MILDEST** not harsh or rough **MILDISH** *adj*

MILDEN *v* **-ED, -ING, -S** to make or become mild

MILDEW *v* **-ED, -ING, -S** to affect with mildew (a whitish growth produced by fungi)

MILDEWY *adj* affected with or resembling mildew

MILDLY *adv* in a mild manner

MILDNESS *n* pl. **-ES** the quality of being mild

MILE *n* pl. **-S** a unit of distance

MILEAGE *n* pl. **-S** total distance expressed in miles

MILEPOST *n* pl. **-S** a post indicating distance in miles

MILER *n* pl. **-S** one that runs a mile race

MILESIAN *adj* pertaining to the native people of Ireland

MILESIMO *n* pl. **-MOS** a former monetary unit of Chile

MILFOIL *n* pl. **-S** a perennial herb

MILIA pl. of milium

MILIARIA *n* pl. **-S** a skin disease

MILIARY *adj* made up of many small projections

MILIEU *n* pl. **-LIEUS** or **-LIEUX** environment

MILING *n* pl. **-S** the activity of running in a one-mile race

MILITANT *n* pl. **-S** a person who is aggressively engaged in a cause

MILITARY *n* pl. **-TARIES** armed forces

MILITATE *v* **-TATED, -TATING, -TATES** to have influence or effect

MILITIA *n* pl. **-S** a citizen army

MILIUM *n* pl. **-IA** a small, whitish lump in the skin

MILK *v* **-ED, -ING, -S** to draw milk (a whitish, nutritious liquid) from the udder of

MILKER *n* pl. **-S** one that milks

MILKFISH *n* pl. **-ES** a marine food fish

MILKIER comparative of milky

MILKIEST superlative of milky

MILKILY *adv* in a milky manner

MILKLESS *adj* lacking milk

MILKMAID *n* pl. **-S** a woman who milks cows

MILKMAN *n* pl. **-MEN** a man who sells or delivers milk

MILKSHED *n* pl. **-S** a region supplying milk to a particular community

MILKSOP *n* pl. **-S** an effeminate man

MILKWEED *n* pl. **-S** a plant that secretes a milky juice

MILKWOOD *n* pl. **-S** a tropical tree

MILKWORT *n* pl. **-S** a flowering plant

MILKY *adj* **MILKIER, MILKIEST** resembling or suggestive of milk

MILL *v* **-ED, -ING, -S** to grind by mechanical means **MILLABLE** *adj*

MILLAGE *n* pl. **-S** a type of monetary rate

MILLCAKE *n* pl. **-S** a residue from pressed linseed

MILLDAM *n* pl. **-S** a dam built to form a millpond

MILLE *n* pl. **-S** a thousand

MILLEPED *n* pl. **-S** milliped

MILLER *n* pl. **-S** one that mills

MILLET *n* pl. **-S** a cereal grass

MILLIAMP *n* pl. **-S** one thousandth of an ampere

MILLIARD *n* pl. **-S** a billion

MILLIARE *n* pl. **-S** a unit of area

MILLIARY *n* pl. **-ARIES** an ancient Roman milestone

MILLIBAR *n* pl. **-S** a unit of atmospheric pressure

MILLIEME *n* pl. **-S** unit of value of Egypt and Sudan

MILLIER *n* pl. **-S** a unit of weight

MILLIGAL *n* pl. **-S** a unit of acceleration

MILLILUX *n* pl. **-LUXES** or **-LUCES** a unit of illumination

MILLIME *n* pl. **-S** a coin of Tunisia

MILLIMHO *n* pl. **-MHOS** a unit of electrical conductance

MILLINE *n* pl. **-S** a unit of advertising space

MILLINER *n* pl. **-S** one who makes or sells women's hats

MILLING *n* pl. **-S** a corrugated edge on a coin

MILLIOHM *n* pl. **-S** a unit of electrical resistance

MILLION *n* pl. **-S** a number

MILLIPED *n* pl. **-S** a multi-legged arthropod

MILLIREM *n* pl. **-S** a quantity of ionizing radiation

MILLPOND *n* pl. **-S** a pond for supplying water to run a mill wheel (a type of waterwheel)

MILLRACE *n* pl. **-S** the current of water that drives a mill wheel

MILLRUN *n* pl. **-S** a millrace

MILLWORK *n* pl. **-S** woodwork produced by milling

MILNEB *n* pl. **-S** a fungicide

MILO *n* pl. **-LOS** a cereal grass

MILORD *n* pl. **-S** an English gentleman

MILPA *n* pl. **-S** a field that is cleared from a jungle for farming purposes

MILREIS *n* pl. **MILREIS** a former monetary unit of Portugal

MILT *v* **-ED, -ING, -S** to impregnate with milt (fish sperm)

MILTER *n* pl. **-S** a male fish at breeding time

MILTY *adj* **MILTIER, MILTIEST** full of milt

MIM *adj* primly demure

MIMBAR *n* pl. **-S** minbar

MIME *v* **MIMED, MIMING, MIMES** to mimic

MIMEO *v* **-ED, -ING, -S** to make copies of by use of a mimeograph

MIMER *n* pl. **-S** one that mimes

MIMESIS *n* pl. **-MESISES** or **-MESES** mimicry **MIMETIC** *adj*

MIMETITE *n* pl. **-S** an ore of lead

MIMIC *v* **-ICKED, -ICKING, -ICS** to imitate closely

MIMICAL *adj* of the nature of mimicry

MIMICKER *n* pl. **-S** one that mimics

MIMICKING present participle of mimic

MIMICRY *n* pl. **-RIES** an instance of mimicking

MIMING present participle of mime

MIMOSA *n* pl. **-S** a tropical plant

MIMULUS *n* pl. **-ES** a flowering plant

MINA *n* pl. **-NAS** or **-NAE** an ancient unit of weight and value

MINABLE *adj* capable of being mined

MINACITY *n* pl. **-TIES** the state of being threatening

MINAE a pl. of mina

MINARET *n* pl. **-S** a slender tower attached to a mosque

MINATORY *adj* threatening

MINBAR *n* pl. **-S** a Muslim pulpit

MINCE *v* **MINCED, MINCING, MINCES** to cut into very small pieces

MINCER *n* pl. **-S** one that minces

MINCY *adj* **MINCIER, MINCIEST** affectedly dainty

MIND *v* **-ED, -ING, -S** to heed

MINDEDLY *adv* in the manner of one with a specified kind of mind

MINDER *n* pl. **-S** one that minds

MINDFUL *adj* heedful

MINDLESS *adj* lacking intelligence

MINDSET *n* pl. **-S** a fixed mental attitude

MINE *v* **MINED, MINING, MINES** to dig into for valuable materials

MINEABLE *adj* minable

MINER *n* pl. **-S** one that mines

MINERAL *n* pl. **-S** a naturally occurring inorganic substance having a characteristic set of physical properties

MINGIER comparative of mingy

MINGIEST superlative of mingy

MINGLE *v* **-GLED, -GLING, -GLES** to mix together

MINGLER *n pl.* **-S** one that mingles

MINGY *adj* **-GIER, -GIEST** mean and stingy **MINGILY** *adv*

MINI *n pl.* **-S** something distinctively smaller than others of its kind

MINIBAR *n pl.* **-S** a small refrigerator stocked with beverages

MINIBIKE *n pl.* **-S** a small motorcycle

MINIBUS *n pl.* **-BUSES** or **-BUSSES** a small bus

MINICAB *n pl.* **-S** a small taxicab

MINICAM *n pl.* **-S** a small portable television camera

MINICAMP *n pl.* **-S** a short training camp for football players

MINICAR *n pl.* **-S** a small automobile

MINIDISC *n pl.* **-S** a miniature compact disc

MINIFY *v* **-FIED, -FYING, -FIES** to make small or smaller

MINIGOLF *n pl.* **-S** a game similar to golf played on a small obstacle course

MINIKIN *n pl.* **-S** a small or dainty creature

MINILAB *n pl.* **-S** a retail outlet offering rapid on-site film development

MINIM *n pl.* **-S** a unit of liquid measure

MINIMA a pl. of minimum

MINIMAL *n pl.* **-S** an element of a mathematical set that precedes all others

MINIMAX *n pl.* **-ES** the minimum of a set of maxima

MINIMILL *n pl.* **-S** a small-scale steel mill

MINIMISE *v* **-MISED, -MISING, -MISES** to minimize

MINIMIZE *v* **-MIZED, -MIZING, -MIZES** to make as small as possible

MINIMUM *n pl.* **-MUMS** or **-MA** the least possible amount, quantity, or degree

MINING *n pl.* **-S** the process or business of working mines (excavations in the earth)

MINION *n pl.* **-S** a servile follower

MINIPARK *n pl.* **-S** a small city park

MINIPILL *n pl.* **-S** a birth control pill containing no estrogen

MINISH *v* **-ED, -ING, -ES** to diminish

MINISKI *n pl.* **-S** a short ski

MINISTER *v* **-ED, -ING, -S** to give aid or service

MINISTRY *n pl.* **-TRIES** the act of ministering

MINIUM *n pl.* **-S** a red pigment

MINIVAN *n pl.* **-S** a small van

MINIVER *n pl.* **-S** a white fur

MINK *n pl.* **-S** a carnivorous mammal

MINKE *n pl.* **-S** a small whale

MINNEOLA *n pl.* **-S** a reddish tangelo

MINNOW *n pl.* **-S** a small fish

MINNY *n pl.* **-NIES** minnow

MINOR *v* **-ED, -ING, -S** to pursue a specific subordinate course of study

MINORCA *n pl.* **-S** any of a breed of large domestic fowls

MINORITY *n pl.* **-TIES** the smaller number or part

MINSTER *n pl.* **-S** a large or important church

MINSTREL *n pl.* **-S** a medieval musician

MINT *v* **-ED, -ING, -S** to produce by stamping metal, as coins

MINTAGE *n pl.* **-S** the act of minting

MINTER *n pl.* **-S** one that mints

MINTY *adj* **MINTIER, MINTIEST** having the flavor of mint (an aromatic herb)

MINUEND *n pl.* **-S** a number from which another is to be subtracted

MINUET *v* **-ED, -ING, -S** to dance a minuet (a slow, stately dance)

MINUS *n pl.* **-ES** a negative quantity

MINUTE *adj* **-NUTER, -NUTEST** very small **MINUTELY** *adv*

MINUTE *v* **-UTED, -UTING, -UTES** to make a brief note of

MINUTIA *n pl.* **-TIAE** a small detail **MINUTIAL** *adj*

MINX *n pl.* **-ES** a pert girl **MINXISH** *adj*

MINYAN *n pl.* **-YANS** or **-YANIM** the minimum number required to be present for the conduct of a Jewish service

MIOSIS *n pl.* **-OSES** excessive contraction of the pupil of the eye

MIOTIC *n pl.* **-S** an agent that causes miosis

MIQUELET *n pl.* **-S** a former Spanish or French soldier

MIR *n pl.* **MIRS** or **MIRI** a Russian peasant commune

MIRACLE	*n* pl. **-S** an event ascribed to supernatural or divine origin
MIRADOR	*n* pl. **-S** an architectural feature designed to afford an extensive view
MIRAGE	*n* pl. **-S** a type of optical illusion
MIRE	*v* **MIRED, MIRING, MIRES** to cause to stick in swampy ground
MIREPOIX	*n* pl. **MIREPOIX** a sauteed mixture of diced vegetables
MIREX	*n* pl. **-ES** an insecticide
MIRI	a pl. of mir
MIRID	*n* pl. **-S** a variety of leaf bug
MIRIER	comparative of miry
MIRIEST	superlative of miry
MIRIN	*n* pl. **-S** a sweet Japanese cooking wine
MIRINESS	*n* pl. **-ES** the state of being miry
MIRING	present participle of mire
MIRK	*adj* **MIRKER, MIRKEST** murk
MIRK	*n* pl. **-S** murk
MIRKY	*adj* **MIRKIER, MIRKIEST** murky **MIRKILY** *adv*
MIRLITON	*n* pl. **-S** a chayote
MIRROR	*v* **-ED, -ING, -S** to reflect an image of
MIRTH	*n* pl. **-S** spirited gaiety **MIRTHFUL** *adj*
MIRY	*adj* **MIRIER, MIRIEST** swampy
MIRZA	*n* pl. **-S** a Persian title of honor
MISACT	*v* **-ED, -ING, -S** to act badly
MISADAPT	*v* **-ED, -ING, -S** to adapt wrongly
MISADD	*v* **-ED, -ING, -S** to add incorrectly
MISAGENT	*n* pl. **-S** a bad agent
MISAIM	*v* **-ED, -ING, -S** to aim badly
MISALIGN	*v* **-ED, -ING, -S** to align improperly
MISALLOT	*v* **-LOTTED, -LOTTING, -LOTS** to allot wrongly
MISALLY	*v* **-LIED, -LYING, -LIES** to ally badly
MISALTER	*v* **-ED, -ING, -S** to alter wrongly
MISANDRY	*n* pl. **-DRIES** hatred of men
MISAPPLY	*v* **-PLIED, -PLYING, -PLIES** to apply wrongly
MISASSAY	*v* **-ED, -ING, -S** to attempt unsuccessfully
MISATE	past tense of miseat
MISATONE	*v* **-ATONED, -ATONING, -ATONES** to atone wrongly
MISAVER	*v* **-AVERRED, -AVERRING, -AVERS** to speak erroneously
MISAWARD	*v* **-ED, -ING, -S** to award wrongly
MISBEGIN	*v* **-GAN, -GUN, -GINNING, -GINS** to begin wrongly
MISBEGOT	*adj* born out of wedlock
MISBIAS	*v* **-ASED, -ASING, -ASES** or **-ASSED, -ASSING, -ASSES** to bias wrongly
MISBILL	*v* **-ED, -ING, -S** to bill wrongly
MISBIND	*v* **-BOUND, -BINDING, -BINDS** to bind imperfectly
MISBRAND	*v* **-ED, -ING, -S** to brand incorrectly
MISBUILD	*v* **-BUILT, -BUILDING, -BUILDS** to build imperfectly
MISCALL	*v* **-ED, -ING, -S** to call by a wrong name
MISCARRY	*v* **-RIED, -RYING, -RIES** to be unsuccessful
MISCAST	*v* **-CAST, -CASTING, -CASTS** to cast in an unsuitable role
MISCHIEF	*n* pl. **-S** action that causes irritation, harm, or trouble
MISCHOSE	past tense of mischoose (to select improperly)
MISCIBLE	*adj* capable of being mixed
MISCITE	*v* **-CITED, -CITING, -CITES** to misquote
MISCLAIM	*v* **-ED, -ING, -S** to claim wrongfully
MISCLASS	*v* **-ED, -ING, -ES** to put in the wrong class
MISCODE	*v* **-CODED, -CODING, -CODES** to code wrongly
MISCOIN	*v* **-ED, -ING, -S** to coin improperly
MISCOLOR	*v* **-ED, -ING, -S** to color incorrectly
MISCOOK	*v* **-ED, -ING, -S** to cook badly
MISCOPY	*v* **-COPIED, -COPYING, -COPIES** to copy incorrectly
MISCOUNT	*v* **-ED, -ING, -S** to count incorrectly
MISCUE	*v* **-CUED, -CUING** or **-CUEING, -CUES** to make a faulty stroke in billiards
MISCUT	*v* **-CUT, -CUTTING, -CUTS** to cut incorrectly
MISDATE	*v* **-DATED, -DATING, -DATES** to date incorrectly
MISDEAL	*v* **-DEALT, -DEALING, -DEALS** to deal cards incorrectly
MISDEED	*n* pl. **-S** an evil act
MISDEEM	*v* **-ED, -ING, -S** to judge unfavorably

MISDIAL v **-DIALED, -DIALING, -DIALS** or **-DIALLED, -DIALLING, -DIALS** to dial wrongly

MISDO v **-DID, -DONE, -DOING, -DOES** to do wrongly

MISDOER n pl. **-S** one that misdoes

MISDOING n pl. **-S** an instance of doing wrong

MISDONE past participle of misdo

MISDOUBT v **-ED, -ING, -S** to doubt

MISDRAW v **-DREW, -DRAWN, -DRAWING, -DRAWS** to draw incorrectly

MISDRIVE v **-DROVE, -DRIVEN, -DRIVING, -DRIVES** to drive wrongly or improperly

MISE n pl. **-S** an agreement or settlement

MISEASE n pl. **-S** discomfort

MISEAT v **-ATE, -EATEN, -EATING, -EATS** to eat improperly

MISEDIT v **-ED, -ING, -S** to edit incorrectly

MISENROL v **-ROLLED, -ROLLING, -ROLS** to enroll improperly

MISENTER v **-ED, -ING, -S** to enter erroneously

MISENTRY n pl. **-TRIES** an erroneous entry

MISER n pl. **-S** one who hoards money greedily

MISERERE n pl. **-S** a part of a church seat

MISERLY adj characteristic of a miser

MISERY n pl. **-ERIES** a state of great suffering

MISEVENT n pl. **-S** a mishap

MISFAITH n pl. **-S** lack of faith; disbelief

MISFEED v **-FED, -FEEDING, -FEEDS** to feed wrongly

MISFIELD v **-ED, -ING, -S** to field badly

MISFILE v **-FILED, -FILING, -FILES** to file in the wrong place

MISFIRE v **-FIRED, -FIRING, -FIRES** to fail to fire

MISFIT v **-FITTED, -FITTING, -FITS** to fit badly

MISFOCUS v **-CUSED, -CUSING, -CUSES** or **-CUSSED, -CUSSING, -CUSSES** to focus badly

MISFOLD v **-ED, -ING, -S** to fold wrongly

MISFORM v **-ED, -ING, -S** to misshape

MISFRAME v **-FRAMED, -FRAMING, -FRAMES** to frame badly

MISGAUGE v **-GAUGED, -GAUGING, -GAUGES** to gauge wrongly or inaccurately

MISGIVE v **-GAVE, -GIVEN, -GIVING, -GIVES** to make doubtful or fearful

MISGRADE v **-GRADED, -GRADING, -GRADES** to grade incorrectly

MISGRAFT v **-ED, -ING, -S** to graft wrongly

MISGROW v **-GREW, -GROWN, -GROWING, -GROWS** to grow abnormally

MISGUESS v **-ED, -ING, -ES** to guess wrongly

MISGUIDE v **-GUIDED, -GUIDING, -GUIDES** to guide wrongly

MISHAP n pl. **-S** an unfortunate accident

MISHEAR v **-HEARD, -HEARING, -HEARS** to hear incorrectly

MISHIT v **-HIT, -HITTING, -HITS** to hit poorly

MISHMASH n pl. **-ES** a confused mixture

MISHMOSH n pl. **-ES** mishmash

MISHUGAS n pl. **-ES** crazy or foolish behavior

MISINFER v **-FERRED, -FERRING, -FERS** to infer wrongly

MISINTER v **-TERRED, -TERRING, -TERS** to inter improperly

MISJOIN v **-ED, -ING, -S** to join improperly

MISJUDGE v **-JUDGED, -JUDGING, -JUDGES** to judge wrongly

MISKAL n pl. **-S** an Oriental unit of weight

MISKEEP v **-KEPT, -KEEPING, -KEEPS** to keep wrongly

MISKEY v **-ED, -ING, -S** to key into a machine incorrectly

MISKICK v **-ED, -ING, -S** to kick badly

MISKNOW v **-KNEW, -KNOWN, -KNOWING, -KNOWS** to fail to understand or recognize

MISLABEL v **-BELED, -BELING, -BELS** or **-BELLED, -BELLING, -BELS** to label incorrectly or falsely

MISLABOR v **-ED, -ING, -S** to labor badly

MISLAIN past participle of mislie

MISLAY v **-LAID, -LAYING, -LAYS** to put in a forgotten place

MISLAYER n pl. **-S** one that mislays

MISLEAD v **-LED, -LEADING, -LEADS** to lead astray

MISLEARN v **-LEARNED** or **-LEARNT, -LEARNING, -LEARNS** to learn wrongly

MISLIE v **-LAY, -LAIN, -LYING, -LIES** to lie in a wrong position

MISLIGHT v **-LIGHTED** or **-LIT, -LIGHTING, -LIGHTS** to lead astray by its light

MISLIKE	*v* **-LIKED, -LIKING, -LIKES** to dislike
MISLIKER	*n* pl. **-S** one that mislikes
MISLIT	a past tense of mislight
MISLIVE	*v* **-LIVED, -LIVING, -LIVES** to live a bad life
MISLODGE	*v* **-LODGED, -LODGING, -LODGES** to lodge in a wrong place
MISLYING	present participle of mislie
MISMAKE	*v* **-MADE, -MAKING, -MAKES** to make incorrectly
MISMARK	*v* **-ED, -ING, -S** to mark wrongly
MISMATCH	*v* **-ED, -ING, -ES** to match badly
MISMATE	*v* **-MATED, -MATING, -MATES** to mate unsuitably
MISMEET	*v* **-MET, -MEETING, -MEETS** to meet under unfortunate circumstances
MISMOVE	*v* **-MOVED, -MOVING, -MOVES** to move wrongly
MISNAME	*v* **-NAMED, -NAMING, -NAMES** to call by a wrong name
MISNOMER	*n* pl. **-S** a name wrongly used
MISO	*n* pl. **-SOS** a type of food paste
MISOGAMY	*n* pl. **-MIES** a hatred of marriage
MISOGYNY	*n* pl. **-NIES** a hatred of women
MISOLOGY	*n* pl. **-GIES** a hatred of debate or reasoning
MISORDER	*v* **-ED, -ING, -S** to order incorrectly
MISPAGE	*v* **-PAGED, -PAGING, -PAGES** to page incorrectly
MISPAINT	*v* **-ED, -ING, -S** to paint wrongly
MISPARSE	*v* **-PARSED, -PARSING, -PARSES** to parse incorrectly
MISPART	*v* **-ED, -ING, -S** to part badly
MISPATCH	*v* **-ED, -ING, -ES** to patch badly
MISPEN	*v* **-PENNED, -PENNING, -PENS** to write incorrectly
MISPLACE	*v* **-PLACED, -PLACING, -PLACES** to put in a wrong place
MISPLAN	*v* **-PLANNED, -PLANNING, -PLANS** to plan badly
MISPLANT	*v* **-ED, -ING, -S** to plant wrongly
MISPLAY	*v* **-ED, -ING, -S** to make a bad play in a game
MISPLEAD	*v* **-PLEADED** or **-PLED, -PLEADING, -PLEADS** to plead wrongly or falsely
MISPOINT	*v* **-ED, -ING, -S** to point improperly
MISPOISE	*v* **-POISED, -POISING, -POISES** to poise incorrectly
MISPRICE	*v* **-PRICED, -PRICING, -PRICES** to price incorrectly
MISPRINT	*v* **-ED, -ING, -S** to print incorrectly
MISPRIZE	*v* **-PRIZED, -PRIZING, -PRIZES** to despise
MISQUOTE	*v* **-QUOTED, -QUOTING, -QUOTES** to quote incorrectly
MISRAISE	*v* **-RAISED, -RAISING, -RAISES** to raise wrongly
MISRATE	*v* **-RATED, -RATING, -RATES** to rate incorrectly
MISREAD	*v* **-READ, -READING, -READS** to read incorrectly
MISREFER	*v* **-FERRED, -FERRING, -FERS** to refer incorrectly
MISRELY	*v* **-LIED, -LYING, -LIES** to rely wrongly
MISROUTE	*v* **-ROUTED, -ROUTING, -ROUTES** to route incorrectly
MISRULE	*v* **-RULED, -RULING, -RULES** to rule unwisely or unjustly
MISS	*v* **-ED, -ING, -ES** to fail to make contact with
MISSABLE	*adj* able to be missed
MISSAL	*n* pl. **-S** a prayer book
MISSAY	*v* **-SAID, -SAYING, -SAYS** to say incorrectly
MISSEAT	*v* **-ED, -ING, -S** to seat wrongly
MISSEL	*n* pl. **-S** a European thrush
MISSEND	*v* **-SENT, -SENDING, -SENDS** to send incorrectly
MISSENSE	*n* pl. **-S** a form of genetic mutation
MISSET	*v* **-SET, -SETTING, -SETS** to set incorrectly
MISSHAPE	*v* **-SHAPED, -SHAPEN, -SHAPING, -SHAPES** to shape badly
MISSHOD	*adj* improperly shod
MISSIES	pl. of missy
MISSILE	*n* pl. **-S** an object or weapon that is thrown or projected
MISSILRY	*n* pl. **-RIES** the science of designing and operating guided missiles
MISSION	*v* **-ED, -ING, -S** to send to perform a specific task
MISSIS	*n* pl. **-SISES** a wife
MISSIVE	*n* pl. **-S** a written communication

MISSORT *v* **-ED, -ING, -S** to sort badly or improperly

MISSOUND *v* **-ED, -ING, -S** to sound wrongly

MISSOUT *n* pl. **-S** a losing throw of dice

MISSPACE *v* **-SPACED, -SPACING, -SPACES** to space incorrectly

MISSPEAK *v* **-SPOKE, -SPOKEN, -SPEAKING, -SPEAKS** to speak incorrectly

MISSPELL *v* **-SPELLED** or **-SPELT, -SPELLING, -SPELLS** to spell incorrectly

MISSPEND *v* **-SPENT, -SPENDING, -SPENDS** to spend wrongly

MISSPOKE past tense of misspeak

MISSPOKEN past participle of misspeak

MISSTAMP *v* **-ED, -ING, -S** to stamp wrongly

MISSTART *v* **-ED, -ING, -S** to start off badly

MISSTATE *v* **-STATED, -STATING, -STATES** to state wrongly

MISSTEER *v* **-ED, -ING, -S** to steer wrongly

MISSTEP *v* **-STEPPED, -STEPPING, -STEPS** to step wrongly

MISSTOP *v* **-STOPPED, -STOPPING, -STOPS** to stop wrongly

MISSTYLE *v* **-STYLED, -STYLING, -STYLES** to style or call wrongly

MISSUIT *v* **-ED, -ING, -S** to suit badly

MISSUS *n* pl. **-ES** missis

MISSY *n* pl. **MISSIES** a young girl

MIST *v* **-ED, -ING, -S** to become blurry

MISTAKE *v* **-TOOK** or **-TEUK, -TAKEN, -TAKING, -TAKES** to interpret wrongly

MISTAKER *n* pl. **-S** one that mistakes

MISTBOW *n* pl. **-S** a fogbow

MISTEACH *v* **-TAUGHT, -TEACHING, -TEACHES** to teach wrongly or badly

MISTEND *v* **-ED, -ING, -S** to tend to improperly

MISTER *n* pl. **-S** sir

MISTERM *v* **-ED, -ING, -S** to call by a wrong name

MISTEUK a past tense of mistake

MISTHINK *v* **-THOUGHT, -THINKING, -THINKS** to think wrongly

MISTHROW *v* **-THREW, -THROWN, -THROWING, -THROWS** to throw errantly

MISTIER comparative of misty

MISTIEST superlative of misty

MISTILY *adv* in a misty manner

MISTIME *v* **-TIMED, -TIMING, -TIMES** to time wrongly

MISTITLE *v* **-TLED, -TLING, -TLES** to call by a wrong title

MISTOOK a past tense of mistake

MISTOUCH *v* **-ED, -ING, -ES** to touch improperly

MISTRACE *v* **-TRACED, -TRACING, -TRACES** to trace wrongly

MISTRAIN *v* **-ED, -ING, -S** to train improperly

MISTRAL *n* pl. **-S** a cold, dry wind

MISTREAT *v* **-ED, -ING, -S** to treat badly

MISTRESS *n* pl. **-ES** a woman in a position of authority

MISTRIAL *n* pl. **-S** a trial made invalid because of some error in procedure

MISTRUST *v* **-ED, -ING, -S** to distrust

MISTRUTH *n* pl. **-S** a lie

MISTRYST *v* **-ED, -ING, -S** to fail to keep an appointment with

MISTUNE *v* **-TUNED, -TUNING, -TUNES** to tune incorrectly

MISTUTOR *v* **-ED, -ING, -S** to instruct or bring up badly

MISTY *adj* **MISTIER, MISTIEST** blurry

MISTYPE *v* **-TYPED, -TYPING, -TYPES** to type incorrectly

MISUNION *n* pl. **-S** a bad union

MISUSAGE *n* pl. **-S** incorrect use

MISUSE *v* **-USED, -USING, -USES** to use incorrectly

MISUSER *n* pl. **-S** one that misuses

MISVALUE *v* **-UED, -UING, -UES** to value incorrectly

MISWORD *v* **-ED, -ING, -S** to word wrongly

MISWRITE *v* **-WROTE** or **-WRIT, -WRITTEN, -WRITING, -WRITES** to write incorrectly

MISYOKE *v* **-YOKED, -YOKING, -YOKES** to yoke improperly

MITE *n* pl. **-S** a small arachnid

MITER *v* **-ED, -ING, -S** to raise to the rank of a bishop

MITERER *n* pl. **-S** one that miters

MITHER *n* pl. **-S** mother

MITICIDE *n* pl. **-S** a substance used to kill mites

MITIER	comparative of mity
MITIEST	superlative of mity
MITIGANT	n pl. **-S** something that mitigates
MITIGATE	v **-GATED, -GATING, -GATES** to make less severe
MITIS	n pl. **-TISES** a type of wrought iron
MITOGEN	n pl. **-S** a substance that induces mitosis
MITOSIS	n pl. **-TOSES** a type of cell division **MITOTIC** adj
MITRAL	adj pertaining to a valve of the heart
MITRE	v **-TRED, -TRING, -TRES** to miter
MITSVAH	n pl. **-VAHS** or **-VOTH** mitzvah
MITT	n pl. **-S** a type of baseball glove
MITTEN	n pl. **-S** a type of covering for the hand **MITTENED** adj
MITTIMUS	n pl. **-ES** a warrant committing a person to prison
MITY	adj **MITIER, MITIEST** infested with mites
MITZVAH	n pl. **-VAHS** or **-VOTH** a commandment of Jewish law
MIX	v **MIXED** or **MIXT, MIXING, MIXES** to put together into one mass **MIXABLE, MIXIBLE** adj **MIXEDLY** adv
MIXDOWN	n pl. **-S** the process of combining soundtracks to make a recording
MIXER	n pl. **-S** one that mixes
MIXOLOGY	n pl. **-GIES** the art of making mixed drinks
MIXTAPE	n pl. **-S** a compilation of songs recorded from various sources
MIXTURE	n pl. **-S** something produced by mixing
MIXUP	n pl. **-S** a state of confusion
MIZEN	n pl. **-S** mizzen
MIZUNA	n pl. **-S** a Japanese mustard
MIZZEN	n pl. **-S** a type of sail
MIZZLE	v **-ZLED, -ZLING, -ZLES** to rain in fine droplets
MIZZLY	adj **-ZLIER, -ZLIEST** characterized by a fine rain
MM	interj — used to express assent or satisfaction
MMM	interj mm
MNEMONIC	n pl. **-S** a device to assist the memory
MO	n pl. **MOS** a moment

MOA	n pl. **-S** an extinct flightless bird
MOAN	v **-ED, -ING, -S** to utter a low, mournful sound
MOANER	n pl. **-S** one that moans
MOANFUL	adj moaning
MOAT	v **-ED, -ING, -S** to surround with a moat (a water-filled trench)
MOATLIKE	adj suggestive of a moat
MOB	v **MOBBED, MOBBING, MOBS** to crowd about
MOBBER	n pl. **-S** one that mobs
MOBBISH	adj characteristic of a mob (a disorderly crowd of people)
MOBBISM	n pl. **-S** mobbish conduct
MOBCAP	n pl. **-S** a woman's cap
MOBILE	n pl. **-S** a form of sculpture
MOBILISE	v **-LISED, -LISING, -LISES** to mobilize
MOBILITY	n pl. **-TIES** the ability to move
MOBILIZE	v **-LIZED, -LIZING, -LIZES** to put into movement
MOBLED	adj wrapped in or as if in a hood
MOBLOG	n pl. **-S** a weblog with data posted from a cell phone
MOBOCRAT	n pl. **-S** a supporter of mob rule
MOBSTER	n pl. **-S** a gangster
MOC	n pl. **-S** a moccasin
MOCCASIN	n pl. **-S** a type of shoe
MOCHA	n pl. **-S** a choice, pungent coffee
MOCHI	n pl. **-S** a Japanese confection made with rice flour and sweetened bean paste
MOCHILA	n pl. **-S** a leather covering for a saddle
MOCK	v **-ED, -ING, -S** to ridicule **MOCKABLE** adj
MOCKER	n pl. **-S** one that mocks
MOCKERY	n pl. **-ERIES** the act of mocking
MOCKTAIL	n pl. **-S** a cocktail with no alcohol
MOCKUP	n pl. **-S** a full-sized model
MOD	n pl. **-S** one who wears boldly stylish clothes
MODAL	n pl. **-S** a verb used with other verbs to express mood or tense
MODALISM	n pl. **-S** the doctrine that members of the Trinity are not distinct persons but modes of divine revelation
MODALIST	n pl. **-S** an adherent of modalism

MODALITY *n pl.* **-TIES** the state of being modal

MODALLY *adv* in a manner pertaining to a mode

MODE *n pl.* **-S** a method of doing or acting

MODEL *v* **-ELED, -ELING, -ELS** or **-ELLED, -ELLING, -ELS** to plan or form after a pattern

MODELER *n pl.* **-S** one that models

MODELING *n pl.* **-S** the treatment of volume in sculpture

MODELIST *n pl.* **-S** one who makes models

MODELLED a past tense of model

MODELLER *n pl.* **-S** modeler

MODELLING a present participle of model

MODEM *v* **-ED, -ING, -S** to transmit by modem (a device for converting signals from one form to another)

MODERATE *v* **-ATED, -ATING, -ATES** to make less extreme

MODERATO *n pl.* **-TOS** a musical passage played at a medium tempo

MODERN *adj* **-ERNER, -ERNEST** pertaining to present or recent time **MODERNLY** *adv*

MODERN *n pl.* **-S** a person of modern times or views

MODERNE *n pl.* **-S** a design style of the 1920s and 1930s

MODEST *adj* **-ESTER, -ESTEST** having a moderate regard for oneself **MODESTLY** *adv*

MODESTY *n pl.* **-TIES** the quality of being modest

MODI pl. of modus

MODICUM *n pl.* **-CUMS** or **-CA** a small amount

MODIFIER *n pl.* **-S** one that modifies

MODIFY *v* **-FIED, -FYING, -FIES** to change in form or character

MODIOLUS *n pl.* **-LI** a bony shaft of the inner ear

MODISH *adj* stylish **MODISHLY** *adv*

MODISTE *n pl.* **-S** a dealer in stylish women's clothing

MODULAR *n pl.* **-S** something built in self-contained units

MODULATE *v* **-LATED, -LATING, -LATES** to adjust to a certain proportion

MODULE *n pl.* **-S** a standard of measurement

MODULO *adv* with respect to a modulus

MODULUS *n pl.* **-LI** a number that produces the same remainder when divided into each of two numbers

MODUS *n pl.* **-DI** a mode

MOFETTE *n pl.* **-S** a noxious emanation from a fissure in the earth

MOFFETTE *n pl.* **-S** mofette

MOG *v* **MOGGED, MOGGING, MOGS** to move away

MOGGIE *n pl.* **-S** moggy

MOGGY *n pl.* **-GIES** a cat

MOGHUL *n pl.* **-S** mogul

MOGUL *n pl.* **-S** an important person

MOGULED *adj* provided with bumps of hard snow

MOHAIR *n pl.* **-S** the long, silky hair of the Angora goat

MOHAWK *n pl.* **-S** a hairstyle marked by a stiff ridge of long hair from front to back

MOHEL *n pl.* **-HELS** or **-HELIM** or **-HALIM** a person who performs Jewish ritual circumcisions

MOHO *n pl.* **MOHOS** a boundary separating the earth's crust and mantle (the region between the crust and the core)

MOHUR *n pl.* **-S** a former gold coin of India

MOI *interj* — used instead of "me?" to feign surprise when accused of something

MOIDORE *n pl.* **-S** a former gold coin of Portugal

MOIETY *n pl.* **-ETIES** a half

MOIL *v* **-ED, -ING, -S** to work hard

MOILER *n pl.* **-S** one that moils

MOIRA *n pl.* **-RAI** fate or destiny, in ancient Greek religion

MOIRE *n pl.* **-S** a fabric having a wavy pattern

MOIST *adj* **MOISTER, MOISTEST** slightly wet

MOISTEN *v* **-ED, -ING, -S** to make or become moist

MOISTFUL *adj* moist

MOISTLY *adv* in a moist manner

MOISTURE *n pl.* **-S** condensed or diffused liquid

MOJARRA *n pl.* **-S** a marine fish

MOJITO *n pl.* **-TOS** a cocktail made of rum, sugar, mint, and lime juice

MOJO	*n* pl. **-JOS** or **-JOES** a magic charm
MOKE	*n* pl. **-S** a donkey
MOKSHA	*n* pl. **-S** the final release of the soul from reincarnations in Hinduism
MOL	*n* pl. **-S** mole
MOLA	*n* pl. **-S** a marine fish
MOLAL	*adj* pertaining to a mole
MOLALITY	*n* pl. **-TIES** the number of moles of solute per 1,000 grams of solvent
MOLAR	*n* pl. **-S** a grinding tooth
MOLARITY	*n* pl. **-TIES** the number of moles of solute per liter of solution
MOLASSES	*n* pl. **-LASSESES** a thick syrup
MOLD	*v* **-ED, -ING, -S** to work into a particular shape **MOLDABLE** *adj*
MOLDER	*v* **-ED, -ING, -S** to turn to dust by natural decay
MOLDIER	comparative of moldy
MOLDIEST	superlative of moldy
MOLDING	*n* pl. **-S** a long, narrow strip used to decorate a surface
MOLDWARP	*n* pl. **-S** a burrowing mammal
MOLDY	*adj* **MOLDIER, MOLDIEST** musty
MOLE	*n* pl. **-S** the quantity of a compound that has a weight equal to the compound's molecular weight
MOLECULE	*n* pl. **-S** the smallest physical unit of an element
MOLEHILL	*n* pl. **-S** a small mound of earth
MOLESKIN	*n* pl. **-S** a cotton fabric
MOLEST	*v* **-ED, -ING, -S** to disturb or annoy
MOLESTER	*n* pl. **-S** one that molests
MOLIES	pl. of moly
MOLINE	*adj* having arms forked and curved at the ends — used of a heraldic cross
MOLL	*n* pl. **-S** a gangster's girlfriend
MOLLAH	*n* pl. **-S** mullah
MOLLIE	*n* pl. **-S** a tropical fish
MOLLIES	pl. of molly
MOLLIFY	*v* **-FIED, -FYING, -FIES** to soothe
MOLLUSC	*n* pl. **-S** mollusk
MOLLUSCA	*n/pl* skin diseases
MOLLUSK	*n* pl. **-S** any of a phylum of soft-bodied invertebrates
MOLLY	*n* pl. **-LIES** mollie
MOLOCH	*n* pl. **-S** a spiny lizard
MOLT	*v* **-ED, -ING, -S** to cast off an outer covering
MOLTEN	*adj* made liquid by heat **MOLTENLY** *adv*
MOLTER	*n* pl. **-S** one that molts
MOLTO	*adv* very — used in musical directions
MOLY	*n* pl. **-LIES** a wild garlic
MOLY	*n* pl. **MOLYS** molybdenum
MOLYBDIC	*adj* pertaining to a certain metallic element
MOM	*n* pl. **-S** mother
MOME	*n* pl. **-S** a fool
MOMENT	*n* pl. **-S** a brief period of time
MOMENTA	a pl. of momentum
MOMENTLY	*adv* from moment to moment
MOMENTO	*n* pl. **-TOS** or **-TOES** memento
MOMENTUM	*n* pl. **-TUMS** or **-TA** force of movement
MOMI	a pl. of momus
MOMISM	*n* pl. **-S** an excessive dependence on mothers
MOMMA	*n* pl. **-S** mother
MOMMY	*n* pl. **-MIES** mother
MOMSER	*n* pl. **-S** a bastard
MOMUS	*n* pl. **-MUSES** or **-MI** a carping person
MOMZER	*n* pl. **-S** momser
MON	*n* pl. **MEN** man
MONACHAL	*adj* pertaining to monks
MONACID	*n* pl. **-S** monoacid
MONAD	*n* pl. **-S** a single-celled organism **MONADAL, MONADIC** *adj*
MONADES	pl. of monas
MONADISM	*n* pl. **-S** a philosophical doctrine
MONAMINE	*n* pl. **-S** an amine containing only one amino group
MONANDRY	*n* pl. **-DRIES** the condition of having one husband at a time
MONARCH	*n* pl. **-S** an absolute ruler
MONARCHY	*n* pl. **-CHIES** rule by a monarch
MONARDA	*n* pl. **-S** an aromatic herb
MONAS	*n* pl. **MONADES** a monad
MONASTIC	*n* pl. **-S** a monk
MONAURAL	*adj* pertaining to sound transmission, recording, or reproduction involving a single transmission path

MONAXIAL	*adj* having one axis
MONAXON	*n* pl. **-S** a straight spicule in sponges
MONAZITE	*n* pl. **-S** a mineral
MONDE	*n* pl. **-S** the world
MONDO	*n* pl. **-DOS** a rapid question and answer technique employed in Zen Buddhism
MONECIAN	*adj* having both male and female sex organs in the same individual
MONELLIN	*n* pl. **-S** a protein extracted from a West African red berry
MONERAN	*n* pl. **-S** a cellular organism that does not have a distinct nucleus
MONETARY	*adj* pertaining to money
MONETISE	*v* **-TISED, -TISING, -TISES** to monetize
MONETIZE	*v* **-TIZED, -TIZING, -TIZES** to coin into money
MONEY	*n* pl. **MONEYS** or **MONIES** an official medium of exchange and measure of value
MONEYBAG	*n* pl. **-S** a bag for holding money
MONEYED	*adj* having much money
MONEYER	*n* pl. **-S** one that coins money
MONEYMAN	*n* pl. **-MEN** a person who invests large sums of money
MONGEESE	a pl. of mongoose
MONGER	*v* **-ED, -ING, -S** to peddle
MONGO	*n* pl. **-GOS** mungo
MONGOE	*n* pl. **-S** mungo
MONGOL	*n* pl. **-S** a person affected with a form of mental deficiency
MONGOOSE	*n* pl. **-GOOSES** or **-GEESE** a carnivorous mammal
MONGREL	*n* pl. **-S** an animal or plant of mixed breed
MONGST	*prep* amongst
MONIC	*adj* denoting a type of polynomial
MONICKER	*n* pl. **-S** moniker
MONIE	*adj* many
MONIED	*adj* moneyed
MONIES	a pl. of money
MONIKER	*n* pl. **-S** a name
MONILIA	*n* pl. **-IAE** a type of parasitic fungus
MONISH	*v* **-ED, -ING, -ES** to warn
MONISM	*n* pl. **-S** a philosophical theory
MONIST	*n* pl. **-S** an adherent of monism **MONISTIC** *adj*
MONITION	*n* pl. **-S** a warning
MONITIVE	*adj* giving warning
MONITOR	*v* **-ED, -ING, -S** to keep track of
MONITORY	*n* pl. **-RIES** a letter of warning
MONK	*n* pl. **-S** a man who is a member of a secluded religious order
MONKERY	*n* pl. **-ERIES** the mode of life of monks
MONKEY	*v* **-ED, -ING, -S** to mimic
MONKFISH	*n* pl. **-ES** a marine fish
MONKHOOD	*n* pl. **-S** the state of being a monk
MONKISH	*adj* pertaining to monks
MONO	*n* pl. **MONOS** an infectious disease
MONOACID	*n* pl. **-S** a type of acid
MONOBLOC	*adj* made in a single casting
MONOCARP	*n* pl. **-S** a plant that yields fruit only once before dying
MONOCLE	*n* pl. **-S** an eyeglass for one eye **MONOCLED** *adj*
MONOCOT	*n* pl. **-S** a type of seed plant
MONOCRAT	*n* pl. **-S** an autocrat
MONOCROP	*n* pl. **-S** the same crop in the same field year after year
MONOCYTE	*n* pl. **-S** a type of white blood cell
MONODIST	*n* pl. **-S** one who writes monodies
MONODY	*n* pl. **-DIES** an elegy performed by one person **MONODIC** *adj*
MONOECY	*n* pl. **-CIES** the condition of being monecian
MONOFIL	*n* pl. **-S** a single filament of synthetic fiber
MONOFUEL	*n* pl. **-S** a type of rocket propellant
MONOGAMY	*n* pl. **-MIES** marriage with one person at a time
MONOGENY	*n* pl. **-NIES** asexual reproduction
MONOGERM	*adj* being a fruit that produces a single plant
MONOGLOT	*n* pl. **-S** a person speaking or writing only one language
MONOGRAM	*v* **-GRAMED, -GRAMING, -GRAMS** or **-GRAMMED, -GRAMMING, -GRAMS** to mark with a design of one's initials
MONOGYNY	*n* pl. **-NIES** the condition of having one wife at a time
MONOHULL	*n* pl. **-S** a vessel with a single hull
MONOKINE	*n* pl. **-S** a substance secreted by white blood cells

MONOKINI *n* pl. **-S** the lower half of a bikini

MONOLITH *n* pl. **-S** a large block of stone

MONOLOG *v* **-LOGGED, -LOGGING, -LOGS** to deliver a monolog (a lengthy speech by one person)

MONOLOGY *n* pl. **-GIES** the act of uttering a monolog

MONOMER *n* pl. **-S** a type of chemical compound

MONOMIAL *n* pl. **-S** an algebraic expression consisting of a single term

MONOPOD *n* pl. **-S** a one-legged support for a camera

MONOPODE *n* pl. **-S** a creature having one foot

MONOPODY *n* pl. **-DIES** a measure consisting of a single metrical foot

MONOPOLE *n* pl. **-S** a type of radio antenna

MONOPOLY *n* pl. **-LIES** exclusive control of a commodity or service in a particular market

MONORAIL *n* pl. **-S** a single rail serving as a track for a wheeled vehicle

MONOSKI *n* pl. **-S** a single broad ski for both feet

MONOSOME *n* pl. **-S** an unpaired chromosome

MONOSOMY *n* pl. **-MIES** a condition of having one unpaired chromosome

MONOTINT *n* pl. **-S** a painting done in different shades of one color

MONOTONE *n* pl. **-S** a vocal utterance in one unvaried tone

MONOTONY *n* pl. **-NIES** tedious sameness

MONOTYPE *n* pl. **-S** the only representative of its group

MONOXIDE *n* pl. **-S** a type of oxide

MONS *n* pl. **MONTES** a protuberance of the body

MONSIEUR *n* pl. **MESSIEURS** a French title of courtesy for a man

MONSOON *n* pl. **-S** a seasonal wind

MONSTER *n* pl. **-S** a strange or terrifying creature

MONSTERA *n* pl. **-S** a tropical American plant

MONTAGE *v* **-TAGED, -TAGING, -TAGES** to combine into a composite picture

MONTANE *n* pl. **-S** the lower vegetation belt of a mountain

MONTE *n* pl. **-S** a card game

MONTEITH *n* pl. **-S** a large punch bowl

MONTERO *n* pl. **-ROS** a type of cap

MONTES pl. of mons

MONTH *n* pl. **-S** a period of approximately 30 days

MONTHLY *n* pl. **-LIES** a publication issued once a month

MONTY *n* pl. **-TIES** the full amount expected or possible

MONUMENT *n* pl. **-S** a structure built as a memorial

MONURON *n* pl. **-S** an herbicide

MONY *adj* many

MOO *v* **-ED, -ING, -S** to make the deep, moaning sound of a cow

MOOCH *v* **-ED, -ING, -ES** to obtain without paying

MOOCHER *n* pl. **-S** one that mooches

MOOD *n* pl. **-S** a person's emotional state at a particular moment

MOODY *adj* **MOODIER, MOODIEST** given to changing moods **MOODILY** *adv*

MOOK *n* pl. **-S** a foolish or contemptible person

MOOL *n* pl. **-S** soft soil

MOOLA *n* pl. **-S** moolah

MOOLAH *n* pl. **-S** money

MOOLEY *n* pl. **-EYS** muley

MOON *v* **-ED, -ING, -S** to spend time idly

MOONBEAM *n* pl. **-S** a ray of light from the moon (the earth's natural satellite)

MOONBOW *n* pl. **-S** a rainbow formed by light from the moon

MOONCALF *n* pl. **-CALVES** a foolish person

MOONDOG *n* pl. **-S** a bright spot in the sky formed by moonlight

MOONDUST *n* pl. **-S** dust on the moon

MOONER *n* pl. **-S** one that moons

MOONEYE *n* pl. **-S** a freshwater fish

MOONFISH *n* pl. **-ES** a marine fish

MOONGATE *n* pl. **-S** a circular gateway in a wall

MOONIER comparative of moony

MOONIEST superlative of moony

MOONILY *adv* in a moony manner

MOONISH *adj* fickle

MOONLESS *adj* lacking the light of the moon

MOONLET *n* pl. **-S** a small satellite

MOONLIKE *adj* resembling the moon

MOONLIT *adj* lighted by the moon

MOONPORT *n* pl. **-S** a facility for launching spacecraft to the moon

MOONRISE *n* pl. **-S** the rising of the moon above the horizon

MOONROOF *n* pl. **-S** a glass panel in an automobile roof

MOONSAIL *n* pl. **-S** a light, square sail

MOONSEED *n* pl. **-S** a climbing plant

MOONSET *n* pl. **-S** the setting of the moon below the horizon

MOONSHOT *n* pl. **-S** the launching of a spacecraft to the moon

MOONWALK *v* **-ED, -ING, -S** to walk on the moon

MOONWARD *adv* toward the moon

MOONWORT *n* pl. **-S** a flowering plant

MOONY *adj* **MOONIER, MOONIEST** resembling the moon

MOOR *v* **-ED, -ING, -S** to secure a vessel by means of cables

MOORAGE *n* pl. **-S** the act of mooring

MOORCOCK *n* pl. **-S** the male moorfowl

MOORFOWL *n* pl. **-S** a game bird

MOORHEN *n* pl. **-S** the female moorfowl

MOORIER comparative of moory

MOORIEST superlative of moory

MOORING *n* pl. **-S** a place where a vessel may be moored

MOORISH *adj* marshy

MOORLAND *n* pl. **-S** a tract of marshy land

MOORWORT *n* pl. **-S** a marsh plant

MOORY *adj* **MOORIER, MOORIEST** marshy

MOOSE *n* pl. **MOOSE** a ruminant mammal

MOOT *v* **-ED, -ING, -S** to bring up for discussion

MOOTER *n* pl. **-S** one that moots

MOOTNESS *n* pl. **-ES** the state of being without legal significance

MOP *v* **MOPPED, MOPPING, MOPS** to wipe with a mop (an implement for cleaning floors)

MOPBOARD *n* pl. **-S** a board at the base of a wall

MOPE *v* **MOPED, MOPING, MOPES** to act in a dejected or gloomy manner

MOPED *n* pl. **-S** a type of motorbike

MOPER *n* pl. **-S** one that mopes

MOPERY *n* pl. **-PERIES** an act of dawdling

MOPEY *adj* **MOPIER, MOPIEST** dejected **MOPILY** *adv*

MOPHEAD *n* pl. **-S** a person with thick shaggy hair

MOPIER comparative of mopy

MOPIEST superlative of mopy

MOPINESS *n* pl. **-ES** the state of being mopey

MOPING present participle of mope

MOPINGLY *adv* in a moping manner

MOPISH *adj* given to moping **MOPISHLY** *adv*

MOPOKE *n* pl. **-S** an Australian bird

MOPPED past tense of mop

MOPPER *n* pl. **-S** one that mops

MOPPET *n* pl. **-S** a child

MOPPING present participle of mop

MOPPY *adj* **-PIER, -PIEST** resembling a mop

MOPY *adj* **MOPIER, MOPIEST** mopey

MOQUETTE *n* pl. **-S** a woolen fabric

MOR *n* pl. **-S** a forest humus

MORA *n* pl. **-RAS** or **-RAE** a unit of metrical time in prosody

MORAINE *n* pl. **-S** an accumulation of debris deposited by a glacier **MORAINAL, MORAINIC** *adj*

MORAL *adj* pertaining to principles of right and wrong

MORALE *n* pl. **-S** the state of the spirits of an individual or group

MORALISE *v* **-ISED, -ISING, -ISES** to moralize

MORALISM *n* pl. **-S** the practice of moralizing

MORALIST *n* pl. **-S** a teacher of morality

MORALITY *n* pl. **-TIES** conformity to the rules of right conduct

MORALIZE *v* **-IZED, -IZING, -IZES** to explain in a moral sense

MORALLY *adv* in a moral manner

MORALS *n/pl* rules of conduct with respect to right and wrong

MORASS *n* pl. **-ES** a marsh **MORASSY** *adj*

MORATORY *adj* authorizing delay of payment

MORAY *n* pl. **-RAYS** a tropical eel

MORBID *adj* gruesome **MORBIDLY** *adv*

MORBIFIC *adj* causing disease

MORBILLI *n/pl* a virus disease

MORCEAU *n* pl. **-CEAUX** a short literary or musical composition

MORDANCY *n* pl. **-CIES** a sarcastic quality

MORDANT	*v* **-ED, -ING, -S** to treat with a caustic substance
MORDENT	*n* pl. **-S** a melodic embellishment
MORE	*adj* greater, additional
MOREEN	*n* pl. **-S** a heavy fabric
MOREISH	*adj* so good that you want to have more
MOREL	*n* pl. **-S** an edible mushroom
MORELLE	*n* pl. **-S** a flowering plant
MORELLO	*n* pl. **-LOS** a variety of sour cherry
MORENESS	*n* pl. **-ES** the state of being more
MOREOVER	*adv* in addition
MORES	*n/pl* the customs of a particular group
MORESQUE	*n* pl. **-S** an ancient decorative style
MORGAN	*n* pl. **-S** a unit of distance between genes
MORGEN	*n* pl. **-S** a Dutch unit of land area
MORGUE	*n* pl. **-S** a place where dead bodies are kept for identification
MORIBUND	*adj* being about to die
MORION	*n* pl. **-S** a type of helmet
MORISH	*adj* moreish
MORN	*n* pl. **-S** morning
MORNAY	*n* pl. **-NAYS** a cheese-flavored white sauce
MORNING	*n* pl. **-S** the early part of the day
MOROCCO	*n* pl. **-COS** a soft leather
MORON	*n* pl. **-S** a mentally deficient person **MORONIC** *adj*
MORONISM	*n* pl. **-S** the condition of being a moron
MORONITY	*n* pl. **-TIES** moronism
MOROSE	*adj* sullen **MOROSELY** *adv*
MOROSITY	*n* pl. **-TIES** the state of being morose
MORPH	*v* **-ED, -ING, -S** to be transformed
MORPHEME	*n* pl. **-S** a linguistic unit
MORPHIA	*n* pl. **-S** morphine
MORPHIC	*adj* pertaining to form
MORPHIN	*n* pl. **-S** morphine
MORPHINE	*n* pl. **-S** a narcotic alkaloid
MORPHING	*n* pl. **-S** the transformation of one form into another
MORPHO	*n* pl. **-PHOS** a tropical butterfly
MORRION	*n* pl. **-S** morion
MORRIS	*n* pl. **-RISES** an English folk dance
MORRO	*n* pl. **-ROS** a rounded elevation
MORROW	*n* pl. **-S** the next day
MORSE	*adj* designating a code used in telegraphy
MORSEL	*v* **-SELED, -SELING, -SELS** or **-SELLED, -SELLING, -SELS** to divide into small pieces
MORT	*n* pl. **-S** a note sounded on a hunting horn to announce the killing of an animal
MORTAL	*n* pl. **-S** a human being
MORTALLY	*adv* fatally
MORTAR	*v* **-ED, -ING, -S** to secure with mortar (a type of cement)
MORTARY	*adj* containing or resembling mortar
MORTGAGE	*v* **-GAGED, -GAGING, -GAGES** to pledge to a creditor as security
MORTICE	*v* **-TICED, -TICING, -TICES** to mortise
MORTICER	*n* pl. **-S** mortiser
MORTIFY	*v* **-FIED, -FYING, -FIES** to humiliate
MORTISE	*v* **-TISED, -TISING, -TISES** to join or fasten securely
MORTISER	*n* pl. **-S** one that mortises
MORTMAIN	*n* pl. **-S** perpetual ownership of land
MORTUARY	*n* pl. **-ARIES** a place where dead bodies are kept until burial
MORULA	*n* pl. **-LAS** or **-LAE** an embryonic mass of cells **MORULAR** *adj*
MOSAIC	*v* **-ICKED, -ICKING, -ICS** to form into a mosaic (a type of inlaid surface decoration)
MOSASAUR	*n* pl. **-S** an extinct lizard
MOSCATO	*n* pl. **-TOS** a sweet dessert wine
MOSCHATE	*adj* musky
MOSELLE	*n* pl. **-S** a medium-dry white wine
MOSEY	*v* **-ED, -ING, -S** to saunter
MOSH	*v* **-ED, -ING, -ES** to engage in frenzied dancing with others at a rock concert
MOSHAV	*n* pl. **-SHAVIM** a cooperative settlement of small farms in Israel
MOSHER	*n* pl. **-S** one that moshes
MOSHING	*n* pl. **-S** frenzied dancing at a rock concert
MOSK	*n* pl. **-S** mosque
MOSQUE	*n* pl. **-S** a Muslim house of worship

MOSQUITO   *n* pl. **-TOS** or **-TOES** a winged insect

MOSS   *v* **-ED, -ING, -ES** to cover with moss (a growth of small, leafy-stemmed plants)

MOSSBACK   *n* pl. **-S** a large, old fish

MOSSER   *n* pl. **-S** one that gathers or works with moss

MOSSLIKE   *adj* resembling moss

MOSSO   *adv* rapidly — used as a musical direction

MOSSY   *adj* **MOSSIER, MOSSIEST** covered with moss

MOST   *n* pl. **-S** the greatest amount

MOSTE   past tense of mote

MOSTEST   *n* pl. **-S** most

MOSTLY   *adv* mainly

MOT   *n* pl. **-S** a witty saying

MOTE   *n* pl. **-S** a small particle

MOTE   *v* past tense **MOSTE** may

MOTEL   *n* pl. **-S** a roadside hotel

MOTET   *n* pl. **-S** a type of choral composition

MOTEY   *adj* full of motes

MOTH   *n* pl. **-S** a winged insect

MOTHBALL   *v* **-ED, -ING, -S** to put into storage

MOTHER   *v* **-ED, -ING, -S** to give birth to

MOTHERLY   *adj* maternal

MOTHERY   *adj* slimy

MOTHLIKE   *adj* resembling a moth

MOTHY   *adj* **MOTHIER, MOTHIEST** full of moths

MOTIF   *n* pl. **-S** a recurring thematic element in an artistic work **MOTIFIC** *adj*

MOTILE   *n* pl. **-S** one whose mental imagery consists chiefly of inner feelings of action

MOTILITY   *n* pl. **-TIES** the ability to move

MOTION   *v* **-ED, -ING, -S** to signal by a bodily movement

MOTIONAL   *adj* pertaining to movement

MOTIONER   *n* pl. **-S** one that motions

MOTIVATE   *v* **-VATED, -VATING, -VATES** to provide with an incentive

MOTIVE   *v* **-TIVED, -TIVING, -TIVES** to motivate

MOTIVIC   *adj* pertaining to a musical motif

MOTIVITY   *n* pl. **-TIES** the ability to move

MOTLEY   *adj* **-LEYER, -LEYEST** or **-LIER, -LIEST** composed of diverse elements

MOTLEY   *n* pl. **-LEYS** a garment of various colors

MOTMOT   *n* pl. **-S** a tropical bird

MOTOR   *v* **-ED, -ING, -S** to travel by automobile

MOTORBUS   *n* pl. **-BUSES** or **-BUSSES** a bus

MOTORCAR   *n* pl. **-S** an automobile

MOTORDOM   *n* pl. **-S** the motor vehicle industry

MOTORIC   *adj* pertaining to muscular movement

MOTORING   *n* pl. **-S** the recreation of traveling by automobile

MOTORISE   *v* **-ISED, -ISING, -ISES** to motorize

MOTORIST   *n* pl. **-S** one who travels by automobile

MOTORIZE   *v* **-IZED, -IZING, -IZES** to equip with motor vehicles

MOTORMAN   *n* pl. **-MEN** one who operates an electric streetcar or subway train

MOTORWAY   *n* pl. **-WAYS** a type of highway

MOTT   *n* pl. **-S** motte

MOTTE   *n* pl. **-S** a small growth of trees on a prairie

MOTTLE   *v* **-TLED, -TLING, -TLES** to mark with spots or streaks of different colors

MOTTLER   *n* pl. **-S** one that mottles

MOTTLING   *n* pl. **-S** an irregular arrangement of spots

MOTTO   *n* pl. **-TOS** or **-TOES** a short expression of a guiding principle

MOUCH   *v* **-ED, -ING, -ES** to mooch

MOUCHOIR   *n* pl. **-S** a small handkerchief

MOUE   *n* pl. **-S** a pouting grimace

MOUFFLON   *n* pl. **-S** mouflon

MOUFLON   *n* pl. **-S** a wild sheep

MOUILLE   *adj* pronounced with the front of the tongue against the palate

MOUJIK   *n* pl. **-S** muzhik

MOULAGE   *n* pl. **-S** the making of a cast or mold of a mark for use in a criminal investigation

MOULD   *v* **-ED, -ING, -S** to mold

MOULDER   *v* **-ED, -ING, -S** to molder

MOULDING   *n* pl. **-S** molding

MOULDY   *adj* **MOULDIER, MOULDIEST** moldy

MOULIN	*n* pl. **-S** a vertical cavity in a glacier
MOULT	*v* **-ED, -ING, -S** to molt
MOULTER	*n* pl. **-S** molter
MOUND	*v* **-ED, -ING, -S** to pile
MOUNT	*v* **-ED, -ING, -S** to get up on
MOUNTAIN	*n* pl. **-S** a large, natural elevation of the earth's surface
MOUNTER	*n* pl. **-S** one that mounts
MOUNTING	*n* pl. **-S** something that provides a backing or appropriate setting for something else
MOURN	*v* **-ED, -ING, -S** to feel or express grief or sorrow
MOURNER	*n* pl. **-S** one that mourns
MOURNFUL	*adj* **-FULLER, -FULLEST** expressing grief or sorrow
MOURNING	*n* pl. **-S** an outward sign of grief
MOUSAKA	*n* pl. **-S** moussaka
MOUSE	*n* pl. **MICE** a small rodent
MOUSE	*v* **MOUSED, MOUSING, MOUSES** to catch mice
MOUSEPAD	*n* pl. **-S** a flat pad on which a computer mouse is used
MOUSER	*n* pl. **-S** an animal that catches mice
MOUSEY	*adj* **MOUSIER, MOUSIEST** mousy
MOUSIER	comparative of mousy
MOUSIEST	superlative of mousy
MOUSILY	*adv* in a mousy manner
MOUSING	*n* pl. **-S** a wrapping around the shank end of a hook
MOUSSAKA	*n* pl. **-S** a Middle Eastern dish of meat and eggplant
MOUSSE	*v* **MOUSSED, MOUSSING, MOUSSES** to style with mousse (foamy preparation used in styling hair)
MOUSSEUX	*n* pl. **MOUSSEUX** a sparkling wine
MOUSY	*adj* **MOUSIER, MOUSIEST** resembling a mouse
MOUTH	*v* **-ED, -ING, -S** to put into the mouth
MOUTHER	*n* pl. **-S** a speaker
MOUTHFUL	*n* pl. **-S** as much as the mouth can hold
MOUTHY	*adj* **MOUTHIER, MOUTHIEST** very talkative **MOUTHILY** *adv*
MOUTON	*n* pl. **-S** sheepskin processed to resemble seal or beaver
MOVABLE	*n* pl. **-S** something that can be moved
MOVABLY	*adv* so as to be capable of being moved
MOVANT	*n* pl. **-S** a person who applies to a court for a favorable ruling
MOVE	*v* **MOVED, MOVING, MOVES** to change from one position to another
MOVEABLE	*n* pl. **-S** movable
MOVEABLY	*adv* movably
MOVED	past tense of move
MOVELESS	*adj* incapable of movement
MOVEMENT	*n* pl. **-S** the act of moving
MOVER	*n* pl. **-S** one that moves
MOVIE	*n* pl. **-S** a motion picture
MOVIEDOM	*n* pl. **-S** filmdom
MOVIEOLA	*n* pl. **-S** a device for viewing and editing film
MOVING	present participle of move
MOVINGLY	*adv* so as to affect the emotions
MOVIOLA	*n* pl. **-S** movieola
MOW	*v* **MOWED, MOWN, MOWING, MOWS** to cut down standing herbage
MOWER	*n* pl. **-S** one that mows
MOWING	*n* pl. **-S** the act of cutting down standing herbage
MOXA	*n* pl. **-S** a Chinese plant
MOXIE	*n* pl. **-S** spirit or courage
MOZETTA	*n* pl. **-TAS** or **-TE** mozzetta
MOZO	*n* pl. **-ZOS** a manual laborer
MOZZETTA	*n* pl. **-TAS** or **-TE** a hooded cape worn by bishops
MRIDANGA	*n* pl. **-S** a drum of India
MU	*n* pl. **-S** a Greek letter
MUCH	*n* pl. **-ES** a great amount
MUCHACHA	*n* pl. **-S** a young woman
MUCHACHO	*n* pl. **-CHOS** a young man
MUCHLY	*adv* very much
MUCHNESS	*n* pl. **-ES** the quality of being great
MUCHO	*adj* much, many
MUCID	*adj* musty
MUCIDITY	*n* pl. **-TIES** the state of being mucid
MUCILAGE	*n* pl. **-S** an adhesive substance

MUCIN	*n* pl. **-S** a protein secreted by the mucous membranes **MUCINOID, MUCINOUS** *adj*
MUCK	*v* **-ED, -ING, -S** to fertilize with manure
MUCKER	*n* pl. **-S** a vulgar person
MUCKIER	comparative of mucky
MUCKIEST	superlative of mucky
MUCKILY	*adv* in a mucky manner
MUCKLE	*n* pl. **-S** a large amount
MUCKLUCK	*n* pl. **-S** mukluk
MUCKRAKE	*v* **-RAKED, -RAKING, -RAKES** to search for and expose corruption
MUCKWORM	*n* pl. **-S** a worm found in manure
MUCKY	*adj* **MUCKIER, MUCKIEST** filthy
MUCLUC	*n* pl. **-S** mukluk
MUCOID	*n* pl. **-S** a complex protein **MUCOIDAL** *adj*
MUCOR	*n* pl. **-S** a type of fungus
MUCOSA	*n* pl. **-SAS** or **-SAE** a mucous membrane **MUCOSAL** *adj*
MUCOSE	*adj* mucous
MUCOSITY	*n* pl. **-TIES** the state of being mucous
MUCOUS	*adj* secreting or containing mucus
MUCRO	*n* pl. **-CRONES** or **-CROS** a sharp point at the end of certain plant and animal organs
MUCUS	*n* pl. **-ES** a viscid bodily fluid
MUD	*v* **MUDDED, MUDDING, MUDS** to cover with mud (soft, wet earth)
MUDBANK	*n* pl. **-S** a sloping area of mud alongside a body of water
MUDBUG	*n* pl. **-S** a crayfish
MUDCAP	*v* **-CAPPED, -CAPPING, -CAPS** to cover an explosive with mud before detonating
MUDCAT	*n* pl. **-S** a type of catfish
MUDDER	*n* pl. **-S** a racehorse that runs well on a muddy track
MUDDIED	past tense of muddy
MUDDIER	comparative of muddy
MUDDIES	present 3d person sing. of muddy
MUDDIEST	superlative of muddy
MUDDILY	*adv* in a muddy manner
MUDDING	present participle of mud
MUDDLE	*v* **-DLED, -DLING, -DLES** to mix in a disordered manner
MUDDLER	*n* pl. **-S** one that muddles
MUDDLY	*adj* disordered
MUDDY	*adj* **-DIER, -DIEST** covered or filled with mud
MUDDY	*v* **-DIED, -DYING, -DIES** to make or become muddy
MUDFISH	*n* pl. **-ES** a fish found in mud or muddy water
MUDFLAP	*n* pl. **-S** a flap hung behind a rear wheel of a vehicle to prevent splashing
MUDFLAT	*n* pl. **-S** a level tract alternately covered and left bare by the tide
MUDFLOW	*n* pl. **-S** a moving mass of mud
MUDGUARD	*n* pl. **-S** a fender
MUDHEN	*n* pl. **-S** a bird that lives in marshes
MUDHOLE	*n* pl. **-S** a hole or hollow place full of mud
MUDLARK	*n* pl. **-S** a street urchin
MUDPACK	*n* pl. **-S** cosmetic paste for the face
MUDPIE	*n* pl. **-S** a small mass of mud formed into a pie shape
MUDPUPPY	*n* pl. **-PIES** a large salamander
MUDRA	*n* pl. **-S** a hand gesture in East Indian classical dancing
MUDROCK	*n* pl. **-S** pelite
MUDROOM	*n* pl. **-S** a room for shedding muddy clothing or footwear
MUDSILL	*n* pl. **-S** the lowest supporting timber of a structure
MUDSLIDE	*n* pl. **-S** a mudflow down a slope
MUDSLING	*v* **-SLUNG, -SLINGING, -SLINGS** to use insults and accusations against a rival candidate
MUDSTONE	*n* pl. **-S** a type of rock
MUEDDIN	*n* pl. **-S** muezzin
MUENSTER	*n* pl. **-S** a mild cheese
MUESLI	*n* pl. **-S** a breakfast cereal
MUEZZIN	*n* pl. **-S** a Muslim crier who calls the faithful to prayer
MUFF	*v* **-ED, -ING, -S** to bungle
MUFFIN	*n* pl. **-S** a small, round bread
MUFFLE	*v* **-FLED, -FLING, -FLES** to wrap with something to deaden sound
MUFFLER	*n* pl. **-S** a device for deadening sound
MUFTI	*n* pl. **-S** a judge who interprets Muslim religious law
MUG	*v* **MUGGED, MUGGING, MUGS** to assault with intent to rob

MUGFUL	*n* pl. **-S** as much as a mug can hold
MUGG	*v* **-ED, -ING, -S** to make funny faces
MUGGAR	*n* pl. **-S** mugger
MUGGED	past tense of mug
MUGGEE	*n* pl. **-S** one who is mugged
MUGGER	*n* pl. **-S** a large Asian crocodile
MUGGIER	comparative of muggy
MUGGIEST	superlative of muggy
MUGGILY	*adv* in a muggy manner
MUGGING	*n* pl. **-S** a street assault or beating
MUGGINS	*n* pl. **-ES** a stupid or foolish person
MUGGUR	*n* pl. **-S** mugger
MUGGY	*adj* **-GIER, -GIEST** warm and humid
MUGHAL	*n* pl. **-S** mogul
MUGSHOT	*n* pl. **-S** a photograph of a person's face for official records
MUGWORT	*n* pl. **-S** a flowering plant
MUGWUMP	*n* pl. **-S** a political independent
MUHLY	*n* pl. **MUHLIES** a perennial grass
MUJIK	*n* pl. **-S** muzhik
MUKHTAR	*n* pl. **-S** the head of the government of a town in Arabic countries
MUKLUK	*n* pl. **-S** a soft boot worn by Inuits
MUKTUK	*n* pl. **-S** whale skin used for food
MULBERRY	*n* pl. **-RIES** a tree bearing an edible, berrylike fruit
MULCH	*v* **-ED, -ING, -ES** to provide with a protective covering for the soil
MULCT	*v* **-ED, -ING, -S** to defraud
MULE	*v* **MULED, MULING, MULES** to strike from dies belonging to two different issues, as a coin
MULETA	*n* pl. **-S** a red cloth used by a matador
MULETEER	*n* pl. **-S** one who drives mules (hoofed work animals)
MULEY	*n* pl. **-LEYS** a hornless cow
MULIE	*n* pl. **-S** a western North American deer
MULING	present participle of mule
MULISH	*adj* stubborn **MULISHLY** *adv*
MULL	*v* **-ED, -ING, -S** to ponder
MULLA	*n* pl. **-S** mullah
MULLAH	*n* pl. **-S** a Muslim religious leader or teacher
MULLEIN	*n* pl. **-S** a Eurasian herb
MULLEN	*n* pl. **-S** mullein
MULLER	*n* pl. **-S** a grinding implement
MULLET	*n* pl. **-S** an edible fish
MULLEY	*n* pl. **-LEYS** muley
MULLIGAN	*n* pl. **-S** a stew of various meats and vegetables
MULLION	*v* **-ED, -ING, -S** to provide with vertical dividing strips
MULLITE	*n* pl. **-S** a mineral
MULLOCK	*n* pl. **-S** waste earth or rock from a mine **MULLOCKY** *adj*
MULLOWAY	*n* **-WAYS** a large fish
MULTIAGE	*adj* including people of various ages
MULTICAR	*adj* owning or involving several cars
MULTIDAY	*adj* lasting or usable for many days
MULTIFID	*adj* divided into many parts
MULTIJET	*adj* having more than two jets
MULTIPED	*n* pl. **-S** an animal having many feet
MULTIPLE	*n* pl. **-S** the product of a quantity by an integer
MULTIPLY	*v* **-PLIED, -PLYING, -PLIES** to increase in number
MULTITON	*adj* weighing many tons
MULTIUSE	*adj* having many uses
MULTIWAY	*adj* having several paths or routes
MULTURE	*n* pl. **-S** a fee paid to a miller for grinding grain
MUM	*v* **MUMMED, MUMMING, MUMS** to act in a disguise
MUMBLE	*v* **-BLED, -BLING, -BLES** to speak unclearly
MUMBLER	*n* pl. **-S** one that mumbles
MUMBLING	*n* pl. **-S** the act of speaking unclearly
MUMBLY	*adj* given to mumbling
MUMM	*v* **-ED, -ING, -S** to mum
MUMMED	past tense of mum and mumm
MUMMER	*n* pl. **-S** one that mums
MUMMERY	*n* pl. **-MERIES** a performance by mummers
MUMMIED	past tense of mummy
MUMMIES	present 3d person sing. of mummy
MUMMIFY	*v* **-FIED, -FYING, -FIES** to preserve by embalming

MUMMING *n* pl. **-S** a performance of a folk play by mummers

MUMMY *v* **-MIED, -MYING, -MIES** to mummify

MUMP *v* **-ED, -ING, -S** to beg

MUMPER *n* pl. **-S** one that mumps

MUMPISH *adj* sullen

MUMSY *adj* **MUMSIER, MUMSIEST** maternal

MUMU *n* pl. **-S** muumuu

MUN *n* pl. **-S** man; fellow

MUNCH *v* **-ED, -ING, -ES** to chew with a crackling sound

MUNCHER *n* pl. **-S** one that munches

MUNCHIE *n* pl. **-S** a small amount of food eaten between meals

MUNCHKIN *n* pl. **-S** a small friendly person

MUNCHY *adj* **MUNCHIER, MUNCHIEST** suitable for snacking

MUNDANE *adj* ordinary

MUNDUNGO *n* pl. **-GOS** a foul-smelling tobacco

MUNG *n* pl. **-S** a round green bean

MUNGO *n* pl. **-GOS** or **-GOES** a low-quality wool

MUNGOOSE *n* pl. **-S** mongoose

MUNI *n* pl. **-S** a security issued by a state or local government

MUNIMENT *n* pl. **-S** a means of defense

MUNITION *v* **-ED, -ING, -S** to furnish with war materiel

MUNNION *n* pl. **-S** a muntin

MUNSTER *n* pl. **-S** muenster

MUNTIN *n* pl. **-S** a dividing strip for window panes **MUNTINED** *adj*

MUNTING *n* pl. **-S** muntin

MUNTJAC *n* pl. **-S** a small Asian deer

MUNTJAK *n* pl. **-S** muntjac

MUON *n* pl. **-S** a subatomic particle **MUONIC** *adj*

MUONIUM *n* pl. **-S** an electron and a positive muon bound together

MURA *n* pl. **-S** a Japanese village

MURAENID *n* pl. **-S** a moray

MURAGE *n* pl. **-S** a tax levied for repairing the walls of a town

MURAL *n* pl. **-S** a painting applied directly to a wall or ceiling **MURALED, MURALLED** *adj*

MURALIST *n* pl. **-S** a painter of murals

MURDER *v* **-ED, -ING, -S** to kill unlawfully with premeditated malice

MURDEREE *n* pl. **-S** one that is murdered

MURDERER *n* pl. **-S** one that murders

MURE *v* **MURED, MURING, MURES** to immure

MUREIN *n* pl. **-S** a type of polymer

MUREX *n* pl. **-REXES** or **-RICES** a marine mollusk

MURIATE *n* pl. **-S** chloride

MURIATED *adj* pickled

MURICATE *adj* covered with short, sharp points

MURICES a pl. of murex

MURID *n* pl. **-S** a murine

MURINE *n* pl. **-S** any of a family of small rodents

MURING present participle of mure

MURK *adj* **MURKER, MURKEST** dark **MURKLY** *adv*

MURK *n* pl. **-S** darkness

MURKY *adj* **MURKIER, MURKIEST** dark **MURKILY** *adv*

MURMUR *v* **-ED, -ING, -S** to speak unclearly

MURMURER *n* pl. **-S** one that murmurs

MURPHY *n* pl. **-PHIES** a potato

MURR *n* pl. **-S** murre

MURRA *n* pl. **-S** a substance used to make fine vases and cups in ancient Rome

MURRAIN *n* pl. **-S** a disease of cattle

MURRE *n* pl. **-S** a diving bird

MURRELET *n* pl. **-S** a small diving bird

MURREY *n* pl. **-REYS** a dark purple color

MURRHA *n* pl. **-S** murra **MURRHINE** *adj*

MURRINE *adj* pertaining to murra

MURRY *n* pl. **-RIES** a moray

MURTHER *v* **-ED, -ING, -S** to murder

MUSCA *n* pl. **-CAE** any of a genus of flies

MUSCADEL *n* pl. **-S** muscatel

MUSCADET *n* pl. **-S** a dry white French wine

MUSCAT *n* pl. **-S** a sweet, white grape

MUSCATEL *n* pl. **-S** a wine made from muscat grapes

MUSCID *n* pl. **-S** musca

MUSCLE *v* **-CLED, -CLING, -CLES** to proceed by force

MUSCLY *adj* **-CLIER, -CLIEST** composed of muscle (tissue that produces bodily movement)

MUSCULAR *adj* pertaining to muscle

MUSE *v* **MUSED, MUSING, MUSES** to ponder

MUSEFUL *adj* pensive

MUSER *n* pl. **-S** one that muses

MUSETTE *n* pl. **-S** a small bagpipe

MUSEUM *n* pl. **-S** a place where objects of lasting interest or value are cared for and exhibited

MUSH *v* **-ED, -ING, -ES** to travel over snow with a dog sled

MUSHER *n* pl. **-S** one that mushes

MUSHING *n* pl. **-S** the act of one that mushes

MUSHRAT *n* pl. **-S** muskrat

MUSHROOM *v* **-ED, -ING, -S** to grow or spread rapidly

MUSHY *adj* **MUSHIER, MUSHIEST** pulpy **MUSHILY** *adv*

MUSIC *n* pl. **-S** vocal or instrumental sounds organized to produce a unified composition

MUSICAL *n* pl. **-S** a play in which dialogue is interspersed with songs and dances

MUSICALE *n* pl. **-S** a program of music performed at a social gathering

MUSICIAN *n* pl. **-S** one who performs or composes music

MUSICK *v* **-ED, -ING, -S** to compose music for

MUSING *n* pl. **-S** contemplation

MUSINGLY *adv* in a pensive manner

MUSJID *n* pl. **-S** a mosque

MUSK *n* pl. **-S** a strongly odorous substance secreted by certain animals

MUSKEG *n* pl. **-S** a marsh

MUSKET *n* pl. **-S** a type of firearm

MUSKETRY *n* pl. **-RIES** the technique of firing small arms

MUSKIE *n* pl. **-S** a freshwater fish

MUSKIER comparative of musky

MUSKIEST superlative of musky

MUSKILY *adv* in a musky manner

MUSKIT *n* pl. **-S** mesquite

MUSKOX *n* pl. **-OXEN** a large bovid of arctic regions

MUSKRAT *n* pl. **-S** an aquatic rodent

MUSKROOT *n* pl. **-S** a perennial herb

MUSKY *adj* **MUSKIER, MUSKIEST** resembling musk

MUSLIN *n* pl. **-S** a cotton fabric **MUSLINED** *adj*

MUSO *n* pl. **MUSOS** a musician

MUSPIKE *n* pl. **-S** a freshwater fish

MUSQUASH *n* pl. **-ES** a muskrat

MUSS *v* **-ED, -ING, -ES** to mess

MUSSEL *n* pl. **-S** a bivalve mollusk

MUSSY *adj* **MUSSIER, MUSSIEST** messy **MUSSILY** *adv*

MUST *v* **-ED, -ING, -S** to become musty

MUSTACHE *n* pl. **-S** a growth of hair on the upper lip

MUSTANG *n* pl. **-S** a wild horse

MUSTARD *n* pl. **-S** a pungent seasoning

MUSTARDY *adj* resembling mustard

MUSTEE *n* pl. **-S** an octoroon

MUSTELID *n* pl. **-S** a mammal of the weasel family

MUSTER *v* **-ED, -ING, -S** to summon or assemble

MUSTH *n* pl. **-S** a state of frenzy occurring in male elephants

MUSTY *adj* **MUSTIER, MUSTIEST** having a stale odor **MUSTILY** *adv*

MUT *n* pl. **-S** mutt

MUTABLE *adj* capable of change **MUTABLY** *adv*

MUTAGEN *n* pl. **-S** a substance that causes biological mutation

MUTANT *n* pl. **-S** something that undergoes mutation

MUTASE *n* pl. **-S** an enzyme

MUTATE *v* **-TATED, -TATING, -TATES** to change or cause to change in form

MUTATION *n* pl. **-S** the act of changing in form **MUTATIVE** *adj*

MUTATOR *n* pl. **-S** one that causes a change in form

MUTCH *n* pl. **-ES** a close-fitting cap

MUTCHKIN *n* pl. **-S** a Scottish unit of liquid measure

MUTE *adj* **MUTER, MUTEST** characterized by an absence of speech **MUTELY** *adv*

MUTE *v* **MUTED, MUTING, MUTES** to deaden the sound of **MUTEDLY** *adv*

MUTENESS *n* pl. **-ES** the state of being mute

MUTER comparative of mute

MUTEST superlative of mute

MUTICOUS *adj* lacking a point

MUTILATE *v* **-LATED, -LATING, -LATES** to deprive of a limb or other essential part

MUTINE *v* **-TINED, -TINING, -TINES** to mutiny

MUTINEER *v* **-ED, -ING, -S** to mutiny

MUTING present participle of mute

MUTINIED past tense of mutiny

MUTINIES present 3d person sing. of mutiny

MUTINING present participle of mutine

MUTINOUS *adj* disposed to mutiny

MUTINY *v* **-NIED, -NYING, -NIES** to revolt against constituted authority

MUTISM *n* pl. **-S** muteness

MUTON *n* pl. **-S** a unit of nucleic acid

MUTT *n* pl. **-S** a mongrel dog

MUTTER *v* **-ED, -ING, -S** to speak unclearly

MUTTERER *n* pl. **-S** one that mutters

MUTTON *n* pl. **-S** the flesh of sheep used as food **MUTTONY** *adj*

MUTUAL *n* pl. **-S** a mutual fund

MUTUALLY *adv* in a manner shared in common

MUTUEL *n* pl. **-S** a system of betting on races

MUTULE *n* pl. **-S** an ornamental block used in classical Greek architecture **MUTULAR** *adj*

MUUMUU *n* pl. **-S** a long, loose dress

MUX *v* **-ED, -ING, -ES** to transmit several messages simultaneously along a single channel

MUZAK *n* pl. **-S** recorded background music

MUZHIK *n* pl. **-S** a Russian peasant

MUZJIK *n* pl. **-S** muzhik

MUZZIER comparative of muzzy

MUZZIEST superlative of muzzy

MUZZILY *adv* in a muzzy manner

MUZZLE *v* **-ZLED, -ZLING, -ZLES** to put a covering over the mouth of to prevent biting or eating

MUZZLER *n* pl. **-S** one that muzzles

MUZZY *adj* **-ZIER, -ZIEST** confused

MY *pron* the possessive form of the pronoun I

MYALGIA *n* pl. **-S** muscular pain **MYALGIC** *adj*

MYASIS *n* pl. **MYASES** myiasis

MYC *n* pl. **-S** a gene that transforms a normal cell into a cancerous cell

MYCELE *n* pl. **-S** mycelium

MYCELIUM *n* pl. **-LIA** the vegetative portion of a fungus **MYCELIAL, MYCELIAN, MYCELOID** *adj*

MYCETOMA *n* pl. **-MAS** or **-MATA** a fungous infection

MYCOLOGY *n* pl. **-GIES** the branch of botany dealing with fungi

MYCOSIS *n* pl. **-COSES** a disease caused by a fungus **MYCOTIC** *adj*

MYELIN *n* pl. **-S** a fatty substance that encases certain nerve fibers **MYELINIC** *adj*

MYELINE *n* pl. **-S** myelin

MYELITIS *n* pl. **-LITIDES** inflammation of the bone marrow

MYELOID *adj* pertaining to bone marrow

MYELOMA *n* pl. **-MAS** or **-MATA** a tumor of the bone marrow

MYIASIS *n* pl. **MYIASES** infestation of human tissue by fly maggots

MYLODON *n* pl. **-S** an extinct giant sloth

MYLONITE *n* pl. **-S** a type of rock

MYNA *n* pl. **-S** an Asian bird

MYNAH *n* pl. **-S** myna

MYNHEER *n* pl. **-S** a Dutch title of courtesy for a man

MYOBLAST *n* pl. **-S** a cell capable of giving rise to muscle cells

MYOGENIC *adj* originating in muscle tissue

MYOGRAPH *n* pl. **-S** an instrument for recording muscular contractions

MYOID *adj* resembling muscle

MYOLOGY *n* pl. **-GIES** the study of muscles **MYOLOGIC** *adj*

MYOMA *n* pl. **-MAS** or **-MATA** a tumor composed of muscle tissue

MYOMERE *n* pl. **-S** part of a vertebrate embryo

MYOPATHY *n* pl. **-THIES** a disorder of muscle tissue

MYOPE *n* pl. **-S** one who is affected with myopia

MYOPIA *n* pl. **-S** a visual defect **MYOPIC** *adj*

MYOPY *n* pl. **-PIES** myopia

MYOSCOPE *n* pl. **-S** an instrument for observing muscular contractions

MYOSIN *n* pl. **-S** a protein found in muscle tissue

MYOSIS *n* pl. **MYOSES** miosis

MYOSITIS *n* pl. **-TISES** muscular pain from infection

MYOSOTE *n* pl. **-S** myosotis

MYOSOTIS *n* pl. **-TISES** a flowering plant

MYOTIC *n* pl. **-S** miotic

MYOTOME *n* pl. **-S** a portion of an embryonic somite

MYOTONIA *n* pl. **-S** temporary muscular rigidity **MYOTONIC** *adj*

MYRIAD *n* pl. **-S** a very large number

MYRIAPOD *n* pl. **-S** a multi-legged arthropod

MYRICA *n* pl. **-S** a medicinal tree bark

MYRIOPOD *n* pl. **-S** myriapod

MYRMIDON *n* pl. **-S** or **-ES** a loyal follower

MYRRH *n* pl. **-S** an aromatic gum resin **MYRRHIC** *adj* **MYRRHY** *adj*

MYRTLE *n* pl. **-S** an evergreen shrub

MYSELF *pron* a form of the 1st person sing. pronoun

MYSID *n* pl. **-S** a small crustacean

MYSOST *n* pl. **-S** a mild cheese

MYSTAGOG *n* pl. **-S** a teacher of religious mysteries

MYSTERY *n* pl. **-TERIES** something that is not or cannot be known, understood, or explained

MYSTIC *n* pl. **-S** one who professes to have had mystical experiences

MYSTICAL *adj* spiritually significant or symbolic

MYSTICLY *adv* in a mystical manner

MYSTIFY *v* **-FIED, -FYING, -FIES** to perplex

MYSTIQUE *n* pl. **-S** an aura of mystery or mystical power surrounding a particular person or thing

MYTH *n* pl. **-S** a type of traditional story

MYTHIC *adj* mythical

MYTHICAL *adj* based on or described in a myth

MYTHOS *n* pl. **-THOI** a myth

MYTHY *adj* **MYTHIER, MYTHIEST** resembling myth

MYXAMEBA *n* pl. **-BAS** or **-BAE** a slime mold that resembles an amoeba

MYXEDEMA *n* pl. **-S** a disease caused by decreased activity of the thyroid gland

MYXOCYTE *n* pl. **-S** a large cell found in mucous tissue

MYXOID *adj* containing mucus

MYXOMA *n* pl. **-MAS** or **-MATA** a tumor composed of mucous tissue

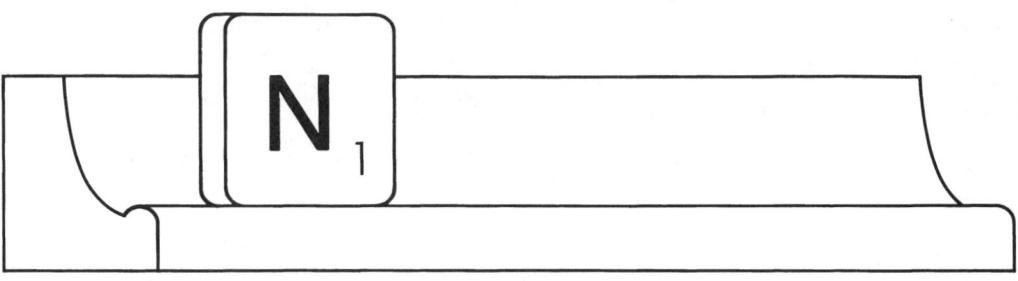

NA	*adv* no; not
NAAN	*n* pl. **-S** nan
NAB	*v* **NABBED, NABBING, NABS** to capture or arrest
NABBER	*n* pl. **-S** one that nabs
NABE	*n* pl. **-S** a neighborhood movie theater
NABIS	*n* pl. **NABIS** a group of French artists
NABOB	*n* pl. **-S** one who becomes rich and prominent **NABOBISH** *adj*
NABOBERY	*n* pl. **-ERIES** the state of being a nabob
NABOBESS	*n* pl. **-ES** a female nabob
NABOBISM	*n* pl. **-S** great wealth and luxury
NACELLE	*n* pl. **-S** a shelter on an aircraft
NACHAS	*n* pl. **NACHAS** pride in another's accomplishments
NACHES	*n* pl. **NACHES** nachas
NACHO	*n* pl. **-CHOS** a tortilla chip topped with cheese and a savory mixture and broiled
NACRE	*n* pl. **-S** the pearly internal layer of certain shells **NACRED, NACREOUS** *adj*
NADA	*n* pl. **-S** nothing
NADIR	*n* pl. **-S** a point on the celestial sphere **NADIRAL** *adj*
NAE	*n* pl. **-S** no
NAETHING	*n* pl. **-S** nothing
NAEVUS	*n* pl. **-VI** nevus **NAEVOID** *adj*
NAFF	*v* **-ED, -ING, -S** to fool around
NAFF	*adj* **NAFFER, NAFFEST** lacking taste or style
NAFFNESS	*n* pl. **-ES** the quality of lacking taste or style
NAG	*v* **NAGGED, NAGGING, NAGS** to find fault incessantly
NAGA	*n* pl. **-S** a half-snake, half-human creature in Hinduism
NAGANA	*n* pl. **-S** a disease of horses in Africa
NAGGER	*n* pl. **-S** one that nags
NAGGING	*n* pl. **-S** the act of finding fault incessantly
NAGGY	*adj* **-GIER, -GIEST** given to nagging
NAGWARE	*n* pl. **-S** software that is at first free but often reminds the user to pay for it
NAH	*adv* no
NAIAD	*n* pl. **-S** or **-ES** a water nymph
NAIF	*n* pl. **-S** a naive person
NAIL	*v* **-ED, -ING, -S** to fasten with a nail (a slender piece of metal)
NAILER	*n* pl. **-S** one that nails
NAILFOLD	*n* pl. **-S** a fold of skin around the fingernail
NAILHEAD	*n* pl. **-S** the top of a nail
NAILLESS	*adj* lacking nails
NAILSET	*n* pl. **-S** a steel rod for driving a nail into something
NAINSOOK	*n* pl. **-S** a cotton fabric
NAIRA	*n* pl. **-S** a monetary unit of Nigeria
NAIRU	*n* pl. **-S** the lowest rate of unemployment at which there is no inflation
NAIVE	*adj* **NAIVER, NAIVEST** lacking sophistication **NAIVELY** *adv*
NAIVE	*n* pl. **-S** a naive person
NAIVETE	*n* pl. **-S** the quality of being naive
NAIVETY	*n* pl. **-TIES** naivete
NAKED	*adj* **-KEDER, -KEDEST** being without clothing or covering **NAKEDLY** *adv*
NAKFA	*n* pl. **-S** a monetary unit of Eritrea
NALA	*n* pl. **-S** nullah

NALED	*n* pl. **-S** an insecticide
NALOXONE	*n* pl. **-S** a chemical compound
NAM	a past tense of nim
NAME	*v* **NAMED, NAMING, NAMES** to give a title to **NAMABLE, NAMEABLE** *adj*
NAMELESS	*adj* lacking distinction or fame
NAMELY	*adv* that is to say
NAMER	*n* pl. **-S** one that names
NAMESAKE	*n* pl. **-S** one who is named after another
NAMETAG	*n* pl. **-S** a tag bearing one's name worn for identification
NAMETAPE	*n* pl. **-S** a tape bearing one's name worn for identification
NAMING	present participle of name
NAN	*n* pl. **-S** a round flat bread
NANA	*n* pl. **-S** a grandmother
NANDIN	*n* pl. **-S** an evergreen shrub
NANDINA	*n* pl. **-S** an Asian shrub
NANISM	*n* pl. **-S** abnormal smallness
NANKEEN	*n* pl. **-S** a cotton fabric
NANKIN	*n* pl. **-S** nankeen
NANNA	*n* pl. **-S** nana
NANNIE	*n* pl. **-S** nanny
NANNY	*v* **-NIED, -NYING, -NIES** to be overprotective toward
NANNYISH	*adj* resembling a children's nurse
NANO	*n* pl. **-NOS** science that deals with materials on an atomic or molecular scale
NANOBOT	*n* pl. **-S** a very small self-propelled machine
NANOGRAM	*n* pl. **-S** a unit of mass and weight
NANOTECH	*n* pl. **-S** the technology of building electronic devices from individual atoms and molecules
NANOTUBE	*n* pl. **-S** a microscopic tube
NANOWATT	*n* pl. **-S** a unit of power
NAOS	*n* pl. **NAOI** an ancient temple
NAP	*v* **NAPPED, NAPPING, NAPS** to sleep briefly
NAPA	*n* pl. **-S** a soft leather
NAPALM	*v* **-ED, -ING, -S** to assault with a type of incendiary bomb
NAPE	*n* pl. **-S** the back of the neck
NAPERY	*n* pl. **-PERIES** table linen
NAPHTHA	*n* pl. **-S** a volatile liquid
NAPHTHOL	*n* pl. **-S** a chemical compound
NAPHTHYL	*n* pl. **-S** a radical derived from naphthalene
NAPHTOL	*n* pl. **-S** naphthol
NAPIFORM	*adj* shaped like a turnip
NAPKIN	*n* pl. **-S** a piece of material used to wipe the hands and mouth
NAPLESS	*adj* threadbare
NAPOLEON	*n* pl. **-S** a type of pastry
NAPPA	*n* pl. **-S** napa
NAPPE	*n* pl. **-S** a type of rock formation
NAPPED	past tense of nap
NAPPER	*n* pl. **-S** one that naps
NAPPIE	*n* pl. **-S** a diaper
NAPPING	present participle of nap
NAPPY	*adj* **-PIER, -PIEST** kinky
NAPROXEN	*n* pl. **-S** an anti-inflammatory drug
NARC	*n* pl. **-S** an undercover drug agent
NARCEIN	*n* pl. **-S** narceine
NARCEINE	*n* pl. **-S** an opium derivative
NARCISM	*n* pl. **-S** excessive love of oneself
NARCISSI	*n/pl* bulbous flowering plants
NARCIST	*n* pl. **-S** one given to narcism
NARCO	*n* pl. **-COS** narc
NARCOMA	*n* pl. **-MAS** or **-MATA** a stupor induced by a narcotic
NARCOSE	*adj* characterized by stupor
NARCOSIS	*n* pl. **-COSES** a drug-induced stupor
NARCOTIC	*n* pl. **-S** a drug that dulls the senses
NARD	*n* pl. **-S** a fragrant ointment **NARDINE** *adj*
NARDOO	*n* pl. **-DOOS** a clover-like plant
NARES	pl. of naris
NARGHILE	*n* pl. **-S** a hookah
NARGILE	*n* pl. **-S** narghile
NARGILEH	*n* pl. **-S** narghile
NARIS	*n* pl. **NARES** a nostril **NARIAL, NARIC, NARINE** *adj*
NARK	*v* **-ED, -ING, -S** to spy or inform
NARKY	*adj* **NARKIER, NARKIEST** irritable
NARRATE	*v* **-RATED, -RATING, -RATES** to tell a story
NARRATER	*n* pl. **-S** narrator
NARRATOR	*n* pl. **-S** one that narrates

NARROW	*adj* **-ROWER, -ROWEST** of little width **NARROWLY** *adv*
NARROW	*v* **-ED, -ING, -S** to make narrow
NARTHEX	*n* pl. **-ES** a vestibule in a church
NARWAL	*n* pl. **-S** narwhal
NARWHAL	*n* pl. **-S** an arctic aquatic mammal
NARWHALE	*n* pl. **-S** narwhal
NARY	*adj* not one
NASAL	*n* pl. **-S** a sound uttered through the nose
NASALISE	*v* **-ISED, -ISING, -ISES** to nasalize
NASALISM	*n* pl. **-S** nasality
NASALITY	*n* pl. **-TIES** the quality or an instance of being produced nasally
NASALIZE	*v* **-IZED, -IZING, -IZES** to produce sounds nasally
NASALLY	*adv* through the nose
NASCENCE	*n* pl. **-S** nascency
NASCENCY	*n* pl. **-CIES** birth; origin
NASCENT	*adj* coming into existence
NASION	*n* pl. **-S** a point in the skull **NASIAL** *adj*
NASTIC	*adj* pertaining to an automatic response of plants
NASTY	*adj* **-TIER, -TIEST** offensive to the senses **NASTILY** *adv*
NASTY	*n* pl. **-TIES** something that is nasty
NATAL	*adj* pertaining to one's birth
NATALITY	*n* pl. **-TIES** birth rate
NATANT	*adj* floating or swimming **NATANTLY** *adv*
NATATION	*n* pl. **-S** the act of swimming
NATATORY	*adj* pertaining to swimming
NATCH	*adv* naturally
NATES	*n/pl* the buttocks
NATHLESS	*adv* nevertheless
NATION	*n* pl. **-S** a politically organized people who share a territory, customs, and history
NATIONAL	*n* pl. **-S** a citizen of a nation
NATIVE	*n* pl. **-S** an original inhabitant of an area
NATIVELY	*adv* in an inborn manner
NATIVISM	*n* pl. **-S** a policy of favoring the interests of native inhabitants
NATIVIST	*n* pl. **-S** an advocate of nativism
NATIVITY	*n* pl. **-TIES** the process of being born
NATRIUM	*n* pl. **-S** sodium
NATRON	*n* pl. **-S** a chemical compound
NATTER	*v* **-ED, -ING, -S** to chatter
NATTERER	*n* pl. **-S** one that natters
NATTY	*adj* **-TIER, -TIEST** neatly dressed **NATTILY** *adv*
NATURAL	*n* pl. **-S** a type of musical note
NATURE	*n* pl. **-S** the essential qualities of a person or thing **NATURED** *adj*
NATURISM	*n* pl. **-S** nudism
NATURIST	*n* pl. **-S** a nudist
NAUGHT	*n* pl. **-S** a zero
NAUGHTY	*n* pl. **-TIES** one that is naughty
NAUGHTY	*adj* **-TIER, -TIEST** disobedient
NAUMACHY	*n* pl. **-CHIES** a mock sea battle
NAUPLIUS	*n* pl. **-PLII** a form of certain crustaceans **NAUPLIAL** *adj*
NAUSEA	*n* pl. **-S** a stomach disturbance
NAUSEANT	*n* pl. **-S** an agent that induces nausea
NAUSEATE	*v* **-ATED, -ATING, -ATES** to affect with nausea
NAUSEOUS	*adj* affected with nausea
NAUTCH	*n* pl. **-ES** a dancing exhibition in India
NAUTICAL	*adj* pertaining to ships
NAUTILUS	*n* pl. **-LUSES** or **-LI** a spiral-shelled mollusk
NAV	*n* pl. **-S** navigation
NAVAID	*n* pl. **-S** a navigational device
NAVAL	*adj* pertaining to ships **NAVALLY** *adv*
NAVAR	*n* pl. **-S** a system of air navigation
NAVARIN	*n* pl. **-S** lamb stew with vegetables
NAVE	*n* pl. **-S** the main part of a church
NAVEL	*n* pl. **-S** a depression in the abdomen
NAVETTE	*n* pl. **-S** a gem cut in a pointed oval form
NAVICERT	*n* pl. **-S** a document permitting a vessel passage through a naval blockade
NAVIES	pl. of navy
NAVIGATE	*v* **-GATED, -GATING, -GATES** to plan and control the course of
NAVVY	*n* pl. **-VIES** a manual laborer
NAVY	*n* pl. **-VIES** a nation's warships
NAW	*adv* no

NAWAB	*n* pl. **-S** a nabob
NAY	*n* pl. **NAYS** a negative vote
NAYSAY	*v* **-SAID, -SAYING, -SAYS** to oppose or deny
NAYSAYER	*n* pl. **-S** one that denies or opposes something
NAZI	*n* pl. **-S** a type of fascist
NAZIFY	*v* **-FIED, -FYING, -FIES** to cause to be like a nazi
NE	*adj* born with the name of
NEAP	*n* pl. **-S** a tide of lowest range
NEAR	*adj* **NEARER, NEAREST** situated within a short distance **NEARISH** *adj*
NEAR	*v* **-ED, -ING, -S** to approach
NEARBY	*adj* near
NEARLY	*adv* **-LIER, -LIEST** with close approximation
NEARNESS	*n* pl. **-ES** the state of being near
NEARSIDE	*n* pl. **-S** the left side
NEAT	*adj* **NEATER, NEATEST** being in a state of cleanliness and order
NEAT	*n* pl. **-S** a bovine
NEATEN	*v* **-ED, -ING, -S** to make neat
NEATH	*prep* beneath
NEATHERD	*n* pl. **-S** a cowherd
NEATLY	*adv* in a neat manner
NEATNESS	*n* pl. **-ES** the state of being neat
NEATNIK	*n* pl. **-S** a compulsively neat person
NEB	*n* pl. **-S** the beak of a bird
NEBBISH	*n* pl. **-ES** a meek person **NEBBISHY** *adj*
NEBULA	*n* pl. **-LAS** or **-LAE** a cloud-like interstellar mass **NEBULAR** *adj*
NEBULE	*adj* composed of successive short curves
NEBULISE	*v* **-LISED, -LISING, -LISES** to nebulize
NEBULIZE	*v* **-LIZED, -LIZING, -LIZES** to reduce to a fine spray
NEBULOSE	*adj* nebulous
NEBULOUS	*adj* unclear
NEBULY	*adj* nebule
NECK	*v* **-ED, -ING, -S** to kiss and caress in lovemaking
NECKBAND	*n* pl. **-S** a band worn around the neck (the part of the body joining the head to the trunk)
NECKER	*n* pl. **-S** one that necks
NECKING	*n* pl. **-S** a small molding near the top of a column
NECKLACE	*v* **-LACED, -LACING, -LACES** to kill by placing a tire around the neck and setting it on fire
NECKLESS	*adj* having no neck
NECKLET	*n* pl. **-S** a close-fiting ornament worn around the neck
NECKLIKE	*adj* resembling the neck
NECKLINE	*n* pl. **-S** the line formed by the neck opening of a garment
NECKTIE	*n* pl. **-S** a strip of fabric worn around the neck
NECKWEAR	*n* pl. **NECKWEAR** something that is worn around the neck
NECROPSY	*v* **-SIED, -SYING, -SIES** to perform an autopsy on
NECROSE	*v* **-CROSED, -CROSING, -CROSES** to affect with necrosis
NECROSIS	*n* pl. **-CROSES** the death of living tissue **NECROTIC** *adj*
NECTAR	*n* pl. **-S** a delicious drink
NECTARY	*n* pl. **-TARIES** a plant gland
NEDDY	*n* pl. **-DIES** a donkey
NEE	*adj* born with the name of
NEED	*v* **-ED, -ING, -S** to have an urgent or essential use for
NEEDER	*n* pl. **-S** one that needs
NEEDFUL	*n* pl. **-S** something that is needed
NEEDIER	comparative of needy
NEEDIEST	superlative of needy
NEEDILY	*adv* in a needy manner
NEEDLE	*v* **-DLED, -DLING, -DLES** to sew with a slender, pointed instrument
NEEDLER	*n* pl. **-S** one that needles
NEEDLESS	*adj* not necessary
NEEDLING	*n* pl. **-S** the act of one who needles
NEEDY	*adj* **NEEDIER, NEEDIEST** in a state of poverty
NEEM	*n* pl. **-S** an East Indian tree
NEEP	*n* pl. **-S** a turnip
NEG	*n* pl. **-S** a photographic negative
NEGATE	*v* **-GATED, -GATING, -GATES** to nullify
NEGATER	*n* pl. **-S** one that negates
NEGATION	*n* pl. **-S** the act of negating
NEGATIVE	*v* **-TIVED, -TIVING, -TIVES** to veto
NEGATON	*n* pl. **-S** negatron
NEGATOR	*n* pl. **-S** negater

NEGATORY	*adj* expressing negation
NEGATRON	*n* pl. **-S** an electron
NEGLECT	*v* **-ED, -ING, -S** to fail to pay attention to
NEGLIGE	*n* pl. **-S** negligee
NEGLIGEE	*n* pl. **-S** a woman's dressing gown
NEGROID	*n* pl. **-S** member of the black race
NEGRONI	*n* pl. **-S** an alcoholic beverage
NEGUS	*n* pl. **-ES** an alcoholic beverage
NEIF	*n* pl. **-S** nieve
NEIGH	*v* **-ED, -ING, -S** to utter the cry of a horse
NEIGHBOR	*v* **-ED, -ING, -S** to live close to
NEIST	*adj* next
NEITHER	*adj* not one or the other
NEKTON	*n* pl. **-S** free-swimming marine animals **NEKTONIC** *adj*
NELLIE	*n* pl. **-S** an effeminate male
NELLY	*n* pl. **-LIES** nellie
NELSON	*n* pl. **-S** a wrestling hold
NELUMBO	*n* pl. **-BOS** an aquatic herb
NEMA	*n* pl. **-S** a nematode
NEMATIC	*n* pl. **-S** a liquid crystal in a particular phase
NEMATODE	*n* pl. **-S** a kind of worm
NEMESIA	*n* pl. **-S** a flowering African plant
NEMESIS	*n* pl. **NEMESES** a formidable opponent
NENE	*n* pl. **-S** a Hawaiian goose
NEOCON	*n* pl. **-S** a neoconservative
NEOLITH	*n* pl. **-S** an ancient stone implement
NEOLOGY	*n* pl. **-GIES** a new word or phrase **NEOLOGIC** *adj*
NEOMORPH	*n* pl. **-S** a type of biological structure
NEOMYCIN	*n* pl. **-S** an antibiotic drug
NEON	*n* pl. **-S** a gaseous element **NEONED** *adj*
NEONATE	*n* pl. **-S** a newborn child **NEONATAL** *adj*
NEOPAGAN	*n* pl. **-S** one who practices a modern form of paganism
NEOPHYTE	*n* pl. **-S** a novice
NEOPLASM	*n* pl. **-S** a tumor
NEOPRENE	*n* pl. **-S** a synthetic rubber
NEOTENY	*n* pl. **-NIES** attainment of sexual maturity in the larval stage **NEOTENIC** *adj*
NEOTERIC	*n* pl. **-S** a modern author
NEOTYPE	*n* pl. **-S** a specimen of a species
NEPENTHE	*n* pl. **-S** a drug that induces forgetfulness
NEPETA	*n* pl. **-S** catnip
NEPHEW	*n* pl. **-S** a son of one's brother or sister
NEPHRIC	*adj* renal
NEPHRISM	*n* pl. **-S** ill health caused by a kidney disease
NEPHRITE	*n* pl. **-S** a mineral
NEPHRON	*n* pl. **-S** an excretory unit of a kidney
NEPOTISM	*n* pl. **-S** favoritism shown to a relative **NEPOTIC** *adj*
NEPOTIST	*n* pl. **-S** one who practices nepotism
NERD	*n* pl. **-S** a socially inept person **NERDISH** *adj*
NERDY	*adj* **NERDIER, NERDIEST** socially inept
NEREID	*n* pl. **-S** a sea nymph
NEREIS	*n* pl. **-REIDES** a marine worm
NERITIC	*adj* pertaining to shallow water
NEROL	*n* pl. **-S** a fragrant alcohol
NEROLI	*n* pl. **-S** a fragrant oil
NERTS	*interj* — used to express defiance
NERTZ	*interj* nerts
NERVATE	*adj* having veins
NERVE	*v* **NERVED, NERVING, NERVES** to give courage to
NERVIER	comparative of nervy
NERVIEST	superlative of nervy
NERVILY	*adv* in a nervy manner
NERVINE	*n* pl. **-S** a soothing medicine
NERVING	*n* pl. **-S** a type of veterinary operation
NERVOUS	*adj* easily excited
NERVULE	*n* pl. **-S** nervure
NERVURE	*n* pl. **-S** a vascular ridge on a leaf
NERVY	*adj* **NERVIER, NERVIEST** impudent
NESCIENT	*n* pl. **-S** one who is ignorant
NESS	*n* pl. **-ES** a headland
NEST	*v* **-ED, -ING, -S** to build a nest (a structure for holding bird eggs)

NESTABLE	adj capable of being fitted closely within another container	**NEUME**	n pl. **-S** a sign used in musical notation **NEUMATIC, NEUMIC** adj
NESTER	n pl. **-S** one that nests	**NEURAL**	adj pertaining to the nervous system **NEURALLY** adv
NESTFUL	n pl. **-S** as much as a nest can hold	**NEURAXON**	n pl. **-S** a part of a neuron
NESTLE	v **-TLED, -TLING, -TLES** to lie snugly	**NEURINE**	n pl. **-S** a ptomaine poison
		NEURITIC	n pl. **-S** one affected with neuritis
NESTLER	n pl. **-S** one that nestles	**NEURITIS**	n pl. **-RITISES** or **-RITIDES** inflammation of a nerve
NESTLIKE	adj resembling a nest		
NESTLING	n pl. **-S** a young bird	**NEUROID**	adj resembling a nerve
NESTMATE	n pl. **-S** a bird sharing a nest with another	**NEUROMA**	n pl. **-MAS** or **-MATA** a type of tumor
NESTOR	n pl. **-S** a wise old man	**NEURON**	n pl. **-S** the basic cellular unit of the nervous system **NEURONAL, NEURONIC** adj
NET	v **NETTED, NETTING, NETS** to catch in a net (a type of openwork fabric)		
		NEURONE	n pl. **-S** neuron
NETBALL	n pl. **-S** a team game similar to basketball	**NEUROSIS**	n pl. **-ROSES** a type of emotional disturbance **NEUROSAL** adj
NETBOOK	n pl. **-S** a small portable computer	**NEUROTIC**	n pl. **-S** one affected with a neurosis
NETFUL	n pl. **-S** as much as a net can hold		
NETHER	adj situated below	**NEURULA**	n pl. **-LAS** or **-LAE** a vertebrate embryo **NEURULAR** adj
NETIZEN	n pl. **-S** a frequent user of the Internet		
		NEUSTON	n pl. **-S** an aggregate of small aquatic organisms **NEUSTIC** adj
NETLESS	adj having no net		
NETLIKE	adj resembling a net	**NEUTER**	v **-ED, -ING, -S** to castrate
NETOP	n pl. **-S** friend; companion	**NEUTRAL**	n pl. **-S** one that is impartial
NETROOTS	n/pl political activists at the basic level of society who communicate via the Internet	**NEUTRINO**	n pl. **-NOS** a subatomic particle
		NEUTRON	n pl. **-S** a subatomic particle
		NEVE	n pl. **-S** a granular snow
NETSUKE	n pl. **-S** a button-like fixture on Japanese clothing	**NEVER**	adv at no time
		NEVUS	n pl. **-VI** a birthmark **NEVOID** adj
NETSURF	v **-ED, -ING, -S** to browse the Internet for information	**NEW**	adj **NEWER, NEWEST** existing only a short time
NETT	v **-ED, -ING, -S** to net		
NETTABLE	adj capable of being netted	**NEW**	n pl. **-S** something that is new
NETTED	past tense of net, nett	**NEWB**	n pl. **-S** a newbie
NETTER	n pl. **-S** one that nets	**NEWBIE**	n pl. **-S** a newcomer
NETTIER	comparative of netty	**NEWBORN**	n pl. **-S** a recently born infant
NETTIEST	superlative of netty	**NEWCOMER**	n pl. **-S** one that has recently arrived
NETTING	n pl. **-S** a net		
NETTLE	v **-TLED, -TLING, -TLES** to make angry	**NEWEL**	n pl. **-S** a staircase support
		NEWFOUND	adj newly found
NETTLER	n pl. **-S** one that nettles	**NEWIE**	n pl. **-S** something new
NETTLY	adj **-TLIER, -TLIEST** prickly	**NEWISH**	adj somewhat new
NETTY	adj **-TIER, -TIEST** resembling a net	**NEWLY**	adv recently
NETWORK	v **-ED, -ING, -S** to cover with or as if with crossing lines	**NEWLYWED**	n pl. **-S** a person recently married
		NEWMOWN	adj recently mown
NEUK	n pl. **-S** nook	**NEWNESS**	n pl. **-ES** the state of being new
NEUM	n pl. **-S** neume	**NEWS**	n/pl a report of recent events

NEWSBEAT *n* pl. **-S** a news source that a reporter is assigned to cover

NEWSBOY *n* pl. **-BOYS** a boy who delivers or sells newspapers

NEWSCAST *n* pl. **-S** a news broadcast

NEWSDESK *n* pl. **-S** the department that receives late-breaking news

NEWSFEED *n* pl. **-S** a service that provides news articles for distribution

NEWSGIRL *n* pl. **-S** a girl who delivers or sells newspapers

NEWSHAWK *n* pl. **-S** a newspaper reporter

NEWSIE *n* pl. **-S** newsy

NEWSIER comparative of newsy

NEWSIES pl. of newsy

NEWSIEST superlative of newsy

NEWSLESS *adj* having no news

NEWSMAN *n* pl. **-MEN** a news reporter

NEWSPEAK *n* pl. **-S** a deliberately ambiguous language

NEWSREEL *n* pl. **-S** a short movie presenting current events

NEWSROOM *n* pl. **-S** a room where the news is gathered

NEWSWIRE *n* pl. **-S** a news agency that transmits news copy to subscribers

NEWSY *adj* **NEWSIER, NEWSIEST** full of news

NEWSY *n* pl. **NEWSIES** a newsboy

NEWT *n* pl. **-S** a small salamander

NEWTON *n* pl. **-S** a unit of force

NEWWAVER *n* pl. **-S** a member of a new-wave movement

NEXT *n* pl. **-S** the one that comes immediately after

NEXTDOOR *adj* located in the next building or room

NEXUS *n* pl. **-ES** a connection or link

NGULTRUM *n* pl. **-S** a monetary unit of Bhutan

NGWEE *n* pl. **-S** a monetary unit of Zambia

NIACIN *n* pl. **-S** a B vitamin

NIAGARA *n* pl. **-S** an outpouring or deluge

NIB *v* **NIBBED, NIBBING, NIBS** to provide with a penpoint

NIBBLE *v* **-BLED, -BLING, -BLES** to eat with small bites

NIBBLER *n* pl. **-S** one that nibbles

NIBBLY *n* pl. **-BLIES** a small food item

NIBLET *n* pl. **-S** a small piece of food

NIBLICK *n* pl. **-S** a golf club

NIBLIKE *adj* resembling a penpoint

NICAD *n* pl. **-S** nickel cadmium

NICE *adj* **NICER, NICEST** pleasing to the senses **NICELY** *adv*

NICENESS *n* pl. **-ES** the quality of being nice

NICETY *n* pl. **-TIES** a fine point or distinction

NICHE *v* **NICHED, NICHING, NICHES** to place in a receding space or hollow

NICK *v* **-ED, -ING, -S** to make a shallow cut in

NICKEL *v* **-ELED, -ELING, -ELS** or **-ELLED, -ELLING, -ELS** to plate with nickel (a metallic element)

NICKELIC *adj* pertaining to or containing nickel

NICKER *v* **-ED, -ING, -S** to neigh

NICKLE *v* **-LED, -LING, -LES** to nickel

NICKNACK *n* pl. **-S** a trinket

NICKNAME *v* **-NAMED, -NAMING, -NAMES** to give an alternate name to

NICOISE *adj* served with black olives, tomatoes, olive oil, and often anchovies

NICOL *n* pl. **-S** a type of prism

NICOTIN *n* pl. **-S** nicotine

NICOTINE *n* pl. **-S** a poisonous alkaloid in tobacco

NICTATE *v* **-TATED, -TATING, -TATES** to wink

NIDAL *adj* pertaining to a nidus

NIDATE *v* **-DATED, -DATING, -DATES** to become implanted in the uterus

NIDATION *n* pl. **-S** the act of nidating

NIDE *v* **NIDED, NIDING, NIDES** to nest

NIDERING *n* pl. **-S** a coward

NIDGET *n* pl. **-S** an idiot

NIDI a pl. of nidus

NIDIFY *v* **-FIED, -FYING, -FIES** to nest

NIDING present participle of nide

NIDUS *n* pl. **NIDUSES** or **NIDI** a nest or breeding place

NIECE *n* pl. **-S** a daughter of one's brother or sister

NIELLIST *n* pl. **-S** one that niellos

NIELLO *n* pl. **-LOS** or **-LI** a black metallic substance

NIELLO   *v* **-ED, -ING, -S** to decorate with niello

NIENTE   *adv* softly fading away — used as a musical direction

NIEVE   *n* pl. **-S** the fist or hand

NIFF   *v* **-ED, -ING, -S** to stink

NIFFER   *v* **-ED, -ING, -S** to barter

NIFFY   *adj* **NIFFIER, NIFFIEST** stinky

NIFTY   *adj* **-TIER, -TIEST** stylish; pleasing **NIFTILY** *adv*

NIFTY   *n* pl. **-TIES** something that is nifty

NIGELLA   *n* pl. **-S** an annual herb

NIGGARD   *v* **-ED, -ING, -S** to act stingily

NIGGLE   *v* **-GLED, -GLING, -GLES** to worry over petty details

NIGGLER   *n* pl. **-S** one that niggles

NIGGLING   *n* pl. **-S** petty or meticulous work

NIGGLY   *adj* **-GLIER, -GLIEST** petty

NIGH   *adj* **NIGHER, NIGHEST** near

NIGH   *v* **-ED, -ING, -S** to approach

NIGHNESS   *n* pl. **-ES** the state of being nigh

NIGHT   *n* pl. **-S** the period from sunset to sunrise

NIGHTCAP   *n* pl. **-S** a cap worn to bed

NIGHTIE   *n* pl. **-S** a nightgown

NIGHTJAR   *n* pl. **-S** a nocturnal bird

NIGHTLY   *adv* every night; at night

NIGHTY   *n* pl. **NIGHTIES** nightie

NIGRIFY   *v* **-FIED, -FYING, -FIES** to make black

NIGROSIN   *n* pl. **-S** a type of dye

NIHIL   *n* pl. **-S** nothing

NIHILISM   *n* pl. **-S** a doctrine that denies traditional values

NIHILIST   *n* pl. **-S** an adherent of nihilism

NIHILITY   *n* pl. **-TIES** the state of being nothing

NIKAH   *n* pl. **-S** a Muslim marriage ceremony

NIL   *n* pl. **-S** nothing

NILGAI   *n* pl. **-S** a large antelope

NILGAU   *n* pl. **-S** nilgai

NILGHAI   *n* pl. **-S** nilgai

NILGHAU   *n* pl. **-S** nilgai

NILL   *v* **-ED, -ING, -S** to be unwilling

NIM   *v* **NIMMED** or **NAM, NIMMING, NIMS** to steal

NIMBLE   *adj* **-BLER, -BLEST** agile **NIMBLY** *adv*

NIMBUS   *n* pl. **-BUSES** or **-BI** a luminous cloud **NIMBUSED** *adj*

NIMIETY   *n* pl. **-ETIES** excess **NIMIOUS** *adj*

NIMMED   past tense of nim

NIMMING   present participle of nim

NIMROD   *n* pl. **-S** a hunter

NINE   *n* pl. **-S** a number

NINEBARK   *n* pl. **-S** a flowering shrub

NINEFOLD   *adj* nine times as great

NINEPIN   *n* pl. **-S** a wooden pin used in a bowling game

NINER   *n* pl. **-S** a student in the ninth grade

NINETEEN   *n* pl. **-S** a number

NINETY   *n* pl. **-TIES** a number

NINJA   *n* pl. **-S** a feudal Japanese warrior

NINJUTSU   *n* pl. **-S** the traditional Japanese method of spying

NINNY   *n* pl. **-NIES** a fool **NINNYISH** *adj*

NINON   *n* pl. **-S** a sheer fabric

NINTH   *n* pl. **-S** one of nine equal parts

NINTHLY   *adv* in the ninth place

NIOBATE   *n* pl. **-S** a chemical salt

NIOBITE   *n* pl. **-S** the mineral columbite

NIOBIUM   *n* pl. **-S** a metallic element **NIOBIC, NIOBOUS** *adj*

NIP   *v* **NIPPED, NIPPING, NIPS** to pinch

NIPA   *n* pl. **-S** a palm tree

NIPPER   *n* pl. **-S** one that nips

NIPPIER   comparative of nippy

NIPPIEST   superlative of nippy

NIPPILY   *adv* in a nippy manner

NIPPING   present participle of nip

NIPPLE   *n* pl. **-S** a protuberance on the breast **NIPPLED** *adj*

NIPPY   *adj* **-PIER, -PIEST** sharp or biting

NIQAAB   *n* pl. **-S** niqab

NIQAB   *n* pl. **-S** a veil worn by some Muslim women

NIRVANA   *n* pl. **-S** a blessed state in Buddhism **NIRVANIC** *adj*

NISEI   *n* pl. **-S** one born in America of immigrant Japanese parents

NISI   *adj* not yet final

NISUS   *n* pl. **NISUS** an effort

NIT	*n* pl. **-S** the egg of a parasitic insect	**NOB**	*n* pl. **-S** a wealthy person
NITE	*n* pl. **-S** night	**NOBBIER**	comparative of nobby
NITER	*n* pl. **-S** a chemical salt	**NOBBIEST**	superlative of nobby
NITERIE	*n* pl. **-S** nitery	**NOBBILY**	*adv* in a nobby manner
NITERY	*n* pl. **-ERIES** a nightclub	**NOBBLE**	*v* **-BLED, -BLING, -BLES** to disable a racehorse
NITID	*adj* bright	**NOBBLER**	*n* pl. **-S** one that nobbles
NITINOL	*n* pl. **-S** an alloy of nickel and titanium	**NOBBY**	*adj* **-BIER, -BIEST** elegant
NITON	*n* pl. **-S** radon	**NOBELIUM**	*n* pl. **-S** a radioactive element
NITPICK	*v* **-ED, -ING, -S** to fuss over petty details	**NOBILITY**	*n* pl. **-TIES** the social class composed of nobles
NITPICKY	*adj* **-PICKIER, -PICKIEST** tending to nitpick	**NOBLE**	*adj* **-BLER, -BLEST** possessing qualities of excellence
NITRATE	*v* **-TRATED, -TRATING, -TRATES** to treat with nitric acid	**NOBLE**	*n* pl. **-S** a person of high birth, rank, or title
NITRATOR	*n* pl. **-S** one that nitrates	**NOBLEMAN**	*n* pl. **-MEN** a noble
NITRE	*n* pl. **-S** niter	**NOBLER**	comparative of noble
NITRIC	*adj* containing nitrogen	**NOBLESSE**	*n* pl. **-S** the nobility
NITRID	*n* pl. **-S** nitride	**NOBLEST**	superlative of noble
NITRIDE	*v* **-TRIDED, -TRIDING, -TRIDES** to convert into a nitride (a compound of nitrogen)	**NOBLY**	*adv* in a noble manner
NITRIFY	*v* **-FIED, -FYING, -FIES** to combine with nitrogen	**NOBODY**	*n* pl. **-BODIES** an unimportant person
NITRIL	*n* pl. **-S** nitrile	**NOCEBO**	*n* pl. **-BOS** a harmless substance that induces harmful effects in patients having negative expectations
NITRILE	*n* pl. **-S** a chemical compound		
NITRITE	*n* pl. **-S** a salt of nitrous acid	**NOCENT**	*adj* harmful
NITRO	*n* pl. **-TROS** a nitrated product	**NOCK**	*v* **-ED, -ING, -S** to notch a bow or arrow
NITROGEN	*n* pl. **-S** a gaseous element	**NOCTUID**	*n* pl. **-S** a night-flying moth **NOCTUOID** *adj*
NITROLIC	*adj* pertaining to a class of acids		
NITROSO	*adj* containing nitrosyl	**NOCTULE**	*n* pl. **-S** a large bat
NITROSYL	*n* pl. **-S** a univalent radical	**NOCTURN**	*n* pl. **-S** a religious service
NITROUS	*adj* containing nitrogen	**NOCTURNE**	*n* pl. **-S** a musical composition
NITTY	*adj* **-TIER, -TIEST** full of nits	**NOCUOUS**	*adj* harmful
NITWIT	*n* pl. **-S** a stupid person	**NOD**	*v* **NODDED, NODDING, NODS** to briefly lower the head forward
NIVAL	*adj* pertaining to snow		
NIVEOUS	*adj* resembling snow	**NODAL**	*adj* of the nature of a node **NODALLY** *adv*
NIX	*n* pl. **NIXES** or **NIXE** a water sprite	**NODALITY**	*n* pl. **-TIES** the state of being nodal
NIX	*v* **-ED, -ING, -ES** to veto	**NODDED**	past tense of nod
NIXIE	*n* pl. **-S** a female water sprite	**NODDER**	*n* pl. **-S** one that nods
NIXY	*n* pl. **NIXIES** an undeliverable piece of mail	**NODDIES**	pl. of noddy
		NODDING	present participle of nod
NIZAM	*n* pl. **-S** a former sovereign of India	**NODDLE**	*v* **-DLED, -DLING, -DLES** to nod frequently
NIZAMATE	*n* pl. **-S** the territory of a nizam	**NODDY**	*n* pl. **-DIES** a fool
NO	*n* pl. **NOS** or **NOES** a negative reply	**NODE**	*n* pl. **-S** a swollen enlargement

NODI	pl. of nodus
NODICAL	*adj* pertaining to an astronomical point
NODOSE	*adj* having nodes
NODOSITY	*n* pl. **-TIES** the state of being nodose
NODOUS	*adj* nodose
NODULE	*n* pl. **-S** a small node **NODULAR, NODULOSE, NODULOUS** *adj*
NODUS	*n* pl. **-DI** a difficulty
NOEL	*n* pl. **-S** a Christmas carol
NOES	a pl. of no
NOESIS	*n* pl. **-SISES** the process of reason
NOETIC	*adj* pertaining to reason
NOG	*v* **NOGGED, NOGGING, NOGS** to fill in a space in a wall with bricks
NOGG	*n* pl. **-S** a strong ale
NOGGIN	*n* pl. **-S** a small cup
NOGGING	*n* pl. **-S** a type of masonry
NOH	*n* pl. **NOH** the classical drama of Japan
NOHOW	*adv* in no manner
NOIL	*n* pl. **-S** a kind of short fiber **NOILY** *adj*
NOIR	*n* pl. **-S** a bleak type of crime fiction **NOIRISH** *adj*
NOISE	*v* **NOISED, NOISING, NOISES** to spread as a rumor or report
NOISETTE	*n* pl. **-S** a small round piece of meat
NOISOME	*adj* disgusting; harmful
NOISY	*adj* **NOISIER, NOISIEST** making loud sounds **NOISILY** *adv*
NOLO	*n* pl. **-LOS** a type of legal plea
NOM	*n* pl. **-S** a name
NOMA	*n* pl. **-S** a severe inflammation of the mouth
NOMAD	*n* pl. **-S** a wanderer **NOMADIC** *adj*
NOMADISM	*n* pl. **-S** the mode of life of a nomad
NOMARCH	*n* pl. **-S** the head of a nome
NOMARCHY	*n* pl. **-ARCHIES** a nome
NOMBLES	*n/pl* numbles
NOMBRIL	*n* pl. **-S** a point on a heraldic shield
NOME	*n* pl. **-S** a province of modern Greece
NOMEN	*n* pl. **-MINA** the second name of an ancient Roman
NOMINAL	*n* pl. **-S** a word used as a noun
NOMINATE	*v* **-NATED, -NATING, -NATES** to name as a candidate
NOMINEE	*n* pl. **-S** one that is nominated
NOMISM	*n* pl. **-S** strict adherence to moral law **NOMISTIC** *adj*
NOMOGRAM	*n* pl. **-S** a type of graph
NOMOLOGY	*n* pl. **-GIES** the science of law
NOMOS	*n* pl. **NOMOI** law
NONA	*n* pl. **-S** a virus disease
NONACID	*n* pl. **-S** a substance that is not an acid
NONACTOR	*n* pl. **-S** a person who is not an actor
NONADULT	*n* pl. **-S** a person who is not an adult
NONAGE	*n* pl. **-S** a period of immaturity
NONAGON	*n* pl. **-S** a nine-sided polygon
NONANE	*n* pl. **-S** a colorless liquid hydrocarbon
NONART	*n* pl. **-S** something that is not art
NONARY	*n* pl. **-ARIES** a group of nine
NONAVIAN	*adj* not of or relating to birds
NONBANK	*n* pl. **-S** a business that is not a bank
NONBASIC	*adj* not basic
NONBEING	*n* pl. **-S** lack of being
NONBLACK	*n* pl. **-S** one that is not black
NONBODY	*n* pl. **-BODIES** a person's nonphysical nature
NONBOOK	*n* pl. **-S** a book of little literary merit
NONBRAND	*adj* lacking a brand name
NONCASH	*adj* other than cash
NONCE	*n* pl. **-S** the present occasion
NONCLASS	*n* pl. **-ES** a lack of class
NONCLING	*adj* not clinging
NONCOLA	*n* pl. **-S** a beverage that is not a cola
NONCOLOR	*n* pl. **-S** a lack of color
NONCOM	*n* pl. **-S** a noncommissioned officer
NONCORE	*adj* not being in or relating to a central part
NONCOUNT	*adj* not capable of being counted
NONCRIME	*n* pl. **-S** something that is not a crime
NONDAIRY	*adj* having no milk products
NONDANCE	*n* pl. **-S** an unrhythmic dance
NONDRIP	*adj* that does not drip
NONDRUG	*adj* not involving drugs

NONE *n* pl. **-S** one of seven canonical daily periods for prayer and devotion

NONEGO *n* pl. **-GOS** all that is not part of the ego

NONELECT *adj* not chosen

NONELITE *adj* not belonging to an elite group

NONEMPTY *adj* not empty

NONENTRY *n* pl. **-TRIES** the fact of not entering

NONEQUAL *n* pl. **-S** one that is not equal

NONESUCH *n* pl. **-ES** a person or thing without an equal

NONET *n* pl. **-S** a composition for nine instruments or voices

NONEVENT *n* pl. **-S** an expected event that does not occur

NONFACT *n* pl. **-S** a statement not based on fact

NONFAN *n* pl. **-S** a person who is not a fan (an enthusiast)

NONFARM *adj* not pertaining to the farm

NONFAT *adj* having no fat solids

NONFATAL *adj* not fatal

NONFATTY *adj* not fatty

NONFINAL *adj* not being the last

NONFLUID *n* pl. **-S** a substance that is not a fluid

NONFOCAL *adj* not focal

NONFOOD *adj* pertaining to something other than food

NONFUEL *adj* not used as a fuel

NONGAME *adj* not hunted for food, sport, or fur

NONGAY *n* pl. **-S** a person who is not a homosexual

NONGLARE *n* pl. **-S** a lack of glare (harsh brilliant light)

NONGREEN *adj* not green

NONGUEST *n* pl. **-S** one who is not a guest

NONGUILT *n* pl. **-S** the absence of guilt

NONHARDY *adj* not hardy

NONHEME *adj* not containing iron that is bound like that of heme

NONHERO *n* pl. **-ROES** an antihero

NONHOME *adj* not taking place in the home

NONHUMAN *n* pl. **-S** one that is not a human

NONI *n* pl. **-S** a small tree

NONIDEAL *adj* not ideal

NONIMAGE *n* pl. **-S** one having no celebrity status

NONINERT *adj* not inactive

NONIONIC *adj* not ionic

NONIRON *adj* not needing to be ironed

NONISSUE *n* pl. **-S** a topic that is not controversial

NONJUROR *n* pl. **-S** one who refuses to take a required oath

NONJURY *n* pl. **-RIES** a case not involving a jury

NONKIN *n* pl. **-S** those who are not kin

NONLABOR *adj* not pertaining to labor

NONLEAFY *adj* not having leaves

NONLEGAL *adj* not legal

NONLEVEL *adj* not flat or even

NONLIFE *n* pl. **-LIVES** the absence of life

NONLOCAL *n* pl. **-S** one that is not local

NONLOYAL *adj* not loyal

NONLYRIC *adj* not lyrical

NONMAJOR *n* pl. **-S** a student who is not majoring in a specified subject

NONMAN *n* pl. **-MEN** a being that is not a man

NONMEAT *adj* not containing meat

NONMETAL *n* pl. **-S** an element that lacks metallic properties

NONMETRO *adj* not metropolitan

NONMODAL *adj* not modal

NONMONEY *adj* not involving money

NONMORAL *adj* not pertaining to morals

NONMUSIC *n* pl. **-S** inferior music

NONNASAL *adj* not involving the nose

NONNAVAL *adj* not naval

NONNEWS *adj* not being news

NONNOBLE *adj* not noble

NONNOVEL *n* pl. **-S** a literary work that is not a novel

NONOBESE *adj* not obese

NONOHMIC *adj* not measured in ohms

NONOILY *adj* not oily

NONORAL *adj* not involving the mouth

NONOWNER *n* pl. **-S** one who is not the owner

NONPAGAN *n* pl. **-S** one who is not a pagan

NONPAID *adj* not paid

NONPAPAL *adj* not papal

NONPAR *adj* being a stock that has no face value

NONPARTY *n* pl. **-TIES** one not belonging to a party

NONPAST *n* pl. **-S** a verb form that lacks an inflection for a past tense

NONPEAK *adj* being a time when something is not at its highest level

NONPLAY *n* pl. **-PLAYS** a theatrical work that is not a play

NONPLUS *v* **-PLUSED, -PLUSING, -PLUSES** or **-PLUSSED, -PLUSSING, -PLUSSES** to baffle

NONPOINT *adj* not occurring at a definite single site

NONPOLAR *adj* not polar

NONPOOR *adj* not being poor

NONPRINT *adj* not involving printed material

NONPROS *v* **-PROSSED, -PROSSING, -PROSSES** to enter a judgment against a plaintiff who fails to prosecute

NONQUOTA *adj* not included in or subject to a quota

NONRATED *adj* not rated

NONRIGID *adj* not rigid

NONRIVAL *n* pl. **-S** an unimportant rival

NONROYAL *adj* not royal

NONRURAL *adj* not rural

NONSELF *n* pl. **-SELVES** foreign material in a body

NONSENSE *n* pl. **-S** behavior or language that is meaningless or absurd

NONSKED *n* pl. **-S** an airline without scheduled flying times

NONSKID *adj* designed to inhibit skidding

NONSKIER *n* pl. **-S** one that does not ski

NONSLIP *adj* designed to prevent slipping

NONSOLAR *adj* not solar

NONSOLID *n* pl. **-S** a substance that is not a solid

NONSTICK *adj* allowing of easy removal of cooked food particles

NONSTOP *n* pl. **-S** a flight without a stop en route

NONSTORY *n* pl. **-RIES** an insignificant news story

NONSTYLE *n* pl. **-S** a style that is not identifiable

NONSUCH *n* pl. **-ES** nonesuch

NONSUGAR *n* pl. **-S** a substance that is not a sugar

NONSUIT *v* **-ED, -ING, -S** to dismiss the lawsuit of

NONTAX *n* pl. **-ES** a tax of little consequence

NONTIDAL *adj* not tidal

NONTITLE *adj* pertaining to an athletic contest in which a title is not at stake

NONTONAL *adj* lacking tonality

NONTONIC *adj* not based on the first tone of a scale

NONTOXIC *n* pl. **-S** a substance that is not toxic

NONTRUMP *adj* not having a trump

NONTRUTH *n* pl. **-S** something that is not true

NONUNION *n* pl. **-S** failure of a broken bone to heal

NONUPLE *n* pl. **-S** a number nine times as great as another

NONURBAN *adj* not urban

NONUSE *n* pl. **-S** failure to use

NONUSER *n* pl. **-S** one that is not a user

NONUSING *adj* not using

NONVALID *adj* not valid

NONVIRAL *adj* not viral

NONVITAL *adj* not vital

NONVOCAL *n* pl. **-S** one that does not involve the voice

NONVOTER *n* pl. **-S** one that does not vote

NONWAGE *adj* not including or involving wages (money paid for work or services)

NONWAR *n* pl. **-S** a war that is not officially declared

NONWHITE *n* pl. **-S** a person who is not of the white race

NONWOODY *adj* not woody

NONWOOL *adj* not made of wool

NONWORD *n* pl. **-S** a word that has no meaning

NONWORK *adj* not involving work

NONWOVEN *n* pl. **-S** a fabric not made by weaving

NONYL *n* pl. **-S** an alkyl radical

NONZERO *adj* having a value other than zero

NOO *adv* now

NOODGE *v* **NOODGED, NOODGING, NOODGES** to nag

NOODLE	v **-DLED, -DLING, -DLES** to play idly on a musical instrument	**NORTHER**	n pl. **-S** a wind or storm from the north
NOODLING	n pl. **-S** the action of idly playing a musical instrument	**NORTHERN**	n pl. **-S** a person living in the north
NOOGIE	n pl. **-S** a playful rubbing of one's knuckles on another's head	**NORTHING**	n pl. **-S** movement toward the north
NOOK	n pl. **-S** a corner, as in a room **NOOKLIKE** adj	**NOSE**	v **NOSED, NOSING, NOSES** to sniff with the nose (the organ of smell)
NOON	n pl. **-S** midday	**NOSEBAG**	n pl. **-S** a feedbag
NOONDAY	n pl. **-DAYS** noon	**NOSEBAND**	n pl. **-S** a part of a horse's bridle
NOONER	n pl. **-S** an event that occurs during the middle of the day	**NOSEDIVE**	v **-DIVED** or **-DOVE, -DIVING, -DIVES** to go into a sudden steep drop
NOONING	n pl. **-S** a meal eaten at noon	**NOSEGAY**	n pl. **-GAYS** a bouquet
NOONTIDE	n pl. **-S** noon	**NOSELESS**	adj having no nose
NOONTIME	n pl. **-S** noon	**NOSELIKE**	adj resembling a nose
NOOSE	v **NOOSED, NOOSING, NOOSES** to secure with a type of loop	**NOSEY**	adj **NOSIER, NOSIEST** nosy
NOOSER	n pl. **-S** one that nooses	**NOSH**	v **-ED, -ING, -ES** to eat snacks between meals
NOPAL	n pl. **-S** or **-ES** a cactus of Mexico and Central America	**NOSHER**	n pl. **-S** one that noshes
NOPALITO	n pl. **-TOS** the stem of the nopal used as food	**NOSIER**	comparative of nosy
		NOSIEST	superlative of nosy
NOPE	adv no	**NOSILY**	adv in a nosy manner
NOPLACE	adv not in or at any place	**NOSINESS**	n pl. **-ES** the quality of being nosy
NOR	conj and not	**NOSING**	n pl. **-S** a projecting edge
NORDIC	adj pertaining to cross-country ski racing and ski jumping	**NOSOLOGY**	n pl. **-GIES** a classification of diseases
NORI	n pl. **-S** dried seaweed pressed into sheets	**NOSTOC**	n pl. **-S** a freshwater alga
NORIA	n pl. **-S** a type of waterwheel	**NOSTRIL**	n pl. **-S** an external opening of the nose
NORITE	n pl. **-S** a granular rock **NORITIC** adj	**NOSTRUM**	n pl. **-S** a medicine of one's own invention
NORLAND	n pl. **-S** a region in the north	**NOSY**	adj **NOSIER, NOSIEST** unduly curious
NORM	n pl. **-S** a standard regarded as typical for a specific group	**NOT**	adv in no way
		NOTA	pl. of notum
NORMAL	n pl. **-S** the usual or expected state or form	**NOTABLE**	n pl. **-S** a person of distinction
NORMALCY	n pl. **-CIES** conformity with the norm	**NOTABLY**	adv in a distinguished manner
		NOTAL	adj pertaining to a notum
NORMALLY	adv as a rule; usually	**NOTARIAL**	adj pertaining to a notary
NORMANDE	adj prepared with foods associated with Normandy	**NOTARISE**	v **-RISED, -RISING, -RISES** to notarize
NORMED	adj having a norm	**NOTARIZE**	v **-RIZED, -RIZING, -RIZES** to certify through a notary
NORMLESS	adj having no norm	**NOTARY**	n pl. **-RIES** a public officer who certifies documents
NORTENA	n pl. **-S** a style of folk music of northern Mexico and Texas		
NORTENO	n pl. **-NOS** an inhabitant of northern Mexico	**NOTATE**	v **-TATED, -TATING, -TATES** to put into notation
NORTH	n pl. **-S** a point of the compass	**NOTATION**	n pl. **-S** a system of symbols
		NOTATOR	n pl. **-S** one that notates

NOTCH	*v* **-ED, -ING, -ES** to make an angular cut in
NOTCHER	*n* pl. **-S** one that notches
NOTCHY	*adj* **NOTCHIER, NOTCHIEST** having angular cuts
NOTE	*v* **NOTED, NOTING, NOTES** to write down
NOTEBOOK	*n* pl. **-S** a book in which to write
NOTECARD	*n* pl. **-S** a card used for sending short messages
NOTECASE	*n* pl. **-S** a billfold
NOTED	past tense of note
NOTEDLY	*adv* in a famous manner
NOTELESS	*adj* undistinguished
NOTELET	*n* pl. **-S** a small sheet of paper for an informal letter
NOTEPAD	*n* pl. **-S** a number of sheets of paper glued together at one end
NOTER	*n* pl. **-S** one that notes
NOTHER	*adj* different
NOTHING	*n* pl. **-S** the absence of all quantity or magnitude
NOTICE	*v* **-TICED, -TICING, -TICES** to become aware of
NOTICER	*n* pl. **-S** one that notices
NOTIFIER	*n* pl. **-S** one that notifies
NOTIFY	*v* **-FIED, -FYING, -FIES** to inform
NOTING	present participle of note
NOTION	*n* pl. **-S** a general idea **NOTIONAL** *adj*
NOTORNIS	*n* pl. **NOTORNIS** a flightless bird
NOTTURNO	*n* pl. **-NI** a nocturne
NOTUM	*n* pl. **-TA** a part of the thorax of an insect
NOUGAT	*n* pl. **-S** a chewy candy
NOUGHT	*n* pl. **-S** naught
NOUMENON	*n* pl. **-MENA** an object of intellectual intuition **NOUMENAL** *adj*
NOUN	*n* pl. **-S** a word used to denote the name of something **NOUNAL, NOUNLESS** *adj* **NOUNALLY** *adv*
NOURISH	*v* **-ED, -ING, -ES** to sustain with food
NOUS	*n* pl. **-ES** mind, reason, or intellect
NOUVEAU	*adj* newly arrived or developed
NOUVELLE	*n* pl. **-S** a style of French cooking
NOVA	*n* pl. **-VAS** or **-VAE** a type of star **NOVALIKE** *adj*
NOVATE	*v* **-VATED, -VATING, -VATES** to replace an old contract with a new one
NOVATION	*n* pl. **-S** the substitution of a new legal obligation for an old one
NOVEL	*n* pl. **-S** a fictional prose narrative
NOVELISE	*v* **-ISED, -ISING, -ISES** to novelize
NOVELIST	*n* pl. **-S** a writer of novels
NOVELIZE	*v* **-IZED, -IZING, -IZES** to put into the form of a novel
NOVELLA	*n* pl. **-LAS** or **-LE** a short novel
NOVELLY	*adv* in a new or unusual manner
NOVELTY	*n* pl. **-TIES** something new or unusual
NOVENA	*n* pl. **-NAS** or **-NAE** a religious devotion lasting nine days
NOVERCAL	*adj* pertaining to a stepmother
NOVICE	*n* pl. **-S** a person new to any field or activity
NOW	*n* pl. **-S** the present time
NOWADAYS	*adv* in these times
NOWAY	*adv* in no way
NOWAYS	*adv* noway
NOWHERE	*n* pl. **-S** a nonexistent place
NOWISE	*adv* not at all
NOWNESS	*n* pl. **-ES** the state of existing at the present time
NOWT	*n* pl. **-S** naught
NOXIOUS	*adj* harmful to health
NOYADE	*n* pl. **-S** an execution by drowning
NOYAU	*n* pl. **-YAUX** a liqueur made of brandy and fruit kernels
NOZZLE	*n* pl. **-S** a projecting spout
NTH	*adj* pertaining to an indefinitely large ordinal number
NU	*n* pl. **-S** a Greek letter
NUANCE	*v* **NUANCED, NUANCING, NUANCES** to give a subtle shade of meaning to
NUB	*n* pl. **-S** a protuberance or knob
NUBBER	*n* pl. **-S** a weakly hit ball
NUBBIER	comparative of nubby
NUBBIEST	superlative of nubby
NUBBIN	*n* pl. **-S** an undeveloped fruit
NUBBLE	*n* pl. **-S** a small nub
NUBBLY	*adj* **-BLIER, -BLIEST** having nubbles
NUBBY	*adj* **-BIER, -BIEST** having nubs

NUBIA   *n* pl. **-S** a woman's scarf

NUBILE   *adj* suitable for marriage

NUBILITY   *n* pl. **-TIES** the quality of being nubile

NUBILOSE   *adj* nubilous

NUBILOUS   *adj* cloudy

NUBUCK   *n* pl. **-S** soft sueded leather

NUCELLUS   *n* pl. **-LI** the essential part of a plant ovule **NUCELLAR** *adj*

NUCHA   *n* pl. **-CHAE** the nape of the neck

NUCHAL   *n* pl. **-S** an anatomical part lying in the region of the nape

NUCLEAL   *adj* nuclear

NUCLEAR   *adj* pertaining to a nucleus

NUCLEASE   *n* pl. **-S** an enzyme

NUCLEATE   *v* **-ATED, -ATING, -ATES** to form into a nucleus

NUCLEI   a pl. of nucleus

NUCLEIN   *n* pl. **-S** a protein found in nuclei

NUCLEOID   *n* pl. **-S** the DNA-containing area of certain cells

NUCLEOLE   *n* pl. **-S** a part of a nucleus

NUCLEOLI   *n/pl* nucleoles

NUCLEON   *n* pl. **-S** a subatomic particle

NUCLEUS   *n* pl. **-CLEUSES** or **-CLEI** an essential part of a cell

NUCLIDE   *n* pl. **-S** a species of atom **NUCLIDIC** *adj*

NUDE   *adj* **NUDER, NUDEST** being without clothing or covering **NUDELY** *adv*

NUDE   *n* pl. **-S** a nude figure

NUDENESS   *n* pl. **-ES** nudity

NUDGE   *v* **NUDGED, NUDGING, NUDGES** to push gently

NUDGER   *n* pl. **-S** one that nudges

NUDICAUL   *adj* having leafless stems

NUDIE   *n* pl. **-S** a movie featuring nude performers

NUDISM   *n* pl. **-S** the practice of going nude

NUDIST   *n* pl. **-S** an advocate of nudism

NUDITY   *n* pl. **-TIES** the state of being nude

NUDNICK   *n* pl. **-S** nudnik

NUDNIK   *n* pl. **-S** an annoying person

NUDZH   *v* **-ED, -ING, -ES** to noodge

NUFF   *n* pl. **-S** enough

NUG   *n* pl. **-S** a chunk of wood sawn from a log

NUGATORY   *adj* having no power

NUGGET   *n* pl. **-S** a mass of solid matter **NUGGETY** *adj*

NUISANCE   *n* pl. **-S** a source of annoyance

NUKE   *v* **NUKED, NUKING, NUKES** to attack with nuclear weapons

NULL   *v* **-ED, -ING, -S** to reduce to nothing

NULLAH   *n* pl. **-S** a ravine

NULLIFY   *v* **-FIED, -FYING, -FIES** to make useless or ineffective

NULLITY   *n* pl. **-TIES** something of no legal force

NUMB   *adj* **NUMBER, NUMBEST** lacking sensation

NUMB   *v* **-ED, -ING, -S** to make numb

NUMBAT   *n* pl. **-S** a small Australian mammal

NUMBER   *v* **-ED, -ING, -S** to count

NUMBERER   *n* pl. **-S** one that numbers

NUMBFISH   *n* pl. **-ES** a fish capable of emitting electric shocks

NUMBLES   *n/pl* animal entrails

NUMBLY   *adv* in a numb manner

NUMBNESS   *n* pl. **-ES** the state of being numb

NUMCHUCK   *n* pl. **-S** nunchaku

NUMDAH   *n* pl. **-S** an embroidered rug of India

NUMEN   *n* pl. **-MINA** a deity

NUMERACY   *n* pl. **-CIES** the ability to understand basic mathematics

NUMERAL   *n* pl. **-S** a symbol that expresses a number

NUMERARY   *adj* pertaining to numbers

NUMERATE   *v* **-ATED, -ATING, -ATES** to count

NUMERIC   *n* pl. **-S** a numeral

NUMEROUS   *adj* many

NUMINA   pl. of numen

NUMINOUS   *adj* supernatural

NUMMARY   *adj* pertaining to coins

NUMMULAR   *adj* shaped like a coin

NUMMY   *adj* **NUMMIER, NUMMIEST** delicious

NUMNAH   *n* pl. **-S** a pad placed under a saddle

NUMSKULL   *n* pl. **-S** a dunce

NUN   *n* pl. **-S** a woman belonging to a religious order

NUNATAK *n* pl. **-S** a mountain peak completely surrounded by glacial ice

NUNCHAKU *n* pl. **-S** a Japanese weapon

NUNCHUCK *n* pl. **-S** nunchaku

NUNCHUK *n* pl. **-S** nunchaku

NUNCIO *n* pl. **-CIOS** an ambassador from the pope

NUNCLE *n* pl. **-S** an uncle

NUNLIKE *adj* resembling a nun

NUNNERY *n* pl. **-NERIES** a religious house for nuns

NUNNISH *adj* of, pertaining to, or characteristic of a nun

NUPTIAL *n* pl. **-S** a wedding

NURD *n* pl. **-S** nerd

NURL *v* **-ED, -ING, -S** to knurl

NURSE *v* **NURSED, NURSING, NURSES** to care for the sick or infirm

NURSER *n* pl. **-S** a baby's bottle

NURSERY *n* pl. **-ERIES** a room for young children

NURSING *n* pl. **-S** the profession of one who nurses

NURSLING *n* pl. **-S** an infant

NURTURAL *adj* pertaining to the process of nurturing

NURTURE *v* **-TURED, -TURING, -TURES** to nourish

NURTURER *n* pl. **-S** one that nurtures

NUT *v* **NUTTED, NUTTING, NUTS** to gather nuts (hard-shelled dry fruits)

NUTANT *adj* drooping

NUTATE *v* **-TATED, -TATING, -TATES** to exhibit nutation

NUTATION *n* pl. **-S** an oscillatory movement of the axis of a rotating body

NUTBAR *n* pl. **-S** a bar made from chopped nuts

NUTBROWN *adj* of a dark brown

NUTCASE *n* pl. **-S** a crazy person

NUTGALL *n* pl. **-S** a gallnut

NUTGRASS *n* pl. **-ES** a perennial herb

NUTHATCH *n* pl. **-ES** a small bird

NUTHOUSE *n* pl. **-S** an insane asylum

NUTJOB *n* pl. **-S** a crazy person

NUTLET *n* pl. **-S** a small nut

NUTLIKE *adj* resembling a nut

NUTMEAT *n* pl. **-S** the edible kernel of a nut

NUTMEG *n* pl. **-S** an aromatic seed used as a spice **NUTMEGGY** *adj*

NUTPICK *n* pl. **-S** a device for extracting the kernels from nuts

NUTRIA *n* pl. **-S** the coypu

NUTRIENT *n* pl. **-S** a nourishing substance

NUTSEDGE *n* pl. **-S** nutgrass

NUTSHELL *n* pl. **-S** the shell of a nut

NUTSO *n* pl. **-SOS** a crazy person

NUTSY *adj* **NUTSIER, NUTSIEST** crazy

NUTTED past tense of nut

NUTTER *n* pl. **-S** one that gathers nuts

NUTTING *n* pl. **-S** the act of gathering nuts

NUTTY *adj* **-TIER, -TIEST** silly; crazy **NUTTILY** *adv*

NUTWOOD *n* pl. **-S** a nut-bearing tree

NUZZLE *v* **-ZLED, -ZLING, -ZLES** to push with the nose

NUZZLER *n* pl. **-S** one that nuzzles

NYAH *interj* — used to express contempt for another

NYALA *n* pl. **-S** an antelope

NYLGHAI *n* pl. **-S** nilgai

NYLGHAU *n* pl. **-S** nilgai

NYLON *n* pl. **-S** a synthetic material **NYLONED** *adj*

NYMPH *n* pl. **-S** a female spirit **NYMPHAL, NYMPHEAN** *adj*

NYMPH *v* **-ED, -ING, -S** to fish using a fly (a hook with silk or feathers) that looks like a larva

NYMPHA *n* pl. **-PHAE** a fold of the vulva

NYMPHET *n* pl. **-S** a young nymph

NYMPHO *n* pl. **-PHOS** a woman obsessed by sexual desire

NYSTATIN *n* pl. **-S** an antibiotic

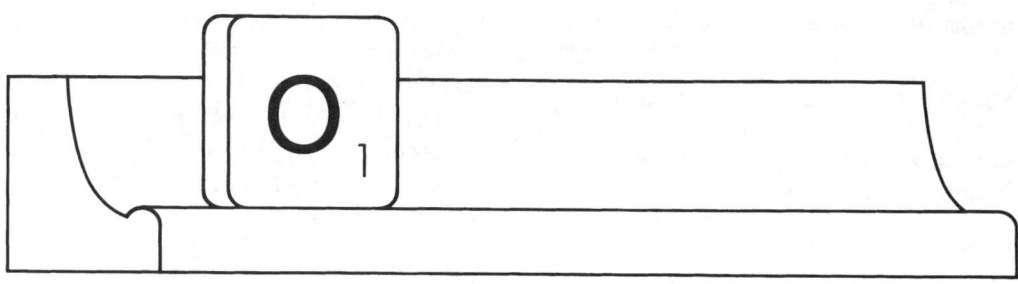

OAF	*n* pl. **OAFS** or **OAVES** a clumsy, stupid person **OAFISH** *adj* **OAFISHLY** *adv*
OAK	*n* pl. **-S** a hardwood tree or shrub **OAKEN, OAKLIKE** *adj*
OAKED	*adj* matured in an oak container
OAKINESS	*n* pl. **-ES** the quality or state of being oaky
OAKMOSS	*n* pl. **-ES** a lichen that grows on oak trees
OAKUM	*n* pl. **-S** loosely twisted hemp fiber
OAKY	*adj* **OAKIER, OAKIEST** tasting of oak sap
OAR	*v* **-ED, -ING, -S** to propel with oars (long, broad-bladed poles)
OARFISH	*n* pl. **-ES** a marine fish
OARLESS	*adj* having no oars
OARLIKE	*adj* resembling an oar
OARLOCK	*n* pl. **-S** a device for holding an oar in place
OARSMAN	*n* pl. **-MEN** a person who rows a boat
OASIS	*n* pl. **OASES** a green area in a desert region
OAST	*n* pl. **-S** a type of kiln
OAT	*n* pl. **-S** a cereal grass
OATCAKE	*n* pl. **-S** a cake made of oatmeal
OATEN	*adj* pertaining to oats
OATER	*n* pl. **-S** a cowboy movie
OATH	*n* pl. **-S** a formal declaration or promise to fulfill a pledge
OATLIKE	*adj* resembling oats
OATMEAL	*n* pl. **-S** meal made from oats
OATY	*adj* **OATIER, OATIEST** tasting or smelling of oats
OAVES	a pl. of oaf
OBA	*n* pl. **-S** a hereditary chief in Benin and Nigeria
OBCONIC	*adj* conical with the apex below
OBDURACY	*n* pl. **-CIES** the quality or an instance of being obdurate
OBDURATE	*adj* stubborn
OBE	*n* pl. **-S** obeah
OBEAH	*n* pl. **-S** a form of sorcery of African origin
OBEAHISM	*n* pl. **-S** the use of obeah
OBEDIENT	*adj* obeying or willing to obey
OBEISANT	*adj* showing reverence or respect
OBELI	pl. of obelus
OBELIA	*n* pl. **-S** a marine hydroid
OBELISE	*v* **-LISED, -LISING, -LISES** to obelize
OBELISK	*n* pl. **-S** a four-sided shaft of stone with a pyramidal top
OBELISM	*n* pl. **-S** the act of obelizing
OBELIZE	*v* **-LIZED, -LIZING, -LIZES** to mark with an obelus
OBELUS	*n* pl. **-LI** a symbol used in ancient manuscripts to indicate a doubtful passage
OBENTO	*n* pl. **-TOS** a Japanese meal packed in a box
OBESE	*adj* very fat **OBESELY** *adv*
OBESITY	*n* pl. **-TIES** the state or condition of being obese
OBEY	*v* **-ED, -ING, -S** to follow the commands or guidance of **OBEYABLE** *adj*
OBEYER	*n* pl. **-S** one that obeys
OBI	*n* pl. **-S** obeah
OBIA	*n* pl. **-S** obeah
OBIISM	*n* pl. **-S** obeahism
OBIT	*n* pl. **-S** an obituary
OBITUARY	*n* pl. **-ARIES** a published notice of a death
OBJECT	*v* **-ED, -ING, -S** to argue in opposition
OBJECTOR	*n* pl. **-S** one that objects

OBJET	*n* pl. **-S** an article of artistic value
OBLAST	*n* pl. **-LASTS** or **-LASTI** an administrative division of Russia
OBLATE	*n* pl. **-S** a layman residing in a monastery
OBLATELY	*adv* elliptically
OBLATION	*n* pl. **-S** the act of making a religious offering **OBLATORY** *adj*
OBLIGATE	*v* **-GATED, -GATING, -GATES** to oblige
OBLIGATO	*n* pl. **-TOS** or **-TI** an important musical part
OBLIGE	*v* **OBLIGED, OBLIGING, OBLIGES** to put in one's debt by a favor or service
OBLIGEE	*n* pl. **-S** one that is obliged
OBLIGER	*n* pl. **-S** one that obliges
OBLIGING	present participle of oblige
OBLIGOR	*n* pl. **-S** one who is bound by a legal obligation
OBLIQUE	*v* **OBLIQUED, OBLIQUING, OBLIQUES** to slant
OBLIVION	*n* pl. **-S** the state of being forgotten; the act of forgetting
OBLONG	*n* pl. **-S** something that is oblong (elongated)
OBLONGLY	*adv* in an oblong manner
OBLOQUY	*n* pl. **-QUIES** abusive language
OBOE	*n* pl. **-S** a woodwind instrument
OBOIST	*n* pl. **-S** one who plays the oboe
OBOL	*n* pl. **-S** a coin of ancient Greece
OBOLE	*n* pl. **-S** a coin of medieval France
OBOLUS	*n* pl. **-LI** an obol
OBOVATE	*adj* ovate with the narrow end at the base
OBOVOID	*adj* ovoid with the narrow end at the base
OBSCENE	*adj* **-SCENER, -SCENEST** indecent
OBSCURE	*adj* **-SCURER, -SCUREST** dark or indistinct
OBSCURE	*v* **-SCURED, -SCURING, -SCURES** to make obscure
OBSEQUY	*n* pl. **-QUIES** a funeral rite
OBSERVE	*v* **-SERVED, -SERVING, -SERVES** to look attentively
OBSERVER	*n* pl. **-S** one that observes
OBSESS	*v* **-ED, -ING, -ES** to dominate the thoughts of
OBSESSOR	*n* pl. **-S** something that obsesses

OBSIDIAN	*n* pl. **-S** a volcanic glass
OBSOLETE	*v* **-LETED, -LETING, -LETES** to make out-of-date
OBSTACLE	*n* pl. **-S** something that obstructs
OBSTRUCT	*v* **-ED, -ING, -S** to get in the way of
OBTAIN	*v* **-ED, -ING, -S** to gain possession of
OBTAINER	*n* pl. **-S** one that obtains
OBTECT	*adj* covered by a hardened secretion
OBTECTED	*adj* obtect
OBTEST	*v* **-ED, -ING, -S** to beseech
OBTRUDE	*v* **-TRUDED, -TRUDING, -TRUDES** to thrust forward
OBTRUDER	*n* pl. **-S** one that obtrudes
OBTUND	*v* **-ED, -ING, -S** to deaden
OBTURATE	*v* **-RATED, -RATING, -RATES** to close or stop up
OBTUSE	*adj* **-TUSER, -TUSEST** dull **OBTUSELY** *adv*
OBTUSITY	*n* pl. **-TIES** the state of being obtuse
OBVERSE	*n* pl. **-S** the side of a coin bearing the main design
OBVERT	*v* **-ED, -ING, -S** to turn so as to show a different surface
OBVIATE	*v* **-ATED, -ATING, -ATES** to prevent or eliminate by effective measures **OBVIABLE** *adj*
OBVIATOR	*n* pl. **-S** one that obviates
OBVIOUS	*adj* easily perceived or understood
OBVOLUTE	*adj* rolled or turned in
OCA	*n* pl. **-S** a South American herb
OCARINA	*n* pl. **-S** a wind instrument
OCCASION	*v* **-ED, -ING, -S** to cause
OCCIDENT	*n* pl. **-S** the west
OCCIPUT	*n* pl. **-PUTS** or **-PITA** the back part of the skull
OCCLUDE	*v* **-CLUDED, -CLUDING, -CLUDES** to close or stop up
OCCLUSAL	*adj* pertaining to the biting surface of a tooth
OCCULT	*v* **-ED, -ING, -S** to conceal
OCCULTER	*n* pl. **-S** one that occults
OCCULTLY	*adv* secretly
OCCUPANT	*n* pl. **-S** a resident
OCCUPIER	*n* pl. **-S** one that occupies
OCCUPY	*v* **-PIED, -PYING, -PIES** to engage the attention or energies of

OCCUR	*v* **-CURRED, -CURRING, -CURS** to take place
OCEAN	*n* pl. **-S** the vast body of salt water that covers most of the earth's surface **OCEANIC** *adj*
OCEANAUT	*n* pl. **-S** an aquanaut
OCELLAR	*adj* pertaining to an ocellus
OCELLATE	*adj* having ocelli
OCELLUS	*n* pl. **-LI** a minute simple eye
OCELOT	*n* pl. **-S** an American wildcat **OCELOID** *adj*
OCH	*interj* — used to express surprise or regret
OCHE	*n* pl. **-S** a line behind which players stand when throwing darts
OCHER	*v* **-ED, -ING, -S** to color with ocher (a red or yellow iron ore used as a pigment)
OCHERISH	*adj* resembling ocher
OCHEROID	*adj* ocherous
OCHEROUS	*adj* containing or resembling ocher
OCHERY	*adj* ocherous
OCHONE	*interj* — used to express grief
OCHRE	*v* **OCHRED, OCHRING, OCHRES** to ocher
OCHREA	*n* pl. **-REAE** or **-REAS** ocrea
OCHREOUS	*adj* ocherous
OCHRING	present participle of ochre
OCHROID	*adj* ocherous
OCHROUS	*adj* ocherous
OCHRY	*adj* ochery
OCICAT	*n* pl. **-S** a domestic cat having a short spotted coat
OCKER	*n* pl. **-S** a boorish person
OCOTILLO	*n* pl. **-LOS** a Mexican shrub
OCREA	*n* pl. **-REAE** or **-REAS** a sheathing plant part
OCREATE	*adj* having ocreae
OCTAD	*n* pl. **-S** a group of eight **OCTADIC** *adj*
OCTAGON	*n* pl. **-S** an eight-sided polygon
OCTAL	*adj* pertaining to a number system with a base of eight
OCTAN	*n* pl. **-S** a fever recurring every eighth day
OCTANE	*n* pl. **-S** a liquid hydrocarbon
OCTANGLE	*n* pl. **-S** an octagon
OCTANOL	*n* pl. **-S** an alcohol
OCTANT	*n* pl. **-S** an eighth of a circle **OCTANTAL** *adj*
OCTARCHY	*n* pl. **-TARCHIES** a government by eight persons
OCTAVE	*n* pl. **-S** a type of musical interval **OCTAVAL** *adj*
OCTAVO	*n* pl. **-VOS** a page size
OCTET	*n* pl. **-S** a group of eight
OCTETTE	*n* pl. **-S** octet
OCTONARY	*n* pl. **-NARIES** a stanza of eight lines
OCTOPOD	*n* pl. **-S** any of an order of eight-armed mollusks
OCTOPOID	*adj* resembling an octopus
OCTOPUS	*n* pl. **-PUSES** or **-PI** or **-PODES** a nocturnal octopod
OCTOROON	*n* pl. **-S** a person of one-eighth black ancestry
OCTROI	*n* pl. **-S** a tax on certain articles brought into a city
OCTUPLE	*v* **-PLED, -PLING, -PLES** to multiply by eight
OCTUPLET	*n* pl. **-S** a group of eight related items
OCTUPLEX	*adj* being eight times as great
OCTUPLING	present participle of octuple
OCTUPLY	*adv* to eight times the degree
OCTYL	*n* pl. **-S** a univalent radical
OCULAR	*n* pl. **-S** an eyepiece
OCULARLY	*adv* by means of the eyes or sight
OCULIST	*n* pl. **-S** a physician who treats diseases of the eye
OCULUS	*n* pl. **-LI** a circular window
OD	*n* pl. **-S** a hypothetical force of natural power
ODA	*n* pl. **-S** a room in a harem
ODAH	*n* pl. **-S** oda
ODALISK	*n* pl. **-S** a female slave in a harem
ODD	*adj* **ODDER, ODDEST** unusual
ODD	*n* pl. **-S** one that is odd
ODDBALL	*n* pl. **-S** an eccentric person
ODDISH	*adj* somewhat odd
ODDITY	*n* pl. **-TIES** one that is odd
ODDLY	*adv* in an odd manner
ODDMENT	*n* pl. **-S** a remnant
ODDNESS	*n* pl. **-ES** the state of being odd
ODE	*n* pl. **-S** a lyric poem
ODEON	*n* pl. **-S** odeum

ODEUM   *n* pl. **ODEUMS** or **ODEA** a theater or concert hall

ODIC   *adj* pertaining to an ode

ODIOUS   *adj* deserving or causing hatred **ODIOUSLY** *adv*

ODIST   *n* pl. **-S** one who writes odes

ODIUM   *n* pl. **-S** hatred

ODOGRAPH   *n* pl. **-S** an odometer

ODOMETER   *n* pl. **-S** a device for measuring distance traveled

ODOMETRY   *n* pl. **-TRIES** the process of using an odometer

ODONATA   *n/pl* insects of an order of predacious insects

ODONATE   *n* pl. **-S** any of an order of predacious insects

ODONTOID   *n* pl. **-S** a toothlike vertebral projection

ODOR   *n* pl. **-S** the property of a substance that affects the sense of smell **ODORED, ODORFUL** *adj*

ODORANT   *n* pl. **-S** an odorous substance

ODORIZE   *v* **-IZED, -IZING, -IZES** to make odorous

ODORIZER   *n* pl. **-S** one that odorizes

ODORLESS   *adj* having no odor

ODOROUS   *adj* having an odor

ODOUR   *n* pl. **-S** odor **ODOURFUL** *adj*

ODYL   *n* pl. **-S** an od

ODYLE   *n* pl. **-S** odyl

ODYSSEY   *n* pl. **-SEYS** a long, wandering journey **ODYSSEAN** *adj*

OE   *n* pl. **-S** a whirlwind off the Faeroe islands

OECOLOGY   *n* pl. **-GIES** ecology

OEDEMA   *n* pl. **-MAS** or **-MATA** edema

OEDIPAL   *adj* pertaining to the libidinal feelings in a child toward the parent of the opposite sex

OEDIPEAN   *adj* oedipal

OEILLADE   *n* pl. **-S** an amorous look

OENOLOGY   *n* pl. **-GIES** the study of wines

OENOMEL   *n* pl. **-S** an ancient Greek beverage of wine and honey

OERSTED   *n* pl. **-S** a unit of magnetic intensity

OESTRIN   *n* pl. **-S** estrin

OESTRIOL   *n* pl. **-S** estriol

OESTRONE   *n* pl. **-S** estrone

OESTROUS   *adj* estrous

OESTRUAL   *adj* estrual

OESTRUM   *n* pl. **-S** estrum

OESTRUS   *n* pl. **-ES** estrus

OEUVRE   *n* pl. **-S** a work of art

OF   *prep* coming from

OFF   *v* **-ED, -ING, -S** to go away

OFFAL   *n* pl. **-S** waste material

OFFBEAT   *n* pl. **-S** an unaccented beat in a musical measure

OFFCAST   *n* pl. **-S** a castoff

OFFCUT   *n* pl. **-S** something that is cut off

OFFENCE   *n* pl. **-S** offense

OFFEND   *v* **-ED, -ING, -S** to commit an offense

OFFENDER   *n* pl. **-S** one that offends

OFFENSE   *n* pl. **-S** a violation of a moral or social code

OFFER   *v* **-ED, -ING, -S** to present for acceptance or rejection

OFFEREE   *n* pl. **-S** one to whom an offer is made

OFFERER   *n* pl. **-S** one that offers

OFFERING   *n* pl. **-S** a contribution

OFFEROR   *n* pl. **-S** offerer

OFFHAND   *adv* without preparation

OFFICE   *n* pl. **-S** a position of authority

OFFICER   *v* **-ED, -ING, -S** to furnish with officers (persons holding positions of authority)

OFFICIAL   *n* pl. **-S** one that holds a position of authority

OFFING   *n* pl. **-S** the near future

OFFISH   *adj* aloof **OFFISHLY** *adv*

OFFKEY   *adj* pitched higher or lower than the correct musical tone

OFFLINE   *adj* not connected to a computer network

OFFLOAD   *v* **-ED, -ING, -S** to unload

OFFPRINT   *v* **-ED, -ING, -S** to reprint an excerpt

OFFRAMP   *n* pl. **-S** a road leading off an expressway

OFFSET   *v* **-SET, -SETTING, -SETS** to compensate for

OFFSHOOT   *n* pl. **-S** a lateral shoot from a main stem

OFFSHORE   *n* pl. **-S** an area of submerged land out from the shore

OFFSIDE   *n* pl. **-S** an improper football play

OFFSTAGE	*n* pl. **-S** a part of a stage not visible to the audience	**OILCUP**	*n* pl. **-S** a closed cup for supplying lubricant
OFFTRACK	*adj* away from a racetrack	**OILER**	*n* pl. **-S** one that oils
OFT	*adv* **OFTER, OFTEST** often	**OILFIELD**	*n* pl. **-S** an area that yields petroleum
OFTEN	*adv* **-ENER, -ENEST** frequently	**OILHOLE**	*n* pl. **-S** a hole through which lubricating oil is injected
OFTTIMES	*adv* often		
OGAM	*n* pl. **-S** ogham	**OILIER**	comparative of oily
OGDOAD	*n* pl. **-S** a group of eight	**OILIEST**	superlative of oily
OGEE	*n* pl. **-S** an S-shaped molding **OGEED** *adj*	**OILILY**	*adv* in an oily manner
OGHAM	*n* pl. **-S** an Old Irish alphabet **OGHAMIC** *adj*	**OILINESS**	*n* pl. **-ES** the state of being oily
		OILMAN	*n* pl. **-MEN** one who owns or operates oil wells
OGHAMIST	*n* pl. **-S** one who writes in ogham		
OGIVE	*n* pl. **-S** a pointed arch **OGIVAL** *adj*	**OILPAPER**	*n* pl. **-S** a water-resistant paper
OGLE	*v* **OGLED, OGLING, OGLES** to stare at	**OILPROOF**	*adj* impervious to oil
		OILSEED	*n* pl. **-S** a seed from which oil is pressed out
OGLER	*n* pl. **-S** one that ogles	**OILSKIN**	*n* pl. **-S** a waterproof fabric
OGRE	*n* pl. **-S** a monster	**OILSTONE**	*n* pl. **-S** a stone for sharpening tools
OGREISH	*adj* resembling an ogre		
OGREISM	*n* pl. **-S** the state of being ogreish	**OILTIGHT**	*adj* being so tight as to prevent the passage of oil
OGRESS	*n* pl. **-ES** a female ogre	**OILWAY**	*n* pl. **-WAYS** a channel for the passage of oil
OGRISH	*adj* ogreish **OGRISHLY** *adv*		
OGRISM	*n* pl. **-S** ogreism	**OILY**	*adj* **OILIER, OILIEST** covered or soaked with oil
OH	*v* **-ED, -ING, -S** to exclaim in surprise, pain, or desire	**OINK**	*v* **-ED, -ING, -S** to utter the natural grunt of a hog
OHIA	*n* pl. **-S** lehua		
OHM	*n* pl. **-S** a unit of electrical resistance **OHMIC** *adj*	**OINOLOGY**	*n* pl. **-GIES** oenology
		OINOMEL	*n* pl. **-S** oenomel
OHMAGE	*n* pl. **-S** electrical resistance expressed in ohms	**OINTMENT**	*n* pl. **-S** a viscous preparation applied to the skin as a medicine or cosmetic
OHMMETER	*n* pl. **-S** an instrument for measuring ohmage		
		OITICICA	*n* pl. **-S** a South American tree
OHO	*interj* — used to express surprise or exultation	**OK**	*adj* all right
		OKA	*n* pl. **-S** a Turkish unit of weight
OI	*interj* oy	**OKAPI**	*n* pl. **-S** an African ruminant mammal
OIDIUM	*n* pl. **OIDIA** a type of fungus **OIDIOID** *adj*		
		OKAY	*v* **-ED, -ING, -S** to approve
OIK	*n* pl. **-S** a very rude or stupid person	**OKE**	*n* pl. **-S** oka
		OKEH	*n* pl. **-S** approval
OIL	*v* **-ED, -ING, -S** to supply with oil (a greasy liquid used for lubrication, fuel, or illumination)	**OKEYDOKE**	*adj* perfectly all right
		OKRA	*n* pl. **-S** a tall annual herb
OILBIRD	*n* pl. **-S** a tropical bird	**OLD**	*adj* **OLDER, OLDEST** or **ELDER, ELDEST** living or existing for a relatively long time
OILCAMP	*n* pl. **-S** a living area for workers at an oil well		
OILCAN	*n* pl. **-S** a can for applying lubricating oil	**OLD**	*n* pl. **-S** an individual of a specified age
OILCLOTH	*n* pl. **-S** a waterproof fabric	**OLDE**	*adj* old

OLDEN	*adj* pertaining to a bygone era
OLDIE	*n* pl. **-S** a popular song of an earlier day
OLDISH	*adj* somewhat old
OLDNESS	*n* pl. **-ES** the state of being old
OLDSQUAW	*n* pl. **-S** a sea duck
OLDSTER	*n* pl. **-S** an old person
OLDSTYLE	*n* pl. **-S** a style of printing type
OLDWIFE	*n* pl. **-WIVES** a marine fish
OLDY	*n* pl. **OLDIES** oldie
OLE	*n* pl. **-S** a shout of approval
OLEA	pl. of oleum
OLEANDER	*n* pl. **-S** a flowering shrub
OLEASTER	*n* pl. **-S** a flowering shrub
OLEATE	*n* pl. **-S** a chemical salt
OLEFIN	*n* pl. **-S** an alkene **OLEFINIC** *adj*
OLEFINE	*n* pl. **-S** olefin
OLEIC	*adj* pertaining to oil
OLEIN	*n* pl. **-S** the liquid portion of a fat
OLEINE	*n* pl. **-S** olein
OLEO	*n* pl. **OLEOS** margarine
OLESTRA	*n* pl. **-S** a noncaloric fat substitute
OLEUM	*n* pl. **-S** a corrosive liquid
OLEUM	*n* pl. **OLEA** oil
OLIBANUM	*n* pl. **-S** a fragrant resin
OLICOOK	*n* pl. **-S** a doughnut
OLIGARCH	*n* pl. **-S** a ruler in a government by the few
OLIGOMER	*n* pl. **-S** a type of polymer
OLIGURIA	*n* pl. **-S** reduced excretion of urine **OLIGURIC** *adj*
OLINGO	*n* pl. **-GOS** a small mammal of Central and South America
OLIO	*n* pl. **OLIOS** a miscellaneous collection
OLIVARY	*adj* shaped like an olive
OLIVE	*n* pl. **-S** the small oval fruit of a Mediterranean tree
OLIVINE	*n* pl. **-S** a mineral **OLIVINIC** *adj*
OLLA	*n* pl. **-S** a wide-mouthed pot or jar
OLLIE	*v* **OLLIED, OLLIEING, OLLIES** to perform a maneuver in skateboarding or snowboarding
OLOGIST	*n* pl. **-S** an expert in a particular ology
OLOGY	*n* pl. **-GIES** a branch of knowledge
OLOROSO	*n* pl. **-SOS** a dark sherry
OLYMPIAD	*n* pl. **-S** a celebration of the Olympic Games
OM	*n* pl. **-S** a mantra used in contemplation of ultimate reality
OMA	*n* pl. **-S** grandmother
OMADHAUN	*n* pl. **-S** a foolish person
OMASUM	*n* pl. **-SA** the third stomach of a ruminant
OMBER	*n* pl. **-S** ombre
OMBRE	*n* pl. **-S** a card game
OMEGA	*n* pl. **-S** a Greek letter
OMELET	*n* pl. **-S** a dish of beaten eggs cooked and folded around a filling
OMELETTE	*n* pl. **-S** omelet
OMEN	*v* **-ED, -ING, -S** to be an omen (a prophetic sign) of
OMENTUM	*n* pl. **-TUMS** or **-TA** a fold in an abdominal membrane **OMENTAL** *adj*
OMER	*n* pl. **-S** a Hebrew unit of dry measure
OMERTA	*n* pl. **-S** a code of silence about criminal activity
OMICRON	*n* pl. **-S** a Greek letter
OMIKRON	*n* pl. **-S** omicron
OMINOUS	*adj* portending evil
OMISSION	*n* pl. **-S** something left undone
OMISSIVE	*adj* marked by omission
OMIT	*v* **OMITTED, OMITTING, OMITS** to leave out
OMITTER	*n* pl. **-S** one that omits
OMNIARCH	*n* pl. **-S** an almighty ruler
OMNIBUS	*n* pl. **-BUSES** or **-BUSSES** a bus
OMNIFIC	*adj* unlimited in creative power
OMNIFORM	*adj* of all forms
OMNIMODE	*adj* of all modes
OMNIVORA	*n/pl* omnivores
OMNIVORE	*n* pl. **-S** an animal that eats all kinds of food
OMOPHAGY	*n* pl. **-GIES** the eating of raw flesh
OMPHALOS	*n* pl. **-LI** or **-LOI** a central point
ON	*n* pl. **-S** the side of the wicket where a batsman stands in cricket
ONAGER	*n* pl. **-GERS** or **-GRI** a wild ass of central Asia
ONANISM	*n* pl. **-S** coitus deliberately interrupted to prevent insemination
ONANIST	*n* pl. **-S** one who practices onanism

ONBOARD *v* **-ED, -ING, -S** to train a new person to do a job

ONCE *adv* one single time

ONCET *adv* once

ONCIDIUM *n* pl. **-S** a tropical orchid

ONCOGENE *n* pl. **-S** a gene that causes a cell to become cancerous

ONCOLOGY *n* pl. **-GIES** the science of tumors

ONCOMING *n* pl. **-S** an approach

ONDOGRAM *n* pl. **-S** a graph of electric wave forms

ONE *n* pl. **-S** a number

ONEFOLD *adj* constituting a single, undivided whole

ONEIRIC *adj* pertaining to dreams

ONENESS *n* pl. **-ES** unity

ONEROUS *adj* burdensome or oppressive

ONERY *adj* **-ERIER, -ERIEST** ornery

ONESELF *pron* a person's self

ONETIME *adj* former

ONGOING *adj* continuing without interruption

ONION *n* pl. **-S** the edible bulb of a cultivated herb **ONIONY** *adj*

ONIUM *adj* characterized by a complex cation

ONLAY *n* pl. **-S** something laid over something else

ONLIEST *adj* only

ONLINE *adj* connected to a computer network

ONLOAD *v* **-ED, -ING, -S** to load a vehicle or container

ONLOOKER *n* pl. **-S** a spectator

ONLY *adv* with nothing or no one else

ONO *n* pl. **ONOS** a large mackerel

ONOMAST *n* pl. **-S** a person who studies proper names

ONRUSH *n* pl. **-ES** a forward rush or flow

ONSCREEN *adj* shown on a movie, television, or display screen

ONSET *n* pl. **-S** a beginning

ONSHORE *adv* toward the shore

ONSIDE *adj* not offside

ONSTAGE *adj* being on a part of the stage visible to the audience

ONSTREAM *adv* in or into production

ONTIC *adj* having real being or existence

ONTO *prep* to a position upon

ONTOGENY *n* pl. **-NIES** the development of an individual organism

ONTOLOGY *n* pl. **-GIES** the branch of philosophy that deals with being

ONUS *n* pl. **-ES** a burden or responsibility

ONWARD *adv* toward a point ahead or in front

ONWARDS *adv* onward

ONYX *n* pl. **-ES** a variety of quartz

OOCYST *n* pl. **-S** a zygote

OOCYTE *n* pl. **-S** an egg before maturation

OODLES *n* pl. **OODLES** a large amount

OODLINS *n* pl. **OODLINS** oodles

OOF *interj* — used to express discomfort

OOGAMETE *n* pl. **-S** a female gamete of certain protozoa

OOGAMOUS *adj* having structurally dissimilar gametes

OOGAMY *n* pl. **-MIES** the state of being oogamous

OOGENY *n* pl. **-NIES** the development of ova

OOGONIUM *n* pl. **-NIUMS** or **-NIA** a female sexual organ in certain algae and fungi **OOGONIAL** *adj*

OOH *v* **-ED, -ING, -S** to exclaim in amazement, joy, or surprise

OOLACHAN *n* pl. **-S** eulachon

OOLICHAN *n* pl. **-S** eulachon

OOLITE *n* pl. **-S** a variety of limestone **OOLITIC** *adj*

OOLITH *n* pl. **-S** oolite

OOLOGIST *n* pl. **-S** an expert in oology

OOLOGY *n* pl. **-GIES** the study of birds' eggs **OOLOGIC** *adj*

OOLONG *n* pl. **-S** a dark Chinese tea

OOMIAC *n* pl. **-S** umiak

OOMIACK *n* pl. **-S** umiak

OOMIAK *n* pl. **-S** umiak

OOMPAH *v* **-ED, -ING, -S** to play a repeated rhythmic bass accompaniment

OOMPH *n* pl. **-S** spirited vigor

OOPHYTE *n* pl. **-S** a stage of development in certain plants **OOPHYTIC** *adj*

OOPS *interj* — used to express mild apology, surprise, or dismay

OORALI *n* pl. **-S** curare

OORIE *adj* ourie

OOSPERM *n* pl. **-S** a fertilized egg

OOSPHERE   *n* pl. **-S** an unfertilized egg within an oogonium

OOSPORE   *n* pl. **-S** a fertilized egg within an oogonium **OOSPORIC** *adj*

OOT   *n* pl. **-S** out

OOTHECA   *n* pl. **-CAE** an egg case of certain insects **OOTHECAL** *adj*

OOTID   *n* pl. **-S** one of the four sections into which a mature ovum divides

OOZE   *v* **OOZED, OOZING, OOZES** to flow or leak out slowly

OOZINESS   *n* pl. **-ES** the state of being oozy

OOZY   *adj* **OOZIER, OOZIEST** containing or resembling soft mud or slime **OOZILY** *adv*

OP   *n* pl. **-S** a style of abstract art

OPA   *n* pl. **-S** grandfather

OPACIFY   *v* **-FIED, -FYING, -FIES** to make opaque

OPACITY   *n* pl. **-TIES** something that is opaque

OPAH   *n* pl. **-S** a marine fish

OPAL   *n* pl. **-S** a mineral

OPALESCE   *v* **-ESCED, -ESCING, -ESCES** to emit an iridescent shimmer of colors

OPALINE   *n* pl. **-S** an opaque white glass

OPAQUE   *adj* **OPAQUER, OPAQUEST** impervious to light **OPAQUELY** *adv*

OPAQUE   *v* **OPAQUED, OPAQUING, OPAQUES** to make opaque

OPE   *v* **OPED, OPING, OPES** to open

OPEN   *adj* **OPENER, OPENEST** affording unobstructed access, passage, or view

OPEN   *v* **-ED, -ING, -S** to cause to become open **OPENABLE** *adj*

OPENCAST   *adj* worked from a surface open to the air

OPENER   *n* pl. **-S** one that opens

OPENING   *n* pl. **-S** a vacant or unobstructed space

OPENLY   *adv* in an open manner

OPENNESS   *n* pl. **-ES** the state of being open

OPENWORK   *n* pl. **-S** ornamental or structural work containing numerous openings

OPERA   *n* pl. **-S** a form of musical drama

OPERABLE   *adj* usable **OPERABLY** *adv*

OPERAND   *n* pl. **-S** a quantity on which a mathematical operation is performed

OPERANT   *n* pl. **-S** one that operates

OPERATE   *v* **-ATED, -ATING, -ATES** to perform a function

OPERATIC   *n* pl. **-S** the technique of staging operas

OPERATOR   *n* pl. **-S** a symbol that represents a mathematical function

OPERCELE   *n* pl. **-S** opercule

OPERCULA   *n/pl* opercules

OPERCULE   *n* pl. **-S** an anatomical part that serves as a lid or cover

OPERETTA   *n* pl. **-S** a light musical drama with spoken dialogue

OPERON   *n* pl. **-S** a type of gene cluster

OPEROSE   *adj* involving great labor

OPHIDIAN   *n* pl. **-S** a snake

OPHITE   *n* pl. **-S** a green mottled igneous rock **OPHITIC** *adj*

OPIATE   *v* **-ATED, -ATING, -ATES** to treat with opium

OPINE   *v* **OPINED, OPINING, OPINES** to hold or state as an opinion

OPING   present participle of ope

OPINION   *n* pl. **-S** a conclusion or judgment one holds to be true

OPIOID   *n* pl. **-S** a peptide that acts like opium

OPIUM   *n* pl. **-S** an addictive narcotic

OPIUMISM   *n* pl. **-S** opium addiction

OPOPANAX   *n* pl. **-ES** a strong-smelling gum resin

OPOSSUM   *n* pl. **-S** an arboreal mammal

OPPIDAN   *n* pl. **-S** a townsman

OPPILATE   *v* **-LATED, -LATING, -LATES** to obstruct **OPPILANT** *adj*

OPPONENS   *n* pl. **OPPONENS** a muscle of the thumb

OPPONENT   *n* pl. **-S** one that opposes another

OPPOSE   *v* **-POSED, -POSING, -POSES** to be in contention or conflict with

OPPOSER   *n* pl. **-S** one that opposes

OPPOSITE   *n* pl. **-S** one that is radically different from another in some related way

OPPRESS   *v* **-ED, -ING, -ES** to burden by abuse of power or authority

OPPUGN   *v* **-ED, -ING, -S** to assail with argument

OPPUGNER *n* pl. **-S** one that oppugns

OPSIMATH *n* pl. **-S** a person who learns only late in life

OPSIN *n* pl. **-S** a type of protein

OPSONIC *adj* pertaining to opsonin

OPSONIFY *v* **-FIED, -FYING, -FIES** to opsonize

OPSONIN *n* pl. **-S** an antibody of blood serum

OPSONISE *v* **-NISED, -NISING, -NISES** opsonize

OPSONIZE *v* **-NIZED, -NIZING, -NIZES** to form opsonins in

OPT *v* **-ED, -ING, -S** to choose

OPTATIVE *n* pl. **-S** a mood of verbs that expresses a wish or desire

OPTIC *n* pl. **-S** an eye

OPTICAL *adj* pertaining to sight

OPTICIAN *n* pl. **-S** one who makes or deals in optical goods

OPTICIST *n* pl. **-S** one engaged in the study of light and vision

OPTIMA a pl. of optimum

OPTIMAL *adj* most desirable

OPTIME *n* pl. **-S** an honor student in mathematics at Cambridge University

OPTIMISE *v* **-MISED, -MISING, -MISES** to optimize

OPTIMISM *n* pl. **-S** a disposition to look on the favorable side of things

OPTIMIST *n* pl. **-S** one who exhibits optimism

OPTIMIZE *v* **-MIZED, -MIZING, -MIZES** to make as perfect, useful, or effective as possible

OPTIMUM *n* pl. **-MUMS** or **-MA** the most favorable condition for obtaining a given result

OPTION *v* **-ED, -ING, -S** to grant an option (a right to buy or sell something at a specified price within a specified time) on

OPTIONAL *n* pl. **-S** an elective course of study

OPTIONEE *n* pl. **-S** one who holds a legal option

OPTRONIC *adj* pertaining to the science concerned with electronics and light

OPULENCE *n* pl. **-S** wealth

OPULENCY *n* pl. **-CIES** opulence

OPULENT *adj* wealthy

OPUNTIA *n* pl. **-S** an American cactus

OPUS *n* pl. **OPUSES** or **OPERA** a literary or musical work

OPUSCULA *n/pl* opuscules

OPUSCULE *n* pl. **-S** a minor work

OQUASSA *n* pl. **-S** a small lake trout

OR *n* pl. **-S** the heraldic color gold

ORA pl. of os

ORACH *n* pl. **-ES** a cultivated plant

ORACHE *n* pl. **-S** orach

ORACLE *n* pl. **-S** a person through whom a deity is believed to speak **ORACULAR** *adj*

ORACY *n* pl. **-CIES** skill in oral expression and comprehension

ORAD *adv* toward the mouth

ORAL *n* pl. **-S** an examination requiring spoken answers

ORALISM *n* pl. **-S** the use of oral methods of teaching the deaf

ORALIST *n* pl. **-S** an advocate of oralism

ORALITY *n* pl. **-TIES** the state of being produced orally

ORALLY *adv* through the mouth

ORANG *n* pl. **-S** a large ape

ORANGE *n* pl. **-S** a citrus fruit

ORANGERY *n* pl. **-RIES** a place where orange trees are cultivated

ORANGEY *adj* **-ANGIER, -ANGIEST** orangy

ORANGISH *adj* of a somewhat orange color

ORANGY *adj* **-ANGIER, -ANGIEST** resembling or suggestive of an orange

ORATE *v* **ORATED, ORATING, ORATES** to speak formally

ORATION *n* pl. **-S** a formal speech

ORATOR *n* pl. **-S** one that orates

ORATORIO *n* pl. **-RIOS** a type of musical composition

ORATORY *n* pl. **-RIES** the art of public speaking

ORATRESS *n* pl. **-ES** oratrix

ORATRIX *n* pl. **-TRICES** a female orator

ORATURE *n* pl. **-S** oral forms of literature, such as folklore

ORB *v* **-ED, -ING, -S** to form into a circle or sphere

ORBIER comparative of orby

ORBIEST superlative of orby

ORBIT	*v* **-ED, -ING, -S** to move or revolve around
ORBITAL	*n* pl. **-S** a subdivision of a nuclear shell
ORBITER	*n* pl. **-S** one that orbits
ORBLESS	*adj* lacking an orb
ORBY	*adj* **ORBIER, ORBIEST** resembling a circle or sphere
ORC	*n* pl. **-S** a marine mammal
ORCA	*n* pl. **-S** orc
ORCEIN	*n* pl. **-S** a reddish brown dye
ORCHARD	*n* pl. **-S** an area for the cultivation of fruit trees
ORCHID	*n* pl. **-S** a flowering plant
ORCHIL	*n* pl. **-S** a purple dye
ORCHILLA	*n* pl. **-S** orchil
ORCHIS	*n* pl. **-CHISES** an orchid
ORCHITIS	*n* pl. **-TISES** inflammation of the testicle **ORCHITIC** *adj*
ORCIN	*n* pl. **-S** orcinol
ORCINOL	*n* pl. **-S** a chemical compound
ORDAIN	*v* **-ED, -ING, -S** to invest with holy authority
ORDAINER	*n* pl. **-S** one that ordains
ORDEAL	*n* pl. **-S** a severely difficult or painful experience
ORDER	*v* **-ED, -ING, -S** to give a command or instruction to
ORDERER	*n* pl. **-S** one that orders
ORDERLY	*n* pl. **-LIES** a male attendant
ORDINAL	*n* pl. **-S** a number designating position in a series
ORDINAND	*n* pl. **-S** a person about to be ordained
ORDINARY	*adj* **-NARIER, -NARIEST** of a kind to be expected in the normal order of events
ORDINARY	*n* pl. **-NARIES** something that is ordinary
ORDINATE	*n* pl. **-S** a particular geometric coordinate
ORDNANCE	*n* pl. **-S** artillery; a cannon
ORDO	*n* pl. **-DOS** or **-DINES** a calendar of religious directions
ORDURE	*n* pl. **-S** manure **ORDUROUS** *adj*
ORE	*n* pl. **-S** a mineral or rock containing a valuable metal
OREAD	*n* pl. **-S** a mountain nymph in Greek mythology
OREBODY	*n* pl. **-BODIES** a mass of ore in a mine
ORECTIC	*adj* pertaining to appetites or desires
ORECTIVE	*adj* orectic
OREGANO	*n* pl. **-NOS** an aromatic herb used as a seasoning
OREIDE	*n* pl. **-S** oroide
OREODONT	*n* pl. **-S** an extinct sheep-sized mammal
ORFRAY	*n* pl. **-FRAYS** orphrey
ORG	*n* pl. **-S** an organization
ORGAN	*n* pl. **-S** a differentiated part of an organism performing a specific function
ORGANA	a pl. of organon and organum
ORGANDIE	*n* pl. **-S** organdy
ORGANDY	*n* pl. **-DIES** a cotton fabric
ORGANIC	*n* pl. **-S** a substance of animal or vegetable origin
ORGANISE	*v* **-NISED, -NISING, -NISES** to organize
ORGANISM	*n* pl. **-S** any form of animal or plant life
ORGANIST	*n* pl. **-S** one who plays the organ (a keyboard musical instrument)
ORGANIZE	*v* **-NIZED, -NIZING, -NIZES** to form into an orderly whole
ORGANON	*n* pl. **-GANONS** or **-GANA** a system of rules for scientific investigation
ORGANUM	*n* pl. **-GANUMS** or **-GANA** organon
ORGANZA	*n* pl. **-S** a sheer fabric
ORGASM	*v* **-ED, -ING, -S** to experience an orgasm (the climax of sexual excitement) **ORGASMIC, ORGASTIC** *adj*
ORGEAT	*n* pl. **-S** an almond-flavored syrup
ORGIAC	*adj* of the nature of an orgy
ORGIAST	*n* pl. **-S** one who participates in an orgy
ORGIC	*adj* orgiac
ORGONE	*n* pl. **-S** a postulated energy pervading the universe
ORGULOUS	*adj* proud
ORGY	*n* pl. **-GIES** a party marked by unrestrained sexual indulgence
ORIBATID	*n* pl. **-S** any of a family of eyeless mites
ORIBI	*n* pl. **-S** an African antelope
ORICHALC	*n* pl. **-S** a yellow metal

ORIEL *n* pl. **-S** a type of projecting window

ORIENT *v* **-ED, -ING, -S** to adjust in relation to something else

ORIENTAL *n* pl. **-S** an inhabitant of an eastern country

ORIENTER *n* pl. **-S** one who helps another to adjust to surroundings

ORIFICE *n* pl. **-S** a mouth or mouthlike opening

ORIGAMI *n* pl. **-S** the Japanese art of paper folding

ORIGAN *n* pl. **-S** marjoram

ORIGANUM *n* pl. **-S** an aromatic herb

ORIGIN *n* pl. **-S** a coming into being

ORIGINAL *n* pl. **-S** the first form of something

ORINASAL *n* pl. **-S** a sound pronounced through both the mouth and nose

ORIOLE *n* pl. **-S** an American songbird

ORISHA *n* pl. **-S** a Yoruba deity

ORISON *n* pl. **-S** a prayer

ORLE *n* pl. **-S** a heraldic border

ORLOP *n* pl. **-S** the lowest deck of a ship

ORMER *n* pl. **-S** an abalone

ORMOLU *n* pl. **-S** an alloy used to imitate gold

ORNAMENT *v* **-ED, -ING, -S** to decorate

ORNATE *adj* elaborately or excessively ornamented **ORNATELY** *adv*

ORNERY *adj* **-NERIER, -NERIEST** stubborn and mean-spirited

ORNIS *n* pl. **ORNITHES** avifauna

ORNITHIC *adj* pertaining to birds

OROGEN *n* pl. **-S** a belt of the earth's crust involved in orogeny

OROGENY *n* pl. **-NIES** the process of mountain formation **OROGENIC** *adj*

OROIDE *n* pl. **-S** an alloy used to imitate gold

OROLOGY *n* pl. **-GIES** the study of mountains

OROMETER *n* pl. **-S** a type of barometer

OROTUND *adj* full and clear in sound

ORPHAN *v* **-ED, -ING, -S** to deprive of both parents

ORPHIC *adj* mystical

ORPHICAL *adj* orphic

ORPHISM *n* pl. **-S** a style of art

ORPHREY *n* pl. **-PHREYS** an ornamental band or border

ORPIMENT *n* pl. **-S** a yellow dye

ORPIN *n* pl. **-S** orpine

ORPINE *n* pl. **-S** a perennial herb

ORRA *adj* occasional

ORRERY *n* pl. **-RERIES** a mechanical model of the solar system

ORRICE *n* pl. **-S** orris

ORRIS *n* pl. **-RISES** a flowering plant

ORT *n* pl. **-S** a scrap of food

ORTHICON *n* pl. **-S** a type of television camera tube

ORTHO *adj* pertaining to reproduction in a photograph of the full range of colors in nature

ORTHODOX *n* pl. **-ES** one holding traditional beliefs

ORTHOEPY *n* pl. **-EPIES** the study of correct pronunciation

ORTHOSIS *n* pl. **-THOSES** an orthotic

ORTHOTIC *n* pl. **-S** a brace for weak joints or muscles

ORTOLAN *n* pl. **-S** a European bird

ORYX *n* pl. **-ES** an African antelope

ORZO *n* pl. **-ZOS** rice-shaped pasta

OS *n* pl. **ORA** an orifice

OS *n* pl. **OSAR** an esker

OS *n* pl. **OSSA** a bone

OSCAR *n* pl. **-S** a South American fish

OSCINE *n* pl. **-S** any of a family of songbirds **OSCININE** *adj*

OSCITANT *adj* yawning

OSCULA pl. of osculum

OSCULANT *adj* adhering closely

OSCULAR *adj* pertaining to the mouth

OSCULATE *v* **-LATED, -LATING, -LATES** to kiss

OSCULE *n* pl. **-S** osculum

OSCULUM *n* pl. **-LA** an opening in a sponge

OSE *n* pl. **-S** an esker

OSETRA *n* pl. **-S** a golden or brownish caviar

OSIER *n* pl. **-S** a European tree **OSIERED** *adj*

OSMATIC *adj* depending mainly on the sense of smell

OSMICS *n/pl* the study of the sense of smell

OSMIUM *n* pl. **-S** a metallic element **OSMIC, OSMIOUS** *adj*

OSMOL *n* pl. **-S** a unit of osmotic pressure **OSMOLAL** *adj*

OSMOLAR *adj* osmotic

OSMOLE *n* pl. **-S** osmol

OSMOSE *v* **-MOSED, -MOSING, -MOSES** to undergo osmosis

OSMOSIS *n* pl. **-MOSES** a form of diffusion of a fluid through a membrane

OSMOTIC *adj* pertaining to osmosis

OSMOUS *adj* containing osmium

OSMUND *n* pl. **-S** any of a genus of large ferns

OSMUNDA *n* pl. **-S** osmund

OSNABURG *n* pl. **-S** a cotton fabric

OSPREY *n* pl. **-PREYS** an American hawk

OSSA pl. of os

OSSATURE *n* pl. **-S** a framework

OSSEIN *n* pl. **-S** a protein substance in bone

OSSEOUS *adj* resembling bone

OSSETRA *n* pl. **-S** osetra

OSSIA *conj* or else — used as a musical direction

OSSICLE *n* pl. **-S** a small bone

OSSIFIC *adj* pertaining to the formation of bone

OSSIFIER *n* pl. **-S** one that ossifies

OSSIFY *v* **-FIED, -FYING, -FIES** to convert into bone

OSSOBUCO *n* pl. **-COS** a dish of veal shanks braised with vegetables and white wine

OSSUARY *n* pl. **-ARIES** a receptacle for the bones of the dead

OSTEAL *adj* osseous

OSTEITIS *n* pl. **-ITIDES** inflammation of bone **OSTEITIC** *adj*

OSTEOID *n* pl. **-S** uncalcified bone matrix

OSTEOMA *n* pl. **-MAS** or **-MATA** a tumor of bone tissue

OSTEOSIS *n* pl. **-OSISES** or **-OSES** the formation of bone

OSTIA pl. of ostium

OSTIARY *n* pl. **-ARIES** a doorkeeper at a church

OSTINATO *n* pl. **-TOS** or **-TI** a constantly recurring musical phrase

OSTIOLE *n* pl. **-S** a small bodily opening **OSTIOLAR** *adj*

OSTIUM *n* pl. **OSTIA** an opening in a bodily organ

OSTLER *n* pl. **-S** hostler

OSTMARK *n* pl. **-S** a former East German monetary unit

OSTOMATE *n* pl. **-S** one who has had an ostomy

OSTOMY *n* pl. **-MIES** a type of surgical operation

OSTOSIS *n* pl. **-TOSISES** or **-TOSES** the formation of bone

OSTRACOD *n* pl. **-S** a minute freshwater crustacean

OSTRACON *n* pl. **-CA** a fragment containing an inscription

OSTRAKON *n* pl. **-KA** ostracon

OSTRICH *n* pl. **-ES** a large, flightless bird

OTAKU *n/pl* young people in Japan who are highly skilled in computer technology

OTALGIA *n* pl. **-S** pain in the ear **OTALGIC** *adj*

OTALGY *n* pl. **-GIES** otalgia

OTHER *v* **-ED, -ING, -S** to treat a person as being very different from oneself

OTIC *adj* pertaining to the ear

OTIOSE *adj* lazy **OTIOSELY** *adv*

OTIOSITY *n* pl. **-TIES** the state of being otiose

OTITIS *n* pl. **OTITISES** or **OTITIDES** inflammation of the ear **OTITIC** *adj*

OTOCYST *n* pl. **-S** an organ of balance in many invertebrates

OTOLITH *n* pl. **-S** a hard mass that forms in the inner ear

OTOLOGY *n* pl. **-GIES** the science of the ear **OTOLOGIC** *adj*

OTOSCOPE *n* pl. **-S** an instrument for examining the ear

OTOSCOPY *n* pl. **-PIES** the use of an otoscope

OTOTOXIC *adj* adversely affecting hearing or balance

OTTAR *n* pl. **-S** attar

OTTAVA *n* pl. **-S** an octave

OTTER *n* pl. **-S** a carnivorous mammal

OTTO *n* pl. **-TOS** attar

OTTOMAN *n* pl. **-S** a type of sofa

OUABAIN *n* pl. **-S** a cardiac stimulant

OUCH   *v* **-ED, -ING, -ES** to ornament with ouches (settings for precious stones)

OUD   *n* pl. **-S** a stringed instrument of northern Africa

OUGHT   *v* **-ED, -ING, -S** to owe

OUGIYA   *n* pl. **-S** ouguiya

OUGUIYA   *n* pl. **-S** a monetary unit of Mauritania

OUISTITI   *n* pl. **-S** a South American monkey

OUNCE   *n* pl. **-S** a unit of weight

OUPH   *n* pl. **-S** ouphe

OUPHE   *n* pl. **-S** an elf

OUR   *pron* a possessive form of the pronoun we

OURANG   *n* pl. **-S** orang

OURARI   *n* pl. **-S** curare

OUREBI   *n* pl. **-S** oribi

OURIE   *adj* shivering with cold

OURS   *pron* a possessive form of the pronoun we

OURSELF   *pron* myself — used in formal or regal contexts

OUSEL   *n* pl. **-S** ouzel

OUST   *v* **-ED, -ING, -S** to expel or remove from a position or place

OUSTER   *n* pl. **-S** the act of ousting

OUT   *v* **-ED, -ING, -S** to be revealed

OUTACT   *v* **-ED, -ING, -S** to surpass in acting

OUTADD   *v* **-ED, -ING, -S** to surpass in adding

OUTAGE   *n* pl. **-S** a failure or interruption in use or functioning

OUTARGUE   *v* **-GUED, -GUING, -GUES** to get the better of by arguing

OUTASK   *v* **-ED, -ING, -S** to surpass in asking

OUTATE   past tense of outeat

OUTBACK   *n* pl. **-S** isolated rural country

OUTBAKE   *v* **-BAKED, -BAKING, -BAKES** to surpass in baking

OUTBARK   *v* **-ED, -ING, -S** to surpass in barking

OUTBAWL   *v* **-ED, -ING, -S** to surpass in bawling

OUTBEAM   *v* **-ED, -ING, -S** to surpass in beaming

OUTBEG   *v* **-BEGGED, -BEGGING, -BEGS** to surpass in begging

OUTBID   *v* **-BID, -BIDDEN, -BIDDING, -BIDS** to bid higher than

OUTBITCH   *v* **-ED, -ING, -ES** to surpass in bitching

OUTBLAZE   *v* **-BLAZED, -BLAZING, -BLAZES** to surpass in brilliance of light

OUTBLEAT   *v* **-ED, -ING, -S** to surpass in bleating

OUTBLESS   *v* **-ED, -ING, -ES** to surpass in blessing

OUTBLOOM   *v* **-ED, -ING, -S** to surpass in blooming

OUTBLUFF   *v* **-ED, -ING, -S** to surpass in bluffing

OUTBLUSH   *v* **-ED, -ING, -ES** to surpass in blushing

OUTBOARD   *n* pl. **-S** a type of motor

OUTBOAST   *v* **-ED, -ING, -S** to surpass in boasting

OUTBOUGHT   past tense of outbuy

OUTBOUND   *adj* outward bound

OUTBOX   *v* **-ED, -ING, -ES** to surpass in boxing

OUTBRAG   *v* **-BRAGGED, -BRAGGING, -BRAGS** to surpass in bragging

OUTBRAVE   *v* **-BRAVED, -BRAVING, -BRAVES** to surpass in courage

OUTBRAWL   *v* **-ED, -ING, -S** to surpass in brawling

OUTBREAK   *n* pl. **-S** a sudden eruption

OUTBREED   *v* **-BRED, -BREEDING, -BREEDS** to interbreed relatively unrelated stocks

OUTBRIBE   *v* **-BRIBED, -BRIBING, -BRIBES** to surpass in bribing

OUTBUILD   *v* **-BUILT, -BUILDING, -BUILDS** to surpass in building

OUTBULGE   *v* **-BULGED, -BULGING, -BULGES** to surpass in size

OUTBULK   *v* **-ED, -ING, -S** to surpass in bulking

OUTBULLY   *v* **-LIED, -LYING, -LIES** to surpass in bullying

OUTBURN   *v* **-BURNED** or **-BURNT, -BURNING, -BURNS** to burn longer than

OUTBURST   *n* pl. **-S** a sudden and violent outpouring

OUTBUY   *v* **-BOUGHT, -BUYING, -BUYS** to surpass in buying

OUTBY   *adv* outdoors

OUTBYE   *adv* outby

OUTCALL   *n* pl. **-S** a house call by a professional person

OUTCAPER   *v* **-ED, -ING, -S** to surpass in capering

OUTCAST   *n* pl. **-S** one that is cast out

OUTCASTE   *v* **-CASTED, -CASTEING, -CASTES** to expel from one's caste

OUTCATCH   *v* **-CAUGHT, -CATCHING, -CATCHES** to surpass in catching

OUTCAVIL   *v* **-ILED, -ILING, -ILS** or **-ILLED, -ILLING, -ILS** to surpass in caviling

OUTCHARM   *v* **-ED, -ING, -S** to surpass in charming

OUTCHEAT   *v* **-ED, -ING, -S** to surpass in cheating

OUTCHIDE   *v* **-CHIDED** or **-CHID, -CHIDDEN, -CHIDING, -CHIDES** to surpass in chiding

OUTCITY   *n* pl. **-TIES** a city on the outskirts of a larger city

OUTCLASS   *v* **-ED, -ING, -ES** to surpass so decisively as to appear of a higher class

OUTCLIMB   *v* **-CLIMBED** or **-CLOMB, -CLIMBING, -CLIMBS** to surpass in climbing

OUTCOACH   *v* **-ED, -ING, -ES** to surpass in coaching

OUTCOME   *n* pl. **-S** a result

OUTCOOK   *v* **-ED, -ING, -S** to surpass in cooking

OUTCOUNT   *v* **-ED, -ING, -S** to surpass in counting

OUTCRAWL   *v* **-ED, -ING, -S** to surpass in crawling

OUTCRIED   past tense of outcry

OUTCRIES   present 3d person sing. of outcry

OUTCROP   *v* **-CROPPED, -CROPPING, -CROPS** to protrude above the soil

OUTCROSS   *v* **-ED, -ING, -ES** to cross with a relatively unrelated individual

OUTCROW   *v* **-ED, -ING, -S** to surpass in crowing

OUTCROWD   *v* **-ED, -ING, -S** to cause to be too crowded

OUTCRY   *v* **-CRIED, -CRYING, -CRIES** to cry louder than

OUTCURSE   *v* **-CURSED, -CURSING, -CURSES** to surpass in cursing

OUTCURVE   *n* pl. **-S** a type of pitch in baseball

OUTDANCE   *v* **-DANCED, -DANCING, -DANCES** to surpass in dancing

OUTDARE   *v* **-DARED, -DARING, -DARES** to surpass in daring

OUTDATE   *v* **-DATED, -DATING, -DATES** to make out-of-date

OUTDO   *v* **-DID, -DONE, -DOING, -DOES** to exceed in performance

OUTDODGE   *v* **-DODGED, -DODGING, -DODGES** to surpass in dodging

OUTDOER   *n* pl. **-S** one that outdoes

OUTDOOR   *adj* pertaining to the open air

OUTDOORS   *adv* in the open air

OUTDRAG   *v* **-DRAGGED, -DRAGGING, -DRAGS** to surpass in drag racing

OUTDRANK   past tense of outdrink

OUTDRAW   *v* **-DREW, -DRAWN, -DRAWING, -DRAWS** to attract a larger audience than

OUTDREAM   *v* **-DREAMED** or **-DREAMT, -DREAMING, -DREAMS** to surpass in dreaming

OUTDRESS   *v* **-ED, -ING, -ES** to surpass in dressing

OUTDRINK   *v* **-DRANK, -DRUNK, -DRINKING, -DRINKS** to surpass in drinking

OUTDRIVE   *v* **-DROVE, -DRIVEN, -DRIVING, -DRIVES** to drive a golf ball farther than

OUTDROP   *v* **-DROPPED, -DROPPING, -DROPS** to surpass in dropping

OUTDUEL   *v* **-DUELED, -DUELING, -DUELS** or **-DUELLED, -DUELLING, -DUELS** to surpass in dueling

OUTEARN   *v* **-ED, -ING, -S** to surpass in earning

OUTEAT   *v* **-ATE, -EATEN, -EATING, -EATS** to surpass in eating

OUTECHO   *v* **-ED, -ING, -ES** to surpass in echoing

OUTER   *n* pl. **-S** a part of a target

OUTFABLE   *v* **-BLED, -BLING, -BLES** to surpass in fabling

OUTFACE   *v* **-FACED, -FACING, -FACES** to confront unflinchingly

OUTFALL   *n* pl. **-S** the outlet of a body of water

OUTFAST   *v* **-ED, -ING, -S** to surpass in fasting

OUTFAWN   *v* **-ED, -ING, -S** to surpass in fawning

OUTFEAST   *v* **-ED, -ING, -S** to surpass in feasting

OUTFEEL   *v* **-FELT, -FEELING, -FEELS** to surpass in feeling

OUTFENCE	*v* **-FENCED, -FENCING, -FENCES** to surpass in fencing	**OUTGROSS**	*v* **-ED, -ING, -ES** to surpass in gross earnings
OUTFIELD	*n* pl. **-S** a part of a baseball field	**OUTGROUP**	*n* pl. **-S** a group of people outside one's own group
OUTFIGHT	*v* **-FOUGHT, -FIGHTING, -FIGHTS** to defeat	**OUTGROW**	*v* **-GREW, -GROWN, -GROWING, -GROWS** to grow too large for
OUTFIND	*v* **-FOUND, -FINDING, -FINDS** to surpass in finding	**OUTGUESS**	*v* **-ED, -ING, -ES** to anticipate the actions of
OUTFIRE	*v* **-FIRED, -FIRING, -FIRES** to surpass in firing	**OUTGUIDE**	*v* **-GUIDED, -GUIDING, -GUIDES** to surpass in guiding
OUTFISH	*v* **-ED, -ING, -ES** to surpass in fishing	**OUTGUN**	*v* **-GUNNED, -GUNNING, -GUNS** to surpass in firepower
OUTFIT	*v* **-FITTED, -FITTING, -FITS** to equip	**OUTGUSH**	*v* **-ED, -ING, -ES** to surpass in gushing
OUTFLANK	*v* **-ED, -ING, -S** to gain a tactical advantage over	**OUTHAUL**	*n* pl. **-S** a rope for extending a sail along a spar
OUTFLOAT	*v* **-ED, -ING, -S** to float longer than	**OUTHEAR**	*v* **-HEARD, -HEARING, -HEARS** to surpass in hearing
OUTFLOW	*v* **-ED, -ING, -S** to flow out	**OUTHIT**	*v* **-HIT, -HITTING, -HITS** to get more hits than
OUTFLY	*v* **-FLEW, -FLOWN, -FLYING, -FLIES** to surpass in speed of flight	**OUTHOMER**	*v* **-ED, -ING, -S** to surpass in hitting home runs
OUTFOOL	*v* **-ED, -ING, -S** to surpass in fooling	**OUTHOUSE**	*n* pl. **-S** a toilet housed in a small structure
OUTFOOT	*v* **-ED, -ING, -S** to surpass in speed	**OUTHOWL**	*v* **-ED, -ING, -S** to surpass in howling
OUTFOUGHT	past tense of outfight	**OUTHUMOR**	*v* **-ED, -ING, -S** to surpass in humoring
OUTFOUND	past tense of outfind	**OUTHUNT**	*v* **-ED, -ING, -S** to surpass in hunting
OUTFOX	*v* **-ED, -ING, -ES** to outwit	**OUTING**	*n* pl. **-S** a short pleasure trip
OUTFROWN	*v* **-ED, -ING, -S** to frown more than	**OUTJINX**	*v* **-ED, -ING, -ES** to surpass in jinxing
OUTGAIN	*v* **-ED, -ING, -S** to gain more than	**OUTJUMP**	*v* **-ED, -ING, -S** to surpass in jumping
OUTGAS	*v* **-GASSED, -GASSING, -GASSES** or **-GASES** to remove gas from	**OUTJUT**	*v* **-JUTTED, -JUTTING, -JUTS** to stick out
OUTGAZE	*v* **-GAZED, -GAZING, -GAZES** to surpass in gazing	**OUTKEEP**	*v* **-KEPT, -KEEPING, -KEEPS** to surpass in keeping
OUTGIVE	*v* **-GAVE, -GIVEN, -GIVING, -GIVES** to give more than	**OUTKICK**	*v* **-ED, -ING, -S** to surpass in kicking
OUTGLARE	*v* **-GLARED, -GLARING, -GLARES** to surpass in glaring	**OUTKILL**	*v* **-ED, -ING, -S** to surpass in killing
OUTGLEAM	*v* **-ED, -ING, -S** to surpass in gleaming	**OUTKISS**	*v* **-ED, -ING, -ES** to surpass in kissing
OUTGLOW	*v* **-ED, -ING, -S** to surpass in glowing	**OUTLAID**	past tense of outlay
OUTGNAW	*v* **-GNAWED, -GNAWN, -GNAWING, -GNAWS** to surpass in gnawing	**OUTLAIN**	past participle of outlie
OUTGO	*v* **-WENT, -GONE, -GOING, -GOES** to go beyond	**OUTLAND**	*n* pl. **-S** a foreign land
OUTGOING	*n* pl. **-S** a departure	**OUTLAST**	*v* **-ED, -ING, -S** to last longer than
OUTGREW	past tense of outgrow	**OUTLAUGH**	*v* **-ED, -ING, -S** to surpass in laughing
OUTGRIN	*v* **-GRINNED, -GRINNING, -GRINS** to surpass in grinning	**OUTLAW**	*v* **-ED, -ING, -S** to prohibit

OUTLAWRY *n* pl. **-RIES** habitual defiance of the law

OUTLAY *v* **-LAID, -LAYING, -LAYS** to pay out

OUTLEAD *v* **-LED, -LEADING, -LEADS** to surpass in leading

OUTLEAP *v* **-LEAPED** or **-LEAPT, -LEAPING, -LEAPS** to surpass in leaping

OUTLEARN *v* **-LEARNED** or **-LEARNT, -LEARNING, -LEARNS** to surpass in learning

OUTLET *n* pl. **-S** a passage for escape or discharge

OUTLIE *v* **-LAY, -LAIN, -LYING, -LIES** to lie beyond

OUTLIER *n* pl. **-S** an outlying area or portion

OUTLINE *v* **-LINED, -LINING, -LINES** to indicate the main features or different parts of

OUTLINER *n* pl. **-S** one that outlines

OUTLIVE *v* **-LIVED, -LIVING, -LIVES** to live longer than

OUTLIVER *n* pl. **-S** one that outlives

OUTLOOK *n* pl. **-S** a point of view

OUTLOVE *v* **-LOVED, -LOVING, -LOVES** to surpass in loving

OUTLYING present participle of outlie

OUTMAN *v* **-MANNED, -MANNING, -MANS** to surpass in manpower

OUTMARCH *v* **-ED, -ING, -ES** to surpass in marching

OUTMATCH *v* **-ED, -ING, -ES** to outdo

OUTMODE *v* **-MODED, -MODING, -MODES** to outdate

OUTMOST *adj* farthest out

OUTMOVE *v* **-MOVED, -MOVING, -MOVES** to move faster or farther than

OUTPACE *v* **-PACED, -PACING, -PACES** to surpass in speed

OUTPAINT *v* **-ED, -ING, -S** to surpass in painting

OUTPASS *v* **-ED, -ING, -ES** to excel in passing a football

OUTPITCH *v* **-ED, -ING, -ES** to surpass in pitching

OUTPITY *v* **-PITIED, -PITYING, -PITIES** to surpass in pitying

OUTPLACE *v* **-PLACED, -PLACING, -PLACES** to discontinue the employment of

OUTPLAN *v* **-PLANNED, -PLANNING, -PLANS** to surpass in planning

OUTPLAY *v* **-ED, -ING, -S** to excel or defeat in a game

OUTPLOD *v* **-PLODDED, -PLODDING, -PLODS** to surpass in plodding

OUTPLOT *v* **-PLOTTED, -PLOTTING, -PLOTS** to surpass in plotting

OUTPOINT *v* **-ED, -ING, -S** to score more points than

OUTPOLL *v* **-ED, -ING, -S** to get more votes than

OUTPORT *n* pl. **-S** a port of export or departure

OUTPOST *n* pl. **-S** a body of troops stationed at a distance from the main body

OUTPOUR *v* **-ED, -ING, -S** to pour out

OUTPOWER *v* **-ED, -ING, -S** to surpass in power

OUTPRAY *v* **-ED, -ING, -S** to surpass in praying

OUTPREEN *v* **-ED, -ING, -S** to surpass in preening

OUTPRESS *v* **-ED, -ING, -ES** to surpass in pressing

OUTPRICE *v* **-PRICED, -PRICING, -PRICES** to surpass in pricing

OUTPSYCH *v* **-ED, -ING, -S** to defeat by psychological means

OUTPULL *v* **-ED, -ING, -S** to attract a larger audience or following than

OUTPUNCH *v* **-ED, -ING, -ES** to surpass in punching

OUTPUPIL *n* **-S** a pupil who lives off campus

OUTPUSH *v* **-ED, -ING, -ES** to surpass in pushing

OUTPUT *v* **-PUTTED, -PUTTING, -PUTS** to produce

OUTQUOTE *v* **-QUOTED, -QUOTING, -QUOTES** to surpass in quoting

OUTRACE *v* **-RACED, -RACING, -RACES** to run faster or farther than

OUTRAGE *v* **-RAGED, -RAGING, -RAGES** to arouse anger or resentment in

OUTRAISE *v* **-RAISED, -RAISING, -RAISES** to surpass in raising

OUTRAN past tense of outrun

OUTRANCE *n* pl. **-S** the last extremity

OUTRANG past tense of outring

OUTRANGE *v* **-RANGED, -RANGING, -RANGES** to surpass in range

OUTRANK *v* **-ED, -ING, -S** to rank higher than

OUTRATE *v* **-RATED, -RATING, -RATES** to surpass in a rating

OUTRAVE   *v* **-RAVED, -RAVING, -RAVES** to surpass in raving

OUTRE   *adj* deviating from what is usual or proper

OUTREACH   *v* **-ED, -ING, -ES** to reach beyond

OUTREAD   *v* **-READ, -READING, -READS** to surpass in reading

OUTRIDE   *v* **-RODE, -RIDDEN, -RIDING, -RIDES** to ride faster or better than

OUTRIDER   *n* pl. **-S** a mounted attendant who rides before or beside a carriage

OUTRIG   *v* **-RIGGED, -RIGGING, -RIGS** to equip (a boat) with outriggers (projections having floats)

OUTRIGHT   *adj* being without limit or reservation

OUTRING   *v* **-RANG, -RUNG, -RINGING, -RINGS** to ring louder than

OUTRIVAL   *v* **-VALED, -VALING, -VALS** or **-VALLED, -VALLING, -VALS** to outdo in a competition or rivalry

OUTRO   *n* pl. **-S** a concluding passage of a piece of music

OUTROAR   *v* **-ED, -ING, -S** to roar louder than

OUTROCK   *v* **-ED, -ING, -S** to surpass in rocking

OUTRODE   past tense of outride

OUTROLL   *v* **-ED, -ING, -S** to roll out

OUTROOT   *v* **-ED, -ING, -S** to pull up by the roots

OUTROW   *v* **-ED, -ING, -S** to surpass in rowing

OUTRUN   *v* **-RAN, -RUNNING, -RUNS** to run faster than

OUTRUNG   past participle of outring

OUTRUSH   *v* **-ED, -ING, -ES** to surpass in rushing

OUTSAID   past tense of outsay

OUTSAIL   *v* **-ED, -ING, -S** to sail faster than

OUTSANG   past tense of outsing

OUTSAT   past tense of outsit

OUTSAVOR   *v* **-ED, -ING, -S** to surpass in a distinctive taste or smell

OUTSAW   past tense of outsee

OUTSAY   *v* **-SAID, -SAYING, -SAYS** to surpass in saying

OUTSCOLD   *v* **-ED, -ING, -S** to surpass in scolding

OUTSCOOP   *v* **-ED, -ING, -S** to surpass in scooping

OUTSCORE   *v* **-SCORED, -SCORING, -SCORES** to score more points than

OUTSCORN   *v* **-ED, -ING, -S** to surpass in scorning

OUTSEE   *v* **-SAW, -SEEN, -SEEING, -SEES** to see beyond

OUTSELL   *v* **-SOLD, -SELLING, -SELLS** to sell more than

OUTSERT   *n* pl. **-S** a folded sheet placed around a folded section of printed matter

OUTSERVE   *v* **-SERVED, -SERVING, -SERVES** to surpass in serving

OUTSET   *n* pl. **-S** a beginning

OUTSHAME   *v* **-SHAMED, -SHAMING, -SHAMES** to surpass in shaming

OUTSHINE   *v* **-SHONE** or **-SHINED, -SHINING, -SHINES** to shine brighter than

OUTSHOOT   *v* **-SHOT, -SHOOTING, -SHOOTS** to shoot better than

OUTSHOUT   *v* **-ED, -ING, -S** to shout louder than

OUTSIDE   *n* pl. **-S** the outer side, surface, or part

OUTSIDER   *n* pl. **-S** one that does not belong to a particular group

OUTSIGHT   *n* pl. **-S** the power of perceiving external things

OUTSIN   *v* **-SINNED, -SINNING, -SINS** to surpass in sinning

OUTSING   *v* **-SANG, -SUNG, -SINGING, -SINGS** to surpass in singing

OUTSIT   *v* **-SAT, -SITTING, -SITS** to remain sitting or in session longer than

OUTSIZE   *n* pl. **-S** an unusual size **OUTSIZED** *adj*

OUTSKATE   *v* **-SKATED, -SKATING, -SKATES** to surpass in skating

OUTSKIRT   *n* pl. **-S** an outlying area

OUTSLEEP   *v* **-SLEPT, -SLEEPING, -SLEEPS** to sleep later than

OUTSLICK   *v* **-ED, -ING, -S** to get the better of by trickery or cunning

OUTSMART   *v* **-ED, -ING, -S** to outwit

OUTSMELL   *v* **-SMELLED** or **-SMELT, -SMELLING, -SMELLS** to surpass in smelling

OUTSMILE   *v* **-SMILED, -SMILING, -SMILES** to surpass in smiling

OUTSMOKE   *v* **-SMOKED, -SMOKING, -SMOKES** to surpass in smoking

OUTSNORE   v **-SNORED, -SNORING, -SNORES** to surpass in snoring

OUTSOAR   v **-ED, -ING, -S** to soar beyond

OUTSOLD   past tense of outsell

OUTSOLE   n pl. **-S** the outer sole of a boot or shoe

OUTSPAN   v **-SPANNED, -SPANNING, -SPANS** to unharness a draft animal

OUTSPEAK   v **-SPOKE, -SPOKEN, -SPEAKING, -SPEAKS** to outdo in speaking

OUTSPEED   v **-SPED** or **-SPEEDED, -SPEEDING, -SPEEDS** to go faster than

OUTSPELL   v **-SPELLED** or **-SPELT, -SPELLING, -SPELLS** to surpass in spelling

OUTSPEND   v **-SPENT, -SPENDING, -SPENDS** to exceed the limits of in spending

OUTSPOKE   past tense of outspeak

OUTSPOKEN   past participle of outspeak

OUTSTAND   v **-STOOD, -STANDING, -STANDS** to endure beyond

OUTSTARE   v **-STARED, -STARING, -STARES** to outface

OUTSTART   v **-ED, -ING, -S** to get ahead of at the start

OUTSTATE   v **-STATED, -STATING, -STATES** to surpass in stating

OUTSTAY   v **-ED, -ING, -S** to surpass in staying power

OUTSTEER   v **-ED, -ING, -S** to surpass in steering

OUTSTEP   v **-STEPPED, -STEPPING, -STEPS** to step beyond

OUTSTOOD   past tense of outstand

OUTSTRIP   v **-STRIPPED, -STRIPPING, -STRIPS** to go faster or farther than

OUTSTUDY   v **-STUDIED, -STUDYING, -STUDIES** to surpass in studying

OUTSTUNT   v **-ED, -ING, -S** to surpass in stunting

OUTSULK   v **-ED, -ING, -S** to surpass in sulking

OUTSUNG   past participle of outsing

OUTSWEAR   v **-SWORE** or **-SWARE, -SWORN, -SWEARING, -SWEARS** to surpass in swearing

OUTSWEEP   v **-SWEPT, -SWEEPING, -SWEEPS** to surpass in sweeping

OUTSWIM   v **-SWAM, -SWUM, -SWIMMING, -SWIMS** to swim faster or farther than

OUTSWING   v **-SWUNG, -SWINGING, -SWINGS** to surpass in swinging

OUTTAKE   n pl. **-S** a passage outwards

OUTTALK   v **-ED, -ING, -S** to surpass in talking

OUTTASK   v **-ED, -ING, -S** to surpass in tasking

OUTTELL   v **-TOLD, -TELLING, -TELLS** to say openly

OUTTHANK   v **-ED, -ING, -S** to surpass in thanking

OUTTHINK   v **-THOUGHT, -THINKING, -THINKS** to get the better of by thinking

OUTTHROB   v **-THROBBED, -THROBBING, -THROBS** to surpass in throbbing

OUTTHROW   v **-THREW, -THROWN, -THROWING, -THROWS** to throw farther or more accurately than

OUTTOLD   past tense of outtell

OUTTOWER   v **-ED, -ING, -S** to tower above

OUTTRADE   v **-TRADED, -TRADING, -TRADES** to get the better of in a trade

OUTTRICK   v **-ED, -ING, -S** to get the better of by trickery

OUTTROT   v **-TROTTED, -TROTTING, -TROTS** to surpass in trotting

OUTTRUMP   v **-ED, -ING, -S** to outplay

OUTTURN   n pl. **-S** a quantity produced

OUTVALUE   v **-UED, -UING, -UES** to be worth more than

OUTVAUNT   v **-ED, -ING, -S** to surpass in vaunting

OUTVIE   v **-VIED, -VYING, -VIES** to surpass in a competition

OUTVOICE   v **-VOICED, -VOICING, -VOICES** to surpass in loudness of voice

OUTVOTE   v **-VOTED, -VOTING, -VOTES** to defeat by a majority of votes

OUTWAIT   v **-ED, -ING, -S** to exceed in patience

OUTWALK   v **-ED, -ING, -S** to surpass in walking

OUTWAR   v **-WARRED, -WARRING, -WARS** to surpass in warring

OUTWARD   adv toward the outside

OUTWARDS   adv outward

OUTWASH   n pl. **-ES** detritus washed from a glacier

OUTWASTE v -**WASTED, -WASTING, -WASTES** to surpass in wasting

OUTWATCH v -**ED, -ING, -ES** to watch longer than

OUTWEAR v -**WORE, -WORN, -WEARING, -WEARS** to last longer than

OUTWEARY v -**RIED, -RYING, -RIES** to surpass in wearying

OUTWEEP v -**WEPT, -WEEPING, -WEEPS** to weep more than

OUTWEIGH v -**ED, -ING, -S** to weigh more than

OUTWENT past tense of outgo

OUTWHIRL v -**ED, -ING, -S** to surpass in whirling

OUTWILE v -**WILED, -WILING, -WILES** to surpass in wiling

OUTWILL v -**ED, -ING, -S** to surpass in willpower

OUTWIND v -**ED, -ING, -S** to cause to be out of breath

OUTWISH v -**ED, -ING, -ES** to surpass in wishing

OUTWIT v -**WITTED, -WITTING, -WITS** to get the better of by superior cleverness

OUTWITH prep beyond the limits of

OUTWORE past tense of outwear

OUTWORK v -**WORKED** or -**WROUGHT, -WORKING, -WORKS** to work faster or better than

OUTWORN past participle of outwear

OUTWRITE v -**WROTE** or -**WRIT, -WRITTEN, -WRITING, -WRITES** to write better than

OUTYELL v -**ED, -ING, -S** to yell louder than

OUTYELP v -**ED, -ING, -S** to surpass in yelping

OUTYIELD v -**ED, -ING, -S** to surpass in yield

OUZEL n pl. -**S** a European bird

OUZO n pl. -**ZOS** a Greek liqueur

OVA pl. of ovum

OVAL n pl. -**S** an oval (egg-shaped) figure or object

OVALITY n pl. -**TIES** ovalness

OVALLY adv in the shape of an oval

OVALNESS n pl. -**ES** the state of being oval

OVARIAL adj ovarian

OVARIAN adj pertaining to an ovary

OVARIES pl. of ovary

OVARIOLE n pl. -**S** one of the tubes of which the ovaries of most insects are composed

OVARITIS n pl. -**RITIDES** inflammation of an ovary

OVARY n pl. -**RIES** a female reproductive gland

OVATE adj egg-shaped **OVATELY** adv

OVATION n pl. -**S** an expression or demonstration of popular acclaim

OVEN n pl. -**S** an enclosed compartment in which substances are heated **OVENLIKE** adj

OVENBIRD n pl. -**S** an American songbird

OVENWARE n pl. -**S** heat-resistant dishes for baking and serving food

OVER v -**ED, -ING, -S** to leap above and to the other side of

OVERABLE adj excessively able

OVERACT v -**ED, -ING, -S** to act with exaggeration

OVERAGE n pl. -**S** an amount in excess

OVERAGED adj too old to be useful

OVERALL n pl. -**S** a loose outer garment

OVERAPT adj excessively apt

OVERARCH v -**ED, -ING, -ES** to form an arch over

OVERARM v -**ED, -ING, -S** to supply with an excess of weaponry

OVERATE past tense of overeat

OVERAWE v -**AWED, -AWING, -AWES** to subdue by inspiring awe

OVERBAKE v -**BAKED, -BAKING, -BAKES** to bake too long

OVERBEAR v -**BORE, -BORNE** or -**BORN, -BEARING, -BEARS** to bring down by superior weight or force

OVERBEAT v -**BEAT, -BEATEN, -BEATING, -BEATS** to beat too much

OVERBED adj spanning a bed

OVERBET v -**BET** or -**BETTED, -BETTING, -BETS** to bet too much

OVERBID v -**BID, -BID** or -**BIDDEN, -BIDDING, -BIDS** to bid higher than

OVERBIG adj too big

OVERBILL v -**ED, -ING, -S** to bill too much

OVERBITE n pl. -**S** a faulty closure of the teeth

OVERBLOW v -**BLEW, -BLOWN, -BLOWING, -BLOWS** to give excessive importance to

OVERBOIL	*v* **-ED, -ING, -S** to boil too long
OVERBOLD	*adj* excessively bold or forward
OVERBOOK	*v* **-ED, -ING, -S** to issue reservations in excess of the space available
OVERBOOT	*n* pl. **-S** a boot worn over a shoe or another boot
OVERBORE	past tense of overbear
OVERBORN	a past participle of overbear
OVERBORNE	a past participle of overbear
OVERBOUGHT	past tense of overbuy
OVERBRED	*adj* bred too finely or to excess
OVERBURN	*v* **-BURNED** or **-BURNT, -BURNING, -BURNS** to burn too long
OVERBUSY	*adj* too busy
OVERBUY	*v* **-BOUGHT, -BUYING, -BUYS** to buy in quantities exceeding need or demand
OVERCALL	*v* **-ED, -ING, -S** to overbid
OVERCAME	past tense of overcome
OVERCAST	*v* **-CAST** or **-CASTED, -CASTING, -CASTS** to become cloudy or dark
OVERCOAT	*n* pl. **-S** a warm coat worn over indoor clothing
OVERCOLD	*adj* too cold
OVERCOME	*v* **-CAME, -COMING, -COMES** to get the better of
OVERCOOK	*v* **-ED, -ING, -S** to cook too long
OVERCOOL	*v* **-ED, -ING, -S** to make too cool
OVERCOY	*adj* too coy
OVERCRAM	*v* **-CRAMMED, -CRAMMING, -CRAMS** to stuff or cram to excess
OVERCROP	*v* **-CROPPED, -CROPPING, -CROPS** to exhaust the fertility of by cultivating to excess
OVERCURE	*v* **-CURED, -CURING, -CURES** to cure too long
OVERCUT	*v* **-CUT, -CUTTING, -CUTS** to cut too much
OVERDARE	*v* **-DARED, -DARING, -DARES** to become too daring
OVERDEAR	*adj* too dear; too costly
OVERDECK	*v* **-ED, -ING, -S** to adorn extravagantly
OVERDO	*v* **-DID, -DONE, -DOING, -DOES** to do to excess
OVERDOER	*n* pl. **-S** one that overdoes
OVERDOG	*n* pl. **-S** one that is dominant or victorious
OVERDOSE	*v* **-DOSED, -DOSING, -DOSES** to give an excessive dose to
OVERDRAW	*v* **-DREW, -DRAWN, -DRAWING, -DRAWS** to draw checks on in excess of the balance
OVERDRY	*v* **-DRIED, -DRYING, -DRIES** to dry too much
OVERDUB	*v* **-DUBBED, -DUBBING, -DUBS** to add sound to an existing recording
OVERDUE	*adj* not paid when due
OVERDYE	*v* **-DYED, -DYEING, -DYES** to dye with too much color
OVERDYER	*n* pl. **-S** one that overdyes
OVEREASY	*adj* too easy
OVEREAT	*v* **-ATE, -EATEN, -EATING, -EATS** to eat to excess
OVEREDIT	*v* **-ED, -ING, -S** to edit more than necessary
OVERFAR	*adj* too great in distance, extent, or degree
OVERFAST	*adj* too fast
OVERFAT	*adj* too fat
OVERFEAR	*v* **-ED, -ING, -S** to fear too much
OVERFEED	*v* **-FED, -FEEDING, -FEEDS** to feed too much
OVERFILL	*v* **-ED, -ING, -S** to fill to overflowing
OVERFINE	*adj* excessively fine or particular
OVERFISH	*v* **-ED, -ING, -ES** to deplete the supply of fish in an area by fishing to excess
OVERFIT	*adj* fitted to excess
OVERFLOW	*v* **-FLOWED, -FLOWN, -FLOWING, -FLOWS** to flow over the top of
OVERFLY	*v* **-FLEW, -FLOWN, -FLYING, -FLIES** to fly over
OVERFOND	*adj* too fond or affectionate
OVERFOUL	*adj* too foul
OVERFREE	*adj* too free
OVERFULL	*adj* too full
OVERFUND	*v* **-ED, -ING, -S** to fund more than required
OVERGILD	*v* **-GILDED** or **-GILT, -GILDING, -GILDS** to gild over
OVERGIRD	*v* **-GIRDED** or **-GIRT, -GIRDING, -GIRDS** to gird to excess
OVERGLAD	*adj* too glad
OVERGOAD	*v* **-ED, -ING, -S** to goad too much
OVERGROW	*v* **-GREW, -GROWN, -GROWING, -GROWS** to grow over

OVERHAND *v* **-ED, -ING, -S** to sew with short, vertical stitches

OVERHANG *v* **-HUNG, -HANGING, -HANGS** to hang or project over

OVERHARD *adj* too hard

OVERHATE *v* **-HATED, -HATING, -HATES** to hate to excess

OVERHAUL *v* **-ED, -ING, -S** to examine carefully for needed repairs

OVERHEAD *n pl.* **-S** the general cost of running a business

OVERHEAP *v* **-ED, -ING, -S** to heap up or accumulate to excess

OVERHEAR *v* **-HEARD, -HEARING, -HEARS** to hear without the speaker's knowledge or intention

OVERHEAT *v* **-ED, -ING, -S** to heat to excess

OVERHIGH *adj* too high

OVERHOLD *v* **-HELD, -HOLDING, -HOLDS** to rate too highly

OVERHOLY *adj* too holy

OVERHOPE *v* **-HOPED, -HOPING, -HOPES** to hope exceedingly

OVERHOT *adj* too hot

OVERHUNG past tense of overhang

OVERHUNT *v* **-ED, -ING, -S** to deplete the supply of game in an area by hunting to excess

OVERHYPE *v* **-HYPED, -HYPING, -HYPES** to hype to excess

OVERIDLE *adj* too idle

OVERJOY *v* **-ED, -ING, -S** to fill with great joy

OVERJUST *adj* too just

OVERKEEN *adj* too keen

OVERKILL *v* **-ED, -ING, -S** to destroy with more nuclear force than required

OVERKIND *adj* too kind

OVERLADE *v* **-LADED, -LADEN, -LADING, -LADES** to load with too great a burden

OVERLAID past tense of overlay

OVERLAIN past participle of overlie

OVERLAND *n pl.* **-S** a train or stagecoach that travels over land

OVERLAP *v* **-LAPPED, -LAPPING, -LAPS** to extend over and cover a part of

OVERLATE *adj* too late

OVERLAX *adj* too lax

OVERLAY *v* **-LAID, -LAYING, -LAYS** to lay over

OVERLEAF *adv* on the other side of the page

OVERLEAP *v* **-LEAPED** or **-LEAPT, -LEAPING, -LEAPS** to leap over

OVERLEND *v* **-LENT, -LENDING, -LENDS** to lend too much

OVERLET *v* **-LET, -LETTING, -LETS** to let to excess

OVERLEWD *adj* too lewd

OVERLIE *v* **-LAY, -LAIN, -LYING, -LIES** to lie over

OVERLIT a past tense of overlight

OVERLIVE *v* **-LIVED, -LIVING, -LIVES** to outlive

OVERLOAD *v* **-ED, -ING, -S** to load to excess

OVERLONG *adj* too long

OVERLOOK *v* **-ED, -ING, -S** to fail to notice

OVERLORD *v* **-ED, -ING, -S** to rule tyrannically

OVERLOUD *adj* too loud

OVERLOVE *v* **-LOVED, -LOVING, -LOVES** to love to excess

OVERLUSH *adj* excessively lush

OVERLY *adv* to an excessive degree

OVERLYING present participle of overlie

OVERMAN *n pl.* **-MEN** a foreman

OVERMAN *v* **-MANNED, -MANNING, -MANS** to provide with more men than are needed

OVERMANY *adj* too many

OVERMEEK *adj* excessively meek

OVERMELT *v* **-ED, -ING, -S** to melt too much

OVERMEN pl. of overman

OVERMILD *adj* too mild

OVERMILK *v* **-ED, -ING, -S** to milk to excess

OVERMINE *v* **-MINED, -MINING, -MINES** to mine to excess

OVERMIX *v* **-ED, -ING, -ES** to mix too much

OVERMUCH *n pl.* **-ES** an excess

OVERNEAR *adj* too near

OVERNEAT *adj* too neat

OVERNEW *adj* too new

OVERNICE *adj* excessively nice

OVERPACK *v* **-ED, -ING, -S** to pack to excess

OVERPASS *v* **-PASSED** or **-PAST, -PASSING, -PASSES** to pass over

OVERPAY *v* **-PAID, -PAYING, -PAYS** to pay too much

OVERPERT *adj* too pert

OVERPLAN *v* **-PLANNED, -PLANNING, -PLANS** to plan to excess

OVERPLAY *v* **-ED, -ING, -S** to exaggerate

OVERPLOT *v* **-PLOTTED, -PLOTTING, -PLOTS** to devise an overly complex plot for

OVERPLUS *n* pl. **-ES** a surplus

OVERPLY *v* **-PLIED, -PLYING, -PLIES** to ply to excess; overwork

OVERPUMP *v* **-ED, -ING, -S** to pump to excess

OVERRAN past tense of overrun

OVERRANK *adj* too luxuriant in growth

OVERRASH *adj* too rash

OVERRATE *v* **-RATED, -RATING, -RATES** to rate too highly

OVERRICH *adj* too rich

OVERRIDE *v* **-RODE, -RIDDEN, -RIDING, -RIDES** to ride over

OVERRIFE *adj* too rife

OVERRIPE *adj* too ripe

OVERRUDE *adj* excessively rude

OVERRUFF *v* **-ED, -ING, -S** to trump with a higher trump card than has already been played

OVERRULE *v* **-RULED, -RULING, -RULES** to disallow the arguments of

OVERRUN *v* **-RAN, -RUNNING, -RUNS** to spread or swarm over

OVERSAD *adj* excessively sad

OVERSALE *n* pl. **-S** the act of overselling

OVERSALT *v* **-ED, -ING, -S** to salt to excess

OVERSAVE *v* **-SAVED, -SAVING, -SAVES** to save too much

OVERSEA *adv* overseas

OVERSEAS *adv* beyond or across the sea

OVERSEE *v* **-SAW, -SEEN, -SEEING, -SEES** to watch over and direct

OVERSEED *v* **-ED, -ING, -S** to seed to excess

OVERSEER *n* pl. **-S** one that oversees

OVERSELL *v* **-SOLD, -SELLING, -SELLS** to sell more of than can be delivered

OVERSET *v* **-SET, -SETTING, -SETS** to turn or tip over

OVERSEW *v* **-SEWED, -SEWN, -SEWING, -SEWS** to overhand

OVERSHOE *n* pl. **-S** a protective outer shoe

OVERSHOT *n* pl. **-S** a type of fabric weave

OVERSICK *adj* too sick

OVERSIDE *n* pl. **-S** the other side of a phonograph record

OVERSIZE *n* pl. **-S** an unusually large size

OVERSLIP *v* **-SLIPPED** or **-SLIPT, -SLIPPING, -SLIPS** to leave out

OVERSLOW *adj* too slow

OVERSOAK *v* **-ED, -ING, -S** to soak too much

OVERSOFT *adj* too soft

OVERSOLD past tense of oversell

OVERSOON *adv* too soon

OVERSOUL *n* pl. **-S** a supreme reality or mind in transcendentalism

OVERSPIN *n* pl. **-S** a forward spin imparted to a ball

OVERSTAY *v* **-ED, -ING, -S** to stay beyond the limits or duration of

OVERSTEP *v* **-STEPPED, -STEPPING, -STEPS** to go beyond

OVERSTIR *v* **-STIRRED, -STIRRING, -STIRS** to stir too much

OVERSUDS *v* **-ED, -ING, -ES** to form an excessive amount of suds

OVERSUP *v* **-SUPPED, -SUPPING, -SUPS** to sup to excess

OVERSURE *adj* too sure

OVERT *adj* open to view

OVERTAKE *v* **-TOOK, -TAKEN, -TAKING, -TAKES** to catch up with

OVERTALK *v* **-ED, -ING, -S** to talk to excess

OVERTAME *adj* too tame

OVERTART *adj* too tart

OVERTASK *v* **-ED, -ING, -S** to task too severely

OVERTAX *v* **-ED, -ING, -ES** to tax too heavily

OVERTHIN *v* **-THINNED, -THINNING, -THINS** to make too thin

OVERTIME *v* **-TIMED, -TIMING, -TIMES** to exceed the desired timing for

OVERTIP *v* **-TIPPED, -TIPPING, -TIPS** to tip more than what is customary

OVERTIRE *v* **-TIRED, -TIRING, -TIRES** to tire excessively

OVERTLY *adv* in an overt manner

OVERTOIL *v* **-ED, -ING, -S** to wear out or exhaust by excessive toil

OVERTONE *n* pl. **-S** a higher partial tone

OVERTOOK past tense of overtake

OVERTOP *v* **-TOPPED, -TOPPING, -TOPS** to rise above the top of

OVERTRIM *v* **-TRIMMED, -TRIMMING, -TRIMS** to trim too much

OVERTURE *v* **-TURED, -TURING, -TURES** to propose

OVERTURN *v* **-ED, -ING, -S** to turn over

OVERURGE *v* **-URGED, -URGING, -URGES** to urge too much

OVERUSE *v* **-USED, -USING, -USES** to use too much

OVERVIEW *n* pl. **-S** a summary

OVERVOTE *v* **-VOTED, -VOTING, -VOTES** to defeat by a majority of votes

OVERWARM *v* **-ED, -ING, -S** to warm too much

OVERWARY *adj* too wary

OVERWEAK *adj* too weak

OVERWEAR *v* **-WORE, -WORN, -WEARING, -WEARS** to wear out

OVERWEEN *v* **-ED, -ING, -S** to be arrogant

OVERWET *v* **-WETTED, -WETTING, -WETS** to wet too much

OVERWIDE *adj* too wide

OVERWILY *adj* too wily

OVERWIND *v* **-WOUND, -WINDING, -WINDS** to wind too much, as a watch

OVERWISE *adj* too wise

OVERWORD *n* pl. **-S** a word or phrase repeated at intervals in a song

OVERWORE past tense of overwear

OVERWORK *v* **-WORKED** or **-WROUGHT, -WORKING, -WORKS** to cause to work too hard

OVERWORN past participle of overwear

OVERWOUND past tense of overwind

OVERZEAL *n* pl. **-S** excess of zeal

OVIBOS *n* pl. **OVIBOS** a wild ox

OVICIDE *n* pl. **-S** an agent that kills eggs **OVICIDAL** *adj*

OVIDUCT *n* pl. **-S** a tube through which ova travel from an ovary **OVIDUCAL** *adj*

OVIFORM *adj* shaped like an egg

OVINE *n* pl. **-S** a sheep or a closely related animal

OVIPARA *n/pl* egg-laying animals

OVIPOSIT *v* **-ED, -ING, -S** to lay eggs

OVISAC *n* pl. **-S** a sac containing an ovum or ova

OVOID *n* pl. **-S** an egg-shaped body

OVOIDAL *n* pl. **-S** an ovoid

OVOLO *n* pl. **-LOS** or **-LI** a convex molding

OVONIC *n* pl. **-S** an electronic device

OVULATE *v* **-LATED, -LATING, -LATES** to produce ova

OVULE *n* pl. **-S** a rudimentary seed **OVULAR, OVULARY** *adj*

OVUM *n* pl. **OVA** the female reproductive cell of animals

OW *interj* — used to express sudden pain

OWE *v* **OWED, OWING, OWES** to be under obligation to pay or repay

OWIE *n* pl. **-S** an injury that is not serious

OWL *n* pl. **-S** a nocturnal bird

OWLERY *n* pl. **-ERIES** a place that owls inhabit

OWLET *n* pl. **-S** a young owl

OWLISH *adj* resembling an owl **OWLISHLY** *adv*

OWLLIKE *adj* owlish

OWLY *adj* **OWLIER, OWLIEST** owlish

OWN *v* **-ED, -ING, -S** to have as a belonging **OWNABLE** *adj*

OWNER *n* pl. **-S** one that owns

OWSE *n* pl. **OWSEN** ox

OWT *n* pl. **-S** anything

OX *n* pl. **-ES** a clumsy person

OX *n* pl. **OXEN** a hoofed mammal

OXALATE *v* **-LATED, -LATING, -LATES** to treat with an oxalate (a chemical salt)

OXALIS *n* pl. **-ALISES** a flowering plant **OXALIC** *adj*

OXAZEPAM *n* pl. **-S** a tranquilizing drug

OXAZINE *n* pl. **-S** a chemical compound

OXAZOLE *n* pl. **-S** a liquid chemical compound

OXBLOOD *n* pl. **-S** a deep red color

OXBOW *n* pl. **-S** a U-shaped piece of wood in an ox yoke

OXCART *n* pl. **-S** an ox-drawn cart

OXEN pl. of ox

OXER *n* pl. **-S** a fence for keeping in cattle

OXEYE *n* pl. **-S** a flowering plant

OXFORD *n* pl. **-S** a type of shoe

OXHEART *n* pl. **-S** a variety of sweet cherry

OXHERD *n* pl. **-S** one who tends oxen

OXHIDE *n* pl. **-S** leather made from the skin of an ox

OXIC	*adj* denoting a process in which oxygen in involved
OXID	*n* pl. **-S** oxide
OXIDABLE	*adj* capable of being oxidized
OXIDANT	*n* pl. **-S** an oxidizing agent
OXIDASE	*n* pl. **-S** an oxidizing enzyme **OXIDASIC** *adj*
OXIDATE	*v* **-DATED, -DATING, -DATES** to oxidize
OXIDE	*n* pl. **-S** a binary compound of oxygen with another element or radical **OXIDIC** *adj*
OXIDISE	*v* **-DISED, -DISING, -DISES** to oxidize
OXIDISER	*n* pl. **-S** oxidizer
OXIDIZE	*v* **-DIZED, -DIZING, -DIZES** to combine with oxygen
OXIDIZER	*n* pl. **-S** an oxidant
OXIM	*n* pl. **-S** oxime
OXIME	*n* pl. **-S** a chemical compound
OXIMETER	*n* pl. **-S** an instrument for measuring the amount of oxygen in the blood
OXIMETRY	*n* pl. **-TRIES** the use of an oximeter
OXLIKE	*adj* resembling an ox
OXLIP	*n* pl. **-S** a flowering plant
OXO	*adj* containing oxygen
OXPECKER	*n* pl. **-S** an African bird
OXTAIL	*n* pl. **-S** the tail of an ox
OXTER	*n* pl. **-S** the armpit
OXTONGUE	*n* pl. **-S** a European herb
OXY	*adj* containing oxygen
OXYACID	*n* pl. **-S** an acid that contains oxygen
OXYGEN	*n* pl. **-S** a gaseous element **OXYGENIC** *adj*
OXYMORON	*n* pl. **-MORONS** or **-MORA** a combination of contradictory or incongruous words
OXYPHIL	*n* pl. **-S** oxyphile
OXYPHILE	*n* pl. **-S** an organism that thrives in a relatively acid environment
OXYSALT	*n* pl. **-S** a salt of an oxyacid
OXYSOME	*n* pl. **-S** a structural unit of cellular cristae
OXYTOCIC	*n* pl. **-S** a drug that hastens the process of childbirth
OXYTOCIN	*n* pl. **-S** a pituitary hormone
OXYTONE	*n* pl. **-S** a word having heavy stress on the last syllable
OXYTROPE	*n* pl. **-S** a flowering plant
OY	*interj* — used to express dismay or pain
OYER	*n* pl. **-S** a type of legal writ
OYES	*n* pl. **OYESSES** oyez
OYEZ	*n* pl. **OYEZES** a cry used to introduce the opening of a court of law
OYSTER	*v* **-ED, -ING, -S** to gather oysters (edible mollusks)
OYSTERER	*n* pl. **-S** one that gathers or sells oysters
OZONATE	*v* **-ATED, -ATING, -ATES** to treat or combine with ozone
OZONE	*n* pl. **-S** a form of oxygen **OZONIC** *adj*
OZONIDE	*n* pl. **-S** a compound of ozone
OZONISE	*v* **-ISED, -ISING, -ISES** to ozonize
OZONIZE	*v* **-IZED, -IZING, -IZES** to convert into ozone
OZONIZER	*n* pl. **-S** a device for converting oxygen into ozone
OZONOUS	*adj* pertaining to ozone

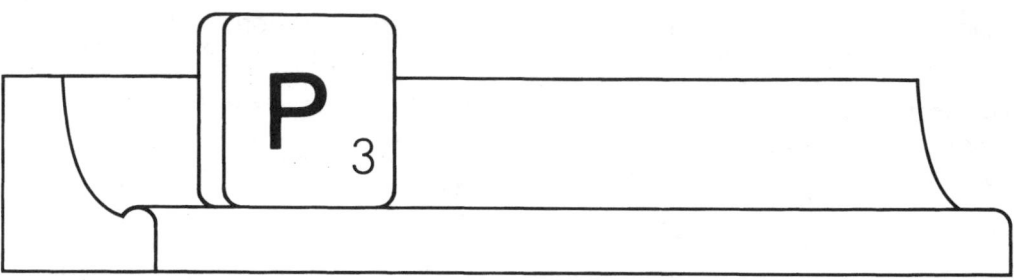

PA   *n* pl. **-S** a father

PAAN   *n* pl. **-S** a betel leaf folded round pieces of betel nut and spices

PABLUM   *n* pl. **-S** insipid writing or speech

PABULUM   *n* pl. **-S** food **PABULAR** *adj*

PAC   *n* pl. **-S** a shoe like a moccasin

PACA   *n* pl. **-S** a large rodent

PACE   *v* **PACED, PACING, PACES** to walk with a regular step

PACER   *n* pl. **-S** a horse whose gait is a pace

PACEY   *adj* **PACIER, PACIEST** keeping a fast pace (rate of speed)

PACHA   *n* pl. **-S** pasha

PACHADOM   *n* pl. **-S** pashadom

PACHALIC   *n* pl. **-S** pashalik

PACHINKO   *n* pl. **-KOS** a Japanese pinball game

PACHISI   *n* pl. **-S** a board game of India

PACHOULI   *n* pl. **-S** an East Indian herb

PACHUCO   *n* pl. **-COS** a flashy Mexican-American youth

PACIER   comparative of pacey and pacy

PACIEST   superlative of pacey and pacy

PACIFIC   *adj* peaceful

PACIFIED   past tense of pacify

PACIFIER   *n* pl. **-S** one that pacifies

PACIFISM   *n* pl. **-S** opposition to war or violence

PACIFIST   *n* pl. **-S** an advocate of pacifism

PACIFY   *v* **-FIED, -FYING, -FIES** to make peaceful

PACING   *n* pl. **-S** the speed at which an event takes place

PACK   *v* **-ED, -ING, -S** to put into a receptacle for transportation or storage **PACKABLE** *adj*

PACKAGE   *v* **-AGED, -AGING, -AGES** to make into a package (a wrapped or boxed object)

PACKAGER   *n* pl. **-S** one that packages

PACKER   *n* pl. **-S** one that packs

PACKET   *v* **-ED, -ING, -S** to make into a small package

PACKING   *n* pl. **-S** material used to pack

PACKLY   *adv* intimately

PACKMAN   *n* pl. **-MEN** a peddler

PACKNESS   *n* pl. **-ES** intimacy

PACKSACK   *n* pl. **-S** a carrying bag to be worn on the back

PACKWAX   *n* pl. **-ES** paxwax

PACT   *n* pl. **-S** an agreement

PACTION   *n* pl. **-S** a pact

PACY   *adj* **PACIER, PACIEST** pacey

PACZKI   *n* pl. **-S** a round doughnut with a filling

PAD   *v* **PADDED, PADDING, PADS** to line or stuff with soft material

PADAUK   *n* pl. **-S** a tropical tree

PADDER   *n* pl. **-S** one that pads

PADDIES   pl. of paddy

PADDING   *n* pl. **-S** material with which to pad

PADDLE   *v* **-DLED, -DLING, -DLES** to propel with a broad-bladed implement

PADDLER   *n* pl. **-S** one that paddles

PADDLING   *n* pl. **-S** the act of one who paddles

PADDOCK   *v* **-ED, -ING, -S** to confine in an enclosure for horses

PADDY   *n* pl. **-DIES** a rice field

PADI   *n* pl. **-S** paddy

PADISHAH   *n* pl. **-S** a sovereign

PADLE   *n* pl. **-S** a hoe

PADLOCK   *v* **-ED, -ING, -S** to secure with a type of lock

PADNAG	*n* pl. **-S** a horse that moves along at an easy pace	**PAID**	a past tense of pay
PADOUK	*n* pl. **-S** padauk	**PAIK**	*v* **-ED, -ING, -S** to beat or strike
PADRE	*n* pl. **-DRES** or **-DRI** a Christian clergyman	**PAIL**	*n* pl. **-S** a watertight cylindrical container
PADRONA	*n* pl. **-S** a female boss or employer	**PAILFUL**	*n* pl. **PAILFULS** or **PAILSFUL** as much as a pail can hold
PADRONE	*n* pl. **-NES** or **-NI** a master or boss	**PAILLARD**	*n* pl. **-S** a slice of meat pounded thin and grilled
PADSHAH	*n* pl. **-S** padishah		
PADUASOY	*n* pl. **-SOYS** a strong silk fabric	**PAIN**	*v* **-ED, -ING, -S** to cause pain (suffering or distress)
PAEAN	*n* pl. **-S** a song of joy	**PAINCH**	*n* pl. **-ES** paunch
PAEANISM	*n* pl. **-S** the chanting of a paean	**PAINFUL**	*adj* **-FULLER, -FULLEST** causing pain
PAELLA	*n* pl. **-S** a saffron-flavored stew		
PAEON	*n* pl. **-S** a metrical foot of four syllables **PAEONIC** *adj*	**PAINLESS**	*adj* not causing pain
		PAINT	*v* **-ED, -ING, -S** to make a representation of with paints (coloring substances)
PAESAN	*n* pl. **-S** paesano		
PAESANO	*n* pl. **-NOS** or **-NI** a fellow countryman	**PAINTBOX**	*n* pl. **-ES** a box holding dry paints
PAGAN	*n* pl. **-S** a follower of a polytheistic religion	**PAINTER**	*n* pl. **-S** one that paints
		PAINTING	*n* pl. **-S** a picture made with paints
PAGANDOM	*n* pl. **-S** the realm of pagans	**PAINTY**	*adj* **PAINTIER, PAINTIEST** covered with paint
PAGANISE	*v* **-ISED, -ISING, -ISES** to paganize		
PAGANISH	*adj* resembling a pagan	**PAIR**	*v* **-ED, -ING, -S** to arrange in sets of two
PAGANISM	*n* pl. **-S** an irreligious attitude		
PAGANIST	*n* pl. **-S** a pagan	**PAIRING**	*n* pl. **-S** a matching of two opponents in a tournament
PAGANIZE	*v* **-IZED, -IZING, -IZES** to make irreligious		
		PAIRWISE	*adv* in sets of two
PAGE	*v* **PAGED, PAGING, PAGES** to summon by calling out the name of	**PAISA**	*n* pl. **PAISAS** or **PAISE** a coin of Pakistan
PAGEANT	*n* pl. **-S** an elaborate public spectacle	**PAISAN**	*n* pl. **-S** paisano
		PAISANA	*n* pl. **-S** a female compatriot
PAGEBOY	*n* pl. **-BOYS** a woman's hairstyle	**PAISANO**	*n* pl. **-NOS** a fellow countryman
PAGEFUL	*n* pl. **-S** as much as a page can hold	**PAISE**	a pl. of paisa
		PAISLEY	*n* pl. **-LEYS** a patterned wool fabric
PAGER	*n* pl. **-S** a beeper		
PAGINAL	*adj* pertaining to the pages of a book	**PAJAMA**	*n* pl. **-S** a garment for sleeping or lounging
PAGINATE	*v* **-NATED, -NATING, -NATES** to number the pages of	**PAJAMAED**	*adj* wearing pajamas
		PAK	*n* pl. **-S** pack
PAGING	*n* pl. **-S** a transfer of computer pages	**PAKEHA**	*n* pl. **-S** a person who is not of Maori descent
PAGOD	*n* pl. **-S** pagoda	**PAKORA**	*n* pl. **-S** a small spicy cake of fried batter with vegetables or meat
PAGODA	*n* pl. **-S** a Far Eastern temple		
PAGURIAN	*n* pl. **-S** a hermit crab	**PAL**	*v* **PALLED, PALLING, PALS** to associate as friends
PAGURID	*n* pl. **-S** pagurian		
PAH	*interj* — used as an exclamation of disgust	**PALABRA**	*n* pl. **-S** a word
		PALACE	*n* pl. **-S** a royal residence **PALACED** *adj*
PAHLAVI	*n* pl. **-S** a former coin of Iran	**PALADIN**	*n* pl. **-S** a knightly champion
PAHOEHOE	*n* pl. **-S** smooth solidified lava	**PALAIS**	*n* pl. **PALAIS** a palace

PALAPA *n* pl. **-S** an open-sided dwelling with a roof of palm leaves

PALATAL *n* pl. **-S** a bone of the palate

PALATE *n* pl. **-S** the roof of the mouth

PALATIAL *adj* resembling a palace

PALATINE *n* pl. **-S** a high officer of an empire

PALAVER *v* **-ED, -ING, -S** to chatter

PALAZZO *n* pl. **-ZI** an impressive building

PALAZZOS *n/pl* wide-legged pants for women

PALE *adj* **PALER, PALEST** lacking intensity of color

PALE *v* **PALED, PALING, PALES** to make or become pale

PALEA *n* pl. **-LEAE** a small bract **PALEAL** *adj*

PALEATE *adj* covered with scales

PALEFACE *n* pl. **-S** a white person

PALELY *adv* in a pale manner

PALENESS *n* pl. **-ES** the quality of being pale

PALEOCON *n* pl. **-S** an extremely right-wing conservative

PALEOSOL *n* pl. **-S** a layer of ancient soil

PALER comparative of pale

PALEST superlative of pale

PALESTRA *n* pl. **-TRAS** or **-TRAE** a school for athletics in ancient Greece

PALET *n* pl. **-S** a palea

PALETOT *n* pl. **-S** a loose overcoat

PALETTE *n* pl. **-S** a board on which an artist mixes colors

PALEWAYS *adv* palewise

PALEWISE *adv* vertically

PALFREY *n* pl. **-FREYS** a riding horse

PALI *n* pl. **-S** a cliff in Hawaii

PALIER comparative of paly

PALIEST superlative of paly

PALIKAR *n* pl. **-S** a Greek soldier

PALIMONY *n* pl. **-NIES** an allowance paid to one member of an unmarried couple who have separated

PALING *n* pl. **-S** a picket fence

PALINODE *n* pl. **-S** a formal retraction

PALISADE *v* **-SADED, -SADING, -SADES** to fortify with a heavy fence

PALISH *adj* somewhat pale

PALL *v* **-ED, -ING, -S** to become insipid

PALLADIA *n/pl* safeguards

PALLADIC *adj* pertaining to the metallic element palladium

PALLED past tense of pal

PALLET *v* **-ED, -ING, -S** to place on platforms for storage or moving

PALLETTE *n* pl. **-S** a piece of armor protecting the armpit

PALLIA a pl. of pallium

PALLIAL *adj* pertaining to a part of the brain

PALLIATE *v* **-ATED, -ATING, -ATES** to conceal the seriousness of

PALLID *adj* **PALLIDER, PALLIDEST** pale **PALLIDLY** *adv*

PALLIER comparative of pally

PALLIEST superlative of pally

PALLING present participle of pal or pall

PALLIUM *n* pl. **-LIUMS** or **-LIA** a cloak worn in ancient Rome

PALLOR *n* pl. **-S** paleness

PALLY *adj* **-LIER, -LIEST** marked by close friendship

PALM *v* **-ED, -ING, -S** to touch with the palm (inner surface) of the hand

PALMAR *adj* pertaining to the palm

PALMARY *adj* worthy of praise

PALMATE *adj* resembling an open hand

PALMATED *adj* palmate

PALMBALL *n* pl. **-S** a baseball pitched from the palm and thumb

PALMER *n* pl. **-S** a religious pilgrim

PALMETTE *n* pl. **-S** a type of ornament

PALMETTO *n* pl. **-TOS** or **-TOES** a tropical tree

PALMFUL *n* pl. **-S** as much as a palm can hold

PALMIER *n* pl. **-S** a pastry shaped like a palm leaf

PALMIEST superlative of palmy

PALMIST *n* pl. **-S** a fortune-teller

PALMITIN *n* pl. **-S** a chemical compound

PALMLIKE *adj* resembling a palm tree

PALMTOP *n* pl. **-S** a small computer that fits in the palm of the hand

PALMY *adj* **PALMIER, PALMIEST** marked by prosperity

PALMYRA *n* pl. **-S** a tropical tree

PALOMINO *n* pl. **-NOS** a horse with a golden coat and white mane

PALOOKA *n* pl. **-S** an inferior boxer

PALP *v* **-ED, -ING, -S** to touch

PALPABLE   *adj* capable of being felt **PALPABLY** *adv*

PALPAL   *adj* pertaining to a palpus

PALPATE   *v* **-PATED, -PATING, -PATES** to examine by touch

PALPATOR   *n* pl. **-S** one that palpates

PALPEBRA   *n* pl. **-BRAS** or **-BRAE** an eyelid

PALPUS   *n* pl. **-PI** a sensory organ of an arthropod

PALSA   *n* pl. **-S** a landform of subarctic regions

PALSHIP   *n* pl. **-S** the relation existing between close friends

PALSY   *v* **-SIED, -SYING, -SIES** to paralyze

PALSY   *adj* **-SIER, -SIEST** friendly in a way that is not proper or sincere

PALTER   *v* **-ED, -ING, -S** to talk or act insincerely

PALTERER   *n* pl. **-S** one that palters

PALTRY   *adj* **-TRIER, -TRIEST** petty **PALTRILY** *adv*

PALUDAL   *adj* pertaining to a marsh

PALUDISM   *n* pl. **-S** malaria

PALY   *adj* **PALIER, PALIEST** somewhat pale

PAM   *n* pl. **-S** the jack of clubs in certain card games

PAMPA   *n* pl. **-S** a grassland of South America

PAMPEAN   *n* pl. **-S** a native of the pampas

PAMPER   *v* **-ED, -ING, -S** to treat with extreme or excessive indulgence

PAMPERER   *n* pl. **-S** one that pampers

PAMPERO   *n* pl. **-ROS** a cold, dry wind

PAMPHLET   *n* pl. **-S** a printed work with a paper cover

PAN   *v* **PANNED, PANNING, PANS** to criticize harshly

PANACEA   *n* pl. **-S** a remedy for all diseases or ills **PANACEAN** *adj*

PANACHE   *n* pl. **-S** an ornamental tuft of feathers

PANADA   *n* pl. **-S** a thick sauce

PANAMA   *n* pl. **-S** a lightweight hat

PANATELA   *n* pl. **-S** a long, slender cigar

PANBROIL   *v* **-ED, -ING, -S** to fry in a pan with little or no fat

PANCAKE   *v* **-CAKED, -CAKING, -CAKES** to land an airplane in a certain manner

PANCETTA   *n* pl. **-S** unsmoked Italian bacon

PANCHAX   *n* pl. **-ES** a tropical fish

PANCREAS   *n* pl. **-ES** a large gland

PANDA   *n* pl. **-S** an herbivorous mammal

PANDAN   *n* pl. **-S** pandanus

PANDANUS   *n* pl. **-NUSES** or **-NI** a tropical plant

PANDECT   *n* pl. **-S** a complete body of laws

PANDEMIC   *n* pl. **-S** a widespread disease

PANDER   *v* **-ED, -ING, -S** to provide gratification for others' desires

PANDERER   *n* pl. **-S** one that panders

PANDIED   past tense of pandy

PANDIES   present 3d person sing. of pandy

PANDIT   *n* pl. **-S** a wise or learned man in India

PANDOOR   *n* pl. **-S** pandour

PANDORA   *n* pl. **-S** bandore

PANDORE   *n* pl. **-S** bandore

PANDOUR   *n* pl. **-S** a marauding soldier

PANDOWDY   *n* pl. **-DIES** an apple dessert

PANDURA   *n* pl. **-S** bandore

PANDY   *v* **-DIED, -DYING, -DIES** to punish by striking the hand

PANE   *n* pl. **-S** a sheet of glass for a window **PANED** *adj*

PANEER   *n* pl. **-S** a milk curd cheese

PANEL   *v* **-ELED, -ELING, -ELS** or **-ELLED, -ELLING, -ELS** to decorate with thin sheets of material

PANELESS   *adj* lacking panes

PANELING   *n* pl. **-S** material with which to panel

PANELIST   *n* pl. **-S** a member of a discussion or advisory group

PANELLED   a past tense of panel

PANELLING   a present participle of panel

PANETELA   *n* pl. **-S** panatela

PANFISH   *v* **-ED, -ING, -ES** to fish for any small fish that can be fried whole

PANFORTE   *n* pl. **-S** a hard spicy cake

PANFRY   *v* **-FRIED, -FRYING, -FRIES** to fry in a frying pan

PANFUL   *n* pl. **-S** as much as a pan will hold

PANG   *v* **-ED, -ING, -S** to cause to have spasms of pain

PANGA   *n* pl. **-S** a large knife

PANGEN *n* pl. **-S** a hypothetical heredity-controlling particle of protoplasm

PANGENE *n* pl. **-S** pangen

PANGOLIN *n* pl. **-S** a toothless mammal

PANGRAM *n* pl. **-S** a sentence that includes all the letters of the alphabet

PANHUMAN *adj* pertaining to all humanity

PANIC *v* **-ICKED, -ICKING, -ICS** to be overwhelmed by fear

PANICKY *adj* **-ICKIER, -ICKIEST** tending to panic

PANICLE *n* pl. **-S** a loosely branched flower cluster **PANICLED** *adj*

PANICUM *n* pl. **-S** a grass

PANIER *n* pl. **-S** pannier

PANINO *n* pl. **PANINI** or **PANINIS** a sandwich made with a small bread roll

PANLIKE *adj* resembling a pan (a container used for cooking)

PANMIXIA *n* pl. **-S** random mating within a breeding population

PANMIXIS *n* pl. **-MIXES** panmixia

PANNE *n* pl. **-S** a lustrous velvet

PANNED past tense of pan

PANNER *n* pl. **-S** one that pans

PANNIER *n* pl. **-S** a large basket

PANNIKIN *n* pl. **-S** a small saucepan

PANNING present participle of pan

PANNIST *n* pl. **-S** a person who plays a steel drum

PANOCHA *n* pl. **-S** a coarse Mexican sugar

PANOCHE *n* pl. **-S** panocha

PANOPLY *n* pl. **-PLIES** a suit of armor

PANOPTIC *adj* including everything visible in one view

PANORAMA *n* pl. **-S** a complete view

PANPIPE *n* pl. **-S** a musical instrument

PANSOPHY *n* pl. **-PHIES** universal knowledge

PANSY *n* pl. **-SIES** a flowering plant

PANT *v* **-ED, -ING, -S** to breathe quickly and with difficulty

PANTALET *n* pl. **-S** long underpants trimmed with ruffles

PANTHEON *n* pl. **-S** a temple dedicated to all the gods

PANTHER *n* pl. **-S** a leopard

PANTIE *n* pl. **-S** a woman's or child's undergarment

PANTIES pl. of panty

PANTILE *n* pl. **-S** a roofing tile **PANTILED** *adj*

PANTO *n* pl. **-TOS** a pantomime

PANTOFLE *n* pl. **-S** a slipper

PANTOUM *n* pl. **-S** a verse form

PANTRY *n* pl. **-TRIES** a closet or room for storing kitchen utensils

PANTSUIT *n* pl. **-S** a type of woman's suit

PANTY *n* pl. **PANTIES** pantie

PANZER *n* pl. **-S** an armored combat vehicle

PAP *n* pl. **-S** a soft food for infants

PAPA *n* pl. **-S** a father

PAPACY *n* pl. **-CIES** the office of the pope

PAPADAM *n* pl. **-S** papadum

PAPADOM *n* pl. **-S** papadum

PAPADUM *n* pl. **-S** a thin, crisp bread of India

PAPAIN *n* pl. **-S** an enzyme

PAPAL *adj* pertaining to the pope **PAPALLY** *adv*

PAPALIST *n* pl. **-S** an advocate of papal supremacy

PAPASAN *n* pl. **-S** a chair shaped like a bowl

PAPAW *n* pl. **-S** a fleshy fruit

PAPAYA *n* pl. **-S** a melon-like fruit **PAPAYAN** *adj*

PAPER *v* **-ED, -ING, -S** to cover or wrap with paper (a thin sheet of material made of cellulose pulp)

PAPERBOY *n* pl. **-BOYS** a newsboy

PAPERER *n* pl. **-S** one that papers

PAPERY *adj* resembling paper

PAPHIAN *n* pl. **-S** a prostitute

PAPILLA *n* pl. **-LAE** a nipple-like projection **PAPILLAR** *adj*

PAPILLON *n* pl. **-S** a small dog having large ears

PAPOOSE *n* pl. **-S** a Native American baby

PAPPADAM *n* pl. **-S** papadum

PAPPADUM *n* pl. **-S** papadum

PAPPI a pl. of pappus

PAPPIER comparative of pappy

PAPPIES pl. of pappy

PAPPOOSE *n* pl. **-S** papoose

PAPPUS *n* pl. **-PI** a tuft of bristles on the achene of certain plants **PAPPOSE, PAPPOUS** *adj*

PAPPY *adj* **-PIER, -PIEST** resembling pap

PAPPY *n* pl. **-PIES** a father

PAPRICA *n* pl. **-S** paprika

PAPRIKA *n* pl. **-S** a seasoning made from red peppers

PAPULA *n* pl. **-LAE** or **-LAS** papule

PAPULE *n* pl. **-S** a pimple **PAPULAR, PAPULOSE, PAPULOUS** *adj*

PAPYRUS *n* pl. **-RUSES** or **-RI** a tall aquatic plant **PAPYRAL, PAPYRIAN, PAPYRINE** *adj*

PAR *v* **PARRED, PARRING, PARS** to shoot in a standard number of strokes in golf

PARA *n* pl. **PARAS** or **PARAE** a woman's status regarding the bearing of offspring

PARABLE *n* pl. **-S** a simple story conveying a moral or religious lesson

PARABOLA *n* pl. **-LAS** or **-LAE** a conic section

PARACHOR *n* pl. **-S** a mathematical constant that relates molecular volume to surface tension

PARADE *v* **-RADED, -RADING, -RADES** to march in a public procession

PARADER *n* pl. **-S** one that parades

PARADIGM *n* pl. **-S** a pattern or example

PARADISE *n* pl. **-S** a place of extreme beauty or delight

PARADOR *n* pl. **-DORS** or **-DORES** an inn in Spain

PARADOS *n* pl. **-ES** a protective embankment

PARADOX *n* pl. **-ES** a statement seemingly contradictory or absurd yet perhaps true

PARADROP *v* **-DROPPED, -DROPPING, -DROPS** to deliver by parachute

PARAFFIN *v* **-ED, -ING, -S** to coat with a waxy substance

PARAFOIL *n* pl. **-S** a fabric device that resembles a parachute

PARAFORM *n* pl. **-S** a substance used as an antiseptic

PARAGOGE *n* pl. **-S** the addition of a sound or sounds at the end of a word

PARAGON *v* **-ED, -ING, -S** to compare with

PARAKEET *n* pl. **-S** a small parrot

PARAKITE *n* pl. **-S** a parachute kite for towing a person through the air by a motorboat

PARALLAX *n* pl. **-ES** an apparent optical displacement of an object

PARALLEL *v* **-LELED, -LELING, -LELS** or **-LELLED, -LELLING, -LELS** to be similar or analogous to

PARALYSE *v* **-LYSED, -LYSING, -LYSES** to paralyze

PARALYZE *v* **-LYZED, -LYZING, -LYZES** to render incapable of movement

PARAMENT *n* pl. **-MENTS** or **-MENTA** an ornamental vestment

PARAMO *n* pl. **-MOS** a plateau region of South America

PARAMOUR *n* pl. **-S** an illicit lover

PARANG *n* pl. **-S** a heavy knife

PARANOEA *n* pl. **-S** paranoia

PARANOIA *n* pl. **-S** a mental disorder

PARANOIC *n* pl. **-S** a paranoid

PARANOID *n* pl. **-S** one affected with paranoia

PARAPET *n* pl. **-S** a protective wall

PARAPH *n* pl. **-S** a flourish at the end of a signature

PARAQUAT *n* pl. **-S** a weed killer

PARAQUET *n* pl. **-S** parakeet

PARASAIL *v* **-ED, -ING, -S** to soar while harnessed to a parachute towed by a car or boat

PARASANG *n* pl. **-S** a Persian unit of distance

PARASHAH *n* pl. **-SHAHS** or **-SHOTH** or **-SHOT** a portion of the Torah read on the Sabbath

PARASITE *n* pl. **-S** an organism that lives and feeds on or in another organism

PARASOL *n* pl. **-S** a small, light umbrella

PARATHA *n* pl. **-S** a piece of unleavened bread fried on a griddle

PARAVANE *n* pl. **-S** an underwater device used to cut cables

PARAWING *n* pl. **-S** a winglike parachute

PARAZOAN *n* pl. **-S** any of a major division of multicellular animals

PARBAKE *v* **-BAKED, -BAKING, -BAKES** to bake partially

PARBOIL *v* **-ED, -ING, -S** to cook partially by boiling for a short time

PARCEL *v* **-CELED, -CELING, -CELS** or **-CELLED, -CELLING, -CELS** to divide into parts or shares

PARCENER *n* pl. **-S** a joint heir

PARCH *v* **-ED, -ING, -ES** to make very dry

PARCHESI *n* pl. **-S** pachisi

PARCHISI *n* pl. **-S** pachisi

PARCLOSE *n* pl. **-S** a screen dividing areas in a church

PARD *n* pl. **-S** a leopard

PARDAH *n* pl. **-S** purdah

PARDEE *interj* pardi

PARDI *interj* — used as a mild oath

PARDIE *interj* pardi

PARDINE *adj* pertaining to a leopard

PARDNER *n* pl. **-S** chum; friend

PARDON *v* **-ED, -ING, -S** to release from liability for an offense

PARDONER *n* pl. **-S** one that pardons

PARDY *interj* pardi

PARE *v* **PARED, PARING, PARES** to cut off the outer covering of

PARECISM *n* pl. **-S** the state of having the male and female sexual organs beside or near each other

PAREIRA *n* pl. **-S** a medicinal plant root

PAREN *n* pl. **-S** a parenthesis

PARENT *v* **-ED, -ING, -S** to exercise the functions of a parent (a father or mother)

PARENTAL *adj* pertaining to a parent

PAREO *n* pl. **-REOS** pareu

PARER *n* pl. **-S** one that pares

PARERGON *n* pl. **-GA** a composition derived from a larger work

PARESIS *n* pl. **-RESES** partial loss of the ability to move

PARETIC *n* pl. **-S** one affected with paresis

PAREU *n* pl. **-S** a Polynesian garment

PAREVE *adj* parve

PARFAIT *n* pl. **-S** a frozen dessert

PARFLESH *n* pl. **-ES** a rawhide soaked in lye to remove the hair and dried

PARFOCAL *adj* having lenses with the corresponding focal points in the same plane

PARGE *v* **PARGED, PARGING, PARGES** to parget

PARGET *v* **-GETED, -GETING, -GETS** or **-GETTED, -GETTING, -GETS** to cover with plaster

PARGING *n* pl. **-S** a thin coat of mortar or plaster for sealing masonry

PARGO *n* pl. **-GOS** a food fish

PARHELIA *n/pl* bright circular spots appearing on a solar halo

PARHELIC *adj* pertaining to parhelia

PARIAH *n* pl. **-S** a social outcast

PARIAN *n* pl. **-S** a hard, white porcelain

PARIES *n* pl. **PARIETES** the wall of an organ

PARIETAL *n* pl. **-S** a bone of the skull

PARING *n* pl. **-S** something pared off

PARIS *n* pl. **-ISES** a European herb

PARISH *n* pl. **-ES** an ecclesiastical district

PARITY *n* pl. **-TIES** equality

PARK *v* **-ED, -ING, -S** to leave a vehicle in a location for a time

PARKA *n* pl. **-S** a hooded garment

PARKADE *n* pl. **-S** a multilevel structure for parking vehicles

PARKER *n* pl. **-S** one that parks

PARKETTE *n* pl. **-S** a small public park

PARKIER comparative of parky

PARKIEST superlative of parky

PARKIN *n* pl. **-S** a kind of bread made with molasses and oatmeal

PARKING *n* pl. **-S** an area in which vehicles may be left

PARKLAND *n* pl. **-S** a grassland region with isolated or grouped trees

PARKLIKE *adj* resembling an outdoor recreational area

PARKOUR *n* pl. **-S** the sport of traversing environmental obstacles by running, climbing, or leaping

PARKWAY *n* pl. **-WAYS** a wide highway

PARKY *adj* **PARKIER, PARKIEST** chilly

PARLANCE *n* pl. **-S** a manner of speaking

PARLANDO *adj* sung in a manner suggestive of speech

PARLANTE *adj* parlando

PARLAY *v* **-ED, -ING, -S** to bet an original wager and its winnings on a subsequent event

PARLE *v* **PARLED, PARLING, PARLES** to parley

PARLEY *v* **-LEYED, -LEYING, -LEYS** to discuss terms with an enemy

PARLEYER *n* pl. **-S** one that parleys

PARLOR *n* pl. **-S** a room for the entertainment of visitors

PARLOUR *n* pl. **-S** parlor

PARLOUS *adj* dangerous

PARMESAN *n* pl. **-S** a hard, dry Italian cheese

PARODIC *adj* comically imitative

PARODIST *n pl.* **-S** one who parodies

PARODOS *n pl.* **-DOI** an ode sung in ancient Greek drama

PARODY *v* **-DIED, -DYING, -DIES** to imitate a serious literary work for comic effect

PAROL *n pl.* **-S** an utterance

PAROLE *v* **-ROLED, -ROLING, -ROLES** to release from prison before completion of the imposed sentence

PAROLEE *n pl.* **-S** one who is paroled

PARONYM *n pl.* **-S** a word having the same root as another

PARONYMY *n pl.* **-MIES** the state of being a paronym

PAROQUET *n pl.* **-S** parakeet

PAROSMIA *n pl.* **-S** a distortion of the sense of smell

PAROTIC *adj* situated near the ear

PAROTID *n pl.* **-S** a salivary gland

PAROTOID *n pl.* **-S** a gland of certain toads and frogs

PAROUS *adj* having produced offspring

PAROXYSM *n pl.* **-S** a sudden fit or attack

PARQUET *v* **-ED, -ING, -S** to furnish with a floor of inlaid design

PARR *n pl.* **-S** a young salmon

PARRAL *n pl.* **-S** parrel

PARRED past tense of par

PARREL *n pl.* **-S** a sliding loop of rope or chain used on a ship

PARRIDGE *n pl.* **-S** porridge

PARRIED past tense of parry

PARRIER *n pl.* **-S** one that parries

PARRIES present 3d person sing. of parry

PARRING present participle of par

PARRITCH *n pl.* **-ES** porridge

PARROKET *n pl.* **-S** parakeet

PARROT *v* **-ED, -ING, -S** to repeat or imitate without thought or understanding

PARROTER *n pl.* **-S** one that parrots

PARROTY *adj* resembling a parrot (a hook-billed tropical bird)

PARRY *v* **-RIED, -RYING, -RIES** to ward off a blow

PARSE *v* **PARSED, PARSING, PARSES** to describe and analyze grammatically **PARSABLE** *adj*

PARSEC *n pl.* **-S** a unit of astronomical distance

PARSER *n pl.* **-S** one that parses

PARSLEY *n pl.* **-LEYS** a cultivated herb **PARSLEYED, PARSLIED** *adj*

PARSNIP *n pl.* **-S** a European herb

PARSON *n pl.* **-S** a clergyman **PARSONIC** *adj*

PART *v* **-ED, -ING, -S** to divide or break into separate pieces

PARTAKE *v* **-TOOK, -TAKEN, -TAKING, -TAKES** to participate

PARTAKER *n pl.* **-S** one that partakes

PARTAN *n pl.* **-S** an edible crab

PARTER *n pl.* **-S** one that parts

PARTERRE *n pl.* **-S** a section of a theater

PARTIAL *n pl.* **-S** a simple component of a complex tone

PARTIBLE *adj* divisible

PARTICLE *n pl.* **-S** a very small piece or part

PARTIED past tense of party

PARTIER *n pl.* **-S** partyer

PARTIES present 3d person sing. of party

PARTING *n pl.* **-S** a division or separation

PARTISAN *n pl.* **-S** a firm supporter of a person, party, or cause

PARTITA *n pl.* **-S** a set of related instrumental pieces

PARTITE *adj* divided into parts

PARTIZAN *n pl.* **-S** partisan

PARTLET *n pl.* **-S** a woman's garment

PARTLY *adv* in some measure or degree

PARTNER *v* **-ED, -ING, -S** to associate with in some activity of common interest

PARTON *n pl.* **-S** a hypothetical atomic particle

PARTOOK past tense of partake

PARTWAY *adv* to some extent

PARTY *v* **-TIED, -TYING, -TIES** to attend a social gathering

PARTYER *n pl.* **-S** one that parties

PARTYING *n pl.* **-S** participation in a party

PARURA *n pl.* **-S** parure

PARURE *n pl.* **-S** a set of matched jewelry

PARVE *adj* made without milk or meat

PARVENU *n pl.* **-S** one who has suddenly risen above his or her class

PARVENUE *n pl.* **-S** a woman who is a parvenu

PARVIS *n pl.* **-VISES** an enclosed area in front of a church

PARVISE *n pl.* **-S** parvis

PARVO *n pl.* **-VOS** a contagious disease of dogs

PARVOLIN *n pl.* **-S** an oily liquid obtained from fish

PASCAL *n pl.* **-S** a unit of pressure

PASCHAL *n pl.* **-S** a candle used in certain religious ceremonies

PASE *n pl.* **-S** a movement of a matador's cape

PASEO *n pl.* **-SEOS** a leisurely stroll

PASH *v* **-ED, -ING, -ES** to strike violently

PASHA *n pl.* **-S** a former Turkish high official

PASHADOM *n pl.* **-S** the rank of a pasha

PASHALIC *n pl.* **-S** pashalik

PASHALIK *n pl.* **-S** the territory of a pasha

PASHKA *n pl.* **-S** paskha

PASHM *n pl.* **-S** the inner fur of some Tibetan animals

PASHMINA *n pl.* **-S** wool obtained from Himalayan goats

PASKA *n pl.* **-S** paskha

PASKHA *n pl.* **-S** a Russian dessert eaten at Easter

PASQUIL *n pl.* **-S** a satire or lampoon

PASS *v* **-ED, -ING, -ES** to go by

PASSABLE *adj* fairly good or acceptable **PASSABLY** *adv*

PASSADE *n pl.* **-S** a turn of a horse backward or forward on the same ground

PASSADO *n pl.* **-DOS** or **-DOES** a forward thrust in fencing

PASSAGE *v* **-SAGED, -SAGING, -SAGES** to make a voyage

PASSANT *adj* walking with the farther forepaw raised — used of a heraldic animal

PASSBAND *n pl.* **-S** a frequency band that permits transmission with maximum efficiency

PASSBOOK *n pl.* **-S** a bankbook

PASSE *adj* outmoded

PASSEE *adj* passe

PASSEL *n pl.* **-S** a large quantity or number

PASSER *n pl.* **-S** one that passes

PASSERBY *n pl.* **PASSERSBY** one who passes by

PASSIBLE *adj* capable of feeling or suffering

PASSIM *adv* here and there

PASSING *n pl.* **-S** a death

PASSION *n pl.* **-S** an intense emotion

PASSIVE *n pl.* **-S** a verb form

PASSKEY *n pl.* **-KEYS** a key that opens several different locks

PASSLESS *adj* incapable of being traveled over or through

PASSOVER *n pl.* **-S** the lamb eaten at the feast of a Jewish holiday

PASSPORT *n pl.* **-S** a document allowing travel from one country to another

PASSUS *n pl.* **-ES** a section of a story or poem

PASSWORD *n pl.* **-S** a secret word that must be spoken to gain admission

PAST *n pl.* **-S** time gone by

PASTA *n pl.* **-S** a food made of dough

PASTE *v* **PASTED, PASTING, PASTES** to fasten with a sticky mixture

PASTEL *n pl.* **-S** a soft, delicate hue

PASTER *n pl.* **-S** one that pastes

PASTERN *n pl.* **-S** a part of a horse's foot

PASTEUP *n pl.* **-S** a finished copy to be photographed for making a printing plate

PASTICCI *n/pl* pastiches

PASTICHE *n pl.* **-S** an artistic work made of fragments from various sources

PASTIE *n pl.* **-S** pasty

PASTIER comparative of pasty

PASTIES pl. of pasty

PASTIEST superlative of pasty

PASTIL *n pl.* **-S** pastille

PASTILLE *n pl.* **-S** a lozenge

PASTILY *adv* in a manner that is pasty

PASTIME *n pl.* **-S** a recreational activity

PASTINA *n pl.* **-S** a type of macaroni

PASTING *n pl.* **-S** a beating

PASTIS *n pl.* **-TISES** a French liqueur

PASTITSO *n pl.* **-TSOS** a Greek dish of ground meat, pasta, white sauce, and cheese

PASTLESS *adj* having no past

PASTNESS *n pl.* **-ES** the state of being past or gone by

PASTOR *v* **-ED, -ING, -S** to serve as the spiritual overseer of

PASTORAL	n pl. **-S** a literary or artistic work that depicts country life
PASTORLY	adj befitting a pastor (a spiritual overseer)
PASTRAMI	n pl. **-S** a highly seasoned smoked beef
PASTROMI	n pl. **-S** pastrami
PASTRY	n pl. **-TRIES** a sweet baked food
PASTURAL	adj pertaining to a pasture
PASTURE	v **-TURED, -TURING, -TURES** to put in a pasture (a grazing area)
PASTURER	n pl. **-S** one that pastures livestock
PASTY	adj **PASTIER, PASTIEST** pale and unhealthy in appearance
PASTY	n pl. **PASTIES** a meat pie
PAT	v **PATTED, PATTING, PATS** to touch lightly
PAT	adj **PATTER, PATTEST** known thoroughly
PATACA	n pl. **-S** a monetary unit of Macao
PATAGIAL	adj pertaining to a patagium
PATAGIUM	n pl. **-GIA** a wing membrane of a bat
PATAMAR	n pl. **-S** a sailing vessel
PATCH	v **-ED, -ING, -ES** to mend or cover a hole or weak spot in
PATCHER	n pl. **-S** one that patches
PATCHY	adj **PATCHIER, PATCHIEST** uneven in quality **PATCHILY** adv
PATE	n pl. **-S** the top of the head **PATED** adj
PATELLA	n pl. **-LAS** or **-LAE** the flat movable bone at the front of the knee **PATELLAR** adj
PATEN	n pl. **-S** a plate
PATENCY	n pl. **-CIES** the state of being obvious
PATENT	v **-ED, -ING, -S** to obtain a patent (a government grant protecting the rights of an inventor) on
PATENTEE	n pl. **-S** one that holds a patent
PATENTLY	adv obviously
PATENTOR	n pl. **-S** one that grants a patent
PATER	n pl. **-S** a father
PATERNAL	adj pertaining to a father
PATH	n pl. **-S** a trodden way or track
PATHETIC	adj arousing pity
PATHLESS	adj having no path
PATHNAME	n pl. **-S** a description of where a file is to be found
PATHOGEN	n pl. **-S** any disease-producing organism
PATHOS	n pl. **-ES** a quality that arouses feelings of pity or compassion
PATHWAY	n pl. **-WAYS** a path
PATIENCE	n pl. **-S** the quality of being patient
PATIENT	adj **-TIENTER, -TIENTEST** able to endure disagreeable circumstances without complaint
PATIENT	n pl. **-S** one who is under medical treatment
PATIN	n pl. **-S** paten
PATINA	n pl. **-NAS** or **-NAE** a green film that forms on bronze **PATINAED** adj
PATINATE	v **-NATED, -NATING, -NATES** to give a patina to
PATINE	v **-TINED, -TINING, -TINES** to cover with a patina
PATINIZE	v **-NIZED, -NIZING, -NIZES** to patinate
PATIO	n pl. **-TIOS** an outdoor paved area adjoining a house
PATLY	adv suitably
PATNESS	n pl. **-ES** suitability
PATOIS	n pl. **PATOIS** a dialect
PATONCE	adj having the arms broaden from the center and end in three-pointed lobes — used of a heraldic cross
PATOOT	n pl. **-S** patootie
PATOOTIE	n pl. **-S** the buttocks
PATRIATE	v **-ATED, -ATING, -ATES** to transfer (power of legislation) to an autonomous country
PATRIOT	n pl. **-S** one who loves his or her country
PATROL	v **-TROLLED, -TROLLING, -TROLS** to pass through an area for the purposes of observation or security
PATRON	n pl. **-S** a regular customer **PATRONAL, PATRONLY** adj
PATROON	n pl. **-S** a landowner with manorial rights under old Dutch law
PATSY	n pl. **-SIES** a person who is easily fooled
PATTAMAR	n pl. **-S** patamar
PATTED	past tense of pat
PATTEE	adj paty
PATTEN	n pl. **-S** a shoe having a thick wooden sole **PATTENED** adj

PATTER	v **-ED, -ING, -S** to talk glibly or rapidly	**PAVILION**	v **-ED, -ING, -S** to cover with a large tent
PATTERER	n pl. **-S** one that patters	**PAVILLON**	n pl. **-S** the bell of a wind instrument
PATTERN	v **-ED, -ING, -S** to make according to a prescribed design	**PAVIN**	n pl. **-S** pavan
PATTEST	superlative of pat	**PAVING**	n pl. **-S** pavement
PATTIE	n pl. **-S** patty	**PAVIOR**	n pl. **-S** a paver
PATTING	present participle of pat	**PAVIOUR**	n pl. **-S** a paver
PATTY	n pl. **-TIES** a small, flat cake of chopped food	**PAVIS**	n pl. **-ISES** a large medieval shield
		PAVISE	n pl. **-S** pavis
PATTYPAN	n pl. **-S** a pan in which patties are baked	**PAVISER**	n pl. **-S** a soldier carrying a pavis
		PAVISSE	n pl. **-S** pavis
PATULENT	adj patulous	**PAVLOVA**	n pl. **-S** a meringue dessert
PATULOUS	adj spreading; open	**PAVONINE**	adj resembling a peacock
PATY	adj formee	**PAW**	v **-ED, -ING, -S** to strike or scrape with a beating motion
PATZER	n pl. **-S** an inept chess player		
PAUA	n pl. **-S** a large New Zealand shellfish	**PAWER**	n pl. **-S** one that paws
		PAWKY	adj **PAWKIER, PAWKIEST** sly **PAWKILY** adv
PAUCITY	n pl. **-TIES** smallness of number or quantity		
		PAWL	n pl. **-S** a hinged mechanical part
PAUGHTY	adj arrogant	**PAWN**	v **-ED, -ING, -S** to give as security for something borrowed **PAWNABLE** adj
PAULDRON	n pl. **-S** a piece of armor for the shoulder		
PAULIN	n pl. **-S** a sheet of waterproof material	**PAWNAGE**	n pl. **-S** an act of pawning
		PAWNEE	n pl. **-S** one to whom something is pawned
PAUNCH	n pl. **-ES** the belly or abdomen **PAUNCHED** adj		
		PAWNER	n pl. **-S** one that pawns something
PAUNCHY	adj **PAUNCHIER, PAUNCHIEST** having a protruding belly	**PAWNOR**	n pl. **-S** pawner
		PAWNSHOP	n pl. **-S** a place where things are pawned
PAUPER	v **-ED, -ING, -S** to reduce to poverty		
		PAWPAW	n pl. **-S** papaw
PAURAQUE	n pl. **-S** a long-tailed nocturnal bird	**PAX**	n pl. **-ES** a ceremonial embrace given to signify Christian love and unity
PAUROPOD	n pl. **-S** any of a class of minute many-legged animals		
		PAXWAX	n pl. **-ES** the nuchal ligament of a quadruped
PAUSAL	adj pertaining to a break or rest in speaking or writing		
PAUSE	v **PAUSED, PAUSING, PAUSES** to stop temporarily	**PAY**	v **PAID** or **PAYED, PAYING, PAYS** to give money or something of value in exchange for goods or services
PAUSER	n pl. **-S** one that pauses		
PAVAN	n pl. **-S** a slow, stately dance		
PAVANE	n pl. **-S** pavan	**PAYABLE**	adj profitable **PAYABLY** adv
PAVE	v **PAVED, PAVING, PAVES** to cover with material that forms a firm, level surface	**PAYABLES**	n/pl accounts payable
		PAYBACK	n pl. **-S** a return on an investment equal to the original capital outlay
PAVEED	adj set close together to conceal a metal base	**PAYCHECK**	n pl. **-S** a check in payment of wages or salary
PAVEMENT	n pl. **-S** a paved surface	**PAYDAY**	n pl. **-DAYS** the day on which wages are paid
PAVER	n pl. **-S** one that paves		
PAVID	adj timid	**PAYDOWN**	n pl. **-S** the reduction of debt through repayment

PAYEE	*n* pl. **-S** one to whom money is paid	**PEAGE**	*n* pl. **-S** peag
PAYER	*n* pl. **-S** one that pays	**PEAHEN**	*n* pl. **-S** a female peafowl
PAYESS	*n/pl* uncut sideburns worn by some Jews	**PEAK**	*v* **-ED, -ING, -S** to reach a maximum
PAYGRADE	*n* pl. **-S** the grade of military personnel according to a base pay scale	**PEAKIER**	comparative of peaky
		PEAKIEST	superlative of peaky
		PEAKISH	*adj* somewhat sickly
PAYLOAD	*n* pl. **-S** the part of a cargo producing income	**PEAKLESS**	*adj* having no peak (a pointed top)
		PEAKLIKE	*adj* resembling a peak
PAYMENT	*n* pl. **-S** something that is paid	**PEAKY**	*adj* **PEAKIER, PEAKIEST** sickly
PAYNIM	*n* pl. **-S** a pagan	**PEAL**	*v* **-ED, -ING, -S** to ring out
PAYOFF	*n* pl. **-S** the act of distributing gains	**PEALIKE**	*adj* resembling a pea
PAYOLA	*n* pl. **-S** a secret payment for favors	**PEAN**	*n* pl. **-S** paean
PAYOR	*n* pl. **-S** payer	**PEANUT**	*n* pl. **-S** the nutlike seed or pod of an annual vine
PAYOUT	*n* pl. **-S** money that is paid out	**PEANUTTY**	*n* **-NUTTIER, -NUTTIEST** having the taste of peanuts
PAYROLL	*n* pl. **-S** a list of employees entitled to payment	**PEAR**	*n* pl. **-S** a fleshy fruit
PAYSLIP	*n* pl. **-S** a brief record of an employee's wages indicating deductions	**PEARL**	*v* **-ED, -ING, -S** to adorn with pearls (smooth, rounded masses formed in certain mollusks)
PAYWALL	*n* pl. **-S** a system that prevents access to a website without a paid subscription	**PEARLASH**	*n* pl. **-ES** an alkaline compound
		PEARLER	*n* pl. **-S** one that dives for pearls
PAZAZZ	*n* pl. **-ES** pizazz	**PEARLIES**	*n/pl* teeth
PE	*n* pl. **-S** a Hebrew letter	**PEARLITE**	*n* pl. **-S** a cast-iron alloy
PEA	*n* pl. **-S** the edible seed of an annual herb	**PEARLY**	*adj* **PEARLIER, PEARLIEST** resembling a pearl
PEABERRY	*n* pl. **-RIES** a coffee berry having a single round seed	**PEARMAIN**	*n* pl. **-S** a variety of apple
PEABRAIN	*n* pl. **-S** a stupid person	**PEART**	*adj* **PEARTER, PEARTEST** lively **PEARTLY** *adv*
PEACE	*v* **PEACED, PEACING, PEACES** to be or become silent	**PEARWOOD**	*n* pl. **-S** the wood of the pear tree
PEACEFUL	*adj* **-FULLER, -FULLEST** undisturbed; calm	**PEASANT**	*n* pl. **-S** a person of inferior social rank **PEASANTY** *adj*
PEACENIK	*n* pl. **-S** one who demonstrates against a war	**PEASCOD**	*n* pl. **-S** peasecod
PEACH	*v* **-ED, -ING, -ES** to inform against someone	**PEASE**	*n* pl. **PEASES** or **PEASEN** a pea
		PEASECOD	*n* pl. **-S** a pea pod
PEACHER	*n* pl. **-S** one that peaches	**PEAT**	*n* pl. **-S** a substance composed of partially decayed vegetable matter
PEACHICK	*n* pl. **-S** a young peafowl	**PEATLAND**	*n* pl. **-S** land consisting mostly of peat
PEACHY	*adj* **PEACHIER, PEACHIEST** dandy	**PEATY**	*adj* **PEATIER, PEATIEST** resembling or containing peat
PEACING	present participle of peace	**PEAVEY**	*n* pl. **-VEYS** a lever used to move logs
PEACOAT	*n* pl. **-S** a heavy woolen jacket	**PEAVY**	*n* pl. **-VIES** peavey
PEACOCK	*v* **-ED, -ING, -S** to strut vainly	**PEBBLE**	*v* **-BLED, -BLING, -BLES** to cover with pebbles (small, rounded stones)
PEACOCKY	*adj* **-COCKIER, -COCKIEST** flamboyant, showy		
PEAFOWL	*n* pl. **-S** a large pheasant		
PEAG	*n* pl. **-S** wampum		

PEBBLY   *adj* **-BLIER, -BLIEST** resembling pebbles

PEC   *n* pl. **-S** a chest muscle

PECAN   *n* pl. **-S** a nut-bearing tree

PECCABLE   *adj* liable to sin

PECCANCY   *n* pl. **-CIES** the state of being peccant

PECCANT   *adj* sinful

PECCARY   *n* pl. **-RIES** a piglike hoofed mammal

PECCAVI   *n* pl. **-S** a confession of sin

PECH   *v* **-ED, -ING, -S** to pant

PECHAN   *n* pl. **-S** the stomach

PECK   *v* **-ED, -ING, -S** to strike with the beak or something pointed

PECKER   *n* pl. **-S** one that pecks

PECKISH   *adj* irritable

PECKY   *adj* **PECKIER, PECKIEST** marked by decay caused by fungi

PECORINO   *n* pl. **-NOS** or **-NI** a hard cheese made from sheep's milk

PECTASE   *n* pl. **-S** an enzyme

PECTATE   *n* pl. **-S** a chemical salt

PECTEN   *n* pl. **-TENS** or **-TINES** a comblike anatomical part

PECTIN   *n* pl. **-S** a carbohydrate derivative **PECTIC** *adj*

PECTIZE   *v* **-TIZED, -TIZING, -TIZES** to change into a jelly

PECTORAL   *n* pl. **-S** something worn on the breast

PECULATE   *v* **-LATED, -LATING, -LATES** to embezzle

PECULIAR   *n* pl. **-S** something belonging exclusively to a person

PECULIUM   *n* pl. **-LIA** private property

PED   *n* pl. **-S** a natural soil aggregate

PEDAGOG   *n* pl. **-S** a teacher

PEDAGOGY   *n* pl. **-GIES** the work of a teacher

PEDAL   *v* **-ALED, -ALING, -ALS** or **-ALLED, -ALLING, -ALS** to operate by means of foot levers

PEDALER   *n* pl. **-S** one that pedals

PEDALFER   *n* pl. **-S** a type of soil

PEDALIER   *n* pl. **-S** the pedal keyboard of an organ

PEDALLER   *n* pl. **-S** pedaler

PEDALO   *n* pl. **-LOS** a paddleboat powered by pedals

PEDANT   *n* pl. **-S** one who flaunts his or her knowledge **PEDANTIC** *adj*

PEDANTRY   *n* pl. **-RIES** ostentatious display of knowledge

PEDATE   *adj* resembling a foot **PEDATELY** *adv*

PEDDLE   *v* **-DLED, -DLING, -DLES** to travel about selling wares

PEDDLER   *n* pl. **-S** one that peddles

PEDDLERY   *n* pl. **-RIES** the trade of a peddler

PEDERAST   *n* pl. **-S** a man who engages in sexual activities with boys

PEDES   pl. of pes

PEDESTAL   *v* **-TALED, -TALING, -TALS** or **-TALLED, -TALLING, -TALS** to provide with an architectural support or base

PEDICAB   *n* pl. **-S** a passenger vehicle that is pedaled

PEDICEL   *n* pl. **-S** a slender basal part of an organism

PEDICLE   *n* pl. **-S** pedicel **PEDICLED** *adj*

PEDICURE   *v* **-CURED, -CURING, -CURES** to administer a cosmetic treatment to the feet and toenails

PEDIFORM   *adj* shaped like a foot

PEDIGREE   *n* pl. **-S** a line of ancestors

PEDIMENT   *n* pl. **-S** a triangular architectural part

PEDIPALP   *n* pl. **-S** an appendage of an arachnid

PEDLAR   *n* pl. **-S** peddler

PEDLARY   *n* pl. **-LARIES** peddlery

PEDLER   *n* pl. **-S** peddler

PEDLERY   *n* pl. **-LERIES** peddlery

PEDOCAL   *n* pl. **-S** a type of soil

PEDOLOGY   *n* pl. **-GIES** the scientific study of the behavior and development of children

PEDRO   *n* pl. **-DROS** a card game

PEDUNCLE   *n* pl. **-S** a flower stalk

PEDWAY   *n* pl. **-WAYS** a walkway for pedestrians only

PEE   *n* pl. **-S** the letter P

PEEBEEN   *n* pl. **-S** a large hardwood evergreen tree

PEEK   *v* **-ED, -ING, -S** to look furtively or quickly

PEEKABOO   *n* pl. **-BOOS** a children's game

PEEKAPOO	*n* pl. **-POOS** a dog that is a cross between a Pekingese and a poodle
PEEL	*v* **-ED, -ING, -S** to strip off an outer covering of **PEELABLE** *adj*
PEELER	*n* pl. **-S** one that peels
PEELING	*n* pl. **-S** a piece or strip that has been peeled off
PEEN	*v* **-ED, -ING, -S** to beat with the non-flat end of a hammerhead
PEENING	*n* pl. **-S** the action of treating sheet metal with metal shot in order to shape it
PEEP	*v* **-ED, -ING, -S** to utter a short, shrill cry
PEEPBO	*n* pl. **-BOS** the game of peekaboo
PEEPER	*n* pl. **-S** one that peeps
PEEPHOLE	*n* pl. **-S** a small opening through which one may look
PEEPSHOW	*n* pl. **-S** an exhibition viewed through a small opening
PEEPUL	*n* pl. **-S** pipal
PEER	*v* **-ED, -ING, -S** to look narrowly or searchingly
PEERAGE	*n* pl. **-S** the rank of a nobleman
PEERESS	*n* pl. **-ES** a noblewoman
PEERIE	*n* pl. **-S** peery
PEERLESS	*adj* having no equal
PEERY	*n* pl. **PEERIES** a child's toy
PEESWEEP	*n* pl. **-S** a lapwing
PEETWEET	*n* pl. **-S** a wading bird
PEEVE	*v* **PEEVED, PEEVING, PEEVES** to annoy
PEEVISH	*adj* irritable
PEEWEE	*n* pl. **-S** an unusually small person or thing
PEEWIT	*n* pl. **-S** pewit
PEG	*v* **PEGGED, PEGGING, PEGS** to fasten with a peg (a wooden pin)
PEGBOARD	*n* pl. **-S** a board with holes for pegs
PEGBOX	*n* pl. **-ES** a part of a stringed instrument
PEGLESS	*adj* lacking a peg
PEGLIKE	*adj* resembling a peg
PEGTOP	*n* pl. **-S** a spinning top having a peg wound with string
PEH	*n* pl. **-S** pe
PEIGNOIR	*n* pl. **-S** a woman's gown
PEIN	*v* **-ED, -ING, -S** to peen

PEISE	*v* **PEISED, PEISING, PEISES** to weigh
PEKAN	*n* pl. **-S** a carnivorous mammal
PEKE	*n* pl. **-S** a small, long-haired dog
PEKEPOO	*n* pl. **-POOS** peekapoo
PEKIN	*n* pl. **-S** a silk fabric
PEKOE	*n* pl. **-S** a black tea
PELAGE	*n* pl. **-S** the coat or covering of a mammal **PELAGIAL** *adj*
PELAGIC	*n* pl. **-S** an inhabitant of the ocean
PELAU	*n* pl. **-S** a dish made with meat, rice, and pigeon peas
PELE	*n* pl. **-S** a medieval fortified tower
PELERINE	*n* pl. **-S** a woman's cape
PELF	*n* pl. **-S** money or wealth
PELHAM	*n* pl. **-S** a type of a horse's mouthpiece
PELICAN	*n* pl. **-S** a large, web-footed bird
PELISSE	*n* pl. **-S** a long outer garment
PELITE	*n* pl. **-S** a rock composed of fine fragments **PELITIC** *adj*
PELLAGRA	*n* pl. **-S** a niacin-deficiency disease
PELLET	*v* **-ED, -ING, -S** to strike with pellets (small rounded masses)
PELLETAL	*adj* resembling a pellet
PELLICLE	*n* pl. **-S** a thin skin or film
PELLMELL	*n* pl. **-S** a jumbled mass
PELLUCID	*adj* transparent
PELMET	*n* pl. **-S** a decorative cornice
PELON	*adj* hairless
PELORIA	*n* pl. **-S** abnormal regularity of a flower form **PELORIAN, PELORIC** *adj*
PELORUS	*n* pl. **-ES** a navigational instrument
PELOTA	*n* pl. **-S** a court game of Spanish origin
PELOTON	*n* pl. **-S** the main body of riders in a bicycle race
PELT	*v* **-ED, -ING, -S** to strike repeatedly with blows or missiles
PELTAST	*n* pl. **-S** a soldier of ancient Greece
PELTATE	*adj* shaped like a shield
PELTER	*v* **-ED, -ING, -S** to pelt
PELTLESS	*adj* lacking a pelt (the skin of an animal)
PELTRY	*n* pl. **-RIES** an animal skin
PELVIC	*n* pl. **-S** a bone of the pelvis

PELVIS *n* pl. **-VISES** or **-VES** a part of the skeleton

PEMBINA *n* pl. **-S** a variety of cranberry

PEMICAN *n* pl. **-S** pemmican

PEMMICAN *n* pl. **-S** a food prepared by Native Americans

PEMOLINE *n* pl. **-S** a drug used as a stimulant

PEMPHIX *n* pl. **-ES** a skin disease

PEN *v* **PENNED, PENNING, PENS** to write with a pen (an instrument for writing with fluid ink)

PENAL *adj* pertaining to punishment

PENALISE *v* **-ISED, -ISING, -ISES** to penalize

PENALITY *n* pl. **-TIES** liability to punishment

PENALIZE *v* **-IZED, -IZING, -IZES** to subject to a penalty

PENALLY *adv* in a penal manner

PENALTY *n* pl. **-TIES** a punishment imposed for violation of a law, rule, or agreement

PENANCE *v* **-ANCED, -ANCING, -ANCES** to impose a type of punishment upon

PENANG *n* pl. **-S** a cotton fabric

PENATES *n/pl* the Roman gods of the household

PENCE a pl. of penny

PENCEL *n* pl. **-S** a small flag

PENCHANT *n* pl. **-S** a strong liking for something

PENCIL *v* **-CILED, -CILING, -CILS** or **-CILLED, -CILLING, -CILS** to produce by using a pencil (a writing and drawing implement)

PENCILER *n* pl. **-S** one that pencils

PEND *v* **-ED, -ING, -S** to remain undecided or unsettled

PENDANT *n* pl. **-S** a hanging ornament

PENDENCY *n* pl. **-CIES** a pending state

PENDENT *n* pl. **-S** pendant

PENDULUM *n* pl. **-S** a type of free swinging body **PENDULAR** *adj*

PENES a pl. of penis

PENGO *n* pl. **-GOS** a former monetary unit of Hungary

PENGUIN *n* pl. **-S** a flightless, aquatic bird

PENICIL *n* pl. **-S** a small tuft of hairs

PENIS *n* pl. **-NISES** or **-NES** the male organ of copulation **PENIAL, PENILE** *adj*

PENITENT *n* pl. **-S** a person who repents his or her sins

PENKNIFE *n* pl. **-KNIVES** a small pocketknife

PENLIGHT *n* pl. **-S** a small flashlight

PENLITE *n* pl. **-S** penlight

PENMAN *n* pl. **-MEN** an author

PENNA *n* pl. **-NAE** any of the feathers that determine a bird's shape

PENNAME *n* pl. **-S** a name used by an author instead of his or her real name

PENNANT *n* pl. **-S** a long, narrow flag

PENNATE *adj* having wings or feathers

PENNATED *adj* pennate

PENNE *n* pl. **-S** short tubular pasta

PENNED past tense of pen

PENNER *n* pl. **-S** one that pens

PENNI *n* pl. **-NIS** or **-NIA** a formerly used Finnish coin

PENNIES a pl. of penny

PENNINE *n* pl. **-S** a mineral

PENNING present participle of pen

PENNON *n* pl. **-S** a pennant **PENNONED** *adj*

PENNY *n* pl. **PENNIES** or **PENCE** a coin of the United Kingdom

PENOCHE *n* pl. **-S** penuche

PENOLOGY *n* pl. **-GIES** the science of the punishment of crime

PENONCEL *n* pl. **-S** a small pennon

PENPOINT *n* pl. **-S** the point of a pen

PENSEE *n* pl. **-S** a thought

PENSIL *n* pl. **-S** pencel

PENSILE *adj* hanging loosely

PENSION *v* **-ED, -ING, -S** to grant a retirement allowance to

PENSIONE *n* pl. **-ONES** or **-ONI** a boarding house

PENSIVE *adj* engaged in deep thought

PENSTER *n* pl. **-S** a writer

PENSTOCK *n* pl. **-S** a conduit for conveying water to a waterwheel

PENT *adj* confined

PENTACLE *n* pl. **-S** a five-pointed star

PENTAD *n* pl. **-S** a group of five

PENTAGON *n* pl. **-S** a five-sided polygon

PENTANE *n* pl. **-S** a volatile liquid

PENTANOL *n* pl. **-S** an alcohol

PENTARCH *n* pl. **-S** one of five joint rulers

PENTENE	*n* pl. **-S** a liquid hydrocarbon
PENTODE	*n* pl. **-S** a type of electron tube
PENTOMIC	*adj* made up of five battle groups
PENTOSAN	*n* pl. **-S** a complex carbohydrate
PENTOSE	*n* pl. **-S** a sugar having five carbon atoms per molecule
PENTYL	*n* pl. **-S** amyl
PENUCHE	*n* pl. **-S** a fudge-like candy
PENUCHI	*n* pl. **-S** penuche
PENUCHLE	*n* pl. **-S** pinochle
PENUCKLE	*n* pl. **-S** pinochle
PENULT	*n* pl. **-S** the next to last syllable in a word
PENUMBRA	*n* pl. **-BRAS** or **-BRAE** a partial shadow
PENURY	*n* pl. **-RIES** extreme poverty
PEON	*n* pl. **-S** or **-ES** an unskilled laborer
PEONAGE	*n* pl. **-S** the condition of being a peon
PEONISM	*n* pl. **-S** peonage
PEONY	*n* pl. **-NIES** a flowering plant
PEOPLE	*v* **-PLED, -PLING, -PLES** to furnish with inhabitants
PEOPLER	*n* pl. **-S** one that peoples
PEP	*v* **PEPPED, PEPPING, PEPS** to fill with energy
PEPERONI	*n* pl. **-S** a highly seasoned sausage
PEPINO	*n* pl. **-NOS** a bushy perennial plant with edible fruit
PEPITA	*n* pl. **-S** the edible dried seed of a pumpkin or squash
PEPLOS	*n* pl. **-ES** a garment worn by women in ancient Greece
PEPLUM	*n* pl. **-LUMS** or **-LA** a short section attached to the waistline of a garment **PEPLUMED** *adj*
PEPLUS	*n* pl. **-ES** peplos
PEPO	*n* pl. **-POS** a fruit having a fleshy interior and a hard rind
PEPONIDA	*n* pl. **-S** pepo
PEPONIUM	*n* pl. **-S** pepo
PEPPED	past tense of pep
PEPPER	*v* **-ED, -ING, -S** to season with pepper (a pungent condiment)
PEPPERER	*n* pl. **-S** one that peppers
PEPPERY	*adj* resembling pepper
PEPPING	present participle of pep
PEPPY	*adj* **-PIER, -PIEST** full of energy **PEPPILY** *adv*

PEPSIN	*n* pl. **-S** a digestive enzyme of the stomach
PEPSINE	*n* pl. **-S** pepsin
PEPTALK	*v* **-ED, -ING, -S** to inspire enthusiasm in by an intense, emotional talk
PEPTIC	*n* pl. **-S** a substance that promotes digestion
PEPTID	*n* pl. **-S** peptide
PEPTIDE	*n* pl. **-S** a combination of amino acids **PEPTIDIC** *adj*
PEPTIZE	*v* **-TIZED, -TIZING, -TIZES** to increase the colloidal dispersion of
PEPTIZER	*n* pl. **-S** one that peptizes
PEPTONE	*n* pl. **-S** a protein compound **PEPTONIC** *adj*
PER	*prep* for each
PERACID	*n* pl. **-S** a type of acid
PERC	*n* pl. **-S** a chemical used in dry cleaning
PERCALE	*n* pl. **-S** a cotton fabric
PERCEIVE	*v* **-CEIVED, -CEIVING, -CEIVES** to become aware of through the senses
PERCENT	*n* pl. **-S** one part in a hundred
PERCEPT	*n* pl. **-S** something that is perceived
PERCH	*v* **-ED, -ING, -ES** to sit or rest on an elevated place
PERCHER	*n* pl. **-S** one that perches
PERCID	*n* pl. **-S** a freshwater fish of the perch family
PERCOID	*n* pl. **-S** any of a large suborder of spiny-finned fishes
PERCUSS	*v* **-ED, -ING, -ES** to strike with force
PERDIE	*interj* pardi
PERDU	*n* pl. **-S** a soldier sent on a dangerous mission
PERDUE	*n* pl. **-S** perdu
PERDURE	*v* **-DURED, -DURING, -DURES** to continue to exist
PERDY	*interj* pardi
PERE	*n* pl. **-S** father
PEREGRIN	*n* pl. **-S** a swift falcon much used in falconry
PEREION	*n* pl. **-REIONS** or **-REIA** the thorax of some crustaceans
PEREON	*n* pl. **-REONS** or **-REA** pereion
PEREOPOD	*n* pl. **-S** an appendage of the pereion

PERFECT	*adj* **-FECTER, -FECTEST** lacking fault or defect; of an extreme kind	**PERINEUM**	*n* pl. **-NEA** a region of the body at the lower end of the trunk **PERINEAL** *adj*
PERFECT	*v* **-ED, -ING, -S** to make perfect	**PERIOD**	*n* pl. **-S** a portion of time
PERFECTA	*n* pl. **-S** a system of betting	**PERIODIC**	*adj* recurring at regular intervals
PERFECTO	*n* pl. **-TOS** a medium-sized cigar	**PERIODID**	*n* pl. **-S** an iodide
PERFIDY	*n* pl. **-DIES** deliberate breach of faith or trust	**PERIOTIC**	*adj* surrounding the ear
PERFORCE	*adv* of necessity	**PERIPETY**	*n* pl. **-TIES** a sudden change in a course of events
PERFORM	*v* **-ED, -ING, -S** to begin and carry through to completion	**PERIPTER**	*n* pl. **-S** a structure with a row of columns around all sides
PERFUME	*v* **-FUMED, -FUMING, -FUMES** to fill with a fragrant odor	**PERIQUE**	*n* pl. **-S** a dark tobacco
PERFUMER	*n* pl. **-S** one that perfumes	**PERISARC**	*n* pl. **-S** a protective covering of certain hydrozoans
PERFUMY	*adj* scented		
PERFUSE	*v* **-FUSED, -FUSING, -FUSES** to spread over or through something	**PERISH**	*v* **-ED, -ING, -ES** to die
		PERISHER	*n* pl. **-S** an annoying person
PERGOLA	*n* pl. **-S** a shaded shelter or passageway	**PERITUS**	*n* pl. **-TI** an expert theologian
PERHAPS	*n* pl. **-ES** something open to doubt or conjecture	**PERIWIG**	*n* pl. **-S** a wig
		PERJURE	*v* **-JURED, -JURING, -JURES** to make a perjurer of
PERI	*n* pl. **-S** a supernatural being of Persian mythology	**PERJURER**	*n* pl. **-S** one guilty of perjury
PERIANTH	*n* pl. **-S** an outer covering of a flower	**PERJURY**	*n* pl. **-RIES** the willful giving of false testimony under oath in a judicial proceeding
PERIAPT	*n* pl. **-S** an amulet		
PERIBLEM	*n* pl. **-S** a region of plant tissue	**PERK**	*v* **-ED, -ING, -S** to prepare (coffee) in a percolator
PERICARP	*n* pl. **-S** the wall of a ripened plant ovary or fruit		
		PERKISH	*adj* somewhat perky
PERICOPE	*n* pl. **-PES** or **-PAE** a selection from a book	**PERKY**	*adj* **PERKIER, PERKIEST** jaunty **PERKILY** *adv*
PERIDERM	*n* pl. **-S** an outer layer of plant tissue	**PERLITE**	*n* pl. **-S** a volcanic glass **PERLITIC** *adj*
PERIDIUM	*n* pl. **-DIA** the covering of the spore-bearing organ in many fungi **PERIDIAL** *adj*	**PERM**	*v* **-ED, -ING, -S** to give hair a permanent wave
		PERMEANT	*adj* that permeates
PERIDOT	*n* pl. **-S** a mineral	**PERMEASE**	*n* pl. **-S** a catalyzing agent
PERIGEE	*n* pl. **-S** the point in the orbit of a celestial body which is nearest to the earth **PERIGEAL, PERIGEAN** *adj*	**PERMEATE**	*v* **-ATED, -ATING, -ATES** to spread through
		PERMIT	*v* **-MITTED, -MITTING, -MITS** to allow
PERIGON	*n* pl. **-S** an angle equal to 360 degrees	**PERMUTE**	*v* **-MUTED, -MUTING, -MUTES** to change the order of
PERIGYNY	*n* pl. **-NIES** the state of being situated on a cuplike organ surrounding the pistil	**PERNIO**	*n* pl. **-NIONES** an inflammation on the hands or feet caused by exposure to cold
PERIL	*v* **-ILED, -ILING, -ILS** or **-ILLED, -ILLING, -ILS** to imperil		
		PEROGI	*n* pl. **-ES** or **-S** pierogi
PERILLA	*n* pl. **-S** an Asian herb	**PEROGIE**	*n* pl. **-S** pierogi
PERILOUS	*adj* dangerous	**PEROGY**	*n* pl. **-GIES** pierogi
PERILUNE	*n* pl. **-S** the point in the orbit of a celestial body which is nearest to the moon	**PERONEAL**	*adj* pertaining to the fibula
		PERORAL	*adj* occurring through the mouth

PERORATE   *v* **-RATED, -RATING, -RATES** to make a lengthy speech

PEROXID   *n* pl. **-S** peroxide

PEROXIDE   *v* **-IDED, -IDING, -IDES** to treat with peroxide (a bleaching agent)

PEROXY   *adj* containing the bivalent group O_2

PERP   *n* pl. **-S** a person who commits a crime

PERPEND   *v* **-ED, -ING, -S** to ponder

PERPENT   *n* pl. **-S** a large building stone

PERPLEX   *v* **-ED, -ING, -ES** to make mentally uncertain

PERRON   *n* pl. **-S** an outdoor stairway

PERRY   *n* pl. **-RIES** a beverage of pear juice often fermented

PERSALT   *n* pl. **-S** a chemical salt

PERSE   *n* pl. **-S** a blue color

PERSIST   *v* **-ED, -ING, -S** to continue resolutely in some activity

PERSON   *n* pl. **-S** a human being

PERSONA   *n* pl. **-NAE** a character in a literary work

PERSONA   *n* pl. **-S** the public role that a person assumes

PERSONAL   *n* pl. **-S** a brief, private notice in a newspaper

PERSPIRE   *v* **-SPIRED, -SPIRING, -SPIRES** to give off moisture through the pores of the skin **PERSPIRY** *adj*

PERSUADE   *v* **-SUADED, -SUADING, -SUADES** to cause to do something by means of argument, reasoning, or entreaty

PERT   *adj* **PERTER, PERTEST** impudent **PERTLY** *adv*

PERTAIN   *v* **-ED, -ING, -S** to have reference or relation

PERTNESS   *n* pl. **-ES** the quality of being pert

PERTURB   *v* **-ED, -ING, -S** to disturb greatly

PERUKE   *n* pl. **-S** a wig **PERUKED** *adj*

PERUSAL   *n* pl. **-S** the act of perusing

PERUSE   *v* **-RUSED, -RUSING, -RUSES** to read

PERUSER   *n* pl. **-S** one that peruses

PERV   *n* pl. **-S** one who is sexually perverted

PERVADE   *v* **-VADED, -VADING, -VADES** to spread through every part of

PERVADER   *n* pl. **-S** one that pervades

PERVERSE   *adj* willfully deviating from desired or expected conduct

PERVERT   *v* **-ED, -ING, -S** to turn away from the right course of action

PERVIOUS   *adj* capable of being penetrated

PERVO   *n* pl. **-VOS** a perv

PERVY   *adj* **PERVIER, PERVIEST** sexually perverted

PES   *n* pl. **PEDES** a foot or footlike part

PESADE   *n* pl. **-S** the position of a horse when rearing

PESETA   *n* pl. **-S** a former monetary unit of Spain

PESEWA   *n* pl. **-S** a monetary unit of Ghana

PESKY   *adj* **-KIER, -KIEST** annoying **PESKILY** *adv*

PESO   *n* pl. **-SOS** a monetary unit of various Spanish-speaking countries

PESSARY   *n* pl. **-RIES** a contraceptive device worn in the vagina

PEST   *n* pl. **-S** an annoying person or thing

PESTER   *v* **-ED, -ING, -S** to bother

PESTERER   *n* pl. **-S** one that pesters

PESTHOLE   *n* pl. **-S** a place liable to epidemic disease

PESTLE   *v* **-TLED, -TLING, -TLES** to crush with a club-shaped hand tool

PESTO   *n* pl. **-TOS** a sauce of basil, garlic, and olive oil

PESTY   *adj* **PESTIER, PESTIEST** annoying

PET   *v* **PETTED, PETTING, PETS** to caress with the hand

PETABYTE   *n* pl. **-S** one quadrillion bytes

PETAL   *n* pl. **-S** a leaflike part of a corolla **PETALED, PETALLED** *adj*

PETALINE   *adj* resembling a petal

PETALODY   *n* pl. **-DIES** the metamorphosis of various floral organs into petals

PETALOID   *adj* resembling a petal

PETALOUS   *adj* having petals

PETANQUE   *n* pl. **-S** a French form of lawn bowling

PETARD   *n* pl. **-S** an explosive device

PETASOS   *n* pl. **-ES** petasus

PETASUS   *n* pl. **-ES** a broad-brimmed hat worn in ancient Greece

PETCOCK   *n* pl. **-S** a small valve or faucet

PETECHIA _n_ pl. **-CHIAE** a small hemorrhagic spot on a body surface

PETER _v_ **-ED, -ING, -S** to diminish gradually

PETIOLAR _adj_ pertaining to a petiole

PETIOLE _n_ pl. **-S** the stalk of a leaf **PETIOLED** _adj_

PETIT _adj_ small; minor

PETITE _n_ pl. **-S** a clothing size for short women

PETITION _v_ **-ED, -ING, -S** to make a formal request

PETNAP _v_ **-NAPPED, -NAPPING, -NAPS** to steal a pet for profit

PETNAPER _n_ pl. **-S** one who steals a pet

PETRALE _n_ pl. **-S** a food fish

PETREL _n_ pl. **-S** a small seabird

PETRIFY _v_ **-FIED, -FYING, -FIES** to convert into stone

PETROL _n_ pl. **-S** gasoline

PETROLIC _adj_ derived from petroleum

PETRONEL _n_ pl. **-S** a portable firearm

PETROSAL _n_ pl. **-S** a part of the temporal bone

PETROUS _adj_ resembling stone in hardness

PETSAI _n_ pl. **-S** Chinese cabbage

PETTABLE _adj_ capable of being petted

PETTED past tense of pet

PETTEDLY _adv_ peevishly

PETTER _n_ pl. **-S** one that pets

PETTI pl. of petto

PETTIER comparative of petty

PETTIEST superlative of petty

PETTIFOG _v_ **-FOGGED, -FOGGING, -FOGS** to quibble

PETTILY _adv_ in a petty manner

PETTING _n_ pl. **-S** amorous caressing and kissing

PETTISH _adj_ peevish

PETTLE _v_ **-TLED, -TLING, -TLES** to caress

PETTO _n_ pl. **-TI** the breast

PETTY _adj_ **-TIER, -TIEST** insignificant

PETULANT _adj_ peevish

PETUNIA _n_ pl. **-S** a tropical herb

PETUNTSE _n_ pl. **-S** a mineral

PETUNTZE _n_ pl. **-S** petuntse

PEW _n_ pl. **-S** a bench in church

PEWEE _n_ pl. **-S** a small bird

PEWIT _n_ pl. **-S** the lapwing

PEWTER _n_ pl. **-S** a tin alloy **PEWTERY** _adj_

PEWTERER _n_ pl. **-S** one that makes articles of pewter

PEYOTE _n_ pl. **-S** a cactus

PEYOTISM _n_ pl. **-S** the Native American ritual in which peyote is used

PEYOTL _n_ pl. **-S** peyote

PEYTRAL _n_ pl. **-S** a piece of armor for the breast of a horse

PEYTREL _n_ pl. **-S** peytral

PFENNIG _n_ pl. **-NIGS** or **-NIGE** a formerly used bronze coin of Germany

PFFT _interj_ — used to express a sudden ending

PFUI _interj_ phooey

PHAETON _n_ pl. **-S** a light carriage

PHAGE _n_ pl. **-S** an organism that destroys bacteria

PHALANGE _n_ pl. **-S** any bone of a finger or toe

PHALANX _n_ pl. **-ES** a formation of infantry in ancient Greece

PHALLI a pl. of phallus

PHALLIC _adj_ pertaining to a phallus

PHALLISM _n_ pl. **-S** worship of the phallus as symbolic of nature's creative power

PHALLIST _n_ pl. **-S** one who practices phallism

PHALLUS _n_ pl. **-LUSES** or **-LI** the penis

PHANTASM _n_ pl. **-S** a creation of the imagination

PHANTAST _n_ pl. **-S** fantast

PHANTASY _v_ **-SIED, -SYING, -SIES** to fantasy

PHANTOM _n_ pl. **-S** something existing in appearance only

PHARAOH _n_ pl. **-S** a ruler of ancient Egypt

PHARISEE _n_ pl. **-S** a hypocritically self-righteous person

PHARMA _n_ pl. **-S** a pharmaceutical company

PHARMACY _n_ pl. **-CIES** a drugstore

PHARMER _n_ pl. **-S** one who participates in pharming

PHARMING _n_ pl. **-S** the production of pharmaceuticals from genetically altered plants or animals

PHAROS _n_ pl. **-ES** a lighthouse or beacon to guide seamen

PHARYNX _n_ pl. **-YNXES** or **-YNGES** a section of the digestive tract

PHASE	*v* **PHASED, PHASING, PHASES** to plan or carry out by phases (distinct stages of development) **PHASEAL, PHASIC** *adj*
PHASEOUT	*n* pl. **-S** a gradual stopping of operations
PHASER	*n* pl. **-S** a type of science-fiction weapon
PHASIS	*n* pl. **PHASES** a phase
PHASMID	*n* pl. **-S** a tropical insect
PHAT	*adj* **PHATTER, PHATTEST** excellent
PHATIC	*adj* sharing feelings rather than ideas
PHEASANT	*n* pl. **-S** a large, long-tailed bird
PHELLEM	*n* pl. **-S** a layer of plant cells
PHELONIA	*n/pl* liturgical vestments
PHENATE	*n* pl. **-S** a salt of carbolic acid
PHENAZIN	*n* pl. **-S** a chemical compound
PHENETIC	*adj* pertaining to a type of classificatory system
PHENETOL	*n* pl. **-S** a volatile liquid
PHENIX	*n* pl. **-ES** phoenix
PHENOL	*n* pl. **-S** a caustic compound
PHENOLIC	*n* pl. **-S** a synthetic resin
PHENOM	*n* pl. **-S** a person of extraordinary ability or promise
PHENOXY	*adj* containing a radical derived from phenol
PHENYL	*n* pl. **-S** a univalent chemical radical **PHENYLIC** *adj*
PHERESIS	*n* pl. **-RESES** withdrawal of blood from a donor, removing some components, and returning the remaining blood to the donor
PHEW	*interj* — used to express relief, fatigue, or disgust
PHI	*n* pl. **-S** a Greek letter
PHIAL	*n* pl. **-S** a vial
PHILABEG	*n* pl. **-S** filibeg
PHILIBEG	*n* pl. **-S** filibeg
PHILOMEL	*n* pl. **-S** a songbird
PHILTER	*v* **-ED, -ING, -S** to put under the spell of a love potion
PHILTRE	*v* **-TRED, -TRING, -TRES** to philter
PHILTRUM	*n* pl. **-TRA** the indentation between the upper lip and the nose
PHIMOSIS	*n* pl. **-MOSES** the abnormal constriction of the opening of the prepuce **PHIMOTIC** *adj*
PHISH	*v* **-ED, -ING, -ES** to engage in phishing
PHISHER	*n* pl. **-S** one that phishes
PHISHING	*n* pl. **-S** the practice of using email illegally to induce people to reveal personal information
PHIZ	*n* pl. **-ES** a face or facial expression
PHIZZ	*n* pl. **-ES** phiz
PHLEGM	*n* pl. **-S** a thick mucus secreted in the air passages
PHLEGMY	*adj* **PHLEGMIER, PHLEGMIEST** resembling phlegm
PHLOEM	*n* pl. **-S** a complex plant tissue
PHLOX	*n* pl. **-ES** a flowering plant
PHO	*n* pl. **PHOS** a Vietnamese soup of rice noodles and vegetables
PHOBIA	*n* pl. **-S** an obsessive or irrational fear
PHOBIC	*n* pl. **-S** one affected with a phobia
PHOCINE	*adj* pertaining to seals
PHOEBE	*n* pl. **-S** a small bird
PHOEBUS	*n* pl. **-ES** the sun
PHOENIX	*n* pl. **-ES** a mythical bird
PHON	*n* pl. **-S** a unit of loudness
PHONAL	*adj* pertaining to speech sounds
PHONATE	*v* **-NATED, -NATING, -NATES** to produce speech sounds
PHONE	*v* **PHONED, PHONING, PHONES** to telephone
PHONEME	*n* pl. **-S** a unit of speech **PHONEMIC** *adj*
PHONER	*n* pl. **-S** one who calls someone on the telephone
PHONETIC	*adj* pertaining to speech sounds
PHONEY	*adj* **-NIER, -NIEST** phony
PHONEY	*v* **-ED, -ING, -S** to phony
PHONIC	*adj* pertaining to the nature of sound
PHONICS	*n/pl* the science of sound
PHONIED	past tense of phony
PHONIER	comparative of phoney and phony
PHONIES	present 3d person sing. of phony
PHONIEST	superlative of phoney and phony
PHONILY	*adv* in a phony manner
PHONING	present participle of phone
PHONO	*n* pl. **-NOS** a record player
PHONON	*n* pl. **-S** a quantum of vibrational energy

PHONY   *adj* **-NIER, -NIEST** not genuine or real

PHONY   *v* **-NIED, -NYING, -NIES** to alter so as to make appear genuine

PHOOEY   *interj* — used as an exclamation of disgust or contempt

PHORATE   *n pl.* **-S** an insecticide

PHORESY   *n pl.* **-SIES** a symbiotic relationship between some arthropods and fishes **PHORETIC** *adj*

PHORONID   *n pl.* **-S** a wormlike marine animal

PHOSGENE   *n pl.* **-S** a poisonous gas

PHOSPHID   *n pl.* **-S** a chemical compound

PHOSPHIN   *n pl.* **-S** a poisonous gas

PHOSPHOR   *n pl.* **-S** a substance that will emit light when exposed to radiation

PHOT   *n pl.* **-S** a unit of illumination

PHOTIC   *adj* pertaining to light

PHOTICS   *n/pl* the science of light

PHOTINO   *n pl.* **-NOS** a hypothetical elementary particle

PHOTO   *v* **-ED, -ING, -S** to photograph

PHOTOG   *n pl.* **-S** one who takes photographs

PHOTOMAP   *v* **-MAPPED, -MAPPING, -MAPS** to map by means of aerial photography

PHOTON   *n pl.* **-S** an elementary particle **PHOTONIC** *adj*

PHOTOPIA   *n pl.* **-S** vision in bright light **PHOTOPIC** *adj*

PHOTOSET   *v* **-SET, -SETTING, -SETS** to prepare for printing by photographic means

PHPHT   *interj* pht

PHRASAL   *adj* pertaining to a group of two or more associated words

PHRASE   *v* **PHRASED, PHRASING, PHRASES** to express in words

PHRASING   *n pl.* **-S** manner or style of verbal expression

PHRATRY   *n pl.* **-TRIES** a tribal unit among primitive peoples **PHRATRAL, PHRATRIC** *adj*

PHREAK   *v* **-ED, -ING, -S** to gain illegal access to a long-distance telephone service to avoid tolls

PHREAKER   *n pl.* **-S** one that phreaks

PHREATIC   *adj* pertaining to underground waters

PHRENIC   *adj* pertaining to the mind

PHRENSY   *v* **-SIED, -SYING, -SIES** to frenzy

PHT   *interj* — used as an expression of mild anger or annoyance

PHTHALIC   *adj* pertaining to a certain acid

PHTHALIN   *n pl.* **-S** a chemical compound

PHTHISIC   *n pl.* **-S** phthisis

PHTHISIS   *n pl.* **PHTHISES** a disease of the lungs

PHUT   *n pl.* **-S** a dull, abrupt sound

PHYLA   pl. of phylon and phylum

PHYLAE   pl. of phyle

PHYLAR   *adj* pertaining to a phylum

PHYLAXIS   *n pl.* **-AXISES** an inhibiting of infection by the body

PHYLE   *n pl.* **-LAE** a political subdivision in ancient Greece **PHYLIC** *adj*

PHYLESIS   *n pl.* **-LESISES** or **-LESES** the course of evolutionary development **PHYLETIC** *adj*

PHYLLARY   *n pl.* **-RIES** a bract of certain plants

PHYLLITE   *n pl.* **-S** a foliated rock

PHYLLO   *n pl.* **-LOS** very thin pastry dough

PHYLLODE   *n pl.* **-S** a flattened petiole that serves as a leaf

PHYLLOID   *n pl.* **-S** a leaflike plant part

PHYLLOME   *n pl.* **-S** a leaf of a plant

PHYLON   *n pl.* **-LA** a genetically related group

PHYLUM   *n pl.* **-LA** a taxonomic division

PHYSALIS   *n pl.* **-LISES** a plant bearing edible yellow fruit

PHYSED   *n pl.* **-S** physical education

PHYSES   pl. of physis

PHYSIC   *v* **-ICKED, -ICKING, -ICS** to treat with medicine

PHYSICAL   *n pl.* **-S** a medical examination of the body

PHYSIO   *n pl.* **PHYSIOS** a physiotherapist

PHYSIQUE   *n pl.* **-S** the form or structure of the body

PHYSIS   *n pl.* **PHYSES** the principle of growth or change in nature

PHYTANE   *n pl.* **-S** a chemical compound

PHYTIN   *n pl.* **-S** a calcium-magnesium salt

PHYTOID   *adj* resembling a plant

PHYTOL   *n pl.* **-S** an alcohol

PHYTON   *n pl.* **-S** a structural unit of a plant **PHYTONIC** *adj*

PI	*n* pl. **-S** a Greek letter
PI	*v* **PIED, PIEING** or **PIING, PIES** to jumble or disorder
PIA	*n* pl. **-S** a membrane of the brain
PIACULAR	*adj* atoning
PIAFFE	*v* **PIAFFED, PIAFFING, PIAFFES** to perform a piaffer
PIAFFER	*n* pl. **-S** a movement in horsemanship
PIAL	*adj* pertaining to a pia
PIAN	*n* pl. **-S** a tropical disease **PIANIC** *adj*
PIANI	*n/pl* music passages to be played softly
PIANISM	*n* pl. **-S** performance on the piano
PIANIST	*n* pl. **-S** one who plays the piano
PIANO	*n* pl. **-NOS** a musical instrument
PIANOLA	*n* pl. **-S** a type of player piano
PIASABA	*n* pl. **-S** piassava
PIASAVA	*n* pl. **-S** piassava
PIASSABA	*n* pl. **-S** piassava
PIASSAVA	*n* pl. **-S** a coarse, stiff fiber
PIASTER	*n* pl. **-S** a monetary unit of several Arab countries
PIASTRE	*n* pl. **-S** piaster
PIAZZA	*n* pl. **-ZAS** or **-ZE** a public square in an Italian town
PIBAL	*n* pl. **-S** a small balloon for determining the direction and speed of the wind
PIBROCH	*n* pl. **-S** a musical piece played on the bagpipe
PIC	*n* pl. **-S** a photograph
PICA	*n* pl. **-S** a craving for unnatural food **PICAL** *adj*
PICACHO	*n* pl. **-CHOS** an isolated peak of a hill
PICADOR	*n* pl. **-S** or **-ES** a horseman in a bullfight
PICANTE	*adj* prepared with a spicy sauce
PICARA	*n* pl. **-S** a female picaro
PICARO	*n* pl. **-ROS** a vagabond
PICAROON	*v* **-ED, -ING, -S** to act as a pirate
PICAYUNE	*n* pl. **-S** a former Spanish-American coin
PICCATA	*n* pl. **-S** a dish of veal cutlets with a sauce of lemon, white wine, and butter
PICCOLO	*n* pl. **-LOS** a small flute

PICE	*n* pl. **PICE** a former coin of India and Pakistan
PICEOUS	*adj* glossy-black in color
PICIFORM	*adj* pertaining to an order of birds
PICK	*v* **-ED, -ING, -S** to select **PICKABLE** *adj*
PICKADIL	*n* pl. **-S** a type of collar
PICKAX	*v* **-ED, -ING, -ES** to use a pickax (a tool for breaking hard surfaces)
PICKAXE	*v* **-AXED, -AXING, -AXES** to pickax
PICKEER	*v* **-ED, -ING, -S** to skirmish in advance of an army
PICKER	*n* pl. **-S** one that picks
PICKEREL	*n* pl. **-S** a freshwater fish
PICKET	*v* **-ED, -ING, -S** to stand outside of some location, as a business, to publicize one's grievances against it
PICKETER	*n* pl. **-S** one who pickets
PICKIER	comparative of picky
PICKIEST	superlative of picky
PICKING	*n* pl. **-S** the act of one that picks
PICKLE	*v* **-LED, -LING, -LES** to preserve or flavor in a solution of brine or vinegar
PICKLER	*n* pl. **-S** a vegetable or fruit suitable for pickling
PICKLOCK	*n* pl. **-S** a tool for opening locks
PICKOFF	*n* pl. **-S** a play in baseball
PICKUP	*n* pl. **-S** a small truck
PICKWICK	*n* pl. **-S** a device for raising wicks in oil lamps
PICKY	*adj* **PICKIER, PICKIEST** fussy
PICLORAM	*n* pl. **-S** an herbicide
PICNIC	*v* **-NICKED, -NICKING, -NICS** to go on a picnic (an outdoor excursion with food)
PICNICKY	*adj* pertaining to a picnic
PICOGRAM	*n* pl. **-S** one trillionth of a gram
PICOLIN	*n* pl. **-S** picoline
PICOLINE	*n* pl. **-S** a chemical compound
PICOMOLE	*n* pl. **-S** one trillionth of a mole
PICOT	*v* **-ED, -ING, -S** to edge with ornamental loops
PICOTEE	*n* pl. **-S** a variety of carnation
PICOWAVE	*v* **-WAVED, -WAVING, -WAVES** to irradiate (food) with gamma rays
PICQUET	*n* pl. **-S** piquet

PICRATE *n* pl. **-S** a chemical salt **PICRATED** *adj*

PICRIC *adj* having a very bitter taste

PICRITE *n* pl. **-S** an igneous rock **PICRITIC** *adj*

PICTURE *v* **-TURED, -TURING, -TURES** to make a visual representation of

PICUL *n* pl. **-S** an Asian unit of weight

PIDDLE *v* **-DLED, -DLING, -DLES** to waste time

PIDDLER *n* pl. **-S** one that piddles

PIDDLY *adj* insignificant

PIDDOCK *n* pl. **-S** a bivalve mollusk

PIDGIN *n* pl. **-S** a mixed language

PIE *v* **PIED, PIEING, PIES** to pi

PIEBALD *n* pl. **-S** a spotted animal

PIECE *v* **PIECED, PIECING, PIECES** to join into a whole

PIECER *n* pl. **-S** one that pieces

PIECING *n* pl. **-S** material to be sewn together

PIECRUST *n* pl. **-S** the crust of a pie

PIED past tense of pie

PIEDFORT *n* pl. **-S** piefort

PIEDMONT *n* pl. **-S** an area lying at the foot of a mountain

PIEFORT *n* pl. **-S** an unusually thick coin

PIEHOLE *n* pl. **-S** a mouth

PIEING *n* pl. **-S** the act of throwing a pie at a public figure

PIEPLANT *n* pl. **-S** a rhubarb

PIER *n* pl. **-S** a structure extending from land out over water

PIERCE *v* **PIERCED, PIERCING, PIERCES** to cut or pass into or through

PIERCER *n* pl. **-S** one that pierces

PIERCING *n* pl. **-S** a piece of jewelry attached to pierced flesh

PIEROGI *n* pl. **-ES** a small dumpling with a filling

PIERROT *n* pl. **-S** a clown

PIETA *n* pl. **-S** a representation of the Virgin Mary mourning over the body of Christ

PIETIES pl. of piety

PIETISM *n* pl. **-S** piety

PIETIST *n* pl. **-S** a pious person

PIETY *n* pl. **-TIES** the quality or state of being pious

PIEZO *adj* pertaining to a type of electricity

PIFFLE *v* **-FLED, -FLING, -FLES** to babble

PIFFLER *n* pl. **-S** one that babbles

PIG *v* **PIGGED, PIGGING, PIGS** to bear pigs (cloven-hoofed mammals)

PIGBOAT *n* pl. **-S** a submarine

PIGEON *n* pl. **-S** a short-legged bird

PIGEONRY *n* pl. **-RIES** a place for keeping pigeons

PIGFISH *n* pl. **-ES** a marine fish

PIGGED past tense of pig

PIGGERY *n* pl. **-GERIES** a pigpen

PIGGIE *n* pl. **-S** piggy

PIGGIER comparative of piggy

PIGGIES pl. of piggy

PIGGIEST superlative of piggy

PIGGIN *n* pl. **-S** a small wooden pail

PIGGING present participle of pig

PIGGISH *adj* greedy or dirty

PIGGY *adj* **-GIER, -GIEST** piggish

PIGGY *n* pl. **-GIES** a small pig

PIGLET *n* pl. **-S** a small pig

PIGLIKE *adj* resembling a pig

PIGMENT *v* **-ED, -ING, -S** to add a coloring matter to

PIGMY *n* pl. **-MIES** pygmy

PIGNOLI *n* pl. **-S** pignolia

PIGNOLIA *n* pl. **-S** the edible seed of nut pines

PIGNUS *n* pl. **-NORA** property held as security for a debt

PIGNUT *n* pl. **-S** a hickory nut

PIGOUT *n* pl. **-S** an instance of eating to excess

PIGPEN *n* pl. **-S** a place where pigs are kept

PIGSKIN *n* pl. **-S** the skin of a pig

PIGSNEY *n* pl. **-NEYS** a darling

PIGSTICK *v* **-ED, -ING, -S** to hunt for wild boar

PIGSTY *n* pl. **-STIES** a pigpen

PIGTAIL *n* pl. **-S** a tight braid of hair

PIGWEED *n* pl. **-S** a weedy plant

PIING a present participle of pi

PIKA *n* pl. **-S** a small mammal

PIKAKE	*n* pl. **-S** an East Indian vine
PIKE	*v* **PIKED, PIKING, PIKES** to pierce with a pike (a long spear)
PIKEMAN	*n* pl. **-MEN** a soldier armed with a pike
PIKER	*n* pl. **-S** a stingy person
PIKI	*n* pl. **-S** thin blue cornmeal bread
PIKING	present participle of pike
PILAF	*n* pl. **-S** a dish made of seasoned rice and often meat
PILAFF	*n* pl. **-S** pilaf
PILAR	*adj* pertaining to hair
PILASTER	*n* pl. **-S** a rectangular column
PILAU	*n* pl. **-S** pilaf
PILAW	*n* pl. **-S** pilaf
PILCHARD	*n* pl. **-S** a small marine fish
PILE	*v* **PILED, PILING, PILES** to lay one upon the other
PILEA	pl. of pileum
PILEATE	*adj* having a pileus
PILEATED	*adj* pileate
PILED	past tense of pile
PILEI	pl. of pileus
PILELESS	*adj* not having a raised surface of yarn
PILEOUS	*adj* pilose
PILEUM	*n* pl. **-LEA** the top of a bird's head
PILEUP	*n* pl. **-S** a collision involving several motor vehicles
PILEUS	*n* pl. **-LEI** the umbrella-shaped portion of a mushroom
PILEWORT	*n* pl. **-S** a medicinal plant
PILFER	*v* **-ED, -ING, -S** to steal
PILFERER	*n* pl. **-S** one that pilfers
PILGRIM	*v* **-ED, -ING, -S** to travel to a holy place for religious reasons
PILI	*n* pl. **-S** a Philippine tree
PILIFORM	*adj* resembling a hair
PILING	*n* pl. **-S** a structure of building supports
PILL	*v* **-ED, -ING, -S** to dose with pills (small, rounded masses of medicine)
PILLAGE	*v* **-LAGED, -LAGING, -LAGES** to plunder
PILLAGER	*n* pl. **-S** one that pillages
PILLAR	*v* **-ED, -ING, -S** to provide with vertical building supports
PILLBOX	*n* pl. **-ES** a small box for pills
PILLBUG	*n* pl. **-S** a wood louse that can roll up into a ball
PILLION	*n* pl. **-S** a pad or cushion for an extra rider on a horse or motorcycle
PILLOCK	*n* pl. **-S** a stupid person
PILLORY	*v* **-RIED, -RYING, -RIES** to expose to public ridicule or abuse
PILLOW	*v* **-ED, -ING, -S** to rest on a pillow (a cushion for the head)
PILLOWY	*adj* **-LOWIER, -LOWIEST** resembling a pillow
PILOSE	*adj* covered with hair
PILOSITY	*n* pl. **-TIES** the state of being pilose
PILOT	*v* **-ED, -ING, -S** to control the course of
PILOTAGE	*n* pl. **-S** the act of piloting
PILOTING	*n* pl. **-S** a branch of navigation
PILOUS	*adj* pilose
PILSENER	*n* pl. **-S** pilsner
PILSNER	*n* pl. **-S** a light beer
PILULE	*n* pl. **-S** a small pill **PILULAR** *adj*
PILUS	*n* pl. **-LI** a hair or hairlike structure
PILY	*adj* divided into a number of wedge-shaped heraldic designs
PIMA	*n* pl. **-S** a strong, high-grade cotton
PIMENTO	*n* pl. **-TOS** pimiento
PIMIENTO	*n* pl. **-TOS** a sweet pepper
PIMP	*v* **-ED, -ING, -S** to solicit clients for a prostitute
PIMPING	*n* pl. **-S** the practice of soliciting clients for a prostitute
PIMPLE	*n* pl. **-S** an inflamed swelling of the skin **PIMPLED** *adj*
PIMPLY	*adj* **-PLIER, -PLIEST** covered with pimples
PIN	*v* **PINNED, PINNING, PINS** to fasten with a pin (a slender, pointed piece of metal)
PINA	*n* pl. **-S** a pineapple
PINAFORE	*n* pl. **-S** a child's apron
PINANG	*n* pl. **-S** a palm tree
PINASTER	*n* pl. **-S** a pine tree
PINATA	*n* pl. **-S** a pottery jar used in a Mexican game
PINBALL	*v* **-ED, -ING, -S** to move abruptly from one place to another
PINBONE	*n* pl. **-S** the hipbone

PINCER   *n* pl. **-S** one of the two pivoted parts of a grasping tool

PINCH   *v* **-ED, -ING, -ES** to squeeze between two edges or surfaces

PINCHBUG   *n* pl. **-S** a large beetle

PINCHECK   *n* pl. **-S** a fabric design

PINCHER   *n* pl. **-S** one that pinches

PINCURL   *n* pl. **-S** a curl held in place with a hairpin

PINDER   *n* pl. **-S** an official who formerly impounded stray animals

PINDLING   *adj* puny or sickly

PINE   *v* **PINED, PINING, PINES** to yearn intensely

PINEAL   *n* pl. **-S** a gland in the brain

PINECONE   *n* pl. **-S** a cone-shaped fruit of a pine tree

PINED   past tense of pine

PINELAND   *n* pl. **-S** land forested with pine

PINELIKE   *adj* resembling a pine (an evergreen tree)

PINENE   *n* pl. **-S** the main constituent of turpentine

PINERY   *n* pl. **-ERIES** an area where pineapples are grown

PINESAP   *n* pl. **-S** a fragrant herb

PINETUM   *n* pl. **-TA** a plantation of pine trees

PINEWOOD   *n* pl. **-S** the wood of a pine tree

PINEY   *adj* **PINIER, PINIEST** piny

PINFISH   *n* pl. **-ES** a small marine fish

PINFOLD   *v* **-ED, -ING, -S** to confine in an enclosure for stray animals

PING   *v* **-ED, -ING, -S** to produce a brief, high-pitched sound

PINGER   *n* pl. **-S** a device for producing pulses of sound

PINGO   *n* pl. **-GOS** or **-GOES** a low mound of earth formed by expansion of underlying frost

PINGRASS   *n* pl. **-ES** a European weed

PINGUID   *adj* greasy

PINHEAD   *n* pl. **-S** the head of a pin

PINHOLE   *n* pl. **-S** a small hole made by a pin

PINIER   comparative of piney and piny

PINIEST   superlative of piney and piny

PINING   present participle of pine

PINION   *v* **-ED, -ING, -S** to remove or bind the wing feathers of to prevent flight

PINITE   *n* pl. **-S** a mineral

PINITOL   *n* pl. **-S** an alcohol

PINK   *adj* **PINKER, PINKEST** of a pale reddish hue

PINK   *v* **-ED, -ING, -S** to cut a saw-toothed edge on cloth

PINKEN   *v* **-ED, -ING, -S** to become pink

PINKER   *n* pl. **-S** one that pinks

PINKEY   *n* pl. **-EYS** a ship with a narrow overhanging stern

PINKEYE   *n* pl. **-S** an inflammation of the eye

PINKIE   *n* pl. **-S** the little finger

PINKING   *n* pl. **-S** a method of cutting or decorating

PINKISH   *adj* somewhat pink

PINKLY   *adv* with a pink hue

PINKNESS   *n* pl. **-ES** the state of being pink

PINKO   *n* pl. **PINKOS** or **PINKOES** a person who holds somewhat radical political views

PINKROOT   *n* pl. **-S** a medicinal plant root

PINKY   *adj* **-KIER, -KIEST** pinkish

PINLESS   *adj* lacking pins

PINNA   *n* pl. **-NAS** or **-NAE** a feather, wing, or winglike part

PINNACE   *n* pl. **-S** a small sailing ship

PINNACLE   *v* **-CLED, -CLING, -CLES** to place on a summit

PINNAL   *adj* pertaining to a pinna

PINNATE   *adj* resembling a feather

PINNATED   *adj* pinnate

PINNED   past tense of pin

PINNER   *n* pl. **-S** one that pins

PINNIES   pl. of pinny

PINNING   present participle of pin

PINNIPED   *n* pl. **-S** a mammal with limbs modified into flippers

PINNULA   *n* pl. **-LAE** pinnule **PINNULAR** *adj*

PINNULE   *n* pl. **-S** a pinnate part or organ

PINNY   *n* pl. **-NIES** a pinafore

PINOCHLE   *n* pl. **-S** a card game

PINOCLE   *n* pl. **-S** pinochle

PINOLE   *n* pl. **-S** a finely ground flour

PINON   *n* pl. **-S** or **-ES** a pine tree

PINOT   *n* pl. **-S** a red or white grape

PINOTAGE   *n* pl. **-S** a variety of red wine grape

PINPOINT   *v* **-ED, -ING, -S** to locate precisely

PINPRICK	*v* **-ED, -ING, -S** to puncture with a pin
PINSCHER	*n* pl. **-S** a large, short-haired dog
PINSPOT	*n* pl. **-S** a small powerful spotlight
PINT	*n* pl. **-S** a liquid and dry measure of capacity
PINTA	*n* pl. **-S** a skin disease
PINTADA	*n* pl. **-S** pintado
PINTADO	*n* pl. **-DOS** or **-DOES** a large food fish
PINTAIL	*n* pl. **-S** a river duck
PINTANO	*n* pl. **-NOS** a tropical fish
PINTLE	*n* pl. **-S** a pin on which something turns
PINTO	*n* pl. **-TOS** or **-TOES** a spotted horse
PINTSIZE	*adj* small
PINTUCK	*n* pl. **-S** a very narrow fold of fabric
PINUP	*n* pl. **-S** a picture that may be pinned up on a wall
PINWALE	*n* pl. **-S** a type of fabric
PINWEED	*n* pl. **-S** a perennial herb
PINWHEEL	*v* **-ED, -ING, -S** to revolve at the end of a stick
PINWORK	*n* pl. **-S** a type of embroidery
PINWORM	*n* pl. **-S** a parasitic worm
PINY	*adj* **PINIER, PINIEST** suggestive of or covered with pine trees
PINYIN	*n* pl. **-S** a system for romanizing Chinese ideograms
PINYON	*n* pl. **-S** pinon
PIOLET	*n* pl. **-S** an ice ax
PION	*n* pl. **-S** a subatomic particle **PIONIC** *adj*
PIONEER	*v* **-ED, -ING, -S** to take part in the beginnings of
PIOSITY	*n* pl. **-TIES** an excessive show of piety
PIOUS	*adj* marked by religious reverence **PIOUSLY** *adv*
PIP	*v* **PIPPED, PIPPING, PIPS** to break through the shell of an egg
PIPA	*n* pl. **-S** a four-stringed Chinese lute
PIPAGE	*n* pl. **-S** a system of pipes
PIPAL	*n* pl. **-S** a fig tree of India
PIPE	*v* **PIPED, PIPING, PIPES** to convey by means of a pipe (a hollow cylinder)
PIPEAGE	*n* pl. **-S** pipage
PIPECLAY	*v* **-ED, -ING, -S** to whiten leather with fine white clay
PIPEFISH	*n* pl. **-ES** a slender fish
PIPEFUL	*n* pl. **-S** a quantity sufficient to fill a tobacco pipe
PIPELESS	*adj* having no pipe
PIPELIKE	*adj* resembling a pipe
PIPELINE	*v* **-LINED, -LINING, -LINES** to convey by a line of pipe
PIPER	*n* pl. **-S** one that plays on a tubular musical instrument
PIPERINE	*n* pl. **-S** a chemical compound
PIPESTEM	*n* pl. **-S** the stem of a tobacco pipe
PIPET	*v* **-PETTED, -PETTING, -PETS** to pipette
PIPETTE	*v* **-PETTED, -PETTING, -PETTES** to measure liquid with a calibrated tube
PIPEWORK	*n* pl. **-S** pipes collectively
PIPIER	comparative of pipy
PIPIEST	superlative of pipy
PIPINESS	*n* pl. **-ES** the quality of being pipy
PIPING	*n* pl. **-S** a system of pipes
PIPINGLY	*adv* shrilly
PIPIT	*n* pl. **-S** a songbird
PIPKIN	*n* pl. **-S** a small pot
PIPLESS	*adj* having no small seeds
PIPPED	past tense of pip
PIPPIN	*n* pl. **-S** any of several varieties of apple
PIPPING	present participle of pip
PIPY	*adj* **PIPIER, PIPIEST** shrill
PIQUANCE	*n* pl. **-S** piquancy
PIQUANCY	*n* pl. **-CIES** the quality of being piquant
PIQUANT	*adj* agreeably sharp in taste
PIQUE	*v* **PIQUED, PIQUING, PIQUES** to arouse anger or resentment in
PIQUET	*n* pl. **-S** a card game
PIRACY	*n* pl. **-CIES** robbery on the high seas
PIRAGUA	*n* pl. **-S** a dugout canoe
PIRANA	*n* pl. **-S** piranha
PIRANHA	*n* pl. **-S** a voracious fish
PIRARUCU	*n* pl. **-S** a large food fish
PIRATE	*v* **-RATED, -RATING, -RATES** to commit piracy
PIRATIC	*adj* pertaining to piracy

PIRAYA	*n* pl. **-S** piranha	**PITAYA**	*n* pl. **-S** pitahaya
PIRIFORM	*adj* pyriform	**PITCH**	*v* **-ED, -ING, -ES** to throw
PIRN	*n* pl. **-S** a spinning-wheel bobbin	**PITCHER**	*n* pl. **-S** a container for holding and pouring liquids
PIROG	*n* pl. **-ROGEN** or **-ROGHI** or **-ROGI** a large Russian pastry	**PITCHIER**	comparative of pitchy
PIROGI	*n* pl. **-ES** pierogi	**PITCHIEST**	superlative of pitchy
PIROGUE	*n* pl. **-S** piragua	**PITCHILY**	*adv* in a very dark manner
PIROQUE	*n* pl. **-S** piragua	**PITCHMAN**	*n* pl. **-MEN** a salesman of small wares
PIROZHOK	*n* pl. **-ROZHKI** or **-ROSHKI** or **-ROJKI** a small Russian pastry	**PITCHOUT**	*n* pl. **-S** a type of pitch in baseball
PISCARY	*n* pl. **-RIES** a place for fishing	**PITCHY**	*adj* **PITCHIER, PITCHIEST** tarry
PISCATOR	*n* pl. **-S** a fisherman	**PITEOUS**	*adj* pitiful
PISCINA	*n* pl. **-NAS** or **-NAE** a basin used in certain church ceremonies **PISCINAL** *adj*	**PITFALL**	*n* pl. **-S** a hidden danger or difficulty
PISCINE	*adj* pertaining to fish	**PITH**	*v* **-ED, -ING, -S** to sever the spinal cord of
PISCO	*n* pl. **-COS** a Peruvian brandy	**PITHEAD**	*n* pl. **-S** a mine entrance
PISH	*v* **-ED, -ING, -ES** to express contempt	**PITHLESS**	*adj* lacking force
PISHER	*n* pl. **-S** a young or inexperienced person	**PITHOS**	*n* pl. **PITHOI** a large ancient storage jar
PISHOGE	*n* pl. **-S** pishogue	**PITHY**	*adj* **PITHIER, PITHIEST** concise **PITHILY** *adv*
PISHOGUE	*n* pl. **-S** an evil spell		
PISIFORM	*n* pl. **-S** a small bone of the wrist	**PITIABLE**	*adj* pitiful **PITIABLY** *adv*
PISMIRE	*n* pl. **-S** an ant	**PITIED**	past tense of pity
PISO	*n* pl. **-SOS** the Philippine peso	**PITIER**	*n* pl. **-S** one that pities
PISOLITE	*n* pl. **-S** a limestone	**PITIES**	present 3d person sing. of pity
PISOLITH	*n* pl. **-S** a small rounded concretion of limestone	**PITIFUL**	*adj* **-FULLER, -FULLEST** arousing pity
PISSOIR	*n* pl. **-S** a public urinal	**PITILESS**	*adj* having no pity
PISTACHE	*n* pl. **-S** a shade of green	**PITMAN**	*n* pl. **-MEN** a mine worker
PISTE	*n* pl. **-S** a downhill ski trail	**PITMAN**	*n* pl. **-S** a connecting rod
PISTIL	*n* pl. **-S** the seed-bearing organ of flowering plants	**PITON**	*n* pl. **-S** a metal spike used in mountain climbing
PISTOL	*v* **-TOLED, -TOLING, -TOLS** or **-TOLLED, -TOLLING, -TOLS** to shoot with a small firearm	**PITOT**	*n* pl. **-S** a tube used to measure the pressure of a fluid stream
PISTOLE	*n* pl. **-S** a formerly used European gold coin	**PITSAW**	*n* pl. **-S** a large saw for cutting logs
		PITTA	*n* pl. **-S** a perching bird of Asia, Australia, and Africa
PISTON	*n* pl. **-S** a part of an engine	**PITTANCE**	*n* pl. **-S** a small allowance of money
PISTOU	*n* pl. **-S** a sauce made of olive oil, garlic, basil, and often cheese	**PITTED**	past tense of pit
PIT	*v* **PITTED, PITTING, PITS** to mark with cavities or depressions	**PITTING**	*n* pl. **-S** an arrangement of cavities or depressions
PITA	*n* pl. **-S** a strong fiber	**PITY**	*v* **PITIED, PITYING, PITIES** to feel pity (sorrow aroused by another's misfortune)
PITAHAYA	*n* pl. **-S** a cactus of southwestern U.S. and Mexico		
PITAPAT	*v* **-PATTED, -PATTING, -PATS** to make a repeated tapping sound	**PIU**	*adv* more — used as a musical direction

PIVOT   *v* **-ED, -ING, -S** to turn on a shaft or rod

PIVOTAL   *adj* critically important

PIVOTMAN   *n* pl. **-MEN** a center on a basketball team

PIX   *n* pl. **-ES** pyx

PIXEL   *n* pl. **-S** a basic unit of a video image

PIXELATE   *v* **-LATED, -LATING, -LATES** to divide an image into pixels for display in a digital format

PIXIE   *n* pl. **-S** pixy **PIXIEISH** *adj*

PIXILATE   *v* **-LATED, -LATING, -LATES** pixelate

PIXINESS   *n* pl. **-ES** the state of being playfully mischievous

PIXY   *n* pl. **PIXIES** a playfully mischievous fairy or elf **PIXYISH** *adj*

PIZAZZ   *n* pl. **-ES** pizzazz

PIZAZZY   *adj* pizzazzy

PIZZA   *n* pl. **-S** an Italian open pie

PIZZAZ   *n* pl. **-ES** pizzazz

PIZZAZZ   *n* pl. **-ES** the quality of being exciting or attractive

PIZZAZZY   *adj* having pizzazz

PIZZELLE   *n* pl. **-S** a thin, crisp Italian cookie

PIZZERIA   *n* pl. **-S** a place where pizzas are made and sold

PIZZLE   *n* pl. **-S** the penis of an animal

PLACABLE   *adj* capable of being placated **PLACABLY** *adv*

PLACARD   *v* **-ED, -ING, -S** to publicize by means of posters

PLACATE   *v* **-CATED, -CATING, -CATES** to soothe or mollify

PLACATER   *n* pl. **-S** one that placates

PLACE   *v* **PLACED, PLACING, PLACES** to set in a particular position

PLACEBO   *n* pl. **-BOS** or **-BOES** a substance containing no medication that is given for its psychological effect

PLACEMAN   *n* pl. **-MEN** a political appointee to a public office

PLACEMAT   *n* pl. **-S** a table mat (a piece of material for protecting a surface) on which a place setting is laid

PLACENTA   *n* pl. **-TAS** or **-TAE** a vascular organ in most mammals

PLACER   *n* pl. **-S** one that places

PLACET   *n* pl. **-S** a vote of assent

PLACID   *adj* calm or peaceful **PLACIDLY** *adv*

PLACING   *n* pl. **-S** the state of being ranked in a race

PLACK   *n* pl. **-S** a former coin of Scotland

PLACKET   *n* pl. **-S** a slit in a garment

PLACOID   *n* pl. **-S** a fish having platelike scales

PLAFOND   *n* pl. **-S** an elaborately decorated ceiling

PLAGAL   *adj* designating a medieval musical mode

PLAGE   *n* pl. **-S** a bright region on the sun

PLAGIARY   *n* pl. **-RIES** the act of passing off another's work as one's own

PLAGUE   *v* **PLAGUED, PLAGUING, PLAGUES** to harass or torment

PLAGUER   *n* pl. **-S** one that plagues

PLAGUEY   *adj* plaguy

PLAGUY   *adj* troublesome **PLAGUILY** *adv*

PLAICE   *n* pl. **-S** a European flatfish

PLAID   *n* pl. **-S** a woolen scarf of a checkered pattern **PLAIDED** *adj*

PLAIN   *adj* **PLAINER, PLAINEST** evident **PLAINLY** *adv*

PLAIN   *v* **-ED, -ING, -S** to complain

PLAINT   *n* pl. **-S** a complaint

PLAISTER   *v* **-ED, -ING, -S** to plaster

PLAIT   *v* **-ED, -ING, -S** to braid

PLAITER   *n* pl. **-S** one that plaits

PLAITING   *n* pl. **-S** something that is plaited

PLAN   *v* **PLANNED, PLANNING, PLANS** to formulate a plan (a method for achieving an end)

PLANAR   *adj* flat

PLANARIA   *n* pl. **-S** an aquatic flatworm

PLANATE   *adj* having a flat surface

PLANCH   *n* pl. **-ES** a plank

PLANCHE   *n* pl. **-S** planch

PLANCHET   *n* pl. **-S** a flat piece of metal for stamping into a coin

PLANE   *v* **PLANED, PLANING, PLANES** to make smooth or even

PLANER   *n* pl. **-S** one that planes

PLANET   *n* pl. **-S** a celestial body

PLANFORM   *n* pl. **-S** the contour of an object as viewed from above

PLANGENT   *adj* resounding loudly

PLANING   present participle of plane

PLANISH *v* **-ED, -ING, -ES** to toughen and smooth by hammering lightly

PLANK *v* **-ED, -ING, -S** to cover with planks (long, flat pieces of lumber)

PLANKING *n* pl. **-S** covering made of planks

PLANKTER *n* pl. **-S** any organism that is an element of plankton

PLANKTON *n* pl. **-S** the minute animal and plant life of a body of water **PLANKTIC** *adj*

PLANLESS *adj* having no plan

PLANNED past tense of plan

PLANNER *n* pl. **-S** one that plans

PLANNING *n* pl. **-S** the establishment of goals or policies

PLANOSOL *n* pl. **-S** a type of soil

PLANT *v* **-ED, -ING, -S** to place in the ground for growing

PLANTAIN *n* pl. **-S** a short-stemmed herb

PLANTAR *adj* pertaining to the sole of the foot

PLANTER *n* pl. **-S** one that plants

PLANTING *n* pl. **-S** an area where plants are grown

PLANTLET *n* pl. **-S** a small plant

PLANULA *n* pl. **-LAE** the free-swimming larva of certain organisms **PLANULAR** *adj*

PLAQUE *n* pl. **-S** an ornamental plate or disk

PLASH *v* **-ED, -ING, -ES** to weave together

PLASHER *n* pl. **-S** one that plashes

PLASHY *adj* **PLASHIER, PLASHIEST** marshy

PLASM *n* pl. **-S** plasma

PLASMA *n* pl. **-S** the liquid part of blood **PLASMIC** *adj*

PLASMID *n* pl. **-S** a hereditary structure of a cell

PLASMIN *n* pl. **-S** an enzyme

PLASMOID *n* pl. **-S** a type of high energy particle

PLASMON *n* pl. **-S** a determinant of inheritance believed to exist in cells

PLASTER *v* **-ED, -ING, -S** to cover with plaster (a mixture of lime, sand, and water)

PLASTERY *adj* resembling plaster

PLASTIC *n* pl. **-S** any of a group of synthetic or natural moldable materials

PLASTID *n* pl. **-S** a structure in plant cells

PLASTRON *n* pl. **-S** a part of the shell of a turtle **PLASTRAL** *adj*

PLASTRUM *n* pl. **-S** plastron

PLAT *v* **PLATTED, PLATTING, PLATS** to plait

PLATAN *n* pl. **-S** a large tree

PLATANE *n* pl. **-S** platan

PLATANNA *n* pl. **-S** an African frog

PLATE *v* **PLATED, PLATING, PLATES** to coat with a thin layer of metal

PLATEAU *n* pl. **-TEAUS** or **-TEAUX** a level stretch of elevated land

PLATEAU *v* **-ED, -ING, -S** to reach a period or condition of stability

PLATEFUL *n* pl. **PLATEFULS** or **PLATESFUL** the quantity that fills a plate (a shallow dish)

PLATELET *n* pl. **-S** a small, flattened body

PLATEN *n* pl. **-S** the roller of a typewriter

PLATER *n* pl. **-S** one that plates

PLATESFUL a pl. of plateful

PLATFORM *n* pl. **-S** a raised floor or flat surface

PLATIER comparative of platy

PLATIES a pl. of platy

PLATIEST superlative of platy

PLATINA *n* pl. **-S** platinum

PLATING *n* pl. **-S** a thin layer of metal

PLATINIC *adj* pertaining to platinum

PLATINUM *n* pl. **-S** a metallic element

PLATONIC *adj* purely spiritual and free from sensual desire

PLATOON *v* **-ED, -ING, -S** to alternate with another player at the same position

PLATTED past tense of plat

PLATTER *n* pl. **-S** a large, shallow dish

PLATTING present participle of plat

PLATY *adj* **PLATIER, PLATIEST** split into thin, flat pieces

PLATY *n* pl. **PLATYS** or **PLATIES** a small tropical fish

PLATYPUS *n* pl. **-PUSES** or **-PI** an aquatic mammal

PLAUDIT *n* pl. **-S** an expression of praise

PLAUSIVE *adj* expressing praise

PLAY *v* **-ED, -ING, -S** to engage in amusement or sport **PLAYABLE** *adj*

PLAYA *n* pl. **-S** the bottom of a desert basin

PLAYACT   *v* **-ED, -ING, -S** to take part in a theatrical performance

PLAYBACK   *n* pl. **-S** the act of replaying a newly made recording

PLAYBILL   *n* pl. **-S** a program for a theatrical performance

PLAYBOOK   *n* pl. **-S** a book containing one or more literary works for the stage

PLAYBOY   *n* pl. **-BOYS** a man devoted to pleasurable activities

PLAYDATE   *n* pl. **-S** the scheduled date for showing a theatrical production

PLAYDAY   *n* pl. **-DAYS** a holiday

PLAYDOWN   *n* pl. **-S** a playoff

PLAYER   *n* pl. **-S** one that plays

PLAYFUL   *adj* frolicsome

PLAYGIRL   *n* pl. **-S** a woman devoted to pleasurable activities

PLAYGOER   *n* pl. **-S** one who attends the theater

PLAYLAND   *n* pl. **-S** a recreational area

PLAYLESS   *adj* lacking playfulness

PLAYLET   *n* pl. **-S** a short theatrical performance

PLAYLIKE   *adj* resembling a theatrical performance

PLAYLIST   *v* **-ED, -ING, -S** to place on a list of recordings to be played on the air

PLAYMATE   *n* pl. **-S** a companion in play

PLAYOFF   *n* pl. **-S** a series of games played to determine a championship

PLAYPEN   *n* pl. **-S** an enclosure in which a young child may play

PLAYROOM   *n* pl. **-S** a recreation room

PLAYSET   *n* pl. **-S** an outdoor apparatus having equipment for children's activities

PLAYSUIT   *n* pl. **-S** a sports outfit for women and children

PLAYTIME   *n* pl. **-S** a time for play or amusement

PLAYWEAR   *n* pl. **PLAYWEAR** clothing worn for leisure activities

PLAZA   *n* pl. **-S** a public square

PLEA   *n* pl. **-S** an entreaty

PLEACH   *v* **-ED, -ING, -ES** to weave together

PLEAD   *v* **PLEADED** or **PLED, PLEADING, PLEADS** to ask for earnestly

PLEADER   *n* pl. **-S** one that pleads

PLEADING   *n* pl. **-S** an allegation in a legal action

PLEASANT   *adj* **-ANTER, -ANTEST** pleasing

PLEASE   *v* **PLEASED, PLEASING, PLEASES** to give enjoyment or satisfaction to

PLEASER   *n* pl. **-S** one that pleases

PLEASURE   *v* **-SURED, -SURING, -SURES** to please

PLEAT   *v* **-ED, -ING, -S** to fold in an even manner

PLEATER   *n* pl. **-S** one that pleats

PLEATHER   *n* pl. **-S** a plastic fabric made to look like leather

PLEATING   *n* pl. **-S** an arrangement of pleats (small folds) in a garment

PLEB   *n* pl. **-S** a commoner

PLEBE   *n* pl. **-S** a freshman at a military or naval academy

PLEBEIAN   *n* pl. **-S** a commoner

PLECTRON   *n* pl. **-TRONS** or **-TRA** plectrum

PLECTRUM   *n* pl. **-TRUMS** or **-TRA** an implement used to pluck the strings of a stringed instrument

PLED   a past tense of plead

PLEDGE   *v* **PLEDGED, PLEDGING, PLEDGES** to give as security for something borrowed

PLEDGEE   *n* pl. **-S** one to whom something is pledged

PLEDGEOR   *n* pl. **-S** pledger

PLEDGER   *n* pl. **-S** one that pledges something

PLEDGET   *n* pl. **-S** a pad of absorbent cotton

PLEDGING   present participle of pledge

PLEDGOR   *n* pl. **-S** pledger

PLEIAD   *n* pl. **-S** or **-ES** a group of seven illustrious persons

PLENA   a pl. of plenum

PLENARY   *n* pl. **-RIES** a session attended by all members

PLENCH   *n* pl. **-ES** a tool serving as pliers and a wrench

PLENISH   *v* **-ED, -ING, -ES** to fill up

PLENISM   *n* pl. **-S** the doctrine that space is fully occupied by matter

PLENIST   *n* pl. **-S** an advocate of plenism

PLENTY   *n* pl. **-TIES** a sufficient or abundant amount

PLENUM   *n* pl. **-NUMS** or **-NA** space considered as fully occupied by matter

PLEON *n* pl. **-S** the abdomen of a crustacean **PLEONAL, PLEONIC** *adj*

PLEONASM *n* pl. **-S** the use of needless words

PLEOPOD *n* pl. **-S** an appendage of crustaceans

PLEROMA *n* pl. **-S** the fullness of the divine powers

PLESSOR *n* pl. **-S** plexor

PLETHORA *n* pl. **-S** an excess

PLEURA *n* pl. **-RAS** or **-RAE** a membrane that envelops the lungs **PLEURAL** *adj*

PLEURISY *n* pl. **-SIES** inflammation of the pleura

PLEURON *n* pl. **-RA** a part of a thoracic segment of an insect

PLEUSTON *n* pl. **-S** aquatic vegetation

PLEW *n* pl. **-S** a beaver skin

PLEX *n* pl. **-ES** a multiplex

PLEXAL *adj* pertaining to a plexus

PLEXOR *n* pl. **-S** a small, hammer-like medical instrument

PLEXUS *n* pl. **-ES** an interlacing of parts

PLIABLE *adj* easily bent **PLIABLY** *adv*

PLIANCY *n* pl. **-CIES** the quality of being pliant

PLIANT *adj* easily bent **PLIANTLY** *adv*

PLICA *n* pl. **-CAE** or **-CAS** a fold of skin **PLICAL** *adj*

PLICATE *adj* pleated

PLICATED *adj* plicate

PLIE *n* pl. **-S** a movement in ballet

PLIED past tense of ply

PLIER *n* pl. **-S** one that plies

PLIES present 3d person sing. of ply

PLIGHT *v* **-ED, -ING, -S** to promise or bind by a solemn pledge

PLIGHTER *n* pl. **-S** one that plights

PLIMSOL *n* pl. **-S** plimsoll

PLIMSOLE *n* pl. **-S** plimsoll

PLIMSOLL *n* pl. **-S** a rubber-soled cloth shoe

PLINK *v* **-ED, -ING, -S** to shoot at random targets

PLINKER *n* pl. **-S** one that plinks

PLINKY *adj* **PLINKIER, PLINKIEST** having or making short, sharp metallic sounds

PLINTH *n* pl. **-S** a stone or slab upon which a column or pedestal rests

PLIOFILM *n* pl. **-S** a transparent sheet of chlorinated rubber used in packaging

PLIOTRON *n* pl. **-S** a type of vacuum tube

PLISKIE *n* pl. **-S** a practical joke

PLISKY *n* pl. **-KIES** pliskie

PLISSE *n* pl. **-S** a puckered texture of cloth

PLOD *v* **PLODDED, PLODDING, PLODS** to walk heavily

PLODDER *n* pl. **-S** one that plods

PLOIDY *n* pl. **-DIES** the extent of repetition of the basic number of chromosomes

PLONK *v* **-ED, -ING, -S** to plunk

PLONKER *n* pl. **-S** a stupid person

PLOP *v* **PLOPPED, PLOPPING, PLOPS** to drop or fall heavily

PLOSION *n* pl. **-S** a release of breath after the articulation of certain consonants

PLOSIVE *n* pl. **-S** a sound produced by plosion

PLOT *v* **PLOTTED, PLOTTING, PLOTS** to plan secretly

PLOTLESS *adj* planless

PLOTLINE *n* pl. **-S** the main story of a book

PLOTTAGE *n* pl. **-S** an area of land

PLOTTED past tense of plot

PLOTTER *n* pl. **-S** one that plots

PLOTTING present participle of plot

PLOTTY *adj* **-TIER, -TIEST** full of intrigue, as a novel

PLOTTY *n* pl. **-TIES** a hot, spiced beverage

PLOTZ *v* **-ED, -ING, -ES** to be overwhelmed by an emotion

PLOUGH *v* **-ED, -ING, -S** to plow

PLOUGHER *n* pl. **-S** one that ploughs

PLOVER *n* pl. **-S** a shore bird

PLOW *v* **-ED, -ING, -S** to turn up land with a plow (a farm implement) **PLOWABLE** *adj*

PLOWBACK *n* pl. **-S** a reinvestment of profits in a business

PLOWBOY *n* pl. **-BOYS** a boy who leads a plow team

PLOWER *n* pl. **-S** one that plows

PLOWHEAD *n* pl. **-S** the clevis of a plow

PLOWLAND *n* pl. **-S** land suitable for cultivation

PLOWMAN	*n* pl. **-MEN** a man who plows	**PLUMMY**	*adj* **-MIER, -MIEST** full of plums
PLOY	*v* **-ED, -ING, -S** to move from a line into a column	**PLUMOSE**	*adj* having feathers
PLOYE	*n* pl. **-S** a buckwheat pancake	**PLUMP**	*adj* **PLUMPER, PLUMPEST** well-rounded and full in form
PLUCK	*v* **-ED, -ING, -S** to pull out or off	**PLUMP**	*v* **-ED, -ING, -S** to make plump
PLUCKER	*n* pl. **-S** one that plucks	**PLUMPEN**	*v* **-ED, -ING, -S** to plump
PLUCKY	*adj* **PLUCKIER, PLUCKIEST** brave and spirited **PLUCKILY** *adv*	**PLUMPER**	*n* pl. **-S** a heavy fall
		PLUMPISH	*adj* somewhat plump
PLUG	*v* **PLUGGED, PLUGGING, PLUGS** to seal or close with a plug (a piece of material used to fill a hole)	**PLUMPLY**	*adv* in a plump way
		PLUMPY	*adj* **PLUMPIER, PLUMPIEST** plumpish
PLUGGER	*n* pl. **-S** one that plugs	**PLUMULE**	*n* pl. **-S** the primary bud of a plant embryo **PLUMULAR** *adj*
PLUGHOLE	*n* pl. **-S** a drain that can be stopped with a plug		
PLUGLESS	*adj* having no plug	**PLUMY**	*adj* **PLUMIER, PLUMIEST** covered with feathers
PLUGOLA	*n* pl. **-S** free incidental advertising on radio or television	**PLUNDER**	*v* **-ED, -ING, -S** to rob of goods by force
PLUGUGLY	*n* pl. **-LIES** a hoodlum	**PLUNGE**	*v* **PLUNGED, PLUNGING, PLUNGES** to throw or thrust suddenly or forcibly into something
PLUM	*n* pl. **-S** a fleshy fruit		
PLUM	*adj* **PLUMMER, PLUMMEST** highly desirable		
		PLUNGER	*n* pl. **-S** one that plunges
PLUMAGE	*n* pl. **-S** the feathers of a bird **PLUMAGED** *adj*	**PLUNK**	*v* **-ED, -ING, -S** to fall or drop heavily
PLUMATE	*adj* resembling a feather	**PLUNKER**	*n* pl. **-S** one that plunks
PLUMB	*v* **-ED, -ING, -S** to determine the depth of	**PLUNKY**	*adj* **PLUNKIER, PLUNKIEST** marked by a quick, hollow, metallic sound
PLUMBAGO	*n* pl. **-GOS** graphite		
PLUMBER	*n* pl. **-S** one who installs and repairs plumbing	**PLUOT**	*n* pl. **-S** a hybrid fruit of plum and apricot
PLUMBERY	*n* pl. **-ERIES** the work of a plumber	**PLURAL**	*n* pl. **-S** a word that expresses more than one
PLUMBIC	*adj* containing lead		
PLUMBING	*n* pl. **-S** the pipe system of a building	**PLURALLY**	*adv* in a manner or form that expresses more than one
PLUMBISM	*n* pl. **-S** lead poisoning	**PLUS**	*n* pl. **PLUSES** or **PLUSSES** an additional quantity
PLUMBOUS	*adj* containing lead		
PLUMBUM	*n* pl. **-S** lead	**PLUSH**	*adj* **PLUSHER, PLUSHEST** luxurious **PLUSHLY** *adv*
PLUME	*v* **PLUMED, PLUMING, PLUMES** to cover with feathers	**PLUSH**	*n* pl. **-ES** a fabric with a long pile
PLUMELET	*n* pl. **-S** a small feather	**PLUSHED**	*adj* showily luxurious
PLUMERIA	*n* pl. **-S** a flowering shrub	**PLUSHY**	*adj* **PLUSHIER, PLUSHIEST** luxurious **PLUSHILY** *adv*
PLUMERY	*n* pl. **-ERIES** the feathers of a bird	**PLUSSAGE**	*n* pl. **-S** an amount over and above another
PLUMIER	comparative of plumy		
PLUMIEST	superlative of plumy	**PLUSSES**	a pl. of plus
PLUMING	present participle of plume	**PLUTEUS**	*n* pl. **-TEI** the larva of a sea urchin
PLUMIPED	*n* pl. **-S** a bird having feathered feet	**PLUTON**	*n* pl. **-S** a formation of igneous rock **PLUTONIC** *adj*
PLUMLIKE	*adj* resembling a plum	**PLUVIAL**	*n* pl. **-S** a prolonged period of wet climate
PLUMMET	*v* **-ED, -ING, -S** to drop straight down	**PLUVIAN**	*adj* characterized by much rain

PLUVIOSE	*adj* pluvious
PLUVIOUS	*adj* pertaining to rain
PLY	*v* **PLIED, PLYING, PLIES** to supply with or offer repeatedly **PLYINGLY** *adv*
PLYER	*n* pl. **-S** plier
PLYWOOD	*n* pl. **-S** a building material
PNEUMA	*n* pl. **-S** the soul or spirit
PO	*n* pl. **POS** a chamber pot
POACEOUS	*adj* pertaining to plants of the grass family
POACH	*v* **-ED, -ING, -ES** to trespass for the purpose of taking game or fish
POACHER	*n* pl. **-S** one that poaches
POACHY	*adj* **POACHIER, POACHIEST** swampy
POBLANO	*n* pl. **-NOS** a mild, dark-green chili pepper
POBOY	*n* pl. **-S** a large sandwich on a long split roll
POCHARD	*n* pl. **-S** a sea duck
POCK	*v* **-ED, -ING, -S** to mark with pocks (pustules caused by an eruptive disease)
POCKET	*v* **-ED, -ING, -S** to place in a pouch sewed into a garment
POCKETER	*n* pl. **-S** one that pockets
POCKMARK	*v* **-ED, -ING, -S** to mark with scars caused by an eruptive disease
POCKY	*adj* **POCKIER, POCKIEST** covered with pocks **POCKILY** *adv*
POCO	*adv* a little — used as a musical direction
POCOSEN	*n* pl. **-S** pocosin
POCOSIN	*n* pl. **-S** an upland swamp
POCOSON	*n* pl. **-S** pocosin
POD	*v* **PODDED, PODDING, PODS** to produce seed vessels
PODAGRA	*n* pl. **-S** gout in the foot **PODAGRAL, PODAGRIC** *adj*
PODCAST	*v* **-CAST** or **-CASTED, -CASTING, -CASTS** to make a program available in digital format for download over the Internet
PODESTA	*n* pl. **-S** an Italian magistrate
PODGY	*adj* **PODGIER, PODGIEST** pudgy **PODGILY** *adv*
PODIA	a pl. of podium
PODIATRY	*n* pl. **-TRIES** the study and treatment of the human foot
PODITE	*n* pl. **-S** a limb segment of an arthropod **PODITIC** *adj*
PODIUM	*n* pl. **-DIUMS** or **-DIA** a small platform
PODLIKE	*adj* resembling a pod (a seed vessel)
PODOCARP	*adj* designating a family of evergreen trees
PODOMERE	*n* pl. **-S** a podite
PODSOL	*n* pl. **-S** podzol **PODSOLIC** *adj*
PODUNK	*n* pl. **-S** a small, unimportant town
PODZOL	*n* pl. **-S** an infertile soil **PODZOLIC** *adj*
POECHORE	*n* pl. **-S** a semiarid region
POEM	*n* pl. **-S** a composition in verse
POESY	*n* pl. **-ESIES** poetry
POET	*n* pl. **-S** one who writes poems
POETESS	*n* pl. **-ES** a female poet
POETIC	*adj* pertaining to poetry
POETICAL	*adj* poetic
POETICS	*n/pl* poetic theory or practice
POETISE	*v* **-ISED, -ISING, -ISES** to poetize
POETISER	*n* pl. **-S** poetizer
POETIZE	*v* **-IZED, -IZING, -IZES** to write poetry
POETIZER	*n* pl. **-S** one that poetizes
POETLESS	*adj* lacking a poet
POETLIKE	*adj* resembling a poet
POETRY	*n* pl. **-RIES** literary work in metrical form
POGEY	*n* pl. **-GEYS** any form of government relief
POGIES	pl. of pogy
POGO	*v* **-GOED, -GOING, -GOES** or **-GOS** to jump up and down as if on a pogo stick
POGONIA	*n* pl. **-S** a small orchid
POGONIP	*n* pl. **-S** a dense fog of suspended ice particles
POGROM	*v* **-ED, -ING, -S** to massacre systematically
POGY	*n* pl. **-GIES** a marine fish
POH	*interj* — used to express disgust
POI	*n* pl. **-S** a Hawaiian food
POIGNANT	*adj* emotionally distressing
POILU	*n* pl. **-S** a French soldier
POIND	*v* **-ED, -ING, -S** to seize and sell the property of to satisfy a debt

POINT   v **-ED, -ING, -S** to indicate direction with the finger

POINTE   n pl. **-S** a ballet position

POINTER   n pl. **-S** one that points

POINTING   n pl. **-S** cement or mortar filling the joints of brickwork

POINTMAN   n pl. **-MEN** a certain player in hockey

POINTY   adj **POINTIER, POINTIEST** coming to a sharp, tapering end

POISE   v **POISED, POISING, POISES** to hold in a state of equilibrium

POISER   n pl. **-S** one that poises

POISHA   n pl. **POISHA** the paisa of Bangladesh

POISON   v **-ED, -ING, -S** to administer a harmful substance to

POISONER   n pl. **-S** one that poisons

POITREL   n pl. **-S** peytral

POKE   v **POKED, POKING, POKES** to push or prod **POKABLE** adj

POKER   n pl. **-S** one that pokes

POKEROOT   n pl. **-S** pokeweed

POKEWEED   n pl. **-S** a perennial herb

POKEY   n pl. **-KEYS** poky

POKIER   comparative of poky

POKIES   pl. of poky

POKIEST   superlative of poky

POKILY   adv in a poky manner

POKINESS   n pl. **-ES** the state of being poky

POKING   present participle of poke

POKY   adj **POKIER, POKIEST** slow

POKY   n pl. **POKIES** a jail

POL   n pl. **-S** a politician

POLAR   n pl. **-S** a straight line related to a point

POLARISE   v **-ISED, -ISING, -ISES** to polarize

POLARITY   n pl. **-TIES** the possession of two opposite qualities

POLARIZE   v **-IZED, -IZING, -IZES** to give polarity to

POLARON   n pl. **-S** a type of electron

POLDER   n pl. **-S** a tract of low land reclaimed from a body of water

POLE   v **POLED, POLING, POLES** to propel with a pole (a long, thin piece of wood or metal)

POLEAX   v **-ED, -ING, -ES** to strike with an axlike weapon

POLEAXE   v **-AXED, -AXING, -AXES** to poleax

POLECAT   n pl. **-S** a carnivorous mammal

POLED   past tense of pole

POLEIS   pl. of polis

POLELESS   adj having no pole

POLEMIC   n pl. **-S** a controversial argument

POLEMIST   n pl. **-S** one who engages in polemics

POLEMIZE   v **-MIZED, -MIZING, -MIZES** to engage in polemics

POLENTA   n pl. **-S** a thick mush of cornmeal

POLER   n pl. **-S** one that poles

POLESTAR   n pl. **-S** a guiding principle

POLEWARD   adv in the direction of either extremity of the earth's axis

POLEYN   n pl. **-S** a protective piece of leather for the knee

POLICE   v **-LICED, -LICING, -LICES** to make clean or orderly

POLICER   n pl. **-S** one that polices

POLICIER   n pl. **-S** a film featuring police investigating crimes

POLICY   n pl. **-CIES** an action or a procedure considered with reference to prudence or expediency

POLING   present participle of pole

POLIO   n pl. **-LIOS** an infectious virus disease

POLIS   n pl. **-LEIS** an ancient Greek city-state

POLISH   v **-ED, -ING, -ES** to make smooth and lustrous by rubbing

POLISHER   n pl. **-S** one that polishes

POLITE   adj **-LITER, -LITEST** showing consideration for others **POLITELY** adv

POLITIC   adj shrewd

POLITICK   v **-ED, -ING, -S** to engage in politics

POLITICO   n pl. **-COS** or **-COES** one who politicks

POLITICS   n/pl the art or science of government

POLITY   n pl. **-TIES** a form or system of government

POLKA   v **-ED, -ING, -S** to perform a lively dance

POLL	*v* **-ED, -ING, -S** to question for the purpose of surveying public opinion
POLLACK	*n* pl. **-S** a marine food fish
POLLARD	*v* **-ED, -ING, -S** to cut the top branches of a tree back to the trunk
POLLEE	*n* pl. **-S** one who is polled
POLLEN	*v* **-ED, -ING, -S** to convey pollen (the fertilizing element in a seed plant) to
POLLER	*n* pl. **-S** one that polls
POLLEX	*n* pl. **-LICES** the innermost digit of the forelimb **POLLICAL** *adj*
POLLING	*n* pl. **-S** the registering or casting of votes
POLLINIA	*n/pl* masses of pollen grains
POLLINIC	*adj* pertaining to pollen
POLLIST	*n* pl. **-S** a poller
POLLIWOG	*n* pl. **-S** a tadpole
POLLOCK	*n* pl. **-S** pollack
POLLSTER	*n* pl. **-S** a poller
POLLUTE	*v* **-LUTED, -LUTING, -LUTES** to make unclean or impure
POLLUTER	*n* pl. **-S** one that pollutes
POLLYWOG	*n* pl. **-S** polliwog
POLO	*n* pl. **-LOS** a game played on horseback
POLOIST	*n* pl. **-S** a polo player
POLONIUM	*n* pl. **-S** a radioactive element
POLTROON	*n* pl. **-S** a base coward
POLY	*n* pl. **POLYS** a type of white blood cell
POLY	*n* pl. **POLIES** a garment made of polyester
POLYADIC	*adj* involving three or more quantities or individuals
POLYBAG	*v* **-BAGGED, -BAGGING, -BAGS** to place something in a polyethylene bag
POLYBRID	*n* pl. **-S** a type of hybrid plant
POLYCOT	*n* pl. **-S** a type of plant
POLYDRUG	*adj* pertaining to the use of several drugs together
POLYENE	*n* pl. **-S** a chemical compound **POLYENIC** *adj*
POLYGALA	*n* pl. **-S** a flowering plant
POLYGAMY	*n* pl. **-MIES** the condition of having more than one spouse at the same time
POLYGENE	*n* pl. **-S** a type of gene
POLYGLOT	*n* pl. **-S** one that speaks or writes several languages
POLYGON	*n* pl. **-S** a closed plane figure bounded by straight lines
POLYGONY	*n* pl. **-NIES** an herb
POLYGYNE	*adj* having more than one egg-laying queen in an insect colony
POLYGYNY	*n* pl. **-NIES** the condition of having more than one wife at the same time
POLYMATH	*n* pl. **-S** a person of great and varied learning
POLYMER	*n* pl. **-S** a complex chemical compound
POLYNYA	*n* pl. **-YAS** or **-YI** an area of open water surrounded by sea ice
POLYOL	*n* pl. **-S** an alcohol containing three or more hydroxyl groups
POLYOMA	*n* pl. **-S** a type of virus
POLYP	*n* pl. **-S** an invertebrate
POLYPARY	*n* pl. **-ARIES** the common supporting structure of a polyp colony
POLYPED	*n* pl. **-S** something having many legs
POLYPI	a pl. of polypus
POLYPIDE	*n* pl. **-S** a polyp
POLYPNEA	*n* pl. **-S** rapid breathing
POLYPOD	*n* pl. **-S** a many-footed organism
POLYPODY	*n* pl. **-DIES** a fern
POLYPOID	*adj* resembling a polyp
POLYPORE	*n* pl. **-S** a type of fungus
POLYPOUS	*adj* pertaining to a polyp
POLYPUS	*n* pl. **-PUSES** or **-PI** a growth protruding from the mucous lining of an organ
POLYSEMY	*n* pl. **-MIES** diversity of meanings
POLYSOME	*n* pl. **-S** a cluster of protein particles
POLYTENE	*adj* having chromosomes of a certain type
POLYTENY	*n* pl. **-NIES** the state of being polytene
POLYTYPE	*n* pl. **-S** a crystal structure
POLYURIA	*n* pl. **-S** excessive urination **POLYURIC** *adj*
POLYZOAN	*n* pl. **-S** a bryozoan
POLYZOIC	*adj* composed of many zooids
POM	*n* pl. **-S** a Pomeranian dog

POMACE	*n* pl. **-S** the pulpy residue of crushed fruits
POMADE	*v* **-MADED, -MADING, -MADES** to apply a perfumed hair dressing to
POMANDER	*n* pl. **-S** a mixture of aromatic substances
POMATUM	*n* pl. **-S** a perfumed hair dressing
POMBE	*n* pl. **-S** an African drink made from grain and fruit
POME	*n* pl. **-S** a fleshy fruit with a core
POMELO	*n* pl. **-LOS** a grapefruit
POMFRET	*n* pl. **-S** a marine fish
POMMEE	*adj* having arms with knoblike ends — used of a heraldic cross
POMMEL	*v* **-MELED, -MELING, -MELS** or **-MELLED, -MELLING, -MELS** to strike with the fists
POMO	*n* pl. **-MOS** the postmodern movement
POMOLOGY	*n* pl. **-GIES** the study of fruits
POMP	*n* pl. **-S** stately or splendid display
POMPANO	*n* pl. **-NOS** a marine food fish
POMPOM	*n* pl. **-S** an antiaircraft cannon
POMPON	*n* pl. **-S** an ornamental tuft or ball
POMPOUS	*adj* marked by exaggerated self-importance
PONCE	*v* **PONCED, PONCING, PONCES** to pimp
PONCHO	*n* pl. **-CHOS** a type of cloak **PONCHOED** *adj*
POND	*v* **-ED, -ING, -S** to collect into a pond (a small body of water)
PONDER	*v* **-ED, -ING, -S** to consider something deeply and thoroughly
PONDERER	*n* pl. **-S** one that ponders
PONDWEED	*n* pl. **-S** an aquatic plant
PONE	*n* pl. **-S** a corn bread
PONENT	*adj* affirmative
PONG	*v* **-ED, -ING, -S** to stink
PONGAL	*n* pl. **-S** a dish of cooked rice in Tamil-speaking India
PONGEE	*n* pl. **-S** a type of silk
PONGID	*n* pl. **-S** an anthropoid ape
PONGO	*n* pl. **-GOS** an anthropoid ape
PONGY	*adj* **PONGIER, PONGIEST** stinky
PONIARD	*v* **-ED, -ING, -S** to stab with a dagger
PONIED	past tense of pony
PONIES	present 3d person sing. of pony

PONS	*n* pl. **PONTES** a band of nerve fibers in the brain
PONTIFEX	*n* pl. **-FICES** an ancient Roman priest
PONTIFF	*n* pl. **-S** a pope or bishop
PONTIFIC	*adj* pertaining to a pope or bishop
PONTIFICES	pl. of pontifex
PONTIL	*n* pl. **-S** a punty
PONTINE	*adj* pertaining to bridges
PONTON	*n* pl. **-S** pontoon
PONTOON	*n* pl. **-S** a flat-bottomed boat
PONY	*v* **-NIED, -NYING, -NIES** to prepare lessons with the aid of a literal translation
PONYTAIL	*n* pl. **-S** a hairstyle
PONZU	*n* pl. **-S** a tangy sauce used chiefly on seafood
POO	*v* **-ED, -ING, -S** to defecate
POOBAH	*n* pl. **-S** an influential person
POOCH	*v* **-ED, -ING, -ES** to bulge
POOD	*n* pl. **-S** a Russian unit of weight
POODLE	*n* pl. **-S** a heavy-coated dog
POOF	*interj* — used to indicate an instantaneous occurrence
POOH	*v* **-ED, -ING, -S** to express contempt for
POOJA	*n* pl. **-S** puja
POOKA	*n* pl. **-S** a hobgoblin in Irish myths
POOL	*v* **-ED, -ING, -S** to combine in a common fund
POOLER	*n* pl. **-S** one that pools
POOLHALL	*n* pl. **-S** a poolroom
POOLROOM	*n* pl. **-S** an establishment for the playing of billiards
POOLSIDE	*n* pl. **-S** the area surrounding a swimming pool
POON	*n* pl. **-S** an East Indian tree
POOP	*v* **-ED, -ING, -S** to tire out
POOPY	*adj* **POOPIER, POOPIEST** stupid or ineffectual
POOR	*adj* **POORER, POOREST** lacking the means of support
POORI	*n* pl. **-S** a light, flat wheat cake
POORISH	*adj* somewhat poor
POORLY	*adv* in a poor manner
POORNESS	*n* pl. **-ES** the state of being poor
POORTITH	*n* pl. **-S** poverty

POORWILL *n* pl. **-S** a small North American bird

POP *v* **POPPED, POPPING, POPS** to make a sharp, explosive sound

POPCORN *n* pl. **-S** a variety of corn

POPE *n* pl. **-S** the head of the Roman Catholic Church **POPELESS, POPELIKE** *adj*

POPEDOM *n* pl. **-S** the office of a pope

POPEYED *adj* having bulging eyes

POPGUN *n* pl. **-S** a toy gun

POPINJAY *n* pl. **-JAYS** a vain person

POPLAR *n* pl. **-S** a fast-growing tree

POPLIN *n* pl. **-S** a durable fabric

POPLITEI *n/pl* muscles at the back of knees

POPLITIC *adj* pertaining to the part of the leg behind the knee

POPOUT *n* pl. **-S** a type of out in baseball

POPOVER *n* pl. **-S** a very light egg muffin

POPPA *n* pl. **-S** papa

POPPADOM *n* pl. **-S** papadum

POPPADUM *n* pl. **-S** papadum

POPPED past tense of pop

POPPER *n* pl. **-S** one that pops

POPPET *n* pl. **-S** a mechanical valve

POPPIED *adj* covered with poppies

POPPIES pl. of poppy

POPPING present participle of pop

POPPLE *v* **-PLED, -PLING, -PLES** to move in a bubbling or rippling manner

POPPLY *adj* **-PLIER, -PLIEST** choppy

POPPY *n* pl. **-PIES** a flowering plant

POPPY *adj* **-PIER, -PIEST** having the characteristics of pop music

POPSIE *n* pl. **-S** popsy

POPSTER *n* pl. **-S** a pop musician

POPSY *n* pl. **-SIES** a girlfriend

POPULACE *n* pl. **-S** the common people

POPULAR *adj* liked by many people

POPULATE *v* **-LATED, -LATING, -LATES** to inhabit

POPULISM *n* pl. **-S** populists' doctrines

POPULIST *n* pl. **-S** a member of a party which represents the common people

POPULOUS *adj* containing many inhabitants

PORCH *n* pl. **-ES** a covered structure at the entrance to a building **PORCHED** *adj*

PORCINE *adj* pertaining to swine

PORCINI *n* pl. **-S** an edible mushroom

PORCINO *n* pl. **-NI** porcini

PORE *v* **PORED, PORING, PORES** to gaze intently

PORGY *n* pl. **-GIES** a marine food fish

PORIN *n* pl. **-S** any of a class of proteins through which molecules can diffuse

PORISM *n* pl. **-S** a type of mathematical proposition

PORK *v* **-ED, -ING, -S** to eat ravenously

PORKER *n* pl. **-S** a pig

PORKIER comparative of porky

PORKIES pl. of porky

PORKIEST superlative of porky

PORKPIE *n* pl. **-S** a man's hat

PORKWOOD *n* pl. **-S** a tropical tree

PORKY *adj* **PORKIER, PORKIEST** resembling pork

PORKY *n* pl. **-KIES** a porcupine

PORN *n* pl. **-S** pornography

PORNO *n* pl. **-NOS** pornography

PORNY *adj* **PORNIER, PORNIEST** pornographic

POROSE *adj* porous

POROSITY *n* pl. **-TIES** the state of being porous

POROUS *adj* having minute openings **POROUSLY** *adv*

PORPHYRY *n* pl. **-RIES** an igneous rock

PORPOISE *v* **-POISED, -POISING, -POISES** to move forward with rising and falling motions

PORRECT *adj* extended forward

PORRIDGE *n* pl. **-S** a soft food **PORRIDGY** *adj*

PORT *v* **-ED, -ING, -S** to shift to the left side

PORTABLE *n* pl. **-S** something that can be carried

PORTABLY *adv* so as to be capable of being carried

PORTAGE *v* **-TAGED, -TAGING, -TAGES** to transport from one navigable waterway to another

PORTAL *n* pl. **-S** a door, gate, or entrance **PORTALED** *adj*

PORTANCE *n* pl. **-S** demeanor

PORTAPAK *n* pl. **-S** a portable combined video recorder and camera

PORTEND   *v* **-ED, -ING, -S** to serve as an omen of

PORTENT   *n* pl. **-S** an omen

PORTER   *v* **-ED, -ING, -S** to carry luggage for pay

PORTHOLE   *n* pl. **-S** a small window in a ship's side

PORTICO   *n* pl. **-COS** or **-COES** a type of porch

PORTIERE   *n* pl. **-S** a curtain for a doorway

PORTION   *v* **-ED, -ING, -S** to divide into shares for distribution

PORTLESS   *adj* having no place for ships to load or unload

PORTLY   *adj* **-LIER, -LIEST** rather heavy or fat

PORTOLAN   *n* pl. **-S** a book of sailing directions

PORTRAIT   *n* pl. **-S** a likeness of a person

PORTRAY   *v* **-ED, -ING, -S** to represent pictorially

PORTRESS   *n* pl. **-ES** a female doorkeeper

PORTSIDE   *adv* on the left side of a ship facing forward

POS   pl. of po

POSADA   *n* pl. **-S** an inn

POSE   *v* **POSED, POSING, POSES** to assume a fixed position **POSABLE, POSEABLE** *adj*

POSER   *n* pl. **-S** one that poses

POSEUR   *n* pl. **-S** an affected or insincere person

POSEY   *adj* **POSIER, POSIEST** pretentious

POSH   *adj* **POSHER, POSHEST** stylish or elegant **POSHLY** *adv*

POSHNESS   *n* pl. **-ES** the quality of being posh

POSIES   pl. of posy

POSING   present participle of pose

POSINGLY   *adv* in a posing manner

POSIT   *v* **-ED, -ING, -S** to place

POSITION   *v* **-ED, -ING, -S** to put in a particular location

POSITIVE   *adj* **-TIVER, -TIVEST** certain

POSITIVE   *n* pl. **-S** a quantity greater than zero

POSITRON   *n* pl. **-S** a subatomic particle

POSOLE   *n* pl. **-S** a thick soup made of pork, corn, garlic, and chili

POSOLOGY   *n* pl. **-GIES** a branch of medicine that deals with drug dosages

POSSE   *n* pl. **-S** a body of men summoned to aid a peace officer

POSSESS   *v* **-ED, -ING, -ES** to have as property

POSSET   *n* pl. **-S** a hot, spiced drink

POSSIBLE   *adj* **-BLER, -BLEST** capable of happening or proving true **POSSIBLY** *adv*

POSSIBLE   *n* pl. **-S** a possibility

POSSUM   *n* pl. **-S** opossum

POST   *v* **-ED, -ING, -S** to affix in a public place

POSTAGE   *n* pl. **-S** the charge for mailing an item

POSTAL   *n* pl. **-S** a postcard

POSTALLY   *adv* in a manner pertaining to the mails

POSTANAL   *adj* situated behind the anus

POSTBAG   *n* pl. **-S** a mailbag

POSTBASE   *adj* following a base word

POSTBOX   *n* pl. **-ES** a mailbox

POSTBOY   *n* pl. **-BOYS** a boy who carries mail

POSTBURN   *adj* following a burn

POSTCARD   *n* pl. **-S** a card for use in the mail

POSTCAVA   *n* pl. **-VAE** a vein in higher vertebrates

POSTCODE   *n* pl. **-S** a code of numbers and letters used in a mailing address

POSTCOUP   *adj* following a coup

POSTDATE   *v* **-DATED, -DATING, -DATES** to give a date later than the actual date to

POSTDIVE   *adj* following a dive

POSTDOC   *n* pl. **-S** one engaged in postdoctoral study

POSTDRUG   *adj* following the taking of a drug

POSTEEN   *n* pl. **-S** an Afghan outer garment

POSTER   *v* **-ED, -ING, -S** to affix public notices on

POSTERN   *n* pl. **-S** a rear door or gate

POSTFACE   *n* pl. **-S** a brief note placed at the end of a publication

POSTFIRE   *adj* following a fire

POSTFIX   *v* **-ED, -ING, -ES** to affix at the end of something

POSTFORM   *v* **-ED, -ING, -S** to shape subsequently

POSTGAME   *adj* following a game

POSTGRAD   *n* pl. **-S** a student continuing formal education after graduation

POSTHEAT *n* pl. **-S** heat applied to a metal after welding

POSTHOLE *n* pl. **-S** a hole for a fence post

POSTICHE *n* pl. **-S** an imitation

POSTIE *n* pl. **-TIES** a letter carrier

POSTIN *n* pl. **-S** posteen

POSTING *n* pl. **-S** the act of transferring to a ledger

POSTIQUE *n* pl. **-S** postiche

POSTLUDE *n* pl. **-S** a closing musical piece

POSTMAN *n* pl. **-MEN** a mailman

POSTMARK *v* **-ED, -ING, -S** to stamp mail with an official mark

POSTOP *n* pl. **-S** a patient after undergoing a surgical operation

POSTORAL *adj* situated behind the mouth

POSTPAID *adv* with the postage prepaid

POSTPONE *v* **-PONED, -PONING, -PONES** to put off to a future time

POSTPOSE *v* **-POSED, -POSING, -POSES** to place (a word or phrase) after a grammatically related word

POSTPUNK *adj* pertaining to music coming after punk rock

POSTRACE *adj* following a race

POSTRIOT *adj* following a riot

POSTSHOW *adj* following a show

POSTSYNC *v* **-ED, -ING, -S** to add sound to a film after a scene has been photographed

POSTTAX *adj* remaining after taxes

POSTTEEN *n* pl. **-S** a person older than 19 years

POSTTEST *n* pl. **-S** a test given after an instructional program

POSTURAL *adj* pertaining to the position of the body

POSTURE *v* **-TURED, -TURING, -TURES** to assume a particular position

POSTURER *n* pl. **-S** one that postures

POSTWAR *adj* occurring or existing after a war

POSY *n* pl. **-SIES** a flower or bouquet

POT *v* **POTTED, POTTING, POTS** to put in a pot (a round, fairly deep container)

POTABLE *n* pl. **-S** a liquid suitable for drinking

POTAGE *n* pl. **-S** a thick soup

POTAMIC *adj* pertaining to rivers

POTASH *n* pl. **-ES** an alkaline compound

POTASSIC *adj* pertaining to potassium (a metallic element)

POTATION *n* pl. **-S** the act of drinking

POTATO *n* pl. **-TOES** the edible tuber of a cultivated plant

POTATORY *adj* pertaining to drinking

POTBELLY *n* pl. **-LIES** a protruding abdominal region

POTBOIL *v* **-ED, -ING, -S** to produce inferior literary or artistic work

POTBOUND *adj* having grown too large for its container

POTBOY *n* pl. **-BOYS** a boy who serves customers in a tavern

POTEEN *n* pl. **-S** Irish whiskey that is distilled unlawfully

POTENCE *n* pl. **-S** potency

POTENCY *n* pl. **-CIES** the quality of being potent

POTENT *adj* powerful **POTENTLY** *adv*

POTFUL *n* pl. **-S** as much as a pot can hold

POTHEAD *n* pl. **-S** one who smokes marijuana

POTHEEN *n* pl. **-S** poteen

POTHER *v* **-ED, -ING, -S** to trouble

POTHERB *n* pl. **-S** any herb used as a food or seasoning

POTHOLE *n* pl. **-S** a deep hole in a road **POTHOLED** *adj*

POTHOLER *n* pl. **-S** one who explores deep underground holes or caves

POTHOOK *n* pl. **-S** a hook for lifting or hanging pots

POTHOS *n* pl. **POTHOS** a climbing plant with glossy variegated leaves

POTHOUSE *n* pl. **-S** a tavern

POTICHE *n* pl. **-S** a type of vase

POTION *n* pl. **-S** a magical or medicinal drink

POTLACH *n* pl. **-ES** a ceremonial feast

POTLACHE *n* pl. **-S** potlach

POTLATCH *v* **-ED, -ING, -ES** to hold a ceremonial feast for

POTLIKE *adj* resembling a pot

POTLINE *n* pl. **-S** a row of electrolytic cells

POTLUCK *n* pl. **-S** food which is incidentally available

POTMAN *n* pl. **-MEN** a man who serves customers in a tavern

POTPIE *n* pl. **-S** a deep-dish pie containing meat and vegetables

POTSHARD *n* pl. **-S** potsherd

POTSHERD *n* pl. **-S** a fragment of broken pottery

POTSHOT *v* **-SHOT, -SHOTTING, -SHOTS** to shoot randomly at

POTSIE *n* pl. **-S** potsy

POTSTONE *n* pl. **-S** a variety of steatite

POTSY *n* pl. **-SIES** a children's game

POTTAGE *n* pl. **-S** a thick soup

POTTED past tense of pot

POTTEEN *n* pl. **-S** poteen

POTTER *v* **-ED, -ING, -S** to putter

POTTERER *n* pl. **-S** one that potters

POTTERY *n* pl. **-TERIES** ware molded from clay and hardened by heat

POTTIER comparative of potty

POTTIES pl. of potty

POTTIEST superlative of potty

POTTING present participle of pot

POTTLE *n* pl. **-S** a drinking vessel

POTTO *n* pl. **-TOS** a lemur of tropical Africa

POTTY *adj* **-TIER, -TIEST** of little importance

POTTY *n* pl. **-TIES** a small toilet seat

POTZER *n* pl. **-S** patzer

POUCH *v* **-ED, -ING, -ES** to put in a pouch (a small, flexible receptacle)

POUCHY *adj* **POUCHIER, POUCHIEST** resembling a pouch

POUF *n* pl. **-S** a loose roll of hair **POUFED, POUFFY** *adj*

POUFF *n* pl. **-S** pouf **POUFFED** *adj*

POUFFE *n* pl. **-S** pouf

POULARD *n* pl. **-S** a spayed hen

POULARDE *n* pl. **-S** poulard

POULT *n* pl. **-S** a young domestic fowl

POULTER *n* pl. **-S** one that deals in poultry

POULTICE *v* **-TICED, -TICING, -TICES** to apply a healing substance to

POULTRY *n* pl. **-TRIES** domestic fowls kept for eggs or meat

POUNCE *v* **POUNCED, POUNCING, POUNCES** to make a sudden assault or approach

POUNCER *n* pl. **-S** one that pounces

POUND *v* **-ED, -ING, -S** to strike heavily and repeatedly

POUNDAGE *n* pl. **-S** the act of impounding

POUNDAL *n* pl. **-S** a unit of force

POUNDER *n* pl. **-S** one that pounds

POUR *v* **-ED, -ING, -S** to cause to flow **POURABLE** *adj*

POURER *n* pl. **-S** one that pours

POUSSIE *n* pl. **-S** pussy

POUT *v* **-ED, -ING, -S** to protrude the lips in ill humor

POUTER *n* pl. **-S** one that pouts

POUTFUL *adj* pouty

POUTINE *n* pl. **-S** a dish of french fries and cheese curds topped with gravy

POUTY *adj* **POUTIER, POUTIEST** tending to pout

POVERTY *n* pl. **-TIES** the state of being poor

POW *n* pl. **-S** an explosive sound

POWDER *v* **-ED, -ING, -S** to reduce to powder (matter in a finely divided state)

POWDERER *n* pl. **-S** one that powders

POWDERY *adj* resembling powder

POWER *v* **-ED, -ING, -S** to provide with means of propulsion

POWERFUL *adj* possessing great force

POWTER *n* pl. **-S** a domestic pigeon

POWWOW *v* **-ED, -ING, -S** to hold a conference

POX *v* **-ED, -ING, -ES** to infect with a pox (a disease marked by skin eruptions)

POXVIRUS *n* pl. **-ES** a type of virus

POXY *adj* **POXIER, POXIEST** afflicted with a pox

POYOU *n* pl. **-S** an armadillo of Argentina

POZOLE *n* pl. **-S** posole

POZZOLAN *n* pl. **-S** a finely divided material used to make cement

PRAAM *n* pl. **-S** pram

PRACTIC *adj* practical

PRACTICE *v* **-TICED, -TICING, -TICES** to perform often so as to acquire skill

PRACTISE *v* **-TISED, -TISING, -TISES** to practice

PRAECIPE *n* pl. **-S** a legal writ

PRAEDIAL *adj* pertaining to land

PRAEFECT *n* pl. **-S** prefect

PRAELECT	*v* **-ED, -ING, -S** to prelect
PRAETOR	*n* pl. **-S** an ancient Roman magistrate
PRAHU	*n* pl. **-S** prau
PRAIRIE	*n* pl. **-S** a tract of grassland
PRAISE	*v* **PRAISED, PRAISING, PRAISES** to express approval or admiration of
PRAISER	*n* pl. **-S** one that praises
PRAJNA	*n* pl. **-S** ultimate knowledge in Buddhism and Hinduism
PRALINE	*n* pl. **-S** a confection made of nuts cooked in sugar
PRAM	*n* pl. **-S** a flat-bottomed boat
PRANA	*n* pl. **-S** breath as a life-giving force in Hinduism
PRANCE	*v* **PRANCED, PRANCING, PRANCES** to spring forward on the hind legs
PRANCER	*n* pl. **-S** one that prances
PRANDIAL	*adj* pertaining to a meal
PRANG	*v* **-ED, -ING, -S** to cause to crash
PRANK	*v* **-ED, -ING, -S** to adorn gaudily
PRANKISH	*adj* mischievous
PRAO	*n* pl. **PRAOS** prau
PRASE	*n* pl. **-S** a mineral
PRAT	*n* pl. **-S** the buttocks
PRATE	*v* **PRATED, PRATING, PRATES** to chatter
PRATER	*n* pl. **-S** one that prates
PRATFALL	*n* pl. **-S** a fall on the buttocks
PRATIE	*n* pl. **-S** a potato
PRATIQUE	*n* pl. **-S** clearance given a ship by the health authority of a port
PRATTLE	*v* **-TLED, -TLING, -TLES** to babble
PRATTLER	*n* pl. **-S** one that prattles
PRAU	*n* pl. **-S** a swift Malaysian sailing vessel
PRAWN	*v* **-ED, -ING, -S** to fish for prawns (edible shellfish)
PRAWNER	*n* pl. **-S** one that prawns
PRAXIS	*n* pl. **PRAXISES** or **PRAXES** practical use of a theory
PRAY	*v* **-ED, -ING, -S** to address prayers to
PRAYER	*n* pl. **-S** a devout petition to a deity
PREACH	*v* **-ED, -ING, -ES** to advocate or recommend urgently
PREACHER	*n* pl. **-S** one that preaches
PREACHY	*adj* **PREACHIER, PREACHIEST** tending to preach
PREACT	*v* **-ED, -ING, -S** to act beforehand
PREADAPT	*v* **-ED, -ING, -S** to adapt beforehand
PREADMIT	*v* **-MITTED, -MITTING, -MITS** to admit beforehand
PREADOPT	*v* **-ED, -ING, -S** to adopt beforehand
PREADULT	*n* pl. **-S** a person not yet an adult
PREAGED	*adj* previously aged
PREALLOT	*v* **-LOTTED, -LOTTING, -LOTS** to allot beforehand
PREALTER	*v* **-ED, -ING, -S** to alter beforehand
PREAMBLE	*n* pl. **-S** an introductory statement
PREAMP	*n* pl. **-S** an amplifier
PREANAL	*adj* situated in front of the anus
PREAPPLY	*v* **-PLIED, -PLYING, -PLIES** to apply beforehand
PREARM	*v* **-ED, -ING, -S** to arm beforehand
PREAUDIT	*n* pl. **-S** an audit made prior to a final settlement of a transaction
PREAVER	*v* **-VERRED, -VERRING, -VERS** to aver or assert beforehand
PREAXIAL	*adj* situated in front of an axis
PREBAKE	*v* **-BAKED, -BAKING, -BAKES** to bake beforehand
PREBASAL	*adj* situated in front of a base
PREBEND	*n* pl. **-S** a clergyman's stipend
PREBID	*v* **-BADE, -BIDDEN, -BIDDING, -BIDS** to bid beforehand
PREBILL	*v* **-ED, -ING, -S** to bill beforehand
PREBIND	*v* **-BOUND, -BINDING, -BINDS** to bind beforehand
PREBIRTH	*n* pl. **-S** the period preceding a child's birth
PREBLESS	*v* **-ED, -ING, -ES** to bless beforehand
PREBOARD	*v* **-ED, -ING, -S** to board before the regular time
PREBOIL	*v* **-ED, -ING, -S** to boil beforehand
PREBOOK	*v* **-ED, -ING, -S** to book beforehand
PREBOOM	*adj* preceding a sudden expansion of business
PREBOUND	past tense of prebind
PREBUILD	*v* **-BUILT, -BUILDING, -BUILDS** to build beforehand
PREBUY	*v* **-BOUGHT, -BUYING, -BUYS** to buy beforehand

PRECAST   *v* **-CAST, -CASTING, -CASTS** to cast before placing into position

PRECAVA   *n* pl. **-VAE** a vein in higher vertebrates **PRECAVAL** *adj*

PRECEDE   *v* **-CEDED, -CEDING, -CEDES** to go before

PRECENT   *v* **-ED, -ING, -S** to lead a church choir in singing

PRECEPT   *n* pl. **-S** a rule of conduct

PRECESS   *v* **-ED, -ING, -ES** to rotate with a complex motion

PRECHECK   *v* **-ED, -ING, -S** to check beforehand

PRECHILL   *v* **-ED, -ING, -S** to chill beforehand

PRECHOSE   past tense of prechoose (to choose beforehand)

PRECIEUX   *adj* excessively refined

PRECINCT   *n* pl. **-S** a subdivision of a city or town

PRECIOUS   *n* pl. **-ES** a darling

PRECIP   *n* pl. **-S** precipitation

PRECIPE   *n* pl. **-S** praecipe

PRECIS   *v* **-ED, -ING, -ES** to make a concise summary of

PRECISE   *adj* **-CISER, -CISEST** sharply and clearly defined or stated

PRECITED   *adj* previously cited

PRECLEAN   *v* **-ED, -ING, -S** to clean beforehand

PRECLEAR   *v* **-ED, -ING, -S** to clear beforehand

PRECLUDE   *v* **-CLUDED, -CLUDING, -CLUDES** to make impossible by previous action

PRECODE   *v* **-CODED, -CODING, -CODES** to code beforehand

PRECOOK   *v* **-ED, -ING, -S** to cook beforehand

PRECOOL   *v* **-ED, -ING, -S** to cool beforehand

PRECOUP   *adj* preceding a coup

PRECRASH   *adj* preceding a crash

PRECURE   *v* **-CURED, -CURING, -CURES** to cure beforehand

PRECUT   *v* **-CUT, -CUTTING, -CUTS** to cut beforehand

PREDATE   *v* **-DATED, -DATING, -DATES** to date before the actual or a specified time

PREDATOR   *n* pl. **-S** one that plunders

PREDAWN   *n* pl. **-S** the time just before dawn

PREDEATH   *n* pl. **-S** the period preceding a person's death

PREDELLA   *n* pl. **-S** the base of an altarpiece

PREDIAL   *adj* praedial

PREDICT   *v* **-ED, -ING, -S** to tell of or about in advance

PREDIVE   *adj* preceding a dive

PREDRAFT   *adj* preceding a draft (a system for selecting players for professional teams)

PREDRILL   *v* **-ED, -ING, -S** to drill beforehand

PREDRY   *v* **-DRIED, -DRYING, -DRIES** to dry beforehand

PREDUSK   *n* pl. **-S** the time just before dusk

PREE   *v* **PREED, PREEING, PREES** to test by tasting

PREEDIT   *v* **-ED, -ING, -S** to edit beforehand

PREELECT   *v* **-ED, -ING, -S** to elect or choose beforehand

PREEMIE   *n* pl. **-S** an infant born prematurely

PREEMPT   *v* **-ED, -ING, -S** to acquire by prior right

PREEN   *v* **-ED, -ING, -S** to smooth or clean with the beak or tongue

PREENACT   *v* **-ED, -ING, -S** to enact beforehand

PREENER   *n* pl. **-S** one that preens

PREERECT   *v* **-ED, -ING, -S** to erect beforehand

PREEXIST   *v* **-ED, -ING, -S** to exist before

PREFAB   *v* **-FABBED, -FABBING, -FABS** to construct beforehand

PREFACE   *v* **-ACED, -ACING, -ACES** to provide with an introductory statement

PREFACER   *n* pl. **-S** one that prefaces

PREFADE   *v* **-FADED, -FADING, -FADES** to fade beforehand

PREFECT   *n* pl. **-S** an ancient Roman official

PREFER   *v* **-FERRED, -FERRING, -FERS** to hold in higher regard or esteem

PREFIGHT   *adj* preceding a fight

PREFILE   *v* **-FILED, -FILING, -FILES** to file beforehand

PREFIRE   *v* **-FIRED, -FIRING, -FIRES** to fire beforehand

PREFIX   *v* **-ED, -ING, -ES** to add as a prefix (a form affixed to the beginning of a root word)

PREFIXAL   *adj* pertaining to or being a prefix

PREFLAME   *adj* preceding a flame

PREFOCUS   *v* **-CUSED, -CUSING, -CUSES** or **-CUSSED, -CUSSING, -CUSSES** to focus beforehand

PREFORM	*v* **-ED, -ING, -S** to form beforehand
PREFRANK	*v* **-ED, -ING, -S** to frank beforehand
PREFUND	*v* **-ED, -ING, -S** to fund beforehand
PREGAME	*v* **-GAMED, -GAMING, -GAMES** to drink alcohol before an event
PREGGERS	*adj* pregnant
PREGNANT	*adj* carrying a developing fetus in the uterus
PREGUIDE	*v* **-GUIDED, -GUIDING, -GUIDES** to guide beforehand
PREHEAT	*v* **-ED, -ING, -S** to heat beforehand
PREHUMAN	*n pl.* **-S** a prototype of man
PREJUDGE	*v* **-JUDGED, -JUDGING, -JUDGES** to judge beforehand
PRELACY	*n pl.* **-CIES** the office of a prelate
PRELATE	*n pl.* **-S** a high-ranking clergyman **PRELATIC** *adj*
PRELAW	*adj* preceding the professional study of law
PRELECT	*v* **-ED, -ING, -S** to lecture
PRELEGAL	*adj* occurring before the commencement of studies in law
PRELIFE	*n pl.* **-LIVES** a life conceived as lived before one's earthly life
PRELIM	*n pl.* **-S** a preliminary match
PRELIMIT	*v* **-ED, -ING, -S** to limit beforehand
PRELOAD	*v* **-ED, -ING, -S** to load beforehand
PRELUDE	*v* **-LUDED, -LUDING, -LUDES** to play a musical introduction
PRELUDER	*n pl.* **-S** one that preludes
PRELUNCH	*adj* preceding lunch
PREMADE	*adj* made beforehand
PREMAN	*n pl.* **-MEN** a hypothetical ancestor of man
PREMEAL	*adj* preceding a meal
PREMED	*n pl.* **-S** a student preparing for the study of medicine
PREMEDIC	*n pl.* **-S** a premed
PREMEET	*adj* preceding a meet
PREMEN	pl. of preman
PREMIE	*n pl.* **-S** preemie
PREMIER	*n pl.* **-S** a prime minister
PREMIERE	*v* **-MIERED, -MIERING, -MIERES** to present publicly for the first time
PREMISE	*v* **-MISED, -MISING, -MISES** to state in advance
PREMISS	*n pl.* **-ES** a proposition in logic
PREMIUM	*n pl.* **-S** an additional payment
PREMIX	*v* **-MIXED** or **-MIXT, -MIXING, -MIXES** to mix before use
PREMOLAR	*n pl.* **-S** a tooth
PREMOLD	*v* **-ED, -ING, -S** to mold beforehand
PREMOLT	*adj* preceding a molt
PREMORAL	*adj* preceding the development of a moral code
PREMORSE	*adj* ending abruptly, as if bitten off
PREMOTOR	*adj* pertaining to a part of the frontal lobe of the brain
PREMUNE	*adj* resistant to a disease
PRENAME	*n pl.* **-S** a forename
PRENATAL	*adj* prior to birth
PRENOMEN	*n pl.* **-MENS** or **-MINA** the first name of an ancient Roman
PRENOON	*adj* preceding noon
PRENTICE	*v* **-TICED, -TICING, -TICES** to place with an employer for instruction in a trade
PRENUP	*n pl.* **-S** an agreement made by a couple before they marry
PREOP	*n pl.* **-S** a patient being prepared for surgery
PREORAL	*adj* situated in front of the mouth
PREORDER	*v* **-ED, -ING, -S** to order beforehand
PREOWNED	*adj* owned beforehand by someone else
PREP	*v* **PREPPED, PREPPING, PREPS** to attend a preparatory school
PREPACK	*v* **-ED, -ING, -S** to package before retail distribution
PREPAID	past tense of prepay
PREPARE	*v* **-PARED, -PARING, -PARES** to put in proper condition or readiness
PREPARER	*n pl.* **-S** one that prepares
PREPASTE	*v* **-PASTED, -PASTING, -PASTES** to paste beforehand
PREPAVE	*v* **-PAVED, -PAVING, -PAVES** to pave beforehand
PREPAY	*v* **-PAID, -PAYING, -PAYS** to pay in advance
PREPENSE	*adj* planned in advance
PREPILL	*adj* preceding the development of a contraceptive pill
PREPLACE	*v* **-PLACED, -PLACING, -PLACES** to place beforehand
PREPLAN	*v* **-PLANNED, -PLANNING, -PLANS** to plan in advance
PREPLANT	*adj* occurring before planting

PREPOSE *v* **-POSED, -POSING, -POSES** to place something in front of another

PREPPED past tense of prep

PREPPIE *n* pl. **-S** one who preps

PREPPING present participle of prep

PREPPY *adj* **-PIER, -PIEST** associated with the style and behavior of preparatory school students **PREPPILY** *adv*

PREPREG *n* pl. **-S** reinforcing material already impregnated with a synthetic resin

PREPRESS *adj* pertaining to the preparation of copy for printing

PREPRICE *v* **-PRICED, -PRICING, -PRICES** to price beforehand

PREPRINT *v* **-ED, -ING, -S** to print in advance

PREPUBIS *n* pl. **-PUBES** a bone situated in front of the pubic bones

PREPUCE *n* pl. **-S** a fold of skin covering the penis

PREPUNCH *v* **-ED, -ING, -ES** to punch in advance

PREPUPA *n* pl. **-PAS** or **-PAE** a stage preceding the pupa

PREPUPAL *adj* preceding the pupal stage

PREQUEL *n* pl. **-S** a book whose story precedes that of an earlier work

PRERACE *adj* preceding a race

PRERADIO *adj* preceding the development of radio

PRERENAL *adj* situated in front of the kidney

PRERINSE *v* **-RINSED, -RINSING, -RINSES** to rinse beforehand

PRERIOT *adj* preceding a riot

PREROCK *adj* preceding the development of rock music

PRESA *n* pl. **-SE** a musical symbol

PRESAGE *v* **-SAGED, -SAGING, -SAGES** to foretell

PRESAGER *n* pl. **-S** one that presages

PRESALE *n* pl. **-S** a sale in advance

PRESCIND *v* **-ED, -ING, -S** to consider separately

PRESCORE *v* **-SCORED, -SCORING, -SCORES** to record the sound of before filming

PRESE pl. of presa

PRESELL *v* **-SOLD, -SELLING, -SELLS** to promote a product not yet being sold to the public

PRESENCE *n* pl. **-S** close proximity

PRESENT *v* **-ED, -ING, -S** to bring into the presence of someone

PRESERVE *v* **-SERVED, -SERVING, -SERVES** to keep free from harm or danger

PRESET *v* **-SET, -SETTING, -SETS** to set beforehand

PRESHAPE *v* **-SHAPED, -SHAPING, -SHAPES** to shape beforehand

PRESHIP *v* **-SHIPPED, -SHIPPING, -SHIPS** to ship beforehand

PRESHOW *v* **-SHOWED, -SHOWN, -SHOWING, -SHOWS** to show beforehand

PRESIDE *v* **-SIDED, -SIDING, -SIDES** to occupy the position of authority

PRESIDER *n* pl. **-S** one that presides

PRESIDIA *n/pl* Soviet executive committees

PRESIDIO *n* pl. **-DIOS** a Spanish fort

PRESIFT *v* **-ED, -ING, -S** to sift beforehand

PRESLEEP *adj* preceding sleep

PRESLICE *v* **-SLICED, -SLICING, -SLICES** to slice beforehand

PRESOAK *v* **-ED, -ING, -S** to soak beforehand

PRESOLD past tense of presell

PRESOLVE *v* **-SOLVED, -SOLVING, -SOLVES** to solve beforehand

PRESONG *adj* preceding a song

PRESORT *v* **-ED, -ING, -S** to sort beforehand

PRESPLIT *adj* preceding a split

PRESS *v* **-ED, -ING, -ES** to act upon with steady force

PRESSER *n* pl. **-S** one that presses

PRESSING *n* pl. **-S** an instance of stamping with a press

PRESSMAN *n* pl. **-MEN** a printing press operator

PRESSOR *n* pl. **-S** a substance that raises blood pressure

PRESSRUN *n* pl. **-S** a continuous operation of a printing press

PRESSURE *v* **-SURED, -SURING, -SURES** to apply force to

PREST *n* pl. **-S** a loan

PRESTAMP *v* **-ED, -ING, -S** to stamp beforehand

PRESTER *n* pl. **-S** a priest

PRESTIGE *n* pl. **-S** distinction or reputation in the eyes of people

PRESTO *n* pl. **-TOS** a musical passage played in rapid tempo

PRESTORE	v **-STORED, -STORING, -STORES** to store beforehand	**PREVERB**	n pl. **-S** a prefix or particle preceding the root of a verb
PRESUME	v **-SUMED, -SUMING, -SUMES** to take for granted	**PREVIEW**	v **-ED, -ING, -S** to view or exhibit in advance
PRESUMER	n pl. **-S** one that presumes	**PREVIOUS**	adj coming or occurring before in time or order
PRETAPE	v **-TAPED, -TAPING, -TAPES** to tape beforehand	**PREVISE**	v **-VISED, -VISING, -VISES** to foresee
PRETASTE	v **-TASTED, -TASTING, -TASTES** to taste beforehand	**PREVISIT**	v **-ED, -ING, -S** to visit beforehand
PRETAX	adj existing before provision for taxes	**PREVISOR**	n pl. **-S** one that previses
PRETEEN	n pl. **-S** a child under the age of thirteen	**PREVUE**	v **-VUED, -VUING, -VUES** to preview
PRETELL	v **-TOLD, -TELLING, -TELLS** to tell beforehand	**PREWAR**	adj occurring or existing before a war
PRETENCE	n pl. **-S** pretense	**PREWARM**	v **-ED, -ING, -S** to warm beforehand
PRETEND	v **-ED, -ING, -S** to assume or display a false appearance of	**PREWARN**	v **-ED, -ING, -S** to warn in advance
PRETENSE	n pl. **-S** the act of pretending	**PREWASH**	v **-ED, -ING, -ES** to wash beforehand
PRETERIT	n pl. **-S** a past tense in grammar	**PREWEIGH**	v **-ED, -ING, -S** to weigh beforehand
PRETERM	n pl. **-S** a child born prematurely		
PRETEST	v **-ED, -ING, -S** to give a preliminary test to	**PREWIRE**	v **-WIRED, -WIRING, -WIRES** to wire beforehand
PRETEXT	v **-ED, -ING, -S** to allege as an excuse	**PREWORK**	v **-ED, -ING, -S** to work beforehand
PRETOLD	past tense of pretell	**PREWORN**	adj previously worn by someone
PRETOR	n pl. **-S** praetor	**PREWRAP**	v **-WRAPPED, -WRAPPING, -WRAPS** to wrap beforehand
PRETRAIN	v **-ED, -ING, -S** to train beforehand	**PREX**	n pl. **-ES** prexy
PRETREAT	v **-ED, -ING, -S** to treat beforehand	**PREXY**	n pl. **PREXIES** a president
PRETRIAL	n pl. **-S** a proceeding that precedes a trial	**PREY**	v **-ED, -ING, -S** to seize and devour animals for food
PRETRIM	v **-TRIMMED, -TRIMMING, -TRIMS** to trim beforehand	**PREYER**	n pl. **-S** one that preys
PRETTIFY	v **-FIED, -FYING, -FIES** to make pretty	**PREZ**	n pl. **-ES** a president
PRETTY	adj **-TIER, -TIEST** pleasing to the eye **PRETTILY** adv	**PREZZIE**	n pl. **-S** a gift
		PRIAPEAN	adj priapic
PRETTY	v **-TIED, -TYING, -TIES** to make pretty	**PRIAPI**	a pl. of priapus
		PRIAPIC	adj phallic
PRETYPE	v **-TYPED, -TYPING, -TYPES** to type beforehand	**PRIAPISM**	n pl. **-S** a persistent erection of the penis
PRETZEL	v **-ZELLED, -ZELLING, -ZELS** to twist, bend, or contort	**PRIAPUS**	n pl. **-PUSES** or **-PI** a representation of the phallus
PREUNION	n pl. **-S** a union beforehand	**PRICE**	v **PRICED, PRICING, PRICES** to set a value on
PREUNITE	v **-UNITED, -UNITING, -UNITES** to unite beforehand	**PRICER**	n pl. **-S** one that prices
PREVAIL	v **-ED, -ING, -S** to triumph	**PRICEY**	adj **PRICIER, PRICIEST** expensive
PREVALUE	v **-UED, -UING, -UES** to value beforehand	**PRICIER**	comparative of pricy
		PRICIEST	superlative of pricy
PREVENT	v **-ED, -ING, -S** to keep from happening	**PRICILY**	adv in a pricey manner
		PRICING	present participle of price

PRICK	*v* **-ED, -ING, -S** to puncture slightly
PRICKER	*n* pl. **-S** one that pricks
PRICKET	*n* pl. **-S** a spike for holding a candle upright
PRICKIER	comparative of pricky
PRICKIEST	superlative of pricky
PRICKING	*n* pl. **-S** a prickly feeling
PRICKLE	*v* **-LED, -LING, -LES** to prick
PRICKLY	*adj* **-LIER, -LIEST** having many sharp points
PRICKY	*adj* **PRICKIER, PRICKIEST** prickly
PRICY	*adj* **PRICIER, PRICIEST** pricey **PRICILY** *adv*
PRIDE	*v* **PRIDED, PRIDING, PRIDES** to feel pride (a feeling of self-esteem)
PRIDEFUL	*adj* full of pride
PRIED	past tense of pry
PRIEDIEU	*n* pl. **-DIEUS** or **-DIEUX** a piece of furniture for kneeling on during prayer
PRIER	*n* pl. **-S** one that pries
PRIES	present 3d person sing. of pry
PRIEST	*v* **-ED, -ING, -S** to ordain as a priest (one authorized to perform religious rites)
PRIESTLY	*adj* **-LIER, -LIEST** characteristic of or befitting a priest
PRIG	*v* **PRIGGED, PRIGGING, PRIGS** to steal
PRIGGERY	*n* pl. **-GERIES** priggism
PRIGGISH	*adj* marked by priggism
PRIGGISM	*n* pl. **-S** prim adherence to convention
PRILL	*v* **-ED, -ING, -S** to convert into pellets
PRIM	*adj* **PRIMMER, PRIMMEST** formally precise or proper
PRIM	*v* **PRIMMED, PRIMMING, PRIMS** to give a prim expression to
PRIMA	*n* pl. **-S** primo
PRIMACY	*n* pl. **-CIES** the state of being first
PRIMAGE	*n* pl. **-S** an amount paid as an addition to freight charges
PRIMAL	*adj* being at the beginning or foundation **PRIMALLY** *adv*
PRIMARY	*n* pl. **-RIES** a preliminary election
PRIMATAL	*n* pl. **-S** a primate
PRIMATE	*n* pl. **-S** any of an advanced order of mammals

PRIME	*v* **PRIMED, PRIMING, PRIMES** to make ready
PRIMELY	*adv* excellently
PRIMER	*n* pl. **-S** a book that covers the basics of a subject
PRIMERO	*n* pl. **-ROS** a card game
PRIMEVAL	*adj* pertaining to the earliest ages
PRIMI	a pl. of primo
PRIMINE	*n* pl. **-S** the outer covering of an ovule
PRIMING	*n* pl. **-S** the act of one that primes
PRIMLY	*adv* in a prim manner
PRIMMED	past tense of prim
PRIMMER	comparative of prim
PRIMMEST	superlative of prim
PRIMMING	present participle of prim
PRIMNESS	*n* pl. **-ES** the state of being prim
PRIMO	*n* pl. **-MOS** or **-MI** the main part in a musical piece
PRIMP	*v* **-ED, -ING, -S** to dress or adorn carefully
PRIMROSE	*n* pl. **-S** a perennial herb
PRIMSIE	*adj* prim
PRIMULA	*n* pl. **-S** primrose
PRIMUS	*n* pl. **-ES** the head bishop of Scotland
PRINCE	*n* pl. **-S** a non-reigning male member of a royal family
PRINCELY	*adj* **-LIER, -LIEST** of or befitting a prince
PRINCESS	*n* pl. **-ES** a non-reigning female member of a royal family
PRINCIPE	*n* pl. **-PI** a prince
PRINCOCK	*n* pl. **-S** a coxcomb
PRINCOX	*n* pl. **-ES** princock
PRINK	*v* **-ED, -ING, -S** to dress or adorn in a showy manner
PRINKER	*n* pl. **-S** one that prinks
PRINT	*v* **-ED, -ING, -S** to produce by pressed type on a surface
PRINTER	*n* pl. **-S** one that prints
PRINTERY	*n* pl. **-ERIES** a place where printing is done
PRINTING	*n* pl. **-S** a reproduction from a printing surface
PRINTOUT	*n* pl. **-S** the printed output of a computer
PRION	*n* pl. **-S** a protein particle
PRIOR	*n* pl. **-S** an officer in a monastery

PRIORATE   *n* pl. **-S** the office of a prior

PRIORESS   *n* pl. **-ES** a nun corresponding in rank to a prior

PRIORITY   *n* pl. **-TIES** precedence established by importance

PRIORLY   *adv* previously

PRIORY   *n* pl. **-RIES** a religious house

PRISE   *v* **PRISED, PRISING, PRISES** to raise or force with a lever

PRISERE   *n* pl. **-S** a succession of vegetational stages

PRISM   *n* pl. **-S** a solid which disperses light into a spectrum

PRISMOID   *n* pl. **-S** a geometric solid

PRISON   *v* **-ED, -ING, -S** to imprison

PRISONER   *n* pl. **-S** one that is imprisoned

PRISS   *v* **-ED, -ING, -ES** to act in a prissy manner

PRISSY   *adj* **-SIER, -SIEST** excessively or affectedly proper **PRISSILY** *adv*

PRISSY   *n* pl. **-SIES** one who is prissy

PRISTANE   *n* pl. **-S** a chemical compound

PRISTINE   *adj* pertaining to the earliest time or state

PRITHEE   *interj* — used to express a wish or request

PRIVACY   *n* pl. **-CIES** the state of being private

PRIVATE   *adj* **-VATER, -VATEST** not for public use or knowledge

PRIVATE   *n* pl. **-S** a soldier of lower rank

PRIVET   *n* pl. **-S** an ornamental shrub

PRIVITY   *n* pl. **-TIES** private knowledge

PRIVY   *adj* **PRIVIER, PRIVIEST** private **PRIVILY** *adv*

PRIVY   *n* pl. **PRIVIES** an outhouse

PRIZE   *v* **PRIZED, PRIZING, PRIZES** to value highly

PRIZER   *n* pl. **-S** one who vies for a reward

PRO   *n* pl. **PROS** an argument or vote in favor of something

PROA   *n* pl. **-S** prau

PROB   *n* pl. **-S** a problem

PROBABLE   *n* pl. **-S** something likely to occur or prove true

PROBABLY   *adv* without much doubt

PROBAND   *n* pl. **-S** one whose reactions or responses are studied

PROBANG   *n* pl. **-S** a surgical rod

PROBATE   *v* **-BATED, -BATING, -BATES** to establish the validity of

PROBE   *v* **PROBED, PROBING, PROBES** to investigate or examine thoroughly

PROBER   *n* pl. **-S** one that probes

PROBIT   *n* pl. **-S** a unit of statistical probability

PROBITY   *n* pl. **-TIES** complete and confirmed integrity

PROBLEM   *n* pl. **-S** a perplexing question or situation

PROCAINE   *n* pl. **-S** a compound used as a local anesthetic

PROCARP   *n* pl. **-S** a female sexual organ in certain algae

PROCEED   *v* **-ED, -ING, -S** to go forward or onward

PROCESS   *v* **-ED, -ING, -ES** to treat or prepare by a special method

PROCHAIN   *adj* prochein

PROCHEIN   *adj* nearest in time, relation, or degree

PROCLAIM   *v* **-ED, -ING, -S** to make known publicly or officially

PROCTOR   *v* **-ED, -ING, -S** to supervise

PROCURAL   *n* pl. **-S** the act of procuring

PROCURE   *v* **-CURED, -CURING, -CURES** to obtain by effort

PROCURER   *n* pl. **-S** one that procures

PROD   *v* **PRODDED, PRODDING, PRODS** to jab with something pointed

PRODDER   *n* pl. **-S** one that prods

PRODIGAL   *n* pl. **-S** one who spends lavishly and foolishly

PRODIGY   *n* pl. **-GIES** a child having exceptional talent or ability

PRODROME   *n* pl. **-DROMES** or **-DROMATA** a sign of impending disease

PRODRUG   *n* pl. **-S** an inactive chemical substance that becomes an active drug in the body

PRODUCE   *v* **-DUCED, -DUCING, -DUCES** to bring into existence

PRODUCER   *n* pl. **-S** one that produces

PRODUCT   *n* pl. **-S** something produced by labor or effort

PROEM   *n* pl. **-S** an introductory statement **PROEMIAL** *adj*

PROETTE   *n* pl. **-S** a female professional athlete

PROF   *n* pl. **-S** a professor

PROFANE   *v* **-FANED, -FANING, -FANES** to treat with irreverence or abuse

PROFANER   *n* pl. **-S** one that profanes

PROFESS   *v* **-ED, -ING, -ES** to affirm openly

PROFFER   *v* **-ED, -ING, -S** to present for acceptance

PROFILE   *v* **-FILED, -FILING, -FILES** to draw an outline of

PROFILER   *n* pl. **-S** one that profiles

PROFIT   *v* **-ED, -ING, -S** to gain an advantage or benefit

PROFITER   *n* pl. **-S** one that profits

PROFORMA   *adj* provided in advance of shipment and showing description and quantity

PROFOUND   *adj* **-FOUNDER, -FOUNDEST** intellectually deep and penetrating

PROFOUND   *n* pl. **-S** something that is very deep

PROFUSE   *adj* pouring forth generously

PROG   *v* **PROGGED, PROGGING, PROGS** to prowl about for food or plunder

PROGENY   *n* pl. **-NIES** a descendant or offspring

PROGERIA   *n* pl. **-S** premature aging

PROGGER   *n* pl. **-S** one that progs

PROGGING   present participle of prog

PROGNOSE   *v* **-NOSED, -NOSING, -NOSES** to forecast the probable course of a disease

PROGRADE   *adj* pertaining to the orbital motion of a body

PROGRAM   *v* **-GRAMED, -GRAMING, -GRAMS** or **-GRAMMED, -GRAMMING, -GRAMS** to arrange in a plan of proceedings

PROGRESS   *v* **-ED, -ING, -ES** to move forward or onward

PROGUN   *adj* favoring the right to own guns without restrictions

PROHIBIT   *v* **-ED, -ING, -S** to forbid by authority

PROJECT   *v* **-ED, -ING, -S** to extend outward

PROJET   *n* pl. **-S** a plan or outline

PROLABOR   *adj* favoring organized labor

PROLAMIN   *n* pl. **-S** a simple protein

PROLAN   *n* pl. **-S** a sex hormone

PROLAPSE   *v* **-LAPSED, -LAPSING, -LAPSES** to fall or slip out of place

PROLATE   *adj* extended lengthwise

PROLE   *n* pl. **-S** a member of the working class

PROLEG   *n* pl. **-S** an abdominal leg of certain insect larvae

PROLIFIC   *adj* producing abundantly

PROLINE   *n* pl. **-S** an amino acid

PROLIX   *adj* tediously long and wordy **PROLIXLY** *adv*

PROLOG   *v* **-ED, -ING, -S** to prologue

PROLOGUE   *v* **-LOGUED, -LOGUING, -LOGUES** to preface

PROLONG   *v* **-ED, -ING, -S** to lengthen in duration

PROLONGE   *n* pl. **-S** a rope used for pulling a gun carriage

PROM   *n* pl. **-S** a formal dance

PROMINE   *n* pl. **-S** a substance that promotes growth

PROMISE   *v* **-ISED, -ISING, -ISES** to make a declaration of assurance

PROMISEE   *n* pl. **-S** one who is promised something

PROMISER   *n* pl. **-S** promisor

PROMISOR   *n* pl. **-S** one that promises

PROMO   *v* **-ED, -ING, -S** to promote

PROMOTE   *v* **-MOTED, -MOTING, -MOTES** to contribute to the progress of

PROMOTER   *n* pl. **-S** one that promotes

PROMOTOR   *n* pl. **-S** a chemical additive that increases the activity of a catalyst

PROMPT   *adj* **PROMPTER, PROMPTEST** quick to act or respond

PROMPT   *v* **-ED, -ING, -S** to induce to action

PROMPTER   *n* pl. **-S** one that prompts

PROMPTLY   *adv* in a prompt manner

PROMULGE   *v* **-MULGED, -MULGING, -MULGES** to proclaim

PRONATE   *v* **-NATED, -NATING, -NATES** to turn the palm downward or backward

PRONATOR   *n* pl. **-S** or **-ES** a forearm or forelimb muscle

PRONE   *adj* lying with the front or face downward **PRONELY** *adv*

PRONG   *v* **-ED, -ING, -S** to pierce with a pointed projection

PRONOTUM   *n* pl. **-NOTA** a hard outer plate of an insect

PRONOUN   *n* pl. **-S** a word that may be used in place of a noun

PRONTO   *adv* quickly

PROOF   *v* **-ED, -ING, -S** to examine for errors

PROOFER   *n* pl. **-S** one that proofs

PROP   *v* **PROPPED, PROPPING, PROPS** to keep from falling

PROPANE   *n* pl. **-S** a flammable gas

PROPANOL   *n* pl. **-S** a liquid alcohol used as a solvent

PROPEL   *v* **-PELLED, -PELLING, -PELS** to cause to move forward or onward

PROPEND   *v* **-ED, -ING, -S** to have a tendency toward

PROPENE   *n* pl. **-S** a flammable gas

PROPENOL   *n* pl. **-S** a flammable liquid

PROPENSE   *adj* tending toward

PROPENYL   *adj* pertaining to a certain chemical group

PROPER   *adj* **-ERER, -EREST** suitable **PROPERLY** *adv*

PROPER   *n* pl. **-S** a portion of the Mass

PROPERTY   *n* pl. **-TIES** something owned

PROPHAGE   *n* pl. **-S** a form of virus

PROPHASE   *n* pl. **-S** the first stage in mitosis

PROPHECY   *n* pl. **-CIES** a prediction

PROPHESY   *v* **-SIED, -SYING, -SIES** to predict

PROPHET   *n* pl. **-S** one who predicts

PROPINE   *v* **-PINED, -PINING, -PINES** to offer as a gift

PROPJET   *n* pl. **-S** a type of airplane

PROPMAN   *n* pl. **-MEN** a man in charge of stage properties

PROPOLIS   *n* pl. **-LISES** a resinous substance used as a cement by bees

PROPONE   *v* **-PONED, -PONING, -PONES** to propose

PROPOSAL   *n* pl. **-S** something that is proposed

PROPOSE   *v* **-POSED, -POSING, -POSES** to put forward for consideration or acceptance

PROPOSER   *n* pl. **-S** one that proposes

PROPOUND   *v* **-ED, -ING, -S** to propose

PROPPED   past tense of prop

PROPPING   present participle of prop

PROPRIUM   *n* pl. **-PRIA** an attribute belonging inseparably to every member of a species

PROPYL   *n* pl. **-S** a univalent radical **PROPYLIC** *adj*

PROPYLON   *n* pl. **-LA** an entrance to a temple

PROPYNE   *n* pl. **-S** a gaseous methyl acetylene

PRORATE   *v* **-RATED, -RATING, -RATES** to divide proportionately

PROROGUE   *v* **-ROGUED, -ROGUING, -ROGUES** to discontinue a session of

PROSAIC   *adj* pertaining to prose

PROSAISM   *n* pl. **-S** a prosaic style

PROSAIST   *n* pl. **-S** a writer of prose

PROSE   *v* **PROSED, PROSING, PROSES** to write prose (writing without metrical structure)

PROSECCO   *n* pl. **-COS** an Italian sparkling wine

PROSECT   *v* **-ED, -ING, -S** to dissect

PROSER   *n* pl. **-S** a prosaist

PROSIER   comparative of prosy

PROSIEST   superlative of prosy

PROSIFY   *v* **-FIED, -FYING, -FIES** to turn into prose

PROSILY   *adv* in a prosy manner

PROSING   present participle of prose

PROSIT   *interj* — used as a drinking toast

PROSO   *n* pl. **-SOS** millet

PROSODY   *n* pl. **-DIES** the study of poetical forms **PROSODIC** *adj*

PROSOMA   *n* pl. **-MAS** or **-MATA** the anterior region of the body of some invertebrates **PROSOMAL** *adj*

PROSPECT   *v* **-ED, -ING, -S** to explore for mineral deposits

PROSPER   *v* **-ED, -ING, -S** to be successful or fortunate

PROSS   *n* pl. **-ES** a prostitute

PROSSIE   *n* pl. **-S** a prostitute

PROST   *interj* prosit

PROSTATE   *n* pl. **-S** a gland in male mammals

PROSTIE   *n* pl. **-S** a prostitute

PROSTYLE   *n* pl. **-S** a building having a row of columns across the front only

PROSUMER   *n* pl. **-S** one who buys electronic products that are in quality between consumer and professional grades

PROSY   *adj* **PROSIER, PROSIEST** prosaic

PROTAMIN   *n* pl. **-S** a simple protein

PROTASIS   *n* pl. **-ASES** the introductory part of a classical drama **PROTATIC** *adj*

PROTEA   *n* pl. **-S** an evergreen shrub

PROTEAN   *n* pl. **-S** a type of protein

PROTEASE   *n* pl. **-S** an enzyme

PROTECT   *v* **-ED, -ING, -S** to keep from harm, attack, or injury

PROTEGE   *n* pl. **-S** one whose career is promoted by an influential person

PROTEGEE   *n* pl. **-S** a female protege

PROTEI   pl. of proteus

PROTEID   *n* pl. **-S** protein

PROTEIDE   *n* pl. **-S** proteid

PROTEIN   *n* pl. **-S** a nitrogenous organic compound

PROTEND   *v* **-ED, -ING, -S** to extend

PROTEOME   *n* pl. **-S** the complement of proteins expressed by a genome

PROTEOSE   *n* pl. **-S** a water-soluble protein

PROTEST   *v* **-ED, -ING, -S** to express strong objection

PROTEUS   *n* pl. **-ES** one that readily changes appearance or principles

PROTEUS   *n* pl. **-TEI** any of a genus of aerobic bacteria

PROTIST   *n* pl. **-S** any of a group of unicellular organisms

PROTIUM   *n* pl. **-S** an isotope of hydrogen

PROTOCOL   *v* **-COLED, -COLING, -COLS** or **-COLLED, -COLLING, -COLS** to form a preliminary draft of an official document

PROTON   *n* pl. **-S** a subatomic particle **PROTONIC** *adj*

PROTOPOD   *n* pl. **-S** a part of a crustacean appendage

PROTOXID   *n* pl. **-S** an oxide

PROTOZOA   *n/pl* unicellular microscopic organisms

PROTRACT   *v* **-ED, -ING, -S** to prolong

PROTRADE   *adj* favoring international trade

PROTRUDE   *v* **-TRUDED, -TRUDING, -TRUDES** to extend beyond the main portion

PROTURAN   *n* pl. **-S** any of an order of white, wingless insects

PROTYL   *n* pl. **-S** protyle

PROTYLE   *n* pl. **-S** a hypothetical substance from which all the elements are supposedly derived

PROUD   *adj* **PROUDER, PROUDEST** having or displaying pride **PROUDLY** *adv*

PROUDFUL   *adj* prideful

PROUNION   *adj* favoring labor unions

PROVE   *v* **PROVED, PROVEN, PROVING, PROVES** to establish the truth or validity of **PROVABLE** *adj* **PROVABLY** *adv*

PROVENLY   *adv* without doubt

PROVER   *n* pl. **-S** one that proves

PROVERB   *v* **-ED, -ING, -S** to make a byword of

PROVIDE   *v* **-VIDED, -VIDING, -VIDES** to supply

PROVIDER   *n* pl. **-S** one that provides

PROVINCE   *n* pl. **-S** an administrative division of a country

PROVING   present participle of prove

PROVIRUS   *n* pl. **-ES** a form of virus **PROVIRAL** *adj*

PROVISO   *n* pl. **-SOS** or **-SOES** a clause in a document introducing a condition or restriction

PROVOKE   *v* **-VOKED, -VOKING, -VOKES** to incite to anger or resentment

PROVOKER   *n* pl. **-S** one that provokes

PROVOST   *n* pl. **-S** a high-ranking university official

PROW   *adj* **PROWER, PROWEST** brave

PROW   *n* pl. **-S** the forward part of a ship

PROWAR   *adj* favoring war

PROWESS   *n* pl. **-ES** exceptional ability

PROWL   *v* **-ED, -ING, -S** to move about stealthily

PROWLER   *n* pl. **-S** one that prowls

PROXEMIC   *adj* pertaining to a branch of environmental study

PROXIMAL   *adj* located near the point of origin

PROXIMO   *adj* of or occurring in the following month

PROXY   *n* pl. **PROXIES** a person authorized to act for another

PRUDE   *n* pl. **-S** a prudish person

PRUDENCE   *n* pl. **-S** the quality of being prudent

PRUDENT   *adj* having, showing, or exercising good judgment

PRUDERY   *n* pl. **-ERIES** excessive regard for propriety, modesty, or morality

PRUDISH   *adj* marked by prudery

PRUINOSE   *adj* having a powdery covering

PRUNE   *v* **PRUNED, PRUNING, PRUNES** to cut off branches or parts from **PRUNABLE** *adj*

PRUNELLA	*n* pl. **-S** a strong woolen fabric
PRUNELLE	*n* pl. **-S** a plum-flavored liqueur
PRUNELLO	*n* pl. **-LOS** prunella
PRUNER	*n* pl. **-S** one that prunes
PRUNEY	*adj* **PRUNIER, PRUNIEST** resembling a prune
PRUNING	present participle of prune
PRUNUS	*n* pl. **-ES** a flowering tree
PRURIENT	*adj* having lustful thoughts or desires
PRURIGO	*n* pl. **-GOS** a skin disease
PRURITUS	*n* pl. **-ES** intense itching **PRURITIC** *adj*
PRUSSIC	*adj* pertaining to a type of acid
PRUTA	*n* pl. **PRUTOT** prutah
PRUTAH	*n* pl. **PRUTOTH** a former monetary unit of Israel
PRY	*v* **PRIED, PRYING, PRIES** to inquire impertinently into private matters **PRYINGLY** *adv*
PRYER	*n* pl. **-S** prier
PRYTHEE	*interj* prithee
PSALM	*v* **-ED, -ING, -S** to praise in psalms (sacred songs)
PSALMIC	*adj* of or pertaining to a psalm
PSALMIST	*n* pl. **-S** a writer of psalms
PSALMODY	*n* pl. **-DIES** the use of psalms in worship
PSALTER	*n* pl. **-S** a book of psalms
PSALTERY	*n* pl. **-TERIES** an ancient stringed musical instrument
PSALTRY	*n* pl. **-TRIES** psaltery
PSAMMITE	*n* pl. **-S** a fine-grained rock
PSAMMON	*n* pl. **-S** a group of microorganisms living in waterlogged sands
PSCHENT	*n* pl. **-S** a crown worn by ancient Egyptian kings
PSEPHITE	*n* pl. **-S** a rock composed of small pebbles
PSEUD	*n* pl. **-S** a person pretending to be an intellectual
PSEUDO	*n* pl. **PSEUDOS** a pseud
PSHAW	*v* **-ED, -ING, -S** to utter an expression of disapproval
PSI	*n* pl. **-S** a Greek letter
PSILOCIN	*n* pl. **-S** a hallucinogenic drug
PSILOSIS	*n* pl. **-LOSES** a tropical disease **PSILOTIC** *adj*

PSIONIC	*adj* pertaining to the practical use of psychic powers
PSOAS	*n* pl. **PSOAI** or **PSOAE** a muscle of the loin **PSOATIC** *adj*
PSOCID	*n* pl. **-S** a minute winged insect
PSORALEA	*n* pl. **-S** a plant of the bean family
PSORALEN	*n* pl. **-S** a drug used to treat psoriasis
PSST	*interj* — used to attract someone's attention
PST	*interj* psst
PSYCH	*v* **-ED, -ING, -S** to put into the proper frame of mind
PSYCHE	*n* pl. **-S** the mental structure of a person
PSYCHIC	*n* pl. **-S** one sensitive to extrasensory phenomena
PSYCHISM	*n* pl. **-S** a belief that there is a fluid that animates all living beings
PSYCHO	*n* pl. **-CHOS** a mentally unstable person
PSYLLA	*n* pl. **-S** any of various plant lice
PSYLLID	*n* pl. **-S** psylla
PSYLLIUM	*n* pl. **-S** the seed of a fleawort
PSYOPS	*n/pl* noncombative military operations to influence the enemy's state of mind
PSYWAR	*n* pl. **-S** psychological warfare
PTERIN	*n* pl. **-S** a chemical compound
PTEROPOD	*n* pl. **-S** a type of mollusk
PTERYGIA	*n/pl* fleshy growths over the cornea
PTERYLA	*n* pl. **-LAE** a feathered area on the skin of a bird
PTISAN	*n* pl. **-S** a tea of herbs or barley
PTOMAIN	*n* pl. **-S** ptomaine
PTOMAINE	*n* pl. **-S** a compound produced by the decomposition of protein
PTOOEY	*interj* ptui
PTOSIS	*n* pl. **PTOSES** a drooping of the upper eyelid **PTOTIC** *adj*
PTUI	*interj* — used to express the sound of spitting
PTYALIN	*n* pl. **-S** a salivary enzyme
PTYALISM	*n* pl. **-S** an excessive flow of saliva
PUB	*n* pl. **-S** a tavern
PUBBING	*n* pl. **-S** the practice of drinking in pubs
PUBERTY	*n* pl. **-TIES** a period of sexual maturation **PUBERAL, PUBERTAL** *adj*

PUBIC   *adj* pertaining to the pubes or pubis

PUBIS   *n* pl. **PUBES** the forward portion of either of the hipbones

PUBLIC   *n* pl. **-S** the community or the people as a whole

PUBLICAN   *n* pl. **-S** one who owns or manages a pub

PUBLICLY   *adv* by the public

PUBLISH   *v* **-ED, -ING, -ES** to print and issue to the public

PUCCOON   *n* pl. **-S** an herb that yields a red dye

PUCE   *n* pl. **-S** a dark red color

PUCK   *n* pl. **-S** a rubber disk used in ice hockey

PUCKA   *adj* pukka

PUCKER   *v* **-ED, -ING, -S** to gather into small wrinkles or folds

PUCKERER   *n* pl. **-S** one that puckers

PUCKERY   *adj* **-ERIER, -ERIEST** having a tendency to pucker

PUCKISH   *adj* impish

PUCKSTER   *n* pl. **-S** a hockey player

PUD   *n* pl. **-S** pudding

PUDDING   *n* pl. **-S** a thick, soft dessert

PUDDINGY   *adj* resembling a pudding

PUDDLE   *v* **-DLED, -DLING, -DLES** to strew with puddles (small pools of water)

PUDDLER   *n* pl. **-S** one who subjects iron to puddling

PUDDLING   *n* pl. **-S** the process of converting pig iron to wrought iron

PUDDLY   *adj* **-DLIER, -DLIEST** full of puddles

PUDENCY   *n* pl. **-CIES** modesty

PUDENDUM   *n* pl. **-DA** the external genital organs of a woman **PUDENDAL** *adj*

PUDEUR   *n* pl. **-S** a sense of shame or embarrassment

PUDGE   *n* pl. **-S** fat on a body

PUDGY   *adj* **PUDGIER, PUDGIEST** short and fat **PUDGILY** *adv*

PUDIBUND   *adj* prudish

PUDIC   *adj* pertaining to the pudendum

PUDU   *n* pl. **-S** a small deer of South America

PUEBLO   *n* pl. **-LOS** a communal dwelling of certain Indian tribes

PUERILE   *adj* childish

PUERPERA   *n* pl. **-PERAE** a woman who has recently given birth to a child

PUFF   *v* **-ED, -ING, -S** to blow in short gusts

PUFFBACK   *n* pl. **-S** a small African bird

PUFFBALL   *n* pl. **-S** any of various globular fungi

PUFFBIRD   *n* pl. **-S** a stocky tropical American bird

PUFFER   *n* pl. **-S** one that puffs

PUFFERY   *n* pl. **-ERIES** excessive public praise

PUFFIN   *n* pl. **-S** a sea bird

PUFFY   *adj* **-FIER, -FIEST** swollen **PUFFILY** *adv*

PUG   *v* **PUGGED, PUGGING, PUGS** to fill in with clay or mortar

PUGAREE   *n* pl. **-S** pugree

PUGGAREE   *n* pl. **-S** pugree

PUGGIER   comparative of puggy

PUGGIEST   superlative of puggy

PUGGING   *n* pl. **-S** the act of preparing clay for making bricks or pottery

PUGGISH   *adj* somewhat stubby

PUGGLE   *n* pl. **-S** a kind of dog

PUGGREE   *n* pl. **-S** pugree

PUGGRY   *n* pl. **-GRIES** pugree

PUGGY   *adj* **-GIER, -GIEST** puggish

PUGH   *interj* — used to express disgust

PUGILISM   *n* pl. **-S** the art or practice of fighting with the fists

PUGILIST   *n* pl. **-S** one who fights with his or her fists

PUGMARK   *n* pl. **-S** a footprint

PUGREE   *n* pl. **-S** a cloth band wrapped around a hat

PUISNE   *n* pl. **-S** one of lesser rank

PUISSANT   *adj* powerful

PUJA   *n* pl. **-S** a Hindu prayer ritual

PUJAH   *n* pl. **-S** puja

PUKE   *v* **PUKED, PUKING, PUKES** to vomit

PUKEY   *adj* **PUKIER, PUKIEST** resembling or suggestive of vomit

PUKKA   *adj* genuine

PUKKAH   *adj* pukka

PUL   *n* pl. **PULS** or **PULI** a coin of Afghanistan

PULA *n* pl. **-S** a monetary unit of Botswana

PULAO *n* pl. **-LAOS** pilaf

PULE *v* **PULED, PULING, PULES** to whine

PULER *n* pl. **-S** one that pules

PULI *n* pl. **-LIS** or **-LIK** a long-haired sheepdog

PULICENE *adj* pertaining to fleas

PULICIDE *n* pl. **-S** an agent used for destroying fleas

PULING *n* pl. **-S** a plaintive cry

PULINGLY *adv* in a whining manner

PULK *n* pl. **-S** a small sled

PULKA *n* pl. **-S** pulk

PULL *v* **-ED, -ING, -S** to exert force in order to cause motion toward the force

PULLBACK *n* pl. **-S** a restraint or drawback

PULLER *n* pl. **-S** one that pulls

PULLET *n* pl. **-S** a young hen

PULLEY *v* **-LEYED, -LEYING, -LEYS** to hoist with a pulley (a device used for lifting weight)

PULLMAN *n* pl. **-S** a railroad sleeping car

PULLOUT *n* pl. **-S** a withdrawal

PULLOVER *n* pl. **-S** a garment that is put on by being drawn over the head

PULLUP *n* pl. **-S** the act of raising oneself while hanging by the hands

PULMONIC *adj* pertaining to the lungs

PULMOTOR *n* pl. **-S** a respiratory device

PULP *v* **-ED, -ING, -S** to reduce to pulp (a soft, moist mass of matter)

PULPAL *adj* pertaining to pulp **PULPALLY** *adv*

PULPER *n* pl. **-S** one that pulps

PULPIER comparative of pulpy

PULPIEST superlative of pulpy

PULPILY *adv* in a pulpy manner

PULPING *n* pl. **-S** the process of reducing to pulp

PULPIT *n* pl. **-S** a platform in a church **PULPITAL** *adj*

PULPLESS *adj* having no pulp

PULPOUS *adj* pulpy

PULPWOOD *n* pl. **-S** soft wood used in making paper

PULPY *adj* **PULPIER, PULPIEST** resembling pulp

PULQUE *n* pl. **-S** a fermented Mexican beverage

PULSANT *adj* pulsating

PULSAR *n* pl. **-S** a celestial source of radio waves

PULSATE *v* **-SATED, -SATING, -SATES** to expand and contract rhythmically

PULSATOR *n* pl. **-S** something that pulsates

PULSE *v* **PULSED, PULSING, PULSES** to pulsate

PULSEJET *n* pl. **-S** a type of engine

PULSER *n* pl. **-S** a device that causes pulsations

PULSING present participle of pulse

PULSION *n* pl. **-S** propulsion

PULSOJET *n* pl. **-S** pulsejet

PULTRUDE *v* **-TRUDED, -TRUDING, -TRUDES** to make a plastic object by drawing resin-coated glass fibers through a die

PULVILLI *n/pl* pads between the claws of an insect's foot

PULVINUS *n* pl. **-NI** a swelling at the base of a leaf **PULVINAR** *adj*

PUMA *n* pl. **-S** a cougar

PUMELO *n* pl. **-LOS** pomelo

PUMICE *v* **-ICED, -ICING, -ICES** to polish with a porous volcanic rock

PUMICER *n* pl. **-S** one that pumices

PUMICITE *n* pl. **-S** a porous volcanic rock

PUMMEL *v* **-MELED, -MELING, -MELS** or **-MELLED, -MELLING, -MELS** to pommel

PUMMELO *n* pl. **-LOS** a shaddock

PUMP *v* **-ED, -ING, -S** to cause to flow by means of a pump (a device for moving fluids) **PUMPABLE** *adj*

PUMPER *n* pl. **-S** one that pumps

PUMPJACK *n* pl. **-S** a pumping apparatus at an oil well

PUMPKIN *n* pl. **-S** a large, edible fruit

PUMPLESS *adj* lacking a pump

PUMPLIKE *adj* resembling a pump

PUN *v* **PUNNED, PUNNING, PUNS** to make a pun (a play on words)

PUNA *n* pl. **-S** a cold, arid plateau

PUNCH *v* **-ED, -ING, -ES** to perforate with a type of tool

PUNCHEON   *n* pl. **-S** a vertical supporting timber

PUNCHER   *n* pl. **-S** one that punches

PUNCHOUT   *n* pl. **-S** a fist fight

PUNCHY   *adj* **PUNCHIER, PUNCHIEST** dazed **PUNCHILY** *adv*

PUNCTATE   *adj* covered with dots

PUNCTUAL   *adj* being on time

PUNCTUM   *n* pl. **-TA** the opening of a tear duct

PUNCTURE   *v* **-TURED, -TURING, -TURES** to pierce with a pointed object

PUNDIT   *n* pl. **-S** a Hindu scholar **PUNDITIC** *adj*

PUNDITRY   *n* pl. **-RIES** the learning of pundits

PUNG   *n* pl. **-S** a box-shaped sleigh

PUNGENCY   *n* pl. **-CIES** the state of being pungent

PUNGENT   *adj* sharply affecting the organs of taste or smell

PUNGLE   *v* **-GLED, -GLING, -GLES** to contribute

PUNIER   comparative of puny

PUNIEST   superlative of puny

PUNILY   *adv* in a puny manner

PUNINESS   *n* pl. **-ES** the state of being puny

PUNISH   *v* **-ED, -ING, -ES** to impose a penalty on in requital for wrongdoing

PUNISHER   *n* pl. **-S** one that punishes

PUNITION   *n* pl. **-S** the act of punishing; punishment

PUNITIVE   *adj* inflicting punishment

PUNITORY   *adj* punitive

PUNJI   *n* pl. **-S** a sharp bamboo stake placed and concealed so as to impale an enemy

PUNK   *adj* **PUNKER, PUNKEST** of inferior quality

PUNK   *n* pl. **-S** dry, decayed wood used as tinder

PUNKA   *n* pl. **-S** a ceiling fan used in India

PUNKAH   *n* pl. **-S** punka

PUNKER   *n* pl. **-S** a punk rock musician

PUNKETTE   *n* pl. **-S** a female punk rocker

PUNKEY   *n* pl. **-KEYS** punkie

PUNKIE   *n* pl. **-S** a biting gnat

PUNKIN   *n* pl. **-S** pumpkin

PUNKISH   *adj* pertaining to a style inspired by punk rock

PUNKY   *adj* **PUNKIER, PUNKIEST** resembling punk

PUNNED   past tense of pun

PUNNER   *n* pl. **-S** a punster

PUNNET   *n* pl. **-S** a small basket

PUNNING   *n* pl. **-S** the act of making a pun

PUNNY   *adj* **-NIER, -NIEST** being or involving a pun

PUNSTER   *n* pl. **-S** one who is given to punning

PUNT   *v* **-ED, -ING, -S** to propel through water with a pole

PUNTER   *n* pl. **-S** one that punts

PUNTO   *n* pl. **-TOS** a hit or thrust in fencing

PUNTY   *n* pl. **-TIES** an iron rod used in glassmaking

PUNY   *adj* **PUNIER, PUNIEST** of inferior size, strength, or significance

PUP   *v* **PUPPED, PUPPING, PUPS** to give birth to puppies

PUPA   *n* pl. **-PAS** or **-PAE** an intermediate stage of a metamorphic insect **PUPAL** *adj*

PUPARIUM   *n* pl. **-IA** a pupal shell **PUPARIAL** *adj*

PUPATE   *v* **-PATED, -PATING, -PATES** to pass through the pupal stage

PUPATION   *n* pl. **-S** the act of pupating

PUPFISH   *n* pl. **-ES** a small, freshwater fish

PUPIL   *n* pl. **-S** a student under the close supervision of a teacher

PUPILAGE   *n* pl. **-S** the state of being a pupil

PUPILAR   *adj* pertaining to a part of the eye

PUPILARY   *adj* pupilar

PUPPED   past tense of pup

PUPPET   *n* pl. **-S** a small figure, as of a person or animal, manipulated by the hand

PUPPETRY   *n* pl. **-RIES** the art of making or manipulating puppets

PUPPING   present participle of pup

PUPPY   *n* pl. **-PIES** a young dog **PUPPYISH** *adj*

PUPPYDOM   *n* pl. **-S** the world of puppies

PUPU   *n* pl. **-S** a dish of Asian foods served as an appetizer

PUR   *v* **PURRED, PURRING, PURS** to purr

PURANA   *n* pl. **-S** a Hindu scripture **PURANIC** *adj*

PURBLIND	*adj* partially blind
PURCHASE	*v* **-CHASED, -CHASING, -CHASES** to acquire by the payment of money
PURDA	*n* pl. **-S** purdah
PURDAH	*n* pl. **-S** a curtain used in India to seclude women
PURE	*adj* **PURER, PUREST** free from anything different, inferior, or contaminating
PUREBRED	*n* pl. **-S** an animal of unmixed stock
PUREE	*v* **-REED, -REEING, -REES** to reduce to a thick pulp by cooking and sieving
PURELY	*adv* in a pure manner
PURENESS	*n* pl. **-ES** the quality of being pure
PURER	comparative of pure
PUREST	superlative of pure
PURFLE	*v* **-FLED, -FLING, -FLES** to decorate the border of
PURFLER	*n* pl. **-S** one that purfles
PURFLING	*n* pl. **-S** an ornamental border
PURGE	*v* **PURGED, PURGING, PURGES** to purify
PURGER	*n* pl. **-S** one that purges
PURGING	*n* pl. **-S** the act of purifying
PURI	*n* pl. **-S** poori
PURIFIER	*n* pl. **-S** one that purifies
PURIFY	*v* **-FIED, -FYING, -FIES** to free from impurities
PURIN	*n* pl. **-S** purine
PURINE	*n* pl. **-S** a chemical compound
PURISM	*n* pl. **-S** strict adherence to traditional correctness
PURIST	*n* pl. **-S** one who practices purism **PURISTIC** *adj*
PURITAN	*n* pl. **-S** a rigorously moral or religious person
PURITY	*n* pl. **-TIES** the quality of being pure
PURL	*v* **-ED, -ING, -S** to knit with a particular stitch
PURLIEU	*n* pl. **-LIEUS** or **-LIEUX** an outlying or neighboring area
PURLIN	*n* pl. **-S** a horizontal supporting timber
PURLINE	*n* pl. **-S** purlin
PURLING	*n* pl. **-S** an inversion of stitches in knitting
PURLOIN	*v* **-ED, -ING, -S** to steal
PURPLE	*adj* **-PLER, -PLEST** of a color intermediate between red and blue
PURPLE	*v* **-PLED, -PLING, -PLES** to make purple
PURPLISH	*adj* somewhat purple
PURPLY	*adj* purplish
PURPORT	*v* **-ED, -ING, -S** to profess or claim
PURPOSE	*v* **-POSED, -POSING, -POSES** to resolve to perform or accomplish
PURPURA	*n* pl. **-S** a disease characterized by purple spots on the skin
PURPURE	*n* pl. **-S** the heraldic color purple
PURPURIC	*adj* pertaining to purpura
PURPURIN	*n* pl. **-S** a reddish dye
PURR	*v* **-ED, -ING, -S** to utter a low, vibrant sound
PURRED	past tense of pur
PURRING	present participle of pur
PURSE	*v* **PURSED, PURSING, PURSES** to pucker
PURSER	*n* pl. **-S** an officer in charge of a ship's accounts
PURSIER	comparative of pursy
PURSIEST	superlative of pursy
PURSILY	*adv* in a pursy manner
PURSING	present participle of purse
PURSLANE	*n* pl. **-S** a common garden herb
PURSUANT	*adv* in accordance
PURSUE	*v* **-SUED, -SUING, -SUES** to follow in order to overtake or capture
PURSUER	*n* pl. **-S** one that pursues
PURSUIT	*n* pl. **-S** the act of pursuing
PURSY	*adj* **PURSIER, PURSIEST** short of breath
PURTY	*adj* **-TIER, -TIEST** pretty
PURULENT	*adj* secreting pus
PURVEY	*v* **-ED, -ING, -S** to supply
PURVEYOR	*n* pl. **-S** one that purveys
PURVIEW	*n* pl. **-S** the extent of operation, authority, or concern
PUS	*n* pl. **-ES** a viscous fluid formed in infected tissue
PUSH	*v* **-ED, -ING, -ES** to exert force in order to cause motion away from the force
PUSHBACK	*n* pl. **-S** a negative or unfavorable response
PUSHBALL	*n* pl. **-S** a type of ball game

PUSHCART	n pl. **-S** a light cart pushed by hand
PUSHDOWN	n pl. **-S** a store of computer data
PUSHER	n pl. **-S** one that pushes
PUSHFUL	adj pushy
PUSHIER	comparative of pushy
PUSHIEST	superlative of pushy
PUSHILY	adv in a pushy manner
PUSHOVER	n pl. **-S** an easily defeated person or team
PUSHPIN	n pl. **-S** a large-headed pin
PUSHROD	n pl. **-S** a rod for operating the valves in an engine
PUSHUP	n pl. **-S** a type of exercise
PUSHY	adj **PUSHIER, PUSHIEST** offensively aggressive
PUSLEY	n pl. **-LEYS** pussley
PUSLIKE	adj resembling pus
PUSS	n pl. **-ES** a cat
PUSSIER	comparative of pussy
PUSSIES	pl. of pussy
PUSSIEST	superlative of pussy
PUSSLEY	n pl. **-LEYS** purslane
PUSSLIKE	adj catlike
PUSSLY	n pl. **-LIES** pussley
PUSSY	adj **-SIER, -SIEST** full of pus
PUSSY	n pl. **PUSSIES** a cat
PUSSYCAT	n pl. **-S** a cat
PUSTULE	n pl. **-S** a small elevation of the skin containing pus **PUSTULAR, PUSTULED** adj
PUT	v **PUT, PUTTING, PUTS** to place in a particular position
PUTAMEN	n pl. **-MINA** or **-MENS** the hard covering of the kernel of certain fruits
PUTATIVE	adj generally regarded as such
PUTDOWN	n pl. **-S** a disparaging or snubbing remark
PUTLOCK	n pl. **-S** putlog
PUTLOG	n pl. **-S** a horizontal supporting timber
PUTOFF	n pl. **-S** an excuse
PUTON	n pl. **-S** a hoax or deception
PUTOUT	n pl. **-S** an act of causing an out in baseball
PUTREFY	v **-FIED, -FYING, -FIES** to make or become putrid

PUTRID	adj being in a decomposed, foul-smelling state **PUTRIDLY** adv
PUTSCH	n pl. **-ES** a suddenly executed attempt to overthrow a government
PUTT	v **-ED, -ING, -S** to hit with a light stroke in golf
PUTTEE	n pl. **-S** a strip of cloth wound around the leg
PUTTER	v **-ED, -ING, -S** to occupy oneself in a leisurely or ineffective manner
PUTTERER	n pl. **-S** one that putters
PUTTI	pl. of putto
PUTTIE	n pl. **-S** puttee
PUTTIED	past tense of putty
PUTTIER	n pl. **-S** one that putties
PUTTING	present participle of put
PUTTO	n pl. **-TI** an infant boy in art
PUTTY	v **-TIED, -TYING, -TIES** to fill with a type of cement
PUTZ	v **-ED, -ING, -ES** to waste time
PUZZLE	v **-ZLED, -ZLING, -ZLES** to cause uncertainty and indecision in
PUZZLER	n pl. **-S** something that puzzles
PYA	n pl. **-S** a copper coin of Myanmar (Burma)
PYAEMIA	n pl. **-S** pyemia **PYAEMIC** adj
PYCNIDIA	n/pl spore-bearing organs of certain fungi
PYCNOSIS	n pl. **-NOSES** pyknosis
PYCNOTIC	adj pyknotic
PYE	n pl. **-S** a book of ecclesiastical rules in the pre-Reformation English church
PYELITIS	n pl. **-TISES** inflammation of the pelvis or the kidney **PYELITIC** adj
PYEMIA	n pl. **-S** the presence of pus in the blood **PYEMIC** adj
PYGIDIUM	n pl. **-IA** the posterior region of certain invertebrates **PYGIDIAL** adj
PYGMY	n pl. **-MIES** a small person **PYGMAEAN, PYGMEAN, PYGMOID, PYGMYISH** adj
PYGMYISM	n pl. **-S** a stunted or dwarfish condition
PYIC	adj pertaining to pus
PYIN	n pl. **-S** a protein compound contained in pus
PYJAMA	n pl. **-S** pajama
PYKNIC	n pl. **-S** a person having a broad, stocky build

PYKNOSIS *n* pl. **-NOSES** a shrinking and thickening of a cell nucleus

PYKNOTIC *adj* exhibiting pyknosis

PYLON *n* pl. **-S** a tall structure marking an entrance or approach

PYLORUS *n* pl. **-RUSES** or **-RI** the opening between the stomach and the duodenum **PYLORIC** *adj*

PYODERMA *n* pl. **-S** a pus-causing skin disease

PYOGENIC *adj* producing pus

PYOID *adj* puslike

PYORRHEA *n* pl. **-S** a discharge of pus

PYOSIS *n* pl. **-OSES** the formation of pus

PYRALID *n* pl. **-S** a long-legged moth

PYRAMID *v* **-ED, -ING, -S** to raise or increase by adding amounts gradually

PYRAN *n* pl. **-S** a chemical compound **PYRANOID** *adj*

PYRANOSE *n* pl. **-S** a simple sugar

PYRE *n* pl. **-S** a pile of combustible material

PYRENE *n* pl. **-S** a putamen

PYRENOID *n* pl. **-S** a protein body of certain lower organisms

PYRETIC *adj* pertaining to fever

PYREXIA *n* pl. **-S** fever **PYREXIAL, PYREXIC** *adj*

PYRIC *adj* pertaining to burning

PYRIDINE *n* pl. **-S** a flammable liquid **PYRIDIC** *adj*

PYRIFORM *adj* pear-shaped

PYRITE *n* pl. **-S** a metallic sulfide **PYRITIC, PYRITOUS** *adj*

PYRITISE *v* **-ISED, -ISING, -ISES** to pyritize

PYRITIZE *v* **-IZED, -IZING, -IZES** to convert into pyrite

PYRO *n* pl. **-ROS** a person who has a compulsion to set fires

PYROGEN *n* pl. **-S** a substance that produces fever

PYROGY *n* pl. **-OGIES** pierogi

PYROHY *n* pl. **-OHIES** pierogi

PYROLA *n* pl. **-S** a perennial herb

PYROLIZE *v* **-LIZED, -LIZING, -LIZES** to pyrolyze

PYROLOGY *n* pl. **-GIES** the scientific examination of materials by heat

PYROLYSE *v* **-LYSED, -LYSING, -LYSES** to pyrolyze

PYROLYZE *v* **-LYZED, -LYZING, -LYZES** to affect compounds by the application of heat

PYRONE *n* pl. **-S** a chemical compound

PYRONINE *n* pl. **-S** a dye

PYROPE *n* pl. **-S** a variety of garnet

PYROSIS *n* pl. **-SISES** heartburn

PYROSTAT *n* pl. **-S** a thermostat

PYROXENE *n* pl. **-S** any of a group of minerals common in igneous rocks

PYRRHIC *n* pl. **-S** a type of metrical foot

PYRROL *n* pl. **-S** pyrrole

PYRROLE *n* pl. **-S** a chemical compound **PYRROLIC** *adj*

PYRUVATE *n* pl. **-S** a chemical salt

PYSANKA *n* pl. **PYSANKY** a hand-painted Ukrainian Easter egg

PYTHON *n* pl. **-S** a large snake **PYTHONIC** *adj*

PYURIA *n* pl. **-S** the presence of pus in the urine

PYX *n* pl. **-ES** a container in which the eucharistic bread is kept

PYXIDIUM *n* pl. **-DIA** a type of seed vessel

PYXIE *n* pl. **-S** an evergreen shrub

PYXIS *n* pl. **PYXIDES** a pyxidium

PZAZZ *n* pl. **-ES** pizazz

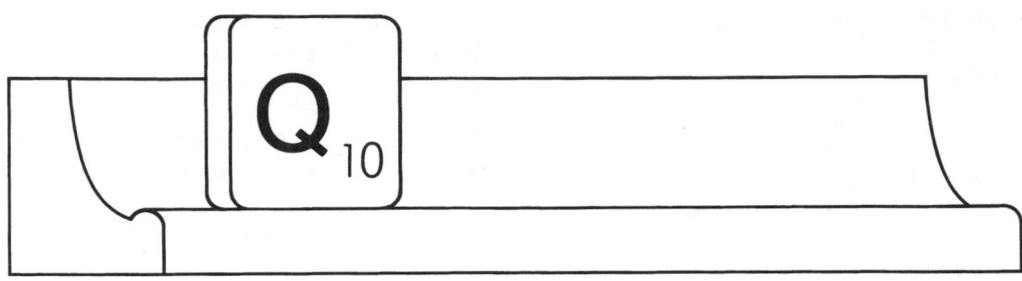

QABALA	*n* pl. **-S** cabala
QABALAH	*n* pl. **-S** cabala
QADI	*n* pl. **-S** cadi
QAID	*n* pl. **-S** caid
QAJAQ	*n* pl. **-S** kayak
QAMUTIK	*n* pl. **-S** komatik
QANAT	*n* pl. **-S** a system of underground tunnels and wells in the Middle East
QAPIK	*n* pl. **-S** gopik
QAT	*n* pl. **-S** kat
QAWWALI	*n* pl. **-S** a style of Muslim music
QI	*n* pl. **-S** the vital force that in Chinese thought is inherent in all things
QIBLA	*n* pl. **-S** kiblah
QIGONG	*n* pl. **-S** a Chinese system of physical exercises
QINDAR	*n* pl. **-DARS** or **-DARKA** qintar
QINTAR	*n* pl. **-S** a monetary unit of Albania
QIVIUT	*n* pl. **-S** the wool of a musk ox
QOPH	*n* pl. **-S** koph
QUA	*adv* in the capacity of
QUAALUDE	*n* pl. **-S** a sedative drug
QUACK	*v* **-ED, -ING, -S** to utter the characteristic cry of a duck
QUACKERY	*n* pl. **-ERIES** fraudulent practice
QUACKISH	*adj* fraudulent
QUACKISM	*n* pl. **-S** quackery
QUACKY	*adj* **QUACKIER, QUACKIEST** resembling the cry of a duck
QUAD	*v* **QUADDED, QUADDING, QUADS** to space out by means of quadrats
QUADPLEX	*n* pl. **-ES** a building having four units
QUADRANS	*n* pl. **-RANTES** an ancient Roman coin
QUADRANT	*n* pl. **-S** a quarter section of a circle

QUADRAT	*n* pl. **-S** a piece of type metal used for filling spaces
QUADRATE	*v* **-RATED, -RATING, -RATES** to correspond or agree
QUADRATI	*n/pl* rectangular muscles
QUADRIC	*n* pl. **-S** a type of geometric surface
QUADRIGA	*n* pl. **-GAE** a chariot drawn by four horses
QUADROON	*n* pl. **-S** a person of one-quarter black ancestry
QUAERE	*n* pl. **-S** a question
QUAESTOR	*n* pl. **-S** an ancient Roman magistrate
QUAFF	*v* **-ED, -ING, -S** to drink deeply
QUAFFER	*n* pl. **-S** one that quaffs
QUAG	*n* pl. **-S** a quagmire
QUAGGA	*n* pl. **-S** an extinct mammal that resembled a zebra
QUAGGY	*adj* **-GIER, -GIEST** marshy
QUAGMIRE	*n* pl. **-S** an area of marshy ground
QUAGMIRY	*adj* **-MIRIER, -MIRIEST** marshy
QUAHAUG	*n* pl. **-S** quahog
QUAHOG	*n* pl. **-S** an edible clam
QUAI	*n* pl. **-S** quay
QUAICH	*n* pl. **-S** or **-ES** a small drinking vessel
QUAIGH	*n* pl. **-S** quaich
QUAIL	*v* **-ED, -ING, -S** to cower
QUAINT	*adj* **QUAINTER, QUAINTEST** pleasingly old-fashioned or unfamiliar **QUAINTLY** *adv*
QUAKE	*v* **QUAKED, QUAKING, QUAKES** to shake or vibrate
QUAKER	*n* pl. **-S** one that quakes
QUAKY	*adj* **QUAKIER, QUAKIEST** tending to quake **QUAKILY** *adv*
QUALE	*n* pl. **-LIA** a property considered apart from things having the property

QUALIFY	*v* **-FIED, -FYING, -FIES** to make suitable or capable
QUALITY	*n* pl. **-TIES** a characteristic or attribute
QUALM	*n* pl. **-S** a feeling of doubt or misgiving
QUALMISH	*adj* having qualms
QUALMY	*adj* **QUALMIER, QUALMIEST** qualmish
QUAMASH	*n* pl. **-ES** camass
QUANDANG	*n* pl. **-S** quandong
QUANDARY	*n* pl. **-RIES** a dilemma
QUANDONG	*n* pl. **-S** an Australian tree
QUANGO	*n* pl. **-GOS** a public administrative board
QUANT	*v* **-ED, -ING, -S** to propel through water with a pole
QUANTA	pl. of quantum
QUANTAL	*adj* pertaining to a quantum
QUANTIC	*n* pl. **-S** a type of mathematical function
QUANTIFY	*v* **-FIED, -FYING, -FIES** to determine the quantity of
QUANTILE	*n* pl. **-S** any of the values of a random variable that divides a frequency distribution
QUANTISE	*v* **-TISED, -TISING, -TISES** to quantize
QUANTITY	*n* pl. **-TIES** a specified or indefinite amount or number
QUANTIZE	*v* **-TIZED, -TIZING, -TIZES** to limit the possible values of to a discrete set
QUANTONG	*n* pl. **-S** quandong
QUANTUM	*n* pl. **-TA** a fundamental unit of energy
QUARE	*adj* queer
QUARK	*n* pl. **-S** a hypothetical atomic particle
QUARREL	*v* **-RELED, -RELING, -RELS** or **-RELLED, -RELLING, -RELS** to engage in an angry dispute
QUARRIER	*n* pl. **-S** one that quarries
QUARRY	*v* **-RIED, -RYING, -RIES** to dig stone from an excavation
QUART	*n* pl. **-S** a liquid measure of capacity
QUARTAN	*n* pl. **-S** a recurrent malarial fever
QUARTE	*n* pl. **-S** a fencing thrust
QUARTER	*v* **-ED, -ING, -S** to divide into four equal parts
QUARTERN	*n* pl. **-S** one-fourth of something
QUARTET	*n* pl. **-S** a group of four
QUARTIC	*n* pl. **-S** a type of mathematical function
QUARTIER	*n* pl. **-S** a district in a French city
QUARTILE	*n* pl. **-S** a portion of a frequency distribution
QUARTO	*n* pl. **-TOS** the size of a piece of paper cut four from a sheet
QUARTZ	*n* pl. **-ES** a mineral
QUASAR	*n* pl. **-S** a distant celestial object emitting strong radio waves
QUASH	*v* **-ED, -ING, -ES** to suppress completely
QUASHER	*n* pl. **-S** one that quashes
QUASI	*adj* similar but not exactly the same
QUASS	*n* pl. **-ES** kvass
QUASSIA	*n* pl. **-S** a tropical tree
QUASSIN	*n* pl. **-S** a medicinal compound obtained from the wood of a quassia
QUATE	*adj* quiet
QUATORZE	*n* pl. **-S** a set of four cards of the same denomination scoring fourteen points
QUATRAIN	*n* pl. **-S** a stanza of four lines
QUATRE	*n* pl. **-S** the four at cards or dice
QUAVER	*v* **-ED, -ING, -S** to quiver
QUAVERER	*n* pl. **-S** one that quavers
QUAVERY	*adj* quivery
QUAY	*n* pl. **QUAYS** a wharf **QUAYLIKE** *adj*
QUAYAGE	*n* pl. **-S** a charge for the use of a quay
QUAYSIDE	*n* pl. **-S** the area adjacent to a quay
QUBIT	*n* pl. **-S** a quantum bit
QUBYTE	*n* pl. **-S** a sequence of eight quantum bits
QUEAN	*n* pl. **-S** a harlot
QUEASY	*adj* **-SIER, -SIEST** easily nauseated **QUEASILY** *adv*
QUEAZY	*adj* **-ZIER, -ZIEST** queasy
QUEEN	*v* **-ED, -ING, -S** to make a queen (a female monarch) of
QUEENCUP	*n* pl. **-S** a flowering plant
QUEENDOM	*n* pl. **-S** the area ruled by a queen
QUEENLY	*adj* **-LIER, -LIEST** of or befitting a queen
QUEENY	*adj* **QUEENIER, QUEENIEST** showily effeminate

QUEER	*adj* **QUEERER, QUEEREST** deviating from the expected or normal
QUEER	*v* **-ED, -ING, -S** to spoil the effect or success of
QUEERISH	*adj* somewhat queer
QUEERLY	*adv* in a queer manner
QUELEA	*n* pl. **-S** an African weaverbird
QUELL	*v* **-ED, -ING, -S** to suppress
QUELLER	*n* pl. **-S** one that quells
QUENCH	*v* **-ED, -ING, -ES** to put out or extinguish
QUENCHER	*n* pl. **-S** one that quenches
QUENELLE	*n* pl. **-S** a type of dumpling
QUERCINE	*adj* pertaining to oaks
QUERIDA	*n* pl. **-S** a female sweetheart
QUERIED	past tense of query
QUERIER	*n* pl. **-S** a querist
QUERIES	present 3d person sing. of query
QUERIST	*n* pl. **-S** one who queries
QUERN	*n* pl. **-S** a hand-turned grain mill
QUERY	*v* **-RIED, -RYING, -RIES** to question
QUEST	*v* **-ED, -ING, -S** to make a search
QUESTER	*n* pl. **-S** one that quests
QUESTION	*v* **-ED, -ING, -S** to put a question (an inquiry) to
QUESTOR	*n* pl. **-S** quaestor
QUETZAL	*n* pl. **-S** or **-ES** a tropical bird
QUEUE	*v* **QUEUED, QUEUING** or **QUEUEING, QUEUES** to line up
QUEUER	*n* pl. **-S** one that queues
QUEY	*n* pl. **QUEYS** a young cow
QUEZAL	*n* pl. **-S** or **-ES** quetzal
QUIBBLE	*v* **-BLED, -BLING, -BLES** to argue over trivialities
QUIBBLER	*n* pl. **-S** one that quibbles
QUICHE	*n* pl. **-S** a custard-filled pastry
QUICK	*adj* **QUICKER, QUICKEST** acting or capable of acting with speed
QUICK	*n* pl. **-S** a sensitive area of flesh
QUICKEN	*v* **-ED, -ING, -S** to speed up
QUICKIE	*n* pl. **-S** something done quickly
QUICKLY	*adv* in a quick manner
QUICKSET	*n* pl. **-S** a plant suitable for hedges
QUID	*n* pl. **-S** a portion of something to be chewed
QUIDDITY	*n* pl. **-TIES** the true nature of a thing
QUIDNUNC	*n* pl. **-S** a nosy person
QUIET	*adj* **-ETER, -ETEST** making little or no noise
QUIET	*v* **-ED, -ING, -S** to cause to be quiet
QUIETEN	*v* **-ED, -ING, -S** to quiet
QUIETER	*n* pl. **-S** one that quiets
QUIETISM	*n* pl. **-S** a form of religious mysticism
QUIETIST	*n* pl. **-S** an advocate of quietism
QUIETLY	*adv* in a quiet manner
QUIETUDE	*n* pl. **-S** a state of tranquillity
QUIETUS	*n* pl. **-ES** a final settlement
QUIFF	*n* pl. **-S** a lock of hair at the front of the head **QUIFFED** *adj*
QUILL	*v* **-ED, -ING, -S** to press small ridges in
QUILLAI	*n* pl. **-S** an evergreen tree
QUILLAIA	*n* pl. **-S** a quillai
QUILLAJA	*n* pl. **-S** a quillai
QUILLET	*n* pl. **-S** a trivial distinction
QUILLING	*n* pl. **-S** material that is quilled
QUILLOW	*n* pl. **-S** a quilt formed into a pillow
QUILT	*v* **-ED, -ING, -S** to stitch together with padding in between
QUILTER	*n* pl. **-S** one that quilts
QUILTING	*n* pl. **-S** material that is used for making quilts
QUIN	*n* pl. **-S** a quintuplet
QUINARY	*n* pl. **-RIES** a group of five
QUINATE	*adj* arranged in groups of five
QUINCE	*n* pl. **-S** an apple-like fruit
QUINCUNX	*n* pl. **-ES** an arrangement of five objects
QUINELA	*n* pl. **-S** quinella
QUINELLA	*n* pl. **-S** a type of bet in horse racing
QUINIC	*adj* pertaining to quinine
QUINIELA	*n* pl. **-S** quinella
QUININ	*n* pl. **-S** quinine
QUININA	*n* pl. **-S** quinine
QUININE	*n* pl. **-S** a medicinal alkaloid
QUINNAT	*n* pl. **-S** a food fish
QUINOA	*n* pl. **-S** a weedy plant
QUINOID	*n* pl. **-S** a chemical compound
QUINOL	*n* pl. **-S** a chemical compound
QUINOLIN	*n* pl. **-S** a chemical compound

QUINONE	*n* pl. **-S** a chemical compound
QUINSY	*n* pl. **-SIES** an inflammation of the tonsils **QUINSIED** *adj*
QUINT	*n* pl. **-S** a group of five
QUINTA	*n* pl. **-S** a country estate in Portugal or Latin America
QUINTAIN	*n* pl. **-S** an object used as a target in a medieval sport
QUINTAL	*n* pl. **-S** a unit of weight
QUINTAN	*n* pl. **-S** a recurrent fever
QUINTAR	*n* pl. **-S** qintar
QUINTE	*n* pl. **-S** a position in fencing
QUINTET	*n* pl. **-S** a group of five
QUINTIC	*n* pl. **-S** a type of mathematical function
QUINTILE	*n* pl. **-S** a portion of a frequency distribution
QUINTIN	*n* pl. **-S** a fine linen
QUINZHEE	*n* pl. **-S** a shelter made by hollowing out a pile of snow
QUINZIE	*n* pl. **-S** quinzhee
QUIP	*v* **QUIPPED, QUIPPING, QUIPS** to make witty remarks
QUIPPER	*n* pl. **-S** one that quips
QUIPPISH	*adj* witty
QUIPPU	*n* pl. **-S** quipu
QUIPPY	*adj* **-PIER, -PIEST** witty
QUIPSTER	*n* pl. **-S** one that quips
QUIPU	*n* pl. **-S** an ancient calculating device
QUIRE	*v* **QUIRED, QUIRING, QUIRES** to arrange sheets of paper in sets of twenty-four
QUIRK	*v* **-ED, -ING, -S** to twist
QUIRKISH	*adj* quirky
QUIRKY	*adj* **QUIRKIER, QUIRKIEST** peculiar **QUIRKILY** *adv*
QUIRT	*v* **-ED, -ING, -S** to strike with a riding whip
QUISLING	*n* pl. **-S** a traitor who aids the invaders of his or her country
QUIT	*v* **QUITTED, QUITTING, QUITS** to end one's engagement in or occupation with
QUITCH	*n* pl. **-ES** a perennial grass
QUITE	*adv* to the fullest extent
QUITRENT	*n* pl. **-S** a fixed rent due from a socage tenant
QUITTED	past tense of quit
QUITTER	*n* pl. **-S** one that quits
QUITTING	present participle of quit
QUITTOR	*n* pl. **-S** an inflammation of an animal's hoof
QUIVER	*v* **-ED, -ING, -S** to shake with a slight but rapid motion
QUIVERER	*n* pl. **-S** one that quivers
QUIVERY	*adj* marked by quivering
QUIXOTE	*n* pl. **-S** a quixotic person
QUIXOTIC	*adj* extremely idealistic
QUIXOTRY	*n* pl. **-TRIES** quixotic action or thought
QUIZ	*v* **QUIZZED, QUIZZING, QUIZZES** to test the knowledge of by asking questions
QUIZZER	*n* pl. **-S** one that quizzes
QULLIQ	*n* pl. **-S** kudlik
QUOD	*n* pl. **-S** a prison
QUOHOG	*n* pl. **-S** quahog
QUOIN	*v* **-ED, -ING, -S** to secure with a type of wedge
QUOINING	*n* pl. **-S** the materials (as stones or bricks) used to form an external corner of a building
QUOIT	*v* **-ED, -ING, -S** to play a throwing game similar to ringtoss
QUOKKA	*n* pl. **-S** a short-tailed wallaby
QUOLL	*n* pl. **-S** a small spotted marsupial
QUOMODO	*n* pl. **-DOS** a means or manner
QUONDAM	*adj* that once was
QUORATE	*adj* having a quorum
QUORUM	*n* pl. **-S** a particularly chosen group
QUOTA	*n* pl. **-S** a proportional part or share
QUOTE	*v* **QUOTED, QUOTING, QUOTES** to repeat the words of **QUOTABLE** *adj* **QUOTABLY** *adv*
QUOTER	*n* pl. **-S** one that quotes
QUOTH	*v* said — QUOTH is the only accepted form of this verb; it cannot be conjugated
QUOTHA	*interj* — used to express surprise or sarcasm
QUOTIENT	*n* pl. **-S** the number resulting from the division of one number by another
QUOTING	present participle of quote
QURSH	*n* pl. **-ES** a monetary unit of Saudi Arabia
QURUSH	*n* pl. **-ES** qursh
QWERTY	*n* pl. **-TYS** a standard keyboard

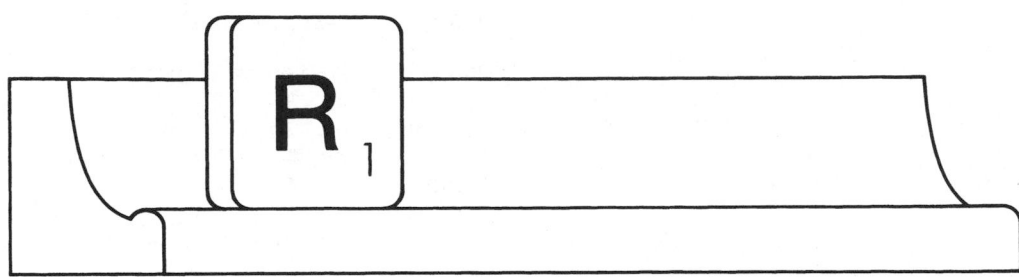

RABASKA	*n* pl. **-S** a large canoe
RABAT	*n* pl. **-S** a dickey attached to a clerical collar
RABATO	*n* pl. **-TOS** a wide, lace-edged collar
RABBET	*v* **-ED, -ING, -S** to cut a groove in
RABBI	*n* pl. **-S** or **-ES** a Jewish spiritual leader
RABBIN	*n* pl. **-S** rabbi
RABBINIC	*adj* pertaining to rabbis
RABBIT	*v* **-ED, -ING, -S** to hunt rabbits (rodent-like mammals)
RABBITER	*n* pl. **-S** one that rabbits
RABBITRY	*n* pl. **-RIES** a place where rabbits are kept
RABBITY	*adj* resembling a rabbit
RABBLE	*v* **-BLED, -BLING, -BLES** to mob
RABBLER	*n* pl. **-S** an iron bar used in puddling
RABBONI	*n* pl. **-S** master; teacher — used as a Jewish title of respect
RABIC	*adj* pertaining to rabies
RABID	*adj* affected with rabies **RABIDLY** *adv*
RABIDITY	*n* pl. **-TIES** the state of being rabid
RABIES	*n* pl. **RABIES** an infectious virus disease **RABIETIC** *adj*
RACCOON	*n* pl. **-S** a carnivorous mammal
RACE	*v* **RACED, RACING, RACES** to compete in a contest of speed
RACEGOER	*n* pl. **-S** one who regularly goes to horse races
RACEMATE	*n* pl. **-S** a chemical salt
RACEME	*n* pl. **-S** a mode of arrangement of flowers along an axis **RACEMED** *adj*
RACEMIC	*adj* pertaining to a racemate
RACEMISM	*n* pl. **-S** the state of being racemic
RACEMIZE	*v* **-MIZED, -MIZING, -MIZES** to convert into a racemic compound
RACEMOID	*adj* pertaining to a raceme
RACEMOSE	*adj* having the form of a raceme
RACEMOUS	*adj* racemose
RACER	*n* pl. **-S** one that races
RACEWALK	*v* **-ED, -ING, -S** to walk for speed while maintaining foot contact with the ground and keeping the supporting leg straight
RACEWAY	*n* pl. **-WAYS** a channel for conducting water
RACHET	*v* **-ED, -ING, -S** ratchet
RACHILLA	*n* pl. **-LAE** the central stalk of a grass spikelet
RACHIS	*n* pl. **-CHISES** or **-CHIDES** the spinal column **RACHIAL** *adj*
RACHITIS	*n* pl. **-TIDES** rickets **RACHITIC** *adj*
RACIAL	*adj* pertaining to an ethnic group **RACIALLY** *adv*
RACIER	comparative of racy
RACIEST	superlative of racy
RACILY	*adv* in a racy manner
RACINESS	*n* pl. **-ES** the quality of being racy
RACING	*n* pl. **-S** the sport of engaging in contests of speed
RACINO	*n* pl. **-NOS** a racetrack at which slot machines are available
RACISM	*n* pl. **-S** a doctrine of racial superiority
RACIST	*n* pl. **-S** an advocate of racism
RACK	*v* **-ED, -ING, -S** to place in a type of framework
RACKER	*n* pl. **-S** one that racks
RACKET	*v* **-ED, -ING, -S** to make a loud noise
RACKETY	*adj* **-ETIER, -ETIEST** noisy
RACKFUL	*n* pl. **-S** as much as a rack can hold

RACKLE *adj* impetuous; rash

RACKWORK *n* pl. **-S** a type of mechanism

RACLETTE *n* pl. **-S** a cheese dish

RACON *n* pl. **-S** a type of radar transmitter

RACOON *n* pl. **-S** raccoon

RACQUET *n* pl. **-S** a lightweight implement used in various ball games

RACY *adj* **RACIER, RACIEST** bordering on impropriety or indecency

RAD *v* **RADDED, RADDING, RADS** to fear

RAD *adj* **RADDER, RADDEST** very appealing or good

RADAR *n* pl. **-S** an electronic locating device

RADDLE *v* **-DLED, -DLING, -DLES** to weave together

RADIABLE *adj* capable of radiating

RADIAL *n* pl. **-S** a part diverging from a center

RADIALE *n* pl. **-LIA** a bone of the carpus

RADIALLY *adv* in a diverging manner

RADIAN *n* pl. **-S** a unit of angular measure

RADIANCE *n* pl. **-S** brightness

RADIANCY *n* pl. **-CIES** radiance

RADIANT *n* pl. **-S** a point from which rays are emitted

RADIATE *v* **-ATED, -ATING, -ATES** to emit rays

RADIATOR *n* pl. **-S** a heating device

RADICAL *n* pl. **-S** a group of atoms that acts as a unit in chemical compounds

RADICAND *n* pl. **-S** a quantity in mathematics

RADICATE *v* **-CATED, -CATING, -CATES** to cause to take root

RADICEL *n* pl. **-S** a rootlet

RADICES a pl. of radix

RADICLE *n* pl. **-S** a part of a plant embryo

RADII a pl. of radius

RADIO *v* **-ED, -ING, -S** or **-ES** to transmit by radio (an apparatus for wireless communication)

RADIOMAN *n* pl. **-MEN** a radio operator or technician

RADISH *n* pl. **-ES** a pungent, edible root

RADIUM *n* pl. **-S** a radioactive element

RADIUS *n* pl. **-DIUSES** or **-DII** a straight line from the center of a circle to the circumference

RADIUS *v* **-ED, -ING, -ES** to give a rounded form to

RADIX *n* pl. **-DIXES** or **-DICES** the root of a plant

RADOME *n* pl. **-S** a domelike device used to shelter a radar antenna

RADON *n* pl. **-S** a radioactive element

RADULA *n* pl. **-LAS** or **-LAE** a tonguelike organ of mollusks **RADULAR** *adj*

RADWASTE *n* pl. **-S** radioactive waste

RAFF *n* pl. **-S** riffraff

RAFFIA *n* pl. **-S** a palm tree

RAFFISH *adj* tawdry

RAFFLE *v* **-FLED, -FLING, -FLES** to dispose of by a form of lottery

RAFFLER *n* pl. **-S** one that raffles

RAFT *v* **-ED, -ING, -S** to transport on a raft (a type of buoyant structure)

RAFTER *n* pl. **-S** a supporting beam

RAFTERED *adj* furnished with rafters

RAFTING *n* pl. **-S** the sport of traveling down a river on a raft

RAFTSMAN *n* pl. **-MEN** one who manages a raft

RAG *v* **RAGGED, RAGGING, RAGS** to scold

RAGA *n* pl. **-S** a Hindu musical form

RAGBAG *n* pl. **-S** a bag for storing scraps of cloth

RAGDOLL *n* pl. **-S** a domestic cat

RAGE *v* **RAGED, RAGING, RAGES** to act or speak with violent anger

RAGEE *n* pl. **-S** ragi

RAGEFUL *adj* full of violent anger

RAGER *n* pl. **-S** one that rages

RAGG *n* pl. **-S** a wool fiber

RAGGA *n* pl. **-S** music that combines reggae and hip hop

RAGGED *adj* **-GEDER, -GEDEST** tattered **RAGGEDLY** *adv*

RAGGEDY *adj* **-GEDIER, -GEDIEST** somewhat ragged

RAGGEE *n* pl. **-S** ragi

RAGGIES pl. of raggy

RAGGING *n* pl. **-S** the technique of decorating a wall by applying paint with a rag

RAGGLE *n* pl. **-S** a groove cut in masonry

RAGGY *n* pl. **-GIES** ragi

RAGI   *n* pl. **-S** an East Indian cereal grass

RAGING   present participle of rage

RAGINGLY   *adv* in a furious manner

RAGLAN   *n* pl. **-S** a type of overcoat

RAGMAN   *n* pl. **-MEN** one who gathers and sells scraps of cloth

RAGOUT   *v* **-ED, -ING, -S** to make into a highly seasoned stew

RAGTAG   *n* pl. **-S** riffraff

RAGTAIL   *adj* ragged, shabby

RAGTIME   *n* pl. **-S** a style of American dance music

RAGTOP   *n* pl. **-S** a convertible automobile

RAGWEED   *n* pl. **-S** a weedy herb

RAGWORM   *n* pl. **-S** an aquatic worm

RAGWORT   *n* pl. **-S** a flowering plant

RAH   *interj* — used to cheer on a team or player

RAI   *n* pl. **-S** a style of popular Algerian music

RAIA   *n* pl. **-S** rayah

RAID   *v* **-ED, -ING, -S** to make a sudden assault on

RAIDER   *n* pl. **-S** one that raids

RAIL   *v* **-ED, -ING, -S** to scold in abusive or insolent language

RAILBED   *n* pl. **-S** a layer of stone or gravel on which a railroad is laid

RAILBIRD   *n* pl. **-S** a racing enthusiast

RAILBUS   *n* pl. **-BUSES** or **-BUSSES** a passenger car equipped for operation on rails

RAILCAR   *n* pl. **-S** a railroad car

RAILCARD   *n* pl. **-S** a card that allows buying railroad tickets at a lower price

RAILER   *n* pl. **-S** one that rails

RAILHEAD   *n* pl. **-S** the end of a railroad line

RAILING   *n* pl. **-S** a fence-like barrier

RAILLERY   *n* pl. **-LERIES** good-natured teasing

RAILMAN   *n* pl. **-MEN** a railroad employee

RAILROAD   *v* **-ED, -ING, -S** to transport by railroad (a type of road on which locomotives are run)

RAILWAY   *n* pl. **-WAYS** a railroad

RAIMENT   *n* pl. **-S** clothing

RAIN   *v* **-ED, -ING, -S** to fall like rain (drops of water condensed from clouds)

RAINBAND   *n* pl. **-S** a dark band in the solar spectrum

RAINBIRD   *n* pl. **-S** a type of bird

RAINBOW   *n* pl. **-S** an arc of spectral colors formed in the sky

RAINCOAT   *n* pl. **-S** a waterproof coat

RAINDROP   *n* pl. **-S** a drop of rain

RAINFALL   *n* pl. **-S** a fall of rain

RAINIER   comparative of rainy

RAINIEST   superlative of rainy

RAINILY   *adv* in a rainy manner

RAINLESS   *adj* having no rain

RAINOUT   *n* pl. **-S** atomic fallout occurring in precipitation

RAINSUIT   *n* pl. **-S** a waterproof jacket and pants

RAINWASH   *v* **-ED, -ING, -ES** to wash material downhill by rain

RAINWEAR   *n* pl. **RAINWEAR** waterproof clothing

RAINY   *adj* **RAINIER, RAINIEST** marked by rain

RAISE   *v* **RAISED, RAISING, RAISES** to move to a higher position **RAISABLE** *adj*

RAISER   *n* pl. **-S** one that raises

RAISIN   *n* pl. **-S** a dried grape **RAISINY** *adj*

RAISING   *n* pl. **-S** an elevation

RAISONNE   *adj* arranged systematically

RAITA   *n* pl. **-S** an Indian salad made with yogurt and chopped vegetables or fruits

RAJ   *n* pl. **-ES** dominion; sovereignty

RAJA   *n* pl. **-S** rajah

RAJAH   *n* pl. **-S** a king or prince in India

RAKE   *v* **RAKED, RAKING, RAKES** to gather with a toothed implement

RAKEE   *n* pl. **-S** raki

RAKEHELL   *n* pl. **-S** a man lacking in moral restraint

RAKEOFF   *n* pl. **-S** a share of profits

RAKER   *n* pl. **-S** one that rakes

RAKI   *n* pl. **-S** a Turkish liqueur

RAKING   present participle of rake

RAKISH   *adj* dapper **RAKISHLY** *adv*

RAKU   *n* pl. **-S** a form of Japanese glazed pottery

RALE   *n* pl. **-S** an abnormal respiratory sound

RALLIER *n* pl. **-S** one that rallies

RALLINE *adj* pertaining to a family of marsh birds

RALLY *v* **-LIED, -LYING, -LIES** to call together for a common purpose

RALLYE *n* pl. **-S** a type of automobile race

RALLYING *n* pl. **-S** the sport of driving in rallyes

RALLYIST *n* pl. **-S** a participant in a rallye

RALPH *v* **-ED, -ING, -S** to vomit

RAM *v* **RAMMED, RAMMING, RAMS** to strike with great force

RAMADA *n* pl. **-S** a roofed, open-sided shelter

RAMAL *adj* pertaining to a ramus

RAMATE *adj* having branches

RAMBLA *n* pl. **-S** a dry ravine

RAMBLE *v* **-BLED, -BLING, -BLES** to wander

RAMBLER *n* pl. **-S** one that rambles

RAMBUTAN *n* pl. **-S** the edible fruit of a Malayan tree

RAMEE *n* pl. **-S** ramie

RAMEKIN *n* pl. **-S** a cheese dish

RAMEN *n* pl. **RAMEN** Japanese noodles in a broth with bits of meat and vegetables

RAMENTUM *n* pl. **-TA** a scale formed on the surface of leaves

RAMEQUIN *n* pl. **-S** ramekin

RAMET *n* pl. **-S** an independent member of a clone

RAMI pl. of ramus

RAMIE *n* pl. **-S** an Asian shrub

RAMIFORM *adj* shaped like a branch

RAMIFY *v* **-FIED, -FYING, -FIES** to divide into branches

RAMILIE *n* pl. **-S** ramillie

RAMILLIE *n* pl. **-S** a type of wig

RAMIN *n* pl. **-S** a Malaysian tree

RAMJET *n* pl. **-S** a type of engine

RAMMED past tense of ram

RAMMER *n* pl. **-S** one that rams

RAMMIER comparative of rammy

RAMMIEST superlative of rammy

RAMMING present participle of ram

RAMMISH *adj* resembling a ram (a male sheep)

RAMMY *adj* **-MIER, -MIEST** rammish

RAMONA *n* pl. **-S** a plant of the mint family

RAMOSE *adj* having many branches **RAMOSELY** *adv*

RAMOSITY *n* pl. **-TIES** the state of being ramose

RAMOUS *adj* ramose

RAMP *v* **-ED, -ING, -S** to rise or stand on the hind legs

RAMPAGE *v* **-PAGED, -PAGING, -PAGES** to move about wildly or violently

RAMPAGER *n* pl. **-S** one that rampages

RAMPANCY *n* pl. **-CIES** the state of being rampant

RAMPANT *adj* unrestrained

RAMPART *v* **-ED, -ING, -S** to furnish with a fortifying embankment

RAMPIKE *n* pl. **-S** a standing dead tree

RAMPION *n* pl. **-S** a European plant

RAMPOLE *n* pl. **-S** rampike

RAMROD *v* **-RODDED, -RODDING, -RODS** to supervise

RAMSHORN *n* pl. **-S** a snail used as an aquarium scavenger

RAMSON *n* pl. **-S** a broad-leaved garlic

RAMTIL *n* pl. **-S** a tropical plant

RAMTILLA *n* pl. **-S** ramtil

RAMULOSE *adj* having many small branches

RAMULOUS *adj* ramulose

RAMUS *n* pl. **-MI** a branch-like part of a structure

RAN past tense of run and rin

RANCE *n* pl. **-S** a variety of marble

RANCH *v* **-ED, -ING, -ES** to work on a ranch (an establishment for raising livestock)

RANCHER *n* pl. **-S** one that owns or works on a ranch

RANCHERA *n* pl. **-S** a type of Mexican country music

RANCHERO *n* pl. **-ROS** a rancher

RANCHING *n* pl. **-S** the work of running a ranch

RANCHMAN *n* pl. **-MEN** a rancher

RANCHO *n* pl. **-CHOS** a ranch

RANCID *adj* having an unpleasant odor or taste **RANCIDLY** *adv*

RANCOR *n* pl. **-S** bitter and vindictive enmity **RANCORED** *adj*

RANCOUR *n* pl. **-S** rancor

RAND   *n* pl. **-S** a strip of leather at the heel of a shoe

RANDAN   *n* pl. **-S** a boat rowed by three persons

RANDIER   comparative of randy

RANDIES   pl. of randy

RANDOM   *n* pl. **-S** a haphazard course

RANDOMLY   *adv* in a haphazard manner

RANDY   *adj* **-DIER, -DIEST** lustful

RANDY   *n* pl. **RANDIES** a rude person

RANEE   *n* pl. **-S** rani

RANG   *n* pl. **-S** a row of long lots along a road

RANGE   *v* **RANGED, RANGING, RANGES** to place in a particular order

RANGER   *n* pl. **-S** an officer supervising the care of a forest

RANGY   *adj* **RANGIER, RANGIEST** tall and slender

RANI   *n* pl. **-S** the wife of a rajah

RANID   *n* pl. **-S** any of a large family of frogs

RANK   *adj* **RANKER, RANKEST** strong and disagreeable in odor or taste

RANK   *v* **-ED, -ING, -S** to determine the relative position of

RANKER   *n* pl. **-S** an enlisted soldier

RANKING   *n* pl. **-S** a listing of ranked individuals

RANKISH   *adj* somewhat rank

RANKLE   *v* **-KLED, -KLING, -KLES** to cause irritation or resentment in

RANKLESS   *adj* having no ranks

RANKLY   *adv* in a rank manner

RANKNESS   *n* pl. **-ES** the state of being rank

RANPIKE   *n* pl. **-S** rampike

RANSACK   *v* **-ED, -ING, -S** to search thoroughly

RANSOM   *v* **-ED, -ING, -S** to obtain the release of by paying a demanded price

RANSOMER   *n* pl. **-S** one that ransoms

RANT   *v* **-ED, -ING, -S** to speak in a loud or vehement manner

RANTER   *n* pl. **-S** one that rants

RANTINGS   *n/pl* loud and angry comments

RANULA   *n* pl. **-S** a cyst formed under the tongue **RANULAR** *adj*

RAP   *v* **RAPPED, RAPPING, RAPS** to strike sharply

RAPACITY   *n* pl. **-TIES** the quality of being ravenous

RAPE   *v* **RAPED, RAPING, RAPES** to force to submit to sexual intercourse

RAPER   *n* pl. **-S** a rapist

RAPESEED   *n* pl. **-S** the seed of a European herb

RAPHE   *n* pl. **RAPHES** or **RAPHAE** a seamlike ridge between two halves of an organ or part

RAPHIA   *n* pl. **-S** raffia

RAPHIDE   *n* pl. **-S** a needle-shaped crystal occurring in plant cells

RAPHIS   *n* pl. **-PHIDES** raphide

RAPID   *adj* **-IDER, -IDEST** fast-moving **RAPIDLY** *adv*

RAPID   *n* pl. **-S** a fast-moving part of a river

RAPIDITY   *n* pl. **-TIES** swiftness

RAPIER   *n* pl. **-S** a long, slender sword **RAPIERED** *adj*

RAPINE   *n* pl. **-S** the taking of property by force

RAPING   present participle of rape

RAPINI   *n/pl* rappini

RAPIST   *n* pl. **-S** one who rapes

RAPPAREE   *n* pl. **-S** a plunderer

RAPPED   past tense of rap

RAPPEE   *n* pl. **-S** a strong snuff

RAPPEL   *v* **-PELED, -PELING, -PELS** or **-PELLED, -PELLING, -PELS** to descend from a steep height by means of a rope

RAPPEN   *n* pl. **RAPPEN** a monetary unit of Switzerland

RAPPER   *n* pl. **-S** one that raps

RAPPING   present participle of rap

RAPPINI   *n/pl* immature turnip plants

RAPPORT   *n* pl. **-S** a harmonious relationship

RAPT   *adj* deeply engrossed **RAPTLY** *adv*

RAPTNESS   *n* pl. **-ES** the state of being rapt

RAPTOR   *n* pl. **-S** a bird of prey

RAPTURE   *v* **-TURED, -TURING, -TURES** to fill with great joy

RARE   *adj* **RARER, RAREST** occurring infrequently

RARE   *v* **RARED, RARING, RARES** to be enthusiastic

RAREBIT	*n* pl. **-S** a cheese dish	**RATAFEE**	*n* pl. **-S** ratafia
RAREFIER	*n* pl. **-S** one that rarefies	**RATAFIA**	*n* pl. **-S** an almond-flavored liqueur
RAREFY	*v* **-EFIED, -EFYING, -EFIES** to make less dense	**RATAL**	*n* pl. **-S** an amount on which rates are assessed
RARELY	*adv* not often	**RATAN**	*n* pl. **-S** rattan
RARENESS	*n* pl. **-ES** the quality of being rare	**RATANY**	*n* pl. **-NIES** rhatany
RARER	comparative of rare	**RATAPLAN**	*v* **-PLANNED, -PLANNING, -PLANS** to make a rapidly repeating sound
RARERIPE	*n* pl. **-S** a fruit that ripens early		
RAREST	superlative of rare	**RATATAT**	*n* pl. **-S** a quick, sharp rapping sound
RARIFY	*v* **-FIED, -FYING, -FIES** to rarefy		
RARING	*adj* full of enthusiasm	**RATBAG**	*n* pl. **-S** an eccentric or disagreeable person
RARITY	*n* pl. **-TIES** rareness		
RAS	*n* pl. **-ES** an Ethiopian prince	**RATCH**	*n* pl. **-ES** a mechanism that allows motion in one direction only
RASBORA	*n* pl. **-S** a tropical fish		
RASCAL	*n* pl. **-S** an unscrupulous or dishonest person	**RATCHET**	*v* **-ED, -ING, -S** to increase or decrease by small amounts
RASCALLY	*adj* characteristic of a rascal	**RATE**	*v* **RATED, RATING, RATES** to estimate the value of
RASE	*v* **RASED, RASING, RASES** to raze		
		RATEABLE	*adj* ratable **RATEABLY** *adv*
RASER	*n* pl. **-S** one that rases	**RATEL**	*n* pl. **-S** a carnivorous mammal
RASH	*adj* **RASHER, RASHEST** acting without due caution or forethought	**RATER**	*n* pl. **-S** one that rates
		RATFINK	*n* pl. **-S** a contemptible person
RASH	*n* pl. **-ES** a skin eruption **RASHLIKE** *adj*	**RATFISH**	*n* pl. **-ES** a marine fish
		RATH	*adj* rathe
RASHER	*n* pl. **-S** a thin slice of meat	**RATHE**	*adj* appearing or ripening early
RASHLY	*adv* in a rash manner	**RATHER**	*adv* preferably
RASHNESS	*n* pl. **-ES** the state of being rash	**RATHOLE**	*n* pl. **-S** a hole made by a rat
RASING	present participle of rase	**RATICIDE**	*n* pl. **-S** a substance for killing rats
RASORIAL	*adj* habitually scratching the ground for food	**RATIFIER**	*n* pl. **-S** one that ratifies
RASP	*v* **-ED, -ING, -S** to rub with something rough	**RATIFY**	*v* **-FIED, -FYING, -FIES** to approve and sanction formally
RASPER	*n* pl. **-S** one that rasps	**RATINE**	*n* pl. **-S** a heavy fabric woven loosely
RASPING	*n* pl. **-S** a tiny piece of wood removed with a coarse file		
		RATING	*n* pl. **-S** relative estimate or evaluation
RASPISH	*adj* irritable		
RASPY	*adj* **RASPIER, RASPIEST** rough	**RATIO**	*n* pl. **-TIOS** a proportional relationship
RASSLE	*v* **-SLED, -SLING, -SLES** to wrestle		
RASSLER	*n* pl. **-S** a wrestler	**RATION**	*v* **-ED, -ING, -S** to distribute in fixed portions
RASTER	*n* pl. **-S** the area reproducing images on the picture tube of a television set	**RATIONAL**	*n* pl. **-S** a number that can be expressed as a quotient of integers
		RATITE	*n* pl. **-S** a flightless bird
RASURE	*n* pl. **-S** erasure	**RATLIKE**	*adj* resembling a rat
RAT	*v* **RATTED, RATTING, RATS** to hunt rats (long-tailed rodents)	**RATLIN**	*n* pl. **-S** ratline
		RATLINE	*n* pl. **-S** one of the ropes forming the steps of a ship's rope ladder
RATABLE	*adj* capable of being rated **RATABLY** *adv*		
		RATO	*n* pl. **-TOS** a rocket-assisted airplane takeoff
RATABLES	*n/pl* taxable properties		

RATOON   v **-ED, -ING, -S** to sprout from a root planted the previous year

RATOONER   n pl. **-S** a plant that ratoons

RATSBANE   n pl. **-S** rat poison

RATTAIL   n pl. **-S** a marine fish

RATTAN   n pl. **-S** a palm tree

RATTED   past tense of rat

RATTEEN   n pl. **-S** a coarse woolen fabric

RATTEN   v **-ED, -ING, -S** to harass

RATTENER   n pl. **-S** one that rattens

RATTER   n pl. **-S** an animal used for catching rats

RATTIER   comparative of ratty

RATTIEST   superlative of ratty

RATTILY   adv in a manner suggestive of rats

RATTING   present participle of rat

RATTISH   adj ratlike

RATTLE   v **-TLED, -TLING, -TLES** to make a quick succession of short, sharp sounds

RATTLER   n pl. **-S** one that rattles

RATTLING   n pl. **-S** ratline

RATTLY   adj **-TLIER, -TLIEST** tending to rattle

RATTON   n pl. **-S** a rat

RATTOON   v **-ED, -ING, -S** to ratoon

RATTRAP   n pl. **-S** a trap for catching rats

RATTY   adj **-TIER, -TIEST** infested with rats

RAUCITY   n pl. **-TIES** the state of being raucous

RAUCOUS   adj loud and unruly

RAUNCH   n pl. **-ES** vulgarity

RAUNCHY   adj **-CHIER, -CHIEST** slovenly

RAVAGE   v **-AGED, -AGING, -AGES** to destroy

RAVAGER   n pl. **-S** one that ravages

RAVE   v **RAVED, RAVING, RAVES** to speak irrationally or incoherently

RAVEL   v **-ELED, -ELING, -ELS** or **-ELLED, -ELLING, -ELS** to separate the threads of

RAVELER   n pl. **-S** one that ravels

RAVELIN   n pl. **-S** a type of fortification

RAVELING   n pl. **-S** a loose thread

RAVELLED   a past tense of ravel

RAVELLER   n pl. **-S** raveler

RAVELLING   a present participle of ravel

RAVELLY   adj tangled

RAVEN   v **-ED, -ING, -S** to eat in a ravenous manner

RAVENER   n pl. **-S** one that ravens

RAVENING   n pl. **-S** rapacity

RAVENOUS   adj extremely hungry

RAVER   n pl. **-S** one that raves

RAVEY   adj **RAVIER, RAVIEST** characteristic of a rave (an all-night dance party with fast electronic music)

RAVIGOTE   n pl. **-S** a spiced vinegar sauce

RAVIN   v **-ED, -ING, -S** to raven

RAVINE   n pl. **-S** a narrow, steep-sided valley

RAVING   n pl. **-S** irrational, incoherent speech

RAVINGLY   adv in a delirious manner

RAVIOLI   n pl. **-S** an Italian pasta dish

RAVISH   v **-ED, -ING, -ES** to seize and carry off by force

RAVISHER   n pl. **-S** one that ravishes

RAW   adj **RAWER, RAWEST** uncooked

RAW   n pl. **-S** a sore or irritated spot

RAWBONED   adj having little flesh

RAWHIDE   v **-HIDED, -HIDING, -HIDES** to beat with a type of whip

RAWIN   n pl. **-S** a wind measurement made by tracking a balloon with radar

RAWISH   adj somewhat raw

RAWLY   adv in a raw manner

RAWNESS   n pl. **-ES** the state of being raw

RAX   v **-ED, -ING, -ES** to stretch out

RAY   v **-ED, -ING, -S** to emit rays (narrow beams of light)

RAYA   n pl. **-S** rayah

RAYAH   n pl. **-S** a non-Muslim inhabitant of Turkey

RAYGRASS   n pl. **-ES** ryegrass

RAYLESS   adj having no rays

RAYLIKE   adj resembling a narrow beam of light

RAYON   n pl. **-S** a synthetic fiber

RAZE   v **RAZED, RAZING, RAZES** to tear down or demolish

RAZEE   v **-ZEED, -ZEEING, -ZEES** to make lower by removing the upper deck, as a ship

RAZER   n pl. **-S** one that razes

RAZOR	*v* **-ED, -ING, -S** to shave or cut with a sharp-edged instrument	**READY**	*adj* **READIER, READIEST** prepared
RAZZ	*v* **-ED, -ING, -ES** to deride	**READY**	*v* **READIED, READYING, READIES** to make ready
RAZZIA	*n* pl. **-S** a hostile and destructive raid	**REAGENT**	*n* pl. **-S** a substance used in a chemical reaction to ascertain the nature or composition of another
RAZZLE	*n* pl. **-S** a flamboyant colorful display	**REAGIN**	*n* pl. **-S** a type of antibody **REAGINIC** *adj*
RE	*n* pl. **-S** the second tone of the diatonic musical scale	**REAL**	*adj* **REALER, REALEST** having actual existence
REACH	*v* **-ED, -ING, -ES** to stretch out or put forth	**REAL**	*n* pl. **-S** or **-ES** a former monetary unit of Spain
REACHER	*n* pl. **-S** one that reaches	**REAL**	*n* pl. **REAIS** or **REIS** a monetary unit of Brazil
REACT	*v* **-ED, -ING, -S** to respond to a stimulus	**REALGAR**	*n* pl. **-S** a mineral
REACTANT	*n* pl. **-S** one that reacts	**REALIA**	*n/pl* objects used by a teacher to illustrate everyday living
REACTION	*n* pl. **-S** the act of reacting	**REALISE**	*v* **-ISED, -ISING, -ISES** to realize
REACTIVE	*adj* tending to react	**REALISER**	*n* pl. **-S** one that realises
REACTOR	*n* pl. **-S** one that reacts	**REALISM**	*n* pl. **-S** concern with fact or reality
READ	*v* **READ, READING, READS** to look at so as to take in the meaning of, as something written or printed **READABLE** *adj* **READABLY** *adv*	**REALIST**	*n* pl. **-S** one who is concerned with fact or reality
READER	*n* pl. **-S** one that reads	**REALITY**	*n* pl. **-TIES** something that is real
READERLY	*adj* typical of a reader	**REALIZE**	*v* **-IZED, -IZING, -IZES** to understand completely
READIED	past tense of ready		
READIER	comparative of ready	**REALIZER**	*n* pl. **-S** one that realizes
READIES	present 3d person sing. of ready	**REALLY**	*adv* actually
READIEST	superlative of ready	**REALM**	*n* pl. **-S** a kingdom
READILY	*adv* in a ready manner	**REALNESS**	*n* pl. **-ES** the state of being real
READING	*n* pl. **-S** material that is read or is for reading	**REALTY**	*n* pl. **-TIES** property in buildings and land
READOUT	*n* pl. **-S** a presentation of computer data	**REAM**	*v* **-ED, -ING, -S** to enlarge with a reamer

 **Following is a list of self-explanatory verbs containing the prefix RE- (again):**

REABSORB	*v* -ED, -ING, -S	**READOPT**	*v* -ED, -ING, -S	**REARM**	*v* -ED, -ING, -S
REACCEDE	*v* -CEDED, -CEDING, -CEDES	**READORN**	*v* -ED, -ING, -S	**REAROUSE**	*v* -AROUSED, -AROUSING, -AROUSES
		REAFFIRM	*v* -ED, -ING, -S		
		REAFFIX	*v* -ED, -ING, -ES		
REACCENT	*v* -ED, -ING, -S	**REALIGN**	*v* -ED, -ING, -S	**REARREST**	*v* -ED, -ING, -S
REACCEPT	*v* -ED, -ING, -S	**REALLOT**	*v* -LOTTED, -LOTTING, -LOTS	**REASCEND**	*v* -ED, -ING, -S
REACCUSE	*v* -CUSED, -CUSING, -CUSES			**REASSAIL**	*v* -ED, -ING, -S
		REALTER	*v* -ED, -ING, -S	**REASSERT**	*v* -ED, -ING, -S
		REANNEX	*v* -ED, -ING, -ES	**REASSESS**	*v* -ED, -ING, -ES
READAPT	*v* -ED, -ING, -S	**REANOINT**	*v* -ED, -ING, -S	**REASSIGN**	*v* -ED, -ING, -S
READD	*v* -ED, -ING, -S	**REAPPEAR**	*v* -ED, -ING, -S	**REASSORT**	*v* -ED, -ING, -S
READDICT	*v* -ED, -ING, -S	**REAPPLY**	*v* -PLIED, -PLYING, -PLIES	**REASSUME**	*v* -SUMED, -SUMING, -SUMES
READJUST	*v* -ED, -ING, -S				
READMIT	*v* -MITTED, -MITTING, -MITS	**REARGUE**	*v* -GUED, -GUING, -GUES		

REAMER	n pl. **-S** a tool used to enlarge holes
REAP	v **-ED, -ING, -S** to cut for harvest **REAPABLE** adj
REAPER	n pl. **-S** one that reaps
REAPHOOK	n pl. **-S** an implement used in reaping
REAR	v **-ED, -ING, -S** to lift upright
REARER	n pl. **-S** one that rears
REARING	n pl. **-S** the act of an animal standing on its rear limbs
REARMICE	n/pl reremice
REARMOST	adj coming or situated last
REARWARD	n pl. **-S** the rearmost division of an army
REASCENT	n pl. **-S** a new or second ascent
REASON	v **-ED, -ING, -S** to derive inferences or conclusions from known or presumed facts
REASONER	n pl. **-S** one that reasons
REATA	n pl. **-S** riata
REAVE	v **REAVED** or **REFT, REAVING, REAVES** to plunder
REAVER	n pl. **-S** one that reaves
REB	n pl. **-S** a Confederate soldier
REBAR	n pl. **-S** a steel rod for use in reinforced concrete
REBASE	v **-BASED, -BASING, -BASES** to set a new foundation for something
REBATE	v **-BATED, -BATING, -BATES** to deduct or return from a payment or bill
REBATER	n pl. **-S** one that rebates

REBATO	n pl. **-TOS** rabato
REBBE	n pl. **-S** a rabbi
REBEC	n pl. **-S** an ancient stringed instrument
REBECK	n pl. **-S** rebec
REBEL	v **-BELLED, -BELLING, -BELS** to oppose the established government of one's land
REBELDOM	n pl. **-S** an area controlled by rebels
REBIRTH	n pl. **-S** a new or second birth
REBOANT	adj resounding loudly
REBOP	n pl. **-S** a type of music
REBORN	adj born again
REBOUND	v **-ED, -ING, -S** to spring back
REBOZO	n pl. **-ZOS** a long scarf
REBRANCH	v **-ED, -ING, -ES** to form secondary branches
REBRAND	v **-ED, -ING, -S** to change the corporate image of a company
REBUFF	v **-ED, -ING, -S** to reject or refuse curtly
REBUKE	v **-BUKED, -BUKING, -BUKES** to criticize sharply
REBUKER	n pl. **-S** one that rebukes
REBURIAL	n pl. **-S** a second burial
REBUS	n pl. **-ES** a type of puzzle
REBUT	v **-BUTTED, -BUTTING, -BUTS** to refute
REBUTTAL	n pl. **-S** argument or proof that rebuts
REBUTTER	n pl. **-S** one that rebuts

List of self-explanatory verbs containing the prefix RE- (continued):

REASSURE	v **-SURED, -SURING, -SURES**	REBID	v **-BID, -BIDDEN, -BIDDING, -BIDS**	REBORE	v **-BORED, -BORING, -BORES**
REATTACH	v **-ED, -ING, -ES**	REBILL	v **-ED, -ING, -S**		
REATTACK	v **-ED, -ING, -S**	REBIND	v **-BOUND, -BINDING, -BINDS**	REBOTTLE	v **-TLED, -TLING, -TLES**
REATTAIN	v **-ED, -ING, -S**			REBOUGHT	past tense of rebuy
REAVAIL	v **-ED, -ING, -S**	REBLEND	v **-BLENDED** or **-BLENT, -BLENDING, -BLENDS**		
REAVOW	v **-ED, -ING, -S**			REBOUND	past tense of rebind
REAWAKE	v **-AWAKED** or **-AWOKE, -AWOKEN, -AWAKING, -AWAKES**	REBLOOM	v **-ED, -ING, -S**	REBREED	v **-BRED, -BREEDING, -BREEDS**
		REBOARD	v **-ED, -ING, -S**		
		REBODY	v **-BODIED, -BODYING, -BODIES**	REBUILD	v **-BUILT** or **-BUILDED, -BUILDING, -BUILDS**
REAWAKEN	v **-ED, -ING, -S**				
REBAIT	v **-ED, -ING, -S**	REBOIL	v **-ED, -ING, -S**		
REBEGIN	v **-GAN, -GUN, -GINNING, -GINS**	REBOOK	v **-ED, -ING, -S**		
		REBOOT	v **-ED, -ING, -S**		

REBUTTING	present participle of rebut	**RECIT**	*n* pl. **-S** the part of a story in which the events are related without enhancement
REC	*n* pl. **-S** recreation		
RECALL	*v* **-ED, -ING, -S** to call back	**RECITAL**	*n* pl. **-S** a detailed account
RECALLER	*n* pl. **-S** one that recalls	**RECITE**	*v* **-CITED, -CITING, -CITES** to declaim or say from memory
RECAMIER	*n* pl. **-S** a backless couch		
RECANT	*v* **-ED, -ING, -S** to make a formal retraction or disavowal of	**RECITER**	*n* pl. **-S** one that recites
		RECK	*v* **-ED, -ING, -S** to be concerned about
RECANTER	*n* pl. **-S** one that recants		
RECAP	*v* **-CAPPED, -CAPPING, -CAPS** to review by a brief summary	**RECKLESS**	*adj* foolishly heedless of danger
		RECKON	*v* **-ED, -ING, -S** to count or compute
RECCE	*v* **RECCED, RECCEING, RECCES** to reconnoiter		
		RECKONER	*n* pl. **-S** one that reckons
RECEDE	*v* **-CEDED, -CEDING, -CEDES** to move back or away	**RECLAIM**	*v* **-ED, -ING, -S** to make suitable for cultivation or habitation
RECEIPT	*v* **-ED, -ING, -S** to mark as having been paid	**RECLAME**	*n* pl. **-S** publicity
		RECLINE	*v* **-CLINED, -CLINING, -CLINES** to lean or lie back
RECEIVE	*v* **-CEIVED, -CEIVING, -CEIVES** to come into possession of		
		RECLINER	*n* pl. **-S** one that reclines
RECEIVER	*n* pl. **-S** one that receives	**RECLUSE**	*n* pl. **-S** one who lives in solitude and seclusion
RECENCY	*n* pl. **-CIES** the state of being recent		
		RECOIL	*v* **-ED, -ING, -S** to draw back in fear or disgust
RECENT	*adj* **-CENTER, -CENTEST** of or pertaining to a time not long past **RECENTLY** *adv*		
		RECOILER	*n* pl. **-S** one that recoils
		RECON	*v* **-CONNED, -CONNING, -CONS** to reconnoiter
RECEPT	*n* pl. **-S** a type of mental image		
RECEPTOR	*n* pl. **-S** a nerve ending specialized to receive stimuli	**RECONVEY**	*v* **-ED, -ING, -S** to convey back to a previous position
RECESS	*v* **-ED, -ING, -ES** to place in a receding space or hollow	**RECORD**	*v* **-ED, -ING, -S** to set down for preservation
RECHEAT	*n* pl. **-S** a hunting call	**RECORDER**	*n* pl. **-S** one that records
RECIPE	*n* pl. **-S** a set of instructions for making something	**RECOUNT**	*v* **-ED, -ING, -S** to relate in detail
		RECOUP	*v* **-ED, -ING, -S** to get back the equivalent of
RECISION	*n* pl. **-S** a cancellation		

List of self-explanatory verbs containing the prefix RE- (continued):

REBURY	*v* **-BURIED, -BURYING, -BURIES**	**RECHANGE**	*v* **-CHANGED, -CHANGING, -CHANGES**	**RECLASP**	*v* **-ED, -ING, -S**
				RECLEAN	*v* **-ED, -ING, -S**
REBUTTON	*v* **-ED, -ING, -S**	**RECHARGE**	*v* **-CHARGED, -CHARGING, -CHARGES**	**RECLOTHE**	*v* **-CLOTHED** or **-CLAD, -CLOTHING, -CLOTHES**
REBUY	*v* **-BOUGHT, -BUYING, -BUYS**				
		RECHART	*v* **-ED, -ING, -S**		
RECANE	*v* **-CANED, -CANING, -CANES**	**RECHECK**	*v* **-ED, -ING, -S**	**RECOAL**	*v* **-ED, -ING, -S**
		RECHEW	*v* **-ED, -ING, -S**	**RECOAT**	*v* **-ED, -ING, -S**
		RECHOOSE	*v* **-CHOSE, -CHOSEN, -CHOOSING, -CHOOSES**	**RECOCK**	*v* **-ED, -ING, -S**
RECARPET	*v* **-ED, -ING, -S**			**RECODE**	*v* **-CODED, -CODING, -CODES**
RECARRY	*v* **-RIED, -RYING, -RIES**				
				RECODIFY	*v* **-FIED, -FYING, -FIES**
RECAST	*v* **-CAST, -CASTING, -CASTS**	**RECIRCLE**	*v* **-CLED, -CLING, -CLES**		
				RECOIN	*v* **-ED, -ING, -S**
		RECLAD	*v* **-CLADDED, -CLADDING, -CLADS**	**RECOLOR**	*v* **-ED, -ING, -S**
RECEMENT	*v* **-ED, -ING, -S**			**RECOLOUR**	*v* **-ED, -ING, -S**
RECENSOR	*v* **-ED, -ING, -S**			**RECOMB**	*v* **-ED, -ING, -S**

RECOUPE	*adj* divided twice
RECOURSE	*n* pl. **-S** a turning or applying to someone or something for aid
RECOVER	*v* **-ED, -ING, -S** to obtain again after losing
RECOVERY	*n* pl. **-ERIES** an economic upturn
RECREANT	*n* pl. **-S** a coward
RECREATE	*v* **-ATED, -ATING, -ATES** to refresh mentally or physically
RECRUIT	*v* **-ED, -ING, -S** to engage for military service
RECTA	a pl. of rectum
RECTAL	*adj* pertaining to the rectum **RECTALLY** *adv*
RECTI	pl. of rectus
RECTIFY	*v* **-FIED, -FYING, -FIES** to correct
RECTO	*n* pl. **-TOS** a right-hand page of a book
RECTOR	*n* pl. **-S** a clergyman in charge of a parish
RECTORY	*n* pl. **-RIES** a rector's dwelling
RECTRIX	*n* pl. **-TRICES** a feather of a bird's tail
RECTUM	*n* pl. **-TUMS** or **-TA** the terminal portion of the large intestine
RECTUS	*n* pl. **-TI** a straight muscle
RECUR	*v* **-CURRED, -CURRING, -CURS** to happen again
RECURVE	*v* **-CURVED, -CURVING, -CURVES** to curve backward or downward
RECUSAL	*n* pl. **-S** the act of recusing
RECUSANT	*n* pl. **-S** one who refuses to accept established authority
RECUSE	*v* **-CUSED, -CUSING, -CUSES** to disqualify or challenge as judge in a particular case
RECYCLE	*v* **-CLED, -CLING, -CLES** to process in order to extract useful materials
RECYCLER	*n* pl. **-S** one that recycles
RED	*adj* **REDDER, REDDEST** of the color of blood
RED	*v* **REDDED, REDDING, REDS** to redd
REDACT	*v* **-ED, -ING, -S** to prepare for publication
REDACTOR	*n* pl. **-S** one that redacts
REDAN	*n* pl. **-S** a type of fortification
REDARGUE	*v* **-GUED, -GUING, -GUES** to disprove
REDBAIT	*v* **-ED, -ING, -S** to denounce as Communist
REDBAY	*n* pl. **-BAYS** a small tree
REDBIRD	*n* pl. **-S** a bird with red plumage
REDBONE	*n* pl. **-S** a hunting dog
REDBRICK	*n* pl. **-S** a modern British university
REDBUD	*n* pl. **-S** a small tree
REDBUG	*n* pl. **-S** a chigger
REDCAP	*n* pl. **-S** a porter
REDCOAT	*n* pl. **-S** a British soldier during the American Revolution
REDD	*v* **-ED, -ING, -S** to put in order
REDDED	past tense of red and redd
REDDEN	*v* **-ED, -ING, -S** to make or become red
REDDER	*n* pl. **-S** one that redds

List of self-explanatory verbs containing the prefix RE- (continued):

RECOMMIT	*v* **-MITTED, -MITTING, -MITS**	**REDAMAGE**	*v* **-AGED, -AGING, -AGES**	**REDIAL**	*v* **-DIALED, -DIALING, -DIALS** or **-DIALLED, -DIALLING, -DIALS**
RECONFER	*v* **-FERRED, -FERRING, -FERS**	**REDATE**	*v* **-DATED, -DATING, -DATES**		
RECOOK	*v* **-ED, -ING, -S**	**REDECIDE**	*v* **-CIDED, -CIDING, -CIDES**	**REDID**	past tense of redo
RECOPY	*v* **-COPIED, -COPYING, -COPIES**	**REDEFEAT**	*v* **-ED, -ING, -S**	**REDIGEST**	*v* **-ED, -ING, -S**
		REDEFECT	*v* **-ED, -ING, -S**	**REDIP**	*v* **-DIPPED** or **-DIPT, -DIPPING, -DIPS**
RECORK	*v* **-ED, -ING, -S**	**REDEFINE**	*v* **-FINED, -FINING, -FINES**		
RECOUPLE	*v* **-PLED, -PLING, -PLES**	**REDEFY**	*v* **-FIED, -FYING, -FIES**	**REDIVIDE**	*v* **-VIDED, -VIDING, -VIDES**
RECRATE	*v* **-CRATED, -CRATING, -CRATES**	**REDEMAND**	*v* **-ED, -ING, -S**	**REDO**	*v* **-DID, -DONE, -DOING, -DOES**
RECROSS	*v* **-ED, -ING, -ES**	**REDENY**	*v* **-NIED, -NYING, -NIES**	**REDOCK**	*v* **-ED, -ING, -S**
RECROWN	*v* **-ED, -ING, -S**	**REDEPLOY**	*v* **-ED, -ING, -S**	**REDON**	*v* **-DONNED, -DONNING, -DONS**
RECUT	*v* **-CUT, -CUTTING, -CUTS**	**REDESIGN**	*v* **-ED, -ING, -S**		

REDDEST	superlative of red	**REDOLENT**	*adj* fragrant
REDDIER	comparative of reddy	**REDOUBLE**	*v* **-BLED, -BLING, -BLES** to double
REDDIEST	superlative of reddy		
REDDING	present participle of red and redd	**REDOUBT**	*n* pl. **-S** an enclosed fortification
REDDISH	*adj* somewhat red	**REDOUND**	*v* **-ED, -ING, -S** to have an effect
REDDLE	*v* **-DLED, -DLING, -DLES** to ruddle	**REDOUT**	*n* pl. **-S** a condition in which blood is driven to the head
REDDY	*adj* **REDDIER, REDDIEST** reddish	**REDOWA**	*n* pl. **-S** a lively dance
REDE	*v* **REDED, REDING, REDES** to advise	**REDOX**	*n* pl. **-ES** a type of chemical reaction
REDEAR	*n* pl. **-S** a common sunfish	**REDPOLL**	*n* pl. **-S** a small finch
REDEEM	*v* **-ED, -ING, -S** to buy back	**REDRAFT**	*v* **-ED, -ING, -S** to make a revised copy of
REDEEMER	*n* pl. **-S** one that redeems		
REDEYE	*n* pl. **-S** a railroad danger signal	**REDRAWER**	*n* pl. **-S** one that redraws
REDFIN	*n* pl. **-S** a freshwater fish	**REDRESS**	*v* **-ED, -ING, -ES** to set right
REDFISH	*n* pl. **-ES** an edible rockfish	**REDROOT**	*n* pl. **-S** a perennial herb
REDHEAD	*n* pl. **-S** a person with red hair	**REDSHANK**	*n* pl. **-S** a shore bird
REDHORSE	*n* pl. **-S** a freshwater fish	**REDSHIFT**	*n* pl. **-S** a displacement of the spectrum of a celestial body toward the longer wavelengths
REDIA	*n* pl. **-DIAS** or **-DIAE** the larva of certain flatworms **REDIAL** *adj*		
REDING	present participle of rede	**REDSHIRT**	*v* **-ED, -ING, -S** to keep a college athlete out of varsity play in order to extend his or her eligibility
REDIRECT	*v* **-ED, -ING, -S** to change the course or direction of		
		REDSKIN	*n* pl. **-S** a variety of peanut
REDLEG	*n* pl. **-S** a bird with red legs	**REDSTART**	*n* pl. **-S** a small songbird
REDLINE	*v* **-LINED, -LINING, -LINES** to withhold loans or insurance from certain neighborhoods	**REDTAIL**	*n* pl. **-S** a type of hawk
		REDTOP	*n* pl. **-S** a type of grass
REDLINER	*n* pl. **-S** one that redlines	**REDUCE**	*v* **-DUCED, -DUCING, -DUCES** to diminish
REDLY	*adv* with red color		
REDNESS	*n* pl. **-ES** the state of being red	**REDUCER**	*n* pl. **-S** one that reduces
REDO	*n* pl. **-DOS** something that is done again	**REDUCTOR**	*n* pl. **-S** an apparatus for the reduction of metallic ions in solution

---

List of self-explanatory verbs containing the prefix RE- (continued):

REDRAW	*v* **-DREW, -DRAWN, -DRAWING, -DRAWS**	**REDYE**	*v* **-DYED, -DYEING, -DYES**	**REENACT**	*v* **-ED, -ING, -S**
				REENDOW	*v* **-ED, -ING, -S**
		REEARN	*v* **-ED, -ING, -S**	**REENGAGE**	*v* **-GAGED, -GAGING, -GAGES**
		REECHO	*v* **-ED, -ING, -ES**		
REDREAM	*v* **-DREAMED** or **-DREAMT, -DREAMING, -DREAMS**	**REEDIT**	*v* **-ED, -ING, -S**		
		REEJECT	*v* **-ED, -ING, -S**	**REENJOY**	*v* **-ED, -ING, -S**
		REELECT	*v* **-ED, -ING, -S**	**REENLIST**	*v* **-ED, -ING, -S**
		REEMBARK	*v* **-ED, -ING, -S**	**REENROLL**	*v* **-ED, -ING, -S**
REDRILL	*v* **-ED, -ING, -S**	**REEMBODY**	*v* **-BODIED, -BODYING, -BODIES**	**REENTER**	*v* **-ED, -ING, -S**
REDRIVE	*v* **-DROVE, -DRIVEN, -DRIVING, -DRIVES**			**REEQUIP**	*v* **-EQUIPPED, -EQUIPPING, -EQUIPS**
		REEMERGE	*v* **-EMERGED, -EMERGING, -EMERGES**		
REDRY	*v* **-DRIED, -DRYING, -DRIES**			**REERECT**	*v* **-ED, -ING, -S**
		REEMIT	*v* **-EMITTED, -EMITTING, -EMITS**	**REEVOKE**	*v* **-EVOKED, -EVOKING, -EVOKES**
REDUB	*v* **-DUBBED, -DUBBING, -DUBS**				
		REEMPLOY	*v* **-ED, -ING, -S**	**REEXPEL**	*v* **-PELLED, -PELLING, -PELS**

REDUVIID	n pl. **-S** a bloodsucking insect	**REEK**	v **-ED, -ING, -S** to give off a strong, unpleasant odor
REDUX	adj brought back		
REDWARE	n pl. **-S** an edible seaweed	**REEKER**	n pl. **-S** one that reeks
REDWATER	n pl. **-S** a blood disease of cattle	**REEKY**	adj **REEKIER, REEKIEST** reeking
REDWING	n pl. **-S** a European thrush	**REEL**	v **-ED, -ING, -S** to wind on a type of rotary device **REELABLE** adj
REDWOOD	n pl. **-S** a very tall evergreen tree		
REE	n pl. **-S** the female Eurasian sandpiper	**REELER**	n pl. **-S** one that reels
		REELING	n pl. **-S** sustained noise
REEBOK	n pl. **-S** rhebok	**REENTRY**	n pl. **-TRIES** a new or second entry
REECHY	adj **REECHIER, REECHIEST** foul, rancid	**REEST**	v **-ED, -ING, -S** to balk
REED	v **-ED, -ING, -S** to fasten with reeds (the stalks of tall grasses)	**REEVE**	v **REEVED** or **ROVE, ROVEN, REEVING, REEVES** to fasten by passing through or around something
REEDBIRD	n pl. **-S** the bobolink		
REEDBUCK	n pl. **-S** an African antelope	**REF**	v **REFFED, REFFING, REFS** to referee
REEDIER	comparative of reedy	**REFACE**	v **-FACED, -FACING, -FACES** to repair the outer surface of
REEDIEST	superlative of reedy		
REEDIFY	v **-FIED, -FYING, -FIES** to rebuild	**REFECT**	v **-ED, -ING, -S** to refresh with food and drink
REEDILY	adv with a thin, piping sound	**REFEL**	v **-FELLED, -FELLING, -FELS** to reject
REEDING	n pl. **-S** a convex molding		
REEDLIKE	adj resembling a reed	**REFER**	v **-FERRED, -FERRING, -FERS** to direct to a source for help or information
REEDLING	n pl. **-S** a marsh bird		
REEDMAN	n pl. **-MEN** one who plays a reed instrument	**REFEREE**	v **-EED, -EEING, -EES** to supervise the play in certain sports
REEDY	adj **REEDIER, REEDIEST** abounding in reeds	**REFERENT**	n pl. **-S** something referred to
		REFERRAL	n pl. **-S** one that is referred
REEF	v **-ED, -ING, -S** to reduce the area of a sail **REEFABLE** adj	**REFERRED**	past tense of refer
		REFERRER	n pl. **-S** one that refers
REEFER	n pl. **-S** one that reefs	**REFERRING**	present participle of refer
REEFY	adj **REEFIER, REEFIEST** abounding in ridges of rock	**REFFED**	past tense of ref

---

List of self-explanatory verbs containing the prefix RE- (continued):

REEXPORT	v **-ED, -ING, -S**	**REFENCE**	v **-FENCED, -FENCING, -FENCES**	**REFLEW**	past tense of refly
REEXPOSE	v **-POSED, -POSING, -POSES**			**REFLIES**	present 3d person sing. of refly
		REFIGHT	v **-FOUGHT, -FIGHTING, -FIGHTS**	**REFLOAT**	v **-ED, -ING, -S**
REFALL	v **-FELL, -FALLEN, -FALLING, -FALLS**			**REFLOOD**	v **-ED, -ING, -S**
		REFIGURE	v **-URED, -URING, -URES**	**REFLOW**	v **-ED, -ING, -S**
				REFLOWER	v **-ED, -ING, -S**
		REFILE	v **-FILED, -FILING, -FILES**	**REFLY**	v **-FLEW, -FLOWN, -FLYING, -FLIES**
REFASTEN	v **-ED, -ING, -S**				
REFEED	v **-FED, -FEEDING, -FEEDS**	**REFILL**	v **-ED, -ING, -S**		
		REFILM	v **-ED, -ING, -S**	**REFOCUS**	v **-CUSED, -CUSING, -CUSES** or **-CUSSED, -CUSSING, -CUSSES**
		REFILTER	v **-ED, -ING, -S**		
		REFIND	v **-FOUND, -FINDING, -FINDS**		
REFEEL	v **-FELT, -FEELING, -FEELS**				
		REFIRE	v **-FIRED, -FIRING, -FIRES**		
REFELL	past tense of refall	**REFIX**	v **-ED, -ING, -ES**	**REFOLD**	v **-ED, -ING, -S**

REFFING	*n* pl. **-S** the work of a referee	**REFRAIN**	*v* **-ED, -ING, -S** to keep oneself back
REFINE	*v* **-FINED, -FINING, -FINES** to free from impurities	**REFRESH**	*v* **-ED, -ING, -ES** to restore the well-being and vigor of
REFINER	*n* pl. **-S** one that refines	**REFT**	a past tense of reave
REFINERY	*n* pl. **-ERIES** a place where crude material is refined	**REFUGE**	*v* **-UGED, -UGING, -UGES** to give or take shelter
REFINING	*n* pl. **-S** the process of removing impurities from something	**REFUGEE**	*n* pl. **-S** one who flees for safety
REFINISH	*v* **-ED, -ING, -ES** to give a new surface to	**REFUGIUM**	*n* pl. **-GIA** a stable area during a period of continental climactic change
REFIT	*v* **-FITTED, -FITTING, -FITS** to prepare and equip for additional use	**REFUND**	*v* **-ED, -ING, -S** to give back
REFLAG	*v* **-FLAGGED, -FLAGGING, -FLAGS** to give a new registered nationality to (a ship)	**REFUNDER**	*n* pl. **-S** one that refunds
		REFUSAL	*n* pl. **-S** the act of refusing
REFLATE	*v* **-FLATED, -FLATING, -FLATES** to inflate again	**REFUSE**	*v* **-FUSED, -FUSING, -FUSES** to express oneself as unwilling to accept, do, or comply with
REFLECT	*v* **-ED, -ING, -S** to turn or throw back from a surface	**REFUSER**	*n* pl. **-S** one that refuses
REFLET	*n* pl. **-S** special brilliance of surface	**REFUSNIK**	*n* pl. **-S** a Soviet citizen who was refused permission to emigrate
REFLEX	*v* **-ED, -ING, -ES** to bend back	**REFUTAL**	*n* pl. **-S** the act of refuting
REFLEXLY	*adv* in a reflexed manner	**REFUTE**	*v* **-FUTED, -FUTING, -FUTES** to prove to be false or erroneous
REFLUENT	*adj* flowing back	**REFUTER**	*n* pl. **-S** one that refutes
REFLUX	*v* **-ED, -ING, -ES** to cause to flow back	**REG**	*n* pl. **-S** a regulation
REFOREST	*v* **-ED, -ING, -S** to replant with trees	**REGAINER**	*n* pl. **-S** one that regains
REFORM	*v* **-ED, -ING, -S** to change to a better state	**REGAL**	*adj* of or befitting a king
		REGALE	*v* **-GALED, -GALING, -GALES** to delight
REFORMER	*n* pl. **-S** one that reforms	**REGALER**	*n* pl. **-S** one that regales
REFRACT	*v* **-ED, -ING, -S** to deflect in a particular manner, as a ray of light	**REGALIA**	*n/pl* the rights and privileges of a king
		REGALITY	*n* pl. **-TIES** regal authority

List of self-explanatory verbs containing the prefix RE- (continued):

REFORGE	*v* **-FORGED, -FORGING, -FORGES**	**REFUEL**	*v* **-ELED, -ELING, -ELS** or **-ELLED, -ELLING, -ELS**	**REGLOSS**	*v* **-ED, -ING, -ES**
				REGLOW	*v* **-ED, -ING, -S**
REFORMAT	*v* **-MATTED, -MATTING, -MATS**	**REGAIN**	*v* **-ED, -ING, -S**	**REGLUE**	*v* **-GLUED, -GLUING, -GLUES**
		REGATHER	*v* **-ED, -ING, -S**		
REFOUGHT	past tense of refight	**REGAUGE**	*v* **-GAUGED, -GAUGING, -GAUGES**	**REGRADE**	*v* **-GRADED, -GRADING, -GRADES**
REFOUND	*v* **-ED, -ING, -S**				
REFRAME	*v* **-FRAMED, -FRAMING, -FRAMES**	**REGEAR**	*v* **-ED, -ING, -S**	**REGRAFT**	*v* **-ED, -ING, -S**
		REGILD	*v* **-GILDED** or **-GILT, -GILDING, -GILDS**	**REGRANT**	*v* **-ED, -ING, -S**
				REGREEN	*v* **-ED, -ING, -S**
REFREEZE	*v* **-FROZE, -FROZEN, -FREEZING, -FREEZES**	**REGIVE**	*v* **-GAVE, -GIVEN, -GIVING, -GIVES**	**REGREW**	past tense of regrow
				REGRIND	*v* **-GROUND, -GRINDING, -GRINDS**
REFRONT	*v* **-ED, -ING, -S**	**REGLAZE**	*v* **-GLAZED, -GLAZING, -GLAZES**		
REFRY	*v* **-FRIED, -FRYING, -FRIES**			**REGROOM**	*v* **-ED, -ING, -S**

REGALLY   *adv* in a regal manner

REGARD   *v* **-ED, -ING, -S** to look upon with a particular feeling

REGATTA   *n* pl. **-S** a boat race

REGELATE   *v* **-LATED, -LATING, -LATES** to refreeze ice by reducing the pressure

REGENCY   *n* pl. **-CIES** the office of a regent

REGENT   *n* pl. **-S** one who rules in the place of a sovereign **REGENTAL** *adj*

REGES   pl. of rex

REGGAE   *n* pl. **-S** a form of popular Jamaican music

REGICIDE   *n* pl. **-S** the killing of a king

REGIE   *n* pl. **-S** a government regulatory body in Quebec

REGIFT   *v* **-ED, -ING, -S** to give a gift one has received to someone else

REGIFTER   *n* pl. **-S** one that regifts

REGIME   *n* pl. **-S** a system of government

REGIMEN   *n* pl. **-S** a systematic plan

REGIMENT   *v* **-ED, -ING, -S** to form into military units

REGINA   *n* pl. **-NAS** or **-NAE** queen **REGINAL** *adj*

REGION   *n* pl. **-S** an administrative area or division

REGIONAL   *n* pl. **-S** something that serves as a region

REGISTER   *v* **-ED, -ING, -S** to record officially

REGISTRY   *n* pl. **-TRIES** the act of registering

REGIUS   *adj* holding a professorship founded by the sovereign

REGLET   *n* pl. **-S** a flat, narrow molding

REGMA   *n* pl. **-MATA** a type of fruit

REGNA   pl. of regnum

REGNAL   *adj* pertaining to a king or his reign

REGNANCY   *n* pl. **-CIES** the state of being regnant

REGNANT   *adj* reigning

REGNUM   *n* pl. **-NA** dominion

REGOLITH   *n* pl. **-S** a layer of loose rock

REGORGE   *v* **-GORGED, -GORGING, -GORGES** to vomit

REGOSOL   *n* pl. **-S** a type of soil

REGRATE   *v* **-GRATED, -GRATING, -GRATES** to buy up in order to sell for a higher price in the same area

REGREET   *v* **-ED, -ING, -S** to greet in return

REGRESS   *v* **-ED, -ING, -ES** to go back

REGRET   *v* **-GRETTED, -GRETTING, -GRETS** to look back upon with sorrow or remorse

REGROWTH   *n* pl. **-S** a new or second growth

REGULAR   *n* pl. **-S** a habitual customer

REGULATE   *v* **-LATED, -LATING, -LATES** to control according to rule

REGULUS   *n* pl. **-LUSES** or **-LI** a mass that forms beneath the slag in a furnace **REGULINE** *adj*

REHAB   *v* **-HABBED, -HABBING, -HABS** to restore to a good condition

REHABBER   *n* pl. **-S** one that rehabs

REHEARSE   *v* **-HEARSED, -HEARSING, -HEARSES** to practice in preparation for a public appearance

---

List of self-explanatory verbs containing the prefix RE- (continued):

REGROOVE	*v* **-GROOVED, -GROOVING, -GROOVES**	**REHASH**	*v* **-ED, -ING, -ES**	**REIMAGE**	*v* **-AGED, -AGING, -AGES**
REGROUND	past tense of regrind	**REHEAR**	*v* **-HEARD, -HEARING, -HEARS**	**REIMPORT**	*v* **-ED, -ING, -S**
REGROUP	*v* **-ED, -ING, -S**	**REHEAT**	*v* **-ED, -ING, -S**	**REIMPOSE**	*v* **-POSED, -POSING, -POSES**
REGROW	*v* **-GREW, -GROWN, -GROWING, -GROWS**	**REHEEL**	*v* **-ED, -ING, -S**		
		REHEM	*v* **-HEMMED, -HEMMING, -HEMS**	**REINCITE**	*v* **-CITED, -CITING, -CITES**
REHAMMER	*v* **-ED, -ING, -S**			**REINCUR**	*v* **-CURRED, -CURRING, -CURS**
REHANDLE	*v* **-DLED, -DLING, -DLES**	**REHINGE**	*v* **-HINGED, -HINGING, -HINGES**		
				REINDEX	*v* **-ED, -ING, -ES**
REHANG	*v* **-HUNG** or **-HANGED, -HANGING, -HANGS**	**REHIRE**	*v* **-HIRED, -HIRING, -HIRES**	**REINDICT**	*v* **-ED, -ING, -S**
		REHUNG	a past tense of rehang	**REINDUCE**	*v* **-DUCED, -DUCING, -DUCES**
REHARDEN	*v* **-ED, -ING, -S**	**REIGNITE**	*v* **-NITED, -NITING, -NITES**	**REINDUCT**	*v* **-ED, -ING, -S**
				REINFECT	*v* **-ED, -ING, -S**

REHEATER	*n* pl. **-S** one that reheats	**REJECTER**	*n* pl. **-S** one that rejects
REHOBOAM	*n* pl. **-S** a wine bottle	**REJECTOR**	*n* pl. **-S** rejecter
REHOUSE	*v* **-HOUSED, -HOUSING, -HOUSES** to establish in a new housing unit	**REJIG**	*v* **-JIGGED, -JIGGING, -JIGS** to rejigger
		REJIGGER	*v* **-ED, -ING, -S** to alter
REI	*n* pl. **-S** an erroneous English form for a former Portuguese coin	**REJOICE**	*v* **-JOICED, -JOICING, -JOICES** to feel joyful
REIF	*n* pl. **-S** robbery	**REJOICER**	*n* pl. **-S** one that rejoices
REIFIER	*n* pl. **-S** one that reifies	**RELAPSE**	*v* **-LAPSED, -LAPSING, -LAPSES** to fall or slip back into a former state
REIFY	*v* **-IFIED, -IFYING, -IFIES** to regard as real or concrete		
REIGN	*v* **-ED, -ING, -S** to exercise sovereign power	**RELAPSER**	*n* pl. **-S** one that relapses
REIKI	*n* pl. **-S** a healing technique involving touching with the hands	**RELATE**	*v* **-LATED, -LATING, -LATES** to give an account of
		RELATER	*n* pl. **-S** one that relates
REIN	*v* **-ED, -ING, -S** to restrain	**RELATION**	*n* pl. **-S** a significant association between two or more things
REINDEER	*n* pl. **-S** a large deer		
REINJURY	*n* pl. **-RIES** a second injury	**RELATIVE**	*n* pl. **-S** one who is connected with another by blood or marriage
REINLESS	*adj* unrestrained		
REINSMAN	*n* pl. **-MEN** a skilled rider of horses	**RELATOR**	*n* pl. **-S** relater
REIS	pl. of real	**RELAX**	*v* **-ED, -ING, -ES** to make less tense or rigid
REISHI	*n* pl. **-S** a mushroom having a shiny cap		
		RELAXANT	*n* pl. **-S** a drug that relieves muscular tension
REISSUER	*n* pl. **-S** one that reissues		
REITBOK	*n* pl. **-S** the reedbuck	**RELAXER**	*n* pl. **-S** one that relaxes
REIVE	*v* **REIVED, REIVING, REIVES** to plunder	**RELAXIN**	*n* pl. **-S** a female hormone
		RELAY	*v* **-ED, -ING, -S** to send along by using fresh sets to replace tired ones
REIVER	*n* pl. **-S** one that reives		
REIVING	*n* pl. **-S** an act or instance of plundering		
		RELEASE	*v* **-LEASED, -LEASING, -LEASES** to set free
REJECT	*v* **-ED, -ING, -S** to refuse to accept, consider, or make use of		
		RELEASEE	*n* pl. **-S** one that is released
REJECTEE	*n* pl. **-S** one that is rejected	**RELEASER**	*n* pl. **-S** one that releases

List of self-explanatory verbs containing the prefix RE- (continued):

REINFORM	*v* **-ED, -ING, -S**	**REINVITE**	*v* **-VITED, -VITING, -VITES**	**REKNIT**	*v* **-KNITTED, -KNITTING, -KNITS**
REINFUSE	*v* **-FUSED, -FUSING, -FUSES**				
		REINVOKE	*v* **-VOKED, -VOKING, -VOKES**		
REINJECT	*v* **-ED, -ING, -S**			**REKNOT**	*v* **-KNOTTED, -KNOTTING, -KNOTS**
REINJURE	*v* **-JURED, -JURING, -JURES**				
		REISSUE	*v* **-SUED, -SUING, -SUES**		
REINK	*v* **-ED, -ING, -S**			**RELABEL**	*v* **-BELED, -BELING, -BELS** or **-BELLED, -BELLING, -BELS**
REINSERT	*v* **-ED, -ING, -S**	**REJACKET**	*v* **-ED, -ING, -S**		
REINSURE	*v* **-SURED, -SURING, -SURES**	**REJOIN**	*v* **-ED, -ING, -S**		
		REJUDGE	*v* **-JUDGED, -JUDGING, -JUDGES**		
REINTER	*v* **-TERRED, -TERRING, -TERS**			**RELACE**	*v* **-LACED, -LACING, -LACES**
		REJUGGLE	*v* **-GLED, -GLING, -GLES**		
REINVADE	*v* **-VADED, -VADING, -VADES**			**RELAND**	*v* **-ED, -ING, -S**
		REKEY	*v* **-ED, -ING, -S**	**RELAUNCH**	*v* **-ED, -ING, -ES**
REINVENT	*v* **-ED, -ING, -S**	**REKINDLE**	*v* **-DLED, -DLING, -DLES**	**RELAY**	*v* **-LAID, -LAYING, -LAYS**
REINVEST	*v* **-ED, -ING, -S**				

RELEASOR	*n* pl. **-S** releaser
RELEGATE	*v* **-GATED, -GATING, -GATES** to assign
RELENT	*v* **-ED, -ING, -S** to become less severe
RELEVANT	*adj* pertaining to the matter at hand
RELEVE	*n* pl. **-S** a raising onto the toe in ballet
RELIABLE	*n* pl. **-S** one that can be relied on
RELIABLY	*adv* in a manner that can be relied on
RELIANCE	*n* pl. **-S** confident or trustful dependence
RELIANT	*adj* showing reliance
RELIC	*n* pl. **-S** a surviving memorial of something past
RELICT	*n* pl. **-S** an organism surviving in a changed environment
RELIED	past tense of rely
RELIEF	*n* pl. **-S** aid in the form of money or necessities
RELIER	*n* pl. **-S** one that relies
RELIES	present 3d person sing. of rely
RELIEVE	*v* **-LIEVED, -LIEVING, -LIEVES** to lessen or free from pain or discomfort
RELIEVER	*n* pl. **-S** one that relieves
RELIEVO	*n* pl. **-VOS** the projection of figures or forms from a flat background
RELIGION	*n* pl. **-S** the worship of a god or the supernatural
RELIQUE	*n* pl. **-S** relic
RELISH	*v* **-ED, -ING, -ES** to enjoy

RELIVE	*v* **-LIVED, -LIVING, -LIVES** to experience again
RELLENO	*n* pl. **-S** a Mexican dish of a stuffed and fried green chile
RELOADER	*n* pl. **-S** one that reloads
RELOCATE	*v* **-CATED, -CATING, -CATES** to establish in a new place
RELUCENT	*adj* reflecting light
RELUCT	*v* **-ED, -ING, -S** to show opposition
RELUME	*v* **-LUMED, -LUMING, -LUMES** to light again
RELUMINE	*v* **-MINED, -MINING, -MINES** to relume
RELY	*v* **-LIED, -LYING, -LIES** to place trust or confidence
REM	*n* pl. **-S** a quantity of ionizing radiation
REMAILER	*n* pl. **-S** an Internet service that forwards email anonymously
REMAIN	*v* **-ED, -ING, -S** to continue in the same state
REMAKER	*n* pl. **-S** one that remakes
REMAN	*v* **-MANNED, -MANNING, -MANS** to furnish with a fresh supply of men
REMAND	*v* **-ED, -ING, -S** to send back
REMANENT	*adj* remaining
REMANNED	past tense of reman
REMANNING	present participle of reman
REMARK	*v* **-ED, -ING, -S** to say or write briefly or casually
REMARKER	*n* pl. **-S** one that remarks
REMARQUE	*n* pl. **-S** a mark made in the margin of an engraved plate

---

List of self-explanatory verbs containing the prefix RE- (continued):

RELEARN	*v* **-LEARNED** or **-LEARNT, -LEARNING, -LEARNS**	**RELIT**	a past tense of relight	**REMATE**	*v* **-MATED, -MATING, -MATES**
RELEND	*v* **-LENT, -LENDING, -LENDS**	**RELOAD**	*v* **-ED, -ING, -S**	**REMEET**	*v* **-MET, -MEETING, -MEETS**
		RELOAN	*v* **-ED, -ING, -S**		
		RELOCK	*v* **-ED, -ING, -S**		
RELET	*v* **-LET, -LETTING, -LETS**	**RELOOK**	*v* **-ED, -ING, -S**	**REMELT**	*v* **-ED, -ING, -S**
		REMAIL	*v* **-ED, -ING, -S**	**REMEND**	*v* **-ED, -ING, -S**
RELETTER	*v* **-ED, -ING, -S**	**REMAKE**	*v* **-MADE, -MAKING, -MAKES**	**REMERGE**	*v* **-MERGED, -MERGING, -MERGES**
RELIGHT	*v* **-LIGHTED** or **-LIT, -LIGHTING, -LIGHTS**	**REMAP**	*v* **-MAPPED, -MAPPING, -MAPS**	**REMET**	past tense of remeet
RELINE	*v* **-LINED, -LINING, -LINES**	**REMARKET**	*v* **-ED, -ING, -S**	**REMIX**	*v* **-MIXED** or **-MIXT, -MIXING, -MIXES**
		REMARRY	*v* **-RIED, -RYING, -RIES**		
RELINK	*v* **-ED, -ING, -S**			**REMODIFY**	*v* **-FIED, -FYING, -FIES**
RELIST	*v* **-ED, -ING, -S**	**REMASTER**	*v* **-ED, -ING, -S**		
RELISTEN	*v* **-ED, -ING, -S**	**REMATCH**	*v* **-ED, -ING, -ES**	**REMOLD**	*v* **-ED, -ING, -S**

REMEDIAL	*adj* intended to correct something	**REMOTE**	*n* pl. **-S** a broadcast originating outside a studio
REMEDY	*v* **-DIED, -DYING, -DIES** to relieve or cure	**REMOTION**	*n* pl. **-S** the act of removing
REMEMBER	*v* **-ED, -ING, -S** to bring to mind again	**REMOVAL**	*n* pl. **-S** the act of removing
REMEX	*n* pl. **REMIGES** a flight feather of a bird's wing **REMIGIAL** *adj*	**REMOVE**	*v* **-MOVED, -MOVING, -MOVES** to take or move away
REMIND	*v* **-ED, -ING, -S** to cause to remember	**REMOVER**	*n* pl. **-S** one that removes
		REMUDA	*n* pl. **-S** a herd of horses
REMINDER	*n* pl. **-S** one that reminds	**RENAL**	*adj* pertaining to the kidneys
REMINT	*v* **-ED, -ING, -S** to melt down and make into new coin	**RENATURE**	*v* **-TURED, -TURING, -TURES** to restore natural qualities
REMISE	*v* **-MISED, -MISING, -MISES** to give up a claim to	**REND**	*v* **RENT** or **RENDED, RENDING, RENDS** to tear apart forcibly
REMISS	*adj* careless **REMISSLY** *adv*	**RENDER**	*v* **-ED, -ING, -S** to cause to be or become
REMIT	*v* **-MITTED, -MITTING, -MITS** to send money in payment	**RENDERER**	*n* pl. **-S** one that renders
REMITTAL	*n* pl. **-S** the act of remitting	**RENDIBLE**	*adj* capable of being rent
REMITTER	*n* pl. **-S** one that remits	**RENDZINA**	*n* pl. **-S** a type of soil
REMITTOR	*n* pl. **-S** remitter	**RENEGADE**	*v* **-GADED, -GADING, -GADES** to become a traitor
REMIXER	*n* pl. **-S** one that remixes (as a recording)	**RENEGADO**	*n* pl. **-DOS** or **-DOES** a traitor
REMNANT	*n* pl. **-S** something remaining	**RENEGE**	*v* **-NEGED, -NEGING, -NEGES** to fail to carry out a promise or commitment
REMODEL	*v* **-ELED, -ELING, -ELS** or **-ELLED, -ELLING, -ELS** to make over	**RENEGER**	*n* pl. **-S** one that reneges
REMOLADE	*n* pl. **-S** a piquant sauce	**RENEGUE**	*v* **-NEGUED, -NEGUING, -NEGUES** to renege
REMORA	*n* pl. **-S** a type of marine fish **REMORID** *adj*	**RENEW**	*v* **-ED, -ING, -S** to make new or as if new again
REMORSE	*n* pl. **-S** deep anguish caused by a sense of guilt	**RENEWAL**	*n* pl. **-S** the act of renewing
		RENEWER	*n* pl. **-S** one that renews
REMOTE	*adj* **-MOTER, -MOTEST** situated far away **REMOTELY** *adv*	**RENIFORM**	*adj* kidney-shaped

---

List of self-explanatory verbs containing the prefix RE- (continued):

REMOULD	*v* **-ED, -ING, -S**	**REOIL**	*v* **-ED, -ING, -S**	**REPARK**	*v* **-ED, -ING, -S**
REMOUNT	*v* **-ED, -ING, -S**	**REOPEN**	*v* **-ED, -ING, -S**	**REPASS**	*v* **-ED, -ING, -ES**
RENAIL	*v* **-ED, -ING, -S**	**REOPPOSE**	*v* **-POSED,**	**REPATCH**	*v* **-ED, -ING, -ES**
RENAME	*v* **-NAMED, -NAMING, -NAMES**		**-POSING, -POSES**	**REPAVE**	*v* **-PAVED, -PAVING, -PAVES**
		REORDAIN	*v* **-ED, -ING, -S**	**REPEG**	*v* **-PEGGED,**
RENEST	*v* **-ED, -ING, -S**	**REORDER**	*v* **-ED, -ING, -S**		**-PEGGING, -PEGS**
RENOTIFY	*v* **-FIED, -FYING, -FIES**	**REORIENT**	*v* **-ED, -ING, -S**		
		REOUTFIT	*v* **-FITTED, -FITTING, -FITS**	**REPEOPLE**	*v* **-PLED, -PLING, -PLES**
RENUMBER	*v* **-ED, -ING, -S**				
REOBJECT	*v* **-ED, -ING, -S**	**REPACIFY**	*v* **-FIED, -FYING, -FIES**	**REPERK**	*v* **-ED, -ING, -S**
REOBTAIN	*v* **-ED, -ING, -S**			**REPHRASE**	*v* **-PHRASED,**
REOCCUPY	*v* **-PIED, -PYING, -PIES**	**REPACK**	*v* **-ED, -ING, -S**		**-PHRASING, -PHRASES**
		REPAINT	*v* **-ED, -ING, -S**		
REOCCUR	*v* **-CURRED, -CURRING, -CURS**	**REPANEL**	*v* **-ELED, -ELING, -ELS** or **-ELLED, -ELLING, -ELS**	**REPIN**	*v* **-PINNED, -PINNING, -PINS**
REOFFEND	*v* **-ED, -ING, -S**	**REPAPER**	*v* **-ED, -ING, -S**		

RENIG	*v* **-NIGGED, -NIGGING, -NIGS** to renege	**REP**	*v* **REPPED, REPPING, REPS** to represent
RENIN	*n* pl. **-S** an enzyme	**REPAID**	past tense of repay
RENITENT	*adj* resisting physical pressure	**REPAIR**	*v* **-ED, -ING, -S** to restore to good condition
RENMINBI	*n* pl. **RENMINBI** currency in the People's Republic of China	**REPAIRER**	*n* pl. **-S** one that repairs
RENNASE	*n* pl. **-S** rennin	**REPAND**	*adj* having a wavy margin **REPANDLY** *adv*
RENNET	*n* pl. **-S** a lining membrane in the stomach of certain young animals	**REPARTEE**	*n* pl. **-S** a quick, witty reply
RENNIN	*n* pl. **-S** an enzyme	**REPAST**	*v* **-ED, -ING, -S** to eat or feast
RENO	*n* pl. **RENOS** a renovated house	**REPAY**	*v* **-PAID, -PAYING, -PAYS** to pay back
RENOGRAM	*n* pl. **-S** a photographic depiction of the course of renal excretion	**REPEAL**	*v* **-ED, -ING, -S** to revoke
RENOUNCE	*v* **-NOUNCED, -NOUNCING, -NOUNCES** to disown	**REPEALER**	*n* pl. **-S** one that repeals
RENOVATE	*v* **-VATED, -VATING, -VATES** to make like new	**REPEAT**	*v* **-ED, -ING, -S** to say or do again
		REPEATER	*n* pl. **-S** one that repeats
RENOWN	*v* **-ED, -ING, -S** to make famous	**REPEL**	*v* **-PELLED, -PELLING, -PELS** to drive back
RENT	*v* **-ED, -ING, -S** to obtain temporary use of in return for compensation **RENTABLE** *adj*	**REPELLER**	*n* pl. **-S** one that repels
		REPENT	*v* **-ED, -ING, -S** to feel remorse or self-reproach for a past action
RENTAL	*n* pl. **-S** an amount paid or collected as rent	**REPENTER**	*n* pl. **-S** one that repents
RENTE	*n* pl. **-S** annual income under French law	**REPETEND**	*n* pl. **-S** a phrase or sound that is repeated
RENTER	*n* pl. **-S** one that rents	**REPINE**	*v* **-PINED, -PINING, -PINES** to express discontent
RENTIER	*n* pl. **-S** one that receives a fixed income	**REPINER**	*n* pl. **-S** one that repines
RENVOI	*n* pl. **-S** the expulsion by a government of an alien	**REPLACE**	*v* **-PLACED, -PLACING, -PLACES** to take the place of
REOFFER	*v* **-ED, -ING, -S** to offer for public sale	**REPLACER**	*n* pl. **-S** one that replaces
		REPLETE	*n* pl. **-S** a worker ant that serves as a living storehouse for liquid food
REORG	*v* **-ED, -ING, -S** to reorganize		
REOVIRUS	*n* pl. **-ES** a type of virus	**REPLEVIN**	*v* **-ED, -ING, -S** to replevy

---

List of self-explanatory verbs containing the prefix RE- (continued):

REPLAN	*v* **-PLANNED, -PLANNING, -PLANS**	**REPLOW**	*v* **-ED, -ING, -S**	**REPROBE**	*v* **-PROBED, -PROBING, -PROBES**
REPLANT	*v* **-ED, -ING, -S**	**REPLUMB**	*v* **-ED, -ING, -S**		
REPLATE	*v* **-PLATED, -PLATING, -PLATES**	**REPLUNGE**	*v* **-PLUNGED, -PLUNGING, -PLUNGES**	**REPUMP**	*v* **-ED, -ING, -S**
				REPURIFY	*v* **-FIED, -FYING, -FIES**
REPLAY	*v* **-ED, -ING, -S**	**REPOINT**	*v* **-ED, -ING, -S**	**REPURSUE**	*v* **-SUED, -SUING, -SUES**
REPLEAD	*v* **-PLEADED** or **-PLED, -PLEADING, -PLEADS**	**REPOLISH**	*v* **-ED, -ING, -ES**		
		REPOLL	*v* **-ED, -ING, -S**	**RERACK**	*v* **-ED, -ING, -S**
		REPOT	*v* **-POTTED, -POTTING, -POTS**	**RERAISE**	*v* **-RAISED, -RAISING, -RAISES**
REPLEDGE	*v* **-PLEDGED, -PLEDGING, -PLEDGES**	**REPOUR**	*v* **-ED, -ING, -S**	**REREAD**	*v* **-READ, -READING, -READS**
		REPOWER	*v* **-ED, -ING, -S**		
REPLOT	*v* **-PLOTTED, -PLOTTING, -PLOTS**	**REPRICE**	*v* **-PRICED, -PRICING, -PRICES**	**RERECORD**	*v* **-ED, -ING, -S**
				REREMIND	*v* **-ED, -ING, -S**
		REPRINT	*v* **-ED, -ING, -S**	**RERENT**	*v* **-ED, -ING, -S**

REPLEVY	*v* **-PLEVIED, -PLEVYING, -PLEVIES** to regain possession of by legal action
REPLICA	*n* pl. **-S** a close copy or reproduction
REPLICON	*n* pl. **-S** a section of nucleic acid that replicates as a unit
REPLIER	*n* pl. **-S** one that replies
REPLY	*v* **-PLIED, -PLYING, -PLIES** to answer
REPO	*n* pl. **-POS** something repossessed
REPORT	*v* **-ED, -ING, -S** to give an account of
REPORTER	*n* pl. **-S** one that reports
REPOSAL	*n* pl. **-S** the act of reposing
REPOSE	*v* **-POSED, -POSING, -POSES** to lie at rest
REPOSER	*n* pl. **-S** one that reposes
REPOSIT	*v* **-ED, -ING, -S** to put away
REPOUSSE	*n* pl. **-S** a raised design hammered in metal
REPP	*n* pl. **-S** a cross-ribbed fabric
REPPED	*adj* resembling repp
REPRESS	*v* **-ED, -ING, -ES** to keep under control
REPRIEVE	*v* **-PRIEVED, -PRIEVING, -PRIEVES** to postpone the punishment of
REPRISAL	*n* pl. **-S** an act of retaliation
REPRISE	*v* **-PRISED, -PRISING, -PRISES** to take back by force
REPRO	*n* pl. **-PROS** a trial sheet of printed material suitable for photographic reproduction
REPROACH	*v* **-ED, -ING, -ES** to find fault with
REPROOF	*n* pl. **-S** criticism for a fault
REPROVAL	*n* pl. **-S** reproof
REPROVE	*v* **-PROVED, -PROVING, -PROVES** to rebuke
REPROVER	*n* pl. **-S** one that reproves
REPTANT	*adj* creeping or crawling
REPTILE	*n* pl. **-S** any of a class of cold-blooded, air-breathing vertebrates
REPTILIA	*n/pl* buildings for housing reptiles
REPUBLIC	*n* pl. **-S** a constitutional form of government
REPUGN	*v* **-ED, -ING, -S** to oppose
REPULSE	*v* **-PULSED, -PULSING, -PULSES** to drive back
REPULSER	*n* pl. **-S** one that repulses
REPUTE	*v* **-PUTED, -PUTING, -PUTES** to consider to be as specified
REQUEST	*v* **-ED, -ING, -S** to express a desire for
REQUIEM	*n* pl. **-S** a musical composition for the dead
REQUIN	*n* pl. **-S** a voracious shark
REQUINTO	*n* pl. **-TOS** a small guitar
REQUIRE	*v* **-QUIRED, -QUIRING, -QUIRES** to have need of
REQUIRER	*n* pl. **-S** one that requires
REQUITAL	*n* pl. **-S** something given in return, compensation, or retaliation
REQUITE	*v* **-QUITED, -QUITING, -QUITES** to make equivalent return for
REQUITER	*n* pl. **-S** one that requites
RERAN	past tense of rerun

List of self-explanatory verbs containing the prefix RE- (continued):

REREPEAT	*v* **-ED, -ING, -S**	**RESAMPLE**	*v* **-PLED, -PLING, -PLES**	**RESECURE**	*v* **-CURED, -CURING, -CURES**
REREVIEW	*v* **-ED, -ING, -S**	**RESAT**	past tense of resit		
RERIG	*v* **-RIGGED, -RIGGING, -RIGS**	**RESAW**	*v* **-SAWED, -SAWN, -SAWING, -SAWS**	**RESEE**	*v* **-SAW, -SEEN, -SEEING, -SEES**
RERISE	*v* **-ROSE, -RISEN, -RISING, -RISES**			**RESEED**	*v* **-ED, -ING, -S**
REROLL	*v* **-ED, -ING, -S**	**RESAY**	*v* **-SAID, -SAYING, -SAYS**	**RESEEK**	*v* **-SOUGHT, -SEEKING, -SEEKS**
REROOF	*v* **-ED, -ING, -S**				
REROSE	past tense of rerise	**RESCHOOL**	*v* **-ED, -ING, -S**		
REROUTE	*v* **-ROUTED, -ROUTING, -ROUTES**	**RESCORE**	*v* **-SCORED, -SCORING, -SCORES**	**RESEEN**	past participle of resee
				RESEIZE	*v* **-SEIZED, -SEIZING, -SEIZES**
RESADDLE	*v* **-DLED, -DLING, -DLES**	**RESCREEN**	*v* **-ED, -ING, -S**		
		RESCULPT	*v* **-ED, -ING, -S**	**RESELECT**	*v* **-ED, -ING, -S**
RESAID	past tense of resay	**RESEAL**	*v* **-ED, -ING, -S**	**RESELL**	*v* **-SOLD, -SELLING, -SELLS**
RESAIL	*v* **-ED, -ING, -S**	**RESEASON**	*v* **-ED, -ING, -S**		
RESALUTE	*v* **-LUTED, -LUTING, -LUTES**	**RESEAT**	*v* **-ED, -ING, -S**		

REREDOS	*n* pl. **-ES** an ornamental screen behind an altar	**RESERVER**	*n* pl. **-S** one that reserves
		RESES	pl. of res
REREMICE	*n/pl* bats (flying mammals)	**RESETTER**	*n* pl. **-S** one that resets
REREWARD	*n* pl. **-S** rearward	**RESH**	*n* pl. **-ES** a Hebrew letter
REROLLER	*n* pl. **-S** one that rerolls	**RESHAPER**	*n* pl. **-S** one that reshapes something
RERUN	*v* **-RAN, -RUNNING, -RUNS** to present a repetition of a recorded performance	**RESID**	*n* pl. **-S** a type of fuel oil
RES	*n* pl. **RESES** a university or college residence	**RESIDE**	*v* **-SIDED, -SIDING, -SIDES** to dwell permanently or continuously
RESALE	*n* pl. **-S** the act of selling again	**RESIDENT**	*n* pl. **-S** one who resides
RESCALE	*v* **-SCALED, -SCALING, -SCALES** to plan on a new scale	**RESIDER**	*n* pl. **-S** a resident
		RESIDUAL	*n* pl. **-S** something left over
RESCIND	*v* **-ED, -ING, -S** to annul	**RESIDUE**	*n* pl. **-S** something remaining after the removal of a part
RESCRIPT	*n* pl. **-S** something rewritten		
RESCUE	*v* **-CUED, -CUING, -CUES** to free from danger	**RESIDUUM**	*n* pl. **-SIDUUMS** or **-SIDUA** residue
		RESIGN	*v* **-ED, -ING, -S** to give up one's office or position
RESCUEE	*n* pl. **-S** one that is rescued		
RESCUER	*n* pl. **-S** one that rescues	**RESIGNER**	*n* pl. **-S** one that resigns
RESEARCH	*v* **-ED, -ING, -ES** to investigate thoroughly	**RESILE**	*v* **-SILED, -SILING, -SILES** to spring back
RESEAU	*n* pl. **-SEAUS** or **-SEAUX** a filter screen for making color films	**RESILIN**	*n* pl. **-S** an elastic substance in the cuticles of many insects
RESECT	*v* **-ED, -ING, -S** to excise part of an organ or structure surgically	**RESIN**	*v* **-ED, -ING, -S** to treat with resin (a viscous substance obtained from certain plants)
RESEDA	*n* pl. **-S** a flowering plant		
RESELLER	*n* pl. **-S** one that resells	**RESINATE**	*v* **-ATED, -ATING, -ATES** to resin
RESEMBLE	*v* **-BLED, -BLING, -BLES** to be similar to	**RESINIFY**	*v* **-FIED, -FYING, -FIES** to convert into resin
RESENT	*v* **-ED, -ING, -S** to feel or express annoyance or ill will at	**RESINOID**	*n* pl. **-S** a resinous substance
		RESINOUS	*adj* resembling resin
		RESINY	*adj* resinous
RESERVE	*v* **-SERVED, -SERVING, -SERVES** to keep back for future use	**RESIST**	*v* **-ED, -ING, -S** to strive against

---

List of self-explanatory verbs containing the prefix RE- (continued):

RESEND	*v* **-SENT, -SENDING, -SENDS**	**RESHINE**	*v* **-SHINED** or **-SHONE, -SHINING, -SHINES**	**RESHOW**	*v* **-SHOWED, -SHOWN, -SHOWING, -SHOWS**
RESET	*v* **-SET, -SETTING, -SETS**	**RESHIP**	*v* **-SHIPPED, -SHIPPING, -SHIPS**	**RESHOWER**	*v* **-ED, -ING, -S**
RESETTLE	*v* **-TLED, -TLING, -TLES**			**RESIFT**	*v* **-ED, -ING, -S**
				RESIGHT	*v* **-ED, -ING, -S**
				RESILVER	*v* **-ED, -ING, -S**
RESEW	*v* **-SEWED, -SEWN, -SEWING, -SEWS**	**RESHOE**	*v* **-SHOD** or **-SHOED, -SHOEING, -SHOES**	**RESIT**	*v* **-SAT, -SITTING, -SITS**
RESHAPE	*v* **-SHAPED, -SHAPING, -SHAPES**			**RESITE**	*v* **-SITED, -SITING, -SITES**
		RESHONE	a past tense of reshine	**RESIZE**	*v* **-SIZED, -SIZING, -SIZES**
RESHAVE	*v* **-SHAVED, -SHAVEN, -SHAVING, -SHAVES**	**RESHOOT**	*v* **-SHOT, -SHOOTING, -SHOOTS**	**RESKETCH**	*v* **-ED, -ING, -ES**
				RESLATE	*v* **-SLATED, -SLATING, -SLATES**

RESISTER	*n* pl. **-S** one that resists
RESISTOR	*n* pl. **-S** a device in an electric circuit
RESKIN	*v* **-SKINNED, -SKINNING, -SKINS** to replace the outermost layer of an aircraft or motor vehicle
RESOJET	*n* pl. **-S** a pulsejet
RESOLUTE	*adj* **-LUTER, -LUTEST** characterized by firmness or determination
RESOLUTE	*n* pl. **-S** one who is resolute
RESOLVE	*v* **-SOLVED, -SOLVING, -SOLVES** to make a firm decision about
RESOLVER	*n* pl. **-S** one that resolves
RESONANT	*n* pl. **-S** a resounding sound
RESONATE	*v* **-NATED, -NATING, -NATES** to resound
RESORB	*v* **-ED, -ING, -S** to absorb again
RESORCIN	*n* pl. **-S** a chemical compound
RESORT	*v* **-ED, -ING, -S** to go frequently or habitually
RESORTER	*n* pl. **-S** one that resorts
RESOUND	*v* **-ED, -ING, -S** to make a loud, long, or echoing sound
RESOURCE	*v* **-SOURCED, -SOURCING, -SOURCES** to provide with supplies
RESPECT	*v* **-ED, -ING, -S** to have a high regard for
RESPIRE	*v* **-SPIRED, -SPIRING, -SPIRES** to breathe
RESPITE	*v* **-SPITED, -SPITING, -SPITES** to relieve temporarily
RESPOND	*v* **-ED, -ING, -S** to say or act in return
RESPONSA	*n/pl* written rabbinic decisions
RESPONSE	*n* pl. **-S** a reply or reaction
REST	*v* **-ED, -ING, -S** to refresh oneself by ceasing work or activity
RESTER	*n* pl. **-S** one that rests
RESTFUL	*adj* **-FULLER, -FULLEST** tranquil
RESTIVE	*adj* difficult to control
RESTLESS	*adj* unable or disinclined to remain at rest
RESTORAL	*n* pl. **-S** the act of restoring
RESTORE	*v* **-STORED, -STORING, -STORES** to bring back to a former or original condition
RESTORER	*n* pl. **-S** one that restores
RESTRAIN	*v* **-ED, -ING, -S** to hold back from action
RESTRICT	*v* **-ED, -ING, -S** to keep within certain boundaries
RESTROOM	*n* pl. **-S** a room furnished with toilets and sinks
RESULT	*v* **-ED, -ING, -S** to occur as a consequence
RESUME	*v* **-SUMED, -SUMING, -SUMES** to take up again after interruption
RESUMER	*n* pl. **-S** one that resumes
RESUPINE	*adj* lying on the back
RESURGE	*v* **-SURGED, -SURGING, -SURGES** to rise again
RET	*v* **RETTED, RETTING, RETS** to soak in order to loosen the fiber from the woody tissue

List of self-explanatory verbs containing the prefix RE- (continued):

RESMELT	*v* **-ED, -ING, -S**	**RESPACE**	*v* **-SPACED, -SPACING, -SPACES**	**RESPLIT**	*v* **-SPLIT, -SPLITTING, -SPLITS**
RESMOOTH	*v* **-ED, -ING, -S**				
RESOAK	*v* **-ED, -ING, -S**				
RESOD	*v* **-SODDED, -SODDING, -SODS**	**RESPADE**	*v* **-SPADED, -SPADING, -SPADES**	**RESPOKE**	past tense of respeak
				RESPOKEN	past participle of respeak
RESOFTEN	*v* **-ED, -ING, -S**	**RESPEAK**	*v* **-SPOKE, -SPOKEN, -SPEAKING, -SPEAKS**		
RESOLD	past tense of resell			**RESPOOL**	*v* **-ED, -ING, -S**
RESOLDER	*v* **-ED, -ING, -S**			**RESPOT**	*v* **-SPOTTED, -SPOTTING, -SPOTS**
RESOLE	*v* **-SOLED, -SOLING, -SOLES**	**RESPELL**	*v* **-SPELLED** or **-SPELT, -SPELLING, -SPELLS**		
RESOUGHT	past tense of reseek			**RESPRANG**	a past tense of respring
RESOW	*v* **-SOWED, -SOWN, -SOWING, -SOWS**	**RESPLICE**	*v* **-SPLICED, -SPLICING, -SPLICES**	**RESPRAY**	*v* **-ED, -ING, -S**
				RESPREAD	*v* **-SPREAD, -SPREADING, -SPREADS**

RETABLE	*n* pl. **-S** a raised shelf above an altar	**RETIFORM**	*adj* arranged like a net
RETABLO	*n* pl. **-BLOS** a retable	**RETINA**	*n* pl. **-NAS** or **-NAE** a membrane of the eye
RETAIL	*v* **-ED, -ING, -S** to sell in small quantities	**RETINAL**	*n* pl. **-S** retinene
RETAILER	*n* pl. **-S** one that retails	**RETINE**	*n* pl. **-S** a substance in cells that retards growth and cell division
RETAIN	*v* **-ED, -ING, -S** to keep possession of	**RETINENE**	*n* pl. **-S** a pigment in the retina
		RETINITE	*n* pl. **-S** a fossil resin
RETAINER	*n* pl. **-S** one that retains	**RETINOID**	*n* pl. **-S** a compound analogous to vitamin A
RETAKE	*v* **-TOOK, -TAKEN, -TAKING, -TAKES** to take back	**RETINOL**	*n* pl. **-S** a liquid hydrocarbon
RETAKER	*n* pl. **-S** one that retakes	**RETINUE**	*n* pl. **-S** a group of attendants **RETINUED** *adj*
RETARD	*v* **-ED, -ING, -S** to slow the progress of	**RETINULA**	*n* pl. **-LAS** or **-LAE** a neural receptor of an arthropod's eye
RETARDER	*n* pl. **-S** one that retards	**RETIRANT**	*n* pl. **-S** a retiree
RETCH	*v* **-ED, -ING, -ES** to make an effort to vomit	**RETIRE**	*v* **-TIRED, -TIRING, -TIRES** to go away or withdraw
RETCHING	*n* pl. **-S** an effort to vomit	**RETIREE**	*n* pl. **-S** one who has retired from his or her vocation
RETE	*n* pl. **-TIA** an anatomical mesh or network	**RETIRER**	*n* pl. **-S** one that retires
RETELLER	*n* pl. **-S** one who tells something again	**RETIRING**	*adj* shy
		RETOOK	past tense of retake
RETEM	*n* pl. **-S** a desert shrub	**RETOOL**	*v* **-ED, -ING, -S** to reequip with tools
RETENE	*n* pl. **-S** a chemical compound	**RETORT**	*v* **-ED, -ING, -S** to answer back sharply
RETIAL	*adj* pertaining to a rete		
RETIARII	*n/pl* ancient Roman gladiators	**RETORTER**	*n* pl. **-S** one that retorts
RETIARY	*adj* resembling a net	**RETOUCH**	*v* **-ED, -ING, -ES** to add new details or touches to
RETICENT	*adj* tending to be silent		
RETICLE	*n* pl. **-S** a network of lines in the eyepiece of an optical instrument	**RETRACE**	*v* **-TRACED, -TRACING, -TRACES** to go back over
RETICULA	*n/pl* netlike structures		
RETICULE	*n* pl. **-S** a woman's handbag	**RETRACER**	*n* pl. **-S** one that retraces

---

List of self-explanatory verbs containing the prefix RE- (continued):

RESPRING	*v* **-SPRANG** or **-SPRUNG, -SPRINGING, -SPRINGS**	**RESTOCK**	*v* **-ED, -ING, -S**	**RESTRUNG**	past tense of restring
		RESTOKE	*v* **-STOKED, -STOKING, -STOKES**	**RESTUDY**	*v* **-STUDIED, -STUDYING, -STUDIES**
RESPROUT	*v* **-ED, -ING, -S**				
RESTABLE	*v* **-BLED, -BLING, -BLES**	**RESTRESS**	*v* **-ED, -ING, -ES**	**RESTUFF**	*v* **-ED, -ING, -S**
		RESTRIKE	*v* **-STRUCK, -STRICKEN, -STRIKING, -STRIKES**	**RESTYLE**	*v* **-STYLED, -STYLING, -STYLES**
RESTACK	*v* **-ED, -ING, -S**				
RESTAFF	*v* **-ED, -ING, -S**				
RESTAGE	*v* **-STAGED, -STAGING, -STAGES**	**RESTRING**	*v* **-STRUNG, -STRINGING, -STRINGS**	**RESUBMIT**	*v* **-MITTED, -MITTING, -MITS**
				RESUMMON	*v* **-ED, -ING, -S**
RESTAMP	*v* **-ED, -ING, -S**	**RESTRIVE**	*v* **-STROVE, -STRIVEN, -STRIVING, -STRIVES**	**RESUPPLY**	*v* **-PLIED, -PLYING, -PLIES**
RESTART	*v* **-ED, -ING, -S**				
RESTATE	*v* **-STATED, -STATING, -STATES**			**RESURVEY**	*v* **-ED, -ING, -S**
		RESTRUCK	past tense of restrike	**RETACK**	*v* **-ED, -ING, -S**
RESTITCH	*v* **-ED, -ING, -ES**			**RETACKLE**	*v* **-LED, -LING, -LES**

RETRACT	v **-ED, -ING, -S** to take back	**REUNION**	n pl. **-S** a reuniting of persons after separation
RETRAL	adj situated toward the back **RETRALLY** adv	**REUNITER**	n pl. **-S** one that reunites
RETREAD	v **-TROD** or **-TREADED, -TRODDEN, -TREADING, -TREADS** to furnish with a new tread	**REUPTAKE**	n pl. **-S** the reabsorption of a chemical into the cell that released it
RETREAT	v **-ED, -ING, -S** to go back or backward	**REUSABLE**	n pl. **-S** something that can be reused
RETRENCH	v **-ED, -ING, -ES** to curtail	**REV**	v **REVVED, REVVING, REVS** to increase the speed of
RETRIAL	n pl. **-S** a second trial	**REVAMP**	v **-ED, -ING, -S** to make over
RETRIEVE	v **-TRIEVED, -TRIEVING, -TRIEVES** to get back	**REVAMPER**	n pl. **-S** one that revamps
RETRO	n pl. **-ROS** a rocket on a spacecraft that produces thrust in a direction opposite to the line of flight	**REVANCHE**	n pl. **-S** a political policy designed to regain lost territory
		REVEAL	v **-ED, -ING, -S** to make known
		REVEALER	n pl. **-S** one that reveals
RETROACT	v **-ED, -ING, -S** to act in return	**REVEHENT**	adj carrying back
RETROD	a past tense of retread	**REVEILLE**	n pl. **-S** a morning bugle call
RETROFIT	v **-FITTED, -FITTING, -FITS** to furnish with new parts not originally available	**REVEL**	v **-ELED, -ELING, -ELS** or **-ELLED, -ELLING, -ELS** to engage in revelry
RETRONYM	n pl. **-S** a term coined to distinguish the original referent from a later development	**REVELER**	n pl. **-S** one that revels
		REVELLER	n pl. **-S** reveler
RETRORSE	adj bent backward	**REVELRY**	n pl. **-RIES** noisy merrymaking
RETSINA	n pl. **-S** a resin-flavored Greek wine	**REVENANT**	n pl. **-S** one that returns
RETTED	past tense of ret	**REVENGE**	v **-VENGED, -VENGING, -VENGES** to inflict injury in return for
RETTING	present participle of ret		
RETURN	v **-ED, -ING, -S** to come or go back	**REVENGER**	n pl. **-S** one that revenges
RETURNEE	n pl. **-S** one that has returned	**REVENUE**	n pl. **-S** the income of a government **REVENUAL, REVENUED** adj
RETURNER	n pl. **-S** one that returns		
RETUSE	adj having a rounded apex with a shallow notch — used of leaves	**REVENUER**	n pl. **-S** a revenue officer

---

List of self-explanatory verbs containing the prefix RE- (continued):

RETAG	v **-TAGGED, -TAGGING, -TAGS**	**RETEAR**	v **-TORE, -TORN, -TEARING, -TEARS**	**RETINT**	v **-ED, -ING, -S**
				RETITLE	v **-TLED, -TLING, -TLES**
RETAILOR	v **-ED, -ING, -S**	**RETELL**	v **-TOLD, -TELLING, -TELLS**	**RETOLD**	past tense of retell
RETALLY	v **-LIED, -LYING, -LIES**			**RETORE**	past tense of retear
RETAPE	v **-TAPED, -TAPING, -TAPES**	**RETEMPER**	v **-ED, -ING, -S**	**RETORN**	past participle of retear
		RETEST	v **-ED, -ING, -S**		
RETARGET	v **-ED, -ING, -S**	**RETHINK**	v **-THOUGHT, -THINKING, -THINKS**	**RETOTAL**	v **-TALED, -TALING, -TALS** or **-TALLED, -TALLING, -TALS**
RETASTE	v **-TASTED, -TASTING, -TASTES**	**RETHREAD**	v **-ED, -ING, -S**		
		RETIE	v **-TIED, -TYING** or **-TIEING, -TIES**	**RETRACK**	v **-ED, -ING, -S**
RETAX	v **-ED, -ING, -ES**			**RETRAIN**	v **-ED, -ING, -S**
RETEACH	v **-TAUGHT, -TEACHING, -TEACHES**	**RETILE**	v **-TILED, -TILING, -TILES**	**RETRIM**	v **-TRIMMED, -TRIMMING, -TRIMS**
RETEAM	v **-ED, -ING, -S**	**RETIME**	v **-TIMED, -TIMING, -TIMES**		

REVERB	*v* **-ED, -ING, -S** to continue in a series of echoes
REVERE	*v* **-VERED, -VERING, -VERES** to regard with great respect
REVEREND	*n* pl. **-S** a clergyman
REVERENT	*adj* deeply respectful
REVERER	*n* pl. **-S** one that reveres
REVERIE	*n* pl. **-S** a daydream
REVERIES	pl. of revery
REVERING	present participle of revere
REVERS	*n* pl. **REVERS** a part of a garment turned back to show the inside
REVERSAL	*n* pl. **-S** the act of reversing
REVERSE	*v* **-VERSED, -VERSING, -VERSES** to turn or move in the opposite direction
REVERSER	*n* pl. **-S** one that reverses
REVERSO	*n* pl. **-VERSOS** verso
REVERT	*v* **-ED, -ING, -S** to return to a former state
REVERTER	*n* pl. **-S** one that reverts
REVERY	*n* pl. **-ERIES** reverie
REVET	*v* **-VETTED, -VETTING, -VETS** to face with masonry
REVIEWAL	*n* pl. **-S** the act of reviewing
REVIEWER	*n* pl. **-S** one that reviews
REVILE	*v* **-VILED, -VILING, -VILES** to denounce with abusive language
REVILER	*n* pl. **-S** one that reviles
REVILING	*n* pl. **-S** the act of denouncing with abusive language
REVISAL	*n* pl. **-S** a revision

REVISE	*v* **-VISED, -VISING, -VISES** to make a new or improved version of
REVISER	*n* pl. **-S** one that revises
REVISION	*n* pl. **-S** a revised version
REVISOR	*n* pl. **-S** reviser
REVISORY	*adj* pertaining to revision
REVIVAL	*n* pl. **-S** renewed attention to or interest in something
REVIVE	*v* **-VIVED, -VIVING, -VIVES** to bring back to life or consciousness
REVIVER	*n* pl. **-S** one that revives
REVIVIFY	*v* **-FIED, -FYING, -FIES** to give new life to
REVOKE	*v* **-VOKED, -VOKING, -VOKES** to annul by taking back
REVOKER	*n* pl. **-S** one that revokes
REVOLT	*v* **-ED, -ING, -S** to rise up against authority
REVOLTER	*n* pl. **-S** one that revolts
REVOLUTE	*adj* rolled backward or downward
REVOLVE	*v* **-VOLVED, -VOLVING, -VOLVES** to turn about an axis
REVOLVER	*n* pl. **-S** a type of handgun
REVUE	*n* pl. **-S** a type of musical show
REVUIST	*n* pl. **-S** a writer of revues
REVULSED	*adj* affected with revulsion
REVVED	past tense of rev
REVVING	present participle of rev
REWARD	*v* **-ED, -ING, -S** to give recompense to for worthy behavior
REWARDER	*n* pl. **-S** one that rewards
REWINDER	*n* pl. **-S** one that rewinds

List of self-explanatory verbs containing the prefix RE- (continued):

RETRY	*v* **-TRIED, -TRYING, -TRIES**	**REVALUE**	*v* **-UED, -UING, -UES**	**REWAN**	a past tense of rewin
RETUNE	*v* **-TUNED, -TUNING, -TUNES**	**REVERIFY**	*v* **-FIED, -FYING, -FIES**	**REWARM**	*v* **-ED, -ING, -S**
RETWIST	*v* **-ED, -ING, -S**	**REVEST**	*v* **-ED, -ING, -S**	**REWASH**	*v* **-ED, -ING, -ES**
RETYING	present participle of retie	**REVIEW**	*v* **-ED, -ING, -S**	**REWAX**	*v* **-ED, -ING, -ES**
		REVISIT	*v* **-ED, -ING, -S**	**REWEAR**	*v* **-WORE, -WORN, -WEARING, -WEARS**
RETYPE	*v* **-TYPED, -TYPING, -TYPES**	**REVOICE**	*v* **-VOICED, -VOICING, -VOICES**	**REWEAVE**	*v* **-WOVE** or **-WEAVED, -WOVEN, -WEAVING, -WEAVES**
REUNIFY	*v* **-FIED, -FYING, -FIES**	**REVOTE**	*v* **-VOTED, -VOTING, -VOTES**		
REUNITE	*v* **-UNITED, -UNITING, -UNITES**	**REWAKE**	*v* **-WAKED** or **-WOKE, -WOKEN, -WAKING, -WAKES**	**REWED**	*v* **-WEDDED, -WEDDING, -WEDS**
REUSE	*v* **-USED, -USING, -USES**			**REWEIGH**	*v* **-ED, -ING, -S**
REUTTER	*v* **-ED, -ING, -S**	**REWAKEN**	*v* **-ED, -ING, -S**	**REWELD**	*v* **-ED, -ING, -S**

REWORD *v* **-ED, -ING, -S** to state again in other words

REWRITER *n* pl. **-S** one that rewrites

REX *n* pl. **-ES** an animal with a single wavy layer of hair

REX *n* pl. **REGES** king

REYNARD *n* pl. **-S** a fox

REZ *n* pl. **REZES** or **REZZES** an area of land set aside for Native Americans

REZERO *v* **-ED, -ING, -ES** or **-S** to reset (a gauge) back to zero

RHABDOM *n* pl. **-S** a rodlike structure in the retinula

RHABDOME *n* pl. **-S** rhabdom

RHACHIS *n* pl. **-CHISES** or **-CHIDES** rachis

RHAMNOSE *n* pl. **-S** a sugar found in plants

RHAMNUS *n* pl. **-ES** a thorny tree or shrub

RHAPHE *n* pl. **-PHES** or **-PHAE** raphe

RHAPSODE *n* pl. **-S** a reciter of epic poetry in ancient Greece

RHAPSODY *n* pl. **-DIES** an exalted expression of feeling

RHATANY *n* pl. **-NIES** a South American shrub

RHEA *n* pl. **-S** a flightless bird

RHEBOK *n* pl. **-S** a large antelope

RHEMATIC *adj* pertaining to a verb

RHEME *n* pl. **-S** a statement of fact or opinion

RHENIUM *n* pl. **-S** a metallic element

RHEOBASE *n* pl. **-S** the smallest amount of electricity required to stimulate a nerve

RHEOLOGY *n* pl. **-GIES** the study of matter in the fluid state

RHEOPHIL *adj* living in flowing water

RHEOSTAT *n* pl. **-S** a resistor used to control electric current

RHESUS *n* pl. **-ES** an Asian monkey

RHETOR *n* pl. **-S** a teacher of rhetoric

RHETORIC *n* pl. **-S** the study of effective speech and writing

RHEUM *n* pl. **-S** a watery discharge from the eyes or nose **RHEUMIC** *adj*

RHEUMY *adj* **RHEUMIER, RHEUMIEST** marked by rheum

RHINAL *adj* pertaining to the nose

RHINITIS *n* pl. **RHINITIDES** inflammation of the mucous membranes of the nose

RHINO *n* pl. **-NOS** a rhinoceros

RHIZOBIA *n/pl* rod-shaped bacteria

RHIZOID *n* pl. **-S** a rootlike structure

RHIZOMA *n* pl. **-MATA** rhizome

RHIZOME *n* pl. **-S** a rootlike, underground stem **RHIZOMIC** *adj*

RHIZOPOD *n* pl. **-S** any of a class of protozoans

RHIZOPUS *n* pl. **-PUSES** or **-PI** any of a genus of mold fungi

RHO *n* pl. **RHOS** a Greek letter

RHODAMIN *n* pl. **-S** a red dye

RHODIUM *n* pl. **-S** a metallic element **RHODIC** *adj*

RHODORA *n* pl. **-S** a flowering shrub

RHOMB *n* pl. **-S** a rhombus

RHOMBIC *adj* having the shape of a rhombus

RHOMBOID *n* pl. **-S** a type of geometric figure

RHOMBUS *n* pl. **-BUSES** or **-BI** a type of geometric figure

---

List of self-explanatory verbs containing the prefix RE- (continued):

REWET	*v* **-WETTED, -WETTING, -WETS**	**REWON**	a past tense of rewin	**REWRAP**	*v* **-WRAPPED** or **-WRAPT, -WRAPPING, -WRAPS**
REWIDEN	*v* **-ED, -ING, -S**	**REWORE**	past tense of rewear		
REWIN	*v* **-WON** or **-WAN, -WINNING, -WINS**	**REWORK**	*v* **-WORKED** or **-WROUGHT, -WORKING, -WORKS**		
REWIND	*v* **-WOUND** or **-WINDED, -WINDING, -WINDS**			**REWRITE**	*v* **-WROTE, -WRITTEN, -WRITING, -WRITES**
		REWORN	past participle of rewear		
REWIRE	*v* **-WIRED, -WIRING, -WIRES**	**REWOUND**	a past tense of rewind	**REWROUGHT**	a past tense of rework
REWOKE	a past tense of rewake	**REWOVE**	a past tense of reweave	**REZONE**	*v* **-ZONED, -ZONING, -ZONES**
REWOKEN	past participle of rewake	**REWOVEN**	past participle of reweave		

RHONCHUS	*n* pl. **-CHI** a rattling respiratory sound **RHONCHAL** *adj*
RHOTIC	*adj* pertaining to a dialect of English in which the letter *r* at the end of a syllable is pronounced
RHUBARB	*n* pl. **-S** a perennial herb
RHUMB	*n* pl. **-S** a point of the mariner's compass
RHUMBA	*v* **-ED, -ING, -S** to rumba
RHUS	*n* pl. **-ES** any of a genus of shrubs and trees
RHYME	*v* **RHYMED, RHYMING, RHYMES** to compose verse with corresponding terminal sounds
RHYMER	*n* pl. **-S** one that rhymes
RHYOLITE	*n* pl. **-S** a volcanic rock
RHYTHM	*n* pl. **-S** movement or procedure with uniform recurrence of strong and weak elements
RHYTHMIC	*n* pl. **-S** the science of rhythm
RHYTON	*n* pl. **-TONS** or **-TA** an ancient Greek drinking horn
RIA	*n* pl. **-S** a long, narrow inlet
RIAL	*n* pl. **-S** a monetary unit of Iran
RIALTO	*n* pl. **-TOS** a marketplace
RIANT	*adj* cheerful **RIANTLY** *adv*
RIATA	*n* pl. **-S** a lasso
RIB	*v* **RIBBED, RIBBING, RIBS** to poke fun at
RIBALD	*n* pl. **-S** one who uses crude language
RIBALD	*adj* **RIBALDER, RIBALDEST** characterized by crude language
RIBALDLY	*adv* crudely
RIBALDRY	*n* pl. **-RIES** crude language
RIBAND	*n* pl. **-S** a ribbon
RIBBAND	*n* pl. **-S** a long, narrow strip used in shipbuilding
RIBBED	past tense of rib
RIBBER	*n* pl. **-S** one that ribs
RIBBIE	*n* pl. **-S** a run batted in
RIBBIER	comparative of ribby
RIBBIEST	superlative of ribby
RIBBING	*n* pl. **-S** the act of one that ribs
RIBBIT	*n* pl. **-S** the sound made by a frog
RIBBON	*v* **-ED, -ING, -S** to decorate with ribbons (narrow strips of fine fabric)
RIBBONY	*adj* resembling ribbon
RIBBY	*adj* **-BIER, -BIEST** marked by prominent ribs (curved bony rods in the body)
RIBES	*n* pl. **RIBES** a flowering shrub
RIBEYE	*n* pl. **-S** a cut of beef
RIBGRASS	*n* pl. **-ES** a weedy plant
RIBIER	*n* pl. **-S** a large, black grape
RIBLESS	*adj* having no ribs
RIBLET	*n* pl. **-S** the rib end in a breast of lamb or veal
RIBLIKE	*adj* resembling a rib
RIBOSE	*n* pl. **-S** a pentose sugar
RIBOSOME	*n* pl. **-S** a particle composed of protein and ribonucleic acid
RIBOZYME	*n* pl. **-S** a molecule of RNA that functions as an enzyme
RIBULOSE	*n* pl. **-S** a type of sugar
RIBWORT	*n* pl. **-S** ribgrass
RICE	*v* **RICED, RICING, RICES** to press through a ricer
RICEBIRD	*n* pl. **-S** the bobolink
RICER	*n* pl. **-S** a kitchen utensil consisting of a container perforated with small holes
RICERCAR	*n* pl. **-S** an instrumental composition
RICH	*adj* **RICHER, RICHEST** having wealth
RICHEN	*v* **-ED, -ING, -S** to make rich
RICHES	*n/pl* wealth
RICHLY	*adv* in a rich manner
RICHNESS	*n* pl. **-ES** the state of being rich
RICHWEED	*n* pl. **-S** a flowering plant
RICIN	*n* pl. **-S** a poisonous protein
RICING	present participle of rice
RICINUS	*n* pl. **-ES** a large-leaved plant
RICK	*v* **-ED, -ING, -S** to pile hay in stacks
RICKETS	*n/pl* a disease resulting from vitamin D deficiency
RICKETY	*adj* **-ETIER, -ETIEST** likely to fall or collapse
RICKEY	*n* pl. **-EYS** an alcoholic beverage containing lime juice, sugar, and soda water
RICKRACK	*n* pl. **-S** a flat braid used as a trimming
RICKSHA	*n* pl. **-S** rickshaw
RICKSHAW	*n* pl. **-S** a small, two-wheeled passenger vehicle

RICOCHET *v* **-CHETED, -CHETING, -CHETS** or **-CHETTED, -CHETTING, -CHETS** to rebound from a surface

RICOTTA *n* pl. **-S** an Italian cheese

RICRAC *n* pl. **-S** rickrack

RICTUS *n* pl. **-ES** the expanse of the open mouth **RICTAL** *adj*

RID *v* **RID** or **RIDDED, RIDDING, RIDS** to free from something objectionable

RIDABLE *adj* capable of being ridden

RIDDANCE *n* pl. **-S** deliverance

RIDDEN past participle of ride

RIDDER *n* pl. **-S** one that rids

RIDDING present participle of rid

RIDDLE *v* **-DLED, -DLING, -DLES** to pierce with many holes

RIDDLER *n* pl. **-S** one that riddles

RIDE *v* **RODE, RIDDEN, RIDING, RIDES** to sit on, control, and be conveyed by an animal or machine

RIDEABLE *adj* ridable

RIDENT *adj* laughing

RIDER *n* pl. **-S** one that rides

RIDGE *v* **RIDGED, RIDGING, RIDGES** to form into ridges (long, narrow elevations)

RIDGEL *n* pl. **-S** a ridgling

RIDGETOP *n* pl. **-S** the crest of a ridge

RIDGEWAY *n* pl. **-WAYS** a road or track along a ridge

RIDGIER comparative of ridgy

RIDGIEST superlative of ridgy

RIDGIL *n* pl. **-S** a ridgling

RIDGING present participle of ridge

RIDGLING *n* pl. **-S** a male animal with undescended testicles

RIDGY *adj* **RIDGIER, RIDGIEST** having ridges

RIDICULE *v* **-CULED, -CULING, -CULES** to make fun of

RIDING *n* pl. **-S** the act of one that rides

RIDLEY *n* pl. **-LEYS** a sea turtle

RIDOTTO *n* pl. **-TOS** a public musical entertainment in 18th century England

RIEL *n* pl. **-S** a monetary unit of Cambodia

RIESLING *n* pl. **-S** a white Rhine wine

RIEVER *n* pl. **-S** reaver

RIF *v* **RIFFED, RIFFING, RIFS** to dismiss from employment

RIFAMPIN *n* pl. **-S** an antibiotic

RIFE *adj* **RIFER, RIFEST** abundant **RIFELY** *adv*

RIFENESS *n* pl. **-ES** the state of being rife

RIFF *v* **-ED, -ING, -S** to riffle

RIFFAGE *n* pl. **-S** a series of musical phrases

RIFFED past tense of rif

RIFFING present participle of rif

RIFFLE *v* **-FLED, -FLING, -FLES** to flip through hastily

RIFFLER *n* pl. **-S** a filing and scraping tool

RIFFRAFF *n* pl. **-S** the disreputable element of society

RIFLE *v* **-FLED, -FLING, -FLES** to search through and rob

RIFLEMAN *n* pl. **-MEN** a soldier armed with a rifle (a type of firearm)

RIFLER *n* pl. **-S** one that rifles

RIFLERY *n* pl. **-RIES** the practice of shooting at targets with a rifle

RIFLING *n* pl. **-S** the system of grooves in a gun barrel

RIFLIP *n* pl. **-S** a fragment of DNA

RIFT *v* **-ED, -ING, -S** to form rifts (clefts)

RIFTLESS *adj* having no rift

RIG *v* **RIGGED, RIGGING, RIGS** to put in proper condition for use

RIGADOON *n* pl. **-S** a lively dance

RIGATONI *n* pl. **-S** a tubular pasta

RIGAUDON *n* pl. **-S** rigadoon

RIGGED past tense of rig

RIGGER *n* pl. **-S** one that rigs

RIGGING *n* pl. **-S** the system of lines, chains, and tackle used aboard a ship

RIGHT *adj* **RIGHTER, RIGHTEST** being in accordance with what is good, proper, or just

RIGHT *v* **-ED, -ING, -S** to put in proper order or condition

RIGHTER *n* pl. **-S** one that rights

RIGHTFUL *adj* just or proper

RIGHTIER comparative of righty

RIGHTIES pl. of righty

RIGHTIEST superlative of righty

RIGHTISH *adj* somewhat right

RIGHTISM *n* pl. **-S** a conservative political philosophy

RIGHTIST	*n* pl. **-S** an advocate of rightism
RIGHTLY	*adv* in a right manner
RIGHTO	*interj* — used to express cheerful consent
RIGHTY	*n* pl. **RIGHTIES** a right-handed person
RIGHTY	*adj* **RIGHTIER, RIGHTIEST** politically conservative
RIGID	*adj* **RIGIDER, RIGIDEST** not flexible; strict, harsh
RIGIDIFY	*v* **-FIED, -FYING, -FIES** to make rigid
RIGIDITY	*n* pl. **-TIES** the state of being rigid
RIGIDLY	*adv* in a rigid manner
RIGOR	*n* pl. **-S** strictness or severity
RIGORISM	*n* pl. **-S** strictness or severity in conduct or attitude
RIGORIST	*n* pl. **-S** one that professes rigorism
RIGOROUS	*adj* characterized by rigor
RIGOUR	*n* pl. **-S** rigor
RIKISHA	*n* pl. **-S** rickshaw
RIKISHI	*n* pl. **RIKISHI** a sumo wrestler
RIKSHAW	*n* pl. **-S** rickshaw
RILE	*v* **RILED, RILING, RILES** to anger
RILEY	*adj* angry
RILIEVO	*n* pl. **-VI** relievo
RILL	*v* **-ED, -ING, -S** to flow like a rill (a small brook)
RILLE	*n* pl. **-S** a valley on the moon's surface
RILLET	*n* pl. **-S** a small rill
RIM	*v* **RIMMED, RIMMING, RIMS** to provide with a rim (an outer edge)
RIME	*v* **RIMED, RIMING, RIMES** to rhyme
RIMER	*n* pl. **-S** one that rimes
RIMESTER	*n* pl. **-S** a rimer
RIMFIRE	*n* pl. **-S** a cartridge having the primer set in the rim of the shell
RIMIER	comparative of rimy
RIMIEST	superlative of rimy
RIMINESS	*n* pl. **-ES** the condition of being rimy
RIMING	present participle of rime
RIMLAND	*n* pl. **-S** an outlying area
RIMLESS	*adj* having no rim
RIMMED	past tense of rim
RIMMER	*n* pl. **-S** a reamer
RIMMING	present participle of rim
RIMOSE	*adj* marked by cracks **RIMOSELY** *adv*
RIMOSITY	*n* pl. **-TIES** the state of being rimose
RIMOUS	*adj* rimose
RIMPLE	*v* **-PLED, -PLING, -PLES** to wrinkle
RIMROCK	*n* pl. **-S** a type of rock formation
RIMSHOT	*n* pl. **-S** a sound made by a drumstick striking the rim and head of a drum
RIMY	*adj* **RIMIER, RIMIEST** frosty
RIN	*v* **RAN, RINNING, RINS** to run or melt
RIND	*n* pl. **-S** a thick and firm outer covering **RINDED, RINDY** *adj*
RIND	*v* **-ED, -ING, -S** to strip the bark from
RINDLESS	*adj* lacking a rind
RING	*v* **-ED, -ING, -S** to form a ring (a circular band) around
RING	*v* **RANG, RUNG, RINGING, RINGS** to give forth a clear, resonant sound
RINGBARK	*v* **-ED, -ING, -S** to make an encircling cut through the bark of
RINGBOLT	*n* pl. **-S** a type of eyebolt
RINGBONE	*n* pl. **-S** a bony growth on a horse's foot
RINGDOVE	*n* pl. **-S** a European pigeon
RINGENT	*adj* having open liplike parts
RINGER	*n* pl. **-S** one that rings
RINGETTE	*n* pl. **-S** a team sport for women played on ice using a rubber ring
RINGGIT	*n* pl. **-S** a monetary unit of Malaysia
RINGHALS	*n* pl. **-ES** a venomous snake
RINGLESS	*adj* being without a ring
RINGLET	*n* pl. **-S** a curly lock of hair
RINGLETY	*adj* resembling or suggestive of a ringlet
RINGLIKE	*adj* resembling a ring
RINGNECK	*n* pl. **-S** a bird having a ring of color around the neck
RINGSIDE	*n* pl. **-S** the area just outside a boxing or wrestling ring (a square enclosure)
RINGSTER	*n* pl. **-S** one of a group of people united for political or economic reasons
RINGTAIL	*n* pl. **-S** an animal having a tail with ringlike markings

RINGTAW	*n* pl. **-S** a game of marbles
RINGTONE	*n* pl. **-S** a sound made by a cell phone when receiving a call
RINGTOSS	*n* pl. **-ES** a game in which the object is to toss a ring onto an upright stick
RINGWORK	*n* pl. **-S** a fortified circular trench around a castle
RINGWORM	*n* pl. **-S** a skin disease
RINK	*n* pl. **-S** a surface of ice for skating
RINKHALS	*n* pl. **-ES** ringhals
RINKSIDE	*n* pl. **-S** the area adjacent to a rink
RINNING	present participle of rin
RINSE	*v* **RINSED, RINSING, RINSES** to cleanse with clear water **RINSABLE, RINSIBLE** *adj*
RINSER	*n* pl. **-S** one that rinses
RINSING	*n* pl. **-S** the act of one that rinses
RIOJA	*n* pl. **-S** a dry red Spanish wine
RIOT	*v* **-ED, -ING, -S** to take part in a violent public disturbance
RIOTER	*n* pl. **-S** one that riots
RIOTING	*n* pl. **-S** a violent public disturbance
RIOTOUS	*adj* characterized by rioting
RIP	*v* **RIPPED, RIPPING, RIPS** to tear or cut apart roughly
RIPARIAN	*adj* pertaining to the bank of a river
RIPCORD	*n* pl. **-S** a cord pulled to release a parachute
RIPE	*adj* **RIPER, RIPEST** fully developed **RIPELY** *adv*
RIPE	*v* **RIPED, RIPING, RIPES** to cleanse
RIPEN	*v* **-ED, -ING, -S** to become ripe
RIPENER	*n* pl. **-S** one that ripens
RIPENESS	*n* pl. **-ES** the state of being ripe
RIPER	comparative of ripe
RIPEST	superlative of ripe
RIPIENO	*n* pl. **-NOS** or **-NI** tutti
RIPING	present participle of ripe
RIPOFF	*n* pl. **-S** an instance of stealing
RIPOST	*v* **-ED, -ING, -S** to riposte
RIPOSTE	*v* **-POSTED, -POSTING, -POSTES** to make a return thrust in fencing
RIPPABLE	*adj* capable of being ripped
RIPPED	past tense of rip
RIPPER	*n* pl. **-S** one that rips
RIPPING	*adj* excellent
RIPPLE	*v* **-PLED, -PLING, -PLES** to form ripples (small waves)
RIPPLER	*n* pl. **-S** a toothed tool for cleaning flax fiber
RIPPLET	*n* pl. **-S** a small ripple
RIPPLING	present participle of ripple
RIPPLY	*adj* **-PLIER, -PLIEST** marked by ripples
RIPRAP	*v* **-RAPPED, -RAPPING, -RAPS** to strengthen with a foundation of broken stones
RIPSAW	*v* **-SAWED, -SAWN, -SAWING, -SAWS** to saw wood by cutting with the grain
RIPSTOP	*n* pl. **-S** a fabric woven so that small tears do not spread
RIPTIDE	*n* pl. **-S** a tide that opposes other tides
RISE	*v* **ROSE, RISEN, RISING, RISES** to move upward
RISER	*n* pl. **-S** one that rises
RISHI	*n* pl. **-S** a Hindu sage
RISIBLE	*adj* inclined to laugh **RISIBLY** *adv*
RISIBLES	*n/pl* a sense of the ridiculous
RISING	*n* pl. **-S** the act of one that rises
RISK	*v* **-ED, -ING, -S** to expose to a risk (a chance of injury or loss)
RISKER	*n* pl. **-S** one that risks
RISKLESS	*adj* free of risk
RISKY	*adj* **RISKIER, RISKIEST** dangerous **RISKILY** *adv*
RISOTTO	*n* pl. **-TOS** a rice dish
RISQUE	*adj* bordering on impropriety or indecency
RISSOLE	*n* pl. **-S** a small roll filled with meat or fish
RISTRA	*n* pl. **-S** a string on which foodstuffs are tied for storage
RISUS	*n* pl. **-ES** a grin or laugh
RITARD	*n* pl. **-S** a musical passage with a gradual slackening in tempo
RITE	*n* pl. **-S** a ceremonial act or procedure
RITTER	*n* pl. **-S** a knight
RITUAL	*n* pl. **-S** a system of rites
RITUALLY	*adv* ceremonially
RITZ	*n* pl. **-ES** pretentious display
RITZY	*adj* **RITZIER, RITZIEST** elegant **RITZILY** *adv*

RIVAGE	*n* pl. **-S** a coast, shore, or bank
RIVAL	*v* **-VALED, -VALING, -VALS** or **-VALLED, -VALLING, -VALS** to strive to equal or surpass
RIVALRY	*n* pl. **-RIES** competition
RIVE	*v* **RIVED, RIVEN, RIVING, RIVES** to tear apart
RIVER	*n* pl. **-S** a large, natural stream of water
RIVERBED	*n* pl. **-S** the area covered or once covered by a river
RIVERINE	*adj* pertaining to a river
RIVERMAN	*n* pl. **-MEN** a man who works on a river
RIVET	*v* **-ETED, -ETING, -ETS** or **-ETTED, -ETTING, -ETS** to fasten with a type of metal bolt
RIVETER	*n* pl. **-S** one that rivets
RIVIERA	*n* pl. **-S** a coastal resort area
RIVIERE	*n* pl. **-S** a necklace of precious stones
RIVING	present participle of rive
RIVULET	*n* pl. **-S** a small stream
RIVULOSE	*adj* having narrow, winding lines
RIVULUS	*n* pl. **-ES** a small tropical American fish
RIYAL	*n* pl. **-S** a monetary unit of Saudi Arabia
ROACH	*v* **-ED, -ING, -ES** to cause to arch
ROAD	*n* pl. **-S** an open way for public passage
ROADBED	*n* pl. **-S** the foundation for a railroad track
ROADEO	*n* pl. **-EOS** a competition for truck drivers
ROADIE	*n* pl. **-S** a person who works for traveling entertainers
ROADKILL	*n* pl. **-S** an animal that has been killed on a road
ROADLESS	*adj* having no roads
ROADSHOW	*n* pl. **-S** a theatrical show on tour
ROADSIDE	*n* pl. **-S** the area along the side of a road
ROADSTER	*n* pl. **-S** a light, open automobile
ROADWAY	*n* pl. **-WAYS** a road
ROADWORK	*n* pl. **-S** outdoor running as a form of physical conditioning
ROAM	*v* **-ED, -ING, -S** to move about without purpose or plan
ROAMER	*n* pl. **-S** one that roams
ROAMING	*n* pl. **-S** the use of a cell phone outside its local area
ROAN	*n* pl. **-S** an animal having a coat sprinkled with white or gray
ROAR	*v* **-ED, -ING, -S** to utter a loud, deep sound
ROARER	*n* pl. **-S** one that roars
ROARING	*n* pl. **-S** a loud, deep sound
ROAST	*v* **-ED, -ING, -S** to cook with dry heat
ROASTER	*n* pl. **-S** one that roasts
ROASTING	*n* pl. **-S** a severe criticism
ROB	*v* **ROBBED, ROBBING, ROBS** to take property from illegally
ROBALO	*n* pl. **-LOS** a marine food fish
ROBAND	*n* pl. **-S** a piece of yarn used to fasten a sail
ROBATA	*n* pl. **-S** a grill used for Japanese cooking
ROBBER	*n* pl. **-S** one that robs
ROBBERY	*n* pl. **-BERIES** the act of one who robs
ROBBIN	*n* pl. **-S** a roband
ROBBING	present participle of rob
ROBE	*v* **ROBED, ROBING, ROBES** to cover with a robe (a long, loose outer garment)
ROBIN	*n* pl. **-S** a songbird
ROBINIA	*n* pl. **-S** a North American tree or shrub
ROBLE	*n* pl. **-S** an oak tree
ROBOCALL	*n* pl. **-S** a telephone call from an automated source that delivers a prerecorded message to a large number of people
ROBORANT	*n* pl. **-S** an invigorating drug
ROBOT	*n* pl. **-S** a humanlike machine that performs various functions **ROBOTIC** *adj*
ROBOTICS	*n/pl* a field of interest concerned with robots
ROBOTISE	*v* **-ISED, -ISING, -ISES** to robotize
ROBOTISM	*n* pl. **-S** the state of being a robot
ROBOTIZE	*v* **-IZED, -IZING, -IZES** to make automatic
ROBOTRY	*n* pl. **-RIES** the science of robots
ROBUST	*adj* **-BUSTER, -BUSTEST** strong and healthy **ROBUSTLY** *adv*
ROBUSTA	*n* pl. **-S** a coffee grown in Africa
ROC	*n* pl. **-S** a legendary bird of prey

ROCAILLE *n* pl. **-S** rococo

ROCHET *n* pl. **-S** a linen vestment

ROCK *v* **-ED, -ING, -S** to move back and forth **ROCKABLE** *adj*

ROCKABY *n* pl. **-BIES** a song used to lull a child to sleep

ROCKABYE *n* pl. **-S** rockaby

ROCKAWAY *n* pl. **-WAYS** a light carriage

ROCKER *n* pl. **-S** a rocking chair

ROCKERY *n* pl. **-ERIES** a rock garden

ROCKET *v* **-ED, -ING, -S** to convey by means of a rocket (a device propelled by the reaction of escaping gases)

ROCKETER *n* pl. **-S** one that designs or launches rockets

ROCKETRY *n* pl. **-RIES** the science of rockets

ROCKFALL *n* pl. **-S** a mass of fallen rocks

ROCKFISH *n* pl. **-ES** a fish living around rocks

ROCKIER comparative of rocky

ROCKIEST superlative of rocky

ROCKILY *adv* in a rocky manner

ROCKLESS *adj* having no rocks

ROCKLIKE *adj* resembling a rock (a large mass of stone)

ROCKLING *n* pl. **-S** a marine fish

ROCKOON *n* pl. **-S** a small rocket

ROCKROSE *n* pl. **-S** a flowering plant

ROCKWEED *n* pl. **-S** a brown seaweed

ROCKWOOL *n* pl. **-S** mineral wool used for insulation

ROCKWORK *n* pl. **-S** a natural mass of rocks

ROCKY *adj* **ROCKIER, ROCKIEST** unsteady

ROCOCO *n* pl. **-COS** a style of architecture and decoration

ROD *v* **RODDED, RODDING, RODS** to provide with a rod (a straight, slender piece of material)

RODE *n* pl. **-S** a cable attached to the anchor of a small boat

RODENT *n* pl. **-S** a gnawing mammal

RODEO *v* **-ED, -ING, -S** to perform cowboy skills in a contest

RODLESS *adj* having no rod

RODLIKE *adj* resembling a rod

RODMAN *n* pl. **-MEN** a surveyor's assistant

RODNEY *n* pl. **-NEYS** a small fishing boat

RODSMAN *n* pl. **-MEN** rodman

ROE *n* pl. **-S** the mass of eggs within a female fish

ROEBUCK *n* pl. **-S** the male of a small Eurasian deer

ROENTGEN *n* pl. **-S** a unit of radiation dosage

ROGATION *n* pl. **-S** the proposal of a law in ancient Rome

ROGATORY *adj* requesting information

ROGER *v* **-ED, -ING, -S** to indicate that a message has been received

ROGUE *v* **ROGUED, ROGUEING** or **ROGUING, ROGUES** to defraud

ROGUERY *n* pl. **-ERIES** roguish conduct

ROGUISH *adj* dishonest

ROIL *v* **-ED, -ING, -S** to make muddy

ROILY *adj* **ROILIER, ROILIEST** muddy

ROISTER *v* **-ED, -ING, -S** to revel

ROLAMITE *n* pl. **-S** a nearly frictionless mechanical device

ROLE *n* pl. **-S** a part played by an actor

ROLF *v* **-ED, -ING, -S** to practice a type of massage

ROLFER *n* pl. **-S** one that rolfs

ROLL *v* **-ED, -ING, -S** to move along by repeatedly turning over **ROLLABLE** *adj*

ROLLAWAY *n* pl. **-WAYS** a piece of furniture that can be rolled away when not in use

ROLLBACK *n* pl. **-S** a return to a lower level of prices or wages

ROLLER *n* pl. **-S** a rotating cylinder

ROLLICK *v* **-ED, -ING, -S** to frolic

ROLLICKY *adj* given to rollicking

ROLLIE *n* pl. **-S** a hand-rolled cigarette

ROLLING *n* pl. **-S** the act of one that rolls

ROLLMOP *n* pl. **-S** a fillet of herring

ROLLOUT *n* pl. **-S** a type of play in football

ROLLOVER *n* pl. **-S** a motor vehicle accident in which the vehicle overturns

ROLLTOP *adj* having a flexible, sliding cover

ROLLUP *n* pl. **-S** something that is rolled into the shape of a tube

ROLLWAY *n* pl. **-WAYS** an incline for rolling logs

ROM *n* pl. **-S** a Gypsy man or boy

ROMAINE *n* pl. **-S** a variety of lettuce

ROMAJI *n* pl. **-S** a system of transliterating Japanese into the Latin alphabet

ROMAN	*n* pl. **-S** a metrical narrative of medieval France
ROMANCE	*v* **-MANCED, -MANCING, -MANCES** to woo
ROMANCER	*n* pl. **-S** one that romances
ROMANISE	*v* **-ISED, -ISING, -ISES** to romanize
ROMANIZE	*v* **-IZED, -IZING, -IZES** to write in the Roman alphabet
ROMANO	*n* pl. **-NOS** an Italian cheese
ROMANTIC	*n* pl. **-S** a fanciful person
ROMAUNT	*n* pl. **-S** a long, medieval tale
ROMEO	*n* pl. **-MEOS** a male lover
ROMP	*v* **-ED, -ING, -S** to play boisterously
ROMPER	*n* pl. **-S** one that romps
ROMPISH	*adj* inclined to romp
RONDE	*n* pl. **-S** a dance in which the dancers move in a circle
RONDEAU	*n* pl. **-DEAUX** a short poem of fixed form
RONDEL	*n* pl. **-S** a rondeau of 14 lines
RONDELET	*n* pl. **-S** a rondeau of 5 or 7 lines
RONDELLE	*n* pl. **-S** rondel
RONDO	*n* pl. **-DOS** a type of musical composition
RONDURE	*n* pl. **-S** a circle or sphere
RONIN	*n* pl. **-S** a wandering samurai
RONION	*n* pl. **-S** a mangy animal or person
RONNEL	*n* pl. **-S** an insecticide
RONTGEN	*n* pl. **-S** roentgen
RONYON	*n* pl. **-S** ronion
ROO	*n* pl. **ROOS** a kangaroo
ROOD	*n* pl. **-S** a crucifix
ROOF	*v* **-ED, -ING, -S** to provide with a roof (the external upper covering of a building)
ROOFER	*n* pl. **-S** one that builds or repairs roofs
ROOFIE	*n* pl. **-S** a tablet of a powerful sedative
ROOFING	*n* pl. **-S** material for a roof
ROOFLESS	*adj* having no roof
ROOFLIKE	*adj* resembling a roof
ROOFLINE	*n* pl. **-S** the profile of a roof
ROOFTOP	*n* pl. **-S** a roof
ROOFTREE	*n* pl. **-S** a horizontal timber in a roof
ROOIBOS	*n* pl. **-ES** a South African evergreen shrub
ROOK	*v* **-ED, -ING, -S** to swindle
ROOKERY	*n* pl. **-ERIES** a colony of rooks (European crows)
ROOKIE	*n* pl. **-S** a novice
ROOKY	*adj* **ROOKIER, ROOKIEST** abounding in rooks
ROOM	*v* **-ED, -ING, -S** to occupy a room (a walled space within a building)
ROOMER	*n* pl. **-S** a lodger
ROOMETTE	*n* pl. **-S** a small room
ROOMFUL	*n* pl. **ROOMFULS** or **ROOMSFUL** as much as a room can hold
ROOMIE	*n* pl. **-S** a roommate
ROOMMATE	*n* pl. **-S** one with whom a room is shared
ROOMY	*adj* **ROOMIER, ROOMIEST** spacious **ROOMILY** *adv*
ROORBACH	*n* pl. **-S** roorback
ROORBACK	*n* pl. **-S** a false story used for political advantage
ROOSE	*v* **ROOSED, ROOSING, ROOSES** to praise
ROOSER	*n* pl. **-S** one that rooses
ROOST	*v* **-ED, -ING, -S** to settle down for rest or sleep
ROOSTER	*n* pl. **-S** a male chicken
ROOT	*v* **-ED, -ING, -S** to put forth a root (an underground portion of a plant)
ROOTAGE	*n* pl. **-S** a system of roots
ROOTBALL	*n* pl. **-S** the mass of a plant's roots and surrounding soil
ROOTCAP	*n* pl. **-S** the loose mass of cells that covers the tip of some roots
ROOTER	*n* pl. **-S** one that gives encouragement or support
ROOTHOLD	*n* pl. **-S** the embedding of a plant to soil through the growing of roots
ROOTIER	comparative of rooty
ROOTIEST	superlative of rooty
ROOTKIT	*n* pl. **-S** software that allows a person to secretly access a computer
ROOTLE	*v* **-TLED, -TLING, -TLES** to dig in the ground as with the snout
ROOTLESS	*adj* having no roots
ROOTLET	*n* pl. **-S** a small root
ROOTLIKE	*adj* resembling a root
ROOTSY	*adj* **ROOTSIER, ROOTSIEST** showing traditional musical origins
ROOTWORM	*n* pl. **-S** a beetle whose larvae feed on the roots of crop plants

ROOTY	*adj* **ROOTIER, ROOTIEST** full of roots
ROPE	*v* **ROPED, ROPING, ROPES** to bind with a rope (a thick line of twisted fibers) **ROPABLE** *adj*
ROPELIKE	*adj* resembling a rope
ROPER	*n* pl. **-S** one that ropes
ROPERY	*n* pl. **-ERIES** a place where ropes are made
ROPEWALK	*n* pl. **-S** a long path where ropes are made
ROPEWAY	*n* pl. **-WAYS** an aerial cable used to transport freight
ROPEY	*adj* **ROPIER, ROPIEST** ropy
ROPIER	comparative of ropy
ROPIEST	superlative of ropy
ROPILY	*adv* in a ropy manner
ROPINESS	*n* pl. **-ES** the quality of being ropy
ROPING	*n* pl. **-S** the act of binding with a rope
ROPY	*adj* **ROPIER, ROPIEST** resembling a rope or ropes
ROQUE	*n* pl. **-S** a form of croquet
ROQUET	*v* **-ED, -ING, -S** to cause one's own ball to hit another in croquet
ROQUETTE	*n* pl. **-S** an arugula
RORQUAL	*n* pl. **-S** a large whale
ROSACE	*n* pl. **-S** an ornamentation resembling a rose
ROSACEA	*n* pl. **-S** a chronic inflammation of parts of the face
ROSARIAN	*n* pl. **-S** a cultivator of roses
ROSARIUM	*n* pl. **-IUMS** or **-IA** a rose garden
ROSARY	*n* pl. **-RIES** a series of prayers in the Roman Catholic Church
ROSCOE	*n* pl. **-S** a pistol
ROSE	*v* **ROSED, ROSING, ROSES** to make the color of a rose (a reddish flower)
ROSEATE	*adj* rose-colored
ROSEBAY	*n* pl. **-BAYS** an evergreen shrub
ROSEBOWL	*n* pl. **-S** a bowl for displaying cut roses
ROSEBUD	*n* pl. **-S** the bud of a rose
ROSEBUSH	*n* pl. **-ES** a shrub that bears roses
ROSED	past tense of rose
ROSEFISH	*n* pl. **-ES** a marine food fish
ROSEHIP	*n* pl. **-S** the aggregate fruit of the rose plant
ROSELIKE	*adj* resembling a rose
ROSELLA	*n* pl. **-S** an Australian parakeet
ROSELLE	*n* pl. **-S** a tropical plant
ROSEMARY	*n* pl. **-MARIES** an evergreen shrub
ROSEOLA	*n* pl. **-S** a rose-colored skin rash **ROSEOLAR** *adj*
ROSEROOT	*n* pl. **-S** a perennial herb
ROSERY	*n* pl. **-ERIES** a place where roses are grown
ROSESLUG	*n* pl. **-S** a larval sawfly that eats rose leaves
ROSET	*n* pl. **-S** resin
ROSETTE	*n* pl. **-S** an ornament resembling a rose **ROSETTED** *adj*
ROSEWOOD	*n* pl. **-S** a tropical tree
ROSHI	*n* pl. **-S** the spiritual leader of a group of Zen Buddhists
ROSIER	comparative of rosy
ROSIEST	superlative of rosy
ROSILY	*adv* in a rosy manner
ROSIN	*v* **-ED, -ING, -S** to treat with rosin (a brittle resin)
ROSINESS	*n* pl. **-ES** the state of being rosy
ROSING	present participle of rose
ROSINOL	*n* pl. **-S** rosin oil
ROSINOUS	*adj* resembling rosin
ROSINY	*adj* rosinous
ROSOLIO	*n* pl. **-LIOS** a liqueur made from raisins and brandy
ROSTELLA	*n/pl* small, beaklike structures
ROSTER	*v* **-ED, -ING, -S** to place in a list of names
ROSTI	*n* pl. **-S** a Swiss dish of fried grated potatoes topped with cheese
ROSTRA	a pl. of rostrum
ROSTRAL	*adj* pertaining to a rostrum
ROSTRATE	*adj* having a rostrum
ROSTRUM	*n* pl. **-TRUMS** or **-TRA** a beaklike process or part
ROSULATE	*adj* arranged in the form of a rosette
ROSY	*adj* **ROSIER, ROSIEST** rose-colored
ROT	*v* **ROTTED, ROTTING, ROTS** to decompose
ROTA	*n* pl. **-S** a roster
ROTARY	*n* pl. **-RIES** a rotating part or device

ROTATE	*v* **-TATED, -TATING, -TATES** to turn about an axis
ROTATION	*n* pl. **-S** the act or an instance of rotating **ROTATIVE** *adj*
ROTATOR	*n* pl. **-ES** or **-S** one that rotates
ROTATORY	*adj* pertaining to rotation
ROTCH	*n* pl. **-ES** rotche
ROTCHE	*n* pl. **-S** a seabird
ROTE	*n* pl. **-S** mechanical routine
ROTELY	*adv* by rote
ROTENONE	*n* pl. **-S** an insecticide
ROTGUT	*n* pl. **-S** inferior liquor
ROTI	*n* pl. **-S** an unleavened bread
ROTIFER	*n* pl. **-S** a microscopic aquatic organism
ROTIFORM	*adj* shaped like a wheel
ROTINI	*n* pl. **-S** pasta in small spirals
ROTL	*n* pl. **ROTLS** or **ARTAL** a unit of weight in Muslim countries
ROTO	*n* pl. **-TOS** a type of printing process
ROTOR	*n* pl. **-S** a rotating part of a machine
ROTOTILL	*v* **-ED, -ING, -S** to till soil with a type of farming implement
ROTTE	*n* pl. **-S** a medieval stringed instrument
ROTTED	past tense of rot
ROTTEN	*adj* **-TENER, -TENEST** being in a state of decay **ROTTENLY** *adv*
ROTTER	*n* pl. **-S** a scoundrel
ROTTING	present participle of rot
ROTUND	*adj* **ROTUNDER, ROTUNDEST** marked by roundness **ROTUNDLY** *adv*
ROTUNDA	*n* pl. **-S** a round building
ROTURIER	*n* pl. **-S** a commoner
ROUBLE	*n* pl. **-S** ruble
ROUCHE	*n* pl. **-S** ruche
ROUE	*n* pl. **-S** a lecherous man
ROUEN	*n* pl. **-S** any of a breed of domestic ducks
ROUGE	*v* **ROUGED, ROUGING, ROUGES** to color with a red cosmetic
ROUGH	*adj* **ROUGHER, ROUGHEST** having an uneven surface
ROUGH	*v* **-ED, -ING, -S** to make rough
ROUGHAGE	*n* pl. **-S** coarse, bulky food

ROUGHDRY	*v* **-DRIED, -DRYING, -DRIES** to dry without ironing, as washed clothes
ROUGHEN	*v* **-ED, -ING, -S** to make rough
ROUGHER	*n* pl. **-S** one that roughs
ROUGHHEW	*v* **-HEWED, -HEWN, -HEWING, -HEWS** to shape roughly
ROUGHING	*n* pl. **-S** an excessive use of force in hockey
ROUGHISH	*adj* somewhat rough
ROUGHLEG	*n* pl. **-S** a large hawk
ROUGHLY	*adv* in a rough manner
ROUGHOUT	*n* pl. **-S** an unfinished roughly shaped artifact
ROUGHY	*n* pl. **ROUGHIES** a small fish having rough scales
ROUGING	present participle of rouge
ROUILLE	*n* pl. **-S** a peppery garlic sauce
ROULADE	*n* pl. **-S** a musical embellishment
ROULEAU	*n* pl. **-LEAUS** or **-LEAUX** a roll of coins wrapped in paper
ROULETTE	*v* **-LETTED, -LETTING, -LETTES** to make tiny slits in
ROUND	*adj* **ROUNDER, ROUNDEST** shaped like a sphere
ROUND	*v* **-ED, -ING, -S** to make round
ROUNDEL	*n* pl. **-S** a round figure or object
ROUNDER	*n* pl. **-S** a tool for rounding
ROUNDISH	*adj* somewhat round
ROUNDLET	*n* pl. **-S** a small circle
ROUNDLY	*adv* in a round manner
ROUNDUP	*n* pl. **-S** the driving together of cattle scattered over a range
ROUP	*v* **-ED, -ING, -S** to auction
ROUPET	*adj* roupy
ROUPY	*adj* **ROUPIER, ROUPIEST** hoarse **ROUPILY** *adv*
ROUSE	*v* **ROUSED, ROUSING, ROUSES** to bring out of a state of sleep or inactivity **ROUSABLE** *adj*
ROUSER	*n* pl. **-S** one that rouses
ROUSSEAU	*n* pl. **-S** fried pemmican
ROUST	*v* **-ED, -ING, -S** to arouse and drive out
ROUSTER	*n* pl. **-S** a wharf laborer and deckhand
ROUT	*v* **-ED, -ING, -S** to defeat overwhelmingly

ROUTE *v* **ROUTED, ROUTING** or **ROUTEING, ROUTES** to send on a particular course

ROUTEMAN *n* pl. **-MEN** one who conducts business on a customary course

ROUTER *n* pl. **-S** a scooping tool

ROUTEWAY *n* pl. **-WAYS** an established course of travel

ROUTH *n* pl. **-S** an abundance

ROUTINE *n* pl. **-S** a regular course of procedure

ROUTING present participle of route

ROUX *n* pl. **ROUX** a mixture of butter and flour

ROVE *v* **ROVED, ROVING, ROVES** to roam

ROVEN a past participle of reeve

ROVER *n* pl. **-S** one that roves

ROVING *n* pl. **-S** a roll of textile fibers

ROVINGLY *adv* in a roving manner

ROW *v* **-ED, -ING, -S** to propel by means of oars **ROWABLE** *adj*

ROWAN *n* pl. **-S** a Eurasian tree

ROWBOAT *n* pl. **-S** a small boat designed to be rowed

ROWDY *adj* **-DIER, -DIEST** disorderly in behavior **ROWDILY** *adv*

ROWDY *n* pl. **-DIES** a rowdy person

ROWDYISH *adj* tending to be rowdy

ROWDYISM *n* pl. **-S** disorderly behavior

ROWEL *v* **-ELED, -ELING, -ELS** or **-ELLED, -ELLING, -ELS** to prick with a spiked wheel in order to urge forward

ROWEN *n* pl. **-S** a second growth of grass

ROWER *n* pl. **-S** one that rows

ROWING *n* pl. **-S** the sport of racing in light, long, and narrow rowboats

ROWLOCK *n* pl. **-S** an oarlock

ROWTH *n* pl. **-S** routh

ROYAL *n* pl. **-S** a size of printing paper

ROYALISM *n* pl. **-S** support of a monarch or monarchy

ROYALIST *n* pl. **-S** a supporter of a monarch or monarchy

ROYALLY *adv* in a kingly manner

ROYALTY *n* pl. **-TIES** the status or power of a monarch

ROYSTER *v* **-ED, -ING, -S** to roister

ROZZER *n* pl. **-S** a policeman

RUANA *n* pl. **-S** a woolen poncho

RUB *v* **RUBBED, RUBBING, RUBS** to move along the surface of a body with pressure

RUBABOO *n* pl. **-BOOS** a type of soup

RUBACE *n* pl. **-S** rubasse

RUBAIYAT *n* pl. **RUBAIYAT** four-lined stanzas in Persian poetry

RUBASSE *n* pl. **-S** a variety of quartz

RUBATO *n* pl. **-TOS** or **-TI** a fluctuation of speed within a musical phrase

RUBBABOO *n* pl. **-BOOS** rubaboo

RUBBED past tense of rub

RUBBER *v* **-ED, -ING, -S** to stretch one's neck in looking at something

RUBBERY *adj* **-BERIER, -BERIEST** resembling rubber (an elastic substance)

RUBBIES pl. of rubby

RUBBING *n* pl. **-S** an image produced by rubbing

RUBBISH *n* pl. **-ES** worthless, unwanted matter **RUBBISHY** *adj*

RUBBISH *v* **-ED, -ING, -ES** to reject as worthless

RUBBLE *v* **-BLED, -BLING, -BLES** to reduce to rubble (broken pieces)

RUBBLY *adj* **-BLIER, -BLIEST** abounding in rubble

RUBBOARD *n* pl. **-S** a corrugated rectangular board used as a percussion instrument

RUBBY *n* pl. **-BIES** an alcoholic given to drinking rubbing alcohol

RUBBYDUB *n* pl. **-S** a rubby

RUBDOWN *n* pl. **-S** a brisk rubbing of the body

RUBE *n* pl. **-S** a rustic

RUBEL *n* pl. **RUBELS** or **RUBLI** a monetary unit of Belarus

RUBELLA *n* pl. **-S** a virus disease

RUBEOLA *n* pl. **-S** a virus disease **RUBEOLAR** *adj*

RUBICUND *adj* ruddy

RUBIDIUM *n* pl. **-S** a metallic element **RUBIDIC** *adj*

RUBIED past tense of ruby

RUBIER comparative of ruby

RUBIES present 3d person sing. of ruby

RUBIEST superlative of ruby

RUBIGO *n* pl. **-GOS** red iron oxide

RUBIOUS	*adj* ruby-colored
RUBLE	*n* pl. **-S** a monetary unit of Russia
RUBOFF	*n* pl. **-S** a deep impression made by close contact
RUBOUT	*n* pl. **-S** an instance of obliterating something
RUBRIC	*n* pl. **-S** a part of a manuscript or book that appears in red **RUBRICAL** *adj*
RUBUS	*n* pl. **RUBUS** a plant of the rose family
RUBY	*adj* **-BIER, -BIEST** of a deep-red color
RUBY	*v* **-BIED, -BYING, -BIES** to tint with the color of a ruby (a deep-red precious stone)
RUBYLIKE	*adj* resembling a ruby
RUCHE	*n* pl. **-S** a pleated strip of fine fabric
RUCHED	*adj* trimmed with a ruche
RUCHING	*n* pl. **-S** a ruche
RUCK	*v* **-ED, -ING, -S** to wrinkle or crease
RUCKLE	*v* **-LED, -LING, -LES** to ruck
RUCKSACK	*n* pl. **-S** a knapsack
RUCKUS	*n* pl. **-ES** a noisy disturbance
RUCOLA	*n* pl. **-S** arugula
RUCTION	*n* pl. **-S** a ruckus
RUCTIOUS	*adj* quarrelsome
RUDD	*n* pl. **-S** a freshwater fish
RUDDER	*n* pl. **-S** a vertical blade used to direct the course of a vessel
RUDDIED	past tense of ruddy
RUDDIER	comparative of ruddy
RUDDIES	present 3d person sing. of ruddy
RUDDIEST	superlative of ruddy
RUDDILY	*adv* in a ruddy manner
RUDDLE	*v* **-DLED, -DLING, -DLES** to color with a red dye
RUDDOCK	*n* pl. **-S** a European bird
RUDDY	*adj* **-DIER, -DIEST** having a healthy, reddish color
RUDDY	*v* **-DIED, -DYING, -DIES** to make ruddy
RUDE	*adj* **RUDER, RUDEST** discourteous or impolite **RUDELY** *adv*
RUDENESS	*n* pl. **-ES** the quality of being rude
RUDERAL	*n* pl. **-S** a plant growing in poor land
RUDERY	*n* pl. **-ERIES** a rude act
RUDESBY	*n* pl. **-BIES** a rude person
RUDEST	superlative of rude
RUDIMENT	*n* pl. **-S** a basic principle or element
RUDIST	*n* pl. **-S** a cone-shaped extinct mollusk
RUDISTID	*n* pl. **-S** a rudist
RUE	*v* **RUED, RUING** or **RUEING, RUES** to feel sorrow or remorse for
RUEFUL	*adj* feeling sorrow or remorse **RUEFULLY** *adv*
RUER	*n* pl. **-S** one that rues
RUFF	*v* **-ED, -ING, -S** to trump
RUFFE	*n* pl. **-S** a freshwater fish
RUFFIAN	*n* pl. **-S** a tough, lawless person
RUFFLE	*v* **-FLED, -FLING, -FLES** to destroy the smoothness of
RUFFLER	*n* pl. **-S** one that ruffles
RUFFLIKE	*adj* resembling a ruff (a pleated collar)
RUFFLING	present participle of ruffle
RUFFLY	*adj* **-FLIER, -FLIEST** not smooth
RUFIYAA	*n* pl. **RUFIYAA** a monetary unit of the Maldives
RUFOUS	*n* pl. **-ES** a reddish-brown color
RUG	*v* **RUGGED, RUGGING, RUGS** to tear roughly
RUGA	*n* pl. **-GAE** an anatomical fold or wrinkle **RUGAL, RUGATE** *adj*
RUGALACH	*n* pl. **RUGALACH** rugelach
RUGBY	*n* pl. **-BIES** a form of football
RUGELACH	*n* pl. **-S** a cookie of cream-cheese dough spread with a filling and rolled up
RUGGED	*adj* **-GEDER, -GEDEST** having an uneven surface **RUGGEDLY** *adv*
RUGGER	*n* pl. **-S** rugby
RUGGING	present participle of rug
RUGLIKE	*adj* resembling a rug (a thick fabric used as a floor covering)
RUGOLA	*n* pl. **-S** arugula
RUGOSA	*n* pl. **-S** a flowering plant
RUGOSE	*adj* full of wrinkles **RUGOSELY** *adv*
RUGOSITY	*n* pl. **-TIES** the state of being rugose
RUGOUS	*adj* rugose
RUGRAT	*n* pl. **-S** a young child

RUGULOSE	*adj* having small wrinkles
RUIN	*v* **-ED, -ING, -S** to destroy **RUINABLE** *adj*
RUINATE	*v* **-ATED, -ATING, -ATES** to ruin
RUINER	*n* pl. **-S** one that ruins
RUING	present participle of rue
RUINOUS	*adj* destructive
RUKH	*n* pl. **-S** a roc
RULE	*v* **RULED, RULING, RULES** to exercise control over **RULABLE** *adj*
RULELESS	*adj* not restrained or regulated by law
RULER	*n* pl. **-S** one that rules
RULING	*n* pl. **-S** an authoritative decision
RULY	*adj* **RULIER, RULIEST** orderly
RUM	*adj* **RUMMER, RUMMEST** odd
RUM	*n* pl. **-S** an alcoholic liquor
RUMAKI	*n* pl. **-S** chicken liver wrapped together with water chestnuts in a bacon slice
RUMBA	*v* **-ED, -ING, -S** to perform a ballroom dance
RUMBLE	*v* **-BLED, -BLING, -BLES** to make a deep, thunderous sound
RUMBLER	*n* pl. **-S** one that rumbles
RUMBLING	*n* pl. **-S** a thunderous sound
RUMBLY	*adj* tending to rumble
RUMDUM	*n* pl. **-S** an alcoholic
RUMEN	*n* pl. **-MENS** or **-MINA** a part of the stomach of a ruminant **RUMINAL** *adj*
RUMINANT	*n* pl. **-S** a hoofed, even-toed mammal
RUMINATE	*v* **-NATED, -NATING, -NATES** to chew again
RUMLY	*adv* in an odd or peculiar way
RUMMAGE	*v* **-MAGED, -MAGING, -MAGES** to search thoroughly through
RUMMAGER	*n* pl. **-S** one that rummages
RUMMER	*n* pl. **-S** a large drinking glass
RUMMEST	superlative of rum
RUMMY	*adj* **-MIER, -MIEST** odd
RUMMY	*n* pl. **-MIES** a card game
RUMNESS	*n* pl. **-ES** the quality or state of being odd or peculiar
RUMOR	*v* **-ED, -ING, -S** to spread by hearsay
RUMOUR	*v* **-ED, -ING, -S** to rumor

RUMP	*n* pl. **-S** the lower and back part of the trunk **RUMPLESS** *adj*
RUMPLE	*v* **-PLED, -PLING, -PLES** to wrinkle
RUMPLY	*adj* **-PLIER, -PLIEST** rumpled
RUMPOT	*n* pl. **-S** an alcoholic
RUMPUS	*n* pl. **-ES** a noisy disturbance
RUN	*v* **RAN, RUNNING, RUNS** to move by rapid steps
RUNABOUT	*n* pl. **-S** a small, open auto
RUNAGATE	*n* pl. **-S** a deserter
RUNAWAY	*n* pl. **-AWAYS** one that runs away
RUNBACK	*n* pl. **-S** a type of run in football
RUNDLE	*n* pl. **-S** a rung
RUNDLET	*n* pl. **-S** a small barrel
RUNDOWN	*n* pl. **-S** a summary
RUNE	*n* pl. **-S** a letter of an ancient alphabet **RUNELIKE** *adj*
RUNG	*n* pl. **-S** a crosspiece forming a step of a ladder **RUNGED** *adj* **RUNGLESS** *adj*
RUNIC	*adj* pertaining to a rune
RUNKLE	*v* **-KLED, -KLING, -KLES** to wrinkle
RUNLESS	*adj* scoring no runs in baseball
RUNLET	*n* pl. **-S** a small stream
RUNNABLE	*adj* capable of being run
RUNNEL	*n* pl. **-S** a small stream
RUNNER	*n* pl. **-S** one that runs
RUNNING	*n* pl. **-S** a race
RUNNY	*adj* **-NIER, -NIEST** tending to drip
RUNOFF	*n* pl. **-S** rainfall that is not absorbed by the soil
RUNOUT	*n* pl. **-S** the end of a film strip
RUNOVER	*n* pl. **-S** matter for publication that exceeds the allotted space
RUNROUND	*n* pl. **-S** evasive action
RUNT	*n* pl. **-S** a small person or animal **RUNTISH** *adj*
RUNTY	*adj* **RUNTIER, RUNTIEST** small
RUNWAY	*n* pl. **-WAYS** a landing and takeoff strip for aircraft
RUPEE	*n* pl. **-S** a monetary unit of India
RUPIAH	*n* pl. **-S** a monetary unit of Indonesia
RUPTURE	*v* **-TURED, -TURING, -TURES** to burst
RURAL	*adj* pertaining to the country
RURALISE	*v* **-ISED, -ISING, -ISES** to ruralize

RURALISM	*n* pl. **-S** the state of being rural
RURALIST	*n* pl. **-S** one who lives in the country
RURALITE	*n* pl. **-S** a ruralist
RURALITY	*n* pl. **-TIES** the state of being rural
RURALIZE	*v* **-IZED, -IZING, -IZES** to make rural
RURALLY	*adv* in a rural manner
RURBAN	*adj* partially rural and urban
RUSE	*n* pl. **-S** a deception
RUSH	*v* **-ED, -ING, -ES** to move swiftly
RUSHEE	*n* pl. **-S** a college student seeking admission to a fraternity or sorority
RUSHER	*n* pl. **-S** one that rushes
RUSHIER	comparative of rushy
RUSHIEST	superlative of rushy
RUSHING	*n* pl. **-S** yardage gained in football by running plays
RUSHLIKE	*adj* resembling a rush (a grasslike marsh plant)
RUSHY	*adj* **RUSHIER, RUSHIEST** abounding in rushes
RUSINE	*adj* pertaining to a genus of deer
RUSK	*n* pl. **-S** a sweetened biscuit
RUSSET	*v* **-ED, -ING, -S** to make or become reddish or yellowish brown in color
RUSSETY	*adj* of a reddish or yellowish brown color
RUSSIFY	*v* **-FIED, -FYING, -FIES** to make Russian
RUSSULA	*n* pl. **-S** a woodland fungus
RUST	*v* **-ED, -ING, -S** to form rust (a reddish coating that forms on iron) **RUSTABLE** *adj*
RUSTIC	*n* pl. **-S** one who lives in the country
RUSTICAL	*n* pl. **-S** a rustic
RUSTICLY	*adv* in a rural manner
RUSTIER	comparative of rusty

RUSTIEST	superlative of rusty
RUSTILY	*adv* in a rusty manner
RUSTLE	*v* **-TLED, -TLING, -TLES** to make a succession of slight, soft sounds
RUSTLER	*n* pl. **-S** one that rustles
RUSTLESS	*adj* free from rust
RUSTY	*adj* **RUSTIER, RUSTIEST** covered with rust
RUT	*v* **RUTTED, RUTTING, RUTS** to make ruts (grooves) in
RUTABAGA	*n* pl. **-S** a plant having a thick, edible root
RUTH	*n* pl. **-S** compassion
RUTHENIC	*adj* pertaining to a rare, metallic element
RUTHFUL	*adj* full of compassion
RUTHLESS	*adj* having no compassion
RUTILANT	*adj* having a reddish glow
RUTILE	*n* pl. **-S** a mineral
RUTIN	*n* pl. **-S** a chemical compound
RUTTED	past tense of rut
RUTTIER	comparative of rutty
RUTTIEST	superlative of rutty
RUTTILY	*adv* in a rutty manner
RUTTING	present participle of rut
RUTTISH	*adj* lustful
RUTTY	*adj* **-TIER, -TIEST** marked by ruts
RYA	*n* pl. **-S** a Scandinavian handwoven rug
RYE	*n* pl. **-S** a cereal grass
RYEGRASS	*n* pl. **-ES** a European grass
RYKE	*v* **RYKED, RYKING, RYKES** to reach
RYND	*n* pl. **-S** an iron support
RYOKAN	*n* pl. **-S** a Japanese inn
RYOT	*n* pl. **-S** a tenant farmer in India
RYU	*n* pl. **-S** a school of Japanese martial arts

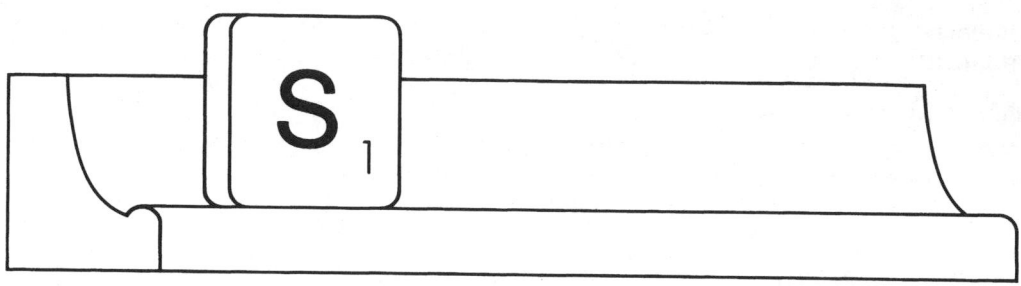

SAB   *v* **SABBED, SABBING, SABS** to sob

SABAL   *n* pl. **-S** a palmetto

SABATON   *n* pl. **-S** a piece of armor for the foot

SABAYON   *n* pl. **-S** a sauce of whipped egg yolks, sugar, and wine

SABBAT   *n* pl. **-S** an assembly of demons and witches

SABBATH   *n* pl. **-S** sabbat

SABBATIC   *n* pl. **-S** a year of release from normal teaching duties

SABBED   past tense of sab

SABBING   present participle of sab

SABE   *v* **SABED, SABEING, SABES** to savvy

SABER   *v* **-ED, -ING, -S** to strike with a saber (a type of sword)

SABICU   *n* pl. **-S** a Caribbean tree

SABIN   *n* pl. **-S** a unit of sound absorption

SABINE   *n* pl. **-S** savin

SABIR   *n* pl. **-S** a French-based pidgin language

SABKHA   *n* pl. **-S** a coastal, flat, periodically flooded area in northern Africa

SABLE   *n* pl. **-S** a carnivorous mammal

SABOT   *n* pl. **-S** a wooden shoe **SABOTED** *adj*

SABOTAGE   *v* **-TAGED, -TAGING, -TAGES** to destroy maliciously

SABOTEUR   *n* pl. **-S** one who sabotages

SABRA   *n* pl. **-S** a native Israeli

SABRE   *v* **-BRED, -BRING, -BRES** to saber

SABULOSE   *adj* sabulous

SABULOUS   *adj* sandy

SAC   *n* pl. **-S** a pouch-shaped structure in an animal or plant

SACATON   *n* pl. **-S** a perennial grass

SACBUT   *n* pl. **-S** sackbut

SACCADE   *n* pl. **-S** a rapid, jerky movement of the eye **SACCADIC** *adj*

SACCATE   *adj* having a sac

SACCULAR   *adj* resembling a sac

SACCULE   *n* pl. **-S** a small sac

SACCULUS   *n* pl. **-LI** saccule

SACHEM   *n* pl. **-S** a Native American chief **SACHEMIC** *adj*

SACHET   *n* pl. **-S** a small bag containing perfumed powder **SACHETED** *adj*

SACK   *v* **-ED, -ING, -S** to put into a sack (a large bag) **SACKABLE** *adj*

SACKBUT   *n* pl. **-S** a medieval trombone

SACKER   *n* pl. **-S** one that sacks

SACKFUL   *n* pl. **SACKFULS** or **SACKSFUL** as much as a sack can hold

SACKING   *n* pl. **-S** material for making sacks

SACKLIKE   *adj* resembling a sack

SACLIKE   *adj* resembling a sac

SACQUE   *n* pl. **-S** a loose-fitting dress

SACRA   pl. of sacrum

SACRAL   *n* pl. **-S** a vertebra or nerve situated near the sacrum

SACRARIA   *n/pl* ancient Roman shrines

SACRED   *adj* **SACREDER, SACREDEST** holy **SACREDLY** *adv*

SACRING   *n* pl. **-S** the consecration of bread and wine of the Eucharist

SACRIST   *n* pl. **-S** a person in charge of a sacristy

SACRISTY   *n* pl. **-TIES** a room in which sacred vessels and vestments are kept

SACRUM   *n* pl. **-CRUMS** or **-CRA** a bone of the pelvis

SAD   *adj* **SADDER, SADDEST** unhappy

SADDEN   *v* **-ED, -ING, -S** to make sad

SADDHU   *n* pl. **-S** sadhu

SADDISH	*adj* somewhat sad
SADDLE	*v* **-DLED, -DLING, -DLES** to put a saddle (a leather seat for a rider) on
SADDLER	*n* pl. **-S** one that makes, repairs, or sells saddles
SADDLERY	*n* pl. **-DLERIES** the shop of a saddler
SADE	*n* pl. **-S** a Hebrew letter
SADHE	*n* pl. **-S** sade
SADHU	*n* pl. **-S** a Hindu holy man
SADI	*n* pl. **-S** sade
SADIRON	*n* pl. **-S** a heavy flatiron
SADISM	*n* pl. **-S** a tendency to take delight in inflicting pain
SADIST	*n* pl. **-S** one marked by sadism **SADISTIC** *adj*
SADLY	*adv* in a sad manner
SADNESS	*n* pl. **-ES** the state of being sad
SAE	*adv* so
SAFARI	*v* **-ED, -ING, -S** to go on a hunting expedition
SAFE	*adj* **SAFER, SAFEST** free from danger **SAFELY** *adv*
SAFE	*n* pl. **-S** a metal receptacle for storing valuables
SAFENESS	*n* pl. **-ES** the quality of being safe
SAFETY	*v* **-TIED, -TYING, -TIES** to protect against failure, breakage, or accident
SAFFRON	*n* pl. **-S** a flowering plant
SAFFRONY	*adj* resembling saffron
SAFRANIN	*n* pl. **-S** a red dye
SAFROL	*n* pl. **-S** safrole
SAFROLE	*n* pl. **-S** a poisonous liquid
SAG	*v* **SAGGED, SAGGING, SAGS** to bend or sink downward from weight or pressure
SAGA	*n* pl. **-S** a medieval Scandinavian narrative
SAGACITY	*n* pl. **-TIES** wisdom
SAGAMAN	*n* pl. **-MEN** a writer of sagas
SAGAMORE	*n* pl. **-S** an Algonquian Indian chief
SAGANASH	*n* pl. **-ES** a white man — an Algonquian Indian term
SAGBUT	*n* pl. **-S** sackbut
SAGE	*adj* **SAGER, SAGEST** wise **SAGELY** *adv*
SAGE	*n* pl. **-S** an aromatic herb used as seasoning
SAGEHOOD	*n* pl. **-S** the state of being wise
SAGENESS	*n* pl. **-ES** wisdom
SAGGAR	*v* **-ED, -ING, -S** to bake in a saggar (a protective clay casing)
SAGGARD	*n* pl. **-S** a saggar
SAGGED	past tense of sag
SAGGER	*v* **-ED, -ING, -S** to saggar
SAGGING	present participle of sag
SAGGY	*adj* **-GIER, -GIEST** characterized by sagging
SAGIER	comparative of sagy
SAGIEST	superlative of sagy
SAGITTAL	*adj* resembling an arrow or arrowhead
SAGO	*n* pl. **-GOS** a tropical tree
SAGUARO	*n* pl. **-ROS** a tall cactus
SAGUM	*n* pl. **-GA** a cloak worn by ancient Roman soldiers
SAGY	*adj* **SAGIER, SAGIEST** flavored with sage
SAHIB	*n* pl. **-S** sir; master — used as a term of respect in colonial India
SAHIWAL	*n* pl. **-S** any of a breed of humped dairy cattle
SAHUARO	*n* pl. **-ROS** saguaro
SAICE	*n* pl. **-S** syce
SAID	*n* pl. **-S** sayyid
SAIGA	*n* pl. **-S** a small antelope
SAIL	*v* **-ED, -ING, -S** to move across the surface of water by the action of wind **SAILABLE** *adj*
SAILBOAT	*n* pl. **-S** a boat that sails
SAILER	*n* pl. **-S** a vessel that sails
SAILFISH	*n* pl. **-ES** a large marine fish
SAILING	*n* pl. **-S** the act of one that sails
SAILLESS	*adj* lacking a sail
SAILOR	*n* pl. **-S** a member of a ship's crew **SAILORLY** *adj*
SAILPAST	*n* pl. **-S** the sailing of ships past a place
SAIMIN	*n* pl. **-S** a Hawaiian noodle soup
SAIN	*v* **-ED, -ING, -S** to make the sign of the cross on
SAINFOIN	*n* pl. **-S** a perennial herb
SAINT	*v* **-ED, -ING, -S** to declare to be a saint (a person of exceptional holiness)
SAINTDOM	*n* pl. **-S** the state of being a saint

SAINTLY *adj* **-LIER, -LIEST** of or befitting a saint

SAITH a present 3d person sing. of say

SAITHE *n* pl. **SAITHE** a marine food fish

SAIYID *n* pl. **-S** sayyid

SAJOU *n* pl. **-S** a capuchin

SAKE *n* pl. **-S** benefit, interest, or advantage

SAKER *n* pl. **-S** a Eurasian falcon

SAKI *n* pl. **-S** a Japanese liquor

SAKTI *n* pl. **-S** the wife of a god in Hinduism

SAL *n* pl. **-S** salt

SALAAM *v* **-ED, -ING, -S** to greet with a low bow

SALABLE *adj* capable of being or fit to be sold **SALABLY** *adv*

SALACITY *n* pl. **-TIES** lewdness

SALAD *n* pl. **-S** a dish of green, raw vegetables

SALADANG *n* pl. **-S** a wild ox

SALAL *n* pl. **-S** a small shrub

SALAMI *n* pl. **-S** a seasoned sausage

SALARIAT *n* pl. **-S** the class of salaried persons

SALARY *v* **-RIED, -RYING, -RIES** to pay a periodic, fixed compensation to

SALAT *n* pl. **-S** the ritual prayer of Muslims

SALCHOW *n* pl. **-S** a figure-skating jump

SALE *n* pl. **-S** the act or an instance of selling

SALEABLE *adj* salable **SALEABLY** *adv*

SALEP *n* pl. **-S** a starchy meal ground from the roots of certain orchids

SALEROOM *n* pl. **-S** a room in which goods are displayed for sale

SALESMAN *n* pl. **-MEN** a man who sells merchandise

SALIC *adj* pertaining to a group of igneous rocks

SALICIN *n* pl. **-S** a chemical compound

SALICINE *n* pl. **-S** salicin

SALIENCE *n* pl. **-S** a projecting feature or detail

SALIENCY *n* pl. **-CIES** salience

SALIENT *n* pl. **-S** the part of a fortification projecting closest to the enemy

SALIFY *v* **-FIED, -FYING, -FIES** to combine with a salt

SALINA *n* pl. **-S** a pond, marsh, or lake containing salt water

SALINE *n* pl. **-S** a salt solution

SALINITY *n* pl. **-TIES** a concentration of salt

SALINIZE *v* **-NIZED, -NIZING, -NIZES** to treat with salt

SALIVA *n* pl. **-S** a fluid secreted by the glands of the mouth **SALIVARY** *adj*

SALIVATE *v* **-VATED, -VATING, -VATES** to secrete saliva

SALL *v* shall — SALL is the only form of this verb; it cannot be conjugated

SALLET *n* pl. **-S** a light medieval helmet

SALLIED past tense of sally

SALLIER *n* pl. **-S** one that sallies

SALLIES present 3d person sing. of sally

SALLOW *adj* **-LOWER, -LOWEST** of a sickly yellowish color **SALLOWLY** *adv*

SALLOW *v* **-ED, -ING, -S** to make sallow

SALLOWY *adj* abounding in willow trees

SALLY *v* **-LIED, -LYING, -LIES** to rush out suddenly

SALMI *n* pl. **-S** a dish of roasted game birds

SALMON *n* pl. **-S** a food fish

SALMONID *n* pl. **-S** a fish of the salmon family

SALMONY *adj* resembling salmon

SALOL *n* pl. **-S** a chemical compound

SALON *n* pl. **-S** a large room in which guests are received

SALOON *n* pl. **-S** a tavern

SALOOP *n* pl. **-S** a hot drink made from an infusion of aromatic herbs

SALP *n* pl. **-S** salpa

SALPA *n* pl. **-PAS** or **-PAE** a free-swimming tunicate

SALPIAN *n* pl. **-S** salpa

SALPICON *n* pl. **-S** a mixture of chopped foods in a sauce used as stuffings

SALPID *n* pl. **-S** salpa

SALPINX *n* pl. **-PINGES** an anatomical tube

SALSA *n* pl. **-S** a spicy sauce of tomatoes, onions, and peppers

SALSIFY *n* pl. **-FIES** a European herb

SALSILLA *n* pl. **-S** a tropical plant

SALT *adj* **SALTER, SALTEST** salty

SALT	*v* **-ED, -ING, -S** to treat with salt (a crystalline compound used as a seasoning and preservative)
SALTANT	*adj* jumping or dancing
SALTBOX	*n* pl. **-ES** a type of house
SALTBUSH	*n* pl. **-ES** a salt-tolerant plant
SALTER	*n* pl. **-S** one that salts
SALTERN	*n* pl. **-S** a place where salt is produced
SALTERY	*n* pl. **-ERIES** a factory where fish is salted for storage
SALTIE	*n* pl. **-S** a deep-sea vessel sailing the Great Lakes
SALTIER	*n* pl. **-S** saltire
SALTIEST	superlative of salty
SALTILY	*adv* in a salty manner
SALTINE	*n* pl. **-S** a salted cracker
SALTING	*n* pl. **-S** land regularly flooded by tides
SALTIRE	*n* pl. **-S** a heraldic design
SALTISH	*adj* somewhat salty
SALTLESS	*adj* having no salt
SALTLIKE	*adj* resembling salt
SALTNESS	*n* pl. **-ES** the state of being salty
SALTPAN	*n* pl. **-S** a large pan for making salt by evaporation
SALTWORK	*n* pl. **-S** a saltern
SALTWORT	*n* pl. **-S** a seaside herb
SALTY	*adj* **SALTIER, SALTIEST** tasting of or containing salt
SALUKI	*n* pl. **-S** a tall, slender dog
SALUT	*interj* — used to express friendship before a drink
SALUTARY	*adj* producing a beneficial effect
SALUTE	*v* **-LUTED, -LUTING, -LUTES** to greet with a sign of welcome or respect
SALUTER	*n* pl. **-S** one that salutes
SALVABLE	*adj* capable of being saved **SALVABLY** *adv*
SALVAGE	*v* **-VAGED, -VAGING, -VAGES** to save from loss or destruction
SALVAGEE	*n* pl. **-S** one in whose favor salvage has been effected
SALVAGER	*n* pl. **-S** one that salvages
SALVE	*v* **SALVED, SALVING, SALVES** to soothe
SALVER	*n* pl. **-S** a tray or serving platter
SALVIA	*n* pl. **-S** a flowering plant
SALVIFIC	*adj* having the power to save
SALVING	present participle of salve
SALVO	*v* **-ED, -ING, -S** or **-ES** to discharge firearms simultaneously
SALVOR	*n* pl. **-S** a salvager
SALWAR	*n* pl. **-S** shalwar
SAMADHI	*n* pl. **-S** a state of concentration in yoga
SAMARA	*n* pl. **-S** a dry, one-seeded fruit
SAMARIUM	*n* pl. **-S** a metallic element
SAMBA	*v* **-ED, -ING, -S** to perform a Brazilian dance
SAMBAL	*n* pl. **-S** a spicy condiment
SAMBAR	*n* pl. **-S** a large Asian deer
SAMBHAR	*n* pl. **-S** sambar
SAMBHUR	*n* pl. **-S** sambar
SAMBO	*n* pl. **-BOS** or **-BOES** a person of mixed ancestry
SAMBUCA	*n* pl. **-S** an ancient stringed instrument
SAMBUKE	*n* pl. **-S** sambuca
SAMBUR	*n* pl. **-S** sambar
SAME	*adj* resembling in every relevant respect
SAMECH	*n* pl. **-S** samek
SAMEK	*n* pl. **-S** a Hebrew letter
SAMEKH	*n* pl. **-S** samek
SAMENESS	*n* pl. **-ES** lack of change or variety
SAMEY	*adj* **SAMIER, SAMIEST** lacking variety
SAMFU	*n* pl. **-S** a casual Chinese outfit of jacket and pants
SAMIEL	*n* pl. **-S** the simoom
SAMISEN	*n* pl. **-S** a Japanese stringed instrument
SAMITE	*n* pl. **-S** a silk fabric
SAMIZDAT	*n* pl. **-S** a system in the Soviet Union for printing and distributing unauthorized literature
SAMLET	*n* pl. **-S** a young salmon
SAMOSA	*n* pl. **-S** a filled pastry turnover
SAMOVAR	*n* pl. **-S** a metal urn for heating water
SAMP	*n* pl. **-S** coarsely ground corn
SAMPAN	*n* pl. **-S** a flat-bottomed Chinese skiff
SAMPHIRE	*n* pl. **-S** a European herb

SAMPLE	*v* **-PLED, -PLING, -PLES** to test a representative portion of a whole
SAMPLER	*n* pl. **-S** one that samples
SAMPLING	*n* pl. **-S** a small part selected for analysis
SAMSARA	*n* pl. **-S** the cycle of birth, death, and rebirth in Buddhism **SAMSARIC** *adj*
SAMSHU	*n* pl. **-S** a Chinese liquor
SAMSKARA	*n* pl. **-S** a Hindu purification ceremony
SAMURAI	*n* pl. **-S** a Japanese warrior
SAN	*n* pl. **-S** a sanatorium
SANATIVE	*adj* having the power to cure or heal
SANCTA	a pl. of sanctum
SANCTIFY	*v* **-FIED, -FYING, -FIES** to make holy
SANCTION	*v* **-ED, -ING, -S** to authorize
SANCTITY	*n* pl. **-TIES** holiness
SANCTUM	*n* pl. **-TUMS** or **-TA** a sacred place
SAND	*v* **-ED, -ING, -S** to smooth by rubbing with an abrasive **SANDABLE** *adj*
SANDAL	*v* **-DALED, -DALING, -DALS** or **-DALLED, -DALLING, -DALS** to provide with sandals (light, open shoes)
SANDARAC	*n* pl. **-S** an aromatic resin
SANDBAG	*v* **-BAGGED, -BAGGING, -BAGS** to surround with bags of sand (loose granular rock material)
SANDBANK	*n* pl. **-S** a large mass of sand
SANDBAR	*n* pl. **-S** a ridge of sand formed in a river or sea
SANDBOX	*n* pl. **-ES** a box containing sand for children to play in
SANDBUR	*n* pl. **-S** an annual herb
SANDBURR	*n* pl. **-S** sandbur
SANDDAB	*n* pl. **-S** a small flatfish
SANDER	*n* pl. **-S** one that sands
SANDFISH	*n* pl. **-ES** a marine fish
SANDFLY	*n* pl. **-FLIES** a biting fly
SANDHI	*n* pl. **-S** a process of phonetic modification
SANDHILL	*n* pl. **-S** a hill of sand
SANDHOG	*n* pl. **-S** a worker who digs or works in sand
SANDIER	comparative of sandy
SANDIEST	superlative of sandy

SANDLESS	*adj* lacking sand
SANDLIKE	*adj* resembling sand
SANDLING	*n* pl. **-S** a marine fish
SANDLOT	*n* pl. **-S** a vacant lot
SANDMAN	*n* pl. **-MEN** a mythical person who makes children sleepy by sprinkling sand in their eyes
SANDPEEP	*n* pl. **-S** a wading bird
SANDPILE	*n* pl. **-S** a pile of sand
SANDPIT	*n* pl. **-S** a pit dug in sandy soil
SANDSHOE	*n* pl. **-S** a lightweight sneaker
SANDSOAP	*n* pl. **-S** a type of soap
SANDSPIT	*n* pl. **-S** a small point of land created by sand dunes
SANDSPUR	*n* pl. **-S** a sandbur
SANDWICH	*v* **-ED, -ING, -ES** to place between two layers or objects
SANDWORM	*n* pl. **-S** a sand-dwelling worm
SANDWORT	*n* pl. **-S** a flowering plant
SANDY	*adj* **SANDIER, SANDIEST** containing or covered with sand
SANDYISH	*adj* somewhat sandy
SANE	*adj* **SANER, SANEST** mentally sound **SANELY** *adv*
SANE	*v* **SANED, SANING, SANES** to sain
SANENESS	*n* pl. **-ES** sanity
SANG	past tense of sing
SANGA	*n* pl. **-S** sangar
SANGAR	*n* pl. **-S** a temporary fortification for two or three men
SANGAREE	*n* pl. **-S** an alcoholic beverage
SANGER	*n* pl. **-S** sangar
SANGH	*n* pl. **-S** an association promoting unity between the different groups in Hinduism
SANGHA	*n* pl. **-S** a Buddhist religious community
SANGRAIL	*n* pl. **-S** the legendary cup used by Christ at the Last Supper
SANGREAL	*n* pl. **-S** sangrail
SANGRIA	*n* pl. **-S** an alcoholic beverage
SANGUINE	*n* pl. **-S** a red color
SANICLE	*n* pl. **-S** a medicinal herb
SANIDINE	*n* pl. **-S** a glassy variety of feldspar
SANIES	*n* pl. **SANIES** a fluid discharged from wounds **SANIOUS** *adj*
SANING	present participle of sane

SANITARY	*n* pl. **-TARIES** a public urinal
SANITATE	*v* **-TATED, -TATING, -TATES** to sanitize
SANITISE	*v* **-TISED, -TISING, -TISES** to sanitize
SANITIZE	*v* **-TIZED, -TIZING, -TIZES** to guard against infection or disease by cleaning or sterilizing
SANITY	*n* pl. **-TIES** the state of being sane
SANJAK	*n* pl. **-S** an administrative district of Turkey
SANK	past tense of sink
SANNOP	*n* pl. **-S** sannup
SANNUP	*n* pl. **-S** a married male Native American
SANNYASI	*n* pl. **-S** a Hindu monk
SANS	*prep* without
SANSAR	*n* pl. **-S** sarsar
SANSEI	*n* pl. **-S** a grandchild of Japanese immigrants to the United States
SANSERIF	*n* pl. **-S** a typeface without serifs
SANTALIC	*adj* pertaining to sandalwood
SANTALOL	*n* pl. **-S** sandalwood oil
SANTERA	*n* pl. **-S** a priestess of santeria
SANTERIA	*n* pl. **-S** a religion of the Caribbean region
SANTERO	*n* pl. **-ROS** a priest of santeria
SANTIM	*n* pl. **-TIMS** or **-TIMI** or **-TIMU** a formerly used coin of Latvia
SANTIR	*n* pl. **-S** a Persian dulcimer
SANTO	*n* pl. **-TOS** a wooden image of a saint
SANTOKU	*n* pl. **-S** a Japanese knife
SANTOL	*n* pl. **-S** a tropical tree
SANTONIN	*n* pl. **-S** a chemical compound
SANTOOR	*n* pl. **-S** santir
SANTOUR	*n* pl. **-S** santir
SANTUR	*n* pl. **-S** santir
SANYASI	*n* pl. **-S** sannyasi
SAP	*v* **SAPPED, SAPPING, SAPS** to deplete or weaken gradually
SAPAJOU	*n* pl. **-S** a capuchin
SAPELE	*n* pl. **-S** a large tropical African tree
SAPHEAD	*n* pl. **-S** a foolish, stupid, or gullible person
SAPHENA	*n* pl. **-NAS** or **-NAE** a vein of the leg
SAPID	*adj* pleasant to the taste
SAPIDITY	*n* pl. **-TIES** the state of being sapid
SAPIENCE	*n* pl. **-S** wisdom
SAPIENCY	*n* pl. **-CIES** sapience
SAPIENS	*adj* pertaining to recent man
SAPIENT	*n* pl. **-S** a wise person
SAPLESS	*adj* lacking vitality
SAPLING	*n* pl. **-S** a young tree
SAPONIFY	*v* **-FIED, -FYING, -FIES** to convert into soap
SAPONIN	*n* pl. **-S** a soapy substance obtained from plants
SAPONINE	*n* pl. **-S** saponin
SAPONITE	*n* pl. **-S** a mineral found in veins and cavities of rocks
SAPOR	*n* pl. **-S** flavor **SAPOROUS** *adj*
SAPOTA	*n* pl. **-S** an evergreen tree
SAPOTE	*n* pl. **-S** a tropical American tree
SAPOUR	*n* pl. **-S** sapor
SAPPED	past tense of sap
SAPPER	*n* pl. **-S** a military engineer
SAPPHIC	*n* pl. **-S** a type of verse form
SAPPHIRE	*n* pl. **-S** a blue gem
SAPPHISM	*n* pl. **-S** lesbianism
SAPPHIST	*n* pl. **-S** a lesbian
SAPPING	*n* pl. **-S** the removal of the foundation of a building so as to weaken it
SAPPY	*adj* **-PIER, -PIEST** silly **SAPPILY** *adv*
SAPREMIA	*n* pl. **-S** a form of blood poisoning **SAPREMIC** *adj*
SAPROBE	*n* pl. **-S** an organism that derives its nourishment from decaying organic matter **SAPROBIC** *adj*
SAPROPEL	*n* pl. **-S** mud consisting chiefly of decaying organic matter
SAPSAGO	*n* pl. **-GOS** a hard green cheese
SAPWOOD	*n* pl. **-S** the newly formed outer wood of a tree
SARABAND	*n* pl. **-S** a stately Spanish dance
SARAN	*n* pl. **-S** a thermoplastic resin
SARANGI	*n* pl. **-S** a stringed instrument of India
SARAPE	*n* pl. **-S** serape
SARCASM	*n* pl. **-S** a sharply mocking or contemptuous remark
SARCENET	*n* pl. **-S** a silk fabric
SARCINA	*n* pl. **-NAS** or **-NAE** a spherical bacterium

SARCOID	n pl. **-S** a disease of horses
SARCOMA	n pl. **-MAS** or **-MATA** a type of tumor
SARCOUS	adj composed of flesh or muscle
SARD	n pl. **-S** a variety of quartz
SARDANA	n pl. **-S** a Spanish folk dance
SARDAR	n pl. **-S** sirdar
SARDINE	v **-DINED, -DINING, -DINES** to pack tightly
SARDIUS	n pl. **-ES** sard
SARDONIC	adj mocking
SARDONYX	n pl. **-ES** a variety of quartz
SAREE	n pl. **-S** sari
SARGASSO	n pl. **-GASSOS** or **-GASSOES** or **-GASSA** a brownish seaweed
SARGE	n pl. **-S** sergeant
SARGO	n pl. **-GOS** a silvery marine fish
SARI	n pl. **-S** an outer garment worn by Hindu women
SARIN	n pl. **-S** a toxic gas
SARK	n pl. **-S** a shirt
SARKY	adj **SARKIER, SARKIEST** sarcastic **SARKILY** adv
SARMENT	n pl. **-S** a type of plant stem
SARMENTA	n/pl sarments
SARNIE	n pl. **-S** a sandwich
SAROD	n pl. **-S** a stringed instrument of India
SARODE	n pl. **-S** sarod
SARODIST	n pl. **-S** one who plays the sarod
SARONG	n pl. **-S** an outer garment worn in the Pacific islands
SAROS	n pl. **-ES** the eclipse cycle of the sun and moon
SARSAR	n pl. **-S** a cold, whistling wind
SARSEN	n pl. **-S** a large sandstone block
SARSENET	n pl. **-S** sarcenet
SARSNET	n pl. **-S** sarcenet
SARTOR	n pl. **-S** a tailor
SARTORII	n/pl flat, narrow thigh muscles
SASANQUA	n pl. **-S** a Japanese camellia
SASH	v **-ED, -ING, -ES** to furnish with a frame in which glass is set
SASHAY	v **-ED, -ING, -S** to flounce
SASHIMI	n pl. **-S** a Japanese dish of sliced raw fish
SASHLESS	adj lacking a sash (a long band worn around the waist)
SASIN	n pl. **-S** an antelope of India
SASS	v **-ED, -ING, -ES** to talk impudently to
SASSABY	n pl. **-BIES** an African antelope
SASSIER	comparative of sassy
SASSIES	pl. of sassy
SASSIEST	superlative of sassy
SASSILY	adv in a sassy manner
SASSWOOD	n pl. **-S** an African tree
SASSY	adj **SASSIER, SASSIEST** impudent
SASSY	n pl. **-SIES** sasswood
SASTRUGA	n pl. **-GI** a ridge of snow formed by the wind in polar regions
SAT	past tense of sit
SATANG	n pl. **-S** a monetary unit of Thailand
SATANIC	adj extremely evil
SATANISM	n pl. **-S** worship of the powers of evil
SATANIST	n pl. **-S** one who practices satanism
SATARA	n pl. **-S** a woolen fabric
SATAY	n pl. **-TAYS** marinated meat that is skewered and broiled and dipped in peanut sauce
SATCHEL	n pl. **-S** a small carrying bag
SATCOM	n pl. **-S** satellite communications
SATE	v **SATED, SATING, SATES** to satiate
SATEEN	n pl. **-S** a cotton fabric
SATEM	adj pertaining to a group of Indo-European languages
SATI	n pl. **-S** suttee
SATIABLE	adj capable of being satiated **SATIABLY** adv
SATIATE	v **-ATED, -ATING, -ATES** to satisfy to or beyond capacity
SATIETY	n pl. **-ETIES** the state of being satiated
SATIN	v **-ED, -ING, -S** to give a glossy surface to
SATINET	n pl. **-S** a thin satin
SATING	present participle of sate
SATINPOD	n pl. **-S** a flowering plant
SATINY	adj resembling satin
SATIRE	n pl. **-S** the use of derisive wit to attack folly or wickedness **SATIRIC** adj

SATIRISE *v* **-RISED, -RISING, -RISES** to satirize

SATIRIST *n* pl. **-S** one who satirizes

SATIRIZE *v* **-RIZED, -RIZING, -RIZES** to subject to satire

SATISFY *v* **-FIED, -FYING, -FIES** to provide fully with what is desired, expected, or needed

SATORI *n* pl. **-S** the illumination of spirit sought by Zen Buddhists

SATRAP *n* pl. **-S** a governor of a province in ancient Persia

SATRAPY *n* pl. **-PIES** the territory of a satrap

SATSANG *n* pl. **-S** a sacred gathering in Hinduism

SATSUMA *n* pl. **-S** a variety of orange

SATURANT *n* pl. **-S** a substance used to saturate

SATURATE *v* **-RATED, -RATING, -RATES** to fill completely with something that permeates

SATYR *n* pl. **-S** a woodland deity of Greek mythology **SATYRIC** *adj*

SATYRID *n* pl. **-S** a brownish butterfly

SAU *n* pl. **SAU** xu

SAUCE *v* **SAUCED, SAUCING, SAUCES** to season with sauce (a flavorful liquid dressing)

SAUCEBOX *n* pl. **-ES** a saucy person

SAUCEPAN *n* pl. **-S** a deep cooking pan with a handle

SAUCEPOT *n* pl. **-S** a deep cooking pot with two handles

SAUCER *n* pl. **-S** a small, shallow dish

SAUCH *n* pl. **-S** saugh

SAUCIER *n* pl. **-S** a chef who specializes in sauces

SAUCING present participle of sauce

SAUCY *adj* **SAUCIER, SAUCIEST** impudent **SAUCILY** *adv*

SAUGER *n* pl. **-S** a freshwater fish

SAUGH *n* pl. **-S** a willow tree **SAUGHY** *adj*

SAUL *n* pl. **-S** soul

SAULT *n* pl. **-S** a waterfall

SAUNA *v* **-ED, -ING, -S** to take a dry heat bath

SAUNTER *v* **-ED, -ING, -S** to walk in a leisurely manner

SAUREL *n* pl. **-S** a marine fish

SAURIAN *n* pl. **-S** any of a suborder of reptiles

SAUROPOD *n* pl. **-S** any of a suborder of large dinosaurs

SAURY *n* pl. **-RIES** a marine fish

SAUSAGE *n* pl. **-S** finely chopped and seasoned meat stuffed into a casing

SAUTE *v* **-TEED** or **-TED, -TEING, -TES** to fry in a small amount of fat

SAUTERNE *n* pl. **-S** a sweet white wine

SAUTOIR *n* pl. **-S** a saltire

SAUTOIRE *n* pl. **-S** sautoir

SAVABLE *adj* capable of being saved

SAVAGE *adj* **-AGER, -AGEST** fierce **SAVAGELY** *adv*

SAVAGE *v* **-AGED, -AGING, -AGES** to attack or treat brutally

SAVAGERY *n* pl. **-RIES** the quality of being savage

SAVAGISM *n* pl. **-S** savagery

SAVANNA *n* pl. **-S** a flat, treeless grassland

SAVANNAH *n* pl. **-S** savanna

SAVANT *n* pl. **-S** a man of profound learning

SAVARIN *n* pl. **-S** a yeast cake baked in a ring mold

SAVATE *n* pl. **-S** a pugilistic sport

SAVE *v* **SAVED, SAVING, SAVES** to rescue from danger, injury, or loss **SAVEABLE** *adj*

SAVELOY *n* pl. **-LOYS** a highly seasoned sausage

SAVER *n* pl. **-S** one that saves

SAVIN *n* pl. **-S** an evergreen shrub

SAVINE *n* pl. **-S** savin

SAVING *n* pl. **-S** the act or an instance of saving

SAVINGLY *adv* in a thrifty manner

SAVIOR *n* pl. **-S** one that saves

SAVIOUR *n* pl. **-S** savior

SAVOR *v* **-ED, -ING, -S** to taste or smell with pleasure

SAVORER *n* pl. **-S** one that savors

SAVOROUS *adj* savory

SAVORY *adj* **-VORIER, -VORIEST** pleasant to the taste or smell **SAVORILY** *adv*

SAVORY *n* pl. **-VORIES** a savory dish served before or after a meal

SAVOUR *v* **-ED, -ING, -S** to savor

SAVOURER *n* pl. **-S** savorer

SAVOURY	*adj* **-VOURIER, -VOURIEST** savory
SAVOURY	*n* pl. **-VOURIES** a savory
SAVOY	*n* pl. **-VOYS** a variety of cabbage
SAVVY	*adj* **-VIER, -VIEST** shrewd
SAVVY	*v* **-VIED, -VYING, -VIES** to understand **SAVVILY** *adv*
SAW	*v* **SAWED, SAWN, SAWING, SAWS** to cut or divide with a saw (a type of cutting tool)
SAWBILL	*n* pl. **-S** a tropical bird
SAWBONES	*n* pl. **-BONESES** a surgeon
SAWBUCK	*n* pl. **-S** a sawhorse
SAWDUST	*n* pl. **-S** small particles of wood produced in sawing **SAWDUSTY** *adj*
SAWER	*n* pl. **-S** one that saws
SAWFISH	*n* pl. **-ES** a marine fish
SAWFLY	*n* pl. **-FLIES** a winged insect
SAWGRASS	*n* pl. **-ES** a sedge with spiny-edged leaves
SAWHORSE	*n* pl. **-S** a rack used to support a piece of wood being sawed
SAWLIKE	*adj* resembling a saw
SAWLOG	*n* pl. **-S** a log large enough to saw into boards
SAWMILL	*n* pl. **-S** a place where logs are sawed
SAWN	a past participle of saw
SAWNEY	*n* pl. **-NEYS** a foolish person
SAWTOOTH	*n* pl. **-TEETH** a cutting edge on a saw
SAWYER	*n* pl. **-S** one that saws wood for a living
SAX	*n* pl. **-ES** a saxophone
SAXATILE	*adj* living or growing among rocks
SAXHORN	*n* pl. **-S** a brass wind instrument
SAXIST	*n* pl. **-S** a saxophone player
SAXMAN	*n* pl. **-MEN** a saxophone player
SAXONY	*n* pl. **-NIES** a woolen fabric
SAXTUBA	*n* pl. **-S** a bass saxhorn
SAY	*v* **SAID, SAYING,** present sing. 2d person **SAY** or **SAYEST** or **SAYST,** 3d person **SAYS** or **SAITH** to utter **SAYABLE** *adj*
SAYED	*n* pl. **-S** sayyid
SAYER	*n* pl. **-S** one that says
SAYID	*n* pl. **-S** sayyid
SAYING	*n* pl. **-S** a maxim
SAYONARA	*n* pl. **-S** goodbye
SAYST	a present 2d person sing. of say
SAYYID	*n* pl. **-S** lord; sir — used as a title of respect for a Muslim dignitary
SCAB	*v* **SCABBED, SCABBING, SCABS** to become covered with a scab (a crust that forms over a healing wound)
SCABBARD	*v* **-ED, -ING, -S** to put into a sheath, as a sword
SCABBLE	*v* **-BLED, -BLING, -BLES** to shape roughly
SCABBY	*adj* **-BIER, -BIEST** covered with scabs **SCABBILY** *adv*
SCABIES	*n* pl. **SCABIES** a skin disease
SCABIOSA	*n* pl. **-S** scabious
SCABIOUS	*n* pl. **-ES** a flowering plant
SCABLAND	*n* pl. **-S** rocky land with little soil cover
SCABLIKE	*adj* resembling a scab
SCABROUS	*adj* roughened with small projections
SCAD	*n* pl. **-S** a marine fish
SCAFFOLD	*v* **-ED, -ING, -S** to provide with a scaffold (a temporary platform for workmen)
SCAG	*n* pl. **-S** heroin
SCALABLE	*adj* capable of being scaled **SCALABLY** *adv*
SCALADE	*n* pl. **-S** an act of scaling the walls of a fortification
SCALADO	*n* pl. **-DOS** scalade
SCALAGE	*n* pl. **-S** a percentage deduction to compensate for shrinkage
SCALAR	*n* pl. **-S** a mathematical quantity possessing only magnitude
SCALARE	*n* pl. **-S** a tropical fish
SCALAWAG	*n* pl. **-S** a rascal
SCALD	*v* **-ED, -ING, -S** to burn with hot liquid or steam
SCALDIC	*adj* skaldic
SCALE	*v* **SCALED, SCALING, SCALES** to climb up or over
SCALENE	*n* pl. **-S** a triangle having no two sides equal
SCALENUS	*n* pl. **-NI** a muscle of the neck
SCALEPAN	*n* pl. **-S** a pan on a weighing scale
SCALER	*n* pl. **-S** one that scales
SCALEUP	*n* pl. **-S** an increase based on a fixed ratio

SCALIER	comparative of scaly	**SCAPHOID**	n pl. **-S** a bone of the wrist
SCALIEST	superlative of scaly	**SCAPOSE**	adj bearing a leafless stalk
SCALING	n pl. **-S** the formation of scales on the skin	**SCAPULA**	n pl. **-LAS** or **-LAE** a bone of the shoulder
SCALL	n pl. **-S** a scaly eruption of the skin	**SCAPULAR**	n pl. **-S** a sleeveless outer garment worn by monks
SCALLION	n pl. **-S** an onion-like plant		
SCALLOP	v **-ED, -ING, -S** to bake in a sauce topped with bread crumbs	**SCAR**	v **SCARRED, SCARRING, SCARS** to form a scar (a mark left by the healing of injured tissue)
SCALP	v **-ED, -ING, -S** to remove an upper part from	**SCARAB**	n pl. **-S** a large, black beetle
SCALPEL	n pl. **-S** a small surgical knife	**SCARCE**	adj **SCARCER, SCARCEST** infrequently seen or found
SCALPER	n pl. **-S** one that scalps		
SCALY	adj **SCALIER, SCALIEST** peeling off in flakes	**SCARCELY**	adv by a narrow margin
		SCARCITY	n pl. **-TIES** the quality of being scarce
SCAM	v **SCAMMED, SCAMMING, SCAMS** to cheat or swindle	**SCARE**	v **SCARED, SCARING, SCARES** to frighten
SCAMMER	n pl. **-S** one that scams		
SCAMMONY	n pl. **-NIES** a climbing plant	**SCARED**	adj **SCAREDER, SCAREDEST** afraid
SCAMP	v **-ED, -ING, -S** to perform in a hasty or careless manner	**SCARER**	n pl. **-S** one that scares
SCAMPER	v **-ED, -ING, -S** to run playfully about	**SCAREY**	adj **SCARIER, SCARIEST** scary
SCAMPI	n pl. **SCAMPI** or **SCAMPIES** large shrimp used in Italian cooking	**SCARF**	n pl. **SCARFS** or **SCARVES** a piece of cloth worn for warmth or protection
SCAMPISH	adj rascally	**SCARF**	v **-ED, -ING, -S** to cover with a scarf
SCAMSTER	n pl. **-S** one that scams		
SCAN	v **SCANNED, SCANNING, SCANS** to examine closely	**SCARFER**	n pl. **-S** one that eats or drinks voraciously
		SCARFPIN	n pl. **-S** a tiepin
SCANDAL	v **-DALED, -DALING, -DALS** or **-DALLED, -DALLING, -DALS** to defame	**SCARIER**	comparative of scarey and scary
		SCARIEST	superlative of scarey and scary
SCANDENT	adj climbing, as a plant	**SCARIFY**	v **-FIED, -FYING, -FIES** to make superficial cuts in
SCANDIA	n pl. **-S** an oxide of scandium		
SCANDIUM	n pl. **-S** a metallic element **SCANDIC** adj	**SCARILY**	adv in a scary manner
		SCARING	present participle of scare
SCANNED	past tense of scan	**SCARIOSE**	adj scarious
SCANNER	n pl. **-S** one that scans	**SCARIOUS**	adj thin, dry, and membranous
SCANNING	n pl. **-S** close examination	**SCARLESS**	adj having no scars
SCANSION	n pl. **-S** the analysis of verse into metrical feet and rhythm patterns	**SCARLET**	n pl. **-S** a red color
SCANT	adj **SCANTER, SCANTEST** meager	**SCARP**	v **-ED, -ING, -S** to cut or make into a steep slope
SCANT	v **-ED, -ING, -S** to provide with a meager portion	**SCARPER**	v **-ED, -ING, -S** to flee
		SCARPH	v **-ED, -ING, -S** to unite by means of a type of joint
SCANTIES	n/pl brief panties for women		
SCANTLY	adv in a scant manner	**SCARRED**	past tense of scar
SCANTY	adj **SCANTIER, SCANTIEST** meager **SCANTILY** adv	**SCARRING**	present participle of scar
		SCARRY	adj **-RIER, -RIEST** marked with scars
SCAPE	v **SCAPED, SCAPING, SCAPES** to escape	**SCART**	v **-ED, -ING, -S** to scratch

SCARVED	*adj* wearing a scarf
SCARVES	a pl. of scarf
SCARY	*adj* **SCARIER, SCARIEST** frightening
SCAT	*v* **SCATTED, SCATTING, SCATS** to leave hastily
SCATBACK	*n* pl. **-S** a type of player in football
SCATHE	*v* **SCATHED, SCATHING, SCATHES** to criticize severely
SCATT	*n* pl. **-S** a tax
SCATTED	past tense of scat
SCATTER	*v* **-ED, -ING, -S** to go or send in various directions
SCATTING	present participle of scat
SCATTY	*adj* **-TIER, -TIEST** crazy **SCATTILY** *adv*
SCAUP	*n* pl. **-S** a sea duck
SCAUPER	*n* pl. **-S** an engraving tool
SCAUR	*n* pl. **-S** a protruding, isolated rock
SCAVENGE	*v* **-ENGED, -ENGING, -ENGES** to search through rubbish for usable items
SCENA	*n* pl. **-S** an elaborate composition for a single voice
SCENARIO	*n* pl. **-IOS** a summary of the plot of a dramatic work
SCEND	*v* **-ED, -ING, -S** to rise upward, as a ship on a wave
SCENE	*n* pl. **-S** the place where some action or event occurs
SCENERY	*n* pl. **-ERIES** a picturesque landscape or view
SCENIC	*n* pl. **-S** a depiction of natural scenery
SCENICAL	*adj* pertaining to scenery
SCENT	*v* **-ED, -ING, -S** to fill with an odor
SCEPTER	*v* **-ED, -ING, -S** to invest with royal authority
SCEPTIC	*n* pl. **-S** skeptic
SCEPTRAL	*adj* pertaining to royal authority
SCEPTRE	*v* **-TRED, -TRING, -TRES** to scepter
SCHAPPE	*n* pl. **-S** a silk fabric
SCHAV	*n* pl. **-S** a chilled soup
SCHEDULE	*v* **-ULED, -ULING, -ULES** to assign to a certain date or time
SCHEMA	*n* pl. **-MAS** or **-MATA** a generalized diagram or plan
SCHEME	*v* **SCHEMED, SCHEMING, SCHEMES** to plan or plot
SCHEMER	*n* pl. **-S** one that schemes
SCHEMING	*n* pl. **-S** the act of planning or plotting
SCHERZO	*n* pl. **-ZOS** or **-ZI** a lively musical movement
SCHILLER	*n* pl. **-S** a brownish luster occurring on certain minerals
SCHISM	*n* pl. **-S** a division into opposing parties
SCHIST	*n* pl. **-S** a rock that readily splits into parallel layers
SCHIZIER	comparative of schizy
SCHIZIEST	superlative of schizy
SCHIZO	*n* pl. **SCHIZOS** a schizoid
SCHIZOID	*n* pl. **-S** a person affected with a type of psychotic disorder
SCHIZONT	*n* pl. **-S** an organism that reproduces by a form of asexual reproduction
SCHIZY	*adj* **SCHIZIER, SCHIZIEST** affected with schizophrenia
SCHIZZY	*adj* **SCHIZZIER, SCHIZZIEST** schizy
SCHLEP	*v* **SCHLEPPED, SCHLEPPING, SCHLEPS** to lug or drag
SCHLEPP	*v* **-ED, -ING, -S** to schlep
SCHLEPPY	*adj* **-PIER, -PIEST** shabby, run-down
SCHLIERE	*n* pl. **-REN** a small streak in an igneous rock
SCHLOCK	*n* pl. **-S** inferior merchandise
SCHLOCKY	*adj* **SCHLOCKIER, SCHLOCKIEST** of inferior quality
SCHLUB	*n* pl. **-S** a stupid or unattractive person
SCHLUMP	*v* **-ED, -ING, -S** to go about lazily or sloppily dressed
SCHLUMPY	*adj* **SCHLUMPIER, SCHLUMPIEST** unattractive, slovenly
SCHMALTZ	*n* pl. **-ES** excessive sentimentality
SCHMALZ	*n* pl. **-ES** schmaltz
SCHMALZY	*adj* **SCHMALZIER, SCHMALZIEST** characterized by schmaltz
SCHMATTE	*n* pl. **-S** a ragged garment
SCHMEAR	*v* **-ED, -ING, -S** to schmeer
SCHMEER	*v* **-ED, -ING, -S** to bribe
SCHMELZE	*n* pl. **-S** a type of decorative glass
SCHMO	*n* pl. **SCHMOES** or **SCHMOS** a stupid person

SCHMOE	*n* pl. **-S** schmo
SCHMOOS	*v* **-ED, -ING, -ES** to schmooze
SCHMOOSE	*v* **SCHMOOSED, SCHMOOSING, SCHMOOSES** to schmooze
SCHMOOZE	*v* **SCHMOOZED, SCHMOOZING, SCHMOOZES** to gossip
SCHMOOZY	*adj* **SCHMOOZIER, SCHMOOZIEST** given to schmoozing
SCHMUCK	*v* **-ED, -ING, -S** to hit or flatten
SCHMUCKY	*adj* **SCHMUCKIER, SCHMUCKIEST** foolish, contemptible
SCHMUTZ	*n* pl. **-ES** dirt, grime
SCHNAPPS	*n* pl. **SCHNAPPS** a strong liquor
SCHNAPS	*n* pl. **SCHNAPS** schnapps
SCHNECKE	*n* pl. **-KEN** a sweet roll
SCHNEID	*n* pl. **-S** a series of losses
SCHNOOK	*n* pl. **-S** an easily deceived person
SCHNOZ	*n* pl. **-ES** the nose
SCHNOZZ	*n* pl. **-ES** schnoz
SCHOLAR	*n* pl. **-S** a learned person
SCHOLIUM	*n* pl. **-LIUMS** or **-LIA** an explanatory marginal note
SCHOOL	*v* **-ED, -ING, -S** to educate in an institution of learning
SCHOONER	*n* pl. **-S** a sailing vessel
SCHORL	*n* pl. **-S** a mineral
SCHRIK	*n* pl. **-S** sudden fright
SCHROD	*n* pl. **-S** scrod
SCHTICK	*n* pl. **-S** shtick
SCHTIK	*n* pl. **-S** shtick
SCHTUM	*adj* silent
SCHUIT	*n* pl. **-S** a Dutch sailing vessel
SCHUL	*n* pl. **SCHULS** or **SCHULN** shul
SCHUSS	*v* **-ED, -ING, -ES** to make a fast, straight run in skiing
SCHUSSER	*n* pl. **-S** one that schusses
SCHVITZ	*v* **-ED, -ING, -ES** to shvitz
SCHWA	*n* pl. **-S** a type of vowel sound
SCIAENID	*n* pl. **-S** a carnivorous fish
SCIATIC	*n* pl. **-S** a nerve, vein, or artery situated near the hip
SCIATICA	*n* pl. **-S** a painful disorder of the hip and adjoining areas
SCIENCE	*n* pl. **-S** a department of systematized knowledge
SCILICET	*adv* namely
SCILLA	*n* pl. **-S** a flowering plant
SCIMETAR	*n* pl. **-S** scimitar
SCIMITAR	*n* pl. **-S** a curved sword used by Arabs and Turks
SCIMITER	*n* pl. **-S** scimitar
SCINCOID	*n* pl. **-S** one of a family of smooth, short-limbed lizards
SCIOLISM	*n* pl. **-S** superficial knowledge
SCIOLIST	*n* pl. **-S** one whose knowledge is superficial
SCION	*n* pl. **-S** a child or descendant
SCIROCCO	*n* pl. **-COS** sirocco
SCIRRHUS	*n* pl. **-RHUSES** or **-RHI** a hard tumor
SCISSILE	*adj* capable of being cut or split easily
SCISSION	*n* pl. **-S** the act of cutting or splitting
SCISSOR	*v* **-ED, -ING, -S** to cut with a two-bladed cutting implement
SCISSURE	*n* pl. **-S** a lengthwise cut
SCIURID	*n* pl. **-S** a sciurine
SCIURINE	*n* pl. **-S** a rodent of the squirrel family
SCIUROID	*adj* resembling a squirrel
SCLAFF	*v* **-ED, -ING, -S** to strike the ground with the club before hitting the ball in golf
SCLAFFER	*n* pl. **-S** one that sclaffs
SCLERA	*n* pl. **-RAS** or **-RAE** the white, fibrous outer coat of the eyeball **SCLERAL** *adj*
SCLEREID	*n* pl. **-S** a type of plant cell
SCLERITE	*n* pl. **-S** one of the hard plates forming the outer covering of an arthropod
SCLEROID	*adj* sclerous
SCLEROMA	*n* pl. **-MAS** or **-MATA** a hardened patch of cellular tissue
SCLEROSE	*v* **-ROSED, -ROSING, -ROSES** to become hard, as tissue
SCLEROUS	*adj* hardened
SCOFF	*v* **-ED, -ING, -S** to express rude doubt or derision
SCOFFER	*n* pl. **-S** one that scoffs
SCOFFLAW	*n* pl. **-S** a habitual law violator
SCOLD	*v* **-ED, -ING, -S** to rebuke harshly
SCOLDER	*n* pl. **-S** one that scolds
SCOLDING	*n* pl. **-S** a harsh reproof

SCOLEX *n* pl. **-LECES** or **-LICES** the knoblike head of a tapeworm

SCOLIOMA *n* pl. **-S** abnormal curvature of the spine

SCOLLOP *v* **-ED, -ING, -S** to scallop

SCOMBRID *n* pl. **-S** a fish of the mackerel family

SCONCE *v* **SCONCED, SCONCING, SCONCES** to fine

SCONE *n* pl. **-S** a flat, round cake

SCOOCH *v* **-ED, -ING, -ES** to slide with short movements

SCOOP *v* **-ED, -ING, -S** to take up with a scoop (a spoon-shaped utensil)

SCOOPER *n* pl. **-S** one that scoops

SCOOPFUL *n* pl. **SCOOPFULS** or **SCOOPSFUL** as much as a scoop will hold

SCOOT *v* **-ED, -ING, -S** to go quickly

SCOOTCH *v* **-ED, -ING, -ES** to scooch

SCOOTER *v* **-ED, -ING, -S** to ride a two-wheeled vehicle

SCOP *n* pl. **-S** an Old English poet

SCOPA *n* pl. **-PAE** a small tuft of hair on the body of an insect

SCOPE *v* **SCOPED, SCOPING, SCOPES** to look at in order to evaluate

SCOPULA *n* pl. **-LAS** or **-LAE** a dense tuft of hairs

SCORCH *v* **-ED, -ING, -ES** to burn slightly so as to alter the color or taste

SCORCHER *n* pl. **-S** one that scorches

SCORE *v* **SCORED, SCORING, SCORES** to make a point in a game or contest

SCOREPAD *n* pl. **-S** a pad on which scored points are recorded

SCORER *n* pl. **-S** one that scores

SCORIA *n* pl. **-RIAE** the refuse of a smelted metal or ore

SCORIFY *v* **-FIED, -FYING, -FIES** to reduce to scoria

SCORING *n* pl. **-S** the act of scoring in a game

SCORN *v* **-ED, -ING, -S** to treat or regard with contempt

SCORNER *n* pl. **-S** one that scorns

SCORNFUL *adj* feeling or expressing contempt

SCORPION *n* pl. **-S** a stinging arachnid

SCOT *n* pl. **-S** a tax

SCOTCH *v* **-ED, -ING, -ES** to put a definite end to

SCOTER *n* pl. **-S** a sea duck

SCOTIA *n* pl. **-S** a concave molding

SCOTOMA *n* pl. **-MAS** or **-MATA** a blind spot in the field of vision

SCOTOPIA *n* pl. **-S** vision in dim light **SCOTOPIC** *adj*

SCOTTIE *n* pl. **-S** a short-legged terrier

SCOUR *v* **-ED, -ING, -S** to cleanse or polish by hard rubbing

SCOURER *n* pl. **-S** one that scours

SCOURGE *v* **SCOURGED, SCOURGING, SCOURGES** to punish severely

SCOURGER *n* pl. **-S** one that scourges

SCOURING *n* pl. **-S** material removed by scouring

SCOUSE *n* pl. **-S** a type of meat stew

SCOUT *v* **-ED, -ING, -S** to observe for the purpose of obtaining information

SCOUTER *n* pl. **-S** one that scouts

SCOUTH *n* pl. **-S** plenty

SCOUTHER *v* **-ED, -ING, -S** to scorch

SCOUTING *n* pl. **-S** the act of one that scouts

SCOW *v* **-ED, -ING, -S** to transport by scow (a flat-bottomed boat)

SCOWDER *v* **-ED, -ING, -S** to scouther

SCOWL *v* **-ED, -ING, -S** to frown angrily

SCOWLER *n* pl. **-S** one that scowls

SCRABBLE *v* **-BLED, -BLING, -BLES** to claw or grope about frantically

SCRABBLY *adj* **-BLIER, -BLIEST** raspy

SCRAG *v* **SCRAGGED, SCRAGGING, SCRAGS** to wring the neck of

SCRAGGLY *adj* **-GLIER, -GLIEST** uneven

SCRAGGY *adj* **-GIER, -GIEST** scrawny

SCRAICH *v* **-ED, -ING, -S** to utter a shrill cry

SCRAIGH *v* **-ED, -ING, -S** to scraich

SCRAM *v* **SCRAMMED, SCRAMMING, SCRAMS** to leave quickly

SCRAMBLE *v* **-BLED, -BLING, -BLES** to move or climb hurriedly

SCRAMJET *n* pl. **-S** a type of aircraft engine

SCRAN *n* pl. **-S** food

SCRANNEL *n* pl. **-S** a thin person

SCRAP *v* **SCRAPPED, SCRAPPING, SCRAPS** to discard

SCRAPE *v* **SCRAPED, SCRAPING, SCRAPES** to rub so as to remove an outer layer

SCRAPER *n pl.* **-S** one that scrapes

SCRAPIE *n pl.* **-S** a disease of sheep

SCRAPING *n pl.* **-S** something scraped off

SCRAPPED past tense of scrap

SCRAPPER *n pl.* **-S** a fighter

SCRAPPING present participle of scrap

SCRAPPLE *n pl.* **-S** a seasoned mixture of ground meat and cornmeal

SCRAPPY *adj* **-PIER, -PIEST** marked by fighting spirit

SCRATCH *v* **-ED, -ING, -ES** to make a thin, shallow cut or mark on

SCRATCHY *adj* **SCRATCHIER, SCRATCHIEST** made by scratching

SCRAVEL *v* **-ED, -ING, -S** to move quickly, scramble

SCRAWB *v* **-ED, -ING, -S** to scrob

SCRAWL *v* **-ED, -ING, -S** to write hastily or illegibly

SCRAWLER *n pl.* **-S** one that scrawls

SCRAWLY *adj* **SCRAWLIER, SCRAWLIEST** written hastily or illegibly

SCRAWNY *adj* **-NIER, -NIEST** extremely thin

SCREAK *v* **-ED, -ING, -S** to screech

SCREAKY *adj* screechy

SCREAM *v* **-ED, -ING, -S** to utter a prolonged, piercing cry

SCREAMER *n pl.* **-S** one that screams

SCREE *n pl.* **-S** a mass of rocks at the foot of a slope

SCREECH *v* **-ED, -ING, -ES** to utter a harsh, shrill cry

SCREECHY *adj* **SCREECHIER, SCREECHIEST** screeching

SCREED *v* **-ED, -ING, -S** to shred

SCREEN *v* **-ED, -ING, -S** to provide with a screen (a device designed to divide, conceal, or protect)

SCREENER *n pl.* **-S** one that screens

SCREW *v* **-ED, -ING, -S** to attach with a screw (a type of metal fastener)

SCREWER *n pl.* **-S** one that screws

SCREWUP *n pl.* **-S** an instance of bungling

SCREWY *adj* **SCREWIER, SCREWIEST** crazy

SCRIBAL *adj* pertaining to a public clerk or secretary

SCRIBBLE *v* **-BLED, -BLING, -BLES** to write hastily or carelessly

SCRIBBLY *adj* consisting of scribbles (careless writings)

SCRIBE *v* **SCRIBED, SCRIBING, SCRIBES** to mark with a scriber

SCRIBER *n pl.* **-S** a pointed instrument used for marking off material to be cut

SCRIED past tense of scry

SCRIES present 3d person sing. of scry

SCRIEVE *v* **SCRIEVED, SCRIEVING, SCRIEVES** to move along swiftly and smoothly

SCRIM *n pl.* **-S** a cotton fabric

SCRIMP *v* **-ED, -ING, -S** to be very or overly thrifty

SCRIMPER *n pl.* **-S** one that scrimps

SCRIMPIT *adj* meager

SCRIMPY *adj* **SCRIMPIER, SCRIMPIEST** meager

SCRIP *n pl.* **-S** a small piece of paper

SCRIPT *v* **-ED, -ING, -S** to prepare a written text for, as a play or motion picture

SCRIPTER *n pl.* **-S** one that scripts

SCRITCH *n pl.* **-ES** a quiet scraping sound

SCRIVE *v* **SCRIVED, SCRIVING, SCRIVES** to engrave

SCROB *v* **SCROBBED, SCROBBING, SCROBS** to scrape with or as with claws

SCROD *n pl.* **-S** a young cod

SCROFULA *n pl.* **-S** a disease of the lymph glands

SCROGGY *adj* **-GIER, -GIEST** of stunted growth

SCROLL *v* **-ED, -ING, -S** to move text across a display screen

SCROLLER *n pl.* **-S** a computer game in which the background scrolls past

SCROOCH *v* **-ED, -ING, -ES** to crouch

SCROOGE *n pl.* **-S** a miserly person

SCROOP *v* **-ED, -ING, -S** to make a harsh, grating sound

SCROOTCH *v* **-ED, -ING, -ES** to scrooch

SCROTUM *n pl.* **-TUMS** or **-TA** the pouch of skin that contains the testes **SCROTAL** *adj*

SCROUGE *v* **SCROUGED, SCROUGING, SCROUGES** to crowd

SCROUNGE *v* **SCROUNGED, SCROUNGING, SCROUNGES** to gather by foraging

SCROUNGY *adj* **SCROUNGIER, SCROUNGIEST** dirty

SCRUB *v* **SCRUBBED, SCRUBBING, SCRUBS** to rub hard in order to clean

SCRUBBER *n* pl. **-S** one that scrubs

SCRUBBY *adj* **-BIER, -BIEST** inferior in size or quality

SCRUFF *v* **-ED, -ING, -S** to make scruffy

SCRUFFY *adj* **-FIER, -FIEST** shabby

SCRUM *v* **SCRUMMED, SCRUMMING, SCRUMS** to engage in a scrummage (a formation around the ball in rugby)

SCRUMMY *adj* **-MIER, -MIEST** delicious

SCRUMPLE *v* **-PLED, -PLING, -PLES** to crumple, wrinkle

SCRUMPY *n* pl. **-PIES** rough cider

SCRUNCH *v* **-ED, -ING, -ES** to crush

SCRUNCHY *n* pl. **SCRUNCHIES** an elastic band for fastening the hair

SCRUPLE *v* **-PLED, -PLING, -PLES** to hesitate because of ethical considerations

SCRUTINY *n* pl. **-NIES** a close examination

SCRY *v* **SCRIED, SCRYING, SCRIES** to foretell the future by using a crystal ball

SCRYER *n* pl. **-S** one that scries

SCUBA *v* **-ED, -ING, -S** to swim underwater using a breathing device with compressed air

SCUD *v* **SCUDDED, SCUDDING, SCUDS** to run or move swiftly

SCUDO *n* pl. **-DI** a former Italian coin

SCUFF *v* **-ED, -ING, -S** to walk without lifting the feet

SCUFFER *n* pl. **-S** one that scuffs

SCUFFLE *v* **-FLED, -FLING, -FLES** to struggle in a rough, confused manner

SCUFFLER *n* pl. **-S** one that scuffles

SCULCH *n* pl. **-ES** clean trash

SCULK *v* **-ED, -ING, -S** to skulk

SCULKER *n* pl. **-S** skulker

SCULL *v* **-ED, -ING, -S** to propel with a type of oar

SCULLER *n* pl. **-S** one that sculls

SCULLERY *n* pl. **-LERIES** a room in which kitchen utensils are cleaned and stored

SCULLION *n* pl. **-S** a kitchen servant who does menial work

SCULP *v* **-ED, -ING, -S** to sculpt

SCULPIN *n* pl. **-S** a freshwater fish

SCULPT *v* **-ED, -ING, -S** to form an image or representation of from solid material

SCULPTOR *n* pl. **-S** one that sculpts

SCULTCH *n* pl. **-ES** sculch

SCUM *v* **SCUMMED, SCUMMING, SCUMS** to remove the scum (impure or extraneous matter) from

SCUMBAG *n* pl. **-S** a dirtbag

SCUMBALL *n* pl. **-S** a dirtbag

SCUMBLE *v* **-BLED, -BLING, -BLES** to soften the outlines or colors of by rubbing lightly

SCUMLESS *adj* having no scum

SCUMLIKE *adj* resembling scum

SCUMMED past tense of scum

SCUMMER *n* pl. **-S** one that scums

SCUMMING present participle of scum

SCUMMY *adj* **-MIER, -MIEST** covered with scum **SCUMMILY** *adv*

SCUNGILE *n* pl. **-GILI** a conch used as food

SCUNNER *v* **-ED, -ING, -S** to feel loathing or disgust

SCUP *n* pl. **-S** a marine food fish

SCUPPAUG *n* pl. **-S** scup

SCUPPER *v* **-ED, -ING, -S** to ambush

SCURF *n* pl. **-S** scaly or shredded dry skin

SCURFY *adj* **SCURFIER, SCURFIEST** covered with scurf

SCURRIL *adj* scurrile

SCURRILE *adj* expressed in coarse and abusive language

SCURRY *v* **-RIED, -RYING, -RIES** to move hurriedly

SCURVY *adj* **-VIER, -VIEST** base or contemptible **SCURVILY** *adv*

SCURVY *n* pl. **-VIES** a disease resulting from vitamin C deficiency

SCUT *n* pl. **-S** a short tail, as of a rabbit

SCUTA pl. of scutum

SCUTAGE *n* pl. **-S** a tax exacted by a feudal lord in lieu of military service

SCUTATE *adj* shaped like a shield

SCUTCH	*v* **-ED, -ING, -ES** to separate the woody fiber from by beating
SCUTCHER	*n* pl. **-S** one that scutches
SCUTE	*n* pl. **-S** a horny plate or scale
SCUTELLA	*n/pl* small, scutate organs or parts
SCUTTER	*v* **-ED, -ING, -S** to scurry
SCUTTLE	*v* **-TLED, -TLING, -TLES** to scurry
SCUTUM	*n* pl. **-TA** scute
SCUTWORK	*n* pl. **-S** tedious or menial work
SCUZZ	*n* pl. **-ES** a dirty or contemptible person
SCUZZBAG	*n* pl. **-S** a dirty or contemptible person
SCUZZY	*adj* **-ZIER, -ZIEST** dirty or shabby
SCYPHATE	*adj* shaped like a cup
SCYPHUS	*n* pl. **-PHI** a Greek cup with two handles
SCYTHE	*v* **SCYTHED, SCYTHING, SCYTHES** to cut with a scythe (a single-bladed cutting implement)
SEA	*n* pl. **-S** the ocean
SEABAG	*n* pl. **-S** a bag used by a sailor
SEABEACH	*n* pl. **-ES** a beach lying along the sea
SEABED	*n* pl. **-S** a seafloor
SEABIRD	*n* pl. **-S** a bird frequenting the ocean or seacoast
SEABOARD	*n* pl. **-S** the seacoast
SEABOOT	*n* pl. **-S** a waterproof boot
SEABORNE	*adj* carried on or over the sea
SEACOAST	*n* pl. **-S** land bordering on the sea
SEACOCK	*n* pl. **-S** a valve in a ship's hull
SEACRAFT	*n* pl. **-S** skill in sea navigation
SEADOG	*n* pl. **-S** a fogbow
SEADROME	*n* pl. **-S** an airport in the sea
SEAFARER	*n* pl. **-S** a sailor
SEAFLOOR	*n* pl. **-S** the bottom of a sea
SEAFOAM	*n* pl. **-S** foam formed on the sea
SEAFOOD	*n* pl. **-S** edible fish or shellfish from the sea
SEAFOWL	*n* pl. **-S** a seabird
SEAFRONT	*n* pl. **-S** an area along the edge of the sea
SEAGIRT	*adj* surrounded by the sea
SEAGOING	*adj* designed for use on the sea
SEAGRASS	*n* pl. **-ES** a grasslike plant living in or close to the sea
SEAGULL	*n* pl. **-S** a gull frequenting the sea
SEAHORSE	*n* pl. **-S** a fish of the pipefish family
SEAKALE	*n* pl. **-S** a coastal plant with edible shoots
SEAL	*v* **-ED, -ING, -S** to close or make secure against access, leakage, or passage **SEALABLE** *adj*
SEALANT	*n* pl. **-S** a sealing agent
SEALER	*n* pl. **-S** one that seals
SEALERY	*n* pl. **-ERIES** the occupation of hunting seals
SEALIFT	*v* **-ED, -ING, -S** to transport by ship (military personnel and equipment)
SEALING	*n* pl. **-S** the act of securing something against leakage, access, or passage
SEALLIKE	*adj* resembling a seal (an aquatic mammal)
SEALSKIN	*n* pl. **-S** the skin of a seal
SEAM	*v* **-ED, -ING, -S** to join with a seam (a line formed by sewing two pieces of fabric together)
SEAMAN	*n* pl. **-MEN** a sailor **SEAMANLY** *adj*
SEAMARK	*n* pl. **-S** a landmark serving as a navigational guide to mariners
SEAMER	*n* pl. **-S** one that seams
SEAMIER	comparative of seamy
SEAMIEST	superlative of seamy
SEAMLESS	*adj* having no seam
SEAMLIKE	*adj* resembling a seam
SEAMOUNT	*n* pl. **-S** an undersea mountain
SEAMSTER	*n* pl. **-S** a person whose occupation is sewing
SEAMY	*adj* **SEAMIER, SEAMIEST** unpleasant
SEANCE	*n* pl. **-S** a meeting of persons seeking spiritualistic messages
SEAPIECE	*n* pl. **-S** a seascape
SEAPLANE	*n* pl. **-S** an airplane designed to take off from or land on the water
SEAPORT	*n* pl. **-S** a harbor or town accessible to seagoing ships
SEAQUAKE	*n* pl. **-S** an undersea earthquake
SEAR	*adj* **SEARER, SEAREST** sere
SEAR	*v* **-ED, -ING, -S** to burn the surface of
SEARCH	*v* **-ED, -ING, -ES** to look through or over carefully in order to find something
SEARCHER	*n* pl. **-S** one that searches
SEAROBIN	*n* pl. **-S** a marine fish

SEASCAPE *n* pl. **-S** a picture of the sea

SEASCOUT *n* pl. **-S** a boy scout trained in water activities

SEASHELL *n* pl. **-S** the shell of a marine mollusk

SEASHORE *n* pl. **-S** land bordering on the sea

SEASICK *adj* affected with nausea caused by the motion of a vessel at sea

SEASIDE *n* pl. **-S** the seashore

SEASON *v* **-ED, -ING, -S** to heighten or improve the flavor of by adding savory ingredients

SEASONAL *n* pl. **-S** an employee or product associated with a time of the year

SEASONER *n* pl. **-S** one that seasons

SEAT *v* **-ED, -ING, -S** to place on a seat (something on which one sits)

SEATBACK *n* pl. **-S** the back of a seat

SEATBELT *n* pl. **-S** an arrangement of straps to keep a person steady in a seat

SEATER *n* pl. **-S** one that seats

SEATING *n* pl. **-S** material for covering seats

SEATLESS *adj* having no seat

SEATMATE *n* pl. **-S** one with whom one shares a seat

SEATRAIN *n* pl. **-S** a ship equipped to carry railroad cars

SEATROUT *n* pl. **-S** a marine fish

SEATWORK *n* pl. **-S** work done at one's seat

SEAWALL *n* pl. **-S** a wall to protect a shoreline from erosion

SEAWAN *n* pl. **-S** wampum

SEAWANT *n* pl. **-S** seawan

SEAWARD *n* pl. **-S** the direction toward the open sea

SEAWARE *n* pl. **-S** seaweed used as fertilizer

SEAWATER *n* pl. **-S** water from the sea

SEAWAY *n* pl. **-WAYS** the headway made by a ship

SEAWEED *n* pl. **-S** a plant growing in the sea **SEAWEEDY** *adj*

SEBACIC *adj* derived from a certain acid

SEBASIC *adj* sebacic

SEBUM *n* pl. **-S** a fatty matter secreted by certain glands of the skin

SEC *n* pl. **-S** secant

SECALOSE *n* pl. **-S** a complex carbohydrate

SECANT *n* pl. **-S** a trigonometric function of an angle

SECANTLY *adv* in an intersecting manner

SECATEUR *n* pl. **-S** a pruning tool

SECCO *n* pl. **-COS** the art of painting on dry plaster

SECEDE *v* **-CEDED, -CEDING, -CEDES** to withdraw formally from an alliance or association

SECEDER *n* pl. **-S** one that secedes

SECERN *v* **-ED, -ING, -S** to discern as separate

SECLUDE *v* **-CLUDED, -CLUDING, -CLUDES** to remove or set apart from others

SECOND *v* **-ED, -ING, -S** to give support or encouragement to

SECONDE *n* pl. **-S** a position in fencing

SECONDEE *n* pl. **-S** a worker who is transferred to another job temporarily

SECONDER *n* pl. **-S** one that seconds

SECONDLY *adv* in the next place after the first

SECONDO *n* pl. **-DI** the lower part in a piano duet

SECPAR *n* pl. **-S** a parsec

SECRECY *n* pl. **-CIES** the condition of being secret

SECRET *adj* **-CRETER, -CRETEST** kept from knowledge or view

SECRET *n* pl. **-S** something kept from the knowledge of others

SECRETE *v* **-CRETED, -CRETING, -CRETES** to generate and separate out from cells or bodily fluids

SECRETIN *n* pl. **-S** a hormone

SECRETLY *adv* in a secret manner

SECRETOR *n* pl. **-S** one that secretes

SECT *n* pl. **-S** a group of people united by common beliefs or interests

SECTARY *n* pl. **-RIES** a member of a sect

SECTILE *adj* capable of being cut smoothly

SECTION *v* **-ED, -ING, -S** to divide into sections (distinct parts)

SECTOR *v* **-ED, -ING, -S** to divide into sectors (sections)

SECTORAL *adj* of or pertaining to a sector

SECULAR *n* pl. **-S** a layman

SECUND *adj* having the parts or organs arranged on one side only **SECUNDLY** *adv*

SECUNDUM *adv* according to

SECURE *adj* **-CURER, -CUREST** free from danger **SECURELY** *adv*

SECURE   v **-CURED, -CURING, -CURES** to make firm or tight

SECURER   n pl. **-S** one that secures something

SECURING   present participle of secure

SECURITY   n pl. **-TIES** the state of being secure

SEDAN   n pl. **-S** a type of automobile

SEDARIM   a pl. of seder

SEDATE   adj **-DATER, -DATEST** calm **SEDATELY** adv

SEDATE   v **-DATED, -DATING, -DATES** to administer a sedative to

SEDATION   n pl. **-S** the reduction of stress or excitement by the use of sedatives

SEDATIVE   n pl. **-S** a drug that induces a calm state

SEDER   n pl. **-DERS** or **-DARIM** a Jewish ceremonial dinner

SEDERUNT   n pl. **-S** a prolonged sitting

SEDGE   n pl. **-S** a marsh plant

SEDGY   adj **SEDGIER, SEDGIEST** abounding in sedge

SEDILE   n pl. **-LIA** one of the seats in a church for the use of the officiating clergy

SEDILIUM   n pl. **-LIA** sedile

SEDIMENT   v **-ED, -ING, -S** to settle to the bottom of a liquid

SEDITION   n pl. **-S** incitement of rebellion against a government

SEDUCE   v **-DUCED, -DUCING, -DUCES** to lead astray **SEDUCIVE** adj

SEDUCER   n pl. **-S** one that seduces

SEDULITY   n pl. **-TIES** the state of being sedulous

SEDULOUS   adj diligent

SEDUM   n pl. **-S** a flowering plant

SEE   v **SAW, SEEN, SEEING, SEES** to perceive with the eyes **SEEABLE** adj

SEECATCH   n pl. **-CATCHIE** an adult male fur seal

SEED   v **-ED, -ING, -S** to plant seeds (propagative plant structures) in

SEEDBED   n pl. **-S** land prepared for seeding

SEEDCAKE   n pl. **-S** a sweet cake containing aromatic seeds

SEEDCASE   n pl. **-S** a pericarp

SEEDER   n pl. **-S** one that seeds

SEEDIER   comparative of seedy

SEEDIEST   superlative of seedy

SEEDILY   adv in a seedy manner

SEEDLESS   adj having no seeds

SEEDLIKE   adj resembling a seed

SEEDLING   n pl. **-S** a young plant

SEEDMAN   n pl. **-MEN** seedsman

SEEDPOD   n pl. **-S** a type of seed vessel

SEEDSMAN   n pl. **-MEN** a dealer in seeds

SEEDTIME   n pl. **-S** the season for sowing seeds

SEEDY   adj **SEEDIER, SEEDIEST** containing seeds; inferior in condition or quality

SEEING   n pl. **-S** the act of one that sees

SEEK   v **SOUGHT, SEEKING, SEEKS** to go in search of

SEEKER   n pl. **-S** one that seeks

SEEL   v **-ED, -ING, -S** to stitch closed the eyes of, as a falcon during training

SEELY   adj frail

SEEM   v **-ED, -ING, -S** to give the impression of being

SEEMER   n pl. **-S** one that seems

SEEMING   n pl. **-S** outward appearance

SEEMLY   adj **-LIER, -LIEST** of pleasing appearance

SEEN   past participle of see

SEEP   v **-ED, -ING, -S** to pass slowly through small openings

SEEPAGE   n pl. **-S** the quantity of fluid that has seeped

SEEPY   adj **SEEPIER, SEEPIEST** soaked or oozing with water

SEER   n pl. **-S** a prophet

SEERESS   n pl. **-ES** a female seer

SEESAW   v **-ED, -ING, -S** to move up and down or back and forth

SEETHE   v **SEETHED, SEETHING, SEETHES** to surge or foam as if boiling

SEG   n pl. **-S** one who advocates racial segregation

SEGETAL   adj growing in fields of grain

SEGGAR   n pl. **-S** a saggar

SEGMENT   v **-ED, -ING, -S** to divide into sections

SEGNO   n pl. **-GNOS** or **-GNI** a musical sign

SEGO   n pl. **-GOS** a perennial herb

SEGUE	*v* **-GUED, -GUEING, -GUES** to proceed without pause from one musical theme to another	**SELAMLIK**	*n* pl. **-S** the portion of a Turkish house reserved for men
SEI	*n* pl. **-S** a rorqual	**SELCOUTH**	*adj* unusual
SEICENTO	*n* pl. **-TOS** the seventeenth century	**SELDOM**	*adj* infrequent **SELDOMLY** *adv*
SEICHE	*n* pl. **-S** an oscillation of the surface of a lake or landlocked sea	**SELECT**	*v* **-ED, -ING, -S** to choose
		SELECTEE	*n* pl. **-S** one that is selected
SEIDEL	*n* pl. **-S** a large beer glass	**SELECTLY**	*adv* by selection
SEIF	*n* pl. **-S** a long, narrow sand dune	**SELECTOR**	*n* pl. **-S** one that selects
SEIGNEUR	*n* pl. **-S** seignior	**SELENATE**	*n* pl. **-S** a chemical salt
SEIGNIOR	*n* pl. **-S** a feudal lord	**SELENIC**	*adj* pertaining to selenium
SEIGNORY	*n* pl. **-GNORIES** the power of a seignior	**SELENIDE**	*n* pl. **-S** a compound of selenium
		SELENITE	*n* pl. **-S** a variety of gypsum
SEINE	*v* **SEINED, SEINING, SEINES** to catch fish with a large, vertically hanging net	**SELENIUM**	*n* pl. **-S** a nonmetallic element **SELENOUS** *adj*
SEINER	*n* pl. **-S** one that seines	**SELF**	*n* pl. **SELVES** the total, essential, or particular being of one person
SEINING	*n* pl. **-S** the act of catching fish with a seine	**SELF**	*v* **-ED, -ING, -S** to inbreed
SEISE	*v* **SEISED, SEISING, SEISES** to seize **SEISABLE** *adj*	**SELFDOM**	*n* pl. **-S** selfhood
		SELFHEAL	*n* pl. **-S** a perennial herb
SEISER	*n* pl. **-S** seizer	**SELFHOOD**	*n* pl. **-S** the state of being an individual person
SEISIN	*n* pl. **-S** seizin	**SELFIE**	*n* pl. **-S** an image of oneself taken by oneself using a phone camera
SEISING	*n* pl. **-S** seizing		
SEISM	*n* pl. **-S** an earthquake **SEISMAL, SEISMIC** *adj*	**SELFISH**	*adj* concerned chiefly or only with oneself
SEISMISM	*n* pl. **-S** the natural activity involved in earthquakes	**SELFLESS**	*adj* unselfish
		SELFNESS	*n* pl. **-ES** selfhood
SEISOR	*n* pl. **-S** seizor	**SELFSAME**	*adj* identical
SEISURE	*n* pl. **-S** seizure	**SELFWARD**	*adv* toward oneself
SEITAN	*n* pl. **-S** a food made from wheat gluten	**SELKIE**	*n* pl. **-S** a creature in Scottish and Irish folklore
SEIZA	*n* pl. **-S** a kneeling position in Japanese martial arts	**SELL**	*v* **SOLD, SELLING, SELLS** to give up to another for money or other valuable consideration **SELLABLE** *adj*
SEIZE	*v* **SEIZED, SEIZING, SEIZES** to take hold of suddenly and forcibly **SEIZABLE** *adj*		
		SELLE	*n* pl. **-S** a saddle
SEIZER	*n* pl. **-S** one that seizes	**SELLER**	*n* pl. **-S** one that sells
SEIZIN	*n* pl. **-S** legal possession of land	**SELLOFF**	*n* pl. **-S** the sale of a large number of stocks, bonds, or commodities
SEIZING	*n* pl. **-S** the act of one that seizes		
SEIZOR	*n* pl. **-S** one that takes seizin	**SELLOUT**	*n* pl. **-S** a performance for which all seats have been sold
SEIZURE	*n* pl. **-S** the act of seizing		
SEJANT	*adj* represented in a sitting position — used of a heraldic animal	**SELSYN**	*n* pl. **-S** a type of remote-control device
SEJEANT	*adj* sejant	**SELTZER**	*n* pl. **-S** carbonated mineral water
SEL	*n* pl. **-S** self	**SELVA**	*n* pl. **-S** a tropical rain forest
SELADANG	*n* pl. **-S** saladang	**SELVAGE**	*n* pl. **-S** the edge of a woven fabric finished to prevent raveling **SELVAGED** *adj*
SELAH	*n* pl. **-S** a word of unknown meaning often marking the end of a verse in the Psalms		
		SELVEDGE	*n* pl. **-S** selvage

SELVES   pl. of self

SEMANTIC   *adj* pertaining to meaning

SEMATIC   *adj* serving as a warning

SEME   *n* pl. **-S** a semee pattern

SEMEE   *adj* covered all over with small heraldic figures

SEMEME   *n* pl. **-S** the meaning of a morpheme **SEMEMIC** *adj*

SEMEN   *n* pl. **-MENS** or **-MINA** a fluid produced in the male reproductive organs

SEMESTER   *n* pl. **-S** a period constituting half of an academic year

SEMI   *n* pl. **-S** a freight trailer

SEMIARID   *adj* characterized by light rainfall

SEMIBALD   *adj* partly bald

SEMIBOLD   *adj* printed in a typeface with strokes not as thick as boldface

SEMICOMA   *n* pl. **-S** a coma from which a person can be aroused

SEMIDEAF   *adj* partly deaf

SEMIDOME   *n* pl. **-S** a half dome

SEMIDRY   *adj* moderately dry

SEMIFIT   *adj* conforming somewhat to the lines of the body

SEMIGALA   *adj* somewhat gala

SEMIHARD   *adj* moderately hard

SEMIHIGH   *adj* moderately high

SEMIHOBO   *n* pl. **-BOS** or **-BOES** a person having some of the characteristics of a hobo

SEMILLON   *n* pl. **-S** a white grape grown in France

SEMILOG   *adj* having one scale logarithmic and the other arithmetic

SEMIMAT   *adj* having a slight luster

SEMIMATT   *adj* semimat

SEMIMILD   *adj* moderately mild

SEMIMUTE   *adj* having partially lost the faculty of speech

SEMINA   a pl. of semen

SEMINAL   *adj* pertaining to semen

SEMINAR   *n* pl. **-S** an advanced study group at a college or university

SEMINARY   *n* pl. **-NARIES** a school for the training of priests, ministers, or rabbis

SEMINOMA   *n* pl. **-MAS** or **-MATA** a malignant tumor of the testis

SEMINUDE   *adj* partly nude

SEMIOPEN   *adj* partly open

SEMIOSIS   *n* pl. **-OSES** a process in which something functions as a sign to an organism

SEMIOTIC   *n* pl. **-S** a general theory of signs and symbolism

SEMIOVAL   *adj* somewhat oval

SEMIPRO   *n* pl. **-PROS** one who is engaged in some field or sport for pay on a part-time basis

SEMIRAW   *adj* somewhat raw

SEMIS   *n* pl. **-MISES** a coin of ancient Rome

SEMISOFT   *adj* moderately soft

SEMITIST   *n* pl. **-S** one who favors Jewish interests

SEMITONE   *n* pl. **-S** a type of musical tone

SEMIWILD   *adj* somewhat wild

SEMOLINA   *n* pl. **-S** a granular product of wheat used for pasta

SEMPLE   *adj* of humble birth

SEMPLICE   *adj* simple — used as a musical direction

SEMPRE   *adv* in the same manner throughout — used as a musical direction

SEN   *n* pl. **SEN** a monetary unit of Japan

SENARIUS   *n* pl. **-NARII** a Greek or Latin verse consisting of six metrical feet

SENARY   *adj* pertaining to the number six

SENATE   *n* pl. **-S** an assembly having high deliberative and legislative functions

SENATOR   *n* pl. **-S** a member of a senate

SEND   *v* **-ED, -ING, -S** to scend

SEND   *v* **SENT, SENDING, SENDS** to cause to go **SENDABLE** *adj*

SENDAL   *n* pl. **-S** a silk fabric

SENDER   *n* pl. **-S** one that sends

SENDOFF   *n* pl. **-S** a farewell celebration

SENDUP   *n* pl. **-S** a parody

SENE   *n* pl. **-S** a monetary unit of Samoa

SENECA   *n* pl. **-S** senega

SENECIO   *n* pl. **-CIOS** a flowering plant

SENEGA   *n* pl. **-S** a medicinal plant root

SENESCE   *v* **-ESCED, -ESCING, -ESCES** to grow old

SENGI   *n* pl. **SENGI** a former monetary unit of Zaire

SENHOR *n* pl. **-S** or **-ES** a Portuguese or Brazilian gentleman

SENHORA *n* pl. **-S** a married Portuguese or Brazilian woman

SENILE *n* pl. **-S** one who exhibits senility

SENILELY *adv* in a senile manner

SENILITY *n* pl. **-TIES** mental and physical infirmity due to old age

SENIOR *n* pl. **-S** a person who is older than another

SENITI *n* pl. **SENITI** a monetary unit of Tonga

SENNA *n* pl. **-S** a medicinal plant

SENNET *n* pl. **-S** a call sounded on a trumpet signaling the entrance or exit of actors

SENNIGHT *n* pl. **-S** a week

SENNIT *n* pl. **-S** braided straw used in making hats

SENOPIA *n* pl. **-S** an improvement of near vision

SENOR *n* pl. **-S** or **-ES** a Spanish gentleman

SENORA *n* pl. **-S** a married Spanish woman

SENORITA *n* pl. **-S** an unmarried Spanish girl or woman

SENRYU *n* pl. **SENRYU** a Japanese poem

SENSA pl. of sensum

SENSATE *v* **-SATED, -SATING, -SATES** to sense

SENSE *v* **SENSED, SENSING, SENSES** to perceive by the senses (any of certain agencies through which an individual receives impressions of the external world)

SENSEFUL *adj* sensible

SENSEI *n* pl. **-S** a teacher of Japanese martial arts

SENSIBLE *adj* **-BLER, -BLEST** having or showing good judgment **SENSIBLY** *adv*

SENSIBLE *n* pl. **-S** something that can be sensed

SENSILLA *n* pl. **-LAE** a simple sense organ

SENSING present participle of sense

SENSOR *n* pl. **-S** a device that receives and responds to a stimulus

SENSORIA *n/pl* the parts of the brain concerned with the reception and interpretation of sensory stimuli

SENSORY *adj* pertaining to the senses or sensation

SENSUAL *adj* pertaining to the physical senses

SENSUM *n* pl. **-SA** an object of perception or sensation

SENSUOUS *adj* pertaining to or derived from the senses

SENT *n* pl. **SENTI** or **SENTS** a monetary unit of Estonia

SENTE *n* pl. **LICENTE** or **LISENTE** a monetary unit of Lesotho

SENTENCE *v* **-TENCED, -TENCING, -TENCES** to declare judicially the extent of punishment to be imposed

SENTI *n* pl. **SENTI** a former monetary unit of Tanzania

SENTIENT *n* pl. **-S** a person or thing capable of sensation

SENTIMO *n* pl. **-MOS** a monetary unit of the Philippines

SENTINEL *v* **-NELED, -NELING, -NELS** or **-NELLED, -NELLING, -NELS** to stand guard

SENTRY *n* pl. **-TRIES** one who stands guard

SEPAL *n* pl. **-S** one of the individual leaves of a calyx **SEPALED, SEPALINE, SEPALLED, SEPALOID, SEPALOUS** *adj*

SEPARATE *v* **-RATED, -RATING, -RATES** to set or keep apart

SEPIA *n* pl. **-S** a brown pigment **SEPIC** *adj*

SEPOY *n* pl. **-POYS** a native of India serving in the British army

SEPPUKU *n* pl. **-S** a Japanese form of suicide

SEPS *n* pl. **-ES** an African lizard

SEPSIS *n* pl. **SEPSES** bacterial invasion of the body

SEPT *n* pl. **-S** a clan

SEPTA pl. of septum

SEPTAGE *n* pl. **-S** the waste in a septic tank

SEPTAL *adj* pertaining to a septum

SEPTARIA *n/pl* limestone nodules

SEPTATE *adj* having a septum

SEPTET *n* pl. **-S** a group of seven

SEPTETTE *n* pl. **-S** septet

SEPTIC *n* pl. **-S** an agent producing sepsis **SEPTICAL** *adj*

SEPTIMAL *adj* based on the number seven

SEPTIME *n* pl. **-S** a position in fencing

SEPTORIA *n* pl. **-S** a type of fungus

SEPTUM *n* pl. **-TUMS** or **-TA** a dividing membrane or partition

SEPTUPLE *v* **-PLED, -PLING, -PLES** to make seven times as great

SEQUEL *n* pl. **-S** something that follows and serves as a continuation

SEQUELA *n* pl. **-QUELAE** an abnormal condition resulting from a preceding disease

SEQUENCE *v* **-QUENCED, -QUENCING, -QUENCES** to arrange in consecutive order

SEQUENCY *n* pl. **-CIES** the following of one thing after another

SEQUENT *n* pl. **-S** something that follows

SEQUIN *v* **-ED, -ING, -S** to affix sequins (shiny ornamental discs) to

SEQUITUR *n* pl. **-S** the conclusion of an inference

SEQUOIA *n* pl. **-S** a large evergreen tree

SER *n* pl. **-S** a unit of weight of India

SERA a pl. of serum

SERAC *n* pl. **-S** a large mass of ice broken off of a glacier

SERAGLIO *n* pl. **-GLIOS** a harem

SERAI *n* pl. **-S** a Turkish palace

SERAIL *n* pl. **-S** a seraglio

SERAL *adj* pertaining to a series of ecological changes

SERAPE *n* pl. **-S** a colorful woolen shawl

SERAPH *n* pl. **-APHS** or **-APHIM** or **-APHIN** a winged celestial being **SERAPHIC** *adj*

SERAPHIM *n* pl. **-S** seraph

SERDAB *n* pl. **-S** a chamber within an ancient Egyptian tomb

SERE *adj* **SERER, SEREST** withered; dry

SERE *v* **SERED, SERING, SERES** to sear

SERE *n* **-S** a natural series of plant or animal communities

SEREIN *n* pl. **-S** a fine rain falling from an apparently clear sky

SERENADE *v* **-NADED, -NADING, -NADES** to perform an honorific evening song for

SERENATA *n* pl. **-TAS** or **-TE** a dramatic cantata

SERENE *adj* **SERENER, SERENEST** calm; tranquil **SERENELY** *adv*

SERENE *n* pl. **-S** a serene condition or expanse

SERENITY *n* pl. **-TIES** the state of being serene

SERER comparative of sere

SEREST superlative of sere

SERF *n* pl. **-S** a feudal slave

SERFAGE *n* pl. **-S** serfdom

SERFDOM *n* pl. **-S** the state of being a serf

SERFHOOD *n* pl. **-S** serfdom

SERFISH *adj* characteristic of a serf

SERFLIKE *adj* serfish

SERGE *v* **SERGED, SERGING, SERGES** to finish (a cut edge of a seam) with overcast stitches

SERGEANT *n* pl. **-S** a noncommissioned military officer

SERGER *n* pl. **-S** a machine for serging

SERGING *n* pl. **-S** a process of finishing the raw edges of a fabric

SERIAL *n* pl. **-S** a literary or dramatic work presented in successive installments

SERIALLY *adv* in the manner or form of a serial

SERIATE *v* **-ATED, -ATING, -ATES** to put into a series

SERIATIM *adv* serially

SERICIN *n* pl. **-S** a kind of protein

SERIEMA *n* pl. **-S** a Brazilian bird

SERIES *n* pl. **SERIES** an arrangement of one after another

SERIF *n* pl. **-S** a fine line used to finish off the main stroke of a letter **SERIFED, SERIFFED** *adj*

SERIN *n* pl. **-S** a European finch

SERINE *n* pl. **-S** an amino acid

SERING present participle of sere

SERINGA *n* pl. **-S** a Brazilian tree

SERIOUS *adj* thoughtful or subdued in appearance or manner

SERJEANT *n* pl. **-S** sergeant

SERMON *n* pl. **-S** a religious discourse **SERMONIC** *adj*

SEROLOGY *n* pl. **-GIES** the science of serums

SEROMA *n* pl. **-S** an abnormal pocket of clear fluid in the body

SEROSA *n* pl. **-SAS** or **-SAE** a thin membrane lining certain bodily cavities **SEROSAL** *adj*

SEROSITY	*n* pl. **-TIES** the quality or state of being serous
SEROTINE	*n* pl. **-S** a European bat
SEROTINY	*n* pl. **-NIES** the condition of having late or gradual seed dispersal
SEROTYPE	*v* **-TYPED, -TYPING, -TYPES** to classify (microorganisms) according to a characteristic set of antigens
SEROUS	*adj* of or resembling serum
SEROVAR	*n* pl. **-S** a group of microorganisms having a characteristic set of antigens
SEROW	*n* pl. **-S** an Asian antelope
SERPENT	*n* pl. **-S** a snake
SERPIGO	*n* pl. **-GOS** or **-GOES** or **-GINES** a spreading skin eruption
SERRANID	*n* pl. **-S** a marine fish
SERRANO	*n* pl. **-NOS** a small hot pepper
SERRATE	*v* **-RATED, -RATING, -RATES** to furnish with toothlike projections
SERRY	*v* **-RIED, -RYING, -RIES** to crowd together
SERUM	*n* pl. **-RUMS** or **-RA** the watery portion of whole blood **SERUMAL** *adj*
SERVABLE	*adj* capable of serving or being served
SERVAL	*n* pl. **-S** an African wildcat
SERVANT	*n* pl. **-S** one that serves others
SERVE	*v* **SERVED, SERVING, SERVES** to work for
SERVER	*n* pl. **-S** one that serves another
SERVERY	*n* pl. **-ERIES** a counter or room from which meals are served
SERVICE	*v* **-VICED, -VICING, -VICES** to repair
SERVICER	*n* pl. **-S** one that services
SERVILE	*adj* slavishly submissive
SERVING	*n* pl. **-S** a portion of food
SERVITOR	*n* pl. **-S** a male servant
SERVO	*n* pl. **-VOS** an automatic device used to control another mechanism
SESAME	*n* pl. **-S** an East Indian plant
SESAMOID	*n* pl. **-S** a nodular mass of bone or cartilage
SESH	*n* pl. **-ES** a session
SESSILE	*adj* permanently attached
SESSION	*n* pl. **-S** a meeting of a legislative or judicial body for the transaction of business

SESSPOOL	*n* pl. **-S** cesspool
SESTERCE	*n* pl. **-S** a coin of ancient Rome
SESTET	*n* pl. **-S** a stanza of six lines
SESTINA	*n* pl. **-S** a type of verse form
SESTINE	*n* pl. **-S** sestina
SET	*v* **SET, SETTING, SETS** to put in a particular position
SETA	*n* pl. **-TAE** a coarse, stiff hair **SETAL** *adj*
SETBACK	*n* pl. **-S** a defeat
SETENANT	*n* pl. **-S** a postage stamp that differs in design from others in the same sheet
SETIFORM	*adj* having the form of a seta
SETLINE	*n* pl. **-S** a strong fishing line
SETOFF	*n* pl. **-S** something that offsets something else
SETON	*n* pl. **-S** a type of surgical thread
SETOSE	*adj* covered with setae
SETOUS	*adj* setose
SETOUT	*n* pl. **-S** a display
SETSCREW	*n* pl. **-S** a type of screw
SETT	*n* pl. **-S** the burrow of a badger
SETTEE	*n* pl. **-S** a long seat with a high back
SETTER	*n* pl. **-S** one that sets
SETTING	*n* pl. **-S** the scenery used in a dramatic production
SETTLE	*v* **-TLED, -TLING, -TLES** to place in a desired state or order
SETTLER	*n* pl. **-S** one that settles
SETTLING	*n* pl. **-S** sediment
SETTLOR	*n* pl. **-S** one that makes a legal settlement
SETULOSE	*adj* covered with seta
SETULOUS	*adj* setulose
SETUP	*n* pl. **-S** the way something is arranged
SEV	*n* pl. **-S** an Indian food of deep-fried strands of flour
SEVEN	*n* pl. **-S** a number
SEVENTH	*n* pl. **-S** one of seven equal parts
SEVENTY	*n* pl. **-TIES** a number
SEVER	*v* **-ED, -ING, -S** to divide or cut into parts
SEVERAL	*n* pl. **-S** a few persons or things
SEVERE	*adj* **-VERER, -VEREST** unsparing in the treatment of others **SEVERELY** *adv*

SEVERITY *n* pl. **-TIES** the quality or state of being severe

SEVERY *n* pl. **-ERIES** a compartment in a vaulted ceiling

SEVICHE *n* pl. **-S** a dish of raw fish

SEVRUGA *n* pl. **-S** caviar from the Caspian Sea

SEW *v* **SEWED, SEWN, SEWING, SEWS** to mend or fasten with a needle and thread **SEWABLE** *adj*

SEWAGE *n* pl. **-S** the waste matter carried off by sewers

SEWAN *n* pl. **-S** seawan

SEWAR *n* pl. **-S** a medieval servant

SEWER *v* **-ED, -ING, -S** to clean or maintain sewers (underground conduits for waste)

SEWERAGE *n* pl. **-S** sewage

SEWING *n* pl. **-S** material that has been or is to be sewed

SEWN a past participle of sew

SEX *v* **-ED, -ING, -ES** to determine the sex (the property by which organisms are classified according to reproductive functions) of

SEXER *n* pl. **-S** one that sexes

SEXIER comparative of sexy

SEXIEST superlative of sexy

SEXILY *adv* in a sexy manner

SEXINESS *n* pl. **-ES** the quality or state of being sexy

SEXISM *n* pl. **-S** prejudice or discrimination against women

SEXIST *n* pl. **-S** one that practices sexism

SEXLESS *adj* lacking sexual characteristics

SEXOLOGY *n* pl. **-GIES** the study of human sexual behavior

SEXPERT *n* pl. **-S** an expert in sexual matters

SEXPOT *n* pl. **-S** a sexually attractive woman

SEXT *n* pl. **-S** one of seven canonical daily periods for prayer and devotion

SEXTAIN *n* pl. **-S** a stanza of six lines

SEXTAN *n* pl. **-S** a recurrent malarial fever

SEXTANT *n* pl. **-S** an instrument for measuring angular distances

SEXTARII *n/pl* ancient Roman units of liquid measure

SEXTET *n* pl. **-S** a group of six

SEXTETTE *n* pl. **-S** sextet

SEXTILE *n* pl. **-S** the position of two celestial bodies when they are sixty degrees apart

SEXTING *n* pl. **-S** the sending of sexually explicit messages or images by cell phone

SEXTO *n* pl. **-TOS** sixmo

SEXTON *n* pl. **-S** a maintenance worker of a church

SEXTUPLE *v* **-PLED, -PLING, -PLES** to make six times as great

SEXTUPLY *adv* to six times as much or as many

SEXUAL *adj* pertaining to sex **SEXUALLY** *adv*

SEXY *adj* **SEXIER, SEXIEST** arousing sexual desire

SFERICS *n/pl* an electronic detector of storms

SFORZATO *n* pl. **-TOS** the playing of a tone or chord with sudden force

SFUMATO *n* pl. **-TOS** a technique used in painting

SH *interj* — used to urge silence

SHA *interj* — used to urge silence

SHABBY *adj* **-BIER, -BIEST** ragged **SHABBILY** *adv*

SHACK *v* **-ED, -ING, -S** to live or dwell

SHACKLE *v* **-LED, -LING, -LES** to confine with metal fastenings placed around the wrists or ankles

SHACKLER *n* pl. **-S** one that shackles

SHACKO *n* pl. **-KOS** or **-KOES** shako

SHACKY *adj* **SHACKIER, SHACKIEST** dilapidated

SHAD *n* pl. **-S** a food fish

SHADBLOW *n* pl. **-S** a shadbush

SHADBUSH *n* pl. **-ES** a flowering tree or shrub

SHADCHAN *n* pl. **-CHANS** or **-CHANIM** a Jewish marriage broker

SHADDOCK *n* pl. **-S** a citrus fruit

SHADDUP *interj* — used to silence someone

SHADE *v* **SHADED, SHADING, SHADES** to screen from light or heat

SHADER *n* pl. **-S** one that shades

SHADFLY *n* pl. **-FLIES** a winged insect

SHADIER comparative of shady

SHADIEST superlative of shady

SHADILY *adv* in a shady manner

SHADING	n pl. **-S** protection against light or heat
SHADKHAN	n pl. **-KHANS** or **-KHANIM** shadchan
SHADOOF	n pl. **-S** a device used in Egypt for raising water for irrigation
SHADOW	v **-ED, -ING, -S** to make dark or gloomy
SHADOWER	n pl. **-S** one that shadows
SHADOWY	adj **-OWIER, -OWIEST** dark
SHADRACH	n pl. **-S** a mass of unfused material in the hearth of a blast furnace
SHADUF	n pl. **-S** shadoof
SHADY	adj **SHADIER, SHADIEST** shaded
SHAFT	v **-ED, -ING, -S** to push or propel with a pole
SHAFTING	n pl. **-S** a system of rods for transmitting motion or power
SHAG	v **SHAGGED, SHAGGING, SHAGS** to make shaggy
SHAGBARK	n pl. **-S** a hardwood tree
SHAGGY	adj **-GIER, -GIEST** covered with long, coarse hair **SHAGGILY** adv
SHAGREEN	n pl. **-S** the rough skin of certain sharks
SHAH	n pl. **-S** an Iranian ruler
SHAHADA	n pl. **-S** the Muslim profession of faith
SHAHADAH	n pl. **-S** shahada
SHAHDOM	n pl. **-S** the territory ruled by a shah
SHAHEED	n pl. **-S** shahid
SHAHID	n pl. **-S** a Muslim martyr
SHAIKH	n pl. **-S** sheik
SHAIRD	n pl. **-S** shard
SHAIRN	n pl. **-S** sharn
SHAITAN	n pl. **-S** an evil spirit
SHAKE	v **SHOOK, SHAKEN, SHAKING, SHAKES** to move to and fro with short, rapid movements **SHAKABLE** adj
SHAKEOUT	n pl. **-S** a minor economic recession
SHAKER	n pl. **-S** one that shakes
SHAKEUP	n pl. **-S** a total reorganization
SHAKIER	comparative of shaky
SHAKIEST	superlative of shaky
SHAKILY	adv in a shaky manner
SHAKING	present participle of shake

SHAKO	n pl. **-KOS** or **-KOES** a type of military hat
SHAKY	adj **SHAKIER, SHAKIEST** shaking
SHALE	n pl. **-S** a fissile rock
SHALED	adj having a shell or husk
SHALEY	adj **SHALIER, SHALIEST** shaly
SHALIER	comparative of shaly
SHALIEST	superlative of shaly
SHALL	v present sing. 2d person **SHALL** or **SHALT,** past sing. 2d person **SHOULD** or **SHOULDST** or **SHOULDEST** — used as an auxiliary to express futurity, inevitability, or command
SHALLOON	n pl. **-S** a woolen fabric
SHALLOP	n pl. **-S** a small, open boat
SHALLOT	n pl. **-S** a plant resembling an onion
SHALLOW	adj **-LOWER, -LOWEST** having little depth
SHALLOW	v **-ED, -ING, -S** to make shallow
SHALOM	n pl. **-S** a word used as a Jewish greeting or farewell
SHALT	a present 2d person sing. of shall
SHALWAR	n pl. **-S** a pair of loose trousers worn by some women of India
SHALY	adj **SHALIER, SHALIEST** resembling shale
SHAM	v **SHAMMED, SHAMMING, SHAMS** to feign
SHAMABLE	adj capable of being shamed **SHAMABLY** adv
SHAMAL	n pl. **-S** a hot, dry wind
SHAMAN	n pl. **-S** a medicine man among certain Native Americans **SHAMANIC** adj
SHAMAS	n pl. **-MOSIM** shammes
SHAMBA	n pl. **-S** a farm in East Africa
SHAMBLE	v **-BLED, -BLING, -BLES** to walk awkwardly
SHAME	v **SHAMED, SHAMING, SHAMES** to cause to feel a painful sense of guilt or degradation
SHAMEFUL	adj disgraceful
SHAMES	n pl. **-MOSIM** shammes
SHAMIANA	n pl. **-S** a large tent in India
SHAMISEN	n pl. **-S** samisen
SHAMMAS	n pl. **-MASIM** shammes
SHAMMASH	n pl. **-MASHIM** shammes
SHAMMED	past tense of sham

SHAMMER	*n* pl. **-S** one that shams
SHAMMES	*n* pl. **-MOSIM** a minor official of a synagogue
SHAMMIED	past tense of shammy
SHAMMIES	present 3d person sing. of shammy
SHAMMING	present participle of sham
SHAMMOS	*n* pl. **-MOSIM** shammes
SHAMMOSIM	pl. of shammes
SHAMMY	*v* **-MIED, -MYING, -MIES** to chamois
SHAMOIS	*n* pl. **SHAMOIS** chamois
SHAMOS	*n* pl. **-MOSIM** shammes
SHAMOSIM	pl. of shames
SHAMOY	*v* **-ED, -ING, -S** to chamois
SHAMPOO	*v* **-ED, -ING, -S** to cleanse with a special preparation
SHAMROCK	*n* pl. **-S** a three-leaved plant
SHAMUS	*n* pl. **-ES** a private detective
SHANDY	*n* pl. **-DIES** an alcoholic drink
SHANGHAI	*v* **-ED, -ING, -S** to kidnap for service aboard a ship
SHANK	*v* **-ED, -ING, -S** to hit sharply to the right, as a golf ball
SHANNY	*n* pl. **-NIES** a marine fish
SHANTEY	*n* pl. **-TEYS** chantey
SHANTI	*n* pl. **-S** peace
SHANTIES	pl. of shanty
SHANTIH	*n* pl. **-S** shanti
SHANTUNG	*n* pl. **-S** a silk fabric
SHANTY	*n* pl. **-TIES** a small, crudely built dwelling
SHAPE	*v* **SHAPED, SHAPEN, SHAPING, SHAPES** to give shape (outward form) to **SHAPABLE** *adj*
SHAPELY	*adj* **-LIER, -LIEST** having a pleasing shape
SHAPER	*n* pl. **-S** one that shapes
SHAPEUP	*n* pl. **-S** a system of hiring a work crew
SHAPING	present participle of shape
SHARD	*n* pl. **-S** a fragment of broken pottery
SHARE	*v* **SHARED, SHARING, SHARES** to have, get, or use in common with another or others **SHARABLE** *adj*
SHARER	*n* pl. **-S** one that shares

SHARIA	*n* pl. **-S** Islamic law based on the Koran
SHARIAH	*n* pl. **-S** sharia
SHARIAT	*n* pl. **-S** sharia
SHARIF	*n* pl. **-S** sherif
SHARING	present participle of share
SHARK	*v* **-ED, -ING, -S** to live by trickery
SHARKER	*n* pl. **-S** one that sharks
SHARKISH	*adj* behaving like a shark (a predatory fish)
SHARN	*n* pl. **-S** cow dung **SHARNY** *adj*
SHARP	*adj* **SHARPER, SHARPEST** suitable for or capable of cutting or piercing
SHARP	*v* **-ED, -ING, -S** to raise in pitch, as a musical tone
SHARPEN	*v* **-ED, -ING, -S** to make sharp
SHARPER	*n* pl. **-S** a swindler
SHARPIE	*n* pl. **-S** a very alert person
SHARPISH	*adj* somewhat sharp
SHARPLY	*adv* in a sharp manner
SHARPY	*n* pl. **SHARPIES** sharpie
SHASHLIK	*n* pl. **-S** kabob
SHASLIK	*n* pl. **-S** shashlik
SHASTA	*n* pl. **-S** a flowering plant
SHATOOSH	*n* pl. **-ES** a fabric made from the wool of the chiru
SHATTER	*v* **-ED, -ING, -S** to break into pieces
SHAUGH	*n* pl. **-S** a thicket
SHAUL	*v* **-ED, -ING, -S** to shoal
SHAVE	*v* **SHAVED, SHAVEN, SHAVING, SHAVES** to sever the hair close to the roots **SHAVABLE** *adj*
SHAVER	*n* pl. **-S** one that shaves
SHAVIE	*n* pl. **-S** a trick or prank
SHAVING	*n* pl. **-S** something shaved off
SHAW	*v* **SHAWED, SHAWN, SHAWING, SHAWS** to show
SHAWARMA	*n* pl. **-S** a sandwich of lamb or chicken, vegetables, and often tahini wrapped in pita bread
SHAWL	*v* **-ED, -ING, -S** to wrap in a shawl (a piece of cloth worn as a covering)
SHAWM	*n* pl. **-S** an early woodwind instrument
SHAY	*n* pl. **SHAYS** a chaise
SHAYKH	*n* pl. **-S** sheik

SHAZAM   *interj* — used to signify a magical occurrence

SHE   *n* pl. **-S** a female person

SHEA   *n* pl. **-S** an African tree

SHEAF   *v* **-ED, -ING, -S** to sheave

SHEAL   *n* pl. **-S** shealing

SHEALING   *n* pl. **-S** a shepherd's hut

SHEAR   *v* **SHEARED** or **SHORE, SHORN, SHEARING, SHEARS** to cut the hair or wool from

SHEARER   *n* pl. **-S** one that shears

SHEARING   *n* pl. **-S** an instance of cutting hair or wool

SHEATH   *v* **-ED, -ING, -S** to sheathe

SHEATHE   *v* **SHEATHED, SHEATHING, SHEATHES** to put into a protective case

SHEATHER   *n* pl. **-S** one that sheathes

SHEAVE   *v* **SHEAVED, SHEAVING, SHEAVES** to gather into a bundle

SHEBANG   *n* pl. **-S** a situation, organization, or matter

SHEBEAN   *n* pl. **-S** shebeen

SHEBEEN   *n* pl. **-S** a place where liquor is sold illegally

SHED   *v* **SHEDDED, SHEDDING, SHEDS** to house in a shed (a small, low structure)

SHEDABLE   *adj* capable of being cast off

SHEDDER   *n* pl. **-S** one that casts off something

SHEDLIKE   *adj* resembling a shed

SHEEN   *v* **-ED, -ING, -S** to shine

SHEENFUL   *adj* shining

SHEENY   *adj* **SHEENIER, SHEENIEST** shining

SHEEP   *n* pl. **SHEEP** a ruminant mammal

SHEEPCOT   *n* pl. **-S** an enclosure for sheep

SHEEPDOG   *n* pl. **-S** a dog trained to guard and herd sheep

SHEEPISH   *adj* embarrassed

SHEEPLE   *n* pl. **-S** people likened to sheep

SHEEPMAN   *n* pl. **-MEN** a person who raises sheep

SHEER   *adj* **SHEERER, SHEEREST** of very thin texture **SHEERLY** *adv*

SHEER   *v* **-ED, -ING, -S** to swerve

SHEESH   *interj* — used to express mild annoyance

SHEET   *v* **-ED, -ING, -S** to cover with a sheet (a thin, rectangular piece of material)

SHEETER   *n* pl. **-S** one that sheets

SHEETFED   *adj* pertaining to a type of printing press

SHEETING   *n* pl. **-S** material in the form of sheets

SHEEVE   *n* pl. **-S** a grooved pulley wheel

SHEHNAI   *n* pl. **-S** a double-reed wind instrument of India

SHEIK   *n* pl. **-S** an Arab chief

SHEIKDOM   *n* pl. **-S** the area ruled by a sheik

SHEIKH   *n* pl. **-S** sheik

SHEILA   *n* pl. **-S** a young woman

SHEITAN   *n* pl. **-S** shaitan

SHEITEL   *n* pl. **-S** a wig worn by a married Jewish woman

SHEKEL   *n* pl. **SHEKELS** or **SHEKELIM** or **SHEKALIM** an ancient unit of weight and money

SHELDUCK   *n* pl. **-S** a European duck

SHELF   *n* pl. **SHELVES** a flat rigid structure used to support articles

SHELFFUL   *n* pl. **-S** as much as a shelf can hold

SHELL   *v* **-ED, -ING, -S** to divest of a shell (a hard outer covering)

SHELLAC   *v* **-LACKED, -LACKING, -LACS** to cover with a thin varnish

SHELLACK   *v* **-ED, -ING, -S** to shellac

SHELLER   *n* pl. **-S** one that shells

SHELLY   *adj* **SHELLIER, SHELLIEST** abounding in seashells

SHELTA   *n* pl. **-S** an esoteric jargon of Gaelic

SHELTER   *v* **-ED, -ING, -S** to provide cover or protection for

SHELTIE   *n* pl. **-S** a small, shaggy pony

SHELTY   *n* pl. **-TIES** sheltie

SHELVE   *v* **SHELVED, SHELVING, SHELVES** to place on a shelf

SHELVER   *n* pl. **-S** one that shelves

SHELVES   pl. of shelf

SHELVING   *n* pl. **-S** material for shelves

SHELVY   *adj* **SHELVIER, SHELVIEST** inclining gradually

SHEN   *n* pl. **SHEN** the spiritual element of a person's psyche

SHENAI   *n* pl. **-S** shehnai

SHEND	*v* **SHENT, SHENDING, SHENDS** to disgrace
SHEOL	*n* pl. **-S** hell
SHEPHERD	*v* **-ED, -ING, -S** to watch over carefully
SHEQEL	*n* pl. **SHEQELS** or **SHEQALIM** shekel
SHERBERT	*n* pl. **-S** sherbet
SHERBET	*n* pl. **-S** a frozen fruit-flavored mixture
SHERD	*n* pl. **-S** shard
SHEREEF	*n* pl. **-S** sherif
SHERIF	*n* pl. **-S** an Arab ruler
SHERIFF	*n* pl. **-S** a law-enforcement officer of a county
SHERLOCK	*n* pl. **-S** a detective
SHERO	*n* pl. **-ROES** a woman regarded as a hero
SHEROOT	*n* pl. **-S** cheroot
SHERPA	*n* pl. **-S** a soft fabric for linings
SHERRIED	*adj* cooked or flavored with sherry
SHERRIS	*n* pl. **-RISES** sherry
SHERRY	*n* pl. **-RIES** a type of wine
SHERWANI	*n* pl. **-S** a knee-length coat worn by some men of India
SHETLAND	*n* pl. **-S** a wool yarn
SHEUCH	*n* pl. **-S** sheugh
SHEUGH	*n* pl. **-S** a ditch
SHEW	*v* **SHEWED, SHEWN, SHEWING, SHEWS** to show
SHEWER	*n* pl. **-S** one that shews
SHH	*interj* sh
SHHH	*interj* sh
SHIATSU	*n* pl. **-S** a massage using finger pressure
SHIATZU	*n* pl. **-S** shiatsu
SHIBAH	*n* pl. **-S** shiva
SHICKER	*n* pl. **-S** a drunkard
SHIED	past tense of shy
SHIEL	*n* pl. **-S** shieling
SHIELD	*v* **-ED, -ING, -S** to provide with a protective cover or shelter
SHIELDER	*n* pl. **-S** one that shields
SHIELING	*n* pl. **-S** shealing
SHIER	*n* pl. **-S** a horse having a tendency to shy
SHIES	present 3d person sing. of shy
SHIEST	a superlative of shy

SHIFT	*v* **-ED, -ING, -S** to move from one position to another
SHIFTER	*n* pl. **-S** one that shifts
SHIFTING	*n* pl. **-S** the act of moving from one place to another
SHIFTY	*adj* **SHIFTIER, SHIFTIEST** tricky **SHIFTILY** *adv*
SHIGELLA	*n* pl. **-LAS** or **-LAE** any of a genus of aerobic bacteria
SHIITAKE	*n* pl. **-S** a dark Oriental mushroom
SHIKAR	*v* **-KARRED, -KARRING, -KARS** to hunt
SHIKARA	*n* pl. **-S** a light, flat-bottomed boat in Kashmir
SHIKAREE	*n* pl. **-S** a big game hunter
SHIKARI	*n* pl. **-S** shikaree
SHIKKER	*n* pl. **-S** shicker
SHIKRA	*n* pl. **-S** a small sparrow hawk
SHILINGI	*n* pl. **SHILINGI** a monetary unit of Tanzania
SHILL	*v* **-ED, -ING, -S** to act as a decoy
SHILLALA	*n* pl. **-S** a short, thick club
SHILLING	*n* pl. **-S** a former monetary unit of Great Britain
SHILPIT	*adj* sickly
SHILY	*adv* in a shy manner
SHIM	*v* **SHIMMED, SHIMMING, SHIMS** to fill out or level by inserting a thin wedge
SHIMMER	*v* **-ED, -ING, -S** to glimmer
SHIMMERY	*adj* shimmering
SHIMMY	*v* **-MIED, -MYING, -MIES** to vibrate or wobble
SHIN	*v* **SHINNED, SHINNING, SHINS** to climb by gripping and pulling alternately with the hands and legs
SHINBONE	*n* pl. **-S** the tibia
SHINDIG	*n* pl. **-S** an elaborate dance or party
SHINDY	*n* pl. **-DYS** or **-DIES** a shindig
SHINE	*v* **SHONE** or **SHINED, SHINING, SHINES** to emit light
SHINER	*n* pl. **-S** one that shines
SHINGLE	*v* **-GLED, -GLING, -GLES** to cover with shingles (thin, oblong pieces of building material)
SHINGLER	*n* pl. **-S** one that shingles
SHINGLY	*adj* covered with small, loose stones
SHINIER	comparative of shiny

SHINIEST superlative of shiny

SHINILY *adv* in a shiny manner

SHINING *adj* emitting or reflecting light

SHINLEAF *n* pl. **-LEAFS** or **-LEAVES** a perennial herb

SHINNED past of shin

SHINNERY *n* pl. **-NERIES** a dense growth of small trees

SHINNEY *v* **-ED, -ING, -S** to play a form of hockey

SHINNING present participle of shin

SHINNY *v* **-NIED, -NYING, -NIES** to shin

SHINTY *n* pl. **-TIES** a Scottish game similar to field hockey

SHINY *adj* **SHINIER, SHINIEST** filled with light

SHIP *v* **SHIPPED, SHIPPING, SHIPS** to transport by ship (a vessel suitable for navigation in deep water)

SHIPLAP *n* pl. **-S** an overlapping joint used in carpentry

SHIPLESS *adj* lacking a ship

SHIPLOAD *n* pl. **-S** as much as a ship can carry

SHIPMAN *n* pl. **-MEN** a sailor

SHIPMATE *n* pl. **-S** a fellow sailor

SHIPMENT *n* pl. **-S** something that is shipped

SHIPPED past tense of ship

SHIPPEN *n* pl. **-S** a cowshed

SHIPPER *n* pl. **-S** one that ships

SHIPPING *n* pl. **-S** the business of one that ships

SHIPPON *n* pl. **-S** shippen

SHIPSIDE *n* pl. **-S** the area alongside a ship

SHIPTIME *n* pl. **-S** the annual arrival of a supply ship

SHIPWAY *n* pl. **-WAYS** a canal deep enough to serve ships

SHIPWORM *n* pl. **-S** a wormlike mollusk

SHIPYARD *n* pl. **-S** a place where ships are built or repaired

SHIRAZ *n* pl. **-ES** a type of wine

SHIRE *n* pl. **-S** a territorial division of Great Britain

SHIRK *v* **-ED, -ING, -S** to avoid work or duty

SHIRKER *n* pl. **-S** one that shirks

SHIRR *v* **-ED, -ING, -S** to draw into three or more parallel rows, as cloth

SHIRRING *n* pl. **-S** a shirred arrangement of cloth

SHIRT *n* pl. **-S** a garment for the upper part of the body **SHIRTED** *adj*

SHIRTING *n* pl. **-S** fabric used for making shirts

SHIRTY *adj* **SHIRTIER, SHIRTIEST** angry **SHIRTILY** *adv*

SHIST *n* pl. **-S** schist

SHITAKE *n* pl. **-S** shiitake

SHITTAH *n* pl. **-S** a hardwood tree

SHITTIM *n* pl. **-S** the wood of the shittah

SHIUR *n* pl. **SHIURIM** a Talmudic study session

SHIV *n* pl. **-S** a knife

SHIVA *n* pl. **-S** a period of mourning

SHIVAH *n* pl. **-S** shiva

SHIVAREE *v* **-REED, -REEING, -REES** to chivaree

SHIVE *n* pl. **-S** a thin fragment

SHIVER *v* **-ED, -ING, -S** to tremble with fear or cold

SHIVERER *n* pl. **-S** one that shivers

SHIVERY *adj* shivering

SHIVITI *n* pl. **-S** a plaque with a Hebrew verse

SHLEMIEL *n* pl. **-S** an unlucky bungler

SHLEP *v* **SHLEPPED, SHLEPPING, SHLEPS** to schlep

SHLEPP *v* **-ED, -ING, -S** to schlep

SHLEPPER *n* pl. **-S** one that schleps

SHLEPPY *adj* **-PIER, -PIEST** schleppy

SHLOCK *n* pl. **-S** schlock

SHLOCKY *adj* **SHLOCKIER, SHLOCKIEST** schlocky

SHLUB *n* pl. **-S** schlub

SHLUMP *v* **-ED, -ING, -S** to schlump

SHLUMPY *adj* slovenly

SHMALTZ *n* pl. **-ES** schmaltz

SHMALTZY *adj* **SHMALTZIER, SHMALTZIEST** schmalzy

SHMATTE *n* pl. **-S** schmatte

SHMEAR *v* **-ED, -ING, -S** to schmeer

SHMEER *v* **-ED, -ING, -S** to schmeer

SHMO *n* pl. **SHMOES** schmo

SHMOE *n* pl. **-S** schmo

SHMOOZE *v* **SHMOOZED, SHMOOZING, SHMOOZES** to schmooze

SHMOOZER   *n* pl. **-S** one that shmoozes

SHMOOZY   *adj* **SHMOOZIER, SHMOOZIEST** schmoozy

SHMUCK   *n* pl. **-S** schmuck

SHMUCKY   *adj* **SHMUCKIER, SHMUCKIEST** schmucky

SHNAPPS   *n* pl. **SHNAPPS** schnapps

SHNAPS   *n* pl. **SHNAPS** schnapps

SHNOOK   *n* pl. **-S** schnook

SHNORRER   *n* pl. **-S** one who takes advantage of the generosity of others

SHO   *n* pl. **SHO** a former monetary unit of Tibet

SHOAL   *adj* **SHOALER, SHOALEST** shallow

SHOAL   *v* **-ED, -ING, -S** to become shallow

SHOALY   *adj* **SHOALIER, SHOALIEST** full of shallow areas

SHOAT   *n* pl. **-S** a young hog

SHOCHET   *n* pl. **-CHETIM** a person who slaughters animals and fowl according to Jewish law

SHOCHU   *n* pl. **-S** a Japanese liquor

SHOCK   *v* **-ED, -ING, -S** to strike with great surprise, horror, or disgust

SHOCKER   *n* pl. **-S** one that shocks

SHOD   a past tense of shoe

SHODDEN   a past participle of shoe

SHODDY   *adj* **-DIER, -DIEST** of inferior quality **SHODDILY** *adv*

SHODDY   *n* pl. **-DIES** a low-quality wool

SHOE   *n* pl. **SHOES** or **SHOON** a covering for the foot

SHOE   *v* **SHOD** or **SHOED, SHODDEN, SHOEING, SHOES** to provide with shoes

SHOEBILL   *n* pl. **-S** a wading bird

SHOEBOX   *n* pl. **-ES** an oblong box for holding a pair of shoes

SHOEHORN   *v* **-ED, -ING, -S** to force into a small space

SHOELACE   *n* pl. **-S** a lace for fastening a shoe

SHOELESS   *adj* having no shoe

SHOEPAC   *n* pl. **-S** a waterproof boot

SHOEPACK   *n* pl. **-S** shoepac

SHOER   *n* pl. **-S** one that shoes horses

SHOETREE   *n* pl. **-S** a device shaped like a foot that is inserted into a shoe to preserve its shape

SHOFAR   *n* pl. **SHOFARS** or **SHOFROTH** a ram's-horn trumpet blown in certain Jewish rituals

SHOG   *v* **SHOGGED, SHOGGING, SHOGS** to move along

SHOGI   *n* pl. **-S** a Japanese game like chess

SHOGUN   *n* pl. **-S** a former military leader of Japan **SHOGUNAL** *adj*

SHOJI   *n* pl. **-S** a paper screen used as a partition or door in a Japanese house

SHOJO   *n* pl. **SHOJO** manga intended primarily for girls

SHOLOM   *n* pl. **-S** shalom

SHONE   a past tense of shine

SHOO   *v* **-ED, -ING, -S** to drive away

SHOOFLY   *n* pl. **-FLIES** a child's rocker

SHOOK   *n* pl. **-S** a set of parts for assembling a barrel or packing

SHOOL   *v* **-ED, -ING, -S** to shovel

SHOON   a pl. of shoe

SHOOSH   *v* **-ED, -ING, -ES** to move with a rushing sound

SHOOT   *v* **SHOT, SHOOTING, SHOOTS** to hit, wound, or kill with a missile discharged from a weapon

SHOOTER   *n* pl. **-S** one that shoots

SHOOTING   *n* pl. **-S** the act of one that shoots

SHOOTIST   *n* pl. **-S** one that is skilled at shooting

SHOOTOUT   *n* pl. **-S** a battle fought with handguns or rifles

SHOP   *v* **SHOPPED, SHOPPING, SHOPS** to examine goods with intent to buy

SHOPBOY   *n* pl. **-BOYS** a salesclerk

SHOPGIRL   *n* pl. **-S** a salesgirl

SHOPHAR   *n* pl. **-PHARS** or **-PHROTH** shofar

SHOPLESS   *adj* having no stores

SHOPLIFT   *v* **-ED, -ING, -S** to steal goods from a store

SHOPMAN   *n* pl. **-MEN** one who owns or operates a small store

SHOPPE   *n* pl. **-S** a small store

SHOPPED   past tense of shop

SHOPPER   *n* pl. **-S** one that shops

SHOPPING   *n* pl. **-S** the act of one that shops

SHOPPY   *adj* **SHOPPIER, SHOPPIEST** conducive to shopping

SHOPTALK *n* pl. **-S** conversation concerning one's business or occupation

SHOPWORN *adj* worn out from being on display in a store

SHORAN *n* pl. **-S** a type of navigational system

SHORE *v* **SHORED, SHORING, SHORES** to prop with a supporting timber

SHORING *n* pl. **-S** a system of supporting timbers

SHORL *n* pl. **-S** schorl

SHORN a past participle of shear

SHORT *adj* **SHORTER, SHORTEST** having little length

SHORT *v* **-ED, -ING, -S** to cause a type of electrical malfunction in

SHORTAGE *n* pl. **-S** an insufficient supply or amount

SHORTCUT *v* **-CUT, -CUTTING, -CUTS** to take a shorter or quicker way

SHORTEN *v* **-ED, -ING, -S** to make or become shorter

SHORTIA *n* pl. **-S** a perennial herb

SHORTIE *n* pl. **-S** shorty

SHORTIES pl. of shorty

SHORTISH *adj* somewhat short

SHORTLY *adv* in a short time

SHORTY *n* pl. **SHORTIES** one that is short

SHOT *v* **SHOTTED, SHOTTING, SHOTS** to load with shot (small lead or steel pellets)

SHOTE *n* pl. **-S** shoat

SHOTGUN *v* **-GUNNED, -GUNNING, -GUNS** to shoot with a type of gun

SHOTHOLE *n* pl. **-S** a hole drilled in rock to hold explosives

SHOTT *n* pl. **-S** chott

SHOTTED past tense of shot

SHOTTEN *adj* having spawned — used of a fish

SHOTTING present participle of shot

SHOULD past tense of shall

SHOULDER *v* **-ED, -ING, -S** to assume the burden or responsibility of

SHOULDEST a 2d person sing. past tense of shall

SHOULDST a 2d person sing. past tense of shall

SHOUT *v* **-ED, -ING, -S** to utter loudly

SHOUTER *n* pl. **-S** one that shouts

SHOUTY *adj* **SHOUTIER, SHOUTIEST** given to or characterized by shouting

SHOVE *v* **SHOVED, SHOVING, SHOVES** to push roughly

SHOVEL *v* **-ELED, -ELING, -ELS** or **-ELLED, -ELLING, -ELS** to take up with a shovel (a digging implement)

SHOVELER *n* pl. **-S** one that shovels

SHOVER *n* pl. **-S** one that shoves

SHOVING present participle of shove

SHOW *v* **SHOWED, SHOWN, SHOWING, SHOWS** to cause or permit to be seen **SHOWABLE** *adj*

SHOWBIZ *n* pl. **-BIZZES** show business

SHOWBOAT *v* **-ED, -ING, -S** to show off

SHOWCASE *v* **-CASED, -CASING, -CASES** to exhibit

SHOWDOWN *n* pl. **-S** an event that forces the conclusion of an issue

SHOWER *v* **-ED, -ING, -S** to bathe in a spray of water

SHOWERER *n* pl. **-S** one that showers

SHOWERY *adj* abounding with brief periods of rain

SHOWGIRL *n* pl. **-S** a chorus girl

SHOWGOER *n* pl. **-S** one that attends a show

SHOWIER comparative of showy

SHOWIEST superlative of showy

SHOWILY *adv* in a showy manner

SHOWING *n* pl. **-S** an exhibition or display

SHOWMAN *n* pl. **-MEN** a theatrical producer

SHOWN past participle of show

SHOWOFF *n* pl. **-S** one given to pretentious display

SHOWRING *n* pl. **-S** a ring where animals are displayed

SHOWROOM *n* pl. **-S** a room used for the display of merchandise

SHOWTIME *n* pl. **-S** the time at which an entertainment is to start

SHOWY *adj* **SHOWIER, SHOWIEST** making a great or brilliant display

SHOYU *n* pl. **-S** soy sauce

SHRANK past tense of shrink

SHRAPNEL *n* pl. **-S** fragments from an exploding bomb, mine, or shell

SHRED *v* **SHREDDED, SHREDDING, SHREDS** to tear into small strips

SHREDDER *n* pl. **-S** one that shreds

SHREW *v* **-ED, -ING, -S** to curse

SHREWD *adj* **SHREWDER, SHREWDEST** having keen insight **SHREWDLY** *adv*

SHREWDIE *n* pl. **-S** a shrewd person

SHREWISH *adj* ill-tempered

SHRI *n* pl. **-S** sri

SHRIEK *v* **-ED, -ING, -S** to utter a shrill cry

SHRIEKER *n* pl. **-S** one that shrieks

SHRIEKY *adj* **SHRIEKIER, SHRIEKIEST** shrill

SHRIEVAL *adj* pertaining to a sheriff

SHRIEVE *v* **SHRIEVED, SHRIEVING, SHRIEVES** to shrive

SHRIFT *n* pl. **-S** the act of shriving

SHRIKE *n* pl. **-S** a predatory bird

SHRILL *adj* **SHRILLER, SHRILLEST** having a high-pitched and piercing quality **SHRILLY** *adv*

SHRILL *v* **-ED, -ING, -S** to utter a shrill sound

SHRIMP *v* **-ED, -ING, -S** to catch shrimps (small marine decapods)

SHRIMPER *n* pl. **-S** a shrimp fisher

SHRIMPY *adj* **SHRIMPIER, SHRIMPIEST** abounding in shrimp

SHRINE *v* **SHRINED, SHRINING, SHRINES** to place in a shrine (a receptacle for sacred relics)

SHRINK *v* **SHRANK, SHRUNK** or **SHRUNKEN, SHRINKING, SHRINKS** to contract or draw back

SHRINKER *n* pl. **-S** one that shrinks

SHRIVE *v* **SHROVE** or **SHRIVED, SHRIVEN, SHRIVING, SHRIVES** to hear the confession of and grant absolution to

SHRIVEL *v* **-ELED, -ELING, -ELS** or **-ELLED, -ELLING, -ELS** to contract into wrinkles

SHRIVER *n* pl. **-S** one that shrives

SHROFF *v* **-ED, -ING, -S** to test the genuineness of, as a coin

SHROOM *n* pl. **-S** a mushroom (a type of fungus)

SHROOMER *n* pl. **-S** one who enjoys eating mushrooms

SHROUD *v* **-ED, -ING, -S** to wrap in burial clothing

SHROVE a past tense of shrive

SHRUB *n* pl. **-S** a low, woody plant

SHRUBBY *adj* **-BIER, -BIEST** covered with shrubs

SHRUG *v* **SHRUGGED, SHRUGGING, SHRUGS** to raise and contract the shoulders

SHRUNK a past tense of shrink

SHRUNKEN a past participle of shrink

SHTETEL *n* pl. **SHTETELS** or **SHTETLACH** a Jewish village

SHTETL *n* pl. **SHTETLS** or **SHTETLACH** shtetel

SHTICK *n* pl. **-S** an entertainment routine

SHTICKY *adj* **SHTICKIER, SHTICKIEST** resembling a shtick

SHTIK *n* pl. **-S** shtick

SHTUM *adj* schtum

SHUCK *v* **-ED, -ING, -S** to remove the husk or shell from

SHUCKER *n* pl. **-S** one that shucks

SHUCKING *n* pl. **-S** the act of one that shucks

SHUDDER *v* **-ED, -ING, -S** to tremble

SHUDDERY *adj* shuddering

SHUFFLE *v* **-FLED, -FLING, -FLES** to walk without lifting the feet

SHUFFLER *n* pl. **-S** one that shuffles

SHUL *n* pl. **SHULS** or **SHULN** a synagogue

SHUMAI *n/pl* Japanese dumplings

SHUN *v* **SHUNNED, SHUNNING, SHUNS** to avoid

SHUNNER *n* pl. **-S** one that shuns

SHUNPIKE *v* **-PIKED, -PIKING, -PIKES** to travel on side roads to avoid expressways

SHUNT *v* **-ED, -ING, -S** to turn aside

SHUNTER *n* pl. **-S** one that shunts

SHURA *n* pl. **-S** an advisory council

SHUSH *v* **-ED, -ING, -ES** to silence

SHUSHER *n* pl. **-S** one that shushes

SHUT *v* **SHUT, SHUTTING, SHUTS** to close

SHUTDOWN *n* pl. **-S** a temporary closing of an industrial plant

SHUTE *v* **SHUTED, SHUTING, SHUTES** to chute

SHUTEYE *n* pl. **-S** sleep

SHUTOFF *n* pl. **-S** a device that shuts something off

SHUTOUT *n* pl. **-S** a game in which one team fails to score

SHUTTER *v* **-ED, -ING, -S** to provide with shutters (hinged window covers)

SHUTTING present participle of shut

SHUTTLE *v* **-TLED, -TLING, -TLES** to move or travel back and forth

SHUTTLER *n* pl. **-S** one that shuttles

SHVITZ *v* **-ED, -ING, -ES** to sweat

SHWA *n* pl. **-S** schwa

SHWANPAN *n* pl. **-S** swanpan

SHY *adj* **SHIER, SHIEST** or **SHYER, SHYEST** timid

SHY *v* **SHIED, SHYING, SHIES** to move suddenly back or aside, as in fear

SHYER *n* pl. **-S** shier

SHYLOCK *v* **-ED, -ING, -S** to lend money at high interest rates

SHYLY *adv* in a shy manner

SHYNESS *n* pl. **-ES** the state of being shy

SHYSTER *n* pl. **-S** an unscrupulous lawyer or politician

SI *n* pl. **-S** ti

SIAL *n* pl. **-S** a type of rock formation **SIALIC** *adj*

SIALID *n* pl. **-S** an alderfly

SIALIDAN *n* pl. **-S** sialid

SIALOID *adj* resembling saliva

SIAMANG *n* pl. **-S** a large, black gibbon

SIAMESE *n* pl. **-S** a water pipe with a connection for two hoses

SIB *n* pl. **-S** a sibling

SIBB *n* pl. **-S** sib

SIBILANT *n* pl. **-S** a speech sound produced by the fricative passage of breath through a narrow orifice

SIBILATE *v* **-LATED, -LATING, -LATES** to hiss

SIBLING *n* pl. **-S** one having the same parents as another

SIBSHIP *n* pl. **-S** a group of children having the same parents

SIBYL *n* pl. **-S** a female prophet **SIBYLIC, SIBYLLIC** *adj*

SIC *v* **SICCED, SICCING, SICS** to urge to attack

SICCAN *adj* such

SICE *n* pl. **-S** syce

SICK *adj* **SICKER, SICKEST** affected with disease or ill health

SICK *v* **-ED, -ING, -S** to sic

SICKBAY *n* pl. **-BAYS** a ship's hospital

SICKBED *n* pl. **-S** a sick person's bed

SICKEE *n* pl. **-S** sickie

SICKEN *v* **-ED, -ING, -S** to make sick

SICKENER *n* pl. **-S** one that sickens

SICKERLY *adv* securely

SICKIE *n* pl. **-S** an emotionally sick person

SICKISH *adj* somewhat sick

SICKLE *v* **-LED, -LING, -LES** to cut with an agricultural implement having a single blade

SICKLY *adj* **-LIER, -LIEST** appearing as if sick **SICKLILY** *adv*

SICKLY *v* **-LIED, -LYING, -LIES** to make sickly

SICKNESS *n* pl. **-ES** the state of being sick

SICKO *n* pl. **SICKOS** sickie

SICKOUT *n* pl. **-S** an organized absence of workers claiming to be sick

SICKROOM *n* pl. **-S** a room occupied by a sick person

SIDALCEA *n* pl. **-S** a North American herb

SIDDHA *n* pl. **-S** one who has attained perfection in Hinduism

SIDDHI *n* pl. **-S** the perfection attained by a siddha

SIDDUR *n* pl. **-DURS** or **-DURIM** a Jewish prayer book

SIDE *v* **SIDED, SIDING, SIDES** to agree with or support

SIDEARM *v* **-ED, -ING, -S** to pitch a ball at or below shoulder level

SIDEBAND *n* pl. **-S** a band of radio frequencies

SIDEBAR *n* pl. **-S** a short news story accompanying a major story

SIDEBURN *n* **-S** either of two strips of hair grown by a man down each side of the face

SIDECAR *n* pl. **-S** a passenger car attached to a motorcycle

SIDED past tense of side

SIDEHILL *n* pl. **-S** a hillside

SIDEKICK *n* pl. **-S** a close friend

SIDELESS *adj* having no sides

SIDELINE *v* **-LINED, -LINING, -LINES** to put out of action

SIDELING *adj* sloping

SIDELOCK *n* pl. **-S** a long lock of hair falling from the side of the head

SIDELONG *adj* directed to one side

SIDEMAN *n* pl. **-MEN** a member of a jazz band

SIDEMEAT *n* pl. **-S** meat cut from the side of the pig

SIDEREAL *adj* pertaining to the stars

SIDERITE *n* pl. **-S** a mineral

SIDEROAD *n* pl. **-S** a rural road

SIDESHOW *n* pl. **-S** a small show offered in addition to a main attraction

SIDESLIP *v* **-SLIPPED, -SLIPPING, -SLIPS** to slip to one side

SIDESMAN *n* pl. **-MEN** a lay assistant at an Anglican church

SIDESPIN *n* pl. **-S** a type of spin imparted to a ball

SIDESTEP *v* **-STEPPED, -STEPPING, -STEPS** to step to one side

SIDEWALK *n* pl. **-S** a paved walk for pedestrians

SIDEWALL *n* pl. **-S** a side surface of a tire

SIDEWARD *adv* toward one side

SIDEWAY *adv* sideways

SIDEWAYS *adv* toward or from one side

SIDEWISE *adv* sideways

SIDH *n* pl. **SIDHE** a hill inhabited by supernatural beings in Irish folklore

SIDING *n* pl. **-S** material used for surfacing a frame building

SIDLE *v* **-DLED, -DLING, -DLES** to move sideways

SIDLER *n* pl. **-S** one that sidles

SIEGE *v* **SIEGED, SIEGING, SIEGES** to attempt to capture or gain

SIEMENS *n* pl. **SIEMENS** a unit of electrical conductance

SIENITE *n* pl. **-S** syenite

SIENNA *n* pl. **-S** a brown pigment

SIEROZEM *n* pl. **-S** a type of soil

SIERRA *n* pl. **-S** a mountain range **SIERRAN** *adj*

SIESTA *n* pl. **-S** an afternoon nap or rest

SIEUR *n* pl. **-S** an old French title of respect for a man

SIEVE *v* **SIEVED, SIEVING, SIEVES** to pass through a sieve (a utensil for separating the coarse parts from the fine parts of loose matter)

SIEVERT *n* pl. **-S** a unit of ionizing radiation

SIFAKA *n* pl. **-S** a lemur of Madagascar

SIFFLEUR *n* pl. **-S** an animal that makes a whistling noise

SIFT *v* **-ED, -ING, -S** to sieve

SIFTER *n* pl. **-S** one that sifts

SIFTING *n* pl. **-S** the work of a sifter

SIG *n* pl. **-S** a short personalized message at the end of an email

SIGANID *n* pl. **-S** any of a family of fishes

SIGH *v* **-ED, -ING, -S** to let out a sigh (a deep, audible breath)

SIGHER *n* pl. **-S** one that sighs

SIGHLESS *adj* uttering no sigh

SIGHLIKE *adj* resembling a sigh

SIGHT *v* **-ED, -ING, -S** to observe or notice

SIGHTER *n* pl. **-S** one that sights

SIGHTING *n* pl. **-S** an observation

SIGHTLY *adj* **-LIER, -LIEST** pleasing to look at

SIGHTSEE *v* **-SAW, -SEEN, -SEEING, -SEES** to visit and view places of interest

SIGIL *n* pl. **-S** an official seal

SIGLOS *n* pl. **-LOI** an ancient Persian coin

SIGLUM *n* pl. **SIGLA** an abbreviation to indicate the source of an edited text

SIGMA *n* pl. **-S** a Greek letter **SIGMATE** *adj*

SIGMOID *n* pl. **-S** an S-shaped curve in a bodily part

SIGN *v* **-ED, -ING, -S** to write one's name on

SIGNA *v* write on the label — no other form of this imperative verb is used

SIGNAGE *n* pl. **-S** a system of signs in a community

SIGNAL *v* **-NALED, -NALING, -NALS** or **-NALLED, -NALLING, -NALS** to notify by a means of communication

SIGNALER *n* pl. **-S** one that signals

SIGNALLY *adv* notably

SIGNEE *n* pl. **-S** a signer of a document

SIGNER *n* pl. **-S** one that signs

SIGNET *v* **-ED, -ING, -S** to mark with an official seal

SIGNIFY *v* **-FIED, -FYING, -FIES** to make known

SIGNING *n* pl. **-S** the act of writing one's signature on a document or in a book

SIGNIOR *n* pl. **-GNIORS** or **-GNIORI** signor

SIGNIORY *n* pl. **-GNIORIES** signory

SIGNOR *n* pl. **-GNORS** or **-GNORI** an Italian title of courtesy for a man

SIGNORA *n* pl. **-GNORAS** or **-GNORE** an Italian title of courtesy for a married woman

SIGNORE *n* pl. **-GNORI** signor

SIGNORY *n* pl. **-GNORIES** seignory

SIGNPOST *v* **-ED, -ING, -S** to provide with signposts (posts bearing signs)

SIKA *n* pl. **-S** a small deer native to Asia

SIKE *n* pl. **-S** syke

SIKER *adj* secure

SIKSIK *n* pl. **-S** the Arctic ground squirrel

SILAGE *n* pl. **-S** fodder that has been preserved in a silo

SILANE *n* pl. **-S** a chemical compound

SILD *n* pl. **-S** a young herring

SILENCE *v* **-LENCED, -LENCING, -LENCES** to make silent

SILENCER *n* pl. **-S** one that silences

SILENI pl. of silenus

SILENT *adj* **-LENTER, -LENTEST** making no sound or noise **SILENTLY** *adv*

SILENTS *n/pl* silent movies

SILENUS *n* pl. **-NI** a woodland deity of Greek mythology

SILESIA *n* pl. **-S** a cotton fabric

SILEX *n* pl. **-ES** silica

SILICA *n* pl. **-S** a form of silicon

SILICATE *n* pl. **-S** a chemical salt

SILICIC *adj* pertaining to silicon

SILICIDE *n* pl. **-S** a silicon compound

SILICIFY *v* **-FIED, -FYING, -FIES** to convert into silica

SILICIUM *n* pl. **-S** silicon

SILICLE *n* pl. **-S** a short, flat silique

SILICON *n* pl. **-S** a nonmetallic element

SILICONE *n* pl. **-S** a silicon compound

SILICULA *n* pl. **-LAE** a silicle

SILIQUA *n* pl. **-QUAE** silique

SILIQUE *n* pl. **-LIQUES** a type of seed capsule

SILK *v* **-ED, -ING, -S** to cover with silk (a soft, lustrous fabric)

SILKEN *adj* made of silk

SILKIE *n* pl. **-S** selkie

SILKIER comparative of silky

SILKIES pl. of silky

SILKIEST superlative of silky

SILKILY *adv* in a silky manner

SILKLIKE *adj* resembling silk

SILKWEED *n* pl. **-S** milkweed

SILKWORM *n* pl. **-S** a caterpillar that spins a cocoon of silk fibers

SILKY *adj* **SILKIER, SILKIEST** resembling silk

SILKY *n* pl. **SILKIES** a glossy-coated terrier

SILL *n* pl. **-S** the horizontal piece at the base of a window

SILLABUB *n* pl. **-S** an alcoholic dessert

SILLER *n* pl. **-S** silver

SILLIBUB *n* pl. **-S** sillabub

SILLY *adj* **-LIER, -LIEST** showing a lack of good sense **SILLILY** *adv*

SILLY *n* pl. **-LIES** a silly person

SILO *v* **-ED, -ING, -S** to store in a silo (a tall, cylindrical structure)

SILOXANE *n* pl. **-S** a chemical compound

SILT *v* **-ED, -ING, -S** to fill with silt (a sedimentary material)

SILTY *adj* **SILTIER, SILTIEST** full of silt

SILURID *n* pl. **-S** any of a family of catfishes

SILUROID *n* pl. **-S** a silurid

SILVA *n* pl. **-VAS** or **-VAE** sylva

SILVAN *n* pl. **-S** sylvan

SILVER *v* **-ED, -ING, -S** to cover with silver (a metallic element)

SILVERER *n* pl. **-S** one that silvers

SILVERIER comparative of silvery

SILVERIEST superlative of silvery

SILVERLY *adv* with a silvery appearance

SILVERN *adj* silvery

SILVERTIP *n* pl. **-S** a grizzly bear with white-tipped hairs

SILVERY *adj* **-VERIER, -VERIEST** resembling silver

SILVEX *n* pl. **-ES** an herbicide

SILVICAL *adj* pertaining to silvics

SILVICS *n/pl* the study of forest trees

SIM	*n* pl. **-S** simulation
SIMA	*n* pl. **-S** an igneous rock
SIMAR	*n* pl. **-S** a woman's light jacket or robe
SIMARUBA	*n* pl. **-S** a tropical tree
SIMAZINE	*n* pl. **-S** an herbicide
SIMCHA	*n* pl. **-S** a Jewish private party
SIMIAN	*n* pl. **-S** an ape or monkey
SIMILAR	*adj* being like but not completely identical to
SIMILE	*n* pl. **-S** a figure of speech
SIMIOID	*adj* simious
SIMIOUS	*adj* pertaining to simians
SIMITAR	*n* pl. **-S** scimitar
SIMLIN	*n* pl. **-S** cymling
SIMMER	*v* **-ED, -ING, -S** to cook below or just at the boiling point
SIMNEL	*n* pl. **-S** a crisp bread
SIMOLEON	*n* pl. **-S** a dollar
SIMONIAC	*n* pl. **-S** one who practices simony
SIMONIES	pl. of simony
SIMONIST	*n* pl. **-S** a simoniac
SIMONIZE	*v* **-NIZED, -NIZING, -NIZES** to polish with wax
SIMONY	*n* pl. **-NIES** the buying or selling of a church office
SIMOOM	*n* pl. **-S** a hot, dry desert wind
SIMOON	*n* pl. **-S** simoom
SIMP	*n* pl. **-S** a foolish person
SIMPER	*v* **-ED, -ING, -S** to smile in a silly manner
SIMPERER	*n* pl. **-S** one that simpers
SIMPLE	*adj* **SIMPLER, SIMPLEST** not complex or complicated
SIMPLE	*n* pl. **-S** something that is simple
SIMPLEX	*n* pl. **-PLEXES** or **-PLICES** or **-PLICIA** a simple word
SIMPLIFY	*v* **-FIED, -FYING, -FIES** to make simple
SIMPLISM	*n* pl. **-S** the tendency to oversimplify an issue or problem
SIMPLIST	*n* pl. **-S** a person given to simplism
SIMPLY	*adv* in a simple manner
SIMULANT	*n* pl. **-S** one that simulates
SIMULAR	*n* pl. **-S** a simulant
SIMULATE	*v* **-LATED, -LATING, -LATES** to take on the appearance of

SIN	*v* **SINNED, SINNING, SINS** to commit a sin (an offense against religious or moral law)
SINAPISM	*n* pl. **-S** a pasty mixture applied to an irritated part of the body
SINCE	*adv* from then until now
SINCERE	*adj* **-CERER, -CEREST** free from hypocrisy or falseness
SINCIPUT	*n* pl. **-CIPUTS** or **-CIPITA** the forehead
SINE	*n* pl. **-S** a trigonometric function of an angle
SINECURE	*n* pl. **-S** an office or position requiring little or no work
SINEW	*v* **-ED, -ING, -S** to strengthen
SINEWY	*adj* lean and muscular
SINFONIA	*n* pl. **-NIAS** or **-NIE** a symphony
SINFUL	*adj* marked by sin **SINFULLY** *adv*
SING	*v* **SANG, SUNG, SINGING, SINGS** to utter with musical inflections of the voice **SINGABLE** *adj*
SINGE	*v* **SINGED, SINGEING, SINGES** to burn slightly
SINGER	*n* pl. **-S** one that sings
SINGING	*n* pl. **-S** the act or sound of one that sings
SINGLE	*v* **-GLED, -GLING, -GLES** to select from a group
SINGLET	*n* pl. **-S** a man's undershirt or jersey
SINGLY	*adv* without the company of others
SINGSONG	*n* pl. **-S** monotonous cadence in speaking or reading
SINGULAR	*n* pl. **-S** a word form that denotes one person or thing
SINH	*n* pl. **-S** a hyperbolic function of an angle
SINICIZE	*v* **-CIZED, -CIZING, -CIZES** to modify by Chinese influence
SINISTER	*adj* threatening or portending evil
SINK	*v* **SANK, SUNK** or **SUNKEN, SINKING, SINKS** to move to a lower level **SINKABLE** *adj*
SINKAGE	*n* pl. **-S** the act, process, or degree of sinking
SINKER	*n* pl. **-S** one that sinks
SINKFUL	*n* pl. **-S** as much as a sink can hold
SINKHOLE	*n* pl. **-S** a natural depression in a land surface
SINLESS	*adj* free from sin
SINNED	past tense of sin

SINNER	*n* pl. **-S** one that sins		**SIRVENTE**	*n* pl. **-S** a satirical medieval song or poem
SINNET	*n* pl. **-S** sennet		**SIS**	*n* pl. **SISES** or **SISSES** sister
SINNING	present participle of sin		**SISAL**	*n* pl. **-S** a strong fiber used for rope
SINOLOGY	*n* pl. **-GIES** the study of the Chinese		**SISKIN**	*n* pl. **-S** a Eurasian finch
SINOPIA	*n* pl. **-PIAS** or **-PIE** a red pigment		**SISSY**	*adj* **SISSIER, SISSIEST** sissyish
SINSYNE	*adv* since		**SISSY**	*n* pl. **-SIES** an effeminate man or boy
SINTER	*v* **-ED, -ING, -S** to make cohesive by the combined action of heat and pressure		**SISSYISH**	*adj* resembling a sissy
			SISTER	*v* **-ED, -ING, -S** to treat like a sister (a female sibling)
SINUATE	*v* **-ATED, -ATING, -ATES** to curve in and out		**SISTERLY**	*adj* of or resembling a sister
SINUOUS	*adj* characterized by curves, bends, or turns		**SISTROID**	*adj* included between the convex sides of two intersecting curves
SINUS	*n* pl. **-ES** a cranial cavity		**SISTRUM**	*n* pl. **-TRUMS** or **-TRA** an ancient Egyptian percussion instrument
SINUSOID	*n* pl. **-S** a mathematical curve		**SIT**	*v* **SAT, SAT** or **SITTEN, SITTING, SITS** to rest on the buttocks
SIP	*v* **SIPPED, SIPPING, SIPS** to drink in small quantities			
SIPE	*v* **SIPED, SIPING, SIPES** to seep		**SITAR**	*n* pl. **-S** a lute of India
SIPHON	*v* **-ED, -ING, -S** to draw off through a siphon (a type of tube)		**SITARIST**	*n* pl. **-S** one who plays the sitar
SIPHONAL	*adj* of or pertaining to a siphon		**SITCOM**	*n* pl. **-S** a television comedy series with continuing characters
SIPHONIC	*adj* siphonal		**SITE**	*v* **SITED, SITING, SITES** to place in position for operation
SIPING	present participle of sipe			
SIPPABLE	*adj* capable of being sipped		**SITH**	*adv* since
SIPPED	past tense of sip		**SITHENCE**	*adv* since
SIPPER	*n* pl. **-S** one that sips		**SITHENS**	*adv* since
SIPPET	*n* pl. **-S** a small piece of bread soaked in gravy		**SITING**	present participle of site
			SITOLOGY	*n* pl. **-GIES** the science of nutrition and diet
SIPPING	present participle of sip			
SIR	*n* pl. **-S** a respectful form of address used to a man		**SITREP**	*n* pl. **-S** a report on the current military situation
SIRDAR	*n* pl. **-S** a person of rank in India		**SITTEN**	a past participle of sit
SIRE	*v* **SIRED, SIRING, SIRES** to beget		**SITTER**	*n* pl. **-S** one that sits
SIREE	*n* pl. **-S** sirree		**SITTING**	*n* pl. **-S** a meeting or session
SIREN	*n* pl. **-S** a device that produces a penetrating warning sound		**SITUATE**	*v* **-ATED, -ATING, -ATES** to place in a certain position
SIRENIAN	*n* pl. **-S** any of an order of aquatic mammals		**SITUP**	*n* pl. **-S** an exercise in which one moves from a lying to a sitting position
SIRING	present participle of sire			
SIRLOIN	*n* pl. **-S** a cut of beef		**SITUS**	*n* pl. **-TUSES** a position or location
SIROCCO	*n* pl. **-COS** a hot, dry wind		**SITZMARK**	*n* pl. **-S** a mark left in the snow by a skier who has fallen backward
SIRRA	*n* pl. **-S** sirrah			
SIRRAH	*n* pl. **-S** a form of address used to inferiors		**SIVER**	*n* pl. **-S** a sewer
			SIX	*n* pl. **-ES** a number
SIRREE	*n* pl. **-S** sir		**SIXER**	*n* pl. **-S** the leader of a group of six Brownies or Cubs
SIRUP	*v* **-ED, -ING, -S** to syrup		**SIXFOLD**	*adj* being six times as great as
SIRUPY	*adj* **-UPIER, -UPIEST** syrupy		**SIXMO**	*n* pl. **-MOS** a paper size

SIXPENCE *n* pl. **-S** a formerly used British coin worth six pennies

SIXPENNY *adj* worth sixpence

SIXTE *n* pl. **-S** a fencing parry

SIXTEEN *n* pl. **-S** a number

SIXTH *n* pl. **-S** one of six equal parts

SIXTHLY *adv* in the sixth place

SIXTIETH *n* pl. **-S** one of sixty equal parts

SIXTY *n* pl. **-TIES** a number

SIXTYISH *adj* being about sixty years old

SIZABLE *adj* of considerable size **SIZABLY** *adv*

SIZAR *n* pl. **-S** a British student who receives financial assistance from his or her college

SIZE *v* **SIZED, SIZING, SIZES** to arrange according to size (physical proportions)

SIZEABLE *adj* sizable **SIZEABLY** *adv*

SIZER *n* pl. **-S** sizar

SIZINESS *n* pl. **-ES** the quality or state of being sizy

SIZING *n* pl. **-S** a substance used as a glaze or filler for porous materials

SIZY *adj* **SIZIER, SIZIEST** viscid

SIZZLE *v* **-ZLED, -ZLING, -ZLES** to burn or fry with a hissing sound

SIZZLER *n* pl. **-S** a very hot day

SJAMBOK *v* **-ED, -ING, -S** to strike with a whip used in South Africa

SKA *n* pl. **-S** a popular music of Jamaica

SKAG *n* pl. **-S** heroin

SKALD *n* pl. **-S** an ancient Scandinavian poet **SKALDIC** *adj*

SKANK *v* **-ED, -ING, -S** to dance in a loose-limbed manner

SKANKER *n* pl. **-S** one that skanks

SKANKY *adj* **SKANKIER, SKANKIEST** filthy or sleazy

SKAT *n* pl. **-S** a card game

SKATE *v* **SKATED, SKATING, SKATES** to glide over ice or the ground on skates (shoes fitted with runners or wheels)

SKATER *n* pl. **-S** one that skates

SKATING *n* pl. **-S** the sport of gliding on skates

SKATOL *n* pl. **-S** skatole

SKATOLE *n* pl. **-S** a chemical compound

SKEAN *n* pl. **-S** a type of dagger

SKEANE *n* pl. **-S** a length of yarn wound in a loose coil

SKED *v* **SKEDDED, SKEDDING, SKEDS** to schedule

SKEE *v* **SKEED, SKEEING, SKEES** to ski

SKEEN *n* pl. **-S** skean

SKEET *n* pl. **-S** the sport of shooting at clay pigeons hurled in the air by spring traps

SKEETER *n* pl. **-S** a skeet shooter

SKEEVY *adj* **SKEEVIER, SKEEVIEST** repulsive, disgusting

SKEG *n* pl. **-S** a timber that connects the keel and sternpost of a ship

SKEIGH *adj* proud

SKEIN *v* **-ED, -ING, -S** to wind into long, loose coils

SKELETON *n* pl. **-S** the supporting or protective framework of a human or animal body **SKELETAL** *adj*

SKELL *n* pl. **-S** a homeless person

SKELLUM *n* pl. **-S** a rascal

SKELM *n* pl. **-S** skellum

SKELP *v* **SKELPED** or **SKELPIT, SKELPING, SKELPS** to slap

SKELTER *v* **-ED, -ING, -S** to scurry

SKENE *n* pl. **-S** skean

SKEP *n* pl. **-S** a beehive

SKEPSIS *n* pl. **-SISES** the attitude or outlook of a skeptic

SKEPTIC *n* pl. **-S** a person who doubts generally accepted ideas

SKERRY *n* pl. **-RIES** a small, rocky island

SKETCH *v* **-ED, -ING, -ES** to make a rough, hasty drawing of

SKETCHER *n* pl. **-S** one that sketches

SKETCHY *adj* **SKETCHIER, SKETCHIEST** lacking in completeness or clearness

SKEW *v* **-ED, -ING, -S** to turn aside

SKEWBACK *n* pl. **-S** a sloping surface against which the end of an arch rests

SKEWBALD *n* pl. **-S** a horse having patches of brown and white

SKEWER *v* **-ED, -ING, -S** to pierce with a long pin, as meat

SKEWNESS *n* pl. **-ES** lack of symmetry

SKI	*v* **-ED, -ING, -S** to travel on skis (long, narrow strips of wood or metal)
SKIABLE	*adj* capable of being skied over
SKIAGRAM	*n* pl. **-S** a picture made up of shadows or outlines
SKIBOB	*v* **-BOBBED, -BOBBING, -BOBS** to ride a bike-like vehicle with skis instead of wheels
SKID	*v* **SKIDDED, SKIDDING, SKIDS** to slide sideways as a result of a loss of traction
SKIDDER	*n* pl. **-S** one that skids
SKIDDING	*n* pl. **-S** the work of hauling logs from a cutting area
SKIDDOO	*v* **-ED, -ING, -S** to go away
SKIDDY	*adj* **-DIER, -DIEST** likely to cause skidding
SKIDOO	*v* **-ED, -ING, -S** to skiddoo
SKIDOOER	*n* pl. **-S** one that rides on a snowmobile
SKIDPAD	*n* pl. **-S** a road surface on which drivers can practice controlling skidding
SKIDWAY	*n* pl. **-WAYS** a platform on which logs are piled for loading or sawing
SKIED	past tense of ski and sky
SKIER	*n* pl. **-S** one that skis
SKIES	present 3d person sing. of sky
SKIEY	*adj* skyey
SKIFF	*n* pl. **-S** a small, open boat
SKIFFLE	*v* **-FLED, -FLING, -FLES** to play a particular style of music
SKIING	*n* pl. **-S** the sport of traveling on skis
SKIJORER	*n* pl. **-S** a skier who is drawn over snow by dogs, a horse, or vehicle
SKILFUL	*adj* skillful
SKILFULL	*adj* skillful
SKILL	*n* pl. **-S** the ability to do something well **SKILLED** *adj*
SKILLESS	*adj* having no skill
SKILLET	*n* pl. **-S** a frying pan
SKILLFUL	*adj* having skill
SKILLING	*n* pl. **-S** a former coin of Scandinavian countries
SKIM	*v* **SKIMMED, SKIMMING, SKIMS** to remove floating matter from the surface of
SKIMMER	*n* pl. **-S** one that skims
SKIMMIA	*n* pl. **-S** an evergreen shrub

SKIMMING	*n* pl. **-S** something that is skimmed from a liquid
SKIMP	*v* **-ED, -ING, -S** to scrimp
SKIMPY	*adj* **SKIMPIER, SKIMPIEST** scanty **SKIMPILY** *adv*
SKIN	*v* **SKINNED, SKINNING, SKINS** to strip or deprive of skin (the membranous tissue covering the body of an animal)
SKINFUL	*n* pl. **-S** as much as a skin container can hold
SKINHEAD	*n* pl. **-S** one whose hair is cut very short
SKINK	*v* **-ED, -ING, -S** to pour out or serve, as liquor
SKINKER	*n* pl. **-S** one that skinks
SKINLESS	*adj* having no skin
SKINLIKE	*adj* resembling skin
SKINNED	past tense of skin
SKINNER	*n* pl. **-S** one that skins
SKINNING	present participle of skin
SKINNY	*adj* **-NIER, -NIEST** very thin
SKINNY	*n* pl. **-NIES** one that is skinny
SKINT	*adj* having no money
SKIORING	*n* pl. **-S** a form of skiing
SKIP	*v* **SKIPPED, SKIPPING, SKIPS** to move with light springing steps
SKIPJACK	*n* pl. **-S** a marine fish
SKIPLANE	*n* pl. **-S** an airplane designed to take off from or land on snow
SKIPPED	past tense of skip
SKIPPER	*v* **-ED, -ING, -S** to act as master or captain of
SKIPPET	*n* pl. **-S** a small box for protecting an official seal
SKIPPING	present participle of skip
SKIRL	*v* **-ED, -ING, -S** to produce a shrill sound
SKIRMISH	*v* **-ED, -ING, -ES** to engage in a minor battle
SKIRR	*v* **-ED, -ING, -S** to move rapidly
SKIRRET	*n* pl. **-S** an Asian herb
SKIRT	*v* **-ED, -ING, -S** to go or pass around
SKIRTER	*n* pl. **-S** one that skirts
SKIRTING	*n* pl. **-S** a board at the base of a wall
SKIT	*n* pl. **-S** a short dramatic scene
SKITE	*v* **SKITED, SKITING, SKITES** to move away quickly

SKITTER   *v* **-ED, -ING, -S** to move lightly or rapidly along a surface

SKITTERY   *adj* **-TERIER, -TERIEST** skittish

SKITTISH   *adj* easily frightened

SKITTLE   *n* pl. **-S** a wooden pin used in a bowling game

SKIVE   *v* **SKIVED, SKIVING, SKIVES** to pare

SKIVER   *n* pl. **-S** one that skives

SKIVVY   *v* **-VIED, -VYING, -VIES** to work as a female servant

SKIWEAR   *n* pl. **SKIWEAR** clothing suitable for wear while skiing

SKLENT   *v* **-ED, -ING, -S** to slant

SKOAL   *v* **-ED, -ING, -S** to drink to the health of

SKOL   *v* **-ED, -ING, -S** to skoal

SKOOKUM   *n* pl. **-S** an evil spirit

SKORT   *n* pl. **-S** a pair of shorts that resembles a skirt

SKOSH   *n* pl. **-ES** a small amount

SKREEGH   *v* **-ED, -ING, -S** to screech

SKREIGH   *v* **-ED, -ING, -S** to screech

SKRY   *v* **SKRIED, SKRYING, SKRIES** to scry

SKUA   *n* pl. **-S** a predatory seabird

SKULK   *v* **-ED, -ING, -S** to move about stealthily

SKULKER   *n* pl. **-S** one that skulks

SKULL   *v* **-ED, -ING, -S** to hit on the head

SKULLCAP   *n* pl. **-S** a close-fitting cap

SKUNK   *v* **-ED, -ING, -S** to defeat overwhelmingly

SKUNKY   *adj* **SKUNKIER, SKUNKIEST** having a smell suggestive of a skunk (a mammal that can spray a foul-smelling liquid)

SKY   *v* **SKIED** or **SKYED, SKYING, SKIES** to hit or throw toward the sky (the upper atmosphere)

SKYBOARD   *n* pl. **-S** a board with foot bindings that is used for skysurfing

SKYBORNE   *adj* airborne

SKYBOX   *n* pl. **-ES** an enclosure of seats situated high in a stadium

SKYCAP   *n* pl. **-S** a porter at an airport

SKYDIVE   *v* **-DIVED** or **-DOVE, -DIVING, -DIVES** to parachute from an airplane for sport

SKYDIVER   *n* pl. **-S** one that skydives

SKYEY   *adj* resembling the sky

SKYGLOW   *n* pl. **-S** a glow in the night sky resulting from urban lights

SKYHOOK   *n* pl. **-S** a hook conceived as being suspended from the sky

SKYJACK   *v* **-ED, -ING, -S** to hijack an airplane

SKYLARK   *v* **-ED, -ING, -S** to frolic

SKYLESS   *adj* having the sky obscured by clouds

SKYLIGHT   *n* pl. **-S** a window in a roof or ceiling

SKYLIKE   *adj* resembling the sky

SKYLINE   *n* pl. **-S** the horizon

SKYLIT   *adj* having a skylight

SKYMAN   *n* pl. **-MEN** an aviator

SKYPHOS   *n* pl. **-PHOI** a drinking vessel used in ancient Greece

SKYSAIL   *n* pl. **-S** a type of sail

SKYSCAPE   *n* pl. **-S** a view of the sky

SKYSURF   *v* **-ED, -ING, -S** to perform maneuvers during free fall while riding on a skyboard

SKYWALK   *n* pl. **-S** an elevated walkway between two buildings

SKYWARD   *adv* toward the sky

SKYWARDS   *adv* skyward

SKYWATCH   *v* **-ED, -ING, -ES** to observe the sky for heavenly bodies or aircraft

SKYWAY   *n* pl. **-WAYS** an elevated highway

SKYWRITE   *v* **-WROTE, -WRITTEN, -WRITING, -WRITES** to write in the sky by releasing a visible vapor from an airplane

SLAB   *v* **SLABBED, SLABBING, SLABS** to remove slabs (broad, flat pieces) from a log

SLABBER   *v* **-ED, -ING, -S** to slobber

SLABBERY   *adj* slobbery

SLABBING   *n* pl. **-S** the act of removing slabs from a log

SLABBY   *adj* **-BIER, -BIEST** covered or paved with slabs

SLABLIKE   *adj* resembling a slab

SLACK   *adj* **SLACKER, SLACKEST** not tight or taut

SLACK   *v* **-ED, -ING, -S** to slacken

SLACKEN   *v* **-ED, -ING, -S** to make less tight or taut

SLACKER   *n* pl. **-S** a shirker

SLACKLY *adv* in a slack manner

SLAG *v* **SLAGGED, SLAGGING, SLAGS** to convert into slag (the fused residue of a smelted ore)

SLAGGING *n* pl. **-S** the process of converting ore into slag

SLAGGY *adj* **-GIER, -GIEST** resembling slag

SLAHAL *n* pl. **-S** lahal

SLAIN past participle of slay

SLAINTE *interj* — used to toast one's health

SLAKE *v* **SLAKED, SLAKING, SLAKES** to quench **SLAKABLE** *adj*

SLAKER *n* pl. **-S** one that slakes

SLALOM *v* **-ED, -ING, -S** to ski in a zigzag course

SLALOMER *n* pl. **-S** one that slaloms

SLAM *v* **SLAMMED, SLAMMING, SLAMS** to shut forcibly and noisily

SLAMMER *n* pl. **-S** a jail

SLAMMING *n* pl. **-S** the practice of switching a person's telephone service from one company to another without permission

SLANDER *v* **-ED, -ING, -S** to defame

SLANG *v* **-ED, -ING, -S** to use slang (extremely informal or vulgar language)

SLANGY *adj* **SLANGIER, SLANGIEST** being or containing slang **SLANGILY** *adv*

SLANK a past tense of slink

SLANT *v* **-ED, -ING, -S** to deviate from the horizontal or vertical

SLANTY *adj* **SLANTIER, SLANTIEST** deviating from the horizontal or vertical **SLANTLY** *adv*

SLAP *v* **SLAPPED, SLAPPING, SLAPS** to strike with the open hand

SLAPDASH *n* pl. **-ES** careless work

SLAPJACK *n* pl. **-S** a pancake

SLAPPER *n* pl. **-S** one that slaps

SLAPPING present participle of slap

SLAPSHOT *n* pl. **-S** a type of shot in hockey

SLASH *v* **-ED, -ING, -ES** to cut with violent sweeping strokes

SLASHER *n* pl. **-S** one that slashes

SLASHING *n* pl. **-S** the act of one that slashes

SLAT *v* **SLATTED, SLATTING, SLATS** to provide with slats (narrow strips of wood or metal)

SLATCH *n* pl. **-ES** a calm between breaking waves

SLATE *v* **SLATED, SLATING, SLATES** to cover with slate (a roofing material)

SLATER *n* pl. **-S** one that slates

SLATEY *adj* **SLATIER, SLATIEST** slaty

SLATHER *v* **-ED, -ING, -S** to spread thickly

SLATIER comparative of slaty

SLATIEST superlative of slaty

SLATING *n* pl. **-S** the act of one that slates

SLATTED past tense of slat

SLATTERN *n* pl. **-S** a slovenly woman

SLATTING *n* pl. **-S** material for making slats

SLATY *adj* **SLATIER, SLATIEST** resembling slate

SLAVE *v* **SLAVED, SLAVING, SLAVES** to work like a slave (one who is owned by another)

SLAVER *v* **-ED, -ING, -S** to drool

SLAVERER *n* pl. **-S** one that slavers

SLAVERY *n* pl. **-ERIES** ownership of one person by another

SLAVEY *n* pl. **-EYS** a female servant

SLAVING present participle of slave

SLAVISH *adj* pertaining to or characteristic of a slave

SLAW *n* pl. **-S** coleslaw

SLAY *v* **SLEW** or **SLAYED, SLAIN, SLAYING, SLAYS** to kill violently **SLAYABLE** *adj*

SLAYER *n* pl. **-S** one that slays

SLAYING *n* pl. **-S** the act or an instance of killing

SLEAVE *v* **SLEAVED, SLEAVING, SLEAVES** to separate into filaments

SLEAZE *v* **SLEAZED, SLEAZING, SLEAZES** to behave in a sleazy manner

SLEAZO *n* pl. **SLEAZOS** a sleazoid

SLEAZOID *n* pl. **-S** a person of low morals or character

SLEAZY *adj* **SLEAZIER, SLEAZIEST** of low quality or character **SLEAZILY** *adv*

SLED *v* **SLEDDED, SLEDDING, SLEDS** to convey on a sled (a vehicle for carrying people or loads over snow or ice)

SLEDDER *n* pl. **-S** one that sleds

SLEDDING *n* pl. **-S** the act of one that sleds

SLEDGE   *v* **SLEDGED, SLEDGING, SLEDGES** to convey on a type of sled

SLEEK   *adj* **SLEEKER, SLEEKEST** smooth and glossy

SLEEK   *v* **-ED, -ING, -S** to make sleek

SLEEKEN   *v* **-ED, -ING, -S** to sleek

SLEEKER   *n* pl. **-S** one that sleeks

SLEEKIT   *adj* sleek

SLEEKLY   *adv* in a sleek manner

SLEEKY   *adj* **SLEEKIER, SLEEKIEST** sleek

SLEEP   *v* **SLEPT, SLEEPING, SLEEPS** to be in a natural, periodic state of rest

SLEEPER   *n* pl. **-S** one that sleeps

SLEEPING   *n* pl. **-S** the act of one that sleeps

SLEEPY   *adj* **SLEEPIER, SLEEPIEST** ready or inclined to sleep **SLEEPILY** *adv*

SLEET   *v* **-ED, -ING, -S** to shower sleet (frozen rain)

SLEETY   *adj* **SLEETIER, SLEETIEST** resembling sleet

SLEEVE   *v* **SLEEVED, SLEEVING, SLEEVES** to furnish with a sleeve (the part of a garment covering the arm)

SLEEVEEN   *n* pl. **-S** a mischievous person

SLEEVING   *n* pl. **-S** tubular insulation for electric cables

SLEIGH   *v* **-ED, -ING, -S** to ride in a sled

SLEIGHER   *n* pl. **-S** one that sleighs

SLEIGHT   *n* pl. **-S** deftness

SLENDER   *adj* **-DERER, -DEREST** thin

SLEPT   past tense of sleep

SLEUTH   *v* **-ED, -ING, -S** to act as a detective

SLEW   *v* **-ED, -ING, -S** to slue

SLICE   *v* **SLICED, SLICING, SLICES** to cut into thin, flat pieces

SLICER   *n* pl. **-S** one that slices

SLICK   *adj* **SLICKER, SLICKEST** smooth and slippery

SLICK   *v* **-ED, -ING, -S** to make slick

SLICKEN   *v* **-ED, -ING, -S** to make slick

SLICKER   *n* pl. **-S** an oilskin raincoat

SLICKLY   *adv* in a slick manner

SLIDE   *v* **SLID, SLIDDEN, SLIDING, SLIDES** to move smoothly along a surface **SLIDABLE** *adj*

SLIDER   *n* pl. **-S** one that slides

SLIDEWAY   *n* pl. **-WAYS** a route along which something slides

SLIER   a comparative of sly

SLIEST   a superlative of sly

SLIEVE   *n* pl. **-S** a mountain

SLIGHT   *adj* **SLIGHTER, SLIGHTEST** small in size or amount **SLIGHTLY** *adv*

SLIGHT   *v* **-ED, -ING, -S** to treat with disregard

SLIGHTER   *n* pl. **-S** one that slights

SLILY   *adv* in a sly manner

SLIM   *adj* **SLIMMER, SLIMMEST** slender

SLIM   *v* **SLIMMED, SLIMMING, SLIMS** to make slim

SLIME   *v* **SLIMED, SLIMING, SLIMES** to cover with slime (viscous mud)

SLIMIER   comparative of slimy

SLIMIEST   superlative of slimy

SLIMILY   *adv* in a slimy manner

SLIMING   present participle of slime

SLIMLINE   *adj* slender in design or build

SLIMLY   *adv* in a slim manner

SLIMMED   past tense of slim

SLIMMER   *n* pl. **-S** a dieter

SLIMMEST   superlative of slim

SLIMMING   *n* pl. **-S** the reducing of one's weight

SLIMNESS   *n* pl. **-ES** the state of being slim

SLIMPSY   *adj* **-SIER, -SIEST** slimsy

SLIMSY   *adj* **-SIER, -SIEST** flimsy

SLIMY   *adj* **SLIMIER, SLIMIEST** resembling slime

SLING   *v* **SLUNG, SLINGING, SLINGS** to throw with a sudden motion

SLINGER   *n* pl. **-S** one that slings

SLINK   *v* **SLUNK** or **SLANK** or **SLINKED, SLINKING, SLINKS** to move stealthily

SLINKY   *adj* **SLINKIER, SLINKIEST** stealthy **SLINKILY** *adv*

SLIP   *v* **SLIPPED** or **SLIPT, SLIPPING, SLIPS** to slide suddenly and accidentally

SLIPCASE   *n* pl. **-S** a protective box for a book

SLIPE   *v* **SLIPED, SLIPING, SLIPES** to peel

SLIPFORM   *v* **-ED, -ING, -S** to construct with the use of a mold in which concrete is placed to set

SLIPKNOT *n* pl. **-S** a type of knot

SLIPLESS *adj* free from errors

SLIPOUT *n* pl. **-S** an insert in a newspaper

SLIPOVER *n* pl. **-S** a pullover

SLIPPAGE *n* pl. **-S** a falling off from a standard or level

SLIPPED a past tense of slip

SLIPPER *n* pl. **-S** a light, low shoe

SLIPPERY *adj* **-PERIER, -PERIEST** causing or tending to cause slipping

SLIPPING present participle of slip

SLIPPY *adj* **-PIER, -PIEST** slippery **SLIPPILY** *adv*

SLIPSHOD *adj* carelessly done or made

SLIPSLOP *n* pl. **-S** watery food

SLIPSOLE *n* pl. **-S** a thin insole

SLIPT a past tense of slip

SLIPUP *n* pl. **-S** a mistake

SLIPWARE *n* pl. **-S** a type of pottery

SLIPWAY *n* pl. **-WAYS** an area sloping toward the water in a shipyard

SLIT *v* **SLITTED, SLITTING, SLITS** to make a slit (a long, narrow cut) in

SLITHER *v* **-ED, -ING, -S** to slide from side to side

SLITHERY *adj* slippery

SLITLESS *adj* having no slits

SLITLIKE *adj* resembling a slit

SLITTED past tense of slit

SLITTER *n* pl. **-S** one that slits

SLITTING present participle of slit

SLITTY *adj* **-TIER, -TIEST** being long and narrow

SLIVER *v* **-ED, -ING, -S** to cut into long, thin pieces

SLIVERER *n* pl. **-S** one that slivers

SLIVOVIC *n* pl. **-ES** a plum brandy

SLOB *n* pl. **-S** a slovenly or boorish person

SLOBBER *v* **-ED, -ING, -S** to drool

SLOBBERY *adj* slobbering

SLOBBISH *adj* resembling a slob

SLOBBY *adj* **SLOBBIER, SLOBBIEST** characteristic of a slob

SLOE *n* pl. **-S** a plumlike fruit

SLOG *v* **SLOGGED, SLOGGING, SLOGS** to plod

SLOGAN *n* pl. **-S** a motto adopted by a group **SLOGANED** *adj*

SLOGGER *n* pl. **-S** one that slogs

SLOID *n* pl. **-S** sloyd

SLOJD *n* pl. **-S** sloyd

SLOMO *n* pl. **-MOS** slow motion

SLOOP *n* pl. **-S** a type of sailing vessel

SLOP *v* **SLOPPED, SLOPPING, SLOPS** to spill or splash

SLOPE *v* **SLOPED, SLOPING, SLOPES** to slant

SLOPER *n* pl. **-S** one that slopes

SLOPPY *adj* **-PIER, -PIEST** messy **SLOPPILY** *adv*

SLOPWORK *n* pl. **-S** the manufacture of cheap clothing

SLOSH *v* **-ED, -ING, -ES** to move with a splashing motion

SLOSHY *adj* **SLOSHIER, SLOSHIEST** slushy

SLOT *v* **SLOTTED, SLOTTING, SLOTS** to cut a long, narrow opening in

SLOTBACK *n* pl. **-S** a type of football player

SLOTH *n* pl. **-S** a slow-moving arboreal mammal

SLOTHFUL *adj* sluggish

SLOTTED past tense of slot

SLOTTER *n* pl. **-S** a machine for slotting

SLOTTING present participle of slot

SLOUCH *v* **-ED, -ING, -ES** to sit, stand, or move with a drooping posture

SLOUCHER *n* pl. **-S** one that slouches

SLOUCHY *adj* **SLOUCHIER, SLOUCHIEST** slouching

SLOUGH *v* **-ED, -ING, -S** to cast off

SLOUGHY *adj* **SLOUGHIER, SLOUGHIEST** miry

SLOVEN *n* pl. **-S** a slovenly person

SLOVENLY *adj* **-LIER, -LIEST** habitually untidy or unclean

SLOW *adj* **SLOWER, SLOWEST** moving with little speed

SLOW *v* **-ED, -ING, -S** to lessen the speed of

SLOWDOWN *n* pl. **-S** a lessening of pace

SLOWISH *adj* somewhat slow

SLOWLY *adv* in a slow manner

SLOWNESS *n* pl. **-ES** the state of being slow

SLOWPOKE *n* pl. **-S** a slow individual

SLOWWORM *n* pl. **-S** a European lizard having no legs

SLOYD *n* pl. **-S** a Swedish system of manual training

SLUB *v* **SLUBBED, SLUBBING, SLUBS** to draw out and twist slightly

SLUBBER *v* **-ED, -ING, -S** to stain or dirty

SLUBBING *n* pl. **-S** a slightly twisted roll of textile fibers

SLUDGE *v* **SLUDGED, SLUDGING, SLUDGES** to form sludge (a muddy mass or sediment)

SLUDGY *adj* **SLUDGIER, SLUDGIEST** covered with sludge

SLUE *v* **SLUED, SLUING, SLUES** to cause to move sideways

SLUFF *v* **-ED, -ING, -S** to discard a card or cards

SLUG *v* **SLUGGED, SLUGGING, SLUGS** to strike heavily

SLUGABED *n* pl. **-S** one inclined to stay in bed out of laziness

SLUGFEST *n* pl. **-S** a vigorous fight

SLUGGARD *n* pl. **-S** a habitually lazy person

SLUGGED past tense of slug

SLUGGER *n* pl. **-S** one that slugs

SLUGGING present participle of slug

SLUGGISH *adj* displaying little movement or activity

SLUICE *v* **SLUICED, SLUICING, SLUICES** to wash with a sudden flow of water

SLUICY *adj* falling in streams

SLUING present participle of slue

SLUM *v* **SLUMMED, SLUMMING, SLUMS** to visit slums (squalid urban areas)

SLUMBER *v* **-ED, -ING, -S** to sleep

SLUMBERY *adj* sleepy

SLUMGUM *n* pl. **-S** the residue remaining after honey is extracted from a honeycomb

SLUMISM *n* pl. **-S** the prevalence of slums

SLUMLORD *n* pl. **-S** a landlord of slum property

SLUMMED past tense of slum

SLUMMER *n* pl. **-S** one that slums

SLUMMING present participle of slum

SLUMMY *adj* **-MIER, -MIEST** resembling a slum

SLUMP *v* **-ED, -ING, -S** to fall or sink suddenly

SLUMPY *adj* **SLUMPIER, SLUMPIEST** characterized by a fall in value or amount

SLUNG past tense of sling

SLUNK a past tense of slink

SLUR *v* **SLURRED, SLURRING, SLURS** to pass over lightly or carelessly

SLURB *n* pl. **-S** a poorly planned suburban area **SLURBAN** *adj*

SLURP *v* **-ED, -ING, -S** to eat or drink noisily

SLURPY *adj* **SLURPIER, SLURPIEST** characterized by the sucking sound made when slurping

SLURRY *v* **-RIED, -RYING, -RIES** to convert into a type of watery mixture

SLURVE *n* pl. **-S** a type of pitch in baseball

SLUSH *v* **-ED, -ING, -ES** to splash with slush (partly melted snow)

SLUSHY *n* pl. **SLUSHIES** a confection consisting of flavored slushy ice

SLUSHY *adj* **SLUSHIER, SLUSHIEST** resembling slush **SLUSHILY** *adv*

SLUT *n* pl. **-S** a slovenly woman **SLUTTISH** *adj*

SLUTTY *adj* **SLUTTIER, SLUTTIEST** characteristic of a slut

SLY *adj* **SLIER, SLIEST** or **SLYER, SLYEST** crafty **SLYLY** *adv*

SLYBOOTS *n* pl. **SLYBOOTS** a sly person

SLYNESS *n* pl. **-ES** the quality or state of being sly

SLYPE *n* pl. **-S** a narrow passage in an English cathedral

SMACK *v* **-ED, -ING, -S** to strike sharply

SMACKER *n* pl. **-S** one that smacks

SMALL *adj* **SMALLER, SMALLEST** of limited size or quantity

SMALL *n* pl. **-S** a small part

SMALLAGE *n* pl. **-S** a wild celery

SMALLISH *adj* somewhat small

SMALLPOX *n* pl. **-ES** a virus disease

SMALT *n* pl. **-S** a blue pigment

SMALTI a pl. of smalto

SMALTINE *n* pl. **-S** smaltite

SMALTITE *n* pl. **-S** a mineral

SMALTO *n* pl. **-TOS** or **-TI** colored glass used in mosaics

SMARAGD *n* pl. **-S** an emerald

SMARAGDE *n* pl. **-S** smaragd

SMARM *v* **-ED, -ING, -S** to use excessive flattery to obtain favors

SMARMY *adj* **SMARMIER, SMARMIEST** marked by excessive flattery **SMARMILY** *adv*

SMART *adj* **SMARTER, SMARTEST** characterized by mental acuity **SMARTISH** *adj*

SMART *v* **-ED, -ING, -S** to cause a sharp, stinging pain

SMARTASS *n* pl. **-ES** a smarty

SMARTEN *v* **-ED, -ING, -S** to improve in appearance

SMARTIE *n* pl. **-S** smarty

SMARTLY *adv* in a smart manner

SMARTY *n* pl. **SMARTIES** an obnoxiously conceited person

SMASH *v* **-ED, -ING, -ES** to shatter violently

SMASHER *n* pl. **-S** one that smashes

SMASHUP *n* pl. **-S** a collision of motor vehicles

SMATTER *v* **-ED, -ING, -S** to speak with little knowledge

SMAZE *n* pl. **-S** an atmospheric mixture of smoke and haze

SMEAR *v* **-ED, -ING, -S** to spread with a sticky, greasy, or dirty substance

SMEARER *n* pl. **-S** one that smears

SMEARY *adj* **SMEARIER, SMEARIEST** smeared

SMECTIC *adj* pertaining to a phase of a liquid crystal

SMECTITE *n* pl. **-S** a clayey mineral

SMEDDUM *n* pl. **-S** ground malt powder

SMEEK *v* **-ED, -ING, -S** to smoke

SMEGMA *n* pl. **-S** sebum

SMELL *v* **SMELLED** or **SMELT, SMELLING, SMELLS** to perceive by means of the olfactory nerves

SMELLER *n* pl. **-S** one that smells

SMELLY *adj* **SMELLIER, SMELLIEST** having an unpleasant odor

SMELT *v* **-ED, -ING, -S** to melt or fuse, as ores

SMELTER *n* pl. **-S** one that smelts

SMELTERY *n* pl. **-ERIES** a place for smelting

SMELTING *n* pl. **-S** the process of melting ores to obtain metal

SMERK *v* **-ED, -ING, -S** to smirk

SMEW *n* pl. **-S** a Eurasian duck

SMIDGE *n* pl. **-S** a smidgen

SMIDGEN *n* pl. **-S** a very small amount

SMIDGEON *n* pl. **-S** smidgen

SMIDGIN *n* pl. **-S** smidgen

SMILAX *n* pl. **-ES** a twining plant

SMILE *v* **SMILED, SMILING, SMILES** to upturn the corners of the mouth in pleasure

SMILER *n* pl. **-S** one that smiles

SMILEY *n* pl. **SMILEYS** or **SMILIES** a representation of a smiling face

SMILEY *adj* **SMILIER, SMILIEST** displaying a smile

SMIRCH *v* **-ED, -ING, -ES** to soil

SMIRK *v* **-ED, -ING, -S** to smile in an affected or smug manner

SMIRKER *n* pl. **-S** one that smirks

SMIRKY *adj* **SMIRKIER, SMIRKIEST** smirking **SMIRKILY** *adv*

SMITE *v* **SMOTE, SMIT** or **SMITTEN, SMITING, SMITES** to strike heavily

SMITER *n* pl. **-S** one that smites

SMITH *n* pl. **-S** a worker in metals

SMITHERS *n/pl* small fragments

SMITHERY *n* pl. **-ERIES** the trade of a smith

SMITHING *n* pl. **-S** the work of a smith

SMITHY *n* pl. **SMITHIES** the workshop of a smith

SMITING present participle of smite

SMITTEN a past participle of smite

SMOCK *v* **-ED, -ING, -S** to furnish with a smock (a loose outer garment)

SMOCKING *n* pl. **-S** a type of embroidery

SMOG *n* pl. **-S** an atmospheric mixture of smoke and fog **SMOGLESS** *adj*

SMOGGY *adj* **-GIER, -GIEST** filled with smog

SMOKE *v* **SMOKED, SMOKING, SMOKES** to emit smoke (the gaseous product of burning materials) **SMOKABLE** *adj*

SMOKEBOX *n* pl. **-ES** a chamber for producing and containing smoke

SMOKEPOT *n* pl. **-S** a container for giving off smoke

SMOKER *n* pl. **-S** one that smokes

SMOKEY *adj* **SMOKIER, SMOKIEST** smoky

SMOKEY *n* pl. **SMOKEYS** or **SMOKIES** a police officer who patrols highways

SMOKIE *n* pl. **-S** a sausage or hot dog

SMOKING	*n* pl. **-S** the inhaling and exhaling of the smoke of tobacco or a drug
SMOKY	*adj* **SMOKIER, SMOKIEST** filled with smoke **SMOKILY** *adv*
SMOLDER	*v* **-ED, -ING, -S** to burn with no flame
SMOLT	*n* pl. **-S** a young salmon
SMOOCH	*v* **-ED, -ING, -ES** to kiss
SMOOCHER	*n* pl. **-S** one that smooches
SMOOCHY	*adj* **SMOOCHIER, SMOOCHIEST** suitable for smooching
SMOOSH	*v* **-ED, -ING, -ES** to squash
SMOOTH	*adj* **SMOOTHER, SMOOTHEST** having a surface that is free from irregularities
SMOOTH	*v* **-ED, -ING, -S** or **-ES** to make smooth
SMOOTHE	*v* **SMOOTHED, SMOOTHING, SMOOTHES** to smooth
SMOOTHEN	*v* **-ED, -ING, -S** to smooth
SMOOTHER	*n* pl. **-S** one that smooths
SMOOTHIE	*n* pl. **-S** a person with polished manners
SMOOTHLY	*adv* in a smooth manner
SMOOTHY	*n* pl. **SMOOTHIES** smoothie
SMORG	*n* pl. **-S** a smorgasbord
SMOTE	past tense of smite
SMOTHER	*v* **-ED, -ING, -S** to prevent from breathing
SMOTHERY	*adj* tending to smother
SMOULDER	*v* **-ED, -ING, -S** to smolder
SMRITI	*n* pl. **-S** a text of Hindu religious teachings
SMUDGE	*v* **SMUDGED, SMUDGING, SMUDGES** to smear or dirty
SMUDGING	*n* pl. **-S** the act of smearing
SMUDGY	*adj* **SMUDGIER, SMUDGIEST** smudged **SMUDGILY** *adv*
SMUG	*adj* **SMUGGER, SMUGGEST** highly self-satisfied
SMUGGLE	*v* **-GLED, -GLING, -GLES** to import or export illicitly
SMUGGLER	*n* pl. **-S** one that smuggles
SMUGLY	*adv* in a smug manner
SMUGNESS	*n* pl. **-ES** the quality or state of being smug
SMUSH	*v* **-ED, -ING, -ES** to smoosh
SMUT	*v* **SMUTTED, SMUTTING, SMUTS** to soil
SMUTCH	*v* **-ED, -ING, -ES** to smudge
SMUTCHY	*adj* **SMUTCHIER, SMUTCHIEST** smudgy
SMUTTY	*adj* **-TIER, -TIEST** obscene **SMUTTILY** *adv*
SNACK	*v* **-ED, -ING, -S** to eat a light meal
SNACKER	*n* pl. **-S** one that snacks
SNACKY	*adj* **SNACKIER, SNACKIEST** suitable as a light meal
SNAFFLE	*v* **-FLED, -FLING, -FLES** to obtain by devious means
SNAFU	*v* **-ED, -ING, -S** to bring into a state of confusion
SNAG	*v* **SNAGGED, SNAGGING, SNAGS** to catch on a snag (a jagged protuberance)
SNAGGER	*n* pl. **-S** a person who uses illegal fishing methods
SNAGGLE	*n* pl. **-S** a tangled or knotted mass
SNAGGY	*adj* **-GIER, -GIEST** full of snags
SNAGLIKE	*adj* resembling a snag
SNAIL	*v* **-ED, -ING, -S** to move slowly
SNAKE	*v* **SNAKED, SNAKING, SNAKES** to move like a snake (a limbless reptile)
SNAKEBIT	*adj* unlucky
SNAKEPIT	*n* pl. **-S** a psychiatric hospital
SNAKEY	*adj* **SNAKIER, SNAKIEST** snaky
SNAKING	present participle of snake
SNAKISH	*adj* resembling a snake
SNAKY	*adj* **SNAKIER, SNAKIEST** resembling a snake **SNAKILY** *adv*
SNAP	*v* **SNAPPED, SNAPPING, SNAPS** to make a sharp cracking sound
SNAPBACK	*n* pl. **-S** a sudden rebound or recovery
SNAPLESS	*adj* lacking a snap (a type of fastening device)
SNAPPER	*n* pl. **-S** one that snaps
SNAPPIER	comparative of snappy
SNAPPIEST	superlative of snappy
SNAPPILY	*adv* in a snappy manner
SNAPPING	present participle of snap
SNAPPISH	*adj* tending to speak in an impatient or irritable manner
SNAPPY	*adj* **-PIER, -PIEST** snappish
SNAPSHOT	*v* **-SHOTTED, -SHOTTING, -SHOTS** to photograph informally and quickly
SNAPWEED	*n* pl. **-S** a flowering plant

SNARE	v **SNARED, SNARING, SNARES** to trap	**SNELL**	adj **SNELLER, SNELLEST** keen
SNARER	n pl. **-S** one that snares	**SNELL**	v **-ED, -ING, -S** to attach a short line to a fishhook
SNARF	v **-ED, -ING, -S** to eat or drink greedily	**SNIB**	v **SNIBBED, SNIBBING, SNIBS** to latch
SNARFLE	v **-FLED, -FLING, -FLES** to snarf	**SNICK**	v **-ED, -ING, -S** to nick
SNARING	present participle of snare	**SNICKER**	v **-ED, -ING, -S** to utter a partly stifled laugh
SNARK	n pl. **-S** an imaginary animal	**SNICKERY**	adj tending to snicker
SNARKY	adj **SNARKIER, SNARKIEST** snappish **SNARKILY** adv	**SNIDE**	adj **SNIDER, SNIDEST** maliciously derogatory **SNIDELY** adv
SNARL	v **-ED, -ING, -S** to growl viciously	**SNIFF**	v **-ED, -ING, -S** to inhale audibly through the nose
SNARLER	n pl. **-S** one that snarls	**SNIFFER**	n pl. **-S** one that sniffs
SNARLY	adj **SNARLIER, SNARLIEST** tangled	**SNIFFIER**	comparative of sniffy
SNASH	n pl. **-ES** abusive language	**SNIFFIEST**	superlative of sniffy
SNATCH	v **-ED, -ING, -ES** to seize suddenly	**SNIFFILY**	adv in a sniffy manner
SNATCHER	n pl. **-S** one that snatches	**SNIFFISH**	adj haughty
SNATCHY	adj **SNATCHIER, SNATCHIEST** occurring irregularly	**SNIFFLE**	v **-FLED, -FLING, -FLES** to sniff repeatedly
SNATH	n pl. **-S** the handle of a scythe	**SNIFFLER**	n pl. **-S** one that sniffles
SNATHE	n pl. **-S** snath	**SNIFFLY**	adj **-FLIER, -FLIEST** that sniffles
SNAW	v **-ED, -ING, -S** to snow	**SNIFFY**	adj **-FIER, -FIEST** sniffish
SNAZZY	adj **-ZIER, -ZIEST** very stylish **SNAZZILY** adv	**SNIFTER**	n pl. **-S** a pear-shaped liquor glass
SNEAK	v **SNEAKED** or **SNUCK, SNEAKING, SNEAKS** to move stealthily	**SNIGGER**	v **-ED, -ING, -S** to snicker
		SNIGGLE	v **-GLED, -GLING, -GLES** to fish for eels
SNEAKBOX	n pl. **-ES** a small boat masked with brush and weeds that is used for wildfowl hunting	**SNIGGLER**	n pl. **-S** one that sniggles
		SNIGLET	n pl. **-S** a word coined for something not having a name
SNEAKER	n pl. **-S** one that sneaks	**SNIP**	v **SNIPPED, SNIPPING, SNIPS** to cut with a short, quick stroke
SNEAKY	adj **SNEAKIER, SNEAKIEST** deceitful **SNEAKILY** adv	**SNIPE**	v **SNIPED, SNIPING, SNIPES** to shoot at individuals from a concealed place
SNEAP	v **-ED, -ING, -S** to chide		
SNECK	n pl. **-S** a latch		
SNED	v **SNEDDED, SNEDDING, SNEDS** to prune	**SNIPER**	n pl. **-S** one that snipes
SNEER	v **-ED, -ING, -S** to curl the lip in contempt	**SNIPING**	n pl. **-S** the act of one that snipes
		SNIPPED	past tense of snip
SNEERER	n pl. **-S** one that sneers	**SNIPPER**	n pl. **-S** one that snips
SNEERFUL	adj given to sneering	**SNIPPET**	n pl. **-S** a small piece snipped off
SNEERY	adj **SNEERIER, SNEERIEST** marked by sneering	**SNIPPETY**	adj **-PETIER, -PETIEST** snippy
SNEESH	n pl. **-ES** snuff	**SNIPPING**	n pl. **-S** a piece of something that has been snipped off
SNEEZE	v **SNEEZED, SNEEZING, SNEEZES** to make a sudden, involuntary expiration of breath	**SNIPPY**	adj **-PIER, -PIEST** snappish **SNIPPILY** adv
		SNIT	n pl. **-S** a state of agitation
SNEEZER	n pl. **-S** one that sneezes	**SNITCH**	v **-ED, -ING, -ES** to tattle
SNEEZY	adj **SNEEZIER, SNEEZIEST** tending to sneeze	**SNITCHER**	n pl. **-S** one that snitches

SNITTY *adj* **-TIER, -TIEST** disagreeably ill-tempered

SNIVEL *v* **-ELED, -ELING, -ELS** or **-ELLED, -ELLING, -ELS** to cry or whine with sniffling

SNIVELER *n* pl. **-S** one that snivels

SNIVELLY *adj* tending to whine with sniffling

SNOB *n* pl. **-S** one who tends to avoid or rebuff those regarded as inferior

SNOBBERY *n* pl. **-BERIES** snobbish behavior

SNOBBIER comparative of snobby

SNOBBIEST superlative of snobby

SNOBBILY *adv* in a snobby manner

SNOBBISH *adj* characteristic of a snob

SNOBBISM *n* pl. **-S** snobbery

SNOBBY *adj* **-BIER, -BIEST** snobbish

SNOCOACH *n* pl. **-ES** a bus-like vehicle with large tires or tracks for traveling on snow

SNOG *v* **SNOGGED, SNOGGING, SNOGS** to kiss

SNOGGER *n* pl. **-S** one that snogs

SNOOD *v* **-ED, -ING, -S** to secure with a snood (a net or fabric cap for the hair)

SNOOK *v* **-ED, -ING, -S** to sniff

SNOOKER *v* **-ED, -ING, -S** to trick

SNOOL *v* **-ED, -ING, -S** to yield meekly

SNOOP *v* **-ED, -ING, -S** to pry about

SNOOPER *n* pl. **-S** one that snoops

SNOOPY *adj* **SNOOPIER, SNOOPIEST** given to snooping **SNOOPILY** *adv*

SNOOSE *n* pl. **-S** chewing tobacco

SNOOT *v* **-ED, -ING, -S** to treat with disdain

SNOOTFUL *n* pl. **-S** enough alcoholic liquor to make one drunk

SNOOTY *adj* **SNOOTIER, SNOOTIEST** snobbish **SNOOTILY** *adv*

SNOOZE *v* **SNOOZED, SNOOZING, SNOOZES** to sleep lightly

SNOOZER *n* pl. **-S** one that snoozes

SNOOZLE *v* **-ZLED, -ZLING, -ZLES** to nuzzle

SNOOZY *adj* **SNOOZIER, SNOOZIEST** drowsy

SNORE *v* **SNORED, SNORING, SNORES** to breathe loudly while sleeping

SNORER *n* pl. **-S** one that snores

SNORING *n* pl. **-S** the act of breathing loudly while sleeping

SNORKEL *v* **-ED, -ING, -S** to swim underwater with a type of breathing device

SNORT *v* **-ED, -ING, -S** to exhale noisily through the nostrils

SNORTER *n* pl. **-S** one that snorts

SNOT *n* pl. **-S** nasal mucus

SNOTTY *adj* **-TIER, -TIEST** arrogant **SNOTTILY** *adv*

SNOUT *v* **-ED, -ING, -S** to provide with a nozzle

SNOUTISH *adj* snouty

SNOUTY *adj* **SNOUTIER, SNOUTIEST** resembling a long, projecting nose

SNOW *v* **-ED, -ING, -S** to fall as snow (precipitation in the form of ice crystals)

SNOWBALL *v* **-ED, -ING, -S** to increase at a rapidly accelerating rate

SNOWBANK *n* pl. **-S** a mound of snow

SNOWBELL *n* pl. **-S** a flowering shrub

SNOWBELT *n* pl. **-S** a region that receives an appreciable amount of snow each year

SNOWBIRD *n* pl. **-S** a small bird

SNOWBUSH *n* pl. **-ES** a flowering shrub

SNOWCAP *n* pl. **-S** a covering of snow

SNOWCAT *n* pl. **-S** a tracklaying vehicle for travel on snow

SNOWDROP *n* pl. **-S** a European herb

SNOWFALL *n* pl. **-S** a fall of snow

SNOWFLEA *n* pl. **-S** a wingless insect appearing on snow in the spring

SNOWIER comparative of snowy

SNOWIEST superlative of snowy

SNOWILY *adv* in a snowy manner

SNOWLAND *n* pl. **-S** an area marked by a great amount of snow

SNOWLESS *adj* having no snow

SNOWLIKE *adj* resembling snow

SNOWMAN *n* pl. **-MEN** a figure of a person that is made of snow

SNOWMELT *n* pl. **-S** water produced by the melting of snow

SNOWMOLD *n* pl. **-S** a fungus disease of grasses near the edge of melting snow

SNOWPACK *n* pl. **-S** an accumulation of packed snow

SNOWPLOW *v* **-ED, -ING, -S** to execute a type of skiing maneuver

SNOWSHED	*n* pl. **-S** a structure built to provide protection against snow
SNOWSHOE	*v* **-SHOED, -SHOEING, -SHOES** to walk on snowshoes (oval frames that allow a person to walk on deep snow)
SNOWSUIT	*n* pl. **-S** a child's garment for winter wear
SNOWY	*adj* **SNOWIER, SNOWIEST** abounding in snow
SNUB	*v* **SNUBBED, SNUBBING, SNUBS** to treat with contempt or neglect
SNUBBER	*n* pl. **-S** one that snubs
SNUBBY	*adj* **-BIER, -BIEST** blunt
SNUBNESS	*n* pl. **-ES** bluntness
SNUCK	a past tense of sneak
SNUFF	*v* **-ED, -ING, -S** to use or inhale snuff (powdered tobacco)
SNUFFBOX	*n* pl. **-ES** a box for holding snuff
SNUFFER	*n* pl. **-S** one that snuffs
SNUFFIER	comparative of snuffy
SNUFFIEST	superlative of snuffy
SNUFFILY	*adv* in a snuffy manner
SNUFFLE	*v* **-FLED, -FLING, -FLES** to sniffle
SNUFFLER	*n* pl. **-S** one that snuffles
SNUFFLY	*adj* **-FLIER, -FLIEST** tending to snuffle
SNUFFY	*adj* **SNUFFIER, SNUFFIEST** dingy
SNUG	*adj* **SNUGGER, SNUGGEST** warmly comfortable
SNUG	*v* **SNUGGED, SNUGGING, SNUGS** to make snug
SNUGGERY	*n* pl. **-GERIES** a snug place
SNUGGEST	superlative of snug
SNUGGIES	*n/pl* women's long underwear
SNUGGING	present participle of snug
SNUGGLE	*v* **-GLED, -GLING, -GLES** to lie or press closely
SNUGGLY	*adj* **SNUGGLIER, SNUGGLIEST** warm and cozy
SNUGLY	*adv* in a snug manner
SNUGNESS	*n* pl. **-ES** the quality or state of being snug
SNYE	*n* pl. **-S** a side channel in a river or creek
SO	*n* pl. **SOS** sol
SOAK	*v* **-ED, -ING, -S** to wet something thoroughly
SOAKAGE	*n* pl. **-S** the act of soaking
SOAKER	*n* pl. **-S** one that soaks
SOAKING	*n* pl. **-S** the act of wetting something thoroughly
SOAP	*v* **-ED, -ING, -S** to treat with soap (a cleansing agent)
SOAPBARK	*n* pl. **-S** a tropical tree
SOAPBOX	*v* **-ED, -ING, -ES** to deliver an informal impassioned speech on the street
SOAPER	*n* pl. **-S** a serial melodrama on radio or television
SOAPFISH	*n* pl. **-ES** a tropical fish that produces toxic mucus
SOAPIER	comparative of soapy
SOAPIEST	superlative of soapy
SOAPILY	*adv* in a soapy manner
SOAPLESS	*adj* having no soap
SOAPLIKE	*adj* resembling soap
SOAPSUDS	*n/pl* suds (soapy water)
SOAPWORT	*n* pl. **-S** a perennial herb
SOAPY	*adj* **SOAPIER, SOAPIEST** containing or resembling soap
SOAR	*v* **-ED, -ING, -S** to fly at a great height
SOARER	*n* pl. **-S** one that soars
SOARING	*n* pl. **-S** the sport of flying in a heavier-than-air craft without power
SOAVE	*n* pl. **-S** an Italian wine
SOB	*v* **SOBBED, SOBBING, SOBS** to cry with a convulsive catching of the breath
SOBA	*n* pl. **-S** a Japanese noodle made from buckwheat flour
SOBBER	*n* pl. **-S** one that sobs
SOBEIT	*conj* provided that
SOBER	*adj* **SOBERER, SOBEREST** having control of one's faculties
SOBER	*v* **-ED, -ING, -S** to make sober
SOBERIZE	*v* **-IZED, -IZING, -IZES** to sober
SOBERLY	*adv* in a sober manner
SOBFUL	*adj* given to sobbing
SOBRIETY	*n* pl. **-ETIES** the quality or state of being sober
SOC	*n* pl. **-ES** a sociology course
SOCA	*n* pl. **-S** a blend of soul and calypso music
SOCAGE	*n* pl. **-S** a form of feudal land tenure
SOCAGER	*n* pl. **-S** a tenant by socage

SOCCAGE	*n* pl. **-S** socage
SOCCER	*n* pl. **-S** a type of ball game
SOCIABLE	*n* pl. **-S** a social
SOCIABLY	*adv* in a friendly manner
SOCIAL	*n* pl. **-S** a friendly gathering
SOCIALLY	*adv* with respect to society
SOCIETY	*n* pl. **-ETIES** an organized group of persons **SOCIETAL** *adj*
SOCK	*n* pl. **SOCKS** or **SOX** a knitted or woven covering for the foot
SOCK	*v* **-ED, -ING, -S** to strike forcefully
SOCKET	*v* **-ED, -ING, -S** to furnish with a socket (an opening for receiving something)
SOCKETTE	*n* pl. **-S** a very short sock
SOCKEYE	*n* pl. **-S** a food fish
SOCKLESS	*adj* having no socks
SOCKMAN	*n* pl. **-MEN** socman
SOCKO	*adj* strikingly impressive
SOCLE	*n* pl. **-S** a block used as a base for a column or pedestal
SOCMAN	*n* pl. **-MEN** a socager
SOD	*v* **SODDED, SODDING, SODS** to cover with sod (turf)
SODA	*n* pl. **-S** a type of chemical compound **SODALESS** *adj*
SODALIST	*n* pl. **-S** a member of a sodality
SODALITE	*n* pl. **-S** a mineral
SODALITY	*n* pl. **-TIES** a society
SODAMIDE	*n* pl. **-S** a chemical compound
SODDED	past tense of sod
SODDEN	*v* **-ED, -ING, -S** to make soggy
SODDENLY	*adv* in a soggy manner
SODDIE	*n* pl. **-S** a soddy
SODDING	present participle of sod
SODDY	*n* pl. **-DIES** a house built of sod
SODIUM	*n* pl. **-S** a metallic element **SODIC** *adj*
SODOM	*n* pl. **-S** a place notorious for vice and corruption
SODOMISE	*v* **-ISED, -ISING, -ISES** to sodomize
SODOMIST	*n* pl. **-S** a sodomite
SODOMITE	*n* pl. **-S** one who practices sodomy
SODOMIZE	*v* **-IZED, -IZING, -IZES** to engage in sodomy with
SODOMY	*n* pl. **-OMIES** unnatural copulation
SOEVER	*adv* at all
SOFA	*n* pl. **-S** a long, upholstered seat
SOFABED	*n* pl. **-S** a sofa that can be made into a bed
SOFAR	*n* pl. **-S** a system for locating underwater explosions
SOFFIT	*n* pl. **-S** the underside of an architectural structure
SOFT	*adj* **SOFTER, SOFTEST** yielding readily to pressure
SOFT	*n* pl. **-S** a soft object or part
SOFTA	*n* pl. **-S** a Muslim theological student
SOFTBACK	*n* pl. **-S** a book bound in a flexible paper cover
SOFTBALL	*n* pl. **-S** a type of ball
SOFTCORE	*adj* less than explicit in depicting sex acts
SOFTEN	*v* **-ED, -ING, -S** to make soft
SOFTENER	*n* pl. **-S** one that softens
SOFTHEAD	*n* pl. **-S** a foolish person
SOFTIE	*n* pl. **-S** softy
SOFTIES	pl. of softy
SOFTISH	*adj* somewhat soft
SOFTLY	*adv* in a soft manner
SOFTNESS	*n* pl. **-ES** the quality or state of being soft
SOFTWARE	*n* pl. **-S** written or printed data used in computer operations
SOFTWOOD	*n* pl. **-S** the soft wood of various trees
SOFTY	*n* pl. **SOFTIES** a sentimental person
SOGGED	*adj* soggy
SOGGY	*adj* **-GIER, -GIEST** heavy with moisture **SOGGILY** *adv*
SOH	*n* pl. **-S** sol
SOIGNE	*adj* carefully done
SOIGNEE	*adj* soigne
SOIL	*v* **-ED, -ING, -S** to make dirty
SOILAGE	*n* pl. **-S** green crops for feeding animals
SOILLESS	*adj* carried on without soil (finely divided rock mixed with organic matter)
SOILURE	*n* pl. **-S** a stain or smudge
SOIREE	*n* pl. **-S** an evening party
SOJA	*n* pl. **-S** the soybean
SOJOURN	*v* **-ED, -ING, -S** to stay temporarily

SOJU *n* pl. **-S** Korean vodka distilled from rice or sweet potato

SOKE *n* pl. **-S** a feudal right to administer justice within a certain territory

SOKEMAN *n* pl. **-MEN** socman

SOKOL *n* pl. **-S** an international group promoting physical fitness

SOL *n* pl. **-S** the fifth tone of the diatonic musical scale

SOLA *n* pl. **-S** a swamp plant of India

SOLACE *v* **-LACED, -LACING, -LACES** to console

SOLACER *n* pl. **-S** one that solaces

SOLAN *n* pl. **-S** a gannet

SOLAND *n* pl. **-S** solan

SOLANDER *n* pl. **-S** a protective box for library materials

SOLANIN *n* pl. **-S** solanine

SOLANINE *n* pl. **-S** a poisonous alkaloid

SOLANO *n* pl. **-NOS** a strong, hot wind

SOLANUM *n* pl. **-S** any of a genus of herbs and shrubs

SOLAR *n* pl. **-S** a solarium

SOLARIA a pl. of solarium

SOLARISE *v* **-ISED, -ISING, -ISES** to solarize

SOLARISM *n* pl. **-S** an interpretation of folk tales as concepts of the nature of the sun

SOLARIUM *n* pl. **-IUMS** or **-IA** a room exposed to the sun

SOLARIZE *v* **-IZED, -IZING, -IZES** to expose to sunlight

SOLATE *v* **-ATED, -ATING, -ATES** to change to a fluid colloidal system

SOLATION *n* pl. **-S** the act of solating

SOLATIUM *n* pl. **-TIA** a compensation given for damage to the feelings

SOLD past tense of sell

SOLDAN *n* pl. **-S** a Muslim ruler

SOLDER *v* **-ED, -ING, -S** to join closely together

SOLDERER *n* pl. **-S** one that solders

SOLDIER *v* **-ED, -ING, -S** to perform military service

SOLDIERY *n* pl. **-DIERIES** the military profession

SOLDO *n* pl. **-DI** a former coin of Italy

SOLE *v* **SOLED, SOLING, SOLES** to furnish with a sole (the bottom surface of a shoe or boot)

SOLECISE *v* **-CISED, -CISING, -CISES** to solecize

SOLECISM *n* pl. **-S** an ungrammatical combination of words in a sentence

SOLECIST *n* pl. **-S** one who solecizes

SOLECIZE *v* **-CIZED, -CIZING, -CIZES** to use solecisms

SOLED past tense of sole

SOLEI a pl. of soleus

SOLELESS *adj* having no sole

SOLELY *adv* singly

SOLEMN *adj* **-EMNER, -EMNEST** serious **SOLEMNLY** *adv*

SOLENESS *n* pl. **-ES** the state of being the only one

SOLENOID *n* pl. **-S** a type of electric coil

SOLERA *n* pl. **-S** a Spanish method of producing wine

SOLERET *n* pl. **-S** solleret

SOLEUS *n* pl. **-LEUSES** or **-LEI** a muscle in the calf of the leg

SOLFEGE *n* pl. **-S** a type of singing exercise

SOLFEGGI *n/pl* solfeges

SOLGEL *adj* involving some changes in the state of a colloidal system

SOLI a pl. of solo

SOLICIT *v* **-ED, -ING, -S** to ask for earnestly

SOLID *adj* **-IDER, -IDEST** having definite shape and volume

SOLID *n* pl. **-S** a solid substance

SOLIDAGO *n* pl. **-GOS** a flowering plant

SOLIDARY *adj* united

SOLIDI pl. of solidus

SOLIDIFY *v* **-FIED, -FYING, -FIES** to make solid

SOLIDITY *n* pl. **-TIES** the quality or state of being solid

SOLIDLY *adv* in a solid manner

SOLIDUS *n* pl. **-DI** a coin of ancient Rome

SOLING present participle of sole

SOLION *n* pl. **-S** an electronic detecting and amplifying device

SOLIQUID *n* pl. **-S** a fluid colloidal system

SOLITARY *n* pl. **-TARIES** one who lives alone

SOLITON *n* pl. **-S** a solitary wave in physics

SOLITUDE *n* pl. **-S** the state of being alone

SOLLERET *n* pl. **-S** a sabaton

SOLO   n pl. **-LOS** or **-LI** a musical composition for a single voice or instrument

SOLO   v **-ED, -ING, -S** or **-ES** to perform alone

SOLOIST   n pl. **-S** one that performs a solo

SOLON   n pl. **-S** a wise lawgiver

SOLONETS   n pl. **-ES** solonetz

SOLONETZ   n pl. **-ES** a type of soil

SOLSTICE   n pl. **-S** the time of the year when the sun is at its greatest distance from the celestial equator

SOLUBLE   n pl. **-S** something that is soluble (capable of being dissolved)

SOLUBLY   adv in a soluble manner

SOLUM   n pl. **-LUMS** or **-LA** a soil layer

SOLUNAR   adj listing the rising and setting times of the sun and moon

SOLUS   adj alone

SOLUTE   n pl. **-S** a dissolved substance

SOLUTION   n pl. **-S** a homogeneous liquid mixture

SOLVABLE   adj capable of being solved

SOLVATE   v **-VATED, -VATING, -VATES** to convert into a type of ion

SOLVE   v **SOLVED, SOLVING, SOLVES** to find the answer or explanation for

SOLVENCY   n pl. **-CIES** the ability to pay all debts

SOLVENT   n pl. **-S** a substance capable of dissolving others

SOLVER   n pl. **-S** one that solves

SOLVING   present participle of solve

SOM   n pl. **SOMS** a monetary unit of Kyrgyzstan

SOMA   n pl. **-MAS** or **-MATA** the body of an organism **SOMATIC** adj

SOMAN   n pl. **-S** a toxic chemical warfare agent

SOMBER   adj **SOMBERER, SOMBEREST** gloomy **SOMBERLY** adv

SOMBRE   adj **SOMBRER, SOMBREST** somber **SOMBRELY** adv

SOMBRERO   n pl. **-ROS** a broad-brimmed hat

SOMBROUS   adj somber

SOME   adj being an unspecified number or part

SOMEBODY   n pl. **-BODIES** an important person

SOMEDAY   adv at some future time

SOMEDEAL   adv to some degree

SOMEHOW   adv by some means

SOMEONE   n pl. **-S** a somebody

SOMERSET   v **-SETED, -SETING, -SETS** or **-SETTED, -SETTING, -SETS** to roll the body in a complete circle, head over heels

SOMETIME   adv at some future time

SOMEWAY   adv somehow

SOMEWAYS   adv someway

SOMEWHAT   n pl. **-S** an unspecified number or part

SOMEWHEN   adv sometime

SOMEWISE   adv somehow

SOMITE   n pl. **-S** a longitudinal segment of the body of some animals **SOMITAL, SOMITIC** adj

SOMONI   n pl. **-S** a monetary unit of Tajikistan

SON   n pl. **-S** a male child

SONANCE   n pl. **-S** sound

SONANT   n pl. **-S** a sound uttered with vibration of the vocal cords **SONANTAL, SONANTIC** adj

SONAR   n pl. **-S** an underwater locating device

SONARMAN   n pl. **-MEN** a person who operates sonar equipment

SONATA   n pl. **-S** a type of musical composition

SONATINA   n pl. **-TINAS** or **-TINE** a short sonata

SONDE   n pl. **-S** a device for observing atmospheric phenomena

SONDER   n pl. **-S** a class of small yachts

SONE   n pl. **-S** a unit of loudness

SONG   n pl. **-S** a musical composition written or adapted for singing

SONGBIRD   n pl. **-S** a bird that utters a musical call

SONGBOOK   n pl. **-S** a book of songs

SONGFEST   n pl. **-S** an informal gathering for group singing

SONGFUL   adj melodious

SONGLESS   adj incapable of singing

SONGLIKE   adj resembling a song

SONGSTER   n pl. **-S** a singer

SONHOOD   n pl. **-S** the state of being a son

SONIC   adj pertaining to sound

SONICATE   v **-CATED, -CATING, -CATES** to disrupt with sound waves

SONICS	*n/pl* the science dealing with the practical applications of sound
SONLESS	*adj* having no son
SONLIKE	*adj* resembling a son
SONLY	*adj* pertaining to a son
SONNET	*v* **-NETED, -NETING, -NETS** or **-NETTED, -NETTING, -NETS** to compose a sonnet (a type of poem)
SONNY	*n* pl. **-NIES** a small boy
SONOBUOY	*n* pl. **-BUOYS** a buoy that detects and transmits underwater sounds
SONOGRAM	*n* pl. **-S** an image produced by ultrasound
SONORANT	*n* pl. **-S** a type of voiced sound
SONORITY	*n* pl. **-TIES** the quality or state of being sonorous
SONOROUS	*adj* characterized by a full and loud sound
SONOVOX	*n* pl. **-ES** a sound effects device
SONSHIP	*n* pl. **-S** the state of being a son
SONSIE	*adj* **-SIER, -SIEST** sonsy
SONSY	*adj* **-SIER, -SIEST** comely
SOOCHONG	*n* pl. **-S** souchong
SOOEY	*interj* — used in calling pigs
SOOK	*n* pl. **-S** souk
SOON	*adv* **SOONER, SOONEST** in the near future **SOONISH** *adj*
SOONER	*n* pl. **-S** one who settles on government land before it is officially opened for settlement
SOOT	*v* **-ED, -ING, -S** to cover with soot (a black substance produced by combustion)
SOOTH	*adj* **SOOTHER, SOOTHEST** true
SOOTH	*n* pl. **-S** truth
SOOTHE	*v* **SOOTHED, SOOTHING, SOOTHES** to restore to a quiet or normal state
SOOTHER	*n* pl. **-S** one that soothes
SOOTHLY	*adv* in truth
SOOTHSAY	*v* **-SAID, -SAYING, -SAYS** to predict
SOOTY	*adj* **SOOTIER, SOOTIEST** covered with soot **SOOTILY** *adv*
SOP	*v* **SOPPED, SOPPING, SOPS** to dip or soak in a liquid
SOPH	*n* pl. **-S** a sophomore
SOPHIES	pl. of sophy
SOPHISM	*n* pl. **-S** a plausible but fallacious argument
SOPHIST	*n* pl. **-S** one that uses sophisms
SOPHY	*n* pl. **-PHIES** a ruler of Persia
SOPITE	*v* **-PITED, -PITING, -PITES** to put to sleep
SOPOR	*n* pl. **-S** an abnormally deep sleep
SOPPED	past tense of sop
SOPPING	*adj* very wet
SOPPY	*adj* **-PIER, -PIEST** very wet **SOPPILY** *adv*
SOPRANO	*n* pl. **-NOS** or **-NI** the highest singing voice
SORA	*n* pl. **-S** a marsh bird
SORB	*v* **-ED, -ING, -S** to take up and hold by absorption or adsorption **SORBABLE** *adj*
SORBATE	*n* pl. **-S** a sorbed substance
SORBENT	*n* pl. **-S** a substance that sorbs
SORBET	*n* pl. **-S** sherbet
SORBIC	*adj* pertaining to a type of fruit
SORBITAN	*n* pl. **-S** a chemical compound
SORBITOL	*n* pl. **-S** a chemical compound
SORBOSE	*n* pl. **-S** a type of sugar
SORCERER	*n* pl. **-S** one who practices sorcery
SORCERY	*n* pl. **-CERIES** alleged use of supernatural powers
SORD	*n* pl. **-S** a flight of mallards
SORDID	*adj* filthy **SORDIDLY** *adv*
SORDINE	*n* pl. **-S** a device used to muffle the tone of a musical instrument
SORDINO	*n* pl. **-NI** sordine
SORDOR	*n* pl. **-S** a sordid state
SORE	*v* **SORED, SORING, SORES** to mutilate the feet of (a horse) so as to force a particular gait
SORE	*adj* **SORER, SOREST** painfully sensitive to the touch
SOREHEAD	*n* pl. **-S** a person who is easily angered or offended
SOREL	*n* pl. **-S** sorrel
SORELY	*adv* in a sore manner
SORENESS	*n* pl. **-ES** the quality or state of being sore
SORER	comparative of sore
SOREST	superlative of sore
SORGHO	*n* pl. **-GHOS** sorgo
SORGHUM	*n* pl. **-S** a cereal grass

SORGO   *n* pl. **-GOS** a variety of sorghum

SORI   pl. of sorus

SORICINE   *adj* belonging to the shrew family of mammals

SORING   *n* pl. **-S** the practice of making a horse's front feet sore to force high stepping

SORITES   *n* pl. **SORITES** a type of argument used in logic **SORITIC** *adj*

SORN   *v* **-ED, -ING, -S** to force oneself on others for food and lodging

SORNER   *n* pl. **-S** one that sorns

SOROCHE   *n* pl. **-S** mountain sickness

SORORAL   *adj* sisterly

SORORATE   *n* pl. **-S** the marriage of a man usually with his deceased wife's sister

SORORITY   *n* pl. **-TIES** a social club for women

SOROSIS   *n* pl. **-ROSISES** or **-ROSES** a women's club or society

SORPTION   *n* pl. **-S** the act or process of sorbing **SORPTIVE** *adj*

SORREL   *n* pl. **-S** a reddish brown color

SORRIER   comparative of sorry

SORRIEST   superlative of sorry

SORRILY   *adv* in a sorry manner

SORROW   *v* **-ED, -ING, -S** to grieve

SORROWER   *n* pl. **-S** one that sorrows

SORRY   *adj* **-RIER, -RIEST** feeling grief or penitence

SORT   *v* **-ED, -ING, -S** to arrange according to kind, class, or size **SORTABLE** *adj* **SORTABLY** *adv*

SORTAL   *n* pl. **-S** a term that classifies an entity as being of a particular kind

SORTER   *n* pl. **-S** one that sorts

SORTES   *n/pl* divination by chance selection of a passage in an authoritative text

SORTIE   *v* **-TIED, -TIEING, -TIES** to attack suddenly from a defensive position

SORTING   *n* pl. **-S** the separating of items into groups

SORUS   *n* pl. **-RI** a cluster of plant reproductive bodies

SOT   *n* pl. **-S** a habitual drunkard

SOTH   *n* pl. **-S** sooth

SOTOL   *n* pl. **-S** a flowering plant

SOTTED   *adj* besotted **SOTTEDLY** *adv*

SOTTISH   *adj* resembling a sot

SOU   *n* pl. **-S** a formerly used French coin

SOUARI   *n* pl. **-S** a tropical tree

SOUBISE   *n* pl. **-S** a sauce of onions and butter

SOUCAR   *n* pl. **-S** a Hindu banker

SOUCHONG   *n* pl. **-S** a Chinese tea

SOUDAN   *n* pl. **-S** soldan

SOUFFLE   *n* pl. **-S** a light, baked dish

SOUFFLED   *adj* made puffy by beating and baking

SOUGH   *v* **-ED, -ING, -S** to make a moaning or sighing sound

SOUGHT   past tense of seek

SOUK   *n* pl. **-S** a marketplace in northern Africa and the Middle East

SOUKOUS   *n* pl. **-ES** a dance music in the Democratic Republic of the Congo

SOUL   *n* pl. **-S** the spiritual aspect of human beings **SOULED, SOULLESS, SOULLIKE** *adj*

SOULFUL   *adj* full of emotion

SOULMATE   *n* pl. **-S** a person with whom one is perfectly suited

SOULSTER   *n* pl. **-S** a singer of soul music

SOUND   *adj* **SOUNDER, SOUNDEST** being in good health or condition

SOUND   *v* **-ED, -ING, -S** to make a sound (something that stimulates the auditory receptors)

SOUNDBOX   *n* pl. **-ES** a resonant cavity in a musical instrument

SOUNDER   *n* pl. **-S** one that sounds

SOUNDING   *n* pl. **-S** a sampling of opinions

SOUNDLY   *adv* in a sound manner

SOUNDMAN   *n* pl. **-MEN** a person who controls the quality of sound being recorded

SOUP   *v* **-ED, -ING, -S** to increase the power or efficiency of

SOUPCON   *n* pl. **-S** a minute amount

SOUPLESS   *adj* having no soup (a liquid food often having solid ingredients)

SOUPLIKE   *adj* resembling soup

SOUPY   *adj* **SOUPIER, SOUPIEST** foggy **SOUPILY** *adv*

SOUR   *adj* **SOURER, SOUREST** sharp or biting to the taste

SOUR   *v* **-ED, -ING, -S** to make or become sour

SOURBALL   *n* pl. **-S** a sour candy

SOURCE	*v* **SOURCED, SOURCING, SOURCES** to obtain from a point of origin
SOURCING	*n* pl. **-S** the act of obtaining something from a point of origin
SOURDINE	*n* pl. **-S** sordine
SOURGUM	*n* pl. **-S** a softwood tree of eastern North America
SOURISH	*adj* somewhat sour
SOURLY	*adv* in a sour manner
SOURNESS	*n* pl. **-ES** the quality or state of being sour
SOURPUSS	*n* pl. **-ES** a grouchy person
SOURSOP	*n* pl. **-S** a tropical tree
SOURWOOD	*n* pl. **-S** a flowering tree
SOUSE	*v* **SOUSED, SOUSING, SOUSES** to immerse something in a liquid
SOUSER	*n* pl. **-S** a drunkard
SOUSLIK	*n* pl. **-S** suslik
SOUTACHE	*n* pl. **-S** a flat, narrow braid
SOUTANE	*n* pl. **-S** a cassock
SOUTER	*n* pl. **-S** a shoemaker
SOUTH	*v* **-ED, -ING, -S** to move toward the south (a cardinal point of the compass)
SOUTHER	*n* pl. **-S** a wind or storm from the south
SOUTHERN	*n* pl. **-S** a person living in the south
SOUTHING	*n* pl. **-S** movement toward the south
SOUTHPAW	*n* pl. **-S** a left-handed person
SOUTHRON	*n* pl. **-S** a southern
SOUVENIR	*n* pl. **-S** a memento
SOUVLAKI	*n* pl. **-S** a Greek shish kebab
SOVIET	*n* pl. **-S** a legislative body in a Communist country
SOVKHOZ	*n* pl. **-KHOZES** or **-KHOZY** a state-owned farm in the former Soviet Union
SOVRAN	*n* pl. **-S** a monarch
SOVRANLY	*adv* supremely
SOVRANTY	*n* pl. **-TIES** a monarchy
SOW	*v* **SOWED, SOWN, SOWING, SOWS** to scatter over land for growth, as seed **SOWABLE** *adj*
SOWANS	*n* pl. **SOWANS** sowens
SOWAR	*n* pl. **-S** a mounted native soldier in India
SOWBACK	*n* pl. **-S** a low ridge of sand
SOWBELLY	*n* pl. **-LIES** pork cured in salt
SOWBREAD	*n* pl. **-S** a flowering plant
SOWBUG	*n* pl. **-S** a wood louse
SOWCAR	*n* pl. **-S** soucar
SOWENS	*n* pl. **SOWENS** porridge made from oat husks
SOWER	*n* pl. **-S** one that sows
SOWING	*n* pl. **-S** the act of scattering seeds
SOWN	past participle of sow
SOX	a pl. of sock
SOY	*n* pl. **SOYS** the soybean
SOYA	*n* pl. **-S** soy
SOYBEAN	*n* pl. **-S** the seed of a cultivated Asian herb
SOYMEAL	*n* pl. **-S** the residue from the extraction of oil from soybean seeds
SOYMILK	*n* pl. **-S** a milk substitute made from soybeans
SOYUZ	*n* pl. **-ES** a manned spacecraft of the former Soviet Union
SOZIN	*n* pl. **-S** a type of protein
SOZINE	*n* pl. **-S** sozin
SOZZLED	*adj* drunk
SPA	*n* pl. **-S** a mineral spring
SPACE	*v* **SPACED, SPACING, SPACES** to set some distance apart
SPACELAB	*n* pl. **-S** a spacecraft equipped with a laboratory
SPACEMAN	*n* pl. **-MEN** an astronaut
SPACER	*n* pl. **-S** one that spaces
SPACEY	*adj* **SPACIER, SPACIEST** weird in behavior
SPACIAL	*adj* spatial
SPACING	*n* pl. **-S** the distance between any two objects
SPACIOUS	*adj* vast or ample in extent
SPACKLE	*v* **-LED, -LING, -LES** to fill cracks or holes in a surface with paste
SPACY	*adj* **SPACIER, SPACIEST** spacey
SPADE	*v* **SPADED, SPADING, SPADES** to take up with a spade (a digging implement)
SPADEFUL	*n* pl. **-S** as much as a spade can hold
SPADER	*n* pl. **-S** one that spades
SPADICES	pl. of spadix
SPADILLE	*n* pl. **-S** the highest trump in certain card games

SPADING	present participle of spade	**SPANK**	v **-ED, -ING, -S** to slap on the buttocks
SPADIX	n pl. **-DIXES** or **-DICES** a flower cluster	**SPANKER**	n pl. **-S** one that spanks
SPADO	n pl. **-DONES** a castrated man or animal	**SPANKING**	n pl. **-S** the act of one that spanks
		SPANLESS	adj having no extent
SPAE	v **SPAED, SPAEING, SPAES** to foretell	**SPANNED**	past tense of span
		SPANNER	n pl. **-S** one that spans
SPAEING	n pl. **-S** the act of foretelling	**SPANNING**	present participle of span
SPAETZLE	n pl. **-S** a tiny dumpling	**SPANWORM**	n pl. **-S** an inchworm
SPAGYRIC	n pl. **-S** a person skilled in alchemy	**SPAR**	v **SPARRED, SPARRING, SPARS** to provide with spars (stout poles used to support rigging)
SPAHEE	n pl. **-S** spahi		
SPAHI	n pl. **-S** a Turkish cavalryman		
SPAIL	n pl. **-S** spale	**SPARABLE**	n pl. **-S** a type of nail
SPAIT	n pl. **-S** spate	**SPARE**	adj **SPARER, SPAREST** meager **SPARELY** adv
SPAKE	a past tense of speak		
SPALDEEN	n pl. **-S** a small hollow rubber ball	**SPARE**	v **SPARED, SPARING, SPARES** to refrain from punishing, harming, or destroying
SPALE	n pl. **-S** a splinter or chip		
SPALL	v **-ED, -ING, -S** to break up into fragments	**SPARER**	n pl. **-S** one that spares
		SPARERIB	n pl. **-S** a cut of pork
SPALLER	n pl. **-S** one that spalls	**SPARGE**	v **SPARGED, SPARGING, SPARGES** to sprinkle
SPALLING	n pl. **-S** a chip of stone or ore		
SPALPEEN	n pl. **-S** a rascal	**SPARGER**	n pl. **-S** one that sparges
SPALTED	adj denoting wood having irregular lines resulting from fungal decay	**SPARID**	n pl. **-S** any of a family of marine fishes
SPAM	v **SPAMMED, SPAMMING, SPAMS** to send unsolicited email to a large number of addresses	**SPARING**	present participle of spare
		SPARK	v **-ED, -ING, -S** to give off sparks (small fiery particles)
SPAMBOT	n pl. **-S** a computer program that sends out unsolicited email	**SPARKER**	n pl. **-S** something that sparks
		SPARKIER	comparative of sparky
SPAMMER	n pl. **-S** one that spams	**SPARKIEST**	superlative of sparky
SPAMMING	n pl. **-S** the practice of sending out unsolicited email	**SPARKILY**	adv in a lively manner
		SPARKISH	adj jaunty
SPAN	v **SPANNED, SPANNING, SPANS** to extend over or across	**SPARKLE**	v **-KLED, -KLING, -KLES** to give off or reflect flashes of light
SPANCEL	v **-CELED, -CELING, -CELS** or **-CELLED, -CELLING, -CELS** to bind or fetter with a rope	**SPARKLER**	n pl. **-S** something that sparkles
		SPARKLET	n pl. **-S** a small spark
SPANDEX	n pl. **-ES** a synthetic elastic fiber **SPANDEXED** adj	**SPARKLY**	adj **-KLIER, -KLIEST** tending to sparkle
SPANDREL	n pl. **-S** a space between two adjoining arches	**SPARKY**	adj **SPARKIER, SPARKIEST** lively
		SPARLIKE	adj resembling a spar
SPANDRIL	n pl. **-S** spandrel	**SPARLING**	n pl. **-S** a young herring
SPANG	adv directly	**SPAROID**	n pl. **-S** a sparid
SPANGLE	v **-GLED, -GLING, -GLES** to adorn with spangles (bits of sparkling metal)	**SPARRED**	past tense of spar
		SPARRING	present participle of spar
SPANGLY	adj **-GLIER, -GLIEST** covered with spangles	**SPARROW**	n pl. **-S** a small bird
		SPARRY	adj **-RIER, -RIEST** resembling spar (a lustrous mineral)
SPANIEL	n pl. **-S** a dog with silky hair		

SPARSE	*adj* **SPARSER, SPARSEST** thinly distributed **SPARSELY** *adv*
SPARSITY	*n* pl. **-TIES** the quality or state of being sparse
SPARTAN	*adj* avoiding luxury and comfort
SPARTINA	*n* pl. **-S** a salt-marsh grass of coastal regions
SPASM	*v* **-ED, -ING, -S** to undergo an involuntary muscular contraction
SPASTIC	*n* pl. **-S** one suffering from a paralysis with muscle spasms
SPAT	*v* **SPATTED, SPATTING, SPATS** to strike lightly
SPATE	*n* pl. **-S** a freshet
SPATHE	*n* pl. **-S** a leaflike organ of certain plants **SPATHAL, SPATHED, SPATHOSE** *adj*
SPATHIC	*adj* sparry
SPATIAL	*adj* of or pertaining to space
SPATTED	past tense of spat
SPATTER	*v* **-ED, -ING, -S** to scatter in drops
SPATTING	present participle of spat
SPATULA	*n* pl. **-S** a mixing implement **SPATULAR** *adj*
SPATZLE	*n* pl. **-S** spaetzle
SPAVIE	*n* pl. **-S** spavin **SPAVIET** *adj*
SPAVIN	*n* pl. **-S** a disease of horses **SPAVINED** *adj*
SPAWN	*v* **-ED, -ING, -S** to deposit eggs
SPAWNER	*n* pl. **-S** one that spawns
SPAY	*v* **-ED, -ING, -S** to remove the ovaries of
SPEAK	*v* **SPOKE** or **SPAKE, SPOKEN, SPEAKING, SPEAKS** to utter words
SPEAKER	*n* pl. **-S** one that speaks
SPEAKING	*n* pl. **-S** a speech or discourse
SPEAN	*v* **-ED, -ING, -S** to wean
SPEAR	*v* **-ED, -ING, -S** to pierce with a spear (a long, pointed weapon)
SPEARER	*n* pl. **-S** one that spears
SPEARGUN	*n* pl. **-S** a gun that shoots a spear
SPEARING	*n* pl. **-S** the act of piercing with a spear
SPEARMAN	*n* pl. **-MEN** a person armed with a spear
SPEC	*v* **SPECCED, SPECCING, SPECS** to write specifications for
SPECIAL	*adj* **-CIALER, -CIALEST** of a distinct kind or character
SPECIAL	*n* pl. **-S** a special person or thing
SPECIATE	*v* **-ATED, -ATING, -ATES** to undergo a type of evolutionary process
SPECIE	*n* pl. **-S** coined money
SPECIFIC	*n* pl. **-S** a remedy intended for a particular disease
SPECIFY	*v* **-FIED, -FYING, -FIES** to state in detail
SPECIMEN	*n* pl. **-S** a part or individual representative of a group or whole
SPECIOUS	*adj* having a false look of truth or authenticity
SPECK	*v* **-ED, -ING, -S** to mark with small spots
SPECKLE	*v* **-LED, -LING, -LES** to speck
SPECKY	*adj* **SPECKIER, SPECKIEST** marked with small spots
SPECTATE	*v* **-TATED, -TATING, -TATES** to attend and view
SPECTER	*n* pl. **-S** a visible disembodied spirit
SPECTRA	a pl. of spectrum
SPECTRAL	*adj* resembling a specter
SPECTRE	*n* pl. **-S** specter
SPECTRUM	*n* pl. **-TRUMS** or **-TRA** an array of the components of a light wave
SPECULUM	*n* pl. **-LUMS** or **-LA** a medical instrument **SPECULAR** *adj*
SPEECH	*n* pl. **-ES** the faculty or act of speaking
SPEED	*v* **SPED** or **SPEEDED, SPEEDING, SPEEDS** to move swiftly
SPEEDER	*n* pl. **-S** one that speeds
SPEEDIER	comparative of speedy
SPEEDIEST	superlative of speedy
SPEEDILY	*adv* in a speedy manner
SPEEDING	*n* pl. **-S** the act of driving faster than the law allows
SPEEDO	*n* pl. **SPEEDOS** a speedometer
SPEEDUP	*n* pl. **-S** an acceleration of production without an increase in pay
SPEEDWAY	*n* pl. **-WAYS** a road designed for rapid travel
SPEEDY	*adj* **SPEEDIER, SPEEDIEST** swift
SPEEL	*v* **-ED, -ING, -S** to climb
SPEER	*v* **-ED, -ING, -S** to inquire
SPEERING	*n* pl. **-S** inquiry
SPEIL	*v* **-ED, -ING, -S** to speel

SPEIR	*v* **-ED, -ING, -S** to speer
SPEISE	*n* pl. **-S** speiss
SPEISS	*n* pl. **-ES** a metallic mixture obtained in smelting certain ores
SPELAEAN	*adj* spelean
SPELEAN	*adj* living in caves
SPELL	*v* **SPELLED** or **SPELT, SPELLING, SPELLS** to name or write the letters of in order
SPELLER	*n* pl. **-S** one that spells words
SPELLING	*n* pl. **-S** a sequence of letters composing a word
SPELT	*n* pl. **-S** a variety of wheat
SPELTER	*n* pl. **-S** zinc in the form of ingots
SPELTZ	*n* pl. **-ES** spelt
SPELUNK	*v* **-ED, -ING, -S** to explore caves
SPENCE	*n* pl. **-S** a pantry
SPENCER	*n* pl. **-S** a trysail
SPEND	*v* **SPENT, SPENDING, SPENDS** to pay out
SPENDER	*n* pl. **-S** one that spends
SPENDY	*adj* **SPENDIER, SPENDIEST** expensive
SPENSE	*n* pl. **-S** spence
SPENT	past tense of spend
SPERM	*n* pl. **-S** a male gamete **SPERMIC** *adj*
SPERMARY	*n* pl. **-RIES** an organ in which sperms are formed
SPERMINE	*n* pl. **-S** a chemical compound
SPERMOUS	*adj* resembling or made up of sperms
SPEW	*v* **-ED, -ING, -S** to vomit
SPEWER	*n* pl. **-S** one that spews
SPHAGNUM	*n* pl. **-S** a grayish moss
SPHENE	*n* pl. **-S** a mineral
SPHENIC	*adj* shaped like a wedge
SPHENOID	*n* pl. **-S** a bone of the skull
SPHERAL	*adj* of, pertaining to, or having the form of a sphere
SPHERE	*v* **SPHERED, SPHERING, SPHERES** to form into a sphere (a type of geometric solid)
SPHERIC	*adj* spheral
SPHERICS	*n/pl* the geometry of figures on the surface of a sphere
SPHERIER	comparative of sphery
SPHERIEST	superlative of sphery
SPHERING	present participle of sphere
SPHEROID	*n* pl. **-S** a type of geometric solid
SPHERULE	*n* pl. **-S** a small sphere
SPHERY	*adj* **SPHERIER, SPHERIEST** resembling a sphere
SPHINGES	a pl. of sphinx
SPHINGID	*n* pl. **-S** the hawkmoth
SPHINX	*n* pl. **SPHINXES** or **SPHINGES** a monster in Egyptian mythology
SPHYGMUS	*n* pl. **-ES** the pulse **SPHYGMIC** *adj*
SPHYNX	*n* pl. **-ES** a cat of a breed of hairless cats
SPICA	*n* pl. **-CAS** or **-CAE** an ear of grain **SPICATE, SPICATED** *adj*
SPICCATO	*n* pl. **-TOS** a method of playing a stringed instrument
SPICE	*v* **SPICED, SPICING, SPICES** to season with a spice (an aromatic vegetable substance)
SPICER	*n* pl. **-S** one that spices
SPICERY	*n* pl. **-ERIES** a spicy quality
SPICEY	*adj* **SPICIER, SPICIEST** spicy
SPICIER	comparative of spicy
SPICIEST	superlative of spicy
SPICILY	*adv* in a spicy manner
SPICING	present participle of spice
SPICULA	*n* pl. **-LAE** spicule **SPICULAR** *adj*
SPICULE	*n* pl. **-S** a needlelike structure
SPICULUM	*n* pl. **-LA** spicule
SPICY	*adj* **SPICIER, SPICIEST** containing spices
SPIDER	*v* **-ED, -ING, -S** to move in a scuttling manner
SPIDERY	*adj* **-DERIER, -DERIEST** resembling a spider (a type of arachnid)
SPIED	past tense of spy
SPIEGEL	*n* pl. **-S** a type of cast iron
SPIEL	*v* **-ED, -ING, -S** to talk at length
SPIELER	*n* pl. **-S** one that spiels
SPIER	*v* **-ED, -ING, -S** to speer
SPIES	present 3d person sing. of spy
SPIFF	*v* **-ED, -ING, -S** to make spiffy
SPIFFING	*adj* spiffy
SPIFFY	*v* **-FIED, -FYING, -FIES** to make stylish
SPIFFY	*adj* **-FIER, -FIEST** stylish **SPIFFILY** *adv*

SPIGOT	*n* pl. **-S** a faucet
SPIKE	*v* **SPIKED, SPIKING, SPIKES** to fasten with a spike (a long, thick nail)
SPIKELET	*n* pl. **-S** a type of flower cluster
SPIKER	*n* pl. **-S** one that spikes
SPIKEY	*adj* **SPIKIER, SPIKIEST** spiky
SPIKING	present participle of spike
SPIKY	*adj* **SPIKIER, SPIKIEST** resembling a spike **SPIKILY** *adv*
SPILE	*v* **SPILED, SPILING, SPILES** to stop up with a wooden plug
SPILIKIN	*n* pl. **-S** a strip of wood used in a game
SPILING	*n* pl. **-S** a piling
SPILITE	*n* pl. **-S** a form of basalt **SPILITIC** *adj*
SPILL	*v* **SPILLED** or **SPILT, SPILLING, SPILLS** to cause to run out of a container
SPILLAGE	*n* pl. **-S** something that is spilled
SPILLER	*n* pl. **-S** one that spills
SPILLWAY	*n* pl. **-WAYS** a channel for surplus water in a reservoir
SPILT	a past tense of spill
SPILTH	*n* pl. **-S** spillage
SPIN	*v* **SPUN, SPINNING, SPINS** to draw out and twist into threads
SPINACH	*n* pl. **-ES** a cultivated herb **SPINACHY** *adj*
SPINAGE	*n* pl. **-S** spinach
SPINAL	*n* pl. **-S** an injection of an anesthetic into the spinal cord
SPINALLY	*adv* with respect to the spine
SPINATE	*adj* bearing thorns
SPINDLE	*v* **-DLED, -DLING, -DLES** to impale on a slender rod
SPINDLER	*n* pl. **-S** one that spindles
SPINDLY	*adj* **-DLIER, -DLIEST** long and slender
SPINE	*n* pl. **-S** the vertebral column **SPINED** *adj*
SPINEL	*n* pl. **-S** a mineral
SPINELLE	*n* pl. **-S** spinel
SPINET	*n* pl. **-S** a small piano
SPINIER	comparative of spiny
SPINIEST	superlative of spiny
SPINIFEX	*n* pl. **-ES** an Australian grass
SPINLESS	*adj* having no rotation
SPINNER	*n* pl. **-S** one that spins
SPINNERY	*n* pl. **-NERIES** a spinning mill
SPINNEY	*n* pl. **-NEYS** a thicket
SPINNING	*n* pl. **-S** the act of one that spins
SPINNY	*n* pl. **-NIES** spinney
SPINNY	*adj* **SPINNIER, SPINNIEST** crazy, foolish
SPINOFF	*n* pl. **-S** a new application or incidental result
SPINOR	*n* pl. **-S** a type of mathematical vector
SPINOSE	*adj* spiny
SPINOUS	*adj* spiny
SPINOUT	*n* pl. **-S** a rotational skid by an automobile
SPINSTER	*n* pl. **-S** an unmarried woman who is past the usual age for marrying
SPINTO	*n* pl. **-TOS** a singing voice that is lyric and dramatic
SPINULA	*n* pl. **-LAE** spinule
SPINULE	*n* pl. **-S** a small thorn
SPINY	*adj* **SPINIER, SPINIEST** bearing or covered with thorns
SPIRACLE	*n* pl. **-S** an orifice through which breathing occurs
SPIRAEA	*n* pl. **-S** spirea
SPIRAL	*v* **-RALED, -RALING, -RALS** or **-RALLED, -RALLING, -RALS** to move like a spiral (a type of plane curve)
SPIRALLY	*adv* in a spiral manner
SPIRANT	*n* pl. **-S** a speech sound produced by the forcing of breath through a narrow passage
SPIRE	*v* **SPIRED, SPIRING, SPIRES** to rise in a tapering manner
SPIREA	*n* pl. **-S** a flowering shrub
SPIREM	*n* pl. **-S** spireme
SPIREME	*n* pl. **-S** a filament forming part of a cell nucleus during mitosis
SPIRIER	comparative of spiry
SPIRIEST	superlative of spiry
SPIRILLA	*n/pl* spirally twisted, aerobic bacteria
SPIRING	present participle of spire
SPIRIT	*v* **-ED, -ING, -S** to carry off secretly
SPIRITUS	*n* pl. **SPIRITUS** spirit
SPIROID	*adj* resembling a spiral
SPIRT	*v* **-ED, -ING, -S** to spurt

SPIRULA *n* pl. **-LAS** or **-LAE** a spiral-shelled mollusk

SPIRY *adj* **SPIRIER, SPIRIEST** tall, slender, and tapering

SPIT *v* **SPITTED, SPITTING, SPITS** to impale on a spit (a pointed rod on which meat is turned)

SPITAL *n* pl. **-S** a hospital

SPITBALL *n* pl. **-S** a type of pitch in baseball

SPITE *v* **SPITED, SPITING, SPITES** to treat with malice

SPITEFUL *adj* **-FULLER, -FULLEST** malicious

SPITFIRE *n* pl. **-S** a quick-tempered person

SPITTED past tense of spit

SPITTER *n* pl. **-S** a spitball

SPITTING present participle of spit

SPITTLE *n* pl. **-S** saliva **SPITTLY** *adj*

SPITTOON *n* pl. **-S** a receptacle for saliva

SPITTY *adj* **-TIER, -TIEST** marked with saliva

SPITZ *n* pl. **-ES** a dog having a heavy coat

SPIV *n* pl. **-S** an unscrupulous petty criminal **SPIVVISH** *adj*

SPIVVY *adj* **SPIVVIER, SPIVVIEST** resembling a spiv in dress or conduct

SPLAKE *n* pl. **-S** a freshwater fish

SPLASH *v* **-ED, -ING, -ES** to scatter a liquid about

SPLASHER *n* pl. **-S** one that splashes

SPLASHY *adj* **SPLASHIER, SPLASHIEST** showy

SPLAT *v* **SPLATTED, SPLATTING, SPLATS** to flatten on impact

SPLATTER *v* **-ED, -ING, -S** to spatter

SPLAY *v* **-ED, -ING, -S** to spread out

SPLEEN *n* pl. **-S** a ductless organ of the body

SPLEENY *adj* **SPLEENIER, SPLEENIEST** peevish

SPLENDID *adj* **-DIDER, -DIDEST** magnificent

SPLENDOR *n* pl. **-S** magnificence

SPLENIAL *adj* pertaining to the splenius

SPLENIC *adj* pertaining to the spleen

SPLENIUM *n* pl. **-NIA** or **-NIUMS** a surgical bandage

SPLENIUS *n* pl. **-NII** a muscle of the neck

SPLENT *n* pl. **-S** a splint

SPLICE *v* **SPLICED, SPLICING, SPLICES** to join at the ends

SPLICER *n* pl. **-S** one that splices

SPLIFF *n* pl. **-S** a marijuana cigarette

SPLINE *v* **SPLINED, SPLINING, SPLINES** to provide with a spline (a key that connects two rotating mechanical parts)

SPLINT *v* **-ED, -ING, -S** to brace with a splint (a thin piece of wood)

SPLINTER *v* **-ED, -ING, -S** to split into sharp, slender pieces

SPLIT *v* **SPLIT, SPLITTING, SPLITS** to separate lengthwise

SPLITTER *n* pl. **-S** one that splits

SPLODGE *v* **SPLODGED, SPLODGING, SPLODGES** to splotch

SPLODGY *adj* **SPLODGIER, SPLODGIEST** splotchy

SPLORE *n* pl. **-S** a carousal

SPLOSH *v* **-ED, -ING, -ES** to splash

SPLOTCH *v* **-ED, -ING, -ES** to mark with large, irregular spots

SPLOTCHY *adj* **SPLOTCHIER, SPLOTCHIEST** splotched

SPLURGE *v* **SPLURGED, SPLURGING, SPLURGES** to spend money lavishly

SPLURGER *n* pl. **-S** one that splurges

SPLURGY *adj* **SPLURGIER, SPLURGIEST** tending to splurge

SPLURT *v* **-ED, -ING, -S** to gush forth in a stream or jet

SPLUTTER *v* **-ED, -ING, -S** to speak rapidly and confusedly

SPODE *n* pl. **-S** a fine china

SPODOSOL *n* pl. **-S** an acidic forest soil

SPOIL *v* **SPOILED** or **SPOILT, SPOILING, SPOILS** to impair the value or quality of

SPOILAGE *n* pl. **-S** something that is spoiled or wasted

SPOILER *n* pl. **-S** one that spoils

SPOKE *v* **SPOKED, SPOKING, SPOKES** to provide with spokes (rods that support the rim of a wheel)

SPOKEN past participle of speak

SPOLIATE *v* **-ATED, -ATING, -ATES** to plunder

SPONDAIC *n* pl. **-S** a spondee

SPONDEE *n* pl. **-S** a type of metrical foot

SPONGE   v **SPONGED, SPONGING** or **SPONGEING, SPONGES** to wipe with a sponge (a mass of absorbent material)

SPONGER   n pl. **-S** one that sponges

SPONGIER   comparative of spongy

SPONGIEST   superlative of spongy

SPONGILY   adv in a spongy manner

SPONGIN   n pl. **-S** a fibrous material

SPONGING   present participle of sponge

SPONGY   adj **SPONGIER, SPONGIEST** resembling a sponge

SPONSAL   adj pertaining to marriage

SPONSION   n pl. **-S** the act of sponsoring

SPONSON   n pl. **-S** a projection from the side of a ship

SPONSOR   v **-ED, -ING, -S** to make oneself responsible for

SPONTOON   n pl. **-S** a spear-like weapon

SPOOF   v **-ED, -ING, -S** to ridicule in fun

SPOOFER   n pl. **-S** one that spoofs

SPOOFERY   n pl. **-ERIES** good-natured ridicule

SPOOFY   adj humorously satiric

SPOOK   v **-ED, -ING, -S** to scare

SPOOKERY   n pl. **-ERIES** something spooky

SPOOKISH   adj spooky

SPOOKY   adj **SPOOKIER, SPOOKIEST** scary **SPOOKILY** adv

SPOOL   v **-ED, -ING, -S** to wind on a small cylinder

SPOOLER   n pl. **-S** one that spools

SPOOLING   n pl. **-S** the temporary storage of data for later output

SPOON   v **-ED, -ING, -S** to take up with a spoon (a type of eating utensil)

SPOONER   n pl. **-S** one that behaves in an amorous way

SPOONEY   adj **SPOONIER, SPOONIEST** spoony

SPOONEY   n pl. **-EYS** a spoony

SPOONFUL   n pl. **SPOONFULS** or **SPOONSFUL** as much as a spoon can hold

SPOONSFUL   a pl. of spoonful

SPOONY   adj **SPOONIER, SPOONIEST** overly sentimental **SPOONILY** adv

SPOONY   n pl. **SPOONIES** a spoony person

SPOOR   v **-ED, -ING, -S** to track an animal

SPOORER   n pl. **-S** one that spoors

SPORADIC   adj occurring at irregular intervals

SPORAL   adj of, pertaining to, or resembling a spore

SPORE   v **SPORED, SPORING, SPORES** to produce spores (asexual, usually single-celled reproductive bodies)

SPOROID   adj resembling a spore

SPOROZOA   n/pl parasitic one-celled animals

SPORRAN   n pl. **-S** a large purse worn by Scottish Highlanders

SPORT   v **-ED, -ING, -S** to frolic

SPORTER   n pl. **-S** one that sports

SPORTFUL   adj sportive

SPORTIF   n pl. **-S** a person who is active or interested in physical competitions

SPORTIVE   adj playful

SPORTY   adj **SPORTIER, SPORTIEST** showy **SPORTILY** adv

SPORULE   n pl. **-S** a small spore **SPORULAR** adj

SPOT   v **SPOTTED, SPOTTING, SPOTS** to mark with spots (small, roundish discolorations)

SPOTLESS   adj perfectly clean

SPOTLIT   a past tense of spotlight

SPOTTER   n pl. **-S** one that spots

SPOTTING   n pl. **-S** the practice of watching for examples of something

SPOTTY   adj **-TIER, -TIEST** marked with spots **SPOTTILY** adv

SPOUSAL   n pl. **-S** marriage

SPOUSE   v **SPOUSED, SPOUSING, SPOUSES** to marry

SPOUT   v **-ED, -ING, -S** to eject in a rapid stream

SPOUTER   n pl. **-S** one that spouts

SPOUTING   n pl. **-S** a channel for draining off water from a roof

SPRADDLE   v **-DLED, -DLING, -DLES** to straddle

SPRAG   n pl. **-S** a device used to prevent a vehicle from rolling backward

SPRAIN   v **-ED, -ING, -S** to weaken by a sudden and violent twisting or wrenching

SPRANG   n pl. **-S** a weaving technique to form an openwork mesh

SPRAT   n pl. **-S** a small herring

SPRATTLE   v **-TLED, -TLING, -TLES** to struggle

SPRAWL *v* **-ED, -ING, -S** to stretch out ungracefully

SPRAWLER *n* pl. **-S** one that sprawls

SPRAWLY *adj* **SPRAWLIER, SPRAWLIEST** tending to sprawl

SPRAY *v* **-ED, -ING, -S** to disperse in fine particles

SPRAYER *n* pl. **-S** one that sprays

SPREAD *v* **SPREAD, SPREADING, SPREADS** to open or expand over a larger area

SPREADER *n* pl. **-S** one that spreads

SPREE *n* pl. **-S** an unrestrained indulgence in an activity

SPRENT *adj* sprinkled over

SPRIER a comparative of spry

SPRIEST a superlative of spry

SPRIG *v* **SPRIGGED, SPRIGGING, SPRIGS** to fasten with small, thin nails

SPRIGGER *n* pl. **-S** one that sprigs

SPRIGGY *adj* **-GIER, -GIEST** having small branches

SPRIGHT *n* pl. **-S** sprite

SPRING *v* **SPRANG** or **SPRUNG, SPRINGING, SPRINGS** to move upward suddenly and swiftly

SPRINGAL *n* pl. **-S** a young man

SPRINGE *v* **SPRINGED, SPRINGEING, SPRINGES** to catch with a type of snare

SPRINGER *n* pl. **-S** one that springs

SPRINGY *adj* **SPRINGIER, SPRINGIEST** resilient

SPRINKLE *v* **-KLED, -KLING, -KLES** to scatter drops or particles on

SPRINT *v* **-ED, -ING, -S** to run at top speed

SPRINTER *n* pl. **-S** one that sprints

SPRIT *n* pl. **-S** a ship's spar

SPRITE *n* pl. **-S** an elf or fairy

SPRITELY *adj* **-LIER, -LIEST** full of energy

SPRITZ *v* **-ED, -ING, -ES** to spray

SPRITZER *n* pl. **-S** a beverage of white wine and soda water

SPRITZY *adj* **SPRITZIER, SPRITZIEST** emitting a spray

SPROCKET *n* pl. **-S** a toothlike projection that engages with the links of a chain

SPROG *n* pl. **-S** a small child

SPROGLET *n* pl. **-S** a sprog

SPROUT *v* **-ED, -ING, -S** to begin to grow

SPRUCE *adj* **SPRUCER, SPRUCEST** neat and trim in appearance **SPRUCELY** *adv*

SPRUCE *v* **SPRUCED, SPRUCING, SPRUCES** to make spruce

SPRUCY *adj* **SPRUCIER, SPRUCIEST** spruce

SPRUE *n* pl. **-S** a tropical disease

SPRUG *n* pl. **-S** a sparrow

SPRUNG a past tense of spring

SPRY *adj* **SPRYER, SPRYEST** or **SPRIER, SPRIEST** nimble **SPRYLY** *adv*

SPRYNESS *n* pl. **-ES** the quality or state of being spry

SPUD *v* **SPUDDED, SPUDDING, SPUDS** to remove with a spade-like tool

SPUDDER *n* pl. **-S** a tool for removing bark from trees

SPUDGEL *n* pl. **-S** a bucket attached to a long pole

SPUE *v* **SPUED, SPUING, SPUES** to spew

SPUMANTE *n* pl. **-S** an Italian sparkling wine

SPUME *v* **SPUMED, SPUMING, SPUMES** to foam

SPUMIER comparative of spumy

SPUMIEST superlative of spumy

SPUMING present participle of spume

SPUMONE *n* pl. **-S** an Italian ice cream

SPUMONI *n* pl. **-S** spumone

SPUMOUS *adj* spumy

SPUMY *adj* **SPUMIER, SPUMIEST** foamy

SPUN past tense of spin

SPUNK *v* **-ED, -ING, -S** to begin to burn

SPUNKIE *n* pl. **-S** a light caused by the combustion of marsh gas

SPUNKY *adj* **SPUNKIER, SPUNKIEST** plucky **SPUNKILY** *adv*

SPUR *v* **SPURRED, SPURRING, SPURS** to urge on with a spur (a horseman's goad)

SPURGALL *v* **-ED, -ING, -S** to injure with a spur

SPURGE *n* pl. **-S** a tropical plant

SPURIOUS *adj* not genuine

SPURLESS *adj* lacking a spur

SPURN *v* **-ED, -ING, -S** to reject with contempt

SPURNER *n* pl. **-S** one that spurns

SPURRED	past tense of spur
SPURRER	*n* pl. **-S** one that spurs
SPURREY	*n* pl. **-REYS** spurry
SPURRIER	*n* pl. **-S** one that makes spurs
SPURRING	present participle of spur
SPURRY	*n* pl. **-RIES** a European weed
SPURT	*v* **-ED, -ING, -S** to gush forth
SPURTER	*n* pl. **-S** one that spurts
SPURTLE	*n* pl. **-S** a stick for stirring porridge
SPUTNIK	*n* pl. **-S** a Soviet artificial earth satellite
SPUTTER	*v* **-ED, -ING, -S** to eject particles in short bursts
SPUTTERY	*adj* ejecting in short bursts
SPUTUM	*n* pl. **-TA** or **-S** saliva
SPY	*v* **SPIED, SPYING, SPIES** to watch secretly
SPYGLASS	*n* pl. **-ES** a small telescope
SPYWARE	*n* pl. **-S** computer software by which personal information is covertly sent to another computer
SQUAB	*n* pl. **-S** a young pigeon
SQUABBLE	*v* **-BLED, -BLING, -BLES** to quarrel
SQUABBY	*adj* **-BIER, -BIEST** short and fat
SQUAD	*v* **SQUADDED, SQUADDING, SQUADS** to form into squads (small organized groups)
SQUADDIE	*n* pl. **-S** a military recruit
SQUADDY	*n* pl. **-DIES** squaddie
SQUADRON	*v* **-ED, -ING, -S** to arrange in squadrons (units of military organization)
SQUALENE	*n* pl. **-S** a chemical compound
SQUALID	*adj* **-IDER, -IDEST** marked by filthiness caused by neglect or poverty
SQUALL	*v* **-ED, -ING, -S** to cry or scream loudly
SQUALLER	*n* pl. **-S** one that squalls
SQUALLY	*adj* **SQUALLIER, SQUALLIEST** gusty
SQUALOR	*n* pl. **-S** the quality or state of being squalid
SQUAMA	*n* pl. **-MAE** a scale **SQUAMOSE, SQUAMOUS** *adj*
SQUAMATE	*n* pl. **-S** any of an order of reptiles
SQUANDER	*v* **-ED, -ING, -S** to spend wastefully
SQUARE	*adj* **SQUARER, SQUAREST** having four equal sides and four right angles; rigidly conventional
SQUARE	*v* **SQUARED, SQUARING, SQUARES** to make square
SQUARELY	*adv* in a straightforward and honest manner
SQUARER	*n* pl. **-S** one that squares
SQUAREST	superlative of square
SQUARING	present participle of square
SQUARISH	*adj* somewhat square
SQUARK	*n* pl. **-S** the hypothetical boson analogue of a quark
SQUASH	*v* **-ED, -ING, -ES** to press into a pulp or flat mass
SQUASHER	*n* pl. **-S** one that squashes
SQUASHY	*adj* **SQUASHIER, SQUASHIEST** soft and moist
SQUAT	*adj* **SQUATTER, SQUATTEST** short and thick **SQUATLY** *adv*
SQUAT	*v* **SQUATTED, SQUATTING, SQUATS** to bend one's knees and sit on one's heels
SQUATTER	*v* **-ED, -ING, -S** to move through water
SQUATTY	*adj* **-TIER, -TIEST** squat
SQUAWK	*v* **-ED, -ING, -S** to utter a loud, harsh cry
SQUAWKER	*n* pl. **-S** one that squawks
SQUEAK	*v* **-ED, -ING, -S** to make a sharp, high-pitched sound
SQUEAKER	*n* pl. **-S** one that squeaks
SQUEAKY	*adj* **SQUEAKIER, SQUEAKIEST** tending to squeak
SQUEAL	*v* **-ED, -ING, -S** to utter a sharp, shrill cry
SQUEALER	*n* pl. **-S** one that squeals
SQUEEGEE	*v* **-GEED, -GEEING, -GEES** to wipe with a squeegee (an implement for removing water from a surface)
SQUEEZE	*v* **SQUEEZED, SQUEEZING, SQUEEZES** to press hard upon
SQUEEZER	*n* pl. **-S** one that squeezes
SQUEG	*v* **SQUEGGED, SQUEGGING, SQUEGS** to oscillate in an irregular manner
SQUELCH	*v* **-ED, -ING, -ES** to squash
SQUELCHY	*adj* **SQUELCHIER, SQUELCHIEST** squashy
SQUIB	*v* **SQUIBBED, SQUIBBING, SQUIBS** to lampoon

SQUIBBER *n pl.* **-S** an infield grounder that becomes a base hit

SQUID *v* **SQUIDDED, SQUIDDING, SQUIDS** to fish for squid (ten-armed marine mollusks)

SQUIDGY *adj* **SQUIDGIER, SQUIDGIEST** squashy, soggy

SQUIFFED *adj* drunk

SQUIFFY *adj* **-FIER, -FIEST** squiffed

SQUIGGLE *v* **-GLED, -GLING, -GLES** to wriggle

SQUIGGLY *adj* **-GLIER, -GLIEST** wriggly

SQUILGEE *v* **-GEED, -GEEING, -GEES** to squeegee

SQUILL *n pl.* **-S** a Eurasian herb

SQUILLA *n pl.* **-LAS** or **-LAE** a burrowing crustacean

SQUINCH *v* **-ED, -ING, -ES** to squint

SQUINNY *adj* **-NIER, -NIEST** squinty

SQUINNY *v* **-NIED, -NYING, -NIES** to squint

SQUINT *adj* **SQUINTER, SQUINTEST** cross-eyed

SQUINT *v* **-ED, -ING, -S** to look with the eyes partly closed

SQUINTER *n pl.* **-S** one that squints

SQUINTY *adj* **SQUINTIER, SQUINTIEST** marked by squinting

SQUIRE *v* **SQUIRED, SQUIRING, SQUIRES** to serve as a squire (an escort)

SQUIREEN *n pl.* **-S** an owner of a small estate

SQUIRELY *adj* of or befitting a squire

SQUIRISH *adj* of, resembling, or befitting a squire

SQUIRL *n pl.* **-S** an ornamental curve in handwriting

SQUIRM *v* **-ED, -ING, -S** to wriggle

SQUIRMER *n pl.* **-S** one that squirms

SQUIRMY *adj* **SQUIRMIER, SQUIRMIEST** wriggly

SQUIRREL *v* **-RELED, -RELING, -RELS** or **-RELLED, -RELLING, -RELS** to store up for future use

SQUIRT *v* **-ED, -ING, -S** to eject in a thin, swift stream

SQUIRTER *n pl.* **-S** one that squirts

SQUISH *v* **-ED, -ING, -ES** to squash

SQUISHY *adj* **SQUISHIER, SQUISHIEST** squashy

SQUITTERS *n/pl* diarrhea

SQUOOSH *v* **-ED, -ING, -ES** to squash

SQUOOSHY *adj* **SQUOOSHIER, SQUOOSHIEST** squashy

SQUUSH *v* **-ED, -ING, -ES** to squash

SRADDHA *n pl.* **-S** sradha

SRADHA *n pl.* **-S** a Hindu ceremonial offering

SRI *n pl.* **-S** mister; sir — used as a Hindu title of respect

SRIRACHA *n pl.* **-S** a spicy pepper sauce

STAB *v* **STABBED, STABBING, STABS** to pierce with a pointed weapon

STABBER *n pl.* **-S** one that stabs

STABBING *n pl.* **-S** the act of piercing someone with a pointed weapon

STABILE *n pl.* **-S** a stationary abstract sculpture

STABLE *adj* **-BLER, -BLEST** resistant to sudden change or position or condition

STABLE *v* **-BLED, -BLING, -BLES** to put in a stable (a shelter for domestic animals)

STABLER *n pl.* **-S** one that keeps a stable

STABLING *n pl.* **-S** accommodation for animals in a stable

STABLISH *v* **-ED, -ING, -ES** to establish

STABLY *adv* in a stable manner

STACCATO *n pl.* **-TOS** or **-TI** a musical passage marked by the short, clear-cut playing of tones

STACK *v* **-ED, -ING, -S** to pile

STACKER *n pl.* **-S** one that stacks

STACKUP *n pl.* **-S** an arrangement of circling airplanes over an airport waiting to land

STACTE *n pl.* **-S** a spice used by the ancient Jews in making incense

STADDLE *n pl.* **-S** a platform on which hay is stacked

STADE *n pl.* **-S** an ancient Greek unit of length

STADIA *n pl.* **-S** a method of surveying distances

STADIUM *n pl.* **-S** a structure in which athletic events are held

STAFF *v* **-ED, -ING, -S** to provide with a staff (a body of assistants)

STAFFER *n pl.* **-S** a member of a staff

STAFFING *n pl.* **-S** the providing with a staff

STAG   v **STAGGED, STAGGING, STAGS** to attend a social function without a female companion

STAGE   v **STAGED, STAGING, STAGES** to produce for public view

STAGEFUL   n pl. **-S** as much or as many as a stage can hold

STAGER   n pl. **-S** an experienced person

STAGETTE   n pl. **-S** an all-female party for a woman about to be married

STAGEY   adj **STAGIER, STAGIEST** stagy

STAGGARD   n pl. **-S** a full-grown male red deer

STAGGART   n pl. **-S** staggard

STAGGED   past tense of stag

STAGGER   v **-ED, -ING, -S** to walk or stand unsteadily

STAGGERY   adj unsteady

STAGGIE   n pl. **-S** a colt

STAGGING   present participle of stag

STAGGY   adj **-GIER, -GIEST** having the appearance of a mature male

STAGHORN   n pl. **-S** a stag's horn used for a knife handle

STAGIER   comparative of stagey and stagy

STAGIEST   superlative of stagey and stagy

STAGILY   adv in a stagy manner

STAGING   n pl. **-S** a temporary platform

STAGNANT   adj not moving or flowing

STAGNATE   v **-NATED, -NATING, -NATES** to become stagnant

STAGY   adj **STAGIER, STAGIEST** having a theatrical quality

STAID   adj **STAIDER, STAIDEST** sober and sedate **STAIDLY** adv

STAIG   n pl. **-S** a colt

STAIN   v **-ED, -ING, -S** to discolor or dirty

STAINER   n pl. **-S** one that stains

STAIR   n pl. **-S** a rest for the foot used in going from one level to another

STAIRWAY   n pl. **-WAYS** a flight of stairs

STAITHE   n pl. **-S** a wharf equipped for transferring coal from railroad cars into ships

STAKE   v **STAKED, STAKING, STAKES** to fasten with a stake (a pointed piece of wood or metal)

STAKEOUT   n pl. **-S** a surveillance of an area especially by the police

STAKER   n pl. **-S** one that marks off an area with stakes

STALAG   n pl. **-S** a German prisoner-of-war camp

STALE   adj **STALER, STALEST** not fresh **STALELY** adv

STALE   v **STALED, STALING, STALES** to become stale

STALK   v **-ED, -ING, -S** to pursue stealthily

STALKER   n pl. **-S** one that stalks

STALKING   n pl. **-S** the act of one that stalks

STALKY   adj **STALKIER, STALKIEST** long and slender **STALKILY** adv

STALL   v **-ED, -ING, -S** to stop the progress of

STALLION   n pl. **-S** an uncastrated male horse

STALWART   n pl. **-S** an unwavering partisan

STAMEN   n pl. **-S** the pollen-bearing organ of flowering plants **STAMENED** adj

STAMINA   n pl. **-S** endurance **STAMINAL** adj

STAMMEL   n pl. **-S** a red color

STAMMER   v **-ED, -ING, -S** to speak with involuntary breaks and pauses

STAMP   v **-ED, -ING, -S** to bring the foot down heavily

STAMPEDE   v **-PEDED, -PEDING, -PEDES** to cause to run away in headlong panic

STAMPER   n pl. **-S** one that stamps

STANCE   n pl. **-S** a manner of standing

STANCH   adj **STANCHER, STANCHEST** staunch

STANCH   v **-ED, -ING, -ES** to stop the flow of blood from

STANCHER   n pl. **-S** one that stanches

STANCHLY   adv in a stanch manner

STAND   v **STOOD, STANDING, STANDS** to assume or maintain an upright position

STANDARD   n pl. **-S** an established measure of comparison

STANDBY   n pl. **-BYS** one that can be relied on

STANDEE   n pl. **-S** one who stands because of the lack of seats

STANDER   n pl. **-S** one that stands

STANDING   n pl. **-S** a position or condition in society

STANDISH   n pl. **-ES** a receptacle for pens and ink

STANDOFF   n pl. **-S** a tie or draw, as in a game

STANDOUT   n pl. **-S** one that shows marked superiority

STANDPAT	*adj* resisting or opposing change
STANDUP	*n* pl. **-S** a comic monologue by a performer alone on a stage
STANE	*v* **STANED, STANING, STANES** to stone
STANG	*v* **-ED, -ING, -S** to sting
STANHOPE	*n* pl. **-S** a light, open carriage
STANINE	*n* pl. **-S** one of the nine classes into which a set of scores are divided
STANING	present participle of stane
STANK	*n* pl. **-S** a pond
STANNARY	*n* pl. **-RIES** a tin-mining region
STANNIC	*adj* pertaining to tin
STANNITE	*n* pl. **-S** an ore of tin
STANNOUS	*adj* pertaining to tin
STANNUM	*n* pl. **-S** tin
STANOL	*n* pl. **-S** a fully saturated phytosterol
STANZA	*n* pl. **-S** a division of a poem **STANZAED, STANZAIC** *adj*
STAPEDES	pl. of stapes
STAPELIA	*n* pl. **-S** an African plant
STAPES	*n* pl. **-PEDES** a bone of the middle ear
STAPH	*n* pl. **-S** any of various spherical bacteria
STAPLE	*v* **-PLED, -PLING, -PLES** to fasten by means of a U-shaped metal loop
STAPLER	*n* pl. **-S** a stapling device
STAR	*v* **STARRED, STARRING, STARS** to shine as a star (a natural luminous body visible in the sky)
STARCH	*v* **-ED, -ING, -ES** to treat with starch (a solid carbohydrate)
STARCHER	*n* pl. **-S** one that starches
STARCHY	*adj* **STARCHIER, STARCHIEST** containing starch
STARDOM	*n* pl. **-S** the status of a preeminent performer
STARDUST	*n* pl. **-S** a romantic quality
STARE	*v* **STARED, STARING, STARES** to gaze fixedly
STARER	*n* pl. **-S** one that stares
STARETS	*n* pl. **STARTSY** a spiritual adviser in the Eastern Orthodox Church
STARFISH	*n* pl. **-ES** a star-shaped marine animal
STARGAZE	*v* **-GAZED, -GAZING, -GAZES** to gaze at the stars
STARING	present participle of stare
STARK	*adj* **STARKER, STARKEST** harsh in appearance **STARKLY** *adv*
STARKERS	*adj* naked
STARLESS	*adj* having no stars
STARLET	*n* pl. **-S** a small star
STARLIKE	*adj* resembling a star
STARLING	*n* pl. **-S** a European bird
STARLIT	*adj* lighted by the stars
STARNOSE	*n* pl. **-S** a burrowing mammal
STARRED	past tense of star
STARRING	present participle of star
STARRY	*adj* **-RIER, -RIEST** abounding with stars **STARRILY** *adv*
STARSHIP	*n* pl. **-S** a spaceship for interstellar travel
START	*v* **-ED, -ING, -S** to set out
STARTER	*n* pl. **-S** one that starts
STARTLE	*v* **-TLED, -TLING, -TLES** to frighten or surprise suddenly
STARTLER	*n* pl. **-S** one that startles
STARTSY	pl. of starets
STARTUP	*n* pl. **-S** the act of starting something
STARVE	*v* **STARVED, STARVING, STARVES** to die from lack of food
STARVER	*n* pl. **-S** one that starves
STARWORT	*n* pl. **-S** a flowering plant
STASES	pl. of stasis
STASH	*v* **-ED, -ING, -ES** to store in a secret place
STASIMON	*n* pl. **-MA** a choral ode in ancient Greek drama
STASIS	*n* pl. **STASES** a stoppage of the normal flow of bodily fluids
STAT	*n* pl. **-S** a statistic
STATABLE	*adj* capable of being stated
STATAL	*adj* pertaining to a national government
STATANT	*adj* standing with all feet on the ground — used of a heraldic animal
STATE	*v* **STATED, STATING, STATES** to set forth in words
STATEDLY	*adv* regularly
STATELET	*n* pl. **-S** a small state (a political community)
STATELY	*adj* **-LIER, -LIEST** dignified
STATER	*n* pl. **-S** one that states

STATIC *n* pl. **-S** random noise produced in a radio or television receiver **STATICAL** *adj*

STATICE *n* pl. **-S** a flowering plant

STATICKY *adj* marked by static

STATIN *n* pl. **-S** any of a class of drugs that reduce serum cholesterol levels

STATING present participle of state

STATION *v* **-ED, -ING, -S** to assign to a position

STATISM *n* pl. **-S** a theory of government

STATIST *n* pl. **-S** an adherent of statism

STATIVE *n* pl. **-S** a verb that expresses a condition

STATOR *n* pl. **-S** the part of a machine about which the rotor revolves

STATUARY *n* pl. **-ARIES** a group of statues

STATUE *n* pl. **-S** a three-dimensional work of art **STATUED** *adj*

STATURE *n* pl. **-S** the natural height of a human or animal body **STATURED** *adj*

STATUS *n* pl. **-ES** relative position

STATUSY *adj* conferring prestige

STATUTE *n* pl. **-S** a law enacted by the legislative branch of a government

STAUMREL *n* pl. **-S** a dolt

STAUNCH *adj* **STAUNCHER, STAUNCHEST** firm and dependable

STAUNCH *v* **-ED, -ING, -ES** to stanch

STAVE *v* **STAVED** or **STOVE, STAVING, STAVES** to drive or thrust away

STAW a past tense of steal

STAY *v* **STAYED** or **STAID, STAYING, STAYS** to continue in a place or condition

STAYER *n* pl. **-S** one that stays

STAYSAIL *n* pl. **-S** a type of sail

STEAD *v* **-ED, -ING, -S** to be of advantage to

STEADIED past tense of steady

STEADIER *n* pl. **-S** one that steadies

STEADING *n* pl. **-S** a small farm

STEADY *adj* **STEADIER, STEADIEST** firm in position **STEADILY** *adv*

STEADY *v* **STEADIED, STEADYING, STEADIES** to make steady

STEAK *n* pl. **-S** a slice of meat

STEAL *v* **STOLE** or **STAW, STOLEN, STEALING, STEALS** to take without right or permission

STEALAGE *n* pl. **-S** theft

STEALER *n* pl. **-S** one that steals

STEALING *n* pl. **-S** the act of one that steals

STEALTH *n* pl. **-S** stealthy procedure

STEALTHY *adj* **STEALTHIER, STEALTHIEST** intended to escape observation

STEAM *v* **-ED, -ING, -S** to expose to steam (water in the form of vapor)

STEAMER *v* **-ED, -ING, -S** to travel by steamship

STEAMIE *n* pl. **-S** a steamed hot dog

STEAMY *adj* **STEAMIER, STEAMIEST** marked by steam **STEAMILY** *adv*

STEAPSIN *n* pl. **-S** an enzyme

STEARATE *n* pl. **-S** a chemical salt

STEARIN *n* pl. **-S** the solid portion of a fat **STEARIC** *adj*

STEARINE *n* pl. **-S** stearin

STEATITE *n* pl. **-S** a variety of talc

STEDFAST *adj* staunch

STEED *n* pl. **-S** a horse

STEEK *v* **-ED, -ING, -S** to shut

STEEL *v* **-ED, -ING, -S** to cover with steel (a tough iron alloy)

STEELIE *n* pl. **-S** a steel playing marble

STEELY *adj* **STEELIER, STEELIEST** resembling steel

STEENBOK *n* pl. **-S** an African antelope

STEEP *adj* **STEEPER, STEEPEST** inclined sharply

STEEP *v* **-ED, -ING, -S** to soak in a liquid

STEEPEN *v* **-ED, -ING, -S** to make steep

STEEPER *n* pl. **-S** one that steeps

STEEPISH *adj* somewhat steep

STEEPLE *n* pl. **-S** a tapering structure on a church tower

STEEPLE *v* **-PLED, -PLING, -PLES** to place the fingers or hands in the form of a steeple

STEEPLY *adv* in a steep manner

STEER *v* **-ED, -ING, -S** to direct the course of

STEERAGE *n* pl. **-S** the act of steering

STEERER *n* pl. **-S** one that steers

STEERING *n* pl. **-S** the act of directing the course of a vehicle or vessel

STEEVE   v **STEEVED, STEEVING, STEEVES** to stow in the hold of a ship

STEEVING   n pl. **-S** the angular elevation of a bowsprit from a ship's keel

STEGODON   n pl. **-S** an extinct elephant-like mammal

STEIN   n pl. **-S** a beer mug

STEINBOK   n pl. **-S** steenbok

STELA   n pl. **-LAE** or **-LAI** an inscribed slab used as a monument **STELAR, STELENE** adj

STELE   n pl. **-S** the central portion of vascular tissue in a plant stem **STELIC** adj

STELLA   n pl. **-S** a formerly used coin of the United States

STELLAR   adj pertaining to the stars

STELLATE   adj shaped like a star

STELLIFY   v **-FIED, -FYING, -FIES** to convert into a star

STEM   v **STEMMED, STEMMING, STEMS** to remove stems (ascending axes of a plant) from

STEMLESS   adj having no stem

STEMLIKE   adj resembling a stem

STEMMA   n pl. **-MAS** or **-MATA** a scroll recording the genealogy of a family in ancient Rome

STEMMED   past tense of stem

STEMMER   n pl. **-S** one that removes stems

STEMMERY   n pl. **-MERIES** a place where tobacco leaves are stripped

STEMMING   present participle of stem

STEMMY   adj **-MIER, -MIEST** abounding in stems

STEMSON   n pl. **-S** a supporting timber of a ship

STEMWARE   n pl. **-S** a type of glassware

STENCH   n pl. **-ES** a foul odor

STENCHY   adj **STENCHIER, STENCHIEST** having a stench

STENCIL   v **-CILED, -CILING, -CILS** or **-CILLED, -CILLING, -CILS** to mark by means of a perforated sheet of material

STENGAH   n pl. **-S** a mixed drink

STENO   n pl. **STENOS** a stenographer

STENOKY   n pl. **-KIES** the ability of an organism to live only under a narrow range of conditions

STENOSED   adj affected with stenosis

STENOSIS   n pl. **-NOSES** a narrowing of a bodily passage **STENOTIC** adj

STENT   n pl. **-S** a tubular device inserted into a blood vessel

STENTOR   n pl. **-S** a person having a very loud voice

STEP   v **STEPPED, STEPPING, STEPS** to move by lifting the foot and setting it down in another place

STEPDAD   n pl. **-S** a stepfather

STEPDAME   n pl. **-S** a stepmother

STEPLESS   adj lacking steps (structures for passing from one level to the next)

STEPLIKE   adj resembling a stair

STEPMOM   n pl. **-S** a stepmother

STEPPE   n pl. **-S** a vast treeless plain

STEPPED   past tense of step

STEPPER   n pl. **-S** one that steps

STEPPING   present participle of step

STEPSON   n pl. **-S** a son of one's spouse by a former marriage

STEPWISE   adj marked by a gradual progression

STERANE   n pl. **-S** a chemical compound

STERE   n pl. **-S** a unit of volume

STEREO   v **-ED, -ING, -S** to make a type of printing plate

STERIC   adj pertaining to the spatial relationships of atoms in a molecule

STERICAL   adj steric

STERIGMA   n pl. **-MAS** or **-MATA** a spore-bearing stalk of certain fungi

STERILE   adj incapable of producing offspring

STERLET   n pl. **-S** a small sturgeon

STERLING   n pl. **-S** British money

STERN   adj **STERNER, STERNEST** unyielding

STERN   n pl. **-S** the rear part of a ship **STERNED** adj

STERNA   a pl. of sternum

STERNAL   adj pertaining to the sternum

STERNITE   n pl. **-S** a somitic sclerite

STERNLY   adv in a stern manner

STERNSON   n pl. **-S** a reinforcing post of a ship

STERNUM   n pl. **-NUMS** or **-NA** a long, flat supporting bone of most vertebrates

STERNWAY *n* pl. **-WAYS** the backward movement of a vessel

STEROID *n* pl. **-S** a type of chemical compound

STEROL *n* pl. **-S** a type of solid alcohol

STERTOR *n* pl. **-S** a deep snoring sound

STET *v* **STETTED, STETTING, STETS** to cancel a previously made printing correction

STEVIA *n* pl. **-S** a South American herb with sweet-tasting leaves

STEW *v* **-ED, -ING, -S** to cook by boiling slowly **STEWABLE** *adj*

STEWARD *v* **-ED, -ING, -S** to manage

STEWBUM *n* pl. **-S** a drunken bum (a vagrant)

STEWPAN *n* pl. **-S** a pan used for stewing

STEWPOT *n* pl. **-S** a large pot for stewing

STEWY *adj* having the characteristics of a stew (food cooked by stewing)

STEY *adj* steep

STHENIA *n* pl. **-S** excessive energy **STHENIC** *adj*

STIBIAL *adj* pertaining to stibium

STIBINE *n* pl. **-S** a poisonous gas

STIBIUM *n* pl. **-S** antimony

STIBNITE *n* pl. **-S** an ore of antimony

STICH *n* pl. **-S** a line of poetry **STICHIC** *adj*

STICK *v* **-ED, -ING, -S** to support with slender pieces of wood

STICK *v* **STUCK, STICKING, STICKS** to pierce with a pointed object

STICKER *n* pl. **-S** an adhesive label **STICKERED** *adj*

STICKFUL *n* pl. **-S** an amount of set type

STICKIE *n* pl. **-S** sticky

STICKIER comparative of sticky

STICKIES pl. of sticky

STICKIEST superlative of sticky

STICKILY *adv* in a sticky manner

STICKIT *adj* unsuccessful

STICKLE *v* **-LED, -LING, -LES** to argue stubbornly

STICKLER *n* pl. **-S** one that stickles

STICKMAN *n* pl. **-MEN** one who supervises the play at a dice table

STICKOUT *n* pl. **-S** one that is conspicuous

STICKPIN *n* pl. **-S** a decorative tiepin

STICKUM *n* pl. **-S** a substance that causes adhesion

STICKUP *n* pl. **-S** a robbery at gunpoint

STICKY *n* pl. **STICKIES** a slip of notepaper having an adhesive strip on the back

STICKY *adj* **STICKIER, STICKIEST** tending to adhere

STICTION *n* pl. **-S** the force required to begin to move a body that is in contact with another body

STIED a past tense of sty

STIES present 3d person sing. of sty

STIFF *adj* **STIFFER, STIFFEST** difficult to bend or stretch

STIFF *v* **-ED, -ING, -S** to cheat someone by not paying

STIFFEN *v* **-ED, -ING, -S** to make stiff

STIFFISH *adj* somewhat stiff

STIFFLY *adv* in a stiff manner

STIFLE *v* **-FLED, -FLING, -FLES** to smother

STIFLER *n* pl. **-S** one that stifles

STIGMA *n* pl. **-MAS** or **-MATA** a mark of disgrace **STIGMAL** *adj*

STILBENE *n* pl. **-S** a chemical compound

STILBITE *n* pl. **-S** a mineral

STILE *n* pl. **-S** a series of steps for passing over a fence or wall

STILETTO *v* **-ED, -ING, -S** or **-ES** to stab with a stiletto (a short dagger)

STILL *adj* **STILLER, STILLEST** free from sound or motion

STILL *v* **-ED, -ING, -S** to make still

STILLAGE *n* pl. **-S** a low platform on which to keep goods off the floor

STILLMAN *n* pl. **-MEN** one who operates a distillery

STILLSON *n* pl. **-S** a large wrench (a tool for gripping and turning)

STILLY *adj* **STILLIER, STILLIEST** still

STILT *v* **-ED, -ING, -S** to raise on stilts (long, slender poles)

STIME *n* pl. **-S** a glimpse

STIMULUS *n* pl. **-LI** something that causes a response

STIMY *v* **-MIED, -MYING, -MIES** to stymie

STING *v* **STUNG, STINGING, STINGS** to prick painfully

STINGE *n* pl. **-S** a mean or stingy person

STINGER   *n* pl. **-S** one that stings

STINGIER   comparative of stingy

STINGIEST   superlative of stingy

STINGILY   *adv* in a stingy manner

STINGO   *n* pl. **-GOS** a strong ale or beer

STINGRAY   *n* pl. **-RAYS** a flat-bodied marine fish

STINGY   *adj* **-GIER, -GIEST** unwilling to spend or give

STINK   *v* **STANK** or **STUNK, STINKING, STINKS** to emit a foul odor

STINKARD   *n* pl. **-S** a despicable person

STINKBUG   *n* pl. **-S** an insect that emits a foul odor

STINKER   *n* pl. **-S** one that stinks

STINKO   *adj* drunk

STINKPOT   *n* pl. **-S** a jar containing foul-smelling combustibles formerly used in warfare

STINKY   *adj* **STINKIER, STINKIEST** emitting a foul odor

STINT   *v* **-ED, -ING, -S** to limit

STINTER   *n* pl. **-S** one that stints

STIPE   *n* pl. **-S** a slender supporting part of a plant **STIPED** *adj*

STIPEL   *n* pl. **-S** a small stipule

STIPEND   *n* pl. **-S** a fixed sum of money paid periodically

STIPES   *n* pl. **STIPITES** a stipe

STIPPLE   *v* **-PLED, -PLING, -PLES** to draw, paint, or engrave by means of dots or short touches

STIPPLER   *n* pl. **-S** one that stipples

STIPULE   *n* pl. **-S** an appendage at the base of a leaf in certain plants **STIPULAR, STIPULED** *adj*

STIR   *v* **STIRRED, STIRRING, STIRS** to pass an implement through in circular motions

STIRK   *n* pl. **-S** a young cow

STIRP   *n* pl. **-S** lineage

STIRPS   *n* pl. **STIRPES** a family or branch of a family

STIRRED   past tense of stir

STIRRER   *n* pl. **-S** one that stirs

STIRRING   *n* pl. **-S** a beginning of motion

STIRRUP   *n* pl. **-S** a support for the foot of a horseman

STITCH   *v* **-ED, -ING, -ES** to join by making in-and-out movements with a threaded needle

STITCHER   *n* pl. **-S** one that stitches

STITHY   *v* **STITHIED, STITHYING, STITHIES** to forge on an anvil

STIVER   *n* pl. **-S** a formerly used Dutch coin

STOA   *n* pl. **STOAE** or **STOAI** or **STOAS** an ancient Greek covered walkway

STOAT   *n* pl. **-S** a weasel with a black-tipped tail

STOB   *v* **STOBBED, STOBBING, STOBS** to stab

STOCCADO   *n* pl. **-DOS** a thrust with a rapier

STOCCATA   *n* pl. **-S** stoccado

STOCK   *v* **-ED, -ING, -S** to keep for future sale or use

STOCKADE   *v* **-ADED, -ADING, -ADES** to build a type of protective fence around

STOCKAGE   *n* pl. **-S** the amount of supplies on hand

STOCKCAR   *n* pl. **-S** a boxcar for carrying livestock

STOCKER   *n* pl. **-S** a young animal suitable for being fattened for market

STOCKIER   comparative of stocky

STOCKIEST   superlative of stocky

STOCKILY   *adv* in a stocky manner

STOCKING   *n* pl. **-S** a knitted or woven covering for the foot and leg

STOCKISH   *adj* stupid

STOCKIST   *n* pl. **-S** one who stocks goods

STOCKMAN   *n* pl. **-MEN** one who owns or raises livestock

STOCKPOT   *n* pl. **-S** a pot in which broth is prepared

STOCKY   *adj* **STOCKIER, STOCKIEST** having a short, thick body

STODGE   *v* **STODGED, STODGING, STODGES** to stuff full with food

STODGY   *adj* **STODGIER, STODGIEST** boring **STODGILY** *adv*

STOGEY   *n* pl. **-GEYS** stogy

STOGIE   *n* pl. **-S** stogy

STOGY   *n* pl. **-GIES** a long, slender cigar

STOIC   *n* pl. **-S** one who is indifferent to pleasure or pain **STOICAL** *adj*

STOICISM   *n* pl. **-S** indifference to pleasure or pain

STOKE   *v* **STOKED, STOKING, STOKES** to supply a furnace with fuel

STOKER	*n* pl. **-S** one that stokes	**STOOD**	past tense of stand
STOKESIA	*n* pl. **-S** a perennial herb	**STOOGE**	*v* **STOOGED, STOOGING,**
STOLE	*n* pl. **-S** a long wide scarf **STOLED** *adj*		**STOOGES** to act as a comedian's straight man
STOLEN	past participle of steal	**STOOK**	*v* **-ED, -ING, -S** to stack (as bundles of grain) upright in a field for drying
STOLID	*adj* **-IDER, -IDEST** showing little or no emotion **STOLIDLY** *adv*	**STOOKER**	*n* pl. **-S** one that stooks
STOLLEN	*n* pl. **-S** a sweet bread	**STOOKING**	*n* pl. **-S** the work of a stooker
STOLON	*n* pl. **-S** a type of plant stem **STOLONIC** *adj*	**STOOL**	*v* **-ED, -ING, -S** to defecate
STOLPORT	*n* pl. **-S** an airport for aircraft needing comparatively short runways	**STOOLIE**	*n* pl. **-S** an informer
		STOOP	*v* **-ED, -ING, -S** to bend the body forward and down
STOMA	*n* pl. **-MAS** or **-MATA** a minute opening in the epidermis of a plant organ	**STOOPER**	*n* pl. **-S** one that stoops
		STOP	*v* **STOPPED** or **STOPT, STOPPING, STOPS** to discontinue the progress or motion of
STOMACH	*v* **-ED, -ING, -S** to tolerate		
STOMACHY	*adj* paunchy	**STOPBAND**	*n* pl. **-S** a band of frequencies limited by a filter
STOMAL	*adj* stomatal		
STOMATA	a pl. of stoma	**STOPBANK**	*n* pl. **-S** an embankment along a river
STOMATAL	*adj* pertaining to a stoma		
STOMATE	*n* pl. **-S** a stoma	**STOPCOCK**	*n* pl. **-S** a type of faucet
STOMATIC	*adj* pertaining to the mouth	**STOPE**	*v* **STOPED, STOPING, STOPES** to excavate in layers, as ore
STOMODEA	*n/pl* embryonic oral cavities		
STOMP	*v* **-ED, -ING, -S** to tread heavily	**STOPER**	*n* pl. **-S** one that stopes
STOMPER	*n* pl. **-S** one that stomps	**STOPGAP**	*n* pl. **-S** a temporary substitute
STOMPY	*adj* **STOMPIER, STOMPIEST** conducive to stomping the feet	**STOPING**	*n* pl. **-S** the process of excavating in layers
		STOPOFF	*n* pl. **-S** a stopover
STONE	*v* **STONED, STONING, STONES** to pelt with stones (pieces of concreted earthy or mineral matter) **STONABLE** *adj*	**STOPOVER**	*n* pl. **-S** a brief stop in the course of a journey
		STOPPAGE	*n* pl. **-S** the act of stopping
		STOPPED	a past tense of stop
STONECUT	*n* pl. **-S** a print made from an image engraved on a stone	**STOPPER**	*v* **-ED, -ING, -S** to plug
		STOPPING	present participle of stop
STONEFLY	*n* pl. **-FLIES** a winged insect	**STOPPLE**	*v* **-PLED, -PLING, -PLES** to stopper
STONER	*n* pl. **-S** one that stones		
STONEY	*adj* **STONIER, STONIEST** stony	**STOPT**	a past tense of stop
STONIER	comparative of stony	**STOPWORD**	*n* pl. **-S** a frequently used word that is not searchable by search engines
STONIEST	superlative of stony		
STONILY	*adv* in a stony manner		
STONING	present participle of stone	**STORABLE**	*n* pl. **-S** something that can be stored
STONISH	*v* **-ED, -ING, -ES** to astonish		
STONK	*v* **-ED, -ING, -S** to bombard with artillery fire	**STORAGE**	*n* pl. **-S** a place for storing
		STORAX	*n* pl. **-ES** a fragrant resin
STONKER	*n* pl. **-S** something very large or impressive of its kind	**STORE**	*v* **STORED, STORING, STORES** to put away for future use
STONKING	*adj* remarkable, exciting	**STOREMAN**	*n* pl. **-MEN** a man who looks after stored goods
STONY	*adj* **STONIER, STONIEST** abounding in stones	**STORER**	*n* pl. **-S** one that stores

STOREY	*n pl.* **-REYS** a horizontal division of a building **STOREYED** *adj*
STORIED	past tense of story
STORIES	present 3d person sing. of story
STORING	present participle of store
STORK	*n pl.* **-S** a wading bird
STORM	*v* **-ED, -ING, -S** to blow violently
STORMY	*adj* **STORMIER, STORMIEST** storming **STORMILY** *adv*
STORY	*v* **-RIED, -RYING, -RIES** to relate as a story (an account of an event or series of events)
STOSS	*adj* facing the direction from which a glacier moves
STOT	*v* **STOTTED, STOTTING, STOTS** to bound with a stiff-legged gait
STOTIN	*n pl.* **-TINS** or **-TINOV** a former monetary unit of Slovenia
STOTINKA	*n pl.* **-KI** a monetary unit of Bulgaria
STOTT	*v* **-ED, -ING, -S** to stot
STOUND	*v* **-ED, -ING, -S** to ache
STOUP	*n pl.* **-S** a basin for holy water
STOUR	*n pl.* **-S** dust
STOURE	*n pl.* **-S** stour
STOURIE	*adj* stoury
STOURY	*adj* dusty
STOUT	*adj* **STOUTER, STOUTEST** fat
STOUT	*n pl.* **-S** a strong, dark ale
STOUTEN	*v* **-ED, -ING, -S** to make stout
STOUTISH	*adj* somewhat stout
STOUTLY	*adv* in a stout manner
STOVE	*v* **STOVED, STOVING, STOVES** to heat something in a heating apparatus
STOVER	*n pl.* **-S** coarse food for cattle
STOVETOP	*n pl.* **-S** the upper surface of a cooking apparatus
STOW	*v* **-ED, -ING, -S** to pack **STOWABLE** *adj*
STOWAGE	*n pl.* **-S** goods in storage
STOWAWAY	*n pl.* **-AWAYS** one who hides aboard a conveyance to obtain free passage
STOWP	*n pl.* **-S** stoup
STRADDLE	*v* **-DLED, -DLING, -DLES** to sit, stand, or walk with the legs wide apart
STRAFE	*v* **STRAFED, STRAFING, STRAFES** to attack with machine-gun fire from an airplane
STRAFER	*n pl.* **-S** one that strafes
STRAGGLE	*v* **-GLED, -GLING, -GLES** to stray
STRAGGLY	*adj* **-GLIER, -GLIEST** irregularly spread out
STRAIGHT	*adj* **STRAIGHTER, STRAIGHTEST** extending uniformly in one direction without bends or irregularities
STRAIGHT	*v* **-ED, -ING, -S** to make straight
STRAIN	*v* **-ED, -ING, -S** to exert to the utmost
STRAINER	*n pl.* **-S** a utensil used to separate liquids from solids
STRAIT	*adj* **STRAITER, STRAITEST** narrow **STRAITLY** *adv*
STRAIT	*n pl.* **-S** a narrow waterway connecting two larger bodies of water
STRAITEN	*v* **-ED, -ING, -S** to make strait
STRAKE	*n pl.* **-S** a line of planking extending along a ship's hull **STRAKED** *adj*
STRAMASH	*n pl.* **-ES** an uproar
STRAMONY	*n pl.* **-NIES** a poisonous weed
STRAND	*v* **-ED, -ING, -S** to leave in an unfavorable situation
STRANDER	*n pl.* **-S** a machine that twists fibers into rope
STRANG	*adj* strong
STRANGE	*n pl.* **-S** a fundamental quark
STRANGE	*adj* **STRANGER, STRANGEST** unusual or unfamiliar
STRANGER	*v* **-ED, -ING, -S** to estrange
STRANGLE	*v* **-GLED, -GLING, -GLES** to choke to death
STRAP	*v* **STRAPPED, STRAPPING, STRAPS** to fasten with a strap (a narrow strip of flexible material)
STRAPPER	*n pl.* **-S** one that straps
STRAPPY	*adj* **STRAPPIER, STRAPPIEST** having straps
STRASS	*n pl.* **-ES** a brilliant glass used in making imitation gems
STRATA	*n pl.* **-S** a dish of alternating layers of food
STRATAL	*adj* pertaining to a stratum
STRATEGY	*n pl.* **-GIES** a plan for obtaining a specific goal
STRATH	*n pl.* **-S** a wide river valley

STRATI	pl. of stratus
STRATIFY	v **-FIED, -FYING, -FIES** to form or arrange in layers
STRATOUS	adj stratal
STRATUM	n pl. **-TUMS** or **-TA** a layer of material
STRATUS	n pl. **-TI** or **-TUSES** a type of cloud
STRAVAGE	v **-VAGED, -VAGING, -VAGES** to stroll
STRAVAIG	v **-ED, -ING, -S** to stravage
STRAW	v **-ED, -ING, -S** to cover with straw (stalks of threshed grain)
STRAWHAT	adj pertaining to a summer theater situated in a resort area
STRAWY	adj **STRAWIER, STRAWIEST** resembling straw
STRAY	v **-ED, -ING, -S** to wander from the proper area or course
STRAYER	n pl. **-S** one that strays
STREAK	v **-ED, -ING, -S** to cover with streaks (long, narrow marks)
STREAKER	n pl. **-S** one that streaks
STREAKY	adj **STREAKIER, STREAKIEST** covered with streaks
STREAM	v **-ED, -ING, -S** to flow in a steady current
STREAMER	n pl. **-S** a long, narrow flag
STREAMY	adj **STREAMIER, STREAMIEST** streaming
STREEK	v **-ED, -ING, -S** to stretch
STREEKER	n pl. **-S** one that streeks
STREEL	v **-ED, -ING, -S** to saunter
STREET	n pl. **-S** a public thoroughfare **STREETED** adj
STRENGTH	n pl. **-S** capacity for exertion or endurance
STREP	n pl. **-S** any of various spherical or oval bacteria
STRESS	v **-ED, -ING, -ES** to place emphasis on
STRESSOR	n pl. **-S** a type of stimulus
STRETCH	v **-ED, -ING, -ES** to draw out or open to full length
STRETCHY	adj **STRETCHIER, STRETCHIEST** having a tendency to stretch
STRETTA	n pl. **-TAS** or **-TE** stretto
STRETTO	n pl. **-TOS** or **-TI** a concluding musical passage played at a faster tempo
STREUSEL	n pl. **-S** a topping for coffee cakes
STREW	v **STREWED, STREWN, STREWING, STREWS** to scatter about
STREWER	n pl. **-S** one that strews
STRIA	n pl. **STRIAE** a thin groove, stripe, or streak
STRIATE	v **-ATED, -ATING, -ATES** to mark with striae
STRIATUM	n pl. **-TA** a mass of nervous tissue within the brain **STRIATAL** adj
STRICK	n pl. **-S** a bunch of flax fibers
STRICKEN	adj strongly affected or afflicted
STRICKLE	v **-LED, -LING, -LES** to shape or smooth with a strickle (an instrument for leveling off grain)
STRICT	adj **STRICTER, STRICTEST** kept within narrow and specific limits **STRICTLY** adv
STRIDE	v **STRODE, STRIDDEN, STRIDING, STRIDES** to walk with long steps
STRIDENT	adj shrill
STRIDER	n pl. **-S** one that strides
STRIDING	present participle of stride
STRIDOR	n pl. **-S** a strident sound
STRIFE	n pl. **-S** bitter conflict or dissension
STRIGIL	n pl. **-S** a scraping instrument
STRIGOSE	adj covered with short, stiff hairs
STRIKE	v **STRUCK** or **STROOK, STRICKEN** or **STRUCKEN, STRIKING, STRIKES** to hit forcibly
STRIKER	n pl. **-S** one that strikes
STRIKING	n pl. **-S** the act of hitting something forcibly
STRINE	n pl. **-S** English as spoken in Australia
STRING	v **STRUNG** or **STRINGED, STRINGING, STRINGS** to provide with strings (slender cords)
STRINGER	n pl. **-S** one that strings
STRINGY	adj **STRINGIER, STRINGIEST** resembling a string or strings
STRIP	v **STRIPPED** or **STRIPT, STRIPPING, STRIPS** to remove the outer covering from
STRIPE	v **STRIPED, STRIPING, STRIPES** to mark with stripes (long, distinct bands)
STRIPER	n pl. **-S** a food and game fish
STRIPEY	adj **STRIPIER, STRIPIEST** stripy
STRIPIER	comparative of stripy

STRIPIEST	superlative of stripy
STRIPING	*n* pl. **-S** the stripes marked or painted on something
STRIPPED	a past tense of strip
STRIPPER	*n* pl. **-S** one that strips
STRIPPING	present participle of strip
STRIPT	a past tense of strip
STRIPY	*adj* **STRIPIER, STRIPIEST** marked with stripes
STRIVE	*v* **STROVE** or **STRIVED, STRIVEN, STRIVING, STRIVES** to exert much effort or energy
STRIVER	*n* pl. **-S** one that strives
STROBE	*v* **STROBED, STROBING, STROBES** to produce brief, high-intensity flashes of light
STROBIC	*adj* spinning
STROBIL	*n* pl. **-S** strobile
STROBILA	*n* pl. **-LAE** the entire body of a tapeworm
STROBILE	*n* pl. **-S** the conical, multiple fruit of certain trees
STROBILI	*n/pl* strobiles
STROBING	*n* pl. **-S** the process of producing high-intensity flashes of light
STRODE	a past tense of stride
STROKE	*v* **STROKED, STROKING, STROKES** to rub gently
STROKER	*n* pl. **-S** one that strokes
STROLL	*v* **-ED, -ING, -S** to walk in a leisurely manner
STROLLER	*n* pl. **-S** one that strolls
STROMA	*n* pl. **-MATA** the substance that forms the framework of an organ or cell **STROMAL** *adj*
STRONG	*adj* **STRONGER, STRONGEST** having great strength **STRONGLY** *adv*
STRONGYL	*n* pl. **-S** a parasitic worm
STRONTIA	*n* pl. **-S** a chemical compound **STRONTIC** *adj*
STROOK	a past tense of strike
STROP	*v* **STROPPED, STROPPING, STROPS** to sharpen on a strip of leather
STROPHE	*n* pl. **-S** a part of an ancient Greek choral ode **STROPHIC** *adj*
STROPPER	*n* pl. **-S** one that strops
STROPPY	*adj* **-PIER, -PIEST** unruly
STROUD	*n* pl. **-S** a coarse woolen blanket

STROVE	a past tense of strive
STROW	*v* **STROWED, STROWN, STROWING, STROWS** to strew
STROY	*v* **-ED, -ING, -S** to destroy
STROYER	*n* pl. **-S** one that stroys
STRUCK	a past tense of strike
STRUCKEN	a past participle of strike
STRUDEL	*n* pl. **-S** a type of pastry
STRUGGLE	*v* **-GLED, -GLING, -GLES** to make strenuous efforts against opposition
STRUM	*v* **STRUMMED, STRUMMING, STRUMS** to play a stringed instrument by running the fingers lightly across the strings
STRUMA	*n* pl. **-MAS** or **-MAE** scrofula
STRUMMER	*n* pl. **-S** one that strums
STRUMMING	present participle of strum
STRUMOSE	*adj* having a struma
STRUMOUS	*adj* having or pertaining to a struma
STRUMPET	*n* pl. **-S** a prostitute
STRUNG	a past tense of string
STRUNT	*v* **-ED, -ING, -S** to strut
STRUT	*v* **STRUTTED, STRUTTING, STRUTS** to walk with a pompous air
STRUTTER	*n* pl. **-S** one that struts
STUB	*v* **STUBBED, STUBBING, STUBS** to strike accidentally against a projecting object
STUBBIER	comparative of stubby
STUBBIEST	superlative of stubby
STUBBILY	*adv* in a stubby manner
STUBBING	present participle of stub
STUBBLE	*n* pl. **-S** a short, rough growth of beard **STUBBLED** *adj*
STUBBLY	*adj* **-BLIER, -BLIEST** covered with stubble
STUBBORN	*adj* **-BORNER, -BORNEST** unyielding
STUBBY	*adj* **-BIER, -BIEST** short and thick **STUBBILY** *adv*
STUBBY	*n* pl. **-BIES** a short squat bottle of beer
STUCCO	*v* **-ED, -ING, -ES** or **-S** to coat with a type of plaster
STUCCOER	*n* pl. **-S** one that stuccoes
STUCK	past tense of stick

STUD   *v* **STUDDED, STUDDING, STUDS** to set thickly with small projections

STUDBOOK   *n* pl. **-S** a record of the pedigree of purebred animals

STUDDIE   *n* pl. **-S** an anvil

STUDDING   *n* pl. **-S** the framework of a wall

STUDENT   *n* pl. **-S** a person formally engaged in learning

STUDFISH   *n* pl. **-ES** a freshwater fish

STUDIED   past tense of study

STUDIER   *n* pl. **-S** one that studies

STUDIES   present 3d person sing. of study

STUDIO   *n* pl. **-DIOS** an artist's workroom

STUDIOUS   *adj* given to study

STUDLY   *adj* **-LIER, -LIEST** muscular and attractive

STUDWORK   *n* pl. **-S** studding

STUDY   *v* **STUDIED, STUDYING, STUDIES** to apply the mind to the acquisition of knowledge

STUFF   *v* **-ED, -ING, -S** to fill or pack tightly

STUFFER   *n* pl. **-S** one that stuffs

STUFFING   *n* pl. **-S** material with which something is stuffed

STUFFY   *adj* **STUFFIER, STUFFIEST** poorly ventilated **STUFFILY** *adv*

STUIVER   *n* pl. **-S** stiver

STULL   *n* pl. **-S** a supporting timber in a mine

STULTIFY   *v* **-FIED, -FYING, -FIES** to cause to appear absurd

STUM   *v* **STUMMED, STUMMING, STUMS** to increase the fermentation of by adding grape juice

STUMBLE   *v* **-BLED, -BLING, -BLES** to miss one's step in walking or running

STUMBLER   *n* pl. **-S** one that stumbles

STUMP   *v* **-ED, -ING, -S** to baffle

STUMPAGE   *n* pl. **-S** uncut marketable timber

STUMPER   *n* pl. **-S** a baffling question

STUMPY   *adj* **STUMPIER, STUMPIEST** short and thick **STUMPILY** *adv*

STUN   *v* **STUNNED, STUNNING, STUNS** to render senseless or incapable of action

STUNG   past tense of sting

STUNK   a past tense of stink

STUNNER   *n* pl. **-S** one that stuns

STUNSAIL   *n* pl. **-S** a type of sail

STUNT   *v* **-ED, -ING, -S** to hinder the normal growth of

STUNTMAN   *n* pl. **-MEN** a person who substitutes for an actor in scenes involving dangerous activities

STUPA   *n* pl. **-S** a Buddhist shrine

STUPE   *n* pl. **-S** a medicated cloth to be applied to a wound

STUPEFY   *v* **-FIED, -FYING, -FIES** to dull the senses of

STUPID   *adj* **-PIDER, -PIDEST** mentally slow **STUPIDLY** *adv*

STUPID   *n* pl. **-S** a stupid person

STUPOR   *n* pl. **-S** a state of reduced sensibility

STURDY   *adj* **-DIER, -DIEST** strong and durable **STURDILY** *adv*

STURDY   *n* pl. **-DIES** a disease of sheep **STURDIED** *adj*

STURGEON   *n* pl. **-S** an edible fish

STURT   *n* pl. **-S** contention

STUTTER   *v* **-ED, -ING, -S** to speak with spasmodic repetition

STY   *v* **STIED** or **STYED, STYING, STIES** to keep in a pigpen

STYE   *n* pl. **-S** an inflamed swelling of the eyelid

STYGIAN   *adj* gloomy

STYLAR   *adj* pertaining to a stylus

STYLATE   *adj* bearing a stylet

STYLE   *v* **STYLED, STYLING, STYLES** to name

STYLER   *n* pl. **-S** one that styles

STYLET   *n* pl. **-S** a small, stiff organ or appendage of certain animals

STYLI   a pl. of stylus

STYLING   *n* pl. **-S** the way in which something is styled

STYLISE   *v* **-ISED, -ISING, -ISES** to stylize

STYLISER   *n* pl. **-S** one that stylises

STYLISH   *adj* fashionable

STYLIST   *n* pl. **-S** one who is a master of a literary or rhetorical style

STYLITE   *n* pl. **-S** an early Christian ascetic **STYLITIC** *adj*

STYLIZE   *v* **-IZED, -IZING, -IZES** to make conventional

STYLIZER   *n* pl. **-S** one that stylizes

STYLOID   *n* pl. **-S** a slender projection of bone

STYLOPID *n* pl. **-S** a stylops

STYLOPS *n* pl. **STYLOPS** an insect that is a parasite of other insects

STYLUS *n* pl. **-LUSES** or **-LI** a pointed instrument for writing, marking, or engraving

STYMIE *v* **-MIED, -MIEING, -MIES** to thwart

STYMY *v* **-MIED, -MYING, -MIES** to stymie

STYPSIS *n* pl. **-SISES** the use of a styptic

STYPTIC *n* pl. **-S** a substance used to check bleeding

STYRAX *n* pl. **-ES** storax

STYRENE *n* pl. **-S** a liquid hydrocarbon

SUABLE *adj* capable of being sued **SUABLY** *adv*

SUASION *n* pl. **-S** persuasion **SUASIVE, SUASORY** *adj*

SUAVE *adj* **SUAVER, SUAVEST** smoothly affable and polite **SUAVELY** *adv*

SUAVITY *n* pl. **-TIES** the state of being suave

SUB *v* **SUBBED, SUBBING, SUBS** to act as a substitute

SUBA *n* pl. **-S** subah

SUBABBOT *n* pl. **-S** a subordinate abbot

SUBACID *adj* slightly sour

SUBACRID *adj* somewhat acrid

SUBACUTE *adj* somewhat acute

SUBADAR *n* pl. **-S** subahdar

SUBADULT *n* pl. **-S** an individual approaching adulthood

SUBAGENT *n* pl. **-S** a subordinate agent

SUBAH *n* pl. **-S** a province of India

SUBAHDAR *n* pl. **-S** a governor of a subah

SUBALAR *adj* situated under the wings

SUBAREA *n* pl. **-S** a subdivision of an area

SUBARID *adj* somewhat arid

SUBATOM *n* pl. **-S** a component of an atom

SUBAURAL *adj* scarcely hearable

SUBAXIAL *adj* somewhat axial

SUBBASE *n* pl. **-S** the lowest part of a base

SUBBASIN *n* pl. **-S** a section of an area drained by a river

SUBBASS *n* pl. **-ES** a pedal stop producing the lowest tones of an organ

SUBBED past tense of sub

SUBBING *n* pl. **-S** a thin coating on the support of a photographic film

SUBBLOCK *n* pl. **-S** a subdivision of a block

SUBBREED *n* pl. **-S** a distinguishable strain within a breed

SUBCASTE *n* pl. **-S** a subdivision of a caste

SUBCAUSE *n* pl. **-S** a subordinate cause

SUBCELL *n* pl. **-S** a subdivision of a cell

SUBCHIEF *n* pl. **-S** a subordinate chief

SUBCLAIM *n* pl. **-S** a subordinate claim

SUBCLAN *n* pl. **-S** a subdivision of a clan

SUBCLASS *v* **-ED, -ING, -ES** to place in a subdivision of a class

SUBCLERK *n* pl. **-S** a subordinate clerk

SUBCODE *n* pl. **-S** a subdivision of a code

SUBCOOL *v* **-ED, -ING, -S** to cool below the freezing point without solidification

SUBCULT *n* pl. **-S** a subdivision of a cult

SUBCUTIS *n* pl. **-CUTISES** or **-CUTES** the deeper part of the dermis

SUBDEAN *n* pl. **-S** a subordinate dean

SUBDEB *n* pl. **-S** a girl the year before she becomes a debutante

SUBDEPOT *n* pl. **-S** a military depot that operates under the jurisdiction of another depot

SUBDUAL *n* pl. **-S** the act of subduing

SUBDUCE *v* **-DUCED, -DUCING, -DUCES** to take away

SUBDUCT *v* **-ED, -ING, -S** to subduce

SUBDUE *v* **-DUED, -DUING, -DUES** to bring under control

SUBDUER *n* pl. **-S** one that subdues

SUBDURAL *adj* situated under the dura mater

SUBDWARF *n* pl. **-S** a small star of relatively low luminosity

SUBECHO *n* pl. **-ECHOES** an inferior echo

SUBEDIT *v* **-ED, -ING, -S** to act as the assistant editor of

SUBENTRY *n* pl. **-TRIES** an entry made under a more general entry

SUBEPOCH *n* pl. **-S** a subdivision of an epoch

SUBER *n* pl. **-S** phellem

SUBERECT *adj* nearly erect

SUBERIC *adj* pertaining to cork

SUBERIN *n* pl. **-S** a substance found in cork cells

SUBERISE *v* **-ISED, -ISING, -ISES** to suberize

SUBERIZE *v* **-IZED, -IZING, -IZES** to convert into cork tissue

SUBEROSE *adj* corky

SUBEROUS *adj* suberose

SUBFIELD *n* pl. **-S** a subset of a mathematical field that is itself a field

SUBFILE *n* pl. **-S** a subdivision of a file

SUBFIX *n* pl. **-ES** a distinguishing symbol or letter written below another character

SUBFLOOR *n* pl. **-S** a rough floor laid as a base for a finished floor

SUBFLUID *adj* somewhat fluid

SUBFRAME *n* pl. **-S** a frame for the attachment of a finish frame

SUBFUSC *n* pl. **-S** dark dull clothing

SUBGENRE *n* pl. **-S** a subdivision of a genre

SUBGENUS *n* pl. **-GENUSES** or **-GENERA** a subdivision of a genus

SUBGOAL *n* pl. **-S** a subordinate goal

SUBGRADE *n* pl. **-S** a surface on which a pavement is placed

SUBGRAPH *n* pl. **-S** a graph contained within a larger graph

SUBGROUP *v* **-ED, -ING, -S** to divide into smaller groups

SUBGUM *n* pl. **-S** a Chinese dish of mixed vegetables

SUBHEAD *n* pl. **-S** the heading of a subdivision

SUBHUMAN *n* pl. **-S** one that is less than human

SUBHUMID *adj* somewhat humid

SUBIDEA *n* pl. **-S** an inferior idea

SUBINDEX *n* pl. **-DEXES** or **-DICES** a subfix

SUBITEM *n* pl. **-S** an item that forms a subdivision of a larger topic

SUBITO *adv* quickly — used as a musical direction

SUBJECT *v* **-ED, -ING, -S** to cause to experience

SUBJOIN *v* **-ED, -ING, -S** to add at the end

SUBLATE *v* **-LATED, -LATING, -LATES** to cancel

SUBLEASE *v* **-LEASED, -LEASING, -LEASES** to sublet

SUBLET *v* **-LET, -LETTING, -LETS** to rent leased property to another

SUBLEVEL *n* pl. **-S** a lower level

SUBLIME *adj* **-LIMER, -LIMEST** of elevated or noble quality

SUBLIME *v* **-LIMED, -LIMING, -LIMES** to make sublime

SUBLIMER *n* pl. **-S** one that sublimes

SUBLIMEST superlative of sublime

SUBLIMIT *n* pl. **-S** a limit within a limit

SUBLINE *n* pl. **-S** an inbred line within a strain

SUBLOT *n* pl. **-S** a subdivision of a lot

SUBLUNAR *adj* pertaining to the earth

SUBMENU *n* pl. **-S** a secondary list of options for a computer

SUBMERGE *v* **-MERGED, -MERGING, -MERGES** to place below the surface of a liquid

SUBMERSE *v* **-MERSED, -MERSING, -MERSES** to submerge

SUBMISS *adj* inclined to submit

SUBMIT *v* **-MITTED, -MITTING, -MITS** to yield to the power of another

SUBNASAL *adj* situated under the nose

SUBNET *n* pl. **-S** a system of interconnections within a communications system

SUBNICHE *n* pl. **-S** a subdivision of a habitat

SUBNODAL *adj* situated under a node

SUBOCEAN *adj* existing below the floor of the ocean

SUBOPTIC *adj* situated under the eyes

SUBORAL *adj* situated under the mouth

SUBORDER *n* pl. **-S** a category of related families within an order

SUBORN *v* **-ED, -ING, -S** to induce to commit perjury

SUBORNER *n* pl. **-S** one that suborns

SUBOVAL *adj* nearly oval

SUBOVATE *adj* nearly ovate

SUBOXIDE *n* pl. **-S** an oxide containing relatively little oxygen

SUBPANEL *n* pl. **-S** a subdivision of a panel

SUBPAR *adj* below par

SUBPART *n* pl. **-S** a subdivision of a part

SUBPENA *v* **-ED, -ING, -S** to subpoena

SUBPHASE *n* pl. **-S** a subdivision of a phase

SUBPHYLA *n/pl* divisions within a phylum

SUBPLOT *n* pl. **-S** a secondary literary plot

SUBPOENA *v* **-ED, -ING, -S** to summon with a type of judicial writ

SUBPOLAR *adj* situated just outside the polar circles

SUBPRIME *adj* denoting a loan that is at a higher interest rate than a prime rate

SUBPUBIC *adj* situated under the pubis

SUBRACE *n* pl. **-S** a subdivision of a race

SUBRENT *n* pl. **-S** rent from a subtenant

SUBRING *n* pl. **-S** a subset of a mathematical ring that is itself a ring

SUBRULE *n* pl. **-S** a subordinate rule

SUBSALE *n* pl. **-S** a resale of purchased goods

SUBSCALE *n* pl. **-S** a subdivision of a scale

SUBSEA *adj* situated below the surface of the sea

SUBSECT *n* pl. **-S** a sect directly derived from another

SUBSENSE *n* pl. **-S** a subdivision of a sense

SUBSERE *n* pl. **-S** a type of ecological succession

SUBSERVE *v* **-SERVED, -SERVING, -SERVES** to serve to promote

SUBSET *n* pl. **-S** a mathematical set contained within a larger set

SUBSHAFT *n* pl. **-S** a shaft that is beneath another shaft

SUBSHELL *n* pl. **-S** one of the orbitals making up an electron shell of an atom

SUBSHRUB *n* pl. **-S** a low shrub

SUBSIDE *v* **-SIDED, -SIDING, -SIDES** to sink to a lower or normal level

SUBSIDER *n* pl. **-S** one that subsides

SUBSIDY *n* pl. **-DIES** a grant or contribution of money

SUBSIST *v* **-ED, -ING, -S** to continue to exist

SUBSITE *n* pl. **-S** a subdivision of a site

SUBSKILL *n* pl. **-S** a subordinate skill

SUBSOIL *v* **-ED, -ING, -S** to plow so as to turn up the subsoil (the layer of earth beneath the surface soil)

SUBSOLAR *adj* situated directly beneath the sun

SUBSONIC *adj* moving at a speed less than that of sound

SUBSPACE *n* pl. **-S** a subset of a mathematical space

SUBSTAGE *n* pl. **-S** a part of a microscope for supporting accessories

SUBSTATE *n* pl. **-S** a subdivision of a state

SUBSTORM *n* pl. **-S** activity that disturbs the magnetic field of a planet

SUBSUME *v* **-SUMED, -SUMING, -SUMES** to include within a larger group

SUBTASK *n* pl. **-S** a subordinate task

SUBTAXON *n* pl. **-TAXONS** or **-TAXA** a subdivision of a taxon

SUBTEEN *n* pl. **-S** a person approaching the teenage years

SUBTEND *v* **-ED, -ING, -S** to extend under or opposite to

SUBTEST *n* pl. **-S** a subdivision of a test

SUBTEXT *n* pl. **-S** written or printed matter under a more general text

SUBTHEME *n* pl. **-S** a subordinate theme

SUBTILE *adj* **-TILER, -TILEST** subtle

SUBTILIN *n* pl. **-S** an antibiotic

SUBTILTY *n* pl. **-TIES** subtlety

SUBTITLE *v* **-TLED, -TLING, -TLES** to give a secondary title to

SUBTLE *adj* **-TLER, -TLEST** so slight as to be difficult to detect **SUBTLY** *adv*

SUBTLETY *n* pl. **-TIES** the state of being subtle

SUBTONE *n* pl. **-S** a low or subdued tone

SUBTONIC *n* pl. **-S** a type of musical tone

SUBTOPIA *n* pl. **-S** the suburbs of a city

SUBTOPIC *n* pl. **-S** a secondary topic

SUBTOTAL *v* **-TALED, -TALING, -TALS** or **-TALLED, -TALLING, -TALS** to total a portion of

SUBTRACT *v* **-ED, -ING, -S** to take away

SUBTRADE *n* pl. **-S** a specialist hired by a general contractor

SUBTREND *n* pl. **-S** a subordinate trend

SUBTRIBE *n* pl. **-S** a subdivision of a tribe

SUBTUNIC *n* pl. **-S** a tunic worn under another tunic

SUBTYPE *n* pl. **-S** a type that is subordinate to or included in another type

SUBULATE *adj* slender and tapering to a point

SUBUNIT *n* pl. **-S** a unit that is a part of a larger unit

SUBURB *n* pl. **-S** a residential area adjacent to a city **SUBURBED** *adj*

SUBURBAN *n* pl. **-S** one who lives in a suburb

SUBURBIA *n* pl. **-S** the suburbs of a city

SUBVENE *v* **-VENED, -VENING, -VENES** to arrive or occur as a support or relief

SUBVERT *v* **-ED, -ING, -S** to destroy completely

SUBVICAR *n* pl. **-S** a subordinate vicar

SUBVIRAL *adj* pertaining to a part of a virus

SUBVIRUS	*n* pl. **-ES** a viral protein smaller than a virus
SUBVOCAL	*adj* mentally formulated as words
SUBWAY	*v* **-ED, -ING, -S** to travel by an underground railroad
SUBWORLD	*n* pl. **-S** a subdivision of a sphere of interest or activity
SUBZERO	*adj* registering less than zero
SUBZONE	*n* pl. **-S** a subdivision of a zone
SUCCAH	*n* pl. **-CAHS** or **-COTH** sukkah
SUCCEED	*v* **-ED, -ING, -S** to accomplish something desired or intended
SUCCESS	*n* pl. **-ES** the attainment of something desired or intended
SUCCINCT	*adj* **-CINCTER, -CINCTEST** clearly expressed in few words
SUCCINIC	*adj* pertaining to amber
SUCCINYL	*n* pl. **-S** a univalent radical
SUCCOR	*v* **-ED, -ING, -S** to go to the aid of
SUCCORER	*n* pl. **-S** one that succors
SUCCORY	*n* pl. **-RIES** chicory
SUCCOTH	a pl. of succah
SUCCOUR	*v* **-ED, -ING, -S** to succor
SUCCUBA	*n* pl. **-BAS** or **-BAE** a succubus
SUCCUBUS	*n* pl. **-BUSES** or **-BI** a female demon
SUCCUMB	*v* **-ED, -ING, -S** to yield to superior force
SUCCUSS	*v* **-ED, -ING, -ES** to shake violently
SUCH	*adj* of that kind
SUCHLIKE	*n* pl. **-S** a thing of such a kind
SUCHNESS	*n* pl. **-ES** essential or characteristic quality
SUCK	*v* **-ED, -ING, -S** to draw in by establishing a partial vacuum
SUCKER	*v* **-ED, -ING, -S** to strip of lower shoots or branches
SUCKFISH	*n* pl. **-ES** a remora
SUCKLE	*v* **-LED, -LING, -LES** to give milk to from the breast
SUCKLER	*n* pl. **-S** one that suckles
SUCKLESS	*adj* having no juice
SUCKLING	*n* pl. **-S** an unweaned mammal
SUCKY	*adj* **SUCKIER, SUCKIEST** extremely objectionable
SUCRASE	*n* pl. **-S** an enzyme
SUCRE	*n* pl. **-S** a former monetary unit of Ecuador
SUCROSE	*n* pl. **-S** a type of sugar
SUCTION	*v* **-ED, -ING, -S** to remove by the process of sucking
SUDARIUM	*n* pl. **-IA** a cloth for wiping the face
SUDARY	*n* pl. **-RIES** sudarium
SUDATION	*n* pl. **-S** excessive sweating
SUDATORY	*n* pl. **-RIES** a hot-air bath for inducing sweating
SUDD	*n* pl. **-S** a floating mass of vegetation
SUDDEN	*adj* happening quickly and without warning **SUDDENLY** *adv*
SUDDEN	*n* pl. **-S** a sudden occurrence
SUDOKU	*n* pl. **-S** a puzzle involving the numbers 1 through 9
SUDOR	*n* pl. **-S** sweat **SUDORAL** *adj*
SUDS	*v* **-ED, -ING, -ES** to wash in soapy water
SUDSER	*n* pl. **-S** a soap opera
SUDSLESS	*adj* having no suds
SUDSY	*adj* **SUDSIER, SUDSIEST** foamy
SUE	*v* **SUED, SUING, SUES** to institute legal proceedings against
SUEDE	*v* **SUEDED, SUEDING, SUEDES** to finish leather with a soft, napped surface
SUER	*n* pl. **-S** one that sues
SUET	*n* pl. **-S** the hard, fatty tissue around the kidneys of cattle and sheep **SUETY** *adj*
SUETE	*n* pl. **-S** a southeasterly wind in areas of Cape Breton Island
SUFFARI	*n* pl. **-S** a safari
SUFFER	*v* **-ED, -ING, -S** to feel pain or distress
SUFFERER	*n* pl. **-S** one that suffers
SUFFICE	*v* **-FICED, -FICING, -FICES** to be adequate
SUFFICER	*n* pl. **-S** one that suffices
SUFFIX	*v* **-ED, -ING, -ES** to add as a suffix (a form affixed to the end of end of word)
SUFFIXAL	*adj* pertaining to or being a suffix
SUFFLATE	*v* **-FLATED, -FLATING, -FLATES** to inflate
SUFFRAGE	*n* pl. **-S** the right to vote
SUFFUSE	*v* **-FUSED, -FUSING, -FUSES** to spread through or over
SUGAR	*v* **-ED, -ING, -S** to cover with sugar (a sweet carbohydrate)
SUGARER	*n* pl. **-S** one that makes sugar

SUGARING	*n* pl. **-S** the process of boiling down maple sap into syrup
SUGARY	*adj* **-ARIER, -ARIEST** containing or resembling sugar
SUGGEST	*v* **-ED, -ING, -S** to bring or put forward for consideration
SUGH	*v* **-ED, -ING, -S** to sough
SUICIDAL	*adj* self-destructive
SUICIDE	*v* **-CIDED, -CIDING, -CIDES** to kill oneself intentionally
SUING	present participle of sue
SUINT	*n* pl. **-S** a natural grease found in the wool of sheep
SUIT	*v* **-ED, -ING, -S** to be appropriate to
SUITABLE	*adj* appropriate **SUITABLY** *adv*
SUITCASE	*n* pl. **-S** a flat, rectangular piece of luggage
SUITE	*n* pl. **-S** a series of things forming a unit
SUITER	*n* pl. **-S** a suitcase holding a specified number of suits (sets of garments)
SUITING	*n* pl. **-S** fabric for making suits
SUITLIKE	*adj* resembling a suit (a set of garments)
SUITOR	*n* pl. **-S** one that is courting a woman
SUK	*n* pl. **-S** souk
SUKH	*n* pl. **-S** a souk
SUKIYAKI	*n* pl. **-S** a Japanese dish
SUKKAH	*n* pl. **-KAHS** or **-KOTH** or **-KOT** a temporary shelter in which meals are eaten during a Jewish festival
SULCATE	*adj* having long, narrow furrows
SULCATED	*adj* sulcate
SULCUS	*n* pl. **-CI** a narrow furrow **SULCAL** *adj*
SULDAN	*n* pl. **-S** soldan
SULFA	*n* pl. **-S** a bacteria-inhibiting drug
SULFATE	*v* **-FATED, -FATING, -FATES** to treat with sulfuric acid
SULFID	*n* pl. **-S** sulfide
SULFIDE	*n* pl. **-S** a sulfur compound
SULFINYL	*n* pl. **-S** a bivalent radical
SULFITE	*n* pl. **-S** a chemical salt **SULFITIC** *adj*
SULFO	*adj* sulfonic
SULFONE	*n* pl. **-S** a sulfur compound
SULFONIC	*adj* containing a certain univalent radical
SULFONYL	*n* pl. **-S** a bivalent radical
SULFUR	*v* **-ED, -ING, -S** to treat with sulfur (a nonmetallic element)
SULFURET	*v* **-RETED, -RETING, -RETS** or **-RETTED, -RETTING, -RETS** to treat with sulfur
SULFURIC	*adj* pertaining to sulfur
SULFURY	*adj* resembling sulfur
SULFURYL	*n* pl. **-S** sulfonyl
SULK	*v* **-ED, -ING, -S** to be sulky
SULKER	*n* pl. **-S** one that sulks
SULKY	*adj* **SULKIER, SULKIEST** sullenly aloof or withdrawn **SULKILY** *adv*
SULKY	*n* pl. **SULKIES** a light horse-drawn vehicle
SULLAGE	*n* pl. **-S** sewage
SULLEN	*adj* **-LENER, -LENEST** showing a brooding ill humor or resentment **SULLENLY** *adv*
SULLY	*v* **-LIED, -LYING, -LIES** to soil
SULPHA	*n* pl. **-S** sulfa
SULPHATE	*v* **-PHATED, -PHATING, -PHATES** to sulfate
SULPHID	*n* pl. **-S** sulfide
SULPHIDE	*n* pl. **-S** sulfide
SULPHITE	*n* pl. **-S** sulfite
SULPHONE	*n* pl. **-S** sulfone
SULPHUR	*v* **-ED, -ING, -S** to sulfur
SULPHURY	*adj* sulfury
SULTAN	*n* pl. **-S** the ruler of a Muslim country **SULTANIC** *adj*
SULTANA	*n* pl. **-S** a sultan's wife
SULTRY	*adj* **-TRIER, -TRIEST** very hot and humid **SULTRILY** *adv*
SULU	*n* pl. **-S** a Melanesian skirt
SUM	*v* **SUMMED, SUMMING, SUMS** to add into one total
SUM	*n* pl. **SUMY** a monetary unit of Uzbekistan
SUMAC	*n* pl. **-S** a flowering tree or shrub
SUMACH	*n* pl. **-S** sumac
SUMI	*n* pl. **-S** a type of black Japanese ink
SUMLESS	*adj* too large for calculation
SUMMA	*n* pl. **-MAS** or **-MAE** a comprehensive work on a topic
SUMMABLE	*adj* capable of being summed

SUMMAND *n* pl. **-S** an addend

SUMMARY *n* pl. **-RIES** a short restatement

SUMMATE *v* **-MATED, -MATING, -MATES** to sum

SUMMED past tense of sum

SUMMER *v* **-ED, -ING, -S** to pass the summer (the warmest season of the year)

SUMMERLY *adj* summery

SUMMERY *adj* **-MERIER, -MERIEST** characteristic of summer

SUMMING present participle of sum

SUMMIT *v* **-ED, -ING, -S** to participate in a highest-level conference

SUMMITAL *adj* pertaining to the highest point

SUMMITRY *n* pl. **-RIES** the use of conferences between chiefs of state for international negotiation

SUMMON *v* **-ED, -ING, -S** to order to appear

SUMMONER *n* pl. **-S** one that summons

SUMMONS *v* **-ED, -ING, -ES** to summon with a court order

SUMO *n* pl. **-MOS** a Japanese form of wrestling

SUMOIST *n* pl. **-S** a sumo wrestler

SUMP *n* pl. **-S** a low area serving as a drain or receptacle for liquids

SUMPTER *n* pl. **-S** a pack animal

SUMPWEED *n* pl. **-S** a marsh plant

SUN *v* **SUNNED, SUNNING, SUNS** to expose to the sun (the star around which the earth revolves)

SUNBACK *adj* cut low to expose the back to sunlight

SUNBAKED *adj* baked by the sun

SUNBATH *n* pl. **-S** an exposure to sunlight

SUNBATHE *v* **-BATHED, -BATHING, -BATHES** to take a sunbath

SUNBEAM *n* pl. **-S** a beam of sunlight **SUNBEAMY** *adj*

SUNBED *n* pl. **-S** a device for acquiring tan skin artificially

SUNBELT *n* pl. **-S** the southern and southwestern states of the U.S.

SUNBIRD *n* pl. **-S** a tropical bird

SUNBLOCK *n* pl. **-S** a preparation to protect the skin from the sun's rays

SUNBOW *n* pl. **-S** an arc of spectral colors formed by the sun shining through a mist

SUNBURN *v* **-BURNED** or **-BURNT, -BURNING, -BURNS** to burn or discolor from exposure to the sun

SUNBURST *n* pl. **-S** a burst of sunlight

SUNCARE *n* pl. **-S** protection of the skin from damage by the sun

SUNCHOKE *n* pl. **-S** a type of sunflower

SUNDAE *n* pl. **-S** a dish of ice cream served with a topping

SUNDECK *n* pl. **-S** a deck that is exposed to the sun

SUNDER *v* **-ED, -ING, -S** to break apart

SUNDERER *n* pl. **-S** one that sunders

SUNDEW *n* pl. **-S** a marsh plant

SUNDIAL *n* pl. **-S** a type of time-telling device

SUNDOG *n* pl. **-S** a small rainbow

SUNDOWN *v* **-ED, -ING, -S** to experience nighttime confusion

SUNDRESS *n* pl. **-ES** a dress with an abbreviated bodice

SUNDRIES *n/pl* miscellaneous items

SUNDROPS *n* pl. **SUNDROPS** a flowering plant

SUNDRY *adj* miscellaneous **SUNDRILY** *adv*

SUNFAST *adj* resistant to fading by the sun

SUNFISH *n* pl. **-ES** a marine fish

SUNG past participle of sing

SUNGLASS *n* pl. **-ES** a lens for concentrating the sun's rays in order to produce heat

SUNGLOW *n* pl. **-S** a glow in the sky caused by the sun

SUNK a past participle of sink

SUNKEN a past participle of sink

SUNKER *n* pl. **-S** a ridge of rock near the surface of the sea

SUNKET *n* pl. **-S** a tidbit

SUNLAMP *n* pl. **-S** a lamp that radiates ultraviolet rays

SUNLAND *n* pl. **-S** an area marked by a great amount of sunshine

SUNLESS *adj* having no sunlight

SUNLIGHT *n* pl. **-S** the light of the sun

SUNLIKE *adj* resembling the sun

SUNLIT *adj* lighted by the sun

SUNN *n* pl. **-S** an East Indian shrub

SUNNA *n* pl. **-S** the body of traditional Muslim law

SUNNAH *n* pl. **-S** sunna

SUNNED	past tense of sun
SUNNING	present participle of sun
SUNNY	*adj* **-NIER, -NIEST** filled with sunlight **SUNNILY** *adv*
SUNPORCH	*n* pl. **-ES** a porch that admits much sunlight
SUNPROOF	*adj* resistant to damage by sunlight
SUNRAY	*n* pl. **-RAYS** a ray of sunlight
SUNRISE	*n* pl. **-S** the ascent of the sun above the horizon in the morning
SUNROOF	*n* pl. **-S** an automobile roof having an openable panel
SUNROOM	*n* pl. **-S** a room built to admit a great amount of sunlight
SUNSCALD	*n* pl. **-S** an injury of woody plants caused by the sun
SUNSET	*v* **-SETTED, -SETTING, -SETS** to come to an end
SUNSHADE	*n* pl. **-S** something used as a protection from the sun
SUNSHINE	*n* pl. **-S** the light of the sun **SUNSHINY** *adj*
SUNSPOT	*n* pl. **-S** a dark spot on the surface of the sun
SUNSTAR	*n* pl. **-S** a type of starfish
SUNSTONE	*n* pl. **-S** a variety of quartz
SUNSUIT	*n* pl. **-S** a type of playsuit
SUNTAN	*v* **-TANNED, -TANNING, -TANS** to become tan
SUNTRAP	*n* pl. **-S** a pleasantly sunny sheltered place
SUNUP	*n* pl. **-S** sunrise
SUNWARD	*adv* toward the sun
SUNWARDS	*adv* sunward
SUNWISE	*adv* from left to right
SUP	*v* **SUPPED, SUPPING, SUPS** to eat supper
SUPE	*n* pl. **-S** an actor without a speaking part
SUPER	*v* **-ED, -ING, -S** to reinforce with a thin cotton mesh, as a book
SUPERADD	*v* **-ED, -ING, -S** to add further
SUPERB	*adj* **-PERBER, -PERBEST** of excellent quality **SUPERBLY** *adv*
SUPERBAD	*adj* exceedingly bad
SUPERBUG	*n* pl. **-S** a strain of bacteria that is resistant to all antibiotics
SUPERCAR	*n* pl. **-S** a superior car
SUPERCOP	*n* pl. **-S** a superior police officer
SUPEREGO	*n* pl. **-EGOS** a part of the psyche

SUPERFAN	*n* pl. **-S** an exceedingly devoted enthusiast
SUPERFIX	*n* pl. **-ES** a recurrent pattern of stress in speech
SUPERFLY	*adj* showily pretentious
SUPERHIT	*n* pl. **-S** something exceedingly successful
SUPERHOT	*adj* exceedingly hot
SUPERIOR	*n* pl. **-S** one of higher rank, quality, or authority than another
SUPERJET	*n* pl. **-S** a type of jet airplane
SUPERLIE	*v* **-LAY, -LAIN, -LYING, -LIES** to lie above
SUPERMAN	*n* pl. **-MEN** a hypothetical superior man
SUPERMOM	*n* pl. **-S** a superior mom
SUPERNAL	*adj* pertaining to the sky
SUPERPRO	*n* pl. **-PROS** a superior professional
SUPERSEX	*n* pl. **-ES** a type of sterile organism
SUPERSPY	*n* pl. **-SPIES** a superior spy
SUPERTAX	*n* pl. **-ES** an additional tax
SUPINATE	*v* **-NATED, -NATING, -NATES** to turn so that the palm is facing upward
SUPINE	*n* pl. **-S** a Latin verbal noun
SUPINELY	*adv* in an inactive manner
SUPPED	past tense of sup
SUPPER	*n* pl. **-S** an evening meal
SUPPING	present participle of sup
SUPPLANT	*v* **-ED, -ING, -S** to take the place of
SUPPLE	*adj* **-PLER, -PLEST** pliant **SUPPLELY** *adv*
SUPPLE	*v* **-PLED, -PLING, -PLES** to make supple
SUPPLIER	*n* pl. **-S** one that supplies
SUPPLY	*v* **-PLIED, -PLYING, -PLIES** to furnish with what is needed
SUPPORT	*v* **-ED, -ING, -S** to hold up or add strength to
SUPPOSAL	*n* pl. **-S** something supposed
SUPPOSE	*v* **-POSED, -POSING, -POSES** to assume to be true
SUPPOSER	*n* pl. **-S** one that supposes
SUPPRESS	*v* **-ED, -ING, -ES** to put an end to forcibly
SUPRA	*adv* above
SUPREME	*n* pl. **-S** a smooth white sauce made with chicken stock

SUPREME *adj* **-PREMER, -PREMEST** highest in power or authority

SUPREMO *n* pl. **-MOS** one who is highest in authority

SUQ *n* pl. **-S** souk

SURA *n* pl. **-S** a chapter of the Koran

SURAH *n* pl. **-S** a silk fabric

SURAL *adj* pertaining to the calf of the leg

SURBASE *n* pl. **-S** a molding or border above the base of a structure **SURBASED** *adj*

SURCEASE *v* **-CEASED, -CEASING, -CEASES** to cease

SURCOAT *n* pl. **-S** an outer coat or cloak

SURD *n* pl. **-S** a voiceless speech sound

SURE *adj* **SURER, SUREST** free from doubt

SUREFIRE *adj* sure to meet expectations

SURELY *adv* certainly

SURENESS *n* pl. **-ES** the state of being sure

SURER comparative of sure

SUREST superlative of sure

SURETY *n* pl. **-TIES** sureness

SURF *v* **-ED, -ING, -S** to ride breaking waves on a long, narrow board **SURFABLE** *adj*

SURFACE *v* **-FACED, -FACING, -FACES** to apply an outer layer to

SURFACER *n* pl. **-S** one that surfaces

SURFBIRD *n* pl. **-S** a shore bird

SURFBOAT *n* pl. **-S** a strong rowboat

SURFEIT *v* **-ED, -ING, -S** to supply to excess

SURFER *n* pl. **-S** one that surfs

SURFFISH *n* pl. **-ES** a marine fish

SURFIER comparative of surfy

SURFIEST superlative of surfy

SURFING *n* pl. **-S** the act or sport of riding the surf (breaking waves)

SURFLIKE *adj* resembling breaking waves

SURFMAN *n* pl. **-MEN** one who is skilled in handling a boat in surf

SURFSIDE *adj* situated near the seashore

SURFY *adj* **SURFIER, SURFIEST** abounding in breaking waves

SURGE *v* **SURGED, SURGING, SURGES** to move in a swelling manner

SURGEON *n* pl. **-S** one who practices surgery

SURGER *n* pl. **-S** one that surges

SURGERY *n* pl. **-GERIES** the treatment of medical problems by operation

SURGICAL *adj* pertaining to surgery

SURGING present participle of surge

SURGY *adj* surging

SURICATE *n* pl. **-S** a burrowing mammal

SURIMI *n* pl. **-S** an inexpensive fish product

SURLY *adj* **-LIER, -LIEST** sullenly rude **SURLILY** *adv*

SURMISE *v* **-MISED, -MISING, -MISES** to infer with little evidence

SURMISER *n* pl. **-S** one that surmises

SURMOUNT *v* **-ED, -ING, -S** to get over or across

SURNAME *v* **-NAMED, -NAMING, -NAMES** to give a family name to

SURNAMER *n* pl. **-S** one that surnames

SURPASS *v* **-ED, -ING, -ES** to go beyond

SURPLICE *n* pl. **-S** a loose-fitting vestment

SURPLUS *v* **-PLUSED, -PLUSING, -PLUSES** or **-PLUSSED, -PLUSSING, -PLUSSES** to treat as being in excess of what is needed

SURPRINT *v* **-ED, -ING, -S** to print over something already printed

SURPRISE *v* **-PRISED, -PRISING, -PRISES** to come upon unexpectedly

SURPRIZE *v* **-PRIZED, -PRIZING, -PRIZES** to surprise

SURRA *n* pl. **-S** a disease of domestic animals

SURREAL *adj* having dreamlike qualities

SURREY *n* pl. **-REYS** a light carriage

SURROUND *v* **-ED, -ING, -S** to extend completely around

SURROYAL *n* pl. **-S** the topmost prong of a stag's antler

SURTAX *v* **-ED, -ING, -ES** to assess with an extra tax

SURTITLE *n* pl. **-S** a translation of a foreign-language dialogue displayed above a screen or stage

SURTOUT *n* pl. **-S** a close-fitting overcoat

SURVEIL *v* **-VEILLED, -VEILLING, -VEILS** to watch closely

SURVEY *v* **-ED, -ING, -S** to determine the boundaries, area, or elevations of by measuring angles and distances

SURVEYOR *n* pl. **-S** one that surveys land

SURVIVAL   *n* pl. **-S** a living or continuing longer than another person or thing

SURVIVE   *v* **-VIVED, -VIVING, -VIVES** to remain in existence

SURVIVER   *n* pl. **-S** survivor

SURVIVOR   *n* pl. **-S** one that survives

SUS   *v* **-ED, -ING, -ES** to suss

SUSHI   *n* pl. **-S** a dish of cold rice cakes topped with strips of raw fish

SUSLIK   *n* pl. **-S** a Eurasian rodent

SUSPECT   *v* **-ED, -ING, -S** to think guilty on slight evidence

SUSPEND   *v* **-ED, -ING, -S** to cause to stop for a period

SUSPENSE   *n* pl. **-S** a state of mental uncertainty or excitement

SUSPIRE   *v* **-PIRED, -PIRING, -PIRES** to sigh

SUSS   *v* **-ED, -ING, -ES** to figure out or check out

SUSTAIN   *v* **-ED, -ING, -S** to maintain by providing with food and drink

SUSURRUS   *n* pl. **-ES** a soft rustling sound

SUTLER   *n* pl. **-S** one that peddles goods to soldiers

SUTRA   *n* pl. **-S** a Hindu aphorism

SUTTA   *n* pl. **-S** sutra

SUTTEE   *n* pl. **-S** a Hindu widow cremated on her husband's funeral pyre to show her devotion to him

SUTURAL   *adj* pertaining to the line of junction between two bones

SUTURE   *v* **-TURED, -TURING, -TURES** to unite by sewing

SUZERAIN   *n* pl. **-S** a feudal lord

SVARAJ   *n* pl. **-ES** swaraj

SVEDBERG   *n* pl. **-S** a unit of time

SVELTE   *adj* **SVELTER, SVELTEST** gracefully slender **SVELTELY** *adv*

SWAB   *v* **SWABBED, SWABBING, SWABS** to clean with a large mop

SWABBER   *n* pl. **-S** one that swabs

SWABBIE   *n* pl. **-S** a sailor

SWABBING   present participle of swab

SWABBY   *n* pl. **-BIES** swabbie

SWACKED   *adj* drunk

SWADDLE   *v* **-DLED, -DLING, -DLES** to wrap in bandages

SWAG   *v* **SWAGGED, SWAGGING, SWAGS** to sway

SWAGE   *v* **SWAGED, SWAGING, SWAGES** to shape with a hammering tool

SWAGER   *n* pl. **-S** one that swages

SWAGGER   *v* **-ED, -ING, -S** to walk with a pompous air

SWAGGIE   *n* pl. **-S** a swagman

SWAGGING   present participle of swag

SWAGING   present participle of swage

SWAGMAN   *n* pl. **-MEN** a hobo

SWAIL   *n* pl. **-S** swale

SWAIN   *n* pl. **-S** a country boy **SWAINISH** *adj*

SWALE   *n* pl. **-S** a tract of low, marshy ground

SWALLOW   *v* **-ED, -ING, -S** to take through the mouth and esophagus into the stomach

SWAM   past tense of swim

SWAMI   *n* pl. **-S** a Hindu religious teacher

SWAMIES   pl. of swamy

SWAMP   *v* **-ED, -ING, -S** to inundate

SWAMPER   *n* pl. **-S** one that lives in a swampy area

SWAMPISH   *adj* swampy

SWAMPY   *adj* **SWAMPIER, SWAMPIEST** marshy

SWAMY   *n* pl. **-MIES** swami

SWAN   *v* **SWANNED, SWANNING, SWANS** to swear

SWANG   a past tense of swing

SWANHERD   *n* pl. **-S** one who tends swans (large aquatic birds)

SWANK   *adj* **SWANKER, SWANKEST** imposingly elegant

SWANK   *v* **-ED, -ING, -S** to swagger

SWANKY   *adj* **SWANKIER, SWANKIEST** swank **SWANKILY** *adv*

SWANLIKE   *adj* resembling a swan

SWANNED   past tense of swan

SWANNERY   *n* pl. **-NERIES** a place where swans are raised

SWANNING   present participle of swan

SWANNY   *v* to declare — used only in the 1st person sing.

SWANPAN   *n* pl. **-S** a Chinese abacus

SWANSKIN   *n* pl. **-S** the skin of a swan

SWAP   *v* **SWAPPED, SWAPPING, SWAPS** to trade

SWAPFILE	*n* pl. **-S** a computer file with space for transferred programs
SWAPPER	*n* pl. **-S** one that swaps
SWARAJ	*n* pl. **-ES** self-government in British India
SWARD	*v* **-ED, -ING, -S** to cover with turf
SWARE	a past tense of swear
SWARF	*n* pl. **-S** material removed by a cutting tool
SWARM	*v* **-ED, -ING, -S** to move in a large group
SWARMER	*n* pl. **-S** one that swarms
SWARMING	*n* pl. **-S** the surrounding of a victim by a group of attackers
SWART	*adj* swarthy
SWARTH	*n* pl. **-S** turf
SWARTHY	*adj* **-THIER, -THIEST** having a dark complexion
SWARTY	*adj* swarthy
SWASH	*v* **-ED, -ING, -ES** to swagger
SWASHER	*n* pl. **-S** one that swashes
SWASTICA	*n* pl. **-S** swastika
SWASTIKA	*n* pl. **-S** a geometrical figure used as a symbol or ornament
SWAT	*v* **SWATTED, SWATTING, SWATS** to hit sharply
SWATCH	*n* pl. **-ES** a sample piece of cloth
SWATH	*n* pl. **-S** a row of cut grass or grain
SWATHE	*v* **SWATHED, SWATHING, SWATHES** to wrap in bandages
SWATHER	*n* pl. **-S** one that swathes
SWATTED	past tense of swat
SWATTER	*n* pl. **-S** one that swats
SWATTING	present participle of swat
SWAY	*v* **-ED, -ING, -S** to move slowly back and forth **SWAYABLE** *adj*
SWAYBACK	*n* pl. **-S** an abnormal sagging of the back
SWAYER	*n* pl. **-S** one that sways
SWAYFUL	*adj* capable of influencing
SWEAR	*v* **SWORE** or **SWARE, SWORN, SWEARING, SWEARS** to utter a solemn oath
SWEARER	*n* pl. **-S** one that swears
SWEARING	*n* pl. **-S** the act of uttering a solemn oath
SWEAT	*v* **-ED, -ING, -S** to perspire
SWEATBOX	*n* pl. **-ES** a small enclosure in which one is made to sweat
SWEATER	*n* pl. **-S** a knitted outer garment **SWEATERED** *adj*
SWEATY	*adj* **SWEATIER, SWEATIEST** covered with perspiration **SWEATILY** *adv*
SWEDE	*n* pl. **-S** a rutabaga
SWEENEY	*n* pl. **-NEYS** sweeny
SWEENY	*n* pl. **-NIES** atrophy of the shoulder muscles in horses
SWEEP	*v* **SWEPT, SWEEPING, SWEEPS** to clear or clean with a brush or broom
SWEEPER	*n* pl. **-S** one that sweeps
SWEEPING	*n* pl. **-S** the act of one that sweeps
SWEEPY	*adj* **SWEEPIER, SWEEPIEST** of wide range or scope
SWEER	*adj* lazy
SWEET	*adj* **SWEETER, SWEETEST** pleasing to the taste
SWEET	*n* pl. **-S** something that is sweet
SWEETEN	*v* **-ED, -ING, -S** to make sweet
SWEETIE	*n* pl. **-S** darling
SWEETING	*n* pl. **-S** a sweet apple
SWEETISH	*adj* somewhat sweet
SWEETLIP	*n* pl. **-S** a fish having a protruding mouth
SWEETLY	*adv* in a sweet manner
SWEETSOP	*n* pl. **-S** a tropical tree
SWELL	*adj* **SWELLER, SWELLEST** stylish
SWELL	*v* **SWELLED, SWOLLEN, SWELLING, SWELLS** to increase in size or volume
SWELLING	*n* pl. **-S** something that is swollen
SWELTER	*v* **-ED, -ING, -S** to suffer from oppressive heat
SWELTRY	*adj* **-TRIER, -TRIEST** oppressively hot
SWEPT	past tense of sweep
SWERVE	*v* **SWERVED, SWERVING, SWERVES** to turn aside suddenly from a straight course
SWERVER	*n* pl. **-S** one that swerves
SWEVEN	*n* pl. **-S** a dream or vision
SWIDDEN	*n* pl. **-S** an agricultural plot produced by burning off the vegetative cover
SWIFT	*adj* **SWIFTER, SWIFTEST** moving with a great rate of motion
SWIFT	*n* pl. **-S** a fast-flying bird
SWIFTER	*n* pl. **-S** a rope on a ship

SWIFTIE	*n* pl. **-S** a person who acts or thinks quickly
SWIFTLET	*n* pl. **-S** a cave-dwelling swift
SWIFTLY	*adv* in a swift manner
SWIG	*v* **SWIGGED, SWIGGING, SWIGS** to drink deeply or rapidly
SWIGGER	*n* pl. **-S** one that swigs
SWILE	*n* pl. **-S** a seal (a marine mammal)
SWILER	*n* pl. **-S** one that hunts seals
SWILING	*n* pl. **-S** the activity of hunting seals
SWILL	*v* **-ED, -ING, -S** to swig
SWILLER	*n* pl. **-S** one that swills
SWIM	*v* **SWAM, SWUM, SWIMMING, SWIMS** to propel oneself in water by natural means
SWIMMER	*n* pl. **-S** one that swims
SWIMMING	*n* pl. **-S** the act of one that swims
SWIMMY	*adj* **-MIER, -MIEST** dizzy **SWIMMILY** *adv*
SWIMSUIT	*n* pl. **-S** a bathing suit
SWIMWEAR	*n* pl. **SWIMWEAR** clothing suitable for swimming
SWINDLE	*v* **-DLED, -DLING, -DLES** to take money or property from by fraudulent means
SWINDLER	*n* pl. **-S** one that swindles
SWINE	*n* pl. **-S** a contemptible person
SWINEPOX	*n* pl. **-ES** a disease of swine
SWING	*v* **SWUNG** or **SWANG, SWINGING, SWINGS** to move freely back and forth
SWINGBY	*n* pl. **-BYS** a mission in which a spacecraft uses a planet's gravitational pull for making course changes
SWINGE	*v* **SWINGED, SWINGEING, SWINGES** to flog
SWINGER	*n* pl. **-S** one that swings
SWINGIER	comparative of swingy
SWINGIEST	superlative of swingy
SWINGING	*adj* **SWINGINGEST** lively and hip
SWINGING	*n* pl. **-S** the practice of swapping sex partners
SWINGLE	*v* **-GLED, -GLING, -GLES** to scutch
SWINGMAN	*n* pl. **-MEN** a basketball player who can play guard or forward
SWINGY	*adj* **SWINGIER, SWINGIEST** marked by swinging
SWINISH	*adj* resembling or befitting a pig

SWINK	*v* **-ED, -ING, -S** to toil
SWINNEY	*n* pl. **-NEYS** sweeny
SWIPE	*v* **SWIPED, SWIPING, SWIPES** to strike with a sweeping blow
SWIPER	*n* pl. **-S** one that swipes
SWIPES	*n/pl* spoiled beer
SWIPLE	*n* pl. **-S** a part of a threshing device
SWIPPLE	*n* pl. **-S** swiple
SWIRL	*v* **-ED, -ING, -S** to move with a whirling motion
SWIRLY	*adj* **SWIRLIER, SWIRLIEST** swirling
SWISH	*v* **-ED, -ING, -ES** to move with a prolonged hissing sound
SWISH	*adj* **SWISHER, SWISHEST** 1. smart, fashionable 2. effeminate
SWISHER	*n* pl. **-S** one that swishes
SWISHY	*adj* **SWISHIER, SWISHIEST** swishing; effeminate
SWISS	*n* pl. **-ES** a cotton fabric
SWITCH	*v* **-ED, -ING, -ES** to beat with a flexible rod
SWITCHEL	*n* pl. **-S** a drink made with water, molasses, and vinegar and often ginger
SWITCHER	*n* pl. **-S** one that switches
SWITH	*adv* quickly
SWITHE	*adv* swith
SWITHER	*v* **-ED, -ING, -S** to doubt
SWITHLY	*adv* swith
SWIVE	*v* **SWIVED, SWIVING, SWIVES** to copulate with
SWIVEL	*v* **-ELED, -ELING, -ELS** or **-ELLED, -ELLING, -ELS** to turn on a pivoted support
SWIVET	*n* pl. **-S** a state of nervous excitement
SWIZZLE	*v* **-ZLED, -ZLING, -ZLES** to drink excessively
SWIZZLER	*n* pl. **-S** one that swizzles
SWOB	*v* **SWOBBED, SWOBBING, SWOBS** to swab
SWOBBER	*n* pl. **-S** swabber
SWOLLEN	past participle of swell
SWOON	*v* **-ED, -ING, -S** to faint
SWOONER	*n* pl. **-S** one that swoons
SWOONY	*adj* **SWOONIER, SWOONIEST** languid, dazed

SWOOP   *v* **-ED, -ING, -S** to make a sudden descent

SWOOPER   *n* pl. **-S** one that swoops

SWOOPY   *adj* **SWOOPIER, SWOOPIEST** having sweeping lines or features

SWOOSH   *v* **-ED, -ING, -ES** to move with a rustling sound

SWOP   *v* **SWOPPED, SWOPPING, SWOPS** to swap

SWOPPER   *n* pl. **-S** swapper

SWORD   *n* pl. **-S** a weapon having a long blade for cutting or thrusting

SWORDMAN   *n* pl. **-MEN** one skilled in the use of a sword

SWORE   a past tense of swear

SWORN   past participle of swear

SWOT   *v* **SWOTTED, SWOTTING, SWOTS** to swat

SWOTTER   *n* pl. **-S** one that swots

SWOUN   *v* **-ED, -ING, -S** to swoon

SWOUND   *v* **-ED, -ING, -S** to swoon

SWUM   past participle of swim

SWUNG   a past tense of swing

SYBARITE   *n* pl. **-S** a person devoted to pleasure and luxury

SYBO   *n* pl. **-BOES** the cibol

SYCAMINE   *n* pl. **-S** the mulberry tree

SYCAMORE   *n* pl. **-S** a North American tree

SYCE   *n* pl. **-S** a male servant in India

SYCEE   *n* pl. **-S** fine uncoined silver formerly used in China as money

SYCOMORE   *n* pl. **-S** sycamore

SYCON   *n* pl. **-S** a type of sponge **SYCONOID** *adj*

SYCONIUM   *n* pl. **-NIA** a fleshy multiple fruit

SYCOSIS   *n* pl. **-COSES** an inflammatory disease of the hair follicles

SYENITE   *n* pl. **-S** an igneous rock **SYENITIC** *adj*

SYKE   *n* pl. **-S** a small stream

SYLI   *n* pl. **-S** a former monetary unit of Guinea

SYLLABI   a pl. of syllabus

SYLLABIC   *n* pl. **-S** a speech sound of high sonority

SYLLABLE   *v* **-BLED, -BLING, -BLES** to pronounce syllables (units of spoken language)

SYLLABUB   *n* pl. **-S** sillabub

SYLLABUS   *n* pl. **-BUSES** or **-BI** an outline of a course of study

SYLPH   *n* pl. **-S** a slender, graceful girl or woman **SYLPHIC, SYLPHISH, SYLPHY** *adj*

SYLPHID   *n* pl. **-S** a young sylph

SYLVA   *n* pl. **-VAS** or **-VAE** the forest trees of an area

SYLVAN   *n* pl. **-S** one that lives in a forest

SYLVATIC   *adj* pertaining to a forest

SYLVIN   *n* pl. **-S** sylvite

SYLVINE   *n* pl. **-S** sylvite

SYLVITE   *n* pl. **-S** an ore of potassium

SYMBION   *n* pl. **-S** symbiont

SYMBIONT   *n* pl. **-S** an organism living in close association with another

SYMBIOT   *n* pl. **-S** symbiont

SYMBIOTE   *n* pl. **-S** symbiont

SYMBOL   *v* **-BOLED, -BOLING, -BOLS** or **-BOLLED, -BOLLING, -BOLS** to serve as a symbol (a representation) of

SYMBOLIC   *adj* pertaining to a symbol

SYMMETRY   *n* pl. **-TRIES** an exact correspondence between the opposite halves of a figure

SYMPATHY   *n* pl. **-THIES** a feeling of compassion for another's suffering

SYMPATRY   *n* pl. **-RIES** the state of occupying the same area without loss of identity from interbreeding

SYMPHONY   *n* pl. **-NIES** an orchestral composition

SYMPODIA   *n/pl* plant stems made up of a series of superposed branches

SYMPOSIA   *n/pl* conferences for the purpose of discussion

SYMPTOM   *n* pl. **-S** an indication of something

SYN   *adv* syne

SYNAGOG   *n* pl. **-S** a building for Jewish worship

SYNANON   *n* pl. **-S** a method of group therapy for drug addicts

SYNAPSE   *v* **-APSED, -APSING, -APSES** to come together in synapsis

SYNAPSID   *n* pl. **-S** one of a group of extinct reptiles

SYNAPSIS   *n* pl. **-APSES** the point at which a nervous impulse passes from one neuron to another **SYNAPTIC** *adj*

SYNC   *v* **-ED, -ING, -S** to cause to operate in unison

SYNCARP   *n* pl. **-S** a fleshy multiple fruit

SYNCARPY   *n* pl. **-PIES** the state of being a syncarp

SYNCH   *v* **-ED, -ING, -S** to sync

SYNCHRO   *n* pl. **-CHROS** a selsyn

SYNCLINE   *n* pl. **-S** a type of rock formation

SYNCOM   *n* pl. **-S** a type of communications satellite

SYNCOPE   *n* pl. **-S** the contraction of a word by omitting one or more sounds from the middle **SYNCOPAL, SYNCOPIC** *adj*

SYNCYTIA   *n/pl* masses of protoplasm resulting from cell fusion

SYNDESIS   *n* pl. **-DESISES** or **-DESES** synapsis

SYNDET   *n* pl. **-S** a synthetic detergent

SYNDETIC   *adj* serving to connect

SYNDIC   *n* pl. **-S** a business agent **SYNDICAL** *adj*

SYNDROME   *n* pl. **-S** a group of symptoms that characterize a particular disorder

SYNE   *adv* since

SYNECTIC   *adj* pertaining to a system of problem solving

SYNERGIA   *n* pl. **-S** synergy

SYNERGID   *n* pl. **-S** a cell found in the embryo sac of a seed plant

SYNERGY   *n* pl. **-GIES** combined action **SYNERGIC** *adj*

SYNESIS   *n* pl. **-SISES** a type of grammatical construction

SYNFUEL   *n* pl. **-S** a fuel derived from fossil fuels

SYNGAMY   *n* pl. **-MIES** the union of two gametes **SYNGAMIC** *adj*

SYNGAS   *n* pl. **-GASES** or **-GASSES** a mixture of carbon monoxide and hydrogen used in chemical synthesis

SYNGENIC   *adj* relating to or being genetically identical individuals with respect to reaction to antigens

SYNKARYA   *n/pl* cell nuclei formed by the fusion of two preexisting nuclei

SYNOD   *n* pl. **-S** a church council **SYNODAL, SYNODIC** *adj*

SYNONYM   *n* pl. **-S** a word having the same meaning as another

SYNONYME   *n* pl. **-S** synonym

SYNONYMY   *n* pl. **-MIES** equivalence of meaning

SYNOPSIS   *n* pl. **-OPSES** a summary **SYNOPTIC** *adj*

SYNOVIA   *n* pl. **-S** a lubricating fluid secreted by certain membranes **SYNOVIAL** *adj*

SYNTAGM   *n* pl. **-S** syntagma

SYNTAGMA   *n* pl. **-MAS** or **-MATA** a syntactic element

SYNTAX   *n* pl. **-ES** the way in which words are put together to form phrases and sentences

SYNTH   *n* pl. **-S** a synthesizer

SYNTHASE   *n* pl. **-S** an enzyme that acts as a catalyst in linking two molecules

SYNTHPOP   *n* pl. **-S** popular music played with synthesizers

SYNTONE   *n* pl. **-S** a person having a syntonic temperament

SYNTONIC   *adj* having a temperament responsive to a given social environment

SYNTONY   *n* pl. **-NIES** the tuning of transmitters and receivers with each other

SYNTYPE   *n* pl. **-S** each of a set of type specimens on which the name of a new species is based

SYNURA   *n* pl. **-RAE** any of a genus of protozoa

SYPH   *n* pl. **-S** syphilis

SYPHER   *v* **-ED, -ING, -S** to overlap so as to make an even surface, as beveled plank edges

SYPHILIS   *n* pl. **-LISES** a venereal disease

SYPHON   *v* **-ED, -ING, -S** to siphon

SYPHONAL   *adj* siphonal

SYPHONIC   *adj* siphonic

SYREN   *n* pl. **-S** siren

SYRETTE   *n* pl. **-S** a small tube fitted with a hypodermic needle containing a single dose of medication

SYRINGA   *n* pl. **-S** an ornamental shrub

SYRINGE   *v* **-RINGED, -RINGING, -RINGES** to cleanse or treat with injected fluid

SYRINX   *n* pl. **-INXES** or **-INGES** the vocal organ of a bird

SYRPHIAN   *n* pl. **-S** syrphid

SYRPHID   *n* pl. **-S** a winged insect

SYRUP   *v* **-ED, -ING, -S** to sweeten with a thick sweet liquid

SYRUPY   *adj* **-UPIER, -UPIEST** resembling a thick, sticky, sweet liquid

SYSADMIN   *n* pl. **-S** a system administrator

SYSOP   *n* pl. **-S** the administrator of a computer bulletin board

SYSTEM   *n* pl. **-S** a group of interacting elements forming a unified whole

SYSTEMIC   *n* pl. **-S** a type of pesticide

SYSTOLE   *n* pl. **-S** the normal rhythmic contraction of the heart **SYSTOLIC** *adj*

SYZYGY   *n* pl. **-GIES** the configuration of the earth, moon, and sun lying in a straight line **SYZYGAL, SYZYGIAL** *adj*

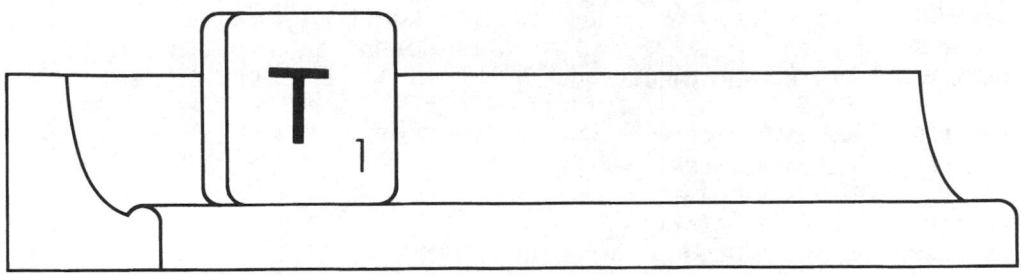

TA	*n* pl. **-S** an expression of gratitude
TAB	*v* **TABBED, TABBING, TABS** to name or designate
TABANID	*n* pl. **-S** a bloodsucking insect
TABARD	*n* pl. **-S** a sleeveless outer garment **TABARDED** *adj*
TABARET	*n* pl. **-S** a silk fabric
TABBED	past tense of tab
TABBING	*n* pl. **-S** the use of the tab key on a keyboard
TABBIS	*n* pl. **-BISES** a silk fabric
TABBY	*v* **-BIED, -BYING, -BIES** to give a wavy appearance to
TABER	*v* **-ED, -ING, -S** to tabor
TABES	*n* pl. **TABES** a syphilitic disease
TABETIC	*n* pl. **-S** one affected with tabes
TABID	*adj* affected with tabes
TABLA	*n* pl. **-S** a small drum
TABLE	*v* **-BLED, -BLING, -BLES** to place on a table (a piece of furniture having a flat upper surface)
TABLEAU	*n* pl. **-LEAUS** or **-LEAUX** a picture
TABLEFUL	*n* pl. **TABLEFULS** or **TABLESFUL** as much as a table can hold
TABLET	*v* **-LETED, -LETING, -LETS** or **-LETTED, -LETTING, -LETS** to inscribe on a small, flat surface
TABLETOP	*n* pl. **-S** the top of a table
TABLING	*n* pl. **-S** the setting of data or information in tables (columns)
TABLOID	*n* pl. **-S** a small newspaper
TABOO	*v* **-ED, -ING, -S** to exclude from use, approach, or mention
TABOOLEY	*n* pl. **-LEYS** tabouli
TABOR	*v* **-ED, -ING, -S** to beat on a small drum
TABORER	*n* pl. **-S** one that tabors
TABORET	*n* pl. **-S** a small drum
TABORIN	*n* pl. **-S** taborine
TABORINE	*n* pl. **-S** a taboret
TABOULEH	*n* pl. **-S** tabouli
TABOULI	*n* pl. **-S** a Lebanese salad containing bulgur wheat, tomatoes, parsley, onions, and mint
TABOUR	*v* **-ED, -ING, -S** to tabor
TABOURER	*n* pl. **-S** taborer
TABOURET	*n* pl. **-S** taboret
TABU	*v* **-ED, -ING, -S** to taboo
TABULAR	*adj* of or pertaining to a list
TABULATE	*v* **-LATED, -LATING, -LATES** to arrange in a list
TABULI	*n* pl. **-S** tabouli
TABUN	*n* pl. **-S** a chemical compound
TACAN	*n* pl. **-S** a navigational system for aircraft
TACE	*n* pl. **-S** a tasset
TACET	*v* be silent — used as a musical direction
TACH	*n* pl. **-S** a device for indicating speed of rotation
TACHE	*n* pl. **-S** a clasp or buckle
TACHINID	*n* pl. **-S** a grayish fly
TACHISM	*n* pl. **-S** action painting
TACHISME	*n* pl. **-S** tachism
TACHIST	*n* pl. **-S** an action painter
TACHISTE	*n* pl. **-S** tachist
TACHYON	*n* pl. **-S** a theoretical subatomic particle
TACIT	*adj* unspoken **TACITLY** *adv*
TACITURN	*adj* habitually silent
TACK	*v* **-ED, -ING, -S** to fasten with tacks (short, sharp-pointed nails)
TACKER	*n* pl. **-S** one that tacks
TACKET	*n* pl. **-S** a hobnail
TACKEY	*adj* **TACKIER, TACKIEST** tacky

TACKIER	comparative of tacky
TACKIEST	superlative of tacky
TACKIFY	*v* **-FIED, -FYING, -FIES** to make tacky
TACKILY	*adv* in a tacky manner
TACKLE	*v* **-LED, -LING, -LES** to seize and throw to the ground
TACKLER	*n* pl. **-S** one that tackles
TACKLESS	*adj* having no tacks
TACKLING	*n* pl. **-S** equipment
TACKY	*adj* **TACKIER, TACKIEST** adhesive
TACNODE	*n* pl. **-S** a point of contact between two curves
TACO	*n* pl. **-COS** a tortilla folded around a filling
TACONITE	*n* pl. **-S** a low-grade iron ore
TACRINE	*n* pl. **-S** a drug for treating Alzheimer's disease
TACT	*n* pl. **-S** skill in dealing with delicate situations
TACTFUL	*adj* having tact
TACTIC	*n* pl. **-S** a maneuver for gaining an objective **TACTICAL** *adj*
TACTILE	*adj* pertaining to the sense of touch
TACTION	*n* pl. **-S** the act of touching
TACTLESS	*adj* lacking tact
TACTUAL	*adj* tactile
TAD	*n* pl. **-S** a small boy
TADPOLE	*n* pl. **-S** the aquatic larva of an amphibian
TAE	*prep* to
TAEL	*n* pl. **-S** a Chinese unit of weight
TAENIA	*n* pl. **-NIAS** or **-NIAE** a tapeworm **TAENIOID** *adj*
TAENITE	*n* pl. **-S** a nickel-iron alloy in meteorites
TAFFAREL	*n* pl. **-S** taffrail
TAFFEREL	*n* pl. **-S** taffrail
TAFFETA	*n* pl. **-S** a lustrous fabric
TAFFIA	*n* pl. **-S** tafia
TAFFRAIL	*n* pl. **-S** a rail around the stern of a ship
TAFFY	*n* pl. **-FIES** a chewy candy
TAFIA	*n* pl. **-S** an inferior rum
TAG	*v* **TAGGED, TAGGING, TAGS** to provide with a tag (an identifying marker)

TAGALONG	*n* pl. **-S** one that follows another
TAGBOARD	*n* pl. **-S** a material for making shipping tags
TAGETES	*n* pl. **TAGETES** a flowering plant
TAGGANT	*n* pl. **-S** a substance added to a product to indicate its source of manufacture
TAGGED	past tense of tag
TAGGER	*n* pl. **-S** one that tags
TAGGING	present participle of tag
TAGINE	*n* pl. **-S** tajine
TAGLIKE	*adj* resembling a tag
TAGLINE	*n* pl. **-S** the final line of a play or joke that makes the point
TAGMEME	*n* pl. **-S** the smallest unit of meaningful grammatical relation
TAGMEMIC	*adj* pertaining to a grammar in which a tagmeme is the basic unit
TAGRAG	*n* pl. **-S** riffraff
TAHINA	*n* pl. **-S** tahini
TAHINI	*n* pl. **-S** a paste of sesame seeds
TAHR	*n* pl. **-S** a goatlike mammal
TAHSIL	*n* pl. **-S** a district in India
TAIGA	*n* pl. **-S** a subarctic evergreen forest
TAIGLACH	*n* pl. **TAIGLACH** teiglach
TAIKO	*n* pl. **-KOS** a barrel-shaped Japanese drum
TAIL	*v* **-ED, -ING, -S** to provide with a tail (a hindmost part)
TAILBACK	*n* pl. **-S** a member of the backfield in some football formations
TAILBONE	*n* pl. **-S** the coccyx
TAILCOAT	*n* pl. **-S** a man's coat
TAILER	*n* pl. **-S** one that secretly follows another
TAILFAN	*n* pl. **-S** a fanlike swimming organ at the rear of some crustaceans
TAILFIN	*n* pl. **-S** a fin at the posterior end of a fish
TAILGATE	*v* **-GATED, -GATING, -GATES** to drive dangerously close behind another vehicle
TAILHOOK	*n* pl. **-S** a hook lowered from the tail of an aircraft to engage a braking cable
TAILING	*n* pl. **-S** the part of a projecting stone or brick that is inserted into a wall
TAILLAMP	*n* pl. **-S** a light at the rear of a vehicle

TAILLE	*n* pl. **-S** a former French tax
TAILLESS	*adj* having no tail
TAILLEUR	*n* pl. **-S** a woman's tailored suit
TAILLIKE	*adj* resembling a tail
TAILOR	*v* **-ED, -ING, -S** to fit with clothes
TAILPIPE	*n* pl. **-S** an exhaust pipe
TAILRACE	*n* pl. **-S** a part of a millrace
TAILSKID	*n* pl. **-S** a support on which the tail of an airplane rests
TAILSPIN	*v* **-SPINNED** or **-SPUN, -SPINNING, -SPINS** to spin headlong down toward earth
TAILWIND	*n* pl. **-S** a wind coming from behind a moving vehicle
TAIN	*n* pl. **-S** a thin plate
TAINT	*v* **-ED, -ING, -S** to touch or affect slightly with something bad
TAIPAN	*n* pl. **-S** a venomous snake
TAJ	*n* pl. **-ES** a tall, conical cap worn in Muslim countries
TAJINE	*n* pl. **-S** an earthenware Moroccan cooking pot
TAKA	*n* pl. **-S** a monetary unit of Bangladesh
TAKAHE	*n* pl. **-S** a flightless bird
TAKE	*v* **TOOK, TAKEN, TAKING, TAKES** to get possession of **TAKABLE, TAKEABLE** *adj*
TAKEAWAY	*n* pl. **-AWAYS** prepared food to be taken away from its place of sale
TAKEDOWN	*n* pl. **-S** an article that can be taken apart easily
TAKEOFF	*n* pl. **-S** the act of rising in flight
TAKEOUT	*n* pl. **-S** the act of removing
TAKEOVER	*n* pl. **-S** the act of assuming control
TAKER	*n* pl. **-S** one that takes
TAKEUP	*n* pl. **-S** the act of taking something up
TAKIN	*n* pl. **-S** a goatlike mammal
TAKING	*n* pl. **-S** a seizure
TAKINGLY	*adv* in an attractive manner
TALA	*n* pl. **-S** a traditional rhythmic pattern of music in India
TALAPOIN	*n* pl. **-S** a small African monkey
TALAR	*n* pl. **-S** a long cloak
TALARIA	*n/pl* winged sandals worn by various figures of classical mythology
TALBOT	*n* pl. **-S** a large dog of an extinct breed

TALC	*v* **TALCKED, TALCKING, TALCS** or **TALCED, TALCING, TALCS** to treat with talc (a soft mineral with a soapy texture) **TALCKY, TALCOSE, TALCOUS, TALCY** *adj*
TALCUM	*v* **-ED, -ING, -S** to treat with a powder made from talc
TALE	*n* pl. **-S** a story
TALEGGIO	*n* pl. **-GIOS** a soft creamy cheese
TALENT	*n* pl. **-S** a special natural ability **TALENTED** *adj*
TALER	*n* pl. **-S** a formerly used German coin
TALESMAN	*n* pl. **-MEN** a person summoned to fill a vacancy on a jury
TALI	pl. of talus
TALION	*n* pl. **-S** a retaliation for a crime
TALIPED	*n* pl. **-S** a person afflicted with clubfoot
TALIPES	*n* pl. **TALIPES** clubfoot
TALIPOT	*n* pl. **-S** a tall palm tree
TALISMAN	*n* pl. **-S** an object believed to possess magical powers
TALK	*v* **-ED, -ING, -S** to communicate by speaking
TALKABLE	*adj* able to be talked about
TALKBACK	*n* pl. **-S** a one-way communications link between a control booth and a recording studio
TALKER	*n* pl. **-S** one that talks
TALKFEST	*n* pl. **-S** a gabfest
TALKIE	*n* pl. **-S** a moving picture with synchronized sound
TALKING	*n* pl. **-S** conversation
TALKY	*adj* **TALKIER, TALKIEST** tending to talk a great deal
TALL	*n* pl. **-S** a garment size for tall persons
TALL	*adj* **TALLER, TALLEST** having great height
TALLAGE	*v* **-LAGED, -LAGING, -LAGES** to tax
TALLBOY	*n* pl. **-BOYS** a highboy
TALLIED	past tense of tally
TALLIER	*n* pl. **-S** one that tallies
TALLIES	present 3d person sing. of tally
TALLIS	*n* pl. **-LISES** or **-LISIM** tallith
TALLISH	*adj* somewhat tall
TALLIT	*n* pl. **-LITOT** or **-LITS** or **-LITIM** tallith

TALLITH *n* pl. **-LITHS** or **-LITHIM** a Jewish prayer shawl

TALLNESS *n* pl. **-ES** the state of being tall

TALLOL *n* pl. **-S** a resinous liquid

TALLOW *v* **-ED, -ING, -S** to smear with tallow (a mixture of animal fats)

TALLOWY *adj* resembling tallow

TALLY *v* **-LIED, -LYING, -LIES** to count

TALLYHO *v* **-HOED, -HOING, -HOS** or **-HOES** to make an encouraging shout to hunting hounds

TALLYMAN *n* pl. **-MEN** a person who tallies

TALMUDIC *adj* pertaining to the body of Jewish civil and religious law

TALON *n* pl. **-S** a claw of a bird of prey **TALONED** *adj*

TALOOKA *n* pl. **-S** taluk

TALUK *n* pl. **-S** an estate in India

TALUKA *n* pl. **-S** taluk

TALUS *n* pl. **-ES** a slope formed by an accumulation of rock debris

TALUS *n* pl. **-LI** a bone of the foot

TAM *n* pl. **-S** a tight-fitting Scottish cap

TAMABLE *adj* capable of being tamed

TAMAL *n* pl. **-S** tamale

TAMALE *n* pl. **-S** a Mexican dish

TAMANDU *n* pl. **-S** tamandua

TAMANDUA *n* pl. **-S** an arboreal anteater

TAMARACK *n* pl. **-S** a timber tree

TAMARAO *n* pl. **-RAOS** tamarau

TAMARAU *n* pl. **-S** a small buffalo of the Philippines

TAMARI *n* pl. **-S** a Japanese soy sauce

TAMARIN *n* pl. **-S** a South American monkey

TAMARIND *n* pl. **-S** a tropical tree

TAMARISK *n* pl. **-S** an evergreen shrub

TAMASHA *n* pl. **-S** a public entertainment in India

TAMBAC *n* pl. **-S** tombac

TAMBAK *n* pl. **-S** tombac

TAMBALA *n* pl. **TAMBALAS** or **MATAMBALA** a monetary unit of Malawi

TAMBOUR *v* **-ED, -ING, -S** to embroider on a round wooden frame

TAMBOURA *n* pl. **-S** tambura

TAMBUR *n* pl. **-S** tambura

TAMBURA *n* pl. **-S** a stringed instrument

TAME *adj* **TAMER, TAMEST** gentle or docile

TAME *v* **TAMED, TAMING, TAMES** to make tame

TAMEABLE *adj* tamable

TAMEIN *n* pl. **-S** a garment worn by Burmese women

TAMELESS *adj* not capable of being tamed

TAMELY *adv* in a tame manner

TAMENESS *n* pl. **-ES** the state of being tame

TAMER *n* pl. **-S** one that tames

TAMEST superlative of tame

TAMING present participle of tame

TAMIS *n* pl. **-ISES** a strainer made of cloth mesh

TAMMIE *n* pl. **-S** tammy

TAMMY *n* pl. **-MIES** a fabric of mixed fibers

TAMP *v* **-ED, -ING, -S** to pack down by tapping

TAMPALA *n* pl. **-S** an annual herb

TAMPAN *n* pl. **-S** a biting insect

TAMPER *v* **-ED, -ING, -S** to interfere in a harmful manner

TAMPERER *n* pl. **-S** one that tampers

TAMPING *n* pl. **-S** the act of packing down by tapping

TAMPION *n* pl. **-S** a plug for the muzzle of a cannon

TAMPON *v* **-ED, -ING, -S** to plug with a cotton pad

TAN *adj* **TANNER, TANNEST** brown from the sun's rays

TAN *v* **TANNED, TANNING, TANS** to convert hide into leather by soaking in chemicals

TANAGER *n* pl. **-S** a brightly colored bird

TANBARK *n* pl. **-S** a tree bark used as a source of tannin

TANDEM *n* pl. **-S** a bicycle built for two

TANDOOR *n* pl. **-DOORS** or **-DOORI** a clay oven

TANDOORI *n* pl. **-S** food cooked in a tandoor

TANG *v* **-ED, -ING, -S** to provide with a pungent flavor

TANGA *n* pl. **TANGA** a former monetary unit of Tajikistan

TANGELO *n* pl. **-LOS** a citrus fruit

TANGENCE *n* pl. **-S** tangency

TANGENCY *n* pl. **-CIES** the state of being in immediate physical contact

TANGENT   *n* pl. **-S** a straight line in contact with a curve at one point

TANGIBLE   *n* pl. **-S** something palpable

TANGIBLY   *adv* palpably

TANGIER   comparative of tangy

TANGIEST   superlative of tangy

TANGLE   *v* **-GLED, -GLING, -GLES** to bring together in intricate confusion

TANGLER   *n* pl. **-S** one that tangles

TANGLY   *adj* **-GLIER, -GLIEST** tangled

TANGO   *v* **-GOED, -GOING, -GOS** or **-GOES** to perform a Latin American dance

TANGRAM   *n* pl. **-S** a Chinese puzzle

TANGY   *adj* **TANGIER, TANGIEST** pungent

TANIST   *n* pl. **-S** the heir apparent to a Celtic chief

TANISTRY   *n* pl. **-RIES** the system of electing a tanist

TANK   *v* **-ED, -ING, -S** to store in a tank (a container usually for liquids)

TANKA   *n* pl. **-S** a Japanese verse form

TANKAGE   *n* pl. **-S** the capacity of a tank

TANKARD   *n* pl. **-S** a tall drinking vessel

TANKER   *n* pl. **-S** a ship designed to transport liquids

TANKFUL   *n* pl. **-S** the amount a tank can hold

TANKINI   *n* pl. **-S** a woman's swimsuit consisting of bikini briefs and a tank top

TANKLESS   *adj* having no tank

TANKLIKE   *adj* resembling a tank

TANKSHIP   *n* pl. **-S** a tanker

TANNABLE   *adj* capable of being tanned

TANNAGE   *n* pl. **-S** the process of tanning

TANNATE   *n* pl. **-S** a chemical salt

TANNED   past tense of tan

TANNER   *n* pl. **-S** one that tans

TANNERY   *n* pl. **-NERIES** a place where hides are tanned

TANNEST   superlative of tan

TANNIC   *adj* pertaining to tannin

TANNIN   *n* pl. **-S** a chemical compound used in tanning

TANNING   *n* pl. **-S** the process of converting hides into leather

TANNISH   *adj* somewhat tan

TANREC   *n* pl. **-S** tenrec

TANSY   *n* pl. **-SIES** a perennial herb

TANTALUM   *n* pl. **-S** a metallic element **TANTALIC** *adj*

TANTALUS   *n* pl. **-ES** a case for wine bottles

TANTARA   *n* pl. **-S** the sound of a trumpet or horn

TANTIVY   *n* pl. **-TIVIES** a hunting cry

TANTO   *n* pl. **-TOS** a short Japanese sword

TANTRA   *n* pl. **-S** one of a class of Hindu religious writings **TANTRIC** *adj*

TANTRISM   *n* pl. **-S** a school of Buddhism incorporating Hindu and pagan elements

TANTRIST   *n* pl. **-S** an adherent of tantrism

TANTRUM   *n* pl. **-S** a fit of rage

TANUKI   *n* pl. **-S** a raccoon dog

TANYARD   *n* pl. **-S** the section of a tannery containing the vats

TAO   *n* pl. **-S** the path of virtuous conduct according to a Chinese philosophy

TAP   *v* **TAPPED, TAPPING, TAPS** to strike gently

TAPA   *n* pl. **-S** a cloth made from tree bark

TAPADERA   *n* pl. **-S** a part of a saddle

TAPADERO   *n* pl. **-ROS** tapadera

TAPALO   *n* pl. **-LOS** a scarf worn in Latin American countries

TAPE   *v* **TAPED, TAPING, TAPES** to fasten with tape (a long, narrow strip or band) **TAPEABLE** *adj*

TAPELESS   *adj* being without tape

TAPELIKE   *adj* resembling tape

TAPELINE   *n* pl. **-S** a tape for measuring distances

TAPENADE   *n* pl. **-S** a spread made with black olives, capers, and anchovies

TAPER   *v* **-ED, -ING, -S** to become gradually narrower toward one end

TAPERER   *n* pl. **-S** one that carries a candle in a religious procession

TAPESTRY   *v* **-TRIED, -TRYING, -TRIES** to decorate with woven wall hangings

TAPETUM   *n* pl. **-TA** a layer of cells in some plants **TAPETAL** *adj*

TAPEWORM   *n* pl. **-S** a parasitic worm

TAPHOLE   *n* pl. **-S** a hole in a blast furnace

TAPHOUSE   *n* pl. **-S** a tavern

TAPING *n* pl. **-S** the act or an instance of recording something on magnetic tape

TAPIOCA *n* pl. **-S** a starchy food

TAPIR *n* pl. **-S** a hoofed mammal

TAPIS *n* pl. **-PISES** material used for wall hangings and floor coverings

TAPLESS *adj* lacking a tap (a device to stop the flow of liquid or gas)

TAPPABLE *adj* capable of being tapped

TAPPED past tense of tap

TAPPER *n* pl. **-S** one that taps

TAPPET *n* pl. **-S** a sliding rod that causes another part of a mechanism to move

TAPPING *n* pl. **-S** the process or means by which something is tapped

TAPROOM *n* pl. **-S** a barroom

TAPROOT *n* pl. **-S** the main root of a plant

TAPSTER *n* pl. **-S** one that dispenses liquor in a barroom

TAQUERIA *n* pl. **-S** a restaurant specializing in tacos and burritos

TAR *v* **TARRED, TARRING, TARS** to cover with tar (a black viscous liquid)

TARABISH *n* pl. **-ES** a type of card game

TARAMA *n* pl. **-S** a Greek paste of fish roe, garlic, lemon juice, and olive oil

TARANTAS *n* pl. **-ES** a Russian carriage

TARBOOSH *n* pl. **-ES** a cap worn by Muslim men

TARBUSH *n* pl. **-ES** tarboosh

TARDIER comparative of tardy

TARDIES pl. of tardy

TARDIVE *adj* having symptoms that develop slowly

TARDO *adj* slow — used as a musical direction

TARDY *adj* **TARDIER, TARDIEST** late **TARDILY** *adv*

TARDY *n* pl. **-DIES** an instance of being late

TARDYON *n* pl. **-S** a subatomic particle that travels slower than the speed of light

TARE *v* **TARED, TARING, TARES** to determine the weight of a container holding goods

TARGA *n* pl. **-S** a type of convertible sports car

TARGE *n* pl. **-S** a small, round shield

TARGET *v* **-ED, -ING, -S** to make a goal of

TARIFF *v* **-ED, -ING, -S** to tax imported or exported goods

TARING present participle of tare

TARLATAN *n* pl. **-S** a cotton fabric

TARLETAN *n* pl. **-S** tarlatan

TARMAC *v* **-MACKED, -MACKING, -MACS** to cause (an aircraft) to sit on a taxiway

TARN *n* pl. **-S** a small mountain lake

TARNAL *adj* damned **TARNALLY** *adv*

TARNISH *v* **-ED, -ING, -ES** to dull the luster of

TARO *n* pl. **-ROS** a tropical plant

TAROC *n* pl. **-S** tarok

TAROK *n* pl. **-S** a card game

TAROT *n* pl. **-S** any of a set of playing cards used for fortune-telling

TARP *n* pl. **-S** a protective canvas covering

TARPAN *n* pl. **-S** an Asian wild horse

TARPAPER *n* pl. **-S** a heavy paper coated with tar

TARPON *n* pl. **-S** a marine game fish

TARRAGON *n* pl. **-S** a perennial herb

TARRE *v* **TARRED, TARRING, TARRES** to urge to action

TARRED past tense of tar

TARRIER *n* pl. **-S** one that tarries

TARRING present participle of tar and tarre

TARRY *adj* **-RIER, -RIEST** resembling tar

TARRY *v* **-RIED, -RYING, -RIES** to delay or be slow in acting or doing

TARSAL *n* pl. **-S** a bone of the foot

TARSI pl. of tarsus

TARSIA *n* pl. **-S** intarsia

TARSIER *n* pl. **-S** a nocturnal primate

TARSUS *n* pl. **TARSI** a part of the foot

TART *adj* **TARTER, TARTEST** having a sharp, sour taste

TART *v* **-ED, -ING, -S** to dress up

TARTAN *n* pl. **-S** a patterned woolen fabric

TARTANA *n* pl. **-S** a Mediterranean sailing vessel

TARTAR *n* pl. **-S** a crust on the teeth **TARTARIC** *adj*

TARTARE *adj* served raw

TARTIER comparative of tarty

TARTIEST superlative of tarty

TARTISH *adj* somewhat tart

TARTLET *n* pl. **-S** a small pie

TARTLY *adv* in a tart manner

TARTNESS *n* pl. **-ES** the state of being tart

TARTRATE *n* pl. **-S** a chemical salt

TARTUFE *n* pl. **-S** tartuffe

TARTUFFE *n* pl. **-S** a hypocrite

TARTUFO *n* pl. **-FI** or **-FOS** a white truffle

TARTY *adj* **TARTIER, TARTIEST** suggestive of a prostitute **TARTILY** *adv*

TARWEED *n* pl. **-S** a flowering plant

TARZAN *n* pl. **-S** a person of superior strength and agility

TASE *v* **TASED, TASING, TASES** to stun with a gun that fires electrified darts

TASK *v* **-ED, -ING, -S** to assign a job to

TASKBAR *n* pl. **-S** a row of graphical controls on a computer screen

TASKWORK *n* pl. **-S** hard work

TASS *n* pl. **-ES** a drinking cup

TASSE *n* pl. **-S** tasset

TASSEL *v* **-SELED, -SELING, -SELS** or **-SELLED, -SELLING, -SELS** to adorn with dangling ornaments

TASSET *n* pl. **-S** a piece of plate armor for the upper thigh

TASSIE *n* pl. **-S** tass

TASSO *n* pl. **-SOS** spicy cured pork

TASTE *v* **TASTED, TASTING, TASTES** to perceive the flavor of by taking into the mouth **TASTABLE** *adj*

TASTEFUL *adj* tasty

TASTER *n* pl. **-S** one that tastes

TASTING *n* pl. **-S** a gathering for sampling wines or foods

TASTY *adj* **TASTIER, TASTIEST** pleasant to the taste **TASTILY** *adv*

TAT *v* **TATTED, TATTING, TATS** to make tatting

TATAMI *n* pl. **-S** straw matting used as a floor covering

TATAR *n* pl. **-S** a ferocious person

TATE *n* pl. **-S** a tuft of hair

TATER *n* pl. **-S** a potato

TATHATA *n* pl. **-S** the ultimate nature of all things in Buddhism

TATOUAY *n* pl. **-AYS** a South American armadillo

TATSOI *n* pl. **-S** an Asian mustard

TATTED past tense of tat

TATTER *v* **-ED, -ING, -S** to become torn and worn

TATTIE *n* pl. **-S** a potato

TATTIER comparative of tatty

TATTIEST superlative of tatty

TATTILY *adv* in a tatty manner

TATTING *n* pl. **-S** delicate handmade lace

TATTLE *v* **-TLED, -TLING, -TLES** to reveal the activities of another

TATTLER *n* pl. **-S** one that tattles

TATTOO *v* **-ED, -ING, -S** to mark the skin with indelible pigments

TATTOOER *n* pl. **-S** one that tattoos

TATTY *adj* **-TIER, -TIEST** shabby

TAU *n* pl. **-S** a Greek letter

TAUGHT past tense of teach

TAUNT *v* **-ED, -ING, -S** to challenge or reproach sarcastically

TAUNTER *n* pl. **-S** one that taunts

TAUON *n* pl. **-S** an unstable lepton

TAUPE *n* pl. **-S** a dark gray color

TAURINE *n* pl. **-S** a chemical compound

TAUT *adj* **TAUTER, TAUTEST** fully stretched, so as not to be slack

TAUT *v* **-ED, -ING, -S** to tangle

TAUTAUG *n* pl. **-S** tautog

TAUTEN *v* **-ED, -ING, -S** to make taut

TAUTLY *adv* in a taut manner

TAUTNESS *n* pl. **-ES** the state of being taut

TAUTOG *n* pl. **-S** a marine fish

TAUTOMER *n* pl. **-S** a type of chemical compound

TAUTONYM *n* pl. **-S** a type of taxonomic designation

TAV *n* pl. **-S** a Hebrew letter

TAVERN *n* pl. **-S** a place where liquor is sold to be drunk on the premises

TAVERNA *n* pl. **-S** a cafe in Greece

TAVERNER *n* pl. **-S** one that runs a tavern

TAW *v* **-ED, -ING, -S** to convert into white leather by the application of minerals

TAWDRY *adj* **-DRIER, -DRIEST** gaudy **TAWDRILY** *adv*

TAWDRY *n* pl. **-DRIES** gaudy finery

TAWER *n* pl. **-S** one that taws

TAWIE *adj* docile

TAWNEY *n* pl. **-NEYS** tawny

TAWNY *adj* **-NIER, -NIEST** light brown **TAWNILY** *adv*

TAWNY *n* pl. **-NIES** a light brown color

TAWPIE *n* pl. **-S** a foolish young person

TAWSE *v* **TAWSED, TAWSING, TAWSES** to flog

TAX *v* **-ED, -ING, -ES** to place a tax (a charge imposed by authority for public purposes) on

TAXA a pl. of taxon

TAXABLE *adj* subject to tax **TAXABLY** *adv*

TAXABLE *n* pl. **-S** a taxable item

TAXATION *n* pl. **-S** the process of taxing

TAXEME *n* pl. **-S** a minimum grammatical feature of selection **TAXEMIC** *adj*

TAXER *n* pl. **-S** one that taxes

TAXI *v* **TAXIED, TAXIING** or **TAXYING, TAXIS** or **TAXIES** to travel in a taxicab

TAXICAB *n* pl. **-S** an automobile for hire

TAXIMAN *n* pl. **-MEN** the operator of a taxicab

TAXINGLY *adv* in an onerous manner

TAXITE *n* pl. **-S** a volcanic rock **TAXITIC** *adj*

TAXIWAY *n* pl. **-WAYS** a paved strip at an airport

TAXLESS *adj* free from taxation

TAXMAN *n* pl. **-MEN** one who collects taxes

TAXOL *n* pl. **-S** a medicinal substance from a yew tree

TAXON *n* pl. **TAXONS** or **TAXA** a unit of scientific classification

TAXONOMY *n* pl. **-MIES** the study of scientific classification

TAXPAID *adj* paid for by taxes

TAXPAYER *n* pl. **-S** one that pays taxes

TAXUS *n* pl. **TAXUS** an evergreen tree or shrub

TAXWISE *adj* pertaining to taxes

TAXYING a present participle of taxi

TAYBERRY *n* pl. **-RIES** a dark red fruit that is a cross between a blackberry and a raspberry

TAYRA *n* pl. **-S** a large mammal of Central and South America

TAZZA *n* pl. **-ZAS** or **-ZE** an ornamental bowl

TE *n* pl. **-S** ti

TEA *n* pl. **-S** a beverage made by infusing dried leaves in boiling water

TEABERRY *n* pl. **-RIES** a North American shrub

TEABOARD *n* pl. **-S** a tray for serving tea

TEABOWL *n* pl. **-S** a teacup having no handle

TEABOX *n* pl. **-ES** a box for tea leaves

TEACAKE *n* pl. **-S** a small cake served with tea

TEACART *n* pl. **-S** a wheeled table used in serving tea

TEACH *v* **TAUGHT, TEACHING, TEACHES** to impart knowledge or skill to

TEACHER *n* pl. **-S** one that teaches

TEACHING *n* pl. **-S** a doctrine

TEACUP *n* pl. **-S** a cup in which tea is served

TEAHOUSE *n* pl. **-S** a public establishment serving tea

TEAK *n* pl. **-S** an East Indian tree

TEAKWOOD *n* pl. **-S** the wood of the teak

TEAL *n* pl. **-S** a river duck

TEALIKE *adj* resembling tea

TEAM *v* **-ED, -ING, -S** to form a team (a group of persons associated in a joint action)

TEAMAKER *n* pl. **-S** one that makes tea

TEAMMATE *n* pl. **-S** a member of the same team

TEAMSTER *n* pl. **-S** a truck driver

TEAMWORK *n* pl. **-S** cooperative effort to achieve a common goal

TEAPOT *n* pl. **-S** a vessel used in making and serving tea

TEAPOY *n* pl. **-POYS** a small table used in serving tea

TEAR *v* **-ED, -ING, -S** to emit tears (drops of saline liquid secreted by a gland of the eye)

TEAR *v* **TORE, TORN, TEARING, TEARS** to pull apart or into pieces **TEARABLE** *adj*

TEARAWAY *n* pl. **-AWAYS** a rebellious person

TEARDOWN *n* pl. **-S** the process of disassembling

TEARDROP *n* pl. **-S** a tear

TEARER *n* pl. **-S** one that tears or rips

TEARFUL *adj* full of tears

TEARGAS *v* **-GASSED, -GASSING, -GASES** or **-GASSES** to subject to a gas that irritates the eyes

TEARIER comparative of teary

TEARIEST superlative of teary

TEARILY *adv* in a teary manner

TEARLESS *adj* being without tears

TEARLIKE *adj* resembling a tear

TEAROOM *n* pl. **-S** a restaurant serving tea

TEARY *adj* **TEARIER, TEARIEST** tearful

TEASE *v* **TEASED, TEASING, TEASES** to make fun of **TEASABLE** *adj*

TEASEL *v* **-SELED, -SELING, -SELS** or **-SELLED, -SELLING, -SELS** to raise a soft surface on fabric with a bristly flower head

TEASELER *n* pl. **-S** one that teasels

TEASER *n* pl. **-S** one that teases

TEASHOP *n* pl. **-S** a tearoom

TEASING present participle of tease

TEASPOON *n* pl. **-S** a small spoon

TEAT *n* pl. **-S** a mammary gland **TEATED** *adj*

TEATIME *n* pl. **-S** the customary time for tea

TEAWARE *n* pl. **-S** a tea service

TEAZEL *v* **-ZELED, -ZELING, -ZELS** or **-ZELLED, -ZELLING, -ZELS** to teasel

TEAZLE *v* **-ZLED, -ZLING, -ZLES** to teasel

TEC *n* pl. **-S** tech

TECH *n* pl. **-S** a technician

TECHED *adj* crazy

TECHIE *n* pl. **-S** a technician

TECHNIC *n* pl. **-S** technique

TECHNO *n* pl. **-NOS** a style of disco music

TECHNOID *n* pl. **-S** a technician

TECHY *adj* **TECHIER, TECHIEST** tetchy **TECHILY** *adv*

TECTA a pl. of tectum

TECTAL *adj* pertaining to a tectum

TECTITE *n* pl. **-S** tektite

TECTONIC *adj* pertaining to construction

TECTRIX *n* pl. **-TRICES** a small feather of a bird's wing

TECTUM *n* pl. **-TUMS** or **-TA** a rooflike structure

TED *v* **TEDDED, TEDDING, TEDS** to spread for drying

TEDDER *v* **-ED, -ING, -S** to ted (hay) with a machine

TEDDY *n* pl. **-DIES** a woman's undergarment

TEDIOUS *adj* causing weariness

TEDIUM *n* pl. **-S** the state of being tedious

TEE *v* **TEED, TEEING, TEES** to place a golf ball on a small peg

TEEL *n* pl. **-S** sesame

TEEM *v* **-ED, -ING, -S** to be full to overflowing

TEEMER *n* pl. **-S** one that teems

TEEN *n* pl. **-S** a teenager

TEENAGE *adj* pertaining to teenagers

TEENAGED *adj* teenage

TEENAGER *n* pl. **-S** a person between the ages of thirteen and nineteen

TEENDOM *n* pl. **-S** teenagers collectively

TEENER *n* pl. **-S** a teenager

TEENFUL *adj* filled with grief

TEENSY *adj* **-SIER, -SIEST** tiny

TEENTSY *adj* **-SIER, -SIEST** tiny

TEENY *adj* **-NIER, -NIEST** tiny

TEENYBOP *adj* pertaining to a young teenager

TEEPEE *n* pl. **-S** tepee

TEETER *v* **-ED, -ING, -S** to move unsteadily

TEETH pl. of tooth

TEETHE *v* **TEETHED, TEETHING, TEETHES** to cut teeth

TEETHER *n* pl. **-S** an object for a baby to bite on during teething

TEETHING *n* pl. **-S** the first growth of teeth

TEETOTAL *v* **-TALED, -TALING, -TALS** or **-TALLED, -TALLING, -TALS** to abstain completely from alcoholic beverages

TEETOTUM *n* pl. **-S** a spinning toy

TEEVEE *n* pl. **-S** a television set

TEFF *n* pl. **-S** a cereal grass

TEFILLIN *n/pl* the phylacteries worn by Jews

TEG *n* pl. **-S** tegg

TEGG *n* pl. **-S** a sheep in its second year

TEGMEN	*n* pl. **-MINA** a covering	**TELEMARK**	*v* **-ED, -ING, -S** to perform a type of turn in skiing
TEGMENTA	*n/pl* anatomical coverings	**TELEOST**	*n* pl. **-S** a bony fish
TEGMINAL	*adj* pertaining to a tegmen	**TELEPATH**	*n* pl. **-S** one who can communicate with another by some means other than the senses
TEGU	*n* pl. **-S** a large lizard of South America		
TEGUA	*n* pl. **-S** a type of moccasin	**TELEPLAY**	*n* pl. **-PLAYS** a play written for television
TEGULA	*n* pl. **-LAE** a flat roof tile used in ancient Rome	**TELEPORT**	*v* **-ED, -ING, -S** to transport by a process that involves no physical means
TEGULAR	*adj* resembling a tile		
TEGUMEN	*n* pl. **-MINA** tegmen		
TEGUMENT	*n* pl. **-S** a covering	**TELERAN**	*n* pl. **-S** a system of air navigation
TEIGLACH	*n* pl. **TEIGLACH** a confection consisting of balls of dough boiled in honey	**TELESHOP**	*v* **-SHOPPED, -SHOPPING, -SHOPS** to shop by interactive telecommunications systems
TEIID	*n* pl. **-S** a tropical American lizard	**TELESIS**	*n* pl. **TELESES** planned progress
TEIN	*n* pl. **-S** a monetary unit of Kazakhstan	**TELESTIC**	*n* pl. **-S** a type of acrostic
TEIND	*n* pl. **-S** a tithe	**TELETEXT**	*n* pl. **-S** a communications system in which printed matter is telecast to subscribers
TEKKIE	*n* pl. **-S** techie		
TEKTITE	*n* pl. **-S** a glassy body believed to be of meteoritic origin **TEKTITIC** *adj*	**TELETHON**	*n* pl. **-S** a fund-raising television program
TEL	*n* pl. **-S** an ancient mound in the Middle East	**TELETYPE**	*v* **-TYPED, -TYPING, -TYPES** to send by teletypewriter
TELA	*n* pl. **-LAE** an anatomical tissue	**TELEVIEW**	*v* **-ED, -ING, -S** to observe by means of television
TELAMON	*n* pl. **-ES** a male figure used as a supporting column	**TELEVISE**	*v* **-VISED, -VISING, -VISES** to broadcast by television (an electronic system of transmitting images and sound)
TELCO	*n* pl. **-COS** a telecommunications company		
TELE	*n* pl. **-S** a television set	**TELEWORK**	*v* **-ED, -ING, -S** to work at home using an electronic linkup with a central office
TELECAST	*v* **-ED, -ING, -S** to broadcast by television		
TELECINE	*n* pl. **-S** the broadcasting of a movie on television	**TELEX**	*v* **-ED, -ING, -ES** to send a message by a type of telegraphic system
TELECOM	*n* pl. **-S** telecommunication	**TELFER**	*v* **-ED, -ING, -S** to telpher
TELECOMM	*n* pl. **-S** telecommunication	**TELFORD**	*n* pl. **-S** a road made of stones
TELEDU	*n* pl. **-S** a carnivorous mammal	**TELIAL**	*adj* pertaining to a telium
TELEFAX	*v* **-ED, -ING, -ES** to transmit graphic material over telephone lines	**TELIC**	*adj* directed toward a goal
		TELICITY	*n* pl. **-TIES** the quality of being telic
TELEFILM	*n* pl. **-S** a motion picture made for television	**TELIUM**	*n* pl. **-LIA** a sorus on the host plant of a rust fungus
TELEGA	*n* pl. **-S** a Russian wagon	**TELL**	*v* **TOLD, TELLING, TELLS** to give a detailed account of **TELLABLE** *adj*
TELEGONY	*n* pl. **-NIES** the supposed influence of a previous sire on the offspring of later matings of the mother with other males		
		TELLER	*n* pl. **-S** one that tells
		TELLIES	*a* pl. of telly
TELEGRAM	*v* **-GRAMMED, -GRAMMING, -GRAMS** to send a message by telegraph	**TELLTALE**	*n* pl. **-S** a tattler
		TELLURIC	*adj* pertaining to the earth
TELEMAN	*n* pl. **-MEN** a naval officer	**TELLY**	*n* pl. **-LYS** or **-LIES** a television set

TELNET   *v* **-NETTED, -NETTING, -NETS** or **-NETED, -NETING, -NETS** to access an account over the Internet using an appropriate procedure

TELOGEN   *n* pl. **-S** a period of hair growth

TELOME   *n* pl. **-S** a structural unit of a vascular plant **TELOMIC** *adj*

TELOMERE   *n* pl. **-S** the natural end of a chromosome

TELOS   *n* pl. **TELOI** an ultimate end

TELPHER   *v* **-ED, -ING, -S** to transport by a system of aerial cable cars

TELSON   *n* pl. **-S** the terminal segment of an arthropod **TELSONIC** *adj*

TEMBLOR   *n* pl. **-S** or **-ES** an earthquake

TEMERITY   *n* pl. **-TIES** foolish boldness

TEMP   *v* **-ED, -ING, -S** to work as a temporary employee

TEMPEH   *n* pl. **-S** an Asian food

TEMPER   *v* **-ED, -ING, -S** to moderate by adding a counterbalancing agent

TEMPERA   *n* pl. **-S** a technique of painting

TEMPERER   *n* pl. **-S** one that tempers

TEMPEST   *v* **-ED, -ING, -S** to agitate violently

TEMPI   a pl. of tempo

TEMPLAR   *n* pl. **-S** a lawyer or student of law in London

TEMPLATE   *n* pl. **-S** a pattern used as a guide in making something

TEMPLE   *n* pl. **-S** a house of worship **TEMPLED** *adj*

TEMPLET   *n* pl. **-S** template

TEMPO   *n* pl. **-POS** or **-PI** the rate of speed of a musical piece

TEMPORAL   *n* pl. **-S** a bone of the skull

TEMPT   *v* **-ED, -ING, -S** to entice to commit an unwise or immoral act

TEMPTER   *n* pl. **-S** one that tempts

TEMPURA   *n* pl. **-S** a Japanese dish

TEN   *n* pl. **-S** a number

TENABLE   *adj* capable of being held **TENABLY** *adv*

TENACE   *n* pl. **-S** a combination of two high cards in some card games

TENACITY   *n* pl. **-TIES** perseverance or persistence

TENACULA   *n/pl* hooked surgical instruments

TENAIL   *n* pl. **-S** tenaille

TENAILLE   *n* pl. **-S** an outer defense

TENANCY   *n* pl. **-CIES** the temporary occupancy of something that belongs to another

TENANT   *v* **-ED, -ING, -S** to inhabit

TENANTRY   *n* pl. **-RIES** tenancy

TENCH   *n* pl. **-ES** a freshwater fish

TEND   *v* **-ED, -ING, -S** to be disposed or inclined

TENDANCE   *n* pl. **-S** watchful care

TENDENCE   *n* pl. **-S** tendance

TENDENCY   *n* pl. **-CIES** an inclination to act or think in a particular way

TENDER   *adj* **-DERER, -DEREST** soft or delicate

TENDER   *v* **-ED, -ING, -S** to present for acceptance

TENDERER   *n* pl. **-S** one that tenders

TENDERLY   *adv* in a tender manner

TENDON   *n* pl. **-S** a band of tough, fibrous tissue

TENDRIL   *n* pl. **-S** a leafless organ of climbing plants

TENDU   *n* pl. **-S** an Asian ebony tree

TENEBRAE   *n/pl* a religious service

TENEMENT   *n* pl. **-S** an apartment house

TENESI   *n* pl. **TENESI** a monetary unit of Turkmenistan

TENESMUS   *n* pl. **-ES** an urgent but ineffectual effort to defecate or urinate **TENESMIC** *adj*

TENET   *n* pl. **-S** a principle, belief, or doctrine held to be true

TENFOLD   *n* pl. **-S** an amount ten times as great as a given unit

TENGE   *n* pl. **-S** a monetary unit of Kazakhstan

TENIA   *n* pl. **-NIAS** or **-NIAE** a tapeworm

TENIASIS   *n* pl. **TENIASES** infestation with tapeworms

TENNE   *n* pl. **-S** an orange-brown color

TENNE   *n* pl. **TENNESI** a monetary unit of Turkmenistan

TENNER   *n* pl. **-S** a ten-dollar bill

TENNIES   *n/pl* low-cut sneakers

TENNIS   *n* pl. **-NISES** an outdoor ball game

TENNIST   *n* pl. **-S** a tennis player

TENNO   *n* pl. **-NOS** the emperor of Japan considered as a divinity

TENNY   *n* pl. **-NIES** tenne

TENON	v **-ED, -ING, -S** to unite by means of a tenon (a projection on the end of a piece of wood)	**TENTPOLE**	n pl. **-S** a big-budget movie whose high earnings are intended to offset the cost of less profitable ones
TENONER	n pl. **-S** one that tenons	**TENTY**	adj **TENTIER, TENTIEST** watchful
TENOR	n pl. **-S** a high male singing voice	**TENUIS**	n pl. **-UES** a voiceless phonetic stop
TENORINO	n pl. **-NI** a high tenor		
TENORIST	n pl. **-S** one who sings tenor or plays a tenor instrument	**TENUITY**	n pl. **-ITIES** lack of substance or strength
TENORITE	n pl. **-S** a mineral	**TENUOUS**	adj having little substance or strength
TENORMAN	n pl. **-MEN** a person who plays tenor saxophone	**TENURE**	v **-URED, -URING, -URES** to grant tenure (the status of holding one's position on a permanent basis) to
TENOTOMY	n pl. **-MIES** the surgical division of a tendon		
TENOUR	n pl. **-S** tenor	**TENURIAL**	adj of or pertaining to tenure
TENPENCE	n pl. **-S** the sum of ten pennies	**TENUTO**	n pl. **-TOS** or **-TI** a musical note or chord held longer than its normal duration
TENPENNY	adj worth tenpence		
TENPIN	n pl. **-S** a bowling pin	**TEOCALLI**	n pl. **-S** an Aztec temple
TENREC	n pl. **-S** a mammal that feeds on insects	**TEOPAN**	n pl. **-S** a teocalli
		TEOSINTE	n pl. **-S** an annual grass
TENSE	adj **TENSER, TENSEST** taut **TENSELY** adv	**TEPA**	n pl. **-S** a chemical compound
TENSE	v **TENSED, TENSING, TENSES** to make tense	**TEPACHE**	n pl. **-S** a Mexican drink made with pineapple, brown sugar, and water
TENSIBLE	adj capable of being stretched **TENSIBLY** adv	**TEPAL**	n pl. **-S** a division of a perianth
		TEPEE	n pl. **-S** a conical tent of some Native Americans
TENSILE	adj tensible		
TENSION	v **-ED, -ING, -S** to make tense	**TEPEFY**	v **-FIED, -FYING, -FIES** to make tepid
TENSITY	n pl. **-TIES** the state of being tense	**TEPHRA**	n pl. **-S** solid material ejected from a volcano
TENSIVE	adj causing tensity		
TENSOR	n pl. **-S** a muscle that stretches a body part	**TEPHRITE**	n pl. **-S** a volcanic rock
		TEPID	adj moderately warm **TEPIDLY** adv
TENT	v **-ED, -ING, -S** to live in a tent (a type of portable shelter)	**TEPIDITY**	n pl. **-TIES** the state of being tepid
TENTACLE	n pl. **-S** an elongated, flexible appendage of some animals	**TEPOY**	n pl. **-POYS** teapoy
		TEQUILA	n pl. **-S** a Mexican liquor
TENTAGE	n pl. **-S** a supply of tents	**TERABYTE**	n pl. **-S** one trillion bytes
TENTER	v **-ED, -ING, -S** to stretch on a type of frame	**TERAFLOP**	n pl. **-S** a measure of computing speed
TENTH	n pl. **-S** one of ten equal parts	**TERAI**	n pl. **-S** a sun hat with a wide brim
TENTHLY	adv in the tenth place	**TERAOHM**	n pl. **-S** one trillion ohms
TENTIE	adj **TENTIER, TENTIEST** tenty	**TERAPH**	n pl. **-APHIM** an image of a Semitic household god
TENTIER	comparative of tenty		
TENTIEST	superlative of tenty	**TERATISM**	n pl. **-S** a malformed fetus **TERATOID** adj
TENTLESS	adj having no tent		
TENTLIKE	adj resembling a tent	**TERATOMA**	n pl. **-MAS** or **-MATA** a type of tumor
TENTORIA	n/pl the internal skeletons of the heads of insects	**TERAWATT**	n pl. **-S** one trillion watts
		TERBIA	n pl. **-S** an oxide of terbium

TERBIUM	n pl. **-S** a metallic element **TERBIC** adj	**TERRAIN**	n pl. **-S** a tract of land
TERCE	n pl. **-S** tierce	**TERRANE**	n pl. **-S** a rock formation
TERCEL	n pl. **-S** a male falcon	**TERRAPIN**	n pl. **-S** a North American tortoise
TERCELET	n pl. **-S** tercel	**TERRARIA**	n/pl glass enclosures for plants or small animals
TERCET	n pl. **-S** a group of three lines of verse	**TERRAS**	n pl. **-ES** trass
TEREBENE	n pl. **-S** a mixture of terpenes	**TERRASSE**	n pl. **TERRASSE** a paved area outside a French cafe
TEREBIC	adj pertaining to an acid derived from oil of turpentine	**TERRAZZO**	n pl. **-ZOS** a mosaic flooring
TEREDO	n pl. **-DOS** or **-DINES** a bivalve mollusk	**TERREEN**	n pl. **-S** terrine
		TERRELLA	n pl. **-S** a spherical magnet
TEREFA	adj tref	**TERRENE**	n pl. **-S** a land area
TEREFAH	adj tref	**TERRET**	n pl. **-S** a metal ring on a harness
TERES	n pl. **TERETES** either of two muscles helping to rotate the arm	**TERRIBLE**	adj very bad **TERRIBLY** adv
TERETE	adj cylindrical and slightly tapering	**TERRIER**	n pl. **-S** a small, active dog
TERGAL	adj pertaining to a tergum	**TERRIES**	pl. of terry
TERGITE	n pl. **-S** a tergum	**TERRIFIC**	adj very good; fine
TERGUM	n pl. **-GA** a back part of a segment of an arthropod	**TERRIFY**	v **-FIED, -FYING, -FIES** to fill with terror
TERIYAKI	n pl. **-S** a Japanese food	**TERRINE**	n pl. **-S** an earthenware jar
TERM	v **-ED, -ING, -S** to give a name to	**TERRIT**	n pl. **-S** terret
TERMER	n pl. **-S** a prisoner serving a specified sentence	**TERROIR**	n pl. **-S** the combination of factors that gives wine grapes their distinctive character
TERMINAL	n pl. **-S** an end or extremity	**TERROR**	n pl. **-S** intense fear
TERMINER	n pl. **-S** a type of court in some states	**TERRY**	n pl. **-RIES** an absorbent fabric
TERMINUS	n pl. **-NUSES** or **-NI** a terminal	**TERSE**	adj **TERSER, TERSEST** succinct **TERSELY** adv
TERMITE	n pl. **-S** an insect resembling an ant **TERMITIC** adj	**TERTIAL**	n pl. **-S** a flight feather of a bird's wing
TERMLESS	adj having no limits	**TERTIAN**	n pl. **-S** a recurrent fever
TERMLY	adv periodically	**TERTIARY**	n pl. **-ARIES** a tertial
TERMOR	n pl. **-S** one that holds land for a certain number of years	**TERZETTO**	n pl. **-TOS** or **-TI** a vocal or instrumental trio
TERMTIME	n pl. **-S** the time when a school or court is in session	**TESLA**	n pl. **-S** a unit of magnetic induction
TERN	n pl. **-S** a seabird	**TESSERA**	n pl. **-SERAE** a small square used in mosaic work **TESSERAL** adj
TERNARY	n pl. **-RIES** a group of three		
TERNATE	adj arranged in groups of three	**TEST**	v **-ED, -ING, -S** to evaluate by an examination **TESTABLE** adj
TERNE	n pl. **-S** an alloy of lead and tin	**TESTA**	n pl. **-TAE** the hard outer coating of a seed
TERNION	n pl. **-S** a group of three		
TERPENE	n pl. **-S** a chemical compound **TERPENIC** adj	**TESTACY**	n pl. **-CIES** the state of having left a will at death
TERPINOL	n pl. **-S** a fragrant liquid	**TESTATE**	n pl. **-S** a testator
TERRA	n pl. **-RAE** earth; land	**TESTATOR**	n pl. **-S** one that makes a will
TERRACE	v **-RACED, -RACING, -RACES** to provide with a terrace (a raised embankment)	**TESTEE**	n pl. **-S** one that is tested
		TESTER	n pl. **-S** one that tests

TESTES	pl. of testis
TESTICLE	n pl. **-S** a testis
TESTIER	comparative of testy
TESTIEST	superlative of testy
TESTIFY	v **-FIED, -FYING, -FIES** to make a declaration of truth under oath
TESTILY	adv in a testy manner
TESTING	n pl. **-S** the act of evaluating one by an examination
TESTIS	n pl. **TESTES** a male reproductive gland
TESTON	n pl. **-S** a former French coin
TESTOON	n pl. **-S** teston
TESTUDO	n pl. **-DOS** or **-DINES** a portable screen used as a shield by the ancient Romans
TESTY	adj **TESTIER, TESTIEST** irritable
TET	n pl. **-S** teth
TETANAL	adj pertaining to tetanus
TETANIC	n pl. **-S** a drug capable of causing convulsions
TETANIES	pl. of tetany
TETANISE	v **-NISED, -NISING, -NISES** to tetanize
TETANIZE	v **-NIZED, -NIZING, -NIZES** to affect with convulsions
TETANUS	n pl. **-ES** an infectious disease **TETANOID** adj
TETANY	n pl. **-NIES** a condition marked by painful muscular spasms
TETCHED	adj crazy
TETCHY	adj **TETCHIER, TETCHIEST** irritable **TETCHILY** adv
TETH	n pl. **-S** a Hebrew letter
TETHER	v **-ED, -ING, -S** to fasten to a fixed object with a rope
TETOTUM	n pl. **-S** teetotum
TETRA	n pl. **-S** a tropical fish
TETRACID	n pl. **-S** a type of acid
TETRAD	n pl. **-S** a group of four **TETRADIC** adj
TETRAGON	n pl. **-S** a four-sided polygon
TETRAMER	n pl. **-S** a type of polymer
TETRAPOD	n pl. **-S** a four-footed animal
TETRARCH	n pl. **-S** one of four joint rulers
TETRI	n pl. **-S** a monetary unit of the Republic of Georgia
TETRODE	n pl. **-S** a type of electron tube

TETROSE	n pl. **-S** a sugar whose molecules contain four carbon atoms
TETROXID	n pl. **-S** a type of oxide
TETRYL	n pl. **-S** a chemical compound
TETTER	n pl. **-S** a skin disease
TEUCH	adj teugh
TEUGH	adj tough **TEUGHLY** adv
TEVATRON	n pl. **-S** a particle accelerator
TEW	v **-ED, -ING, -S** to work hard
TEXAS	n pl. **-ES** the uppermost structure on a steamboat
TEXT	v **-ED, -ING, -S** to send a message from one cell phone to another
TEXTBOOK	n pl. **-S** a book used in the study of a subject
TEXTER	n pl. **-S** one that texts
TEXTILE	n pl. **-S** a woven fabric
TEXTLESS	adj having no text
TEXTUAL	adj pertaining to a text
TEXTUARY	n pl. **-ARIES** a specialist in the study of the Scriptures
TEXTURAL	adj pertaining to the surface characteristics of something
TEXTURE	v **-TURED, -TURING, -TURES** to make by weaving
THACK	v **-ED, -ING, -S** to thatch
THAE	adj these; those
THAIRM	n pl. **-S** tharm
THALAMUS	n pl. **-MI** a part of the brain **THALAMIC** adj
THALER	n pl. **-S** taler
THALI	n pl. **-S** a platter on which food is served in India
THALLIUM	n pl. **-S** a metallic element **THALLIC, THALLOUS** adj
THALLUS	n pl. **-LUSES** or **-LI** a plant body without true root, stem, or leaf **THALLOID** adj
THALWEG	n pl. **-S** the line defining the lowest points along the length of a riverbed
THAN	conj — used to introduce the second element of a comparison
THANAGE	n pl. **-S** the land held by a thane
THANATOS	n pl. **-ES** an instinctual desire for death
THANE	n pl. **-S** a man holding land by military service in Anglo-Saxon England
THANEDOM	n pl. **-S** the domain of a thane

THANK	*v* **-ED, -ING, -S** to express gratitude to	**THEM**	*pron* the objective case of the pronoun they
THANKER	*n* pl. **-S** one that thanks	**THEMATIC**	*n* pl. **-S** a stamp collected according to its subject
THANKFUL	*adj* **-FULLER, -FULLEST** feeling gratitude	**THEME**	*v* **THEMED, THEMING, THEMES** to plan something according to a central subject
THARM	*n* pl. **-S** the belly		
THAT	*pron* pl. **THOSE** the one indicated	**THEMSELF**	*pron* a person of unspecified sex
THATAWAY	*adv* in that direction	**THEN**	*n* pl. **-S** that time
THATCH	*v* **-ED, -ING, -ES** to cover with thatch (plant stalks or foliage)	**THENAGE**	*n* pl. **-S** thanage
		THENAL	*adj* pertaining to the palm of the hand
THATCHER	*n* pl. **-S** one that thatches		
THATCHY	*adj* **THATCHIER, THATCHIEST** resembling thatch	**THENAR**	*n* pl. **-S** the palm of the hand
		THENCE	*adv* from that place
THAW	*v* **-ED, -ING, -S** to melt	**THEOCRAT**	*n* pl. **-S** a person who rules as a representative of a god
THAWER	*n* pl. **-S** one that thaws		
THAWING	*n* pl. **-S** the melting of a frozen substance	**THEODICY**	*n* pl. **-CIES** a defense of God's goodness in respect to the existence of evil
THAWLESS	*adj* never thawing		
THE	*definite article* — used to specify or make particular	**THEOGONY**	*n* pl. **-NIES** an account of the origin of the gods
		THEOLOG	*n* pl. **-S** a student of theology
THEANINE	*n* pl. **-S** an amino acid that has health benefits	**THEOLOGY**	*n* pl. **-GIES** the study of religion
		THEONOMY	*n* pl. **-MIES** rule by a god
THEARCHY	*n* pl. **-CHIES** rule by a god	**THEORBO**	*n* pl. **-BOS** a stringed musical instrument
THEATER	*n* pl. **-S** a building for dramatic presentations **THEATRIC** *adj*		
		THEOREM	*n* pl. **-S** a proposition that is demonstrably true or is assumed to be so
THEATRE	*n* pl. **-S** theater		
THEBAINE	*n* pl. **-S** a poisonous alkaloid		
THEBE	*n* pl. **-S** a monetary unit of Botswana	**THEORIES**	pl. of theory
		THEORISE	*v* **-RISED, -RISING, -RISES** to theorize
THECA	*n* pl. **-CAE** a protective anatomical covering **THECAL, THECATE** *adj*		
		THEORIST	*n* pl. **-S** one that theorizes
THEE	*pron* the objective case of the pronoun thou	**THEORIZE**	*v* **-RIZED, -RIZING, -RIZES** to form theories
THEELIN	*n* pl. **-S** estrone	**THEORY**	*n* pl. **-RIES** a group of propositions used to explain a class of phenomena
THEELOL	*n* pl. **-S** estriol		
THEFT	*n* pl. **-S** the act of stealing		
THEGN	*n* pl. **-S** thane **THEGNLY** *adj*	**THERAPY**	*n* pl. **-PIES** the treatment of illness or disability
THEIN	*n* pl. **-S** theine		
THEINE	*n* pl. **-S** caffeine	**THERE**	*n* pl. **-S** that place
THEIR	*adj* belonging to them	**THEREAT**	*adv* at that place or time
THEIRS	*pron* a possessive form of the pronoun they	**THEREBY**	*adv* by that means
		THEREFOR	*adv* for that
THEISM	*n* pl. **-S** belief in the existence of a god	**THEREIN**	*adv* in that place
		THEREMIN	*n* pl. **-S** a musical instrument
THEIST	*n* pl. **-S** one who believes in the existence of a god **THEISTIC** *adj*	**THEREOF**	*adv* of that
		THEREON	*adv* on that
THELITIS	*n* pl. **-TISES** inflammation of the nipple	**THEREOUT**	*adv* out of that
		THERETO	*adv* to that

THERIAC *n* pl. **-S** molasses

THERIACA *n* pl. **-S** theriac

THERIAN *n* pl. **-S** any of a subclass of mammals

THERM *n* pl. **-S** a unit of quantity of heat

THERMAE *n/pl* hot springs

THERMAL *n* pl. **-S** a rising mass of warm air

THERME *n* pl. **-S** therm

THERMEL *n* pl. **-S** a device for temperature measurement

THERMIC *adj* pertaining to heat

THERMION *n* pl. **-S** an ion emitted by a heated body

THERMITE *n* pl. **-S** a metallic mixture that produces intense heat when ignited

THERMOS *n* pl. **-ES** a container used to keep liquids either hot or cold

THEROID *adj* resembling a beast

THEROPOD *n* pl. **-S** a carnivorous dinosaur

THESAURI *n/pl* dictionaries of synonyms and antonyms

THESE pl. of this

THESIS *n* pl. **THESES** a proposition put forward for discussion

THESP *n* pl. **-S** an actor

THESPIAN *n* pl. **-S** an actor or actress

THETA *n* pl. **-S** a Greek letter

THETIC *adj* arbitrary

THETICAL *adj* thetic

THETRI *n* pl. **-S** tetri

THEURGY *n* pl. **-GIES** divine intervention in human affairs **THEURGIC** *adj*

THEW *n* pl. **-S** a well-developed muscle

THEWLESS *adj* weak

THEWY *adj* **THEWIER, THEWIEST** brawny

THEY *pron* the 3d person pl. pronoun in the nominative case

THIAMIN *n* pl. **-S** thiamine

THIAMINE *n* pl. **-S** a B vitamin

THIAZIDE *n* pl. **-S** a drug used to treat high blood pressure

THIAZIN *n* pl. **-S** thiazine

THIAZINE *n* pl. **-S** a chemical compound

THIAZOL *n* pl. **-S** thiazole

THIAZOLE *n* pl. **-S** a chemical compound

THICK *adj* **THICKER, THICKEST** having relatively great extent from one surface to its opposite

THICK *n* pl. **-S** the thickest part

THICKEN *v* **-ED, -ING, -S** to make thick

THICKET *n* pl. **-S** a dense growth of shrubs or small trees **THICKETY** *adj*

THICKISH *adj* somewhat thick

THICKLY *adv* in a thick manner

THICKSET *n* pl. **-S** a thicket

THIEF *n* pl. **THIEVES** one that steals

THIEVE *v* **THIEVED, THIEVING, THIEVES** to steal

THIEVERY *n* pl. **-ERIES** the act or practice of stealing

THIEVISH *adj* given to stealing

THIGH *n* pl. **-S** a part of the leg **THIGHED** *adj*

THILL *n* pl. **-S** a shaft of a vehicle

THIMBLE *n* pl. **-S** a cap used to protect the fingertip during sewing

THIN *adj* **THINNER, THINNEST** having relatively little density or thickness

THIN *v* **THINNED, THINNING, THINS** to make thin

THINCLAD *n* pl. **-S** a runner on a track team

THINDOWN *n* pl. **-S** a lessening in the number of atomic particles and cosmic rays passing through the earth's atmosphere

THINE *pron* a possessive form of the pronoun thou

THING *n* pl. **-S** an inanimate object

THINGY *n* pl. **THINGIES** something whose name is unknown or forgotten

THINK *v* **THOUGHT, THINKING, THINKS** to formulate in the mind

THINKER *n* pl. **-S** one that thinks

THINKING *n* pl. **-S** an opinion or judgment

THINLY *adv* in a thin manner

THINNED past tense of thin

THINNER *n* pl. **-S** one that thins

THINNESS *n* pl. **-ES** the quality or state of being thin

THINNEST superlative of thin

THINNING present participle of thin

THINNISH *adj* somewhat thin

THIO *adj* containing sulfur

THIOL *n* pl. **-S** a sulfur compound **THIOLIC** *adj*

THIONATE	*n* pl. **-S** a chemical salt
THIONIC	*adj* pertaining to sulfur
THIONIN	*n* pl. **-S** a violet dye
THIONINE	*n* pl. **-S** thionin
THIONYL	*n* pl. **-S** sulfinyl
THIOPHEN	*n* pl. **-S** a chemical compound
THIOTEPA	*n* pl. **-S** a chemical compound
THIOUREA	*n* pl. **-S** a chemical compound
THIR	*pron* these
THIRAM	*n* pl. **-S** a chemical compound
THIRD	*n* pl. **-S** one of three equal parts
THIRDLY	*adv* in the third place
THIRL	*v* **-ED, -ING, -S** to thrill
THIRLAGE	*n* pl. **-S** an obligation requiring feudal tenants to grind grain at a certain mill
THIRST	*v* **-ED, -ING, -S** to feel a desire or need to drink
THIRSTER	*n* pl. **-S** one that thirsts
THIRSTY	*adj* **THIRSTIER, THIRSTIEST** feeling a desire or need to drink
THIRTEEN	*n* pl. **-S** a number
THIRTY	*n* pl. **-TIES** a number
THIS	*pron* pl. **THESE** the person or thing just mentioned
THISAWAY	*adv* this way
THISTLE	*n* pl. **-S** a prickly plant
THISTLY	*adj* **-TLIER, -TLIEST** prickly
THITHER	*adv* in that direction
THO	*conj* though
THOLE	*v* **THOLED, THOLING, THOLES** to endure
THOLEPIN	*n* pl. **-S** a pin that serves as an oarlock
THOLOS	*n* pl. **-LOI** a circular, underground tomb
THONG	*v* **-ED, -ING, -S** to flog with a whip
THONGY	*adj* **THONGIER, THONGIEST** resembling an item of clothing made from a narrow strip of fabric
THORAX	*n* pl. **-RAXES** or **-RACES** the part of the body between the neck and the abdomen **THORACAL, THORACIC** *adj*
THORIA	*n* pl. **-S** an oxide of thorium
THORIC	*adj* pertaining to thorium
THORITE	*n* pl. **-S** a thorium ore
THORIUM	*n* pl. **-S** a metallic element
THORN	*v* **-ED, -ING, -S** to prick with a thorn (a sharp, rigid projection on a plant)
THORNY	*adj* **THORNIER, THORNIEST** full of thorns **THORNILY** *adv*
THORO	*adj* thorough
THORON	*n* pl. **-S** a radioactive isotope of radon
THOROUGH	*adj* **THOROUGHER, THOROUGHEST** complete in all respects
THORP	*n* pl. **-S** a small village
THORPE	*n* pl. **-S** thorp
THOSE	pl. of that
THOU	*v* **-ED, -ING, -S** to address as "thou" (the 2d person sing. pronoun in the nominative case)
THOUGH	*conj* despite the fact that
THOUGHT	*n* pl. **-S** a product of thinking
THOUSAND	*n* pl. **-S** a number
THOWLESS	*adj* listless
THRALDOM	*n* pl. **-S** servitude
THRALL	*v* **-ED, -ING, -S** to enslave
THRASH	*v* **-ED, -ING, -ES** to beat
THRASHER	*n* pl. **-S** one that thrashes
THRASHY	*adj* **THRASHIER, THRASHIEST** characteristic of a style of fast, loud, punk-rock music
THRAVE	*n* pl. **-S** a unit of measure for grain
THRAW	*v* **-ED, -ING, -S** to twist
THRAWART	*adj* stubborn
THRAWN	*adj* twisted **THRAWNLY** *adv*
THREAD	*v* **-ED, -ING, -S** to pass a thread (a very slender cord) through
THREADER	*n* pl. **-S** one that threads
THREADY	*adj* **THREADIER, THREADIEST** resembling a thread
THREAP	*v* **-ED, -ING, -S** to dispute
THREAPER	*n* pl. **-S** one that threaps
THREAT	*v* **-ED, -ING, -S** to threaten
THREATEN	*v* **-ED, -ING, -S** to be a source of danger to
THREE	*n* pl. **-S** a number
THREEP	*v* **-ED, -ING, -S** to threap
THRENODE	*n* pl. **-S** a threnody
THRENODY	*n* pl. **-DIES** a song of lamentation
THRESH	*v* **-ED, -ING, -ES** to separate the grain or seeds from a plant mechanically

THRESHER	*n* pl. **-S** one that threshes
THREW	past tense of throw
THRICE	*adv* three times
THRIFT	*n* pl. **-S** care and wisdom in the management of one's resources
THRIFTY	*adj* **THRIFTIER, THRIFTIEST** displaying thrift
THRILL	*v* **-ED, -ING, -S** to excite greatly
THRILLER	*n* pl. **-S** one that thrills
THRIP	*n* pl. **-S** a British coin
THRIVE	*v* **THROVE** or **THRIVED, THRIVEN, THRIVING, THRIVES** to grow vigorously
THRIVER	*n* pl. **-S** one that thrives
THRO	*prep* through
THROAT	*v* **-ED, -ING, -S** to utter in a hoarse voice
THROATY	*adj* **THROATIER, THROATIEST** hoarse
THROB	*v* **THROBBED, THROBBING, THROBS** to pulsate
THROBBER	*n* pl. **-S** one that throbs
THROE	*n* pl. **-S** a violent spasm of pain
THROMBIN	*n* pl. **-S** an enzyme
THROMBUS	*n* pl. **-BI** a clot occluding a blood vessel
THRONE	*v* **THRONED, THRONING, THRONES** to place on a throne (a royal chair)
THRONG	*v* **-ED, -ING, -S** to crowd into
THROSTLE	*n* pl. **-S** a songbird
THROTTLE	*v* **-TLED, -TLING, -TLES** to strangle
THROUGH	*prep* by way of
THROVE	a past tense of thrive
THROW	*v* **THREW, THROWN, THROWING, THROWS** to propel through the air with a movement of the arm
THROWER	*n* pl. **-S** one that throws
THRU	*prep* through
THRUM	*v* **THRUMMED, THRUMMING, THRUMS** to play a stringed instrument idly or monotonously
THRUMMER	*n* pl. **-S** one that thrums
THRUMMY	*adj* **-MIER, -MIEST** shaggy
THRUPUT	*n* pl. **-S** the amount of raw material processed within a given time
THRUSH	*n* pl. **-ES** a songbird
THRUST	*v* **-ED, -ING, -S** to push forcibly
THRUSTER	*n* pl. **-S** one that thrusts
THRUSTOR	*n* pl. **-S** thruster
THRUWAY	*n* pl. **-WAYS** an express highway
THUD	*v* **THUDDED, THUDDING, THUDS** to make a dull, heavy sound
THUG	*n* pl. **-S** a brutal ruffian or assassin
THUGGEE	*n* pl. **-S** thuggery in India
THUGGERY	*n* pl. **-GERIES** thuggish behavior
THUGGISH	*adj* characteristic of a thug
THUJA	*n* pl. **-S** an evergreen tree or shrub
THULIA	*n* pl. **-S** an oxide of thulium
THULIUM	*n* pl. **-S** a metallic element
THUMB	*v* **-ED, -ING, -S** to leaf through with the thumb (the short, thick digit of the human hand)
THUMBKIN	*n* pl. **-S** a screw that is turned by the thumb and fingers
THUMBNUT	*n* pl. **-S** a nut that is turned by the thumb and fingers
THUMP	*v* **-ED, -ING, -S** to strike so as to make a dull, heavy sound
THUMPER	*n* pl. **-S** one that thumps
THUNDER	*v* **-ED, -ING, -S** to produce a loud, resounding sound
THUNDERY	*adj* accompanied with thunder
THUNK	*v* **-ED, -ING, -S** to make a sudden, muffled sound
THURIBLE	*n* pl. **-S** a censer
THURIFER	*n* pl. **-S** one who carries a thurible in a religious ceremony
THURL	*n* pl. **-S** the hip joint in cattle
THUS	*adv* in this manner
THUSLY	*adv* thus
THUYA	*n* pl. **-S** thuja
THWACK	*v* **-ED, -ING, -S** to strike with something flat
THWACKER	*n* pl. **-S** one that thwacks
THWART	*v* **-ED, -ING, -S** to prevent the accomplishment of
THWARTER	*n* pl. **-S** one that thwarts
THWARTLY	*adv* athwart
THY	*adj* belonging to thou
THYME	*n* pl. **-S** an aromatic herb
THYMEY	*adj* **THYMIER, THYMIEST** thymy
THYMI	a pl. of thymus
THYMIC	*adj* pertaining to thyme
THYMIER	comparative of thymey and thymy
THYMIEST	superlative of thymey and thymy

THYMINE	*n* pl. **-S** a chemical compound
THYMOL	*n* pl. **-S** a chemical compound
THYMOMA	*n* pl. **-MAS** or **-MATA** a tumor arising from thymus tissue
THYMOSIN	*n* pl. **-S** a hormone secreted by the thymus
THYMUS	*n* pl. **-MUSES** or **-MI** a glandular structure in the body
THYMY	*adj* **THYMIER, THYMIEST** abounding in thyme
THYREOID	*adj* pertaining to the thyroid
THYROID	*n* pl. **-S** an endocrine gland
THYROXIN	*n* pl. **-S** an amino acid
THYRSE	*n* pl. **-S** thyrsus
THYRSUS	*n* pl. **-SI** a type of flower cluster **THYRSOID** *adj*
THYSELF	*pron* yourself
TI	*n* pl. **-S** the seventh tone of the diatonic musical scale
TIAN	*n* pl. **-S** a large oval cooking pot
TIARA	*n* pl. **-S** a jeweled headpiece worn by women **TIARAED** *adj*
TIBIA	*n* pl. **-IAS** or **-IAE** a bone of the leg **TIBIAL** *adj*
TIBIALIS	*n* pl. **TIBIALES** a muscle in the calf of the leg
TIC	*v* **TICCED, TICCING, TICS** to have an involuntary muscular contraction
TICAL	*n* pl. **-S** a former Thai unit of weight
TICK	*v* **-ED, -ING, -S** to make a recurrent clicking sound
TICKER	*n* pl. **-S** one that ticks
TICKET	*v* **-ED, -ING, -S** to attach a tag to
TICKING	*n* pl. **-S** a strong cotton fabric
TICKLACE	*n* pl. **-S** a type of small seabird
TICKLE	*v* **-LED, -LING, -LES** to touch lightly so as to produce a tingling sensation
TICKLER	*n* pl. **-S** one that tickles
TICKLISH	*adj* sensitive to tickling
TICKLY	*adj* **-LIER, -LIEST** ticklish
TICKSEED	*n* pl. **-S** a flowering plant
TICKTACK	*v* **-ED, -ING, -S** to ticktock
TICKTOCK	*v* **-ED, -ING, -S** to make the ticking sound of a clock
TICTAC	*v* **-TACKED, -TACKING, -TACS** to ticktock
TICTOC	*v* **-TOCKED, -TOCKING, -TOCS** to ticktock
TIDAL	*adj* pertaining to the tides **TIDALLY** *adv*
TIDBIT	*n* pl. **-S** a choice bit of food
TIDDLER	*n* pl. **-S** a small fish
TIDDLY	*adj* **-DLIER, -DLIEST** slightly drunk
TIDE	*v* **TIDED, TIDING, TIDES** to flow like the tide (the rise and fall of the ocean's waters)
TIDELAND	*n* pl. **-S** land alternately covered and uncovered by the tide
TIDELESS	*adj* lacking a tide
TIDELIKE	*adj* resembling a tide
TIDELINE	*n* pl. **-S** a line on a shore marking the highest point of the tide
TIDEMARK	*n* pl. **-S** a mark showing the highest or lowest point of a tide
TIDERIP	*n* pl. **-S** a riptide
TIDEWAY	*n* pl. **-WAYS** a tidal channel
TIDIED	past tense of tidy
TIDIER	*n* pl. **-S** one that tidies
TIDIES	present 3d person sing. of tidy
TIDIEST	superlative of tidy
TIDILY	*adv* in a tidy manner
TIDINESS	*n* pl. **-ES** the state of being tidy
TIDING	*n* pl. **-S** a piece of news
TIDY	*adj* **-DIER, -DIEST** neat and orderly
TIDY	*v* **-DIED, -DYING, -DIES** to make tidy
TIDYTIPS	*n* pl. **TIDYTIPS** an annual herb
TIE	*v* **TIED, TYING** or **TIEING, TIES** to fasten with a cord or rope
TIEBACK	*n* pl. **-S** a loop for holding a curtain back to one side
TIEBREAK	*n* pl. **-S** a contest to select a winner from among contestants with a tied score
TIECLASP	*n* pl. **-S** a clasp for securing a necktie
TIED	past tense of tie
TIEING	a present participle of tie
TIELESS	*adj* having no necktie
TIEPIN	*n* pl. **-S** a pin for securing a necktie
TIER	*v* **-ED, -ING, -S** to arrange in tiers (rows placed one above another)
TIERCE	*n* pl. **-S** one of seven canonical daily periods for prayer and devotion
TIERCED	*adj* divided into three equal parts

TIERCEL	*n* pl. **-S** tercel
TIFF	*v* **-ED, -ING, -S** to have a petty quarrel
TIFFANY	*n* pl. **-NIES** a thin, mesh fabric
TIFFIN	*v* **-ED, -ING, -S** to lunch
TIGER	*n* pl. **-S** a large feline mammal
TIGEREYE	*n* pl. **-S** a gemstone
TIGERISH	*adj* resembling a tiger
TIGHT	*adj* **TIGHTER, TIGHTEST** firmly or closely fixed in place **TIGHTLY** *adv*
TIGHTEN	*v* **-ED, -ING, -S** to make tight
TIGHTS	*n/pl* a close-fitting garment
TIGHTWAD	*n* pl. **-S** a miser
TIGLON	*n* pl. **-S** the offspring of a male tiger and a female lion
TIGNON	*n* pl. **-S** a piece of cloth worn as a headdress in Louisiana
TIGON	*n* pl. **-S** tiglon
TIGRESS	*n* pl. **-ES** a female tiger
TIGRISH	*adj* tigerish
TIKE	*n* pl. **-S** tyke
TIKI	*n* pl. **-S** a wood or stone image of a Polynesian god
TIKKA	*n* pl. **-S** an Indian dish of meat cooked on a skewer
TIL	*n* pl. **-S** the sesame plant
TILAK	*n* pl. **-S** a mark worn on the forehead by Hindus
TILAPIA	*n* pl. **-S** an African fish
TILBURY	*n* pl. **-BURIES** a carriage having two wheels
TILDE	*n* pl. **-S** a mark placed over a letter to indicate its sound
TILE	*v* **TILED, TILING, TILES** to cover with tiles (thin slabs of baked clay)
TILEFISH	*n* pl. **-ES** a marine food fish
TILELIKE	*adj* resembling a tile
TILER	*n* pl. **-S** one that tiles
TILING	*n* pl. **-S** a surface of tiles
TILL	*v* **-ED, -ING, -S** to prepare land for crops by plowing **TILLABLE** *adj*
TILLAGE	*n* pl. **-S** cultivated land
TILLER	*v* **-ED, -ING, -S** to put forth stems from a root
TILLITE	*n* pl. **-S** rock made up of consolidated clay, sand, gravel, and boulders

TILT	*v* **-ED, -ING, -S** to cause to slant **TILTABLE** *adj*
TILTER	*n* pl. **-S** one that tilts
TILTH	*n* pl. **-S** tillage
TILTYARD	*n* pl. **-S** an area for jousting contests
TIMARAU	*n* pl. **-S** tamarau
TIMBAL	*n* pl. **-S** a large drum
TIMBALE	*n* pl. **-S** a pastry shell shaped like a drum
TIMBER	*v* **-ED, -ING, -S** to furnish with timber (wood used as a building material) **TIMBERY** *adj*
TIMBRE	*n* pl. **-S** the quality given to a sound by its overtones **TIMBRAL** *adj*
TIMBREL	*n* pl. **-S** a percussion instrument
TIME	*v* **TIMED, TIMING, TIMES** to determine the speed or duration of
TIMECARD	*n* pl. **-S** a card for recording an employee's times of arrival and departure
TIMELESS	*adj* having no beginning or end
TIMELINE	*n* pl. **-S** a schedule of events
TIMELY	*adj* **-LIER, -LIEST** occurring at the right moment
TIMEOUS	*adj* timely
TIMEOUT	*n* pl. **-S** a brief suspension of activity
TIMER	*n* pl. **-S** one that times
TIMEWORK	*n* pl. **-S** work paid for by the hour or by the day
TIMEWORN	*adj* showing the effects of long use or wear
TIMID	*adj* **-IDER, -IDEST** lacking courage or self-confidence **TIMIDLY** *adv*
TIMIDITY	*n* pl. **-TIES** the quality of being timid
TIMING	*n* pl. **-S** the selection of the proper moment for doing something
TIMOLOL	*n* pl. **-S** a drug used to treat glaucoma
TIMOROUS	*adj* fearful
TIMOTHY	*n* pl. **-THIES** a European grass
TIMPANO	*n* pl. **-NI** a kettledrum
TIMPANUM	*n* pl. **-NUMS** or **-NA** tympanum
TIN	*v* **TINNED, TINNING, TINS** to coat with tin (a metallic element)
TINAMOU	*n* pl. **-S** a South American game bird
TINCAL	*n* pl. **-S** crude borax

TINCT   v **-ED, -ING, -S** to tinge

TINCTURE   v **-TURED, -TURING, -TURES** to tinge

TINDER   n pl. **-S** readily combustible material **TINDERY** adj

TINE   v **TINED, TINING, TINES** to lose

TINEA   n pl. **-S** a fungous skin disease **TINEAL** adj

TINEID   n pl. **-S** one of a family of moths

TINFOIL   n pl. **-S** a thin metal sheeting

TINFUL   n pl. **-S** as much as a tin container can hold

TING   v **-ED, -ING, -S** to emit a high-pitched metallic sound

TINGE   v **TINGED, TINGEING** or **TINGING, TINGES** to apply a trace of color to

TINGLE   v **-GLED, -GLING, -GLES** to cause a prickly, stinging sensation

TINGLER   n pl. **-S** one that tingles

TINGLY   adj **-GLIER, -GLIEST** tingling

TINHORN   n pl. **-S** a showily pretentious person

TINIER   comparative of tiny

TINIEST   superlative of tiny

TINILY   adv in a tiny manner

TININESS   n pl. **-ES** the quality of being tiny

TINING   present participle of tine

TINKER   v **-ED, -ING, -S** to repair in an unskilled or experimental manner

TINKERER   n pl. **-S** one that tinkers

TINKLE   v **-KLED, -KLING, -KLES** to make slight, sharp, metallic sounds

TINKLER   n pl. **-S** one that tinkles

TINKLING   n pl. **-S** the sound made by something that tinkles

TINKLY   adj **-KLIER, -KLIEST** producing a tinkling sound

TINLIKE   adj resembling tin

TINMAN   n pl. **-MEN** a tinsmith

TINNED   past tense of tin

TINNER   n pl. **-S** a tin miner

TINNIER   comparative of tinny

TINNIEST   superlative of tinny

TINNILY   adv in a tinny manner

TINNING   present participle of tin

TINNITUS   n pl. **-ES** a ringing sound in the ears

TINNY   adj **-NIER, -NIEST** of or resembling tin

TINPLATE   v **-PLATED, -PLATING, -PLATES** to coat an object with tin

TINPOT   adj of little importance

TINSEL   v **-SELED, -SELING, -SELS** or **-SELLED, -SELLING, -SELS** to give a showy or gaudy appearance to

TINSELLY   adj cheaply gaudy

TINSELY   adj tinsely

TINSMITH   n pl. **-S** one who works with tin

TINSNIPS   n/pl a tool for cutting sheet metal

TINSTONE   n pl. **-S** a tin ore

TINT   v **-ED, -ING, -S** to color slightly or delicately

TINTER   n pl. **-S** one that tints

TINTING   n pl. **-S** the process of one that tints

TINTLESS   adj lacking color

TINTYPE   n pl. **-S** a kind of photograph

TINWARE   n pl. **-S** articles made of tinplate

TINWORK   n pl. **-S** something made of tin

TINY   adj **TINIER, TINIEST** very small

TIP   v **TIPPED, TIPPING, TIPS** to tilt

TIPCART   n pl. **-S** a type of cart

TIPCAT   n pl. **-S** a game resembling baseball

TIPI   n pl. **-S** tepee

TIPLESS   adj having no point or extremity

TIPOFF   n pl. **-S** a hint or warning

TIPPABLE   adj capable of being tipped

TIPPED   past tense of tip

TIPPER   n pl. **-S** one that tips

TIPPET   n pl. **-S** a covering for the shoulders

TIPPIER   comparative of tippy

TIPPIEST   superlative of tippy

TIPPING   present participle of tip

TIPPLE   v **-PLED, -PLING, -PLES** to drink alcoholic beverages

TIPPLER   n pl. **-S** one that tipples

TIPPY   adj **-PIER, -PIEST** unsteady

TIPPYTOE   v **-TOED, -TOEING, -TOES** to tiptoe

TIPSHEET   n pl. **-S** a publication with tips for betting on races or investing in stocks

TIPSIER	comparative of tipsy
TIPSIEST	superlative of tipsy
TIPSILY	*adv* in a tipsy manner
TIPSTAFF	*n* pl. **-STAFFS** or **-STAVES** an attendant in a court of law
TIPSTER	*n* pl. **-S** one that sells information to gamblers
TIPSTOCK	*n* pl. **-S** a part of a gun
TIPSY	*adj* **-SIER, -SIEST** slightly drunk
TIPTOE	*v* **-TOED, -TOEING, -TOES** to walk on the tips of one's toes
TIPTOP	*n* pl. **-S** the highest point
TIRADE	*n* pl. **-S** a long, vehement speech
TIRAMISU	*n* pl. **-S** a dessert made with ladyfingers, mascarpone, chocolate, and espresso
TIRE	*v* **TIRED, TIRING, TIRES** to grow tired
TIRED	*adj* **TIREDER, TIREDEST** sapped of strength **TIREDLY** *adv*
TIRELESS	*adj* seemingly incapable of tiring
TIRESOME	*adj* tedious
TIRING	present participle of tire
TIRL	*v* **-ED, -ING, -S** to make a vibrating sound
TIRO	*n* pl. **-ROS** tyro
TIRRIVEE	*n* pl. **-S** a tantrum
TISANE	*n* pl. **-S** a ptisan
TISSUAL	*adj* pertaining to tissue
TISSUE	*v* **-SUED, -SUING, -SUES** to weave into tissue (a fine sheer fabric)
TISSUEY	*adj* resembling tissue
TISSULAR	*adj* affecting an organism's tissue (structural material)
TIT	*n* pl. **-S** a small bird
TITAN	*n* pl. **-S** a person of great size
TITANATE	*n* pl. **-S** a chemical salt
TITANESS	*n* pl. **-ES** a female titan
TITANIA	*n* pl. **-S** a mineral
TITANIC	*adj* of great size
TITANISM	*n* pl. **-S** revolt against social conventions
TITANITE	*n* pl. **-S** a mineral
TITANIUM	*n* pl. **-S** a metallic element
TITANOUS	*adj* pertaining to titanium
TITBIT	*n* pl. **-S** tidbit
TITCH	*n* pl. **-ES** a small amount
TITCHIE	*adj* **TITCHIER, TITCHIEST** titchy
TITCHY	*adj* **TITCHIER, TITCHIEST** very small
TITER	*n* pl. **-S** the strength of a chemical solution
TITFER	*n* pl. **-S** a hat
TITHABLE	*adj* subject to the payment of tithes
TITHE	*v* **TITHED, TITHING, TITHES** to pay a tithe (a small tax)
TITHER	*n* pl. **-S** one that tithes
TITHING	*n* pl. **-S** the act of levying tithes
TITHONIA	*n* pl. **-S** a tall herb
TITI	*n* pl. **-S** an evergreen shrub or tree
TITIAN	*n* pl. **-S** a reddish brown color
TITIVATE	*v* **-VATED, -VATING, -VATES** to dress smartly
TITLARK	*n* pl. **-S** a songbird
TITLE	*v* **-TLED, -TLING, -TLES** to furnish with a title (a distinctive appellation)
TITLIST	*n* pl. **-S** a sports champion
TITMAN	*n* pl. **-MEN** the smallest of a litter of pigs
TITMOUSE	*n* pl. **-MICE** a small bird
TITRABLE	*adj* capable of being titrated
TITRANT	*n* pl. **-S** the reagent used in titration
TITRATE	*v* **-TRATED, -TRATING, -TRATES** to determine the strength of a solution by adding a reagent until a desired reaction occurs
TITRATOR	*n* pl. **-S** one that titrates
TITRE	*n* pl. **-S** titer
TITTER	*v* **-ED, -ING, -S** to utter a restrained, nervous laugh
TITTERER	*n* pl. **-S** one that titters
TITTIE	*n* pl. **-S** a sister
TITTLE	*n* pl. **-S** a very small mark in writing or printing
TITTUP	*v* **-TUPED, -TUPING, -TUPS** or **-TUPPED, -TUPPING, -TUPS** to move in a lively manner
TITTUPPY	*adj* shaky; unsteady
TITTY	*n* pl. **-TIES** a teat
TITUBANT	*adj* marked by wavering
TITULAR	*n* pl. **-S** one who holds a title
TITULARY	*n* pl. **-LARIES** a titular
TIVY	*adv* with great speed
TIX	*n/pl* tickets

TIYIN	*n* pl. **-S** a monetary unit of Kyrgyzstan
TIYN	*n* pl. **-S** a monetary unit of Kazakhstan
TIZ	*n* pl. **-ES** tizzy
TIZZ	*n* pl. **-ES** tizzy
TIZZY	*n* pl. **-ZIES** a state of nervous confusion
TMESIS	*n* pl. **TMESES** the separation of the parts of a compound word by an intervening word or words
TO	*prep* in the direction of
TOAD	*n* pl. **-S** a tailless, jumping amphibian
TOADFISH	*n* pl. **-ES** a marine fish
TOADFLAX	*n* pl. **-ES** a perennial herb
TOADIED	past tense of toady
TOADIES	present 3d person sing. of toady
TOADISH	*adj* resembling a toad
TOADLESS	*adj* having no toads
TOADLET	*n* pl. **-S** a small toad
TOADLIKE	*adj* resembling a toad
TOADY	*v* **TOADIED, TOADYING, TOADIES** to engage in servile flattering
TOADYISH	*adj* characteristic of one that toadies
TOADYISM	*n* pl. **-S** toadyish behavior
TOAST	*v* **-ED, -ING, -S** to brown by exposure to heat
TOASTER	*n* pl. **-S** a device for toasting
TOASTING	*n* pl. **-S** the adding of rhythmic speech to reggae music
TOASTY	*adj* **TOASTIER, TOASTIEST** comfortably warm
TOBACCO	*n* pl. **-COS** or **-COES** an annual herb cultivated for its leaves
TOBOGGAN	*v* **-ED, -ING, -S** to ride on a long, narrow sled
TOBY	*n* pl. **-BIES** a type of drinking mug
TOCCATA	*n* pl. **-TAS** or **-TE** a musical composition usually for an organ
TOCHER	*v* **-ED, -ING, -S** to give a dowry to
TOCK	*n* pl. **-S** a short, hollow sound
TOCO	*n* pl. **-COS** a South American toucan
TOCOLOGY	*n* pl. **-GIES** the branch of medicine dealing with childbirth
TOCSIN	*n* pl. **-S** an alarm sounded on a bell
TOD	*n* pl. **-S** a British unit of weight

TODAY	*n* pl. **-DAYS** the present day
TODDLE	*v* **-DLED, -DLING, -DLES** to walk unsteadily
TODDLER	*n* pl. **-S** one that toddles
TODDY	*n* pl. **-DIES** an alcoholic beverage
TODY	*n* pl. **-DIES** a West Indian bird
TOE	*v* **TOED, TOEING, TOES** to touch with the toe (one of the terminal members of the foot)
TOEA	*n* pl. **-S** a monetary unit of Papua New Guinea
TOECAP	*n* pl. **-S** a covering for the tip of a shoe or boot
TOECLIP	*n* pl. **-S** a device that holds the front of a cyclist's shoe to the pedal
TOEHOLD	*n* pl. **-S** a space that supports the toes in climbing
TOEING	present participle of toe
TOELESS	*adj* having no toes
TOELIKE	*adj* resembling a toe
TOENAIL	*v* **-ED, -ING, -S** to fasten with obliquely driven nails
TOEPIECE	*n* pl. **-S** a piece of a shoe designed to cover the toes
TOEPLATE	*n* pl. **-S** a metal tab attached to the tip of a shoe
TOERAG	*n* pl. **-S** a contemptible person
TOESHOE	*n* pl. **-S** a dance slipper without a heel
TOFF	*n* pl. **-S** a dandy
TOFFEE	*n* pl. **-S** a chewy candy
TOFFY	*n* pl. **-FIES** toffee
TOFT	*n* pl. **-S** a hillock
TOFU	*n* pl. **-S** a soft food product made from soybean milk
TOG	*v* **TOGGED, TOGGING, TOGS** to clothe
TOGA	*n* pl. **-GAS** or **-GAE** an outer garment worn in ancient Rome **TOGAED** *adj*
TOGATE	*adj* pertaining to ancient Rome
TOGATED	*adj* wearing a toga
TOGETHER	*adv* into a union or relationship
TOGGED	past tense of tog
TOGGERY	*n* pl. **-GERIES** clothing
TOGGING	present participle of tog
TOGGLE	*v* **-GLED, -GLING, -GLES** to fasten with a type of pin or short rod
TOGGLER	*n* pl. **-S** one that toggles

TOGROG	*n* pl. **-S** tugrik
TOGUE	*n* pl. **-S** a freshwater fish
TOIL	*v* **-ED, -ING, -S** to work strenuously
TOILE	*n* pl. **-S** a sheer linen fabric
TOILER	*n* pl. **-S** one that toils
TOILET	*v* **-ED, -ING, -S** to dress and groom oneself
TOILETRY	*n* pl. **-TRIES** an article used in dressing and grooming oneself
TOILETTE	*n* pl. **-S** the act of dressing and grooming oneself
TOILFUL	*adj* toilsome
TOILSOME	*adj* demanding much exertion
TOILWORN	*adj* worn by toil
TOIT	*v* **-ED, -ING, -S** to saunter
TOKAMAK	*n* pl. **-S** a doughnut-shaped nuclear reactor
TOKAY	*n* pl. **-KAYS** a Malaysian gecko
TOKE	*v* **TOKED, TOKING, TOKES** to take a puff on a marijuana cigarette
TOKEN	*v* **-ED, -ING, -S** to serve as a sign of
TOKENISM	*n* pl. **-S** the policy of making only a superficial effort
TOKER	*n* pl. **-S** one that tokes
TOKING	present participle of toke
TOKOLOGY	*n* pl. **-GIES** tocology
TOKOMAK	*n* pl. **-S** tokamak
TOKONOMA	*n* pl. **-S** a small alcove in a Japanese house
TOLA	*n* pl. **-S** a unit of weight used in India
TOLAN	*n* pl. **-S** a chemical compound
TOLANE	*n* pl. **-S** tolan
TOLAR	*n* pl. **-LARS** or **-LARJEV** a former monetary unit of Slovenia
TOLBOOTH	*n* pl. **-S** a prison
TOLD	past tense of tell
TOLE	*v* **TOLED, TOLING, TOLES** to allure
TOLEDO	*n* pl. **-DOS** a finely tempered sword
TOLERANT	*adj* inclined to tolerate
TOLERATE	*v* **-ATED, -ATING, -ATES** to allow without active opposition
TOLEWARE	*n* pl. **-S** objects made of elaborately decorated sheet metal
TOLIDIN	*n* pl. **-S** tolidine
TOLIDINE	*n* pl. **-S** a chemical compound

TOLING	present participle of tole
TOLL	*v* **-ED, -ING, -S** to collect or impose a toll (a fixed charge for a service or privilege)
TOLLAGE	*n* pl. **-S** a toll
TOLLBAR	*n* pl. **-S** a tollgate
TOLLER	*n* pl. **-S** a collector of tolls
TOLLGATE	*v* **-GATED, -GATING, -GATES** to block a business deal pending payment of a bribe
TOLLING	*n* pl. **-S** the collecting of tolls
TOLLMAN	*n* pl. **-MEN** a toller
TOLLWAY	*n* pl. **-WAYS** a road on which tolls are collected
TOLT	*n* pl. **-S** an isolated hill
TOLU	*n* pl. **-S** a fragrant resin
TOLUATE	*n* pl. **-S** a chemical salt
TOLUENE	*n* pl. **-S** a flammable liquid
TOLUIC	*adj* pertaining to any of four isomeric acids derived from toluene
TOLUID	*n* pl. **-S** toluide
TOLUIDE	*n* pl. **-S** an amide
TOLUIDIN	*n* pl. **-S** an amine
TOLUOL	*n* pl. **-S** toluene
TOLUOLE	*n* pl. **-S** toluol
TOLUYL	*n* pl. **-S** a univalent chemical radical
TOLYL	*n* pl. **-S** a univalent chemical radical
TOM	*n* pl. **-S** the male of various animals
TOMAHAWK	*v* **-ED, -ING, -S** to strike with a light ax
TOMALLEY	*n* pl. **-LEYS** the liver of a lobster
TOMAN	*n* pl. **-S** a formerly used coin of Iran
TOMATO	*n* pl. **-TOES** the fleshy, edible fruit of a perennial plant **TOMATOEY** *adj*
TOMB	*v* **-ED, -ING, -S** to place in a tomb (a burial vault or chamber)
TOMBAC	*n* pl. **-S** an alloy of copper and zinc
TOMBACK	*n* pl. **-S** tombac
TOMBAK	*n* pl. **-S** tombac
TOMBAL	*adj* pertaining to a tomb
TOMBLESS	*adj* having no tomb
TOMBLIKE	*adj* resembling a tomb
TOMBOLA	*n* pl. **-S** a gambling game that is a type of lottery

TOMBOLO *n* pl. **-LOS** a sandbar connecting an island to the mainland

TOMBOY *n* pl. **-BOYS** a girl who prefers boyish activities

TOMCAT *v* **-CATTED, -CATTING, -CATS** to engage in sexually promiscuous behavior — used of a male

TOMCOD *n* pl. **-S** a marine fish

TOME *n* pl. **-S** a large book

TOMENTUM *n* pl. **-TA** a network of small blood vessels

TOMFOOL *n* pl. **-S** a foolish person

TOMMY *n* pl. **-MIES** a loaf of bread

TOMMYCOD *n* pl. **-S** tomcod

TOMMYROT *n* pl. **-S** nonsense

TOMOGRAM *n* pl. **-S** a photograph made with X-rays

TOMORROW *n* pl. **-S** the day following today

TOMPION *n* pl. **-S** tampion

TOMTIT *n* pl. **-S** any of various small active birds

TON *n* pl. **-S** a unit of weight

TONAL *adj* pertaining to tone **TONALLY** *adv*

TONALITY *n* pl. **-TIES** a system of tones

TONDO *n* pl. **-DOS** or **-DI** a circular painting

TONE *v* **TONED, TONING, TONES** to give a particular tone (a sound of definite pitch and vibration) to

TONEARM *n* pl. **-S** the pivoted part of a record player that holds the needle

TONELESS *adj* lacking in tone

TONEME *n* pl. **-S** a tonal unit of speech **TONEMIC** *adj*

TONER *n* pl. **-S** one that tones

TONETICS *n/pl* the phonetic study of tone in language **TONETIC** *adj*

TONETTE *n* pl. **-S** a simple flute

TONEY *adj* **TONIER, TONIEST** tony

TONG *v* **-ED, -ING, -S** to lift with a type of grasping device

TONGA *n* pl. **-S** a light cart used in India

TONGER *n* pl. **-S** one that tongs

TONGMAN *n* pl. **-MEN** a member of a Chinese secret society

TONGUE *v* **TONGUED, TONGUING, TONGUES** to touch with the tongue (an organ of the mouth)

TONGUING *n* pl. **-S** the use of the tongue in articulating notes on a wind instrument

TONIC *n* pl. **-S** something that invigorates or refreshes

TONICITY *n* pl. **-TIES** normal, healthy bodily condition

TONIER comparative of toney and tony

TONIEST superlative of toney and tony

TONIFY *v* **-FIED, -FYING, -FIES** to give tone to

TONIGHT *n* pl. **-S** the present night

TONING present participle of tone

TONISH *adj* stylish **TONISHLY** *adv*

TONLET *n* pl. **-S** a skirt of plate armor

TONNAGE *n* pl. **-S** total weight in tons

TONNE *n* pl. **-S** a unit of weight

TONNEAU *n* pl. **-NEAUS** or **-NEAUX** the rear seating compartment of an automobile

TONNER *n* pl. **-S** an object having a specified tonnage

TONNISH *adj* tonish

TONSIL *n* pl. **-S** a lymphoid organ **TONSILAR** *adj*

TONSURE *v* **-SURED, -SURING, -SURES** to shave the head of

TONTINE *n* pl. **-S** a form of collective life insurance

TONUS *n* pl. **-ES** a normal state of tension in muscle tissue

TONY *adj* **TONIER, TONIEST** stylish

TOO *adv* in addition

TOODLE *v* **-DLED, -DLING, -DLES** to tootle

TOOK past tense of take

TOOL *v* **-ED, -ING, -S** to form or finish with a tool (an implement used in manual work)

TOOLBAR *n* pl. **-S** a row of icons on a computer screen that activate functions

TOOLBOX *n* pl. **-ES** a box for tools

TOOLER *n* pl. **-S** one that tools

TOOLHEAD *n* pl. **-S** a part of a machine

TOOLING *n* pl. **-S** ornamentation done with tools

TOOLLESS *adj* having no tools

TOOLPUSH *n* pl. **-ES** a worker who directs the drilling on an oil rig

TOOLROOM	*n* pl. **-S** a room where tools are stored	**TOPICAL**	*n* pl. **-S** a postage stamp in a collection with designs relating to the same subject
TOOLSET	*n* pl. **-S** a set of tools	**TOPING**	present participle of tope
TOOLSHED	*n* pl. **-S** a building where tools are stored	**TOPKICK**	*n* pl. **-S** a first sergeant
TOOM	*adj* empty	**TOPKNOT**	*n* pl. **-S** an ornament for the hair
TOON	*n* pl. **-S** an East Indian tree	**TOPLESS**	*adj* having no top
TOONIE	*n* pl. **-S** a Canadian two-dollar coin	**TOPLINE**	*n* pl. **-S** the outline of the top of an animal's body
TOOT	*v* **-ED, -ING, -S** to sound a horn or whistle in short blasts	**TOPLOFTY**	*adj* **-LOFTIER, -LOFTIEST** haughty
TOOTER	*n* pl. **-S** one that toots	**TOPMAST**	*n* pl. **-S** a mast of a ship
TOOTH	*n* pl. **TEETH** one of the hard structures attached in a row to each jaw	**TOPMOST**	*adj* highest
		TOPNOTCH	*adj* excellent
TOOTH	*v* **-ED, -ING, -S** to furnish with toothlike projections	**TOPO**	*adj* topographic
		TOPOI	pl. of topos
TOOTHY	*adj* **TOOTHIER, TOOTHIEST** having or showing prominent teeth **TOOTHILY** *adv*	**TOPOLOGY**	*n* pl. **-GIES** a branch of mathematics
		TOPONYM	*n* pl. **-S** the name of a place
TOOTLE	*v* **-TLED, -TLING, -TLES** to toot softly or repeatedly	**TOPONYMY**	*n* pl. **-MIES** the study of toponyms
		TOPOS	*n* pl. **-POI** a stock rhetorical theme
TOOTLER	*n* pl. **-S** one that tootles	**TOPOTYPE**	*n* pl. **-S** a specimen selected from a locality typical of a species
TOOTS	*n* pl. **-ES** a woman or girl — usually used as a form of address		
		TOPPED	past tense of top
TOOTSIE	*n* pl. **-S** tootsy	**TOPPER**	*n* pl. **-S** one that tops
TOOTSY	*n* pl. **-SIES** a foot	**TOPPING**	*n* pl. **-S** something that forms a top
TOP	*v* **TOPPED, TOPPING, TOPS** to cut off the top (the highest part, point, or surface) of	**TOPPLE**	*v* **-PLED, -PLING, -PLES** to fall forward
		TOPSAIL	*n* pl. **-S** a sail of a ship
TOPAZ	*n* pl. **-ES** a mineral **TOPAZINE** *adj*	**TOPSIDE**	*n* pl. **-S** the upper portion of a ship
TOPCOAT	*n* pl. **-S** a lightweight overcoat	**TOPSIDER**	*n* pl. **-S** one who is at the highest level of authority
TOPCROSS	*n* pl. **-ES** a cross between a purebred male and inferior female stock	**TOPSOIL**	*v* **-ED, -ING, -S** to remove the surface layer of soil from
		TOPSPIN	*n* pl. **-S** a forward spin imparted to a ball
TOPE	*v* **TOPED, TOPING, TOPES** to drink liquor to excess	**TOPSTONE**	*n* pl. **-S** the stone at the top of a structure
TOPEE	*n* pl. **-S** topi		
TOPER	*n* pl. **-S** one that topes	**TOPWATER**	*adj* floating on or near the top of the water
TOPFUL	*adj* topfull		
TOPFULL	*adj* full to the top	**TOPWORK**	*v* **-ED, -ING, -S** to graft scions of another variety of plant on the main branches of
TOPH	*n* pl. **-S** tufa		
TOPHE	*n* pl. **-S** tufa	**TOQUE**	*n* pl. **-S** a close-fitting woman's hat
TOPHUS	*n* pl. **-PHI** a deposit of urates in the tissue around a joint	**TOQUET**	*n* pl. **-S** toque
		TOQUILLA	*n* pl. **-S** a palmlike plant of South America
TOPI	*n* pl. **-S** a sun helmet		
TOPIARY	*n* pl. **-ARIES** the art of trimming shrubs into shapes	**TOR**	*n* pl. **-S** a high, craggy hill
TOPIC	*n* pl. **-S** a subject of discourse	**TORA**	*n* pl. **-S** torah

TORAH	*n* pl. **-RAHS** or **-ROTH** or **-ROT** a law or precept
TORC	*n* pl. **-S** a metal collar or necklace
TORCH	*v* **-ED, -ING, -ES** to set on fire
TORCHERE	*n* pl. **-S** a type of electric lamp
TORCHIER	*n* pl. **-S** torchere
TORCHLIT	*adj* lighted by torches (poles with a burning end)
TORCHON	*n* pl. **-S** a coarse lace
TORCHY	*adj* **TORCHIER, TORCHIEST** characteristic of a torch song
TORE	*n* pl. **-S** a torus
TOREADOR	*n* pl. **-S** a bullfighter
TORERO	*n* pl. **-ROS** a bullfighter
TOREUTIC	*adj* pertaining to a type of metalwork
TORI	pl. of torus
TORIC	*n* pl. **-S** a lens designed to correct astigmatism
TORIES	pl. of tory
TORII	*n* pl. **TORII** the gateway of a Japanese temple
TORMENT	*v* **-ED, -ING, -S** to inflict with great bodily or mental suffering
TORN	past participle of tear
TORNADO	*n* pl. **-DOS** or **-DOES** a violent windstorm **TORNADIC** *adj*
TORNILLO	*n* pl. **-LOS** a flowering shrub
TORO	*n* pl. **-ROS** a bull
TOROID	*n* pl. **-S** a type of geometric surface **TOROIDAL** *adj*
TOROSE	*adj* cylindrical and swollen at intervals
TOROSITY	*n* pl. **-TIES** the quality or state of being torose
TOROT	a pl. of torah
TOROTH	a pl. of torah
TOROUS	*adj* torose
TORPEDO	*v* **-ED, -ING, -ES** or **-S** to damage or sink with an underwater missile
TORPEFY	*v* **-FIED, -FYING, -FIES** to make sluggish
TORPID	*n* pl. **-S** a racing boat
TORPIDLY	*adv* in a sluggish manner
TORPOR	*n* pl. **-S** mental or physical inactivity
TORQUATE	*adj* having a torques
TORQUE	*v* **TORQUED, TORQUING, TORQUES** to cause to twist
TORQUER	*n* pl. **-S** one that torques
TORQUES	*n* pl. **-QUESES** a band of feathers, hair, or coloration around the neck
TORQUEY	*adj* **-QUIER, -QUIEST** providing force to cause rotation
TORR	*n* pl. **-S** a unit of pressure
TORREFY	*v* **-FIED, -FYING, -FIES** to subject to intense heat
TORRENT	*n* pl. **-S** a rapid stream of water
TORRID	*adj* **-RIDER, -RIDEST** extremely hot **TORRIDLY** *adv*
TORRIFY	*v* **-FIED, -FYING, -FIES** to torrefy
TORSADE	*n* pl. **-S** a twisted cord
TORSE	*n* pl. **-S** a wreath of twisted silks
TORSI	a pl. of torso
TORSION	*n* pl. **-S** the act of twisting
TORSK	*n* pl. **-S** a marine food fish
TORSO	*n* pl. **-SOS** or **-SI** the trunk of the human body
TORT	*n* pl. **-S** a civil wrong
TORTA	*n* pl. **-S** an elaborate dessert
TORTE	*n* pl. **TORTES** or **TORTEN** a rich cake
TORTELLI	*n/pl* pieces of pasta stuffed with cheese, meat, or vegetables
TORTILE	*adj* twisted; coiled
TORTILLA	*n* pl. **-S** a round, flat cake of unleavened cornmeal
TORTIOUS	*adj* of the nature of a tort
TORTOISE	*n* pl. **-S** any of an order of reptiles having the body enclosed in a bony shell
TORTONI	*n* pl. **-S** a type of ice cream
TORTRIX	*n* pl. **-TRIXES** or **-TRICES** a small moth
TORTUOUS	*adj* marked by repeated turns or bends
TORTURE	*v* **-TURED, -TURING, -TURES** to subject to severe physical pain
TORTURER	*n* pl. **-S** one that tortures
TORULA	*n* pl. **-LAS** or **-LAE** a type of fungus
TORUS	*n* pl. **-RI** or **-RUSES** a large convex molding
TORY	*n* pl. **-RIES** a political conservative
TOSA	*n* pl. **-S** a dog of a breed of mastiff
TOSH	*n* pl. **-ES** nonsense
TOSS	*v* **TOSSED** or **TOST, TOSSING, TOSSES** to throw lightly

TOSSER	*n* pl. **-S** one that tosses
TOSSPOT	*n* pl. **-S** a drunkard
TOSSUP	*n* pl. **-S** an even choice or chance
TOST	a past tense of toss
TOSTADA	*n* pl. **-S** a tortilla fried in deep fat
TOSTADO	*n* pl. **-DOS** tostada
TOSTONE	*n* pl. **-S** a Mexican dish of fried plantains
TOT	*v* **TOTTED, TOTTING, TOTS** to total
TOTABLE	*adj* capable of being toted
TOTAL	*v* **-TALED, -TALING, -TALS** or **-TALLED, -TALLING, -TALS** to ascertain the entire amount of
TOTALISE	*v* **-ISED, -ISING, -ISES** to totalize
TOTALISM	*n* pl. **-S** centralized control by an autocratic authority
TOTALIST	*n* pl. **-S** one who tends to regard things as a unified whole
TOTALITY	*n* pl. **-TIES** the quality or state of being complete
TOTALIZE	*v* **-IZED, -IZING, -IZES** to make complete
TOTALLED	a past tense of total
TOTALLING	a present participle of total
TOTALLY	*adv* completely
TOTE	*v* **TOTED, TOTING, TOTES** to carry by hand **TOTEABLE** *adj*
TOTEM	*n* pl. **-S** a natural object serving as the emblem of a family or clan **TOTEMIC** *adj*
TOTEMISM	*n* pl. **-S** a system of tribal division according to totems
TOTEMIST	*n* pl. **-S** a specialist in totemism
TOTEMITE	*n* pl. **-S** a totemist
TOTER	*n* pl. **-S** one that totes
TOTHER	*pron* the other
TOTING	present participle of tote
TOTTED	past tense of tot
TOTTER	*v* **-ED, -ING, -S** to walk unsteadily
TOTTERER	*n* pl. **-S** one that totters
TOTTERY	*adj* shaky
TOTTING	present participle of tot
TOUCAN	*n* pl. **-S** a tropical bird
TOUCH	*v* **-ED, -ING, -ES** to be in or come into contact with
TOUCHE	*interj* — used to acknowledge a hit in fencing
TOUCHER	*n* pl. **-S** one that touches
TOUCHPAD	*n* pl. **-S** a keypad sensitized to finger movement or pressure
TOUCHUP	*n* pl. **-S** an act of finishing by adding minor improvements
TOUCHY	*adj* **TOUCHIER, TOUCHIEST** overly sensitive **TOUCHILY** *adv*
TOUGH	*adj* **TOUGHER, TOUGHEST** strong and resilient
TOUGH	*v* **-ED, -ING, -S** to endure hardship
TOUGHEN	*v* **-ED, -ING, -S** to make tough
TOUGHIE	*n* pl. **-S** a tough person
TOUGHISH	*adj* somewhat tough
TOUGHLY	*adv* in a tough manner
TOUGHY	*n* pl. **TOUGHIES** toughie
TOUPEE	*n* pl. **-S** a wig worn to cover a bald spot
TOUPIE	*n* pl. **-S** a round boneless smoked ham
TOUR	*v* **-ED, -ING, -S** to travel from place to place
TOURACO	*n* pl. **-COS** an African bird
TOURER	*n* pl. **-S** a large, open automobile
TOURING	*n* pl. **-S** cross-country skiing for pleasure
TOURISM	*n* pl. **-S** the practice of touring for pleasure
TOURIST	*n* pl. **-S** one who tours for pleasure **TOURISTY** *adj*
TOURISTA	*n* pl. **-S** turista
TOURNEY	*v* **-ED, -ING, -S** to compete in a tournament
TOUSE	*v* **TOUSED, TOUSING, TOUSES** to tousle
TOUSLE	*v* **-SLED, -SLING, -SLES** to dishevel
TOUT	*v* **-ED, -ING, -S** to solicit brazenly
TOUTER	*n* pl. **-S** one that touts
TOUTON	*n* pl. **-S** a deep-fried round of bread dough
TOUZLE	*v* **-ZLED, -ZLING, -ZLES** to tousle
TOVARICH	*n* pl. **-ES** comrade
TOVARISH	*n* pl. **-ES** tovarich
TOW	*v* **-ED, -ING, -S** to pull by means of a rope or chain **TOWABLE** *adj*
TOWAGE	*n* pl. **-S** the price paid for towing
TOWARD	*prep* in the direction of
TOWARDLY	*adj* favorable
TOWARDS	*prep* toward

TOWAWAY	*n* pl. **-AWAYS** the act of towing away a vehicle
TOWBOAT	*n* pl. **-S** a tugboat
TOWEL	*v* **-ELED, -ELING, -ELS** or **-ELLED, -ELLING, -ELS** to wipe with a towel (an absorbent cloth)
TOWELING	*n* pl. **-S** material used for towels
TOWER	*v* **-ED, -ING, -S** to rise to a great height
TOWERY	*adj* **-ERIER, -ERIEST** very tall
TOWHEAD	*n* pl. **-S** a head of light blond hair
TOWHEE	*n* pl. **-S** a common finch
TOWIE	*n* pl. **-S** a form of contract bridge for three players
TOWLINE	*n* pl. **-S** a line used in towing
TOWMOND	*n* pl. **-S** a year
TOWMONT	*n* pl. **-S** towmond
TOWN	*n* pl. **-S** a center of population smaller than a city
TOWNEE	*n* pl. **-S** a townsman
TOWNFOLK	*n/pl* the inhabitants of a town
TOWNHOME	*n* pl. **-S** one of a series of contiguous houses of two or three stories
TOWNIE	*n* pl. **-S** a nonstudent who lives in a college town
TOWNIES	pl. of towny
TOWNISH	*adj* characteristic of a town
TOWNLESS	*adj* having no towns
TOWNLET	*n* pl. **-S** a small town
TOWNSHIP	*n* pl. **-S** an administrative division of a county
TOWNSITE	*n* pl. **-S** the site of a town
TOWNSMAN	*n* pl. **-MEN** a resident of a town
TOWNWARD	*adv* toward the town
TOWNWEAR	*n* pl. **TOWNWEAR** apparel that is suitable for wear in the city
TOWNY	*n* pl. **TOWNIES** townie
TOWPATH	*n* pl. **-S** a path along a river that is used by animals towing boats
TOWPLANE	*n* pl. **-S** an airplane that tows gliders
TOWROPE	*n* pl. **-S** a rope used in towing
TOWSACK	*n* pl. **-S** a sack made of a coarse fabric
TOWY	*adj* resembling coarse hemp or flax fiber
TOXAEMIA	*n* pl. **-S** toxemia **TOXAEMIC** *adj*

TOXEMIA	*n* pl. **-S** the condition of having toxins in the blood **TOXEMIC** *adj*
TOXIC	*n* pl. **-S** a poisonous substance
TOXICAL	*adj* toxic
TOXICANT	*n* pl. **-S** a poisonous substance
TOXICITY	*n* pl. **-TIES** the quality of being poisonous
TOXIN	*n* pl. **-S** a poisonous substance
TOXINE	*n* pl. **-S** toxin
TOXOID	*n* pl. **-S** a type of toxin
TOY	*v* **-ED, -ING, -S** to amuse oneself as if with a toy (a child's plaything)
TOYER	*n* pl. **-S** one that toys
TOYISH	*adj* frivolous
TOYLAND	*n* pl. **-S** the toy industry
TOYLESS	*adj* having no toy
TOYLIKE	*adj* resembling a toy
TOYO	*n* pl. **-YOS** a smooth straw used in making hats
TOYON	*n* pl. **-S** an ornamental evergreen shrub
TOYSHOP	*n* pl. **-S** a shop where toys are sold
TOYTOWN	*n* pl. **-S** a small model of a town
TRABEATE	*adj* constructed with horizontal beams
TRACE	*v* **TRACED, TRACING, TRACES** to follow the course of
TRACER	*n* pl. **-S** one that traces
TRACERY	*n* pl. **-ERIES** ornamental work of interlaced lines
TRACHEA	*n* pl. **-CHEAS** or **-CHEAE** the passage for conveying air to the lungs **TRACHEAL** *adj*
TRACHEID	*n* pl. **-S** a long, tubular plant cell
TRACHLE	*v* **-LED, -LING, -LES** to draggle
TRACHOMA	*n* pl. **-S** a disease of the eye
TRACHYTE	*n* pl. **-S** a light-colored igneous rock
TRACING	*n* pl. **-S** something that is traced
TRACK	*v* **-ED, -ING, -S** to follow the marks left by an animal, a person, or a vehicle
TRACKAGE	*n* pl. **-S** the track system of a railroad
TRACKBED	*n* pl. **-S** a roadbed for a railroad
TRACKER	*n* pl. **-S** one that tracks
TRACKING	*n* pl. **-S** the placement of students within a curriculum
TRACKMAN	*n* pl. **-MEN** a railroad worker

TRACKPAD *n* pl. **-S** a touchpad

TRACKWAY *n* pl. **-WAYS** a trodden path

TRACT *n* pl. **-S** an expanse of land

TRACTATE *n* pl. **-S** a treatise

TRACTILE *adj* capable of being drawn out in length

TRACTION *n* pl. **-S** the act of pulling or drawing over a surface **TRACTIVE** *adj*

TRACTOR *n* pl. **-S** a motor vehicle used in farming

TRACTRIX *n* pl. **-TRICES** a mathematical curve

TRAD *adj* traditional

TRADE *v* **TRADED, TRADING, TRADES** to give in exchange for another commodity **TRADABLE** *adj*

TRADEOFF *n* pl. **-S** a giving up of one thing in return for another

TRADER *n* pl. **-S** one that trades

TRADING *n* pl. **-S** the action of exchanging commodities

TRADITOR *n* pl. **-ES** a traitor among the early Christians

TRADUCE *v* **-DUCED, -DUCING, -DUCES** to defame

TRADUCER *n* pl. **-S** one that traduces

TRAFFIC *v* **-FICKED, -FICKING, -FICS** to engage in buying and selling

TRAGEDY *n* pl. **-DIES** a disastrous event

TRAGI pl. of tragus

TRAGIC *n* pl. **-S** the element of a drama that produces tragedy

TRAGICAL *adj* of the nature of a tragedy

TRAGOPAN *n* pl. **-S** an Asian pheasant

TRAGUS *n* pl. **-GI** a part of the external opening of the ear

TRAIK *v* **-ED, -ING, -S** to trudge

TRAIL *v* **-ED, -ING, -S** to drag along a surface

TRAILER *v* **-ED, -ING, -S** to transport by means of a trailer (a vehicle drawn by another)

TRAIN *v* **-ED, -ING, -S** to instruct systematically

TRAINEE *n* pl. **-S** a person receiving training

TRAINER *n* pl. **-S** one that trains

TRAINFUL *n* pl. **-S** as much as a railroad train can hold

TRAINING *n* pl. **-S** systematic instruction

TRAINMAN *n* pl. **-MEN** a railroad employee

TRAINWAY *n* pl. **-WAYS** a railway

TRAIPSE *v* **TRAIPSED, TRAIPSING, TRAIPSES** to walk about in an idle or aimless manner

TRAIT *n* pl. **-S** a distinguishing characteristic

TRAITOR *n* pl. **-S** one who betrays another

TRAJECT *v* **-ED, -ING, -S** to transmit

TRAM *v* **TRAMMED, TRAMMING, TRAMS** to convey in a tramcar

TRAMCAR *n* pl. **-S** a streetcar

TRAMEL *v* **-ELED, -ELING, -ELS** or **-ELLED, -ELLING, -ELS** to trammel

TRAMELL *v* **-ED, -ING, -S** to trammel

TRAMLESS *adj* having no tramcar

TRAMLINE *n* pl. **-S** a streetcar line

TRAMMED past tense of tram

TRAMMEL *v* **-MELED, -MELING, -MELS** or **-MELLED, -MELLING, -MELS** to hinder

TRAMMING present participle of tram

TRAMP *v* **-ED, -ING, -S** to walk with a firm, heavy step

TRAMPER *n* pl. **-S** one that tramps

TRAMPISH *adj* resembling a vagabond

TRAMPLE *v* **-PLED, -PLING, -PLES** to tread on heavily

TRAMPLER *n* pl. **-S** one that tramples

TRAMPY *adj* **TRAMPIER, TRAMPIEST** having the characteristics of a vagrant

TRAMROAD *n* pl. **-S** a railway in a mine

TRAMWAY *n* pl. **-WAYS** a tramline

TRANCE *v* **TRANCED, TRANCING, TRANCES** to put into a trance (a semiconscious state)

TRANCHE *n* pl. **-S** a portion

TRANGAM *n* pl. **-S** a gewgaw

TRANK *v* **-ED, -ING, -S** to tranquilize

TRANNIE *n* pl. **-S** tranny

TRANNY *n* pl. **-NIES** a transmission

TRANQ *n* pl. **-S** trank

TRANQUIL *adj* **-QUILER, -QUILEST** or **-QUILLER, -QUILLEST** free from disturbance

TRANS *adj* characterized by the arrangement of different atoms on opposite sides of the molecule

TRANSACT	*v* **-ED, -ING, -S** to carry out	**TRASHER**	*n* pl. **-S** one that destroys or damages
TRANSECT	*v* **-ED, -ING, -S** to cut across	**TRASHMAN**	*n* pl. **-MEN** a person who removes trash
TRANSEPT	*n* pl. **-S** a major transverse part of the body of a church	**TRASHY**	*adj* **TRASHIER, TRASHIEST** resembling trash **TRASHILY** *adv*
TRANSFER	*v* **-FERRED, -FERRING, -FERS** to convey from one source to another	**TRASS**	*n* pl. **-ES** a volcanic rock
TRANSFIX	*v* **-FIXED** or **-FIXT, -FIXING, -FIXES** to impale	**TRAUCHLE**	*v* **-LED, -LING, -LES** to trachle
TRANSHIP	*v* **-SHIPPED, -SHIPPING, -SHIPS** to transfer from one conveyance to another	**TRAUMA**	*n* pl. **-MAS** or **-MATA** a severe emotional shock
TRANSIT	*v* **-ED, -ING, -S** to pass across or through	**TRAVAIL**	*v* **-ED, -ING, -S** to toil
		TRAVE	*n* pl. **-S** a frame for confining a horse
TRANSMIT	*v* **-MITTED, -MITTING, -MITS** to send from one place or person to another	**TRAVEL**	*v* **-ELED, -ELING, -ELS** or **-ELLED, -ELLING, -ELS** to go from one place to another
TRANSOM	*n* pl. **-S** a small window above a door or another window	**TRAVELER**	*n* pl. **-S** one that travels
TRANSUDE	*v* **-SUDED, -SUDING, -SUDES** to pass through a membrane	**TRAVELOG**	*n* pl. **-S** a lecture or film on traveling
TRAP	*v* **TRAPPED** or **TRAPT, TRAPPING, TRAPS** to catch in a trap (a device for capturing and holding animals)	**TRAVERSE**	*v* **-VERSED, -VERSING, -VERSES** to pass across or through
		TRAVESTY	*v* **-TIED, -TYING, -TIES** to parody
TRAPAN	*v* **-PANNED, -PANNING, -PANS** to trephine	**TRAVOIS**	*n* pl. **-ES** a type of sled
		TRAVOISE	*n* pl. **-S** travois
TRAPBALL	*n* pl. **-S** a type of ball game	**TRAWL**	*v* **-ED, -ING, -S** to fish by dragging a net along the sea bottom
TRAPDOOR	*n* pl. **-S** a lifting or sliding door covering an opening	**TRAWLER**	*n* pl. **-S** a boat used for trawling
TRAPES	*v* **-ED, -ING, -ES** to traipse	**TRAWLEY**	*n* pl. **-LEYS** a small truck or car for conveying material
TRAPEZE	*n* pl. **-S** a gymnastic apparatus		
TRAPEZIA	*n/pl* four-sided polygons having no parallel sides	**TRAWLNET**	*n* pl. **-S** the large net used in trawling
TRAPEZII	*n/pl* triangular muscles of the back	**TRAY**	*n* pl. **TRAYS** a flat, shallow receptacle
TRAPLIKE	*adj* resembling a trap	**TRAYF**	*adj* not prepared according to Jewish law
TRAPLINE	*n* pl. **-S** a series of traps		
TRAPNEST	*v* **-ED, -ING, -S** to determine the productivity of hens with a type of nest	**TRAYFUL**	*n* pl. **-S** as much as a tray will hold
		TREACLE	*n* pl. **-S** molasses
TRAPPEAN	*adj* pertaining to traprock	**TREACLY**	*adj* **-CLIER, -CLIEST** cloyingly sweet and sentimental
TRAPPED	a past tense of trap		
TRAPPER	*n* pl. **-S** one that traps	**TREAD**	*v* **TROD** or **TRODE** or **TREADED, TRODDEN, TREADING, TREADS** to walk on, over, or along
TRAPPING	*n* pl. **-S** a covering for a horse		
TRAPPOSE	*adj* trappean	**TREADER**	*n* pl. **-S** one that treads
TRAPPOUS	*adj* trappean	**TREADLE**	*v* **-DLED, -DLING, -DLES** to work a foot lever
TRAPROCK	*n* pl. **-S** an igneous rock		
TRAPT	a past tense of trap	**TREADLER**	*n* pl. **-S** one that treadles
TRAPUNTO	*n* pl. **-TOS** a decorative quilted design	**TREASON**	*n* pl. **-S** violation of allegiance toward one's country
TRASH	*v* **-ED, -ING, -ES** to free from trash (worthless or waste matter)	**TREASURE**	*v* **-SURED, -SURING, -SURES** to value highly

TREASURY   *n* pl. **-URIES** a place where funds are received, kept, and disbursed

TREAT   *v* **-ED, -ING, -S** to behave in a particular way toward

TREATER   *n* pl. **-S** one that treats

TREATING   *n* pl. **-S** the act of providing someone with something pleasurable

TREATISE   *n* pl. **-S** a formal and systematic written account of a subject

TREATY   *n* pl. **-TIES** a formal agreement between two or more nations

TREBLE   *v* **-BLED, -BLING, -BLES** to triple

TREBLY   *adv* triply

TRECENTO   *n* pl. **-TOS** the fourteenth century

TREDDLE   *v* **-DLED, -DLING, -DLES** to treadle

TREE   *v* **TREED, TREEING, TREES** to drive up a tree (a tall, woody plant)

TREELAWN   *n* pl. **-S** the strip of lawn between the street and the sidewalk

TREELESS   *adj* having no tree

TREELIKE   *adj* resembling a tree

TREELINE   *n* pl. **-S** the limit north of which trees do not grow

TREEN   *n* pl. **-S** an article made from wood

TREENAIL   *n* pl. **-S** a wooden peg used for fastening timbers

TREETOP   *n* pl. **-S** the top of a tree

TREF   *adj* unfit for use according to Jewish law

TREFA   *adj* tref

TREFAH   *adj* tref

TREFOIL   *n* pl. **-S** a plant having ternate leaves

TREHALA   *n* pl. **-S** a sweet, edible substance forming the pupal case of certain weevils

TREK   *v* **TREKKED, TREKKING, TREKS** to make a slow or arduous journey

TREKKER   *n* pl. **-S** one that treks

TRELLIS   *v* **-ED, -ING, -ES** to provide with a trellis (a frame used as a support for climbing plants)

TREM   *n* pl. **-S** an electric guitar lever for producing a tremolo

TREMBLE   *v* **-BLED, -BLING, -BLES** to shake involuntarily

TREMBLER   *n* pl. **-S** one that trembles

TREMBLOR   *n* pl. **-S** an earth tremor

TREMBLY   *adj* **-BLIER, -BLIEST** marked by trembling

TREMOLO   *n* pl. **-LOS** a vibrating musical effect

TREMOR   *v* **-ED, -ING, -S** to undergo a shaking or quivering

TRENAIL   *n* pl. **-S** treenail

TRENCH   *v* **-ED, -ING, -ES** to dig a long, narrow excavation in the ground

TRENCHER   *n* pl. **-S** a wooden platter for serving food

TREND   *v* **-ED, -ING, -S** to take a particular course

TRENDIFY   *v* **-FIED, -FYING, -FIES** to make something trendy

TRENDOID   *n* pl. **-S** a trendy person

TRENDY   *adj* **TRENDIER, TRENDIEST** very fashionable **TRENDILY** *adv*

TRENDY   *n* pl. **TRENDIES** a trendy person

TREPAN   *v* **-PANNED, -PANNING, -PANS** to trephine

TREPANG   *n* pl. **-S** a marine animal

TREPHINE   *v* **-PHINED, -PHINING, -PHINES** to operate on with a surgical saw

TREPID   *adj* timorous

TRESPASS   *v* **-ED, -ING, -ES** to enter upon the land of another unlawfully

TRESS   *v* **-ED, -ING, -ES** to arrange the hair in long locks

TRESSEL   *n* pl. **-S** trestle

TRESSOUR   *n* pl. **-S** tressure

TRESSURE   *n* pl. **-S** a type of heraldic design

TRESSY   *adj* **TRESSIER, TRESSIEST** abounding in tresses

TRESTLE   *n* pl. **-S** a framework for supporting a bridge

TRET   *n* pl. **-S** an allowance formerly paid to purchasers for waste incurred in transit

TREVALLY   *n* pl. **-LIES** or **-LYS** an Australian food fish

TREVET   *n* pl. **-S** trivet

TREWS   *n/pl* close-fitting tartan trousers

TREY   *n* pl. **TREYS** a three in cards, dice, or dominoes

TREYF   *adj* trayf

TREYFA   *adj* trayf

TRIABLE   *adj* subject to judicial examination

TRIAC   *n* pl. **-S** an electronic device used to control power

TRIACID	*n* pl. **-S** a type of acid	**TRICITY**	*n* pl. **-TIES** an area that comprises three adjoining independent cities
TRIACTOR	*n* pl. **-S** a trifecta		
TRIAD	*n* pl. **-S** a group of three	**TRICK**	*v* **-ED, -ING, -S** to deceive
TRIADIC	*n* pl. **-S** a member of a triad	**TRICKER**	*n* pl. **-S** one that tricks
TRIADISM	*n* pl. **-S** the quality or state of being a triad	**TRICKERY**	*n* pl. **-ERIES** deception
		TRICKIE	*adj* **TRICKIER, TRICKIEST** tricky
TRIAGE	*v* **-AGED, -AGING, -AGES** to practice a system of treating disaster victims	**TRICKIER**	comparative of tricky
		TRICKIEST	superlative of tricky
		TRICKILY	*adv* in a tricky manner
TRIAL	*v* **-ALED, -ALING, -ALS** or **-ALLED, -ALLING, -ALS** to test something to assess its performance	**TRICKISH**	*adj* tricky
		TRICKLE	*v* **-LED, -LING, -LES** to flow or fall in drops
TRIALIST	*n* pl. **-S** a person who participates in a test of something	**TRICKLY**	*adj* **-LIER, -LIEST** marked by trickling
TRIANGLE	*n* pl. **-S** a polygon having three sides	**TRICKSY**	*adj* **-SIER, -SIEST** mischievous
		TRICKY	*adj* **TRICKIER, TRICKIEST** characterized by deception
TRIARCHY	*n* pl. **-CHIES** government by three persons		
		TRICLAD	*n* pl. **-S** an aquatic flatworm
TRIAXIAL	*adj* having three axes	**TRICOLOR**	*n* pl. **-S** a flag having three colors
TRIAZIN	*n* pl. **-S** triazine	**TRICORN**	*n* pl. **-S** a hat with the brim turned up on three sides
TRIAZINE	*n* pl. **-S** a chemical compound		
TRIAZOLE	*n* pl. **-S** a chemical compound	**TRICORNE**	*n* pl. **-S** tricorn
TRIBADE	*n* pl. **-S** a lesbian **TRIBADIC** *adj*	**TRICOT**	*n* pl. **-S** a knitted fabric
TRIBAL	*n* pl. **-S** a member of an aboriginal people of India	**TRICTRAC**	*n* pl. **-S** a form of backgammon
		TRICYCLE	*v* **-CLED, -CLING, -CLES** to ride a vehicle having three wheels
TRIBALLY	*adv* in a manner characteristic of a tribe	**TRIDENT**	*n* pl. **-S** a spear having three prongs
TRIBASIC	*adj* having three replaceable hydrogen atoms	**TRIDUUM**	*n* pl. **-S** a period of three days of prayer
TRIBE	*n* pl. **-S** a group of people sharing a common ancestry and culture	**TRIED**	past tense of try
TRIBRACH	*n* pl. **-S** a type of metrical foot	**TRIENE**	*n* pl. **-S** a type of chemical compound
TRIBUNAL	*n* pl. **-S** a court of justice	**TRIENNIA**	*n/pl* periods of three years
TRIBUNE	*n* pl. **-S** a defender of the rights of the people	**TRIENS**	*n* pl. **-ENTES** a coin of ancient Rome
TRIBUTE	*n* pl. **-S** something given to show respect, gratitude, or admiration	**TRIER**	*n* pl. **-S** one that tries
		TRIES	present 3d person sing. of try
TRICE	*v* **TRICED, TRICING, TRICES** to haul up with a rope	**TRIETHYL**	*adj* containing three ethyl groups
		TRIFECTA	*n* pl. **-S** a system of betting
TRICEP	*n* pl. **-S** a triceps	**TRIFFID**	*n* pl. **-S** a fictional predatory plant
TRICEPS	*n* pl. **-ES** an arm muscle	**TRIFID**	*adj* divided into three parts
TRICHINA	*n* pl. **-NAS** or **-NAE** a parasitic worm	**TRIFLE**	*v* **-FLED, -FLING, -FLES** to waste time
TRICHITE	*n* pl. **-S** a minute mineral body found in volcanic rocks	**TRIFLER**	*n* pl. **-S** one that trifles
		TRIFLING	*n* pl. **-S** a waste of time
TRICHOID	*adj* hairlike	**TRIFOCAL**	*n* pl. **-S** a type of lens
TRICHOME	*n* pl. **-S** a hairlike outgrowth	**TRIFOLD**	*adj* having three parts
TRICING	present participle of trice		

TRIFORIA	*n/pl* galleries in a church	**TRIMMER**	*n* pl. **-S** one that trims
TRIFORM	*adj* having three forms	**TRIMMEST**	superlative of trim
TRIG	*adj* **TRIGGER, TRIGGEST** neat	**TRIMMING**	*n* pl. **-S** something added as a decoration
TRIG	*v* **TRIGGED, TRIGGING, TRIGS** to make trig	**TRIMNESS**	*n* pl. **-ES** the state of being trim
TRIGAMY	*n* pl. **-MIES** the crime of being married to three people at once	**TRIMORPH**	*n* pl. **-S** a substance existing in three forms
TRIGGER	*v* **-ED, -ING, -S** to actuate	**TRIMOTOR**	*n* pl. **-S** an airplane powered by three engines
TRIGLY	*adv* in a trig manner		
TRIGLYPH	*n* pl. **-S** an architectural ornament	**TRIMPOT**	*n* pl. **-S** a small instrument for adjusting resistance or voltage
TRIGNESS	*n* pl. **-ES** the quality or state of being trig	**TRINAL**	*adj* having three parts
TRIGO	*n* pl. **-GOS** wheat	**TRINARY**	*adj* consisting of three parts
TRIGON	*n* pl. **-S** an ancient stringed instrument	**TRINDLE**	*v* **-DLED, -DLING, -DLES** to trundle
TRIGONAL	*adj* shaped like a triangle	**TRINE**	*v* **TRINED, TRINING, TRINES** to place in a particular astrological position
TRIGRAM	*n* pl. **-S** a cluster of three successive letters		
TRIGRAPH	*n* pl. **-S** a group of three letters representing one sound	**TRINITY**	*n* pl. **-TIES** a group of three
		TRINKET	*v* **-ED, -ING, -S** to deal secretly
TRIHEDRA	*n/pl* figures having three plane surfaces meeting at a point	**TRINKUMS**	*n/pl* small ornaments
		TRINODAL	*adj* having three nodes
TRIJET	*n* pl. **-S** an airplane powered by three jet engines	**TRIO**	*n* pl. **TRIOS** a group of three
		TRIODE	*n* pl. **-S** a type of electron tube
TRIKE	*n* pl. **-S** a tricycle	**TRIOL**	*n* pl. **-S** a type of chemical compound
TRILBY	*n* pl. **-BIES** a soft felt hat **TRILBIED** *adj*		
		TRIOLET	*n* pl. **-S** a short poem of fixed form
TRILITH	*n* pl. **-S** a prehistoric structure of three large stones	**TRIOSE**	*n* pl. **-S** a simple sugar
		TRIOXID	*n* pl. **-S** trioxide
TRILL	*v* **-ED, -ING, -S** to sing or play with a vibrating effect	**TRIOXIDE**	*n* pl. **-S** a type of oxide
		TRIP	*v* **TRIPPED, TRIPPING, TRIPS** to stumble
TRILLER	*n* pl. **-S** one that trills		
TRILLION	*n* pl. **-S** a number	**TRIPACK**	*n* pl. **-S** a type of film pack
TRILLIUM	*n* pl. **-S** a flowering plant	**TRIPART**	*adj* divided into three parts
TRILOBAL	*adj* trilobed	**TRIPE**	*n* pl. **-S** a part of the stomach of a ruminant that is used as food
TRILOBED	*adj* having three lobes		
TRILOGY	*n* pl. **-GIES** a group of three related literary works	**TRIPEDAL**	*adj* having three feet
		TRIPHASE	*adj* having three phases
TRIM	*adj* **TRIMMER, TRIMMEST** neat and orderly	**TRIPLANE**	*n* pl. **-S** a type of airplane
		TRIPLE	*v* **-PLED, -PLING, -PLES** to make three times as great
TRIM	*v* **TRIMMED, TRIMMING, TRIMS** to make trim by cutting		
		TRIPLET	*n* pl. **-S** a group of three of one kind
TRIMARAN	*n* pl. **-S** a sailing vessel		
TRIMER	*n* pl. **-S** a type of chemical compound **TRIMERIC** *adj*	**TRIPLEX**	*v* **-ED, -ING, -ES** to provide something in triplicate
		TRIPLITE	*n* pl. **-S** a mineral
TRIMETER	*n* pl. **-S** a verse of three metrical feet	**TRIPLOID**	*n* pl. **-S** a cell having a chromosome number that is three times the basic number
TRIMLY	*adv* in a trim manner		
TRIMMED	past tense of trim		

TRIPLY *adv* in a triple degree, manner, or number

TRIPMAN *n* pl. **-MEN** a man hired to work on a trip

TRIPOD *n* pl. **-S** a stand having three legs **TRIPODAL, TRIPODIC** *adj*

TRIPODY *n* pl. **-DIES** a verse of three metrical feet

TRIPOLI *n* pl. **-S** a soft, friable rock

TRIPOS *n* pl. **-ES** a tripod

TRIPPANT *adj* walking — used of a heraldic animal

TRIPPED past tense of trip

TRIPPER *n* pl. **-S** one that trips

TRIPPET *n* pl. **-S** a part of a mechanism designed to strike another part

TRIPPING *n* pl. **-S** the act of one that trips

TRIPPY *adj* **-PIER, -PIEST** suggesting a trip on psychedelic drugs

TRIPTAN *n* pl. **-S** a drug for treating migraine attacks

TRIPTANE *n* pl. **-S** a chemical compound

TRIPTYCA *n* pl. **-S** a triptych

TRIPTYCH *n* pl. **-S** an ancient writing tablet

TRIPWIRE *n* pl. **-S** a low-placed hidden wire that sets off an alarm or a trap

TRIREME *n* pl. **-S** an ancient Greek or Roman warship

TRISCELE *n* pl. **-S** triskele

TRISECT *v* **-ED, -ING, -S** to divide into three equal parts

TRISEME *n* pl. **-S** a type of metrical foot **TRISEMIC** *adj*

TRISHAW *n* pl. **-S** a pedicab

TRISKELE *n* pl. **-S** a figure consisting of three branches radiating from a center

TRISMUS *n* pl. **-ES** lockjaw **TRISMIC** *adj*

TRISOME *n* pl. **-S** an organism having one chromosome in addition to the usual diploid number

TRISOMIC *n* pl. **-S** a trisome

TRISOMY *n* pl. **-MIES** the condition of being a trisome

TRISTATE *adj* pertaining to an area made up of three adjoining states

TRISTE *adj* sad

TRISTEZA *n* pl. **-S** a disease of citrus trees

TRISTFUL *adj* sad

TRISTICH *n* pl. **-S** a stanza of three lines

TRITE *adj* **TRITER, TRITEST** used so often as to be made commonplace **TRITELY** *adv*

TRITHING *n* pl. **-S** an administrative division in England

TRITICUM *n* pl. **-S** a cereal grass

TRITIUM *n* pl. **-S** an isotope of hydrogen

TRITOMA *n* pl. **-S** an African herb

TRITON *n* pl. **-S** a marine mollusk

TRITONE *n* pl. **-S** a musical interval of three whole tones

TRIUMPH *v* **-ED, -ING, -S** to be victorious

TRIUMVIR *n* pl. **-VIRS** or **-VIRI** one of a ruling body of three in ancient Rome

TRIUNE *n* pl. **-S** a trinity

TRIUNITY *n* pl. **-TIES** a trinity

TRIVALVE *n* pl. **-S** a type of shell

TRIVET *n* pl. **-S** a small stand having three legs

TRIVIA *n/pl* insignificant matters

TRIVIAL *adj* insignificant

TRIVIUM *n* pl. **-IA** a group of studies in medieval schools

TROAK *v* **-ED, -ING, -S** to troke

TROCAR *n* pl. **-S** a surgical instrument

TROCHAIC *n* pl. **-S** a trochee

TROCHAL *adj* shaped like a wheel

TROCHAR *n* pl. **-S** trocar

TROCHE *n* pl. **-S** a medicated lozenge

TROCHEE *n* pl. **-S** a type of metrical foot

TROCHIL *n* pl. **TROCHILS** or **TROCHILI** an African bird

TROCHLEA *n* pl. **-LEAS** or **-LEAE** an anatomical structure resembling a pulley

TROCHOID *n* pl. **-S** a type of geometric curve

TROCK *v* **-ED, -ING, -S** to troke

TROD a past tense of tread

TRODDEN past participle of tread

TRODE a past tense of tread

TROFFER *n* pl. **-S** a fixture for fluorescent lighting

TROG *n* pl. **-S** a hooligan

TROGON *n* pl. **-S** a tropical bird

TROIKA *n* pl. **-S** a Russian carriage

TROILISM *n* pl. **-S** sexual relations involving three persons

TROILITE *n* pl. **-S** a mineral

TROILUS *n pl.* **-ES** a large butterfly

TROIS *n pl.* **TROIS** the number three

TROKE *v* **TROKED, TROKING, TROKES** to exchange

TROLAND *n pl.* **-S** a unit of measurement of retinal response to light

TROLL *v* **-ED, -ING, -S** to fish with a slowly trailing line

TROLLER *n pl.* **-S** one that trolls

TROLLEY *v* **-ED, -ING, -S** to convey by streetcar

TROLLING *n pl.* **-S** the act of one that trolls

TROLLISH *adj* resembling a troll (a mythological dwarf)

TROLLOP *n pl.* **-S** a prostitute **TROLLOPY** *adj*

TROLLY *v* **-LIED, -LYING, -LIES** to trolley

TROMBONE *n pl.* **-S** a brass wind instrument

TROMMEL *n pl.* **-S** a screen used for sifting rock, ore, or coal

TROMP *v* **-ED, -ING, -S** to tramp

TROMPE *n pl.* **-S** a device used for supplying air to a furnace

TRONA *n pl.* **-S** a mineral

TRONE *n pl.* **-S** a weighing device

TROOP *v* **-ED, -ING, -S** to move or gather in crowds

TROOPER *n pl.* **-S** a cavalryman

TROOPIAL *n pl.* **-S** troupial

TROOZ *n/pl* trews

TROP *adv* too much

TROPE *n pl.* **-S** the figurative use of a word

TROPHIC *adj* pertaining to nutrition

TROPHY *v* **-PHIED, -PHYING, -PHIES** to honor with a trophy (a symbol of victory)

TROPIC *n pl.* **-S** either of two circles of the celestial sphere on each side of the equator

TROPICAL *n pl.* **-S** a plant of the region lying between the tropics

TROPIN *n pl.* **-S** tropine

TROPINE *n pl.* **-S** a poisonous alkaloid

TROPISM *n pl.* **-S** the involuntary response of an organism to an external stimulus

TROPONIN *n pl.* **-S** a protein of muscle

TROPPO *adj* too much — used in musical directions

TROT *v* **TROTTED, TROTTING, TROTS** to go at a gait between a walk and a run

TROTH *v* **-ED, -ING, -S** to betroth

TROTLINE *n pl.* **-S** a strong fishing line

TROTTER *n pl.* **-S** a horse that trots

TROTTING *n pl.* **-S** harness racing

TROTYL *n pl.* **-S** an explosive

TROU *n/pl* trousers

TROUBLE *v* **-BLED, -BLING, -BLES** to distress

TROUBLER *n pl.* **-S** one that troubles

TROUGH *n pl.* **-S** a long, narrow receptacle

TROUNCE *v* **TROUNCED, TROUNCING, TROUNCES** to beat severely

TROUNCER *n pl.* **-S** one that trounces

TROUPE *v* **TROUPED, TROUPING, TROUPES** to tour with a theatrical company

TROUPER *n pl.* **-S** a member of a theatrical company

TROUPIAL *n pl.* **-S** a tropical bird

TROUSER *adj* pertaining to trousers

TROUSERS *n/pl* a garment for the lower part of the body

TROUT *n pl.* **-S** a freshwater fish

TROUTING *n pl.* **-S** the activity of fishing for trout

TROUTY *adj* **TROUTIER, TROUTIEST** abounding in trout

TROUVERE *n pl.* **-S** a medieval poet

TROUVEUR *n pl.* **-S** trouvere

TROVE *n pl.* **-S** a valuable discovery

TROVER *n pl.* **-S** a type of legal action

TROW *v* **-ED, -ING, -S** to suppose

TROWEL *v* **-ELED, -ELING, -ELS** or **-ELLED, -ELLING, -ELS** to smooth with a trowel (a hand tool having a flat blade)

TROWELER *n pl.* **-S** one that trowels

TROWSERS *n/pl* trousers

TROWTH *n pl.* **-S** truth

TROY *n pl.* **TROYS** a system of weights

TRUANCY *n pl.* **-CIES** an act of truanting

TRUANT *v* **-ED, -ING, -S** to stay out of school without permission

TRUANTLY *adv* in a manner of one who shirks duty

TRUANTRY *n pl.* **-RIES** truancy

TRUCE   *v* **TRUCED, TRUCING, TRUCES** to suspend hostilities by mutual agreement

TRUCK   *v* **-ED, -ING, -S** to transport by truck (an automotive vehicle designed to carry loads)

TRUCKAGE   *n* pl. **-S** transportation of goods by trucks

TRUCKER   *n* pl. **-S** a truck driver

TRUCKFUL   *n* pl. **-S** as much as a truck can hold

TRUCKING   *n* pl. **-S** truckage

TRUCKLE   *v* **-LED, -LING, -LES** to yield weakly

TRUCKLER   *n* pl. **-S** one that truckles

TRUCKMAN   *n* pl. **-MEN** a trucker

TRUDGE   *v* **TRUDGED, TRUDGING, TRUDGES** to walk tiredly

TRUDGEN   *n* pl. **-S** a swimming stroke

TRUDGEON   *n* pl. **-S** trudgen

TRUDGER   *n* pl. **-S** one that trudges

TRUDGING   present participle of trudge

TRUE   *adj* **TRUER, TRUEST** consistent with fact or reality

TRUE   *v* **TRUED, TRUING** or **TRUEING, TRUES** to bring to conformity with a standard or requirement

TRUEBLUE   *n* pl. **-S** a person of unwavering loyalty

TRUEBORN   *adj* genuinely such by birth

TRUEBRED   *adj* designating an animal of unmixed stock

TRUED   past tense of true

TRUEING   a present participle of true

TRUELOVE   *n* pl. **-S** a sweetheart

TRUENESS   *n* pl. **-ES** the quality or state of being true

TRUER   comparative of true

TRUEST   superlative of true

TRUFFE   *n* pl. **-S** truffle

TRUFFLE   *n* pl. **-S** an edible fungus **TRUFFLED** *adj*

TRUFFLING   *n* pl. **-S** the activity of hunting for truffles

TRUG   *n* pl. **-S** a gardener's basket

TRUING   a present participle of true

TRUISM   *n* pl. **-S** an obvious truth **TRUISTIC** *adj*

TRULL   *n* pl. **-S** a prostitute

TRULY   *adv* in conformity with fact or reality

TRUMEAU   *n* pl. **-MEAUX** a column supporting part of a doorway

TRUMP   *v* **-ED, -ING, -S** to outdo

TRUMPERY   *n* pl. **-ERIES** worthless finery

TRUMPET   *v* **-ED, -ING, -S** to sound on a trumpet (a brass wind instrument)

TRUNCAL   *adj* affecting the trunk (the central part) of the body

TRUNCATE   *v* **-CATED, -CATING, -CATES** to shorten by cutting off a part

TRUNDLE   *v* **-DLED, -DLING, -DLES** to propel by causing to rotate

TRUNDLER   *n* pl. **-S** one that trundles

TRUNK   *n* pl. **-S** the main stem of a tree **TRUNKED** *adj*

TRUNKFUL   *n* pl. **-S** as much as a trunk (a storage box) can hold

TRUNKING   *n* pl. **-S** a system of electrical or telephone lines

TRUNNEL   *n* pl. **-S** treenail

TRUNNION   *n* pl. **-S** a pin or pivot on which something can be rotated

TRUSS   *v* **-ED, -ING, -ES** to secure tightly

TRUSSER   *n* pl. **-S** one that trusses

TRUSSING   *n* pl. **-S** the framework of a structure

TRUST   *v* **-ED, -ING, -S** to place confidence in

TRUSTEE   *v* **-TEED, -TEEING, -TEES** to commit to the care of an administrator

TRUSTER   *n* pl. **-S** one that trusts

TRUSTFUL   *adj* inclined to trust

TRUSTOR   *n* pl. **-S** one that trustees his or her property

TRUSTY   *adj* **TRUSTIER, TRUSTIEST** worthy of trust **TRUSTILY** *adv*

TRUSTY   *n* pl. **TRUSTIES** one worthy of trust

TRUTH   *n* pl. **-S** conformity to fact or reality

TRUTHER   *n* pl. **-S** one who believes that the truth is being hidden

TRUTHFUL   *adj* telling the truth

TRY   *v* **TRIED, TRYING, TRIES** to attempt

TRYINGLY   *adv* in a distressing manner

TRYMA   *n* pl. **-MATA** a type of nut

TRYOUT   *n* pl. **-S** a test of ability

TRYPSIN   *n* pl. **-S** an enzyme **TRYPTIC** *adj*

TRYSAIL	*n* pl. **-S** a type of sail
TRYST	*v* **-ED, -ING, -S** to agree to meet
TRYSTE	*n* pl. **-S** a market
TRYSTER	*n* pl. **-S** one that trysts
TRYWORKS	*n/pl* a type of furnace
TSADDIK	*n* pl. **-DIKIM** zaddik
TSADE	*n* pl. **-S** sade
TSADI	*n* pl. **-S** sade
TSAR	*n* pl. **-S** czar
TSARDOM	*n* pl. **-S** czardom
TSAREVNA	*n* pl. **-S** czarevna
TSARINA	*n* pl. **-S** czarina
TSARISM	*n* pl. **-S** czarism
TSARIST	*n* pl. **-S** czarist
TSARITZA	*n* pl. **-S** czaritza
TSATSKE	*n* pl. **-S** chachka
TSETSE	*n* pl. **-S** an African fly
TSIMMES	*n* pl. **TSIMMES** tzimmes
TSK	*v* **-ED, -ING, -S** to utter an exclamation of annoyance
TSKTSK	*v* **-ED, -ING, -S** to tsk
TSOORIS	*n* pl. **TSOORIS** tsuris
TSORES	*n* pl. **TSORES** tsuris
TSORIS	*n* pl. **TSORIS** tsuris
TSORRISS	*n* pl. **TSORRISS** tsuris
TSOTSI	*n* pl, **-S** a black African urban criminal
TSOURIS	*n* pl. **TSOURIS** tsuris
TSUBA	*n* pl. **-S** a part of a Japanese sword
TSUBO	*n* pl. **-BOS** a Japanese unit of area
TSUNAMI	*n* pl. **-S** a very large ocean wave **TSUNAMIC** *adj*
TSURIS	*n* pl. **TSURIS** or **TSURISES** a series of misfortunes
TUATARA	*n* pl. **-S** a large reptile
TUATERA	*n* pl. **-S** tuatara
TUB	*v* **TUBBED, TUBBING, TUBS** to wash in a tub (a round, open vessel)
TUBA	*n* pl. **-BAS** or **-BAE** a brass wind instrument
TUBAIST	*n* pl. **-S** a tuba player
TUBAL	*adj* pertaining to a tube
TUBATE	*adj* tubular
TUBBABLE	*adj* suitable for washing in a tub
TUBBED	past tense of tub
TUBBER	*n* pl. **-S** one that tubs
TUBBING	present participle of tub
TUBBY	*adj* **-BIER, -BIEST** short and fat
TUBE	*v* **TUBED, TUBING, TUBES** to provide with a tube (a long, hollow cylinder)
TUBELESS	*adj* having no tube
TUBELIKE	*adj* resembling a tube
TUBENOSE	*n* pl. **-S** a bird having tubular nostrils
TUBER	*n* pl. **-S** a thick underground stem
TUBERCLE	*n* pl. **-S** a small, rounded swelling
TUBEROID	*adj* pertaining to a tuber
TUBEROSE	*n* pl. **-S** a Mexican herb
TUBEROUS	*adj* pertaining to a tuber
TUBEWELL	*n* pl. **-S** a water well in which a long steel tube is bored into an underground aquifer
TUBEWORK	*n* pl. **-S** tubing
TUBEWORM	*n* pl. **-S** a marine worm that builds and lives in a tube
TUBFUL	*n* pl. **-S** as much as a tub will hold
TUBIFEX	*n* pl. **-ES** an aquatic worm
TUBIFORM	*adj* tubular
TUBING	*n* pl. **-S** material in the form of a tube
TUBIST	*n* pl. **-S** a tubaist
TUBLIKE	*adj* resembling a tub
TUBULAR	*n* pl. **-S** a completely enclosed bicycle tire
TUBULATE	*v* **-LATED, -LATING, -LATES** to form into a tube
TUBULE	*n* pl. **-S** a small tube
TUBULIN	*n* pl. **-S** a protein that polymerizes to form tiny tubules
TUBULOSE	*adj* tubulous
TUBULOUS	*adj* having the form of a tube
TUBULURE	*n* pl. **-S** a short cylindrical opening
TUCHIS	*n* pl. **-ES** tuchus
TUCHUN	*n* pl. **-S** a Chinese military governor
TUCHUS	*n* pl. **-ES** the buttocks
TUCK	*v* **-ED, -ING, -S** to fold under
TUCKAHOE	*n* pl. **-S** the edible root of certain arums
TUCKER	*v* **-ED, -ING, -S** to weary
TUCKET	*n* pl. **-S** a trumpet fanfare
TUCKING	*n* pl. **-S** a series of stitched folds in a garment

TUCKSHOP	*n* pl. **-S** a confectioner's shop
TUFA	*n* pl. **-S** a porous limestone
TUFF	*n* pl. **-S** a volcanic rock
TUFFET	*n* pl. **-S** a clump of grass
TUFOLI	*n* pl. **TUFOLI** a large macaroni shell
TUFT	*v* **-ED, -ING, -S** to form into tufts (clusters of flexible outgrowths attached at the base)
TUFTER	*n* pl. **-S** one that tufts
TUFTING	*n* pl. **-S** a cluster of tufts used for decoration
TUFTY	*adj* **TUFTIER, TUFTIEST** abounding in tufts **TUFTILY** *adv*
TUG	*v* **TUGGED, TUGGING, TUGS** to pull with force
TUGBOAT	*n* pl. **-S** a boat built for towing
TUGGER	*n* pl. **-S** one that tugs
TUGGING	present participle of tug
TUGHRIK	*n* pl. **-S** tugrik
TUGLESS	*adj* being without a rope or chain with which to pull
TUGRIK	*n* pl. **-S** a monetary unit of Mongolia
TUI	*n* pl. **-S** a bird of New Zealand
TUILE	*n* pl. **-S** a thin cookie made with almonds
TUILLE	*n* pl. **-S** a tasset
TUITION	*n* pl. **-S** a fee for instruction
TULADI	*n* pl. **-S** a freshwater fish
TULE	*n* pl. **-S** a tall marsh plant
TULIP	*n* pl. **-S** a flowering plant
TULLE	*n* pl. **-S** a silk material
TULLIBEE	*n* pl. **-S** a freshwater fish
TULSI	*n* pl. **-S** a type of basil
TUM	*n* pl. **-S** a person's stomach (an organ of digestion) or abdomen
TUMBLE	*v* **-BLED, -BLING, -BLES** to fall or roll end over end
TUMBLER	*n* pl. **-S** one that tumbles
TUMBLING	*n* pl. **-S** the sport of gymnastics
TUMBREL	*n* pl. **-S** a type of cart
TUMBRIL	*n* pl. **-S** tumbrel
TUMEFY	*v* **-FIED, -FYING, -FIES** to swell
TUMESCE	*v* **-MESCED, -MESCING, -MESCES** to become swollen
TUMID	*adj* swollen **TUMIDLY** *adv*

TUMIDITY	*n* pl. **-TIES** the quality or state of being tumid
TUMMLER	*n* pl. **-S** an entertainer who encourages audience participation
TUMMY	*n* pl. **-MIES** the stomach
TUMOR	*n* pl. **-S** an abnormal swelling **TUMORAL, TUMOROUS** *adj*
TUMOUR	*n* pl. **-S** tumor
TUMP	*v* **-ED, -ING, -S** to tip over
TUMPLINE	*n* pl. **-S** a strap for supporting a load on the back
TUMULAR	*adj* having the form of a mound
TUMULI	a pl. of tumulus
TUMULOSE	*adj* full of mounds
TUMULOUS	*adj* tumulose
TUMULT	*n* pl. **-S** a great din and commotion
TUMULUS	*n* pl. **-LUSES** or **-LI** a mound over a grave
TUN	*v* **TUNNED, TUNNING, TUNS** to store in a large cask
TUNA	*n* pl. **-S** a marine food fish
TUNABLE	*adj* capable of being tuned **TUNABLY** *adv*
TUNDISH	*n* pl. **-ES** a receptacle for molten metal
TUNDRA	*n* pl. **-S** a level, treeless expanse of arctic land
TUNE	*v* **TUNED, TUNING, TUNES** to put into the proper pitch
TUNEABLE	*adj* tunable **TUNEABLY** *adv*
TUNEFUL	*adj* melodious
TUNELESS	*adj* not tuneful
TUNER	*n* pl. **-S** one that tunes
TUNEUP	*n* pl. **-S** an adjustment to ensure efficient operation
TUNG	*n* pl. **-S** a Chinese tree
TUNGSTEN	*n* pl. **-S** a metallic element **TUNGSTIC** *adj*
TUNIC	*n* pl. **-S** a loose-fitting garment
TUNICA	*n* pl. **-CAE** an enveloping membrane or layer of body tissue
TUNICATE	*n* pl. **-S** a small marine animal
TUNICLE	*n* pl. **-S** a type of vestment
TUNING	*n* pl. **-S** the act of adjusting a musical instrument to a correct pitch
TUNKET	*n* pl. **-S** hell
TUNNAGE	*n* pl. **-S** tonnage
TUNNED	past tense of tun

TUNNEL *v* **-NELED, -NELING, -NELS** or **-NELLED, -NELLING, -NELS** to dig a tunnel (an underground passageway)

TUNNELER *n* pl. **-S** one that tunnels

TUNNING present participle of tun

TUNNY *n* pl. **-NIES** a tuna

TUP *v* **TUPPED, TUPPING, TUPS** to copulate with a ewe — used of a ram

TUPELO *n* pl. **-LOS** a softwood tree

TUPIK *n* pl. **-S** an Inuit tent

TUPPENCE *n* pl. **-S** twopence

TUPPENNY *adj* twopenny

TUPPING *n* pl. **-S** the act of a ram copulating with a ewe

TUQUE *n* pl. **-S** a knitted woolen cap

TURACO *n* pl. **-COS** touraco

TURACOU *n* pl. **-S** touraco

TURBAN *n* pl. **-S** a head covering worn by Muslims **TURBANED** *adj*

TURBARY *n* pl. **-RIES** a place where peat can be dug

TURBETH *n* pl. **-S** turpeth

TURBID *adj* thick or opaque with roiled sediment **TURBIDLY** *adv*

TURBINAL *n* pl. **-S** a bone of the nasal passage

TURBINE *n* pl. **-S** a type of engine

TURBIT *n* pl. **-S** a domestic pigeon

TURBITH *n* pl. **-S** turpeth

TURBO *n* pl. **-BOS** a turbine

TURBOCAR *n* pl. **-S** an auto powered by a gas turbine

TURBOFAN *n* pl. **-S** a type of jet engine

TURBOJET *n* pl. **-S** a type of jet engine

TURBOT *n* pl. **-S** a European flatfish

TURDINE *adj* belonging to a large family of singing birds

TUREEN *n* pl. **-S** a large, deep bowl

TURF *n* pl. **TURFS** or **TURVES** a surface layer of earth containing a dense growth of grass

TURF *v* **-ED, -ING, -S** to cover with turf

TURFIER comparative of turfy

TURFIEST superlative of turfy

TURFLESS *adj* having no turf

TURFLIKE *adj* resembling turf

TURFMAN *n* pl. **-MEN** a person who is devoted to horse racing

TURFSKI *n* pl. **-S** a type of ski

TURFY *adj* **TURFIER, TURFIEST** covered with turf

TURGENCY *n* pl. **-CIES** turgor

TURGENT *adj* turgid

TURGID *adj* swollen **TURGIDLY** *adv*

TURGITE *n* pl. **-S** an iron ore

TURGOR *n* pl. **-S** the quality or state of being turgid

TURION *n* pl. **-S** a thick new growth on a plant

TURISTA *n* pl. **-S** intestinal sickness affecting a tourist in a foreign country

TURK *n* pl. **-S** one who eagerly advocates change

TURKEY *n* pl. **-KEYS** a large American bird

TURKOIS *n* pl. **-ES** turquois

TURMERIC *n* pl. **-S** an East Indian herb

TURMOIL *v* **-ED, -ING, -S** to throw into an uproar

TURN *v* **-ED, -ING, -S** to move around a central point **TURNABLE** *adj*

TURNCOAT *n* pl. **-S** a traitor

TURNCOCK *n* pl. **-S** an employee who turns water on or off at the main

TURNDOWN *n* pl. **-S** a rejection

TURNER *n* pl. **-S** one that turns

TURNERY *n* pl. **-ERIES** the process of shaping articles on a lathe

TURNHALL *n* pl. **-S** a building where gymnasts practice

TURNING *n* pl. **-S** a rotation about an axis

TURNIP *n* pl. **-S** an edible plant root **TURNIPY** *adj*

TURNKEY *n* pl. **-KEYS** a person who has charge of a prison's keys

TURNOFF *n* pl. **-S** a road that branches off from a larger one

TURNON *n* pl. **-S** something that arouses interest

TURNOUT *n* pl. **-S** an assemblage of people

TURNOVER *n* pl. **-S** an upset or overthrow

TURNPIKE *n* pl. **-S** a toll road

TURNSOLE *n* pl. **-S** a plant that turns with the sun

TURNSPIT *n* pl. **-S** one that turns a roasting spit

TURNUP   *n* pl. **-S** a part of a garment that is turned up

TURPETH   *n* pl. **-S** a medicinal plant root

TURPS   *n* pl. **TURPS** turpentine

TURQUOIS   *n* pl. **-ES** a greenish blue gem

TURR   *n* pl. **-S** a murre

TURRET   *n* pl. **-S** a small tower **TURRETED** *adj*

TURRICAL   *adj* resembling a turret

TURTLE   *v* **-TLED, -TLING, -TLES** to catch turtles (tortoises)

TURTLER   *n* pl. **-S** one that turtles

TURTLING   *n* pl. **-S** the act of one that turtles

TURVES   a pl. of turf

TUSCHE   *n* pl. **-S** a liquid used in lithography

TUSH   *v* **-ED, -ING, -ES** to tusk

TUSHERY   *n* pl. **-ERIES** pretentious writing

TUSHIE   *n* pl. **-S** the buttocks

TUSHY   *n* pl. **TUSHIES** tushie

TUSK   *v* **-ED, -ING, -S** to gore with a tusk (a long, pointed tooth extending outside of the mouth)

TUSKER   *n* pl. **-S** an animal with tusks

TUSKLESS   *adj* having no tusk

TUSKLIKE   *adj* resembling a tusk

TUSKY   *adj* **TUSKIER, TUSKIEST** having tusks

TUSSAH   *n* pl. **-S** an Asian silkworm

TUSSAL   *adj* pertaining to a cough

TUSSAR   *n* pl. **-S** tussah

TUSSEH   *n* pl. **-S** tussah

TUSSER   *n* pl. **-S** tussah

TUSSIS   *n* pl. **TUSSISES** or **TUSSES** a cough **TUSSIVE** *adj*

TUSSLE   *v* **-SLED, -SLING, -SLES** to struggle

TUSSOCK   *n* pl. **-S** a clump of grass **TUSSOCKY** *adj*

TUSSOR   *n* pl. **-S** tussah

TUSSORE   *n* pl. **-S** tussah

TUSSUCK   *n* pl. **-S** tussock

TUSSUR   *n* pl. **-S** tussah

TUT   *v* **TUTTED, TUTTING, TUTS** to utter an exclamation of impatience

TUTEE   *n* pl. **-S** one who is being tutored

TUTELAGE   *n* pl. **-S** the act of tutoring

TUTELAR   *n* pl. **-S** a tutelary

TUTELARY   *n* pl. **-LARIES** one who has the power to protect

TUTOR   *v* **-ED, -ING, -S** to instruct privately

TUTORAGE   *n* pl. **-S** tutelage

TUTORESS   *n* pl. **-ES** a female who tutors

TUTORIAL   *n* pl. **-S** a session of tutoring

TUTOYER   *v* **-TOYERED** or **-TOYED, -TOYERING, -TOYERS** to address familiarly

TUTTED   past tense of tut

TUTTI   *n* pl. **-S** a musical passage performed by all the performers

TUTTING   present participle of tut

TUTTY   *n* pl. **-TIES** an impure zinc oxide

TUTU   *n* pl. **-S** a short ballet skirt **TUTUED** *adj*

TUX   *n* pl. **-ES** a tuxedo

TUXEDO   *n* pl. **-DOS** or **-DOES** a man's semiformal dinner coat **TUXEDOED** *adj*

TUYER   *n* pl. **-S** tuyere

TUYERE   *n* pl. **-S** a pipe through which air is forced into a blast furnace

TWA   *n* pl. **-S** two

TWADDLE   *v* **-DLED, -DLING, -DLES** to talk foolishly

TWADDLER   *n* pl. **-S** one that twaddles

TWAE   *n* pl. **-S** two

TWAIN   *n* pl. **-S** a set of two

TWANG   *v* **-ED, -ING, -S** to make a sharp, vibrating sound

TWANGER   *n* pl. **-S** one that twangs

TWANGLE   *v* **-GLED, -GLING, -GLES** to twang

TWANGLER   *n* pl. **-S** one that twangles

TWANGY   *adj* **TWANGIER, TWANGIEST** twanging

TWANKY   *n* pl. **-KIES** a variety of green tea

TWASOME   *n* pl. **-S** twosome

TWATTLE   *v* **-TLED, -TLING, -TLES** to twaddle

TWEAK   *v* **-ED, -ING, -S** to pinch and twist sharply

TWEAKY   *adj* **TWEAKIER, TWEAKIEST** twitchy

TWEE   *adj* **TWEER, TWEEST** affectedly cute or dainty

TWEED   *n* pl. **-S** a coarse woolen fabric

TWEEDLE   *v* **-DLED, -DLING, -DLES** to perform casually on a musical instrument

TWEEDY   *adj* **TWEEDIER, TWEEDIEST** resembling or wearing tweed **TWEEDILY** *adv*

TWEEN   *n* pl. **-S** a child typically between the ages of eight and twelve

TWEENER   *n* pl. **-S** a player having some but not all of the qualifications for two or more positions

TWEENESS   *n* pl. **-ES** the state of being twee

TWEENIE   *n* pl. **-S** tweeny

TWEENY   *n* pl. **TWEENIES** a housemaid

TWEEP   *n* pl. **-S** one who uses the Twitter online message service

TWEET   *v* **-ED, -ING, -S** to chirp

TWEETER   *n* pl. **-S** a loudspeaker designed to reproduce high-pitched sounds

TWEEZE   *v* **TWEEZED, TWEEZING, TWEEZES** to pluck with a tweezer

TWEEZER   *n* pl. **-S** a pincerlike tool

TWELFTH   *n* pl. **-S** the number twelve in a series

TWELVE   *n* pl. **-S** a number

TWELVEMO   *n* pl. **-MOS** a page size

TWENTY   *n* pl. **-TIES** a number

TWERK   *v* **-ED, -ING, -S** to dance by shaking the buttocks while squatting

TWERP   *n* pl. **-S** a small, impudent person

TWERPY   *adj* **TWERPIER, TWERPIEST** resembling a twerp

TWIBIL   *n* pl. **-S** a battle-ax with two cutting edges

TWIBILL   *n* pl. **-S** twibil

TWICE   *adv* two times

TWIDDLE   *v* **-DLED, -DLING, -DLES** to play idly with something

TWIDDLER   *n* pl. **-S** one that twiddles

TWIDDLY   *adj* **-DLIER, -DLIEST** having many turns

TWIER   *n* pl. **-S** tuyere

TWIG   *v* **TWIGGED, TWIGGING, TWIGS** to observe

TWIGGEN   *adj* made of twigs (small branches)

TWIGGY   *adj* **-GIER, -GIEST** twiglike

TWIGLESS   *adj* having no twigs

TWIGLIKE   *adj* resembling a twig

TWILIGHT   *n* pl. **-S** the early evening light

TWILIT   *adj* lighted by twilight

TWILL   *v* **-ED, -ING, -S** to weave so as to produce a diagonal pattern

TWILLING   *n* pl. **-S** a twilled fabric

TWIN   *v* **TWINNED, TWINNING, TWINS** to bring together in close association

TWINBORN   *adj* born at the same birth

TWINE   *v* **TWINED, TWINING, TWINES** to twist together

TWINER   *n* pl. **-S** one that twines

TWINGE   *v* **TWINGED, TWINGING** or **TWINGEING, TWINGES** to affect with a sharp pain

TWINIER   comparative of twiny

TWINIEST   superlative of twiny

TWINIGHT   *adj* pertaining to a baseball doubleheader that begins in the late afternoon

TWINING   present participle of twine

TWINJET   *n* pl. **-S** an aircraft with two jet engines

TWINK   *n* pl. **-S** a weak or ineffectual person

TWINKIE   *n* pl. **-S** a twink

TWINKLE   *v* **-KLED, -KLING, -KLES** to shine with a flickering or sparkling light

TWINKLER   *n* pl. **-S** one that twinkles

TWINKLY   *adj* twinkling

TWINKY   *n* pl. **-KIES** a twink

TWINNED   past tense of twin

TWINNING   *n* pl. **-S** the bearing of two children at the same birth

TWINSET   *n* pl. **-S** a matching pair of sweaters to be worn together

TWINSHIP   *n* pl. **-S** close similarity or association

TWINY   *adj* **TWINIER, TWINIEST** resembling twine (a strong string)

TWIRL   *v* **-ED, -ING, -S** to rotate rapidly

TWIRLER   *n* pl. **-S** one that twirls

TWIRLY   *adj* **TWIRLIER, TWIRLIEST** curved

TWIRP   *n* pl. **-S** twerp

TWIST   *v* **-ED, -ING, -S** to combine by winding together

TWISTER   *n* pl. **-S** one that twists

TWISTING   *n* pl. **-S** a form of trickery used in selling life insurance

TWISTOR   *n* pl. **-S** a complex variable in descriptions of space-time

TWISTY   *adj* **TWISTIER, TWISTIEST** full of curves

TWIT	*v* **TWITTED, TWITTING, TWITS** to ridicule	**TYMPANUM**	*n* pl. **-NUMS** or **-NA** the middle ear
TWITCH	*v* **-ED, -ING, -ES** to move or pull with a sudden motion	**TYMPANY**	*n* pl. **-NIES** a swelling of the abdomen
TWITCHER	*n* pl. **-S** one that twitches	**TYNE**	*v* **TYNED, TYNING, TYNES** to tine
TWITCHY	*adj* **TWITCHIER, TWITCHIEST** fidgety	**TYPAL**	*adj* typical
		TYPE	*v* **TYPED, TYPING, TYPES** to write with a typewriter **TYPABLE, TYPEABLE** *adj*
TWITTED	past tense of twit		
TWITTER	*v* **-ED, -ING, -S** to utter a succession of chirping sounds	**TYPEBAR**	*n* pl. **-S** a part of a typewriter
		TYPECASE	*n* pl. **-S** a tray for holding printing type
TWITTERY	*adj* nervously agitated		
TWITTING	present participle of twit	**TYPECAST**	*v* **-CAST, -CASTING, -CASTS** to cast in an acting role befitting one's own nature
TWITTISH	*adj* silly, foolish		
TWIXT	*prep* between	**TYPED**	past tense of type
TWIZZLE	*n* pl. **-S** a maneuver in figure skating	**TYPEFACE**	*n* pl. **-S** the face of printing type
		TYPESET	*v* **-SET, -SETTING, -SETS** to set in type
TWO	*n* pl. **TWOS** a number		
TWOFER	*n* pl. **-S** something sold at the rate of two for the price of one	**TYPEY**	*adj* **TYPIER, TYPIEST** typy
		TYPHOID	*n* pl. **-S** an infectious disease
TWOFOLD	*n* pl. **-S** an amount twice as great as a given unit	**TYPHON**	*n* pl. **-S** a type of signal horn
		TYPHOON	*n* pl. **-S** a tropical hurricane **TYPHONIC** *adj*
TWONESS	*n* pl. **-ES** the state of being two		
TWOONIE	*n* pl. **-S** toonie	**TYPHOSE**	*adj* pertaining to typhoid
TWOPENCE	*n* pl. **-S** a British coin worth two pennies	**TYPHUS**	*n* pl. **-ES** an infectious disease **TYPHOUS** *adj*
TWOPENNY	*adj* worth twopence	**TYPIC**	*adj* typical
TWOSOME	*n* pl. **-S** a group of two	**TYPICAL**	*adj* having the nature of a representative specimen
TWYER	*n* pl. **-S** tuyere		
TYCHISM	*n* pl. **-S** the proposition that chance is operative in the universe	**TYPIER**	comparative of typey and typy
		TYPIEST	superlative of typey and typy
TYCOON	*n* pl. **-S** a wealthy and powerful business person	**TYPIFIER**	*n* pl. **-S** one that typifies
		TYPIFY	*v* **-FIED, -FYING, -FIES** to serve as a typical example of
TYE	*n* pl. **-S** a chain on a ship		
TYEE	*n* pl. **-S** a food fish	**TYPING**	*n* pl. **-S** the activity of writing with a typewriter
TYER	*n* pl. **-S** one that ties		
TYIN	*n* pl. **TYIN** a monetary unit of Kazakhstan	**TYPIST**	*n* pl. **-S** one who types
		TYPO	*n* pl. **-POS** a typographical error
TYING	a present participle of tie	**TYPOLOGY**	*n* pl. **-GIES** the study of classification according to common characteristics
TYIYN	*n* pl. **TYIYN** a monetary unit of Kyrgyzstan		
TYKE	*n* pl. **-S** a small child	**TYPP**	*n* pl. **-S** a unit of yarn size
TYLOSIN	*n* pl. **-S** an antibiotic	**TYPY**	*adj* **TYPIER, TYPIEST** characterized by strict conformance to the characteristics of a group
TYMBAL	*n* pl. **-S** timbal		
TYMPAN	*n* pl. **-S** a drum		
TYMPANA	a pl. of tympanum	**TYRAMINE**	*n* pl. **-S** a chemical compound
TYMPANAL	*adj* tympanic	**TYRANNIC**	*adj* characteristic of a tyrant
TYMPANIC	*adj* pertaining to the tympanum	**TYRANNY**	*n* pl. **-NIES** the rule of a tyrant
TYMPANO	*n* pl. **-NI** timpano	**TYRANT**	*n* pl. **-S** an absolute ruler

TYRE v **TYRED, TYRING, TYRES** to furnish with a covering for a wheel

TYRO n pl. **-ROS** a beginner **TYRONIC** adj

TYROPITA n pl. **-S** a pastry made with layers of phyllo and filled with a cheese-egg mixture

TYROSINE n pl. **-S** an amino acid

TYTHE v **TYTHED, TYTHING, TYTHES** to tithe

TZADDIK n pl. **-DIKIM** zaddik

TZAR n pl. **-S** czar

TZARDOM n pl. **-S** czardom

TZAREVNA n pl. **-S** czarevna

TZARINA n pl. **-S** czarina

TZARISM n pl. **-S** czarism

TZARIST n pl. **-S** czarist

TZARITZA n pl. **-S** czaritza

TZATZIKI n pl. **-S** a dish of yogurt with cucumber, garlic, and sometimes mint

TZEDAKAH n pl. **-S** charitable giving as a moral obligation among Jews

TZETZE n pl. **-S** tsetse

TZIGANE n pl. **-S** a gypsy

TZIMMES n pl. **TZIMMES** a vegetable stew

TZITZIS n/pl zizith

TZITZIT n/pl zizith

TZITZITH n/pl zizith

TZURIS n pl. **TZURIS** or **TZURISES** tsuris

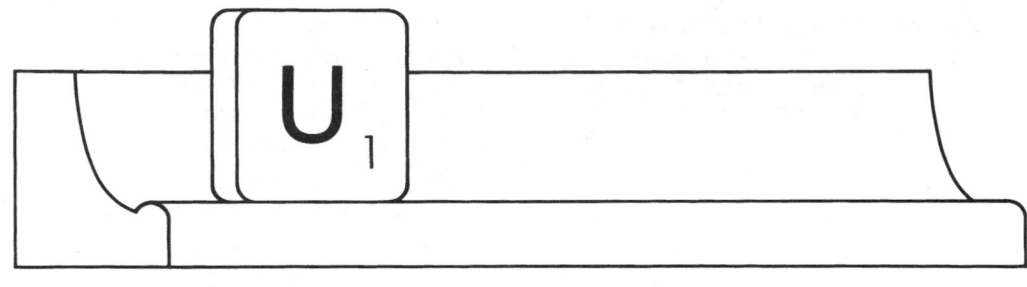

UAKARI	*n* pl. **-S** a South American monkey
UBIETY	*n* pl. **-ETIES** the state of having a definite location
UBIQUE	*adv* everywhere
UBIQUITY	*n* pl. **-TIES** the state of being everywhere at the same time
UDDER	*n* pl. **-S** a mammary gland **UDDERED** *adj*
UDO	*n* pl. **UDOS** a Japanese herb
UDOMETER	*n* pl. **-S** a rain gauge
UDOMETRY	*n* pl. **-TRIES** the measurement of rain
UDON	*n* pl. **-S** a Japanese noodle made with wheat flour
UFOLOGY	*n* pl. **-GIES** the study of unidentified flying objects
UGH	*n* pl. **-S** the sound of a cough or grunt
UGLIER	comparative of ugly
UGLIES	pl. of ugly
UGLIEST	superlative of ugly
UGLIFIER	*n* pl. **-S** one that uglifies
UGLIFY	*v* **-FIED, -FYING, -FIES** to make ugly
UGLINESS	*n* pl. **-ES** the state of being ugly
UGLY	*adj* **-LIER, -LIEST** displeasing to the sight **UGLILY** *adv*
UGLY	*n* pl. **-LIES** one that is ugly
UGSOME	*adj* disgusting
UH	*interj* — used to express hesitation
UHLAN	*n* pl. **-S** one of a body of Prussian cavalry
UINTAITE	*n* pl. **-S** a variety of asphalt
UKASE	*n* pl. **-S** an edict
UKE	*n* pl. **-S** ukelele
UKELELE	*n* pl. **-S** ukulele
UKULELE	*n* pl. **-S** a small guitar-like instrument
ULAMA	*n* pl. **-S** ulema
ULAN	*n* pl. **-S** uhlan
ULCER	*v* **-ED, -ING, -S** to affect with an ulcer (a type of lesion)
ULCERATE	*v* **-ATED, -ATING, -ATES** to ulcer
ULCEROUS	*adj* being or affected with an ulcer
ULEMA	*n* pl. **-S** a Muslim scholar
ULEXITE	*n* pl. **-S** a mineral
ULLAGE	*n* pl. **-S** the amount that a container lacks of being full **ULLAGED** *adj*
ULNA	*n* pl. **-NAS** or **-NAE** a bone of the forearm **ULNAR** *adj*
ULNAD	*adv* toward the ulna
ULPAN	*n* pl. **-PANIM** a school in Israel for teaching Hebrew
ULSTER	*n* pl. **-S** a long, loose overcoat
ULTERIOR	*adj* more remote
ULTIMA	*n* pl. **-S** the last syllable of a word
ULTIMACY	*n* pl. **-CIES** the state of being last or final
ULTIMATA	*n/pl* final proposals
ULTIMATE	*v* **-MATED, -MATING, -MATES** to come to an end
ULTIMO	*adj* of or occurring in the preceding month
ULTISOL	*n* pl. **-S** a reddish-yellow acid soil
ULTRA	*n* pl. **-S** an ultraist
ULTRADRY	*adj* extremely dry
ULTRAHIP	*adj* extremely hip
ULTRAHOT	*adj* extremely hot
ULTRAISM	*n* pl. **-S** advocacy of extreme measures
ULTRAIST	*n* pl. **-S** an advocate of extreme measures
ULTRALOW	*adj* extremely low
ULTRARED	*n* pl. **-S** infrared
ULU	*n* pl. **-S** an Inuit knife
ULULANT	*adj* howling

ULULATE	*v* **-LATED, -LATING, -LATES** to howl
ULVA	*n* pl. **-S** an edible seaweed
UM	*v* **UMMED, UMMING, UMS** to hesitate or pause in speaking
UMAMI	*n* pl. **-S** a taste characteristic of monosodium glutamate
UMANGITE	*n* pl. **-S** a mineral consisting of copper selenide
UMBEL	*n* pl. **-S** a type of flower cluster **UMBELED, UMBELLAR, UMBELLED** *adj*
UMBELLET	*n* pl. **-S** a small umbel
UMBELULE	*n* pl. **-S** a secondary umbel
UMBER	*v* **-ED, -ING, -S** to color with a brown pigment
UMBILICI	*n/pl* navels
UMBLES	*n/pl* the entrails of a deer
UMBO	*n* pl. **-BOS** or **-BONES** the rounded elevation at the center of a shield **UMBONAL, UMBONATE, UMBONIC** *adj*
UMBRA	*n* pl. **-BRAS** or **-BRAE** a dark area **UMBRAL** *adj*
UMBRAGE	*n* pl. **-S** resentment
UMBRELLA	*v* **-ED, -ING, -S** to provide with an umbrella (a portable cover for protection from rain or sun)
UMBRETTE	*n* pl. **-S** a wading bird
UMIAC	*n* pl. **-S** umiak
UMIACK	*n* pl. **-S** umiak
UMIAK	*n* pl. **-S** an open Inuit boat
UMIAQ	*n* pl. **-S** umiak
UMLAUT	*v* **-ED, -ING, -S** to modify a vowel sound by partial assimilation to a succeeding sound

UMM	*interj* um
UMMA	*n* pl. **-S** the whole community of Muslims
UMMAH	*n* pl. **-S** umma
UMP	*v* **-ED, -ING, -S** to umpire
UMPH	*n* pl. **-S** oomph
UMPIRAGE	*n* pl. **-S** the function of an umpire
UMPIRE	*v* **-PIRED, -PIRING, -PIRES** to act as umpire (a person appointed to rule on the plays in a game)
UMPTEEN	*adj* indefinitely numerous
UMPTY	*adj* umpteen
UMTEENTH	*adj* being the last in an indefinitely numerous series
UN	*pron* pl. **-S** one
UNAI	*n* pl. **-S** unau
UNAKITE	*n* pl. **-S** an igneous rock
UNANCHOR	*v* **-ED, -ING, -S** to loosen from an anchor
UNANELED	*adj* not having received the sacrament of anointing of the sick
UNARM	*v* **-ED, -ING, -S** to disarm
UNARY	*adj* consisting of a single element
UNAU	*n* pl. **-S** a two-toed sloth
UNAWARES	*adv* without warning
UNBALE	*v* **-BALED, -BALING, -BALES** to loosen from a compressed bundle
UNBAN	*v* **-BANNED, -BANNING, -BANS** to remove a prohibition against
UNBAR	*v* **-BARRED, -BARRING, -BARS** to remove a bar from
UNBATED	*adj* unabated

Following is a list of self-explanatory adjectives and adverbs containing the prefix UN- (not):

UNABATED	*adj*	**UNAIDED**	*adj*	**UNATONED**	*adj*
UNABLE	*adj*	**UNAIMED**	*adj*	**UNAVOWED**	*adj*
UNABUSED	*adj*	**UNAIRED**	*adj*	**UNAWAKE**	*adj*
UNACIDIC	*adj*	**UNAKIN**	*adj*	**UNAWAKED**	*adj*
UNACTED	*adj*	**UNALIKE**	*adj*	**UNAWARE**	*adj*
UNADDED	*adj*	**UNALLIED**	*adj*	**UNAWED**	*adj*
UNADEPT	*adj*	**UNAMAZED**	*adj*	**UNAXED**	*adj*
UNADULT	*adj*	**UNAMUSED**	*adj*	**UNBACKED**	*adj*
UNAFRAID	*adj*	**UNAPT**	*adj*	**UNBAKED**	*adj*
UNAGED	*adj*	**UNAPTLY**	*adv*	**UNBANDED**	*adj*
UNAGEING	*adj*	**UNARCHED**	*adj*	**UNBANNED**	*adj*
UNAGILE	*adj*	**UNARGUED**	*adj*	**UNBARBED**	*adj*
UNAGING	*adj*	**UNARTFUL**	*adj*	**UNBASED**	*adj*
UNAGREED	*adj*	**UNASKED**	*adj*	**UNBASTED**	*adj*

UNBE	*v* **UNBEING** to cease to have being	**UNBRIDLE**	*v* **-DLED, -DLING, -DLES** to set loose
UNBEAR	*v* **-BEARED, -BEARING, -BEARS** to free from the pressure of a rein	**UNBUCKLE**	*v* **-LED, -LING, -LES** to loosen a buckle
UNBELIEF	*n* pl. **-S** lack of belief	**UNBUILD**	*v* **-BUILT, -BUILDING, -BUILDS** to demolish
UNBELT	*v* **-ED, -ING, -S** to remove the belt of		
UNBEND	*v* **-BENT** or **-BENDED, -BENDING, -BENDS** to make or allow to become straight	**UNBUNDLE**	*v* **-DLED, -DLING, -DLES** to price separately
UNBID	*adj* unbidden	**UNBURDEN**	*v* **-ED, -ING, -S** to free from a burden
UNBIDDEN	*adj* not invited	**UNBURY**	*v* **-BURIED, -BURYING, -BURIES** to remove from the ground after burial
UNBIND	*v* **-BOUND, -BINDING, -BINDS** to free from bindings		
UNBLIND	*v* **-ED, -ING, -S** to free from blindness or illusion	**UNBUTTON**	*v* **-ED, -ING, -S** to unfasten the buttons of
UNBLOCK	*v* **-ED, -ING, -S** to free from being blocked	**UNCAGE**	*v* **-CAGED, -CAGING, -CAGES** to release from a cage
UNBODIED	*adj* having no body	**UNCAKE**	*v* **-CAKED, -CAKING, -CAKES** to break up a cake (a block of compacted matter)
UNBOLT	*v* **-ED, -ING, -S** to open by withdrawing a bolt (a metal bar)		
UNBONNET	*v* **-ED, -ING, -S** to uncover the head	**UNCANNY**	*adj* **-NIER, -NIEST** strange and inexplicable
UNBOSOM	*v* **-ED, -ING, -S** to reveal	**UNCAP**	*v* **-CAPPED, -CAPPING, -CAPS** to remove the cap from
UNBOTTLE	*v* **-TLED, -TLING, -TLES** to release from or as if from a bottle	**UNCARED**	*adj* not properly taken care of
UNBOUND	past tense of unbind	**UNCASE**	*v* **-CASED, -CASING, -CASES** to remove from a case
UNBOX	*v* **-ED, -ING, -ES** to remove from a box	**UNCHAIN**	*v* **-ED, -ING, -S** to free by removing a chain
UNBRACE	*v* **-BRACED, -BRACING, -BRACES** to free from braces	**UNCHAIR**	*v* **-ED, -ING, -S** to remove from a chairmanship
UNBRAID	*v* **-ED, -ING, -S** to separate the strands of	**UNCHANCY**	*adj* unlucky
UNBRAKE	*v* **-BRAKED, -BRAKING, -BRAKES** to release a brake	**UNCHARGE**	*v* **-CHARGED, -CHARGING, -CHARGES** to acquit
UNBREECH	*v* **-ED, -ING, -ES** to remove the breeches of	**UNCHOKE**	*v* **-CHOKED, -CHOKING, -CHOKES** to free from obstruction

---

List of self-explanatory adjectives and adverbs containing the prefix UN- (continued):

UNBATHED	*adj*	**UNBOUGHT**	*adj*	**UNCARING**	*adj*
UNBEATEN	*adj*	**UNBOUNCY**	*adj*	**UNCARTED**	*adj*
UNBENIGN	*adj*	**UNBOWED**	*adj*	**UNCARVED**	*adj*
UNBIASED	*adj*	**UNBOWING**	*adj*	**UNCASHED**	*adj*
UNBILLED	*adj*	**UNBRED**	*adj*	**UNCASKED**	*adj*
UNBITTED	*adj*	**UNBRIGHT**	*adj*	**UNCAST**	*adj*
UNBITTEN	*adj*	**UNBROKE**	*adj*	**UNCATCHY**	*adj*
UNBITTER	*adj*	**UNBROKEN**	*adj*	**UNCAUGHT**	*adj*
UNBLAMED	*adj*	**UNBULKY**	*adj*	**UNCAUSED**	*adj*
UNBLEST	*adj*	**UNBURNED**	*adj*	**UNCEDED**	*adj*
UNBLOODY	*adj*	**UNBURNT**	*adj*	**UNCHARY**	*adj*
UNBOBBED	*adj*	**UNBUSTED**	*adj*	**UNCHASTE**	*adj* **-CHASTER, -CHASTEST**
UNBOILED	*adj*	**UNBUSY**	*adj*		
UNBONDED	*adj*	**UNCALLED**	*adj*	**UNCHEWED**	*adj*
UNBONED	*adj*	**UNCANDID**	*adj*	**UNCHIC**	*adj*
UNBOOTED	*adj*	**UNCANNED**	*adj*	**UNCHICLY**	*adv*
UNBORN	*adj*	**UNCARDED**	*adj*	**UNCHOSEN**	*adj*

UNCHURCH	*v* **-ED, -ING, -ES** to expel from a church
UNCI	pl. of uncus
UNCIA	*n* pl. **-CIAE** a coin of ancient Rome
UNCIAL	*n* pl. **-S** a style of writing
UNCIALLY	*adv* in the uncial style
UNCIFORM	*n* pl. **-S** a bone of the wrist
UNCINAL	*adj* uncinate
UNCINATE	*adj* bent at the end like a hook
UNCINUS	*n* pl. **-NI** an uncinate structure
UNCLAD	a past tense of unclothe
UNCLAMP	*v* **-ED, -ING, -S** to free from a clamp
UNCLASP	*v* **-ED, -ING, -S** to free from a clasp
UNCLE	*n* pl. **-S** the brother of one's father or mother
UNCLENCH	*v* **-ED, -ING, -ES** to open from a clenched position
UNCLINCH	*v* **-ED, -ING, -ES** to unclench
UNCLIP	*v* **-CLIPPED, -CLIPPING, -CLIPS** to remove a clip (a fastening device) from
UNCLOAK	*v* **-ED, -ING, -S** to remove a cloak from
UNCLOG	*v* **-CLOGGED, -CLOGGING, -CLOGS** to free from a difficulty or obstruction
UNCLONED	*adj* not produced by cloning
UNCLOSE	*v* **-CLOSED, -CLOSING, -CLOSES** to open
UNCLOTHE	*v* **-CLOTHED** or **-CLAD, -CLOTHING, -CLOTHES** to divest of clothing
UNCLOUD	*v* **-ED, -ING, -S** to free from clouds
UNCO	*n* pl. **-COS** a stranger
UNCOCK	*v* **-ED, -ING, -S** to remove from a cocked position
UNCOFFIN	*v* **-ED, -ING, -S** to remove from a coffin
UNCOIL	*v* **-ED, -ING, -S** to release from a coiled position
UNCORK	*v* **-ED, -ING, -S** to draw the cork
UNCOUPLE	*v* **-PLED, -PLING, -PLES** to disconnect
UNCOVER	*v* **-ED, -ING, -S** to remove the covering from
UNCRATE	*v* **-CRATED, -CRATING, -CRATES** to remove from a crate
UNCREATE	*v* **-ATED, -ATING, -ATES** to deprive of existence
UNCROSS	*v* **-ED, -ING, -ES** to change from a crossed position
UNCROWN	*v* **-ED, -ING, -S** to deprive of a crown
UNCTION	*n* pl. **-S** the act of anointing
UNCTUOUS	*adj* greasy
UNCUFF	*v* **-ED, -ING, -S** to remove handcuffs from
UNCURB	*v* **-ED, -ING, -S** to remove restraints from
UNCURL	*v* **-ED, -ING, -S** to straighten the curls of
UNCUS	*n* pl. **-CI** a hook-shaped anatomical part
UNDE	*adj* wavy
UNDEAD	*n* pl. **UNDEAD** a vampire
UNDEE	*adj* unde
UNDELETE	*v* **-LETED, -LETING, -LETES** to cancel the deletion of
UNDER	*prep* in a lower position than

List of self-explanatory adjectives and adverbs containing the prefix UN- (continued):

UNCIVIL	*adj*	**UNCOMMON**	*adj* **-MONER, -MONEST**	**UNDECKED**	*adj*
UNCLASSY	*adj*			**UNDENIED**	*adj*
UNCLAWED	*adj*	**UNCOOKED**	*adj*	**UNDENTED**	*adj*
UNCLEAN	*adj* **-CLEANER, -CLEANEST**	**UNCOOL**	*adj*	**UNDEVOUT**	*adj*
		UNCOOLED	*adj*	**UNDIMMED**	*adj*
UNCLEAR	*adj* **-CLEARER, -CLEAREST**	**UNCOUTH**	*adj*	**UNDOABLE**	*adj*
		UNCOY	*adj*	**UNDOCILE**	*adj*
UNCLEFT	*adj*	**UNCRAZY**	*adj* **-ZIER, -ZIEST**	**UNDOTTED**	*adj*
UNCLOUDY	*adj*	**UNCREWED**	*adj*	**UNDREAMT**	*adj*
UNCLOYED	*adj*	**UNCUFFED**	*adj*	**UNDRIED**	*adj*
UNCOATED	*adj*	**UNCURED**	*adj*	**UNDUBBED**	*adj*
UNCODED	*adj*	**UNCURSED**	*adj*	**UNDULLED**	*adj*
UNCOINED	*adj*	**UNCUT**	*adj*	**UNDYED**	*adj*
UNCOMBED	*adj*	**UNCUTE**	*adj*	**UNEAGER**	*adj*
UNCOMELY	*adj* **-LIER, -LIEST**	**UNDAMPED**	*adj*	**UNEARNED**	*adj*
UNCOMIC	*adj*	**UNDARING**	*adj*	**UNEATEN**	*adj*
		UNDATED	*adj*	**UNEDIBLE**	*adj*

UNDERACT	*v* **-ED, -ING, -S** to act subtly and with restraint	**UNDERLIP**	*n* pl. **-S** the lower lip
UNDERAGE	*n* pl. **-S** a shortage	**UNDERLIT**	*adj* lacking adequate light
UNDERARM	*n* pl. **-S** the armpit	**UNDERMAN**	*v* **-MANNED, -MANNING, -MANS** to fail to provide with enough workers
UNDERATE	past tense of undereat		
UNDERBID	*v* **-BID, -BIDDING, -BIDS** to bid lower than	**UNDERPAD**	*n* pl. **-S** a layer of soft foam laid under carpeting
UNDERBUD	*v* **-BUDDED, -BUDDING, -BUDS** to bud from beneath	**UNDERPAY**	*v* **-PAID, -PAYING, -PAYS** to pay less than is deserved
UNDERBUY	*v* **-BOUGHT, -BUYING, -BUYS** to buy at a lower price than	**UNDERPIN**	*v* **-PINNED, -PINNING, -PINS** to support from below
UNDERCUT	*v* **-CUT, -CUTTING, -CUTS** to cut under	**UNDERRUN**	*v* **-RAN, -RUNNING, -RUNS** to pass or extend under
UNDERDO	*v* **-DID, -DONE, -DOING, -DOES** to do insufficiently	**UNDERSEA**	*adv* beneath the surface of the sea
UNDERDOG	*n* pl. **-S** one who is expected to lose	**UNDERSET**	*n* pl. **-S** a current below the surface of the ocean
UNDEREAT	*v* **-ATE, -EATEN, -EATING, -EATS** to eat an insufficient amount	**UNDERSOW**	*v* **-SOWED, -SOWN, -SOWING, -SOWS** to sow land already seeded with a later-growing crop
UNDERFED	*adj* fed an insufficient amount		
UNDERFUR	*n* pl. **-S** the thick, soft fur beneath the outer coat of certain mammals	**UNDERTAX**	*v* **-ED, -ING, -ES** to tax less than the usual amount
UNDERGO	*v* **-WENT, -GONE, -GOING, -GOES** to be subjected to	**UNDERTOW**	*n* pl. **-S** the seaward pull of receding waves breaking on a shore
UNDERGOD	*n* pl. **-S** a lesser god		
UNDERJAW	*n* pl. **-S** the lower jaw	**UNDERUSE**	*v* **-USED, -USING, -USES** to use less than fully
UNDERLAIN	past participle of underlie		
UNDERLAP	*v* **-LAPPED, -LAPPING, -LAPS** to extend partly under	**UNDERWAY**	*adv* in progress
		UNDERWENT	past tense of undergo
UNDERLAY	*v* **-LAID, -LAYING, -LAYS** to place under	**UNDID**	past tense of undo
UNDERLET	*v* **-LET, -LETTING, -LETS** to lease at less than the usual value	**UNDIES**	*n/pl* underwear
		UNDINE	*n* pl. **-S** a female water spirit
UNDERLIE	*v* **-LAY, -LAIN, -LYING, -LIES** to lie under	**UNDO**	*v* **-DID, -DONE, -DOING, -DOES** to bring to ruin

---

List of self-explanatory adjectives and adverbs containing the prefix UN- (continued):

UNEDITED	*adj*	**UNFAIRLY**	*adv*	**UNFLEXED**	*adj*
UNENDED	*adj*	**UNFAKED**	*adj*	**UNFLUTED**	*adj*
UNENDING	*adj*	**UNFALLEN**	*adj*	**UNFOILED**	*adj*
UNENVIED	*adj*	**UNFAMOUS**	*adj*	**UNFOND**	*adj*
UNERASED	*adj*	**UNFANCY**	*adj*	**UNFONDLY**	*adv*
UNEROTIC	*adj*	**UNFAZED**	*adj*	**UNFORCED**	*adj*
UNERRING	*adj*	**UNFEARED**	*adj*	**UNFORGED**	*adj*
UNEVADED	*adj*	**UNFED**	*adj*	**UNFORKED**	*adj*
UNEVEN	*adj* **-EVENER, -EVENEST**	**UNFELT**	*adj*	**UNFORMED**	*adj*
		UNFELTED	*adj*	**UNFOUGHT**	*adj*
UNEVENLY	*adv*	**UNFILIAL**	*adj*	**UNFOUND**	*adj*
UNEXOTIC	*adj*	**UNFILLED**	*adj*	**UNFRAMED**	*adj*
UNEXPERT	*adj*	**UNFILMED**	*adj*	**UNFUNDED**	*adj*
UNFADED	*adj*	**UNFIRED**	*adj*	**UNFUNNY**	*adj* **-NIER, -NIEST**
UNFADING	*adj*	**UNFISHED**	*adj*	**UNFUSED**	*adj*
UNFAIR	*adj* **-FAIRER, -FAIREST**	**UNFLASHY**	*adj*	**UNFUSSED**	*adj*
		UNFLAWED	*adj*		

UNDO	*n* pl. **UNDOS** a computer feature that allows the user to reverse the effect of the last action	**UNEQUAL**	*n* pl. **-S** one that is not equal to another
UNDOCK	*v* **-ED, -ING, -S** to move away from a dock	**UNFAITH**	*n* pl. **-S** lack of faith
		UNFASTEN	*v* **-ED, -ING, -S** to release from fastenings
UNDOER	*n* pl. **-S** one that undoes	**UNFENCE**	*v* **-FENCED, -FENCING, -FENCES** to remove a fence from
UNDOING	*n* pl. **-S** a cause of ruin		
UNDONE	past participle of undo	**UNFETTER**	*v* **-ED, -ING, -S** to free from fetters
UNDOUBLE	*v* **-BLED, -BLING, -BLES** to unfold	**UNFIT**	*v* **-FITTED, -FITTING, -FITS** to make unsuitable
UNDRAPE	*v* **-DRAPED, -DRAPING, -DRAPES** to strip of drapery	**UNFITLY**	*adv* in an unsuitable manner
UNDRAW	*v* **-DREW, -DRAWN, -DRAWING, -DRAWS** to draw open	**UNFIX**	*v* **-FIXED** or **-FIXT, -FIXING, -FIXES** to unfasten
UNDRESS	*v* **-DRESSED** or **-DREST, -DRESSING, -DRESSES** to remove one's clothing	**UNFOLD**	*v* **-ED, -ING, -S** to open something that is folded
		UNFOLDER	*n* pl. **-S** one that unfolds
UNDRUNK	*adj* not swallowed	**UNFORGOT**	*adj* not forgotten
UNDUE	*adj* exceeding what is appropriate or normal	**UNFREE**	*v* **-FREED, -FREEING, -FREES** to deprive of freedom
UNDULANT	*adj* undulating	**UNFREEZE**	*v* **-FROZE, -FROZEN, -FREEZING, -FREEZES** to cause to thaw
UNDULAR	*adj* undulating		
UNDULATE	*v* **-LATED, -LATING, -LATES** to move with a wavelike motion	**UNFRIEND**	*v* **-ED, -ING, -S** to defriend
		UNFROCK	*v* **-ED, -ING, -S** to divest of ecclesiastical authority
UNDULOUS	*adj* undulating		
UNDULY	*adv* in an undue manner	**UNFURL**	*v* **-ED, -ING, -S** to unroll
UNDY	*adj* unde	**UNGAINLY**	*adj* **-LIER, -LIEST** awkward
UNDYING	*adj* not subject to death	**UNGIRD**	*v* **-GIRDED** or **-GIRT, -GIRDING, -GIRDS** to remove a belt from
UNEARTH	*v* **-ED, -ING, -S** to dig up		
UNEASE	*n* pl. **-S** mental or physical discomfort	**UNGLOVE**	*v* **-GLOVED, -GLOVING, -GLOVES** to uncover by removing a glove
UNEASY	*adj* **-EASIER, -EASIEST** marked by mental or physical discomfort **UNEASILY** *adv*	**UNGLUE**	*v* **-GLUED, -GLUING, -GLUES** to disjoin
		UNGODLY	*adj* **-LIER, -LIEST** impious

List of self-explanatory adjectives and adverbs containing the prefix UN- (continued):

UNFUSSY	*adj* **-FUSSIER, -FUSSIEST**	**UNGREEDY**	*adj*	**UNHIP**	*adj* **-HIPPER, -HIPPEST**
UNGALLED	*adj*	**UNGROUND**	*adj*		
UNGARBED	*adj*	**UNGUIDED**	*adj*	**UNHIRED**	*adj*
UNGATED	*adj*	**UNHAILED**	*adj*	**UNHOLILY**	*adv*
UNGAZING	*adj*	**UNHALVED**	*adj*	**UNHOLY**	*adj* **-LIER, -LIEST**
UNGELDED	*adj*	**UNHAPPY**	*adj* **-PIER, -PIEST**	**UNHUMAN**	*adj*
UNGENIAL	*adj*	**UNHARMED**	*adj*	**UNHUNG**	*adj*
UNGENTLE	*adj*	**UNHASTY**	*adj*	**UNHURT**	*adj*
UNGENTLY	*adv*	**UNHEALED**	*adj*	**UNIDEAL**	*adj*
UNGIFTED	*adj*	**UNHEARD**	*adj*	**UNIMBUED**	*adj*
UNGIVING	*adj*	**UNHEATED**	*adj*	**UNIRONED**	*adj*
UNGLAZED	*adj*	**UNHEDGED**	*adj*	**UNIRONIC**	*adj*
UNGLITZY	*adj*	**UNHEEDED**	*adj*	**UNISSUED**	*adj*
UNGOWNED	*adj*	**UNHELPED**	*adj*	**UNJADED**	*adj*
UNGRACED	*adj*	**UNHEROIC**	*adj*	**UNJOINED**	*adj*
UNGRADED	*adj*	**UNHEWN**	*adj*	**UNJOYFUL**	*adj*
				UNJUDGED	*adj*

UNGOT	*adj* ungotten	**UNHEALTH**	*n* pl. **-S** a state of ill health
UNGOTTEN	*adj* not obtained	**UNHELM**	*v* **-ED, -ING, -S** to remove the helmet of
UNGREEN	*adj* **-GREENER, -GREENEST** harmful to the environment	**UNHINGE**	*v* **-HINGED, -HINGING, -HINGES** to remove from hinges
UNGROUP	*v* **-ED, -ING, -S** to separate from a group	**UNHITCH**	*v* **-ED, -ING, -ES** to free from being hitched
UNGUAL	*adj* pertaining to an unguis	**UNHOOD**	*v* **-ED, -ING, -S** to remove a hood from
UNGUARD	*v* **-ED, -ING, -S** to leave unprotected		
UNGUENT	*n* pl. **-S** an ointment	**UNHOOK**	*v* **-ED, -ING, -S** to remove from a hook
UNGUENTA	*n/pl* ointments	**UNHOPED**	*adj* not hoped for or expected
UNGUIS	*n* pl. **-GUES** a nail, claw, or hoof	**UNHORSE**	*v* **-HORSED, -HORSING, -HORSES** to cause to fall from a horse
UNGULA	*n* pl. **-LAE** an unguis **UNGULAR** *adj*		
UNGULATE	*n* pl. **-S** a hoofed mammal	**UNHOUSE**	*v* **-HOUSED, -HOUSING, -HOUSES** to deprive of a protective shelter
UNGULED	*adj* having hoofs of a color that is different from the body — used of a heraldic animal	**UNHUSK**	*v* **-ED, -ING, -S** to remove the husk from
UNHAIR	*v* **-ED, -ING, -S** to remove the hair from	**UNI**	*n* pl. **-S** 1. a uniform 2. university
UNHAIRER	*n* pl. **-S** one that unhairs	**UNIALGAL**	*adj* pertaining to a single algal cell
UNHALLOW	*v* **-ED, -ING, -S** to profane	**UNIAXIAL**	*adj* having one axis
UNHAND	*v* **-ED, -ING, -S** to remove the hand from	**UNIBODY**	*n* pl. **-BODIES** a single molded unit that forms the bodywork and chassis of a vehicle
UNHANDY	*adj* **-HANDIER, -HANDIEST** difficult to handle		
UNHANG	*v* **-HUNG** or **-HANGED, -HANGING, -HANGS** to detach from a hanging support	**UNIBROW**	*n* pl. **-S** a single continuous eyebrow formed when hair grows above the bridge of the nose
		UNICED	*adj* not covered with icing
UNHAPPEN	*v* **-ED, -ING, -S** to become as though never having happened	**UNICOLOR**	*adj* of one color
		UNICOM	*n* pl. **-S** a radio communications system at some airports
UNHASP	*v* **-ED, -ING, -S** to unfasten		
UNHAT	*v* **-HATTED, -HATTING, -HATS** to remove one's hat	**UNICORN**	*n* pl. **-S** a mythical horselike creature

---

List of self-explanatory adjectives and adverbs containing the prefix UN- (continued):

UNJUST	*adj*	**UNLIKE**	*adj*	**UNMAPPED**	*adj*
UNJUSTLY	*adv*	**UNLIKED**	*adj*	**UNMARKED**	*adj*
UNKEELED	*adj*	**UNLIKELY**	*adj* **-LIER, -LIEST**	**UNMARRED**	*adj*
UNKEPT	*adj*	**UNLINED**	*adj*	**UNMATED**	*adj*
UNKIND	*adj* **-KINDER, -KINDEST**	**UNLISTED**	*adj*	**UNMATTED**	*adj*
		UNLIT	*adj*	**UNMEANT**	*adj*
UNKINDLY	*adv* **-LIER, -LIEST**	**UNLIVELY**	*adj*	**UNMELLOW**	*adj*
UNKINGLY	*adj*	**UNLOBED**	*adj*	**UNMELTED**	*adj*
UNKISSED	*adj*	**UNLOVED**	*adj*	**UNMENDED**	*adj*
UNKOSHER	*adj*	**UNLOVELY**	*adj* **-LIER, -LIEST**	**UNMERRY**	*adj* **-RIER, -RIEST**
UNLAWFUL	*adj*	**UNLOVING**	*adj*	**UNMET**	*adj*
UNLEASED	*adj*	**UNLUCKY**	*adj* **-LUCKIER, -LUCKIEST**	**UNMILLED**	*adj*
UNLED	*adj*			**UNMINED**	*adj*
UNLETHAL	*adj*	**UNMACHO**	*adj*	**UNMODISH**	*adj*
UNLETTED	*adj*	**UNMAILED**	*adj*	**UNMOLTEN**	*adj*
UNLEVIED	*adj*	**UNMANFUL**	*adj*	**UNMOVED**	*adj*
UNLICKED	*adj*	**UNMANLY**	*adj* **-LIER, -LIEST**	**UNMOVING**	*adj*

UNICUM *n pl.* **-CA** a unique example or specimen

UNICYCLE *v* **-CLED, -CLING, -CLES** to ride a one-wheeled vehicle

UNIDEAED *adj* lacking ideas

UNIFACE *n pl.* **-S** a coin having a design on only one side

UNIFIC *adj* unifying

UNIFIED past tense of unify

UNIFIER *n pl.* **-S** one that unifies

UNIFIES present 3d person sing. of unify

UNIFILAR *adj* having only one thread, wire, or fiber

UNIFORM *adj* **-FORMER, -FORMEST** unchanging

UNIFORM *v* **-ED, -ING, -S** to make uniform

UNIFY *v* **-FIED, -FYING, -FIES** to make into a coherent whole

UNILOBED *adj* having one lobe

UNIMODAL *adj* having or involving one mode

UNINSTAL *v* **-STALLED, -STALLING, -STALS** to remove a file or an application from a computer

UNION *n pl.* **-S** a number of persons, parties, or political entities united for a common purpose

UNIONISE *v* **-ISED, -ISING, -ISES** to unionize

UNIONISM *n pl.* **-S** the principle of forming a union

UNIONIST *n pl.* **-S** an advocate of unionism

UNIONIZE *v* **-IZED, -IZING, -IZES** to form into a union

UNIPOD *n pl.* **-S** a one-legged support

UNIPOLAR *adj* showing only one kind of polarity

UNIQUE *adj* **UNIQUER, UNIQUEST** existing as the only one of its kind; very unusual **UNIQUELY** *adv*

UNIQUE *n pl.* **-S** something that is unique

UNISEX *n pl.* **-ES** the condition of not being distinguishable as to sex

UNISIZE *adj* made to fit all sizes

UNISON *n pl.* **-S** complete agreement **UNISONAL** *adj*

UNIT *n pl.* **-S** a specific quantity used as a standard of measurement

UNITAGE *n pl.* **-S** amount in units

UNITARD *n pl.* **-S** a leotard that also covers the legs

UNITARY *adj* pertaining to a unit

UNITE *v* **UNITED, UNITING, UNITES** to bring together so as to form a whole **UNITEDLY** *adv*

UNITER *n pl.* **-S** one that unites

UNITIES pl. of unity

UNITIVE *adj* serving to unite

UNITIZE *v* **-IZED, -IZING, -IZES** to divide into units

UNITIZER *n pl.* **-S** one that unitizes

UNITRUST *n pl.* **-S** a type of annuity trust

UNITY *n pl.* **-TIES** the state of being one single entity

UNIVALVE *n pl.* **-S** a mollusk having a single shell

UNIVERSE *n pl.* **-S** the totality of all existing things

UNIVOCAL *n pl.* **-S** a word having only one meaning

List of self-explanatory adjectives and adverbs containing the prefix UN- (continued):

UNMOWN	*adj*	**UNPITIED**	*adj*	**UNPROBED**	*adj*
UNNAMED	*adj*	**UNPITTED**	*adj*	**UNPROVED**	*adj*
UNNEEDED	*adj*	**UNPLACED**	*adj*	**UNPROVEN**	*adj*
UNNOISY	*adj*	**UNPLAYED**	*adj*	**UNPRUNED**	*adj*
UNNOTED	*adj*	**UNPLIANT**	*adj*	**UNPURE**	*adj*
UNOILED	*adj*	**UNPLOWED**	*adj*	**UNPURELY**	*adv*
UNOPEN	*adj*	**UNPOETIC**	*adj*	**UNPURGED**	*adj*
UNOPENED	*adj*	**UNPOISED**	*adj*	**UNQUIET**	*adj* **-ETER,**
UNORNATE	*adj*	**UNPOLITE**	*adj*		**-ETEST**
UNOWNED	*adj*	**UNPOLLED**	*adj*	**UNRAISED**	*adj*
UNPADDED	*adj*	**UNPOSED**	*adj*	**UNRAKED**	*adj*
UNPAID	*adj*	**UNPOSTED**	*adj*	**UNRANKED**	*adj*
UNPAIRED	*adj*	**UNPOTTED**	*adj*	**UNRATED**	*adj*
UNPARTED	*adj*	**UNPRETTY**	*adj* **-TIER, -TIEST**	**UNRAZED**	*adj*
UNPAVED	*adj*	**UNPRICED**	*adj*	**UNREAD**	*adj*
UNPAYING	*adj*	**UNPRIMED**	*adj*	**UNREADY**	*adj* **-READIER,**
UNPEELED	*adj*	**UNPRIZED**	*adj*		**-READIEST**

UNJAM	*v* -JAMMED, -JAMMING, -JAMS to undo things tightly crammed together
UNJOINT	*v* -ED, -ING, -S to separate at a juncture
UNKEMPT	*adj* untidy
UNKEND	*adj* unkenned
UNKENNED	*adj* not known or recognized
UNKENNEL	*v* -NELED, -NELING, -NELS or -NELLED, -NELLING, -NELS to release from a kennel
UNKENT	*adj* unkenned
UNKINK	*v* -ED, -ING, -S to remove curls from
UNKNIT	*v* -KNITTED, -KNITTING, -KNITS to unravel
UNKNOT	*v* -KNOTTED, -KNOTTING, -KNOTS to undo a knot in
UNKNOWN	*n* pl. **-S** one that is not known
UNLACE	*v* -LACED, -LACING, -LACES to unfasten the laces of
UNLADE	*v* -LADED, -LADEN, -LADING, -LADES to unload
UNLASH	*v* -ED, -ING, -ES to untie the lashing (a type of binding) of
UNLATCH	*v* -ED, -ING, -ES to open by lifting the latch (a fastening device)
UNLAY	*v* -LAID, -LAYING, -LAYS to untwist
UNLEAD	*v* -ED, -ING, -S to remove the lead from
UNLEADED	*n* pl. **-S** a product containing no lead
UNLEARN	*v* -LEARNED or -LEARNT, -LEARNING, -LEARNS to put out of one's knowledge or memory
UNLEASH	*v* -ED, -ING, -ES to free from a leash
UNLESS	*conj* except on the condition that
UNLET	*adj* not rented
UNLEVEL	*v* -ELED, -ELING, -ELS or -ELLED, -ELLING, -ELS to make uneven
UNLIMBER	*v* -ED, -ING, -S to prepare for action
UNLINK	*v* -ED, -ING, -S to unfasten the links (connecting devices) of
UNLIVE	*v* -LIVED, -LIVING, -LIVES to live so as to make amends for
UNLOAD	*v* -ED, -ING, -S to remove the load or cargo from
UNLOADER	*n* pl. **-S** one that unloads
UNLOCK	*v* -ED, -ING, -S to unfasten the lock of
UNLOOSE	*v* -LOOSED, -LOOSING, -LOOSES to set free
UNLOOSEN	*v* -ED, -ING, -S to unloose
UNMAKE	*v* -MADE, -MAKING, -MAKES to destroy
UNMAKER	*n* pl. **-S** one that unmakes
UNMAN	*v* -MANNED, -MANNING, -MANS to deprive of courage
UNMASK	*v* -ED, -ING, -S to remove a mask from
UNMASKER	*n* pl. **-S** one that unmasks
UNMEET	*adj* improper **UNMEETLY** *adv*
UNMESH	*v* -ED, -ING, -ES to disentangle
UNMEW	*v* -ED, -ING, -S to set free
UNMINGLE	*v* -GLED, -GLING, -GLES to separate things that are mixed

---

List of self-explanatory adjectives and adverbs containing the prefix UN- (continued):

UNREAL	*adj*		**UNSAFE**	*adj* -SAFER,		**UNSEXUAL**	*adj*
UNREALLY	*adv*			-SAFEST		**UNSEXY**	*adj* -SEXIER,
UNRENTED	*adj*		**UNSAFELY**	*adv*			-SEXIEST
UNREPAID	*adj*		**UNSALTED**	*adj*		**UNSHADED**	*adj*
UNRESTED	*adj*		**UNSATED**	*adj*		**UNSHAKEN**	*adj*
UNRHYMED	*adj*		**UNSAVED**	*adj*		**UNSHAMED**	*adj*
UNRIBBED	*adj*		**UNSAVORY**	*adj*		**UNSHAPED**	*adj*
UNRIDDEN	*adj*		**UNSAWED**	*adj*		**UNSHAPEN**	*adj*
UNRIFLED	*adj*		**UNSAWN**	*adj*		**UNSHARED**	*adj*
UNRIMED	*adj*		**UNSCALED**	*adj*		**UNSHARP**	*adj*
UNRINSED	*adj*		**UNSEARED**	*adj*		**UNSHAVED**	*adj*
UNRISEN	*adj*		**UNSEEDED**	*adj*		**UNSHAVEN**	*adj*
UNROPED	*adj*		**UNSEEMLY**	*adj* -LIER, -LIEST		**UNSHED**	*adj*
UNROUGH	*adj*		**UNSEIZED**	*adj*		**UNSHOD**	*adj*
UNRULED	*adj*		**UNSENT**	*adj*		**UNSHORN**	*adj*
UNRUSHED	*adj*		**UNSERVED**	*adj*		**UNSHOWY**	*adj* -SHOWIER,
UNRUSTED	*adj*		**UNSEXILY**	*adv*			-SHOWIEST

UNMITER v **-ED, -ING, -S** to depose from the rank of bishop

UNMITRE v **-TRED, -TRING, -TRES** to unmiter

UNMIX v **-MIXED** or **-MIXT, -MIXING, -MIXES** to separate from a mixture

UNMOLD v **-ED, -ING, -S** to remove from a mold

UNMOOR v **-ED, -ING, -S** to release from moorings

UNMORAL adj amoral

UNMOULD v **-ED, -ING, -S** to unmold

UNMUFFLE v **-FLED, -FLING, -FLES** to free from something that muffles

UNMUZZLE v **-ZLED, -ZLING, -ZLES** to remove a muzzle from

UNNAIL v **-ED, -ING, -S** to remove the nails from

UNNERVE v **-NERVED, -NERVING, -NERVES** to deprive of courage

UNOAKED adj not matured in an oak container — used of wine

UNPACK v **-ED, -ING, -S** to remove the contents of

UNPACKER n pl. **-S** one that unpacks

UNPAGED adj having no page numbers

UNPEG v **-PEGGED, -PEGGING, -PEGS** to remove the pegs from

UNPEN v **-PENNED** or **-PENT, -PENNING, -PENS** to release from confinement

UNPEOPLE v **-PLED, -PLING, -PLES** to remove people from

UNPERSON n pl. **-S** one who is removed completely from recognition

UNPICK v **-ED, -ING, -S** to remove the stitches from

UNPILE v **-PILED, -PILING, -PILES** to take or disentangle from a pile

UNPIN v **-PINNED, -PINNING, -PINS** to remove the pins from

UNPLAIT v **-ED, -ING, -S** to undo the plaits of

UNPLUG v **-PLUGGED, -PLUGGING, -PLUGS** to take a plug out of

UNPUCKER v **-ED, -ING, -S** to remove the wrinkles from

UNPUZZLE v **-ZLED, -ZLING, -ZLES** to work out the obscured meaning of

UNQUIET n pl. **-S** a state of unrest

UNQUOTE v **-QUOTED, -QUOTING, -QUOTES** to close a quotation

UNRAVEL v **-ELED, -ELING, -ELS** or **-ELLED, -ELLING, -ELS** to separate the threads of

UNREASON v **-ED, -ING, -S** to disrupt the sanity of

UNREEL v **-ED, -ING, -S** to unwind from a reel

UNREELER n pl. **-S** one that unreels

UNREEVE v **-REEVED** or **-ROVE, -ROVEN, -REEVING, -REEVES** to withdraw a rope from an opening

UNRENT adj not torn

UNREPAIR n pl. **-S** lack of repair

UNREST n pl. **-S** a disturbed or uneasy state

UNRETIRE v **-TIRED, -TIRING, -TIRES** to return to work after having taken retirement

UNRIDDLE v **-DLED, -DLING, -DLES** to solve

List of self-explanatory adjectives and adverbs containing the prefix UN- (continued):

UNSHRUNK	adj	**UNSOLID**	adj	**UNSTABLY**	adv
UNSHUT	adj	**UNSOLVED**	adj	**UNSTEADY**	adj -STEADIER, -STEADIEST
UNSIFTED	adj	**UNSORTED**	adj		
UNSIGNED	adj	**UNSOUGHT**	adj	**UNSTONED**	adj
UNSILENT	adj	**UNSOUND**	adj -SOUNDER, -SOUNDEST	**UNSTUFFY**	adj -STUFFIER, -STUFFIEST
UNSINFUL	adj				
UNSIZED	adj	**UNSOURED**	adj	**UNSTUNG**	adj
UNSLAKED	adj	**UNSOWED**	adj	**UNSUBTLE**	adj -TLER, -TLEST
UNSLICED	adj	**UNSOWN**	adj		
UNSLICK	adj	**UNSPENT**	adj	**UNSUBTLY**	adv
UNSMART	adj	**UNSPILT**	adj	**UNSUITED**	adj
UNSMOKED	adj	**UNSPLIT**	adj	**UNSUNG**	adj
UNSOAKED	adj	**UNSPOILT**	adj	**UNSUNK**	adj
UNSOBER	adj	**UNSPRUNG**	adj	**UNSURE**	adj
UNSOCIAL	adj	**UNSPUN**	adj	**UNSURELY**	adv
UNSOILED	adj	**UNSTABLE**	adj -BLER, -BLEST	**UNSWAYED**	adj
UNSOLD	adj			**UNSWEPT**	adj

UNRIG *v* **-RIGGED, -RIGGING, -RIGS** to divest of rigging

UNRIP *v* **-RIPPED, -RIPPING, -RIPS** to rip open

UNRIPE *adj* **-RIPER, -RIPEST** not ripe **UNRIPELY** *adv*

UNRIVET *v* **-ETED, -ETING, -ETS** or **-ETTED, -ETTING, -ETS** to remove rivets (metal bolts) from

UNROBE *v* **-ROBED, -ROBING, -ROBES** to undress

UNROLL *v* **-ED, -ING, -S** to open something that is rolled up

UNROOF *v* **-ED, -ING, -S** to strip off the roof of

UNROOT *v* **-ED, -ING, -S** to uproot

UNROPE *v* **-ROPED, -ROPING, -ROPES** to detach oneself from a rope

UNROUND *v* **-ED, -ING, -S** to articulate without rounding the lips

UNROVE a past tense of unreeve

UNROVEN a past participle of unreeve

UNRULY *adj* **-LIER, -LIEST** difficult to control

UNSADDLE *v* **-DLED, -DLING, -DLES** to remove the saddle from

UNSAFETY *n* pl. **-TIES** lack of safety

UNSAY *v* **-SAID, -SAYING, -SAYS** to retract something said

UNSCREW *v* **-ED, -ING, -S** to remove the screws from

UNSEAL *v* **-ED, -ING, -S** to remove the seal of

UNSEAM *v* **-ED, -ING, -S** to open the seams of

UNSEAT *v* **-ED, -ING, -S** to remove from a seat

UNSEE *v* **-SAW, -SEEN, -SEEING, -SEES** to fail to see

UNSELL *v* **-SOLD, -SELLING, -SELLS** to persuade to change an opinion or belief

UNSET *v* **-SET, -SETTING, -SETS** to unsettle

UNSETTLE *v* **-TLED, -TLING, -TLES** to make unstable

UNSEW *v* **-SEWED, -SEWN, -SEWING, -SEWS** to undo the sewing of

UNSEX *v* **-ED, -ING, -ES** to deprive of sexual power

UNSHELL *v* **-ED, -ING, -S** to remove the shell from

UNSHIFT *v* **-ED, -ING, -S** to release the shift key on a typewriter

UNSHIP *v* **-SHIPPED, -SHIPPING, -SHIPS** to unload from a ship

UNSICKER *adj* unreliable

UNSIGHT *v* **-ED, -ING, -S** to prevent from seeing

UNSLING *v* **-SLUNG, -SLINGING, -SLINGS** to remove from a slung position

UNSNAG *v* **-SNAGGED, -SNAGGING, -SNAGS** to free of snags

UNSNAP *v* **-SNAPPED, -SNAPPING, -SNAPS** to undo the snaps of

UNSNARL *v* **-ED, -ING, -S** to untangle

UNSOLDER *v* **-ED, -ING, -S** to separate

UNSONCY *adj* unsonsie

UNSONSIE *adj* unlucky

UNSONSY *adj* unsonsie

List of self-explanatory adjectives and adverbs containing the prefix UN- (continued):

UNTAGGED	*adj*	UNTINGED	*adj*	UNUNITED	*adj*
UNTAKEN	*adj*	UNTIPPED	*adj*	UNURGED	*adj*
UNTAME	*adj*	UNTIRED	*adj*	UNUSABLE	*adj*
UNTAMED	*adj*	UNTIRING	*adj*	UNUSABLY	*adv*
UNTANNED	*adj*	UNTITLED	*adj*	UNUSED	*adj*
UNTAPPED	*adj*	UNTOLD	*adj*	UNUSUAL	*adj*
UNTASTED	*adj*	UNTORN	*adj*	UNVALUED	*adj*
UNTAXED	*adj*	UNTRACED	*adj*	UNVARIED	*adj*
UNTENDED	*adj*	UNTRENDY	*adj* -TRENDIER,	UNVEINED	*adj*
UNTESTED	*adj*		-TRENDIEST	UNVERSED	*adj*
UNTHAWED	*adj*	UNTRIED	*adj*	UNVESTED	*adj*
UNTIDILY	*adv*	UNTRUE	*adj* -TRUER,	UNVEXED	*adj*
UNTIDY	*adj* -DIER, -DIEST		-TRUEST	UNVEXT	*adj*
UNTILLED	*adj*	UNTRULY	*adv*	UNVIABLE	*adj*
UNTILTED	*adj*	UNTRUSTY	*adj*	UNVOCAL	*adj*
UNTIMED	*adj*	UNTUFTED	*adj*	UNWALLED	*adj*
UNTIMELY	*adj* -LIER, -LIEST	UNTURNED	*adj*	UNWANING	*adj*

UNSPEAK	*v* **-SPOKE, -SPOKEN, -SPEAKING, -SPEAKS** to unsay	**UNTEACH**	*v* **-TAUGHT, -TEACHING, -TEACHES** to cause to unlearn something
UNSPHERE	*v* **-SPHERED, -SPHERING, -SPHERES** to remove from a sphere	**UNTENTED**	*adj* not probed or attended to
		UNTETHER	*v* **-ED, -ING, -S** to free from a tether
UNSPOOL	*v* **-ED, -ING, -S** to unwind from a small cylinder	**UNTHAW**	*v* **-ED, -ING, -S** to thaw
UNSTACK	*v* **-ED, -ING, -S** to remove from a stack	**UNTHINK**	*v* **-THOUGHT, -THINKING, -THINKS** to dismiss from the mind
UNSTATE	*v* **-STATED, -STATING, -STATES** to deprive of status	**UNTHREAD**	*v* **-ED, -ING, -S** to remove the thread from
UNSTAYED	*adj* not secured with ropes or wires	**UNTHRONE**	*v* **-THRONED, -THRONING, -THRONES** to remove from a throne
UNSTEADY	*v* **-STEADIED, -STEADYING, -STEADIES** to make not firm or stable	**UNTIDY**	*v* **-DIED, -DYING, -DIES** to make untidy
UNSTEEL	*v* **-ED, -ING, -S** to make soft	**UNTIE**	*v* **-TIED, -TYING** or **-TIEING, -TIES** to free from something that ties
UNSTEP	*v* **-STEPPED, -STEPPING, -STEPS** to remove from a socket	**UNTIL**	*prep* up to the time of
UNSTICK	*v* **-STUCK, -STICKING, -STICKS** to disjoin	**UNTO**	*prep* to
		UNTONED	*adj* lacking in muscular definition
UNSTITCH	*v* **-ED, -ING, -ES** to remove the stitches from	**UNTOWARD**	*adj* unruly
UNSTOP	*v* **-STOPPED, -STOPPING, -STOPS** to remove a stopper from	**UNTRACK**	*v* **-ED, -ING, -S** to cause to escape from a slump
UNSTRAP	*v* **-STRAPPED, -STRAPPING, -STRAPS** to remove a strap from	**UNTREAD**	*v* **-TROD** or **-TREADED, -TRODDEN, -TREADING, -TREADS** to tread back
UNSTRESS	*n* pl. **-ES** a syllable having relatively weak stress	**UNTRIM**	*v* **-TRIMMED, -TRIMMING, -TRIMS** to strip of trimming
UNSTRING	*v* **-STRUNG, -STRINGING, -STRINGS** to remove from a string	**UNTRUSS**	*v* **-ED, -ING, -ES** to free from a truss
UNSTUCK	past tense of unstick	**UNTRUTH**	*n* pl. **-S** something that is untrue
UNSWATHE	*v* **-SWATHED, -SWATHING, -SWATHES** to unbind	**UNTUCK**	*v* **-ED, -ING, -S** to release from being tucked up
UNSWEAR	*v* **-SWORE, -SWORN, -SWEARING, -SWEARS** to retract something sworn	**UNTUNE**	*v* **-TUNED, -TUNING, -TUNES** to put out of tune
		UNTWINE	*v* **-TWINED, -TWINING, -TWINES** to separate the twisted or tangled parts of
UNTACK	*v* **-ED, -ING, -S** to remove a tack from	**UNTWIST**	*v* **-ED, -ING, -S** to untwine
UNTANGLE	*v* **-GLED, -GLING, -GLES** to free from tangles	**UNTYING**	present participle of untie
		UNUNBIUM	*n* pl. **-S** a synthetic element

List of self-explanatory adjectives and adverbs containing the prefix UN- (continued):

UNWANTED	*adj*	**UNWARY**	*adj* **-WARIER, -WARIEST**	**UNWELDED**	*adj*
UNWARIER	comparative of unwary			**UNWELL**	*adj*
		UNWASTED	*adj*	**UNWEPT**	*adj*
UNWARIEST	superlative of unwary	**UNWAXED**	*adj*	**UNWET**	*adj*
		UNWEANED	*adj*	**UNWETTED**	*adj*
UNWARILY	*adv*	**UNWEARY**	*adj*	**UNWHITE**	*adj*
UNWARMED	*adj*	**UNWED**	*adj*	**UNWIELDY**	*adj* **-WIELDIER, -WIELDIEST**
UNWARNED	*adj*	**UNWEDDED**	*adj*		
UNWARPED	*adj*	**UNWEEDED**	*adj*	**UNWIFELY**	*adj*

UNVEIL	*v* **-ED, -ING, -S** to remove a covering from	**UPBOIL**	*v* **-ED, -ING, -S** to boil up
UNVOICE	*v* **-VOICED, -VOICING, -VOICES** to deprive of voice or vocal quality	**UPBORE**	past tense of upbear
		UPBORNE	past participle of upbear
UNWAGED	*adj* not receiving money for work	**UPBOUND**	past tense of upbind
UNWASHED	*n* pl. **-S** an ignorant or underprivileged group	**UPBOW**	*n* pl. **-S** a type of stroke in playing a bowed instrument
UNWEAVE	*v* **-WOVE, -WOVEN, -WEAVING, -WEAVES** to undo something woven	**UPBRAID**	*v* **-ED, -ING, -S** to reproach severely
UNWEIGHT	*v* **-ED, -ING, -S** to reduce the weight of	**UPBUILD**	*v* **-BUILT, -BUILDING, -BUILDS** to build up
UNWIND	*v* **-WOUND, -WINDING, -WINDS** to reverse the winding of	**UPBY**	*adv* upbye
		UPBYE	*adv* a little farther on
UNWINDER	*n* pl. **-S** one that unwinds	**UPCAST**	*v* **-CAST, -CASTING, -CASTS** to cast up
UNWISDOM	*n* pl. **-S** lack of wisdom	**UPCHUCK**	*v* **-ED, -ING, -S** to vomit
UNWISH	*v* **-ED, -ING, -ES** to cease to wish for	**UPCLIMB**	*v* **-ED, -ING, -S** to climb up
		UPCOAST	*adv* up the coast
UNWIT	*v* **-WITTED, -WITTING, -WITS** to make insane	**UPCOIL**	*v* **-ED, -ING, -S** to coil up
UNWONTED	*adj* unusual	**UPCOMING**	*adj* about to happen or appear
UNWORTHY	*n* pl. **-THIES** an unworthy person	**UPCOURT**	*adv* in the opposite half of a basketball court
UNWOUND	past tense of unwind	**UPCURL**	*v* **-ED, -ING, -S** to curl up
UNWOVE	past tense of unweave	**UPCURVE**	*v* **-CURVED, -CURVING, -CURVES** to curve upward
UNWOVEN	past participle of unweave		
UNWRAP	*v* **-WRAPPED, -WRAPPING, -WRAPS** to remove the wrapping from	**UPCYCLE**	*v* **-CLED, -CLING, -CLES** to make a product of greater value from recycled material
UNYEANED	*adj* unborn	**UPDART**	*v* **-ED, -ING, -S** to dart up
UNYOKE	*v* **-YOKED, -YOKING, -YOKES** to free from a yoke	**UPDATE**	*v* **-DATED, -DATING, -DATES** to bring up to date
UNZIP	*v* **-ZIPPED, -ZIPPING, -ZIPS** to open the zipper of	**UPDATER**	*n* pl. **-S** one that updates
		UPDIVE	*v* **-DIVED** or **-DOVE, -DIVING, -DIVES** to spring upward
UP	*v* **UPPED, UPPING, UPS** to raise		
UPALONG	*n* pl. **-S** a location away from a person or place	**UPDO**	*n* pl. **-DOS** an upswept hairdo
		UPDOMING	*n* pl. **-S** the upward deformation of a rock mass into a dome shape
UPAS	*n* pl. **-ES** an Asian tree		
UPBEAR	*v* **-BORE, -BORNE, -BEARING, -BEARS** to raise aloft	**UPDRAFT**	*n* pl. **-S** an upward movement of air
		UPDRY	*v* **-DRIED, -DRYING, -DRIES** to dry completely
UPBEARER	*n* pl. **-S** one that upbears		
UPBEAT	*n* pl. **-S** an unaccented beat in a musical measure	**UPEND**	*v* **-ED, -ING, -S** to set or stand on end
UPBIND	*v* **-BOUND, -BINDING, -BINDS** to bind completely	**UPFIELD**	*adv* into the part of the field toward which the offensive team is going

---

List of self-explanatory adjectives and adverbs containing the prefix UN- (continued):

UNWILLED	*adj*	**UNWOODED**	*adj*	**UNWORTHY**	*adj* **-THIER, -THIEST**
UNWISE	*adj* **-WISER, -WISEST**	**UNWOOED**	*adj*		
		UNWORKED	*adj*	**UNWRUNG**	*adj*
UNWISELY	*adv*	**UNWORN**	*adj*	**UNYOUNG**	*adj*
UNWON	*adj*			**UNZONED**	*adj*

UPFLING	*v* **-FLUNG, -FLINGING, -FLINGS** to fling up	**UPON**	*prep* on
UPFLOW	*v* **-ED, -ING, -S** to flow up	**UPPED**	past tense of up
UPFOLD	*v* **-ED, -ING, -S** to fold up	**UPPER**	*n* pl. **-S** the part of a boot or shoe above the sole
UPFRONT	*adj* honest; candid	**UPPERCUT**	*v* **-CUT, -CUTTING, -CUTS** to strike an upward blow
UPGATHER	*v* **-ED, -ING, -S** to gather up		
UPGAZE	*v* **-GAZED, -GAZING, -GAZES** to gaze up	**UPPILE**	*v* **-PILED, -PILING, -PILES** to pile up
UPGIRD	*v* **-GIRDED** or **-GIRT, -GIRDING, -GIRDS** to gird completely	**UPPING**	*n* pl. **-S** the process of marking young swans for identification purposes
UPGOING	*adj* going up	**UPPISH**	*adj* uppity **UPPISHLY** *adv*
UPGRADE	*v* **-GRADED, -GRADING, -GRADES** to raise to a higher grade or standard	**UPPITY**	*adj* tending to be snobbish and arrogant
UPGRADER	*n* pl. **-S** one that upgrades	**UPPROP**	*v* **-PROPPED, -PROPPING, -PROPS** to prop up
UPGROW	*v* **-GREW, -GROWN, -GROWING, -GROWS** to grow up	**UPRAISE**	*v* **-RAISED, -RAISING, -RAISES** to raise up
UPGROWTH	*n* pl. **-S** the process of growing up	**UPRAISER**	*n* pl. **-S** one that upraises
UPHEAP	*v* **-ED, -ING, -S** to heap up	**UPRATE**	*v* **-RATED, -RATING, -RATES** to improve the power output of an engine
UPHEAVAL	*n* pl. **-S** the act of upheaving		
UPHEAVE	*v* **-HEAVED** or **-HOVE, -HEAVING, -HEAVES** to heave up	**UPREACH**	*v* **-ED, -ING, -ES** to reach up
UPHEAVER	*n* pl. **-S** one that upheaves	**UPREAR**	*v* **-ED, -ING, -S** to upraise
UPHILL	*n* pl. **-S** an upward slope	**UPRIGHT**	*v* **-ED, -ING, -S** to make vertical
UPHOARD	*v* **-ED, -ING, -S** to hoard up	**UPRISE**	*v* **-ROSE, -RISEN, -RISING, -RISES** to rise up
UPHOLD	*v* **-HELD, -HOLDING, -HOLDS** to hold aloft		
UPHOLDER	*n* pl. **-S** one that upholds	**UPRISER**	*n* pl. **-S** one that uprises
UPHOVE	a past tense of upheave	**UPRISING**	*n* pl. **-S** a revolt
UPHROE	*n* pl. **-S** euphroe	**UPRIVER**	*n* pl. **-S** an area lying toward the source of a river
UPKEEP	*n* pl. **-S** the cost of maintaining something in good condition	**UPROAR**	*n* pl. **-S** a state of noisy excitement and confusion
UPLAND	*n* pl. **-S** the higher land of a region	**UPROOT**	*v* **-ED, -ING, -S** to pull up by the roots
UPLANDER	*n* pl. **-S** an inhabitant of an upland		
UPLEAP	*v* **-LEAPED** or **-LEAPT, -LEAPING, -LEAPS** to leap up	**UPROOTAL**	*n* pl. **-S** the act of uprooting
		UPROOTER	*n* pl. **-S** one that uproots
UPLIFT	*v* **-ED, -ING, -S** to lift up	**UPROSE**	past tense of uprise
UPLIFTER	*n* pl. **-S** one that uplifts	**UPROUSE**	*v* **-ROUSED, -ROUSING, -ROUSES** to rouse up
UPLIGHT	*v* **-LIGHTED** or **-LIT, -LIGHTING, -LIGHTS** to light to a higher degree		
		UPRUSH	*v* **-ED, -ING, -ES** to rush up
UPLINK	*v* **-ED, -ING, -S** to transmit (data) to a spacecraft or satellite	**UPSCALE**	*v* **-SCALED, -SCALING, -SCALES** to make appealing to affluent consumers
UPLOAD	*v* **-ED, -ING, -S** to transfer information from a small computer to a larger computer	**UPSELL**	*v* **-SOLD, -SELLING, -SELLS** to try to sell a customer something more expensive
UPMARKET	*adj* upscale		
UPMOST	*adj* highest	**UPSEND**	*v* **-SENT, -SENDING, -SENDS** to send upward
UPO	*prep* upon	**UPSET**	*v* **-SET, -SETTING, -SETS** to overturn

UPSETTER	*n* pl. **-S** one that upsets		**UPTEAR**	*v* **-TORE, -TORN, -TEARING, -TEARS** to tear out by the roots
UPSHIFT	*v* **-ED, -ING, -S** to shift into a higher gear		**UPTEMPO**	*n* pl. **-POS** a fast or lively tempo
UPSHOOT	*v* **-SHOT, -SHOOTING, -SHOOTS** to shoot upward		**UPTHROW**	*v* **-THREW, -THROWN, -THROWING, -THROWS** to throw upward
UPSHOT	*n* pl. **-S** the final result		**UPTHRUST**	*v* **-ED, -ING, -S** to thrust up
UPSIDE	*n* pl. **-S** a positive aspect		**UPTICK**	*n* pl. **-S** an increase or rise
UPSILON	*n* pl. **-S** a Greek letter		**UPTIGHT**	*adj* nervous
UPSIZE	*v* **-SIZED, -SIZING, -SIZES** to increase in size		**UPTILT**	*v* **-ED, -ING, -S** to tilt upward
UPSKILL	*v* **-ED, -ING, -S** to improve the job skills of someone		**UPTIME**	*n* pl. **-S** the time during which machinery is functioning
UPSLOPE	*n* pl. **-S** an upward slope		**UPTORE**	past tense of uptear
UPSOAR	*v* **-ED, -ING, -S** to soar upward		**UPTORN**	past participle of uptear
UPSPRING	*v* **-SPRANG** or **-SPRUNG, -SPRINGING, -SPRINGS** to spring up		**UPTOSS**	*v* **-ED, -ING, -ES** to toss upward
			UPTOWN	*n* pl. **-S** the upper part of a city
UPSTAGE	*v* **-STAGED, -STAGING, -STAGES** to outdo theatrically		**UPTOWNER**	*n* pl. **-S** one that lives uptown
UPSTAGER	*n* pl. **-S** one that upstages		**UPTREND**	*n* pl. **-S** a tendency upward or toward growth
UPSTAIR	*adj* pertaining to an upper floor		**UPTURN**	*v* **-ED, -ING, -S** to turn up or over
UPSTAIRS	*adv* up the stairs		**UPWAFT**	*v* **-ED, -ING, -S** to waft upward
UPSTAND	*v* **-STOOD, -STANDING, -STANDS** to stand up on one's feet		**UPWARD**	*adv* toward a higher place or position **UPWARDLY** *adv*
UPSTARE	*v* **-STARED, -STARING, -STARES** to stare upward		**UPWARDS**	*adv* upward
UPSTART	*v* **-ED, -ING, -S** to spring up suddenly		**UPWELL**	*v* **-ED, -ING, -S** to well up
UPSTATE	*n* pl. **-S** the northern region of a state		**UPWIND**	*n* pl. **-S** a wind that blows against one's course
UPSTATER	*n* pl. **-S** an inhabitant of an upstate region		**URACIL**	*n* pl. **-S** a chemical compound
			URAEMIA	*n* pl. **-S** uremia **URAEMIC** *adj*
UPSTEP	*v* **-STEPPED, -STEPPING, -STEPS** to step up		**URAEUS**	*n* pl. **URAEUSES** or **URAEI** the figure of the sacred serpent on the headdress of ancient Egyptian rulers
UPSTIR	*v* **-STIRRED, -STIRRING, -STIRS** to stir up			
UPSTOOD	past tense of upstand		**URALITE**	*n* pl. **-S** a mineral **URALITIC** *adj*
UPSTREAM	*adv* toward the source of a stream		**URANIA**	*n* pl. **-S** uranium dioxide
UPSTROKE	*n* pl. **-S** an upward stroke		**URANIC**	*adj* pertaining to uranium
UPSURGE	*v* **-SURGED, -SURGING, -SURGES** to surge up		**URANIDE**	*n* pl. **-S** uranium
			URANISM	*n* pl. **-S** homosexuality
UPSWEEP	*v* **-SWEPT, -SWEEPING, -SWEEPS** to sweep upward		**URANITE**	*n* pl. **-S** a mineral **URANITIC** *adj*
UPSWELL	*v* **-SWELLED, -SWOLLEN, -SWELLING, -SWELLS** to swell up		**URANIUM**	*n* pl. **-S** a radioactive element
			URANOUS	*adj* pertaining to uranium
UPSWING	*v* **-SWUNG, -SWINGING, -SWINGS** to swing upward		**URANYL**	*n* pl. **-S** a bivalent radical **URANYLIC** *adj*
UPTAKE	*n* pl. **-S** an upward ventilating shaft		**URARE**	*n* pl. **-S** curare
UPTALK	*n* pl. **-S** a manner of ending a declarative sentence with a rising intonation		**URARI**	*n* pl. **-S** curare
			URASE	*n* pl. **-S** urease
			URATE	*n* pl. **-S** a chemical salt **URATIC** *adj*

URB	*n* pl. **-S** an urban area	**URIC**	*adj* pertaining to urine
URBAN	*adj* pertaining to a city	**URIDINE**	*n* pl. **-S** a chemical compound
URBANE	*adj* **-BANER, -BANEST** refined and elegant **URBANELY** *adv*	**URINAL**	*n* pl. **-S** a fixture used for urinating
		URINARY	*n* pl. **-NARIES** a urinal
URBANISE	*v* **-ISED, -ISING, -ISES** to urbanize	**URINATE**	*v* **-NATED, -NATING, -NATES** to discharge urine
URBANISM	*n* pl. **-S** the lifestyle of city dwellers		
URBANIST	*n* pl. **-S** a specialist in city planning	**URINATOR**	*n* pl. **-S** one that urinates
URBANITE	*n* pl. **-S** one who lives in a city	**URINE**	*n* pl. **-S** a liquid containing body wastes
URBANITY	*n* pl. **-TIES** the quality of being urbane	**URINEMIA**	*n* pl. **-S** uremia **URINEMIC** *adj*
URBANIZE	*v* **-IZED, -IZING, -IZES** to cause to take on urban characteristics	**URINOSE**	*adj* pertaining to urine
		URINOUS	*adj* pertaining to urine
URBIA	*n* pl. **-S** cities collectively	**URN**	*n* pl. **-S** a type of vase **URNLIKE** *adj*
URCHIN	*n* pl. **-S** a mischievous boy		
URD	*n* pl. **-S** an annual bean grown in India	**UROBOROS**	*n* pl. **-ES** a circular symbol of a snake or dragon swallowing its own tail **UROBORIC** *adj*
UREA	*n* pl. **-S** a chemical compound **UREAL** *adj*	**UROCHORD**	*n* pl. **-S** a rodlike structure in certain lower vertebrates
UREASE	*n* pl. **-S** an enzyme		
UREDIA	pl. of uredium	**URODELE**	*n* pl. **-S** a type of amphibian
UREDIAL	*adj* pertaining to a uredium	**UROGRAM**	*n* pl. **-S** an X-ray of part of the urinary tract
UREDINIA	*n/pl* uredia		
UREDIUM	*n* pl. **-DIA** a spore-producing organ of certain fungi	**UROLITH**	*n* pl. **-S** a concretion in the urinary tract
UREDO	*n* pl. **-DOS** a skin irritation	**UROLOGY**	*n* pl. **-GIES** the branch of medicine dealing with the urinary tract **UROLOGIC** *adj*
UREIC	*adj* pertaining to urea		
UREIDE	*n* pl. **-S** a chemical compound	**UROPOD**	*n* pl. **-S** an abdominal limb of an arthropod **UROPODAL** *adj*
UREMIA	*n* pl. **-S** an abnormal condition of the blood **UREMIC** *adj*	**UROPYGIA**	*n/pl* the humps from which birds' tail feathers grow
URETER	*n* pl. **-S** the duct that conveys urine from the kidney to the bladder **URETERAL, URETERIC** *adj*	**UROSCOPY**	*n* pl. **-PIES** analysis of the urine as a means of diagnosis
		UROSTYLE	*n* pl. **-S** a part of the vertebral column of frogs and toads
URETHAN	*n* pl. **-S** urethane	**URP**	*v* **-ED, -ING, -S** to vomit
URETHANE	*n* pl. **-S** a chemical compound	**URSA**	*n* pl. **-SAE** a female bear
URETHRA	*n* pl. **-THRAS** or **-THRAE** the duct through which urine is discharged from the bladder **URETHRAL** *adj*	**URSID**	*n* pl. **-S** a mammal of the family Ursidae
		URSIFORM	*adj* having the form of a bear
URETIC	*adj* pertaining to urine	**URSINE**	*adj* pertaining to a bear
URGE	*v* **URGED, URGING, URGES** to force forward	**URTEXT**	*n* pl. **-TEXTS** or **-TEXTE** the original text
URGENCY	*n* pl. **-CIES** the quality of being urgent	**URTICANT**	*n* pl. **-S** an urticating substance
URGENT	*adj* requiring immediate attention **URGENTLY** *adv*	**URTICATE**	*v* **-CATED, -CATING, -CATES** to cause itching or stinging
URGER	*n* pl. **-S** one that urges		
URGING	*n* pl. **-S** an attempt to persuade someone to do something	**URUS**	*n* pl. **-ES** an extinct European ox
		URUSHIOL	*n* pl. **-S** a toxic liquid
URGINGLY	*adv* in an urging manner	**US**	*pron* the objective case of the pronoun we
URIAL	*n* pl. **-S** a wild Asian sheep		

USABLE	*adj* capable of being used **USABLY** *adv*
USAGE	*n* pl. **-S** a firmly established and generally accepted practice or procedure
USANCE	*n* pl. **-S** usage
USAUNCE	*n* pl. **-S** usance
USE	*v* **USED, USING, USES** to put into service
USEABLE	*adj* usable **USEABLY** *adv*
USEFUL	*adj* serving a purpose **USEFULLY** *adv*
USELESS	*adj* serving no purpose
USER	*n* pl. **-S** one that uses
USERNAME	*n* pl. **-S** an identifying sequence of characters used for logging on to a computer system
USHER	*v* **-ED, -ING, -S** to conduct to a place
USING	present participle of use
USNEA	*n* pl. **-S** any of a genus of lichens
USQUABAE	*n* pl. **-S** usquebae
USQUE	*n* pl. **-S** usquebae
USQUEBAE	*n* pl. **-S** whiskey
USTULATE	*adj* scorched
USUAL	*n* pl. **-S** something that is usual (ordinary)
USUALLY	*adv* ordinarily
USUFRUCT	*n* pl. **-S** the legal right to use another's property so long as it is not damaged or altered
USURER	*n* pl. **-S** one that practices usury
USURIES	pl. of usury
USURIOUS	*adj* practicing usury
USURP	*v* **-ED, -ING, -S** to seize and hold without legal authority
USURPER	*n* pl. **-S** one that usurps
USURY	*n* pl. **-RIES** the lending of money at an exorbitant interest rate
UT	*n* pl. **-S** the musical tone C in the French solmization system now replaced by do
UTA	*n* pl. **-S** any of a genus of large lizards
UTE	*n* pl. **-S** a utility vehicle

UTENSIL	*n* pl. **-S** a useful implement
UTERUS	*n* pl. **UTERUSES** or **UTERI** an organ of female mammals **UTERINE** *adj*
UTILE	*n* pl. **-S** an African hardwood tree
UTILIDOR	*n* pl. **-S** an insulated system of pipes for use in arctic regions
UTILISE	*v* **-LISED, -LISING, -LISES** to utilize
UTILISER	*n* pl. **-S** utilizer
UTILITY	*n* pl. **-TIES** the quality of being useful
UTILIZE	*v* **-LIZED, -LIZING, -LIZES** to make use of
UTILIZER	*n* pl. **-S** one that utilizes
UTMOST	*n* pl. **-S** the greatest degree or amount
UTOPIA	*n* pl. **-S** a place of ideal perfection
UTOPIAN	*n* pl. **-S** one who believes in the perfectibility of human society
UTOPISM	*n* pl. **-S** the body of ideals or principles of a utopian
UTOPIST	*n* pl. **-S** a utopian
UTRICLE	*n* pl. **-S** a saclike cavity in the inner ear
UTRICULI	*n/pl* utricles
UTTER	*v* **-ED, -ING, -S** to give audible expression to
UTTERER	*n* pl. **-S** one that utters
UTTERLY	*adv* totally
UVEA	*n* pl. **-S** a layer of the eye **UVEAL** *adj*
UVEITIS	*n* pl. **-ITISES** inflammation of the uvea **UVEITIC** *adj*
UVEOUS	*adj* pertaining to the uvea
UVULA	*n* pl. **-LAS** or **-LAE** the pendent, fleshy portion of the soft palate
UVULAR	*n* pl. **-S** a uvularly produced sound
UVULARLY	*adv* with the use of the uvula
UVULITIS	*n* pl. **-TISES** inflammation of the uvula
UXORIAL	*adj* pertaining to a wife
UXORIOUS	*adj* excessively submissive or devoted to one's wife

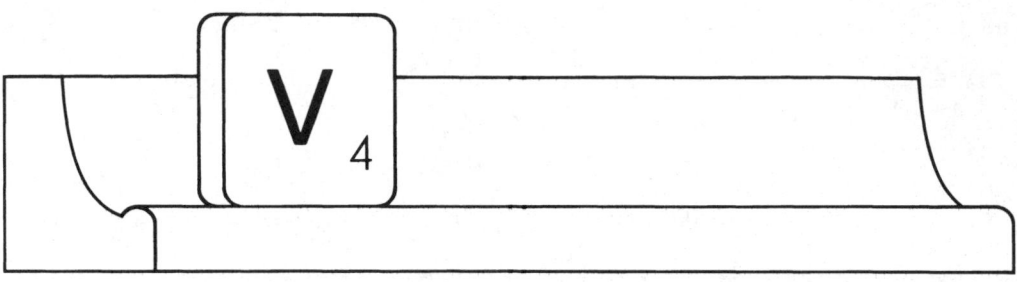

V ₄

VAC	*n* pl. **-S** a vacuum cleaner
VACANCY	*n* pl. **-CIES** the quality or state of being vacant
VACANT	*adj* empty **VACANTLY** *adv*
VACATE	*v* **-CATED, -CATING, -CATES** to make vacant
VACATION	*v* **-ED, -ING, -S** to take a vacation (a period of time devoted to rest and relaxation)
VACCINA	*n* pl. **-S** vaccinia
VACCINE	*n* pl. **-S** a preparation given to produce immunity to a specific disease **VACCINAL** *adj*
VACCINEE	*n* pl. **-S** one that is vaccinated
VACCINIA	*n* pl. **-S** cowpox
VACUA	a pl. of vacuum
VACUITY	*n* pl. **-ITIES** an empty space
VACUOLE	*n* pl. **-S** a small cavity in organic tissue **VACUOLAR** *adj*
VACUOUS	*adj* empty
VACUUM	*n* pl. **VACUUMS** or **VACUA** a space entirely devoid of matter
VACUUM	*v* **-ED, -ING, -S** to use a device that cleans by suction
VADOSE	*adj* located above the permanent groundwater level
VAGABOND	*v* **-ED, -ING, -S** to live like a vagabond (a vagrant)
VAGAL	*adj* pertaining to the vagus nerve **VAGALLY** *adv*
VAGARY	*n* pl. **-RIES** a whim
VAGI	pl. of vagus
VAGILE	*adj* free to move about
VAGILITY	*n* pl. **-TIES** freedom of movement
VAGINA	*n* pl. **-NAS** or **-NAE** the passage leading from the uterus to the vulva **VAGINAL** *adj*
VAGINATE	*adj* enclosed in a sheath
VAGOTOMY	*n* pl. **-MIES** surgical division of the vagus nerve
VAGRANCY	*n* pl. **-CIES** the state of being a vagrant
VAGRANT	*n* pl. **-S** a wanderer with no apparent means of support
VAGROM	*adj* wandering
VAGUE	*adj* **VAGUER, VAGUEST** not clearly expressed or understood **VAGUISH** *adj* **VAGUELY** *adv*
VAGUS	*n* pl. **-GI** a cranial nerve
VAHINE	*n* pl. **-S** wahine
VAIL	*v* **-ED, -ING, -S** to lower
VAIN	*adj* **VAINER, VAINEST** filled with undue admiration for oneself **VAINLY** *adv*
VAINNESS	*n* pl. **-ES** the quality or state of being vain
VAIR	*n* pl. **-S** a fur used for lining and trimming medieval garments
VAKEEL	*n* pl. **-S** a native lawyer in India
VAKIL	*n* pl. **-S** vakeel
VALANCE	*v* **-LANCED, -LANCING, -LANCES** to furnish with a short drapery
VALE	*n* pl. **-S** a valley
VALENCE	*n* pl. **-S** the degree of combining power of an element or radical
VALENCIA	*n* pl. **-S** a woven fabric
VALENCY	*n* pl. **-CIES** valence
VALERATE	*n* pl. **-S** a chemical salt
VALERIAN	*n* pl. **-S** a perennial herb **VALERIC** *adj*
VALET	*v* **-ED, -ING, -S** to act as a personal servant to
VALGUS	*n* pl. **-ES** the position of a joint that is abnormally turned outward **VALGOID** *adj*
VALIANCE	*n* pl. **-S** valor
VALIANCY	*n* pl. **-CIES** valor

VALIANT	*n* pl. **-S** a courageous person
VALID	*adj* based on evidence that can be supported
VALIDATE	*v* **-DATED, -DATING, -DATES** to give legal force to
VALIDITY	*n* pl. **-TIES** the quality or state of being valid
VALIDLY	*adv* in a valid manner
VALINE	*n* pl. **-S** an amino acid
VALISE	*n* pl. **-S** a small piece of hand luggage
VALKYR	*n* pl. **-S** valkyrie
VALKYRIE	*n* pl. **-S** a maiden in Norse mythology
VALLATE	*adj* bordered by a raised edge
VALLEY	*n* pl. **-LEYS** a depression of the earth's surface **VALLEYED** *adj*
VALLUM	*n* pl. **-S** a defensive wall of earth and stone
VALONIA	*n* pl. **-S** a substance obtained from dried acorn cups and used in tanning and dyeing
VALOR	*n* pl. **-S** courage
VALORISE	*v* **-ISED, -ISING, -ISES** to valorize
VALORIZE	*v* **-IZED, -IZING, -IZES** to establish and maintain the price of by governmental action
VALOROUS	*adj* courageous
VALOUR	*n* pl. **-S** valor
VALSE	*n* pl. **-S** a concert waltz
VALUABLE	*n* pl. **-S** a possession of value
VALUABLY	*adv* with value
VALUATE	*v* **-ATED, -ATING, -ATES** to appraise
VALUATOR	*n* pl. **-S** one that valuates
VALUE	*v* **-UED, -UING, -UES** to estimate the value (the quality that renders a thing useful or desirable) of
VALUER	*n* pl. **-S** one that values
VALUTA	*n* pl. **-S** the agreed or exchange value of a currency
VALVAL	*adj* resembling or pertaining to a valve
VALVAR	*adj* valval
VALVATE	*adj* having valves or parts resembling valves
VALVE	*v* **VALVED, VALVING, VALVES** to provide with a valve (a device for controlling the flow of a liquid or gas)
VALVELET	*n* pl. **-S** a small valve
VALVULA	*n* pl. **-LAE** valvule
VALVULAR	*adj* pertaining to a valve
VALVULE	*n* pl. **-S** a small valve
VAMBRACE	*n* pl. **-S** a piece of armor for the forearm
VAMOOSE	*v* **-MOOSED, -MOOSING, -MOOSES** to leave quickly
VAMOSE	*v* **-MOSED, -MOSING, -MOSES** to vamoose
VAMP	*v* **-ED, -ING, -S** to repair or patch
VAMPER	*n* pl. **-S** one that vamps
VAMPIRE	*n* pl. **-S** a reanimated corpse believed to feed on sleeping persons' blood **VAMPIRIC** *adj*
VAMPISH	*adj* seductive
VAMPLATE	*n* pl. **-S** a circular metal plate on a spear or lance for protecting the hand
VAMPY	*adj* **VAMPIER, VAMPIEST** seductive
VAN	*v* **VANNED, VANNING, VANS** to transport in a van (a type of motor vehicle)
VANADATE	*n* pl. **-S** a chemical salt
VANADIUM	*n* pl. **-S** a metallic element **VANADIC, VANADOUS** *adj*
VANDA	*n* pl. **-S** a tropical orchid
VANDAL	*n* pl. **-S** one who willfully destroys or defaces property **VANDALIC** *adj*
VANDYKE	*n* pl. **-S** a short, pointed beard **VANDYKED** *adj*
VANE	*n* pl. **-S** a device for showing the direction of the wind **VANED** *adj*
VANG	*n* pl. **-S** a rope on a ship
VANGUARD	*n* pl. **-S** the forefront of a movement
VANILLA	*n* pl. **-S** a flavoring extract **VANILLIC** *adj*
VANILLIN	*n* pl. **-S** a chemical compound used in flavoring
VANISH	*v* **-ED, -ING, -ES** to disappear
VANISHER	*n* pl. **-S** one that vanishes
VANITAS	*n* pl. **-ES** a still-life painting having symbols of death or change
VANITORY	*n* pl. **-RIES** a combined dressing table and basin
VANITY	*n* pl. **-TIES** inflated pride in oneself **VANITIED** *adj*
VANLOAD	*n* pl. **-S** the quantity that a van can carry

VANMAN *n pl.* **-MEN** a person who drives a van

VANNED past tense of van

VANNER *n pl.* **-S** a person who owns a van

VANNING present participle of van

VANPOOL *n pl.* **-S** an arrangement whereby several commuters travel in one van

VANQUISH *v* **-ED, -ING, -ES** to defeat in battle

VANTAGE *n pl.* **-S** superiority over a competitor

VANWARD *adv* toward the front

VAPE *v* **VAPED, VAPING, VAPES** to inhale vapor from an electronic device

VAPER *n pl.* **-S** a person who vapes

VAPID *adj* insipid **VAPIDLY** *adv*

VAPIDITY *n pl.* **-TIES** the quality or state of being vapid

VAPOR *v* **-ED, -ING, -S** to emit vapor (visible floating moisture)

VAPORER *n pl.* **-S** one that vapors

VAPORING *n pl.* **-S** boastful talk

VAPORISE *v* **-ISED, -ISING, -ISES** to vaporize

VAPORISH *adj* resembling vapor

VAPORIZE *v* **-IZED, -IZING, -IZES** to convert into vapor

VAPOROUS *adj* vaporish

VAPORY *adj* vaporish

VAPOUR *v* **-ED, -ING, -S** to vapor

VAPOURER *n pl.* **-S** vaporer

VAPOURY *adj* vapory

VAQUERO *n pl.* **-ROS** a cowboy

VAR *n pl.* **-S** a unit of reactive power

VARA *n pl.* **-S** a Spanish unit of length

VARACTOR *n pl.* **-S** a capacitor with variable capacitance

VAREC *n pl.* **-S** seaweed

VARENYKY *n/pl* Ukrainian stuffed dumplings

VARIA *n pl.* **-S** a miscellany of literary works

VARIABLE *n pl.* **-S** something that varies

VARIABLY *adv* in a varying manner

VARIANCE *n pl.* **-S** a license to perform an act contrary to the usual rule

VARIANT *n pl.* **-S** a variable

VARIATE *v* **-ATED, -ATING, -ATES** to vary

VARICEAL *adj* pertaining to or involving a varix

VARICES pl. of varix

VARICOSE *adj* abnormally swollen or dilated

VARIED past tense of vary

VARIEDLY *adv* in a varied manner

VARIER *n pl.* **-S** one that varies

VARIES present 3d person sing. of vary

VARIETAL *n pl.* **-S** a wine designated by the variety of grape

VARIETY *n pl.* **-ETIES** something differing from others of the same general kind

VARIFORM *adj* having various forms

VARIOLA *n pl.* **-S** smallpox **VARIOLAR** *adj*

VARIOLE *n pl.* **-S** a foveola

VARIORUM *n pl.* **-S** an edition containing various versions of a text

VARIOUS *adj* of diverse kinds

VARISTOR *n pl.* **-S** a type of electrical resistor

VARIX *n pl.* **VARICES** a varicose vein

VARLET *n pl.* **-S** a knave

VARLETRY *n pl.* **-RIES** a group of common people

VARMENT *n pl.* **-S** varmint

VARMINT *n pl.* **-S** an animal considered to be a pest

VARNA *n pl.* **-S** any of the four main Hindu social classes

VARNISH *v* **-ED, -ING, -ES** to give a glossy appearance to

VARNISHY *adj* glossy

VAROOM *v* **-ED, -ING, -S** to vroom

VARROA *n pl.* **-S** a mite that is a parasite of the honeybee

VARSITY *n pl.* **-TIES** the principal team representing a university, college, or school in any activity

VARUS *n pl.* **-ES** a malformation of a bone or joint

VARVE *n pl.* **-S** a deposit of sedimentary material **VARVED** *adj*

VARY *v* **VARIED, VARYING, VARIES** to become or make different

VAS *n pl.* **VASA** an anatomical duct **VASAL** *adj*

VASCULAR *adj* pertaining to ducts that convey body fluids

VASCULUM *n pl.* **-LUMS** or **-LA** a box used to hold plant specimens

VASE	*n* pl. **-S** a rounded, decorative container **VASELIKE** *adj*
VASEFUL	*n* pl. **-S** as much as a vase can hold
VASIFORM	*adj* having the form of a vase
VASOTOMY	*n* pl. **-MIES** a surgical cutting of the vas deferens
VASSAL	*n* pl. **-S** a person granted the use of land by a feudal lord in return for homage and allegiance
VAST	*adj* **VASTER, VASTEST** of great extent or size
VAST	*n* pl. **-S** a vast space
VASTIER	comparative of vasty
VASTIEST	superlative of vasty
VASTITY	*n* pl. **-ITIES** vastness
VASTLY	*adv* to a vast extent or degree
VASTNESS	*n* pl. **-ES** the quality or state of being vast
VASTY	*adj* **VASTIER, VASTIEST** vast
VAT	*v* **VATTED, VATTING, VATS** to put into a vat (a large container for holding liquids)
VATFUL	*n* pl. **-S** as much as a vat can hold
VATIC	*adj* pertaining to a prophet
VATICAL	*adj* vatic
VATICIDE	*n* pl. **-S** the killing of a prophet
VATTED	past tense of vat
VATTING	present participle of vat
VATU	*n* pl. **-S** a monetary unit of Vanuatu
VAU	*n* pl. **-S** vav
VAULT	*v* **-ED, -ING, -S** to provide with a vault (an arched ceiling)
VAULTER	*n* pl. **-S** one that leaps
VAULTING	*n* pl. **-S** the structure forming a vault
VAULTY	*adj* **VAULTIER, VAULTIEST** resembling a vault
VAUNT	*v* **-ED, -ING, -S** to brag
VAUNTER	*n* pl. **-S** one that vaunts
VAUNTFUL	*adj* boastful
VAUNTIE	*adj* boastful
VAUNTY	*adj* vauntie
VAV	*n* pl. **-S** a Hebrew letter
VAVASOR	*n* pl. **-S** a high-ranking vassal
VAVASORY	*n* pl. **-RIES** the estate of a vavasor
VAVASOUR	*n* pl. **-S** vavasor
VAVASSOR	*n* pl. **-S** vavasor

VAW	*n* pl. **-S** vav
VAWARD	*n* pl. **-S** the foremost part
VAWNTIE	*adj* vaunty
VEAL	*v* **-ED, -ING, -S** to kill and prepare a calf for food
VEALER	*n* pl. **-S** a calf raised for food
VEALY	*adj* **VEALIER, VEALIEST** immature
VECTOR	*v* **-ED, -ING, -S** to guide in flight by means of radioed directions
VEDALIA	*n* pl. **-S** an Australian ladybug
VEDETTE	*n* pl. **-S** a small boat used for scouting
VEE	*n* pl. **-S** the letter V
VEEJAY	*n* pl. **-JAYS** an announcer on a program of music videos
VEENA	*n* pl. **-S** vina
VEEP	*n* pl. **-S** a vice president
VEEPEE	*n* pl. **-S** veep
VEER	*v* **-ED, -ING, -S** to change direction
VEERY	*n* pl. **-RIES** a songbird
VEG	*v* **VEGGED, VEGGING, VEGES** or **VEGGES** to spend time idly
VEGA	*n* pl. **-S** a large plain or valley
VEGAN	*n* pl. **-S** one that eats only plant products
VEGANISM	*n* pl. **-S** the practice of eating only plant products
VEGETAL	*adj* pertaining to plants
VEGETANT	*adj* characteristic of plant life
VEGETATE	*v* **-TATED, -TATING, -TATES** to grow in the manner of a plant
VEGETE	*adj* healthy
VEGETIST	*n* pl. **-S** one that eats only plant products
VEGETIVE	*adj* growing or capable of growing
VEGGIE	*n* pl. **-S** a vegetable
VEGIE	*n* pl. **-S** veggie
VEHEMENT	*adj* ardent
VEHICLE	*n* pl. **-S** a device used as a means of conveyance
VEIL	*v* **-ED, -ING, -S** to provide with a veil (a piece of sheer fabric worn over the face)
VEILEDLY	*adv* in a disguised manner
VEILER	*n* pl. **-S** one that veils
VEILING	*n* pl. **-S** a veil
VEILLESS	*adj* not veiled

VEILLIKE	*adj* resembling a veil
VEIN	*v* **-ED, -ING, -S** to fill with veins (tubular blood vessels)
VEINAL	*adj* of or pertaining to the veins
VEINER	*n* pl. **-S** a tool used in wood carving
VEINIER	comparative of veiny
VEINIEST	superlative of veiny
VEINING	*n* pl. **-S** a network of veins
VEINLESS	*adj* having no veins
VEINLET	*n* pl. **-S** a small vein
VEINLIKE	*adj* resembling a vein
VEINOUS	*adj* having prominent veins
VEINULE	*n* pl. **-S** venule
VEINULET	*n* pl. **-S** venule
VEINY	*adj* **VEINIER, VEINIEST** full of veins
VELA	pl. of velum
VELAMEN	*n* pl. **-MINA** a velum
VELAR	*n* pl. **-S** a kind of speech sound
VELARIUM	*n* pl. **-IA** an awning over an ancient Roman theater
VELARIZE	*v* **-IZED, -IZING, -IZES** to pronounce with the back of the tongue touching the soft palate
VELATE	*adj* having a velum
VELD	*n* pl. **-S** veldt
VELDT	*n* pl. **-S** a grassland of southern Africa
VELIGER	*n* pl. **-S** a larval stage of certain mollusks
VELITES	*n/pl* foot soldiers of ancient Rome
VELLEITY	*n* pl. **-ITIES** a very low degree of desire
VELLUM	*n* pl. **-S** a fine parchment
VELOCE	*adv* rapidly — used as a musical direction
VELOCITY	*n* pl. **-TIES** rapidity of motion
VELOUR	*n* pl. **-S** a fabric resembling velvet
VELOUTE	*n* pl. **-S** a type of sauce
VELUM	*n* pl. **-LA** a thin membranous covering or partition
VELURE	*v* **-LURED, -LURING, -LURES** to smooth with a velvet or silk pad, as a hat
VELVERET	*n* pl. **-S** a fabric resembling velvet
VELVET	*n* pl. **-S** a soft, smooth fabric **VELVETED** *adj*

VELVETY	*adj* **-VETIER, -VETIEST** resembling velvet in texture
VENA	*n* pl. **-NAE** a vein
VENAL	*adj* open to bribery **VENALLY** *adv*
VENALITY	*n* pl. **-TIES** the quality or state of being venal
VENATIC	*adj* pertaining to hunting
VENATION	*n* pl. **-S** an arrangement of veins
VEND	*v* **-ED, -ING, -S** to sell
VENDABLE	*n* pl. **-S** vendible
VENDACE	*n* pl. **-S** a European fish
VENDEE	*n* pl. **-S** a buyer
VENDER	*n* pl. **-S** vendor
VENDETTA	*n* pl. **-S** a feud between two families
VENDEUSE	*n* pl. **-S** a saleswoman
VENDIBLE	*n* pl. **-S** a salable article
VENDIBLY	*adv* salably
VENDOR	*n* pl. **-S** a seller
VENDUE	*n* pl. **-S** a public sale
VENEER	*v* **-ED, -ING, -S** to overlay with thin layers of material
VENEERER	*n* pl. **-S** one that veneers
VENENATE	*v* **-NATED, -NATING, -NATES** to poison
VENENE	*n* pl. **-S** venin
VENENOSE	*adj* poisonous
VENERATE	*v* **-ATED, -ATING, -ATES** to revere
VENEREAL	*adj* involving the genital organs
VENERY	*n* pl. **-ERIES** sexual intercourse
VENETIAN	*n* pl. **-S** a flexible window screen
VENGE	*v* **VENGED, VENGING, VENGES** to avenge
VENGEFUL	*adj* seeking to avenge
VENIAL	*adj* easily excused or forgiven **VENIALLY** *adv*
VENIN	*n* pl. **-S** a toxin found in snake venom
VENINE	*n* pl. **-S** venin
VENIRE	*n* pl. **-S** a type of judicial writ
VENISON	*n* pl. **-S** the edible flesh of a deer
VENOGRAM	*n* pl. **-S** a roentgenogram of a vein
VENOLOGY	*n* pl. **-GIES** the study of veins
VENOM	*v* **-ED, -ING, -S** to inject with venom (a poisonous secretion of certain animals)
VENOMER	*n* pl. **-S** one that venoms

VENOMOUS   *adj* poisonous

VENOSE   *adj* venous

VENOSITY   *n* pl. **-TIES** the quality or state of being venous

VENOUS   *adj* full of veins **VENOUSLY** *adv*

VENT   *v* **-ED, -ING, -S** to provide with a vent (an opening for the escape of gas or liquid)

VENTAGE   *n* pl. **-S** a small opening

VENTAIL   *n* pl. **-S** the adjustable front of a medieval helmet

VENTER   *n* pl. **-S** the abdomen

VENTLESS   *adj* having no vent

VENTRAL   *n* pl. **-S** a fin located on the underside of a fish

VENTURE   *v* **-TURED, -TURING, -TURES** to risk

VENTURER   *n* pl. **-S** one that ventures

VENTURI   *n* pl. **-S** a device for measuring the flow of a fluid

VENUE   *n* pl. **-S** the locale of an event

VENULE   *n* pl. **-S** a small vein **VENULAR, VENULOSE, VENULOUS** *adj*

VERA   *adj* very

VERACITY   *n* pl. **-TIES** conformity to truth

VERANDA   *n* pl. **-S** a type of porch

VERANDAH   *n* pl. **-S** veranda

VERATRIA   *n* pl. **-S** veratrin

VERATRIN   *n* pl. **-S** a poisonous mixture of alkaloids

VERATRUM   *n* pl. **-S** a poisonous herb

VERB   *n* pl. **-S** a word used to express an act, occurrence, or mode of being

VERBAL   *n* pl. **-S** a word derived from a verb

VERBALLY   *adv* in a spoken manner

VERBATIM   *adv* word for word

VERBENA   *n* pl. **-S** a flowering plant

VERBIAGE   *n* pl. **-S** an excess of words

VERBID   *n* pl. **-S** a verbal

VERBIFY   *v* **-FIED, -FYING, -FIES** to use as a verb

VERBILE   *n* pl. **-S** one whose mental imagery consists of words

VERBLESS   *adj* lacking a verb

VERBOSE   *adj* wordy

VERBOTEN   *adj* forbidden

VERDANCY   *n* pl. **-CIES** the quality or state of being verdant

VERDANT   *adj* green with vegetation

VERDERER   *n* pl. **-S** an officer in charge of the royal forests of England

VERDEROR   *n* pl. **-S** verderer

VERDICT   *n* pl. **-S** the decision at the end of a legal proceeding

VERDIN   *n* pl. **-S** a small bird

VERDITER   *n* pl. **-S** a blue or green pigment

VERDURE   *n* pl. **-S** green vegetation **VERDURED** *adj*

VERECUND   *adj* shy

VERGE   *v* **VERGED, VERGING, VERGES** to come near

VERGENCE   *n* pl. **-S** a movement of one eye in relation to the other

VERGER   *n* pl. **-S** a church official

VERGLAS   *n* pl. **-ES** a thin coating of ice on rock

VERIDIC   *adj* truthful

VERIER   comparative of very

VERIEST   superlative of very

VERIFIER   *n* pl. **-S** one that verifies

VERIFY   *v* **-FIED, -FYING, -FIES** to prove to be true

VERILY   *adv* in truth

VERISM   *n* pl. **-S** realism in art or literature **VERISTIC** *adj*

VERISMO   *n* pl. **-MOS** verism

VERIST   *n* pl. **-S** one who practices verism

VERITAS   *n* pl. **-TATES** truth

VERITE   *n* pl. **-S** the technique of filming so as to convey candid realism

VERITY   *n* pl. **-TIES** truth

VERJUICE   *n* pl. **-S** the juice of sour or unripe fruit

VERJUS   *n* pl. **-ES** verjuice

VERMEIL   *n* pl. **-S** a red color

VERMES   pl. of vermis

VERMIAN   *adj* pertaining to worms

VERMIN   *n* pl. **VERMIN** small, common, harmful, or objectionable animals

VERMIS   *n* pl. **-MES** a part of the brain

VERMOULU   *adj* eaten by worms

VERMOUTH   *n* pl. **-S** a liqueur

VERMUTH   *n* pl. **-S** vermouth

VERNACLE   *n* pl. **-S** vernicle

VERNAL   *adj* pertaining to spring **VERNALLY** *adv*

VERNICLE *n* pl. **-S** veronica

VERNIER *n* pl. **-S** an auxiliary scale used with a main scale to obtain fine measurements

VERNIX *n* pl. **-ES** a fatty substance covering the skin of a fetus

VERONAL *n* pl. **-S** a sedative drug

VERONICA *n* pl. **-S** a handkerchief bearing the image of Christ's face

VERRUCA *n* pl. **-CAS** or **-CAE** a wart

VERSAL *n* pl. **-S** an ornate capital letter used to begin a verse or paragraph

VERSANT *n* pl. **-S** the slope of a mountain or mountain chain

VERSE *v* **VERSED, VERSING, VERSES** to versify

VERSELET *n* pl. **-S** a short group of lines that form a unit in a poem or song

VERSEMAN *n* pl. **-MEN** one who versifies

VERSER *n* pl. **-S** a verseman

VERSET *n* pl. **-S** a versicle

VERSICLE *n* pl. **-S** a short line of metrical writing

VERSIFY *v* **-FIED, -FYING, -FIES** to change from prose into metrical form

VERSIN *n* pl. **-S** versine

VERSINE *n* pl. **-S** a trigonometric function of an angle

VERSING present participle of verse

VERSION *v* **-ED, -ING, -S** to create a new account or description from a particular point of view

VERSO *n* pl. **-SOS** a left-hand page of a book

VERST *n* pl. **-S** a Russian measure of distance

VERSTE *n* pl. **-S** verst

VERSUS *prep* against

VERT *n* pl. **-S** the heraldic color green

VERTEBRA *n* pl. **-BRAS** or **-BRAE** any of the bones or segments forming the spinal column

VERTEX *n* pl. **-TEXES** or **-TICES** the highest point of something

VERTICAL *n* pl. **-S** something that is vertical (extending up and down)

VERTICIL *n* pl. **-S** a circular arrangement, as of flowers or leaves, about a point on an axis

VERTIGO *n* pl. **-GOES** or **-GOS** or **-GINES** a disordered state in which the individual or his or her surroundings seem to whirl dizzily

VERTISOL *n* pl. **-S** a type of clayey soil

VERTU *n* pl. **-S** virtu

VERVAIN *n* pl. **-S** a flowering plant

VERVE *n* pl. **-S** vivacity

VERVET *n* pl. **-S** an African monkey

VERY *adj* **VERIER, VERIEST** absolute

VESICA *n* pl. **-CAE** a bladder **VESICAL** *adj*

VESICANT *n* pl. **-S** a chemical warfare agent that induces blistering

VESICATE *v* **-CATED, -CATING, -CATES** to blister

VESICLE *n* pl. **-S** a small bladder

VESICULA *n* pl. **-LAE** a vesicle

VESPER *n* pl. **-S** an evening service, prayer, or song

VESPERAL *n* pl. **-S** a covering for an altar cloth

VESPIARY *n* pl. **-ARIES** a nest of wasps

VESPID *n* pl. **-S** a wasp

VESPINE *adj* pertaining to wasps

VESSEL *n* pl. **-S** a craft for traveling on water **VESSELED** *adj*

VEST *v* **-ED, -ING, -S** to place in the control of

VESTA *n* pl. **-S** a short friction match

VESTAL *n* pl. **-S** a chaste woman

VESTALLY *adv* chastely

VESTEE *n* pl. **-S** a garment worn under a woman's jacket or blouse

VESTIARY *n* pl. **-ARIES** a dressing room

VESTIGE *n* pl. **-S** a visible sign of something that is no longer in existence

VESTIGIA *n/pl* vestiges

VESTING *n* pl. **-S** the right of an employee to share in and withdraw from a pension fund without penalty

VESTLESS *adj* being without a vest

VESTLIKE *adj* resembling a vest (a short, sleeveless garment)

VESTMENT *n* pl. **-S** one of the ceremonial garments of the clergy

VESTRY *n* pl. **-TRIES** a room in which vestments are kept **VESTRAL** *adj*

VESTURAL *adj* pertaining to clothing

VESTURE *v* **-TURED, -TURING, -TURES** to clothe

VESUVIAN	*n* pl. **-S** a mineral	**VIBRATO**	*n* pl. **-TOS** a tremulous or pulsating musical effect
VET	*v* **VETTED, VETTING, VETS** to treat animals medically	**VIBRATOR**	*n* pl. **-S** something that vibrates
VETCH	*n* pl. **-ES** a climbing plant	**VIBRIO**	*n* pl. **-RIOS** any of a genus of bacteria shaped like a comma **VIBRIOID** *adj*
VETERAN	*n* pl. **-S** a former member of the armed forces		
VETIVER	*n* pl. **-S** an Asian grass	**VIBRION**	*n* pl. **-S** vibrio
VETIVERT	*n* pl. **-S** the essential oil of the vetiver	**VIBRISSA**	*n* pl. **-SAE** one of the stiff hairs growing about the mouth of certain mammals
VETO	*v* **-ED, -ING, -ES** to forbid or prevent authoritatively	**VIBRONIC**	*adj* pertaining to changes in molecular energy states resulting from vibrational energy
VETOER	*n* pl. **-S** one that vetoes		
VETTED	past tense of vet	**VIBURNUM**	*n* pl. **-S** a flowering shrub
VETTER	*n* pl. **-S** one that evaluates something for approval	**VICAR**	*n* pl. **-S** a church official
		VICARAGE	*n* pl. **-S** the office of a vicar
VETTING	present participle of vet	**VICARATE**	*n* pl. **-S** vicarage
VEX	*v* **VEXED** or **VEXT, VEXING, VEXES** to annoy	**VICARIAL**	*adj* pertaining to a vicar
VEXATION	*n* pl. **-S** a cause of trouble	**VICARLY**	*adj* vicarial
VEXEDLY	*adv* in a vexed manner	**VICE**	*v* **VICED, VICING, VICES** to vise
VEXER	*n* pl. **-S** one that vexes	**VICELESS**	*adj* having no immoral habits
VEXIL	*n* pl. **-S** vexillum	**VICELIKE**	*adj* viselike
VEXILLUM	*n* pl. **-LA** the web or vane of a feather **VEXILLAR** *adj*	**VICENARY**	*adj* pertaining to the number twenty
VEXINGLY	*adv* in a vexing manner	**VICEROY**	*n* pl. **-ROYS** one who rules as the representative of a sovereign
VEXT	a past tense of vex		
VIA	*prep* by way of	**VICHY**	*n* pl. **-CHIES** a type of mineral water
VIABLE	*adj* capable of living **VIABLY** *adv*		
VIADUCT	*n* pl. **-S** a type of bridge	**VICINAGE**	*n* pl. **-S** vicinity
VIAL	*v* **VIALED, VIALING, VIALS** or **VIALLED, VIALLING, VIALS** to put in a vial (a small container for liquids)	**VICINAL**	*adj* nearby
		VICING	present participle of vice
		VICINITY	*n* pl. **-TIES** the region near or about a place
VIAND	*n* pl. **-S** an article of food	**VICIOUS**	*adj* dangerously aggressive
VIATIC	*adj* pertaining to traveling	**VICOMTE**	*n* pl. **-S** a French nobleman
VIATICAL	*n* pl. **-S** a type of life insurance arrangement	**VICTIM**	*n* pl. **-S** one who suffers from a destructive or injurious action
VIATICUM	*n* pl. **-CUMS** or **-CA** an allowance for traveling expenses	**VICTOR**	*n* pl. **-S** one who defeats an adversary
VIATOR	*n* pl. **-ES** or **-S** a traveler	**VICTORIA**	*n* pl. **-S** a light carriage
VIBE	*n* pl. **-S** a vibration	**VICTORY**	*n* pl. **-RIES** a successful outcome in a contest or struggle
VIBIST	*n* pl. **-S** one who plays the vibraphone	**VICTRESS**	*n* pl. **-ES** a female victor
VIBRANCE	*n* pl. **-S** vibrancy	**VICTUAL**	*v* **-UALED, -UALING, -UALS** or **-UALLED, -UALLING, -UALS** to provide with food
VIBRANCY	*n* pl. **-CIES** the quality or state of being vibrant		
		VICUGNA	*n* pl. **-S** vicuna
VIBRANT	*n* pl. **-S** a sonant	**VICUNA**	*n* pl. **-S** a ruminant mammal
VIBRATE	*v* **-BRATED, -BRATING, -BRATES** to move back and forth rapidly	**VID**	*n* pl. **-S** a video

VIDALIA *n* pl. **-S** a sweet onion of the southern U.S.

VIDE *v* see — used to direct a reader to another item; VIDE is the only form of this verb; it cannot be conjugated

VIDEO *v* **-ED, -ING, -S** to record visual images on magnetic tape or disc

VIDEOCAM *n* pl. **-S** a camera for recording images and usually sound

VIDEOTEX *n* pl. **-ES** an electronic system for transmitting data to a subscriber's video screen

VIDETTE *n* pl. **-S** vedette

VIDICON *n* pl. **-S** a type of television camera tube

VIDIOT *n* pl. **-S** a habitual, undiscriminating viewer of television

VIDUITY *n* pl. **-ITIES** the quality or state of being a widow

VIE *v* **VIED, VYING, VIES** to strive for superiority

VIELLE *n* pl. **-S** a musical instrument played by turning a handle

VIER *n* pl. **-S** one that vies

VIEW *v* **-ED, -ING, -S** to look at **VIEWABLE** *adj*

VIEWBOOK *n* pl. **-S** a promotional booklet with pictures that is published by a college or university

VIEWDATA *n* pl. **VIEWDATA** a videotex

VIEWER *n* pl. **-S** one that views

VIEWIER comparative of viewy

VIEWIEST superlative of viewy

VIEWING *n* pl. **-S** an act of seeing, watching, or looking

VIEWLESS *adj* having no opinions

VIEWPORT *n* pl. **-S** a framed area on a display screen for viewing information

VIEWSHED *n* pl. **-S** the natural environment visible from a viewing point

VIEWY *adj* **VIEWIER, VIEWIEST** showy

VIFF *v* **-ED, -ING, -S** to change direction abruptly of a vertical take-off aircraft

VIG *n* pl. **-S** a vigorish

VIGA *n* pl. **-S** a ceiling beam in Spanish architecture

VIGIA *n* pl. **-S** a warning on a navigational chart

VIGIL *n* pl. **-S** a period of watchfulness maintained during normal sleeping hours

VIGILANT *adj* watchful

VIGNERON *n* pl. **-S** a winegrower

VIGNETTE *v* **-GNETTED, -GNETTING, -GNETTES** to describe briefly

VIGOR *n* pl. **-S** active strength or force

VIGORISH *n* pl. **-ES** a charge paid to a bookie on a bet

VIGOROSO *adv* with emphasis and spirit — used as a musical direction

VIGOROUS *adj* full of vigor

VIGOUR *n* pl. **-S** vigor

VIHUELA *n* pl. **-S** a type of early Spanish guitar

VIKING *n* pl. **-S** a Scandinavian pirate

VILAYET *n* pl. **-S** an administrative division of Turkey

VILE *adj* **VILER, VILEST** morally despicable or physically repulsive **VILELY** *adv*

VILENESS *n* pl. **-ES** the state of being vile

VILIFIER *n* pl. **-S** one that vilifies

VILIFY *v* **-FIED, -FYING, -FIES** to defame

VILIPEND *v* **-ED, -ING, -S** to vilify

VILL *n* pl. **-S** a village

VILLA *n* pl. **-LAS** or **-LAE** an agricultural estate of ancient Rome

VILLADOM *n* pl. **-S** the world constituted by suburban residences and their occupants

VILLAGE *n* pl. **-S** a small community in a rural area

VILLAGER *n* pl. **-S** one who lives in a village

VILLAGEY *adj* pertaining to or characteristic of a village

VILLAIN *n* pl. **-S** a cruelly malicious person

VILLAINY *n* pl. **-LAINIES** conduct characteristic of a villain

VILLATIC *adj* rural

VILLEIN *n* pl. **-S** a type of serf

VILLUS *n* pl. **-LI** one of the hairlike projections found on certain membranes **VILLOSE, VILLOUS** *adj*

VIM *n* pl. **-S** energy

VIMEN *n* pl. **-MINA** a long, flexible branch of a plant **VIMINAL** *adj*

VIN *n* pl. **-S** French wine

VINA	*n* pl. **-S** a stringed instrument of India
VINAL	*n* pl. **-S** a synthetic textile fiber
VINASSE	*n* pl. **-S** a residue left after the distillation of liquor
VINCA	*n* pl. **-S** a flowering plant
VINCIBLE	*adj* capable of being conquered **VINCIBLY** *adv*
VINCULUM	*n* pl. **-LUMS** or **-LA** a unifying bond **VINCULAR** *adj*
VINDALOO	*n* pl. **-LOOS** a curried dish made with meat, garlic, and wine
VINE	*v* **VINED, VINING, VINES** to grow like a vine (a climbing plant)
VINEAL	*adj* vinous
VINEGAR	*n* pl. **-S** a sour liquid used as a condiment or preservative **VINEGARY** *adj*
VINERY	*n* pl. **-ERIES** a place in which grapevines are grown
VINEYARD	*n* pl. **-S** an area planted with grapevines
VINIC	*adj* derived from wine
VINIER	comparative of viny
VINIEST	superlative of viny
VINIFERA	*n* pl. **-S** a European grape
VINIFY	*v* **-FIED, -FYING, -FIES** to convert into wine by fermentation
VINING	present participle of vine
VINO	*n* pl. **-NOS** wine
VINOSITY	*n* pl. **-TIES** the character of a wine
VINOUS	*adj* pertaining to wine **VINOUSLY** *adv*
VINTAGE	*n* pl. **-S** a season's yield of wine from a vineyard
VINTAGER	*n* pl. **-S** one that harvests wine grapes
VINTNER	*n* pl. **-S** a wine merchant
VINY	*adj* **VINIER, VINIEST** covered with vines
VINYL	*n* pl. **-S** a type of plastic **VINYLIC** *adj*
VIOL	*n* pl. **-S** a stringed instrument
VIOLA	*n* pl. **-S** a stringed instrument
VIOLABLE	*adj* capable of being violated **VIOLABLY** *adv*
VIOLATE	*v* **-LATED, -LATING, -LATES** to break or disregard the terms or requirements of
VIOLATER	*n* pl. **-S** violator
VIOLATOR	*n* pl. **-S** one that violates
VIOLENCE	*n* pl. **-S** violent action
VIOLENT	*adj* marked by intense physical force or roughness
VIOLET	*n* pl. **-S** a flowering plant
VIOLIN	*n* pl. **-S** a stringed instrument
VIOLIST	*n* pl. **-S** one who plays the viol or viola
VIOLONE	*n* pl. **-S** a stringed instrument
VIOMYCIN	*n* pl. **-S** an antibiotic
VIPER	*n* pl. **-S** a venomous snake **VIPERINE, VIPERISH, VIPEROUS** *adj*
VIRAEMIA	*n* pl. **-S** viremia **VIRAEMIC** *adj*
VIRAGO	*n* pl. **-GOS** or **-GOES** a noisy, domineering woman
VIRAL	*adj* pertaining to or caused by a virus **VIRALLY** *adv*
VIRELAI	*n* pl. **-S** virelay
VIRELAY	*n* pl. **-LAYS** a medieval French verse form
VIREMIA	*n* pl. **-S** the presence of a virus in the blood **VIREMIC** *adj*
VIREO	*n* pl. **-EOS** a small bird
VIRES	pl. of vis
VIRGA	*n* pl. **-GAS** or **-GAE** wisps of precipitation evaporating before reaching ground
VIRGATE	*n* pl. **-S** an early English measure of land area
VIRGER	*n* pl. **-S** verger
VIRGIN	*n* pl. **-S** a person who has never had sexual intercourse
VIRGINAL	*n* pl. **-S** a musical instrument
VIRGULE	*n* pl. **-S** a diagonal printing mark used to separate alternatives
VIRICIDE	*n* pl. **-S** a substance that destroys viruses
VIRID	*adj* verdant
VIRIDIAN	*n* pl. **-S** a bluish-green pigment
VIRIDITY	*n* pl. **-TIES** verdancy
VIRILE	*adj* having masculine vigor **VIRILELY** *adv*
VIRILISE	*v* **-ISED, -ISING, -ISES** to virilize
VIRILISM	*n* pl. **-S** the development of male secondary sex characteristics in a female
VIRILITY	*n* pl. **-TIES** the quality or state of being virile

VIRILIZE   *v* **-IZED, -IZING, -IZES** to induce male characteristics in (a female)

VIRION   *n* pl. **-S** a virus particle

VIRL   *n* pl. **-S** a metal ring or cap put around a shaft to prevent splitting

VIROID   *n* pl. **-S** a viruslike plant pathogen

VIROLOGY   *n* pl. **-GIES** the study of viruses

VIROSIS   *n* pl. **-ROSES** infection with a virus

VIRTU   *n* pl. **-S** a love or taste for the fine arts

VIRTUAL   *adj* having the effect but not the actual form of what is specified

VIRTUE   *n* pl. **-S** moral excellence

VIRTUOSA   *n* pl. **-SAS** or **-SE** a female virtuoso

VIRTUOSO   *n* pl. **-SOS** or **-SI** a highly skilled artistic performer

VIRTUOUS   *adj* characterized by virtue

VIRUCIDE   *n* pl. **-S** viricide

VIRULENT   *adj* extremely poisonous

VIRUS   *n* pl. **-ES** any of a class of submicroscopic pathogens

VIRUSOID   *n* pl. **-S** a particle of RNA associated with some plant viruses

VIS   *n* pl. **VIRES** force or power

VISA   *v* **-ED, -ING, -S** to put an official endorsement on, as a passport

VISAGE   *n* pl. **-S** the face or facial expression of a person **VISAGED** *adj*

VISARD   *n* pl. **-S** vizard

VISCACHA   *n* pl. **-S** a burrowing rodent

VISCERA   pl. of viscus

VISCERAL   *adj* pertaining to the internal organs

VISCID   *adj* thick and adhesive **VISCIDLY** *adv*

VISCOID   *adj* somewhat viscid

VISCOSE   *n* pl. **-S** a viscous solution

VISCOUNT   *n* pl. **-S** a British nobleman

VISCOUS   *adj* having relatively high resistance to flow

VISCUS   *n* pl. **-CERA** an internal organ

VISE   *v* **VISED, VISING, VISES** to hold in a vise (a clamping device)

VISE   *v* **VISEED, VISEING, VISES** to visa

VISELIKE   *adj* resembling a vise

VISIBLE   *n* pl. **-S** a person or thing that can be seen

VISIBLY   *adv* in a manner capable of being seen

VISION   *v* **-ED, -ING, -S** to imagine

VISIONAL   *adj* imaginary

VISIT   *v* **-ED, -ING, -S** to go or come to see someone or something

VISITANT   *n* pl. **-S** a visitor

VISITER   *n* pl. **-S** visitor

VISITING   *n* pl. **-S** the act or an instance of visiting someone or something

VISITOR   *n* pl. **-S** one that visits

VISIVE   *adj* visible

VISOR   *v* **-ED, -ING, -S** to provide with a visor (a projecting brim)

VISTA   *n* pl. **-S** a distant view **VISTAED** *adj*

VISUAL   *n* pl. **-S** something that illustrates by pictures or diagrams

VISUALLY   *adv* with regard to sight

VITA   *n* pl. **-TAE** a brief, autobiographical sketch

VITAL   *adj* necessary to life

VITALISE   *v* **-ISED, -ISING, -ISES** to vitalize

VITALISM   *n* pl. **-S** a philosophical doctrine

VITALIST   *n* pl. **-S** an advocate of vitalism

VITALITY   *n* pl. **-TIES** exuberant physical strength or mental vigor

VITALIZE   *v* **-IZED, -IZING, -IZES** to give life to

VITALLY   *adv* in a vital manner

VITALS   *n/pl* vital organs

VITAMER   *n* pl. **-S** a type of chemical compound

VITAMIN   *n* pl. **-S** any of various organic substances essential to proper nutrition

VITAMINE   *n* pl. **-S** vitamin

VITELLIN   *n* pl. **-S** a protein found in egg yolk

VITELLUS   *n* pl. **-LUSES** or **-LI** the yolk of an egg

VITESSE   *n* pl. **-S** speed

VITIATE   *v* **-ATED, -ATING, -ATES** to impair the value or quality of **VITIABLE** *adj*

VITIATOR   *n* pl. **-S** one that vitiates

VITILIGO   *n* pl. **-GOS** a skin disease

VITRAIN   *n* pl. **-S** the material in the vitreous layers of banded bituminous coal

VITREOUS   *n* pl. **-ES** the jelly that fills the eyeball

VITRIC	*adj* pertaining to glass	**VLEI**	*n* pl. **-S** a hollow in South Africa in which water collects
VITRICS	*n/pl* the art of making or decorating glass articles	**VLOG**	*v* **VLOGGED, VLOGGING, VLOGS** to blog video material
VITRIFY	*v* **-FIED, -FYING, -FIES** to convert into glass	**VLOGGER**	*n* pl. **-S** one that vlogs
VITRINE	*n* pl. **-S** a glass showcase for art objects	**VOCAB**	*n* pl. **-S** a vocabulary
		VOCABLE	*n* pl. **-S** a word
VITRIOL	*v* **-OLED, -OLING, -OLS** or **-OLLED, -OLLING, -OLS** to treat with sulfuric acid	**VOCABLY**	*adv* in a manner that may be voiced aloud
VITTA	*n* pl. **-TAE** a streak or band of color **VITTATE** *adj*	**VOCAL**	*n* pl. **-S** a sound produced with the voice
VITTLE	*v* **-TLED, -TLING, -TLES** to victual	**VOCALESE**	*n* pl. **-S** a form of jazz singing
VITULINE	*adj* pertaining to a calf	**VOCALIC**	*n* pl. **-S** a vowel sound
VIVA	*n* pl. **-S** a shout or cry used to express approval	**VOCALISE**	*v* **-ISED, -ISING, -ISES** to vocalize
		VOCALISM	*n* pl. **-S** the act of vocalizing
VIVACE	*n* pl. **-S** a musical passage played in a brisk spirited manner	**VOCALIST**	*n* pl. **-S** a singer
VIVACITY	*n* pl. **-TIES** the quality or state of being lively	**VOCALITY**	*n* pl. **-TIES** possession or exercise of vocal powers
VIVARIUM	*n* pl. **-IUMS** or **-IA** a place for raising and keeping live animals	**VOCALIZE**	*v* **-IZED, -IZING, -IZES** to produce with the voice
VIVARY	*n* pl. **-RIES** vivarium	**VOCALLY**	*adv* with the voice
VIVAT	*n* pl. **-S** viva	**VOCATION**	*n* pl. **-S** the work in which a person is regularly employed
VIVE	*interj* — used as an exclamation of approval	**VOCATIVE**	*n* pl. **-S** a grammatical case used in some languages
VIVERRID	*n* pl. **-S** any of a family of small carnivorous mammals	**VOCES**	pl. of vox
VIVERS	*n/pl* food	**VOCODER**	*n* pl. **-S** an electronic device used in transmitting speech signals
VIVID	*adj* **-IDER, -IDEST** strikingly bright or intense **VIVIDLY** *adv*	**VODCAST**	*v* **-CAST** or **-CASTED, -CASTING, -CASTS** to make video files available for download over the Internet
VIVIFIC	*adj* vivifying		
VIVIFIER	*n* pl. **-S** one that vivifies		
VIVIFY	*v* **-FIED, -FYING, -FIES** to give life to	**VODKA**	*n* pl. **-S** a liquor
VIVIPARA	*n/pl* animals that bring forth living young	**VODOU**	*n* pl. **-S** vodun
		VODOUN	*n* pl. **-S** vodun
VIVISECT	*v* **-ED, -ING, -S** to dissect the living body of	**VODUN**	*n* pl. **-S** a primitive religion of the West Indies
VIXEN	*n* pl. **-S** a shrewish woman **VIXENISH, VIXENLY** *adj*	**VOE**	*n* pl. **-S** a small bay, creek, or inlet
		VOG	*n* pl. **-S** air pollution caused by volcanic emissions
VIZARD	*n* pl. **-S** a mask **VIZARDED** *adj*	**VOGIE**	*adj* vain
VIZCACHA	*n* pl. **-S** viscacha	**VOGUE**	*v* **VOGUED, VOGUING** or **VOGUEING, VOGUES** to imitate poses of fashion models
VIZIER	*n* pl. **-S** a high official in some Muslim countries		
VIZIR	*n* pl. **-S** vizier **VIZIRIAL** *adj*	**VOGUEING**	*n* pl. **-S** voguing
VIZIRATE	*n* pl. **-S** the office of a vizir	**VOGUER**	*n* pl. **-S** one that vogues
VIZOR	*v* **-ED, -ING, -S** to visor	**VOGUING**	*n* pl. **-S** a dance consisting of a series of styled poses
VIZSLA	*n* pl. **-S** a Hungarian breed of dog	**VOGUISH**	*adj* fashionable

VOICE	v **VOICED, VOICING, VOICES** to express or utter	**VOLTI**	v turn — used to direct musicians to turn the page
VOICEFUL	adj sonorous	**VOLUBLE**	adj talkative **VOLUBLY** adv
VOICER	n pl. **-S** one that voices	**VOLUME**	v **-UMED, -UMING, -UMES** to send or give out in large quantities
VOICING	n pl. **-S** the tonal quality of an instrument in an ensemble	**VOLUMISE**	v **-ISED, -ISING, -ISES** to volumize
VOID	v **-ED, -ING, -S** to make void (of no legal force or effect) **VOIDABLE** adj	**VOLUMIZE**	v **-IZED, -IZING, -IZES** to give body to (hair)
VOIDANCE	n pl. **-S** the act or process of voiding	**VOLUTE**	n pl. **-S** a spiral architectural ornament **VOLUTED** adj
VOIDER	n pl. **-S** one that voids	**VOLUTIN**	n pl. **-S** a granular substance that is common in microorganisms
VOIDNESS	n pl. **-ES** the quality or state of being void	**VOLUTION**	n pl. **-S** a spiral
VOILA	interj — used to call attention to something	**VOLVA**	n pl. **-S** a membranous sac that encloses certain immature mushrooms **VOLVATE** adj
VOILE	n pl. **-S** a sheer fabric	**VOLVOX**	n pl. **-ES** any of a genus of freshwater protozoa
VOLANT	adj flying or capable of flying		
VOLANTE	adj moving with light rapidity — used as a musical direction	**VOLVULUS**	n pl. **-LUSES** or **-LI** a twisting of the intestine that causes obstruction
VOLAR	adj pertaining to flight	**VOMER**	n pl. **-S** a bone of the skull **VOMERINE** adj
VOLATILE	n pl. **-S** a winged creature		
VOLCANIC	n pl. **-S** a rock produced by a volcano	**VOMICA**	n pl. **-CAE** a cavity in the body containing pus
VOLCANO	n pl. **-NOS** or **-NOES** an opening in the earth's crust through which molten rock and gases are ejected	**VOMIT**	v **-ED, -ING, -S** to eject the contents of the stomach through the mouth
VOLE	v **VOLED, VOLING, VOLES** to win all the tricks in a card game	**VOMITER**	n pl. **-S** one that vomits
		VOMITIVE	n pl. **-S** an emetic
VOLERY	n pl. **-ERIES** a large birdcage	**VOMITO**	n pl. **-TOS** the black vomit of yellow fever
VOLITANT	adj volant		
VOLITION	n pl. **-S** the power of choosing or determining	**VOMITORY**	n pl. **-RIES** an emetic
		VOMITOUS	adj pertaining to vomiting
VOLITIVE	adj pertaining to volition	**VOMITUS**	n pl. **-ES** vomited matter
VOLK	n pl. **-S** the Afrikaner people	**VOMITY**	adj resembling or smelling of vomit
VOLLEY	v **-ED, -ING, -S** to return a tennis ball before it touches the ground	**VOODOO**	v **-ED, -ING, -S** to hex
VOLLEYER	n pl. **-S** one that volleys	**VORACITY**	n pl. **-TIES** the quality or state of being ravenous
VOLOST	n pl. **-S** an administrative district in Russia	**VORLAGE**	n pl. **-S** a position in skiing
VOLPLANE	v **-PLANED, -PLANING, -PLANES** to glide in an airplane	**VORTEX**	n pl. **-TEXES** or **-TICES** a whirling mass of fluid **VORTICAL** adj
VOLT	v **-ED, -ING, -S** to make a quick movement in fencing to avoid a thrust	**VOTABLE**	adj capable of being voted on
		VOTARESS	n pl. **-ES** a female votary
		VOTARIST	n pl. **-S** a votary
VOLTA	n pl. **-TE** a turning	**VOTARY**	n pl. **-RIES** a person who is bound by religious vows
VOLTAGE	n pl. **-S** electromotive force expressed in volts		
		VOTE	v **VOTED, VOTING, VOTES** to cast a vote (a formal expression of will or opinion)
VOLTAISM	n pl. **-S** electricity produced by chemical action **VOLTAIC** adj		
VOLTE	n pl. **-S** a fencing movement	**VOTEABLE**	adj votable

VOTELESS	*adj* having no vote
VOTER	*n* pl. **-S** one that votes
VOTING	present participle of vote
VOTIVE	*n* pl. **-S** a small squat candle
VOTIVELY	*adv* in a manner expressing devotion or gratitude
VOTRESS	*n* pl. **-ES** votaress
VOUCH	*v* **-ED, -ING, -ES** to give one's personal assurance or guarantee
VOUCHEE	*n* pl. **-S** one for whom another vouches
VOUCHER	*v* **-ED, -ING, -S** to establish the authenticity of
VOUDON	*n* pl. **-S** vodun
VOUDOUN	*n* pl. **-S** vodun
VOUSSOIR	*n* pl. **-S** a wedge-shaped building stone
VOUVRAY	*n* pl. **-VRAYS** a French white wine
VOW	*v* **-ED, -ING, -S** to make a vow (a solemn promise)
VOWEL	*n* pl. **-S** a type of speech sound **VOWELED, VOWELLED** *adj*
VOWELIZE	*v* **-IZED, -IZING, -IZES** to provide with symbols used to indicate vowels
VOWER	*n* pl. **-S** one that vows
VOWLESS	*adj* having made no vow
VOX	*n* pl. **VOCES** voice
VOXEL	*n* pl. **-S** each of an array of elements of volume in graphic simulation
VOYAGE	*v* **-AGED, -AGING, -AGES** to travel
VOYAGER	*n* pl. **-S** one that voyages
VOYAGEUR	*n* pl. **-S** a person employed by a fur company to transport goods between distant stations
VOYAGING	*n* pl. **-S** the action of travelling over or across, especially by sea
VOYEUR	*n* pl. **-S** one who is sexually gratified by looking at sexual objects or acts
VROOM	*v* **-ED, -ING, -S** to run an engine at high speed
VROUW	*n* pl. **-S** a Dutch woman
VROW	*n* pl. **-S** vrouw
VUG	*n* pl. **-S** a small cavity in a rock or lode
VUGG	*n* pl. **-S** vug
VUGGY	*adj* **-GIER, -GIEST** abounding in vugs
VUGH	*n* pl. **-S** vug
VUGULAR	*adj* pertaining to vugs
VULCANIC	*adj* pertaining to a volcano
VULGAR	*adj* **-GARER, -GAREST** crude **VULGARLY** *adv*
VULGAR	*n* pl. **-S** a common person
VULGATE	*n* pl. **-S** the common speech of a people
VULGO	*adv* commonly
VULGUS	*n* pl. **-ES** an exercise in Latin formerly required of pupils in some English public schools
VULN	*v* **-ED, -ING, -S** to wound
VULPINE	*adj* pertaining to a fox
VULTURE	*n* pl. **-S** a bird of prey
VULVA	*n* pl. **-VAS** or **-VAE** the external genital organs of a female **VULVAL, VULVAR, VULVATE** *adj*
VULVITIS	*n* pl. **-TISES** inflammation of the vulva
VUM	*interj* — used to express surprise
VYING	present participle of vie
VYINGLY	*adv* in a vying manner

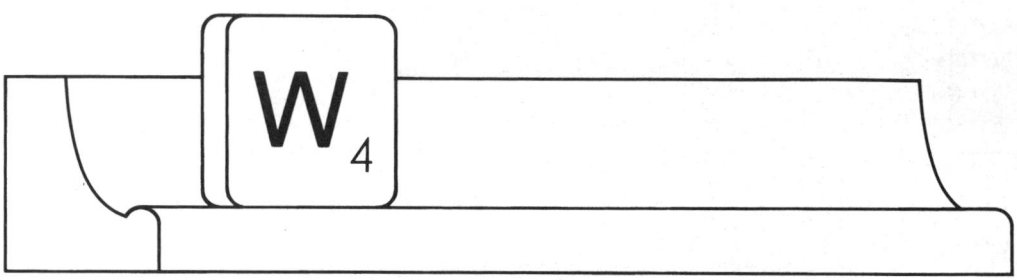

WAAH	*interj* — used to express wailing
WAB	*n* pl. **-S** a web
WABBLE	*v* **-BLED, -BLING, -BLES** to wobble
WABBLER	*n* pl. **-S** one that wabbles
WABBLY	*adj* **-BLIER, -BLIEST** wobbly
WACK	*adj* **WACKER, WACKEST** very bad
WACK	*n* pl. **-S** a wacky person
WACKE	*n* pl. **-S** a type of basaltic rock
WACKED	*adj* whacked
WACKO	*n* pl. **WACKOS** or **WACKOES** a wacky person
WACKY	*adj* **WACKIER, WACKIEST** very irrational **WACKILY** *adv*
WAD	*v* **WADDED, WADDING, WADS** to form into a wad (a small mass of soft material)
WADABLE	*adj* wadeable
WADDER	*n* pl. **-S** one that wads
WADDIE	*n* pl. **-S** a cowboy
WADDIED	past tense of waddy
WADDIES	present 3d person sing. of waddy
WADDING	*n* pl. **-S** a wad
WADDLE	*v* **-DLED, -DLING, -DLES** to walk with short, swaying steps
WADDLER	*n* pl. **-S** one that waddles
WADDLY	*adj* having or being a waddling gait
WADDY	*v* **-DIED, -DYING, -DIES** to strike with a thick club
WADE	*v* **WADED, WADING, WADES** to walk through water
WADEABLE	*adj* capable of being passed through by wading
WADER	*n* pl. **-S** one that wades
WADI	*n* pl. **-S** the bed of a usually dry watercourse
WADIES	pl. of wady
WADING	present participle of wade
WADMAAL	*n* pl. **-S** wadmal
WADMAL	*n* pl. **-S** a thick woolen fabric
WADMEL	*n* pl. **-S** wadmal
WADMOL	*n* pl. **-S** wadmal
WADMOLL	*n* pl. **-S** wadmal
WADSET	*v* **-SET, -SETTING, -SETS** to mortgage
WADY	*n* pl. **-DIES** wadi
WAE	*n* pl. **-S** woe
WAEFUL	*adj* woeful
WAENESS	*n* pl. **-ES** woeness
WAESUCK	*interj* waesucks
WAESUCKS	*interj* — used to express pity
WAFER	*v* **-ED, -ING, -S** to seal with an adhesive disk
WAFERY	*adj* resembling a wafer (a thin, crisp biscuit)
WAFF	*v* **-ED, -ING, -S** to wave
WAFFIE	*n* pl. **-S** a vagabond
WAFFLE	*v* **-FLED, -FLING, -FLES** to talk vaguely or indecisively
WAFFLER	*n* pl. **-S** one that waffles
WAFFLING	*n* pl. **-S** an indecisive statement or position
WAFFLY	*adj* **-FLIER, -FLIEST** indecisive
WAFT	*v* **-ED, -ING, -S** to carry lightly over air or water
WAFTAGE	*n* pl. **-S** the act of wafting
WAFTER	*n* pl. **-S** one that wafts
WAFTURE	*n* pl. **-S** waftage
WAG	*v* **WAGGED, WAGGING, WAGS** to move briskly up and down or to and fro
WAGE	*v* **WAGED, WAGING, WAGES** to engage in or carry on

WAGELESS *adj* unpaid

WAGER *v* **-ED, -ING, -S** to risk on an uncertain outcome

WAGERER *n* pl. **-S** one that wagers

WAGERING *n* pl. **-S** the act of risking something on an uncertain outcome

WAGGED past tense of wag

WAGGER *n* pl. **-S** one that wags

WAGGERY *n* pl. **-GERIES** waggish behavior

WAGGING present participle of wag

WAGGISH *adj* playfully humorous

WAGGLE *v* **-GLED, -GLING, -GLES** to wag

WAGGLY *adj* **-GLIER, -GLIEST** unsteady

WAGGON *v* **-ED, -ING, -S** to wagon

WAGGONER *n* pl. **-S** wagoner

WAGING present participle of wage

WAGON *v* **-ED, -ING, -S** to convey by wagon (a four-wheeled, horse-drawn vehicle)

WAGONAGE *n* pl. **-S** conveyance by wagon

WAGONER *n* pl. **-S** one who drives a wagon

WAGSOME *adj* waggish

WAGTAIL *n* pl. **-S** a songbird

WAHCONDA *n* pl. **-S** wakanda

WAHINE *n* pl. **-S** a Hawaiian woman

WAHOO *n* pl. **-HOOS** a flowering shrub

WAIF *v* **-ED, -ING, -S** to throw away

WAIFISH *adj* waiflike

WAIFLIKE *adj* resembling a waif (a homeless child)

WAIL *v* **-ED, -ING, -S** to utter a long, mournful cry

WAILER *n* pl. **-S** one that wails

WAILFUL *adj* mournful

WAILSOME *adj* wailful

WAIN *n* pl. **-S** a large, open wagon

WAINSCOT *v* **-SCOTED, -SCOTING, -SCOTS** or **-SCOTTED, -SCOTTING, -SCOTS** to line the walls of with wooden paneling

WAIR *v* **-ED, -ING, -S** to spend

WAIST *n* pl. **-S** the part of the body between the ribs and the hips **WAISTED** *adj*

WAISTER *n* pl. **-S** a seaman stationed in the middle section of a ship

WAISTING *n* pl. **-S** a type of dressmaking material

WAIT *v* **-ED, -ING, -S** to stay in expectation of

WAITER *v* **-ED, -ING, -S** to work as a male server in a restaurant

WAITING *n* pl. **-S** the act of one who waits

WAITLIST *v* **-ED, -ING, -S** to put on a list of persons waiting

WAITRESS *v* **-ED, -ING, -ES** to work as a female server in a restaurant

WAITRON *n* pl. **-S** a server in a restaurant

WAIVE *v* **WAIVED, WAIVING, WAIVES** to give up intentionally

WAIVER *n* pl. **-S** the act of waiving something

WAKAME *n* pl. **-S** a brown seaweed native to Asia

WAKANDA *n* pl. **-S** a supernatural force in Sioux beliefs

WAKE *v* **WAKED** or **WOKE, WOKEN, WAKING, WAKES** to rouse from sleep

WAKEFUL *adj* not sleeping or able to sleep

WAKELESS *adj* unbroken — used of sleep

WAKEN *v* **-ED, -ING, -S** to wake

WAKENER *n* pl. **-S** one that wakens

WAKENING *n* pl. **-S** the act of one that wakens

WAKER *n* pl. **-S** one that wakes

WAKERIFE *adj* wakeful

WAKIKI *n* pl. **-S** shell money of the South Sea Islands

WAKING *n* pl. **-S** the state of being awake

WALE *v* **WALED, WALING, WALES** to mark with welts

WALER *n* pl. **-S** an Australian-bred saddle horse

WALI *n* pl. **-S** the governor of a province in an Arab country

WALIE *adj* sturdy

WALIES pl. of waly

WALK *v* **-ED, -ING, -S** to advance on foot **WALKABLE** *adj*

WALKAWAY *n* pl. **-AWAYS** an easy victory

WALKER *n* pl. **-S** one that walks

WALKIES *interj* — used to command a dog to prepare for a walk

WALKING *n* pl. **-S** the act of one that walks

WALKOUT *n* pl. **-S** a strike by workers

WALKOVER *n* pl. **-S** a walkaway

WALKUP *n* pl. **-S** an apartment house having no elevator

WALKWAY	*n* pl. **-WAYS** a passage for walking
WALKYRIE	*n* pl. **-S** valkyrie
WALL	*v* **-ED, -ING, -S** to provide with a wall (an upright structure built to enclose an area)
WALLA	*n* pl. **-S** wallah
WALLABY	*n* pl. **-BIES** a small kangaroo
WALLAH	*n* pl. **-S** a person engaged in a particular occupation or activity
WALLAROO	*n* pl. **-ROOS** a large kangaroo
WALLET	*n* pl. **-S** a flat folding case
WALLEY	*n* pl. **-LEYS** a type of jump in figure skating
WALLEYE	*n* pl. **-S** an eye having a white cornea **WALLEYED** *adj*
WALLIE	*n* pl. **-S** a valet
WALLIES	pl. of wally
WALLOP	*v* **-ED, -ING, -S** to beat soundly
WALLOPER	*n* pl. **-S** one that wallops
WALLOW	*v* **-ED, -ING, -S** to roll about
WALLOWER	*n* pl. **-S** one that wallows
WALLY	*n* pl. **-LIES** waly
WALNUT	*n* pl. **-S** an edible nut
WALRUS	*n* pl. **-ES** a marine mammal
WALTZ	*v* **-ED, -ING, -ES** to perform a ballroom dance
WALTZER	*n* pl. **-S** one that waltzes
WALY	*n* pl. **WALIES** something visually pleasing
WAMBLE	*v* **-BLED, -BLING, -BLES** to move unsteadily
WAMBLY	*adj* **-BLIER, -BLIEST** unsteady
WAME	*n* pl. **-S** the belly
WAMEFOU	*n* pl. **-S** a bellyful
WAMEFUL	*n* pl. **-S** wamefou
WAMMUS	*n* pl. **-ES** wamus
WAMPISH	*v* **-ED, -ING, -ES** to throw about
WAMPUM	*n* pl. **-S** a form of currency formerly used by Native Americans
WAMPUS	*n* pl. **-ES** wamus
WAMUS	*n* pl. **-ES** a heavy outer jacket
WAN	*adj* **WANNER, WANNEST** unnaturally pale
WAN	*v* **WANNED, WANNING, WANS** to become wan
WAND	*n* pl. **-S** a slender rod
WANDER	*v* **-ED, -ING, -S** to move about with no destination or purpose
WANDERER	*n* pl. **-S** one that wanders
WANDEROO	*n* pl. **-ROOS** an Asian monkey
WANDLE	*adj* supple
WANE	*v* **WANED, WANING, WANES** to decrease in size or extent
WANEY	*adj* **WANIER, WANIEST** wany
WANGAN	*n* pl. **-S** wanigan
WANGLE	*v* **-GLED, -GLING, -GLES** to obtain or accomplish by contrivance
WANGLER	*n* pl. **-S** one that wangles
WANGUN	*n* pl. **-S** wanigan
WANIER	comparative of waney and wany
WANIEST	superlative of waney and wany
WANIGAN	*n* pl. **-S** a supply chest used in a logging camp
WANING	present participle of wane
WANION	*n* pl. **-S** vengeance
WANLY	*adv* in a wan manner
WANNABE	*n* pl. **-S** one who aspires to be like someone else
WANNABEE	*n* **-S** wannabe
WANNED	past tense of wan
WANNER	comparative of wan
WANNESS	*n* pl. **-ES** the quality of being wan
WANNEST	superlative of wan
WANNIGAN	*n* pl. **-S** wanigan
WANNING	present participle of wan
WANT	*v* **-ED, -ING, -S** to have a desire for
WANTAGE	*n* pl. **-S** something that is lacking
WANTER	*n* pl. **-S** one that wants
WANTON	*v* **-ED, -ING, -S** to behave immorally
WANTONER	*n* pl. **-S** one that wantons
WANTONLY	*adv* immorally
WANY	*adj* **WANIER, WANIEST** waning in some parts
WAP	*v* **WAPPED, WAPPING, WAPS** to wrap
WAPITI	*n* pl. **-S** a large deer
WAR	*v* **WARRED, WARRING, WARS** to engage in war (a state of open, armed conflict)
WARBIRD	*n* pl. **-S** a vintage military aircraft
WARBLE	*v* **-BLED, -BLING, -BLES** to sing with melodic embellishments
WARBLER	*n* pl. **-S** one that warbles
WARBLY	*adj* **-BLIER, -BLIEST** voiced in a trilling or quavering manner

WARCRAFT   *n* pl. **-S** the art of war

WARD   *v* **-ED, -ING, -S** to turn aside

WARDEN   *n* pl. **-S** the chief officer of a prison

WARDENRY   *n* pl. **-RIES** the office of a warden

WARDER   *n* pl. **-S** a person who guards something

WARDLESS   *adj* having no ward (part of a lock casing)

WARDRESS   *n* pl. **-ES** a female warden

WARDROBE   *n* pl. **-S** a collection of garments

WARDROBE   *v* **-ROBED, -ROBING, -ROBES** to provide with a collection of garments

WARDROOM   *n* pl. **-S** a dining area for officers on a warship

WARDSHIP   *n* pl. **-S** the state of being under a guardian

WARE   *v* **WARED, WARING, WARES** to beware of

WAREROOM   *n* pl. **-S** a room in which goods are displayed for sale

WAREZ   *n* pl. **WAREZ** illegally copied software

WARFARE   *n* pl. **-S** the act of engaging in war

WARFARIN   *n* pl. **-S** a chemical compound

WARGAME   *v* **-GAMED, -GAMING, -GAMES** to engage in simulated military conflicts

WARGAMER   *n* pl. **-S** one that wargames

WARHEAD   *n* pl. **-S** the front part of a missile containing the explosive

WARHORSE   *n* pl. **-S** a musical or dramatic work that has been performed to excess

WARIER   comparative of wary

WARIEST   superlative of wary

WARILY   *adv* in a wary manner

WARINESS   *n* pl. **-ES** the state of being wary

WARING   present participle of ware

WARISON   *n* pl. **-S** a call to attack

WARK   *v* **-ED, -ING, -S** to endure pain

WARLESS   *adj* free from war

WARLIKE   *adj* disposed to engage in war

WARLOCK   *n* pl. **-S** a sorcerer

WARLORD   *n* pl. **-S** a military leader of a warlike nation

WARM   *adj* **WARMER, WARMEST** moderately hot

WARM   *v* **-ED, -ING, -S** to make warm

WARMAKER   *n* pl. **-S** one that wars

WARMER   *n* pl. **-S** one that warms

WARMING   *n* pl. **-S** the act or an instance of making something warm

WARMISH   *adj* somewhat warm

WARMLY   *adv* in a warm manner

WARMNESS   *n* pl. **-ES** the state of being warm

WARMOUTH   *n* pl. **-S** a freshwater fish

WARMTH   *n* pl. **-S** warmness

WARMUP   *n* pl. **-S** a preparatory exercise or procedure

WARN   *v* **-ED, -ING, -S** to make aware of impending or possible danger

WARNER   *n* pl. **-S** one that warns

WARNING   *n* pl. **-S** something that warns

WARP   *v* **-ED, -ING, -S** to turn or twist out of shape

WARPAGE   *n* pl. **-S** the act of warping

WARPAINT   *n* pl. **-S** paint used to decorate the face and body before battle

WARPATH   *n* pl. **-S** the route taken by attacking Native Americans

WARPER   *n* pl. **-S** one that warps

WARPLANE   *n* pl. **-S** an airplane armed for combat

WARPOWER   *n* pl. **-S** the power to make war

WARPWISE   *adv* in a vertical direction

WARRAGAL   *n* pl. **-S** warrigal

WARRANT   *v* **-ED, -ING, -S** to give authority to

WARRANTY   *v* **-TIED, -TYING, -TIES** to provide a written guarantee for

WARRED   past tense of war

WARREN   *n* pl. **-S** a place where rabbits live and breed

WARRENER   *n* pl. **-S** the keeper of a warren

WARRIGAL   *n* pl. **-S** a dingo

WARRING   present participle of war

WARRIOR   *n* pl. **-S** one engaged or experienced in warfare

WARSAW   *n* pl. **-S** a marine fish

WARSHIP   *n* pl. **-S** a ship armed for combat

WARSLE   *v* **-SLED, -SLING, -SLES** to wrestle

WARSLER   *n* pl. **-S** a wrestler

WARSTLE   *v* **-TLED, -TLING, -TLES** to wrestle

WARSTLER   *n* pl. **-S** a wrestler

WART   *n* pl. **-S** a protuberance on the skin **WARTED** *adj*

WARTHOG   *n* pl. **-S** an African wild hog

WARTIER   comparative of warty

WARTIEST	superlative of warty
WARTIME	n pl. **-S** a time of war
WARTLESS	adj having no warts
WARTLIKE	adj resembling a wart
WARTY	adj **WARTIER, WARTIEST** covered with warts
WARWORK	n pl. **-S** work done during a war
WARWORN	adj showing the effects of war
WARY	adj **WARIER, WARIEST** watchful
WAS	1st and 3d person sing. past indicative of be
WASABI	n pl. **-S** a pungent herb
WASH	v **-ED, -ING, -ES** to cleanse by immersing in or applying a liquid
WASHABLE	n pl. **-S** something that can be washed without damage
WASHBAG	n pl. **-S** a small bag for carrying toiletries when traveling
WASHBOWL	n pl. **-S** a bowl used for washing oneself
WASHDAY	n pl. **-DAYS** a day set aside for washing clothes
WASHER	n pl. **-S** one that washes
WASHIER	comparative of washy
WASHIEST	superlative of washy
WASHING	n pl. **-S** articles washed or to be washed
WASHOUT	n pl. **-S** an erosion of earth by the action of water
WASHRAG	n pl. **-S** a small cloth used for washing oneself
WASHROOM	n pl. **-S** a lavatory
WASHTUB	n pl. **-S** a tub used for washing clothes
WASHUP	n pl. **-S** the act of washing clean
WASHY	adj **WASHIER, WASHIEST** overly diluted
WASP	n pl. **-S** a stinging insect **WASPISH, WASPLIKE** adj
WASPY	adj **WASPIER, WASPIEST** resembling a wasp **WASPILY** adv
WASSAIL	v **-ED, -ING, -S** to drink to the health of
WAST	n pl. **-S** west
WASTABLE	adj capable of being wasted
WASTAGE	n pl. **-S** something that is wasted
WASTE	v **WASTED, WASTING, WASTES** to use thoughtlessly
WASTEFUL	adj tending to waste
WASTELOT	n pl. **-S** a vacant lot
WASTER	n pl. **-S** one that wastes
WASTERIE	n pl. **-S** wastry
WASTERY	n pl. **-RIES** wastry
WASTEWAY	n pl. **-WAYS** a channel for excess water
WASTING	present participle of waste
WASTREL	n pl. **-S** one that wastes
WASTRIE	n pl. **-S** wastry
WASTRY	n pl. **-RIES** reckless extravagance
WAT	adj **WATTER, WATTEST** wet
WAT	n pl. **-S** a hare
WATAP	n pl. **-S** a thread made from the roots of various trees
WATAPE	n pl. **-S** watap
WATCH	v **-ED, -ING, -ES** to observe carefully
WATCHCRY	n pl. **-CRIES** a password
WATCHDOG	v **-DOGGED, -DOGGING, -DOGS** to act as a guardian for
WATCHER	n pl. **-S** one that watches
WATCHEYE	n pl. **-S** a walleye
WATCHFUL	adj closely observant or alert
WATCHMAN	n pl. **-MEN** a man employed to stand guard
WATCHOUT	n pl. **-S** the act of looking out for something
WATER	v **-ED, -ING, -S** to sprinkle with water (a transparent, odorless, tasteless liquid)
WATERAGE	n pl. **-S** the conveyance of goods by water
WATERBED	n pl. **-S** a bed whose mattress is a plastic bag filled with water
WATERBUS	n pl. **-BUSES** or **-BUSSES** a large motorboat for carrying passengers
WATERDOG	n pl. **-S** a large salamander
WATERER	n pl. **-S** one that waters
WATERHEN	n pl. **-S** the American coot
WATERIER	comparative of watery
WATERIEST	superlative of watery
WATERILY	adv in a watery manner
WATERING	n pl. **-S** the act of one that waters
WATERISH	adj watery
WATERJET	n pl. **-S** a stream of water forced through a small opening
WATERLOG	v **-LOGGED, -LOGGING, -LOGS** to soak with water

WATERLOO *n* pl. **-LOOS** a decisive defeat

WATERMAN *n* pl. **-MEN** a boatman

WATERSKI *n* pl. **-S** a ski for skiing on water

WATERWAY *n* pl. **-WAYS** a navigable body of water

WATERY *adj* **-TERIER, -TERIEST** containing water

WATT *n* pl. **-S** a unit of power

WATTAGE *n* pl. **-S** an amount of power in terms of watts

WATTAPE *n* pl. **-S** watap

WATTER comparative of wat

WATTEST superlative of wat

WATTHOUR *n* pl. **-S** a unit of energy

WATTLE *v* **-TLED, -TLING, -TLES** to weave into a network

WATTLESS *adj* denoting a type of electric current

WAUCHT *v* **-ED, -ING, -S** to waught

WAUGH *adj* damp

WAUGHT *v* **-ED, -ING, -S** to drink deeply

WAUK *v* **-ED, -ING, -S** to wake

WAUL *v* **-ED, -ING, -S** to cry like a cat

WAUR *adj* worse

WAVE *v* **WAVED, WAVING, WAVES** to move freely back and forth or up and down

WAVEBAND *n* pl. **-S** a range of radio frequencies

WAVEFORM *n* pl. **-S** a type of mathematical graph

WAVELESS *adj* having no waves (moving ridges on the surface of a liquid)

WAVELET *n* pl. **-S** a small wave

WAVELIKE *adj* resembling a wave

WAVEOFF *n* pl. **-S** the act of denying landing permission to an approaching aircraft

WAVER *v* **-ED, -ING, -S** to move back and forth

WAVERER *n* pl. **-S** one that wavers

WAVERY *adj* wavering

WAVEY *n* pl. **-VEYS** the snow goose

WAVICLE *n* pl. **-S** a subatomic particle that can act like both a wave and a particle

WAVIER comparative of wavy

WAVIES pl. of wavy

WAVIEST superlative of wavy

WAVILY *adv* in a wavy manner

WAVINESS *n* pl. **-ES** the state of being wavy

WAVING present participle of wave

WAVY *adj* **WAVIER, WAVIEST** having waves

WAVY *n* pl. **-VIES** wavey

WAW *n* pl. **-S** vav

WAWL *v* **-ED, -ING, -S** to waul

WAX *v* **-ED, -ING, -ES** to coat with wax (a natural, heat-sensitive substance) **WAXABLE** *adj*

WAXBERRY *n* pl. **-RIES** a berry with a waxy coating

WAXBILL *n* pl. **-S** a tropical bird

WAXEN *adj* covered with wax

WAXER *n* pl. **-S** one that waxes

WAXIER comparative of waxy

WAXIEST superlative of waxy

WAXILY *adv* in a waxy manner

WAXINESS *n* pl. **-ES** the quality of being waxy

WAXING *n* pl. **-S** the act of one that waxes

WAXLIKE *adj* resembling wax

WAXPLANT *n* pl. **-S** a tropical plant

WAXWEED *n* pl. **-S** an annual herb

WAXWING *n* pl. **-S** a type of passerine bird

WAXWORK *n* pl. **-S** an effigy made of wax

WAXWORM *n* pl. **-S** a moth that infests beehives

WAXY *adj* **WAXIER, WAXIEST** resembling wax

WAY *n* pl. **WAYS** a method of doing something

WAYANG *n* pl. **-S** a performance featuring puppets or human dancers

WAYBACK *n* pl. **-S** the area in the back of a vehicle

WAYBILL *n* pl. **-S** a list of goods relative to a shipment

WAYFARER *n* pl. **-S** a traveler

WAYGOING *n* pl. **-S** the act of leaving

WAYLAY *v* **-LAID, -LAYING, -LAYS** to ambush

WAYLAYER *n* pl. **-S** one that waylays

WAYLESS *adj* having no road or path

WAYMARK *n* pl. **-S** an object that serves as a guide for travelers

WAYPOINT *n* pl. **-S** a point between major points along a route

WAYSIDE	*n* pl. **-S** the side of a road
WAYWARD	*adj* willful
WAYWORN	*adj* fatigued by travel
WE	*pron* 1st person pl. pronoun in the nominative case
WEAK	*adj* **WEAKER, WEAKEST** lacking strength
WEAKEN	*v* **-ED, -ING, -S** to make weak
WEAKENER	*n* pl. **-S** one that weakens
WEAKFISH	*n* pl. **-ES** a marine fish
WEAKISH	*adj* somewhat weak
WEAKLING	*n* pl. **-S** a weak person
WEAKLY	*adj* **-LIER, -LIEST** weak and sickly
WEAKNESS	*n* pl. **-ES** the state of being weak
WEAKON	*n* pl. **-S** a subatomic particle
WEAKSIDE	*n* pl. **-S** the side of a basketball court with fewer players
WEAL	*n* pl. **-S** a welt
WEALD	*n* pl. **-S** a woodland
WEALTH	*n* pl. **-S** a great quantity of valuable material
WEALTHY	*adj* **WEALTHIER, WEALTHIEST** having wealth
WEAN	*v* **-ED, -ING, -S** to withhold mother's milk from and substitute other nourishment
WEANER	*n* pl. **-S** one that weans
WEANLING	*n* pl. **-S** a recently weaned child or animal
WEAPON	*v* **-ED, -ING, -S** to supply with a weapon (an instrument used in combat)
WEAPONRY	*n* pl. **-RIES** an aggregate of weapons
WEAR	*v* **WORE, WORN, WEARING, WEARS** to have on one's person
WEARABLE	*n* pl. **-S** a garment
WEARER	*n* pl. **-S** one that wears something
WEARIED	past tense of weary
WEARIER	comparative of weary
WEARIES	present 3d person sing. of weary
WEARIFUL	*adj* tiresome
WEARISH	*adj* tasteless
WEARY	*adj* **-RIER, -RIEST** tired **WEARILY** *adv*
WEARY	*v* **-RIED, -RYING, -RIES** to make or become weary
WEASAND	*n* pl. **-S** the throat
WEASEL	*v* **-SELED, -SELING, -SELS** or **-SELLED, -SELLING, -SELS** to act evasively
WEASELLY	*adj* resembling a weasel (a small carnivorous mammal)
WEASELY	*adj* weaselly
WEASON	*n* pl. **-S** weasand
WEATHER	*v* **-ED, -ING, -S** to expose to atmospheric conditions
WEAVE	*v* **WOVE** or **WEAVED, WOVEN, WEAVING, WEAVES** to form by interlacing threads
WEAVER	*n* pl. **-S** one that weaves
WEAVING	*n* pl. **-S** the activity of creating woven materials
WEAZAND	*n* pl. **-S** weasand
WEB	*v* **WEBBED, WEBBING, WEBS** to provide with a web (an interlaced fabric or structure)
WEBBING	*n* pl. **-S** a woven strip of fiber
WEBBY	*adj* **-BIER, -BIEST** weblike
WEBCAM	*n* pl. **-S** a camera used for transmitting live images over the World Wide Web
WEBCAST	*v* **-ED, -ING, -S** to transmit sound and images via the World Wide Web
WEBER	*n* pl. **-S** a unit of magnetic flux
WEBFED	*adj* designed to print a continuous roll of paper
WEBFOOT	*n* pl. **-FEET** a foot having the toes joined by a membrane
WEBINAR	*n* pl. **-S** a live interactive educational presentation conducted on a website
WEBISODE	*n* pl. **-S** an episode of a television show that can be viewed on a website
WEBLESS	*adj* having no webs
WEBLIKE	*adj* resembling a web
WEBLOG	*n* pl. **-S** a website that contains an online personal journal
WEBPAGE	*n* pl. **-S** a single document on the World Wide Web
WEBSITE	*n* pl. **-S** a set of interconnected webpages maintained by an individual or organization
WEBSTER	*n* pl. **-S** a weaver
WEBWORK	*n* pl. **-S** a weblike pattern or structure
WEBWORM	*n* pl. **-S** a web-spinning caterpillar

WEBZINE *n* pl. **-S** a magazine published on the Internet

WECHT *n* pl. **-S** weight

WED *v* **WEDDED, WEDDING, WEDS** to marry

WEDDER *n* pl. **-S** one that weds

WEDDING *n* pl. **-S** a marriage ceremony

WEDEL *v* **-ED, -ING, -S** to perform a wedeln

WEDELN *n* pl. **-S** a skiing technique

WEDGE *v* **WEDGED, WEDGING, WEDGES** to force apart with a wedge (a tapering piece of wood or metal)

WEDGIE *n* pl. **-S** a type of woman's shoe

WEDGY *adj* **WEDGIER, WEDGIEST** resembling a wedge

WEDLOCK *n* pl. **-S** the state of being married

WEE *adj* **WEER, WEEST** very small

WEE *v* **WEED, WEEING, WEES** to urinate

WEED *v* **-ED, -ING, -S** to remove weeds (undesirable plants)

WEEDBED *n* pl. **-S** an area of a body of water having many weeds

WEEDER *n* pl. **-S** one that weeds

WEEDIER comparative of weedy

WEEDIEST superlative of weedy

WEEDILY *adv* in a weedy manner

WEEDLESS *adj* having no weeds

WEEDLIKE *adj* resembling a weed

WEEDLINE *n* pl. **-S** the edge of a weedbed

WEEDY *adj* **WEEDIER, WEEDIEST** resembling a weed

WEEK *n* pl. **-S** a period of seven days

WEEKDAY *n* pl. **-DAYS** any day of the week except Saturday and Sunday

WEEKEND *v* **-ED, -ING, -S** to spend the weekend (the end of the week)

WEEKLONG *adj* continuing for a week

WEEKLY *n* pl. **-LIES** a publication issued once a week

WEEL *adj* well

WEEN *v* **-ED, -ING, -S** to suppose

WEENIE *n* pl. **-S** a wiener

WEENSY *adj* **-SIER, -SIEST** tiny

WEENY *adj* **-NIER, -NIEST** tiny

WEEP *v* **WEPT, WEEPING, WEEPS** to express sorrow by shedding tears

WEEPER *n* pl. **-S** one that weeps

WEEPIE *n* pl. **-S** a very maudlin movie

WEEPING *n* pl. **-S** the act of one that weeps

WEEPY *adj* **WEEPIER, WEEPIEST** tending to weep **WEEPILY** *adv*

WEER comparative of wee

WEEST superlative of wee

WEET *v* **-ED, -ING, -S** to know

WEEVER *n* pl. **-S** a marine fish

WEEVIL *n* pl. **-S** a small beetle **WEEVILED, WEEVILLY, WEEVILY** *adj*

WEEWEE *v* **-WEED, -WEEING, -WEES** to urinate

WEFT *n* pl. **-S** a woven fabric or garment

WEFTWISE *adv* in a horizontal direction

WEIGELA *n* pl. **-S** a flowering shrub

WEIGELIA *n* pl. **-S** weigela

WEIGH *v* **-ED, -ING, -S** to determine the weight of

WEIGHER *n* pl. **-S** one that weighs

WEIGHMAN *n* pl. **-MEN** one whose occupation is weighing goods

WEIGHT *v* **-ED, -ING, -S** to add weight (heaviness) to

WEIGHTER *n* pl. **-S** one that weights

WEIGHTY *adj* **WEIGHTIER, WEIGHTIEST** having great weight

WEINER *n* pl. **-S** wiener

WEIR *n* pl. **-S** a fence placed in a stream to catch fish

WEIRD *v* **-ED, -ING, -S** to cause to experience a strange sensation

WEIRD *adj* **WEIRDER, WEIRDEST** mysteriously strange

WEIRD *n* pl. **-S** destiny

WEIRDIE *n* pl. **-S** a very strange person

WEIRDIES pl. of weirdy

WEIRDLY *adv* in a weird manner

WEIRDO *n* pl. **WEIRDOES** or **WEIRDOS** a weirdie

WEIRDY *n* pl. **WEIRDIES** weirdie

WEKA *n* pl. **-S** a flightless bird

WELCH *v* **-ED, -ING, -ES** to welsh

WELCHER *n* pl. **-S** one that welshes

WELCOME *v* **-COMED, -COMING, -COMES** to greet cordially

WELCOMER *n* pl. **-S** one that welcomes

WELD *v* **-ED, -ING, -S** to join by applying heat **WELDABLE** *adj*

WELDER *n* pl. **-S** one that welds

WELDLESS *adj* having no welded joints

WELDMENT *n* pl. **-S** a unit composed of welded pieces

WELDOR *n* pl. **-S** welder

WELFARE *n* pl. **-S** general well-being

WELKIN *n* pl. **-S** the sky

WELL *v* **-ED, -ING, -S** to rise to the surface and flow forth

WELLADAY *n* pl. **-DAYS** wellaway

WELLAWAY *n* pl. **-WAYS** an expression of sorrow

WELLBORN *adj* of good birth or ancestry

WELLCURB *n* pl. **-S** the stone ring around a well (a hole dug in the ground to obtain water)

WELLDOER *n* pl. **-S** a doer of good deeds

WELLHEAD *n* pl. **-S** the source of a spring or stream

WELLHOLE *n* pl. **-S** the shaft of a well

WELLIE *n* pl. **-S** a Wellington boot

WELLIES pl. of welly

WELLNESS *n* pl. **-ES** the state of being healthy

WELLSITE *n* pl. **-S** a mineral

WELLY *n* pl. **-LIES** wellie

WELSH *v* **-ED, -ING, -ES** to fail to pay a debt

WELSHER *n* pl. **-S** one that welshes

WELT *v* **-ED, -ING, -S** to mark with welts (ridges or lumps raised on the skin)

WELTER *v* **-ED, -ING, -S** to roll about

WELTING *n* pl. **-S** a cord or strip used to reinforce a seam

WEN *n* pl. **-S** a benign tumor of the skin

WENCH *v* **-ED, -ING, -ES** to consort with prostitutes

WENCHER *n* pl. **-S** one that wenches

WEND *v* **-ED, -ING, -S** to proceed along

WENDIGO *n* pl. **-GOS** windigo

WENNISH *adj* wenny

WENNY *adj* **-NIER, -NIEST** resembling a wen

WENT past tense of go

WEPT past tense of weep

WERE a pl. and 2d person sing. past indicative, and past subjunctive of be

WEREGILD *n* pl. **-S** wergeld

WEREWOLF *n* pl. **-WOLVES** a person capable of assuming the form of a wolf

WERGELD *n* pl. **-S** a price paid for the taking of a man's life in Anglo-Saxon law

WERGELT *n* pl. **-S** wergeld

WERGILD *n* pl. **-S** wergeld

WERT a 2d person sing. past tense of be

WERWOLF *n* pl. **-WOLVES** werewolf

WESKIT *n* pl. **-S** a vest

WESSAND *n* pl. **-S** weasand

WEST *n* pl. **-S** a cardinal point of the compass

WESTER *v* **-ED, -ING, -S** to move toward the west

WESTERLY *n* pl. **-LIES** a wind from the west

WESTERN *n* pl. **-S** one who lives in the west

WESTING *n* pl. **-S** a shifting west

WESTMOST *adj* farthest west

WESTWARD *n* pl. **-S** a direction toward the west

WET *adj* **WETTER, WETTEST** covered or saturated with a liquid

WET *v* **WETTED, WETTING, WETS** to make wet

WETA *n* pl. **-S** a large wingless insect of New Zealand

WETHER *n* pl. **-S** a gelded male sheep

WETLAND *n* pl. **-S** land containing much soil moisture

WETLY *adv* in a wet manner

WETNESS *n* pl. **-ES** the state of being wet

WETPROOF *adj* waterproof

WETSUIT *n* pl. **-S** a close-fitting rubberlike suit worn in cold water by skin divers

WETTABLE *adj* capable of being wetted

WETTED past tense of wet

WETTER *n* pl. **-S** one that wets

WETTEST superlative of wet

WETTING *n* pl. **-S** a liquid used in moistening something

WETTISH *adj* somewhat wet

WETWARE *n* pl. **-S** the human brain when considered as functionally equivalent to a computer

WHA *pron* who

WHACK *v* **-ED, -ING, -S** to strike sharply

WHACKED *adj* 1. intoxicated on alcohol or drugs 2. exhausted

WHACKER *n* pl. **-S** one that whacks

WHACKING *n* pl. **-S** the act or an instance of striking something sharply

WHACKO *n* pl. **WHACKOS** wacko

WHACKY *adj* **WHACKIER, WHACKIEST** wacky

WHALE *v* **WHALED, WHALING, WHALES** to engage in the hunting of whales (large marine mammals)

WHALEMAN *n* pl. **-MEN** a whaler

WHALER *n* pl. **-S** a person engaged in whaling

WHALING *n* pl. **-S** the industry of hunting and processing whales

WHAM *v* **WHAMMED, WHAMMING, WHAMS** to hit with a loud impact

WHAMMO *interj* — used to indicate a startling event

WHAMMY *n* pl. **-MIES** a supernatural spell bringing bad luck

WHAMO *interj* whammo

WHANG *v* **-ED, -ING, -S** to beat with a whip

WHANGEE *n* pl. **-S** an Asian grass

WHAP *v* **WHAPPED, WHAPPING, WHAPS** to whop

WHAPPER *n* pl. **-S** whopper

WHARF *v* **-ED, -ING, -S** to moor to a wharf (a docking place for vessels)

WHARFAGE *n* pl. **-S** the use of a wharf

WHARVE *n* pl. **-S** a round piece of wood used in spinning thread

WHAT *n* pl. **-S** the true nature of something

WHATEVER *adj* being what or who it may be

WHATNESS *n* pl. **-ES** the true nature of something

WHATNOT *n* pl. **-S** an ornamental set of shelves

WHATSIS *n* pl. **-SISES** whatsit

WHATSIT *n* pl. **-S** something whose name is unknown or forgotten

WHATSO *pron* what or who it may be

WHAUP *n* pl. **-S** a European bird

WHEAL *n* pl. **-S** a welt

WHEAT *n* pl. **-S** a cereal grass

WHEATEAR *n* pl. **-S** a small bird of northern regions

WHEATEN *n* pl. **-S** a pale yellowish color

WHEE *interj* — used to express delight

WHEEDLE *v* **-DLED, -DLING, -DLES** to attempt to persuade by flattery

WHEEDLER *n* pl. **-S** one that wheedles

WHEEL *v* **-ED, -ING, -S** to convey on wheels (circular frames designed to turn on an axis)

WHEELER *n* pl. **-S** one that wheels

WHEELIE *n* pl. **-S** a maneuver made on a wheeled vehicle

WHEELING *n* pl. **-S** the condition of a road for vehicles

WHEELMAN *n* pl. **-MEN** a helmsman

WHEEN *n* pl. **-S** a fairly large amount

WHEEP *v* **-ED, -ING, -S** to wheeple

WHEEPLE *v* **-PLED, -PLING, -PLES** to give forth a prolonged whistle

WHEEZE *v* **WHEEZED, WHEEZING, WHEEZES** to breathe with a whistling sound

WHEEZER *n* pl. **-S** one that wheezes

WHEEZY *adj* **WHEEZIER, WHEEZIEST** characterized by wheezing **WHEEZILY** *adv*

WHELK *n* pl. **-S** a pustule

WHELKY *adj* **WHELKIER, WHELKIEST** marked with whelks

WHELM *v* **-ED, -ING, -S** to cover with water

WHELP *v* **-ED, -ING, -S** to give birth to

WHEN *n* pl. **-S** the time in which something is done or occurs

WHENAS *conj* at which time

WHENCE *conj* from what place

WHENEVER *conj* at whatever time

WHERE *n* pl. **-S** the place at or in which something is located or occurs

WHEREAS *n* pl. **-ES** an introductory statement of a formal document

WHEREAT *conj* at which

WHEREBY *conj* by which

WHEREIN *conj* in which

WHEREOF *conj* of which

WHEREON *conj* on which

WHERETO *conj* to which

WHEREVER *conj* in or to whatever place

WHERRY *v* **-RIED, -RYING, -RIES** to transport in a light rowboat

WHERVE *n* pl. **-S** wharve

WHET *v* **WHETTED, WHETTING, WHETS** to sharpen by friction

WHETHER *conj* if it be the case that

WHETTER *n* pl. **-S** one that whets

WHEW *n* pl. **-S** a whistling sound

WHEY *n* pl. **WHEYS** the watery part of milk **WHEYEY, WHEYISH** *adj*

WHEYFACE *n* pl. **-S** a pale, sallow face

WHEYLIKE *adj* resembling whey

WHICH *pron* what particular one or ones

WHICKER *v* **-ED, -ING, -S** to whinny

WHID *v* **WHIDDED, WHIDDING, WHIDS** to move rapidly and quietly

WHIDAH *n* pl. **-S** whydah

WHIFF *v* **-ED, -ING, -S** to blow or convey with slight gusts of air

WHIFFER *n* pl. **-S** one that whiffs

WHIFFET *n* pl. **-S** an insignificant person

WHIFFLE *v* **-FLED, -FLING, -FLES** to move or think erratically

WHIFFLER *n* pl. **-S** one that whiffles

WHIFFY *adj* **WHIFFIER, WHIFFIEST** having an unpleasant smell

WHIG *n* pl. **-S** one who interprets history as a continuing victory of progress over reactionary forces

WHILE *v* **WHILED, WHILING, WHILES** to cause to pass pleasantly

WHILOM *adv* formerly

WHILST *conj* during the time that

WHIM *n* pl. **-S** an impulsive idea

WHIMBREL *n* pl. **-S** a shore bird

WHIMPER *v* **-ED, -ING, -S** to cry with plaintive, broken sounds

WHIMSEY *n* pl. **-SEYS** whimsy

WHIMSY *n* pl. **-SIES** a whim **WHIMSIED** *adj*

WHIN *n* pl. **-S** furze

WHINCHAT *n* pl. **-S** a songbird

WHINE *v* **WHINED, WHINING, WHINES** to utter a plaintive, high-pitched sound

WHINER *n* pl. **-S** one that whines

WHINEY *adj* **WHINIER, WHINIEST** whiny

WHINGE *v* **WHINGED, WHINGEING** or **WHINGING, WHINGES** to whine

WHINGER *n* pl. **-S** one that whinges

WHINGY *adj* **WHINGIER, WHINGIEST** tending to whinge

WHINIER comparative of whiney and whiny

WHINIEST superlative of whiney and whiny

WHINING present participle of whine

WHINNY *adj* **-NIER, -NIEST** abounding in whin

WHINNY *v* **-NIED, -NYING, -NIES** to neigh in a low or gentle manner

WHINY *adj* **WHINIER, WHINIEST** tending to whine

WHIP *v* **WHIPPED** or **WHIPT, WHIPPING, WHIPS** to strike with a whip (an instrument for administering corporal punishment)

WHIPCORD *n* pl. **-S** a strong, twisted cord

WHIPLASH *v* **-ED, -ING, -ES** to move like the action of a whip

WHIPLESS *adj* lacking a whip

WHIPLIKE *adj* resembling a whip

WHIPPED a past tense of whip

WHIPPER *n* pl. **-S** one that whips

WHIPPET *n* pl. **-S** a small, swift dog

WHIPPING *n* pl. **-S** material used to whip

WHIPPIT *n* pl. **-S** a small container of nitrous oxide

WHIPPY *adj* **-PIER, -PIEST** pertaining to or resembling a whip

WHIPRAY *n* pl. **-RAYS** a stingray

WHIPSAW *v* **-SAWED, -SAWN, -SAWING, -SAWS** to cut with a narrow, tapering saw

WHIPT a past tense of whip

WHIPTAIL *n* pl. **-S** a lizard having a long, slender tail

WHIPWORM *n* pl. **-S** a parasitic worm

WHIR *v* **WHIRRED, WHIRRING, WHIRS** to move with a buzzing sound

WHIRL *v* **-ED, -ING, -S** to revolve rapidly

WHIRLER *n* pl. **-S** one that whirls

WHIRLY *adj* **WHIRLIER, WHIRLIEST** marked by a whirling motion

WHIRLY *n* pl. **WHIRLIES** a small tornado

WHIRR *v* **-ED, -ING, -S** to whir

WHIRRA *interj* wirra

WHIRRED past tense of whir

WHIRRING present participle of whir

WHIRRY *v* **-RIED, -RYING, -RIES** to hurry

WHISH *v* **-ED, -ING, -ES** to move with a hissing sound

WHISHT *v* **-ED, -ING, -S** to hush

WHISK *v* **-ED, -ING, -S** to move briskly

WHISKER *n* pl. **-S** a hair on a man's face **WHISKERY** *adj*

WHISKEY *n* pl. **-KEYS** a liquor

WHISKY	*n* pl. **-KIES** whiskey
WHISPER	*v* **-ED, -ING, -S** to speak softly
WHISPERY	*adj* resembling a whisper
WHIST	*v* **-ED, -ING, -S** to hush
WHISTLE	*v* **-TLED, -TLING, -TLES** to make a shrill, clear musical sound
WHISTLER	*n* pl. **-S** one that whistles
WHIT	*n* pl. **-S** a particle
WHITE	*adj* **WHITER, WHITEST** of the color of pure snow
WHITE	*v* **WHITED, WHITING, WHITES** to whiten
WHITECAP	*n* pl. **-S** a wave with a crest of foam
WHITEFLY	*n* pl. **-FLIES** a small whitish insect
WHITELY	*adv* in a white manner
WHITEN	*v* **-ED, -ING, -S** to make white
WHITENER	*n* pl. **-S** one that whitens
WHITEOUT	*n* pl. **-S** an arctic weather condition
WHITER	comparative of white
WHITEST	superlative of white
WHITEY	*adj* whity
WHITHER	*adv* to what place
WHITIER	comparative of whity
WHITIEST	superlative of whity
WHITING	*n* pl. **-S** a marine food fish
WHITISH	*adj* somewhat white
WHITLOW	*n* pl. **-S** an inflammation of the finger or toe
WHITRACK	*n* pl. **-S** a weasel
WHITTER	*n* pl. **-S** a large draft of liquor
WHITTLE	*v* **-TLED, -TLING, -TLES** to cut or shave bits from
WHITTLER	*n* pl. **-S** one that whittles
WHITTRET	*n* pl. **-S** a weasel
WHITY	*adj* **WHITIER, WHITIEST** whitish
WHIZ	*v* **WHIZZED, WHIZZING, WHIZZES** to move with a buzzing or hissing sound
WHIZBANG	*n* pl. **-S** a type of explosive shell
WHIZZ	*v* **-ED, -ING, -ES** to whiz
WHIZZER	*n* pl. **-S** one that whizzes
WHIZZES	present 3d person sing. of whiz
WHIZZING	present participle of whiz
WHIZZY	*adj* **-ZIER, -ZIEST** marvelous in construction or operation
WHO	*pron* what or which person or persons
WHOA	*interj* — used to command an animal to stop
WHODUNIT	*n* pl. **-S** a mystery story
WHOEVER	*pron* whatever person
WHOLE	*n* pl. **-S** all the parts or elements entering into and making up a thing
WHOLISM	*n* pl. **-S** holism
WHOLLY	*adv* totally
WHOM	*pron* the objective case of who
WHOMEVER	*pron* the objective case of whoever
WHOMP	*v* **-ED, -ING, -S** to defeat decisively
WHOMSO	*pron* the objective case of whoso
WHOOF	*v* **-ED, -ING, -S** to make a deep snorting sound
WHOOMP	*n* pl. **-S** a sudden loud sound
WHOOMPH	*n* pl. **-S** whoomp
WHOOP	*v* **-ED, -ING, -S** to utter loud cries
WHOOPEE	*n* pl. **-S** boisterous fun
WHOOPER	*n* pl. **-S** one that whoops
WHOOPIE	*n* pl. **-S** whoopee
WHOOPLA	*n* pl. **-S** a noisy commotion
WHOOSH	*v* **-ED, -ING, -ES** to move with a hissing sound
WHOOSIS	*n* pl. **-SISES** an object or person whose name is not known
WHOP	*v* **WHOPPED, WHOPPING, WHOPS** to strike forcibly
WHOPPER	*n* pl. **-S** something unusually large
WHORE	*v* **WHORED, WHORING, WHORES** to consort with prostitutes
WHOREDOM	*n* pl. **-S** prostitution
WHORESON	*n* pl. **-S** a bastard
WHORING	*n* pl. **-S** the use of the services of a prostitute
WHORISH	*adj* lewd
WHORL	*v* **-ED, -ING, -S** to move in a twisted or convoluted fashion
WHORT	*n* pl. **-S** an edible berry
WHORTLE	*n* pl. **-S** whort
WHOSE	*pron* the possessive case of who
WHOSESO	*pron* possessive of whoso
WHOSEVER	*pron* the possessive case of whoever
WHOSIS	*n* pl. **-SISES** whoosis
WHOSIT	*n* pl. **-S** whoosis
WHOSO	*pron* whoever

WHUMP	*v* **-ED, -ING, -S** to thump	**WIDOW**	*v* **-ED, -ING, -S** to deprive of a spouse
WHUP	*v* **WHUPPED, WHUPPING, WHUPS** to defeat decisively	**WIDOWER**	*n* pl. **-S** a man whose spouse has died and who has not remarried
WHY	*n* pl. **WHYS** the reason or cause of something	**WIDTH**	*n* pl. **-S** extent from side to side
WHYDA	*n* pl. **-S** whydah	**WIDTHWAY**	*adv* from side to side
WHYDAH	*n* pl. **-S** an African bird	**WIELD**	*v* **-ED, -ING, -S** to handle or use effectively
WICCA	*n* pl. **-S** a form of nature-oriented witchcraft	**WIELDER**	*n* pl. **-S** one that wields
WICCAN	*n* pl. **-S** one who practices wicca	**WIELDY**	*adj* **WIELDIER, WIELDIEST** easily wielded
WICH	*n* pl. **-ES** wych	**WIENER**	*n* pl. **-S** a frankfurter
WICK	*n* pl. **-S** a bundle of loosely twisted fibers in a candle or oil lamp	**WIENIE**	*n* pl. **-S** a wiener
WICKAPE	*n* pl. **-S** wicopy	**WIFE**	*n* pl. **WIVES** a female partner in a marriage
WICKED	*adj* **-EDER, -EDEST** evil **WICKEDLY** *adv*	**WIFE**	*v* **WIFED, WIFING, WIFES** to wive
WICKER	*n* pl. **-S** a slender, pliant twig or branch	**WIFEDOM**	*n* pl. **-S** the status or function of a wife
WICKET	*n* pl. **-S** a small door or gate	**WIFEHOOD**	*n* pl. **-S** the state of being a wife
WICKING	*n* pl. **-S** material for wicks	**WIFELESS**	*adj* having no wife
WICKIUP	*n* pl. **-S** a Native American hut	**WIFELIKE**	*adj* wifely
WICKLESS	*adj* having no wick	**WIFELY**	*adj* **-LIER, -LIEST** of or befitting a wife
WICKYUP	*n* pl. **-S** wickiup	**WIFEY**	*n* pl. **WIFEYS** a wife
WICOPY	*n* pl. **-PIES** a flowering shrub	**WIFING**	present participle of wife
WIDDER	*n* pl. **-S** a widow	**WIFTY**	*adj* **-TIER, -TIEST** ditsy
WIDDIE	*n* pl. **-S** widdy	**WIG**	*v* **WIGGED, WIGGING, WIGS** to provide with a wig (an artificial covering of hair for the head)
WIDDLE	*v* **-DLED, -DLING, -DLES** to wriggle		
WIDDY	*n* pl. **-DIES** a hangman's noose	**WIGAN**	*n* pl. **-S** a stiff fabric
WIDE	*adj* **WIDER, WIDEST** having great extent from side to side **WIDELY** *adv*	**WIGEON**	*n* pl. **-S** widgeon
		WIGGED	past tense of wig
WIDE	*n* pl. **-S** a type of bowled ball in cricket	**WIGGER**	*n* pl. **-S** an unreliable or eccentric person
WIDEBAND	*adj* operating over a wide band of frequencies	**WIGGERY**	*n* pl. **-GERIES** a wig
WIDEBODY	*n* pl. **-BODIES** a jet aircraft having a wide fuselage	**WIGGIER**	comparative of wiggy
		WIGGIEST	superlative of wiggy
		WIGGING	*n* pl. **-S** a scolding
WIDEN	*v* **-ED, -ING, -S** to make wide or wider	**WIGGLE**	*v* **-GLED, -GLING, -GLES** to move with short, quick movements from side to side
WIDENER	*n* pl. **-S** one that widens		
WIDENESS	*n* pl. **-ES** the state of being wide	**WIGGLER**	*n* pl. **-S** one that wiggles
WIDEOUT	*n* pl. **-S** a receiver in football	**WIGGLY**	*adj* **-GLIER, -GLIEST** tending to wiggle
WIDER	comparative of wide		
WIDEST	superlative of wide	**WIGGY**	*adj* **-GIER, -GIEST** crazy
WIDGEON	*n* pl. **-S** a river duck	**WIGHT**	*n* pl. **-S** a living being
WIDGET	*n* pl. **-S** a gadget	**WIGLESS**	*adj* having no wig
WIDISH	*adj* somewhat wide	**WIGLET**	*n* pl. **-S** a small wig

WIGLIKE	*adj* resembling a wig
WIGMAKER	*n* pl. **-S** one that makes wigs
WIGWAG	*v* **-WAGGED, -WAGGING, -WAGS** to move back and forth
WIGWAM	*n* pl. **-S** a Native American dwelling
WIKI	*n* pl. **-S** a website that allows any user to add or edit content
WIKIUP	*n* pl. **-S** wickiup
WILCO	*interj* — used to indicate that a message received will be complied with
WILD	*v* **-ED, -ING, -S** to go about in a group attacking others
WILD	*adj* **WILDER, WILDEST** living in a natural state
WILDCARD	*n* pl. **-S** a symbol used in a database search to represent unspecified characters
WILDCAT	*v* **-CATTED, -CATTING, -CATS** to search for oil in an area of doubtful productivity
WILDER	*v* **-ED, -ING, -S** to bewilder
WILDFIRE	*n* pl. **-S** a raging, destructive fire
WILDFOWL	*n* pl. **-S** a wild game bird
WILDING	*n* pl. **-S** a wild plant or animal
WILDISH	*adj* somewhat wild
WILDLAND	*n* pl. **-S** uncultivated land
WILDLIFE	*n* pl. **WILDLIFE** wild animals and vegetation
WILDLING	*n* pl. **-S** a wilding
WILDLY	*adv* in a wild manner
WILDNESS	*n* pl. **-ES** the state of being wild
WILDWOOD	*n* pl. **-S** natural forest land
WILE	*v* **WILED, WILING, WILES** to entice
WILFUL	*adj* willful **WILFULLY** *adv*
WILIER	comparative of wily
WILIEST	superlative of wily
WILILY	*adv* in a wily manner
WILINESS	*n* pl. **-ES** the quality of being wily
WILING	present participle of wile
WILL	*v* **-ED, -ING, -S** to decide upon **WILLABLE** *adj*
WILL	*v* past sing. 2d person **WOULD** or **WOULDEST** or **WOULDST** — used as an auxiliary followed by a simple infinitive to express futurity, inclination, likelihood, or requirement
WILLER	*n* pl. **-S** one that wills

WILLET	*n* pl. **-S** a shore bird
WILLFUL	*adj* bent on having one's own way
WILLIED	past tense of willy
WILLIES	present 3d person sing. of willy
WILLING	*adj* **-INGER, -INGEST** inclined or favorably disposed in mind
WILLIWAU	*n* pl. **-S** williwaw
WILLIWAW	*n* pl. **-S** a violent gust of cold wind
WILLOW	*v* **-ED, -ING, -S** to clean textile fibers with a certain machine
WILLOWER	*n* pl. **-S** one that willows
WILLOWY	*adj* **-LOWIER, -LOWIEST** pliant
WILLY	*v* **-LIED, -LYING, -LIES** to willow
WILLYARD	*adj* willful
WILLYART	*adj* willyard
WILLYWAW	*n* pl. **-S** williwaw
WILT	*v* **-ED, -ING, -S** to become limp
WILY	*adj* **WILIER, WILIEST** crafty
WIMBLE	*v* **-BLED, -BLING, -BLES** to bore with a hand tool
WIMP	*v* **-ED, -ING, -S** to act in a timid manner
WIMPISH	*adj* wimpy
WIMPLE	*v* **-PLED, -PLING, -PLES** to pleat
WIMPY	*adj* **WIMPIER, WIMPIEST** weak, ineffectual
WIN	*v* **WINNED, WINNING, WINS** to winnow
WIN	*v* **WON** or **WAN, WINNING, WINS** to be victorious
WINCE	*v* **WINCED, WINCING, WINCES** to flinch
WINCER	*n* pl. **-S** one that winces
WINCEY	*n* pl. **-CEYS** a type of fabric
WINCH	*v* **-ED, -ING, -ES** to raise with a winch (a hoisting machine)
WINCHER	*n* pl. **-S** one that winches
WINCING	present participle of wince
WIND	*v* **WOUND** or **WINDED, WINDING, WINDS** to pass around an object or fixed center **WINDABLE** *adj*
WINDAGE	*n* pl. **-S** the effect of the wind (air in natural motion) on a projectile
WINDBAG	*n* pl. **-S** a talkative person
WINDBELL	*n* pl. **-S** a light bell that can be sounded by the wind

WINDBURN	v **-BURNED** or **-BURNT, -BURNING, -BURNS** to be affected with skin irritation caused by exposure to the wind
WINDER	n pl. **-S** one that winds
WINDFALL	n pl. **-S** a sudden and unexpected gain
WINDFLAW	n pl. **-S** a gust of wind
WINDGALL	n pl. **-S** a swelling on a horse's leg
WINDIER	comparative of windy
WINDIEST	superlative of windy
WINDIGO	n pl. **-GOS** or **-GOES** an evil demon in Algonquian mythology
WINDILY	adv in a windy manner
WINDING	n pl. **-S** material wound about an object
WINDLASS	v **-ED, -ING, -ES** to raise with a windlass (a hoisting machine)
WINDLE	v **-DLED, -DLING, -DLES** to wind
WINDLESS	adj being without wind
WINDLING	n pl. **-S** a bundle of straw
WINDLOAD	n pl. **-S** the force exerted by the wind on a structure
WINDMILL	v **-ED, -ING, -S** to rotate solely under the force of a passing airstream
WINDOW	v **-ED, -ING, -S** to provide with a window (an opening in a wall to admit light and air)
WINDOWY	adj having many windows
WINDPACK	n pl. **-S** snow that has been compacted by the wind
WINDPIPE	n pl. **-S** the trachea
WINDROW	v **-ED, -ING, -S** to arrange as hay or grain in long rows
WINDSAIL	n pl. **-S** a funnel of sailcloth used to convey air down into the lower parts of a ship
WINDSLAB	n pl. **-S** a crust formed on soft snow by the wind
WINDSOCK	n pl. **-S** a device used to indicate wind direction
WINDSURF	v **-ED, -ING, -S** to sail on a sailboard
WINDUP	n pl. **-S** a conclusion
WINDWARD	n pl. **-S** the direction from which the wind blows
WINDWAY	n pl. **-WAYS** a passage for air
WINDY	adj **WINDIER, WINDIEST** marked by strong wind
WINE	v **WINED, WINING, WINES** to provide with wine (the fermented juice of the grape)
WINELESS	adj having no wine
WINERY	n pl. **-ERIES** an establishment for making wine
WINESAP	n pl. **-S** a red apple with somewhat tart flesh
WINESHOP	n pl. **-S** a shop where wine is sold
WINESKIN	n pl. **-S** a goatskin bag for holding wine
WINESOP	n pl. **-S** a food sopped in wine
WINEY	adj **WINIER, WINIEST** winy
WING	v **-ED, -ING, -S** to travel by means of wings (organs of flight)
WINGBACK	n pl. **-S** a certain player in football
WINGBEAT	n pl. **-S** one full set of motions of a wing in flying
WINGBOW	n pl. **-S** a mark on the wing of a domestic fowl
WINGDING	n pl. **-S** a lively party
WINGEDLY	adv swiftly
WINGER	n pl. **-S** a certain player in soccer
WINGIER	comparative of wingy
WINGIEST	superlative of wingy
WINGLESS	adj having no wings
WINGLET	n pl. **-S** a small wing
WINGLIKE	adj resembling a wing
WINGMAN	n pl. **-MEN** a pilot behind the leader of a flying formation
WINGNUT	n pl. **-S** a nut with projections for gripping with the thumb and finger
WINGOVER	n pl. **-S** a flight maneuver
WINGSPAN	n pl. **-S** the distance from the tip of one of a pair of wings to that of the other
WINGTIP	n pl. **-S** a type of man's shoe
WINGY	adj **WINGIER, WINGIEST** swift
WINIER	comparative of winey and winy
WINIEST	superlative of winey and winy
WINING	present participle of wine
WINISH	adj winy
WINK	v **-ED, -ING, -S** to close and open one eye quickly
WINKER	n pl. **-S** one that winks
WINKLE	v **-KLED, -KLING, -KLES** to displace, extract, or evict from a position
WINKLER	n pl. **-S** one that winkles

WINLESS	*adj* having no wins
WINNABLE	*adj* able to be won
WINNED	past tense of win (to winnow)
WINNER	*n* pl. **-S** one that wins
WINNING	*n* pl. **-S** money won in a game or competition
WINNOCK	*n* pl. **-S** a window
WINNOW	*v* **-ED, -ING, -S** to free grain from impurities
WINNOWER	*n* pl. **-S** one that winnows
WINO	*n* pl. **WINOS** or **WINOES** one who is habitually drunk on wine
WINSOME	*adj* **-SOMER, -SOMEST** charming
WINTER	*v* **-ED, -ING, -S** to pass the winter (the coldest season of the year)
WINTERER	*n* pl. **-S** one that winters
WINTERLY	*adj* wintry
WINTERY	*adj* **-TERIER, -TERIEST** wintry
WINTLE	*v* **-TLED, -TLING, -TLES** to stagger
WINTRY	*adj* **-TRIER, -TRIEST** characteristic of winter **WINTRILY** *adv*
WINY	*adj* **WINIER, WINIEST** having the taste or qualities of wine
WINZE	*n* pl. **-S** a steeply inclined mine shaft
WIPE	*v* **WIPED, WIPING, WIPES** to rub lightly in order to clean or dry **WIPEABLE** *adj*
WIPEOUT	*n* pl. **-S** a fall from a surfboard
WIPER	*n* pl. **-S** one that wipes
WIRE	*v* **WIRED, WIRING, WIRES** to fasten with wire (a slender rod, strand, or thread of ductile metal) **WIRABLE** *adj*
WIREDRAW	*v* **-DREW, -DRAWN, -DRAWING, -DRAWS** to draw into wire
WIREHAIR	*n* pl. **-S** a dog having a wiry coat
WIRELESS	*v* **-ED, -ING, -ES** to radio
WIRELIKE	*adj* resembling wire
WIRELINE	*n* pl. **-S** a telegraph or telephone wire
WIREMAN	*n* pl. **-MEN** one who makes or works with wire
WIRER	*n* pl. **-S** one that wires
WIRETAP	*v* **-TAPPED, -TAPPING, -TAPS** to intercept messages by means of a concealed monitoring device
WIREWAY	*n* pl. **-WAYS** a tube for protecting electric wires
WIREWORK	*n* pl. **-S** an article made of wire
WIREWORM	*n* pl. **-S** a wirelike worm
WIRIER	comparative of wiry
WIRIEST	superlative of wiry
WIRILY	*adv* in a wiry manner
WIRINESS	*n* pl. **-ES** the quality of being wiry
WIRING	*n* pl. **-S** a system of electric wires
WIRRA	*interj* — used to express sorrow
WIRY	*adj* **WIRIER, WIRIEST** resembling wire
WIS	*v* past tense **WIST** to know — WIS and WIST are the only accepted forms of this verb; it cannot be conjugated further
WISDOM	*n* pl. **-S** the power of true and right discernment
WISE	*adj* **WISER, WISEST** having wisdom
WISE	*v* **WISED, WISING, WISES** to become aware or informed
WISEACRE	*n* pl. **-S** a pretentiously wise person
WISEASS	*n* pl. **-ES** a wiseacre
WISED	past tense of wise
WISEGUY	*n* pl. **-GUYS** a mobster
WISELY	*adv* **-LIER, -LIEST** in a wise manner
WISENESS	*n* pl. **-ES** wisdom
WISENT	*n* pl. **-S** a European bison
WISER	comparative of wise
WISEST	superlative of wise
WISH	*v* **-ED, -ING, -ES** to feel an impulse toward attainment or possession of something
WISHA	*interj* — used to express surprise
WISHBONE	*n* pl. **-S** a forked bone in front of a bird's breastbone
WISHER	*n* pl. **-S** one that wishes
WISHFUL	*adj* desirous
WISHLESS	*adj* not wishful
WISING	present participle of wise
WISP	*v* **-ED, -ING, -S** to twist into a wisp (a small bunch or bundle)
WISPIER	comparative of wispy
WISPIEST	superlative of wispy
WISPILY	*adv* in a wispy manner
WISPISH	*adj* wispy
WISPLIKE	*adj* wispy

WISPY *adj* **WISPIER, WISPIEST** resembling a wisp

WISS *v* **-ED, -ING, -ES** to wish

WIST *v* **-ED, -ING, -S** to know

WISTARIA *n* pl. **-S** wisteria

WISTERIA *n* pl. **-S** a flowering shrub

WISTFUL *adj* yearning

WIT *n* pl. **-S** intelligence

WIT *v* **WIST, WITING** or **WITTING,** present sing. 1st person **WOT,** 2d **WOST,** 3d **WOT,** present pl. **WITE** to know

WITAN *n* pl. **-S** an Anglo-Saxon council to the king

WITCH *v* **-ED, -ING, -ES** to bewitch

WITCHERY *n* pl. **-ERIES** sorcery

WITCHING *n* pl. **-S** sorcery

WITCHY *adj* **WITCHIER, WITCHIEST** malicious

WITE *v* **WITED, WITING, WITES** to blame

WITH *prep* in the company of

WITHAL *adv* in addition

WITHDRAW *v* **-DREW, -DRAWN, -DRAWING, -DRAWS** to move back or away

WITHE *v* **WITHED, WITHING, WITHES** to bind with flexible twigs

WITHER *v* **-ED, -ING, -S** to dry up and wilt

WITHERER *n* pl. **-S** one that withers

WITHEROD *n* pl. **-S** a North American shrub

WITHHOLD *v* **-HELD, -HOLDING, -HOLDS** to hold back

WITHIER comparative of withy

WITHIES pl. of withy

WITHIEST superlative of withy

WITHIN *n* pl. **-S** an interior place or area

WITHING present participle of withe

WITHOUT *n* pl. **-S** an exterior place or area

WITHY *adj* **WITHIER, WITHIEST** flexible and tough

WITHY *n* pl. **WITHIES** a flexible twig

WITING present participle of wit and wite

WITLESS *adj* lacking intelligence

WITLING *n* pl. **-S** one who considers himself or herself witty

WITLOOF *n* pl. **-S** chicory

WITNESS *v* **-ED, -ING, -ES** to see or know by personal experience

WITNEY *n* pl. **-NEYS** a heavy woolen fabric

WITTED *adj* having intelligence

WITTER *v* **-ED, -ING, -S** to speak at length on trivial matters

WITTIER comparative of witty

WITTIEST superlative of witty

WITTILY *adv* in a witty manner

WITTING *n* pl. **-S** knowledge

WITTOL *n* pl. **-S** a man who tolerates his wife's infidelity

WITTY *adj* **-TIER, -TIEST** humorously clever

WIVE *v* **WIVED, WIVING, WIVES** to marry a woman

WIVER *n* pl. **-S** wivern

WIVERN *n* pl. **-S** a two-legged dragon

WIVES pl. of wife

WIVING present participle of wive

WIZ *n* pl. **WIZZES** or **WIZES** a very clever or skillful person

WIZARD *n* pl. **-S** a sorcerer **WIZARDLY** *adj*

WIZARDRY *n* pl. **-RIES** sorcery

WIZEN *v* **-ED, -ING, -S** to shrivel

WIZZEN *n* pl. **-S** weasand

WO *n* pl. **WOS** woe

WOAD *n* pl. **-S** a blue dye **WOADED** *adj*

WOADWAX *n* pl. **-ES** an ornamental shrub

WOALD *n* pl. **-S** a yellow pigment

WOBBLE *v* **-BLED, -BLING, -BLES** to move unsteadily

WOBBLER *n* pl. **-S** one that wobbles

WOBBLY *adj* **-BLIER, -BLIEST** unsteady

WOBBLY *n* pl. **-BLIES** a member of the Industrial Workers of the World

WOBEGONE *adj* affected with woe

WODGE *n* pl. **-S** a chunk of something

WOE *n* pl. **-S** tremendous grief

WOEFUL *adj* **-FULLER, -FULLEST** full of woe **WOEFULLY** *adv*

WOENESS *n* pl. **-ES** sadness

WOESOME *adj* woeful

WOFUL *adj* **-FULLER, -FULLEST** woeful **WOFULLY** *adv*

WOGGLE *n* pl. **-S** a ring through which a Scout's neckerchief is threaded

WOK *n* pl. **-S** a cooking utensil

WOKE *adj* **WOKER, WOKEST** aware of important facts

WOKEN	a past participle of wake
WOLD	*n* pl. **-S** an elevated tract of open land
WOLF	*n* pl. **WOLVES** a carnivorous mammal
WOLF	*v* **-ED, -ING, -S** to devour voraciously
WOLFER	*n* pl. **-S** one who hunts wolves
WOLFFISH	*n* pl. **-ES** a marine fish
WOLFISH	*adj* wolflike
WOLFLIKE	*adj* resembling a wolf
WOLFRAM	*n* pl. **-S** tungsten
WOLFSKIN	*n* pl. **-S** the skin of a wolf
WOLVER	*n* pl. **-S** wolfer
WOLVES	pl. of wolf
WOMAN	*n* pl. **WOMEN** an adult human female
WOMAN	*v* **-MANED, -MANING, -MANS** or **-MANNED, -MANNING, -MANS** to provide with a staff of women
WOMANISE	*v* **-ISED, -ISING, -ISES** to womanize
WOMANISH	*adj* characteristic of a woman
WOMANISM	*n* pl. **-S** a belief in or respect for women
WOMANIST	*n* pl. **-S** a supporter of womanism
WOMANIZE	*v* **-IZED, -IZING, -IZES** to make effeminate
WOMANLY	*adj* **-LIER, -LIEST** having the qualities of a woman
WOMB	*n* pl. **-S** the uterus **WOMBED** *adj*
WOMBAT	*n* pl. **-S** a nocturnal mammal
WOMBLIKE	*adj* resembling a womb
WOMBY	*adj* **WOMBIER, WOMBIEST** hollow
WOMEN	pl. of woman
WOMERA	*n* pl. **-S** a device used to propel spears
WOMMERA	*n* pl. **-S** womera
WOMYN	*n/pl* women
WON	*v* **WONNED, WONNING, WONS** to dwell
WONDER	*v* **-ED, -ING, -S** to have a feeling of curiosity or doubt
WONDERER	*n* pl. **-S** one that wonders
WONDROUS	*adj* marvelous
WONK	*n* pl. **-S** an overly studious student **WONKISH** *adj*
WONKERY	*n* pl. **-ERIES** the qualities or activities of a wonk
WONKY	*adj* **-KIER, -KIEST** unsteady **WONKILY** *adv*
WONNED	past tense of won
WONNER	*n* pl. **-S** a prodigy
WONNING	present participle of won
WONT	*v* **-ED, -ING, -S** to make accustomed to
WONTEDLY	*adv* in a usual manner
WONTON	*n* pl. **-S** a pork-filled dumpling used in Chinese cooking
WOO	*v* **-ED, -ING, -S** to seek the affection of **WOOABLE** *adj*
WOOD	*v* **-ED, -ING, -S** to furnish with wood (the hard, fibrous substance beneath the bark of a tree or shrub)
WOODBIN	*n* pl. **-S** a bin for holding firewood
WOODBIND	*n* pl. **-S** woodbine
WOODBINE	*n* pl. **-S** a European shrub
WOODBOX	*n* pl. **-ES** a woodbin
WOODCHAT	*n* pl. **-S** a European shrike
WOODCOCK	*n* pl. **-S** a game bird
WOODCUT	*n* pl. **-S** an engraved block of wood
WOODEN	*adj* **-ENER, -ENEST** resembling wood in stiffness **WOODENLY** *adv*
WOODFERN	*n* pl. **-S** an evergreen fern
WOODHEN	*n* pl. **-S** the weka
WOODIE	*n* pl. **-S** woody
WOODIER	comparative of woody
WOODIES	pl. of woody
WOODIEST	superlative of woody
WOODLAND	*n* pl. **-S** land covered with trees
WOODLARK	*n* pl. **-S** a songbird
WOODLESS	*adj* having no wood
WOODLICE	*n/pl* sowbugs
WOODLORE	*n* pl. **-S** knowledge of the forest
WOODLOT	*n* pl. **-S** an area restricted to the growing of forest trees
WOODMAN	*n* pl. **-MEN** woodsman
WOODMICE	*n/pl* field mice
WOODNOTE	*n* pl. **-S** a song or call of a forest bird
WOODPILE	*n* pl. **-S** a pile of wood
WOODRAT	*n* pl. **-S** a North American rat having a well-furred tail and large ears
WOODRUFF	*n* pl. **-S** an aromatic herb

WOODRUSH *n* pl. **-ES** a grasslike plant having leaves fringed with long hairs

WOODSHED *v* **-SHEDDED, -SHEDDING, -SHEDS** to practice on a musical instrument

WOODSIA *n* pl. **-S** a small fern

WOODSMAN *n* pl. **-MEN** one who works or lives in the forest

WOODSY *adj* **WOODSIER, WOODSIEST** suggestive of a forest

WOODTONE *n* pl. **-S** a finish that imitates wood

WOODWASP *n* pl. **-S** a large wasplike insect

WOODWAX *n* pl. **-ES** woadwax

WOODWIND *n* pl. **-S** a musical wind instrument

WOODWORK *n* pl. **-S** work made of wood

WOODWORM *n* pl. **-S** a wood-boring worm

WOODY *adj* **WOODIER, WOODIEST** containing or resembling wood

WOODY *n* pl. **WOODIES** a wood-paneled station wagon

WOODYARD *n* pl. **-S** a yard where wood is chopped or stored

WOOER *n* pl. **-S** one that woos

WOOF *v* **-ED, -ING, -S** to utter a gruff barking sound

WOOFER *n* pl. **-S** a loudspeaker designed to reproduce low-pitched sounds

WOOINGLY *adv* attractively

WOOL *n* pl. **-S** the dense, soft hair forming the coat of certain mammals

WOOLED *adj* having wool of a specified kind

WOOLEN *n* pl. **-S** a fabric made of wool

WOOLER *n* pl. **-S** a domestic animal raised for its wool

WOOLFELL *n* pl. **-S** woolskin

WOOLHAT *n* pl. **-S** one who works a small farm

WOOLIE *n* pl. **-S** a woolly

WOOLIER comparative of wooly

WOOLIES pl. of wooly

WOOLIEST superlative of wooly

WOOLLED *adj* wooled

WOOLLEN *n* pl. **-S** woolen

WOOLLIES pl. of woolly

WOOLLIKE *adj* resembling wool

WOOLLY *adj* **-LIER, -LIEST** consisting of or resembling wool **WOOLLILY** *adv*

WOOLLY *n* pl. **-LIES** a garment made of wool

WOOLMAN *n* pl. **-MEN** a dealer in wool

WOOLPACK *n* pl. **-S** a bag for packing a bale of wool

WOOLSACK *n* pl. **-S** a sack of wool

WOOLSHED *n* pl. **-S** a building in which sheep are sheared

WOOLSKIN *n* pl. **-S** a sheepskin with the wool still on it

WOOLWORK *n* pl. **-S** needlework

WOOLY *adj* **WOOLIER, WOOLIEST** woolly

WOOLY *n* pl. **WOOLIES** a woolly

WOOMERA *n* pl. **-S** womera

WOONERF *n* pl. **-S** a road in the Netherlands primarily for pedestrians and cyclists

WOOPIE *n* pl. **-S** a well-off older person

WOOPS *v* **-ED, -ING, -ES** to vomit

WOOPY *n* pl. **-PIES** woopie

WOORALI *n* pl. **-S** curare

WOORARI *n* pl. **-S** curare

WOOSH *v* **-ED, -ING, -ES** to whoosh

WOOZY *adj* **-ZIER, -ZIEST** dazed **WOOZILY** *adv*

WORD *v* **-ED, -ING, -S** to express in words (speech sounds that communicate meaning)

WORDAGE *n* pl. **-S** the number of words used

WORDBOOK *n* pl. **-S** a dictionary

WORDIE *n* pl. **-S** a lover of words

WORDIER comparative of wordy

WORDIEST superlative of wordy

WORDILY *adv* in a wordy manner

WORDING *n* pl. **-S** the act or style of expressing in words

WORDLESS *adj* being without words

WORDPLAY *n* pl. **-PLAYS** a witty exchange of words

WORDY *adj* **WORDIER, WORDIEST** using many or too many words

WORE past tense of wear

WORK *v* **WORKED** or **WROUGHT, WORKING, WORKS** to exert one's powers of body or mind for some purpose

WORKABLE *adj* capable of being done **WORKABLY** *adv*

WORKADAY *adj* everyday

WORKBAG *n* pl. **-S** a bag for holding work instruments and materials

WORKBOAT *n* pl. **-S** a boat used for commercial purposes

WORKBOOK *n* pl. **-S** an exercise book for a student

WORKBOOT *n* pl. **-S** a sturdy leather boot for workers

WORKBOX *n* pl. **-ES** a box for holding work instruments and materials

WORKDAY *n* pl. **-DAYS** a day on which work is done

WORKER *n* pl. **-S** one that works

WORKFARE *n* pl. **-S** a welfare program that requires recipients to perform public-service work

WORKFLOW *n* pl. **-S** the amount of work to and from an office or employee

WORKFOLK *n/pl* manual laborers

WORKHOUR *n* pl. **-S** any of the hours of the day during which work is done

WORKING *n* pl. **-S** a mining excavation

WORKLESS *adj* unemployed

WORKLOAD *n* pl. **-S** the amount of work assigned to an employee

WORKMAN *n* pl. **-MEN** a male worker

WORKMATE *n* pl. **-S** a fellow worker

WORKOUT *n* pl. **-S** a period of physical exercise

WORKROOM *n* pl. **-S** a room in which work is done

WORKSHOP *v* **-SHOPPED, -SHOPPING, -SHOPS** to perform and discuss (a play) before public performance

WORKSITE *n* pl. **-S** an area where work takes place

WORKSONG *n* pl. **-S** a song sung while doing physical work

WORKTOP *n* pl. **-S** a work surface especially in a kitchen

WORKUP *n* pl. **-S** an intensive diagnostic study

WORKWEAR *n* pl. **WORKWEAR** heavy-duty clothes for physical work

WORKWEEK *n* pl. **-S** the number of hours worked in a week

WORLD *n* pl. **-S** the earth and all its inhabitants

WORLDER *n* pl. **-S** one who belongs to a specified class, time, domain, or sphere of activity

WORLDLY *adj* **-LIER, -LIEST** pertaining to the world

WORM *v* **-ED, -ING, -S** to rid of worms (small, limbless invertebrates)

WORMCAST *n* pl. **-S** a mass of earth left on the surface by a burrowing earthworm

WORMER *n* pl. **-S** one that worms

WORMGEAR *n* pl. **-S** a gear wheel driven by a worm (a rotating shaft with threads)

WORMHOLE *n* pl. **-S** a hole made by a burrowing worm

WORMIER comparative of wormy

WORMIEST superlative of wormy

WORMIL *n* pl. **-S** a lump in the skin of an animal's back

WORMISH *adj* wormlike

WORMLIKE *adj* resembling a worm

WORMROOT *n* pl. **-S** pinkroot

WORMSEED *n* pl. **-S** a tropical plant

WORMWOOD *n* pl. **-S** a European herb

WORMY *adj* **WORMIER, WORMIEST** infested with worms

WORN *adj* affected by wear or use

WORNNESS *n* pl. **-ES** the state of being worn

WORRIER *n* pl. **-S** one that worries

WORRIT *v* **-ED, -ING, -S** to worry

WORRY *v* **-RIED, -RYING, -RIES** to feel anxious and uneasy about something

WORSE *n* pl. **-S** something that is worse (bad in a greater degree)

WORSEN *v* **-ED, -ING, -S** to make or become worse

WORSER *adj* worse

WORSET *n* pl. **-S** worsted

WORSHIP *v* **-SHIPED, -SHIPING, -SHIPS** or **-SHIPPED, -SHIPPING, -SHIPS** to honor and love as a divine being

WORST *v* **-ED, -ING, -S** to defeat

WORSTED *n* pl. **-S** a woolen yarn

WORT *n* pl. **-S** a plant, herb, or vegetable

WORTH *v* **-ED, -ING, -S** to befall

WORTHFUL *adj* worthy

WORTHY *adj* **-THIER, -THIEST** having value or merit **WORTHILY** *adv*

WORTHY *n* pl. **-THIES** a worthy person

WOST a present 2d person sing. of wit

WOT *v* **WOTTED, WOTTING, WOTS** to know

WOTCHER *interj* — used as a casual greeting

WOULD past tense of will

WOULDEST	a 2d person sing. past tense of will
WOULDST	a 2d person sing. past tense of will
WOUND	v **-ED, -ING, -S** to inflict an injury upon
WOVE	a past tense of weave
WOVEN	n pl. **-S** a woven fabric
WOW	v **-ED, -ING, -S** to excite to enthusiastic approval
WOWEE	interj — used to express astonishment or admiration
WOWSER	n pl. **-S** a puritanical person
WRACK	v **-ED, -ING, -S** to wreck
WRACKFUL	adj destructive
WRAITH	n pl. **-S** a ghost
WRANG	n pl. **-S** a wrong
WRANGLE	v **-GLED, -GLING, -GLES** to argue noisily
WRANGLER	n pl. **-S** one that wrangles
WRAP	v **WRAPPED** or **WRAPT, WRAPPING, WRAPS** to enclose in something wound or folded about
WRAPPER	n pl. **-S** one that wraps
WRAPPING	n pl. **-S** the material in which something is wrapped
WRASSE	n pl. **-S** a marine fish
WRASSLE	v **-SLED, -SLING, -SLES** to wrastle
WRASTLE	v **-TLED, -TLING, -TLES** to wrestle
WRATH	v **-ED, -ING, -S** to make wrathful
WRATHFUL	adj extremely angry
WRATHY	adj **WRATHIER, WRATHIEST** wrathful **WRATHILY** adv
WREAK	v **-ED, -ING, -S** to inflict
WREAKER	n pl. **-S** one that wreaks
WREATH	n pl. **-S** a band of flowers **WREATHY** adj
WREATHE	v **WREATHED, WREATHEN, WREATHING, WREATHES** to shape into a wreath
WREATHER	n pl. **-S** one that wreathes
WRECK	v **-ED, -ING, -S** to cause the ruin of
WRECKAGE	n pl. **-S** the act of wrecking
WRECKER	n pl. **-S** one that wrecks
WRECKFUL	adj destructive
WRECKING	n pl. **-S** the occupation of salvaging wrecked objects
WREN	n pl. **-S** a small songbird
WRENCH	v **-ED, -ING, -ES** to twist suddenly and forcibly
WRENCHER	n pl. **-S** one that wrenches
WRENTIT	n pl. **-S** a long-tailed North American songbird
WREST	v **-ED, -ING, -S** to take away by force
WRESTER	n pl. **-S** one that wrests
WRESTLE	v **-TLED, -TLING, -TLES** to engage in a type of hand-to-hand contest
WRESTLER	n pl. **-S** one that wrestles
WRETCH	n pl. **-ES** a wretched person
WRETCHED	adj **-EDER, -EDEST** extremely unhappy
WRICK	v **-ED, -ING, -S** to wrench
WRIED	past tense of wry
WRIER	a comparative of wry
WRIES	present 3d person sing. of wry
WRIEST	a superlative of wry
WRIGGLE	v **-GLED, -GLING, -GLES** to turn or twist in a sinuous manner
WRIGGLER	n pl. **-S** one that wriggles
WRIGGLY	adj **-GLIER, -GLIEST** wriggling
WRIGHT	n pl. **-S** one who constructs or creates
WRING	v **WRUNG** or **WRINGED, WRINGING, WRINGS** to twist so as to compress
WRINGER	n pl. **-S** one that wrings
WRINKLE	v **-KLED, -KLING, -KLES** to make wrinkles (small ridges or furrows) in
WRINKLY	adj **-KLIER, -KLIEST** having wrinkles
WRIST	v **-ED, -ING, -S** to sweep the puck along the ice before shooting it
WRISTER	n pl. **-S** a type of shot in hockey
WRISTLET	n pl. **-S** a band worn around the wrist
WRISTY	adj **WRISTIER, WRISTIEST** using much wrist action
WRIT	n pl. **-S** a written legal order
WRITE	v **WROTE, WRITTEN, WRITING, WRITES** to form characters or symbols on a surface with an instrument **WRITABLE** adj
WRITEOFF	n pl. **-S** an uncollectible debt that is cancelled
WRITER	n pl. **-S** one that writes
WRITERLY	adj characteristic of a writer
WRITHE	v **WRITHED, WRITHING, WRITHES** to squirm or twist in pain

WRITHEN	*adj* twisted
WRITHER	*n* pl. **-S** one that writhes
WRITING	*n* pl. **-S** a written composition
WRITTEN	past participle of write
WRONG	*adj* **WRONGER, WRONGEST** not according to what is right, proper, or correct
WRONG	*v* **-ED, -ING, -S** to treat injuriously or unjustly
WRONGER	*n* pl. **-S** one that wrongs
WRONGFUL	*adj* wrong
WRONGLY	*adv* in a wrong manner
WROTE	past tense of write
WROTH	*adj* very angry
WROTHFUL	*adj* wroth
WROUGHT	a past tense of work
WRUNG	a past tense of wring
WRY	*adj* **WRIER, WRIEST** or **WRYER, WRYEST** contorted **WRYLY** *adv*
WRY	*v* **WRIED, WRYING, WRIES** to contort
WRYNECK	*n* pl. **-S** a European bird
WRYNESS	*n* pl. **-ES** the state of being wry
WUD	*adj* insane
WUDDY	*n* pl. **-DIES** a large loop at the end of a rope
WURST	*n* pl. **-S** sausage
WURTZITE	*n* pl. **-S** a mineral
WURZEL	*n* pl. **-S** a variety of beet
WUSHU	*n* pl. **WUSHU** Chinese martial arts
WUSS	*n* pl. **-ES** a wimp (a weak, ineffectual person)
WUSSY	*adj* **WUSSIER, WUSSIEST** wimpy
WUSSY	*n* pl. **-SIES** a wuss
WUTHER	*v* **-ED, -ING, -S** to blow with a dull roaring sound
WYCH	*n* pl. **-ES** a European elm
WYE	*n* pl. **-S** the letter Y
WYLE	*v* **WYLED, WYLING, WYLES** to beguile
WYN	*n* pl. **-S** wynn
WYND	*n* pl. **-S** a narrow street
WYNN	*n* pl. **-S** the rune for W
WYSIWYG	*adj* denoting the text on a display screen that exactly corresponds to its appearance on a printout
WYTE	*v* **WYTED, WYTING, WYTES** to wite
WYVERN	*n* pl. **-S** wivern

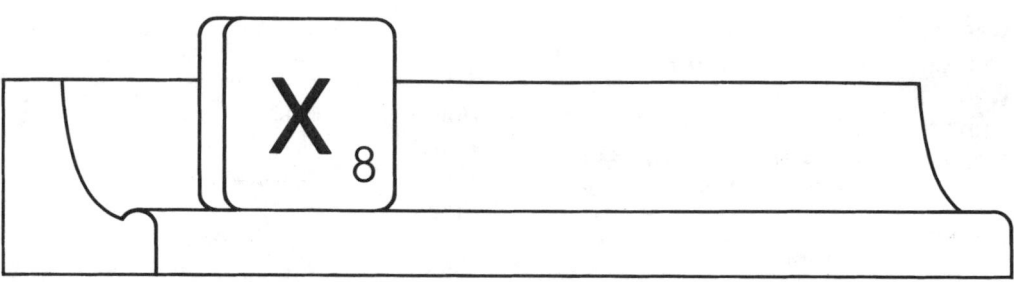

XANTHAN *n* pl. **-S** a gum produced by bacterial fermentation

XANTHATE *n* pl. **-S** a chemical salt

XANTHEIN *n* pl. **-S** the water-soluble part of the coloring matter in yellow flowers

XANTHENE *n* pl. **-S** a chemical compound

XANTHIC *adj* tending to have a yellow color

XANTHIN *n* pl. **-S** a yellow pigment

XANTHINE *n* pl. **-S** a chemical compound

XANTHOMA *n* pl. **-MAS** or **-MATA** a skin disease

XANTHONE *n* pl. **-S** a chemical compound

XANTHOUS *adj* yellow

XEBEC *n* pl. **-S** a Mediterranean sailing vessel

XENIA *n* pl. **-S** the effect of pollen on certain plant structures **XENIAL** *adj*

XENIC *adj* pertaining to a type of culture medium

XENOGAMY *n* pl. **-MIES** the transfer of pollen from one plant to another

XENOGENY *n* pl. **-NIES** the supposed production of offspring totally different from the parent

XENOLITH *n* pl. **-S** a rock fragment included in another rock

XENON *n* pl. **-S** a gaseous element

XENOPUS *n* pl. **-PUSES** a frog native to southern Africa

XENOTIME *n* pl. **-S** a yellowish-brown mineral

XERARCH *adj* developing in a dry area

XERIC *adj* requiring only a small amount of moisture

XEROSERE *n* pl. **-S** a dry-land sere

XEROSIS *n* pl. **-ROSES** abnormal dryness of a body part or tissue **XEROTIC** *adj*

XEROX *v* **-ED, -ING, -ES** to copy on a xerographic copier

XERUS *n* pl. **-ES** an African ground squirrel

XI *n* pl. **-S** a Greek letter

XIPHOID *n* pl. **-S** a part of the sternum

XU *n* pl. **XU** a monetary unit of Vietnam

XYLAN *n* pl. **-S** a substance found in cell walls of plants

XYLEM *n* pl. **-S** a complex plant tissue

XYLENE *n* pl. **-S** a flammable hydrocarbon

XYLIDIN *n* pl. **-S** xylidine

XYLIDINE *n* pl. **-S** a chemical compound

XYLITOL *n* pl. **-S** an alcohol

XYLOCARP *n* pl. **-S** a hard, woody fruit

XYLOID *adj* resembling wood

XYLOL *n* pl. **-S** xylene

XYLOSE *n* pl. **-S** a type of sugar

XYLOTOMY *n* pl. **-MIES** the preparation of sections of wood for microscopic examination

XYLYL *n* pl. **-S** a univalent radical

XYST *n* pl. **-S** xystus

XYSTER *n* pl. **-S** a surgical instrument for scraping bones

XYSTOS *n* pl. **-TOI** xystus

XYSTUS *n* pl. **-TI** a roofed area where athletes trained in ancient Greece

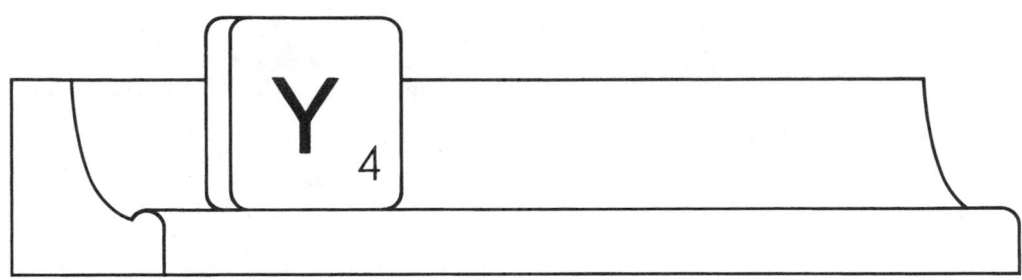

YA	*n* pl. **-S** an Asian pear
YABBER	*v* **-ED, -ING, -S** to jabber
YABBIE	*n* pl. **-S** yabby
YABBY	*n* pl. **-BIES** an Australian crayfish
YACHT	*v* **-ED, -ING, -S** to sail in a yacht (a vessel used for pleasure cruising or racing)
YACHTER	*n* pl. **-S** one who sails a yacht
YACHTIE	*n* pl. **-S** a yachter
YACHTING	*n* pl. **-S** the sport of sailing in yachts
YACHTMAN	*n* pl. **-MEN** a yachter
YACK	*v* **-ED, -ING, -S** to yak
YAFF	*v* **-ED, -ING, -S** to bark
YAFFLE	*n* pl. **-S** the European green woodpecker
YAG	*n* pl. **-S** a synthetic garnet
YAGE	*n* pl. **-S** a tropical vine of the Amazon region
YAGER	*n* pl. **-S** jaeger
YAGI	*n* pl. **-S** a type of shortwave antenna
YAH	*interj* — used as an exclamation of disgust
YAHOO	*n* pl. **-HOOS** a coarse, uncouth person
YAHOOISM	*n* pl. **-S** coarse, uncouth behavior
YAHRZEIT	*n* pl. **-S** an anniversary of the death of a family member observed by Jews
YAIRD	*n* pl. **-S** a garden
YAK	*v* **YAKKED, YAKKING, YAKS** to chatter
YAKITORI	*n* pl. **-S** marinated chicken pieces on skewers
YAKKER	*n* pl. **-S** one that yaks
YAKUZA	*n* pl. **YAKUZA** an alliance of Japanese criminal organizations
YALD	*adj* yauld
YAM	*n* pl. **-S** a plant having an edible root
YAMALKA	*n* pl. **-S** yarmulke
YAMEN	*n* pl. **-S** the residence of a Chinese public official
YAMMER	*v* **-ED, -ING, -S** to whine or complain peevishly
YAMMERER	*n* pl. **-S** one that yammers
YAMULKA	*n* pl. **-S** yarmulke
YAMUN	*n* pl. **-S** yamen
YANG	*n* pl. **-S** the masculine active principle in Chinese cosmology
YANK	*v* **-ED, -ING, -S** to pull suddenly
YANQUI	*n* pl. **-S** a United States citizen
YANTRA	*n* pl. **-S** a geometrical diagram used in meditation
YAP	*v* **YAPPED, YAPPING, YAPS** to bark shrilly
YAPOCK	*n* pl. **-S** an aquatic mammal
YAPOK	*n* pl. **-S** yapock
YAPON	*n* pl. **-S** yaupon
YAPPED	past tense of yap
YAPPER	*n* pl. **-S** one that yaps
YAPPING	present participle of yap
YAPPY	*adj* **-PIER, -PIEST** inclined to yap
YAR	*adj* yare
YARAK	*n* pl. **-S** a fit condition for hunting — used of a hawk
YARD	*v* **-ED, -ING, -S** to put in a yard (a tract of ground adjacent to a building)
YARDAGE	*n* pl. **-S** the use of an enclosure for livestock at a railroad station
YARDARM	*n* pl. **-S** either end of a ship's spar
YARDBIRD	*n* pl. **-S** an army recruit
YARDER	*n* pl. **-S** one having a specified number of yards in length

YARDLAND	*n* pl. **-S** an old English unit of land measure
YARDMAN	*n* pl. **-MEN** a man employed to do outdoor work
YARDWAND	*n* pl. **-S** a measuring stick
YARDWORK	*n* pl. **-S** the work of caring for a lawn
YARE	*adj* **YARER, YAREST** nimble **YARELY** *adv*
YARMELKE	*n* pl. **-S** yarmulke
YARMULKA	*v* pl. **-S** yarmulke
YARMULKE	*n* pl. **-S** a skullcap worn by Jewish males
YARN	*v* **-ED, -ING, -S** to tell a long story
YARNER	*n* pl. **-S** one that yarns
YARROW	*n* pl. **-S** a perennial herb
YASHMAC	*n* pl. **-S** yashmak
YASHMAK	*n* pl. **-S** a veil worn by Muslim women
YASMAK	*n* pl. **-S** yashmak
YATAGAN	*n* pl. **-S** yataghan
YATAGHAN	*n* pl. **-S** a Turkish sword
YATTER	*v* **-ED, -ING, -S** to talk idly
YAUD	*n* pl. **-S** an old mare
YAULD	*adj* vigorous
YAUP	*v* **-ED, -ING, -S** to yawp
YAUPER	*n* pl. **-S** one that yaups
YAUPON	*n* pl. **-S** an evergreen shrub
YAUTIA	*n* pl. **-S** a tropical plant
YAW	*v* **-ED, -ING, -S** to deviate from an intended course
YAWEY	*adj* pertaining to yaws (an infectious disease)
YAWL	*v* **-ED, -ING, -S** to yowl
YAWMETER	*n* pl. **-S** an instrument in an aircraft
YAWN	*v* **-ED, -ING, -S** to open the mouth wide with a deep inhalation of air
YAWNER	*n* pl. **-S** one that yawns
YAWP	*v* **-ED, -ING, -S** to utter a loud, harsh cry
YAWPER	*n* pl. **-S** one that yawps
YAWPING	*n* pl. **-S** a loud, harsh cry
YAY	*n* pl. **YAYS** yea
YCLAD	*adj* clothed
YCLEPED	*adj* yclept
YCLEPT	*adj* called; named
YE	*pron* you
YEA	*n* pl. **-S** an affirmative vote
YEAH	*n* pl. **-S** an affirmative reply
YEALING	*n* pl. **-S** a person of the same age
YEAN	*v* **-ED, -ING, -S** to bear young
YEANLING	*n* pl. **-S** the young of a sheep or goat
YEAR	*n* pl. **-S** a period of time consisting of 365 or 366 days
YEARBOOK	*n* pl. **-S** a book published each year by a graduating class
YEAREND	*n* pl. **-S** the end of a year
YEARLING	*n* pl. **-S** an animal past its first year and not yet two years old
YEARLONG	*adj* lasting through a year
YEARLY	*n* pl. **-LIES** a publication appearing once a year
YEARN	*v* **-ED, -ING, -S** to have a strong or deep desire
YEARNER	*n* pl. **-S** one that yearns
YEARNING	*n* pl. **-S** a strong or deep desire
YEASAYER	*n* pl. **-S** one that affirms something
YEAST	*v* **-ED, -ING, -S** to foam
YEASTY	*adj* **YEASTIER, YEASTIEST** foamy **YEASTILY** *adv*
YECCH	*n* pl. **-S** something disgusting
YECH	*n* pl. **-S** yecch
YECHY	*adj* disgusting
YEELIN	*n* pl. **-S** yealing
YEESH	*interj* — used to express frustration
YEGG	*n* pl. **-S** a burglar
YEGGMAN	*n* pl. **-MEN** a yegg
YEH	*adv* — used to express assent or agreement
YELD	*adj* not giving milk
YELK	*n* pl. **-S** yolk
YELL	*v* **-ED, -ING, -S** to cry out loudly
YELLER	*n* pl. **-S** one that yells
YELLING	*n* pl. **-S** the act or an instance of making a loud cry
YELLOW	*adj* **-LOWER, -LOWEST** of a bright color like that of ripe lemons **YELLOWLY** *adv*
YELLOW	*v* **-ED, -ING, -S** to make or become yellow
YELLOWY	*adj* somewhat yellow
YELP	*v* **-ED, -ING, -S** to utter a sharp, shrill cry
YELPER	*n* pl. **-S** one that yelps

YEN	*v* **YENNED, YENNING, YENS** to yearn
YENTA	*n* pl. **-S** a gossipy woman
YENTE	*n* pl. **-S** yenta
YEOMAN	*n* pl. **-MEN** an independent farmer **YEOMANLY** *adj*
YEOMANRY	*n* pl. **-RIES** the collective body of yeomen
YEOW	*interj* — used to express pain or shock
YEP	*n* pl. **-S** an affirmative reply
YERBA	*n* pl. **-S** a South American beverage resembling tea
YERK	*v* **-ED, -ING, -S** to beat vigorously
YES	*v* **YESSED, YESSING, YESSES** or **YESES** to give an affirmative reply to
YESHIVA	*n* pl. **-VAS** or **-VOT** or **-VOTH** an orthodox Jewish school
YESHIVAH	*n* pl. **-S** yeshiva
YESSIR	*interj* — used to express assent
YESSIREE	*interj* yessir
YESSUM	*interj* — used to express assent to a woman
YESTER	*adj* pertaining to yesterday
YESTERN	*adj* yester
YESTREEN	*n* pl. **-S** the previous evening
YET	*adv* up to now
YETI	*n* pl. **-S** the abominable snowman
YETT	*n* pl. **-S** a gate
YEUK	*v* **-ED, -ING, -S** to itch
YEUKY	*adj* itchy
YEW	*n* pl. **-S** an evergreen tree or shrub
YIELD	*v* **-ED, -ING, -S** to give up
YIELDER	*n* pl. **-S** one that yields
YIKES	*interj* — used to express fear or pain
YILL	*n* pl. **-S** ale
YIN	*n* pl. **-S** the feminine passive principle in Chinese cosmology
YINCE	*adv* once
YIP	*v* **YIPPED, YIPPING, YIPS** to yelp
YIPE	*interj* — used to express fear or surprise
YIPES	*interj* yipe
YIPPEE	*interj* — used to express joy
YIPPIE	*n* pl. **-S** a politically radical hippie
YIPPING	present participle of yip
YIRD	*n* pl. **-S** earth
YIRR	*v* **-ED, -ING, -S** to snarl
YIRTH	*n* pl. **-S** yird
YLEM	*n* pl. **-S** hypothetical matter from which the elements are derived
YO	*interj* — used to call attention or to express affirmation
YOB	*n* pl. **-S** a hooligan
YOBBERY	*n* pl. **-BERIES** the behavior of a yob
YOBBISH	*adj* characteristic of a yob
YOBBO	*n* pl. **-BOS** or **-BOES** a yob
YOBBY	*adj* **-BIER, -BIEST** resembling a yob
YOCK	*v* **-ED, -ING, -S** to laugh boisterously
YOD	*n* pl. **-S** a Hebrew letter
YODEL	*v* **-DELED, -DELING, -DELS** or **-DELLED, -DELLING, -DELS** to sing with a fluctuating voice
YODELER	*n* pl. **-S** one that yodels
YODELLER	*n* pl. **-S** yodeler
YODH	*n* pl. **-S** yod
YODLE	*v* **-DLED, -DLING, -DLES** to yodel
YODLER	*n* pl. **-S** yodeler
YOGA	*n* pl. **-S** a Hindu philosophy involving physical and mental disciplines
YOGEE	*n* pl. **-S** yogi
YOGH	*n* pl. **-S** a Middle English letter
YOGHOURT	*n* pl. **-S** yogurt
YOGHURT	*n* pl. **-S** yogurt
YOGI	*n* pl. **-S** a person who practices yoga
YOGIC	*adj* pertaining to yoga
YOGIN	*n* pl. **-S** yogi
YOGINI	*n* pl. **-S** a female yogi
YOGISM	*n* pl. **-S** the practice or system of yoga
YOGOURT	*n* pl. **-S** yogurt
YOGURT	*n* pl. **-S** a food made from milk
YOHIMBE	*n* pl. **-S** a topical African tree
YOICKS	*interj* — used to encourage hunting hounds
YOK	*n* pl. **-S** a boisterous laugh
YOKE	*v* **YOKED, YOKING, YOKES** to fit with a yoke (a wooden frame for joining together draft animals)
YOKEL	*n* pl. **-S** a naive or gullible rustic

YOKELESS	*adj* having no yoke
YOKELISH	*adj* resembling a yokel
YOKEMATE	*n* pl. **-S** a companion in work
YOKING	present participle of yoke
YOKOZUNA	*n* pl. **-S** a champion sumo wrestler
YOLK	*n* pl. **-S** the yellow portion of an egg **YOLKED** *adj*
YOLKLESS	*adj* lacking a yolk
YOLKY	*adj* **YOLKIER, YOLKIEST** resembling a yolk
YOM	*n* pl. **YOMIM** day
YOMP	*v* **-ED, -ING, -S** to march with heavy equipment over difficult terrain
YON	*adv* over there
YOND	*adv* over there
YONDER	*n* pl. **-S** the far distance
YONI	*n* pl. **-S** a symbol for the vulva in Hindu religion **YONIC** *adj*
YONKER	*n* pl. **-S** younker
YONKS	*n/pl* a very long time
YOOF	*n* pl. **-S** youth
YORE	*n* pl. **-S** time past
YOU	*n* pl. **-S** something identified with the person addressed
YOUNG	*adj* **YOUNGER, YOUNGEST** being in the early period of life or growth
YOUNG	*n* pl. **-S** offspring
YOUNGER	*n* pl. **-S** an inferior in age
YOUNGISH	*adj* somewhat young
YOUNKER	*n* pl. **-S** a young gentleman
YOUPON	*n* pl. **-S** yaupon
YOUR	*adj* a possessive form of the pronoun you
YOURN	*pron* yours
YOURS	*pron* a possessive form of the pronoun you
YOURSELF	*pron* pl. **-SELVES** a form of the 2d person pronoun
YOUSE	*pron* you
YOUTH	*n* pl. **-S** a young person
YOUTHEN	*v* **-ED, -ING, -S** to make youthful
YOUTHFUL	*adj* young
YOW	*v* **-ED, -ING, -S** to yowl
YOWE	*n* pl. **-S** a ewe
YOWIE	*n* pl. **-S** a small ewe
YOWL	*v* **-ED, -ING, -S** to utter a loud, long, mournful cry
YOWLER	*n* pl. **-S** one that yowls
YOWZA	*interj* — used to express surprise
YPERITE	*n* pl. **-S** a poisonous gas
YTTERBIA	*n* pl. **-S** a chemical compound **YTTERBIC** *adj*
YTTRIA	*n* pl. **-S** a chemical compound
YTTRIUM	*n* pl. **-S** a metallic element **YTTRIC** *adj*
YUAN	*n* pl. **-S** a monetary unit of China
YUCA	*n* pl. **-S** yucca
YUCCA	*n* pl. **-S** a tropical plant
YUCCH	*interj* — used to express disgust
YUCH	*interj* yucch
YUCK	*v* **-ED, -ING, -S** to yuk
YUCKY	*adj* **YUCKIER, YUCKIEST** disgusting
YUGA	*n* pl. **-S** an age of time in Hinduism
YUK	*v* **YUKKED, YUKKING, YUKS** to laugh loudly
YUKATA	*n* pl. **-S** a light cotton kimono
YUKE	*v* **YUKED, YUKING, YUKES** yeuk
YUKKY	*adj* **YUKKIER, YUKKIEST** yucky
YULAN	*n* pl. **-S** a Chinese tree
YULE	*n* pl. **-S** Christmas time
YULETIDE	*n* pl. **-S** yule
YUM	*interj* — used to express pleasurable satisfaction
YUMMY	*adj* **-MIER, -MIEST** delicious
YUMMY	*n* pl. **-MIES** something delicious
YUP	*n* pl. **-S** a yuppie
YUPON	*n* pl. **-S** yaupon
YUPPIE	*n* pl. **-S** a young professional person working in a city
YUPPIFY	*v* **-FIED, -FYING, -FIES** to make appealing to yuppies
YUPPY	*n* pl. **-PIES** yuppie
YUPPYDOM	*n* pl. **-S** the state of being a yuppie
YURT	*n* pl. **YURTS** or **YURTA** a portable tent
YUTZ	*n* pl. **-ES** a stupid, foolish, or ineffectual person
YUZU	*n* pl. **-S** a sour Japanese citrus fruit
YWIS	*adv* iwis

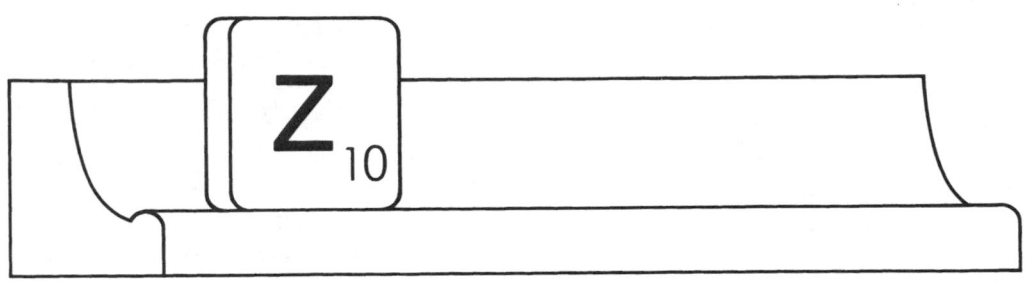

ZA	*n* pl. **-S** a pizza	**ZANY**	*n* pl. **-NIES** a zany person
ZABAIONE	*n* pl. **-S** a dessert resembling custard	**ZANYISH**	*adj* somewhat zany
ZABAJONE	*n* pl. **-S** zabaione	**ZANZA**	*n* pl. **-S** an African musical instrument
ZACATON	*n* pl. **-S** a Mexican grass	**ZAP**	*v* **ZAPPED, ZAPPING, ZAPS** to kill or destroy instantaneously
ZADDICK	*n* pl. **-DIKIM** zaddik	**ZAPATEO**	*n* pl. **-TEOS** a Spanish dance
ZADDIK	*n* pl. **-DIKIM** a virtuous person by Jewish religious standards	**ZAPPER**	*n* pl. **-S** a device that zaps
ZAFFAR	*n* pl. **-S** zaffer	**ZAPPY**	*adj* **-PIER, -PIEST** zippy
ZAFFER	*n* pl. **-S** a blue ceramic coloring	**ZAPTIAH**	*n* pl. **-S** a Turkish policeman
ZAFFIR	*n* pl. **-S** zaffer	**ZAPTIEH**	*n* pl. **-S** zaptiah
ZAFFRE	*n* pl. **-S** zaffer	**ZARATITE**	*n* pl. **-S** a chemical compound
ZAFTIG	*adj* full-bosomed	**ZAREBA**	*n* pl. **-S** an improvised stockade
ZAG	*v* **ZAGGED, ZAGGING, ZAGS** to turn sharply	**ZAREEBA**	*n* pl. **-S** zareba
ZAIBATSU	*n* pl. **ZAIBATSU** a powerful family combine in Japan	**ZARF**	*n* pl. **-S** a metal holder for a coffee cup
ZAIDA	*n* pl. **-S** zeda	**ZARIBA**	*n* pl. **-S** zareba
ZAIDEH	*n* pl. **-S** zeda	**ZARZUELA**	*n* pl. **-S** a Spanish operetta
ZAIDY	*n* pl. **-DIES** zeda	**ZASTRUGA**	*n* pl. **-GI** sastruga
ZAIKAI	*n* pl. **-S** the business community of Japan	**ZAX**	*n* pl. **-ES** a tool for cutting roof slates
ZAIRE	*n* pl. **-S** a former monetary unit of Zaire	**ZAYIN**	*n* pl. **-S** a Hebrew letter
ZAKAT	*n* pl. **-S** payment made annually under Islamic law on certain kinds of property	**ZAZEN**	*n* pl. **-S** meditation in Zen Buddhism
ZAMARRA	*n* pl. **-S** a sheepskin coat	**ZEAL**	*n* pl. **-S** enthusiastic devotion
ZAMARRO	*n* pl. **-ROS** zamarra	**ZEALOT**	*n* pl. **-S** one who is zealous
ZAMIA	*n* pl. **-S** a tropical plant	**ZEALOTRY**	*n* pl. **-RIES** excessive zeal
ZAMINDAR	*n* pl. **-S** a tax collector in precolonial India	**ZEALOUS**	*adj* filled with zeal
ZANANA	*n* pl. **-S** zenana	**ZEATIN**	*n* pl. **-S** a chemical compound found in maize
ZANDER	*n* pl. **-S** a freshwater fish	**ZEBEC**	*n* pl. **-S** xebec
ZANINESS	*n* pl. **-ES** the quality or state of being zany	**ZEBECK**	*n* pl. **-S** xebec
ZANY	*adj* **ZANIER, ZANIEST** ludicrously comical **ZANILY** *adv*	**ZEBRA**	*n* pl. **-S** an African mammal that is related to the horse **ZEBRAIC** *adj*
		ZEBRANO	*n* pl. **-BRANOS** a tree having striped wood

ZEBRASS	*n* pl. **-ES** the offspring of a zebra and an ass
ZEBRINE	*n* pl. **-S** the offspring of a male horse and a female zebra
ZEBROID	*adj* resembling a zebra
ZEBU	*n* pl. **-S** an Asian ox
ZECCHIN	*n* pl. **-S** zecchino
ZECCHINO	*n* pl. **-NOS** or **-NI** a former gold coin of Italy
ZECHIN	*n* pl. **-S** zecchino
ZED	*n* pl. **-S** the letter Z
ZEDA	*n* pl. **-S** grandfather
ZEDOARY	*n* pl. **-ARIES** the medicinal root of a tropical plant
ZEE	*n* pl. **-S** the letter Z
ZEIN	*n* pl. **-S** a simple protein
ZEK	*n* pl. **-S** an inmate in a Soviet labor camp
ZELKOVA	*n* pl. **-S** a Japanese tree
ZEMINDAR	*n* pl. **-S** zamindar
ZEMSTVO	*n* pl. **-VOS** or **-VA** an elective council in czarist Russia
ZEN	*n* a state of calm attentiveness
ZENAIDA	*n* pl. **-S** a wild dove
ZENANA	*n* pl. **-S** the section of a house in India reserved for women
ZENDO	*n* pl. **-DOS** a place where Zen Buddhists meditate and study
ZENITH	*n* pl. **-S** the highest point **ZENITHAL** *adj*
ZEOLITE	*n* pl. **-S** a mineral **ZEOLITIC** *adj*
ZEP	*n* pl. **-S** a long sandwich
ZEPHYR	*n* pl. **-S** a gentle breeze
ZEPPELIN	*n* pl. **-S** a long, rigid airship
ZEPPOLE	*n* pl. **-POLES** or **-POLI** a deep-fried pastry
ZERK	*n* pl. **-S** a grease fitting
ZERO	*v* **-ED, -ING, -ES** or **-S** to aim at the exact center of a target
ZEROTH	*adj* being numbered zero in a series
ZEST	*v* **-ED, -ING, -S** to fill with zest (invigorating excitement)
ZESTER	*n* pl. **-S** a utensil for peeling citrus rind
ZESTFUL	*adj* full of zest
ZESTLESS	*adj* lacking zest
ZESTY	*adj* **ZESTIER, ZESTIEST** marked by zest **ZESTILY** *adv*
ZETA	*n* pl. **-S** a Greek letter
ZETETIC	*adj* proceeding by inquiry
ZEUGMA	*n* pl. **-S** the use of a word to modify or govern two or more words, while applying to each in a different sense
ZIBELINE	*n* pl. **-S** a soft fabric
ZIBET	*n* pl. **-S** an Asian civet
ZIBETH	*n* pl. **-S** zibet
ZIG	*v* **ZIGGED, ZIGGING, ZIGS** to turn sharply
ZIGGURAT	*n* pl. **-S** an ancient Babylonian temple tower
ZIGZAG	*v* **-ZAGGED, -ZAGGING, -ZAGS** to proceed on a course marked by sharp turns
ZIGZAGGY	*adj* marked by sharp turns
ZIKKURAT	*n* pl. **-S** ziggurat
ZIKURAT	*n* pl. **-S** ziggurat
ZILCH	*n* pl. **-ES** nothing
ZILL	*n* pl. **-S** one of a pair of finger cymbals
ZILLAH	*n* pl. **-S** an administrative district in India
ZILLION	*n* pl. **-S** an indeterminately large number
ZIN	*n* pl. **-S** a dry red wine
ZINC	*v* **ZINCED, ZINCING, ZINCS** or **ZINCKED, ZINCKING, ZINCS** to coat with zinc (a metallic element)
ZINCATE	*n* pl. **-S** a chemical salt
ZINCIC	*adj* pertaining to zinc
ZINCIFY	*v* **-FIED, -FYING, -FIES** to coat with zinc
ZINCITE	*n* pl. **-S** an ore of zinc
ZINCKED	a past tense of zinc
ZINCKING	a present participle of zinc
ZINCKY	*adj* resembling zinc
ZINCO	*n* pl. **-COS** a letterpress printing plate made of zinc
ZINCOID	*adj* zincic
ZINCOUS	*adj* zincic
ZINCY	*adj* zincky
ZINE	*n* pl. **-S** a magazine
ZINEB	*n* pl. **-S** an insecticide
ZING	*v* **-ED, -ING, -S** to move with a high-pitched humming sound
ZINGANO	*n* pl. **-NI** zingaro
ZINGARA	*n* pl. **-RE** a female gypsy
ZINGARO	*n* pl. **-RI** a gypsy

ZINGER	*n* pl. **-S** a pointed witty retort or remark
ZINGY	*adj* **ZINGIER, ZINGIEST** enjoyably exciting
ZINKIFY	*v* **-FIED, -FYING, -FIES** to zincify
ZINKY	*adj* zincky
ZINNIA	*n* pl. **-S** a tropical plant
ZIP	*v* **ZIPPED, ZIPPING, ZIPS** to move with speed and vigor
ZIPLESS	*adj* lacking vigor or energy
ZIPLOCK	*adj* having a groove and ridge that form a tight seal when joined
ZIPOLA	*n* pl. **-S** zippo
ZIPPER	*v* **-ED, -ING, -S** to fasten with a zipper (a fastener consisting of two rows of interlocking teeth)
ZIPPO	*n* pl. **-POS** nothing
ZIPPY	*adj* **-PIER, -PIEST** full of energy **ZIPPILY** *adv*
ZIRAM	*n* pl. **-S** a chemical salt
ZIRCALOY	*n* pl. **-S** a zirconium alloy
ZIRCON	*n* pl. **-S** a mineral
ZIRCONIA	*n* pl. **-S** a chemical compound
ZIRCONIC	*adj* pertaining to the metallic element zirconium
ZIT	*n* pl. **-S** a pimple
ZITHER	*n* pl. **-S** a stringed instrument
ZITHERN	*n* pl. **-S** zither
ZITI	*n* pl. **-S** a tubular pasta
ZIZIT	*n/pl* zizith
ZIZITH	*n/pl* the tassels on the four corners of a Jewish prayer shawl
ZIZZ	*v* **-ED, -ING, -ES** to make a buzzing sound
ZIZZLE	*v* **-ZLED, -ZLING, -ZLES** to sizzle
ZLOTY	*n* pl. **ZLOTE** or **ZLOTIES** or **ZLOTYCH** or **ZLOTYS** a monetary unit of Poland
ZOA	a pl. of zoon
ZOARIUM	*n* pl. **-IA** a colony of bryozoans **ZOARIAL** *adj*
ZOCALO	*n* pl. **-LOS** the public square in a Mexican city or town
ZODIAC	*n* pl. **-S** an imaginary belt encircling the celestial sphere **ZODIACAL** *adj*
ZOEA	*n* pl. **ZOEAS** or **ZOEAE** a larval form of certain crustaceans **ZOEAL** *adj*
ZOECIUM	*n* pl. **-CIA** zooecium

ZOETROPE	*n* pl. **-S** an optical toy in which a series of pictures rotates to give the illusion of motion
ZOFTIG	*adj* zaftig
ZOIC	*adj* pertaining to animals or animal life
ZOISITE	*n* pl. **-S** a mineral
ZOMBI	*n* pl. **-S** zombie
ZOMBIE	*n* pl. **-S** a will-less human capable only of automatic movement
ZOMBIFY	*v* **-FIED, -FYING, -FIES** to turn into a zombie
ZOMBIISM	*n* pl. **-S** the system of beliefs connected with a West African snake god
ZOMBOID	*adj* resembling zombies
ZONA	*n* pl. **-NAE** a transparent substance surrounding the ovum of mammals
ZONAL	*adj* pertaining to a zone **ZONALLY** *adv*
ZONARY	*adj* zonal
ZONATE	*adj* arranged in zones
ZONATED	*adj* zonate
ZONATION	*n* pl. **-S** arrangement in zones
ZONE	*v* **ZONED, ZONING, ZONES** to arrange in zones (areas distinguished from other adjacent areas)
ZONELESS	*adj* having no zone or belt
ZONER	*n* pl. **-S** one that zones
ZONETIME	*n* pl. **-S** standard time used at sea
ZONING	*n* pl. **-S** the division of a city or land into areas subject to planning restrictions
ZONK	*v* **-ED, -ING, -S** to stupefy
ZONULA	*n* pl. **-LAS** or **-LAE** zonule
ZONULE	*n* pl. **-S** a small zone **ZONULAR** *adj*
ZOO	*n* pl. **ZOOS** a place where animals are kept for public exhibition
ZOOCHORE	*n* pl. **-S** a plant dispersed by animals
ZOOECIUM	*n* pl. **-CIA** a sac secreted and lived in by an aquatic organism
ZOOEY	*adj* **ZOOIER, ZOOIEST** resembling a zoo
ZOOGENIC	*adj* caused by animals or their activities
ZOOGENY	*n* pl. **-NIES** the development or evolution of animals

ZOOGLEA *n* pl. **-GLEAS** or **-GLEAE** a jellylike mass of bacteria **ZOOGLEAL** *adj*

ZOOGLOEA *n* pl. **-GLOEAS** or **-GLOEAE** zooglea

ZOOID *n* pl. **-S** an organic cell or body capable of independent movement **ZOOIDAL** *adj*

ZOOKS *interj* — used as a mild oath

ZOOLATER *n* pl. **-S** one that worships animals

ZOOLATRY *n* pl. **-TRIES** the worship of animals

ZOOLOGY *n* pl. **-GIES** the science that deals with animals **ZOOLOGIC** *adj*

ZOOM *v* **-ED, -ING, -S** to move with a loud humming sound

ZOOMABLE *adj* capable of being viewed at various levels of detail and magnification

ZOOMANIA *n* pl. **-S** an excessive interest in animals

ZOOMETRY *n* pl. **-TRIES** the measurement of animals or animal parts

ZOOMORPH *n* pl. **-S** something in the form of an animal

ZOON *n* pl. **ZOONS** or **ZOA** the whole product of one fertilized egg **ZOONAL** *adj*

ZOON *v* **-ED, -ING, -S** to zoom

ZOONOSIS *n* pl. **-NOSES** a disease that can be transmitted from animals to humans **ZOONOTIC** *adj*

ZOOPHILE *n* pl. **-S** a lover of animals

ZOOPHILY *n* pl. **-LIES** a love of animals

ZOOPHOBE *n* pl. **-S** one who fears or hates animals

ZOOPHYTE *n* pl. **-S** an invertebrate animal

ZOOSPERM *n* pl. **-S** the male fertilizing element of an animal

ZOOSPORE *n* pl. **-S** a type of spore

ZOOTOMY *n* pl. **-MIES** the dissection of animals **ZOOTOMIC** *adj*

ZOOTY *adj* **ZOOTIER, ZOOTIEST** flashy in manner or style

ZORI *n* pl. **-S** a type of sandal

ZORIL *n* pl. **-S** a small African mammal

ZORILLA *n* pl. **-S** zoril

ZORILLE *n* pl. **-S** zoril

ZORILLO *n* pl. **-LOS** zoril

ZOSTER *n* pl. **-S** a virus disease

ZOUAVE *n* pl. **-S** a French infantryman

ZOUK *n* pl. **-S** a dance music of the French West Indies

ZOUNDS *interj* — used as a mild oath

ZOWEE *interj* zowie

ZOWIE *interj* — used to express surprise or pleasure

ZOYSIA *n* pl. **-S** a perennial grass

ZUCCHINI *n* pl. **-S** a vegetable

ZUGZWANG *n* pl. **-S** a situation in chess that forces a disadvantageous move

ZUPPA *n* pl. **-S** a fish soup

ZUZ *n* pl. **ZUZIM** an ancient Hebrew silver coin

ZWIEBACK *n* pl. **-S** a sweetened bread

ZYDECO *n* pl. **-COS** popular music of southern Louisiana

ZYGOID *adj* pertaining to a zygote

ZYGOMA *n* pl. **-MAS** or **-MATA** the cheekbone

ZYGOSIS *n* pl. **-GOSES** the union of two gametes **ZYGOSE** *adj*

ZYGOSITY *n* pl. **-TIES** the makeup of a particular zygote

ZYGOTE *n* pl. **-S** a cell formed by the union of two gametes **ZYGOTIC** *adj*

ZYGOTENE *n* pl. **-S** a stage in meiosis

ZYMASE *n* pl. **-S** an enzyme

ZYME *n* pl. **-S** an enzyme

ZYMOGEN *n* pl. **-S** a substance that develops into an enzyme when suitably activated

ZYMOGENE *n* pl. **-S** zymogen

ZYMOGRAM *n* pl. **-S** a record of separated proteins after electrophoresis

ZYMOLOGY *n* pl. **-GIES** the science of fermentation

ZYMOSAN *n* pl. **-S** an insoluble fraction of yeast cell walls

ZYMOSIS *n* pl. **-MOSES** fermentation **ZYMOTIC** *adj*

ZYMURGY *n* pl. **-GIES** a branch of chemistry dealing with fermentation

ZYZZYVA *n* pl. **-S** a tropical weevil

ZZZ *interj* — used to suggest the sound of snoring

A SELECTION OF USEFUL WORDS FOR PLAYERS

Letter values

A is worth 1	G is worth 2	M is worth 3	S is worth 1	Y is worth 4
B is worth 3	H is worth 4	N is worth 1	T is worth 1	Z is worth 10
C is worth 3	I is worth 1	O is worth 1	U is worth 1	
D is worth 2	J is worth 8	P is worth 3	V is worth 4	
E is worth 1	K is worth 5	Q is worth 10	W is worth 4	
F is worth 4	L is worth 1	R is worth 1	X is worth 8	

Q words not followed by U

BUQSHA	NIQAABS	QAMUTIK	QIBLAS	QULLIQS
BUQSHAS	NIQAB	QAMUTIKS	QIGONG	QWERTY
BURQA	NIQABS	QANAT	QIGONGS	QWERTYS
BURQAS	QABALA	QANATS	QINDAR	SHEQEL
CINQ	QABALAS	QAPIK	QINDARS	SHEQELS
CINQS	QABALAH	QAPIKS	QINDARKA	SHEQALIM
FAQIR	QABALAHS	QAT	QINTAR	SUQ
FAQIRS	QADI	QATS	QINTARS	SUQS
KAMOTIQ	QADIS	QAWWALI	QIVIUT	TRANQ
KAMOTIQS	QAID	QAWWALIS	QIVIUTS	TRANQS
MBAQANGA	QAIDS	QI	QOPH	UMIAQ
MBAQANGAS	QAJAQ	QIS	QOPHS	UMIAQS
NIQAAB	QAJAQS	QIBLA	QULLIQ	

2- to 7-letter words with no AEIOU vowels

BY	SLY	SCRY	LYNCH	FLYSCH
HM	SPY	SHHH	MYRRH	GHYLLS
MM	STY	SKRY	MYTHS	GLYCYL
MY	SYN	SPRY	MYTHY	GLYPHS
SH	THY	SYNC	NYMPH	GRRRLS
	TRY	SYPH	PHPHT	LYMPHS
BRR	TSK	TSKS	PSYCH	MYRRHS
BYS	WHY	TYPP	PYGMY	MYRRHY
CRY	WRY	TYPY	RYNDS	NYMPHS
CWM	WYN	WHYS	SHYLY	PSYCHS
DRY	ZZZ	WYCH	SLYLY	RHYTHM
FLY		WYND	STYMY	SPHYNX
FRY	BRRR	WYNN	SYLPH	SPRYLY
GRR	BYRL	WYNS	SYNCH	SYLPHS
GYM	CWMS	XYST	SYNCS	SYLPHY
GYP	CYST		SYNTH	SYNCHS
HMM	DRYS	BYRLS	SYPHS	SYNTHS
HYP	GYMS	CRWTH	THYMY	SYZYGY
MMM	GYPS	CRYPT	TRYST	TRYSTS
MYC	HWYL	CYSTS	TYPPS	TSKTSK
NTH	HYMN	DRYLY	WRYLY	XYLYLS
PHT	HYPS	FLYBY	WYNDS	
PLY	LYCH	GHYLL	WYNNS	GLYCYLS
PRY	LYNX	GLYPH	XYLYL	RHYTHMS
PST	MYCS	GRRRL	XYSTS	TSKTSKS
PYX	MYTH	GYPSY		
SHH	PFFT	HWYLS	CRWTHS	
SHY	PSST	HYMNS	CRYPTS	
SKY	RYND	LYMPH	FLYBYS	

2- to 6-letter words containing J, Q, X, or Z

AX	PYX	CALX	JAMS	JOYS
EX	QAT	CAZH	JANE	JUBA
JO	QIS	CHEZ	JAPE	JUBE
OX	QUA	CINQ	JARL	JUCO
QI	RAJ	COAX	JARS	JUDO
XI	RAX	COXA	JATO	JUDY
XU	REX	COZY	JAUK	JUGA
ZA	REZ	CRUX	JAUP	JUGS
	SAX	CZAR	JAVA	JUJU
ADZ	SEX	DAZE	JAWS	JUKE
AJI	SIX	DEXY	JAYS	JUKU
AXE	SOX	DITZ	JAZZ	JUMP
AZO	SUQ	DJIN	JEAN	JUNK
BIZ	TAJ	DOJO	JEED	JUPE
BOX	TAX	DOUX	JEEP	JURA
COX	TIX	DOXY	JEER	JURY
COZ	TIZ	DOZE	JEES	JUST
CUZ	TUX	DOZY	JEEZ	JUTE
DEX	VEX	EAUX	JEFE	JUTS
FAX	VOX	EXAM	JEHU	KOJI
FEZ	WAX	EXEC	JELL	LAZE
FIX	WIZ	EXED	JEON	LAZY
FIZ	XIS	EXES	JERK	LUTZ
FOX	ZAG	EXIT	JESS	LUXE
GOX	ZAP	EXON	JEST	LYNX
HAJ	ZAS	EXPO	JETE	MAXI
HEX	ZAX	FALX	JETS	MAZE
JAB	ZED	FAUX	JEUX	MAZY
JAG	ZEE	FAZE	JIAO	MEZE
JAM	ZEK	FIXT	JIBB	MINX
JAR	ZEN	FIZZ	JIBE	MIXT
JAW	ZEP	FLAX	JIBS	MOJO
JAY	ZIG	FLEX	JIFF	MOXA
JEE	ZIN	FLUX	JIGS	MOZO
JET	ZIP	FOXY	JILL	NAZI
JEU	ZIT	FOZY	JILT	NEXT
JIB	ZOA	FRIZ	JIMP	NIXE
JIG	ZOO	FUJI	JINK	NIXY
JIN	ZUZ	FUTZ	JINN	ONYX
JOB	ZZZ	FUZE	JINS	OOZE
JOE		FUZZ	JINX	OOZY
JOG	ADZE	GAZE	JIRD	ORYX
JOT	AJAR	GEEZ	JIVE	ORZO
JOW	AJEE	GOJI	JIVY	OUZO
JOY	AJIS	GRIZ	JOBS	OXEN
JUG	APEX	HADJ	JOCK	OXER
JUN	AQUA	HAJI	JOES	OXES
JUS	AXAL	HAJJ	JOEY	OXIC
JUT	AXED	HAZE	JOGS	OXID
KEX	AXEL	HAZY	JOHN	OXIM
LAX	AXES	HOAX	JOIN	OYEZ
LEX	AXIL	IBEX	JOKE	PHIZ
LOX	AXIS	ILEX	JOKY	PIXY
LUX	AXLE	IXIA	JOLE	PLEX
MAX	AXON	IZAR	JOLT	POXY
MIX	AZAN	JABS	JOOK	PREX
MUX	AZON	JACK	JOSH	PREZ
NIX	BAZZ	JADE	JOSS	PUJA
OXO	BIZE	JAGG	JOTA	PUTZ
OXY	BOXY	JAGS	JOTS	QADI
PAX	BOZO	JAIL	JOUK	QAID
PIX	BRUX	JAKE	JOWL	QATS
POX	BUZZ	JAMB	JOWS	QOPH

QUAD	ZOON	BORTZ	EQUAL	GIZMO
QUAG	ZOOS	BOXED	EQUES	GLAZE
QUAI	ZORI	BOXER	EQUID	GLAZY
QUAY	ZOUK	BOXES	EQUIP	GLITZ
QUEY	ZYME	BOXLA	EXACT	GLOZE
QUID		BOZOS	EXALT	GOJIS
QUIN	ABUZZ	BRAXY	EXAMS	GONZO
QUIP	ADDAX	BRAZA	EXCEL	GOXES
QUIT	ADMIX	BRAZE	EXECS	GRAZE
QUIZ	ADOZE	BURQA	EXERT	GROSZ
QUOD	ADZED	BUXOM	EXILE	GYOZA
RAJA	ADZES	BUZZY	EXINE	HADJI
RAZE	AFFIX	CAJON	EXING	HAFIZ
RAZZ	AGAZE	CALIX	EXIST	HAJES
RITZ	AJIES	CALYX	EXITS	HAJIS
ROUX	AJIVA	CAPIZ	EXOME	HAJJI
SEXT	AJUGA	CAREX	EXONS	HAMZA
SEXY	AMAZE	CIMEX	EXPAT	HAPAX
SIZE	ANNEX	CINQS	EXPEL	HAZAN
SIZY	AQUAE	CLOZE	EXPOS	HAZED
SOJA	AQUAS	CODEX	EXTOL	HAZEL
SOJU	ARROZ	COLZA	EXTRA	HAZER
SUQS	ATAXY	COMIX	EXUDE	HAZES
TAXA	AUXIN	COQUI	EXULT	HEEZE
TAXI	AXELS	COXAE	EXURB	HELIX
TEXT	AXIAL	COXED	FAQIR	HERTZ
TIZZ	AXILE	COXES	FAXED	HEXAD
TZAR	AXILS	COZEN	FAXES	HEXED
VEXT	AXING	COZES	FAZED	HEXER
WAXY	AXIOM	COZEY	FAZES	HEXES
WHIZ	AXION	COZIE	FEAZE	HEXYL
XYST	AXITE	CRAZE	FEDEX	HIJAB
YUTZ	AXLES	CRAZY	FEEZE	HIJRA
YUZU	AXMAN	CROZE	FEZES	HUZZA
ZAGS	AXMEN	CULEX	FIQUE	HYRAX
ZANY	AXONE	CYLIX	FIXED	IMMIX
ZAPS	AXONS	CZARS	FIXER	INBOX
ZARF	AZANS	DAZED	FIXES	INDEX
ZEAL	AZIDE	DAZES	FIXIT	INFIX
ZEBU	AZINE	DEOXY	FIZZY	IXIAS
ZEDA	AZLON	DESEX	FJELD	IXNAY
ZEDS	AZOIC	DETOX	FJORD	IXORA
ZEES	AZOLE	DEWAX	FLAXY	IXTLE
ZEIN	AZONS	DEXES	FOREX	IZARD
ZEKS	AZOTE	DEXIE	FOXED	IZARS
ZEPS	AZOTH	DIAZO	FOXES	JABOT
ZERK	AZUKI	DITZY	FRITZ	JACAL
ZERO	AZURE	DIXIT	FRIZZ	JACKS
ZEST	BAIZA	DIZEN	FROZE	JACKY
ZETA	BAIZE	DIZZY	FUJIS	JADED
ZIGS	BANJO	DJINN	FURZE	JADES
ZILL	BAZAR	DJINS	FURZY	JAGER
ZINC	BAZOO	DOJOS	FUZED	JAGGS
ZINE	BEAUX	DOOZY	FUZEE	JAGGY
ZING	BEMIX	DOXIE	FUZES	JAGRA
ZINS	BEZEL	DOZED	FUZIL	JAILS
ZIPS	BEZIL	DOZEN	FUZZY	JAKES
ZITI	BHAJI	DOZER	GALAX	JALAP
ZITS	BIJOU	DOZES	GANJA	JALOP
ZIZZ	BIZES	EEJIT	GAUZE	JAMBE
ZOEA	BLAZE	EJECT	GAUZY	JAMBS
ZOIC	BLITZ	EJIDO	GAZAR	JAMMY
ZONA	BONZE	EMOJI	GAZED	JANES
ZONE	BOOZE	ENJOY	GAZER	JANNY
ZONK	BOOZY	ENZYM	GAZES	JANTY
ZOOM	BORAX	EPOXY	GHAZI	JAPAN

JAPED	JOKER	KYLIX	OXIMS	QUIDS
JAPER	JOKES	LATEX	OXLIP	QUIET
JAPES	JOKEY	LAXER	OXTER	QUIFF
JARLS	JOLES	LAXES	OZONE	QUILL
JATOS	JOLLY	LAXLY	PAXES	QUILT
JAUKS	JOLTS	LAZAR	PHIZZ	QUINS
JAUNT	JOLTY	LAZED	PHLOX	QUINT
JAUPS	JOMON	LAZES	PIEZO	QUIPS
JAVAS	JONES	LEXES	PIQUE	QUIPU
JAWAN	JOOKS	LEXIS	PIXEL	QUIRE
JAWED	JORAM	LOXED	PIXES	QUIRK
JAZZY	JORUM	LOXES	PIXIE	QUIRT
JEANS	JOTAS	LUXES	PIZZA	QUITE
JEBEL	JOTTY	MAIZE	PLAZA	QUITS
JEEPS	JOUAL	MAJOR	PLOTZ	QUODS
JEERS	JOUKS	MAQUI	PONZU	QUOIN
JEEZE	JOULE	MATZA	POOJA	QUOIT
JEFES	JOUST	MATZO	POXED	QUOLL
JEHAD	JOWAR	MAUZY	POXES	QUOTA
JEHUS	JOWED	MAXED	PREXY	QUOTE
JELLS	JOWLS	MAXES	PRIZE	QUOTH
JELLY	JOWLY	MAXIM	PROXY	QURSH
JEMMY	JOYED	MAXIS	PUJAH	RADIX
JENNY	JUBAS	MAZED	PUJAS	RAJAH
JERID	JUBES	MAZER	PUNJI	RAJAS
JERKS	JUCOS	MAZES	PYXES	RAJES
JERKY	JUDAS	MEZES	PYXIE	RAXED
JERRY	JUDGE	MEZZO	PYXIS	RAXES
JESSE	JUDGY	MIREX	PZAZZ	RAZED
JESTS	JUDOS	MIRZA	QADIS	RAZEE
JETES	JUGAL	MIXED	QAIDS	RAZER
JETON	JUGUM	MIXER	QAJAQ	RAZES
JETTY	JUICE	MIXES	QANAT	RAZOR
JEWEL	JUICY	MIXUP	QAPIK	REDOX
JIBBA	JUJUS	MIZEN	QIBLA	REDUX
JIBBS	JUKED	MOJOS	QOPHS	REFIX
JIBED	JUKES	MOXAS	QUACK	REJIG
JIBER	JUKUS	MOXIE	QUADS	RELAX
JIBES	JULEP	MOZOS	QUAFF	REMEX
JIFFS	JUMAR	MUJIK	QUAGS	REMIX
JIFFY	JUMBO	MUREX	QUAIL	RETAX
JIGGY	JUMPS	MUXED	QUAIS	REWAX
JIHAD	JUMPY	MUXES	QUAKE	REXES
JILLS	JUNCO	MUZZY	QUAKY	REZES
JILTS	JUNKS	NAZIS	QUALE	RIOJA
JIMMY	JUNKY	NERTZ	QUALM	RITZY
JIMPY	JUNTA	NEXUS	QUANT	ROQUE
JINGO	JUNTO	NINJA	QUARE	SAJOU
JINKS	JUPES	NIQAB	QUARK	SAXES
JINNI	JUPON	NIXED	QUART	SCUZZ
JINNS	JURAL	NIXES	QUASH	SEIZA
JIRDS	JURAT	NIXIE	QUASI	SEIZE
JIVED	JUREL	NIZAM	QUASS	SEXED
JIVER	JUROR	NUDZH	QUATE	SEXER
JIVES	JUSTS	OBJET	QUAYS	SEXES
JIVEY	JUTES	OOZED	QUBIT	SEXTO
JNANA	JUTTY	OOZES	QUEAN	SEXTS
JOCKO	JUVIE	ORZOS	QUEEN	SHOJI
JOCKS	KANJI	OUZEL	QUEER	SHOJO
JOCKY	KANZU	OUZOS	QUELL	SILEX
JOEYS	KAZOO	OXBOW	QUERN	SIXER
JOHNS	KEXES	OXERS	QUERY	SIXES
JOINS	KLUTZ	OXEYE	QUEST	SIXMO
JOINT	KOJIS	OXIDE	QUEUE	SIXTE
JOIST	KOPJE	OXIDS	QUEYS	SIXTH
JOKED	KUDZU	OXIME	QUICK	SIXTY

SIZAR	WHIZZ	ZONER	AZLONS	BOXLAS
SIZED	WINZE	ZONES	AZOLES	BRAIZE
SIZER	WIZEN	ZONKS	AZONAL	BRAZAS
SIZES	WIZES	ZOOEY	AZONIC	BRAZED
SLOJD	WOOZY	ZOOID	AZOTES	BRAZEN
SMAZE	XEBEC	ZOOKS	AZOTHS	BRAZER
SOJAS	XENIA	ZOOMS	AZOTIC	BRAZES
SOJUS	XENIC	ZOONS	AZUKIS	BRAZIL
SOYUZ	XENON	ZOOTY	AZURES	BREEZE
SOZIN	XERIC	ZORIL	AZYGOS	BREEZY
SPITZ	XEROX	ZORIS	BAIZAS	BRONZE
SQUAB	XERUS	ZOUKS	BAIZES	BRONZY
SQUAD	XYLAN	ZOWEE	BANJAX	BRUXED
SQUAT	XYLEM	ZOWIE	BANJOS	BRUXES
SQUEG	XYLOL	ZUPPA	BANZAI	BUQSHA
SQUIB	XYLYL	ZUZIM	BARQUE	BURQAS
SQUID	XYSTI	ZYMES	BASQUE	BUZUKI
TAJES	XYSTS		BAZAAR	BUZZED
TAXED	YOWZA	ABJECT	BAZARS	BUZZER
TAXER	YUZUS	ABJURE	BAZOOS	BUZZES
TAXES	ZAIDA	ABLAZE	BAZZED	BYZANT
TAXIS	ZAIDY	ACAJOU	BAZZES	CAIQUE
TAXOL	ZAIRE	ACQUIT	BEEZER	CAJOLE
TAXON	ZAKAT	ADIEUX	BEGAZE	CALQUE
TAXUS	ZAMIA	ADJOIN	BEMIXT	CALXES
TAZZA	ZANZA	ADJURE	BENZAL	CASQUE
TAZZE	ZAPPY	ADJUST	BENZIN	CAUDEX
TELEX	ZARFS	ADMIXT	BENZOL	CERVIX
TEXAS	ZAXES	ADNEXA	BENZYL	CHAZAN
TEXTS	ZAYIN	ADZING	BEZANT	CHEQUE
THUJA	ZAZEN	ADZUKI	BEZAZZ	CHINTZ
TIZES	ZEALS	AFFLUX	BEZELS	CINQUE
TIZZY	ZEBEC	AGNIZE	BEZILS	CIRQUE
TOPAZ	ZEBRA	AJIVAS	BEZOAR	CLAQUE
TOQUE	ZEBUS	AJOWAN	BHAJIS	CLAXON
TOXIC	ZEDAS	AJUGAS	BIAXAL	CLIMAX
TOXIN	ZEINS	ALEXIA	BIFLEX	CLIQUE
TRANQ	ZENDO	ALEXIN	BIJOUS	CLIQUY
TROOZ	ZERKS	ALKOXY	BIJOUX	CLOQUE
TUQUE	ZEROS	AMAZED	BISQUE	CLOZES
TUXES	ZESTS	AMAZES	BIZJET	COAXAL
TWIXT	ZESTY	AMAZON	BIZONE	COAXED
TZARS	ZETAS	ANNEXE	BIZZES	COAXER
UMIAQ	ZIBET	ANOXIA	BLAZED	COAXES
UNBOX	ZILCH	ANSATZ	BLAZER	COCCYX
UNFIX	ZILLS	APEXES	BLAZES	COJOIN
UNJAM	ZINCO	ASSIZE	BLAZON	COLZAS
UNMIX	ZINCS	ATAXIA	BLINTZ	COMMIX
UNSEX	ZINCY	ATAXIC	BLOWZY	CONVEX
UNZIP	ZINEB	AUSPEX	BOLLIX	COQUET
USQUE	ZINES	AUXINS	BOLLOX	COQUIS
VARIX	ZINGS	AXEMAN	BOMBAX	COROZO
VEXED	ZINGY	AXEMEN	BOMBYX	CORTEX
VEXER	ZINKY	AXENIC	BONZER	CORYZA
VEXES	ZIPPO	AXILLA	BONZES	COTIJA
VEXIL	ZIPPY	AXIOMS	BOOJUM	COWPOX
VIXEN	ZIRAM	AXIONS	BOOZED	COXING
VIZIR	ZITIS	AXISES	BOOZER	COZENS
VIZOR	ZIZIT	AXITES	BOOZES	COZEYS
VOXEL	ZLOTY	AXLIKE	BORZOI	COZIED
WALTZ	ZOEAE	AXONES	BOSQUE	COZIER
WAREZ	ZOEAS	AXONIC	BOXCAR	COZIES
WAXED	ZOMBI	AXSEED	BOXERS	COZZES
WAXEN	ZONAE	AZALEA	BOXFUL	CRAZED
WAXER	ZONAL	AZIDES	BOXIER	CRAZES
WAXES	ZONED	AZINES	BOXING	CROJIK

CROZER	EUTAXY	FAZING	GEEZER	INJURE
CROZES	EVZONE	FEAZED	GHAZAL	INJURY
CRUXES	EXACTA	FEAZES	GHAZIS	INKJET
CUZZES	EXACTS	FEEZED	GIZMOS	IODIZE
DAZING	EXALTS	FEEZES	GLAZED	IONIZE
DAZZLE	EXAMEN	FEIJOA	GLAZER	IXODID
DEEJAY	EXARCH	FEZZES	GLAZES	IXORAS
DEFUZE	EXCEED	FIQUES	GLITZY	IXTLES
DEIXIS	EXCELS	FIXATE	GLOZED	IZARDS
DEJECT	EXCEPT	FIXERS	GLOZES	IZZARD
DELUXE	EXCESS	FIXING	GRAZED	JABBED
DESOXY	EXCIDE	FIXITS	GRAZER	JABBER
DEXIES	EXCISE	FIXITY	GRAZES	JABIRU
DEXTER	EXCITE	FIXURE	GROSZE	JABOTS
DEXTRO	EXCUSE	FIZGIG	GROSZY	JACALS
DEZINC	EXEDRA	FIZZED	GUZZLE	JACANA
DIAZIN	EXEMPT	FIZZER	GYOZAS	JACKAL
DIAZOS	EXEQUY	FIZZES	GYTTJA	JACKED
DIOXAN	EXERTS	FIZZLE	HADJEE	JACKER
DIOXID	EXEUNT	FJELDS	HADJES	JACKET
DIOXIN	EXHALE	FJORDS	HADJIS	JADING
DIPLEX	EXHORT	FLAXEN	HAJJES	JADISH
DIQUAT	EXHUME	FLAXES	HAJJIS	JAEGER
DITZES	EXILED	FLEXED	HALLUX	JAGERS
DIXITS	EXILER	FLEXES	HALUTZ	JAGGED
DIZENS	EXILES	FLEXOR	HAMZAH	JAGGER
DJEBEL	EXILIC	FLOOZY	HAMZAS	JAGRAS
DJEMBE	EXINES	FLUXED	HANDAX	JAGUAR
DJIBBA	EXISTS	FLUXES	HATBOX	JAILED
DJINNI	EXITED	FOOZLE	HAZANS	JAILER
DJINNS	EXODOI	FORNIX	HAZARD	JAILOR
DJINNY	EXODOS	FOXIER	HAZELS	JALAPS
DONJON	EXODUS	FOXILY	HAZERS	JALOPS
DONZEL	EXOGEN	FOXING	HAZIER	JALOPY
DOOZER	EXOMES	FOZIER	HAZILY	JAMBED
DOOZIE	EXONYM	FRAZIL	HAZING	JAMBES
DOXIES	EXOTIC	FREEZE	HAZMAT	JAMMED
DOZENS	EXPAND	FRENZY	HAZZAN	JAMMER
DOZERS	EXPATS	FRIEZE	HEEZED	JANGLE
DOZIER	EXPECT	FRIJOL	HEEZES	JANGLY
DOZILY	EXPELS	FRIZED	HEJIRA	JANNEY
DOZING	EXPEND	FRIZER	HEXADE	JAPANS
DUPLEX	EXPERT	FRIZES	HEXADS	JAPERS
EARWAX	EXPIRE	FRIZZY	HEXANE	JAPERY
ECZEMA	EXPIRY	FROUZY	HEXERS	JAPING
EEJITS	EXPORT	FROWZY	HEXING	JARFUL
EFFLUX	EXPOSE	FROZEN	HEXONE	JARGON
EJECTA	EXSECT	FURZES	HEXOSE	JARINA
EJECTS	EXSERT	FUTZED	HEXYLS	JARRAH
EJIDOS	EXTANT	FUTZES	HIJABS	JARRED
ELIXIR	EXTEND	FUZEES	HIJACK	JARVEY
EMOJIS	EXTENT	FUZILS	HIJRAH	JASMIN
ENJAMB	EXTERN	FUZING	HIJRAS	JASPER
ENJOIN	EXTOLL	FUZZED	HOAXED	JASSID
ENJOYS	EXTOLS	FUZZES	HOAXER	JAUKED
ENZYME	EXTORT	GAIJIN	HOAXES	JAUNCE
ENZYMS	EXTRAS	GALAXY	HOTBOX	JAUNTS
EPIZOA	EXUDED	GANJAH	HUTZPA	JAUNTY
EQUALS	EXUDES	GANJAS	HUZZAH	JAUPED
EQUATE	EXULTS	GAUZES	HUZZAS	JAWANS
EQUIDS	EXURBS	GAZABO	IBEXES	JAWING
EQUINE	FAJITA	GAZARS	ICEBOX	JAYGEE
EQUIPS	FANJET	GAZEBO	ILEXES	JAYVEE
EQUITY	FAQIRS	GAZERS	INFLUX	JAZZBO
ERSATZ	FAQUIR	GAZING	INJECT	JAZZED
ETHOXY	FAXING	GAZUMP	INJERA	JAZZER

JAZZES	JIVERS	JUGUMS	LIQUOR	MYXOMA
JEBELS	JIVIER	JUICED	LIZARD	NAZIFY
JEEING	JIVING	JUICER	LOGJAM	NINJAS
JEEPED	JNANAS	JUICES	LOQUAT	NIQAAB
JEERED	JOBBED	JUJUBE	LOXING	NIQABS
JEERER	JOBBER	JUKING	LUMMOX	NIXIES
JEESLY	JOBBIE	JULEPS	LUTZES	NIXING
JEEZLY	JOCKEY	JUMARS	LUXATE	NIZAMS
JEHADI	JOCKOS	JUMBAL	LUXURY	NONTAX
JEHADS	JOCOSE	JUMBIE	LYNXES	NOYAUX
JEJUNA	JOCUND	JUMBLE	MAGNOX	NOZZLE
JEJUNE	JOGGED	JUMBOS	MAHZOR	NUTJOB
JELLED	JOGGER	JUMPED	MAIZES	NUZZLE
JENNET	JOGGLE	JUMPER	MAJLIS	OBJECT
JERBOA	JOHNNY	JUNCOS	MAJORS	OBJETS
JEREED	JOINED	JUNGLE	MAMZER	ONYXES
JERIDS	JOINER	JUNGLY	MANQUE	OOZIER
JERKED	JOINTS	JUNIOR	MAQUIS	OOZING
JERKER	JOISTS	JUNKED	MARQUE	OPAQUE
JERKIN	JOJOBA	JUNKER	MASJID	ORYXES
JERRID	JOKERS	JUNKET	MASQUE	OUTBOX
JERSEY	JOKIER	JUNKIE	MASTIX	OUTFOX
JESSED	JOKING	JUNTAS	MATRIX	OUTJUT
JESSES	JOLTED	JUNTOS	MATZAH	OUZELS
JESTED	JOLTER	JUPONS	MATZAS	OXALIS
JESTER	JORAMS	JURANT	MATZOH	OXBOWS
JETLAG	JORDAN	JURATS	MATZOS	OXCART
JETONS	JORUMS	JURELS	MATZOT	OXEYES
JETSAM	JOSEPH	JURIED	MAXIMA	OXFORD
JETSOM	JOSHED	JURIES	MAXIMS	OXHERD
JETTED	JOSHER	JURIST	MAXING	OXHIDE
JETTON	JOSHES	JURORS	MAXIXE	OXIDES
JEWELS	JOSSES	JUSTED	MAZARD	OXIMES
JEZAIL	JOSTLE	JUSTER	MAZERS	OXLIKE
JIBBAH	JOTTED	JUSTLE	MAZIER	OXLIPS
JIBBAS	JOTTER	JUSTLY	MAZILY	OXTAIL
JIBBED	JOUALS	JUTTED	MAZING	OXTERS
JIBBER	JOUKED	JUVIES	MAZUMA	OXYGEN
JIBERS	JOULES	KAIZEN	MENINX	OYEZES
JIBING	JOUNCE	KAMEEZ	MEZCAL	OZONES
JICAMA	JOUNCY	KANJIS	MEZUZA	PACZKI
JIGGED	JOURNO	KANZUS	MEZZOS	PAJAMA
JIGGER	JOUSTS	KAZOOS	MINXES	PANZER
JIGGLE	JOVIAL	KHAZEN	MIRZAS	PATZER
JIGGLY	JOWARS	KIBITZ	MIXERS	PAXWAX
JIGSAW	JOWING	KLAXON	MIXING	PAZAZZ
JIHADI	JOYFUL	KLUTZY	MIXUPS	PEGBOX
JIHADS	JOYING	KOLHOZ	MIZENS	PEROXY
JILTED	JOYOUS	KOLKOZ	MIZUNA	PHENIX
JILTER	JOYPAD	KOPJES	MIZZEN	PHIZES
JIMINY	JOYPOP	KUDZUS	MIZZLE	PIAZZA
JIMMIE	JUBBAH	KUVASZ	MIZZLY	PIAZZE
JIMPER	JUBHAH	KWANZA	MOJITO	PICKAX
JIMSON	JUBILE	LARYNX	MOJOES	PIQUED
JINGAL	JUDDER	LAXEST	MOMZER	PIQUES
JINGKO	JUDGED	LAXITY	MOSQUE	PIQUET
JINGLE	JUDGER	LAZARS	MOUJIK	PIXELS
JINGLY	JUDGES	LAZIED	MOXIES	PIXIES
JINKED	JUDGEY	LAZIER	MUJIKS	PIZAZZ
JINKER	JUDIES	LAZIES	MUSJID	PIZZAS
JINNEE	JUDOKA	LAZILY	MUSKOX	PIZZAZ
JINNIS	JUGATE	LAZING	MUXING	PIZZLE
JINXED	JUGFUL	LAZULI	MUZHIK	PLAQUE
JINXES	JUGGED	LEXEME	MUZJIK	PLAZAS
JITNEY	JUGGLE	LEXICA	MUZZLE	PLEXAL
JITTER	JUGULA	LIQUID	MYXOID	PLEXES

PLEXOR	QUARTZ	RAZING	SIXTES	TAXITE
PLEXUS	QUASAR	RAZORS	SIXTHS	TAXMAN
PODZOL	QUATRE	RAZZED	SIZARS	TAXMEN
POLEAX	QUAVER	RAZZES	SIZERS	TAXOLS
POLLEX	QUBITS	RAZZIA	SIZIER	TAXONS
PONZUS	QUBYTE	RAZZLE	SIZING	TAZZAS
POOJAS	QUEANS	REBOZO	SIZZLE	TEABOX
POTZER	QUEASY	REFLEX	SKYBOX	TEAZEL
POXIER	QUEAZY	REFLUX	SLEAZE	TEAZLE
POXING	QUEENS	REJECT	SLEAZO	TEXTED
POZOLE	QUEENY	REJIGS	SLEAZY	TEXTER
PRAJNA	QUEERS	REJOIN	SLOJDS	THORAX
PRAXES	QUELEA	REMIXT	SMAZES	THUJAS
PRAXIS	QUELLS	REQUIN	SMILAX	TIZZES
PREFIX	QUENCH	RESIZE	SNAZZY	TOQUES
PREMIX	QUERNS	REZERO	SNEEZE	TOQUET
PRETAX	QUESTS	REZONE	SNEEZY	TORQUE
PREXES	QUEUED	REZZES	SNOOZE	TOUZLE
PREZES	QUEUER	RIOJAS	SNOOZY	TOXICS
PRIZED	QUEUES	RISQUE	SOZINE	TOXINE
PRIZER	QUEZAL	RITZES	SOZINS	TOXINS
PRIZES	QUICHE	ROMAJI	SPADIX	TOXOID
PROJET	QUICKS	ROQUES	SPELTZ	TRANQS
PROLIX	QUIETS	ROQUET	SPHINX	TRIJET
PUJAHS	QUIFFS	ROZZER	SPHYNX	TUQUES
PULQUE	QUILLS	SACQUE	SPRITZ	TUXEDO
PUNJIS	QUILTS	SAJOUS	SQUABS	TWEEZE
PUTZED	QUINCE	SANJAK	SQUADS	TZETZE
PUTZES	QUINIC	SAXIST	SQUALL	TZURIS
PUZZLE	QUININ	SAXMAN	SQUAMA	UBIQUE
PYJAMA	QUINOA	SAXMEN	SQUARE	UMIAQS
PYXIES	QUINOL	SAXONY	SQUARK	UNAXED
QABALA	QUINSY	SCHIZO	SQUASH	UNFIXT
QAJAQS	QUINTA	SCHIZY	SQUATS	UNIQUE
QANATS	QUINTE	SCHNOZ	SQUAWK	UNISEX
QAPIKS	QUINTS	SCOLEX	SQUEAK	UNJAMS
QIBLAS	QUIPPU	SCUZZY	SQUEAL	UNJUST
QIGONG	QUIPPY	SEIZAS	SQUEGS	UNMIXT
QINDAR	QUIPUS	SEIZED	SQUIBS	UNSEXY
QINTAR	QUIRED	SEIZER	SQUIDS	UNVEXT
QIVIUT	QUIRES	SEIZES	SQUILL	UNZIPS
QUACKS	QUIRKS	SEIZIN	SQUINT	UPGAZE
QUACKY	QUIRKY	SEIZOR	SQUIRE	UPSIZE
QUAERE	QUIRTS	SEJANT	SQUIRL	URTEXT
QUAFFS	QUITCH	SEQUEL	SQUIRM	USQUES
QUAGGA	QUIVER	SEQUIN	SQUIRT	VEEJAY
QUAGGY	QULLIQ	SEXERS	SQUISH	VERJUS
QUAHOG	QUOHOG	SEXIER	SQUUSH	VERNIX
QUAICH	QUOINS	SEXILY	STANZA	VERTEX
QUAIGH	QUOITS	SEXING	STORAX	VEXERS
QUAILS	QUOKKA	SEXISM	STYRAX	VEXILS
QUAINT	QUOLLS	SEXIST	SUBFIX	VEXING
QUAKED	QUORUM	SEXPOT	SUFFIX	VIXENS
QUAKER	QUOTAS	SEXTAN	SURTAX	VIZARD
QUAKES	QUOTED	SEXTET	SVARAJ	VIZIER
QUALIA	QUOTER	SEXTON	SWARAJ	VIZIRS
QUALMS	QUOTES	SEXTOS	SYNTAX	VIZORS
QUALMY	QUOTHA	SEXUAL	SYRINX	VIZSLA
QUANGO	QURUSH	SHAZAM	SYZYGY	VOLVOX
QUANTA	QWERTY	SHEQEL	TAJINE	VORTEX
QUANTS	RAJAHS	SHIRAZ	TARZAN	VOXELS
QUARKS	RAMJET	SHOJIS	TAXEME	WAXERS
QUARRY	RAXING	SHVITZ	TAXERS	WAXIER
QUARTE	RAZEED	SILVEX	TAXIED	WAXILY
QUARTO	RAZEES	SIXERS	TAXIES	WAXING
QUARTS	RAZERS	SIXMOS	TAXING	WHEEZE

WHEEZY	YUTZES	ZAZENS	ZINCKY	ZOMBIS
WHIZZY	ZADDIK	ZEALOT	ZINCOS	ZONARY
WINZES	ZAFFAR	ZEATIN	ZINEBS	ZONATE
WIZARD	ZAFFER	ZEBECK	ZINGED	ZONERS
WIZENS	ZAFFIR	ZEBECS	ZINGER	ZONING
WIZZEN	ZAFFRE	ZEBRAS	ZINNIA	ZONKED
WIZZES	ZAFTIG	ZECHIN	ZIPOLA	ZONULA
WURZEL	ZAGGED	ZENANA	ZIPPED	ZONULE
XEBECS	ZAIDAS	ZENDOS	ZIPPER	ZOOIDS
XENIAS	ZAIDEH	ZENITH	ZIPPOS	ZOOIER
XENONS	ZAIKAI	ZEPHYR	ZIRAMS	ZOOMED
XYLANS	ZAIRES	ZEROED	ZIRCON	ZOONED
XYLEMS	ZAKATS	ZEROES	ZITHER	ZORILS
XYLENE	ZAMIAS	ZEROTH	ZIZITH	ZOSTER
XYLOID	ZANANA	ZESTED	ZIZZED	ZOUAVE
XYLOLS	ZANDER	ZESTER	ZIZZES	ZOUNDS
XYLOSE	ZANIER	ZEUGMA	ZIZZLE	ZOYSIA
XYLYLS	ZANIES	ZIBETH	ZLOTYS	ZUPPAS
XYSTER	ZANZAS	ZIBETS	ZOARIA	ZYDECO
XYSTOI	ZAPPED	ZIGGED	ZOCALO	ZYGOID
XYSTOS	ZAPPER	ZIGZAG	ZODIAC	ZYGOMA
XYSTUS	ZAREBA	ZILLAH	ZOECIA	ZYGOTE
YAKUZA	ZARIBA	ZINCED	ZOFTIG	ZYMASE
YANQUI	ZAYINS	ZINCIC	ZOMBIE	

North American SCRABBLE Players Association

Making words, building friendships

Established in 2009, the North American SCRABBLE Players Association — NASPA — is a community of tournament, club and avid home players of the SCRABBLE Brand Crossword Game. We foster an atmosphere for people of all skill levels to play their favorite game, improve their abilities and above all, meet people who share a similar love of the game.

To learn more about the world of official competition and our:

WORDS... our members have access to the full *Official Tournament and Club Word List* with every acceptable word of up to 15 letters.

PEOPLE... make lifelong friendships with other players near you and always have someone that you can play your favorite game with.

RULES... learn how to use a game timer, how to challenge a play, and when to call for one of our certified tournament directors for a ruling.

RATINGS... are you a world-championship contender rated above 2,000, or a 500-rated novice? Test your skills and find out.

EVENTS... how serious is your game? Do you want to play weekly at your local club, monthly at one-day tournaments, or compete at multi-day regionals or even the North American SCRABBLE Championship?

Please find us at:

Web: http://www.scrabbleplayers.org

Email: info@scrabbleplayers.org

Twitter: @NASPA

Facebook: scrbblplyrs